AMERICAN DECADES
PRIMARY SOURCES

1900–1909

CYNTHIA ROSE, PROJECT EDITOR

Detroit • New York • San Diego • San Francisco • Cleveland • New Haven, Conn. • Waterville, Maine • London • Munich

American Decades Primary Sources, 1900–1909

Project Editor
Cynthia Rose

Editorial
Jason M. Everett, Rachel J. Kain, Pamela A. Dear, Andrew C. Claps, Thomas Carson, Kathleen Droste, Christy Justice, Lynn U. Koch, Michael D. Lesniak, Nancy Matuszak, John F. McCoy, Michael Reade, Rebecca Parks, Mark Mikula, Polly A. Rapp, Mark Springer

Data Capture
Civie A. Green, Beverly Jendrowski, Gwendolyn S. Tucker

Permissions
Margaret Abendroth, Margaret A. Chamberlain, Lori Hines, Jacqueline Key, Mari Masalin-Cooper, William Sampson, Shalice Shah-Caldwell, Kim Smilay, Sheila Spencer, Ann Taylor

Indexing Services
Lynne Maday, John Magee

Imaging and Multimedia
Randy Bassett, Dean Dauphinais, Leitha Etheridge-Sims, Mary K. Grimes, Lezlie Light, Daniel W. Newell, David G. Oblender, Christine O'Bryan, Kelly A. Quin, Luke A. Rademacher, Denay Wilding, Robyn V. Young

Product Design
Michelle DiMercurio

Composition and Electronic Prepress
Evi Seoud

Manufacturing
Rita Wimberley

For more information, contact
The Gale Group, Inc.
27500 Drake Rd.
Farmington Hills, MI 48331-3535
Or you can visit our Internet site at
http://www.gale.com

Cover photographs reproduced by permission of Corbis (President Theodore Roosevelt and educator Booker T. Washington, center), Hulton-Deutsch Collection/Corbis (Two suffragettes, left; writer Upton Sinclair, right), The Kobal Collection (Film still from *A Trip to the Moon,* spine), and The Library of Congress (Homestead Steel Works, Homestead, Pennsylvania, background).

LIBRARY OF CONGRESS CATALOGING-IN-PUBLICATION DATA

American decades primary sources / edited by Cynthia Rose.
v. cm.
Includes bibliographical references and index.
Contents: [1] 1900-1909 — [2] 1910-1919 — [3] 1920-1929 — [4] 1930-1939 — [5] 1940-1949 — [6] 1950-1959 — [7] 1960-1969 — [8] 1970-1979 — [9] 1980-1989 — [10] 1990-1999.
ISBN 0-7876-6587-8 (set : hardcover : alk. paper) — ISBN 0-7876-6588-6 (v. 1 : hardcover : alk. paper) — ISBN 0-7876-6589-4 (v. 2 : hardcover : alk. paper) — ISBN 0-7876-6590-8 (v. 3 : hardcover : alk. paper) — ISBN 0-7876-6591-6 (v. 4 : hardcover : alk. paper) — ISBN 0-7876-6592-4 (v. 5 : hardcover : alk. paper) — ISBN 0-7876-6593-2 (v. 6 : hardcover : alk. paper) — ISBN 0-7876-6594-0 (v. 7 : hardcover : alk. paper) — ISBN 0-7876-6595-9 (v. 8 : hardcover : alk. paper) — ISBN 0-7876-6596-7 (v. 9 : hardcover : alk. paper) — ISBN 0-7876-6597-5 (v. 10 : hardcover : alk. paper)
1. United States—Civilization—20th century—Sources. I. Rose, Cynthia.
E169.1.A471977 2004
973.91—dc21

2002008155

Printed in the United States of America
10 9 8 7 6 5 4 3 2 1

CONTENTS

Entries are arranged in chronological order by date of primary source. For entries with one primary source, the entry title is the primary source title. Entries with more than one primary source have an overall entry title, followed by the titles of the primary sources.

Business and the Economy

Education

Fashion and Design

Government and Politics

Law and Justice

Medicine and Health

Religion

Science and Technology

Sports

ADVISORS AND CONTRIBUTORS

Advisors

CARL A. ANTONUCCI, JR. has spent the past ten years as a reference librarian at various colleges and universities. Currently director of library services at Capital Community College, he holds two master's degrees and is a doctoral candidate at Providence College. He particularly enjoys researching Rhode Island political history during the 1960's and 1970's.

KATHY ARSENAULT is the dean of library at the University of South Florida, St. Petersburg's Poynter Library. She holds a master's degree in library science. She has written numerous book reviews for *Library Journal,* and has published articles in such publications as the *Journal of the Florida Medical Association,* and *Collection Management.*

JAMES RETTIG holds two master's degrees. He has written numerous articles and has edited *Distinguished Classics of Reference Publishing* (1992). University librarian at the University of Richmond, he is the recipient of three American Library Association awards: the Isadore Gibert Mudge Citation (1988), the G.K. Hall Award for Library Literature (1993), and the Louis Shores-Oryx Press Award (1995).

HILDA K. WEISBURG is the head library media specialist at Morristown High School Library and specializes in building school library media programs. She has several publications to her credit, including: *The School Librarians Workshop, Puzzles, Patterns, and Problem Solving: Creative Connections to Critical Thinking,* and *Learning, Linking & Critical Thinking: Information Strategies for the K-12 Library Media Curriculum.*

Contributors

PETER J. CAPRIOGLIO is a professor emeritus at Middlesex Community College, where he taught social sciences for thirty years prior to his retirement. He has a master's in sociology, and he is currently at work on a book entitled, *The Glory of God's Religions: A Beginner's Guide to Exploring the Beauty of the World's Faiths.*

Chapter: Religion.

PAUL G. CONNORS earned a doctorate in American history from Loyola University in Chicago. He has a strong interest in Great Lakes maritime history, and has contributed the article "Beaver Island Ice Walkers" to *Michigan History.* He has worked for the Michigan Legislative Service Bureau as a research analyst since 1996.

Essay: Using Primary Sources. ***Chronologies:*** Selected World Events Outside the United States; Government and Politics, Sports Chapters. ***General Resources:*** General, Government and Politics, Sports.

JAMES N. CRAFT has been the president and owner of Southill, LLC in Royal Oak, Michigan, since 1999. He is also a senior consultant for Lee Hecht Harrision. He has previously worked as a history teacher and as a curriculum consultant for the Detroit Historical Museum and the Detroit 300 Committee. His research interests include the nineteenth century (particularly the 1840s), the Progressive Era, and primary source–based curriculum material.

Chapters: Business and Economy, Government and Politics, Lifestyles and Social Trends.

CHRISTOPHER CUMO is a staff writer for *The Adjunct Advocate Magazine*. Formerly an adjunct professor of history at Walsh University, he has written two books, *A History of the Ohio Agricultural Experiment Station, 1882–1997* and *Seeds of Change,* and has contributed to numerous scholarly journals. He holds a doctorate in history from the University of Akron.

Chapters: Medicine and Health, Science and Technology. ***Chapter Chronologies and General Resources:*** Business and the Economy, Education, Medicine and Health, Science and Technology.

JENNIFER HELLER holds bachelor's degrees in religious studies and English education, as well as a master's in curriculum and instruction, all from the University of Kansas. She has been an adjunct associate professor at Johnson County Community College in Kansas since 1998. She is currently at work on a dissertation on contemporary women's religious literature.

Chapter Chronology and General Resources: Religion.

DAVID M. HOLFORD has worked as an adjunct instructor at Ohio University, Park College, and Columbus State Community College; education curator for the Ohio Historical Society; and held editorial positions at Glencoe/McGraw Hill and Holt, Rinehard, and Winston. He also holds a doctorate in history from Ohio State University. A freelance writer/editor since 1996, he as published *Herbert Hoover* (1999) and *Abraham Lincoln and the Emancipation Proclamation (2002).*

Chapter Chronologies and General Resources: Lifestyles and Social Trends, The Media.

SCOTT A. MERRIMAN currently works as a part-time instructor at the University of Kentucky and is finishing his doctoral dissertation on Espionage and Sedition Acts in the Sixth Court of Appeals. He has contributed to *The History Highway* and *History.edu,* among others. He is a resident of Lexington, Kentucky.

Chapter: Law and Justice.

KRISTINA PETERSON earned her bachelor's degree in psychology from Northland College. She also holds a master's in education from the College of William and Mary, as well as a doctorate in history and philosophy of education from the University of Minnesota.

Chapter: Education.

JESSIE BISHOP POWELL is a librarian assistant at the Lexington Public Library and a cataloger at Book Wholesaler's Inc. She resides in Lexington, Kentucky.

Chapter: Sports.

DAN PROSTERMAN is an adjunct professor of history at St. Francis College, as well as an adjunct lecturer at Pace University. He holds a master's in history at New York University and is working on his doctoral dissertation on the subject of anti-Communism in New York City during the Great Depression and World War II.

Chapter: The Media.

LORNA BIDDLE RINEAR is the editor and co-author of *The Complete Idiot's Guide to Women's History*. A Ph.D. candidate at Rutger's University, she holds a bachelor's from Wellesley College and a master's degree from Boston College. She resides in Bellingham, Massachusetts.

Chapter Chronologies and General Resources: The Arts, Fashion and Design.

MARY HERTZ SCARBROUGH earned both her bachelor's in English and German and her J.D. from the University of South Dakota. Prior to becoming a freelance writer in 1996, she worked as a law clerk in the Federal District Court for the District of South Dakota and as legal counsel for the Immigration and Naturalization Service. She lives in Storm Lake, Iowa.

Chapter Chronology and General Resources: Law and Justice.

ANITA MILLER STAMPER spent twenty-five years on the University of Southern Mississippi faculty, serving ten of those years as the Director of the School of Family and Consumer and Apparel Studies. Currently a professor of Family and Consumer Sciences at Lambuth University in Jackson, Tennessee, her primary field of interest is nineteenth-century Southern dress and textile production. She has contributed to numerous books, including *Mississippi Homespun: Nineteenth-century Textiles and the Women Who Made Them.*

Chapter: Fashion.

ALICE WU holds a bachelor's in English from Wellesley College, as well as a master's of fine art in sculpture from Yale University. An artist and fashion designer, she lives in New York City.

Chapter: The Arts.

Acknowledgments

Following is a list of the copyright holders who have granted us permission to reproduce material in this volume of American Decades Primary Sources. *Every effort has been made to trace copyright, but if omissions have been made, please let us know.*

Copyrighted material in *American Decades Primary Sources, 1900–1909* was reproduced from the following books: Baum, L. Frank. From *Baum's Road to Oz: The Dakota Years*, edited by Nancy Tystad Koupal. South Dakota State Historical Society Press, 2000. © by the South Dakota State Historical Society. Reproduced by permission. —Brown, Estelle Aubrey. From *Stubborn Fool: A Narrative*. The Caxton Publishers, Ltd., 1952. Copyright 1952 by The Caxton Printers, Ltd., renewed 1980 by Sarah McWhirt Johnson. Reproduced by permission. —Cobb, Ty. From "How to Hit," in *Famous Slugger Year Book*. Hillerich & Bradsby, 1950. Reproduced by permission. —Cobb, Ty, with Al Stump. From *My Life in Baseball: The True Record*. Doubleday & Company, Inc., 1961. Copyright © 1961 by Doubleday, a division of Bantam Doubleday Dell Publishing Group, Inc. Reproduced by permission of Doubleday, a division of Random House, Inc. —Duncan, Isadora. From *My Life*. Copyright, 1927 by Horace Liveright, Inc., renewed © 1955 by Liveright Publishing Corporation. Reproduced by permission of Liveright Publishing Corporation. —Flexner, Abraham. From *Abraham Flexner: An Autobiography*. Simon & Schuster, 1960. Edited by Allan Nevins, Copyright © 1960. Copyright © 1940 by Abraham Flexner. Copyright renewed 1960 by Jean Flexner and Eleanor Flexner. Reproduced by permission of Simon & Schuster. —Fuess, Claude M. and Emory S. Basford. From "The School Readers," in *Unseen Harvests: A Treasury of Teaching*. The McMillan Company, 1947. Copyright © 1947 by The McMillan Company; copyright renewed © 1975 by Emory S. Bradford and Cora Frances Fuess. All rights reserved. Reproduced by permission of Scribner, an imprint of Simon & Schuster & Schuster Adult Publishing Group. —Pickford, Mary. From *Sunshine and Shadow*. Doubleday & Company, Inc., 1955. Copyright © 1955, by Mary Pickford Rogers; copyright, 1954, by McCall Corporation. Reproduced by permission. —Reid, Bill. From *Big-Time Football at Harvard, 1905: The Diary of Coach Bill Reid*. Edited by Ronald A. Smith. University of Illinois Press, 1994. © 1994 by Ronald A. Smith. Courtesy of the Harvard University Archives. Reproduced by permission. —Robinson, Edwin Arlington. From *Selected Letters of Edwin Arlington Robinson*. The Macmillan Company, 1940. Copyright © 1940 by The MacMillan Company; copyright renewed © by Mrs. Ruth Nivison and Mrs. Barbara W. Holt. Reproduced by permission of Scribner, an imprint of Simon & Schuster Adult Publishing Group. —Stave, Bruce M., John F. Sutherland with Aldo Salerno. From *From the Old Country: An Oral History of the European Migration to America*. Twayne Publishers, 1994. © 1994 by Twayne Publishers. Reproduced by permission. —Toscanini, Arturo. From *The Letters of Arturo Toscanini*. Edited by Harvey Sachs. Alfred A. Knopf, 2002. Copyright © 2002 by Alfred A. Knopf, a division of Random House, Inc. Reproduced by permission of Alfred A. Knopf, a division of Random House, Inc.

About the Set

American Decades Primary Sources is a ten-volume collection of more than two thousand primary sources on twentieth-century American history and culture. Each volume comprises about two hundred primary sources in 160–170 entries. Primary sources are enhanced by informative context, with illustrative images and sidebars—many of which are primary sources in their own right—adding perspective and a deeper understanding of both the primary sources and the milieu from which they originated.

Designed for students and teachers at the high school and undergraduate levels, as well as researchers and history buffs, *American Decades Primary Sources* meets the growing demand for primary source material.

Conceived as both a stand-alone reference and a companion to the popular *American Decades* set, *American Decades Primary Sources* is organized in the same subject-specific chapters for compatibility and ease of use.

Primary Sources

To provide fresh insights into the key events and figures of the century, thirty historians and four advisors selected unique primary sources far beyond the typical speeches, government documents, and literary works. Screenplays, scrapbooks, sports box scores, patent applications, college course outlines, military codes of conduct, environmental sculptures, and CD liner notes are but a sampling of the more than seventy-five types of primary sources included.

Diversity is shown not only in the wide range of primary source types, but in the range of subjects and opinions, and the frequent combination of primary sources in entries. Multiple perspectives in religious, political, artistic, and scientific thought demonstrate the commitment of *American Decades Primary Sources* to diversity, in addition to the inclusion of considerable content displaying ethnic, racial, and gender diversity. *American Decades Primary Sources* presents a variety of perspectives on issues and events, encouraging the reader to consider subjects more fully and critically.

American Decades Primary Sources' innovative approach often presents related primary sources in an entry. The primary sources act as contextual material for each other—creating a unique opportunity to understand each and its place in history, as well as their relation to one another. These may be point-counterpoint arguments, a variety of diverse opinions, or direct responses to another primary source. One example is President Franklin Delano Roosevelt's letter to clergy at the height of the Great Depression, with responses by a diverse group of religious leaders from across the country.

Multiple primary sources created by particularly significant individuals—Dr. Martin Luther King Jr., for example—reside in *American Decades Primary Sources*. Multiple primary sources on particularly significant subjects are often presented in more than one chapter of a volume, or in more than one decade, providing opportunities to see the significance and impact of an event or figure from many angles and historical perspectives. For example, seven primary sources on the controversial Scopes "monkey" trial are found in five chapters of the

1920s volume. Primary sources on evolutionary theory may be found in earlier and later volumes, allowing the reader to see and analyze the development of thought across time.

Entry Organization

Contextual material uses standardized rubrics that will soon become familiar to the reader, making the entries more accessible and allowing for easy comparison. Introduction and Significance essays—brief and focused—cover the historical background, contributing factors, importance, and impact of the primary source, encouraging the reader to think critically—not only about the primary source, but also about the way history is constructed. Key Facts and a Synopsis provide quick access and recognition of the primary sources, and the Further Resources are a stepping-stone to additional study.

Additional Features

Subject chronologies and thorough tables of contents (listing titles, authors, and dates) begin each chapter. The main table of contents assembles this information conveniently at the front of the book. An essay on using primary sources, a chronology of selected events outside the United States during the twentieth century, substantial general and subject resources, and primary source-type and general indexes enrich *American Decades Primary Sources.*

The ten volumes of *American Decades Primary Sources* provide a vast array of primary sources integrated with supporting content and user-friendly features. This value-laden set gives the reader an unparalleled opportunity to travel into the past, to relive important events, to encounter key figures, and to gain a deep and full understanding of America in the twentieth century.

Acknowledgments

A number of people contributed to the successful completion of this project. The editor wishes to acknowledge them with thanks: Eugenia Bradley, Luann Brennan, Neva Carter, Katrina Coach, Pamela S. Dear, Nikita L. Greene, Madeline Harris, Alesia James, Cynthia Jones, Pamela M. Kalte, Arlene Ann Kevonian, Frances L. Monroe, Charles B. Montney, Katherine H. Nemeh, James E. Person, Tyra Y. Phillips, Elizabeth Pilette, Noah Schusterbauer, Andrew Specht, Susan Strickland, Karissa Walker, Tracey Watson, and Jennifer M. York.

Contact Us

The editors of *American Decades Primary Sources* welcome your comments, suggestions, and questions. Please direct all correspondence to:

Editor, *American Decades Primary Sources*
The Gale Group, Inc.
27500 Drake Road
Farmington Hills, MI 48331-3535
(800) 877-4253

For email inquiries, please visit the Gale website at www.gale.com, and click on the Contact Us tab.

About the Volume

The 1900s began a century of advancement, invention, and progress in the United States. The automobile was just beginning to make what would become an indelible mark on the U.S. economy and way of life, and the Wright brothers made their first air flight. From federal regulations of the food industry to the advent of the first cartoon, the United States saw a wide spectrum of events and issues during the first decade of the twentieth century. The following documents are just a sampling of the offerings available in this volume.

Highlights of Primary Sources, 1900–1909

- Diary entry of December 17, 1903, by Orville Wright
- "The Man with the Muck Rake, speech given by President Theodore Roosevelt, April 15, 1906
- *Fundamentals of Basketball,* handbook written by James Naismith, creator of the game
- "To the Person Sitting in Darkness," an article by Mark Twain
- *Ford Price List of Parts for Models "N," "R," "S" and "S" Roadster,* manual written for Ford car dealers
- Drawings by Charles Dana Gibson, creator of the "Gibson Girl"
- "Lynch Law in America," an article by Ida B. Wells-Barnett, founding member of the NAACP
- Letter to Commissioner of Indian Affairs Francis E. Leupp from Susan La Flesche Picotte, the first American Indian woman physician
- "The Little Schoolboy," from *The New McGuffey Second Reader*
- "Humorous Phases of Funny Faces," one of the first cartoons
- Lecture by philosopher William James, "The Varieties of Religious Experience"
- "The Memphis Blues," by W.C. Handy
- Speech on "The Road Problem," by William Jennings Bryan

Volume Structure and Content

Front matter

- Table of Contents—lists primary sources, authors, and dates of origin, by chapter and chronologically within chapters.
- About the Set, About the Volume, About the Entry essays—guide the reader through the set and promote ease of use.
- Highlights of Primary Sources—a quick look at a dozen or so primary sources gives the reader a feel for the decade and the volume's contents.
- Using Primary Sources—provides a crash course in reading and interpreting primary sources.

- Chronology of Selected World Events Outside the United States—lends additional context in which to place the decade's primary sources.

Chapters:

- The Arts
- Business and the Economy
- Education
- Fashion and Design
- Government and Politics
- Law and Justice
- Lifestyles and Social Trends
- The Media
- Medicine and Health
- Religion
- Science and Technology
- Sports

Chapter structure

- Chapter table of contents—lists primary sources, authors, and dates of origin chronologically, showing each source's place in the decade.
- Chapter chronology—highlights the decade's important events in the chapter's subject.
- Primary sources—displays sources surrounded by contextual material.

Back matter

- General Resources—promotes further inquiry with books, periodicals, websites, and audio and visual media, all organized into general and subject-specific sections.
- General Index—provides comprehensive access to primary sources, people, events, and subjects, and cross-referencing to enhance comparison and analysis.
- Primary Source Type Index—locates primary sources by category, giving readers an opportunity to easily analyze sources across genres.

About the Entry

The primary source is the centerpiece and main focus of each entry in *American Decades Primary Sources.* In keeping with the philosophy that much of the benefit from using primary sources derives from the reader's own process of inquiry, the contextual material surrounding each entry provides access and ease of use, as well as giving the reader a springboard for delving into the primary source. Rubrics identify each section and enable the reader to navigate entries with ease.

Entry structure

- Key Facts—essential information pertaining to the primary source, including full title, author, source type, source citation, and notes about the author.
- Introduction—historical background and contributing factors for the primary source.
- Significance—importance and impact of the primary source, at the time and since.
- Primary Source—in text, text facsimile, or image format; full or excerpted.
- Synopsis—encapsulated introduction to the primary source.
- Further Resources—books, periodicals, websites, and audio and visual material.

Navigating an Entry

Entry elements are numbered and reproduced here, with an explanation of the data contained in these elements explained immediately thereafter according to the corresponding numeral.

Entry Title, Primary Source Type

•1• "Ego"

•2• **Magazine article**

•1• ENTRY TITLE The entry title is the primary source title for entries with one primary source. Entry titles appear as catchwords at the top outer margin of each page.

•2• PRIMARY SOURCE TYPE The type of primary source is listed just below the title. When assigning source types, great weight was given to how the author of the primary source categorized it. If a primary source comprised more than one type—for example, an article about art in the United States that included paintings, or a scientific essay that included graphs and photographs—each primary source type included in the entry appears below the title.

Composite Entry Title

•3• Debate Over *The Birth of a Nation*

•1• **"Capitalizing Race Hatred"**

•2• **Editorial**

•1• "Reply to the *New York Globe*"

•2• Letter

•3• **COMPOSITE ENTRY TITLE** An overarching entry title is used for entries with more than one primary source, with the primary source titles and types below.

Key Facts

•4• **By:** Norman Mailer

•5• **Date:** March 19, 1971

•6• **Source:** Mailer, Norman. "Ego." *Life* 70, March 19, 1971, 30, 32–36.

•7• **About the Author:** Norman Mailer (1923–) was born in Long Branch, New Jersey. After graduating from Harvard and military service in World War II (1939–1945), Mailer began writing, publishing his first book, the best-selling novel *The Naked and the Dead,* in 1948. Mailer has written over thirty books, including novels, plays, political commentary, and essay collections, as well as numerous magazine articles. He won the Pulitzer Prize in 1969 and 1979. ■

•4• **AUTHOR OR ORIGINATOR** The name of the author or originator of the primary source begins the Key Facts section.

•5• **DATE OF ORIGIN** The date of origin of the primary source appears in this field, and may differ from the date of publication in the source citation below it; for example, speeches are often given before they are published.

•6• **SOURCE CITATION** The source citation is a full bibliographic citation, giving original publication data as well as reprint and/or online availability (usually both the deep-link and home-page URLs).

•7• **ABOUT THE AUTHOR** A brief bio of the author or originator of the primary source gives birth and death dates and a quick overview of the person's life. This rubric has been customized in some cases. If the primary source is the autobiography of an artist, the term "author" appears; however, if the primary source is a work of art, the term "artist" is used, showing the person's direct relationship to the primary source. Terms like "inventor" and "designer" are used similarly. For primary sources created by a group, "organization" may have been used instead of "author." If an author is anonymous or unknown, a brief "About the Publication" sketch may appear.

Introduction and Significance Essays

•8• Introduction

. . . As images from the Vietnam War (1964–1975) flashed onto television screens across the United States in the late 1960s, however, some reporters took a more active role in questioning the pronouncements of public officials. The broad cultural changes of the 1960s, including a sweeping suspicion of authority figures by younger people, also encouraged a more restive spirit in the reporting corps. By the end of the decade, the phrase "Gonzo Journalism" was coined to describe the new breed of reporter: young, rebellious, and unafraid to get personally involved in the story at hand. . . .

•8• **INTRODUCTION** The introduction is a brief essay on the contributing factors and historical context of the primary source. Intended to promote understanding and jump-start the reader's curiosity, this section may also describe an artist's approach, the nature of a scientific problem, or the struggles of a sports figure. If more than one primary source is included in the entry, the introduction and significance address each one, and often the relationship between them.

•9• Significance

Critics of the new style of journalism maintained that the emphasis on personalities and celebrity did not necessarily lead to better reporting. As political reporting seemed to focus more on personalities and images and less on substantive issues, some observers feared that the American public was ill-served by the new style of journalism. Others argued that the media had also encouraged political apathy among the public by superficial reporting. . . .

•9• **SIGNIFICANCE** The significance discusses the importance and impact of the primary source. This section may touch on how it was regarded at the time and since, its place in history, any awards given, related developments, and so on.

Primary Source Header, Synopsis, Primary Source

•10• Primary Source

The Boys on the Bus [excerpt]

•11• **SYNOPSIS:** A boisterous account of Senator George McGovern's ultimately unsuccessful 1972 presidential bid, Crouse's work popularized the term "pack journalism," describing the herd mentality that gripped reporters focusing endlessly on the same topic. In later years, political advisors would become more adept at "spinning" news stories to their candidates' advantage, but the essential dynamics of pack journalism remain in place.

•12• The feverish atmosphere was halfway between a high school bus trip to Washington and a gambler's jet junket to Las Vegas, where small-time Mafiosi were lured into betting away their restaurants. There was giddy camaraderie mixed with fear and low-grade hysteria. To file a story late, or to make one glaring factual error, was to chance losing everything—one's job, one's expense account, one's drinking buddies, one's mad-dash existence, and the methedrine buzz that comes from knowing stories that the public would not know for hours and secrets that the public would never know. Therefore reporters channeled their gambling instincts into late-night poker games and private bets on the outcome of the elections. When it came to writing a story, they were as cautious as diamond-cutters. . . .

•10• **PRIMARY SOURCE HEADER** The primary source header signals the beginning of the primary source, and "[excerpt]" is attached if the source does not appear in full.

•11• **SYNOPSIS** The synopsis gives a brief overview of the primary source.

•12• **PRIMARY SOURCE** The primary source may appear excerpted or in full, and may appear as text, text facsimile (photographic reproduction of the original text), image, or graphic display (such as a table, chart, or graph).

Text Primary Sources

The majority of primary sources are reproduced as plain text. The font and leading of the primary sources are distinct from that of the context—to provide a visual clue to the change, as well as to facilitate ease of reading. Often, the original formatting of the text was preserved in order to more accurately represent the original (screenplays, for example). In order to respect the integrity of the primary sources, content some readers may consider sensitive was retained where it was deemed to be integral to the source. Text facsimile formatting was used sparingly and where the original provided additional value (for example, Aaron Copland's typing and handwritten notes on "Notes for a Cowboy Ballet").

Narrative Break

•13• I told him I'd rest and then fix him something to eat when he got home. I could hear someone enter his office then, and Medgar laughed at something that was said. "I've got to go, honey. See you tonight. I love you." "All right," I said. "Take care." Those were our last words to each other.

■ ■ ■

Medgar had told me that President Kennedy was speaking on civil rights that night, and I made a mental note of the time. We ate alone, the children and I. It had become a habit now to set only four places for supper. Medgar's chair stared at us, and the children, who had heard about the President's address to the nation, planned to watch it with me. There was something on later that they all wanted to see, and they begged to be allowed to wait up for Medgar to return home. School was out, and I knew that Van would fall asleep anyway, so I agreed.

•13• **NARRATIVE BREAK** A narrative break appears where there is a significant amount of elided material, beyond what ellipses would indicate (for example, excerpts from a nonfiction work's introduction and second chapter, or sections of dialogue from two acts of a play).

Image Primary Sources

Primary source images (whether photographs, text facsimiles, or graphic displays) are bordered with a distinctive double rule. The Primary Source header and Synopsis appear under the image, with the image reduced in size to accommodate the synopsis. For multipart images, the synopsis appears only under the first part of the image; subsequent parts have brief captions.

•14• "Art: U.S. Scene": *The Tornado* by John Steuart Curry **(2 OF 4)**

•14• **PRIMARY SOURCE IMAGE HEADER** The primary source image header assists the reader in tracking the images in a series. Also, the primary source header listed here indicates a primary source with both text and image components. The text of the *Time* magazine article "Art: U.S. Scene," appears with four of the paintings from the article. Under each painting, the title of the article appears first, followed by a colon, then the title of the painting. The header for the text component has a similar structure, with the term "magazine article" after the colon. Inclusion of images or graphic elements from primary sources, and their designation in the entry as main primary sources, is discretionary.

Further Resources

•15• **Further Resources**

BOOKS

Dixon, Phil. *The Negro Baseball Leagues, 1867–1955: A Photographic History.* Mattituck, N.Y.: Amereon House, 1992.

PERIODICALS

"Steven Spielberg: The Director Says It's Good-Bye to Spaceships and Hello to Relationships." *American Film* 13, no. 8, June 1988, 12–16.

WEBSITES

Architecture and Interior Design for 20th Century America, 1935–1955. American Memory digital primary source collection, Library of Congress. Available online at http://memory.loc.gov/ammem/gschtml/gotthome

.html; website home page: http://memory.loc.gov/ammem/ammemhome.html (accessed March 27, 2003).

AUDIO AND VISUAL MEDIA

E.T.: The Extra-Terrestrial. Original release, 1982, Universal. Directed by Steven Spielberg. Widescreen Collector's Edition DVD, 2002, Universal Studios.

•15• FURTHER RESOURCES A brief list of resources provides a stepping stone to further study. If it's known that a resource contains additional primary source material specifically related to the entry, a brief note in italics appears at the end of the citation. For websites, both the deep link and home page usually appear.

Using Primary Sources

The philosopher R.G. Collingwood once said, "Every new generation must rewrite history in its own way." What Collingwood meant is that new events alter our perceptions of the past and necessitate that each generation interpret the past in a different light. For example, since September 11, 2001, and the "War on Terrorism," the collapse of the Soviet Union seemingly is no longer as historically important as the rise of Islamic fundamentalism, which was once only a minor concern. Seen from this viewpoint, history is not a rigid set of boring facts, but a fascinating, ever-changing field of study. Much of this fascination rests on the fact that historical interpretation is based on the reading of primary sources. To historians and students alike, primary sources are ambiguous objects because their underlying meanings are often not crystal clear. To learn a primary document's meaning(s), students must identify its main subject and recreate the historical context in which the document was created. In addition, students must compare the document with other primary sources from the same historical time and place. Further, students must cross-examine the primary source by asking of it a series of probing investigative questions.

To properly analyze a primary source, it is important that students become "active" rather than "casual" readers. As in reading a chemistry or algebra textbook, historical documents require students to analyze them carefully and extract specific information. In other words, history requires students to read "beyond the text" and focus on what the primary source tells us about the person or group and the era in which they lived. Unlike chemistry and algebra, however, historical primary sources have the additional benefit of being part of a larger, interesting story full of drama, suspense, and hidden agendas. In order to detect and identify key historical themes, students need to keep in mind a set of questions. For example, Who created the primary source? Why did the person create it? What is the subject? What problem is being addressed? Who was the intended audience? How was the primary source received and how was it used? What are the most important characteristics of this person or group for understanding the primary source? For example, what were the authors' biases? What was their social class? Their race? Their gender? Their occupation? Once these questions have been answered reasonably, the primary source can be used as a piece of historical evidence to interpret history.

In each *American Decades Primary Sources* volume, students will study examples of the following categories of primary sources:

- Firsthand accounts of historic events by witnesses and participants. This category includes diary entries, letters, newspaper articles, oral-history interviews, memoirs, and legal testimony.
- Documents representing the official views of the nation's leaders or of their political opponents. These include court decisions, policy statements, political speeches, party platforms, petitions, legislative debates, press releases, and federal and state laws.

- Government statistics and reports on such topics as birth, employment, marriage, death, and taxation.
- Advertisers' images and jingles. Although designed to persuade consumers to purchase commodities or to adopt specific attitudes, advertisements can also be valuable sources of information about popular beliefs and concerns.
- Works of art, including paintings, symphonies, play scripts, photographs, murals, novels, and poems.
- The products of mass culture: cartoons, comic books, movies, radio scripts, and popular songs.
- Material artifacts. These are everyday objects that survived from the period in question. Examples include household appliances and furnishings, recipes, and clothing.
- Secondary sources. In some cases, secondary sources may be treated as primary sources. For example, from 1836 to 1920, public schools across America purchased 122 million copies of a series of textbooks called the McGuffey Reader. Although current textbooks have more instructional value, the Reader is an invaluable primary source. It provides important insights into the unifying morals and cultural values that shaped the worldview of several generations of Americans, who differed in ethnicity, race, class, and religion.

Each of the above-mentioned categories of primary sources reveals different types of historical information. A politician's diary, memoirs, or collection of letters, for example, often provide students with the politicians' unguarded, private thoughts and emotions concerning daily life and public events. Though these documents may be a truer reflection of the person's character and aspirations, students must keep in mind that when people write about themselves, they tend to put themselves at the center of the historical event or cast themselves in the best possible light. On the other hand, the politician's public speeches may be more cautious, less controversial, and limited to advancing his or her political party's goals or platform.

Like personal diaries, advertisements reveal other types of historical information. What information does the WAVES poster on this page reveal?

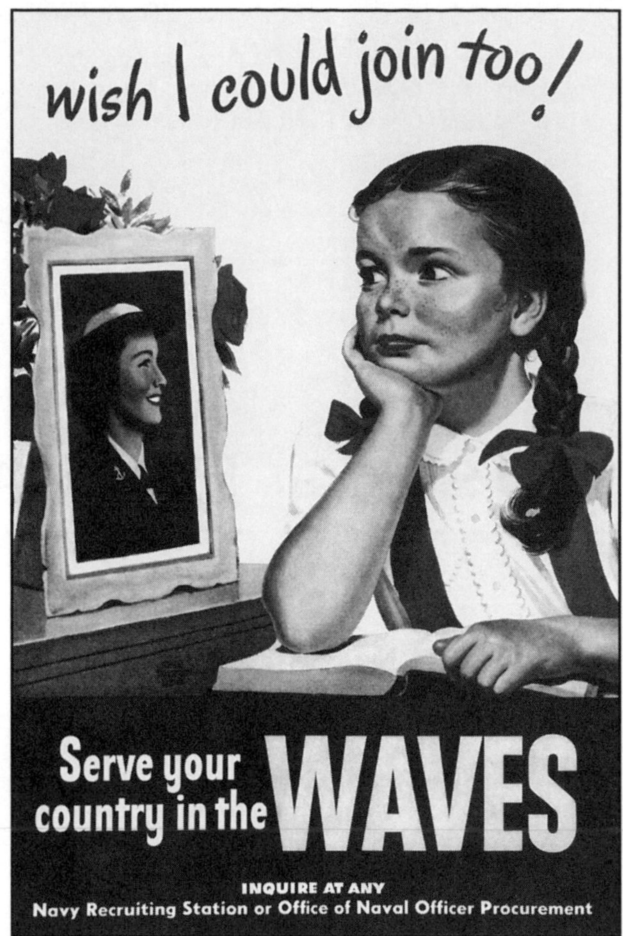

COURTESY OF THE NAVAL HISTORICAL FOUNDATION. REPRODUCED BY PERMISSION.

John Phillip Faller, a prolific commercial artist known for his *Saturday Evening Post* covers, designed this recruitment poster in 1944. It was one of over three hundred posters he produced for the U.S. Navy while enrolled in that service during World War II. The purpose of the poster was to encourage women to enlist in the WAVES (Women Accepted for Volunteer Emergency Service), a women's auxiliary to the Navy established in 1942. It depicts a schoolgirl gazing admiringly at a photograph of a proud, happy WAVE (perhaps an older sister), thus portraying the military service as an appropriate and admirable aspiration for women during wartime. However, what type of military service? Does the poster encourage women to enlist in military combat like World War II male recruitment posters? Does it reflect gender bias? What does this poster reveal about how the military and society in general feel about women in the military? Does the poster reflect current military and societal attitudes toward women in the military? How many women joined the WAVES? What type of duties did they perform?

Like personal diaries, photographs reveal other types of historical information. What information does the next photograph reveal?

Today, we take electricity for granted. However, in 1935, although 90 percent of city dwellers in America had electricity, only 10 percent of rural Americans did. Private utility companies refused to string electric lines

THE LIBRARY OF CONGRESS.

to isolated farms, arguing that the endeavor was too expensive and that most farmers were too poor to afford it anyway. As part of the Second New Deal, President Franklin Delano Roosevelt issued an executive order creating the Rural Electrification Administration (REA). The REA lent money at low interest rates to utility companies to bring electricity to rural America. By 1950, 90 percent of rural America had electricity. This photograph depicts a 1930s tenant farmer's house in Greene County, Georgia. Specifically, it shows a brand-new electric meter on the wall. The picture presents a host of questions: What was rural life like without electricity? How did electricity impact the lives of rural Americans, particularly rural Georgians? How many rural Georgians did not have electricity in the 1930s? Did Georgia have more electricity-connected farms than other Southern states? What was the poverty rate in rural Georgia, particularly among rural African Americans? Did rural electricity help lift farmers out of poverty?

Like personal diaries, official documents reveal other types of historical information. What information does the next document, a memo, reveal?

From the perspective of the early twenty-first century, in a democratic society, integration of the armed services seems to have been inevitable. For much of American history, however, African Americans were prevented from joining the military, and when they did enlist they were segregated into black units. In 1940, of the nearly 170,000-man Navy, only 4,007, or 2.3 percent, were African American personnel. The vast majority of these men worked in the mess halls as stewards—or, as labeled by the black press, "seagoing bellhops." In this official document, the chairman of the General Board refers to compliance with a directive that would enlist African Americans into positions of "unlimited general service." Who issued the directive? What was the motivation behind the new directive? Who were the members of the General Board? How much authority did they wield? Why did the Navy restrict African Americans to the "messman branch"? Notice the use of the term "colored race." Why was this term used and what did it imply? What did the board conclude? When did the Navy become integrated? Who was primarily responsible for integrating the Navy?

G.B. No. 421
(Serial No. 201)
SECRET

Feb 3, 1942

From: Chairman General Board.
To: Secretary of the Navy.

Subject: Enlistment of men of colored race to other than Messman branch.

Ref: (a) SecNav let. (SC)P14-4/MM (03200A)/Gen of Jan 16, 1942.

1. The General Board, complying with the directive contained in reference (a), has given careful attention to the problem of enlisting in the Navy, men of the colored race in other than the messman branch.

2. The General Board has endeavored to examine the problem placed before it in a realistic manner.

A. Should negroes be enlisted for unlimited general service?

(a) Enlistment for general service implies that the individual may be sent anywhere, - to any ship or station where he is needed. Men on board ship live in particularly close association; in their messes, one man sits beside another; their hammocks or bunks are close together; in their common tasks they work side by side; and in particular tasks such as those of a gun's crew, they form a closely knit, highly coordinated team. How many white men would choose, of their own accord, that their closest associates in sleeping quarters, at mess, and in a gun's crew should be of another race? How many would accept such conditions, if required to do so, without resentment and just as a matter of course? The General Board believes that the answer is "Few, if any," and further believes that if the issue were forced, there would be a lowering of contentment, teamwork and discipline in the service.

(b) One of the tennets of the recruiting service is that each recruit for general service is potentially a leading petty officer. It is true that some men never do become petty officers, and that when recruiting white men, it is not possible to establish which will be found worthy of and secure promotion and which will not. If negroes are recruited for general service, it can be said at once that few will obtain advancement to petty officers. With every desire to be fair, officers and leading petty officers in general will not recommend negroes for promotion to positions of authority over white men.

- 1 -

The General Board is convinced that the enlistment of negroes for unlimited general service is unadvisable.

B. Should negroes be enlisted in general service but detailed in special ratings or for special ships or units?

(a) The ratings now in use in the naval service cover every phase of naval activity, and no new ratings are deemed necessary merely to promote the enlistment of negroes.

(b) At first thought, it might appear that assignment of negroes to certain vessels, and in particular to small vessels of the patrol type, would be feasible. In this connection, the following table is of interest:

Type of Ship	Total Crew	Men in Pay Grades 1 to 4	Men in Pay Grades 5 to 7 (Non-rated)
Battleship	1892	666	1226
Light Cruiser (10,000 ton)	988	365	623
Destroyer (1630 ton)	206	109	97
Submarine	54	47	7
Patrol Boat (180 foot)	55	36	19
Patrol Boat (110 foot)	20	15	5

NOTE: Pay grades 1 to 4 include Chief Petty Officers and Petty Officers, 1st, 2nd and 3rd Class; also Firemen, 1st Class and a few other ratings requiring length of service and experience equal to that required for qualification of Petty Officers, 3rd class. Pay grades 5 to 7 include all other non-rated men and recruits.

There are no negro officers and so few negro petty officers in the Navy at present that any vessels to which negroes might be assigned must have white officers and white petty officers. Examination of the table shows the small number of men in other than petty officer ratings that might be assigned to patrol vessels and indicates to the General Board that such assignments would not be happy ones. The assignment of negroes to the larger ships, where well over one-half of the crews are non-rated men, with mixture of whites and negroes, would inevitably lead to discontent on the part of one or the other, resulting in clashes and lowering of the efficiency of the vessels and of the Navy.

DOWNGRADED AT 3 YEAR INTERVALS;
DECLASSIFIED AFTER 12 YEARS
DOD DIR 5200.10 NARS-NT

DOWNGRADED AND DECLASSIFIED

- 2 -

COURTESY OF THE HARRY S. TRUMAN LIBRARY. REPRODUCED BY PERMISSION.

The material collected in these volumes of *American Decades Primary Sources* are significant because they will introduce students to a wide variety of historical sources that were created by those who participated in or witnessed the historical event. These primary sources not only vividly describe historical events, but also reveal the subjective perceptions and biases of their authors. Students should read these documents "actively," and with the contextual assistance of the introductory material, history will become relevant and entertaining.

—Paul G. Connors

Chronology of Selected World Events Outside the United States, 1900–1909

1900

- Marie Curie discovers that an atom can spontaneously break apart, releasing energy, in what becomes known as radiation.
- Sigmund Freud publishes *Die Traumdeutung,* later translated as *The Interpretation of Dreams.*
- José Enrique Rodó publishes *Ariel,* a work that heightens anti-U.S. sentiment among South American intellectuals.
- At the Paris Exposition, the elevator is unveiled to the public.
- On January 1, Britain declares northern Nigeria a protectorate, meaning that Britain governed northern Nigeria but did not allow its people to govern themselves.
- On January 31, John Sholto Douglas, eighth Marquess of Queensbury, dies. In 1867, Douglas had established a set of rules for the sport of boxing: the Queensbury rules.
- On February 27, a group of liberals found the British Labour Representation Labour Committee, which would become the Labour Party.
- On February 28, British forces under the command of Redvers Buller relieve the Boer siege of Ladysmith in South Africa.
- On April 7, the ministers of Germany, France, Britain, and the United States issue an ultimatum to the Chinese government, giving it two months to suppress the Boxer uprising.
- On April 14, the president of France opens the Paris International Exhibition, which covers 547 acres.
- On April 22, the French defeat Rabah Zubayr, conqueror of the Sudan, in the Battle of Kusseri, in present-day Chad.
- On April 26, fire destroys the Canadian cities of Ottawa and Hull. Fire ravages five square miles of buildings, causes $15 million in damage, and leaves twelve thousand people homeless.
- In May, the Police Regulations ban collective bargaining and the right to strike in Japan.
- In May, the Russians occupy Manchuria, and their forces massacre forty-five thousand Chinese inhabitants.
- On May 17, British forces break the siege of Mafeking, South Africa, after 217 days.
- On May 20, the second Olympic Games of the modern era open in Paris. More than one thousand athletes from twenty-two nations compete.
- On May 24, Great Britain annexes the Orange Free State in South Africa.
- On June 12, the German Reichstag announces its intent to expand its naval fleet by thirty-eight battleships over twenty years.
- On June 13, the Boxer Rebellion in China expands into an attack against foreigners within China.
- On July 2, a Zeppelin airship lifts off on its maiden voyage.
- On July 9, Britain establishes the Commonwealth of Australia, effective January 1, 1901.
- On July 29, Umberto of Italy, king since 1878, is assassinated and is succeeded by his son, Victor Emmanuel III, who will remain titular ruler of Italy until 1946, though the fascists will erode his power in the 1920s.
- On August 31, British troops occupy Johannesburg in southern Africa.
- On October 18, Bernhard von Bülow becomes chancellor of Germany, succeeding Chlodwig Karl Hohenlohe, who resigned two days earlier.
- On December 14, German physicist Max Planck announces the quantum theory: energy is not a continuum but instead comes in discrete units called quanta.

1901

- The Trans-Siberian railway links Moscow with the Pacific at Port Arthur in Manchuria, stimulating trade east and west.
- Britain annexes Baluchistan, parts of present-day Pakistan and Iran.
- On March 23, U.S. Marines capture Emilio Aguinaldo, leader of an insurrection in the Philippines against U.S. rule.
- In June, the Cuban Congress adopts a new constitution under Platt Amendment, which grants the United States a naval base and trade rights.
- In September, Vladimir Lenin founds the Socialist Revolutionary Party of Russia.
- On September 7, the Boxer Rebellion in China ends with the signing of the Peace of Peking between China and Britain, France, Russia and the U.S.
- On November 18, the U.S. and Britain negotiate the Hay-Pauncefote Treaty, authorizing construction of the Panama Canal by the United States and ending British treaty rights in the region.
- In December, the Royal Academy of Sweden awards the first Nobel Prizes, which engineer Alfred Nobel had established with a bequest, in physics (Wilhelm Röntgen), chemistry (Jacobus Hendricus van't Hoff), and physiology or medicine (Emil von Behring).
- On December 10, French poet and writer Sully Prudhomme receives the first Nobel Prize in literature.
- On December 10, Jean-Henri Dunant, Swiss founder of the International Red Cross, and Frédéric Passy, French founder of the International League of Peace, share the first Nobel Peace Prize.

1902

- French composer Claude Debussy composes *Pelléas et Mélisande.*
- In 1902 Dutch physician Eugene Dubois withdraws Java Man from scientific scrutiny, stung by criticism from Henry Fairfield Osborn at the American Museum of Natural History that Java Man is the ancestor of the gibbon rather than of humans.
- Polish-born novelist Joseph Conrad publishes "Heart of Darkness.," a novella that exposes the savagery of European colonialism.
- The *Times Literary Supplement* of London is founded.
- In separate experiments, English physicist Oliver Heaviside and British American electrical engineer Arthur Kennelly discover the existence of an electrified layer of the earth's atmosphere.
- In April, Russia agrees to remove its forces from Manchuria under the terms of the Russo-Japanese Convention.
- On April 15, troops loyal to Czar Nicholas II crush a peasant uprising in Russia.
- On April 20, at an exhibition of La Société Nationale des Beaux Arts in Paris, the Art Nouveau style, whose influence will pervade everything from painting to interior design to the subway entrances of the Paris Métro, is on display.
- In May, British physicists Ernest Rutherford and Frederick Soddy publish an article that describes radioactivity as the release of energy from the nucleus of an atom.
- On May 7, a volcanic eruption on the island of Saint Vincent, in the Windward Islands, kills two thousand inhabitants.
- On May 8, the eruption of Mount Pelée, on the island of Martinique in the Windward Islands, sends a cloud of ash, steam, and gas onto the city of Saint Pierre, killing thirty thousand people.
- On May 20, voters elect Tomás Estrada Palma first president of the independent Republic of Cuba, marking the end of U.S. occupation following the Spanish-American War.
- On May 31, the Peace of Vereeniging ends the Boer War in South Africa.
- In December, British engineers complete the Aswan Dam in Egypt.
- On December 7, Great Britain and Germany demand reparations from Venezuela following a violent takeover of the government in 1899.
- On December 10, German historian Theodor Mommsen, a scholar of ancient Rome, receives the Nobel Prize in literature.
- On December 13, Germany and Britain blockade Venezuela and begin bombarding its forts as punishment for Venezuela's failure to make payments on its international debt.
- On December 18, the Education Act extends primary education to all children in England and Wales.

1903

- Willem Einthoven, a Dutch physiologist, develops the string galvanometer, a forerunner of his electrocardiogram (EKG).
- In January, Canada and the United States settle their border dispute over Alaska.
- On January 19, the first radio message is transmitted from the United States to England.
- On March 20, French painter Henri Matisse exhibits his paintings at the Salon des Indépendants in Paris.
- In April, Russian physiologist Ivan Pavlov reports his experiments in behavior and "conditioned reflexes."
- In April, Russian anti-Semites kill forty-five Russian Jews and destroy fifteen hundred Jewish homes in a three-day pogrom in Kishinev, Bessarabia.
- In May, Norwegian explorer Roald Amundsen begins the first successful voyage through the Northwest Passage, the narrow sea connecting the Atlantic and Pacific Oceans.
- In July, Leo XIII, elected Pope in 1878, dies. In August, the College of the Cardinals elect Pius X his successor.
- On July 30, the Russian Social Democratic Party splits into two wings, the Mensheviks and the more radical Bolsheviks, during a meeting in London. Vladimir Lenin, Leon Trotsky and Joseph Stalin jockey for power among the Bolsheviks.
- In August, Marcel Garin of France wins the first Tour de France, the world's most prestigious bicycle race.
- In October, British feminist Emmeline Pankhurst founds the Women's Social and Political Union.

- On November 3, the U.S. warship *Nashville* arrives off the coast of Colón, Colombia. Colombia refuses President Theodore Roosevelt permission to construct the Panama Canal.
- On November 6, Panama declares its independence from Colombia as a U.S. protectorate.
- On November 18, the Hay-Bunau-Varilla Treaty between Panama and the United States cedes control of the Panama Canal Zone to the United States.
- On December 10, Norwegian writer Bjørnstjerne Bjørnson wins the Nobel Prize in literature.
- On December 17, the Wright brothers fly successfully at Kitty Hawk, North Carolina.

1904

- Joseph Conrad publishes *Nostromo.*
- The Rolls-Royce automobile company begins manufacturing cars in Britain.
- The Abbey Theatre opens in Dublin, Ireland.
- Russian playwright Anton Chekhov writes *The Cherry Orchard.*
- Chemist Francis S. Kipping develops the polymer silicone.
- In January, British scientist John A. Fleming invents the diode vacuum tube, a crucial step in the development of radio.
- From February 8 to February 9, the Russo-Japanese War begins when the Japanese attack the Russian fleet. Japan declares war on 10 February.
- On April 8, France and Britain sign the Entente Cordiale after resolving territorial disagreements over Egypt, Newfoundland, Morocco, and Siam.
- On May 17, France and the Vatican quarrel over who controls the Catholic Church in France.
- On June 2, Henri Matisse stages an exhibit at Galeries Vollard, Paris.
- In July, French sculptor Auguste Rodin creates one of his best-known works, *The Thinker.*
- From July 1 to November 23, Saint Louis, Missouri, hosts the Summer Olympic Games.
- On July 4, U.S. military and civil engineers begin to dig the Panama Canal.
- On July 7, France prohibits religious orders from teaching in schools and universities.
- In August, Italian Giacomo Puccini composes his opera *Madame Butterfly.*
- On September 7, Britain forces the Dalai Lama, the ruler of Tibet, to sign a treaty granting Britain trading rights in three cities.
- On October 3, the Hottentots and Herero, the indigenous peoples of southwest Africa, rebel against German colonial rule.
- On October 18, France establishes Dakar as the capital of French West Africa.
- On October 21, the Russian navy fires on British fishing vessels in the North Sea, mistaking them for Japanese ships.
- On December 10, French writer Frédéric Mistral and Spanish writer José Echegaray y Eizaguirre share the Nobel Prize in literature.
- On December 12, Ivan Pavlov receives the Nobel Prize in physiology or medicine for describing the physiology of digestion.

1905

- French composer Claude Debussy composes *La Mer.*
- The Fauves (wild beasts), a group of painters led by Henri Matisse and André Derain, stages an exhibition at the Salon d'Automne in Paris.
- On January 1, the Japanese capture the Russian city of Port Arthur.
- On January 22, troops loyal to Czar Nicholas II fire on demonstrators in Saint Petersburg, Russia, in the "Bloody Sunday" massacre, sparking the Russian Revolution of 1905.
- On February 17, Grand Duke Serge, the governor of Moscow, is assassinated in the Kremlin.
- On March 3, Czar Nicholas II of Russia promises religious reforms.
- On May 27, Japan destroys the Russian navy in the Battle of Tsushima.
- On June 7, Norway's parliament dissolves the union of Norway and Sweden under Oscar II, king of Sweden.
- From June 27 to June 28, the crew of the Russian ship *Potemkin* mutiny in the harbor at Odessa.
- On June 30, Albert Einstein publishes a paper announcing his special theory of relativity.
- In July, Muslims (Maji-Maji) in German East Africa revolt against German control.
- On July 3, both houses of the French legislature endorse a law separating church and state.
- In August, engineers complete the Trans-Siberian Railroad between Moscow and Vladivostok on the Pacific coast.
- On August 20, Chinese nationalist leader Sun Yat-Sen issues his Three People's Principles—nationalism, democracy, and livelihood for the people—in his first public statement of his philosophy after a decade of secret activities.
- On September 1, Britain establishes Alberta and Saskatchewan as provinces of Canada.
- On September 5, the Treaty of Portsmouth, brokered by U.S. President Theodore Roosevelt, gives Japan control of Korea and rights to Port Arthur and Sakhalin Island in recognition of Japan's victory over Russia in the Russo-Japanese War.
- On September 27, Norway gains independence from Sweden.
- On September 27, Albert Einstein publishes a paper announcing that mass and energy can transpose one into the other according to the equation: energy equals mass times the speed of light squared ($E = mc^2$).
- In October, Bolshevik leader Leon Trotsky establishes the first Russian soviet, a council of workers, in Saint Petersburg.

- On October 17, Czar Nicholas II issues the October Manifesto, promising civil liberties and democratic institutions in Russia.
- On November 28, Irish nationalists establish the Sinn Féin (Ourselves Alone) Party, which aims to end British rule in Ireland.
- In December, Albert Einstein publishes two papers, one on the photoelectric effect and the other on Brownian motion.
- On December 4, Arthur Balfour, Britain's Conservative prime minister, resigns after his party splits between protectionists and advocates of free trade.
- From December 4 to December 5, a congress meeting in Vilnius declares Lithuania independent from Russia.
- On December 5, police loyal to Czar Nicholas II arrest all 230 members of the Saint Petersburg Soviet in an attempt to silence opposition to the czar.
- On December 9, the law in France separating church and state takes effect.
- On December 10, Polish writer Henryk Sienkiewicz receives the Nobel Prize in literature.
- On December 12, German physician Robert Koch receives the Nobel Prize in physiology or medicine for discovering that a microbe causes tuberculosis.
- On December 15, Russian troops crush a citizen uprising in Moscow.

1906

- Explorer Roald Amundsen determines the position of the magnetic North Pole.
- Spanish architect Antonio Gaudi begins constructing Casa Milá in Barcelona.
- The Simplon Tunnel, running 12.3 miles between Brig, Switzerland, and Isella, Italy, opens as the world's longest railway tunnel.
- *Tears of Blood* by Yi Injik, generally recognized as the first modern novel in Korean, is published in serialized form in a Korean newspaper.
- Le Mans, France, hosts that country's first Grand Prix auto race.
- On January 12, the Liberal Party wins in a landslide in Britain, and, led by Prime Minister Henry Campbell-Bannerman, inaugurates a period of social reforms.
- In February, German physicist Walther Hermann Nernst develops the third law of thermodynamics, which states that the entropy (the amount of disorder) of a crystal is zero at zero degrees Kelvin.
- In February, Pope Pius X, in the encyclical *Vehementer Nos,* condemns the separation of church and state in France.
- On February 10, Britain launches the HMS *Dreadnought,* prototype of the battleship.
- In March, Britain agrees to pay Dutch residents of South Africa compensation for damages from the Boer War.
- On March 7, Finland allows everyone older than twenty-four to vote, becoming the first nation to grant women the vote.
- On March 10, a coal-mine explosion in Courières, France, kills more than one thousand miners.
- On April 6, Mount Vesuvius erupts, destroying several towns near Naples, Italy.
- On April 7, France and Spain agree at the Algeciras Conference, which had begun on January 16, to split Morocco between them.
- On May 6, Czar Nicholas II issues the Fundamental Laws, which restore most of the imperial powers he had surrendered in the October Manifesto.
- On May 10, the Duma, the Russian parliament, first meets.
- On May 19, King Carlos I of Portugal names Jõao Franco, a monarchist, prime minister.
- In June, anti-Semites attack Jews throughout Russia.
- In July, a peace treaty ends war between Guatemala, El Salvador, and Honduras in Central America.
- On July 4, Britain, France, and Italy agree to guarantee the independence of Ethiopia.
- On July 9, troops loyal to Czar Nicholas II prevent the Russian Duma from meeting. Nicholas declares martial law.
- On July 12, France's Supreme Court of Appeals acquits French officer Alfred Dreyfus of treason.
- On July 22, Nicholas II dissolves the Duma and begins a crackdown on dissenters.
- On August 16, an earthquake in Valparaiso and Santiago, Chile, kills twenty thousand people and causes $300 million in property damage.
- In September, the Chinese Imperial Court agrees to the gradual adoption of a constitution.
- On September 29, U.S. troops occupy Cuba and repress a liberal uprising against the government of Tomás Estrada Palma.
- In October, German bacteriologist August von Wassermann and dermatologist Albert Neisser develop a test for diagnosing syphilis.
- In October, the U.S. installs in Cuba a provisional government led by Charles Magoon.
- On October 1, Great Britain, Egypt, and Turkey settle their boundary dispute over the Sinai Peninsula, most of which remains under Turkish control.
- On October 18, Georges Clemenceau becomes premier of France for the first time.
- In November, British physicist Joseph John Thomson discovers gamma rays, a type of light invisible to humans.
- In November, Czar Nicholas II exiles Leon Trotsky, one of the leaders of the 1905 Russian Revolution, to Siberia.
- In December, Aga Khan forms the All-India Muslim League, demanding representative government and separate electorates for Muslims in India.
- In December, Giosuè Carducci of Italy receives the Nobel Prize in literature.
- On December 21, the Trade Disputes Act limits the liability of trade unions for damages resulting from strikes and makes picketing legal in Britain.
- On December 30, the shah of Persia (Iran), Muzaffer-ed-Din, grants the country its first constitution.

1907

- Austrian Gustav Mahler composes his Eighth Symphony, the "Symphony of a Thousand."
- Spaniard Pablo Picasso paints *Les Demoiselles d'Avignon,* an early work of the Cubist movement led by Pablo Picasso and Georges Braque.
- A secret Russo-Japanese agreement divides Manchuria between Russia and Japan and acknowledges Japanese control of Korea.
- On January 1, Austria grants universal suffrage.
- On January 14, an earthquake in Kingston, Jamaica, kills fourteen hundred people.
- On January 26, the premiere of Irish playwright John Millington Synge's *The Playboy of the Western World* at the Abbey Theatre in Dublin provokes public outrage.
- On February 26, Louis Botha, a Dutch settler, is elected prime minister of the Transvaal in southern Africa.
- On March 22, Morocco revolts against French rule.
- In June, Britain launches the *Mauritania,* the fastest ocean liner of the era, with a top speed of twenty-five knots, ushering in the age of elegant cruise ships.
- On June 14, Norway grants women the vote.
- In July, Britain grants the Orange Free State, settled by the Dutch, autonomy in South Africa.
- On August 10, the world's most grueling automobile race to date ends when Italy's Prince Borghese arrives in Paris, having driven eight thousand miles in sixty-two days from Peking (Beijing), China.
- On August 31, Russia and Britain agree to divide central Asia and Persia (Iran) into seperate "spheres of influence".
- In September, Maria Montessori, who had earlier pioneered the education of children with low capabilities, opens in Rome her first school for average children.
- On September 6, Pope Pius X in the encyclical *Pascendi Gregis* condemns modernism.
- On September 26, Britain elevates New Zealand from colony to dominion.
- On October 18, the Second International Peace Conference (which had begun on June 15) ends without accomplishing its main objective: the reduction of armaments.
- In December, British writer Rudyard Kipling receives the Nobel Prize in literature.
- On December 16, the "Great White Fleet," a flotilla of sixteen U.S. warships, begins a cruise around the world to demonstrate American naval power.

1908

- Hungarian composer Béla Bartók composes his First String Quartet.
- *Ecce Homo,* the autobiography of German philosopher and poet Friedrich Nietzsche, is published posthumously.
- Charles Pathé shows the first newsreel in a Paris theater.
- German chemist Fritz Haber synthesizes ammonia.
- On January 24, Robert Stephenson Smyth Baden-Powell forms the Boy Scouts.
- On February 20, Emilio Marinetti publishes the *Futurist Manifesto,* galvanizing a school of Italian artists fascinated with movement and action and scornful of past artistic achievements.
- On April 8, Herbert Asquith, chancellor of the exchequer, becomes prime minister of Britain following the resignation of Henry Campbell-Bannerman.
- From April 27 to October 31, London, England, hosts the fourth Summer Olympic Games of the modern era.
- On May 26, geologists discover oil in Persia (Iran), igniting an oil boom is western Asia and leading to the discovery of other oil deposits.
- On June 7, an earthquake kills eighty-three thousand Italians in Calabria and Sicily.
- On July 24, the "Young Turks" force Abdülhamid II, sultan of the Ottoman Empire, to restore the constitution of 1876.
- On July 25, Louis Blériot achieves the first crossing of the English Channel in a heavier-than-air machine.
- In August, Cuba holds the first general elections under U.S. supervision.
- In September, a cholera epidemic claims more than seventy-one hundred lives in Russia, with nearly two thousand deaths in Saint Petersburg alone.
- On October 5, Bulgaria declares independence from the Ottoman Empire.
- On October 6, Austria annexes the former Turkish provinces of Bosnia and Herzegovina, where tensions will precipitate the First World War in 1914.
- On October 12, the Cape Colony and Natal meet with the former Boer states of the Transvaal and Orange Free State to form the Union of South Africa.
- On October 18, Leopold II gives the Belgian parliament control over the Belgian Congo (in Africa), which he had held as a personal possession.
- On November 14, the Chinese government announces the deaths of Kuang Hsü, the Chinese emperor since 1875, and his empress, Tzu Hsi. Hsüan-T'ung, the emperor's infant nephew, becomes the last emperor of the Manchu dynasty.
- On November 30, Japan and the United States sign the Root-Takahira Agreement. Both nations pledge not to establish colonies in China and to respect each other's Pacific possessions.
- On December 11, German bacteriologist Paul Ehrlich shares the Nobel Prize in medicine with immunologist Elie Metchnikoff.
- On December 28, French Impressionist painter Henri Matisse publishes "Notes d'un peintre" in *La Grande Revue,* setting forth his principles of art.

1909

- Rafael Reyes Prieto is ousted as president of Colombia, following his recognition of the independence of Panama in a treaty with the United States.

- On January 1, astronomers in London report the possibility of a planet in the solar system beyond Neptune.
- On January 9, British explorer Ernest Henry Shackleton misses reaching the South Pole by one hundred miles.
- On January 18, brewers in New Zealand decide to abolish barmaids and to ban women from purchasing alcohol in bars.
- On February 9, a British court forbids a wife from divorcing her husband, even if he leaves her.
- On March 27, German writer Rudolf C. Eucken delivers his Nobel lecture. He won the 1908 Nobel Prize for literature but did not receive the award until 1909.
- On April 6, Robert Peary reaches the North Pole, though his achievement will remain in dispute for decades.
- On April 13, Armenians rebel against Ottoman rule following a massacre by the sultan's troops at Adana in southern Turkey.
- On April 18, Pope Pius X beatifies Joan of Arc in Rome.
- On May 18, Sergey Diaghilev's Ballets Russes perform for the first time in Paris.
- On May 25, a Russian court jails the publisher of Leo Tolstoy's "Thou Shalt Not Kill" but does not prosecute Tolstoy, whose eminence as a novelist makes him unassailable.
- On June 11, an earthquake in Provence, in southern France, kills sixty people.
- On June 26, the shah of Persia (Iran) annuls a new election law and postpones adoption of a constitution.
- In August Dutch zoologist Wilhelm Johannsen defines *gene, genotype,* and *phenotype.*
- In August, troops crush an uprising in Barcelona, Spain.
- On August 28, American Glenn Curtiss wins the first airplane race for the Gordon Bennett Cup in Rheims, France, with an average speed of 47 mph.
- On October 10, the execution of Spanish anarchist Francisco Ferrer ignites protests across Europe.
- On November 28, the French national assembly endorses a law granting pregnant women an eight-week leave from their jobs.
- On December 10, Selma Lagerlöf of Sweden receives the Nobel Prize in literature.

1

The Arts

Alice Wu

Entries are arranged in chronological order by date of primary source. For entries with one primary source, the entry title is the same as the primary source title. Entries with more than one primary source have an overall entry title, followed by the titles of the primary sources.

CHRONOLOGY

PRIMARY SOURCES

Important Events in The Arts, 1900–1909

1900

- *To Have and to Hold,* by Mary Johnston, and *Eben Holden* by Irving Bacheller are the best-sellers of 1900.
- The approval of the New York City audience has become the standard by which theater professionals measure their work—the rest of the nation is merely "the Road." More than five hundred New York shows go on the road in 1900.
- *Theatre Magazine,* edited by Arthur Hornblow, begins publication.
- The novelty of the "moving picture" phenomenon of the 1890s has worn off. The public is bored with the uninspired menu of news events, sight gags, panoramas, and camera tricks.
- Eastman Kodak introduces the Brownie Box camera at one dollar; Americans embrace the new hobby of amateur photography.
- The trademark and painting *His Master's Voice* first appears on record labels of the firm that later becomes the Victor Company.
- Brothers James Weldon and J. Rosamond Johnson compose "Lift Every Voice and Sing," a musical inspiration for African Americans.
- On January 3, Giuseppe Verdi's opera *Aida* (1871) is performed in New York.
- On February 5, Clyde Fitch's drama *Sappho* premieres in New York; police close it after twenty-nine performances, citing "immorality."
- On April 23, Buffalo Bill Cody's *Wild West Show* opens at Madison Square Garden.
- On April 30, railroad engineer Casey Jones is killed when he jams on the brakes of his wreck-bound train. His passengers' lives are saved, and Jones' exploit becomes the stuff of immediate legend when Wallace Saunders, an African American fellow worker, composes a song about him.
- In May, poet-dramatist William Vaughn Moody publishes "An Ode in Time of Hesitation" in *Atlantic Monthly* magazine. It is a thoughtful comment on American imperialism.
- On May 22, inventor Edwin S. Voter patents the "pneumatic piano attachment"; the Pianola, or player piano, soon becomes popular.
- On May 28, a posthumous exhibit of American landscape painter Frederic Church's works is mounted at the Metropolitan Museum of Art, New York.
- On June 15, Ignacy Paderewski, Polish pianist, composer, and statesman, sets up a ten thousand dollar fund for best orchestral works by American composers.
- On October 15, Mark Twain returns from a nine-year journey abroad. Five days later, he receives an honorary degree from Yale University.
- Boston's 2,500-seat Symphony Hall opens.
- On November 12, *Florodora,* one of the most popular stage musicals of the decade, debuts in New York. It has a run of 505 performances.
- On November 16, German conductor Fritz Scheel directs the first concert of the newly formed Philadelphia Orchestra at the Philadelphia Academy of Music.
- On November 20, Sarah Bernhardt arrives for her first American tour since 1886. At age fifty-six, she plays Hamlet.

MOVIES: *Adventures of Jones* (series), produced, directed and acted by James White for Edison; *Battle of Mafeking, Filipinos Retreat from the Trenches,* and *Panorama of the Paris Exposition from the Seine,* filmed and produced by James White for Edison; *Beheading a Chinese Prisoner* and *Chinese Massacring Christians,* produced by Sigmund Lubin; *Cinderella,* produced and directed by Georges Méliès; *The Clown and the Alchemist* and *A Visit to the Spiritualist,* produced and filmed by J. Stuart Blackton and Albert E. Smith for Vitagraph; *The Downward Path,* produced by Wallace McCutcheon and filmed by Arthur Marvin for Biograph; *Faust and Marguerite,* produced and directed by Edwin S. Porter; *Fire Engines at Work, The Gans-McGovern Fight,* and *Something Good—Negro Kiss,* produced by William Selig; *Love in the Suburbs,* filmed by G. W. "Billy" Bitzer for Biograph; *Maude's Naughty Little Brother,* produced and filmed by J. Stuart Blackton and Albert E. Smith for Vitagraph.

FICTION: L. Frank Baum, *The Wonderful Wizard of Oz*; Charles Waddell Chesnutt, *The House Behind the Cedars*; Joseph Conrad, *Lord Jim*; Stephen Crane, *Whilomville Stories*; Theodore Dreiser, *Sister Carrie*; Paul Laurence Dunbar, *The Strength of Gideon and Other Stories*; Finley Peter Dunne, *Mr. Dooley's Philosophy*; Pauline Elizabeth Hopkins, *Contending Forces: A Romance Illustrative of Negro Life North and South*; Booth Tarkington, *Monsieur Beaucaire*; Harriet Prescott Spofford, *Old Madame and Other Stories*; Mark Twain, *The Man that Corrupted Hadleyburg.*

POPULAR SONGS: "A Bird in a Gilded Cage," music by Harry von Tilzer, lyrics by Arthur Lamb; "I Can't Tell Why I Love You, But I Do," music by Charles Previn, lyrics by Gus Edwards; "Rosie, You Are My Posie (Ma Blushin' Rosie)," music by John Stromberg, lyrics by Edgar Smith; "Voodoo Man," music and lyrics by Bert Williams and George Walker, "The Maple Leaf Rag," music by Scott Joplin.

1901

- *Gaustark* by George Barr McCutcheon, *Mrs. Wiggs of the Cabbage Patch* by Alice Hegan Rice, and *The Crisis* by Winston Churchill are the best-sellers of 1901.

- As Scott Joplin's popular "The Entertainer" helps to create an original American musical art form, the American Federation of Musicians passes an anti-ragtime resolution, calling for "every effort to suppress and discourage . . . such musical trash."
- The Harvard Theatre Collection is opened; it is the first dance and theater-research collection in the world.
- The Rudolf Wurlitzer Company announces a new coin-operated music machine, the Tonophone.
- Thomas Edison adds a device to his motion picture camera that allows it to "pan".
- Clyde Fitch, the first American playwright to become a millionaire in his profession, has five plays appearing on Broadway in 1901.
- Autobiographies of African American leader Booker T. Washington *(Up From Slavery)* and of immigrant reformer Jacob Riis *(The Making of an American)* are published.
- Experimental composer Charles Ives (1874–1954) continues work on his *Songs* and completes his *Symphony No. 2*; it does not premier for sixty years.
- On February 2, Giacomo Puccini's opera *Tosca* (1900) debuts in New York.
- On February 4, Clyde Fitch's *Captain Jinks of the Horse Marines* opens on Broadway for 192 performances, making twenty-one-year-old Ethel Barrymore a star.
- On February 21, vaudeville performers organize and strike to protest the inclusion of moving pictures on vaudeville bills. The Eastern Association of Vaudeville Managers adds more films to replace the striking acts.
- On March 13, Andrew Carnegie, steel baron and philanthropist, gives $5.2 million to fund a New York public library system.
- On April 14, police enforce New York City's blue laws by arresting actors at the Academy of Music for appearing in costume on Sunday.
- On May 1, the Pan-American Exposition, an exhibition of the trends, developments, inventions and attitudes of the McKinley era, opens in Buffalo, New York.
- On October 16, new President Theodore Roosevelt invites author Booker T. Washington to dinner at the White House. Much of the nation is shocked; within two weeks race riots occur in New Orleans. Thirty-four people are killed.
- On October 20, *The New York Times* celebrates fifty years in publication.

MOVIES: *Bluebeard,* produced by Georges Méliès; *Couche Dance on the Midway* and *Wedding Procession in Cairo,* produced by Sigmund Lubin; *Coaching Party* and *Yosemite Valley,* filmed by Robert K. Bonine for Biograph; *The Finish of Bridget McKeen, Kansas Saloon Smashers,* and *Laura Comstock's Bag-Punching Dog,* filmed and designed by Edwin S. Porter and George S. Fleming for Edison; *In the Forbidden City,* filmed by C. Fred Ackerman for Biograph; *Opening—Pan-American Exposition, President McKinley's Speech at the Pan-American Exposition,* and *Complete Funeral Cortege [McKinley] at Canton, Ohio,* produced by James White for Edison; *Stock Yard Series (Stunning Cattle, Koshering Cattle, Dressing Beef etc.),* produced by William Selig.

FICTION: Gertrude Bonnin (Zitkala-Sa) *Old Indian Legends*; Charles Waddell Chesnutt, *The Marrow of Tradition*; Paul Laurence Dunbar, *The Fanatics*; Finley Peter Dunne, *Mr. Dooley's Opinions*; Henry James, *The Sacred Font*; Frank Norris, *The Octopus*; Alice Hegan Race, *Mrs. Wiggs of the Cabbage Patch.*

POPULAR SONGS: "Boola Boola," music and lyrics by Allan M. Hirsch; "Hello Central, Give Me Heaven, For My Mama's There," music and lyrics by Charles K. Harris; "I'm Captain Jinks of the Horse Marines," music by T. MacLaglen, lyrics by William H. Lingard; "Just A-Wearyin' For You," music and lyrics by Carrie Jacobs Bond; "The Maiden With the Dreamy Eyes" and "My Castle on the Nile," music by J. Rosamond Johnson, lyrics by Robert Cole and James Weldon Johnson; "Mighty Lak a Rose," music by Ethelbert Nevin, lyrics by Frank L. Stanton; "Tell Me Pretty Maiden," music by Leslie Stuart, lyrics by Owen Hall and Frank Pixley.

1902

- *The Virginian* by Owen Wister is the best-seller of 1902.
- For the first time, a well-known stage actor, Kyrle Bellew, agrees to appear in a motion picture.
- Helen Keller publishes *The Story of My Life.* The autobiography of the twenty-two-year-old woman, blind and deaf since the age of nineteen months, becomes a best-seller.
- *McClure's* magazine begins publishing Ida Tarbell's and Lincoln Steffens's "muckraking" treatments of the oil industry and municipal corruption.
- *Appalachia,* a musical composition by British American Frederick Delius, introduces American folk-song motifs.
- Frederic Remington completes his *Comin' Through the Rye,* a bronze sculptural tribute to the American cowboy.
- Sheet music and player pianos gain nationwide popularity; Broadway scores and ragtime songs reach a wide market.
- Photographer Edouard (later Edward) Steichen opens a one-man show in Paris.
- Works such as *The Hand of Man* and *The Flat-Iron Building* establish Alfred Stieglitz as the foremost art photographer in America.
- On January 4, the Carnegie Institute is founded for research in the humanities and sciences.
- On January 13, the well-known British actress Mrs. Patrick Campbell makes her first performance in America in *Magda.*
- On March 7, J. Pierpont Morgan purchases the Garland collection of oriental porcelain, keeping it in the United States.
- On March 18, Italian opera singer Enrico Caruso and U.S. recording engineer Fred Gaisberg produce the tenor's first phonograph recording.
- On April 16, Tally's Electric Theater, the first theater expressly for the purpose of showing motion pictures, opens in Los Angeles.
- On April 30, Claude Debussy's *Pelleas et Melisande* premieres in Paris with Scots American Mary Garden singing the soprano lead.

- On September 29, Emile Zola (b. 1840), whose writing influenced American naturalist writers, dies in Paris.
- On October 4, Chicago's New Orpheon Theatre opens with the musical *Chow-Chow.*
- On October 23, Charles Dana Gibson, creator of the "Gibson Girl," whose looks dominate women's fashion in the early part of the decade, accepts a one hundred thousand-dollar contract to draw for *Life* and *Collier's* magazines.
- On November 8, Barnum and Bailey's Circus returns to the United States after a European triumph.
- On December 3, David Belasco premieres his spectacular melodrama *The Darling of the Gods* in New York at a cost of seventy-eight thousand dollars.
- On December 21, Chicago's La Salle Theatre opens.
- On December 29, *The Sultan of Sulu,* a George Ade musical, is one of the few shows to move successfully from Chicago to Broadway. The spoof of U.S. cultural imperialism enjoys an eight-month run.

MOVIES: *Alphonse and Gaston* (series), filmed by Robert K. Bonine for Biograph; *Appointment by Telephone* and *How They Do Things on the Bowery,* filmed by Edwin S. Porter for Edison; *Cake Walking Horse* and *Feeding the Rhinoceros,* produced by Sigmund Lubin; *"Foxy Grandpa"* (series), starring Joseph Hart and Carrie De Mar for Biograph; *The Great Sword Combat on the Stairs* (excerpt from the stage play *A Gentleman of France*), starring Kyrle Bellew, filmed by J. Stuart Blackton and Albert E. Smith for Vitagraph; *Prizefight in Coontown,* produced by William Selig; *Robinson Crusoe* and *A Trip to the Moon,* produced and filmed by Georges Méliès.

FICTION: Paul Laurence Dunbar, *The Sport of the Gods*; Finley Peter Dunne, *Observations by Mr. Dooley*; Hamlin Garland, *The Captain of the Gray-Horse Troop*; Ellen Glasgow, *The Battleground*; Joel Chandler Harris, *Gabriel Tolliver, A Story of Reconstruction*; Pauline Elizabeth Hopkins, *Hagar's Daughter: A Story of Southern Caste Prejudice* and *Winona: A Tale of Negro Life in the South and Southwest*; Henry James, *The Wings of the Dove*; Jack London, "To Light a Fire" and *A Daughter of the Snows*; Edith Wharton, *The Valley of Decision*; Owen Wister, *The Virginian.*

POPULAR SONGS: "Bill Bailey, Won't You Please Come Home?," music and lyrics by Hughie Cannon; "Down Where the Wurzburger Flows," music by Harry von Tilzer, lyrics by Vincent P. Bryan; "In the Good Old Summer Time," music by George Evans, lyrics by Ren Shields; "In the Sweet Bye and Bye," music by Harry von Tilzer, lyrics by Vincent P. Bryan; "The Mansion of Broken Hearts," music by Harry von Tilzer, lyrics by Arthur J. Lamb; "Please Go 'Way and Let Me Sleep," music and lyrics by Harry von Tilzer; "Under the Bamboo Tree," music by J. Rosamond Johnson, lyrics by Bob Cole.

1903

- The Columbia Company and Thomas Edison begin to release music recordings regularly.
- The sixteen-story Ingalls building in Cincinnati is the first skyscraper built with a reinforced concrete infrastructure.
- Author Gertrude Stein moves to Paris.
- W. E. B. Du Bois publishes *The Souls of Black Folk.*
- The Manhattan Opera House is completed.
- John Knowles Paine composes an American opera, *Azora.*
- British American designer Frederick Carder founds the Steuben Glass Works. Carder's coloring techniques soon rival Louis Comfort Tiffany's work.
- *The Great Train Robbery,* a twelve-minute, nine-scene film by Edwin S. Porter, shows audiences the potential of the moving picture. Its effective narrative and cinematic techniques make it the most popular movie of the decade and revitalize the motion picture industry.
- Professor George Pierce Baker offers the first playwriting and theater classes at Radcliffe College.
- In January, the first issue of Alfred Stieglitz's photography journal, *Camera Work,* appears.
- On January 21, the musical version of *The Wizard of Oz* debuts on Broadway; it runs for 293 performances.
- On February 18, *In Dahomey,* a musical with lyrics written by Paul Laurence Dunbar and acted by African Americans, opens at the New York Theater and scores a hit on Broadway.
- On May 6, Emma Lazarus's poem "The New Colossus" (1883) is affixed to the Statue of Liberty.
- On August 6, twenty-eight circus people are killed when two railroad cars collide in Durand, Michigan.
- On August 15, publisher Joseph Pulitzer gives $2 million to establish the Columbia University School of Journalism; a portion of the donation is used to establish the Pulitzer Prizes, which are first awarded for literature in 1918.
- On September 12, Scott Joplin's ragtime opera, *A Guest of Honor,* begins a Midwest tour. Internal difficulties cause cancellation in less than six weeks.
- On October 13, Victor Herbert's operetta *Babes In Toyland* opens in New York; it becomes one of the season's biggest hits.
- On October 27, Richard Jose, former minstrel singer, records "Silver Threads Among the Gold" for the Victor Talking Machine Company.
- On November 11, *Hiawatha,* a cantata composed by English composer Samuel Coleridge Taylor and based on Henry Wadsworth Longfellow's poem, premieres in Washington, D.C.
- On November 21, Italian tenor Enrico Caruso debuts at the Metropolitan Opera in New York; he appears regularly at the Met until 1920.
- On December 30, the Iroquois Theatre fire in Chicago claims 602 lives, prompting improved safety regulations throughout the country.

MOVIES: *American Soldier in Love and War,* produced by Biograph; *The Divorce,* produced by Wallace McCutcheon and Frank Marion for Biograph; *Don Quixote,* produced by Pathé; *The Great Train Robbery,* starring G. M. Anderson and Justus D. Barnes, produced and filmed by Edwin S. Porter for Edison; *Kit Carson* and *The Pioneers,* starring Kit Carson and produced by Wallace McCutcheon for Biograph; *"I Want My Dinner,"* starring Ross McCutcheon (age two), produced by Wallace McCutcheon and Frank Marion for Biograph; *The Kingdom of the Fairies,* produced by Georges Méliès; *Panoramic View of Multnomah Falls,* produced by William Selig; *Rip Van Winkle,* starring Joseph Jefferson, produced by Biograph; *The Runaway Match; or, Marriage by Motorcar,* produced by British Gaumont; *Sorting Refuse at Incinerating Plant, New York City,* produced and filmed by Edwin S. Porter and J. Blair Smith for Edison; *Uncle Tom's Cabin,* produced and filmed by Edwin S. Porter for Edison.

FICTION: Pauline Elizabeth Hopkins, *Of One Blood, or, The Hidden Self*; Paul Laurence Dunbar, *In Old Plantation Days*; Henry James, *The Ambassadors*; Frank Norris, *The Pit*; Jack London, *The Call of the Wild* and *People of the Abyss*; Kate Douglas Wiggin, *Rebecca of Sunnybrook Farm.*

POPULAR SONGS: "Bedelia," music by Jean Schwartz, lyrics by William Jerome; "Congo Love Song," music by J. Rosamond Johnson, lyrics by Robert Cole; "Dear Old Girl," music by Theodore F. Morse, lyrics by Richard and Henry Buck; "Good-Bye Eliza Jane," music by Harry von Tilzer, lyrics by Andrew B. Sterling; "Ida, Sweet as Apple Cider," music and lyrics by Eddie Leonard; "Something Doing," music by Scott Joplin, lyrics by Scott Hayden; "Sweet Adeline," music by Harry Armstrong, lyrics by Richard H. Gerard; "Under the Anheuser Busch," music by Harry von Tilzer, lyrics by Andrew B. Sterling.

1904

- *The Sea Wolf* by Jack London and *Freckles* by Gene Stratton Porter are the best-sellers of 1905.
- The "kickapoo" dance craze sweeps the nation.
- Sculptor Augustus Saint-Gaudens creates the General Sherman Memorial for Central Park, New York City.
- The National Academy of Arts and Letters is established; many creative artists oppose its conservative views.
- Ruth St. Denis abandons a theater career to concentrate on achievements in modern dance.
- The first two-sided record disks are put on the American market by Columbia; they retail at $1.50.
- On January 5, Owen Wister's stage adaptation of *The Virginian,* starring Dustin Farnum, opens in Manhattan. It runs more than seventeen weeks.
- On February 1, Enrico Caruso makes his first phonograph recording in the United States.
- On April 2, the musical *Piff! Paff! Pouf!,* starring popular comic actor Eddie Foy, opens on Broadway.
- On April 30, the Saint Louis World's Fair opens.
- On May 23, the musical play *The Southerners,* score by African American composer Will Marion Cook, premieres in New York with a mixed-race cast.
- On September 1, Helen Keller graduates from Radcliffe College.
- On September 3, *Mrs. Wiggs of the Cabbage Patch* opens on the New York stage, proving to be as popular a play as it was a novel.
- On October 4, French sculptor Frédéric-Auguste Bartholdi, designer of the Statue of Liberty, dies in Paris.
- Chicago's $1 million Orchestra Hall, completed October 14 in the French Renaissance style by architect Daniel Burnham, opens with a dedicatory concert.

MOVIES: *Annie's Love Story, Cowboys and Indians, Barnum's Trunk,* and *In the Strike,* produced by Pathé; *Avenging a Crime, or, Burned at the Stake, Just Like a Girl,* and *Trials and Troubles of an Automobilist,* produced by William Paley and William F. Stiener; *The Barber of Sevilla and An Impossible Voyage,* produced by Georges Méliès; *Boxing Horses—Luna Park, Coney Island, Elephants Shooting the Chutes at Luna Park, Opening Ceremonies, New York Subway, October 27, 1904,* produced by Edison; *Buster Brown and His Dog Tige* (series), filmed and produced by Edwin S. Porter for Edison; *The Child Stealers,* produced by British Gaumont; *The Ex-Convict,* produced by Edwin S. Porter for Edison; *Girls in Overalls, Tracked by Bloodhounds, or, A Lynching at Cripple Creek,* and *The Hold-Up of the Leadville Stage,* produced by William Selig; *The Hero of Liao-Yang, The Moonshiner, Personal, The Suburbanite,* and *The Widow and the Only Man,* produced by Biograph; *The Kidnapped Child* and *Meet Me at the Fountain,* produced by Sigmund Lubin.

FICTION: Paul Laurence Dunbar, *The Heart of Happy Hollow*; Charles Alexander Eastman (Ohiyesa), *Red Hunters and the Animal People*; Henry James, *The Golden Bowl*; O. Henry, *Cabbages and Kings*; Jack London, *The Sea-Wolf*; Gene Stratton Porter, *Freckles*; Edith Wharton, *The Descent of Man.*

POPULAR SONGS: "Alexander, Don't You Love Your Baby No More?" music by Harry von Tilzer, lyrics by Andrew B. Sterling; "Give My Regards to Broadway" and "The Yankee Doodle Boy," music and lyrics by George M. Cohan; "Good Bye My Lady Love," music and lyrics by Joe Howard; "He Done Me Wrong, or, the Death of Bill Bailey," music and lyrics by Hughie Cannon; "Meet Me in St. Louis," music by Kerry Mills, lyrics by Andrew B. Sterling.

1905

- William Randolph Hearst acquires *Cosmopolitan* magazine for four hundred thousand dollars.
- The Institute of Musical Art, later renamed the Juilliard School, is established in New York.
- Isadora Duncan opens an academy of modern dance in Berlin.
- *Variety,* the show-business weekly, begins publication in New York.
- The player piano which could be played manually or with rolls of pre-encoded music is introduced.
- Gertrude "Ma" Rainey gains fame as the first African American minstrel star to sing "the blues."
- L. A. Coernes's *Zenobia* is the first American opera produced in Europe.
- On January 9, George Bernard Shaw's *You Never Can Tell* succeeds in New York; three other Shaw plays, *Man and Superman, John Bull's Other Island,* and *Mrs. Warren's*

Profession, open in New York this year as well as a revival of *How He Lied to Her Husband.*

- On May 3, the Metropolitan Opera chorus strikes.
- On May 5, the *Chicago Defender,* the first important African American newspaper, begins publication.
- On May 13, Broadway entrepreneur Sam Shubert dies in a railway accident outside Harrisburg, Pennsylvania.
- In June, the nickelodeon era gets under way when entrepreneur Harry Davis's Pittsburgh movie theater offers continuous showings and frequent program changes. By 1909, eight thousand nickel-admission movie theaters are in operation.
- On June 6, real estate at Broadway and Wall Street in New York City is offered at four dollars per square inch.
- On October 23, Edwin Milton Royle's *The Squaw Man,* a drama attempting serious treatment of the American Indian, premieres in New York City.
- On October 31, Bernard Shaw's play *Mrs. Warren's Profession* opens and closes in New York; critics call its treatment of prostitution "unfit," "indecent," and "vicious."
- *The Earl and the Girl,* a musical featuring songs by Jerome Kern and starring Eddie Foy, opens on Broadway at the Casino Theater.
- On November 14, David Belasco's atmospheric melodrama *The Girl of the Golden West* opens on Broadway; it plays for three years.
- On November 25, in New York Alfred Stieglitz inaugurates the first show at the "Little Galleries of the Photo-Secession." The avant-garde gallery soon exhibits a variety of advanced art and comes to be known by its address, 291.
- On December 23, Joseph Stella's drawings of immigrants at Ellis Island are published in *Outlook* magazine.

MOVIES: *Adventures of Sherlock Holmes, Escape from Sing-Sing, Monsieur Beaucaire,* and *The Servant Girl Problem,* produced by Vitagraph; *The Burglar's Slide for Life,* produced by Edison and featuring Mannie the Edison dog; *The Bold Bank Robbery; Dog, Lost, Strayed or Stolen, The Sign of the Cross, A Policeman's Love Affair,* and *Tramp's Revenge,* produced by Sigmund Lubin; *Everybody Works but Father, The Miller's Daughter, On a Good Old Five Cent Trolley Ride,* and *The Whole Dam Family and the Dam Dog,* filmed by Edwin S. Porter for Edison; *The Faithless Lover, A Father's Honor, The Pastry Cook's Practical Jokes,* and *The Mining District,* produced by Pathé; *The Gentle Highwayman, The Lost Child,* and *Tom, and Tom the Piper's Son,* produced by Biograph; *The Launching of the USS "Connecticut,"* filmed by Wallace McCutcheon, G. W. "Billy" Bitzer, and A. E. Weed for Biograph; *The Palace of the Arabian Knights* and *Rip's Dream,* produced by Georges Méliès.

FICTION: Willa Cather, *The Troll Garden*; Charles Waddell Chesnutt, *The Colonel's Dream*; Thomas Dixon, *The Clansman*; Ellen Glasgow, *The Deliverance*; Mary J. Holmes, *Lucy Harding*; Grace King, *Stories from Louisiana History*; Jack London, *White Fang*; Edith Wharton, *The House of Mirth.*

POPULAR SONGS: "Daddy's Little Girl," music by Theodore F. Morse, lyrics by Edward Madden; "Everybody Works but Father," music and lyrics by Jean Havez; "Give My Regards to Broadway" and "Mary's A Grand Old Name," music and lyrics by George M. Cohan; "I Don't Care," music by Harry O. Sutton, lyrics by Jean Lenox; "In My Merry Oldsmobile," music by Gus Edwards, lyrics by Vincent Bryan; "In the Shade of the Old Apple Tree," music by Egbert Van Alstyne, lyrics by Henry Williams; "I Want What I Want When I Want It" and "Kiss Me Again," music by Victor Herbert, lyrics by Henry Blossom; "My Gal Sal," music and lyrics by Paul Dresser; "Wait 'Til the Sun Shines, Nellie," and "What You Gonna Do When the Rent Comes 'Round?" music by Albert von Tilzer, lyrics by Andrew B. Sterling; "Will You Love Me in December as You Do in May?," music by Ernest R. Ball, lyrics by James J. Walker.

1906

- Zane Grey's *The Sea Wolf* is the best-seller of 1906.
- Photographer Arnold Genthe records the aftermath of the San Francisco earthquake. Although his own studio and library are demolished, his photographs of Chinese immigrant life are saved.
- The American stage is host to foreign talent in 1906: Russian actress and recent immigrant Alla Nazimova debuts in Norwegian playwright Henrik Ibsen's *Hedda Gabler,* and Irish dramatist Bernard Shaw has four plays on Broadway.
- Nickelodeons proliferate across the country; the storefront theaters are expressly for showing films and charge a nickel admission. Among the those who succeed in the nickelodeon business are William Fox and the Warner brothers, who later found the Hollywood movie studios named after them.
- The first radio program of voice and music is broadcast in the United States by R. A. Fessenden.
- On January 8, protesters distribute pamphlets at the opening of the play *The Clansman* (based on the novel by Thomas Dixon) at New York's Liberty Theater. The pamphlets call attention to the play's racism; distributors are dispersed by police.
- On April 11, Russian novelist Maksim Gorky arrives in the United States to raise money for Russia's revolution; Mark Twain heads a funding committee.
- On April 14, President Theodore Roosevelt publicly chastises journalists he calls "muckrakers." He takes this term from *Pilgrim's Progress,* in which John Bunyan wrote of the man who never looked up to finer things because he was intent on applying his muckrake to the ground.
- In July, Ruth St. Denis introduces modern dance to the United States; she begins her American tour with the Eastern-inspired *Radha.* The young dancer, who has had little formal training, is praised for her artistic vision.
- On July 7, courts rule that Bernard Shaw's play *Mrs. Warren's Profession* is appropriate for New York audiences.
- On August 28, President Roosevelt proposes that "simplified spelling" be used in federal documents. The proposal, if accepted, would alter the mechanics of American English to achieve a spelling more synchronous with pronunciation; thus, for example, *through* would be spelled *thru.*

- On October 30, the U.S. Supreme Court bans "simplified spelling" in federal documents.
- On November 3, French composer Camille Saint-Saëns makes his New York debut.

MOVIES: *And the Villain Still Pursued Her; or The Author's Dream, Automobile Thieves, Foul Play,* and *The Jailbird and How He Flew,* produced by Vitagraph; *The Bank Defaulter* and *The Secret of Death Valley,* produced by Sigmund Lubin; *The Black Hand, The Lone Highwayman, The Silver Wedding, The Subpoena Server, Trial Marriages,* and *Wanted: A Nurse,* produced by Biograph; *Daniel Boone; or, Pioneer Days in America* and *Kathleen Mavourneen,* filmed by Edwin S. Porter and produced by Edison; *Dream of a Rarebit Fiend,* produced by Edwin S. Porter and Wallace McCutcheon for Edison; *Dr. Dippy's Sanatorium, Mr. Butt-In,* and *Married for Millions,* produced by Biograph; *The Female Highwayman* and *The Tomboys,* produced by William Selig; *The Female Spy,* produced by Pathé; *Humorous Phases of Funny Faces* (animation experiment), filmed by J. Stuart Blackton, produced by Vitagraph; *The Life of Christ,* produced by British Gaumont; *Oh! That Limburger: the Story of a Piece of Cheese* and *Please Help the Blind; or, A Game of Graft,* produced by Vitagraph; *Terrible Kids* and *Three American Beauties,* produced by Edison; *Venetian Tragedy,* produced by Pathé; *World Series Baseball,* produced by William Selig.

FICTION: Rex Beach, *The Spoilers*; Ambrose Bierce, *The Cynic's Word Book*; O. Henry, *The Four Million* and "The Gift of the Magi"; Finley Peter Dunne, *Dissertations by Mr. Dooley*; Mary E. Wilkins Freeman, *By the Light of the Soul*; Upton Sinclair, *The Jungle*; Harriet Prescott Spofford, *Old Washington*; Booth Tarkington, *The Conquest of Canaan*; Owen Wister, *Lady Baltimore.*

POPULAR SONGS: "The Bird on Nellie's Hat," music by Alfred Solman, lyrics by Arthur J. Lamb; "I Just Can't Make My Eyes Behave," music by Will D. Cobb, lyrics by Gus Edwards; "I'm a Yankee Doodle Dandy" and "You're a Grand Old Flag," music and lyrics by George M. Cohan; "Love Me and the World is Mine," music by Dave Reed Jr., lyrics by Ernest R. Ball; "Mandy," music by Bob Cole, lyrics by James Weldon and J. Rosamond Johnson; "Rosalie," music by Jerome Kern, lyrics by George Grossmith; "Virginia Song," music and lyrics by George M. Cohan; "Won't You Come Over to My House," music by Egbert Van Alstyne, lyrics by Harry H. Williams.

1907

- *The Shepherd of the Hills* by Harold Bell Wright is the best-seller of 1907.
- Alfred Stieglitz produces his best-known photograph, *The Steerage.*
- Wealthy arts patron and sculptress Gertrude Vanderbilt Whitney opens her Greenwich Village studio to exhibits by fellow artists.
- Author Mark Twain receives an honorary degree from Oxford University.
- John Sloan paints *The Haymarket, The Wake of the Ferry,* and *The Hairdresser's Window.*
- Hungarian composer Franz Lehar's experimental opera *The Merry Widow* is produced in New York; among its nontraditional elements are the waltz and the cancan.
- The De Forest Radio Company begins New York broadcasts.
- Edwin S. Porter hires D. W. Griffith as an actor at ten dollars a day.
- On January 26, J. P. Morgan's daughter, a member of the New York Metropolitan Opera Board of Directors, advocates the closing of the Oscar Wilde-Richard Strauss opera *Salome* for indecency.
- On March 18, in San Francisco the Alcazar Theater, designed by G. H. Corwin, opens; it is one of many theaters that are rebuilt or reopened after the devastating earthquake of 1906.
- On July 8, Florenz Ziegfeld's musical revue, the *Ziegfeld Follies,* opens at the New York Roof Theater; the *Follies* become an annual theater event, continuing until 1927.
- On August 24, New York galleries are featuring the works of Mary Cassatt, American Impressionist.
- On September 7, Oscar Hammerstein announces he will build four opera houses in New York City.
- On November 8, photographs can now be reproduced by cable, owing to new advances in the field.
- On December 3, Mary Pickford makes her stage debut in *The Warrens of Virginia.*

MOVIES: *All's Well That Ends Well* and *What a Pipe Did,* produced by Selig Polyscope; *An Awful Skate* and *His First Ride,* produced by Essanay; *The Bandit King, The Girl from Montana,* and *Western Justice,* directed by G. M. Anderson for Selig Polyscope; *Athletic American Girls, "The Bad Man"—A Tale of the West,* produced by Vitagraph; *Bargain Fiend; or, Shopping A La Mode,* starring Florence Lawrence and Florence Turner, produced by Vitagraph; *The Boy, the Bust and the Bath,* produced by Vitagraph; *College Chums,* directed by Edwin S. Porter, produced by Edison; *The Doings of a Poodle* and *The Policeman's Little Run,* produced by Pathé; *Dolls in Dreamland, Crayono,* and *The Tired Tailor's Dream* (all with object animation) directed by Joseph A. Golden, produced by Biograph; *The Hypnotist's Revenge* and *Terrible Ted,* directed by Joseph A. Golden, produced by Biograph; *John D. and the Reporter, The Unwritten Law: A Thrilling Drama Based on the Thaw-White Tragedy, Too Much Mother-in-Law,* and *When Women Vote,* produced by Sigmund Lubin; *The Masher* and *The Matinee Idol,* produced by Selig Polyscope; *The Rivals* and *"Teddy" Bears,* produced by Edison; *The Wrong Flat,* starring William Delany, produced by Vitagraph; *Work for Your Grub,* produced by Filmograph.

FICTION: Henry Brooks Adams, *The Education of Henry Adams* (autobiography); F. Marion Crawford, *A Lady of Rome*; Charles Alexander Eastman, *Old Indian Days*; Ellen Glasgow, *The Wheel of Life*; Elinor Glyn, *Three Weeks*; O. Henry, "The Last Leaf"; Frances Little, *The Lady of the Decoration*; George Barr McCutcheon, *Jane Cable*; John Milton Oskison, "The Problem of Old Harjo"; Edith Wharton, *Madame de Treymes*; Kate Douglas Wiggin, *New Chronicles of Rebecca.*

POPULAR SONGS: "Harrigan," music and lyrics by George M. Cohan; "You're a Grand Old Flag," music and lyrics by George M. Cohan; "Heart of My Heart," music and lyrics by Andrew Mack; "Honey Boy," music by Albert von Tilzer, lyrics by Jack Norworth; "The Little Church Around the Corner," music by Jerome Kern, lyrics by M. E. Rourke; "Marie from Sunny Italy," music by Nick Nicholson, lyrics by Irving Berlin; "School Days," music by Will D. Cobb, lyrics by Gus Edwards.

1908

- *The Trail of the Lonesome Pine* by John Fox, Jr. and *The Circular Staircase* by Mary Roberts Rinehart are the best-sellers of 1908.
- D. W. Griffith directs his first one-reel film, *The Adventures of Dolly*; his cameraman is the expert G. W. "Billy" Bitzer. Griffith directs one hundred films in the next year.
- The Motion Picture Patents Company, the first movie monopoly, is formed. Edison, Lubin, Selig, and other producers believe films should be limited to one reel because audience attention span falters after ten minutes.
- Female ushers, orange drink, and drinking-cup dispensers are introduced at the Shubert-owned Casino Theater in New York City.
- Canadian writer Lucy Maud Montgomery publishes the novel soon to be among America's favorites, *Anne of Green Gables.*
- The New Society of American Artists is founded in Paris by Edward Steichen and others.
- Movie actress Florence Lawrence quits Vitagraph Studios and goes to work for Biograph; her salary goes up ten dollars to twenty-five dollars a week.
- The first "documentary" records are released by Edison, who has recorded the campaign speeches of William Jennings Bryan and William Howard Taft.
- On January 11, Italian soprano Louisa Tetrazinni makes her U.S. debut.
- On January 14, a theater fire in Boyertown, Pennsylvania, kills 150.
- In February, "The Eight," painters Robert Henri, George Luks, John Sloan, William Glackens, Everett Shinn, Maurice Prendergast, Ernest Lawson, and Arthur B. Davies, exhibit together in New York, protesting the conservative National Academy of Design.
- On February 11, Thomas Edison and his film-producing partners win a series of patent-infringement lawsuits.
- On February 20, Thomas Edison sends Russian writer Leo Tolstoy a phonograph; Tolstoy later sends Edison a recording of his voice.
- In March, the Original Independent Show, organized in New York, includes works by painters George Bellows, Edward Hopper, and Rockwell Kent.
- On March 30, Louisa Tetrazinni signs a five-year contract with Oscar Hammerstein; she appears at the new Manhattan Opera House.
- On May 5, courts rule that moving pictures be placed under copyright laws; royalties will be paid to the owners of the copyrights.
- On September 6, Israel Zangwill's play *The Melting Pot* opens in New York City; the title becomes an internationally recognized description of the United States.
- On October 5, *The American Idea,* a George M. Cohan musical, opens in New York.
- On November 16, Italian opera conductor Arturo Toscanini makes his American debut with Verdi's *Aida* at New York's Metropolitan Opera.
- On December 22, New York's Herald Square Theater is damaged by fire; the successful run of *Three Twins,* starring Bessie McCoy, is halted until a new location is found.

MOVIES: *After Many Years, Behind the Scenes,* and *The Fatal Hour,* directed by D. W. Griffith, produced by Edison; *As You Like It,* adapted from William Shakespeare, produced by Kalem; *The Cattle Rustlers* and *The Count of Monte Cristo,* filmed by Francis Boggs for Selig; *A Christmas Carol,* adapted from Charles Dickens, produced by Essanay; *The Cowboy Escapade,* produced by David Horsely's Centaur Film Manufacturing Company; *The Devil* and *Dr. Jekyll and Mr. Hyde,* produced by Edison; *Fireside Reminiscences,* directed by Edwin S. Porter for Edison; *The Girl and the Outlaw, The Greaser's Gauntlet, The Fight for Freedom,* and *The Red Girl,* directed by D. W. Griffith, produced by Biograph; *Julius Caesar, Richard III, Romeo and Juliet,* and *Macbeth,* produced by Vitagraph; *The Music Master,* produced by Biograph; *Old Isaacs the Pawnbroker,* scripted by D. W. Griffith, directed by Wallace McCutcheon, produced by Biograph; *Saved by Love,* produced by Edison; *The Welcome Burglar,* directed by D. W. Griffith, produced by Edison.

FICTION: Rex Beach, *The Barrier*; Frances Hodgson Burnett, *The Shuttle*; John Fox Jr., *The Trail of the Lonesome Pine*; Ellen Glasgow, *The Ancient Law*; Zane Grey, *The Last of the Plainsmen*; O. Henry, *The Voice of the City*; Jack London, *The Iron Heel*; Mary Roberts Rinehart, *The Circular Staircase*; Edith Wharton, *The Fruit of the Tree.*

POPULAR SONGS: "I Wonder Who's Kissing Her Now," music by Will M. Hough and Frank R. Adams, lyrics by Joseph E. Howard and Harold Orlob; "Cuddle Up A Little Closer," music by Karl Hoschna, lyrics by Otto Hauerbach; "She Was a Dear Little Girl," music by Ted Snyder, lyrics by Irving Berlin; "Shine On Harvest Moon," music and lyrics by Nora Bayes and Jack Norworth; "Smarty," music by Albert von Tilzer, lyrics by Jack Norworth; "Sunbonnet Sue," music by Will D. Cobb, lyrics by Gus Edwards; "Take Me Out to the Ball Game," music by Albert von Tilzer, lyrics by Jack Norworth; "The Yama Yama Man," music by Karl Hoschna, lyrics by Collin Davis.

1909

- *A Girl of the Limberlost* by Gene Stratton Porter and *The Calling of Dan Matthews* by Harold Bell Wright are the best-sellers of 1909.
- Modernist poets Ezra Pound and William Carlos Williams publish collections.
- George Bellows paints *Both Members of the Club.*
- W. C. Handy's "Memphis Blues" is the first published American blues song. Reworked later, it becomes "The Saint Louis Blues."

- D. W. Griffith features sixteen-year-old Mary Pickford in his films. The former Gladys Smith now makes forty dollars a week starring in Biograph pictures.
- "The movies" are now a $40-million-a-year industry employing more than one hundred thousand artists and craftspeople. There are ten thousand moving-picture theaters in the United States.
- Mack Sennett is employed by Biograph as an actor-writer; he tries to convince D. W. Griffith that a film about comic policemen would be successful; years later his Keystone Kops prove him right.
- The first fully animated film, made from 10,300 drawings by newspaper cartoonist Windsor McCay, is released; Gertie the Dinosaur stars.
- On January 19, Eugene Walter's controversial drama *The Easiest Way,* about a woman who chooses to live "immorally," opens at the Belasco-Stuyvesant Theater in New York. *The New York Times* defends the play.
- On March 1, an adaptation of American author Bret Harte's *The Luck of the Roaring Camp* opens in London.
- On April 9, Enrico Caruso makes a radio broadcast from the Metropolitan Opera House to the home of Lee De Forest, the inventor of the vacuum tube.
- On May 1, the works of American expatriate painter John Singer Sargent are among the most impressive to be seen at the 141st annual Royal Academy of Art Show in London.
- On June 15, the *Ziegfeld Follies* features chorus girls costumed as glittering mosquitoes; Nora Bayes introduces "Shine On Harvest Moon."
- On October 11, George M. Cohan premieres *The Man Who Owned Broadway* at the New York Theater.
- On October 28, the nine-hundred-seat Cort Theater opens in Chicago; the theater's Italianate design is by E. O. Pridmore.
- On November 4, composer Sergei Rachmaninoff makes his American debut at Smith College.
- On December 29, the first known "goddamn" is uttered on the American stage. Clyde Fitch's *The City* has been banned in Boston but plays in New York without police interference. Several people, including a theater critic, are said to have fainted on hearing the words "You're a goddamn liar."

MOVIES: *The Aborigine's Devotion,* produced by World Pictures; *An Alpine Echo,* produced by Vitagraph; *The Bride of the Lamermoor,* adapted from Sir Walter Scott, produced by Vitagraph; *Brother Against Brother,* produced by Selig; *A Change of Complexion,* produced by the Powers Company; *The Convict's Sacrifice,* directed by D. W. Griffith, starring Stephanie Longfellow, Gladys Egan, James Kirkwood, and Henry Walthall, produced by Biograph; *A Corner in Wheat,* directed by D. W. Griffith, produced by Biograph; *The Escape from Andersonville,* produced by Kalem; *Faust,* produced by Edison; *The Girl Spy,* scripted by and starring in by Gene Gautier, produced by Kalem; *Hiawatha,* produced by Carl Laemmle's Independent Moving Picture Company; *King Lear* and *A Midsummer Night's Dream,* produced by Vitagraph; *The Lonely Villa,* directed by D. W. Griffith, starring Mary Pickford, Gladys Egan, and Adele De Garde, produced by Biograph; *Napoleon, Man of Destiny, The Life of George Washington,* and *The Life of Moses,* produced by Vitagraph; *Pippa Passes,* produced by Biograph; *The Prince and the Pauper,* starring Miss Cecil Spooner in the double role, produced by Edison.

FICTION: Mary Austin, *Lost Borders; The Collected Works of Ambrose Bierce*; Charles Alexander Eastman and Elaine Goodale Eastman, *Wigwam Evenings*; Edith Maude Eaton, "Leaves from the Mental Portfolio of a Eurasian" and *Mrs. Spring Fragrance*; Frank Norris, *The Third Circle* (posthumous); Jack London, *Martin Eden*; Gene Stratton Porter, *Girl of the Limberlost*; Gertrude Stein, *Three Lives.*

POPULAR SONGS: "By the Light of the Silvery Moon," music by Edward Madden, lyrics by Gus Edwards; "Casey Jones," lyrics by Wallace Saunders; "Every Little Movement," music by Karl Hoschna, lyrics by Otto Harbach; "That Mesmerizing Mendelssohn Tune," music and lyrics by Irving Berlin; "Put on Your Old Grey Bonnet," music by Stanley Murphy, lyrics by Percy Wenrich; "Yiddle on Your Fiddle, Play Some Ragtime," music and lyrics by Irving Berlin.

Poems by Paul Laurence Dunbar

"Trouble in de Kitchen"; "When Malindy Sings"; "We Wear the Mask"

Poems

By: Paul Laurence Dunbar

Date: 1896–1906

Source: Dunbar, Paul Laurence. "Trouble in de Kitchen"; "When Malindy Sings"; "We Wear the Mask." Reprinted in *The Collected Poetry of Paul Laurence Dunbar.* Charlottesville: The University Press of Virginia, 1994. Available online at http://www2.scc.rutgers.edu/~triggs/AAP/foo13.pdf; website home page: http://www2.scc.rutgers.edu/~triggs/AAP/ (accessed May 19, 2003).

About the Author: Paul Laurence Dunbar (1872–1906), one of the first African Americans to receive national recognition as a poet and novelist, was born in Dayton, Ohio. The son of former slaves, Dunbar published his first volume of verse, *Oak and Ivy,* at twenty-one. In his lifetime, he was best known for his dialect verse, but he wrote in standard English as well. ■

Introduction

When he was twelve, Paul Laurence Dunbar's father died, and his mother raised him alone. As an adult, many of Dunbar's writings were inspired by the stories of slave life that she told him. However, she never spoke of the horrific aspects of her experiences. As a result, Dunbar tended toward a romantic view of plantation life, an aspect of his writing that has been much criticized.

He expressed early interest in a literary career. As a high school student—the only African American in his school—Dunbar published his verse in the *Dayton Herald.* Dunbar had hoped to become a lawyer, but he could not afford to attend college. He finally found work as an elevator operator, and he used the time between calls to continue writing. In addition to poetry, Dunbar wrote articles and short stories for small newspapers throughout the Midwest, often for little or no pay.

In 1892, one of Dunbar's former teachers invited him to address the annual Western Association of Writers, held in Dayton that year. This gave Dunbar his first opportunity to connect with other writers. An attendee wrote to an Illinois newspaper describing the talents of the young poet. Soon Dunbar's reputation spread beyond Dayton. The WAOW invited Dunbar to join, and he gained popularity as a speaker. He self-published *Oak and Ivy* in 1893, and sold copies from his elevator post. One reader, Toledo attorney Charles Thatcher, was so impressed by the volume that he offered to sponsor Dunbar's college education. Although Dunbar turned down the opportunity because his mother depended on his elevator job earnings, Thatcher supported Dunbar throughout his career. With Thatcher's influence, Dunbar published another collection of poetry in 1896, *Majors and Minors.* This volume was praised in *Harper's Weekly* by William Dean Howells, one of the most influential American literary critics at the time. *Majors and Minors* included one of his most powerful poems, "We Wear the Mask."

Significance

Dunbar, like his contemporary, Mark Twain, used dialect to depict American life. Most readers remember Dunbar for his verse written in turn-of-the-century black dialect. However, Dunbar, who loved to experiment with language, wrote in other American dialects as well. His writings captured the speech of Midwesterners, German Americans, and Irish Americans, among others. In contrast to his writings featuring fictitious characters, Dunbar also wrote in standard English—particularly for poetry reflecting his personal anguish. His dialect poems appealed to readers for their humor, as well as their realism and tenderness. Both African American and white audiences preferred Dunbar's dialect poetry to his works in standard English. Dunbar had hoped that his more serious work would eventually gain wider acceptance if he continued to please publishers and readers with his dialect poetry. But publishers returned his standard English manuscripts, requesting further dialect poetry instead.

Dunbar married poet and teacher, Alice Ruth Moore, in 1898. Around the same period, he collaborated with Will Marion Cook on *Clorindy; or The Origin of the Cakewalk,* a musical that was a huge financial success in New York. But the press dubbed Dunbar the "king of the coon shows," and he was extremely distressed by this. He also contracted tuberculosis, and developed alcoholism after he began using alcohol to alleviate his physical pain. Health concerns necessitated trips to more temperate climates, creating intermittent separations from his wife. Finally, at his mother's house, Dunbar died at only 34.

In his short life, Dunbar was extremely prolific. While most famous for his poetry, he also wrote short stories, novels, librettos, plays, songs, and essays. Dunbar died believing his work and career were failures. After his death, white critics largely ignored his work. With some African American audiences, he had been unpopular for propagating the minstrel tradition and racial stereotypes. More recently, scholars have begun to reexamine Dunbar's work and career.

Paul Laurence Dunbar, one of the first African American poets to have success with a white American audience. **THE LIBRARY OF CONGRESS.**

Primary Source

"Trouble in de Kitchen"; "When Malindy Sings"; "We Wear the Mask"

SYNOPSIS: Dunbar's last volume of poetry was *Lyrics of Sunshine and Shadow* (1906). Like his other collections, this volume included poems written in each of his distinct styles.

"Trouble in de Kitchen"

Dey was oncet a awful quoil 'twixt de skillet an' de pot;
De pot was des a-bilin' an' de skillet sho' was hot.
Dey slurred each othah's colah an' dey called each othah names.
W'ile de coal-oil can des gu-gled, po'in oil erpon de flames.

De pot, hit called de skillet des a flat, disfiggered t'ing,
An' de skillet 'plied dat all de pot could do was set an' sing.
An' he 'lowed dat dey was 'lusions dat he wouldn't stoop to mek
'Case he reckernize his juty, an' he had too much at steak.

Well, at dis de pot biled ovah, case his tempah gittin' highah,
An' de skillet got to sputterin', den de fat was in de fiah.
Mistah fiah lay daih smokin' an' a-t'inkin' to hisse'f,
W'ile de peppah-box us nudgin' of de gingah on de she'f.

Den dey all des lef' hit to 'im, 'bout de trouble an' de talk;
An' howevah he decided, w'y dey bofe 'u'd walk de chalk;
But de fiah uz so 'sgusted how dey quoil an' dey shout
Dat he cooled 'em off, I reckon, w'en he puffed an' des went out.

"When Malindy Sings"

G'way an' quit dat noise, Miss Lucy—
Put dat music book away;
What's de use to keep on tryin'?
Ef you practise twell you're gray,
You cain't sta't no notes a-flyin'
Lak de ones dat rants and rings
F'om de kitchen to be big woods
When Malindy sings.

You ain't got de nachel o'gans
Fu' to make de soun' come right,
You ain't got de tu'ns an' twistin's
Fu' to make it sweet an' light.
Tell you one thing now, Miss Lucy,
An' I'm tellin' you fu' true,
When hit comes to raal right singin',
'T ain't no easy thing to do.

Easy 'nough fu' folks to hollah,
Lookin' at de lines an' dots,
When dey ain't no one kin sence it,
An' de chune comes in, in spots;
But fu' real melojous music,
Dat jes' strikes you' hea't and clings,
Jes' you stan' an' listen wif me
When Malindy sings.

Ain't you nevah hyeahd Malindy?
Blessed soul, tek up de cross!
Look hyeah, ain't you jokin', honey?
Well, you don't know whut you los'.
Y' ought to hyeah dat gal a-wa'blin',
Robins, la'ks, an' all dem things,
Heish dey moufs an' hides dey faces
When Malindy sings.

Fiddlin' man jes' stop his fiddlin',
Lay his fiddle on de she'f;
Mockin'-bird quit tryin' to whistle,
'Cause he jes' so shamed hisse'f.

Folks a-playin' on de banjo
   Draps dey fingahs on de strings—
Bless yo' soul—fu'gits to move'em,
   When Malindy sings.

She jes' spreads huh mouf and hollahs,
   "Come to Jesus," twell you hyeah
Sinnah's tremblin' steps and voices,
   Timid-lak a-drawin' neah;
Den she tu'ns to "Rock of Ages,"
   Simply to de cross she clings,
An' you fin' yo' teahs a-drappin'
   When Malindy sings.

Who dat says dat humble praises
   Wif de Master nevah counts?
Heish yo' mouf, I hyeah dat music,
   Ez hit rises up an' mounts—
Floatin' by de hills an' valleys,
   Way above dis buryin' sod,
Ez hit makes its way in glory
   To de very gates of God!

Oh, hit's sweetah dan de music
   Of an edicated band;
An' hit's dearah dan de battle's
   Song o' triumph in de lan'.
It seems holier dan evenin'
   When de solemn chu'ch bell rings,
Ez I sit an' ca'mly listen
   While Malindy sings.

Towsah, stop dat ba'kin', hyeah me!
   Mandy, mek dat chile keep still;
Don't you hyeah de echoes callin'
   F'om de valley to de hill?
Let me listen, I can hyeah it,
   Th'oo de bresh of angels' wings,
Sof' an' sweet, "Swing Low, Sweet Chariot,"
   Ez Malindy sings.

"We Wear the Mask"

We wear the mask that grins and lies,
It hides our cheeks and shades our eyes,—
This debt we pay to human guile;
With torn and bleeding hearts we smile,
And mouth with myriad subtleties.

Why should the world be overwise,
In counting all our tears and sighs?
Nay, let them only see us, while
   We wear the mask.

We smile, but, O great Christ, our cries
To thee from tortured souls arise.
We sing, but oh the clay is vile
Beneath our feet, and long the mile;
But let the world dream otherwise,
   We wear the mask!

Further Resources

BOOKS

Brawley, Benjamin Griffith. *Paul Laurence Dunbar, Poet of His People.* Port Washington, N.Y.: Kennicat Press, 1967.

Dunbar, Paul Laurence. *The Complete Poems of Paul Laurence Dunbar.* New York: Dodd, Mead, 1980.

Martin, Herbert Woodward, and Ronald Primeau, ed. *In His Own Voice: The Dramatic and Other Uncollected Works of Paul Laurence Dunbar.* Athens: Ohio University Press, 2002.

Martin, Jay. *A Singer in the Dawn: Reinterpretations of Paul Laurence Dunbar.* New York: Dodd, Mead & Co., 1975.

Wiggins, Lida Keck. *The Life and Works of Paul Laurence Dunbar.* Millwood, N.Y.: Kraus Reprint Co., 1975.

PERIODICALS

Allen, Caffilene. "The Caged Bird Sings: The Ellison-Dunbar Connection. *CLA Journal* 40, no. 1, December 1996, 178.

Wilson, Matthew. "The Advent of 'The Nigger': The Careers of Paul Laurence Dunbar, Henry O. Tanner, and Charles W. Chesnutt." *American Studies* 43, no. 1, Spring 2002, 5.

WEBSITES

Columbus, Tom. "Paul Laurence Dunbar." University of Dayton. Available online at http://www.plethoreum.org/dunbar/links.asp; website home page http://www.plethoreum.org (accessed March 24, 2003).

Nelson, Cary, ed. "Paul Laurence Dunbar." Modern American Poetry. Available online at http://www.english.uiuc.edu/maps/poets/a_f/dunbar/dunbar.htm; website home page http://www.english.uiuc.edu (accessed March 24, 2003).

Paul Laurence Dunbar Digital Text Collection. Available online at http://www.libraries.wright.edu/dunbar/#Biblio; website home page http://www.libraries.wright.edu (accessed March 24, 2003).

Art of Frederic Remington

"Western Types: The Cow-boy and The Half-breed"

Illustrations

By: Frederic Remington

Date: October 19, 1902

Source: Remington, Frederic. "Western Types: The Cow-boy and The Half-breed." *Scribner's,* October 19, 1902. Reprinted in Samuels, Peggy, and Harold Samuels, eds. *The Collected Writings of Frederic Remington.* Garden City, N.Y.: Doubleday, 1979, 450–454.

"A Few Words From Mr. Remington"

Magazine article

By: Frederic Remington

Date: March 18, 1905

Source: Remington, Frederic. "A Few Words From Mr. Remington." *Collier's Magazine,* March 18, 1905. Reprinted in Samuels, Peggy, and Harold Samuels, eds. *The Collected Writings of Frederic Remington.* Garden City, N.Y.: Doubleday, 1979, 550–551.

About the Artist: Frederic Remington (1861–1909) was a painter, illustrator, and sculptor famous for his romantic depictions of the Old West. He created archetypal images of cowboys, soldiers, and American Indians. Remington was born in upstate New York. Although he never actually lived in the West, he made frequent trips there—taking photographs and gathering props to enable him to work from his studio. He was also a popular writer, even publishing a best-selling novel, *John Ermine of the Yellowstone* (1902). ■

Introduction

Remington made his first trip to the West in 1881, vacationing in the Montana Territory. In 1883, he used his inheritance to buy a sheep ranch in Kansas. He also invested in a hardware store, and then a saloon. Each of these ventures failed. Broke, Remington returned east in 1885, settling in Brooklyn, New York, where he studied drawing at the Art Students League. He continued to take summer trips throughout the Americas, including Arizona, Mexico, North Dakota, Wyoming, and Western Canada. To support himself, Remington sold his Western sketches to high-paying magazines. His work began to appear in major publications of the day, including *Scribner's, Harper's Weekly, Century, Collier's,* and *Boys' Life.* He created reporting missions for himself, providing both the text and illustrations for articles. In 1888, Remington began illustrating Theodore Roosevelt's serialized great-outdoors articles for *Century Magazine.* Although Remington's primary interest was Western imagery, he drew other subjects as well. He was a war correspondent, and traveled to Cuba to cover the Spanish-American War (1898) for *Harper's* and the *New York Journal.*

Remington's popularity peaked at the beginning of the twentieth century, his work seen by hundreds of thousands of Americans. His art reflected an era that glorified the strenuous life and the cultivation of personal character, an attitude appealing to turn-of-the-century Americans. This gave Remington's work tremendous popular appeal. When *Harper's* released him due to financial constraints, Remington defected to *Collier's* in 1903. *Collier's* even placed a large advertisement in *Harper's* to announce Remington's change in publishers.

Remington had a great influence on the look of future Western movies; John Ford's 1949 film *She Wore a Yellow Ribbon* was inspired directly by Remington's work.

Significance

Even a century later, Remington still is considered the premier illustrator of Western lore. Less well-known is his successful, secondary career as a writer. His magazine articles were so widely acclaimed that they were collected and published as books. Remington wrote short fiction and novels, including *Pony Tracks* (1895), *Stories of Peace and War* (1899), and *The Way of an Indian* (1906). Remington published his best-selling novel *John Ermine of the Yellowstone* in the same year that his friend Owen Wister's *The Virginians* (1902) appeared. Remington would come to immortalize the Old West through visual representations, while Wister would be the one to do so with language.

Artist and author Frederic Remington, best known for his romantic depictions of the Old West. © CORBIS. REPRODUCED BY PERMISSION.

Magazines were ideal for gaining exposure for Remington's art. But Remington bristled at criticism from other artists who maintained that he was merely an illustrator, rather than a painter. A member of the National Academy pointed out that to Remington, "the subject is more to him than the purely artistic qualities." It was true, on close inspection, that some of Remington's many drawings were not always so believable. In "Bringing Home the New Cook," chaotic image of horses in action, seen by thousands of Americans when it was published as a full-color feature in *Collier's,* Remington himself later admitted that one of the horse's legs was impossibly bunched.

After 1902, Remington gave up writing to devote himself full-time to painting and sculpture. However, he agreed to submit an essay to the all-Remington issue of *Collier's Magazine* on March 18, 1905. This tribute represented an artistic triumph, and it provided a

Primary Source

"Western Types": *The Cow-boy*

SYNOPSIS: *Author's photoengraving.* "No longer strange, and become conventional, the Cowboy is merely trying to get mountain-bred ponies to go where he wants them to go. Knowing the 'Irish Pig' of their nature, he has to be fast and insistent; all of which represents a type of riding and pony 'footing' easier to delineate than to perform." SCRIBNER'S MAGAZINE, OCTOBER, 1902.

Primary Source

"Western Types": *The Half-breed* (2 OF 2)

Author's photoengraving. "One of the relics of the old fur company days—the descendant of the white employees and Indian squaws. In great numbers of the half-breeds led a nomad existence on the plains of the Northwest, and at one time bid fair to become a separate and peculiar people. Our government through the army deported large bands from the then territory of Montana to Canada, and their expiring effort was the Louis Riel rebellion. The passing of the buffalo left them stranded, and their predatory habits made their suppression necessary, but they still exist, though robbed of their picturesque apparel and characteristic traits." SCRIBNER'S MAGAZINE, OCTOBER, 1902.

major opportunity for the artist to express himself in prose again. In "A Few Words From Mr. Remington," the artist eloquently describes how his boyhood fascination with the West led to a lifelong career in illustration. Although he loved writing, Remington's personal vision of the disappearing frontier truly was expressed best by his visual work. Dedicated to Remington's art and life story, the magazine's pages included several full-color reproductions of his paintings and photographs of his bronze sculptures of bucking broncos, previously unseen by most readers.

Primary Source

"A Few Words From Mr. Remington"

SYNOPSIS: Remington created the artwork for his black and white magazine illustrations using pen and ink, ink wash and gouache, or black and white oil. The drawings then were reproduced as photoengravings—a common photomechanical process where the subject is photographed, and the image is recorded on a metal plate specially treated with a resist. The plate is dipped in an acid bath to create an etching of the image, and the plate may then be used on a printing press. It was an ideal method for reproducing Remington's illustrations, as it produced subtle tonal gradations and a velvety, tactile quality.

From behind the breastworks of his big desk the editor is banging at me to write about myself. I find the thought very chilly out here in the garish light, but his last shot says, "If you don't, I will send a person to interview you, and he will probably misquote you." Quite so—one doesn't need that character of help when about to play the fool; so if you find the going heavy, gentle reader, camp here.

I had brought more than ordinary schoolboy enthusiasm to Catlin, Irving, Gregg, Lewis and Clark, and others on their shelf, and youth found me sweating along their tracks. I was in the grand silent country following my own inclinations, but there was a heavy feel in the atmosphere. I did not immediately see what it portended, but it gradually obtruded itself. The times had changed.

Evening overtook me one night in Montana, and I by good luck made the campfire of an old wagon freighter who shared his bacon and coffee with me. I was nineteen years of age and he was a very old man. Over the pipes he developed that he was born in Western New York and had gone West at an early age. His West was Iowa. Thence during his long life he had followed the receding frontiers, always further and further West. "And now," said he, "there is no more West. In a few years the railroad will come along the Yellowstone and a poor man can not make a living at all."

There he was, my friend of the open, sleeping in a blanket on the ground (it snowed that night), eating his own villanies out of his frying-pan, wearing a cotton shirt open at the throat, and hunting his horses through the bleak hills before daylight; and all for enough money to mend harness and buy wagon grease. He had his point of view and he made a new one for me.

The old man had closed my very entrancing book almost at the first chapter. I knew the railroad was coming—I saw men already swarming into the land. I knew the derby hat, the smoking chimneys, the cord-binder, and the thirty-day note were upon us in a resistless surge. I knew the wild riders and the vacant land were about to vanish forever, and the more I considered the subject the bigger the Forever loomed.

Without knowing exactly how to do it, I began to try to record some facts around me, and the more I looked the more the panorama unfolded. Youth is never appalled by the insistent demands of a great profession, because it is mostly unconscious of their existence. Time unfolds these abruptly enough. Art is a she-devil of a mistress, and, if at times in earlier days she would not even stoop to my way of thinking, I have persevered and will so continue. Some day, who knows, she may let me tell you some of my secrets. Meanwhile be patient, and if the recording of a day which is past infringes on the increasing interest of the present, be assured there are those who will set this down in turn and everything will be right in the end. Besides, artists must follow their own inclinations unreservedly. It's more a matter of heart than head, with nothing perfunctory about it. I saw the living, breathing end of three American centuries of smoke and dust and sweat, and I now see quite another thing where it all took place, but it does not appeal to me.

Further Resources

BOOKS

Giesecke, Ernestine. *Frederic Remington.* Des Plaines, Ill.: Heinemann Library, 2001.

Manley, Atwood, and Margaret Manley Mangum. *Frederic Remington and the North Country.* New York: E.P. Dutton, 1988.

Nemerov, Alexander. *Frederic Remington and Turn-of-the Century America.* New Haven, Conn.: Yale University Press, 1995.

Remington, Frederic. *Pony Tracks.* New York: Random House, 1983.

Samuels, Peggy, and Harold Samuels. *Frederic Remington: A Biography*. Austin: University of Texas Press, 1985.

PERIODICALS

Buscombe, Edward. "Painting the Legend: Frederic Remington and the Western." *Cinema Journal* 23, no. 4, Summer 1984.

Hassrick, Peter H. "Frederic Remington's Studio: A Reflection." *Magazine Antiques* 146, no. 5, November 1994, 666–674.

Nemerov, A. "Frederic Remington." *American Art* 5, no. 1/2, Winter/Spring 1991, 36–60.

WEBSITES

Frederic Remington Art Museum. Available online at http://www.fredericremington.org (accessed March 20, 2003).

"Frederic Remington." The Artchive. Available online at http://www.artchive.com/artchive/R/remington.html; website home page www.artchive.com (accessed March 20, 2003).

AUDIO AND VISUAL MEDIA

Frederic Remington: "The Truth of Other Days." Public Media Home Vision, 1990, VHS.

"What Children Want"

Essay

By: L. Frank Baum

Date: November 27, 1902

Source: Baum, Frank. "What Children Want," *Chicago Evening Post,* November 27, 1902. Reprinted in Tystad Koupal, Nancy, ed. *Baum's Road to Oz: The Dakota Years.* Pierre: South Dakota State Historical Society Press. 166–170.

About the Author: L.(yman) Frank Baum (1856–1919), creator of the beloved Wizard of Oz stories, spent much of his adult life moving—from New York to South Dakota to Chicago, and finally California. He worked as a journalist, shopkeeper, traveling salesman, playwright, and magazine editor, each with varying degrees of success. The phenomenal popularity of the first Oz book, *The Wonderful Wizard of Oz* (1900) gave Baum financial stability for the first time in his life, and it enabled him to continuing writing for children until his death. ■

Introduction

The Wonderful Wizard of Oz, one of the most enduring stories in modern literature, nearly was never published. Baum had difficulty finding a publisher for his story of an ordinary child from the American Midwest transported to an imaginary land, as European fairy tales were in vogue at the time. Baum had introduced the character of Dorothy in his first children's book, *Mother Goose in Prose* (1897), illustrated by Maxfield Parrish. Even the success of Baum's previous book did not convince publishers. That volume, *Father Goose, His Book,* a collection of light verse written by Baum and illustrated by W.W. Denslow, had been the nation's best-selling children's book in 1899. Finally, Hill Company agreed to publish Baum's manuscript, and *The Wonderful Wizard of Oz* met with immediate success.

L. (Lyman) Frank Baum, author of the 1900 classic *The Wonderful Wizard of Oz,* c. 1908. THE LIBRARY OF CONGRESS.

At the same time, Baum wrote another children's book series, the *Aunt Jane's Nieces* series, under the pseudonym Edith Van Dyne. These were just as popular as the Oz books. He also wrote for children under other aliases, including Laura Bancroft, S.S. Gardons, Floyd Akers, Captain Hugh Fitzgerald, and Suzanne Metcalf. Under the male pseudonyms, Baum often wrote adventure stories, especially for boys.

At the turn of the century, in literature, as with many of the arts, Americans were looking still to European tradition. Baum admired the classic fairy tales by Hans Christian Andersen and the Brothers Grimm, but felt that it was time for beginning the tradition of the American fairy tale. Baum tried to write stories that did not contain stock characters like the genie, dwarf, and fairy. Earlier fairy tales attempted to be morally instructive. However, they often frightened children with their bloody episodes and cruel punishments. With *The Wonderful Wizard of Oz,* Baum hoped to create a modernized fairy tale in which "all the wonderment and joy are retained and the heartaches and nightmares are left out." Although the Wizard of Oz contains a fascinating allegorical under-

The title page of the first (1900) edition of *The Wonderful Wizard of Oz.* © BETTMANN/CORBIS. REPRODUCED BY PERMISSION.

current, Baum always insisted that his primary intent was to please and entertain his young audience.

Significance

In his 1902 essay, "What Children Want," Baum advises would-be authors of children's books. Baum felt that children's literature should be updated for modern times. He praises illustrators in their role of stimulating the reader's imagination. Baum believed stories were essential to developing young children's minds. In his own youth, Baum had been very sickly and entertained himself by creating fantastic stories. His published stories were often based on those he told to his four sons and other children. Having published under male and female pseudonyms, writing specifically for neither boys nor girls, Baum demonstrated with the Oz books that great children's stories transcend gender, as well as age.

At the time, Baum was unaware of brewing controversy over *The Wonderful Wizard of Oz.* Some librarians banned the Oz books because they believed they could not be considered important juvenile literature. The book's critics complained that the book was poorly written; it was true that the Oz stories were written in simple language, intended for young readers. Opponents to the book felt that it was dangerous to expose young children to a tale of such imaginary adventures, for fear that they might be unable to distinguish between reality and fantasy. Still others felt that the book was simply too sanitized and sentimental.

Baum's young readers felt otherwise, and they sent letters to the author clamoring for more Oz stories. He acquiesced to his reader's requests, producing thirteen more sequels. After his death in 1919, other writers, including Baum's son, continued the series. Additionally, there was an Oz Sunday comic strip, a young readers' edition of the Oz books, and the classic 1939 film version of *The Wizard of Oz,* starring Judy Garland. The Oz series ended in 1951, having sold over seven million copies.

Primary Source

"What Children Want"

SYNOPSIS: Baum was a prolific writer; besides his children's literature, he frequently published essays and articles for various periodicals. "What Children Want" originally appeared in the *Chicago Evening Post,* on November 27, 1902. By this time, Baum had already published two best-selling children's books (*Father Goose, His Book* and *The Wonderful Wizard of Oz*). The musical version of the Wizard of Oz had just begun a successful run in both New York and Chicago theaters, with Baum himself writing the lyrics.

Many authors have an idea that to write a story about children is to write a children's story. No notion could be more erroneous. Perhaps one out of a hundred alleged children's stories possesses elements of interest to the real child—but that is a liberal estimate. Not that the writers are not competent, nor possessed of kindliest intent to interest the little ones; but to them child life is a sweet memory, idealized by lapse of years, and more or less their stories are infected by the life experiences that led them to regard childhood retrospectively and to color each humdrum incident of youth with absurdly sentimental rose tints. There is nothing humdrum about the average child. You cannot interest it by telling how little Angelina washed her face and curled her hair. The things that frequently interest adults in children often have no interest whatever to the children themselves.

It is said that a child learns more during the first five years of its life than in the succeeding fifty years. This may well be true, for all the marvels of life and the wonders of the universe are brought to its notice and registered upon the sensitive film of its mind in those years when it first begins to understand it is a component part of mighty creation. The very realization of existence is sufficient to set every childish nerve tingling with excitement, and when the mind has absorbed the astonishing circumstances of its environments there comes a time when comprehension pauses, to resume more deliberately the practical details of worldly experience. Thus the amazed child, wide-eyed, eager, nervous and filled with unalloyed vigor, steps upon the threshold of real life. Remembering this, is it strange that children indulge in mischievous pranks; that they whoop and romp and are well-nigh irrepressible? Then is it small wonder that the passive tales of their sedate elders fail to afford them amusement. The real surprise, in this connection, is that adults fail so evidently to grasp the physical or mental condition of the little one that is taking its first peep at the world's wonderland.

Positively the child cannot be satisfied with inanities in its story books. It craves marvels—fairy tales, adventures, surprising and unreal occurrences; gorgeousness, color and kaleidoscopic succession of inspiring incident. Give it these for mental refreshment and the child's nervous energy is soothed and rested; its heart beats become normal; the eager eyes take on a dreamy and contented look, while above the throbbing course of rich lifeblood the glowing cheeks wear a happy smile of satisfaction.

Nearly every great writer, at one time or another in his or her experience, has written a book for children. Scarcely can we name one that has written a children's book. The old nurse's tales—the folklore of peoples who were close to nature—are the ideal thing in children's stories. They will live forever, preserved to us in their wise consideration for the coming child by John Newbury, the Brothers Grimm, Andrew Lang and other collectors. And above all stands the one great author of fairy tales—the revered Hans Christian Andersen—who knew well the child heart and child requirements and gave to all future ages the wonder tales that have been so instrumental in gladdening and soothing our restless little ones. These people lived with children and knew them; nor did they feed their minds with chaff.

No Distinction Between Sexes

In childish requirements sex is not clearly defined. There is little excuse for giving namby-pamby books to girls and adventurous ones to boys. The girls as eagerly demand and absorb the marvelous as their brothers; aye, and need it as much. Kindly maiden ladies and reverend grandmothers write many "sweet" stories for girls; and dignified, conservative publishers print them as "children's literature;" and scholarly reviewers commend them as most excellent for the childish mind. But, oh, if the little girls could only tell in print what they think of these stories, what an astonished lot of writers and publishers and reviewers there would be! And in many cases the boy child is as grossly misunderstood as the girl.

I am aware that many placid parents prefer to force "nice" and "gentle" tales upon their children to giving them the exciting stories their natures demand, but you will observe that the children of these placid ones grow up to occupy very placid positions in life, their youthful vigor having been sapped in many ways by attempts to engraft the conservatism of maturity upon the riotous bud of childhood. And I have never known a boy less manly for having read wonder books nor a girl less tender and womanly through reading of fairies and nymphs. The child seldom errs by believing such stories true; nor is it misguided in after life by the marvels it has read of in books. But the wonderment, the joy, the satisfaction in these tales at a period when their earnest natures crave hearty food lend to their lives a vigor and strength that is all-abiding. And, as one of our great writers truly says, the child that can be influenced to evil by reading a wholesome fairy tale or a book of stirring adventure is not worth considering.

Until four or five years ago there has been a great dearth in America of new stories for children, outside the inevitable "goody-goody" books. But the liberal spirit fast permeating every branch of literature has at length reached the child story, and the child itself is beginning to be better understood. Therefore the modern juvenile book is not nearly so apt to prove inane and unsatisfying to its youthful readers as formerly and the gorgeousness of modern illustration lends an irresistible charm to most of the recent publications for children. Indeed, I am not sure that the great modern illustrators of children's books, such as Peter Newell, Oliver Herford, Fanny Y. Cory, and W. W. Denslow, are not worthy as much love and reverence as the great story-writers themselves.

There seems no plausible reason why another Hans Christian Andersen should not arise to bless children with a modern collection of original fairy tales; and, indeed, some of the fairy stories of today seem to me to equal those of the glorious Dane in their marvelous construction and directness. Yet there still remains a lamentable failure on the part of many otherwise able authors to comprehend the child requirements in literature. Children do not relish descriptive passages, however beautiful they may be. They want their dialogue decisive and crisp. The action of the story must not lag—it should be a swift current whirling ever onward to the end. And the language employed should be simple and unadorned. As for a moral, children are quick to discover and absorb one, provided it is not tacked up like a warning on a signpost.

Further Resources

BOOKS

Baum, Frank Joslyn, and Russell P. MacFall. *To Please a Child: A Biography of L. Frank Baum, Royal Historian of Oz.* Chicago: Reilly & Lee Co., 1961.

Carpenter, Angelica Shirley and Jean Shirley. *L. Frank Baum: Royal Historian of Oz.* Minneapolis: Lerner Publications Co., 1992.

Riley, Michael O'Neal. *Oz and Beyond: The Fantasy World of L. Frank Baum.* Lawrence: University Press of Kansas, 1997.

Greene, Douglas G., and Michael Patrick Hearn. *W. W. Denslow.* Mount Pleasant: Central Michigan University, 1976.

PERIODICALS

Hearn, Michael Patrick. "Toto, I've A Feeling We're Not In Kansas City Anymore . . . Or Detroit . . . Or Washington, DC!" *Horn Book Magazine* 77, no. 1, January/February 2001, 16–33.

Gardner, Martin. "Why Librarians Dislike Oz."*American Book Collector* 13, no. 4, December 1962, 14–16.

Lurie, Alison. "The Oddness of Oz." *The New York Review of Books* 47, no. 20, December 21, 2000, 16–21.

Ritter, Gretchen. "The Real Meaning of Oz." *Wilson Quarterly* 22, no. 1, Winter 1998, 136–138.

WEBSITES

Gjovaag, Eric P. *The Wonderful Wizard of Oz* Website. Available online at http://www.eskimo.com/~tiktok/index.html; website home page http://www.eskimo.com (accessed March 25, 2003).

Kennedy, Elizabeth. "L. Frank Baum and '*The Wonderful Wizard of Oz*'." About.com. Available online at http://childrensbooks.about.com/library/weekly/aa052900a.htm; website home page http://childrensbooks.about.com (accessed March 25, 2003).

McGovern, Linda. "The Man Behind the Curtain: L. Frank Baum and the Wizard of Oz ." Literary Traveler. http://www.literarytraveler.com/spring/west/baum.htm; website home page http://www.literarytraveler.com (accessed March 25, 2003).

The Project Gutenberg E-text of *The Marvelous Land of Oz* by L. Frank Baum. Available online at http://www-2.cs.cmu.edu/People/rgs/ozland-table.html; website home page http://www-2.cs.cmu.edu (accessed March 25, 2003).

The Project Gutenberg E-text of *The Wonderful Wizard of Oz* by L. Frank Baum. Available online at http://www-2.cs.cmu.edu/People/rgs/wizoz10.html; website home page http://www-2.cs.cmu.edu (accessed March 25, 2003).

"To Please a Child: L. Frank Baum and the Land of Oz." Library of Congress. Available online at http://www.loc.gov/exhibits/oz/; website home page http://www.loc.gov (accessed March 25, 2003).

Whitcomb, James. R. Jim's Wizard of Oz Website. Available online at http://www.geocities.com/Hollywood/Hills/6396/index.html; website home page http://www.geocities.com (accessed March 25, 2003).

A Trip to the Moon

Manuscript

By: Georges Méliès

Date: c. 1902

Source: Méliès, Georges. *A Trip to the Moon* [manuscript]. Reprinted in Bessy, Maurice, and G.M. Lo Duca. *Georges Méliès: Mage et "Mes Memoires" par Méliès.* Paris: Prisma, 1945, 80; The Kobal Collection.

About the Author: Georges Méliès (1861–1938) was a French stage magician whose expansive imagination and fascination with optical illusions led to *A Trip to the Moon* (1902), a landmark in cinematic history. Méliès, a prodigiously talented artist, built Europe's first film studio in Montreuil, France. There he constructed elaborate sets for his fantastic short films. He produced over one thousand films and invented many special effects techniques before bankruptcy ended his film career in 1913. ■

Introduction

Méliès studied painting, drawing, and sculpture in his youth, and sold his share in his family's footwear business to become a stage magician. In 1895 a demonstration of the Lumière brothers' cinematograph sparked Méliès' interest in cinema. He eventually constructed his own camera and founded a production company, Star Films. Star Films was housed in a specially designed greenhouse-like structure, where Méliès created more than five hundred films between 1896 and 1912. These included reels of conjuring tricks, burlesques, newsreels, melodramas, adventure voyages, fairy tales, literary adaptations, and even advertisements.

Méliès painted magnificent sets for his films, and costumed his actors in the finest fashions and fabrics. He told stories of impossible adventures, mermaids, and fairies. As he used special effects in the narrative, Méliès is often considered the first filmmaker to bring storytelling to cinema. Before the popularity of story films, early audiences watched "actuality" films—depicting landscapes and news events; these films might show busy

A scene from the 1902 silent film *Le Voyage dans la lune* (A Trip to the Moon). A giant shell capsule is being loaded into a cannon that will fire it all the way to the Moon. **THE KOBAL COLLECTION/MELIES. REPRODUCED BY PERMISSION.**

downtown intersections in major American cities or important current events, such as the Pan American Exposition of 1901.

A Trip to the Moon (in French, *Le Voyage dans la lune*) was the most complex film of its time. It depicts the adventures of a group of scientists. The film even features dancers from the famous Parisian entertainment revue, The Folies Bergere. Méliès premiered *A Trip to the Moon* in a free showing in August 1902 at Paris's Olympia Theater. He sold the film to theaters throughout Europe, where it drew crowds and became highly profitable for theater owners. Méliès offered two versions of the film: a black and white print costing 560 francs ($126.75 at the time); and for twice that price, a colorized version—each frame was hand-tinted individually—was available.

The first part of *A Trip to the Moon* is believed to be based on a Jules Verne story and its illustrations by Alfred de Neuville. And its second half is believed to be based on H.G. Wells' *The First Men on the Moon.*

Significance

A Trip to the Moon often has been called the world's first science-fiction film, as well as its first popular narrative film. Some of the techniques Méliès invented for *A Trip to the Moon* revolutionized cinematography: fade-outs to black (to signify a passage of time); stop motion (advancing the film frame by frame to enable optical illusions by substituting props between frames—for example, chairs turning into telescopes); dissolves (overlapping two frames to indicate a passage of time or a change of location); double exposures (he accidentally discovered that two superimposed images could create a "ghostly" effect); filming small-scale models to give the illusion of full-scale objects; and the use of scenes to tell a story occurring in multiple locations.

Méliès planned to bring one hundred copies of *A Trip to the Moon* to New York, but discovered that Americans already were enjoying a bootleg copy of the film. Thomas A. Edison had pirated the prints that Méliès sold to London theater owners. Thus, Méliès, whose film career ended in bankruptcy, never realized any profit from his landmark film. To combat future piracy, Star Films opened a branch office in New York City in 1903. Méliès' brother, Gaston, oversaw its operations. Star Films took advantage of United States copyright laws and sold prints directly to the American market. Meanwhile, Georges continued to work

A scene from the 1902 silent film *Le Voyage dans la lune* (A Trip to the Moon). The Moon, in the form of a face, grimaces as a shell fired from Earth containing a scientific expedition hits it in the eye. **THE KOBAL COLLECTION. REPRODUCED BY PERMISSION.**

from France. Eventually, Gaston, also a film producer, moved the business west—first to Chicago in 1908, and then to San Antonio to make "cowboy movies" under the imprint, "American Wildwest," and eventually to California. The films of American Wildwest were profitable and helped keep Star Films afloat for a time.

Eventually, Star Films could not keep up. Just a few years after the success of *A Trip to the Moon,* the United States witnessed a boom in the cinema market. It was a major blow to Star Films when early industry regulators decided that films would be rented, rather than purchased. Additionally, Méliès' expensive, elaborate productions could not compete with the cheap and popular "Westerns" his competitors typically filmed in New Jersey.

Primary Source

A Trip to the Moon [excerpt]

SYNOPSIS: *A Trip to the Moon* is one of approximately fifty remaining films by Méliès. He destroyed many of his cinematic works, believing that they had no artistic or commercial value. *A Trip to the Moon* is regarded as Méliès' masterpiece. It was his most lucrative film, although he did not consider it his personal best. The existing prints vary in length from eight to fourteen minutes. Some prints omit the final scene in the town square, which is included in Méliès' handwritten manuscript for the film.

Outline

1. The Scientific Congress of the Astronomers Club.
2. The plan of the voyage is explained to the scientists with general enthusiasm.
3. The monstrous factory. Construction of the projectile.
4. Foundries, blast furnaces. Casting of the giant gun.
5. The astronomers embark in the shell.

6. The loading of the gun.
7. A signal with a flag. Fire!!
8. The race in space. The moon approaches.
9. Fully right into the eye!!
10. The shell falls to the moon. The Earth Light.
11. The plain of craters. Volcanic eruptions.
12. The dream (meteors, the Great Bear, Phoebe, twin stars, Saturn, etc.)
13. The snowstorm.
14. At forty degrees below zero. The descent into one of the craters.
15. Within the interior of the moon. The cave with giant mushrooms.
16. Meeting of the Selenites. Homeric combat.
17. Prisoners!
18. The king of the moon. The army of Selenites.
19. Escape.
20. Devilish pursuit.
21. The astronomers find the shell. Departure from the moon.
22. A vertical fall in the vacuum.
23. The shell falls into the ocean.
24. In the maritime depths.
25. Rescue. Return to port.
26. A large fete. A triumphal function.
27. Crowning and decoration of the heroes of the voyage.
28. A grand procession of "marines" and the men fired from the gun.
29. Inauguration of the commemorative statue by the Mayor and the city councilmen.
30. Large public rejoicing. A Selenite, captive from the moon, is exhibited in public as a phenomenon.

Narrative

The astronomers are assembled in a large hall embellished with instruments.

The president and members of the committee enter.

Everybody takes his seat.

. . . entrance of six man-servants carrying the telescopes of the astronomers.

The president takes his chair and explains to the members his plan of a Trip to the Moon.

His schemes are approved by many.

But one member violently opposes same.

After some argument, the president throws his papers and books at his head.

Upon order being restored, the trip proposed by the president is voted by acclamation.

Five learned men make up their mind to go with him.

The man-servants bring travelling suits.

President Barbenfouillis selects five colleagues to accompany him . . .

. . . Nostadamus, Alcofrisbas, Omega, Micromegas and Parafaragamus.

■ ■ ■

We enter the interior of the workshops where smiths, mechanics, weighers, carpenters, upholsterers, etc . . . are working hard at the completion of the machine.

Micromegas accidentally falls into a tub of nitric acid.

A workman informs the astronomers that if they would ascend to the roof, they would witness a splendid spectacle . . . the casting of the gun.

■ ■ ■

The astronomers ascend to a ladder and climb on the roof . . .

. . . where they finally arrive.

Against the horizon, the chimneys are seen belching forth volumes of smoke.

Suddenly, a flag is hoisted.

At the signal, a mass of molten steel is directed from each furnace into the mold for the gun.

The mold puts forth flames and vapor.

This causes much rejoicing among the enthusiastic astronomers.

■ ■ ■

On the top of the roofs of the town, pompous preparations have been made.

The shell is in position, ready to receive the travelers.

These arrive . . .

. . . respond to the acclamations of the crowd . . .

. . . and enter the shell.

Marine close the bridge through which they have passed.

A number of gunners are now pushing the shell up an incline into the mouth of the gun.

■ ■ ■

The cannon is loaded.

The bridge is closed.

Everyone is enthusiastically waiting for the signal which starts the shell on its voyage.

The officer gives the signal.

The gun is fired . . .

■ ■ ■

. . . and the shell disappears into space.

■ ■ ■

The shell coming closer every minute . . .

. . . the moon magnifies rapidly . . .

. . . and until finally it attains colossal dimensions.

Suddenly, the shell kisses the "eye" of the moon.

■ ■ ■

The shell comes down with a crash.

The astronomers get out and are delighted at the landscape which is new to them.

Against the horizon, the Earth is rising slowly into space . . .

. . . illuminating the picture with a fantastic light.

The astronomers, inspecting the strange country, see craters everywhere.

Just as they are about to explore, an explosion throws the unfortunate men violently in all directions.

The astronomers show signs of fatigue . . . after the rough trip they have just had.

They stretch themselves out on the ground and go to sleep.

Seven gigantic stars representing the Great Bear appear slowly . . .

. . . and out of the stars come faces of women whom seem annoyed at the presence of these intruders in the moon.

. . . in their dreams, they see passing in space: comets, meteors, etc.

Then, the stars are replaced by a lovely vision of Phoebes on the crescent, of Saturn in his globe surrounded by a ring and of charming young girls holding up a star.

They decide to punish the terrestrials in an exemplary manner.

By order of Phoebes, snow is falling from all quarters . . .

. . . covering the ground with its white coat. The cold becomes terrible.

The unfortunate voyagers wake up half-frozen.

They decide without hesitation (and in spite of the danger) to descend into the interior of the great crater . . .

. . . in which they disappear one-by-one whilst the snowstorm is still raging.

■ ■ ■

The astronomers arrive in the interior of a most curious grotto.

Here we see enormous mushrooms of every kind.

One of them opens his umbrella to compare its size with the mushroom . . .

. . . but the umbrella suddenly takes root and transforming itself into a mushroom starts growing gradually into gigantic proportions.

The astronomers suddenly notice strange beings coming out from underneath the mushrooms . . . while making singular contortions.

These are the Selenites . . . or inhabitants of the Moon.

A fantastical being rushes on an astronomer . . . who defends himself . . . and with a stroke of his umbrella the Selenite bursts into a thousand pieces.

A second suffers the same fate.

But the Selenites are arriving in numbers.

The terrified astronomers, to save themselves, take flight with the Selenites in pursuit.

■ ■ ■

Succumbing to numbers, the astronomers are captured, bound and taken to the palace of the King of the Selenites.

On a splendid throne, surrounded by living stars, the Selenite king is sitting.

President Barbenfouillis makes a dash for the King of the Selenites . . . and lifting him like a feather throws him violently on the ground.

The unfortunate king bursts like a bombshell.

■ ■ ■

The astronomers run away in the midst of the general disorder.

The Selenite army is pursuing them.

The astronomers run at full speed turning around each time they are pressed too closely . . . and reducing the fragile beings to dust.

The still increasing number of Selenites obliges the astronomer to take desperation to flight again.

■ ■ ■

At last, the astronomers have found the shell and quickly shove themselves in the interior.

Thanks to the advance, they have succeeded in gaining over their adversaries . . . only one, the president, has been left behind.

He rushes to the rope which hangs on the front of the shell . . . and letting himself slide down the rope he gives it a push which causes the shell to fall off the edge of the Moon.

A Selenite clinging to the shell to hold it back is drawn with it . . .

. . . and hanging on the projectile accompanies it in its drop.

■ ■ ■

The shell falls with sickening rapidity.

■ ■ ■

The Sea appears.

We're currently following the course of the shell into the bottom of the ocean.

The shell balances . . . and thanks to the hermetically sealed air in its interior rises slowly to the surface . . . to the puzzlement of the fishes.

■ ■ ■

The shell is picked up by a steamer which tows it to port . . .

. . . where a general ovation awaits the happy return.

nnn

(additional tableaux)

The Selenite is still seen clinging to the shell.

In the market place of the town the authorities are assembled . . .

. . . the crowd awaiting the appearance of the astronomers.

The procession arrives.

The municipal band advances . . .

. . . followed by marines drawing the decorated shell.

The Mayor congratulates the astronomers on their happy return.

Crowning them, he confers upon them the Order of the Moon.

The march past of the fire brigade and marines takes place.

On the square appears the commemorative statue of the trip . . .

. . . representing President Barbenfouillis vanquishing the moon, with this device:

"Labor Omnia Vincit."

The marines, the astronomers, the crowd, the Mayor and councillors join in chorus dancing around the statue to the President.

Further Resources

BOOKS

Barnouw, Erik. *The Magician and the Cinema.* New York: Oxford University Press, 1981.

Brakhage, Stan. *The Brakhage Lectures: Georges Méliès, David Wark Griffith, Carl Theodore Dreyer, Sergei Eisenstein.* Chicago: The GoodLion, 1972.

Cook, David A. *A History of Narrative Film.* New York: W.W. Norton, 1996.

Ezra, Elizabeth. *George Méliès: the Birth of the Auteur.* Manchester, England: St. Martin's Press, 2000.

Frazer, John. *Artificially Arranged Scenes: The Films of George Méliès.* Boston: G.K. Hall & Co., 1979.

Hammond, Paul. *Marvelous Méliès* . London: Gordon Fraser Gallery, 1974.

PERIODICALS

Boddy, William. "The Rhetoric and Economic Roots of the American Broadcasting Industry." *Cine-Tracts 6* 2, no. 2, Spring 1979, 28–36.

Helman, A. "An Appraisal of the Work of Georges Méliès as Compared to that of Lumière." *Kino,* January 9, 1974.

Jefferson, Margo. "Moonstruck Magic by the Grandfather of Film Fantasies." *New York Times,* November 15, 1997, B7.

WEBSITES

Dirks, Tim. "*Le Voyage Dans La Lune (A Trip To The Moon).*" The Greatest Films. http://www.filmsite.org/voya.html; website home page http://www.filmsite.org (accessed March 20, 2003).

"Foreign Films: Georges Méliès." 3to6.com. http://www.3to6.com/final_foreignfilm/foreign1_dir.asp?vid=3; website home page http://www.3to6.com (accessed March 20, 2003).

Larson, E.H. "Georges Méliès." Silent Movie Personalities. Available online at http://www.nwlink.com/~erick/silentera/Melies/melies.html; website home page http://www.nwlink.com (accessed March 20, 2003).

AUDIO AND VISUAL MEDIA

"Part 12: Le Voyage Dans La Lune." *From The Earth To The Moon.* HBO Home Video Release, 1998, VHS.

Méliès the Magician. Facets Video, 1997, VHS, DVD.

Selected Letters of Edwin Arlington Robinson

Letters

By: Edwin Arlington Robinson

Date: 1905, 1908

Source: Robinson, Edwin Arlington. *Selected Letters of Edwin Arlington Robinson.* New York: Macmillan, 1940, 59–65.

About the Author: Edwin Arlington Robinson (1869–1935) was one of the most acclaimed American poets during his lifetime. Robinson's mature poetry had a dark, direct tone. This made his writing popular, even though he refused to adopt the developing modernist style of American verse. Robinson famously eschewed the comforts of traditional life, embracing poverty for the freedom to write. Even after he achieved recognition for his writing, he continued to work from Gardiner, Maine, where he was raised. During the 1920s, he was awarded a Pulitzer Prize three times. ■

Introduction

In his early twenties, Edwin Arlington Robinson dedicated himself to a literary career. In 1896, he self-published his first pamphlet-sized volume of poetry, *The Torrent and the Night Before.* He sent out copies, and he received some favorable responses. Encouraged, he published *The Children of the Night* in 1897. He then moved to New York to be among other writers. Unable to make a living by writing, he took a job as a time-checker for the New York subway system.

Robinson developed his poetic reputation through his fictional characters inspired by his bleak New England upbringing; he renamed Gardiner as "Tilbury Town." Among his best-known poems are "Richard Cory," "Miniver Cheevy," and "Mr. Flood's Last Party." Although he acknowledged Wordsworth and Kipling as his influences, he wrote in colloquial language, rather than with "poetic diction." Many of Robinson's poems are dramatic monologues by anti-heroes. Robinson was most interested in characters that struggled to gain spiritual wisdom. These characters either failed spiritually or appeared as failures in the eyes of the world.

Robinson was disinterested in descriptive poetry, or poetry about nature. He chose to write poems about subjects that might have been just as easily written in prose. But he delighted in the verse tradition—such as the sonnet, quatrain, or eight-line stanza—and he allowed the form of the poem to carry his narratives. When asked why he did not try free verse, Robinson dryly replied, "I write badly enough as it is."

Significance

His third volume of poetry, *Captain Craig* (1902) received little fanfare. But *The Children of the Night* had captured the attention of President Theodore Roosevelt (served 1901–1909). Roosevelt was so impressed that he wrote a magazine article praising Robinson's poetry, coerced Scribner's Sons to reprint the book, and procured Robinson a job at the New York Customs House. In 1905, Robinson accepted the post. As his responsibilities were minimal, the position afforded him an excellent salary and plenty of time to write. Robinson later complained that during this time of relative affluence, he produced his worst work ever.

At the time, critics did not agree with the President's assessment of Robinson's poetry. Even with Roosevelt's patronage, major magazines still refused to publish Robinson's works. When Roosevelt left the White House in 1909, Robinson resigned from his post—after being ordered to do his job, wear a uniform, and keep regular hours. Robinson returned to Gardiner, and he began to write full time. He revised older work and wrote new poems. The following year, he published *The Town Down the River,* dedicated to his former benefactor, Roosevelt.

For the first time, Robinson received an energetic response to his poetry from literary critics, who had been previously lukewarm to his writing. *The New York Times* gave *The Town Down the River* a positive review, but it was *The Boston Transcript* that boldly hailed Robinson (in a large headline) as "America's Foremost Poet." *The Boston Transcript's* editor, William Stanley Braithwaite, was an established poet and literary critic. After this, Robinson's literary reputation began to grow.

Primary Source

Selected Letters of Edwin Arlington Robinson [excerpt]

SYNOPSIS: Edward Arlington Robinson frequently corresponded with numerous friends, including Richard Watson Gilder (1844–1909)—one of the most influential figures in American publishing, a poet and editor-in-chief of *The Century* monthly magazine for three decades. Gilder was an elder figure to Robinson, who greatly admired his work; at the time of these letters, Gilder was nearing the end of his life. Craven Langstroth Betts was another of Robinson's writer friends, as was Laura E. Richards (1850–1943), a popular children's author, also from Gardiner, Maine. Daniel Gregory Mason (1873–1953) was an important composer, writer, and lecturer of the period. Like his poetry, Robinson's letters reveal a self-deprecating humor.

To Richard Watson Gilder

April 11, 1905

1 Yarmouth Street (Boston)

Some time ago I was surprised to receive a pleasant note from President Roosevelt, speaking well of my books and showing clearly that someone had been at work upon him. This note was soon followed by offers of employment in strange lands—to wit, in Montreal and Mexico—which I could not see my way to accept. Now he understands my situation, and I may or may not hear from him again. In many respects I am placed fortunately as I am, in that I have about two-thirds of my time to myself. I have told him this, making it clear at the same time that if I could have more congenial work, with more pay and the same amount of leisure, I should be happy to get it. Were I not cursed with the poetical microbe, of course everything would be different. In fact, I should never have heard from him at all.

All this is in the way of saying that I thank you very much for what you have done in the matter. I cannot find out from Mr. Moody just how far he is implicated, as he contents himself with being facetious at my expense, after the manner of one who can well afford to do so. Will you kindly see that he gets his share of my gratitude? For even though nothing should come of it, I shall always remember this episode as one of those pleasant and unexpected things that come about as frequently as the Phoenix. I am quoting Schopenhauer apropos of the critic. He adds that the Phoenix comes once every five hundred years. All of which is amusing, but not to the purpose.

Acclaimed American poet Edwin Arlington Robinson. AP/WIDE WORLD PHOTOS. REPRODUCED BY PERMISSION.

To Craven Langstroth Betts

April 18, 1905

1 Yarmouth Street, Boston

I have just received a letter from Mrs. C. in which she tells me that you are thinking of closing your establishment and living by yourself. I wonder if you will pardon me if I venture to hope that you will not spend too much time in thinking about it? You deserve your freedom, if ever a man did and you ought to have it. I have thought about it a great deal during the past two or three years and very likely I have been remiss sometimes in letting you know it. All this is only in the hope that you may soon have a den of your own and another for your sister. I have two cousins, brother and sister, who have lived together so long that I don't like to think about them. They are so much like married mummies that the thought of them makes me weep. I have no fear of your becoming like one of them, but I have a great fear of your losing that simple joy of living for which you have—or at any rate appear to have—such a God-given genius. Don't throw away the rest of your life, even if the change does make some disturbance in the lives of others. There is nothing in the law or the prophets that says a man must crucify himself to please his relations. I suppose I ought not to write this but I'm damned if I can help it.—If ever I get hold of any money, and there are small symptoms of such a thing, my first selfish dissipation will be to pay back (I don't like that way of putting it) some of the life that I owe to you. The opportunity may never come but we'll wait and see. If T. Roosevelt keeps on offering me two thousand dollar jobs that I don't want, I can't say what may happen. The trouble with me is that I want to live in New York. I can't feel at home anywhere else. I have more than half a mind to get my shoes tapped and go to Washington as soon as T.R. comes back from the bear country. He says he wants to see me, and that he doesn't want me to leave the country; so perhaps he can land me in New York. Also, perhaps I may never hear from him again. . . .

To Mrs. Laura E. Richards

June 5, 1905

United States Customs Service, Port of New York

Madam:

In reply to your letter of the second instant I have to say that bananas and skeletons may be imported free of duty. I regret to inform you that there is a duty of ten (10) per centum on baked ant's eggs.

Respectfully,
E. A. Robinson

P. S. I am not in buttons—nor am I a Special Agent. I don't yet see why I should be, but that may be explained.

To Mrs. Laura E. Richards

New York, August 7, 1905

Special Agent Treasury Department

The soulless Secretary of the Treasury has taken away my steamboat and given me poor quality of paper in the bargain. That steamboat was more than half of all that I had in the world—in fact it was the only thing connected with the United States Customs Service that was at all worth while. Therefore the Secretary removed it. His dinner disagreed with him sometime ago and since then he has been dreaming that he is going to be the next President. All this is pretty nice on my part, for I assume it to be true that there is in him something that is as human as a stomach. You may think from my literary style that I have been reading the Holy Scriptures for relief, but I have not been reading them. On the contrary, I have been reading Torrence's monumental poem for the September *Atlantic,* by means of which he hopes to leap into immortal glory and leave Moody in the shadow, swearing. I don't think that he will quite do it, but he will do enough to make some thousands of people rub their eyes.

To Mrs. Laura E. Richards

[1905, undated]

The strenuous man has given me some of the most powerful loafing that has ever come my way. Sometime there is going to be something to do—otherwise there would be no Custom House. As it is I look out upon Wall Street and see men going to their ruin and to their luncheons. It is a sad life. If my next book turns out pessimistic you are to attribute the fact to T. R., not to me. By nature I am jovial and sunny but I can't continue so unless there is crime in the world to cheer me up and give me something to do. I am (along with 13 others) the victim of other men's good conduct. If you are really a friend of mine you will go abroad at once and smuggle something. There is a duty of twenty cents a pound on nails.

Yours Very Truly

[Postscript]

I live at 450 West 23rd Street.

To Daniel Gregory Mason

July 22, 1908

United States Customs Service, Port of New York

Under a new system and a new Boss my chief duty as a pillar of the government appears to consist in remaining a prisoner in Room 408. This is particularly rotten just now, as I am in a mood for work (work with me means studying the ceiling and my navel for four hours and then writing down perhaps four lines—sometimes as many as seven and again none at all) while there is just enough going on here, not to mention all hell outside, to keep my poor relic of a brain in a state that suggests nothing to me at the moment unless it be a state of semi-agitated punk. Yes, punk's the word with me; and it will be for some time to come unless I can contrive to hypnotize my chief officer into an appreciation of my place in nature. If I come in some afternoon and find him waving a "phony" invoice in one hand and Old Doctor Moody's *Masque of Judgment* in the other, I shall know that I have the right kind of an eye for him. Don't let my apparent inertness lead you into supposing that I am as mud in the hands of my immediate superiors, for there are other elements at work. As a matter of fact my three years in this business have not been, for the most part, years to make a fellow grow young. There is no need of my going into particulars. On the other hand don't you make the mistake of supposing that I have failed, or do fail, to appreciate my devilish good luck in landing here. My chief concern is a fear that I may turn out a disappointment to my friends and to T. R., who must be wondering—if he finds time—how long it takes a man to write a hundred pages of verse. It does not, in fact, take long to write a hundred pages of verse, but unfortunately, there is only a visual resemblance between verse and the other thing. For quantity (I mean size) I do not myself care a damn; but a fellow has to be dead before the public understands that a dozen titles are quite enough to string wires on that will reach through ten times as many centuries—perhaps. I don't know about my metaphor, nor do I know that I have ever done anything that the future will require, but I do know that those things I have done are my own (to use the world's nonsense) and that they have to be done in my way. If they go by the board, they will go because I could not build them any better.—Now that this exquisite bit of drivel is out of my system, I'll have a smoke.

Hurrah for crime—as Burnham used to say,

Yours to command

To Richard Watson Gilder

December 22, 1908

United States Customs Service, Port of New York,

Since writing my hurried note of something like a fortnight ago I have been living with your book; and I wish now to repeat my sincere thanks to you for sending it. While nearly everything in it was familiar in a general way, I found, as a result of a more leisurely and intimate acquaintance with your work, now brought together in one volume, that the distinction and originality of the poems are perhaps even more apparent and satisfying than when they were scattered. It must give you a sense of comfortable triumph to know that your position in literature is assured beyond all question and that it is so honorable and so high. You will remember that I am writing as a younger man to his elder, and I am sure that you will excuse anything that may seem like naiveté in my attempt to express an admiration that is to be taken for what you think it worth, and in no sense as an accompaniment of my natural gratitude to you for your friendliness on many occasions in the past.

When I used to read your poems twenty years ago in Maine I little supposed that I was ever to meet the man who wrote them—still less did I suspect that I was ever to be under such pleasant and life-long obligations to him as I have lately experienced—in more ways than one.

Putting aside your past-mastery of technique—the praise of which would at this late date be banal—I admire most your willingness to look life in the face without resorting to the nauseating evasions of the uncompromising "optimist." The predominance of this willingness to be honest, with never the suggestion of surrender—or even of weariness—is to my mind the most admirable thing in life or in art—provided always that the artist has the faculty of being interesting. To be more concrete I will say I have long thought "Non Sine Dolore" not only interesting but exciting—and this is only one poem of thirty or forty of which I could say as much.

Yours sincerely, and always with gratitude and admiration,

Further Resources

BOOKS

Bloom, Harold, ed. *Edwin Arlington Robinson.* New York: Chelsea House Publishers, 1988.

Boswell, Jeanetta. *Edwin Arlington Robinson and the Critics.* Metuchen, N.J.: Scarecrow Press, 1988.

Ellsworth, Barnard. *Edwin Arlington Robinson: A Critical Study.* New York: Octagon Books, 1969.

Hagedorn, Hermann. *Edwin Arlington Robinson: A Biography.* New York, The Macmillan Company, 1938.

Smith, Chard Powers. *Where the Light Falls: A Portrait of Edwin Arlington Robinson.* New York: Macmillan, 1965.

PERIODICALS

Branscomb, Jack. "Edwin Arlington Robinson's Wretched Wight: 'Miniver Cheevy' and 'La Belle Dame Sans Merci.'" *ANQ* 9, no. 1, Winter 1996, 17.

Dauner, Louise. "Edwin Arlington Robinson: Tilbury Town Revisited." *Modern Age* 39, no. 3, Summer 1997, 256.

WEBSITES

Edwin Arlington Robinson. Available online at http://robinson.bokardo.com/index.phtml; website home page http://robinson.bokardo.com (accessed March 24, 2003).

Justice, Donald. "Benign Obscurity: Edward Arlington Robinson." The New Criterion Online. Available online at http://www.newcriterion.com/archive/15/feb97/justice.htm; website home page http://www.newcriterion.com (accessed March 24, 2003).

Nelson, Cary, ed. "Edwin Arlington Robinson." Modern American Poetry. http://www.english.uiuc.edu/maps/poets/m_r/robinson/robinson.htm; website home page http://www.english.uiuc.edu (accessed March 24, 2003).

The Letters of Arturo Toscanini

Letters

By: Arturo Toscanini

Date: 1905–1909

Source: Sachs, Harvey. ed., trans. *The Letters of Arturo Toscanini.* New York: Alfred A. Knopf, 2002, 69–80.

About the Author: Arturo Toscanini (1867–1957) was one of the world's most legendary conductors. Under his leadership, he elicited some of the most breathtaking and energetic orchestral performances of the twentieth century. He introduced radical changes to the way operas and orchestras were run. In addition to his musical accomplishments, Toscanini was outspoken in his opposition to fascism in Italy and Germany. Born in Parma, Italy, Toscanini first came to the United States to lead New York City's Metropolitan Opera in 1908. But there resistance to his demands for artistic control ultimately led to his departure in 1914, although his reforms had been instrumental in bringing a new level of professionalism to the music world. Toscanini returned to La Scala from 1921 to 1929, and returned to the U.S. to lead the New

York Philharmonic Orchestra from 1928 to 1936. Beginning in 1937 he conducted the NBC Symphony Orchestra (formed especially for him) until his retirement in 1954. Throughout his career, Toscanini appeared internationally, serving as guest conductor for some of the world's greatest orchestras. He also conducted numerous recordings, most notably his versions of Beethoven's symphonies, as well as the works of Brahms, Wagner, Verdi, and many others. He died in Riverdale, New York. ■

Introduction

Arturo Toscanini began his career as a cellist. After graduating from music school with top honors, he worked as a cellist playing in minor orchestras. He began his international music career by joining a touring opera orchestra. In Brazil, Toscanini made an impromptu debut as a conductor. In 1886, the opera company presented Verdi's *Aida.* On the second night of the engagement, the performers dismissed the principal conductor for incompetence. When the assistant conductor attempted to ascend the podium, the audience heckled him off. Amidst the chaos, several fellow musicians urged Toscanini to take the conductor's baton, as they knew he had memorized the music thoroughly. As the young Toscanini assumed the conductor's position, the curious audience fell into silence. By the end of the performance, Toscanini had won the respect of both the orchestra and the audience. He was only nineteen.

Toscanini was asked to lead the orchestra for the remainder of its season. The following year, he returned to Italy to devote himself to conducting, taking apprenticeships in provincial theaters. Despite his impressive debut, Toscanini drifted from orchestra to orchestra. At the time, orchestras were poorly organized. Musicians could not count on a regular salary, since few theater houses had permanent orchestras. In opera, the situation was even worse. In Italy, famously passionate about opera, even the smallest town had its own theater. However, too often, patrons chose leading performers for reasons other than vocal ability. Orchestras were poorly prepared, as rehearsal occurred infrequently and inconsistently.

As a conductor, Toscanini was consistently in demand. He developed a reputation for bringing out the best in his musicians. In 1898, he was appointed principal conductor of Milan's La Scala, Europe's most prestigious and famous opera house. By this time, he had already led 113 productions of fifty-eight operas all over Italy, including premieres of major works like Puccini's *La Boheme* (1896). He would conduct La Scala until resigning in 1903. He retook his part in 1906 but departed for the United States in 1908.

Significance

Toscanini was notorious for his volatile temper, particularly during rehearsals. Many called him "Maestro," meaning master or leader. On the conductor's podium, he demanded absolute perfection from his performers, throwing tantrums if they failed to play up to his standards. He even canceled performances if dress rehearsals went poorly. He often conducted from memory. Unlike other conductors, he wanted total artistic control over the whole opera production: Toscanini chose his repertoire, performers, stage design, rehearsal schedules, and performance dates. He insisted on auditions for orchestra musicians and performers to ensure that parts were cast according to merit, rather than patronage—a common practice, especially in opera. He eliminated the tradition of performing amusing ballet shorts after tragic operas (done so that the audience would not leave depressed). He put the orchestra in a pit, and dimmed the house lights to allow audiences to focus their attentions onstage. Toscanini refused to do encores. Toscanini was confrontational and unyielding, yet often successful in making substantive changes. He garnered enormous respect from his performers and was emulated by other conductors.

Toscanini's letters to his friends, family, and lovers provide valuable insight into the dynamic personality behind his musical accomplishments. Toscanini was proud, and he had an artistic conscience that made even the smallest musical mistake intolerable; he could not bear the thought of undeserved praise. He was fastidious and hardworking. During his lifetime, he allowed some of his private letters to be published, including the January 1, 1905 letter to Enrico Polo—in which Toscanini deplored Mahler's supposed lack of originality—as well as other correspondence regarding artistic matters. A cache of pornographic letters from Toscanini to his numerous lovers was discovered soon after his death, but is considered of little musical-historical value. In the mid-1990s, another batch of letters surfaced, revealing the conductor's thoughts and feelings on many subjects including his musical career, literature, his political beliefs, love and sex, and travel.

Primary Source

The Letters of Arturo Toscanini [excerpt]

SYNOPSIS: By 1903, Toscanini had departed La Scala. But in 1906 he went back to La Scala for another two years. He already had an international reputation; that year, the Metropolitan Opera in New York began urging Toscanini to take on its leadership, but he did not accept the invitation until 1908. Prior to joining the Met, Toscanini was a guest conductor in Buenos Aires, Argentina, and conducted concerts throughout Italy in Bologna, Rome, Turin, and Milan. Giuseppe Martucci (1856–1909) was a conductor, pianist, and composer much admired by Toscanini. In the first letter to Martucci, Toscanini refers to Martucci's Second Symphony in F Major, opus 81 and the orchestra of the Accademia di

Santa Cecilia. (At the time Martucci conducted concerts at La Scala, but Toscanini could not attend due to his eye problems.) Enrico Polo (1868–1953) was a violinist and former classmate of Toscanini's at the Parma Conservatory. Toscanini met his wife, Carla de Martini (1887–1951) during his preparations for the first Italian production of Wagner's Gotterdammerung in Turin in 1895. Her sister Ida, who would later marry Enrico Polo, was in the cast. Carla and Toscanini married in 1897. He affectionately calls her Bocchietto here, writing from the Ansonia, the hotel where he stayed in New York. These letters were written in Italian, appearing here in translation.

Letter to Giuseppe Martucci, February 15, 1905

. . . Yesterday I began rehearsing the symphony and after two hours of assiduous study I was not able to get through the first movement. What a horrid orchestra! How badly they sight-read! And they play even worse! I haven't conducted their like in years. I have to think back to a rather remote period in order to remind myself of impressions similar to the ones revived in me by this Roman orchestra. These people have lost the feel for playing—I won't even say well, but at least correctly. I nearly slaughtered myself trying to put together the first concert, which the public and *magna critica* deemed highly successful. And here it is really the case that he who is satisfied enjoys himself. I was disgusted by it.

Today I was able to read through the first movement better and to run through the Scherzo, which turned out to be less difficult than the first movement. Tomorrow I shall dedicate to the Scherzo again and I shall read through the Adagio. I can already hear those cellos and those wretched double basses wreaking havoc on those poor notes. Enough—I've armed myself with patience. I hope it will serve to achieve everything that these not good, but good-hearted players (since that is how they have been with me) can give. And to think that you read through the whole symphony in two rehearsals in Bologna!

I told Count di San Martino that eight rehearsals will be necessary for this concert; I am sure that he will be able to satisfy my request, somehow or other. . . .

Letter to Mr. Fano, March 8, 1905

Dear Mr. Fano

I beg your pardon for having taken so long to reply to your very kind letter, but a series of doubts, of ifs, of buts, made me and continues to make me

Conductor Arturo Toscanini at age 28. © **CORBIS. REPRODUCED BY PERMISSION.**

hesitate as to whether or not to accept your proposal, which is an extremely kind one in many respects. I fear working abroad because of the dizzying rush in the preparation of both opera productions and concerts, but I especially fear London because I remember a performance of *Götterdämmerung* in which the orchestra, under the direction of Felix Mottl, was sight-reading the opera's final scene before an audience. The audience noticed nothing, and the press found the performance superb. Of course! An eminent maestro was conducting, and he was German to boot.

Now, under no circumstances would I want to find myself in such a situation, in the first place out of self-respect; in the second, because I would despair if I were to be treated in such a way by the English public and press—and this is why I would like to know what the terms for these two concerts would be—how many rehearsals would be granted me for each of them, and of what length, and what criteria I would have to apply in working out the programs.

As to my fee for each concert, you may bear in mind that the Bologna Quartet Society usually gives me 1,500 lire [roughly $300 or £60 at the time] and that, as a special favor on my part, I accept a thousand lire from the Turin Concert Society. If these negotiations haven't already fallen through, as a result of my delay in replying, I hope that you will be so kind as to refer my questions to London and to let me know the outcome as soon as you can. For the time being, I thank you with all my heart and I greet you cordially.

Your Dev. A Toscanini

Letter to Richard Strauss, October 9 or 10, 1906

Dear Master,

I want to tell you immediately that I am not at all angry with you: I am only very astonished that when I expressed my simple and more than natural personal wish to give *Salome* in Milan on the 26th [of December], you didn't interpret this wish according to its true meaning but rather brought the matter onto commercial terrain. I repeat that it's not La Scala's administration that is requesting permission to move up the opening date in Milan, because in any case the administration could never give more than 15 performances of your opera; it is I, rather, [who request this permission] for entirely personal and artistic satisfaction. But in the end, dear Master, if you intend to continue in your determination to change the conditions of the contract [in order to grant] the favor that I had asked, then I am obliged to ask you to leave things as they are: we will give *Salome* in Milan at the time already decided upon, because I cannot allow the administration of La Scala to make a sacrifice in order to do me a favor.

In any case, I shall be at Mr. Fürstner's at 11 o'clock. Sincerely,

Your
A. Toscanini

Letter to Richard Strauss, November 12, 1906

12 November 1906

Highly esteemed Master!

I received your letter from Frankfurt just when I wanted to give you news of La Scala's *Salome*—news that will spare further annoyances to both you and me, and for which you need not thank me for my compliance—I felt no obligation at all to be so (notice my free declaration)—but rather a situation that hadn't been sufficiently anticipated and that now turns the matter to your advantage. I began the piano rehearsals of *Salome* several days ago, and you cannot imagine what a titanic, superhuman effort the singers have to make to try to overcome the colossal difficulties, which are made even worse by a bad translation. This convinced me that I had been perfectly stupid in settling on a date for the performance of an opera without having taken its difficulties into consideration—an opera in which, for the ears of our Italian singers, there are extraordinary harmonic contrasts and great difficulties to be overcome.

I considered it my duty to inform the administration of La Scala of all this: consequently, *Salome* cannot be performed before early January, the more so inasmuch as I have to prepare the opera *Carmen* at the same time.

As you see, esteemed Master, the matter has taken a good turn, not thanks to me but thanks to your luck, as you and the Turin impresa desired. I hope that it won't be necessary to add anything else to all that has already been said and argued on this subject.

Please believe always in my admiration for your art, and accept my devoted greetings.

Your
Arturo Toscanini

Letter to Giuseppe Martucci, April or May, 1907 or 1908

My dear Maestro

My brother-in-law Polo will have told you about the monastic isolation that the doctor has imposed on me for two weeks. I can't begin to tell you how superirritable I've become as a result of this hard-and-fast requirement to wander around the house all day, in the dark, like a ghost, without being able to read and without being able to work at anything at all! I can't describe my displeasure over not having been able to spend a few hours in your and your good wife's company. You can surely imagine how I feel. I was hoping that the doctor would allow me to come to La Scala for a moment this evening to say hello, but he is sticking inexorably to his orders, for the health of my eyes. Therefore I'm sending you in writing my most affectionate greetings, and I beg you to present my most devoted salutations to your good wife.

Your Affectionate A Toscanini

Letter to Bocchietto, December 12, 1909

My dearest Bocchietto

. . . when I have nothing to do at the theater I stay home. I study, and from time to time I read in

English, but . . . unfortunately, I don't speak it. And to think that I could do so rather well. As I've already written, on Sundays I have dinner with the Amatos, excepting the two occasions on which I was invited by the De Macchis and Dr. Castelli's fiancée. I went to Alda's a couple of times, but some time ago. The other day Marchesi's landlady's little girl came to lunch, and in fact she asked me to write and tell you that she would like to have a photograph of you together with the children. . . . Last week Marchesi came to my place almost every day for either lunch or supper. Setti and Romei haven't yet been here. I'll invite them soon. Tomorrow is the Orfeo dress rehearsal, in the evening a performance of But[terfly; rest of letter missing]

Further Resources

BOOKS

Frank, Mortimer H. *Arturo Toscanini: The NBC Years* Portland, Ore.: Amadeus Press, 2002.

Freeman, John W., and Walfredo Toscanini. *Portraits of Greatness: Toscanini.* New York: Treves Publishing Company, 1987.

Haggin, B. H. *Conversations with Toscanini.* New York: Da Capo Press, 1989.

Marsh, Robert C. *Toscanini and the Art of Orchestral Performance.* Westport, Colo.: Greenwood Press, 1973.

Sachs, Harvey. *Reflections on Toscanini.* Rocklin, Calif. Prima Publishing, 1993.

PERIODICALS

Epperson, Gordon. "At the Hands of the Mighty." *Strad* 108, no. 1287, July 1997, 744–748.

Teachout, Terry. "Toscanini Lives." *Commentary* 114, no. 1, July–August 2002, 58–63.

WEBSITES

Arturo Toscanini Foundation. Available online at http://www.fondazione-toscanini.it/ (accessed March 25, 2003).

Gutmann, Peter. "Toscanini, the Recorded Legend." Classical Notes. Available online at http://www.classicalnotes.net/features/toscaweb.html; website home page http://www.classicalnotes.net (accessed March 25, 2003).

"History: An Introduction to the Metropolitan Opera." The Metropolitan Opera. Available online at http://www.metopera.org/history/intro.html; website home page http://www.metopera.org (accessed March 25, 2003).

Harry Houdini's Magic

Advertisement for *The Conjuror's Monthly Magazine; "Harry Houdini Performs the Amazing Milk Can Escape"*

Advertisement; Photograph

By: Harry Houdini

Date: 1906–1908

Source: "Advertisement for *The Conjurors' Monthly Magazine;*" "Harry Houdini Performs the Amazing Milk Can Eascape." *The American Variety Stage: Vaudeville and Popular Entertainment, 1870–1920: Houdini.* American Memory digital primary source collection. Library of Congress. Available online at http://memory.loc.gov/ammem/vshtml/vshdini.html; website home page: http://memory.loc.gov (accessed May 19, 2003).

"Hogan Envelope Company Employees Challenge to the Famous Houdini;" "Houdini Defied!!"

Posters

By: Hogan Envelope Company; Alliance Dairy

Date: 1907–1908

Source: "Hogan Envelope Company Employees Challenge to the Famous Houdini;" "Houdini Defied!!" 1907; 1908. Reprinted in Gibson, Walter B. *The Original Houdini Scrapbook.* New York: Corwin Sterling, 1976, 33, 35.

Primary Source

Advertisement for *The Conjuror's Monthly Magazine*

SYNOPSIS: An advertisement for Houdini's publication *The Conjuror's Monthly Magazine.* A master self-promoter, Houdini was constantly engaged in a variety of pursuits besides his magic and escape acts to keep in the public eye, including writing, films, and stunts. THE LIBRARY OF CONGRESS.

Primary Source

"Harry Houdini Performs the Amazing Milk Can Escape"

SYNOPSIS: Photograph of Harry Houdini in a milk can, preparing to make an escape. He is surrounded by policemen and officials there to ensure that his escape attempt is genuine. Houdini's Giant Milk Can escape became one of his most popular tricks on his tour through the United States, England, and Germany. THE LIBRARY OF CONGRESS.

Hogan Envelope Company

EMPLOYEES

CHALLENGE TO THE

FAMOUS HOUDINI

Manager.

Majestic Theatre, Chicago.

Dear Sir:

We believe a giant Envelope can be made by us which will enclose Houdini and successfully prevent his escape therefrom under the following conditions.

His hands and feet to be securly tied with strong rope, after which he is to be placed in the Envelope, tieing the top of Envelope with rope and sealing same.

The Envelope will be the largest ever made, being constructed of the toughest heaviest rope fibre manila paper obtainable.

It will be open on the end with an 18 inch flap.

150 inches high by 54 inches wide and will contain 16,000 square inches of stock. The sides will be securly sealed also being riveted with our Tension fasteners. the bottom being of the Satchel variety. Weight 15 pounds. Kindly let us know if the great Houdini will accept our challenge.

Employees,
HOGAN ENVELOPE COMPANY.

EMPLOYEES,
Hogan Envelope Company,
86-96 E. Ohio St., Chicago.

Gentlemen:

I accept your extraordinary challenge and will endeavor to make my escape from your Envelope Friday Evening, December 13th, 1907, on the stage of the Majestic Theatre.

HOUDINI.

Primary Source

"Hogan Envelope Company Employees Challenge to the Famous Houdini"

SYNOPSIS: A poster challenges Harry Houdini to escape from a giant envelope. Houdini accepted the challenge and performed the stunt in 1907. Many companies devised special restraints and challenged Houdini to escape them. REPRINTED FROM WALTER BROWN GIBSON, *THE ORIGINAL HOUDINI SCRAPBOOK.* NEW YORK: CORWIN STERLING PUBLISHING CO. INC., 1976.

HOUDINI DEFIED!!

[COPY OF LETTER.]

H. HOUDINI, ESQ.,
The "Oxford"
Oxford Street, W.

Sir,

Having witnessed your new "Can" Trick, we believe that the main secret is your ability to see through the water, and we would like to know if you will allow us to send along 60 Gallons of Milk, and fill up the Can; the liquid in which you are immersed on this occasion being opaque our opinion is that you will be unable to make your escape in the usual fashion.

If you will agree to our test, we will send along the Milk any time you select but insist that our men fill the Can as well as lock you in.

Awaiting your reply,
We remain, yours faithfully,
ALLIANCE DAIRY Co., Ltd.

HOUDINI has accepted the above Challenge for FRIDAY EVENING

November 13, 1908

Test to take place at the

OXFORD

Music Hall.

Tribes' Printing Works, 108, Albion Road, Stoke Newington.

Primary Source

"Houdini Defied!!"

SYNOPSIS: This poster announces a challenge to Houdini to escape from a locked and full milk can. This would be become one of Houdini's most popular escape acts during the 1900s. REPRINTED FROM WALTER BROWN GIBSON, *THE ORIGINAL HOUDINI SCRAPBOOK*. NEW YORK: CORWIN STERLING PUBLISHING CO. INC., 1976.

About the Artist: Harry Houdini (1874–1926), the legendary master magician and escape artist, was born as Erich Weiss in Budapest, Hungary. His talents and interest were wide ranging: in addition to achieving international fame for his escape acts, Houdini also pursued filmmaking, writing, publishing, and aviation. In 1910, he was the first to fly a plane across Australia. Houdini died on October 31, 1926, in Detroit, Michigan. ■

Introduction

Erich Weiss arrived in America with his family in 1878. His father was a rabbi invited to lead the congregation in Appleton, Wisconsin. After a few years, however, he was dismissed. The family moved east, settling in Manhattan. The family struggled financially; by age eleven, Erich was working in a necktie factory. Erich had little formal education, but, at seventeen, he became fascinated by magic after reading the autobiography of French conjuror, Robert Houdin.

After his father's death, Erich Weiss felt free to pursue a career as a professional magician. He adopted a version of his hero's surname, and it is believed that he derived Harry from "Eiri," his nickname. Thus "Harry Houdini" was born. He and his brother, Theo, known professionally as "Hardeen," performed as "The Brothers Houdini." They traveled and worked in dime museums, circuses, medicine shows, and theaters. They did not earn much money, and labored in relative obscurity for nearly seven years. Then vaudeville impresario, Martin Beck, saw one of their shows and invited them to join his Orpheum circuit. Beck urged Harry Houdini to alter the act by eliminating magic and concentrating, instead, on escapes. This new approach distinguished Houdini from the other vaudeville magicians. In 1899, Houdini became a vaudeville headliner and made a fortune.

The following year, Harry Houdini and his wife, Bess Rahner, sailed for England. There he was such a sensation as "The Handcuff King" that he stayed for five years touring Europe. Upon returning to the United States in 1906, Houdini decided to abandon handcuff-escapes in favor of more dangerous, high-profile restraint stunts. A master of publicity, Houdini had been sending American newspapers accounts of his exploits in Europe. American audiences were excited about his homecoming. He often received challenges from various companies, which created special restraints for Houdini—including an iron-bound hamper by the Wakefield Rattan Company, a giant leather mail pouch by the W.L. Douglas Shoe Company, and a large manila envelope by the Hogan Envelope Company.

Significance

Houdini was fascinated by the history of magic. He amassed a vast library of books containing the greatest secrets of the conjuring arts. Houdini also was interested in the history of witchcraft, which the Western world lacked in its guise of performance art. He left behind written records of his craft, documenting how his own tricks were modern versions of ancient illusions. He was especially proud to own a copy of *The Conjuror's Magazine,* the first English-language serial literature on magic. This eighteenth century periodical included articles on alchemy, astrology, legerdemain, and card tricks. Houdini named his own magazine *The Conjuror's Monthly Magazine,* in homage to this earlier publication. He edited the magazine from 1906 to 1908, and wrote many of its articles. Geared toward magic enthusiasts, the articles related the history of magic, exposed conjuring tricks, and reviewed books of interest to magicians. It also included letters and anecdotes from fellow conjurors, as well as dispatches from Hardeen in Europe.

As his international fame grew, Houdini turned his attention to his own publishing activities. Houdini himself revealed the methods he used to escape from handcuffs and other restraints. These articles were readily available in the books and magazine articles he published. What was incomparable, however, was Houdini's brilliant showmanship. His escape acts were performed with such brio that he became a folk hero. He wrote sensationalized, autobiographical short stories that often provided the basis for his film work, such as "The Marvelous Adventures of Houdini, the Justly Celebrated Elusive American." He wrote an expose of his former hero, *The Unmasking of Robert Houdin* (1908). Houdini also had developed a secondary reputation as an exposer of psychic frauds, publishing such titles as *Miracle Mongers and Their Methods* (1920) and *A Magician Among the Spirits* (1924).

In 1923, J.C. Henneberger invited Harry Houdini to write for the debut issue of his *Weird Tales,* an American pulp magazine featuring fiction pieces by influential fantasy and horror writers. That year, Houdini supplied the magazine with a column, "Ask Houdini," and provided stories of his life (ghost-written by H. P. Lovecraft).

Further Resources

BOOKS

Brandon, Ruth. *The Life and Many Deaths of Harry Houdini.* New York: Random House, 1993.

Christopher, Milbourne. *Houdini: A Pictorial Life.* New York: Thomas Crowell Company, 1976.

Fitz Simons, Raymund. *Death and the Magician.* New York: Athenum, 1985.

Gibson, Walter. *The Original Houdini Scrapbook.* New York: Sterling Publishing, 1976.

Silverman, Kenneth. *Houdini!!! The Career of Ehrich Weiss.* New York: HarperCollins, 1996.

PERIODICALS

Pain, Stephanie. "The Great Escape." *New Scientist* 166, no. 2244, June 24, 2000, 44.

Stashower, Daniel. "The Medium & the Magician." *American History* 34, no. 3, August 1999, 38.

WEBSITES

Houdini Historical Center. Available online at http://www.foxvalleyhistory.org/houdini/index.html; website home page http://www.foxvalleyhistory.org (accessed May 19, 2003).

Houdini Museum. Available online at http://www.microserve.net/~magicusa/officialseance.html (accessed March 24, 2003).

The Largest Electronic Archive in the World on Houdini. Available online at http://www.houdiniana.com (accessed March 24, 2003).

"The Old-Maid Aunt"

Short story

By: Mary Eleanor Wilkins Freeman

Date: 1908

Source: Freeman, Mary Eleanor Wilkins. "The Old-Maid Aunt." In *The Whole Family: A Novel by Twelve Authors.* New York: Harper & Brothers Publishers, 1908.

About the Author: Mary Eleanor Wilkins Freeman (1852–1930), born in Vermont and based in New England for much of her life, began her writing career with occasional poems for children. In a time of financial need, she published adult stories in important national magazines including *Harper's,* garnering a reputation for her depictions of New England life. Freeman also wrote popular ghost stories. She received the Howells Medal by the American Academy of Arts and Letters in 1926, and was one of the first four women elected to the National Institute of Letters. ■

Introduction

Mary Eleanor Wilkins Freeman's work demonstrated early American realist literature. She earned a reputation for her vivid portrayals of New Englanders in stories such as "The Revolt of Mother" (1891). Employing regional dialect and first person narratives, she wrote of the bleak lives of women in small villages and towns. Freeman's stories often examined the divided self that resulted from a constant struggle against social restrictions. Her later female characters were more forceful and outspoken.

In the early 1900s, Freeman increasingly dedicated herself to writing novels. One of her first, *Pembroke* (1894), is considered her best. *By the Light of the Soul* (1906) received mixed reviews, and *The Shoulders of Atlas* (1908) won an award in a transatlantic writing contest. Following the success of her latest novel, William Dean Howells, a writer and influential critic, invited Freeman to participate in a multi-author project called *The Whole Family.* Twelve popular writers were asked to contribute a first-person narrative of a particular family member—each installment to be published in

Author Mary Eleanor Wilkins Freeman, in the 1890s.

Harper's Bazaar. This was a prime opportunity to bring Freeman's talent for short fiction to the forefront again.

Howells began the series with his contribution, "The Father," and Freeman followed with "The Old Maid Aunt." However, much to Howells' dismay, Freeman transformed her minor character into a major one: Lily Talbot, the thirty-four-year-old unmarried aunt became a sophisticated, worldly, wealthy, and beautiful woman. Freeman's narrative even revealed that Lily was the woman Ned Temple (Howells' subject) wished he had married. Even though her relatives thought of her as "unfortunate" and treated her with condescension, Lily looked upon them with amusement at their ignorance of her real happiness. They expected her to wear only black and enjoy knitting. Instead, Lily Talbot wore bright pink dresses, read voraciously, and was desirable to men half her age, causing a scandal when her niece's fiancée began to fall in love with her. Lily Talbot's narrative is written with brisk, understated irony. The story unfolded largely through dialogue, typical of many Freeman stories.

Significance

The Whole Family was conceived as a simple novel, centering on the romantic adventures of Peggy. Freeman transformed the mawkish tale into an exploration of family tensions by making her character the young girl's rival. Extremely upset, Howells attempted to halt publication of Freeman's installment. In a protest letter to the editor of *Harper's Bazaar,* Freeman stated that Lily Talbot was a thoroughly modern character—to hold to the notion that it was unacceptable for women to be anything other than married with children by a certain age was old-fashioned, and harkened to attitudes found in literature of the previous century. Publication went ahead, and, although the other writers were divided on their opinion of Freeman's chapter, they followed her lead in turning their chapters toward a racier exploration of family tensions and jealousies.

"The Old-Maid Aunt" may have its precedent in an undated fragment Freeman called "Jane Lennox." Lennox's first person narrative begins similarly to Lily Talbot's, but with a far more bitter tone. Mary Eleanor Wilkins herself had been long pressured to marry, and did so at age forty in 1902. Her marriage to Dr. Charles Freeman, seven years her junior, began happily, but soured, as her husband developed a drinking problem; he died in an institution in 1922. In "The Old Maid Aunt," Freeman explored the various societal pressures women faced, no matter their marriage status: whether past the marriageable age, and, thus, rendered "invisible" and supposedly undesirable (Lily Talbot), about to be married (Peggy), or married, but "dowdy" (Mrs. Temple). Lily is determined to turn her perceived role into an advantage; because she is ignored, she does as she pleases.

Even though "The Old-Maid Aunt" technically was not a short story, it demonstrated Freeman's ability to create a quick portrait of a believable, modern character, and represents some of Freeman's best writing at the time. *The Whole Family* was later published as a book, and readers and critics agreed that Freeman's contribution was its strongest and most amusing chapter. *The New York Times* gave positive mention of Freeman's part; however, the book generally was perceived as a mere literary gimmick. Nevertheless, Freeman's participation in this project and its ensuing notoriety helped her literary reputation early in the new century.

Primary Source

"The Old-Maid Aunt" [excerpt]

SYNOPSIS: Mary E. Wilkins Freeman's "The Old-Maid Aunt" was the second in a series of twelve short stories, each about a different member of a single family. Freeman's aunt character, Lily Talbot, was anything but an old maid, as demonstrated by this passage in which she is accused of trying to steal another woman's husband.

Nobody, not even another woman, can tell what a woman really is. I thought I had estimated Ned Temple's wife correctly. I had taken her for a monotonous, orderly, dull sort of creature, quite incapable of extremes; but in reality she has in her rather large, flabby body the characteristics of a kitten, with the possibilities of a tigress. The tigress was uppermost when I entered the room. The woman was as irresponsible as a savage. I was disgusted and sorry and furious at the same time. I cannot imagine myself making such a spectacle over any mortal man. She was weeping frantically into a mussy little ball of handkerchief, and when she saw me she rushed at me and gripped me by the arm like a mad thing.

"If you can't get a husband for yourself," said she, "you might at least let other women's husbands alone!"

She was vulgar, but she was so wild with jealousy that I suppose vulgarity ought to be forgiven her.

I hardly know myself how I managed it, but, somehow, I got the poor thing out of the room and the house and into the cool night air, and then I talked to her, and fairly made her be quiet and listen. I told her that Ned Temple had made love to me when he was just out of petticoats and I was in short dresses. I stretched or shortened the truth a little, but it was a case of necessity. Then I intimated that I never would have married Ned Temple, anyway, and that worked beautifully. She turned upon me in such a delightfully inconsequent fashion and demanded to know what I expected, and declared her husband was good enough for any woman. Then I said I did not doubt that, and hinted that other women might have had their romances, even if they did not marry. That immediately interested her. She stared at me, and said, with the most innocent impertinence, that my brother's wife had intimated that I had had an unhappy love-affair when I was a girl. I did not think that Cyrus had told Ada, but I suppose a man has to tell his wife everything.

I hedged about the unhappy love-affair, but the first thing I knew the poor, distracted woman was sobbing on my shoulder as we stood in front of her gate, and saying that she was so sorry, but her whole life was bound up in her husband, and I was so beautiful and had so much style, and she knew what a dowdy she was, and she could not blame poor Ned if—But I hushed her.

"Your husband has no more idea of caring for another woman besides you than that moon has of travelling around another world," said I; "and you are a fool if you think so; and if you are dowdy it is your own fault. If you have such a good husband you owe it to him not to be dowdy. I know you keep his house beautifully, but any man would rather have his wife look well than his house, if he is worth anything at all."

Then she gasped out that she wished she knew how to do up her hair like mine. It was all highly ridiculous, but it actually ended in my going into the Temple house and showing Ned's wife how to do up her hair like mine. She looked like another woman when it was puffed softly over her forehead—she has quite pretty brown hair. Then I taught her how to put on her corset and pin her shirt-waist taut in front and her skirt behind. Ned was not to be home until late, and there was plenty of time. It ended in her fairly purring around me, and saying how sorry she was, and ashamed, that she had been so foolish, and all the time casting little covert, conceited glances at herself in the looking-glass. Finally I kissed her and she kissed me, and I went home. I don't really see what more a woman could have done for a rival who had supplanted her. But this revelation makes me more sorry than ever for poor Ned. I don't know, though; she may be more interesting than I thought. Anything is better than the dead level of small books on large ones, and meals on time. It cannot be exactly monotonous never to know whether you will find a sleek, purry cat, or an absurd kitten, or a tigress, when you come home. Luckily, she did not tell Ned of her jealousy, and I have cautioned all in my family to hold their tongues, and I think they will. I infer that they suspect that I must have been guilty of some unbecoming elderly prank to bring about such a state of affairs, unless, possibly, Maria's husband and Billy are exceptions. I find that Billy, when Alice lets him alone, is a boy who sees with his own eyes. He told me yesterday that I was handsomer in my pink dress than any girl in his school.

"Why, Billy Talbert!" I said, "talking that way to your old aunt!"

"I suppose you are awful old," said Billy, bless him! "but you are enough-sight prettier than a girl. I hate girls. I hope I can get away from girls when I am a man."

I wanted to tell the dear boy that was exactly the time when he would not get away from girls, but I thought I would not frighten him, but let him find it out for himself.

Further Resources

BOOKS

Glasser, Leah Blatt. *In a Closet Hidden: The Life and Work of Mary E. Wilkins Freeman.* Amherst: University of Massachusetts Press, 1996.

Howells, William Dean et al. *The Whole Family: A Novel by Twelve Authors* New York: Ungar Publishing Co., 1986.

Kendrick, Brent L. *The Infant Sphinx: Collected Letters of Mary E. Wilkins Freeman.* Metuchen, N.J.: Scarecrow, 1985.

Reichardt, Mary R. *A Mary Wilkins Freeman Reader.* Lincoln, Neb.: University of Nebraska Press, 1997.

PERIODICALS

Camfield, Gregg. "'I never saw anything at once so pathetic and funny': Humor in the Stories of Mary Wilkins Freeman." *ATQ*13, no.3, September 1999, 215–32.

Maik, Thomas A. "Dissent and Affirmation: Conflicting Voices of Female Roles in Selected Stories by Mary Wilkins Freeman." *Colby Quarterly* 26, 1990, 59–68.

"The Whole Family and Its Troubles." *The New York Times,* October 24, 1908.

WEBSITES

Mary Eleanor Wilkins Freeman. Available online at http://guweb2.gonzaga.edu/faculty/campbell/enl311/freeman.htm; website home page http://guweb2.gonzaga.edu (accessed March 25, 2003).

Reuben, Paul P. "Chapter 6: Late Nineteenth Century—Mary Wilkins Freeman." PAL: Perspectives in American Literature—A Research and Reference Guide. Available online at http://www.csustan.edu/english/reuben/pal/chap6/freeman.html; website home page http://www.csustan.edu (accessed March 25, 2003).

Miss Innocence

Musical Composition

By: Florenz Ziegfeld

Date: April 12, 1909

Source: "My Pony Boy" Sheet music, 1909, cover. *Historic American Sheet Music, 1850–1920.* American Memory digital primary source collection, Library of Congress. Available online at http://memory.loc.gov/ammem/award97/ncdhtml/hasmhome.html; website home page: http://memory.loc.gov. (accessed May 19, 2003).

About the Author: Broadway impressario Florenz Ziegfeld Jr. (1869–1932) was born in Chicago and growing up, he helped his father manage a variety hall called the Trocadero. His first wife, Anna Held (1868?–1918), a French actress, created the legendary Ziegfeld Follies. Anna Held was already a famous showgirl in Paris when she met Ziegfeld in America in 1896. She contracted to perform with Ziegfeld's company. Their relationship evolved into a domestic and creative partnership that resulted in numerous hit shows—in no small part due to each having an extraordinary gift for publicity. Held was the singular inspiration for the Follies, which featured performers who would go on to become the first stars of the modern entertainment industry. ■

Introduction

Although Anna Held and Flo Ziegfeld were never formally married, by 1904 they were considered common law husband and wife. The two separated around 1913, but each continued their successes: Anna Held performed in both America and Europe until her premature death from bone cancer; Ziegfeld produced *Showboat* (1927), one of the most influential musicals of the twentieth century, and his Ziegfeld Follies continued until the Great Depression. The Held-Ziegfeld years of partnership, however, transformed the world of live entertainment in America. They brought the glamour and excitement of Parisian clubs to the American stage.

Anna Held grew up in poverty before becoming a music hall star in Paris. Although she claimed to be native Parisian, Held actually was born in Warsaw, Poland, the daughter of a German Jewish glove maker and his French wife. Her family fled to Paris during anti-Semitic pogroms in 1881. A few years later, she moved to London, where she secured leading parts in Yiddish musicals and polished her stagecraft. Upon her return to Paris, she became a popular café singer. She was an even bigger celebrity in America, where she became the new darling of the theatrical world. She spoke English with a charming French accent; she had an air of fashionable sophistication, as well as naughtiness. Miss Held created a scandal by being one of the first women to appear in public riding a bicycle, and riding a horse straddled, (rather than side-saddle, as was considered properly lady-like at the time). The image of her tiny waist made the hourglass figure desirable at the beginning of the twentieth century. Held was famous for supposedly indulging in milk baths, and she was also one of the first performers to appear in previously anonymous national advertisements for cigars and other products.

Significance

Held and Ziegfeld collaborated on numerous musicals. The scripts and songs, full of double entendres that audiences found titillating, were box office hits. However, in spite of her love of the stage, Anna Held did not require that the spotlight always be on her. Without Anna Held, there would have been no Ziegfeld's Follies. She suggested to Ziegfeld that if his beautiful chorus girls were fantastically outfitted, his revue would be even better than the famed Parisian Folies Bergere. The first of these annual shows opened in 1907, with the chorus girls called "The Anna Held Girls." Miss Held herself did not appear in the show, but the following year she would have her own star vehicle, *Miss Innocence.*

Miss Innocence would be the last and greatest of the Held-Ziegfeld collaborations. Audiences and critics agreed that *Miss Innocence* showed Anna Held at the apex of her art and Ziegfeld's theatrical genius. Absent was much of the formulaic raciness that characterized earlier Ziegfeld productions, in favor of a more childlike, fairy-tale atmosphere. There was still some innuendo, but

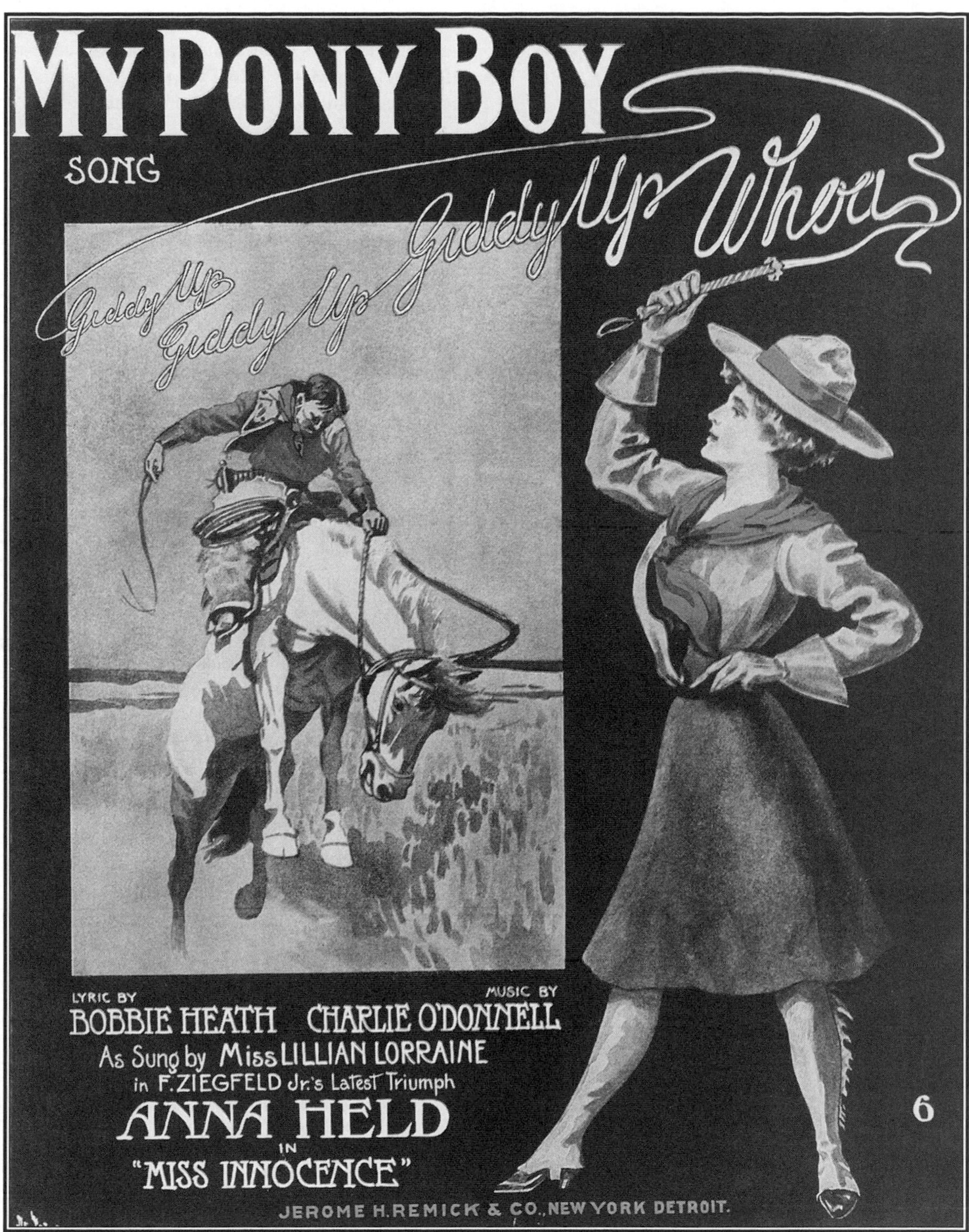

Primary Source

"Miss Innocence"

SYNOPSIS: While the Ziegfeld Follies was a fantasy world of women that created an instant box office hit for Ziegfeld, he considered it still only one of his side projects. He instead poured all of his artistic energies into *Miss Innocence.* Like their previous shows, including *The French Maid* (1898), *The Parisian Model* (1905) or *Papa's Wife* (1899), this new musical showcased Held's good looks and charisma. The show opened in New York on November 30, 1908 at the New York Theater. It was a smashing success, and it would eventually go on tour until 1913. "My Pony Boy" was a popular song from the revue. Its sheet music was later published by Jerome H. Remick & Co. RARE BOOK, MANUSCRIPT, AND SPECIAL COLLECTIONS LIBRARY, DUKE UNIVERSITY, DURHAM, NORTH CAROLINA.

Anna Held was America's most popular musical comedy actress in the two decades preceding World War I. THE LIBRARY OF CONGRESS.

Miss Innocence featured light-hearted music, fabulous costumes, sets painted by the best scenic artists of the day, and a fantastic story. Miss Held played "Anna," a pupil in a school for young girls on the Isle of Innocence; comedienne Emma Janvier was "Miss Sniffens," the old-maid headmistress with a shady past. Charles Bigelow played the role of "The Greatest Detective in the World." The Detective believed that Anna was a missing heiress; he fled with her to Paris where she was introduced to the big city life, traveled to further mythical lands, and eventually ended up, happily, in "The Land of Peach Blossoms." There was even a musical number featuring Miss Held and Leo Mars, "We Two in an Aeroplane," which contained a full-size biplane hung against a backdrop of Paris at night.

Further Resources

BOOKS

Golden, Eve. *Anna Held and the Birth of Ziegfeld's Broadway.* Lexington: The University Press of Kentucky, 2000.

Mizejewski, Linda. *Ziegfeld Girl: Image and Icon in Culture and Cinema.* Durham, N.C.: Duke University Press, 1999.

McEvoy, Joseph Patrick. *Simon and Schuster Present Show Girl.* New York: Simon and Schuster, 1928.

McGaffey, Kenneth. *The Sorrows of a Show Girl: A Story of the Great "White Way."* Chicago: J.I. Austen Co., 1908.

Ziegfeld, Patricia. *The Ziegfelds' Girl: Confessions of an Abnormally Happy Childhood.* Boston: Little, Brown, 1964.

PERIODICALS

Wilson, Victoria. "Follies' Specialty Girl: Doris Eaton Travis, a Former Ziegfeld Follies Dancer." *Interview Magazine,* January 1999.

WEBSITES

Kenrick, John. " The Life and Legacy of Florenz Ziegfeld." Musicals101.com. Available online at http://www.musicals101.com/ziegfeld.htm; website home page www.musicals101.com (accessed March 24, 2003).

The Ziegfeld Girls of Florida. Available online at http://www.showbizmall.com/ziegfeld/zieg_p17.htm; website home page http://www.showbizmall.com (accessed March 24, 2003).

"The Memphis Blues"

Musical composition

By: W.C. Handy

Date: 1912

Source: Handy, William Christopher. "The Memphis Blues." New York: Joe Morris Music Co., 1912. *Historic American Sheet Music: 1850–1920.* American Memory digital primary source collection, Library of Congress. Available online at http://memory.loc.gov/ammem/award97/ncdhtml/hasmhome.html; website home page: http://memory.loc.gov/ammem (accessed May 12, 2003).

About the Author: William Christopher Handy (1873–1958) was born in Florence, Alabama. Handy showed musical talent at an early age, and he took cornet lessons. As a teenager, he left home to join a minstrel show. As a performer, bandleader, and songwriter, Handy rose to musical prominence. Although he did not invent the blues, his 1912 composition "Memphis Blues" became the first blues ever published. W.C. Handy was one of the earliest musicians to make a successful living from the blues. ■

Primary Source

"The Memphis Blues"

SYNOPSIS: The original sheet music of W.C. Handy's "The Memphis Blues." It was the first blues song ever published. RARE BOOK, MANUSCRIPT, AND SPECIAL COLLECTIONS LIBRARY, DUKE UNIVERSITY, DURHAM, NORTH CAROLINA.

Musician, songwriter, composer, and bandleader W.C. Handy. **HULTON ARCHIVE/GETTY IMAGES. REPRODUCED BY PERMISSION.**

Introduction

As a teenager, W.C. Handy once spent money earned from odd jobs to buy a guitar. Dismayed, his parents made Handy return and exchange it for a dictionary. They felt that the guitar was an evil thing to bring into their Christian home—his father was a minister. They signed him up for organ lessons, instead, so Handy could use his vast musical talents in the church. Bored with the organ, Handy ran off to seek the life of a musician. He toured with minstrel shows, joined a band, and sang tenor in a quartet. And he taught himself to play the guitar after all. At the age of twenty-three, he became the bandmaster of Mahara's Colored Minstrels, an experience that helped him eventually to lead his own band.

It was in Memphis, Tennessee, that Handy began writing songs in earnest. Harry H. Pace was a local legend, as both a lyricist and vocalist at church programs. Pace worked as a cashier at the Solvent Savings Bank, where Handy was a customer. They struck a friendship, and together wrote "In the Cotton Fields of Dixie" in 1907. The song was published later that year by a Cincinnati firm. They formed a partnership, Pace & Handy Music Company Publishers.

Although Pace and Handy disbanded in 1920, Handy continued publishing both his own compositions and those of other black composers. Handy wrote about sixty blues tunes and more than 150 compositions and folk song arrangements. He also wrote and edited *Blues: An Anthology* (1926), *Negro Authors and Composers of the United States* (1935), *W.C. Handy's Collection of Negro Spirituals* (1938), *Negro Authors and Composers of the United States* (1938), and *Unsung Americans Sung* (1944). Handy taught music at Alabama Agricultural and Mechanical College for Negroes from 1900 to 1902.

Significance

Handy authored an autobiography entitled *Father of the Blues* in 1944. The work is a reflection on the origins of the blues (as he experienced them) and details his slow, steady climb to success. Until recently, Handy's autobiography had been underrecognized as "blues literature." Earlier scholars dismissed the volume as too upbeat—having less to do with Handy's musical innovations than with his business acumen. Handy's financial success hardly exemplified the down-and-out lyrics so typical of blues songs. Contemporary studies point out, however, that while Handy's tone may be generally optimistic, his politics are an ever-present force within the narrative. Paradoxically, along with widespread acclaim for the music he and his bands brought to audiences, there was the ever-looming "nightmare of those minstrel days," as Handy referred to them. Handy recounted how young black men had to navigate the Jim Crow South, dodging lynch mobs merely to realize their professional ambitions.

In *Father of the Blues* Handy recounts that he initially had doubted that blues music would be widely accepted. He wrote that:

> ...I took up with low folk forms hesitantly ... I had picked up a fair training in the music of the modern world and had assumed that the correct manner to compose was to develop simples into grandissimos and not to repeat them monotonously. As a director of many respectable, conventional bands, it was not easy for me to concede that a simple slow-drag and repeat could be rhythm itself. Neither was I ready to believe that this was just what the public wanted. But we live to learn.

Later, however, after moving to Mississippi in 1903, Handy and his band played at an event where they were asked to step aside for a rhythm and guitar band. The crowd took that band's music much more enthusiastically than they had Handy's more sophisticated music. The other band was treated to a shower of silver dollars from the dancing crowd. Handy wrote:

> Then I saw the beauty of primitive music. They had the stuff the people wanted. It touched the spot.

Their music wanted polishing, but it contained the essence.

In 1909, Handy's band was hired to play at political rallies for Memphis mayoral candidate Edward H. Crump. Handy composed an instrumental tune known as "Mr. Crump." It was never published, but its unexpected, enormous popularity inspired Handy to rework the song as "Memphis Blues," becoming America's first published blues song in 1912. In 1913, George A. Norton supplied new lyrics for the song, replacing the references to Edward Crump.

The original "Mr. Crump" was actually an amalgam of the blues and the popular style of the day, ragtime. It had an up-tempo beat suited for rousing the crowds. The original composition did not have lyrics. However, derogatory comments overheard from a skeptical crowd during one of Crump's campaign speeches soon became the lyrics:

Mr. Crump won't 'low no easy riders here
Mr. Crump won't 'low no easy riders here
We don't care what Mr. Crump don't 'low
We gon' to bar'l-house anyhow—
Mr. Crump can go and catch hisself some air!

The candidate was unaware of the lyrics to his commissioned campaign song, though he was elected as mayor of Memphis in spite of it. Handy wrote in *Father of the Blues*, "I was now embarrassed by the words. With Mr. Crump holding forth as mayor, I couldn't get the consent of mind to keep telling his honor to catch hisself some air." To disassociate its origin as a campaign tune, the song was reincarnated as "The Memphis Blues." Handy's new version was more solemn and "bluesy." Handy wanted a more direct acknowledgement of the anonymous folk singers who had influenced him musically. He named the song in honor of the city that had given him so much favorable attention.

Handy published "Memphis Blues," and it appeared in stores on September 28, 1912. One thousand copies sold out in just three days. However, Handy's dishonest publisher lied to the composer, and led him to believe that the song was a flop. The publisher offered fifty dollars for the rights to this song that he claimed nobody wanted. Handy agreed, only to discover later that another man was making profits from his work; he swore to never be cheated again. Handy went on to write other hits that afforded him a life of comfort unknown to most blues musicians.

W. C. Handy made it his priority to bring the music he loved to a wider audience. As the "Father of the Blues," he did not claim to have invented the blues. However, he was the first to transcribe and publish this music that he first heard on his travels throughout the South. Handy died on March 28, 1958. A film based on his life was released later that year. *St. Louis Blues,* named for Handy's greatest hit, starred musical luminaries Nat "King" Cole, Pearl Bailey, Mahalia Jackson, Cab Calloway, and Eartha Kitt, among others.

Further Resources

BOOKS

Lee, George W. *Beale Street, Where the Blues Began.* New York: R.O. Ballou, 1934.

Handy, W.C. *Father of the Blues.* Arna Bontemps, ed. New York: Macmillan, 1944.

Oliver, Paul. *Conversation with the Blues.* 2nd ed. Cambridge: Cambridge University Press, 1997.

Pomerance, Alan. *Repeal of the Blues: How Black Entertainers Influenced Civil Rights.* New York: Citadel, 1988.

PERIODICALS

Gussow, Adam. "'Make My Getaway': The Blues Lives of Black Minstrels in W. C. Handy's *Father of the Blues.*" *African American Review,* March 22, 2001.

"The Beethoven of Beale Street." *Newsweek,* July 7, 1941, 46.

WEBSITES

Edwards, William "Perfessor" Bill Edwards, Professional Patriotic Purveyor of Pianistic Pyrotechnics. Available online at http://www.perfessorbill.com (accessed March 25, 2003).

"Father of the Blues: Today in History, September 28." American Memory Collection, Library of Congress. Available online at http://memory.loc.gov/ammem/today/sep28.html; website home page http://memory.loc.gov (accessed March 25, 2003)

Morgan, Thomas L. "W.C. Handy." Jazz Roots. Available online at http://www.jass.com/Others/wchandy.html; website home page http://www.jass.com (accessed March 25, 2003).

Oliver, Phillip. "W. C. Handy, 'Father of the Blues.'" University of North Alabama Special Collections. Available online at http://www2.una.edu/library/handy/index.html; website home page http://www2.una.edu (accessed March 25, 2003).

Songs of Ma Rainey

"Slow Drivin' Moan"; "Moonshine Blues"

Songs

By: Ma Rainey

Date: 1923

Source: Rainey, Ma. "Slow Drivin' Moan"; "Moonshine Blues." Reprinted in Lieb, Sandra. *Mother of the Blues: A Study of Ma Rainey.* University of Massachusetts Press, 1998, 68, 91.

About the Author: Gertrude Pridgett (1886–1939) became known as "Ma Rainey" when she married performer William "Pa" Rainey in 1904. She was born in Georgia. By fourteen,

Gertrude "Ma" Rainey and her Georgia Jazz Band in Chicago, Illinois, 1923. Ma Rainey was one of the most successful early blues singers. **ARCHIVE PHOTOS. REPRODUCED BY PERMISSION.**

she was already singing and dancing in minstrel and vaudeville stage revues. "Ma and Pa Rainey" went on tour together, calling themselves "The Assassinators of the Blues." Ma Rainey performed solo after her split with Pa Rainey, becoming the most influential female blues singer of her day. ■

Introduction

"The Assassinators of the Blues" performed mostly with tent shows in the South. These were popular with both black and white audiences (although they sat on opposite sides of the tent). Some of the best known of these variety shows were Tolliver's Circus, The Musical Extravaganza, and The Rabbit Foot Minstrels. The blues songs comprised only part of her repertoire; Ma Rainey often sang songs in the context of a spoken-word skit. She also performed comedy and dancing routines.

Ma Rainey, known in her day as "the ugliest woman in show business," nevertheless exuded a raw sexuality that appealed to her audiences. She made a fortune from her in-demand performances. After her split with Pa Rainey, she became a solo star of TOBA (Theatre Owners Booking Agency), the African American theater circuit. Ma Rainey was an imposing figure on the stage. She was short and dark, with wild hair and gold teeth—flamboyantly dressed to dramatize the colorful protagonists she portrayed in her songs. After she became famous and rich, she wore her wealth in gold chains—loading herself with diamonds in her ears and wearing a tiara on her head. She was called "The Paramount Wildcat," as well as "The Gold Necklace Woman of the Blues." She performed throughout the South, and eventually moved north to Chicago. She also made appearances in Cleveland, Cincinnati, Detroit, Philadelphia, Newark, and New York. Her popularity even spread to Europe.

Ma Rainey bought a large bus to take her show on tour. She performed nonstop until 1923, when she signed a recording contract with Paramount. She went back to touring until her retirement in the mid-1930s. She had a wide-ranging repertoire of songs, but her most memorable were blues tunes such as "See, See Rider" and "Bo Weavil Blues." With the release of her first track, "Moonshine Blues," Paramount claimed that they had "discovered" Ma Rainey, although African Americans had enjoyed her performances for years.

Significance

Ma Rainey did not invent the blues, but she was one of its first recognizable performers. Rooted in the culture of rural southern African Americans that emerged from slavery, the first blues songs descended from work songs and spirituals. Ma Rainey herself was born only one generation removed from slavery. Spending most of her career on the road, she played a major role in popularizing the blues.

Ma Rainey claimed to have been singing the blues in her acts since 1902, after hearing them while touring in a small Mississippi town. The music came to be personified by the lone black man and his guitar, wandering through the South in search of work and singing about his life; this became known as the country blues. Ma Rainey's songs borrowed liberally from this "wandering" tradition. In "Slow Driving Moan," it is the woman who wants to take to the road, yet promises her man that she will eventually return home. As an entertainer who was constantly touring, Ma Rainey defied normal social expectations of women.

Ma Rainey was a pioneer on the African American entertainment circuit, influencing women's blues for generations to follow. Rainey's songs were typically assertive, exploring various perspectives on its themes; she sang of women as cavalier as men, boasting of conquests and leaving lovers behind. Ma Rainey's music provided a crucial link between country blues and popular blues, the more "sophisticated" versions later sung by performers like Bessie Smith and Ethel Waters.

Primary Source

"Slow Driving Moan"; "Moonshine Blues"

SYNOPSIS: Paramount billed Ma Rainey as "The Mother of the Blues." These recordings are the only remaining form of Ma Rainey's artistic legacy. She did not write down most of her songs. Even in her live performances, Rainey changed or improvised her lyrics and phrasing of songs. The blues element of her songs often lay in the vocal delivery of the tune; she would moan, hum, and draw out notes to create an emotional pitch.

"Slow Drivin' Moan"

I've traveled 'Til I'm tired
And I ain't satisfied
I've traveled 'til I'm tired
And I ain't satisfied
If I don't find my sweet man
I'll ramble til I die.

Ah Lawdy Lawd Lawd Lawdy
Lawd Lawdy Lawd lawd Lawd
Ah Lawdy Lawd Lawd Lawdy
Lawd Lawdy Lawd Lawd Lawd
Lawd Lawdy Lawd Lawd Lawd
Lawd Lawdy Lawd Lawd Lawd.

I've got slow drivin' blues
I'm blue as I can be
I've got the slow drivin' blues
I'm blue as I can be
Don't play that Old band music
Just play the blues for me.

"Moon Shine Blues"

Now I've been drinking all night babe
 and the night before
But when I get sober I ain't a-gonna drink no more
Because my best friend has left me,
 I mean standing at my door

My head goes round and around babe
 since my baby left town
And I don't know if the river is up or down
Now I know one thing that's certain,
 mama's gonna leave this town.

You find me reeling and rocking
 howlin' like a houn'
And I'm gonna catch the first train
 that's goin' south bound
Cause mama don't mean to stay here
 and be treated like a hound.

Now mister conductor man please
 won't you stop that train
Mister conductor man won't you please sir,
 please sir, stop that train
So I can go back to my home again.

I'm gonna stop running
 'round and settle down
Cause I'm tired running around and
 now I've got no time to lose
Tell everyone that you meet
 that I've got the moonshine blues.

Further Resources

BOOKS

Barlow, William. *Looking Up at Down: The Emergence of Blues Culture.* Philadelphia: Temple University Press, 1989.

Bogle, Donald. *Brown Sugar: Eighty Years of America's Black Female Superstars.* New York: Harmony Books, 1980.

Lieb, Sandra. *Mother of the Blues: A Study of Ma Rainey.* Amherst: University of Massachusetts Press, 1981

Oakley, Giles. *The Devil's Music: A History of the Blues.* New York: Taplinger Publishing Co., 1977.

Oliver, Paul. *Savannah Syncopators: African Retentions in the Blues.* New York: Stein and Day, 1970.

———. *Songsters and Saints: Vocal Traditions on Race Records.* New York: Cambridge University Press, 1984.

Stewart-Baxter, Derrick. *Ma Rainey and The Classic Blues Singers.* New York: Stein and Day Press, 1970.

PERIODICALS

Hirshey, Gerri and Anthony Bozza. "Women Who Rocked the World." *Rolling Stone* 773, November 13, 1997, 41.

Shannon, Sandra G. "The Long Wait: August Wilson's *Ma Rainey's Black Bottom.*" *Black American Literature Forum* 25, no. 1, Spring 1991, 135.

WEBSITES

Alexander, Scott. "Gertrude 'Ma' Rainey." The Red Hot Jazz Archive. Available online at http://www.redhotjazz.com/rainey.html; website home page http://www.redhotjazz.com (accessed March 24, 2003).

White, Alan, and Max Haymes. The Early Blues Website. Available online at http://www.earlyblues.com (accessed March 24, 2003).

Robert Henri

The Art Spirit

Handbook

By: Robert Henri

Date: 1923

Source: Henri, Robert. *The Art Spirit*, ed. Margery Ryerson, Philadelphia: Lippincott, 1923. Reprint, Boulder, Colo.: Westview Press, 1984, 15–19, 102–105.

Snow in New York

Painting

By: Robert Henri

Date: 1902

Source: Henri, Robert. *Snow in New York.* From the collection of the National Museum of Art, Washington, D.C. Available online at The National Gallery of Art. http://www.nga.gov/ (accessed May 19, 2003).

About the Artist: Robert Henri (1865–1929), artist and teacher, was born Robert Henry Cozad in Cincinnati, Ohio. However, a family scandal forced him to assume a new identity in his teen years. He studied painting at Pennsylvania Academy and at the Ecole des Beaux Arts in Paris. He returned to the United States and became the leader of the Ash Can artists, who helped to establish an identity for American art. He had a long, distinguished teaching career. ■

Introduction

Robert Henri took a teaching position at the Women's School of Design in Philadelphia in 1891. Henri had recently returned to the United States after studying art in France, where he had been highly influenced by impressionism. Impressionism is a style of painting that developed in France in the 1870s. Although it was heavily criticized in its earliest days for disregarding traditional artistic conventions, its concepts have become the norms of painting. Impressionist painting was characterized by landscape scenes without specific content or meaning, and it used textured brushstrokes to imply, rather than delineate, light and form. Impressionist painters included Claude Monet and Pierre-August Renoir, as well as American Mary Cassatt.

The influential realist artist Robert Henri, c. 1907. **THE LIBRARY OF CONGRESS.**

Henri promoted impressionism at first, but later turned to the work of his predecessor, Thomas Eakins, a leader of American naturalist painting from Pennsylvania. Like Henri, Eakins studied painting in Europe, but returned to the United States, believing American art could only progress by American artists staying at home. Inspired, Henri looked to the urban reality of Philadelphia. He and his artist friends viewed art as a means of describing the world outside of the artist's studio.

Many artists worked as "artist reporters." At the time, newspaper stories were often accompanied by artists' illustrations, instead of photographs. Cameras were available readily, but film developing processes were not refined enough to produce quality images in a timely manner. So artists accompanied news reporters and created on-the-spot drawings, documenting the events of everyday lives.

Significance

By the beginning of the twentieth century, Henri was known as the leading voice of these artists identifying with realism. He left Philadelphia to join the faculty of the New York School of Art in 1902. Two years later, he opened his own school, inviting artist friends from Philadelphia to come and teach, as well as two of the new generation of American realist artists, Reginald Marsh and George Bellows. Henri also taught at the Ferrer Center (1911–1918) and the Arts Students League (1915–1928).

Henri taught his students that art could be used as a tool of social reform by looking to the distinct character of the American city, instead of merely mimicking European painting traditions. Paintings should not always depict picturesque scenes, but also could illustrate the ugly realities of modern life, such as slum overcrowding in the ghettoes.

Henri was a dynamic teacher, as well as a charismatic leader. He spoke about art in everyday language, not in theoretical terms. His book *The Art Spirit* provided both practical and technical advice for the art student of any age, and it also could be used as a guide to art appreciation. First published in 1923, Henri's timeless text is readily available and still read widely in art schools.

Primary Source

The Art Spirit [excerpt]

SYNOPSIS: *The Art Spirit: Notes, Articles, Fragments of Letters and Talks to Students, Bearing on the Concept and Technique of Picture Making, the Study of Art* was compiled by Robert Henri's student, Margery Ryerson (1886–1989). In it are Henri's thoughts on art, artists, and their place in the world. Ryerson became a successful artist, also particularly noted for portraiture.

Art when really understood is the province of every human being.

It is simply a question of doing things, anything, well. It is not an outside, extra thing.

When the artist is alive in any person, whatever his kind of work may be, he becomes an inventive, searching, daring, self-expressing creature. He becomes interesting to other people. He disturbs, upsets, enlightens, and he opens ways for a better understanding. Where those who are not artists are trying to close the book, he opens it, shows there are still more pages possible.

The world would stagnate without him, and the world would be beautiful with him; for he is interesting to himself and he is interesting to others. He does not have to be a painter or sculptor to be an artist. He can work in any medium. He simply has to find the gain in the work itself, not outside it.

Museums of art will not make a country an art country. But where there is the art spirit there will be precious works to fill museums. Better still, there will be the happiness that is in the making. Art tends towards balance, order, judgment of relative values, the laws of growth, the economy of living—very good things for anyone to be interested in.

■ ■ ■

The work of the art student is no light matter. Few have the courage and stamina to see it through. You have to make up your mind to be alone in many ways. We like sympathy and we like to be in company. It is easier than going it alone. But alone one gets acquainted with himself, grows up and on, not stopping with the crowd. It costs to do this. If you succeed somewhat you may have to pay for it as well as enjoy it all your life.

Primary Source

Snow in New York

SYNOPSIS: An oil on canvas painting by Robert Henri. Henri's realistic depictions of American cities were an influential break from the artistic traditions of his day. NATIONAL GALLERY OF ART, WASHINGTON DC, USA/BRIDGEMAN ART LIBRARY.

■ ■ ■

Cherish your own emotions and never undervalue them.

■ ■ ■

We are not here to do what has already been done.

■ ■ ■

I have little interest in teaching you what I know. I wish to stimulate you to tell me what *you* know. In my office toward you I am simply trying to improve my own environment.

■ ■ ■

Know what the old masters did. Know how they composed their pictures, but do not fall into the conventions they established. These conventions were right for them, and they are wonderful. They made their language. You make yours. They can help you. All the past can help you....

■ ■ ■

It is not enough to have thought great things *before* doing the work. The brush stroke at the moment of contact carries inevitably the exact state of being of the artist at that exact moment into the work, and there it is, to be seen and read by those who can read such signs, and to be read later by the artist himself, with perhaps some surprise, as a revelation of himself.

For an artist to be interesting to us he must have been interesting to himself. He must have been capable of intense feeling, and capable of profound contemplation.

He who has contemplated has met with himself, is in a state to see into the realities beyond the surfaces of his subject. Nature reveals to him, and, seeing and feeling intensely, he paints, and whether he wills it or not each brush stroke is an exact record of such as he was at the exact moment the stroke was made. . . .

■ ■ ■

When the motives of artists are profound, when they are at their work as a result of deep consideration, when they believe in the importance of what they are doing, their work creates a stir in the world.

The stir may not be one of thanks or compliment to the artist. It may be that it will rouse two kinds of men to bitter antagonism, and the artist may be more showered with abuse than praise, just as Darwin was in the start, because he introduced a new idea into the world.

The complaint that "the public do not come to our exhibitions—they are not interested in art!" is heard with a bias to the effect that it is *all* the public's fault, and that there could not possibly be anything the matter with art. A thoughtful person may ponder the question and finally ask if the fault is totally on the public's side.

There are two classes of people in the world: students and non-students. In each class there are elements of the other class so that it is possible to develop or to degenerate and thus effect a passage from one class to the other.

The true character of the student is one of great mental and spiritual activity. He arrives at conclusions and he searches to express his findings. He goes to the market place, to the exhibition place, wherever he can reach the people, to lay before them his new angle on life. He creates a disturbance, wins attention from those who have in them his kind of blood—the student blood. These are stirred into activity. Camps are established. Discussion runs high. There is life in the air.

The non-student element says it is heresy. Let us have "peace!" Put the disturber in jail.

In this, we have two ideas of life, motion and non-motion.

If the art students who enter the schools today believe in the greatness of their profession, if they believe in self-development and courage of vision and expression, and conduct their study accordingly, they will not find the audience wanting when they go to the market place with expressions of their ideas.

They will find a crowd there ready to tear them to pieces; to praise them and to ridicule them.

Julian's Academy, as I knew it, was a great cabaret with singing and huge practical jokes, and as such, was a wonder. It was a factory, too, where thousands of drawings of human surfaces were turned out.

It is true, too, that among the great numbers of students there were those who searched each other out and formed little groups which met independently of the school, and with art as the central interest talked, and developed ideas about everything under the sun. But these small groups of true students were exceptional.

An art school should be a boiling, seething place. And such it would be if the students had a fair idea of the breadth of knowledge and the general per-

"The Eight"

When Henri and his friends arrived in New York, they became known as the New York Realists. Henri won much acclaim for his paintings, particularly his portraiture. In 1906, he was elected to the National Academy of Design, a highly influential honorary association of artists at the time. When his friends Wiliam Glackens, John Sloan, George Luks, and Everett Shinn were rejected by the Academy's annual juried exhibition in 1907, Henri withdrew his own paintings from the Academy. Their peers Arthur B. Davies and Ernest Lawson were rejected the following month, and Henri proposed that they should stage their own exhibition, to protest the rigid conventions that entities like the Academy insisted upon. Henri organized an exhibition for Glackens, Sloan, Shinn, Luks, and invited Ernest Lawson, Arthur B. Davies, and Maurice Prendergast to join. The artists varied in subject matter and technique. On opening day, February 3, 1908, about 7,000 people came to see the show at Macbeth Gallery. The exhibit received mixed reviews. Many viewers, used to genteel portraiture in the European tradition, were shocked by these new paintings of machinery, apartment buildings, and ordinary people at work and leisure. The group of artists was referred to as "The Eight," and the association of some of these artists led to the emergence of the Ash Can School, a major force in American painting. Artists associated with the Ash Can School are George Bellows, William Glackens, Robert Henri, George Luks, Everett Shinn, and John Sloan.

Henri's ideas also inspired the International Exhibition of Modern Art held in New York. Organized by Henri and several members of "The Eight," this was the first major exhibition designed to show the newest and avant-garde art from both Europe and America. Held at the 69th Regiment Armory in February 1913, the exhibition (known as the Armory Show) included over 1,300 works. The exhibition received around 250,000 visitors. Since 1999, the Armory Show has been reincarnated as an annual event showcasing international contemporary art.

sonal development necessary to the man who is to carry his news to the market place.

When a thing is put down in such permanent mediums as paint or stone it should be a thing well worthy of record. It must be the work of one who has looked at all things, has interested himself in all life.

Art has relations to science, religions and philosophies. The artist must be a student.

The value of a school should be in the meeting of students. The art school should be the life-centre of a city. Ideas should radiate from it.

I can see such a school as a vital power; stimulating without and within. Everyone would know of its existence, would feel its hand in all affairs.

I can hear the song, the humor, of such a school, putting its vitality into play at moments of play, and having its say in every serious matter of life.

Such a school can only develop through the will of the students. Some such thing happened in Greece. It only lasted for a short time, but long enough to stock the world with beauty and knowledge which is fresh to this day.

Further Resources

BOOKS

Altshuler, Bruce. *The Avant-Garde in Exhibition: New Art in the 20th Century.* New York: Abrams, 1994.

de Shavo, Edith. *Everett Shinn: A Figure in His Time.* New York: Clarkson N. Potter, Inc., 1974.

Perlman, Bennard B. *Painters of the Ashcan School: The Immortal Eight.* New York: Dover Publications, 1988.

———, ed. *Revolutionaries of Realism: The Letters of John Sloan and Robert Henri.* Princeton, N.J.: Princeton University Press, 1997.

St. John, Bruce, ed. *John Sloan's New York Scene.* New York: Harper & Row, 1965.

PERIODICALS

Townsend, James B. "'The Eight' Arrive." *Art News* 91, no. 9, November 1992, 102.

WEBSITES

"Metropolitan Lives: The Ashcan Artists and Their New York." Smithsonian American Art Museum. Available online at http://nmaa-ryder.si.edu/collections/exhibits/metlives/index2.html; website home page http://nmaa-ryder.si.edu (accessed March 24, 2003).

Schiff, Richard. SoHo Art.com. "The Ashcan School." Available online at http://www.sohoart.com/ashcan.htm; website home page http://sohoart.com (accessed March 24, 2003).

AUDIO AND VISUAL MEDIA

Robert Henri and the Art Spirit. Cornfed Video. 1990, DVD.

Twenty Years on Broadway

Memoir

By: George M. Cohan

Date: 1924

Source: Cohan, George M. *Twenty Years on Broadway.* New York: Harper & Brothers, 1924, 93–99.

About the Author: George Michael Cohan (1878–1942) was an actor, playwright, director, author, composer, director, and star of more than twenty musicals. Many of his songs are still heard today, such as "You're a Grand Old Flag," "Give My Regards to Broadway," and "Over There." Cohan built his reputation on patriotic songs full of flag-waving optimism. He claimed his birthday was on July 4, but it was actually July 3; he was born in Providence, Rhode Island. ■

Introduction

George M. Cohan spent most of his life in the theater. His parents, Jerry and Nellie Cohan, were traveling vaudevillians. At age three, George made his debut. By nine, he and his older sister, Josephine, began to perform with their parents as The Four Cohans. Cohan started writing songs at age thirteen, publishing his first, "Why Did Nellie Leave Her Home?" at age sixteen. By age twenty, he was writing the family act and managing The Four Cohans. Backstage, the arrogant young man was a troublemaker. His brashness consistently would be reflected in his later hit songs. Cohan composed over 500 songs, many of them national hits. He received a Congressional Gold Medal of Honor for "Over There," a rousing battle cry written for America's entrance into World War I (1914–1919).

Cohan's hit shows were typically fast-paced, upbeat musicals with inspirational characters modeled after real persons. Cohan was also adept at doctoring plays, proudly describing his adaptations as "Cohanized." He also wrote popular non-musical comedies, such as *Seven Keys to Baldpate* (1913). Cohan was an acclaimed actor, especially for his appearance in Eugene O'Neill's *Ah, Wilderness!* (1934) and in *I'd Rather Be Right* (1937). (This last performance, in which he portrayed Franklin D. Roosevelt, was the first time Cohan appeared in a musical that he had not written himself.)

Cohan's first musical was *The Governor's Son* (1901), a mild success. The second, *Running for Office* (1903) reworked one of his old vaudeville skits into a three-act musical play. It was favorably received in New York at the Fourteenth Street Theater in Union Square. With *Little Johnny Jones* (1904), Cohan finally struck a winning formula. Cohan was the show's writer, producer, composer, and star. The title character was an extension of Cohan's personality. A newspaper article about London jockey, Todd Sloane, inspired Cohan to recreate the character as Johnny Jones, an American jockey who goes to England, only to be wrongly accused of accepting a bribe to lose a big race. Cohan adopted the familiar tune "Yankee Doodle" for the song "I'm a Yankee Doodle Dandy." Cohan's wife, Ethel Levey, played Goldie, who follows Jones to London disguised as a man to find out if Jones really loves her. At the end, Jones is declared innocent, and marries Goldie.

Significance

The premiere of *Little Johnny Jones* in 1904 marked the birth of the American musical play and made George M. Cohan a household name. At the time, live theater was still the chief form of entertainment, but Broadway was dominated by European-style musical operettas. Cohan took a completely different approach, eschewing genteel manners in favor of bold melodrama matched with songs that reflected the speech of the American audience. Cohan was the first in a tradition of great American songwriters including Cole Porter, George Gershwin, Rodgers and Hammerstein, Leonard Bernstein, and Steven Sondheim.

Cohan was careful not to give Johnny Jones too much stage time. But when Cohan appeared onstage, he dazzled audiences with his singing and his signature dance move, a strange, stiff-legged cocky strut. *Little Johnny Jones* appealed to audiences for its catchy tunes, fancy stage sets, and distinctly patriotic theme. It marked the first collaboration between Cohan and Sam H. Harris, Cohan's only partner throughout his long stage career. Cohan & Harris had signed a contract with A.L. "Abe" Erlanger of the Theatrical Syndicate to ensure that their new production would play in the country's best theaters. At the time, Erlanger was the most powerful figure in show business. He and his partner Marc Klaw held a monopoly of bookings for almost every theater in the United States. They financed dozens of important productions, including Cohan's next hit, *Forty-Five Minutes from Broadway* (1906).

Reviewers, even if they did not like the musical, admitted that Cohan had introduced a new dramatic form to the American stage, calling *Little Johnny Jones* a "musical melodrama." Although highbrow music critics deplored the "tin-pan" quality of Cohan's songs, the audiences kept coming and giving him standing ovations. After a short stint on Broadway, Cohan took the show on the road beginning 1905, believing that he had a major hit. Cohan revised and reworked the music while touring across America. Cohan brought the show back to Broadway in the summer of 1905 and, again, in the fall. He appeared in another *Little Johnny Jones* revival in 1907.

Cohan called his memoirs *Twenty Years On Broadway and the Years It Took To Get There: The True Story Of A Trouper's Life From the Cradle to the "Closed Shop."* By the time of its publication in 1924, Cohan realized he was falling out of step with the current fashions on Broadway. Jazz was growing in popularity, and Cohan did not write jazz songs. Both his music and his plot lines were beginning to seem old-fashioned. A biographical film, *Yankee Doodle Dandy* (1942), starred James Cagney as George M. Cohan. The film was released soon after America entered World War II (1939–1945). Sequences from *Little Johnny Jones* were incorporated into the film, with sets based on the origi-

George Cohan began his enormously successful showbusiness career in his family's vaudeville acts while only a child. This poster from around 1900 shows (left to right) father Jerry, mother Nellie, sister Josephine, and George Cohan. © **BETTMANN/CORBIS. REPRODUCED BY PERMISSION.**

nal 1904 production. More recent attempts to bring *Little Johnny Jones* to the stage have not been as successful. A 1982 Broadway revival of *Little Johnny Jones,* starring Donny Osmond, opened and closed on the same night.

Primary Source

Twenty Years on Broadway [excerpt]

SYNOPSIS: Cohan's book concentrates on the glory days of his career, giving little mention of his family, his wife, Ethel Levey, the Actor's Equity strike, or the breakup of his partnership with Sam H. Harris in 1919. Cohan's attempts to revive his flailing career often included revisiting his first hit. *Little Johnny Jones* was filmed as a silent in 1923, and again in 1930. Cohan recorded live versions of its songs "I'm a Yankee Doodle Dandy" and "Give My Regards to Broadway." These songs are still widely heard today, even though many listeners have forgotten the composer's name.

The season of 1903–04 we toured the country with "Running for Office," playing all the principal cities from New York to San Francisco.

Josie had been married now for over two years, and she and her husband (who was also a performer) had decided that being separated was a hardship they could no longer endure. The result was that they had signed a joint contract to appear in one of Klaw and Erlanger's attractions the following season. This arrangement naturally meant the breaking up of the trade mark.

"Why don't you write a play and star yourself, Georgie?" Josie suggested. "Mother and dad would be tickled to pieces to play two parts for you." Then to them, "Wouldn't you, folks?"

"I think that's what you should do," agreed dad.

"So do I," echoed mother, and so it was settled that the season of 1904–05 would find me an individual star.

On the way back from the Coast, I slipped a chorus boy into my part, left the troupe in Vancouver, and got into New York during the early part of April, to lay my plans for the new play.

After a short consultation with A. L. Erlanger, it was understood that I was to open in a Broadway theater the following September.

"What's the name of the piece?" asked Erlanger.

"'Little Johnny Jones,'" I replied.

"What's it all about?" he inquired.

George Cohan in costume for his first hit musical, "Little Johnny Jones," in 1905. Cohan played the title role. © BETTMANN/CORBIS. REPRODUCED BY PERMISSION.

"Wait till you see it. It's the best thing I've ever done." As a matter of fact, I hadn't done it at all. All I'd thought of so far was the title, and that struck me as being a hundred per cent "box office."

I took desk room in the Miner Lithographing Company's offices in the Sheridan Building at Broadway and Thirty-fifth Street, engaged a cast and chorus, signed agreements with scenic artists and carpenters for the painting and building of the production, ordered costumes, props, and printing, and inside of two weeks' time was all set and ready, with the exception of writing the play. I'd been to London the summer before and had conceived the idea of using the Cecil Hotel courtyard for one scene and the Southampton pier for another, but beyond that I had given no thought to story, situations, or musical numbers, and was far too busy to get down to actual writing until about ten days before the rehearsal call.

"What you ought to have around you is some fellow who could take the business burdens off your mind," suggested Walter Moore, of the Miner Company, one afternoon as he hopped on the side of my desk for a pow-wow.

"Do you happen to know any manager with a whole lot of money who wants to buy in on a surefire hit?" I was half kidding when I said this, but he took it seriously.

"Sure I do. There's a little guy right over there that'll take a chance," and he pointed to Sam Harris, who was at another end of the room, looking over a scene model with A. H. Woods, who was a partner of his in several melodramas at the time.

"Hey, Sam!" Walter called out. "Come over here a minute."

Harris and I started a joke conversation about the matter. It seemed that as we talked along we sort of warmed up to each other. That evening we went to dinner together. The next day we both attended a song writers' outing given by a crowd known as the Words and Music Club. Crossing the ferry on the way back from Staten Island that night, we shook hands (which was the only contract ever existing between us) and formed the partnership of Cohan and Harris.

The Spotlight

When I got through with the manuscript of "Little Johnny Jones" I had an old-fashioned comedy melodrama "all dressed up" in songs and dances.

"You can't play a mob scene, shoot off guns, and dash from heroics into a musical number. The public will never stand for it," said Theodore Kreamer, a writer of popular melodramas, after witnessing my dress rehearsal.

"Well, it's new, isn't it?"

"Yes, it's new, of course, but—"

"Then at least they'll have to give me credit for trying."

That was the only argument I had to offer.

I was superstitious enough to book Hartford as the opening stand, hoping to follow along the luck of "The Governor's Son." "Little Johnny Jones" was a smashing hit, possibly one of the biggest in the history of American musical comedy.

Our first New York engagement with the piece, nevertheless, was a queer experience. We came into the Liberty Theater, and the opening performance was apparently a sensational success. The indifference of both press and public, however, was so pronounced that after seven weeks of half-filled houses we took to the road, pretty well convinced that New York would have none of it.

We moved to Philadelphia, where the play proved such a popular hit that we were immediately recalled to Broadway, where we reopened at the New York Theater and ran to capacity audiences for weeks and weeks. Of course, this was to a scale of popular prices, but the speculators were on the sidewalk collecting fancy premiums just the same. It was the one and only Broadway "comeback" I have ever known or heard of.

We got busy at once and organized a second "Johnny Jones" troupe and sent it throughout the country while I continued to play New York and Philadelphia, and later on Boston and Chicago. It was what is known as a "freak attraction" from a box-office standpoint, but the critics didn't take very kindly to my personal performance of the title role.

"A swaggering, impudent, noisy vaudevillian, entirely out of place in first-class theaters," was the opinion of one of New York's foremost dramatic experts. Another prominent critic characterized me as "the musical-comedy nuisance." I thought back to the days of the Buffalo *Advertiser,* when I could write my own notices.

An idea struck me. "Why not publish my own sheet and tell the world what a truly great 'author-composer-actor-manager' I really am?" No sooner thought of than done.

In two weeks' time I was shooting throughout the country copies of a four-page, illustrated, bright and snappy, full-fledged newspaper which I named *The Spotlight.*

Walter Kingsley, who was then our press representative, had dug up a mailing list three thousand miles long, so we claimed "the largest free circulation of any theatrical publication in the world."

This little sheet was devoted to the interests of George M. Cohan's plays and productions, with a weekly attack on all unfriendly critics in a column which I wrote and signed myself.

Further Resources

BOOKS

Gilbert, Douglas. *American Vaudeville: Its Life and Times.* New York, Dover Publications, 1963.

McCabe, John. *George M. Cohan: The Man Who Owned Broadway.* New York: Doubleday & Co., 1973.

Morehouse, Ward. *George M. Cohan: Prince of the American Theater.* Philadelphia: J.B. Lippencott, 1943.

PERIODICALS

Andersen, Fred. "'My God What an Act to Follow!'" *American Heritage* 48, no. 4, July-August 1997, 66–77.

Lyman, Rick. "You Never Get Over Yankee Doodle Fever." *The New York Times,* November 30, 2001, E1.

WEBSITES

Collins, David. "George M. Cohan in America's Theater." Available online at http://members.tripod.com/davecol8/index.htm; website home page http://members.tripod.com (accessed March 25, 2003).

Kenrick, John. "George M. Cohan 101." Musicals101.com. Available online at http://www.musicals101.com/cohan.htm; website host page http://www.musicals101.com (accessed March 25, 2003).

My Life

Autobiography

By: Isadora Duncan

Date: 1927

Source: Duncan, Isadora. *My Life.* New York: Liveright Publishing Co., 1927; 1995, 154–163.

About the Artist: Isadora Duncan (1878–1927) is regarded as the mother of modern dance, famous for dancing barefoot in simple Greek robes. She was born in 1878 in San Francisco, California, as Dora Angela Duncan. Performing for audiences by age twelve, she made her dazzling New York debut in 1899. She became famous in Europe, and she died as spectacularly as she lived. In 1927, while speeding along in a Bugatti sports car in Nice, France, her long scarf became entangled in the car's wheels and strangled her. ■

Introduction

Isadora Duncan's sensational life was marked by much hardship and tragedy. In her childhood, her father, in a state of financial ruin, abandoned the family and left Isadora's mother to raise three young children by herself. Duncan was encouraged in the arts of dance, theater, and literature. The family lived a life of genteel poverty; her mother gave music lessons. By age six, Isadora was helping to support the household by dancing for money, and she and her sister, Elizabeth, taught dance to other young children. Although she had little formal education, Duncan was an avid reader. She particularly was moved by

A group of early twentieth century dancers performing in the fluid, interpretive style pioneered by Isadora Duncan. © HULTON-DEUTSCH COLLECTION/CORBIS. REPRODUCED BY PERMISSION.

the works of Walt Whitman, William Shakespeare, and Friedrich Nietzsche, and in her later years became a frequent writer herself.

In 1895, Isadora Duncan's mother moved the family to Chicago in hopes of a better life. Duncan's professional stage career began to blossom. In 1899, August Daly, a Broadway producer, invited her to tour with his company in New York, where she debuted as a fairy in Shakespeare's *A Midsummer Night's Dream.* Duncan also gave private concerts for wealthy New Yorkers, providing the family with significant income. In 1898, the Duncans once again sought to enhance their fortunes by traveling to London on a cattle boat. Duncan's first professional performance, for which she received raucous acclaim, was at London's Lyceum Theater on February 22, 1900. Turning down other substantial offers, Duncan instead decided to join her heroine, Loie Fuller, and her touring company. Duncan conquered Budapest, Vienna, Munich, and Berlin before embarking on a solo career.

Isadora Duncan's new dancing was an extreme departure from the conventions of ballet. Instead, she developed interpretive dance, characterized by free-form movements inspired by poetry, music, and nature (such as swaying arms to symbolize the branches of trees; and swooping spinal movements to evoke breaking ocean waves). Duncan was interested in dance as a form of expression. Her ideas helped to free dance from rigid formulas and mere displays of technical prowess—conveying meaning and feeling through naturalistic movements. Her acolytes recognized Duncan for her passionate dancing, and she ultimately came to be the most famous dancer of her time. Although her style of dancing may now be considered outdated, Isadora Duncan paved the way for other modern dance pioneers, such as Martha Graham.

Significance

Duncan's autobiography, *My Life,* chronicles her childhood years in San Francisco, her introduction to classical music and poetry by her mother, and her year of intense study of classical Greek art in Athens. The poses of the ancient sculptures inspired her for years to come. Isadora did not believe in marriage, and shocked many of her contemporaries with her notorious love affairs with high-profile individuals of the day, including stage designer Gordon Graig and millionaire Paris Eugene Singer (heir to the sewing machine empire). These and many other passionate encounters are retold in frank and passionate detail. Duncan had two children, Deirdre and Patrick, who both accidentally drowned in 1913 while with their governess.

Duncan expressed an increasingly passionate desire to teach dance throughout the world. Her dream was to open a dancing school. She opened her first dance school in Grunwald, Germany, in 1904. She chose six of its students, called "The Isadorables" after her own image, to tour with her. However, the school floundered. To make ends meet, Duncan left her school behind—finally returning to the American stage for a tour to raise money. There, she reconnected with other artists and writers whom she had admired when first arriving on the artistic scene in New York. She came to be managed by Broadway mogul, Charles Frohman, who failed to realize that the marketing techniques for popular musical shows were ill-suited for Duncan's avant-garde dance performances. While the first of these performances produced by Frohman received favorable reviews, Duncan's ticket sales were unremarkable. Duncan wanted to return to Europe. However, her sculptor friend George Barnard convinced her to stay, and introduced her to conductor, Walter Damrosch. Damrosch had admired Duncan's interpretation of Beethoven's Seventh Symphony—Duncan was fond of choreographing her work to classical music, including Strauss's Blue Danube and Chopin's Funeral March. The conductor offered to represent her at the Metropolitan Opera House for a month. Much better publicized, these concerts frequently sold out and helped to solidify Duncan's artistic reputation in America. Still, she desired to return to Europe.

In spite of the financial success of the American tour, Duncan still did not have enough money for her schools. None of her several endeavors to open dancing schools in Germany, Russia, and the United States succeeded. Duncan's narrative in *My Life* stops in 1921, just before she is to embark on another attempt to open a dance school in Moscow. She had just received a letter from the Russian government, promising to provide her with classrooms, and room and board for herself. Unfortunately, after the school is built, the Russian government will withdraw its support. However, today, Isadora Duncan's art, now in its third generation, lives on in the schools and dance companies formed by her students.

Isadora Duncan, a pioneer of modern dance, performing around 1910. © BETTMANN/CORBIS. REPRODUCED BY PERMISSION.

Primary Source

My Life [excerpt]

SYNOPSIS: In addition to her teaching and performing activities, Isadora Duncan frequently wrote on dance. Her articles appeared in numerous periodicals. Her other books include *The Dance* (1909), *The Philosopher's Stone of Dancing* (1920), and *The Art of the Dance,* published posthumously in 1928. Her autobiography *My Life* was published in 1927, the year of her death. The following excerpt recounts Duncan's attempts to finance her dancing school by returning to America for a tour in 1908.

It became clearer and clearer to me that in Germany I would not find the support I needed for my school. . . .

As always, the expenses of my little flock were enormous. Once more my bank account was nil, and so, in the end, my school was forced to return to Grünewald, while I signed a contract with Charles Frohman for an American tour.

It cost me many pangs to part from my school, from Elizabeth, and Craig, but, most of all, to forgo the big bond between myself and my baby, Deirdre, who was now almost a year old, and grown into a blonde, rosy-cheeked child, with blue eyes.

And so it happened that one day in July I found myself all alone on a big ship bound for New York—just eight years since I had left there on a cattle boat. I was already famous in Europe. I had created an Art, a School, a Baby. Not so bad. But, as far as finances went, I was not much richer than before.

Charles Frohman was a great manager, but he failed to realise that my art was not of the nature of a theatrical venture. It could only appeal to a certain restricted public. He presented me in the heat of August, and as a Broadway attraction, with a small and insufficient orchestra, attempting to play the "Iphigenia" of Gluck and the Seventh Symphony of Beethoven. The result was, as might have been expected, a flat failure. The few people who wandered into the theatre on those torrid nights, when the temperature was ninety degrees and more, were bewildered, and, most of them, not pleased with what they saw. The critics were few, and wrote badly. On the whole I could not but feel that my return to my native country was a great mistake.

One evening when I was sitting in my dressing-room, feeling particularly discouraged, I heard a fine, hearty voice greeting me, and saw, standing in the doorway, a man, not tall, but of beautiful frame, with a shock of brown curly hair and a winning smile. He held out his hand to me in spontaneous affection, and said so many beautiful things about the effect that my art had upon him, that I felt recompensed for all I had suffered since my arrival in New York. This man was George Grey Barnard, the great American sculptor. Thereafter he came every night to the performance, and often brought with him artists, poets, and other friends of his, among them David Belasco, the genial theatrical producer, the painters Robert Henri and George Bellows, Percy MacKaye, Max Eastman—in fact, all the young revolutionaries of Greenwich Village. I remember, too, the three inseparable poets who lived together in a tower below Washington Square—E. A. Robinson, Ridgeley Torrence, and William Vaughn Moody.

This friendly greeting and enthusiasm from the poets and artists cheered me immensely, and made up for the meagreness and coldness of the New York audiences. . . .

Charles Frohman, finding that the stay on Broadway was disastrous, attempted a tour in the smaller towns, but this tour was also so badly arranged that it was even more of a failure than the New York performances. Finally I lost patience, and went to see Charles Frohman. I found him in a very disconcerted state, thinking over all the money he had lost. "America does not understand your Art," he said. "It is considerably over the heads of Americans, and they will never understand it. It would be better for you to return to Europe."

I had a contract with Frohman, calling for a six months' tour, with a guarantee, whether or not it made a success. Nevertheless, from a feeling of hurt pride, and also out of contempt for his lack of sportsmanship, I took this contract and tore it up before his eyes, saying, "At any rate this leaves you free from all responsibility."

Following the counsels of George Barnard, who told me repeatedly that he was proud of me, as a product of American soil, and that it would be a great sorrow to him if America did not appreciate my art, I decided to stay in New York. So I took a studio in the Beaux Arts Building, fitted it up with my blue curtains and my carpet, and proceeded to create some new work, dancing every evening for the poets and artists. . . .

George Grey Barnard had counselled me to stay in America, and I was glad I had listened to him. For, one day, there arrived in the studio a man who was to be instrumental in gaining for me the enthusiasm of the American public. This was Walter Damrosch. He had seen me dancing an interpretation of the Seventh Symphony of Beethoven at the Criterion Theatre, with a small, bad orchestra, and he had had the understanding to realise what would be the effect of this dancing when inspired by his own fine orchestra and glorious conducting.

My studies of the piano and of the theory of orchestral composition, as a child, must have remained in my subsconsciousness. Whenever I lie quiet and shut my eyes, I can hear the whole orchestra as plainly as if they were playing before me, and for each instrument I see a god-like figure in movement of fullest expression. This orchestra of shadows danced always in my inner vision.

Damrosch proposed to me a series of representations at the Metropolitan Opera House for the month of December, to which I joyfully assented.

The result was just as he had predicted. At the first performance, Charles Frohman, who had sent for a box, was astonished to learn that not a seat remained in the theatre. This experience proves that, no matter how great the artist, without the proper setting even the greatest art can be lost. This was the case with Eleanora Duse on her first tour in America, when, because of poor management, she played to almost empty houses and felt that America could never appreciate her. Whereas, when she returned in 1924, she was greeted from New York to San Francisco with one continual ovation, simply because, this time, Morris Gest had had the artistic intelligence to understand her.

I was very proud to travel with an orchestra of eighty men, conducted by the great Walter Damrosch. This tour was particularly successful, as there reigned throughout the orchestra such a feeling of good-will towards the chief and towards myself. Indeed, I felt such sympathy with Walter Damrosch that it seemed to me when I stood in the centre of the stage to dance, I was connected by every nerve in my body with the orchestra and with the great conductor.

How can I describe the joy of dancing with this orchestra? It is there before me—Walter Damrosch raises his baton—I watch it, and, at the first stroke there surges within me the combined symphonic chord of all the instruments in one. The mighty reverberation rushes over me and I become the medium to condense in unified expression the joy of Brünnhilde awakened by Siegfried, or the soul of Isolde seeking in Death her realisation. Voluminous, vast, swelling like sails in the wind, the movements of my dance carry me onward—onward and upward, and I feel the presence of a mighty power within me which listens to the music and then reaches out through all my body, trying to find an outlet for this listening. Sometimes this power grew furious, sometimes it raged and shook me until my heart nearly burst from its passion, and I thought my last moments on earth had surely arrived. At other times it brooded heavily, and I would suddenly feel such anguish that, through my arms stretched to the Heavens, I implored help from where no help came. Often I thought to myself, what a mistake to call me a dancer—I am the magnetic centre to convey the emotional expression of the orchestra. From my soul sprang fiery rays to connect me with my trembling, vibrating orchestra.

There was a flutist who played so divinely the solo of the Happy Spirits in "Orpheus" that I often found myself immobile on the stage with the tears flowing from my eyes, just from the ecstasy of listening to him, and the singing of the violins and the whole orchestra soaring upwards, inspired by the wonderful conductor.

Louis of Bavaria used to sit alone listening to the orchestra at Bayreuth, but if he had danced to this orchestra, he would have known an even greater delight.

There was a marvellous sympathy between Damrosch and me, and to each one of his gestures I instantly felt the answering vibration. As he augmented the crescendo in volume, so the life in me mounted and overflowed in gesture—for each musical phrase translated into a musical movement, my whole being vibrated in harmony with his.

Sometimes when I looked down from the stage and saw the great brow of Damrosch bent over the score, I felt that my dance really resembled the birth of Athena, springing full-armed from the head of Zeus.

This tour in America was probably the happiest time of my life, only, naturally, I suffered from homesickness, and when I danced the Seventh Symphony, I pictured about me the forms of my pupils when they should have grown to an age to interpret it with me. So it was not a complete joy, but the hope of a future, greater joy. Perhaps there is no complete joy in life, but only hope. The last note of Isolde's love song seems complete, but that means Death.

In Washington I was met by a perfect storm. Some of the ministers had protested against my dance in violent terms.

And then, suddenly, to the astonishment of everyone, who should appear in the stage-box on the afternoon of a matinée, but President Roosevelt himself. He seemed to enjoy the performance, and led the applause after every item of the programme. He afterwards wrote to a friend:

> What harm can these ministers find in Isadora's dances? She seems to me as innocent as a child dancing through the garden in the morning sunshine and picking the beautiful flowers of her fantasy.

This saying of Roosevelt's, which was quoted in the newspapers, considerably abashed the preachers, and aided our tournée. In fact, the entire tournée was most happy and propitious in every way, and no one could have asked for a kinder director or more charming comrade than Walter Damrosch, who had the temperament of a really great artist. In his moments of relaxation he could enjoy a good supper and play upon the piano for hours, never tired, always genial, lighthearted, and delightful.

When we returned to New York, I had the satisfaction of hearing from my bank that I had a goodly deposit to my account. If it had not been for the pulling at my heart-strings to see my baby and my school I would never have left America. But one morning I left the little group of friends on the pier—Mary and Billy Roberts, my poets, my artists—and returned to Europe.

Further Resources

BOOKS

Blair, Fredrika. *Isadora: Portrait of the Artist as a Woman.* New York: McGraw-Hill, 1986.

Daly, Ann. *Done into Dance: Isadora Duncan in America.* Indianapolis: Indiana University Press, 1995.

Dillan, Millicent. *After Egypt: Isadora Duncan and Mary Cassatt.* New York: Dutton, 1990.

Isadora, Rachel. *Isadora Dances.* New York: Viking, 1998.

Kendall, Elizabeth. *Where She Danced: The Birth of American Art Dance.* Berkeley: University of California Press, 1984

Kurth, Peter. *Isadora: A Sensational Life.* Boston: Little, Brown and Company, 2001.

MacDougall, Allan Ross. *Isadora; a Revolutionary in Art and Love.* New York: T. Nelson, 1960.

Wagenknecht, Edward. *Seven Daughters of the Theatre.* Norman: University of Oklahoma Press, 1964.

PERIODICALS

Eley, Susie Eisner. " Dancing Through History." *Dance Spirit* 6, no. 3, March 2002, 57.

Fanger, Iris. " Isadora Duncan." *Dance Magazine,* May, 1999.

WEBSITES

Dickson, Samuel. Isadora Duncan. Museum of the City of San Francisco. Available online at http://www.sfmuseum.org/bio/isadora.html; website home page http://www.sfmuseum.org (accessed March 24, 2003).

Isadora Duncan Foundation for Contemporary Dance, Inc. Available online at http://www.isadoraduncan.org/ (accessed March 24, 2003).

AUDIO AND VISUAL MEDIA

Isadora Duncan: Movement from the Soul. Geller/Goldfine, 1987, VHS.

Sunshine and Shadow

Autobiography

By: Mary Pickford

Date: 1955

Source: Pickford, Mary. *Sunshine and Shadow.* Garden City, NY: Doubleday & Company, Inc. 1955, 63–71.

About the Author: Mary Pickford (1892–1979) was one of the first powerful women in film. Originally from Toronto, Ontario, Canada, Gladys Louise Smith began her acting career to support her family after her father's death. By fourteen, she was on Broadway, starring in David Belasco's *The Warrens of Virginia.* Belasco gave Pickford her stage name. She made her screen debut two years later, in 1909. She became known as "America's Sweetheart" for the little girl roles she played well into adulthood. In addition to acting, she was also a film producer, writer, and director. In 1919, she formed United Artists with Charlie Chaplin, D.W. Griffith, and Douglas Fairbanks. ■

Introduction

Early films were shown in theater houses called "nickelodeons"—named for "odeon," the Greek word for "music"—and the admission of a nickel. A program consisted of six ten-minute film reels, which might include an adventure, a comedy, an information film, a chase, and a melodrama. Although the films were silent, a piano player often provided musical accompaniment. Nickelodeons became a popular form of entertainment for many working class and immigrant families.

By the turn of the twentieth century, filmgoers, who had been watching "actuality films" since the 1890s, began to enjoy the availability of fiction films. In these early films, many actors received no credits, as appearing in motion pictures generally was regarded as a low profession. Professional stage actors were often disdainful of "the flickers," a derogatory nickname. Many preferred not to use their stage names in association with this cheap form of entertainment, while film producers felt that advertising the names of actors would inflate egos and salaries. The idea of the movie star had not yet been born.

Mary Pickford was simply known as "The Biograph Girl," "Little Mary," or "The Girl with the Golden Curls," until she began to get billing for her performances. She demanded high salaries for her performances. She was one of the first actors to act in a naturalistic manner, rather than with exaggerated movements. Pickford's wide-eyed portrayals of young female heroines entranced audiences worldwide. Some of her most memorable roles were in *The New York Hat* (1912), *Poor Little Rich Girl* (1917), *Rebecca of Sunnybrook Farm* (1917), and *Pollyanna* (1920). Pickford's siblings also developed successful careers in cinema; Lottie Pickford as an actor, and Jack Pickford as an actor and director.

Significance

When sixteen-year-old Mary Pickford entered the Biograph studios, director D. W. Griffith had been making films for the company for a year. Griffith had appeared in Edwin S. Porter's groundbreaking *The Great Train Robbery* in 1902. In his films after that appearance, Griffith continued experimenting with cinematic narrative techniques. Griffith's *Pippa Passes,* in which Pickford undergoes a "screen test," became the first film to be reviewed in *The New York Times.*

That year, 1909, Pickford appeared in about 50 more shorts—each shoot taking a day or two. Owen Moore, the young man she describes in the following passage about her first days at Biograph, would become Mary Pickford's first husband. The marriage did not last. They

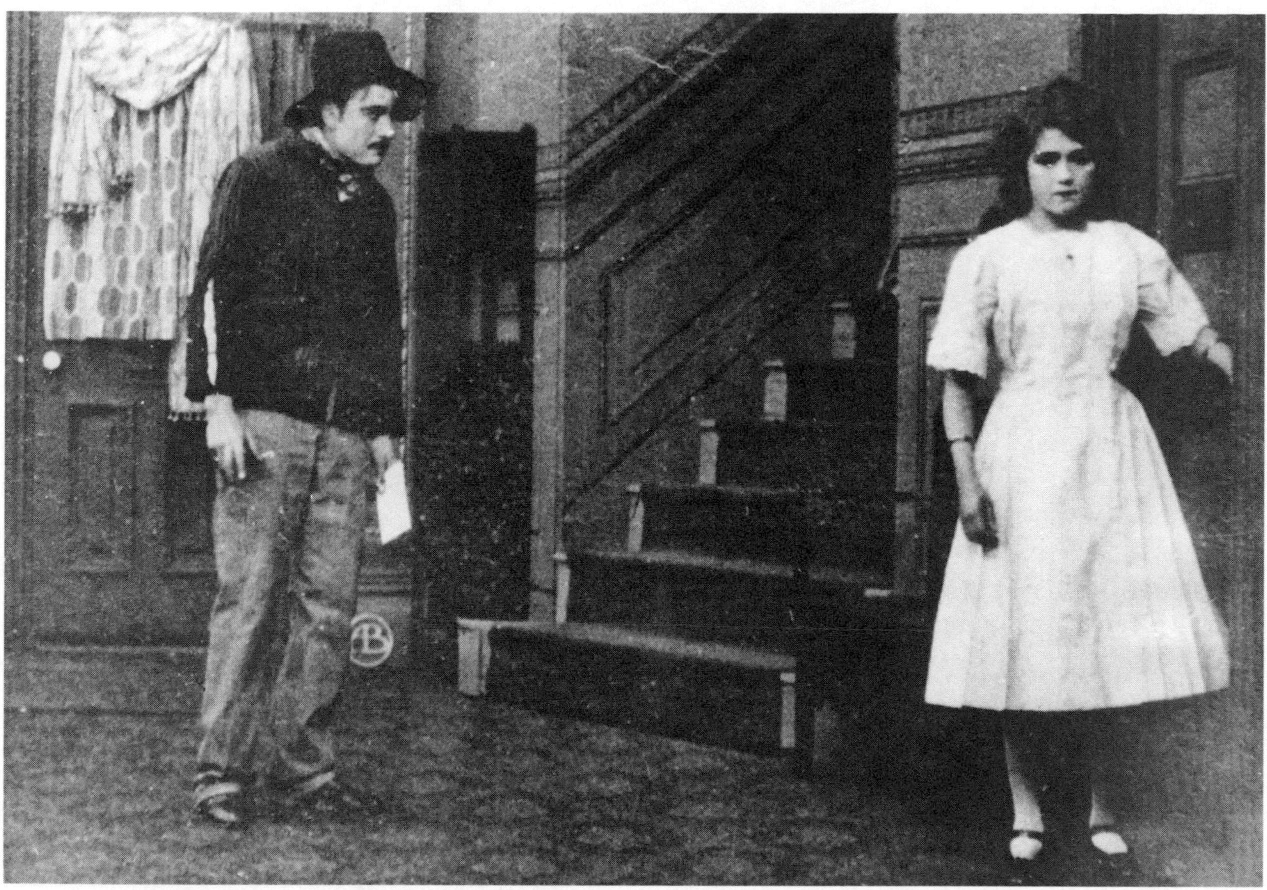

Mary Pickford at age sixteen in one of her earliest roles, the 1909 film *Lonely Villa.* Pickford would go on to become one of Hollywood's first stars. © BETTMANN/CORBIS. REPRODUCED BY PERMISSION.

divorced, and she married Douglas Fairbanks and, later, Buddy Rogers.

Mary Pickford's success on the silent screen led to the rise of the star system. She realized that although her name and off-screen personality were unknown to audiences, they were buying tickets to see the films because of her. In Griffith's *Friends* (1912), she appeared in the earliest close-up shot in filmmaking; Pickford encouraged the cameraman to come closer to her face. At the time, this cinematic move was considered outrageous because it was believed that audiences were paying to see all of her, "including her feet—not just half of her." Pickford knew that her talented performances deserved a higher salary and name recognition. She was a brilliant, ambitious young businesswoman. She demanded and received veto power over her scripts, exercised creative input in her films, and chose her directors and co-stars. Though she sometimes rebelled against the child roles that audiences loved, Pickford portrayed a young girl as late as 1926, at age thirty-three. This film, *Sparrows,* was Pickford's last silent movie, and it is considered one of her finest performances. Pickford transitioned to the "talkies," winning an Academy Award for her role in *Coquette* (1929). In 1933, she retired from film.

Primary Source

Sunshine and Shadow [excerpt]

SYNOPSIS: Mary Pickford was already an acclaimed stage actress before entering the film world. At the time, it was considered degrading for a stage actress to appear in films. However, the prospect of a daily salary convinced Pickford to try to secure some work at American Biograph Company, a fledgling film studio. Mary Pickford quickly became the film industry's first major international star.

It was in Chicago, while touring with *The Warrens* that I had my first taste of the "flickers." The makeshift movie house was a long, narrow store on State Street, outfitted with train and streetcar seats. The camera was mounted on an engine that sped through tunnels and around tracks. The illusion of actually being on a train was so vivid that I became violently carsick. This gave me a horror of the "flickers," and I vowed never to go back. Not Lottie and Jack, however. They became hopeless addicts of the new fad very early, and I remember beseeching Mother to keep them away from this fearful iniquity. Every time they could raise five or ten cents, they would rush off to a store on West Twenty-third Street to see a film. . . .

■ ■ ■

That particular spring after *The Warrens of Virginia* closed our funds got so low that Mother made what seemed to me a very shocking proposal.

"Would you be very much against applying for work at the Biograph Studios, Gladdie?" she said one day.

"Oh no, not that, Mama!"

"Well, now, it's not what I would want for you, either, dear. I thought if you could make enough money we could keep the family together. I'm sure it would make up for the lowering of our standard."

I wanted to argue with her, but I knew better. I agreed.

"I knew you would, dear," said Mother. "It's only to tide us over. They say the pay is good . . ."

. . . In my secret heart I was disappointed in Mother: permitting a Belasco actress, and her own daughter at that, to go into one of those despised, cheap, loathsome motion-picture studios. It was beneath my dignity as an artist, which I most certainly considered myself at the time. . . .

. . . But on that March day of 1909, on East Fourteenth Street in New York, Gladys was sent back to Canada and Mary Pickford was to embark on a great and thrilling career.

■ ■ ■

As I crossed the marble-floored foyer of the old mansion occupied by the Biograph Studio, a man came through the swinging door opposite me and began to look me over in a manner that was too jaunty and familiar for my taste.

"Are you an actress?" he demanded at once.

"I most certainly am," I retorted.

"What, if any, experience have you had, may I ask?"

"Only ten years in the theater, sir, and two of them with David Belasco," I said icily.

"You're too little and too fat, but I may give you a chance. My name is Griffith. What's yours?"

The name meant nothing to me at all. I thought him a pompous and insufferable creature and I wanted more than ever to escape. Instead I found myself being led through two swinging doors and into the ladies' dressing room. . . . No one paid the slightest attention to Mr. Griffith and me as we walked by. The dressing room was deserted. He sat me down and told me to wait. . . .

. . . I was hastily tiptoeing out of the dressing room when Mr. Griffith reappeared. He told me that I was to be given a test, the first, and, I may add, the *only* test that I was ever subjected to at Biograph. It was for *Pippa Passes,* and Mr. Griffith himself put on my make-up. The result seemed more appropriate for Pancho Villa than for Pippa. A makeshift costume was rounded up in the wardrobe department—a tiny cellar alcove set aside for the Biograph costume rack.

Wearing this grotesque make-up, I was led on the stage and, without any introduction to the cast, given a quick briefing on what I was to do. . . .

. . . I was handed a guitar and told to act as if I were singing and strumming!

During the filming of this scene in which everyone improvised his own lines, a handsome young man, with a melodious Irish voice, stepped forth and nonchalantly said:

"Who's the dame?"

That was going too far. I forgot all about the guitar, the scene, my grotesque make-up, and Mr. Griffith, and turned the full force of my indignation on this boor.

"How dare you, sir, insult me? I'll have you understand I'm a perfectly respectable young girl, and don't you dare call me a bad name!"

With that Mr. Griffith let out a roar that would have done the M.G.M. lion credit.

"Miss . . . Miss . . . what the devil is your name? But no matter . . . Never, do you hear, never stop in the middle of a scene. Do you know how much film costs per foot? You've ruined it! Start from the beginning!"

In those days "dame" meant to me just one thing—a loose woman. I had just never heard a girl publicly referred to as "a dame." Of course that young Irishman had meant no offense and was simply ad-libbing as they all did in the early movies. . . .

Why Mr. Griffith asked me to come back the next day is still a matter of amazement to me. I was positive this was the end of my career in the "flickers." I knew it in my heart. I had put ten years in the theater, and I knew whether a performance was good or bad. Mine that day at the Biograph Studio was distinctly bad.

It was well past eight o'clock when I returned to the dressing room and removed my hated make-up. Mr. Griffith was waiting for me outside.

"Will you dine with me?"

"I'm sorry, Mr. Griffith, I've never dined with any boy, let alone a man, and besides I have to leave immediately for Brooklyn. My mother and sister are playing there with Mr. Olcott."

"Will you come back tomorrow? Our pay for everybody is five dollars a day. We pay only by the day."

Already my Scotch blood was coming to the fore.

"I'm a Belasco actress, Mr. Griffith, and I must have ten."

He laughed.

"Agreed! Five dollars for today and ten for tomorrow. But keep it to yourself. No one is paid that much, and there will be a riot if it leaks out." . . .

The next morning, promptly at 7:30, an alarm clock shimmied off the table onto the floor of my bedroom. Sleepy and aching all over, I never was so reluctant to rise in my life. But I got to the studio at nine o'clock on the dot, walking all the way this time, to save the five cents. I remember praying that no one from the theater would see me going up the Biograph steps. That day I played a ten-year-old girl in a picture entitled *Her First Biscuits*. . . .

. . . I found the work less irksome that day, and before I knew it I was back in the dressing room removing my make-up and getting into my street clothes. I was going through the swinging doors into the foyer when Mr. Griffith called out to me.

"Will you play the lead tomorrow?"

"Why, yes, sir!"

"Do you know anything about love-making?"

After several inaudible gulps I assured him I did.

At that moment a carpenter passed by us, carrying a papier-mâché pillar.

Mr. Griffith asked him to set the pillar down.

"All right, Pickford, make love to that pillar."

I was fifteen years old. I had never gone on a date, much less been kissed by a boy. Hoping to escape, I said:

"Please, Mr. Griffith, how could I make love to a cold pillar?"

I had no sooner said that than Owen Moore stepped out of the men's dressing room.

"Come here, Moore!" Griffith shouted to him.

Moore walked over to us, a puzzled smile on his handsome Irish face.

"Stand there!" Mr. Griffith directed him. "Miss Pickford doesn't like to make love to a lifeless pillar. See if she can do any better with you."

Panic-stricken, I was ready to rebel and walk out on the whole sickening business, when I remembered the ten dollars Mr. Griffith had promised me. I pulled myself together and tried to recall how I had seen people make love in the theater. I decided that the way to do it was to look lovingly into the man's eyes. I made up my mind right then and there that there would be no kissing. I had been taught to regard kissing in public as vulgar in the extreme and completely unnecessary in the theater, where one could pretend without actually kissing.

Whatever the merits of my pathetic attempt at love-making that evening, it must have satisfied Mr. Griffith. I was given the leading role opposite Owen Moore in *The Violin Maker of Cremona*. . . .

Making a picture in those days generally took one day indoors and one day outdoors. *The Violin Maker of Cremona* was apparently successful, and Mr. Griffith seemed to be very happy over his latest acquisition. In fact he announced to the heads of the Biograph company that he intended to put me under contract at a guaranteed weekly salary of twenty-five dollars for the first three days, and five for the remaining three. . . .

Even though I was only a child, I gave considerable thought to the problem of acting in those early days. One day I made a vow that I tried never to break. I swore that, whatever the temptation, I would never overact. This was revolutionary in the early movies where the actors were using the elaborate gestures of the French school of pantomime.

"I will not exaggerate, Mr. Griffith," I would say in a firm voice. "I think it's an insult to the audience."

This was only one of many things over which the great director and I squabbled. The argument usually ended with my quitting and being rehired a few hours later.

Further Resources

BOOKS

Brownlow, Kevin. *Mary Pickford Rediscovered: Rare Pictures of a Hollywood Legend.* New York: Harry N. Abrams, 1999.

Eyman, Scott. *Mary Pickford: America's Sweetheart.* New York: D.I. Fine, 1990.

Lee, Raymond. *The Films of Mary Pickford.* South Brunswick, N.J.: A. S. Barnes, 1971.

Niver, Kemp R. *Mary Pickford, Comedienne.* Los Angeles: Locane Research Group, 1969.

Whitfield, Eileen. *Pickford: The Woman Who Made Hollywood.* Lexington, Ky.: The University Press of Kentucky, 1997.

Windeler, Robert. *Sweetheart: The Story of Mary Pickford.* London, W.H. Allen, 1973.

PERIODICALS

Croce, Arlene. "Golden Girl: The Return of Mary Pickford." *The New Yorker,* September 25, 1997, 130–138.

Corliss, Richard. "Queen of the Movies."*Film Comment* 34.2, March-April 1998, 53–62.

WEBSITES

Griffith, Linda. "How Mary Pickford Got Her Start in the Pictures." Available online at http://www.2020site.org/marypickford/firstrole.html; website home page http://www.2020site.org (accessed March 25, 2003).

The Mary Pickford Foundation. Available online at http://www.marypickford.com (accessed March 25, 2003).

AUDIO AND VISUAL MEDIA

Mary Pickford: A Life on Film. Directed by Hugh Munro Neely. Milestone Video, 1997, VHS.

2

Business and the Economy

James N. Craft

Entries are arranged in chronological order by date of primary source. For entries with one primary source, the entry title is the same as the primary source title. Entries with more than one primary source have an overall entry title, followed by the titles of the primary sources.

Important Events in Business and the Economy, 1900–1909

1900

- In January, 250,000 U.S. children under age 15 worked in mines and factories rather than attending school.
- On January 10, the National Civic Federation is established in Chicago to promote labor-management relations with representatives from business, labor, and the public.
- In February, the Alabama State Federation of Labor becomes the first U.S. union to integrate African American and white workers.
- On March 14, Congress passes the Gold Standard Act, empowering the U.S. Treasury to use gold in its transactions.
- On March 18, veteran train engineer John Luther "Casey" Jones, thirty-six, is killed when his train crashes near Vaughan, Mississippi. His heroic efforts to save as many lives as possible are later immortalized by another railroad worker in the ballad "Casey Jones."
- On March 31, *The Saturday Evening Post* carries the first national advertisement for automobiles.
- On May 1, more than two hundred miners die in an explosion in Scofield, Utah.
- On May 26, the horsecar era ends as the last horsecar in the United States makes its final run in Washington, D.C.
- On June 3, the American Federation of Labor (AFL) organizes the International Ladies Garment Workers Union in New York City.
- In September, the National Metal Trades Association and the Machinists' Union agree to reduce the workday from ten to nine hours.
- On September 17, nearly one hundred thousand miners in the new United Mine Workers (UMW) stage their first strike in Pennsylvania.
- On October 29, the Republican Party pressures the mine owners to grant a small pay raise and the United Mine Workers return to work. Negotiations between the mine owners and the UMW continue throughout 1901.
- On November 3, the first U.S. National Automobile Show opens at New York's Madison Square Garden and lasts a week. The show features fifty-one exhibitors and numerous contests on starting, stopping, turning, and obstacle-course proficiency.
- On November 6, voters reelect Republican candidate William McKinley president with a percentage of the popular vote exceeding his previous election.
- On November 15, steel magnate Andrew Carnegie founds the Carnegie Institute of Technology in Pittsburgh, Pennsylvania. The institute personifies his belief that philanthropists should enrich economic and cultural institutions throughout their lives.

1901

- On January 10, the oil gusher Spindletop blasts near Beaumont, Texas, establishing the petroleum industry in Texas.
- On February 25, U.S. Steel forms from a merger of ten companies and is the world's largest industrial corporation.
- On May 9, the stock market declines the most since 1803, with some stocks dropping twenty points.

1902

- On February 19, the U.S. Justice Department prosecutes the Northern Securities Company, formed by a railroad merger, as a violation of the Sherman Antitrust Act. This prosecution is the first use of the act, which forbids businesses from monopolizing the production or distribution of a commodity or service.
- On May 12, the Anthracite Coal Strike begins and lasts five months, nearly crippling the nation. The United Mine Workers demand union representation, a wage increase of 20 percent, and an eight-hour workday.
- On June 1, the state of Maryland passes a workers' compensation law, the nation's first.
- On June 17, Congress passes the National Reclamation Act, also called the Newlands Act or the Irrigation Bill. The act, which authorizes the federal government to build dams in the West for irrigation, is vital to westward expansion and farming.
- On October 3, President Theodore Roosevelt gathers representatives of labor and management in Washington, D.C. to confer with him in settling the Anthracite Coal Strike.
- On October 16, President Theodore Roosevelt appoints a special commission to mediate the Anthracite Coal Strike.
- On October 21, the head of the United Mine Workers, John Mitchell, calls off the twenty-three-week strike as negotiations begin, though a settlement is not reached until the following March.
- On November 16, the famous "Drawing the Line in Mississippi" political cartoon appears in the *Washington Post* and the *Washington Evening Star.* The cartoon, which depicts Theodore Roosevelt's refusal to participate in the staged killing of a bear on a hunting expedition, is the impetus for the creation of the teddy bear.

1903

- On February 4, Congress passes the Elkins Act to regulate interstate commerce by railroads. The act strengthens the power of the Interstate Commerce Commission to investigate charges that railroad companies are increasing rates to artificial levels and stifling competition.

- On February 11, Congress passes the Expedition Act, giving antitrust suits precedence over other docketed cases.
- On February 14, Congress creates the U.S. Department of Commerce and Labor. Among its bureaus is a Bureau of Corporations that will investigate the organization, conduct, or management of any company.
- On February 25, Congress passes the Immunity Provision Act, protecting witnesses, especially employees of corporations, who testify in antitrust cases.
- On March 22, the Anthracite Mediation Commission, appointed by Roosevelt the previous October, grants concessions to both the mine operators and the United Mine Workers.
- On May 6, President Theodore Roosevelt, in a speech at the Grand Canyon, promises Americans a "Square Deal." By the phrase, Roosevelt means that corporations, workers, and consumers will benefit from a federal government strong enough to prevent any one of the three from abusing the others.
- On July 14, President Theodore Roosevelt declares that the civil service is an "open" shop—that is, workers are allowed to decide for themselves whether they want to join a union, rather than being required to join one.
- On August 8, nearly four thousand miners of the Western Federation of Miners (WFM) strike in Cripple Creek, Colorado, to gain a shorter workday and lower wages.
- On September 4, federal troops arrive in Colorado to stop the WFM strike, and a few of the mines reopen.
- In October, AFL President Samuel Gompers warned that Asian immigrants were taking jobs from Americans.
- On October 22, the Electrical Vehicle Company and George B. Selden file suit against the Ford Motor Company for infringement of the Selden patent on engines. The case, known as the Selden Patent Case, will not go to trial for six years.
- On November 30, the U.S. Supreme Court rules in *Atkin* v. *Kansas* that an eight-hour workday for government-employed construction workers is constitutional.

1904

- On January 1, three hundred U.S. firms controlled 40 percent of U.S. capital. As early as the eighteenth century Alexander Hamilton had anticipated and Thomas Jefferson had feared this accumulation of wealth in few hands.
- On February 7, the business center of Baltimore burns for more than a day, causing $85 million in damage and the destruction of more than 140 acres encompassing 75 square blocks.
- On March 14, the U.S. Supreme Court rules in *Northern Securities* v. *United States* that Northern Securities, a conglomeration of railroad companies, violates the Sherman Antitrust Act of 1890. The court orders Northern Securities to dissolve into several railroad companies, with the aim of restoring competition and innovation to the industry.
- On April 30, the World's Fair, called the Louisiana Purchase Exposition, begins in Saint Louis after a dedication by Roosevelt and is open for seven months.
- On June 4, an explosion destroys the Independence railroad station in Colorado, killing fourteen nonunion miners. Police charge the WFM with the crime, though a spy working for the Mine Owners' Association will later confess.
- On October 27, the first rapid transit system, the New York City subway system, opens.
- In December, a fifteen-month WFM strike that began in August 1903 at the gold mine in Cripple Creek, Colorado ends with concessions from the Mine Owners' Association, including a three-dollar-a-day minimum wage for an eight-hour day.
- In December, membership in U.S. unions reaches 2 million.
- On December 1, *American Industries*, a publication of the National Association of Manufacturers, denounces labor's request for a shorter workday as communistic.

1905

- In January, the price of admission to a movie theater is five cents. Americans call these theaters "nickelodeons."
- On January 8, a strike lasting more than five months by textile workers in Fall River, Massachusetts, ends with labor winning concessions.
- On January 30, the U.S. Justice Department, in *Swift and Company* v. *United States,* charges Swift and Company, the largest producer and distributor of meat, with creating a monopoly in violation of the Sherman Antitrust Act.
- On February 23, the Rotary Club, the first business-related service organization, is founded in Chicago.
- On April 17, the U.S. Supreme Court rules in *Lochner* v. *New York* that limiting the maximum number of hours an employee works is unconstitutional.
- On June 27, the Industrial Workers of the World (IWW) is created as an international union. The "Wobblies," as IWW members are called, seek to unite all industrial workers in a single union.
- On December 30, a bomb kills former Idaho governor Frank Steunenberg in his home in Caldwell, Idaho. Police arrest prominent union organizers from the WFM, including William D. "Big Bill" Haywood. The case, settled in 1907, becomes one of the most notorious labor trials of the century.

1906

- On February 21, Congress passes the Heyburn Bill, regulating the producers and sellers of food.
- On March 12, the U.S. Supreme Court rules in *Hale* v. *Henkel* that employees called as witnesses in antitrust cases can be forced to testify against their employers.
- On April 18, the San Francisco earthquake destroys the business district and much of the city. Fire consumes more than 500 blocks, kills 500 people, leaves 250,000 homeless, and destroys 25,000 buildings.
- On May 3, the First Annual Advertising Show opens in New York City.

- On June 4, a presidential commission issues the Neill-Reynolds report, documenting the unsanitary conditions in the meatpacking industry. President Theodore Roosevelt had appointed the commission after Upton Sinclair exposed the industry's filth in his novel *The Jungle.*
- On June 29, Congress passes the Hepburn Act. Like the Elkins Act, the Hepburn Act strengthens the Interstate Commerce Commission (ICC)'s power to investigate collusion and price fixing among railroad companies.
- On June 30, Congress passes the Meat Inspection Act, empowering the U.S. Department of Agriculture to inspect all meat for quality and wholesomeness.
- On June 30, Congress passes the Pure Food and Drug Act, prohibiting the mislabeling or adulteration of food and drugs.

1907

- On March 13, the stock market drops, causing a financial panic, unemployment, high food prices, and bank failures by the end of the year.
- In June, Congress bars Japanese immigrants from the U.S. for fear they were taking jobs from Americans.
- In June, Andrew Carnegie laments in a speech the growing gap between rich and poor. It remains a characteristic of the U.S. economy.
- On July 29, a jury acquits William D. "Big Bill" Haywood in the murder of former Idaho governor Frank Steunenberg. The killer, who worked for the Mine Owners' Association, confessed he had planted the bomb to frame union organizers, a revelation that shocked the public.
- On October 21, a run on the Knickerbocker Trust Company ruins the bank. In the coming weeks, other banks and trusts fail, requiring an infusion of money from the U.S. Treasury and from private corporations under the leadership of financier and industrialist J. P. Morgan.
- On December 6, 361 coal miners die in an explosion in Monongah, West Virginia.
- On December 19, 239 coal miners die in an explosion in Jacobs Creek, Pennsylvania.

1908

- In January, a survey estimates that more than three hundred thousand people in New York City go to the movies every day.
- On January 27, the U.S. Supreme Court rules in *Adair* v. *United States* that the portion of the Erdman Act of 1898 outlawing yellow-dog contracts is unconstitutional.
- On February 3, the U.S. Supreme Court rules in the Danbury Hatters case, *Loewe* v. *Lawlor,* that a nationwide boycott of an industry is a restraint of trade under the Sherman Antitrust Act, and thus a violation of the act.
- On February 10, the Wright brothers sign their first U.S. Army contract for the delivery of a plane, establishing the record of a bid-to-contract time of five days. The contract will be finalized upon successful operation of the plane.
- On February 24, the U.S. Supreme Court rules in *Muller* v. *Oregon* that laws limiting the maximum number of hours that women can work to ten hours a day are constitutional.
- On March 16, the U.S. Supreme Court upholds the Elkins Act (1903) in *Armour Packing Company* v. *United States.* The court affirms the ICC's power to investigate railroad rates.
- On May 30, Congress passes the Aldrich-Vreeland Act to correct deficiencies in the banking system that created the Panic of 1907.
- On July 26, Congress creates the precursor to the Federal Bureau of Investigation as a branch of the Justice Department to investigate organized labor, fight the greed of big business, and prevent theft of public lands.
- On October 1, the Ford Motor Company unveils the Model T at $825, a price many Americans could afford.

1909

- On May 28, the Selden Patent Case, filed in 1903, opens with arguments about the nature of Selden's patent. The court rules the patent nonrestrictive, allowing Selden to claim royalties on the thousands of cars made since the U.S. Patent Office granted the patent in 1879. The case is instrumental in reforming patent laws.
- On July 12, Congress passes the Sixteenth Amendment to the Constitution, authorizing an income tax.
- On August 2, the Wright brothers deliver their first plane to the U.S. Army Signal Corps at a cost of thirty thousand dollars.
- On August 5, President William Howard Taft signs the Payne-Aldrich Tariff Act, reducing tariffs in hopes that other countries will reciprocate and thereby open foreign markets to U.S. goods.
- On November 13, more than 250 miners die in an explosion at the Saint Paul Mine in Cherry, Illinois.
- On November 22, the International Ladies Garment Workers Union begins a three-month strike in New York City.
- In December, the Cambria Steel Factory in Johnstown, Pennsylvania employs twenty thousand workers, making it among the world's largest factories.

First Annual Report of the United States Steel Corporation for the Fiscal Year Ended December 31, 1902

Report

By: United States Steel Corporation

Date: 1902

Source: United States Steel Corporation. *First Annual Report of the United States Steel Corporation for the Fiscal Year Ended December 31, 1902.* Pittsburgh: United States Steel Corporation, 1902, 13–20.

About the Organization: When it was founded in 1901, the United States Steel Corporation, better known as U.S. Steel, was the largest business enterprise ever launched, with more than $1 billion in capital. Formed through the dealings of legendary businessmen including J.P. Morgan, Andrew Carnegie, Charles Schwab, and Elbert H. Gary (the company's first chairman), U.S. Steel quickly became the country's largest producer of steel, a title it still holds today. ■

Introduction

The late–nineteenth century was a period of unparalleled industrial growth in America. It was marked by the emergence of new industries, the expansion of established industries, consolidation of capital, and the rise of powerful, wealthy business leaders. It was also a time of cutthroat competition, which many business leaders found harmful to business and to the country as a whole. No one better represented the drive for order, discipline, and economic stability than the powerful banker and financier, J.P. Morgan. First in the railroad industry and later in other industries, Morgan drove consolidation and the creation of great trusts to help bring order to an economy that he considered little more than a barroom brawl. Personally controlling or influencing vast sums of investment capital, Morgan was able to force compliance by creating large business consolidations and trusts. His greatest creation was the United States Steel Corporation.

U.S. Steel was the result of the ambition of two giants of American business—Morgan and steel magnate, Andrew Carnegie. Morgan and his associates had been acquiring steel-related businesses since the late 1890s, but an entity on the scale of U.S. Steel became possible only as a result of the personal aspirations of Andrew Carnegie. By 1900, Carnegie had gone into semiretirement, leaving the operation of his vast company to his lieutenants, including Charles Schwab. Carnegie spent much of his time in his native Scotland and wanted to fully retire, but he also wanted to extract as much capital as possible from his business in order to pursue his philanthropic activities. He also wanted the business he had built to continue to grow and prosper.

In Carnegie's mind, the only option was to sell out to Morgan, so in 1900, he authorized Schwab to float the idea by Morgan. Morgan immediately saw the potential and quickly assembled the necessary resources. Another giant of American business, John D. Rockefeller, also took part in the deal. Within days, the deal was put together, and the syndicate bought out Carnegie for the then enormous sum of $400 million.

Significance

Organized in March 1901, U.S. Steel became the world's first billion-dollar company. Upon its formation, it controlled sixty-five percent of the steel-producing capacity in the United States. Huge though the company was, its long-term strategy lay not in capturing more market share through internal growth or the acquisition of competing firms, but in vertical integration. That is, U.S. Steel not only produced steel, but also owned coal and iron ore mines, railroad and shipping companies, as well as production facilities that turned out finished steel products. Within a few years, though, U.S. Steel became concerned with the antitrust temper of the country and the trust-busting tendencies of Presidents Roosevelt (served 1901–1909), Taft (served 1909–1913), and Wilson (served 1913–1921). Thereafter, it concentrated on operating efficiencies and profits, rather than monopolizing the industry.

Primary Source

First Annual Report of the United States Steel Corporation for the Fiscal Year Ended December 31, 1902 [excerpt]

SYNOPSIS: The following excerpt from U.S. Steel's first annual report includes portions from the partial year of operation, 1901, and the first full year, 1902. It describes the major component companies and future prospects. Note the prominent members of the board of directors.

Acquired by the Carnegie Steel Company in 1883, the massive Homestead Steel Works in Pennsylvania became part of U.S. Steel in 1901. An area called "the Ward," just south of the plant, housed hundreds of steel workers and their families. THE LIBRARY OF CONGRESS.

Organization and the Issue of Stocks and Bonds

The United States Steel Corporation was incorporated under the laws of the State of New Jersey, the original certificate of incorporation having been filed at Trenton, February 25, 1901, and the amended certificate, April 1, 1901. By the amended certificate, the authorized capital stock of the Corporation was fixed at 11,000,000 shares of the par value of $100 each, equally divided into 5,500,000 shares of seven per cent. cumulative preferred stock (preferred as to both dividends and capital), and 5,500,000 shares of common stock.

Of the total authorized capital stock, there have been issued, and at this date (January 10, 1902) are outstanding 5,102,056 shares of preferred stock, and 5,082,273 shares of common stock. The Corporation also has issued $303,450,000 of five per cent. bonds secured by a Trust Indenture, dated April 1, 1901, to the United States Trust Company of New York as Trustee.

Substantially all of these bonds and shares have been issued to acquire the bonds and stocks of the subsidiary companies which were held by the public, as well as considerable amounts thereof, which belonged to members of the Syndicate and to the Syndicate Managers, viz.: (1) the bonds and stock of the Carnegie Company and the capital stocks of the several other companies under the original agreement of March 1, 1901, with J. P. Morgan & Co., Managers of a Syndicate which includes among its members and participants officers and directors of this Corporation; (2) the stocks of the American Bridge Company and the Lake Superior Consolidated Iron Mines under the agreement of April 1, 1901, with J.P. Morgan & Co.; (3) the stocks of the Oliver Iron Mining Company and of the Pittsburg Steamship Company; and (4) the stocks of the Shelby Steel Tube Company, for which a contract was negotiated in June, 1901, with representatives of the stockholders of that company.

Details of Issue of Stocks and Bonds

(1) 4,247,688 shares of the common stock and 4,249,716 shares of the preferred stock and $303,450,000 face value of bonds of the Corporation were issued in payment for the $25,000,000 in cash, paid to the Corporation by the Syndicate Managers, and for the stocks and bonds set forth in the following table, excepting 1,644 shares otherwise acquired, and directors' qualifying shares, viz.:

Federal Steel Company	Common Stock	$46,483,700
	Preferred Stock	53,260,200
National Steel Company	Common	31,970,000
	Preferred	26,966,000
National Tube Company	Common	40,000,000
	Preferred	40,000,000
American Steel and Wire Company of New Jersey	Common	49,981,400
	Preferred	39,999,000
American Tin Plate Company	Common	28,000,000
	Preferred	18,325,000
American Steel Hoop Company	Common	19,000,000
	Preferred	14,000,000
American Sheet Steel Company	Common	24,499,600
	Preferred	24,499,600
Carnegie Company	Common Stock	160,000,000
	Bonds	159,450,000

(2) 722,025 shares of common stock, and 741,915 shares of preferred stock of the Corporation were issued for the acquisition of $29,413,905 par value of stock of the Lake Superior Consolidated Iron Mines and $30,946,400 of common stock and $31,348,000 of preferred stock par values of the American Bridge Company;

(3) 92,500 shares each of common and preferred stock of the Corporation were issued for the acquisition of an outstanding one-sixth interest in the Oliver Iron Mining Company and in the Pittsburgh Steamship Company, thus securing the ownership of all of the stock of those two companies not owned by the Carnegie Company except directors' qualifying shares; and

(4) 20,045 shares of common stock and 17,910 shares of preferred stock of the Corporation were issued for the acquisition of $8,018,200 of common stock and $4,776,100 shares of preferred stock, par values, of the Shelby Steel Tube Company under the contract above mentioned.

The Aragon Iron Mines leasehold and the stock of the Bessemer Steamship Company have been purchased for cash paid and payable by this Corporation or by some of the subsidiary companies above mentioned.

All of the bonds of the Carnegie Company and all of the stocks of the companies acquired as above mentioned by the United States Steel Corporation, have been lodged with the United States Trust Company, as Trustee, for the benefit of the Corporation and its stockholders, and to secure the payment of the $304,000,000 bonds of the Corporation authorized by the deed of trust of April 1, 1901. This deposit affords security to stockholders as well as bondholders against diversion or depletion of these important assets of the corporation.

Circulars, dated March 2, and April 2, and 8, 1901, addressed to the holders of shares of the several companies therein specified were issued and published by the Syndicate Managers. At the rates offered in the circular dated March 2, 1901, the Syndicate acquired the common stocks and preferred stocks of the seven companies (other than the Carnegie Company) as above mentioned (see p. 15), and thereupon sold and transferred the same to this Corporation under the contract of March 1, 1901. The Syndicate delivered to the holders of such stocks of said seven companies in the aggregate 2,694,909 shares of common stock and 2,616,957 shares of preferred stock of this Corporation. The Syndicate acquired sixty per cent. ($96,000,000) of the stock of the Carnegie Company, and $159,450,000 face value of the five per cent. bonds of the Carnegie Company by delivering to the holders thereof said $303,450,000 of bonds of this Corporation and $1,200,000 in cash; and the Syndicate acquired the remaining forty per cent. ($64,000,000) of the stock of the Carnegie Company by delivering to the holders thereof 982,771 shares of preferred stock and 902,790 shares of the common stock of this Corporation.

The residue of the common and preferred stock of this Corporation delivered to the Syndicate under the contract of March 1, 1901, and not used for the acquisition by it of the stocks of the specified companies, being the shares which, as stated in the Syndicate circular of March 2, 1901, were to be retained by and to belong to the Syndicate, amounted to 649,987 shares of preferred stock, and 649,988 shares of common stock. This residue of stock or the proceeds thereof, after reimbursing the Syndicate the $25,000,000 in cash which it paid to the Corporation, and approximately $3,000,000 for other syndicate obligations and expenses, constituted surplus or profit of the Syndicate.

The transactions between this Corporation and the Syndicate having been concluded, an agreement of final settlement and mutual release, dated Janu-

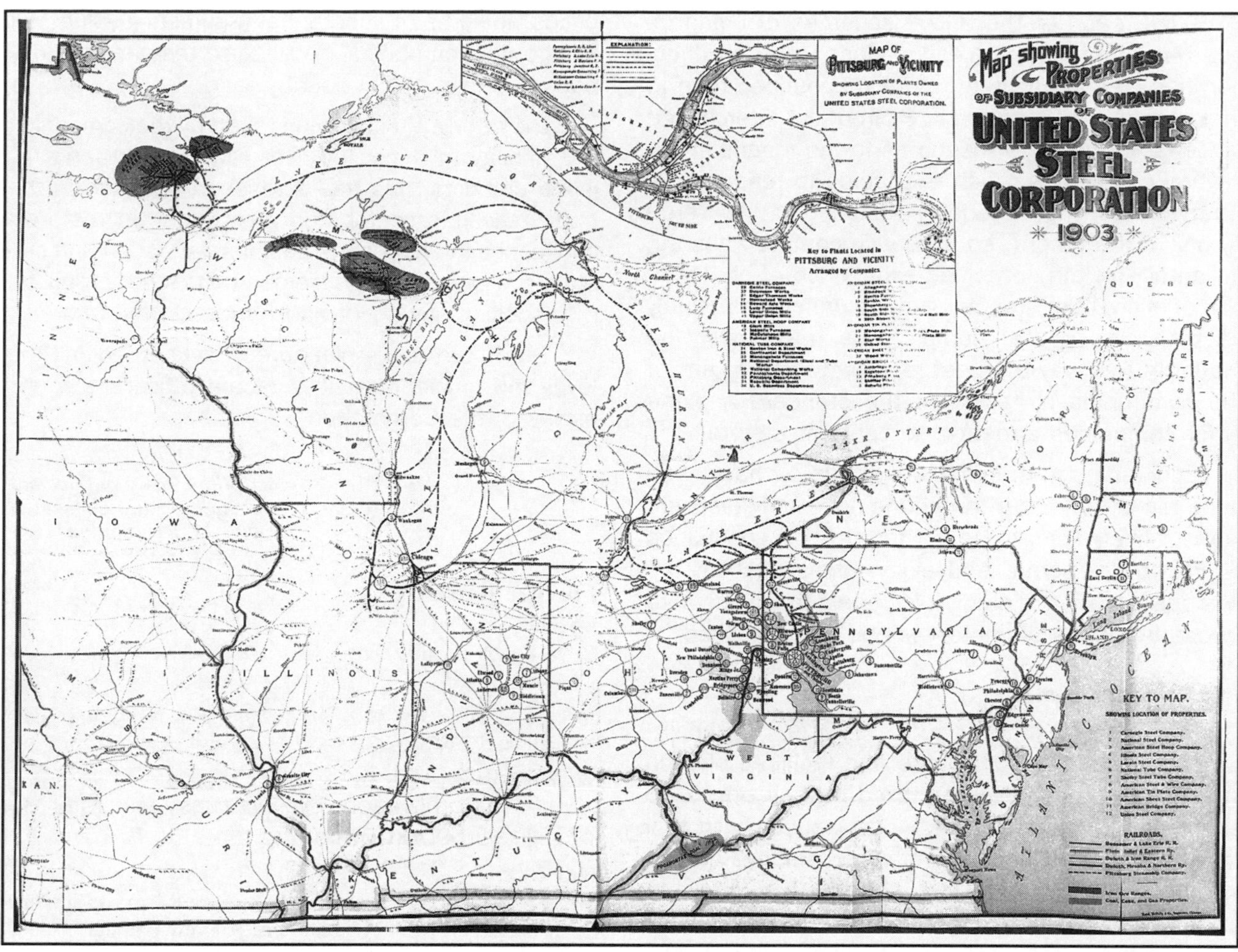

A map of U.S. Steel's business holdings in 1903. U.S. Steel was the world's largest business enterprise when it was formed in 1901. UNITED STATES STEEL CORPORATION.

ary 3, 1902, was executed between this Corporation and the Syndicate Managers.

It will be noted that this Corporation has received and now owns in the aggregate more than ninety-nine and three-fourths per cent. of the shares of all the specified companies. The acquisition of so large a proportion of the shares has enabled the Corporation promptly to enter upon the accomplishment of the principal objects which induced its formation, and has facilitated the fulfilment of the original expectations of large reductions in expenditures for improvements, of increased earnings applicable to dividends, and of greater stability of investment, without increasing the prices of manufactured products. . . .

General Results in Organization and Manufacturing

It was expected that by harmonious co-operation of the several companies great economies in manufacturing would be accomplished, and such expectations have been fully realized. Diversified management has been dispensed with as far as possible, and the several companies have endeavored to adopt similar methods as far as suited to their respective businesses. Great departments like Ore Mining, Coal Mining, Manufacture of Coke and Lake Transportation, have been thoroughly systematized, and the managements of the manufacturing plants in the same locality have been brought into closer relations.

The companies have endeavored to concentrate the manufacture of their various products at the point most favorable to their production, thus insuring to each ultimate economy in manufacturing costs and in the assembling of material. The effort also is made by the different companies to regulate their manufacture of various products so that the fullest advantage can be taken of the economical production of any special article and its cheapest distribution to the consumer.

While each of the above schemes of organization has effected great economies, yet in no direction has this result been more pronounced than in that of manufacturing itself. By frequent interchange of views and full information as to the results in the several companies, each is enabled to reap the advantage of any new economy practiced or discovered by any of the others, so that each company has the advantage of the combined experience of all. Methods of accounting are being made uniform as rapidly as possible so that comparisons may readily be made. In this way the best result attained by any of the companies is taken as the standard and the other companies endeavor to conform thereto.

Economies in manufacturing thus far have been quite remarkable, but the end is not nearly reached, nor is it likely soon to be, for through the continuous efforts to co-operate and aid in bringing about the best results at each plant, it is certain that even more favorable results ultimately will be accomplished.

The Business Outlook

The outlook for the year 1902 is very bright. Everything indicates that all of the facilities of each subsidiary company will be taxed to their utmost to supply the demand that is being made. The actual business now booked, and of which shipment is being called for faster than it can be supplied, amounts to more than half the total combined annual capacity of all the companies. The heavier products, like rails, billets, plates and structural material are sold up to the productive capacity of the Mills, until nearly the end of the year. In the more highly finished products, the consumption in each case is greater now than at the corresponding period in 1901, which, it should be remembered, was an abnormally heavy year. The expectation, therefore, of those closely connected with the manufacture and sale of these highly finished products, is for a demand even larger than that of 1901, and up to the limit of production.

Policy as to Prices

The demand for the products of the several companies has been so great that prices could easily have been advanced. Indeed, higher prices have been voluntarily offered by consumers who were anxious for immediate execution of orders, but the companies have firmly maintained the position of not advancing prices, believing that the existing prices were sufficient to yield a fair return on capital and maintain the properties in satisfactory physical condition, and that the many collateral advantages to be gained in the long run by refusing to advance prices would be of substantial and lasting value, not only to the companies, but also to the general business interests of the country.

The strong position thus taken by the companies for stability in prices both of raw material and finished products, has had a reassuring effect on the trade, and has contributed greatly toward restoring confidence in the general business situation and creating the present large demand for steel products, by dispelling any doubt as to prices in the future.

The Board takes pleasure in acknowledging the loyal and efficient services of the officers and employes of the Corporation.

By order of the Board of Directors,
Elbert H. Gary, Chairman Executive Committee.
Charles M. Schwab, President.

Further Resources

BOOKS

Hoyt, Edwin P., Jr. *The House of Morgan.* New York: Dodd, Mead, 1966.

Jackson, Stanley. *J.P. Morgan: A Biography.* New York: Stein and Day, 1983.

Warren, Kenneth. *Big Steel: The First Century of the United States Steel Corporation, 1901–2001.* Pittsburgh: University of Pittsburgh Press, 2001.

WEBSITES

"History of Andrew Carnegie and Carnegie Libraries: The Life of Industrialist and Philanthropist Andrew Carnegie (1835–1919)." Available online at http://andrewcarnegie.tripod.com/acbio.html; website home page http://andrewcarnegie.tripod.com (accessed December 24, 2002). *This website includes numerous links to biographies of Carnegie and information about U.S. Steel.*

"J.P. Morgan." Brad DeLong's Website. Available online at http://econ161.berkeley.edu/TCEH/j.p.morgan.html; website home page http://econ161.berkeley.edu (accessed December 24, 2002).

Report to the President on the Anthracite Coal Strike of May–October, 1902

Report

By: Anthracite Coal Strike Commission

Date: 1903

Source: Anthracite Coal Strike Commission. *Report to the President on the Anthracite Coal Strike of May–October, 1902* Washington, D.C.: Government Printing Office, 1903, 80–87.

About the Author: The Anthracite Coal Strike Commission was created in October 1902 to arbitrate the dispute between miners and mine owners in the ongoing strike in the anthracite coal region of eastern Pennsylvania. An outgrowth of a preliminary investigation performed by Commissioner of Labor Carroll D. Wright, the seven-person commission included a mine engineer, a U.S. Army engineer, a Catholic bishop, "a businessman familiar with the coal industry," the president of the Brotherhood of Railroad Conductors, a federal judge, and Commissioner Wright. ■

Introduction

In May 1902, the coal miners of the anthracite region in eastern Pennsylvania went on strike. Led by the young John L. Mitchell, president of the United Mine Workers (UMW) union, the miners sought a twenty percent wage increase, an eight-hour workday, revised practices for weighing their daily output, and recognition of the union. A strike in 1900 had achieved a ten percent wage increase, but, beginning in 1901, Lewis made numerous efforts to bring the mine owners to the bargaining table to address other unresolved issues. The owners refused to deal with the UMW, so the miners walked out. The 1900 strike had been settled because of the influence of Marcus Hanna, President William McKinley's (served 1897–1901) political friend. Fearful of the negative results of a long strike during a presidential election year, Hanna had put pressure on the mine operators, including the railroads that owned seventy to eighty percent of the mines in the region, to settle. Reluctantly, they did so, but by 1902 they were determined to crush the workers.

The strike had ramifications for the entire nation. Anthracite (hard coal) was superior to bituminous (soft coal) because it was more efficient and much cleaner, so it had become the staple for heating homes and buildings, particularly in large cities. With winter approaching, the nation became increasingly agitated over the violence in the coalfields and the possibility of a fuel shortage. As prices began to rise, some, President Roosevelt (served 1901–1909) among them, were concerned that a coal shortage would cause riots, pitting the poor against the established order. Others were concerned that a prolonged strike would raise the clamor for public ownership of the mines. Gradually public opinion began to favor some form of government intervention.

Worried more about the consequences of a coal shortage than the rights of the workers, Roosevelt searched for an excuse to intervene. Although the federal government lacked the constitutional basis to take action, Roosevelt argued that the nation's interests took precedence.

Significance

On October 3, 1902, Roosevelt called mine owners and labor representatives to the White House, hoping to broker a settlement. Lewis, pleased with the implicit acceptance by the President of the union's right to represent the workers, adopted a conciliatory stance. The mine owners were intransigent, so much so that many Americans, even conservative business leaders, considered them to be overbearing and irresponsible. The conference accomplished nothing. Roosevelt was incensed by what he felt was the "arrogant stupidity" of the mine owners. More determined than ever to get the coalmines operating, he persuaded the governor of Pennsylvania to ask that federal troops be brought in to control the situation. Roosevelt let it be known that he was considering seizing and operating the mines in the public interest.

Two anthracite coal miners on strike in 1902. The strike caused a national crisis, and was resolved through one of the first instances of labor arbitration by the federal government. THEODORE ROOSEVELT COLLECTION, HARVARD COLLEGE COLLECTION.

This prospect was sufficient to induce J.P. Morgan, the country's most powerful financier, to step in. Morgan agreed to persuade the mine operators to accept the findings of a presidential commission, as Roosevelt had suggested at the earlier White House conference. The miners also agreed to the proposal, and, on October 23, agreed to return to work. Following an exhaustive examination, in which the commission heard over 500 witnesses and took over 10,000 pages of testimony, its report was made public in March 1903. Adopting a middle ground between workers and owners, the commission proposed increasing wages by ten percent and cutting hours from ten to nine per day. The operators were not compelled to recognize the union, and a ten percent increase in coal prices was recommended.

Although the United Mine Workers was not officially recognized by the mine owners, the settlement was widely regarded as a union victory. It was a major stimulus for growth of unions and union membership; from one million at the turn of the century, union membership grew to over two million by 1904. More importantly, Roosevelt's actions helped establish the federal government as a neutral arbitrator in labor disputes. It was consistent with the president's view, and that of many Progressives, that the government needed to play a proactive, balanced role in managing the country's economic affairs.

Primary Source

Report to the President on the Anthracite Coal Strike of May–October, 1902

SYNOPSIS: What follows are excerpts from the Recapitulation of Awards and the commission's General Recommendations. It provides a description of the wages and hours by major classification of employee and a mechanism to resolve disputes that arise under the agreement. The commission also commented on the employment by the mines of private police and child labor and on the need for government authority to investigate disputes. This investigative power would ensure that the public had sufficient information to judge the merits of labor disputes that affected the public interest.

Recapitulation of Awards

I. The Commission adjudges and awards: That an increase of 10 per cent over and above the rates paid in the month of April, 1902, be paid to all contract miners for cutting coal, yardage, and other work for which standard rates or allowances existed at that time, from and after November 1, 1902, and during the life of this award; and also to the legal representatives of such contract miners as may have died since November 1, 1902. The amount of increase under the award due for work done between November 1, 1902, and April 1, 1903, to be paid on or before June 1, 1903. . . .

III. The Commission adjudges and awards: That during the life of this award the present methods of payment for coal mined, shall be adhered to, unless changed by mutual agreement.

IV. The Commission adjudges and awards: That any difficulty or disagreement arising under this award, either as to its interpretation or application, or in any way growing out of the relations of the employers and employed, which can not be settled or adjusted by consultation between the superintendent or manager of the mine or mines, and the miner or miners directly interested, or is of a scope too large to be so settled or adjusted, shall be referred to a permanent joint committee, to be called a board of conciliation, to consist of six persons, appointed as hereinafter provided. . . .

V. The Commission adjudges and awards: That whenever requested by a majority of the contract miners of any colliery, check weighmen or check docking bosses, or both, shall be employed. The wages of said check weighmen and check docking bosses shall be fixed, collected, and paid by the miners in such manner as the said miners shall by a majority vote elect; and when requested by a majority of said miners, the operators shall pay the wages fixed for check weighmen and check docking bosses, out of deductions made proportionately from the earnings of the said miners, on such basis as the majority of said miners shall determine.

VI. The Commission adjudges and awards: That mine cars shall be distributed among miners, who are at work, as uniformly and as equitably as possible, and that there shall be no concerted effort on the part of the miners or mine workers of any colliery or collieries, to limit the output of the mines or to detract from the quality of the work performed, unless such limitation of output be in conformity to an agreement between an operator or operators, and an organization representing a majority of said miners in his or their employ.

VII. The Commission adjudges and awards: That in all cases where miners are paid by the car, the increase awarded to the contract miners is based upon the cars in use, the topping required, and the rates paid per car which were in force on April 1, 1902. Any increase in the size of car, or in the topping required, shall be accompanied by a proportionate increase in the rate paid per car. . . .

IX. The Commission adjudges and awards: That no person shall be refused employment, or in any way discriminated against, on account of membership or nonmembership in any labor organization; and that there shall be no discrimination against, or interference with, any employee who is not a member of any labor organization by members of such organization.

X. The Commission adjudges and awards: That all contract miners be required to furnish within a reasonable time before each pay day, a statement of the amount of money due from them to their laborers, and such sums shall be deducted from the amount due the contract miner, and paid directly to each laborer by the company. All employees when paid shall be furnished with an itemized statement of account.

XI. The Commission adjudges and awards: That the awards herein made shall continue in force until March 31, 1906; and that any employee, or group of employees, violating any of the provisions thereof, shall be subject to reasonable discipline by the employer; and, further, that the violation of any provision of these awards, either by employer or employees, shall not invalidate any of the provisions thereof.

General Recommendations

Enforcement of Law and Protection of Property

The Commission thinks that the practice of employing deputies, upon the request and at the expense of employers, instead of throwing the whole responsibility of preserving peace and protecting property upon the county and State officers, is one of doubtful wisdom, and perhaps tends to invite conflicts between such officers and idle men, rather than to avert them. Peace and order should be maintained at any cost, but should be maintained by regularly appointed and responsible officers and deputies, at the expense of the public, and reenforced as strongly as may be necessary by public authorities, rather than by guards hired by corporations or individuals. The fact that deputies are, to all intents and purposes the employees of one of the parties, usually works injury to the cause in which they are engaged—that of preserving peace and protecting property.

The employment of what are known as "coal and iron policemen," by the coal-mining companies, while a necessity as things are, militates against the very purpose for which they are employed. Although the testimony before the Commission proved that, as a whole, the coal and iron policemen were men of good character, there were a sufficient number of bad characters, taken from cities, to discredit the efforts of the whole body. The employment of this body of police is authorized by law, but they are really the employees of the coal companies, and thus do not secure the respect and obedience to which officers of the law are entitled. Their presence is an irritant, and many of the disturbances in the coal regions during the late strike grew out of their presence. Should this matter be remedied by legislation, so that the laws could be enforced and peace preserved by a regularly constituted constabulary, appointed and paid by the county or State, the Commission believes that much of the disorder which accompanies strikes would be avoided.

Employment of Children

Another subject, not a matter of submission, but concerning which much testimony was offered, is that of the employment of children. Boys are employed in the breakers. The attention of the Commission was called to the painful fact that in other industries boys and girls are employed, and work long hours both day and night. While the law prescribes the ages at which boys may be employed in and around the mines, and at which children may be employed in factories or mills, it appears, from the evidence, that the age is not placed sufficiently high. Infancy should be protected against the physical and moral influences of such employment, and there ought to be a more rigid enforcement of the laws which now exist.

Compulsory Investigation

Your letter of October 23, 1902, stated that you had appointed the undersigned "a Commission to inquire into, consider, and pass upon the questions in controversy in connection with the strike in the anthracite region, and the causes out of which the controversy arose," and also enjoined upon us to make the "endeavor to establish the relations between the employers and the wage workers in the anthracite fields on a just and permanent basis, and, as far as possible, to do away with any causes for the recurrence of such difficulties as those which you have been called in to settle."

We believe that the awards we have made, and which are herewith submitted, will accomplish, certainly during their life, the high aims contemplated in your letter. Faithful adherence to the terms of the awards can not fail to accomplish this; but in order to secure the public against long-continued controversy, and to make a coal famine or a famine in any other direction practically impossible, we deem it essential that there should be some authority to conduct just such investigations as that you called upon us to make.

There are some who have urged the Commission to recommend the adoption of compulsory arbitration, so called, as the means of securing this desired result, but we can not see our way to recommend any such drastic measure. We do not believe that in the United States such a system would meet with general approval or with success. Apart from the apparent lack of constitutional power to enact laws providing for compulsory arbitration, our industries are too vast and too complicated for the practical application of such a system.

We do believe, however, that the State and Federal governments should provide the machinery for what may be called the compulsory investigation of controversies when they arise. The States can do this, whatever the nature of the controversy. The Federal Government can resort to some such measure when difficulties arise by reason of which the transportation of the United States mails, the operations, civil or military, of the Government of the United States, or the free and regular movement of commerce among the several States and with foreign nations, are interrupted or directly affected, or are threatened with being interrupted or affected.

The Federal Government has already recognized the propriety of action under the circumstances just cited, as evidenced in the act creating boards of arbitration or commission for settling controversies and differences between railroad corporations and other common carriers engaged in interstate or territorial transportation of property or persons, and their employees, approved October 1, 1888. Under that act, when such controversies and differences arose, the President was authorized, on the application of either of the contestants, to appoint a commission of three members to investigate the causes surrounding the difficulty. That act was cumbersome in its provisions and was repealed by an act approved June 1, 1898, entitled "An act concerning carriers engaged in interstate commerce and their employees."

The provisions of the act first cited were applied at the time of the Chicago strike, so called, of 1894. There has been no resort to the act of June 1, 1898, which simply provides, so far as the Federal Government is concerned, that the chairman of the Interstate Commerce Commission and the Commissioner of Labor shall, upon the request of either party to a controversy coming under the terms of the act, with all practicable expedition put themselves in communication with the parties to such controversy, and shall use their best efforts, by mediation and conciliation, to settle the same amicably; and that if such effort shall be unsuccessful, they shall at once endeavor to bring about an arbitration of the controversy in accordance with the provisions of the act. The duties of these officials then cease, except where there is no choice of a referee by the parties selected as arbitrators. Then the commissioners named have power to designate the third arbitrator. Thus the principle of Federal interference, through investigation, has been established by these acts of Congress.

We print in the appendix a paper by Charles Francis Adams, read before the American Civic Federation in New York December 8, 1902, in which he outlined a proposed "act to provide for the investigation of controversies affecting interstate commerce, and for other purposes." *(a)* This proposition is that the President, whenever within any State or States, Territory or Territories of the United States a controversy concerning wages, hours of labor, or conditions of employment shall arise between an employer and the employees or association or combination of employees of an employer, by which the free and regular movement of commerce among the several States and with foreign nations, is in his judgment interrupted or directly affected, or threatened with being so interrupted or directly affected, shall, in his discretion, inquire into the same and investigate the causes thereof, and to this end may appoint a special commission, not exceeding seven in number, of persons in his judgment specially qualified to conduct such an investigation. The proposed act consists of eleven sections, and makes provision for all methods of procedure, rules, etc., requisite for its being carried into effect.

With a few slight modifications such an act would, in the opinion of the Commission, meet just such an emergency as that which arose last summer in the anthracite coal regions, and we submit it to you for your consideration. A similar act might be passed by the States not now having the machinery for the rigid investigation of labor troubles. Some of the State boards of arbitration have the right to make such investigation, but others are limited simply to the consideration of controversies when voluntarily submitted to them by the parties concerned.

These suggestions are reenforced through the consideration of a matter, somewhat without the scope of our inquiries, but which during their progress has pressed itself upon the attention of the Commission, and that is the apparent lack of a sense of responsibility to the public at large, manifested by both operators and mine workers, in allowing the controversy between them to go to such an extent as to entail upon millions of their fellow-citizens the cruel suffering of a fuel famine.

In the opinion of the Commission the questions involved in this controversy were not of such importance as to justify forcing upon the public consequences so fraught with danger to the peace and good order as well as to the well-being and comfort of society. If neither party could have made concessions to avoid a result so serious, an arbitration would have prevented the extremity which was reached. Undoubtedly the proposition that the men who own the property and carry on the business must control it, is generally true, and its maintenance is necessary to the political and economical welfare of society; but it is also true that where a business is of such magnitude, and its physical conditions are such as to constitute a natural monopoly, it is affected with a public interest that can not be ignored by those who control it.

The Commission trusts that when the time during which its awards are to remain in force shall have elapsed, the relations of operator and employee will have so far improved, as to make impossible such a condition as existed throughout the country in consequence of the strike in the anthracite region. Nevertheless the public has the right, when controversies like that of last year cause it serious loss and suffering, to know all the facts, and so be able to fix the responsibility. In order to do this power must be given the authorized representatives of the people to act for them by conducting a thorough investigation into all the matters involved in the controversy. This, of course, applies only to those cases where great public interests are at stake. It should not apply to petty difficulties or local strikes.

The chief benefit to be derived from the suggestion herein made lies in placing the real facts and the responsibility for such condition authoritatively before the people, that public opinion may crystallize and make its power felt. Could such a commission as that suggested have been brought into existence in June last, we believe that the coal famine might have been averted—certainly the suffering and deprivation might have been greatly mitigated.

All of which is respectfully submitted.

Geo. Gray.
Carroll D. Wright.
John M. Wilson.
John L. Spalding.
Edgar E. Clark.
Thomas H. Watkins.
Edward W. Parker.

Further Resources

BOOKS

Dubofsky, Melvyn, and Warren Van Tine. *John L. Lewis: A Biography.* New York: Quadrangle/New York Times, 1977.

Foner, Philip S. *History of the Labor Movement in the United States: Vol. 3. The Policies and Practices of the American Federation of Labor, 1900–1909.* New York: International Publishers, 1964.

Long, Priscilla. *Where the Sun Never Shines: A History of America's Bloody Coal Industry.* New York: Paragon House, 1989.

WEBSITES

Grossman, Jonathan. "The Coal Strike of 1902—Turning Point in U.S. Policy." Available online at http://www.dol.gov/asp/programs/history/coalstrike.htm; website home page http://www.dol.gov (accessed December 24, 2002).

International Association of Labour Institutions News Service. "The Great Strike." Available online at http://www.ialhi.org/news/i0203_21.html; website home page: http://www.ialhi.org (accessed December 24, 2002).

The History of the Standard Oil Company

Nonfiction work

By: Ida M. Tarbell

Date: 1904

Source: Tarbell, Ida M. *The History of the Standard Oil Company,* vol. 2. New York: McClure, Phillips, 1904, 267–269, 274–277, 287–288, 292. Available online at http://www.history.rochester.edu/fuels/tarbell/main.htm; website home page http://www.history.rochester.edu (accessed January 6, 2003).

About the Author: Ida M. Tarbell (1857–1944) was a prominent investigative journalist who achieved her greatest fame as the author of *The History of the Standard Oil Company.* Originally published as a series of articles in *McClure's Magazine* beginning in November 1902, the book exposed Standard Oil's sometimes ruthless business practices. In 1906, Tarbell became co-owner of *American Magazine.* She wrote several biographies, including an eight-volume study of Abraham Lincoln, and was a popular lecturer. ■

Introduction

Standard Oil Company was the quintessential business trust, and its founder, John D. Rockefeller, the quintessential "robber baron" of the Gilded Age. Through sound management, operating efficiencies, shrewdness, and sometimes highly unethical business practices, Standard Oil ruthlessly eliminated competition. By 1880, it

John D. Rockefeller in 1911. Founder of Standard Oil, Rockefeller was one of the wealthiest and most powerful businessmen of his era. AP/WIDE WORLD PHOTOS. REPRODUCED BY PERMISSION.

controlled up to ninety-five percent of the nation's oil-refining capacity.

Rockefeller was an extremely capable businessman who made Standard Oil the most efficient oil refiner in the industry. When he entered the newly emerging oil industry, whose then primary product was kerosene, it was a highly competitive business susceptible to wild market fluctuations that could wipe out companies overnight. Rockefeller was determined to bring order out of the chaos. He detested the unbridled competition that disrupted the smooth operation of the economy. His mission was to bring rivals into the sphere of Standard Oil, or destroy them. Rockefeller and his lieutenants were not above employing dubious practices to achieve their objectives. Most notably, he persuaded railroads to ship the company's oil at rates less than those they charged Standard Oil's competitors, and even to remit a portion of the difference to Standard Oil. Faced with ruin, competitors sold to or joined Rockefeller—or were driven out of business.

To help bring stability to the industry, Rockefeller's attorneys refined the legal device known as a trust. Essentially, the stockholders in Standard Oil's twenty-seven leading competitors were persuaded to exchange their stock in these firms for stock in the new Standard Oil Trust Company, created in 1879. This gave the nine directors of the Standard Oil Trust, led by Rockefeller, practical control over the entire oil industry. The Standard Oil model was soon emulated by other industries. Fearing, with good reason, the abuse of such monopolistic power and its corruptive influence on the political system, many people demanded legislation limiting the growth and influence of trusts.

State legislation failed to curb the trusts's growing influence. In 1890, the federal government passed the Sherman Anti-Trust Act. It, too, proved ineffective, and as the new century began, a new wave of trusts, holding companies, and other large corporations raised anew fears that the nation's economic and political systems were falling under the influence of a small group of extraordinarily wealthy business leaders.

Significance

Into this setting came Tarbell's eloquent and extensive critique of Standard Oil, *The History of the Standard Oil Company,* stimulating the public's demand for action against trusts. Buoyed by popular support, Presidents Theodore Roosevelt (served 1901–1909), William Howard Taft (served 1909–1913), and Woodrow Wilson (served 1913–1921) initiated successful antitrust action against a number of trusts, including the Standard Oil Company. In the years following the publication of Tarbell's book, Standard Oil became the object of sustained federal, state, and local government legal action. In a suit brought in 1906 by the Roosevelt administration, the federal government sought the breakup of the company under the provisions of the Sherman Anti-Trust Act. The dissolution finally took place in 1911, when the company was broken into thirty-three separate companies, including some that exist today, such as Exxon, Mobil, Conoco, Amoco, Pennzoil, Marathon, and Atlantic Richfield.

Primary Source

The History of the Standard Oil Company [excerpt]

SYNOPSIS: In the conclusion to her book *The History of the Standard Oil Company,* Tarbell emphasizes the great power that Standard Oil holds over the oil industry, and its ability to acquire influence in a dizzying array of other industries. Tarbell also argues that Standard's stranglehold on the transportation network—railroads, pipelines, and shipping—is its greatest advantage. Unless those transportation systems can be made to serve the public interests through regulation, she says, Standard Oil's power will not be broken.

The profits of the present Standard Oil Company are enormous. For five years the dividends have

A cartoon by Udo Keppler, published in 1904, shows a Standard Oil tank as an octopus whose tentacles grip the steel, copper, and shipping industries, as well as the Capitol, while another tentacle reaches out for the White House. **THE LIBRARY OF CONGRESS.**

been averaging about forty-five million dollars a year, or nearly fifty per cent. on its capitalisation, a sum which capitalised at five per cent. would give $900,000,000. Of course this is not all that the combination makes in a year. It allows an annual average of 5.77 per cent. for deficit, and it carries always an ample reserve fund. When we remember that probably one-third of this immense annual revenue goes into the hands of John D. Rockefeller, that probably ninety per cent of it goes to the few men who make up the "Standard Oil family," and that it must every year be invested, the Standard Oil Company becomes a much more serious public matter than it was in 1872, when it stamped itself as willing to enter into a conspiracy to raid the oil business—as a much more serious concern than in the years when it openly made warfare of business, and drove from the oil industry by any means it could invent all who had the hardihood to enter it. For, consider what must be done with the greater part of this $45,000,000. It must be invested. The oil business does not demand it. There is plenty of reserve for all of its ventures. It must go into other industries. Naturally, the interests sought will be allied to oil. They will be gas, and we have the Standard Oil crowd steadily acquiring the gas interests of the country. They will be railroads, for on transportation all industries depend, and, besides, railroads are one of the great consumers of oil products and must be kept in line as buyers. And we have the directors of the Standard Oil Company acting as directors on nearly all of the great railways of the country, the New York Central, New York, New Haven and Hartford, Chicago, Milwaukee and St. Paul, Union Pacific, Northern Pacific, Delaware, Lackawanna and Western, Missouri Pacific, Missouri, Kansas and Texas, Boston and Maine, and other lesser roads. They will go into copper, and we have the Amalgamated scheme. They will go into steel, and we have Mr. Rockefeller's enormous holdings in the Steel Trust. They will go into banking, and we have the National City Bank and its allied institutions in New York City and Boston, as well as a long chain running over the country. No one who has followed this history can expect these holdings will be acquired on a rising market. Buy cheap and sell high is a rule of business, and when you control enough money and enough banks you can always manage that a stock you want shall be temporarily cheap. No value is destroyed for you—only for the original owner. This has been one of Mr. Rockefeller's most successful manœuvres in doing business from the day he scared his twenty Cleveland competitors until they sold to him at half price. You can also sell high, if you have a reputation of a great financier, and control of money and banks. Amalgamated Copper is an excellent example. The names of certain Standard Oil officials would float the most worthless property on earth a few years ago. It might be a little difficult for them to do so to-day with Amalgamated so fresh in mind. Indeed, Amalgamated seems to-day to be the worst "break," as it certainly was one of the most outrageous performances of the Standard Oil crowd. But that will soon be forgotten! The result is that the Standard Oil Company is probably in the strongest financial position of any aggregation in the world. And every year its position grows stronger, for every year there is pouring in another $45,000,000 to be used in wiping up the property most essential to preserving and broadening its power. . . .

Altogether the most important question concerning the Standard Oil Company to-day is how far it is sustaining its power by the employment of the peculiar methods of the South Improvement Company. It should never be forgotten that Mr. Rockefeller never depended on these methods alone for securing power in the oil trade. From the beginning the Standard Oil Company has studied thoroughly everything connected with the oil business. It has known, not guessed at conditions. It has had a keen authoritative sight. It has applied itself to its tasks with indefatigable zeal. It has been as courageous as it has been cautious. Nothing has been too big to undertake, as nothing has been too small to neglect. These facts have been repeatedly pointed out in this narrative. But these are the American industrial qualities. . . .

These qualities alone would have made a great business, and unquestionably it would have been along the line of combination, for when Mr. Rockefeller undertook to work out the good of the oil business the tendency to combination was marked throughout the industry, but it would not have been the combination whose history we have traced. To the help of these qualities Mr. Rockefeller proposed to bring the peculiar aids of the South Improvement Company. He secured an alliance with the railroads to drive out rivals. For fifteen years he received rebates of varying amounts on at least the greater part of his shipments, and for at least a portion of that time he collected drawbacks of the oil other people shipped; at the same time he worked with the railroads to prevent other people getting oil to manufacture, or if they got it he worked with the railroads to prevent the shipment of the product. If it reached a dealer, he did his utmost to bully or wheedle him to countermand his order. If he failed in that, he undersold until the dealer, losing on his purchase, was glad enough to buy thereafter of Mr. Rockefeller. How much of this system remains in force to-day? The spying on independent shipments, the effort to have orders countermanded, the predatory competition prevailing, are well enough known. Contemporaneous documents, showing how these practices have been worked into a very perfect and practically universal system, have already been printed in this work.[See Chapter X] As for the rebates and drawbacks, if they do not exist in the forms practised up to 1887, as the Standard officials have repeatedly declared, it is not saying that the Standard enjoys no special transportation privileges. As has been pointed out, it controls the great pipeline handling all but perhaps ten per cent. of the oil produced in the Eastern fields. This system is fully 35,000 miles long. It goes to the wells of every producer, gathers his oil into its storage tanks, and from there transports it to Philadelphia, Baltimore, New York, Chicago, Buffalo, Cleveland, or any other refining point where it is needed. This pipe-line is a common carrier by virtue of its use of the right of eminent domain, and, as a common carrier, is theoretically obliged to carry and deliver the oil of all comers, but in practice this does not always work. It has happened more than once in the history of the Standard pipes that they have refused to gather or deliver oil. Pipes have been taken up from wells belonging to individuals running or working with independent refiners. Oil has been refused delivery at points practical for independent refiners. For many years the supply of oil has been so great that the Standard could not refuse oil to the independent refiner on the ground of scarcity. However, a shortage in Pennsylvania oil occurred in 1903. A very interesting situation arose as a result. There are in Ohio and Pennsylvania several independent refiners who, for a number of years, have depended on the Standard lines (the National Transit Company) for their supply of crude. In the fall of 1903 these refiners were informed that thereafter the Standard could furnish them with only fifty per cent. of their refining capacity. It was a serious matter to the independents, who had their own markets, and some of whom were increasing their plants. Supposing we buy oil directly from the producers, they asked one another, must not the Standard as a common carrier gather and deliver it? The experienced in the business said: "Yes. But what will happen? The producer rash enough to sell you oil may be cut off by the National Transit Company. Of course, if he wants to fight in the courts he may eventually force the Standard to reconnect, but they could delay the suit until he was ruined. Also, if you go over Mr. Seep's head"—Mr. Seep is the Standard Oil buyer, and all oil going into the National Transit system goes through his hands—"you will antagonise him." Now, "antagonise" in Standard circles may mean a variety of things. The independent refiners decided to compromise, and an agreement terminable by either party at short notice was made between them and the Standard, by which the members of the former were each to have eighty per cent. of their capacity of crude oil, and were to give to the Standard all of their export oil to market. As a matter of fact, the Standard's ability to cut off crude supplies from the outside refiners is much greater than in the days before the Interstate Commerce Bill, when it depended on its alliance with the railroads to prevent its rival getting oil. It goes without saying that this is an absurd power to allow in the hands of any manufacturer of a great necessity of life. It is exactly as if one corporation aiming at manufacturing all the flour of the country owned all but ten per cent. of the entire railroad system collecting and transporting wheat. They could, of course, in time of shortage, prevent any would-be competitor from getting grain to grind, and they could and would make it difficult and expensive at all times for him to get it.

It is not only in the power of the Standard to cut off outsiders from it, it is able to keep up transportation prices. Mr. Rockefeller owns the pipe system—a common carrier—and the refineries of the Standard Oil Company pay in the final accounting cost for transporting their oil, while outsiders pay just what they paid twenty-five years ago. There are lawyers who believe that if this condition were tested in the courts, the National Transit Company would be obliged to give the same rates to others as the Standard refineries ultimately pay. It would be interesting to see the attempt made. . . .

Very often people who admit the facts, who are willing to see that Mr. Rockefeller has employed force and fraud to secure his ends, justify him by declaring, "It's business." That is, "it's business" has to come to be a legitimate excuse for hard dealing, sly tricks, special privileges. It is a common enough thing to hear men arguing that the ordinary laws of morality do not apply in business. Now, if the Standard Oil Company were the only concern in the country guilty of the practices which have given it monopolistic power, this story never would have been written. Were it alone in these methods, public scorn would long ago have made short work of the Standard Oil Company. But it is simply the most conspicuous type of what can be done by these practices. The methods it employs with such acumen, persistency, and secrecy are employed by all sorts of business men, from corner grocers up to bankers. If exposed, they are excused on the ground that this is business. If the point is pushed, frequently the defender of the practice falls back on the Christian doctrine of charity, and points that we are erring mortals and must allow for each other's weaknesses!—an excuse which if carried to its legitimate conclusion, would leave our business men weeping on one another's shoulders over human frailty, while they picked one another's pockets.

One of the most depressing features of the ethical side of the matter is that instead of such methods arousing contempt they are more or less openly admired. And this is logical Canonise "business success," and men who make a success like that of the Standard Oil Trust become national heroes! The history of its organisation is studied as a practical lesson in money-making. It is the most startling feature of the case to one who would like to feel that it is possible to be a commercial people and yet a race of gentlemen. Of course such practices exclude men by all the codes from the rank of gentlemen, just as such practices would exclude men from the sporting world or athletic field. There is no gaming table in the world where loaded dice are tolerated, no athletic field where men must not start fair. Yet Mr. Rockefeller has systematically played with loaded dice, and it is doubtful if there has ever been a time since 1872 when he has run a race with a competitor and started fair. Business played in this way loses all its sportsmanlike qualities. It is fit only for tricksters. . . .

And what are we going to do about it? for it is *our* business. We, the people of the United States, and nobody else must cure whatever is wrong in the industrial situation, typified by this narrative of the growth of the Standard Oil Company. That our first task is to secure free and equal transportation privileges by rail, pipe and waterway is evident. It is not an easy matter. It is one which may require operations which will seem severe; but the whole system of discrimination has been nothing but violence, and those who have profited by it cannot complain if the curing of the evils they have wrought bring hardship in turn on them. At all events, until the transportation matter is settled, and settled right, the monopolistic trust will be with us, a leech on our pockets, a barrier to our free efforts.

As for the ethical side, there is no cure but in an increasing scorn of unfair play—an increasing sense that a thing won by breaking the rules of the game is not worth the winning. When the business man who fights to secure special privileges, to crowd his competitor off the track by other than fair competitive methods, receives the same summary disdainful ostracism by his fellows that the doctor or lawyer who is "unprofessional," the athlete who abuses the rules, receives, we shall have gone a long way toward making commerce a fit pursuit for our young men.

Further Resources

BOOKS

Nevins, Allan. *John D. Rockefeller: The Heroic Age of American Enterprise.* New York: Scribner's, 1940.

Segall, Grant. *John D. Rockefeller: Anointed With Oil.* New York: Oxford University Press, 2001.

Tarbell, Ida M. *All in the Day's Work: An Autobiography.* Washington, D.C.: Zenger, 1939.

Manifesto of the Industrial Workers of the World

Declaration

By: Industrial Workers of the World

Date: January 1905

Source: Manifesto of the International Workers of the World. Adopted January 1905. Reprinted in Haywood, William D. *Bill Haywood's Book: The Autobiography of William D. Haywood.* New York: International Publishers, 1929, 175–179.

About the Organization: The Industrial Workers of the World, a radical labor organization, was organized in Chicago in January 1905. Prominent among the organizing members were William D. Haywood of the Western Federation of Miners, Daniel De Leon of the Socialist Labor Party, Eugene V. Debs of the Socialist Party, and fiery labor agitator, Mother Jones. ■

Introduction

The economic order that emerged in the post–Civil War era was dominated by ever larger business concerns. The industrial laborer who provided the muscle that drove these enterprises had become part of a permanent underclass. Increasingly labor saw its future not in rising up the economic and social scale through individual achievement, but rather in improving its condition through collective action.

Within the labor movement, two primary schools of thought had evolved by 1900. The first, best represented by Samuel Gompers and the craft unions that made up the American Federation of Labor (AFL), essentially sought an accommodation with capitalism. Its proponents attempted to improve the lot of workers through collective bargaining, but were content with the basic premises of capitalism. The other school of thought was more radical. Its proponents believed that capitalism needed to be abolished. According to this view capitalism could not be reformed; the inherent incompatibility between capitalism and the interests of workers precluded long-term accommodation. There were many variations on this theme. Some were content to work toward a socialist state within the existing system. Others—anarchists, for example—were prepared to use violence to destroy all government. Perhaps the most successful of the radical labor organizations was the Industrial Workers of the World (IWW).

Significance

Formed in 1905, the IWW, or Wobblies, thought of themselves as the economic arm of the Socialist Party's efforts to reform society through the ballot. Within a few years, however, more radical elements led by burly William D. Haywood had driven out the more politically oriented members, such as Eugene Debs. Thereafter, IWW relied on direct action by workers to press its goals. The IWW was not a timid group, and its history is marked by frequent violent confrontations with mill owners, their hired private police, local police, and even state militia.

The founders of the IWW hoped to create a single great union of all workers for the purpose of destroying capitalism and establishing a socialist society. While the AFL favored craft unions of skilled workers, the IWW attempted to organize unskilled and often foreign-born workers through strikes, boycotts, and unvarnished propaganda. Especially strong in the West among miners, lumbermen, dockworkers, and migrant farmworkers, the Wobblies also gained a considerable following in the textile mills of New England. They led a number of well-known labor actions, including a miner's strike in Goldfield, Nevada; textile strikes in Lowell, Massachusetts, and Patterson, New Jersey; and a general strike in Seattle in 1919.

While the membership in the IWW was never large, its willingness to support workers in every labor struggle possible made the organization particularly appealing to struggling workers. This radicalism attracted the special wrath of business and government leaders. The IWW's opposition to the First World War (1914–1918)

A group of workers outside their New England factory in 1905. The International Workers of the World union gained a considerable following in the textile mills of New England. **HULTON ARCHIVE. REPRODUCED BY PERMISSION.**

pushed it to the fringes of the labor movement. The IWW was also a target of the postwar–Red Scare—the fear of communists—in which radical ideas lost much of their popularity, even among workers. As a result, by the early 1920s it had lost most of its influence and had become a marginal organization.

Primary Source

Manifesto of the Industrial Workers of the World [excerpt]

SYNOPSIS: *Bill Haywood's Book* is the 1929 autobiography of radical labor leader William D. Haywood. In this excerpt, he reproduces the manifesto that brought the Industrial Workers of the World into existence in 1905.

Industrial Workers of the World

Social relations and groupings only reflect mechanical and industrial conditions. The great facts of present industry are the displacement of human skill by machines and the increase of capitalist power through concentration in the possession of the tools with which wealth is produced and distributed.

Because of these facts trade divisions among laborers and competition among capitalists are alike disappearing. Class divisions grow ever more fixed and class antagonisms more sharp. Trade lines have been swallowed up in a common servitude of all workers to the machines which they tend. New machines, ever replacing less productive ones, wipe out whole trades and plunge new bodies of workers into the ever-growing army of tradeless, hopeless unemployed. As human beings and human skill are displaced by mechanical progress, the capitalists need use the workers only during the brief period when muscles and nerves respond most intensely. The moment the laborer no longer yields the maximum of profits, he is thrown upon the scrap-pile, to starve alongside the discarded machine. A dead-line has been drawn, and an age-limit established, to cross which, in this world of monopolized opportunities, means condemnation to industrial death.

The worker, wholly separated from the land and the tools, with his skill of craftsmanship rendered useless, is sunk in the uniform mass of wage slaves. He sees his power of resistance broken by craft divisions, perpetuated from outgrown industrial stages. His wages constantly grow less as his hours grow longer and monopolized prices grow higher. Shifted hither and thither by the demands of profit-takers the laborer's home no longer exists. In this helpless condition he is forced to accept whatever humiliating conditions his master may impose. He is submitted to a physical and intellectual examination more searching than was the chattel slave when sold from the auction block. Laborers are no longer classified by differences in trade skill, but the employer assigns them according to the machines to which they are attached. These divisions, far from representing differences in skill or interests among the laborers, are imposed by the employers that workers may be pitted against one another and spurred to greater exertion in the shop, and that all resistance to capitalist tyranny may be weakened by artificial distinctions.

While encouraging these outgrown divisions among the workers the capitalists carefully adjust themselves to the new conditions. They wipe out all differences among themselves and present a united front in their war upon labor. Through employers' associations they seek to crush with brutal force, by the injunctions of the judiciary and the use of military power, all efforts at resistance. Or when the other policy seems more profitable, they conceal their daggers beneath the Civic Federation and hoodwink and betray those whom they would rule and exploit. Both methods depend for success upon the blindness and internal dissensions of the working class. The employers' line of battle and methods of warfare correspond to the solidarity of the mechanical and industrial concentration, while laborers still form their fighting organizations on lines of long-gone trade divisions. The battles of the past emphasize this lesson. The textile workers of Lowell, Philadelphia, and Fall River; the butchers of Chicago, weakened by the disintegrating effects of trade divisions; the machinists of the Santa Fe, unsupported by their fellow-workers subject to the same masters; the long struggling miners of Colorado, hampered by lack of unity and solidarity upon the industrial battle-field, all bear witness to the helplessness and impotency of labor as at present organized.

This worn out and corrupt system offers no promise of improvement and adaptation. There is no silver lining to the clouds of darkness and despair settling down upon the world of labor.

This system offers only a perpetual struggle for slight relief within wage slavery. It is blind to the possibility of establishing an industrial democracy, wherein there shall be no wage slavery, but where the workers will own the tools which they operate, and the product of which they alone will enjoy.

It shatters the ranks of the workers into fragments, rendering them helpless and impotent on the industrial battle-field.

Separation of craft from craft renders industrial and financial solidarity impossible.

Union men scab upon union men; hatred of worker for worker is engendered, and the workers are delivered helpless and disintegrated into the hands of the capitalists.

Craft jealousy leads to the attempt to create trade monopolies.

Prohibitive initiation fees are established that force men to become scabs against their will. Men whom manliness or circumstances have driven from one trade are thereby fined when they seek to transfer membership to the union of the new craft.

Craft divisions foster political ignorance among the workers, thus dividing their class at the ballot box as well as in the shop, mine and factory.

Craft unions may be and have been used to assist employers in the establishment of monopolies and the raising of prices. One set of workers is thus used to make harder the conditions of life of another body of workers.

Craft divisions hinder the growth of class consciousness of the workers, foster the idea of harmony of interests between employing exploiter and employed slave. They permit the association of the misleaders of the workers with the capitalists in the Civic Federation, where plans are made for the perpetuation of capitalism and the permanent enslavement of the workers through the wage system.

Previous efforts for the betterment of the working class have proven abortive because limited in scope and disconnected in action.

Universal economic evils afflicting the working class can be eradicated only by a universal working-class movement. Such a movement of the working class is impossible while separate craft and wage agreements are made favoring the employer against other crafts in the same industry, and while energies are wasted in fruitless jurisdiction struggles which serve only to further the personal aggrandizement of union officials.

A movement to fulfill these conditions must consist of one great industrial union embracing all industries,—providing for craft autonomy locally, industrial autonomy internationally, and working-class unity generally.

It must be founded on the class struggle, and its general administration must be conducted in harmony with the recognition of the irrepressible conflict between the capitalist class and the working class.

It should be established as the economic organization of the working class, without affiliation to any political party.

All power should rest in a collective membership.

Local, national and general administration, including union labels, buttons, badges, transfer cards, initiation fees, and per capita tax, should be uniform throughout.

All members must hold membership in the local, national or international union covering the industry in which they are employed, but transfers of membership between unions should be universal.

Workingmen bringing union cards from industrial unions in foreign countries should be freely admitted into the organization.

The general administration should issue a publication representing the entire union and its principles which should reach all members in every industry at regular intervals.

A central defense fund, to which all members contribute equally, should be established and maintained.

All workers, therefore, who agree with the principles herein set forth, will meet in convention at Chicago the 27th day of June, 1905, for the purpose of forming an economic organization of the working class along the lines marked out in this Manifesto.

Representation to the convention should be based upon the number of workers the delegate represents. No delegate, however, shall be given representation in the convention on the numerical basis of an organization unless he has credentials—bearing the seal of his union, local, national or international, and the signatures of the officers thereof,—authorizing him to install his union as a working part of the proposed economic organization in the industrial department in which it logically belongs in the general plan of the organization. Lacking this authority the delegate shall represent himself as an individual.

Adopted at Chicago, January 2, 3, and 4, 1905

. . . .

A. G. Swing
A. M. Simons
W. Shurtleff
Frank McCabe
John M. O'Neill
Geo. Estes
Wm. D. Haywood
Mother Jones
Ernest Untermann
W. L. Hall
Chas. H. Moyer
Clarence Smith
Wm. E. Trautmann
Jos. Schmidt
John Guild
Daniel McDonald
Eugene V. Debs
Thos. J. DeYoung
Thos. J. Hagerty
Fred D. Henion
W. J. Bradley
Chas. O. Sherman
M. E. White
Wm. J. Pinkerton
Frank Krafft
J. E. Fitzgerald
Frank Bohn

[Requirements for an Industrial Organization of the Workers:]

A labor organization to correctly represent the working class must have two things in view.

First—It must combine the wage workers in such a way that it can most successfully fight the battles and protect the interests of the working people of to-day in their struggle for fewer hours, more wages and better conditions.

Secondly—It must offer a final solution of the labor problem—an emancipation from strikes, injunctions and bull-pens.

Study the chart and observe how this organization will give recognition to trade and craft divisions, yet provide perfect Industrial Unionism and converge the strength of all organized workers to a common center, from which any weak point can be strengthened and protected.

Observe, also, how the growth and development of this organization will build up within itself the structure of an Industrial Democracy—a Workers' Cooperative Republic—which must finally burst the shell of capitalist government, and be the agency by which the working people will operate the industries and appropriate the products to themselves.

One obligation for all.

A union man once and in one industry, a union man always and in all industries.

Universal transfers.

Universal label.

An open union and a closed shop.

Further Resources

BOOKS

Archer, Jules. *Strikes, Bombs and Bullets: Big Bill Haywood and the IWW.* New York: J. Messner, 1972.

Foner, Philip S. *History of the Labor Movement in the United States: Vol. 4. The Industrial Workers of The World, 1905–1917.* New York: International Publishers, 1987.

WEBSITES

Flemming, Marcy, and Josh Thomason. "A Brief History of the IWW." Available online at http://www.ou.edu/student/ucurrent/archives/volVno2/articles/HistoryIWW.html; website home page http://www.ou.edu (accessed December 24, 2002).

Flynn, Elizabeth Gurley. "Memories of the Industrial Workers of the World (IWW)." Available online at http://www.geocities.com/CapitolHill/5202/rebelgirl.html; website home page http://www.geocities.com (accessed December 24, 2002).

Conditions in Chicago Stock Yards: Message from the President of the United States

Message

By: James Bronson Reynolds and Charles P. Neill

Date: June 4, 1906

Source: Reynolds, James Bronson, and Charles P. Neill. *Conditions in Chicago Stock Yards: Message from the President of the United States,* 59th Congress, 1st sess., June 4, 1906, document no. 873, 3–8.

About the Author: Charles Patrick Neill (1865–1942) received a Ph.D. in economics from Johns Hopkins University. He taught at the Catholic University of America before being appointed by President Theodore Roosevelt (served 1901–1909) to serve as assistant recorder at federal hearings into the anthracite coal strike in 1902. He was appointed Commissioner of Labor in 1905, but he resigned in 1913 to pursue a career in business. He served as a referee in labor-management disputes in the coal and railroad industries throughout his professional career. James B. Reynolds (1861–1924) was a social worker who played an active role in a wide range of reform activities. A graduate of Yale University (1884), Reynolds became head of the Columbia University Settlement in New York's Lower East Side in 1894. In addition to serving with Charles Neill in the investigation of the meatpacking industry, he also served on commissions concerned with immigration, working conditions on the construction of the Panama Canal, and municipal affairs in Washington, D.C. ■

Introduction

The last quarter of the nineteenth century witnessed a dramatic change in the way Americans provided themselves with food. The development of refrigeration and chemical preservatives, combined with an extensive railroad network, created a nationwide system for the preparation and distribution of food. This was essential for the growth of great cities, but it also dramatically altered the eating habits of small-town and rural America. As packaged foods and the mechanization of the dairy and meatpacking industries replaced home production and the local supplier, Americans became increasingly removed from the original source of food and increasingly dependent on larger and larger enterprises for their daily nourishment. Mark Sullivan described the difference between the local butcher and the meat trust in this way: "He [the local butcher] looked across the counter into the eyes of customers who knew him, who had known his father before him, whose children went to school with his children. He had to hold his head up in his own community." (*Our Times, The United States, 1900–1925,* Vol. 2, *America Finding Herself.* New York: Scribner's, 1927.)

The American consumer was at the mercy of food corporations. But the temptation for those who did not look "across the counter into the eyes of customers" often proved too great, and corporations profited by producing and selling many products that were blatantly harmful. As the nineteenth century ended, states had already begun to pass legislation to address some of the problems related to adulterated food, drink, and patent medicines. Several notable articles critical of the meatpacking industry appeared in magazines. These reinforced the disgust much of the country felt when the poor quality of canned meat distributed to soldiers during the Spanish-American War came to light.

In response, federal pure food and drug legislation was introduced to Congress in 1902. While it passed the House on several occasions, the Senate, influenced by the food, drug, and liquor lobbies as well as states-rights proponents, tied up the proposed legislation for several years. The logjam was finally broken by the publication of *The Jungle,* Upton Sinclair's emotional account of an immigrant family's struggle to survive in a thinly disguised Chicago at the turn of the century. Sinclair intended to write a novel about the horrors of capitalism, but instead disgusted the public with graphic descriptions of conditions inside the meatpacking plants.

Significance

Despite the popular storm raised by *The Jungle,* the Senate still refused to act. It was not until President Theodore Roosevelt (who had read the novel) entered the fray that Congress moved forward. Appalled by what he had read, Roosevelt ordered an independent examination of the Chicago meatpacking plants, selecting James Bronson Reynolds and Charles P. Neill to perform the study. The Reynolds-Neill report confirmed the accuracy of *The Jungle.* Presented with this evidence, Roosevelt was determined to push the proposed legislation through Congress. Conservative elements in the Senate, however, continued to hold out. Reluctantly, Roosevelt released the first part of the Reynolds-Neill report. He also threatened to publish the second and more damning part unless the Congress passed the pending Pure Food and Drug Act, as well as a stronger Meat Inspection Act. After weeks of wrangling, both bills were passed.

Primary Source

Conditions in Chicago Stock Yards: Message from the President of the United States [excerpt]

SYNOPSIS: Reynolds and Neill spent two-and-a-half weeks in Chicago observing conditions in the meat-packing plants. In this portion of the report, they were concerned primarily with cleanliness and the physical condition of the plants. The section describing the use of chemicals in meat processing was withheld. Roosevelt shrewdly determined that he could accomplish his ends—the passage of the Pure Food and Drug Act and a strengthened Meat Inspection Act—by threatening to release it if the reluctant senators did not support the new legislation.

The President:

As directed by you, we investigated the conditions in the principal establishments in Chicago engaged in the slaughter of cattle, sheep, and hogs and in the preparation of dressed meat and meat food products. Two and a half weeks were spent in the investigation in Chicago, and during this time we went through the principal packing houses in the stock-yards district, together with a few of the smaller ones. A day was spent by Mr. Reynolds in New York City in the investigation of several of its leading slaughterhouses. . . .

I. Condition of the Yards

Before entering the buildings we noted the condition of the yards themselves as shown in the pavement, pens, viaducts, and platforms. The pavement is mostly of brick, the bricks laid with deep grooves between them, which inevitably fill with manure and refuse. Such pavement can not be properly cleaned and is slimy and malodorous when wet, yielding clouds of ill-smelling dust when dry. The pens are generally uncovered except those for sheep; these latter are paved and covered. The viaducts and platforms are of wood. Calves, sheep, and hogs that have died en route are thrown out upon the platforms where cars are unloaded. On a single platform on one occasion we counted 15 dead hogs, on the next 10 dead hogs. The only excuse given for delay in removal was that so often heard—the expense.

II. Buildings

Sanitary Conveniences

Nothing shows more strikingly the general indifference to matters of cleanliness and sanitation than do the privies for both men and women. The prevailing type is made by cutting off a section of the workroom by a thin wooden partition rising to within a few feet of the ceiling. These privies usually ventilate into the workroom, though a few are found with a window opening into the outer air. Many are located in the inside corners of the work rooms, and thus have no outside opening whatever. They are furnished with a row of seats, generally without even side partitions. These rooms are sometimes used as cloakrooms by the employees. Lunch rooms constructed in the same manner, by boarding off a section of the workroom, often adjoin the privies, the odors of which add to the generally insanitary state of the atmosphere.

Abominable as the above-named conditions are, the one that affects most directly and seriously the cleanliness of the food products is the frequent absence of any lavatory provisions in the privies. Washing sinks are either not furnished at all or are small and dirty. Neither are towels, soap, or toilet paper provided. Men and women return directly from these places to plunge their unwashed hands into the meat to be converted into such food products as sausages, dried beef, and other compounds. Some of the privies are situated at a long distance from the workrooms, and men relieve themselves on the killing floors or in a corner of the workrooms. Hence, in some cases the fumes of the urine swell the sum of nauseating odors arising from the dirty-blood-soaked, rotting wooden floors, fruitful culture beds for the disease germs of men and animals.

New Buildings

It is stated that many of the unsanitary conditions are due to the fact that these buildings are old and have been built by piecemeal, and that in the newer buildings, being erected from time to time, the defects of the earlier structures are being remedied. This contention is not borne out by the facts. One of the large plants erected within recent years has most of the defects of the older buildings. It is true that three large model buildings have been erected, but one is an office building, while the other two contain only cooling, storage, and sales rooms. No model building for the preparation of food products has been built in the stock yards of Chicago. . . .

Men work with sheep carcasses at the Armour company's meat packing plant in the Union Stock Yards in Chicago. THE LIBRARY OF CONGRESS.

IV.—Treatment of Meats and Prepared Food Products

Uncleanliness in Handling Products

An absence of cleanliness was also found everywhere in the handling of meat being prepared for the various meat-food products. After killing, carcasses are well washed, and up to the time they reach the cooling room are handled in a fairly sanitary and cleanly manner. The parts that leave the cooling room for treatment in bulk are also handled with regard to cleanliness, but the parts that are sent from the cooling room to those departments of the packing houses in which various forms of meat products are prepared are handled with no regard whatever for cleanliness. In some of the largest establishments sides that are sent to what is known as the boning room are thrown in a heap upon the floor. The workers climb over these heaps of meat, select the pieces they wish, and frequently throw them down upon the dirty floor beside their working bench. Even in cutting the meat upon the bench, the work is usually held pressed against their aprons, and these aprons were, as a rule, indescribably filthy. They were made in most cases of leather or of rough sacking and bore long accumulated grease and dirt. In only a few places were suitable oilcloth aprons worn. Moreover, men were seen to climb from the floor and stand, with shoes dirty with the refuse of the floors, on the tables upon which the meat was handled. They were seen at the lunch hour sitting on the tables on the spot on which the meat product was handled, and all this under the very eye of the superintendent of the room, showing that this was the common practice.

Meat scraps were also found being shoveled into receptacles from dirty floors where they were left to lie until again shoveled into barrels or into machines for chopping. These floors, it must be noted, were in most cases damp and soggy, in dark, ill-ventilated rooms, and the employees in utter ignorance of cleanliness or danger to health expectorated at will upon them. In a word, we saw meat shoveled from filthy wooden floors, piled on tables rarely washed, pushed from room to room in rotten box carts, in all of which processes it was in the way of gathering dirt, splinters, floor filth, and the expectoration of tuberculous and other diseased workers. Where comment was made to floor superintendents about these matters, it was always the reply that this meat would afterwards be cooked, and that this sterilization would prevent any danger from its use. Even this, it may be pointed out in passing, is not wholly true. A very considerable portion of the meat so handled is sent out as smoked products and in the form of sausages, which are prepared to be eaten without being cooked.

A particularly glaring instance of uncleanliness was found in a room where the best grade of sausage was being prepared for export. It was made from carefully selected meats, and was being prepared to be eaten uncooked. In this case the employee carted the chopped-up meat across a room in a barrow, the handles of which were filthy with grease. The meat was then thrown out upon tables, and the employee climbed upon the table, handled the meat with his unwashed hands, knelt with his dirty apron and trousers in contact with the meat he was spreading out, and, after he had finished his operation, again took hold of the dirty handles of the wheelbarrow, went back for another load, and repeated this process indefinitely. Inquiry developed the fact that there was no water in this room at all, and the only method the man adopted for cleaning his hands was to rub them against his dirty apron or on his still filthier trousers.

As an extreme example of the entire disregard on the part of employees of any notion of cleanliness in handling dressed meat, we saw a hog that had just been killed, cleaned, washed, and started on its way to the cooling room fall from the sliding rail to a dirty wooden floor and slide part way into a filthy men's privy. It was picked up by two employees, placed upon a truck, carried into the cooling room and hung up with other carcasses, no effort being made to clean it.

Treatment of Meat After Inspection

The radical defect in the present system of inspection is that it does not go far enough. It is confined at present by law to passing on the healthfulness of animals at the time of killing; but the meat that is used in sausage and in the various forms of canned products and other prepared meat foods goes through many processes, in all of which there is possibility of contamination through insanitary handling, and further danger through the use of chemicals. During all these processes of preparation there is no Government inspection and no assurance whatever that these meat-food products are wholesome and fit for food—despite the fact that all these products, when sent out, bear a label stating they have been passed upon by Government inspectors.

As to the investigation of the alleged use of dyes, preservatives, or chemicals in the preparation of cured meats, sausages, and canned goods we are not yet prepared to report. We did look into the matter of sanitary handling of the meats being prepared for the various food products. The results of our observations have already been partly given. Other instances of how products may be made up, and still secure the stamp of Government inspection are here given. In one well-known establishment we came upon fresh meat being shoveled into barrels, and a regular proportion being added of stale scraps that had lain on a dirty floor in the corner of a room for some days previous. In another establishment, equally well known, a long table was noted covered with several hundred pounds of cooked scraps of beef and other meats. Some of these meat scraps were dry, leathery, and unfit to be eaten; and in the heap were found pieces of pigskin, and even some bits of rope strands and other rubbish. Inquiry evoked the frank admission from the man in charge that this was to be ground up and used in making "potted ham."

All of these canned products bear labels of which the following is a sample:

ABATTOIR NO.–.

The contents of this package have been inspected according to the act of Congress of March 3, 1891.

QUALITY GUARANTEED.

The phraseology of these labels is wholly unwarranted. The Government inspectors pass only upon the healthfulness of the animal at the time of killing. They know nothing of the processes through which the meat has passed since this inspection. They do not know what else may have been placed in the cans in addition to "inspected meat." As a matter of fact, they know nothing about the "contents" of the can upon which the packers place these labels—do not even know that it contains what it purports to contain. The legend "Quality guaranteed" immediately following the statement as to Government inspection is wholly unjustifiable. It deceives and is plainly designed to deceive the average purchaser, who naturally infers from the label that the Government guarantees the contents of the can to be what it purports to be.

In another establishment piles of sausages and dry moldy canned meats, admittedly several years old, were found, which the superintendent stated to us would be tanked and converted into grease. The disposition to be made of this was wholly optional with the superintendents or representatives of the packers, as the Government does not concern itself with the disposition of meats after they have passed inspection on the killing floor. It might all be treated with chemicals, mixed with other meats, turned out in any form of meat product desired, and yet the packages or receptacles in which it was to be shipped out to the public would be marked with a label that their contents had been "Government inspected." It is not alleged here that such use was to be made of this stuff. The case is pointed out as one showing the glaring opportunity for the misuse of a label bearing the name and the implied guaranty of the United States Government.

Another instance of abuse in the use of the labels came to our notice. In two different establishments great stocks of old canned goods were being put through a washing process to remove the old labels. They were then subjected to sufficient heat to "liven up" the contents—to use the phrase of the room superintendent. After this, fresh labels, with the Government name on them, were to be placed upon the cans, and they were to be sent out bearing all the evidence of being a freshly put up product. In one of these instances, by the admission of the superintendent, the stock thus being relabeled was over two years old. In the other case the superintendent evaded a statement of how old the goods were.

Further Resources

BOOKS

Burrow, James G. *Organized Medicine in the Progressive Era.* Baltimore, Md.: Johns Hopkins University Press, 1977.

Weinberg, Arthur, and Lila Weinberg, eds. *The Muckrakers: The Era in Journalism That Moved America to Reform: The Most Significant Magazine Articles of 1902–1912.* New York: Simon and Schuster, 1961.

WEBSITES

"Pure Food and Drug Act of 1906." Available online at http://www.hs1.hst.msu.edu/~hst203/documents/pure.html; website home page http://www.hs1.hst.msu.edu (accessed December 26, 2002).

Harcourt College Publishing. "Tainted Foods and Fake Drugs." Available online at http://www.azimuth.harcourtcollege.com/history/ayers/chapter20/20.3.module.html; website home page http://www.azimuth.harcourtcollege.com (accessed December 26, 2002). This site contains links to information about the food industry in the early twentieth century.

Court Injunctions and Labor Unions

The Abuses of Organized Labor and Their Remedy

Speech

By: Frederick R. Boocock

Date: October 17, 1906

Source: Boocock, Frederick R. *The Abuses of Organized Labor and Their Remedy: Address Delivered before the National Association of Hardware Manufacturers, October 17, 1906.* Pamphlets in American History: Labor 114.

About the Author: Frederick R. Boocock was secretary of the American Anti-Boycott Association. Established in 1902, the association was a leader in the effort to destroy labor unions, particularly through court-ordered injunctions supported by restraint-of-trade provisions of the Sherman Anti-Trust Act.

"Free Press and Free Speech Invaded by Injunction Against the A.F. of L.: A Review and Protest"

Journal article

By: Samuel Gompers

Date: February 1908

Source: Gompers, Samuel. "Free Press and Free Speech Invaded by Injunction Against the A.F. of L.: A Review and Protest." *American Federationist.* Washington, D.C.: American Federation of Labor, 1908, 1–5.

About the Author: Samuel Gompers (1850–1924), a leading figure in the American labor movement for over forty years, helped found the American Federation of Labor in 1886, and was president of the organization until his death (except for 1895). Generally a conservative, Gompers avoided involvement with radical reform movements and shunned partisan politics, preferring direct economic action by unions in the form of strikes, boycotts, and picketing. ■

Introduction

The 1890s were a period of great labor unrest and conflict. In the first years of the new century, unions grew dramatically. From fewer than one million in 1900, union membership grew to two and a half million by 1904. Soon, though, a number of business organizations emerged with the primary purpose of destroying unions, including the Employers' Association (formed in 1901), the Citizens' Alliance (1901), the National Association of Manufacturers (1895), and the American Anti-Boycott Association (1902). With local branches all over the country, these organizations were well supported by Wall Street and leading business concerns. Their stated objective was to guarantee to workers an "open shop," that is, to prevent them from being compelled to join a union, but their real goal was to weaken unions.

The philosophical justification for union busting was the inalienable right of individual workers to sell their labor where they wished, for whatever wages they could negotiate. Compelling workers to join a union (a "closed shop"), they argued, was regarded as both un-American and a restraint of trade. In reality, business leaders, often with financial backing from antilabor organizations, used spies, bribery, physical violence, strike breakers, yellow dog contracts, and blacklists to defeat unions.

The most effective weapon against unions, however, was the court-ordered injunction. Anti-union forces successfully argued in court that the Sherman Anti-Trust Act, which prohibited restraint of trade, applied to labor unions. This interpretation made boycotts, strikes, and picketing illegal. The effect of this assault on unions was a steady deterioration of union strength. By 1910, the labor movement was reeling from a series of unfavorable judicial decisions, especially court rulings against unions in strikes against the Bucks Stove and Range Company in St. Louis and D. E. Loewe and Company in Danbury, Connecticut (the *Danbury Hatters'* case.)

Significance

One common AFL tactic was to boycott the target company's products. The AFL, for example, published a "We Don't Patronize" list, but in *Bucks Stove* the court outlawed such lists. Gompers and other AFL leaders spoke out against the ruling and in support of the boycott against the company. As a result, they were convicted of contempt by Judge Ashley M. Gould and sentenced to up to one year in jail, though the case was eventually dismissed. Then in the midst of the *Bucks Stove* case, the U.S. Supreme Court handed down a devastating decision in *Danbury Hatters* in February 1908, holding that unions were trusts, and, therefore, fell under the restraint-of-trade provisions of the Sherman Anti-Trust Act. The ruling said that labor union strikes, boycotts, and pickets were illegal conspiracies in restraint of trade.

Until this time, Gompers had kept the AFL out of partisan politics, but the increasing use of injunctions following *Danbury Hatters* and *Bucks Stove* gave the AFL little choice but to enter politics to seek legislation reversing the hostile interpretation of the Sherman Anti-Trust Act. The AFL's first great political battle came during the 1908 presidential election. Republican candidate William Howard Taft had a reputation as being anti-labor. Democratic candidate William Jennings Bryan recognized Taft's vulnerability and used the opportunity to bring labor into the party's camp by supporting revisions to the Sherman Anti-Trust Act stating that unions "should not be regarded as illegal combinations in restraint of trade." Gompers supported Bryan and the Democrats.

The results were disheartening for labor, for Taft (served 1909–1913) won easily. In 1912, though, the labor cause received a boost when Democratic nominee Woodrow Wilson (served 1913–21), campaigning on a progressive, prolabor platform, was elected and lived up to his campaign promises: The 1914 Clayton Act specifically excluded labor unions from the antitrust provisions of the Sherman Act, and limited the use of court injunctions in labor conflicts. While Gompers and the AFL rejoiced at this apparent victory, conservative court rulings undercut the anticipated gains. It was not until Depression-era legislation was passed in the 1930s that labor's rights to organize were finally secured.

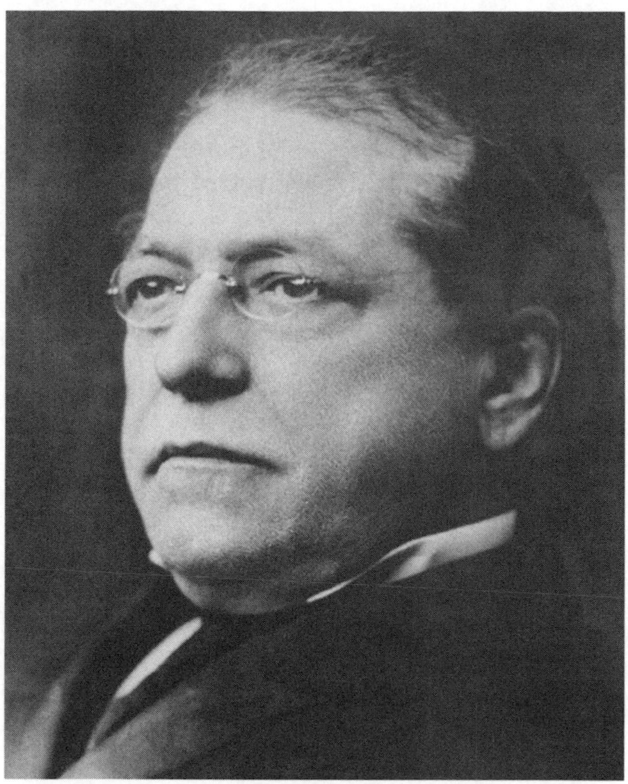

Samuel Gompers, founder and leader of the American Federation of Labor, supported direct action by unions in the form of strikes, boycotts, and picketing. **THE LIBRARY OF CONGRESS.**

Primary Source

The Abuses of Organized Labor and Their Remedy [excerpt]

SYNOPSIS: The following address was given by Secretary Boocock to the National Association of Hardware Manufacturers. To a sympathetic audience, he explained that the Anti-Boycott Association policy was to support companies fighting unions. Their most important tactic was to obtain court injunctions enforcing existing laws, particularly the Sherman Anti-Trust Act, in effect making collective bargaining impossible.

Corporation abuse is the howling clap trap of every demagogue who would utilize popular prejudice as the stepping stone to the attainment of his own ambitions. An audience composed of men, each of whom carried in his pocket a union card, would wildly applaud sentiments denouncing the misuse of corporate power, and would immediately after assemble in trade union councils and vote to boycott a given concern because it has refused to unionize its factory. I presume it is the inconsistency of human nature that accounts for these vagaries of thought.

Labor unions have a worthy purpose fundamentally. They premise their function upon the social, fraternal and intellectual needs of the laborer. Surely a most exalted intention, in the development of which there should be great promise for the individual. . . .

It never was originally intended that the union should develop into an organization employing coercion, intimidation, conspiracy, picketing, violence, and the boycott in the achievement of its desires. It was not originally intended to resort to unmanly and un-American practices in the accomplishment of selfish demands. These are the eruptions of a polluted system. They are the excesses of misdirected power. They have been instigated and propagated by those officials whose tenure of office and degree of usefulness depends upon their seeming shrewdness and brilliancy. They have been ratified and sustained by that unthinking and irresponsible class of union membership, which seems for the time to be in control, and whose scale of wages and actual employment often depends more upon the union than upon inherent qualities of workmanship. Let us not confuse the issue for the employers of the country are not opposed to unions, but are simply opposed to their abuses. . . .

The only remedy for the correction of the abuses of organized labor, is exactly the same remedy that is being sought and applied in correcting the excesses of organized capital. That is, law. The government may be intrusted to apply the remedy in the one case. The employers of labor must insure its application in the other. There can be little doubt but what this is the proper method of dealing with these abuses. The only question is as to the best plan of insuring its application. . . .

Such an institution is the American Anti-Boycott Association. It has been living, growing, working and winning for some three years and over. It exists for the purpose of defining, enforcing and preserving law as it relates to the problem of capital and labor. . . .

The judicial opinions of to-day become the accepted rules of practice to-morrow. What a power it would be, if this organization was so financially strong, that any attempt upon the part of a labor union anywhere to enforce its desires by methods which have been held, or are believed to be contrary to law, would be promptly contested through our instrumentality. Such an overwhelming volume of judicial opinion should be created that there can be no possible misunderstanding of the intent or scope of the law. As this is more and more accomplished it will serve to increasingly diminish the practice of coercion, conspiracy, picketing, violence and the boycott, and may possibly lead to the reorganization of trade unionism on a basis that will emphasize the individual rather than the mass.

This will not be consumated, however, until every effort has been exhausted on the part of organized labor to secure the passage of new laws that will permit those very practices which the courts now forbid. Interpretation and enforcement of law are basic activities of our association, but so also is preservation of law and the future is going to acquire the finest exhibition of diplomacy logic and energy in the achievement of this result. Under no circumstances would I wish to be an alarmist, but I say to you with all emphasis that the situation requires deliberate thought and united action. There is no need of my dwelling upon the character of laws which organized labor wants. They are revolutionary in substance and dangerous in detail. Organized labor will stop at nothing in an effort to have these laws passed. The leaders are playing upon the prejudices and passions of workmen in an effort to arouse them to vote as a unit against any candidate for a legislative position who is unwilling to bind himself to labor's chariot. . . .

And if organized labor finally obtains anti-injunction, conspiracy, eight hour and picketing laws, they will only be suggestive of still broader concessions that will later be demanded. Organized labor has never been satisfied with any concession for long. Neither will it be in the question of law. Not only will the demands be made of Congress, but there is evidence to show a concerted determination to move upon State legislatures. The American Anti-Boycott Association proposes to fight these efforts to the very last hour, and if our resistance proves futile, we shall simply thank God we have a United States Supreme Court and proceed to invoke such relief. . . .

For every onward movement that enriches labor and contributes to the comfort and happiness of the American workman let us be grateful. The prosperity of the one must be the prosperity of all. Let us make certain, however, that such developments shall be the result of peaceable practices, and shall be insured as the conditions of trade and the untrammeled judgment of employers will permit. But to organized efforts to coerce by conspiracy picketing, violence, and the boycott into the granting of concessions which neither reason or industrial conditions justify, let the American manufacturer stand as a unit in defence of oppression and in defence of liberty and right.

Primary Source

"Free Press and Free Speech Invaded by Injunction Against the A.F. of L.: A Review and Protest"

SYNOPSIS: The Gompers article appeared in *American Federationist,* the official organ of the AFL. Gompers presented labor's case against Judge Gould's order for the union to refrain from speaking out in favor of the boycott against Bucks Stove Company.

Justice Gould, of the Supreme Court of the District of Columbia, issued an injunction, on December 18, 1907, against the American Federation of Labor and its officers, and all persons within the jurisdiction of the court.

This injunction enjoins them as officials, or as individuals, from any reference whatsoever to the

Buck's Stove and Range Co.'s relations to organized labor, to the fact that the said company is regarded as unfair; that it is on an "unfair" list, or on the "We Don't Patronize" list of the American Federation of Labor. The injunction orders that the facts in controversy between the Buck's Stove and Range Co. and organized labor must not be referred to, either by printed or written word or orally. The American Federation of Labor and its officers are each and severally named in the injunction. This injunction is the most sweeping ever issued.

IT IS AN INVASION OF THE LIBERTY OF THE PRESS AND THE RIGHT OF FREE SPEECH.

On account of its invasion of these two fundamental liberties, this injunction should be seriously considered by every citizen of our country.

It is the American Federation of Labor and the *American Federationist* that are now enjoined. To-morrow it may be another publication or some other class of equally law-abiding citizens, and the present injunction may then be quoted as a sacred precedent for future encroachments upon the liberties of the people.

With all due respect to the court it is impossible for us to see how we can comply with all the terms of this injunction. We would not be performing our duty to labor and to the public without discussion of this injunction. A great principle is at stake. Our forefathers sacrificed even life in order that these fundamental constitutional rights of free press and free speech might be forever guaranteed to our people. We would be recreant to our duty did we not do all in our power to point out to the people the serious invasion of their liberties which has taken place. . . .

The publication of the Buck's Stove and Range Co. on the "We Don't Patronize" list of the American Federation of Labor is the exercise of a plain right. To enjoin its publication is to invade and deny the freedom of the press—a right which is guaranteed under our constitution.

The right to print which has grown up through the centuries of freedom, has its basis in the fundamental guarantees of human liberty. It has been defended and upheld by the ablest minds. It ought not to be forbidden by judicial order. . . .

The plaintiff for the Buck's Stove and Range Co., also its president, is no other than Mr. Van Cleave, also president of the National Association of Manufacturers. The recent contemptible attacks of the manufacturers' association's hirelings upon the character of the men of labor are still fresh in the public mind. The application for an injunction against the publication as "unfair" of the Buck's Stove and Range Co. by the American Federation of Labor, savored very much of an attempt to use the courts in the prosecution of the manufacturers' association's avowed union-crushing campaign. . . .

If the champions of the non-union shop are so proud of their stand in the matter and so convinced of their own fairness, and wisdom we really fail to see why they should object to the publication of that fact.

If, as they claim, the public is with *them* and disapproves of unions and their method of "collective bargaining," we should think that the publication of the fact of a firm declining to pay union wages or concede union hours would be its best possible advertisement and one that would be eagerly sought. Not so it seems. The Buck's Stove and Range Co. judging from the terms of the injunction desires to stifle the voice of labor and enforce a continuous and unbroken silence on the subject of its bad standing with union workmen.

In the application for the injunction it was alleged by the Buck's Stove and Range Co. that its business had suffered seriously from the refusal of union workmen and their friends to purchase its stoves and ranges. But would not absolute silence on our part as to its hostile attitude toward certain union employes be dishonest? Why should we encourage our members and friends to buy the Buck's Stoves and Ranges under the apprehension that this company deals fairly with union labor? Could not union employers then accuse us of unfair discrimination, of trickery and humbug?

If Mr. Van Cleave's opposition to the union shop is a matter of honest and conscientious conviction we should think he would writhe in pain under an injunction which prevents the publication of that fact.

The injunction is printed in full in this issue of the *American Federationist.* We hope our readers will study carefully every word and every phrase. It is a most remarkable injunction.

Justice Gould seems to base this injunction on the *assumption* that there has been a combination of numbers of wage-earners "conspiring" to commit unlawful acts. Such is not the fact. The public should understand clearly the difference between combinations for unlawful purposes and the voluntary associations of wage-earners for entirely lawful and proper purposes.

Let us for a moment consider what are some of the aims and purposes of our labor movement; to render means and opportunity of employment less precarious; to improve the standard of life; to uproot ignorance and foster education: to establish a normal workday; instill character, manhood, and an independent spirit among our people; to establish the recognition of the interdependence of man upon man, and that no man can be sufficient unto himself; that he must not shirk a duty to his fellows; to take children from the factory and the workshop, the mill, the mine; and to give them the opportunity of the school, the home and the playground. In a word, to lighten toil, brighten man, to cheer the home and the fireside, to contribute our effort to make life the better worth living. To achieve these ends, all honorable and lawful means are not only justifiable, but commendable, and should receive the sympathetic support of every right-thinking American, rather than bitter, relentless antagonism. . . .

The members of organized labor are not themselves *obliged* to refrain from dealing with the firms on the "We Don't Patronize" list of the American Federation of Labor. The information is given them. There is no compulsion. They are entirely free to use their own judgment.

It must be remembered, however, that for the one firm which declines to employ union labor there are probably a score in the same business which prefer it on account of its greater skill and reliability, and for many other sound, economic reasons. Such firms are conceded to turn out a higher quality of product than non-union concerns. The members of organized labor naturally desire to expend their earnings to the best advantage when purchasing and wish to be informed as to what firms do and do not employ union labor. In purchasing, it is often a question of the *quality* of the goods offered. The "boycott" is a letting alone of undesirable goods.

Further Resources

BOOKS

Brooks, Thomas R. *Toil and Trouble: A History of American Labor.* New York: Delta, 1971.

Ernst, Daniel R. *Lawyers Against Labor: From Individual Rights to Corporate Liberalism.* Urbana: University of Illinois Press, 1995.

Foner, Philip S. *History of the Labor Movement in the United States: Vol. 3. The Policies and Practices of The American Federation of Labor, 1900–1909.* New York: International Publishers, 1987.

WEBSITES

"Democrat Platform." Available online at http://1912.history.ohio-state.edu/labor/democrat1.htm; website home page http://www.1912.history.ohio-state.edu (accessed December 26, 2002).

Marot, Helen. "The Boycott." In *American Labor Unions.* Available online at http://www.boondocksnet.com/editions/marot/marot10.html; website home page http://www.boondocksnet.com (accessed December 26, 2002).

The Western Federation of Miners on the Mesabi Range: An Address at a Social Entertainment of Hibbing Mine Workers

Speech

By: Teofilo Petriella

Date: November 26, 1906

Source: Petriella, Teofilo. *The Western Federation of Miners on the Mesabi Range: An Address at a Social Entertainment of Hibbing Mine Workers.* Pamphlets in American History. L1644, pp. 1–4, 7–9, 10, 12.

About the Author: Teofilo Petriella was an Italian-born socialist and labor organizer for the Western Federation of Miners (WFM). In addition to his activities in the iron-mining region of Minnesota, he was also active in efforts to organize copper miners on the Keweenaw Peninsula in northern Michigan. ■

Introduction

The Western Federation of Miners, organized in 1893, represented metal miners. It was particularly successful in the Rocky Mountain states, although it also launched serious organizing efforts in the Minnesota iron mines and the Michigan copper mines, and briefly attempted to organize miners in the coal industry. The WFM was the primary organizer of the Industrial Workers of the World (IWW) and the Western (later American) Labor Union. Business leaders regarded the WFM as radical, militant, and violent. Certainly it was radical and militant and made no apologies for its opposition to capitalism and support of socialism—a position that attracted the special enmity of the mine owners and much of the country.

It is inaccurate, however, to say that the WFM was revolutionary or particularly violent, for it advocated peaceful resolution of labor issues. Nonetheless, violence was a feature of labor-management disputes, and the WFM saw no contradiction in defending itself against the aggressive tactics frequently used by owners to break the union and crush strikes. In reality, the supposed violent

A man surveys the open pit iron mine in Hibbing, Minnesota, where steam shovels and a steam locomotive traverse the bottom. © CORBIS. REPRODUCED BY PERMISSION.

character of the WFM was largely a pretext for mine owners to use force to destroy it.

The socialist character of the WFM also led to an irreconcilable split with the nation's dominant labor organization, the American Federation of Labor. Although the WFM had briefly affiliated with the AFL in 1896, the two organizations had fundamentally different views on the goals of the labor movement, making a lasting alliance impossible. Led by Samuel Gompers, the AFL was primarily an association of craft unions that accepted the reality of the American economic system. It sought to use its leverage as an essential part of that system to achieve practical objectives: better wages, shorter hours, and better working conditions. Ignoring the interests of unskilled (and often foreign-born, black, or female) workers who made up much of the workforce, the AFL often found itself at odds with the WFM.

Significance

By the turn of the century, the two labor organizations were irreconcilable. Gompers, opposed to the WFM's socialist aspirations, used that as a rationale to limit his support for and, at times, undermined the WFM's labor actions. To the miners, Gompers and the AFL were tools of the capitalists. This split seriously undermined the labor movement, and occasionally resulting with the AFL allied with business against the more radical union by, for example, organizing strikebreakers to thwart WFM strikes. It is little wonder that by 1906

Teofilo Petriella, the WFM organizer who delivered the following speech, regarded the AFL and Gompers as enemies of workers.

The AFL had little interest in organizing the iron miners of the Mesabi Range and avoided northern Minnesota for a number of reasons. The workforce was dominated by recent immigrants from eastern and southern Europe. These immigrants were largely unskilled or semiskilled. There was a strong undercurrent of radicalism. Furthermore, success seemed unlikely, for the miners were isolated in company-controlled mining camps, and after 1901, eighty percent of the mines were owned by the powerful and virulently anti-union United States Steel Corporation. But while the AFL was unwilling to invest in the Mesabi Range miners, the WFM launched a serious organizing effort in 1906. By July 1907, they felt strong enough to risk a strike over wages, working conditions, safety, and union recognition.

United States Steel was determined to crush the strike. It brought in armed guards and trainloads of strikebreakers and exerted tremendous economic pressure on the strikers. Isolated, outgunned, and lacking the financial resources to sustain a long walkout, the union had little chance of success. By mid-September, it collapsed, and soon after the WFM abandoned the region.

Primary Source

The Western Federation of Miners on the Mesabi Range: An Address at a Social Entertainment of Hibbing Mine Workers [excerpt]

SYNOPSIS: The following speech, given by labor organizer Teofilo Petriella, highlights the differences between the Western Federation of Miners and the American Federation of Labor. Petriella paints the AFL as pawns of the capitalists, while the WFM is described as working in the true interests of the worker. He clearly states the socialist objectives of the WFM, but points out that the WFM does not compel members to support the Socialist Party, and that they are free to vote their conscience.

Ladies and Fellow Workers:

The Hibbing Miners Union has invited you to share an hour of recreation with it tonight and has charged me with explaining to you the fundamental principles of our organization.

To accomplish my task I need not take much of your time: neither do I need to make a speech. It will suffice to call your attention to the condition of our everyday life, as the Western Federation of Miners is nothing but the natural outcome of the appalling conditions under which live, we slaves of the mines. For a moment go with me to the main streets of Hibbing. Look into every open door as we pass by; then recall the house in which you live: cast a glance into the nasty shanties of the various locations swarming with human beings. It will not be hard for you to notice the glaring contrast which exists between the stores piled with merchandise that the dealers do not know how to sell, and the shacks of an immense army of workers who need everything and can buy very little.. . .

In all the lands, with very little difference, our lot is common to all the lemurs of the mines, to all the workers of the mills and shelters, factories and shops. Everywhere the man who toils for a wage becomes maimed, dumb or blind when he does not die of starvation or consumption: while the idle masters, besides living in mansions, get abundant and wholesome food, pure water and fresh air: making good blood, strong muscles and sound bones.

From the review of this sad condition of affairs comes spontaneously a question which I leave with you, while I sketch briefly the attitude of others interested in it.

The question is the following: "Is it natural and honest that at one pole of society be accumulated so much wealth and luxury, and at the other pole so much misery and want?" Or, in other words, "Is it fair and possible to rise to the standard of a decent human life the existence of those who do the hard work of the world and who today are allowed to eat only a meagre pittance and to inhabit houses which are nothing but ice box in winter and hot oven in summer?". . .

There are workers who think social disparities are natural and eternal. However, they organize themselves into a union of their craft, and hope, by so doing, prevent the evils caused by the development of economical extreme anomalies. Craft unionism believes in the possibility of a fair wage system, and endeavors to better the conditions of the workers by fastening a tie of friendship between capital and labor.

Craft unions, when they are not piloted by paid agents of the capitalist, are blinded by some "good objects and good deeds," of the employers. The pure and simple craft union man overlook to consider that the case of our more liberal exploiters is like that of the more rapacious robber-barons in former ages, who wished to signify their penitence by giving part of their booty to the church and to charity. Appearances very easily hide the fact that the employer's willingness to give is the expression of his soul's moments of unrest. It is not belated passion for justice, or for learning, or for religion, but it is a somewhat fear to loose everything. It is, I should say, a longing to avoid trouble and to continue to suck the best blood at the veins of those who toil and produce the wealth of the world.

We of the Western Federation of Miners have an opinion altogether different from that of the gentlemen named. We believe that the hideous social disparities and contrasts are unnatural and dishonest. We believe that wealth today is unjustly and ignobly distributed. We believe that the cause of our misery lies in the fact that the masters appropriate the product of our labor; and we unite not to graft our fellow-workers, but to fight those who own the means of livelihood and happiness; but to get gradual possession of what the capitalist class has taken and is taking from us.

The Western Federation of Miners is one of the most progressive labor organizations in the world, its fundamental principles being the struggle of classes, the workers unity on the industrial battlefield, the membership direct rule, and last but not least the collective ownership of the sources and machinery of production as a final object.

We adhere to the principle that the interests of the working class and those of the capitalist are irreconcilably opposed. In accepting this principle we give the lie to the notion dominating the craft unions—the Brotherhood of Steam Shovel Men, for instance—which in spite of the bitter experience of daily life, still claims that the interests of the two classes are identical or mutual.. . .

Don't be conceited and think that you have a special capacity which makes it impossible for an untrained person to relieve you. You will be bitterly disappointed in that. The man who makes $2.25 a day while working never misses a chance to watch you who make $3.50 and $5.00 a day. He may run the steam shovel as good as, or he may run it worse than you did but he will run it. For as sure as you get off, the pitman will jump on. He will be satisfied with less than what you get now. He has a grudge against you who barred him out of your organization and helped the employer to keep low his wage.

Neither must you believe that the affiliation of your Brotherhood with the American Federation of Labor will help you any. The A.F.L. is good for the masters, not for you. Should you continue in the organization in which you are now, in time of trouble, you would find yourselves helpless and isolated. Remember what I tell you now. It is part of an historical document containing many indictments against the A.F.L. When the members of the American Flint Glass Workers were on strike in Olean N.Y., D.A. Hayes, president of the Green Bottle Blowers Association, and sixth vice president of the American Federation of Labor, sent an executive officer to Washington, Pa., who installed a crew of non-unionists into the G.B.B.A., and paid their transportation to Olean, at which place the newly elected members of the G.B.B.A. were put to work, taking the places of the striking members of the A.F.G.W.U. The officers of the last named organization preferred charges against Mr. Hayes, of the A.F.L., and the case was brought before the executive council and officers of the Federation in Washington, D.C. Upon hearing the evidence, the council rendered the following decision: "We find D.A. Hayes not guilty. He simply sent an officer to a non-union locality and converted a crew of non-union men into union men and transported them to another locality to fill the complements of men required at that factory."

Isn't this enough for you to realize the necessity of a single and compact organization as advocated by us? We take in drillmen, pitmen, pumpmen, engineers, firemen, cranemen. For us, there is no discrimination between the dinkey crew and the steam shovel crew, or between the workers of the underground mines and those of the surface. We all have the same interests: then why shouldn't you come with us? Think for a moment what will happen on the Mesaba Range the day in which all the twenty–five thousand workers connected with the iron mining industry will be organized under the glorious banner of the Western Federation of Miners. Think of a strike. We do not organize for strikes. We want to reduce them to a minimum. Yet our miserable conditions—you know, we are the most overworked and the worst paid men working in and around the mines—our miserable conditions. I say might compel us to lay down the tools and leave our places. The complete paralysis of the industry, the deterioration of the mines and machinery left uncared for would cost the companies in a week more than a fifty per cent increase of wages to all of us for a year.

Another cardinal point, which makes our organization without a peer in the world of organized labor, is that the rank and file are the only law-makers and managers of their own affairs. Our officers, local and national, have a very limited power. The collective will of the membership is supreme. It is not so with your Brotherhood or with others of the same kind. There is no time now to go into details. I will be satisfied to point out to you that in our organization any local may enter upon a strike when ordered by three–fourths of its resident members in good standing, after having received the approval of the Executive Board of the Western Federation of Miners. The Local Union calls the stike and the Local Union will conduct it directly. Our general office will do nothing but to advise, but to give all the material and moral support. . . .

The ultimate and never-to-be-forgotten object of industrial unionism as advocated by the Western Federation of Miners is to seize and hold as our own collective property all the means of production and distribution. Our continuous struggle for an increase of wages will end only when our wage will represent the value of the whole product of our labor. That day the mine will be ours. It will be a great and necessary attainment, as capitalism is nothing but a system of robbery and social crime. Private ownership of the materials and machinery of production is a theft, the result of a slow process of human skinning and slaughtering.

When once we have got hold of fields and mines, mills and factories, there will be no more production for profit, no more wage system, no more class exploitation. We will all be workers, all free, all happy. That will be the dawning of the Socialist republic. Yes, I want to tell you the truth. We work for Socialism; our organization, among other things, does prepare the way for, and lays the foundations of a co-operative society, whose administration will be entirely industrial. Under such a regime, the social authority will be invested in an elective house of representatives of the various departments of production and distribution. The consumers will be the producers, and the producers will also make the organic law of the community. . . .

Forget the difference of occupation and of nationalities, and join hands with us. We are oppressed by the same master; let us react against him united and harmoniously. A unified action means victory, and we must win out for ourselves and our children.

Join the Western Federation of Miners, sure that by so doing you fall in line with those who work to emancipate our class from the thraldom of capitalist slavery.

Make up your mind tonight; drop in your application now, and be confident that the future will be ours, that the sun of better days will appear on the horizon of our life and that of the generations who will succeed us on the face of earth.

No matter the obstacles, so far we have succeeded to organize a Local Union in almost every mining camp of Minnesota. We have parted the bushes and opened our way ahead. The banner of the miners of the West has been hoisted on this Range and there it will remain unfurled until the inhabitants of the shacks, now stripped of all the habiliments of man, all united have blown into the whistles of the mines a tremendous blast which, piercing the veins of the masters, will find its echo among the tallowy faced sweaters of the slums in the industrial cities. That will be the eve of the proclamation of the Brotherhood of Man, ushered in by the Social Revolution in the name of the workers of the world.

Further Resources

BOOKS

Foner, Philip S. *History of the Labor Movement in the United States: Vol. 4. The Industrial Workers of the World, 1905–1917.* New York: International Publishers, 1987.

WEBSITES

Kostiainen, Auvo. "A Dissenting Voice of Finnish Radicals in America: The Formative Years of the *Socialisti-Industrialisti* in the 1910s." Available online at http://www.genealogia.fi/emi/art/article256e.htm; website home page http://www.genealogia.fi (accessed December 26, 2002).

Linder, Douglas. "Famous American Trials: Bill Haywood Trial, 1907." Available online at www.law.umkc.edu/faculty/projects/ftrials/haywood/HAYWOOD.htm; website home page: http://www.law.umkc.edu (accessed December 26, 2002).

Rate Wars in the Railroad Industry

From the Directors of the Standard Oil Company to Its Employees and Stockholders

Pamphlet

By: James A. Moffett

Date: August 1907

Source: Standard Oil Company. *From the Directors of the Standard Oil Company to Its Employees and Stockholders.* August 1907.

About the Author: James A. Moffett (1851–1913) entered the oil-refining business as a young man in Parkersburg, West Virginia, and joined Standard Oil in 1883. In 1888, he took charge of building a major refinery at Whiting, Indiana.

The next year he became president of the Standard Oil Company of Indiana. He later became a director and vice president of the Standard Oil Trust Company.

Statement in Answer to the Allegations of the Standard Oil Company Regarding Its Conviction at Chicago.

Statement

By: Herbert Knox Smith

Date: October 11, 1907

Source: United States Bureau of Corporations. *Statement in Answer to the Allegations of the Standard Oil Company Regarding its Conviction at Chicago.* Washington, D.C.: U.S. Government Printing Office, 1907.

About the Author: Herbert Knox Smith (1869–1931) practiced corporate law in Hartford, Connecticut, before being appointed to the newly formed Bureau of Corporations. He was instrumental in the investigations against Standard Oil that led to the rate-fixing case at Alton and eventually the company's dissolution in 1911. ■

Introduction

The popular hostility against business trusts and monopolies often played itself out in battles over railroad rates. For a generation, the railroads had been justifiably accused of discriminatory rate setting. The industry was highly competitive, so the railroads offered favorable rates to large shippers in competitive markets. In contrast, along routes where railroad companies held a monopoly and for small shippers, they pushed rates "as high as the market would bear." The outcry against rate manipulation led to the passage of the Interstate Commerce Act in 1887. The act forbade price fixing and required railroads to set "reasonable and just" published rates, but like many initial legislative attempts to regulate the economy, the act achieved little.

In the first decade of the twentieth century, rate manipulation once again became a major political issue. The apparent ability of powerful trusts to force railroads to grant special rates and rebates helped focus attention on shipping rates. Furthermore, the consolidation of railroads in the 1890s, under the leadership of J. P. Morgan, created larger, more powerful railroad combinations. This consolidation put the complex process of ratemaking into the hands of a few business leaders who had the ability to unilaterally establish transportation rates for the entire country, usually secretly and without any evident logic. Faced both with growing public concern and evidence of abuse, President Theodore Roosevelt (served 1901–1909) and his administration supported additional regulatory measures to ensure that "reasonable and just" rates were available to all shippers. The Elkins Act (1903) prohibited railroads from granting rebates to shippers, a common means of circumventing published rates. The Hepburn Act (1906) expanded the power of the Interstate Commerce Commission to establish rates, subject to court review. A third piece of legislation created the Bureau of Corporations in 1903. It gave the president a powerful new agency able to gather information to influence public opinion and guide government policy. The Roosevelt administration used these powers to investigate rate discrimination.

Federal judge Kenesaw Mountain Landis reads at a desk.

Significance

Because of its monopolistic power, blatant rate manipulation, and high profile, the Standard Oil Company became a special target of government investigation. By the middle of the decade, both the federal government and various states had initiated major legal proceedings against the giant holding company. One of the most dramatic suits, initiated by the Bureau of Corporations, accused Standard of fixing rates in shipping oil from its refinery at Whiting, Indiana, to East St. Louis. The government charged that the Chicago and Alton Railroad had given Standard rebates in violation of the Elkins Act on hundreds of shipments over the line. In a dramatic and highly publicized case tried before flamboyant federal judge Kenesaw Mountain Landis, Standard Oil was found guilty of 1,462 counts of rate manipulation and fined an astounding $29,240,000.

Popular reaction was mixed. While many were overjoyed, others were appalled at the apparently vindictive assault by the government. Criticism increased when, on the heels of Landis's verdict, the stock market began to slump, setting off the Panic of 1907. While the panic was actually caused by stock manipulators, Roosevelt's opponents blamed the stock market collapse on his antibusiness policies.

Standard Oil appealed the fine, and, in August 1908, it was set aside and a new trial ordered. By this time, however, Standard's attention was fixed on a trial of even greater importance. Under the provisions of the Sherman Anti-Trust Act, the federal government sought the dissolution of the company. The case, initially tried in the Federal Circuit of Eastern Missouri, resulted in a victory for the government in November 1909. On May 15, 1911, the U.S. Supreme Court affirmed this judgment and Standard Oil dissolved.

Primary Source

From the Directors of the Standard Oil Company to Its Employees and Stockholders [excerpt]

SYNOPSIS: Almost immediately after Landis's ruling in the Alton case, the Standard Oil public relations department distributed a forty-page brochure to newspapers, stockholders, and influential people all across the country. Composed largely of sharp criticisms of the ruling, it also included comments by Standard Oil of Indiana's president, James A. Moffet.

A Word in Advance

The Directors of the Standard Oil Company, in printing this pamphlet, desire to emphasize for the half million of people directly-interested in its welfare the assurance of the Company's absolute innocence of wrongdoing in any of the prosecutions lately instituted against it in the Federal Courts. Particularly is this so in the recent Chicago & Alton R. R. case, made notorious by the sensational fine of $29,240,000 imposed on the Standard Oil Company of Indiana. . . .

Statement of James A. Moffett, President, Standard Oil Company, of Indiana

The Court having pronounced its judgment in the case of the *United States vs. Standard Oil Company, of Indiana,* there can now be no impropriety in stating our position to the American people.

The facts in this case are simple and easily understood. The Standard Oil Company, of Indiana, was convicted of receiving what the Government claimed was a concession from the Chicago & Alton in the shipment of oil from its refinery at Whiting, Indiana, to East St. Louis, Illinois. It must be borne in mind that there is no question of rebate or discrimination in this case. The contention of the Government was that the lawful rate was 18 cents per one hundred pounds between these two points. The defendant claims: First, that the lawful rate was 6 cents; and, secondly, if 6 cents was not the lawful rate it was the rate issued to the Standard by the Alton as the lawful rate, and the Standard was justified in believing from its own investigation and from the information received from the Railroad Company that 6 cents was the lawful rate.

The 18-cent rate was a "class" and not a "commodity" rate, and the chairman of the Chicago & St. Louis Traffic Association, the association issuing the 18 cent class rate, under oath testified that it was never applied and was never intended to apply to oil.

The period of time covered by the indictment in this case was from September 1st, 1903, to March 1st, 1905. The rate on oil between Chicago and East St. Louis over the Alton for fourteen years, from 1891 to 1905, was always 6 cents per one hundred pounds. This was an open published rate known to everyone concerned in the shipment of oil and generally known in all railroad circles in Chicago. Both Chicago and East St. Louis being in Illinois, the railroad company was under no legal obligation to file this rate with the Interstate Commerce Commission at Washington, but Whiting, being in Indiana, shipments from Whiting to East St. Louis were technically, at least, interstate and hence the Alton filed with the Interstate Commerce Commission what is known as an "application sheet" applying to Whiting the Chicago rate, and deemed the filing of the application sheet all that was necessary under the law.

For over thirty years, by custom, all of the little industrial towns grouped about Chicago, and which are in reality an essential part of Chicago and go to make up its industrial strength, have been given the same freight rates as Chicago. The reason for this is, of course, apparent, and it is because of this uniformity of freight rates that Chicago as the center of this group is to-day a city of over two millions of inhabitants. If Whiting, Pullman, Hegewisch and South Chicago did not get the same freight rates as

Chicago, manufacturing establishments in these towns would be compelled to close their doors. Because of this condition and situation railroads created what is known as the Chicago Switching District, which includes Whiting and all of these other little manufacturing towns in and around Chicago. These towns are further unified by a belt line railroad which encircles Chicago and connects this entire industrial system with the trunk lines radiating from Chicago.

Thousands of tons of freight have been shipped from these points during the past fifteen years under the same circumstances as the Standard shipments, and if the Standard is guilty in this case, so is practically every other shipper in this great manufacturing territory. Is there a purpose in selecting the Standard as the victim?

The Chicago & Eastern Illinois Railroad also runs between Whiting and East St. Louis. The Standard Oil Company shipped about one-third of all the oil that went from Whiting to East St. Louis over the Eastern Illinois, the other two-thirds going over the Alton and the Burlington. On the trial of the case the defendant offered to show by witnesses who were on the stand that not only during the period of time covered by the indictment, but continuously from 1895, the Eastern Illinois had a lawful published and filed rate between Whiting and East St. Louis on oil of 6 cents per one hundred pounds and that the Standard Oil Company shipped at such rate over the Eastern Illinois more than two thousand cars of oil each year during said period. To this offer the Government through its attorneys strenuously objected and the Court sustained the objection. The defendant contended, and still does contend, that this proof would have conclusively shown that the Standard Oil Company had no possible motive in shipping over the Alton, and thereby violating the law, when it might just as readily and conveniently have shipped all of its oil over the Eastern Illinois and not have violated any law. . . .

Under such circumstances, and in view of the fact that petroleum had been openly carried over the three roads from Whiting to East St. Louis for from ten to fourteen years for 6 cents, what a draft it is on human credulity for the prosecution to assert that 18 cents was the only possible lawful rate!

The uncontradicted evidence also showed that the Standard Oil Company was advised by the Rate Clerk of the Chicago & Alton that this 6 cent rate *was* filed with the Interstate Commerce Commission.

Knowing that the rate on the Eastern Illinois was but 6 cents; having no reason for shipping over the Alton in preference to the Eastern Illinois, and able to ship all of its oil over the latter road, we insist that the facts, many of which the Court did not permit us to show, not alone demonstrate innocence but inherently forbid the idea of guilt.

We further insist that whatever may be one's technical view of the law relating to the above question, every equitable consideration is with the defendant, and if the only desire was to give this defendant a "square deal" this prosecution would never have been instituted.

The American public not only believes in fair play in the abstract, but, with all the facts before it, it has the capacity to determine whether a defendant, rich or poor, has received a "square deal."

For all these reasons the Standard Oil Company asserts that it is not even technically guilty and that it ought never to have been prosecuted because of the claimed failure of a railroad company—which has neither been indicated nor prosecuted—to file its tariff, and that the prosecution of this defendant under the circumstances of this case is a prostitution of the spirit and the high purpose of the Interstate Commerce Act.

Primary Source

Statement in Answer to the Allegations of the Standard Oil Company Regarding Its Conviction at Chicago [excerpt]

SYNOPSIS: A few weeks after the Standard Oil pamphlet was released, the Bureau of Corporations produced a rebuttal laying out the case against Standard Oil. It was prepared by Herbert Knox Smith, commissioner of the Bureau of Corporations, at the request of Secretary of Commerce and Labor Oscar S. Straus.

On August 3, 1907, at Chicago, the Standard Oil Company of Indiana was fined $29,240,000 for the violation of the Elkins anti-rebate law. This was the so-called "Alton case." Various statements have since appeared, one in particular signed by the president of that company, James A. Moffett, others in the public press, and also a series of confidential circular "trade letters," all endeavoring to throw doubt on the legality and equity of that conviction.

The report of the Commissioner of Corporations on the Transportation of Petroleum, published in May, 1906, on which this and all other pending rebate indictments of the Standard (except one) were based, set forth in detail the deliberate, long-continued conduct on the part of the Standard in violating the antirebate laws. But these recent statements have made it necessary to show once more that the transactions which form the basis of this conviction at Chicago were such as struck at the very life and spirit of the Elkins antirebate law and of the policy of Congress in forbidding unfairness as between shippers.

The question in this case was one of a published 18-cent rate to East St. Louis, as against a secret 6-cent rate. The oil shipments involved in this so-called "Alton" conviction started from Whiting, Ind., the great refinery of the Standard near Chicago, and were delivered at St. Louis, Mo., or at East St. Louis, Ill., just across the river from St. Louis, by the Chicago and Alton Railroad. They covered a period from September 1, 1903, to March 1, 1905.

The law requires that all interstate railway rates be filed with the Interstate Commerce Commission. During this entire time there was on file with the Interstate Commerce Commission a joint "tariff" or rate sheet to which the Alton road was a party, showing that the rate on fifth-class freight from Whiting and Chicago to East St. Louis was 18 cents per hundred pounds. Fifth-class freight includes petroleum oil. This joint tariff was a large printed document distributed to many shippers of all sorts of freight.

During the time so stated, 1,462 cars of oil were carried from Whiting, Ind., to East St. Louis over the Alton road for the Standard Oil Company at the rate of 6 cents per hundred pounds, just one-third of the said published rate. This same secret 6-cent rate had been used by the Standard Oil Company, and by no one else, for many years prior to this period. It was not filed with the Interstate Commerce Commission, and was absolutely secret and unknown to independent oil refiners, or to shippers generally.

The said statement of James A. Moffett uses the following remarkable language:

> It must be borne in mind that there is no question of rebate or discrimination in this case.

Whether it was a "rebate" or not is a mere question of words. Apparently the position of Mr. Moffett is that if he had actually paid the Alton railroad 18 cents per hundred pounds and received back 12 cents, so as to make a net rate of 6 cents, this would have been a "rebate." But that because the lawful rate was 18 cents and his company only paid 6, and the balance (12 cents) never physically passed back and forth between his company and the Alton railroad, although the result was exactly the same, it was not a "rebate." This statement is simply an evasion.

The other proposition of Mr. Moffett is that there was "no discrimination in this case." Apparently his position is that, because no one else is known to have paid the published 18-cent rate from Whiting to East St. Louis while his company was paying 6 cents, therefore there was no discrimination. On the contrary, this very situation proves that not only was there discrimination, but that this discrimination had worked out its logical result, so that no one else could ship at 18 cents in competition with the Standard's 6-cent rate. Precisely this, and other secret discriminations in shipments from Whiting, produced that complete state of monopoly in the vicinity of Chicago which the Standard now calmly designates as "absence of discrimination."

This 6-cent Alton rate was a "rebate" in essence, if not in form, and both in essence and in form it was a discrimination of the most severe and successful type.

The Standard Oil Company of Indiana has tried to excuse its use of the 6-cent rate on two grounds. It admits that the 6-cent rate over the Alton railroad was never filed with the Interstate Commerce Commission, as the law required. But the Standard tries to remedy this fatal defect by referring to a certain "application sheet," which was on file with the Commission. This sheet merely stated that the rates from Chicago should apply also from Whiting, enumerated the tariffs referred to by it, and named specifically the tariff containing the 18-cent oil rate; but it made no mention of the unfiled "Special Billing Order" containing the 6-cent rate, nor did it give any information as to any 6-cent rate on oil. Of course, this sort of thing was absolutely no notice to anyone of the unpublished 6-cent rate, nor was it intended to be.

But the chief ground upon which the Standard defends itself is the so-called "Chicago and Eastern Illinois rate." The claim is that while the shipments of oil were going on at 6 cents over the Alton railroad there existed at the same time over the Chicago and Eastern Illinois Railroad a rate of 6¼ cents from Whiting to East St. Louis. The Standard claims that this 6¼-cent rate was a legal rate, and that therefore, inasmuch as the Standard could have shipped all its oil at this alleged legal rate over the Chicago and Eastern Illinois, it was justified in accepting a like rate over the Alton, and thus that even if these shipments over the Alton were technically illegal there was no moral wrong about them.

So far from this "Chicago and Eastern Illinois rate" being a justification for the Alton shipments, it was an additional wrong in itself. The Chicago and

Eastern Illinois rate was quite as secret as the Alton rate and was merely one more instance of the ingenious and deliberate attempts of the Standard to evade, or violate with impunity, the whole spirit of the antidiscrimination law. . . .

The grand jury, on instructions from Judge Landis, thereupon summoned Mr. Moffett before it, and reported to Judge Landis on October 4, in part, as follows:

> He [Mr. Moffett] was also unable to give to the grand jury information as to the shipment of a single pound of freight except by the Standard Oil Company from the points in question at a rate less than the lawfully published and filed rate. . . .

Why were these unique and elaborate measures of concealment taken if the rates were lawful?

The grand jury, in the report above mentioned, refer to this point also as follows:

> The representatives of the Chicago and Alton Railway Company stated to the grand jury that the case of the Standard Oil Company was the only one where the tariff naming the rate collected had not been regularly sent to the local freight agent, and that so far as they knew, this was the only case in which shipments had been made at a rate less than that named in the lawful tariff.

The officers of both these railroads admitted that this 6-cent rate was secret. One phrased it as "semiprivate." . . .

These rates were all exposed by this Bureau in May, 1906. Within three months after that date every such rate criticised by the Bureau as illegal had been canceled by the railroads making the said rates. This voluntary action of the railroads themselves more than justified the conclusion of the Bureau that there had been in existence for a long time a system of railway discriminations in favor of the Standard Oil Company in almost every section of the country.

Considerations like these become highly material when the Standard Oil Company appeals, as it has, from a question of strict legality to a question of equity and good faith, and claims that in this specific case, though it may have been technically guilty, nevertheless it was morally innocent. As Judge Landis remarked, in imposing the fine, this was by no means "its virgin offense."

This Alton rate, therefore, was substantially a rebate; was the most effective kind of discrimination, because it killed out all competition; was secret and was concealed by secret methods; is sought to be justified only by another like secret rate which also was covered by secret methods; was only one of a great system of discriminatory rates practically covering the country (which the railroads dared not maintain in the light of publicity), and in its ingenuity, secrecy, and complete effectiveness constitutes as extreme a violation of both the letter and spirit of the antirebate laws as could well be imagined. . . .

The Standard undersold competitors in the great Southwest by means of this 6-cent rate to the St. Louis gateway, and, having undersold them and driven them out of that territory, it then raised prices to a monopoly figure, so that its marketing concern there was making over 690 per cent on its capital stock in 1904, and for a long series of years had been making profits extortionately high. These profits were thus based on this secret discrimination which had been in existence over fifteen years. The enjoyment of this discriminatory rate was well worth many millions of dollars to the Standard, and most emphatically justified the imposition of a great fine when that rate was finally discovered and conviction was secured thereon.

Further Resources

BOOKS

Chernow, Ron. *Titan: The Life of John D. Rockefeller, Sr.* New York: Vintage Books, 1999.

Giddens, Paul Henry. *Standard Oil Company (Indiana): Oil Pioneer of the Middle West.* New York: Appleton-Century-Crofts, 1955.

WEBSITES

Crotty, Charles R. "Crotty vs Standard Oil Company." Available online at http://home.nycap.rr.com/crcrotty/Standard%20Oil/Crotty%20vs%20Standard%20Oil.htm; website home page: http://www.home.nycap.rr.com (accessed December 27, 2002).

Explosion at Darr Mine

"Over Four Hundred Men Entombed by Explosion at Darr Mine"; "Only Six Bodies Are Recovered at Darr"

Newpaper articles

By: United Press

Date: December 20, 1907; December 21, 1907

Source: United Press. "Over Four Hundred Men Entombed by Explosion at Darr Mine." *Washington (Pa.) Reporter,*

December 20, 1907; "Only Six Bodies Are Recovered at Darr." *Washington (Pa.) Reporter,* December 21, 1907.

About the Organization: United Press was a news service created by Edward W. Scripps in 1907. Scripps had, by this time, acquired a group of newspapers that would later form the basis for the Scripps-Howard chain. The United Press merged with the Hearst-owned International News Service in 1956 to form United Press International (UPI).

Darr Mine Rescue Team at Van Meter, Pennsylvania

Photograph

By: Anonymous

Date: December 19, 1907

Source: "Darr Mine Rescue Team at Van Meter, Pennsylvania." From the personal collection of Anna Toth, Bobtown, Penn. Available online at http://patheoldminer.rootsweb.com /darr2.html; website home page http://patheoldminer.rootsweb .com/ (accessed May 8, 2003). ■

Introduction

Coal was the fuel that made the industrial age possible. It powered trains and steamships, generated the electricity found in most cities, and fueled the engines that drove the belt-driven machinery almost universally found in turn-of-the-century factories. In 1910, eighty-eight percent of all energy generated in the United States came from coal. About 700,000 coal miners toiled to bring nearly 500 million tons of coal to the surface each year. An item so critical to the economy came at a steep price. In an age when job-related injuries and fatalities were common, coal mining was the country's most dangerous occupation. Coal miners faced special dangers from working thousands of feet underground. Most dangerous were the accumulation of methane gas and the presence of highly explosive coal dust. These resulted in horrific explosions that, with terrible regularity, cost scores of miners their lives. In the decade ending in 1909, over 21,000 miners lost their lives on the job. In the twentieth century, over 100,000 coal miners were killed.

The danger of coal mining led to efforts to improve mine safety. Beginning in the late–nineteenth century, states passed legislation to improve safety. Such early legislation dealt with such matters as roofing supports and banning miners from riding in mine cars. Insufficient in scope and laxly enforced, this legislation was largely ineffective. Worker safety was also high on the agenda of the unions, and in 1910 the Federal Bureau of Mines was established, in part to promote mine safety. Despite these efforts, fatality rates in American mines remained high.

Significance

In 1907, 3,242 coal miners died on the job—the worst year in American mine history. It had already been a disastrous year when, in a two-week period, three separate explosions claimed 658 lives. The worst occurred on December 6 at Monongah, West Virgina, where 362 miners died. A week later, fifty-seven miners perished in Yolande, Alabama. The third incident was at the Darr mine, located about twenty-five miles southeast of Pittsburgh near the town of Van Meter. The mine was one of several in the area owned by the Pittsburgh Coal Company, whose chief stockholder was Andrew Mellon. Also a founder of the Aluminum Company of America, Mellon later served as secretary of the treasury under Presidents Harding (served 1921–1923), Coolidge (served 1923–1929), and Hoover (served 1929–1933).

On December 19, 1907, disaster struck at the Darr mine when a methane gas and coal dust explosion killed 239 miners. The cause of the explosion remained uncertain, although it is likely that an open-flame miner's lamp ignited a gas and dust pocket that was insufficiently ventilated. Although rescue attempts were launched immediately, there was little hope of saving lives. Rescuers did, however, make one of the first uses in the United States of a self-contained breathing apparatus, allowing rescue workers to operate in a mine section filled with deadly gases.

Following the explosion, the Darr mine was closed for several years. It reopened under a different name in 1910 and continued production until 1920, when the seam played out. The Pittsburgh Coal Company continued to operate nearby mines until the late 1940s.

Primary Source

"Over Four Hundred Men Entombed by Explosion at Darr Mine"; "Only Six Bodies Are Recovered at Darr"

SYNOPSIS: The following United Press releases describe the early hours following the December 19 explosion at the Darr mine. As with most such on-the-spot reporting, the information is sketchy and speculative.

"Over Four Hundred Men Entombed by Explosion at Darr Mine"

Another Terrible Fatality Today in the Pittsburg District The Mine is On Fire.

In an explosion at the Darr mine at 11:30 this morning, 400 men were entombed. The mine is on fire, and it is believed all are dead. The Darr mine is operated by the Pittsburg Coal company and is located at Jacob's Creek, on the Pittsburg and Lake Erie Railroad. Of the miners entombed 100 are Americans, and the rest principally Italians. Immediately after the explosion smoke poured from the mouth

Primary Source

Darr Mine Rescue Team

SYNOPSIS: The only photo in existence of the Darr Mine rescue. Members of the rescue team prepare to enter the slope entry to the Darr Mine in Van Meter, Pennsylvania. The explosion on December 19, 1907 killed 239 miners. DARR MINE RESCUE TEAM AT VAN METER PA, DECEMBER 19, 1907. COURTESY OF ANN TOTH, BOBTOWN, PA.

of the mine, which is of the slope variety. Most of the mine is wrecked, and up to 1 o'clock no one was able to enter to search for the entombed men. The cause of the explosion is unknown.

■ ■ ■

"Only Six Bodies Are Recovered at Darr"

Rescuers Have Not Yet Reached the Point Where the Diggers Were Employed.

The recovery of bodies from the ill-fated Darr mine is now in progress. It is believed that the death list will reach 200. On account of the Greek holiday yesterday, and the fact that many of the Greek Catholics were at church, the usual number of men were not at work, or the death list would have more than equaled the Monongah disaster. At 9:30 this morning there six bodies had been recovered. Among them is Mine Foreman, W.S. Campbell.

The fans have been started and the fire is now believed to be out. It will take hours to reach the bodies and to tell the extent of the disaster. Pitiful scenes are to be noticed today about the little town that lies nearby, as wives and children of the unfortunate men anxiously wait the recovery of their loved ones.

Six members of the state constabulary arrived from Greensburg this morning and have taken charge. Ten mine inspectors arrived on the scenes this morning. Many have been attracted here by morbid curiosity.

Rescuers have gone 5,000 feet into the mine, it will be necessary to go three-fourths of a mile farther before coming to where the diggers will be found.

Superintendent Black, who was in charge of the mine, recently resigned, as did David Wingrove, former fire boss, on account of the gaseous nature of the mine. It is said they notified the officials the mine was unsafe for the men to work in. There are many such reports current here.

Jacob's Creek, Pa. Dec. 20. Death to at least 200 miners and the accompanying suffering and bereavement to their families came yesterday between 11:15 and 11:30, with all that sadness and fatality characteristic of subterranean eruptions when a combination of gas and coal dust cause a terrible explosion in the Darr mines of the Pittsburg Coal company, located just across the Youghiogheny at Van Meter. There was but one explosion and it was accompanied by a flaming detonation. While the surface indications do not show that it came with great force, residents of both sides of the river say that their houses shook and the earth fairly rumbles as the gas and dust made a fruitless effort to belch itself forth through any entrance, all of which were too confined for its purpose. This was the warning to the neighborhood and it was not mistaken.

Wrought up by the death bearing calamities in other parts, wives, sisters, and sweethearts had lived in dread of a like fate, and when the explosion came it was as both a warning and a death knell. Survivors Are Brave. Last night in two little hamlets, weeping women, many with babes in their arms, tell the tale of happy homes bereft and springing hope blighted. Survivors, be it said, are bearing up bravely and most of them seem resigned to the fate of those who knew too well the risk their loved ones took, but who had fondly hoped that they might be exempted. . . .

Arrangements were completed last night by which all the dead will be buried by the company. This was decided on after a consultation among the officials here and the Pittsburg office. The place of burial and the time of interment will, of course, be subject to the wishes of the bereaved. After bodies have been taken out and identified they will be encased in shrouds and caskets ordered by the company, tonight. Representatives of the National Casket company and the United States Casket company of Pittsburg were here and secured the order for the caskets and supplies. It was impressed on these men when the order was given that it was the intention to accord the victims of the disaster a respectable interment and the selections were made accordingly. Two hundred and fifty caskets were ordered to be shipped on request. Rescuers Promptly at Work. With all the sadness that the accident took on, in the same ratio of sobriety was the work of rescue begun. Men seemed to fairly spring from the ground, anxious to pull down the barriers between their unfortunate fellowmen and liberty, which in this case meant life.

Workmen from the other mines of the company in this section, the Wickhaven and the Banning, rushed from their places without instructions from their superiors. Fifteen minutes after the explosion occurred the debris from the entrance had been cleared away, and the first rescue party entered. As nearly as can be ascertained, through the company officials refuse to go on record at the present time, either as the cause or effect, the point of the explosion was located about two miles from the entrance.

By 7 o'clock last evening penetration had been made to the twenty-first entrance, fully 5,000 feet from the entrance to the mine. First Bodies Found. It was here that the first bodies were found. Right at this point is located the shanty in which the pit boss makes his headquarters while in the mine. As it hove in view it presented an uncanny appearance with a grave-like stillness about it. Here within the four walls of this little wooden structure were huddled five dead bodies. Four of them rested on an improvised bench and the fifth, headless, believed to be that of the mine foreman, W.S. Campbell, lay on the floor. Stout-hearted enough to dare death themselves in any form, the rescue party stood trembling at this ghastly find. This discovery was made about 7 o'clock and the rescue party returned to the entrance. When their find was reported to General Manager J.M. Armstrong he gave instructions that no bodies be brought out until the crowd, which besieged the entrance, had departed.

The rescue work was greatly helped in two ways. The brattice work in the mine, with few exceptions, was in good condition, and in addition to this the fan used to force air into the mine was not injured. The Darr mine, which is one of the oldest in the field, the first coal having been taken out 65 years ago, is located on the riverbank, with a slope entrance. On either side lie the Banning and Wickhaven mines, also operated by the Pittsburg Coal Company.

While officials of the company assert that there is absolutely no connection between these mines, several of the miners assert that this is not true, and that in several places at different points augur holes have been bored through the connection walls on both sides, and in this and through these entrances, it would be an easy matter for the gas in both the others to congregate in the Darr.

In the Port Royal mine which lies only a short distance off, and which produced the only fatal explosion in this section in the past, there is also supposed to be an entrance to the Darr. The Darr lies higher than the others and as gas naturally rises to the surface, it is asserted that it became the receiving chamber for the other three.

News Summary

Town and County. W.S. Campbell, foreman at the Darr mine, and among the dead, a former resident of McDonald and Finleyville. Walter Shepherd, also formerly located in this county, among the dead.

Further Resources

BOOK

Long, Priscilla. *Where the Sun Never Shines: A History of America's Bloody Coal Industry.* New York: Paragon House, 1989.

WEBSITES

Centers for Disease Control and Prevention. "Improvements in Workplace Safety: United States, 1900–1999." Available online at http://jama.ama-assn.org/issues/v282n4/ffull/jwr0728-3.html; website home page http://jama.ama-assn.org/ (accessed December 27, 2002).

"Coal Mining in the Gilded Age and Progressive Era." Available online at http://www.cohums.ohio-state.edu/history/projects/Lessons_US/Gilded_Age/; website home page http://www.cohums.ohio-state.edu (accessed December 27, 2002). This site consists of links to articles about coal mining in the early twentieth century.

"Mine Disasters in PA." Available online at http://www.ncpenn.com/pa_mineaccidents.html; website home page http://www.ncpenn.com (accessed December 27, 2002).

National Institute for Occupational Safety and Health. "Historical Mine Disasters." Available online at http://www.cdc.gov/niosh/mining/data/gt_disaster.html; website home page: http://www.cdc.gov (accessed December 27, 2002).

Ford Price List of Parts for Models "N," "R," "S" and "S" Roadster

Manual

By: Ford Motor Company

Date: 1908

Source: Ford Motor Company. *Ford Price List of Parts for Models "N," "R," "S" and "S" Roadster.* Detroit: Ford Motor Company, 1908, 1, 54, 55, 56–57, 58, 59, 61.

About the Author: Henry Ford (1863–1947) led a social and economic revolution in the United States with the introduction of the Model T automobile in October 1908. While working as an engineer in Detroit, he built his first automobile in 1896, but it was not until 1903 that the Ford Motor Company became a going concern. Ford was one of many auto manufacturers, but the introduction of the Model T and his improvement of mass production techniques pushed the company into a class of its own. ■

Introduction

"I will build a car for the masses," Henry Ford said on announcing the Model T. It will allow them, he said, to "enjoy the blessing of hours of pleasure in God's great open spaces." Few prognostications have been more accurate. When he spoke those words, the automobile was regarded as a rich person's toy. Some automakers, Ransom E. Olds, for example, had visions similar to Ford, but most clung to the belief that the automobile would appeal only to a small elite, and they built cars for that market.

Ford's objective was different. He wanted to build a car that would be affordable for average people and would give them unparalleled personal mobility. Farmers would be able escape the isolation of the farm and more easily bring products to market. The urban worker would be able to find refuge from the unhealthy conditions of the city in regular trips to the therapeutic countryside. Ford planned to design a rugged, easily serviced vehicle using high-quality, mass-produced components.

In 1900, however, this was just a dream. Ford and hundreds of other backyard mechanics struggled to build and sell automobiles. Over the course of the decade more than a thousand auto companies were born, but most had brief lives. Ford, too, struggled. More concerned with technical matters than sales, he was unsuccessful in his first two manufacturing attempts. By 1903, however, he had a design that met his expectations. Despite his disappointing track record in business, Ford's technical reputation attracted backing from local businessmen and the Ford Motor Company came into existence.

Significance

The first decade of the twentieth century began with the automobile barely on the radar screen. In 1900, there were only 8,000 automobiles in the entire country, and they were generally regarded as a curiosity or a nuisance. Only the dreamers saw the potential. In 1910, there were 470,000 automobiles, and, by 1920, the number had grown to over nine million. The country had fallen in love with the automobile.

Leading this growth was the Ford Motor Company. Even before the Model T, Ford was producing fifteen percent of the cars made in the United States. The Model T, which Ford put into production in October 1908, revolutionized American society and the economy. By the time Ford ceased production of the Model T in 1926, over 15.5 million had been sold in the United States. Nearly half the vehicles in the world were Model T's. Originally, they were priced at around $850, but Ford steadily dropped the price, eventually selling them for as little as $290. As production techniques improved, particularly between 1910 and 1914, Ford passed these savings onto the consumer and his workers, paying them what in those years was the princely sum of $5 per day.

Following Ford's lead, the industry exploded, becoming the major stimulus to the America economy. Steel production, the oil industry, road construction, and dozens of other support businesses prospered in the wake of the auto sales. Just as dramatic was the social impact. The personal mobility the automobile provided changed how Americans lived. The auto ended the isolation of the farmer, stimulated the growth of suburbs, and opened up access to every corner of the country. People could go where they wanted, when they wanted, and in the privacy of their own vehicle. This freedom of movement became a deeply ingrained trait of Americans.

Primary Source

Ford Price List of Parts for Model "N," "R," "S" and "S" Roadster

SYNOPSIS: The automobile was initially sold to a population almost totally ignorant of its inner workings. Further, at least in the early years, a service infrastructure did not exist. If drivers did not, as one song went, "get out and get under," there was no one else to do it. The following excerpt from the 1908 parts manual for Ford's pre-Model T offerings gives an interesting perspective on the owner's responsibilities as a driver and mechanic—expectations vastly different from those found in modern owner's manuals.

Foreword

Human ingenuity has never been able to produce perpetual motion, to invent a machine that did not require adjustment, discover a metal that would not break or a bearing alloy that would not wear.

Science has enabled us to determine with wonderful accuracy the factor of safety required in different parts and experience has enabled us to reduce wear and probable breakages to a minimum.

Next to performing the impossible—making a perfect car—that manufacturer performs the most valuable service to his patrons who makes every part absolutely interchangeable—absolutely accurate—and who makes it possible for owners to procure replacements instantly and at a fair price. This is our aim in furnishing Ford owners with this parts price list in which every part of Models N, R and S is illustrated, numbered and priced.

The wise motorist is the one who understands that frequent inspection is essential to safety and that prompt replacements of worn parts is the truest economy.

We have endeavored herein to forecast the troubles which the novice may expect and to guard him against them.

Then we have revised our parts price list making it conform to the newer order of things and reducing prices to the lowest figure practicable—a figure made possible by our unrivalled facilities for quantity production.

Few persons appreciate how much money the manufacturer must keep tied up in parts, machinery, dies, jigs and tools for making them, if he would give his patrons prompt service. The Ford Company keeps on hand at all times every part of every model it has ever sold—and of those parts most likely to be called for, several hundred sets are always in stock. Many parts may never be called for—but they must be kept nevertheless. It is our boast that any Ford owner can get any part of any Ford car ever made at a moment's notice. . . .

General

Persons who have an imperfect understanding of the principles of the light weight, high powered gas engine, which alone is suitable for and capable of meeting the exacting service of motor car usage, frequently inquire why the maker does not "gear the car lower" and thus guard the driver against his own recklessness in the matter of speeding.

The aim of the designer is to make every part as light as possible so as to reduce the yearly tire bill—the most expensive item of motoring—and at the same time to equip the car with surplus power to meet the most severe road condition—sand, mud, soft clay, or hills—and to navigate such roads without having to change gears. If you have this surplus power available for the above conditions, there is no way to prevent you applying it under the most favorable conditions—and that gives you forty-five miles an hour. There is no law but common sense to prevent reckless driving any more than there is to prevent the use of fire arms or other necessary though dangerous agents by foolish persons.

It should be remembered, however, that driving a car at its limit of speed is most expensive. An athlete may run a hundred yards in eleven seconds, but the strain is so severe it will show up in a prematurely aged man a few years later. Just because it is made of metal instead of flesh and bone and muscle, is no reason why extreme effort is not injurious to a motor or a chassis. As a matter of fact, racing machines, though built most carefully and of the best

Henry Ford (right) and friend David Gray cruise by Ford's Piquette Avenue Plant in a 1905 Model N, a precursor to the Model T. © BETTMANN/CORBIS. REPRODUCED BY PERMISSION.

materials obtainable regardless of cost, are very short lived.

Every time you send your car to its limit you apply all the power the motor can develop and you strain every part severely. If you are willing to pay the price, it is your own affair, but one hour's driving at forty to forty-five miles an hour—and your car will do that if properly adjusted—will take more out of it than several months of reasonable driving. . . .

Odometer

Every car should be equipped with a small odometer so that an account of the exact mileage can be kept. This will prove a very profitable investment in more ways than one. First, you will be surprised at the mileage your car makes in a year, and you will be able to more accurately gauge your gasoline, oil and battery consumption and tire cost. We have known owners of Ford runabouts to claim they could not get 100 miles out of a set of 6 Columbia Dry Cells, and yet we have letters from other owners who have driven their cars over a year—some of the very earliest ones—and who claim they average 600 miles on a set.

Weak Batteries

When your car develops an apparent looseness everywhere—so noisy and rattley it seems as if every part of the machine is hopelessly worn, try recharging your storage battery or installing a fresh set of dry cells—you will find the trouble was due to irregular firing of the cylinders—lagging, so that the interval between impulses causes back lash in gears, excessive vibration and jerky running of the car. It's remarkable what a lot of ills a fresh battery will cure.

Tires

Tires not in use should be kept in some dark place where the atmosphere is moist, preferably in a cellar. When the car is laid up for the winter the wheels should be raised off the floor and the air pressure in the tires reduced sufficiently to just keep the tires distended. It should be borne in mind that tires deteriorate less under moderate usage than when stored away. It should also be remembered that tires are one of the chief items of expense in the maintenance of a car and that proper care will more than double the life of a set of them. Every owner should, therefore, study the peculiarities of rubber and learn how best to treat his tires to retain their resiliency. . . .

Common Sources of Trouble

There are a few common sources of trouble which may affect the operation of a gasoline-driven carriage and which we have mentioned in the order of their possible occurrence. Following these will be noted the remedy. In dealing with common sources of trouble the operator should remember that the difference between a comprehensive understanding of his automobile and the superficial knowledge possessed by many owners is the difference between success and failure. Familiarity with an automobile does not call for special mechanical ability; only a careful study of the directions and explanations contained in this book and a common-sense application of them to your car.

Imperfect Vibrator Action

The vibrator can be seen by opening the top of the spark coil box; and this trouble can generally be corrected by changing the position of the adjusting screw on the top of the coil or by cleaning the platinum points. The indications of this trouble are uncertainty in starting, skipping of explosions and irregular action when running.

Dirty Spark Plug

This trouble can be corrected by removing the spark plug with an ordinary monkey wrench. The plug can then be cleaned, using brush or emery cloth together with some clean gasoline. If the spark plug points are badly burned, they may be cleaned with very fine emery paper or cloth, or fine sandpaper. The points on the spark plug should be 1–32 of an inch apart.

Exhausted Batteries

The remedy is obvious.

Loose or Broken Wires

Troubles Nos. 4 and 5 must be discovered by inspection. In an engine well cared for and properly adjusted so as to turn easily, nearly all failures to start promptly and run regularly are electrical, easily found and quicky remedied. Do not waste time and patience in cranking an engine, for, if in proper condition, it will start as surely and run as regularly as a locomotive. One of the most annoying troubles to locate is a wire which is broken in the insulation. This can only be discovered by taking the cable in each hand between the forefingers and thumbs, and going over the wiring inch by inch.

A Weak Commutator Spring

This will give all the symptoms of No. 1. That is, uncertainty in starting, skipping of explosions, and irregular action when running. It is the least liable to occur and the easiest to discover. If this trouble is suspected remove the cover on the commutator, when it can be easily located.

Worn Commutator

The symptoms of this are similar to Nos. 1 and 5. It results from failure to keep a supply of lubricant in the commutator. The are formed by the break in the current as the roller leaves the bronze segments, gradually burns the metal away, causing uncertainty of conduct and hence weak or uneven explosions. Take off the commutator, put in a lathe and turn about 1–64 inch or less off from the inside—being careful to turn it evenly.

Water or Dirt in Gasoline

A globular trap is provided below the gasoline tank to catch sediment or water and prevent it getting into the carburetor. This will arrest a limited amount of water or sediment, but it should be drained frequently. This should never happen if the gasoline is strained through a chamois skin. The remedy is to disconnect gasoline pipe from the carburetor and drain thoroughly. It may be well to completely drain the tank and refill with fresh clear gasoline.

Frozen Water in Circulating Pipes and Pumps

This must never be permitted to occur as the operator should use an anti-freezing mixture in cold weather, or else drain the tanks and water system after the return from every run. No attempt should be made to run the engine when in a frozen condition as it is liable to break the pump and damage the engine beyond repair. The water cooling system must be thawed out by the use of warm water. . . .

Inspection and Care of Car

No matter how carefully locked with spring washers, or cotter pins, every nut and bolt in an automobile will work loose from time to time. This is due to the vibration and the various strains to which a car is subjected. Every nut and bolt should be inspected at least once every two weeks to see that all are tight. Bolts which hold engine and transmission in the frame, spring clips and steering connections especially should be frequently inspected. It would seem that if the nuts were thoroughly tightened when the car was built, and fixed with cotter pins through castellated nuts, they should not require further attention unless purposely disturbed. This is erroneous. You can turn on a new nut until you twist the head off the bolt, but after running a few days the bolts will seat themselves and you will find the nut will require at least a part of a turn. This will occur frequently during the season. Intake and exhaust pipe clamps should be tightened occasionally. These will work loose even though the nut cannot turn on the thread.

Inspection

Immediately after coming in from a drive, and not just before starting on a pleasure trip, is the time to inspect every part of a car for loose nuts, spring clips, injury to tires or other parts, and then is the time to correct them.

It is well to remember that the only other person in your city who is vitally interested in the satisfactory performance of your car is—the Ford representative. Agents for competing cars are as vitally interested in its non-performance, and so serious a factor has this car become we have known of many cases of malicious tampering with the motor, coil and other parts to "put the car out of business."

Wherever possible, therefore, your car should be kept in the garage of the Ford agent—better still, at your own home—and it should be taken to him for all repairs and adjustments you cannot make yourself. So notorious is the tendency of competing garage men to tamper with Ford cars, some of our agents positively refuse to make the slightest adjustment, gratis, if they know the car has passed through the hands of other agents.

When an agent tells you he "threw up the Ford agency," take it with a grain of salt. More likely his treatment of customers or his methods of dealing did not meet with our strict ideas and rules in these matters. Anyway, it will be well to have all future repairs made by the man who is still interested in the good performance of your car—the present Ford agent or branch manager. . . .

Repainting

Once a year every car should have a thorough inspection and overhauling, replacing worn bushings and other parts. This is a good time to enhance the outward appearance of your equipage by repainting. A properly painted car looks as good as new, and if properly used during the preceding months it actually is.

Avoid flashy colors and freakish combinations, especially if you wish to sell or exchange your car for a later model. Stick to standard colors as these will always command a higher price than any other. The same may be said with regard to changes of body, fenders or other details—the standard car just as turned out of the factory will always more readily appeal to the average taste and command a higher figure than any "improvement" you can make. Every Ford agent should be prepared to repaint your car for you and the cost should not exceed $35.00. Time is the chief essential—time to let each coat dry thoroughly. Lack of time—the necessity for hurrying the output to satisfy impatient customers was the reason Ford cars were not more highly finished this season—you can correct that during the winter. . . .

Warning

Owing to a large number of unscrupulous concerns who have already begun to prey upon Ford owners (tempted by the fact that there are now 10,000 possible purchasers for their wares) we feel it due to Ford owners to warn them against the wiles of gentlemen who, for their own good reasons, advocate the substitution of carburetors, magnetos, coils, commutators and other accessories, as well as tops, and even bodies, of their make in place of those that came with the car.

The habit of putting on extra seats is also quite prevalent in some sections, and while this is not so serious, inasmuch as the axles have ample strength to sustain the extra weight, it should not be done without changing the spring suspension; nor should extra holes be drilled in the frame for the application of other types of fenders or running boards without exercising extreme care as to where they are placed or what relation they bear to other holes. We have, so far, had no trouble with Model N. or S.

frames on this score, but with former models, frames have been so weakened by careless drilling of holes as to be unsafe.

The only safe rules to follow in this matter is to positively refuse to substitute or to add any accessory to the Ford car without first obtaining the advice and sanction of the factory. The slightest change from the standard construction cancels the manufacturer's guarantee.

We are constantly improving details of Ford cars and these improvements are substituted for the original construction only after the most careful and exhaustive tests to determine their superiority. In buying such you have the backing of the maker, as well as the benefit of his greater experience.

The man who can sell you a "better top" for less than the Ford Company charges, or who tells you that his device has been tried by the Ford Company but the price was prohibitive, may be set down as a plain everyday falsifier. You will consult your own best interests by ignoring his advice and his wares.

The enormous quantities we buy enables us to get anything we want at prices well within our reach; and you can rest assured that you cannot buy a top or any other article of automobile equipment of equal quality at retail, as cheaply as we can sell it to you after making a good profit, because of our quantity purchases.

We would like to feel that every Ford agent has the best interests of the Ford Company and his customers at heart, but we feel it necessary to advise Ford owners even against some of these. Tempted by the profits to be gained by selling carburetors, magnetos, coils and other accessories, we sometimes find agents so shortsighted as to recommend extras other than standard equipment of the car. In all such cases we would esteem it a favor if the customer will notify us before making the purchase.

Further Resources

BOOKS

Lacey, Robert. *Ford, the Men and the Machine.* Boston: Little, Brown, 1986.

McCalley, Bruce W. *Model T Ford: The Car That Changed the World.* Iola, Wisc.: Krause, 1994.

Rae, John B. *The American Automobile: A Brief History.* Chicago: University of Chicago Press, 1965.

WEBSITES

Frontenac Motor Company. "The Ford Model T: A Short History of Ford's Innovation." Available online at http://www.modelt.ca/background.html; website home page http://www.modelt.ca/ (accessed December 27, 2002).

"The History of Ford Motor Company." Available online at http://www.54youth.com.cn/gb/paper111/5/class011100001/hwz160863.htm; website home page: http://www.54youth.com.cn (accessed December 27, 2002).

Showroom of Automotive History. "The Model T." Available online at http://www.hfmgv.org/exhibits/showroom/1908/model.t.html; website home page http://www.hfmgv.org (accessed December 27, 2002).

"A Protective vs. a Competitive Tariff"

Essay

By: Home Market Club

Date: 1909?

Source: Home Market Club. "A Protective vs. a Competitive Tariff." 1909? Reproduced in *Pamphlets in American History,* T1315. Microform. Microfilming Corp. of America.

About the Author: The Home Market Club, organized in Boston in the 1880s, was a leading advocate for protective tariffs. It published a monthly magazine *The Protectionist,* from 1899 to 1942. The club frequently hosted prominent figures for major addresses, including President William McKinley (served 1897–1901) and President Warren G. Harding (served 1921–1923), who in 1920 coined his famous phrase calling for a "return to normalcy." This referred to a return to high protective tariffs and a reduction in taxes following the administration of Woodrow Wilson (served 1913–1921). ■

Introduction

The debate over tariffs is as old as the Republic itself. They were the chief source of revenue for the new federal government in 1789, but one segment of the country, best represented by Alexander Hamilton, believed that tariffs should be used not just to raise revenue, but also to protect American industry from foreign competition. Opponents felt that protective tariffs raised prices, and, in effect, taxed of one segment of the population for the benefit of another.

The tariff controversy became increasingly heated and sectional as the Northern states industrialized, while the South remained almost entirely agricultural. As industry grew, the demand for protection from foreign, chiefly British, competition increased. During the Civil War (1861–1865), Northern industrialists, heavily taxed to help pay for the war, successfully argued for a dramatic increase in tariff rates. These high rates became a basic tenet of Republican policy, and by the late–nineteenth century, American tariff rates had climbed to record highs. The resulting higher cost of consumer goods and the belief that the trusts were the primary beneficiaries of high tariffs led reformers to launch more aggressive efforts to reduce them. They were backed by farmers, organized labor, and opponents of trusts.

Supporters of a protective tariff were generally able to win enough support to beat back serious reform efforts. They argued that without protective tariffs, the economy would collapse, and workers would be thrown out of work or forced to accept wage cuts. Only with high tariffs would American industry remain competitive with the lower wages paid in other parts of the world.

Significance

Despite the growing public pressure for tariff reform, President Theodore Roosevelt (served 1901–1909) was largely indifferent. He was politically astute enough to know that his party generally remained committed to a strong protective tariff stance, but he kept his position to himself. He backed off tariff reform in exchange for support for the Hepburn Act, which gave the federal government power to set railroad rates.

Although Roosevelt managed to avoid a battle over tariff reform, his successor could not. As pressure increased for tariff reform, both Democrats and Republicans supported tariff revision during the election campaign of 1908. The Democrats expressly called for the gradual elimination of protective tariffs. The Republican platform was more ambiguous, but implied favoring lower tariffs. William Howard Taft (served 1909–1913), the winner, stayed out of the congressional battle over the tariff early in his term. An initial House version of a tariff reform bill contained modest reforms. In the Senate, reformers, led by midwestern progressives, were unable to overcome the conservative, protectionist bloc. The resulting Payne-Aldrich tariff was a bitter disappointment to advocates of lower tariffs.

The resulting split between the Progressive and conservative wings of the Republican Party over the tariff was the opening round in the temporary breakup of the Republican Party in 1912, ensuring the election of Democrat Woodrow Wilson. One of Wilson's first steps was to actively push for tariff revision. The Underwood tariff, while still protectionist, passed only a few months after Wilson's inauguration and significantly reduced overall rates. To offset the anticipated loss in revenue, the same bill included the country's first graduated income tax, legalized by the recent passage of the Sixteenth Amendment in March 1913.

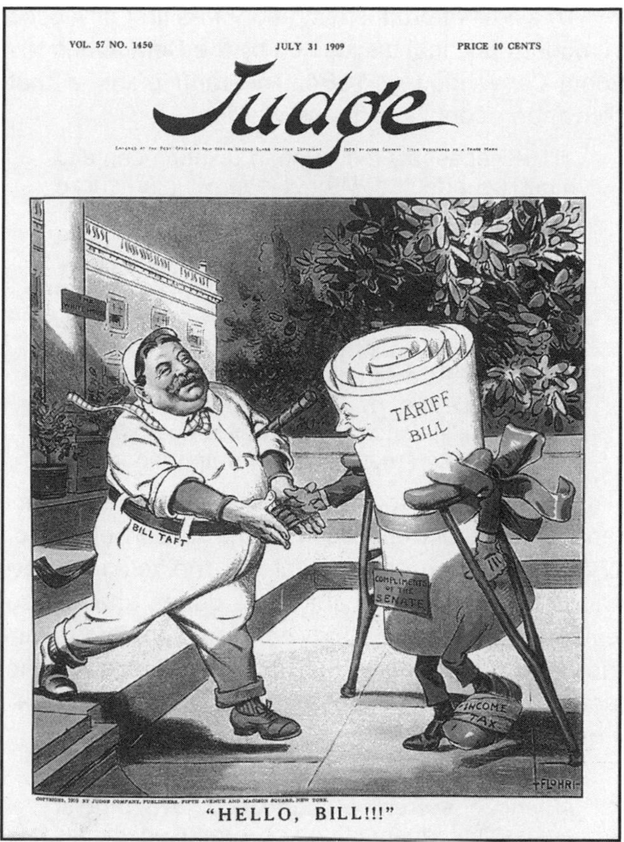

Cover of *Judge* magazine featuring a cartoon of President Taft coming from the White House to greet a crippled Payne-Aldrich tariff bill, 1909. Initially intended to reform tariff rates downwards, businessmen and conservative politicians managed to weaken its reforms and in fact raise many tariffs, angering reformers. THE LIBRARY OF CONGRESS.

Primary Source

"A Protective vs. A Competitive Tariff"

SYNOPSIS: The debate over the tariff often centered around the proposition that tariffs should be lowered to a point that offset the difference between the labor rates in the United States and those in other countries. In other words, tariffs should only ensure that American goods would be competitive with foreign goods in the home market despite the higher wages of American workers. The following Home Market Club essay refutes this view. It argues unabashedly for a protective tariff high enough to ensure dominance of American products in the domestic market.

Amount of Imports Not Difference in Cost of Protection, the True Measure of Tariff Duties

The committee appointed by the Home Market Club to urge the National Republican Convention to adopt a plank in favor of such protection to American industries as will promote the widest possible employment of American labor at the high standard of American wages, strongly protests against the incorporation in the tariff plank of any such standard of tariff duties as "the difference in cost of production at home and abroad."

This cost of production theory was first advanced in modern political discussion by the Democratic National Convention of 1884. The tariff plank of that convention contained these words:

> The necessary reduction in taxation can and must be effected without depriving American labor of the ability to compete successfully with foreign labor and without imposing lower rates of duty than will be ample to cover any increased cost of production which may exist in consequence of the higher rate of wages prevailing in this country.The Democratic Convention of 1888 declared that the interests of labor will be benefited by "a revision of our tax laws, with due allowance for the difference between the wages of American and foreign labor."

In opposition to the tariff theory of the Democratic party, the Republican National Convention of 1884 demanded "that in raising the requisite revenues for the Government, such duties shall be so levied as to afford security to our diversified industries and protection to the rights and wages of the laborers"; and in 1888 met the Democratic challenge by declaring:

> We are uncompromisingly in favor of the American system of protection. We protest against its destruction, as proposed by the President (Cleveland) and his party. They serve the interest of Europe: we will support the interests of America. The protective system must be maintained. Its abandonment has always been followed by disaster to all interests except those of the usurer and the sheriff.

Four year later, however, the Republican National Convention of 1892, voiced practically the same demand as the Democratic Conventions of '84 and '88 when it said that "on all imports coming into competition with the products of American labor there should be levied duties equal to the difference between wages abroad and at home."

But in 1896 the Republican Convention renewed and emphasized "our allegiance to the policy of protection as the bulwark of American industrial independence and the foundation of American development and prosperity. This true American policy taxes foreign products and encourages home industry; it puts the burden of revenue on foreign goods; it secures the American market for the American producer; it upholds the American standard of wages."

In 1900 the Republican National Convention renewed "our faith in the policy of protection in American labor. In that policy our industries have been established, diversified and maintained. By protecting the home market competition has been stimulated and production cheapened."

In 1904 the Republican National Convention declared:

> Protection, which guards and develops our industries, is a cardinal policy of the Republican Party. The measure of protection should always at least equal the difference in the cost of production at home and abroad. We insist upon the maintenance of the principles of protection, and therefore, rates of duty should be readjusted only when conditions have so changed that the public interest demands their alteration.

In 1908 the Republican party declared unequivocally for revision of the tariff and declared that "in all tariff legislation the true principle of protection is best maintained by the imposition of such duties as will equal the difference between the cost of production at home and abroad, together with a reasonable profit to American industries."

This brief review of the political history of "the cost of production" theory shows that it was first advocated by the Democrats and when abandoned by them was taken up with varying qualifications by the Republicans.

That the theory has proven impracticable is demonstrated by recent experience.

President Taft in a speech at Winona said referring to the Ways and Means Committee:

> They found that the determination of the question what was the actual cost of production and whether an industry in this country could live under a certain rate and withstand threatened competition from abroad was most difficult.

To supplement their investigations the Tariff Board was appointed and this Board found great difficulty in obtaining full and reliable information as to the cost of production in foreign mills, difficulties which could not be overcome in the time which they had at their disposal or by the expenditure of large sums of money.

The lack of full and reliable data in regard to foreign costs of production has been pointed out repeatedly by the critics of the Tariff Board's reports. Hon William C. Redfield, in a speech in the House of Representatives June 4, 1912 said, "Many examples could be given from the report (of the Tariff Board) to show that even within its meager scope the fact comes clearly out that any attempt to cover by a fixed tariff the difference in labor costs is absurd."

President Taft said in his speech at Winona, "I have never known a subject that will evoke so much contradictory evidence as the question of tariff rates and the question of cost of production at home and abroad."

As a reliable standard for adjusting tariff rates, the difference in the cost of production at home and abroad has been demonstrated to be unsound and impracticable. It cannot be obtained with efficient accuracy; it is varying and changeable; it is not margin enough, even could it be obtained with precision, to prevent this country from becoming the dumping ground of foreign manufacturers, and it grossly discriminates against our manufacturers by publishing to the world details of our manufacturing processes which are much more complete than any information which can be obtained in regard to foreign countries.

The cost of production theory is inconsistent with the American policy of protection and it should be abandoned now for good and all.

To consistent protectionists who believe that the American market belongs to the American producers, the amount of competition not the cost of production is the true measure of tariff duties. The constitutional justification of protection is found in the clause which empowers Congress "To regulate commerce with other nations" and "provide for the general welfare of the United States." If the welfare of the country is promoted by diversified industries and a prosperous industrious people, then commerce with foreign nations should be so regulated as to establish and maintain those manufacturing and agricultural industries which are indispensable to our existence as an independent nation.

To base our tariff duties on the difference in the cost of production at home and abroad, even if it were possible to establish a definite standard of foreign costs where they vary so in different countries, and even in the same country, would give us an equalizing not a protective tariff. Such a policy were it possible to enforce it, would place American goods on an equality with foreign goods, and foreign goods on an equality with American made goods. Protection gives to American made goods an advantage in the American market. In one case American goods are subjected to foreign competition, in the other they are protected from it. One policy leads to a competitive tariff the other to a protective tariff. That the cost of production theory as a basis for tariff rates results in a competitive not a protective tariff was claimed in a speech in the House of Representatives on April 9, 1900, by Champ Clark, who in speaking in favor of an amendment to the Payne-Aldrich Bill said:

> Amend by reducing and adjusting rates in all schedules so that the duties shall not exceed the difference in the cost of labor in America and abroad and shall be upon a basis to produce increased revenue for the Government, and competitive prices for the American consumer.It was a protective and not a competitive tariff upon which the industries of the United States have expanded until we are the foremost agricultural and manufacturing nation of the world.

It is not necessary to subject American industries to an inrush of foreign goods to secure that degree of competition which will prevent extortionate prices and the "plundering of the consumer." The business of the United States is conducted under the keenest competition and the products of our mills and factories are sold on a low margin of profit. This condition of mammoth production and low factory prices was the aim and object of the advocates of protection from the days of Alexander Hamilton to the present time and is a complete justification of the protective policy. The policy which has produced such beneficial results should be maintained and the party which has won its most notable victories as an advocate of protection should not fail now when the enemies of the "American system" are fighting as they have not fought for years to overthrow it.

The committee of the Home Market Club firmly believes that protection is essential to the welfare and prosperity of the country, and earnestly requests you to exert your influence to have the Republican National Conference adopt a strong plank in favor of ample protection for American industries.

Respectfully,
Wm. B. H. Dawes
Franklin W Hobbs
Richard S. Russell
R. P. Snelling
Thomas O. Marvin, Secy.
Executive Committee Home Market Club.

Further Resources

BOOKS

Kaplan, Edward S. *Prelude to Trade Wars: American Tariff Policy, 1890–1922.* Westport, Conn.: Greenwood, 1994.

Taussig, F. W. *The Tariff History of the United States.* New York: Capricorn, 1964.

WEBSITES

"The Payne-Aldrich Tariff." Available online at http://1912.history.ohio-state.edu/Tariff/PayneAldrich1.htm; website home page http://1912.history.ohio-state.edu (accessed December 27, 2002).

"Tariff Site Map." Available online at http://1912.history.ohio-state.edu/Tariff/tariff_site_map.htm; website home page http://1912.history.ohio-state.edu (accessed December 27, 2002). This website consists of links to numerous articles about tariff issues.

Shop Management

Handbook

By: Frederick Winslow Taylor

Date: 1911

Source: Taylor, Frederick Winslow. *Shop Management.* New York: Harper & Brothers, 1911, 49–56.

About the Author: Frederick Winslow Taylor (1856–1915), a Philadelphia-born engineer and inventor, is best known for helping modernize industrial management techniques. Taylor was obsessively organized and constantly looked for ways to bring order and discipline to his affairs. As a young engineer, he began a series of studies designed to improve operations in his own plants. By the early 1890s, he had started working as an independent consultant showing manufacturing companies how to improve operations. ■

Introduction

The development of technology, increased productive capacity, and sophisticated business organizations after the Civil War (1861–1865) were not accompanied by a comparable improvement in the day-to-day operations of manufacturing plants, which stumbled along in much the same way as they had in the premechanized world of preceding generations. As the nineteenth century came to a close, some industrialists, like Frederick Taylor, came to realize that the old, inefficient ways needed to change. Mechanization had replaced handicraft, and management in these new conditions needed to adapt.

Taylor felt driven to thoroughly understand the most minute details of how a job was performed. Operating on the belief that there was "one best way" to perform a given task, Taylor analyzed the minutia of each job, broke each task into simple and repetitive steps, redesigned it to ensure the "best way" was being followed, and offered financial incentives to workers to perform their assigned duties in accordance with the design process. The results were often significant increases in productivity. This justified wage increases for the participating worker and was, in part, why Taylor saw his system as a broad benefit to society.

Steel workers wait for their pay at the Homestead steel works in Pennsylvania, 1907. THE LIBRARY OF CONGRESS.

Significance

One of Taylor's best known projects was at Bethlehem Steel, where he worked as a consultant from 1898 to 1901. There he applied his famous time-and-motion system of analysis and an adjusted piece-rate worker compensation scheme to dramatically improve productivity in the department that handled raw materials being brought into the plant.

Under Taylor's direction, the process was broken into narrow and specialized tasks, simplifying the jobs and making them easier to complete and to teach to new workers. Workers were compelled to follow strict guidelines as to how each task should be performed. They were required to use, for example, shovels of various sizes depending on the item being shoveled. They were also instructed on how to use the shovel most efficiently. Those who did not comply were removed. Those who did and who achieved the desired level of productivity saw their wages increase by sixty percent. The improvement was dramatic. Bethlehem's material-handling costs were cut in half, and Taylor's system attracted more and more converts. Taylor, though, was a difficult man to get along with, and he made many enemies within the Bethlehem management team. Despite the considerable efficiencies Taylor and his team implemented, he was dismissed in 1901.

One of the benefits of Taylor's approach was that it reduced the influence of foremen. Shop floor operations had traditionally been under the control of the foreman and skilled craftsman. As enterprises grew, these men became virtually autonomous. This affected upper management's ability to change or improve operations and was a source of considerable frustration to management. Taylor's methods created a system that allowed better top-down control of operations. Teams of unskilled workers could be rapidly trained to perform complex jobs. While individual workers may have lacked the skill to build, for example, an automobile engine, each could be assigned one step in the process, master it quickly, and, in combination with other workers, each performing single tasks, complete complex projects faster than one highly skilled worker.

Despite the obvious advantages of Taylor's ideas, they met stiff resistance. Simple inertia prevented some business leaders from adopting Taylor's ideas. Others saw little point in paying workers more money. Workers, and particularly such union leaders as Samuel Gompers, feared the dehumanizing potential of Taylor's methods. Required to perform more and more specific tasks, workers, Gompers feared, would become mere extensions of machines.

Primary Source

Shop Management [excerpt]

SYNOPSIS: Taylor describes his famous study of material handlers begun in 1899 at the Bethlehem Steel Works in Pennsylvania. He used this as a classic demonstration of the effectiveness of his methods.

Up to the spring of the year 1899, all of the materials in the yard of the Bethlehem Steel Company had been handled by gangs of men working by the day, and under the foremanship of men who had themselves formerly worked at similar work as laborers. Their management was about as good as the average of similar work, although it was bad; all of the men being paid the ruling wages of laborers in this section of the country, namely, $1.15 per day, the only means of encouraging or disciplining them being either talking to them or discharging them; occasionally, however, a man was selected from among these men and given a better class of work with slightly higher wages in some of the companies' shops, and this had the effect of slightly stimulating them. From four to six hundred men were employed on this class of work throughout the year.

The work of these men consisted mainly of unloading from railway cars and shoveling on to piles, and from these piles again loading as required, the raw materials used in running three blast furnaces and seven large open-hearth furnaces, such as ore of various kinds, varying from fine, gravelly ore to that which comes in large lumps, coke, limestone, special pig, sand, etc., unloading hard and soft coal for boilers gas-producers, etc., and also for storage and again loading the stored coal as required for use, loading the pig-iron produced at the furnaces for shipment, for storage, and for local use, and handling billets, etc., produced by the rolling mills. The work covered a large variety as laboring work goes, and it was not usual to keep a man continuously at the same class of work.

Before undertaking the management of these men, the writer was informed that they were steady workers, but slow and phlegmatic, and that nothing would induce them to work fast.

The first step was to place an intelligent, college-educated man in charge of progress in this line. This man had not before handled this class of labor, although he understood managing workmen. He was not familiar with the methods pursued by the writer, but was soon taught the art of determining how much work a first-class man can do in a day. This was done by timing with a stop watch a first-class man while he was working fast. The best way to do this, in fact almost the only way in which the timing can be done with certainty, is to divide the man's work into its elements and time each element separately. For example, in the case of a man loading pig-iron on to a car, the elements should be: (a) picking up the pig from the ground or pile (time in hundredths of a minute); (b) walking with it on a level (time per foot walked); (c) walking with it up an incline to car (time per foot walked); (d) throwing the pig down (time in hundredths of a minute), or laying it on a pile (time in hundredths of a minute); (e) walking back empty to get a load (time per foot walked).

In case of important elements which were to enter into a number of rates, a large number of observations were taken when practicable on different first-class men, and at different times, and they were averaged.

The most difficult elements to time and decide upon in this, as in most cases, are the percentage of the day required for rest, and the time to allow for accidental or unavoidable delays.

In the case of the yard labor at Bethlehem, each class of work was studied as above, each element being timed separately, and, in addition, a record was kept in many cases of the total amount of work done by the man in a day. The record of the gross work of the man (who is being timed) is, in most cases, not necessary after the observer is skilled in his work. As the Bethlehem time observer was new to this work, the gross time was useful in checking his detailed observations and so gradually educating him and giving him confidence in the new methods.

The writer had so many other duties that his personal help was confined to teaching the proper methods and approving the details of the various changes which were in all cases outlined in written reports before being carried out.

As soon as a careful study had been made of the time elements entering into one class of work, a single first-class workman was picked out and started on ordinary piece work on this job. His task required him to do between *three and one-half* and *four times* as much work in a day as had been done in the past on an average.

Between twelve and thirteen tons of pig-iron per man had been carried from a pile on the ground, up an inclined plank, and loaded on to a gondola car by the average pig-iron handler while working by the day. The men in doing this work had worked in gangs of from five to twenty men.

The man selected from one of these gangs to make the first start under the writer's system was called upon to load on piece work from forty-five to forty-eight tons (2,240 lbs. each) per day.

He regarded this task as an entirely fair one, and earned on an average, from the start, $1.85 per day, which was 60 per cent. more than he had been paid by the day. This man happened to be considerably lighter than the average good workman at this class of work. He weighed about 130 pounds. He proved, however, to be especially well suited to this job, and was kept at it steadily throughout the time that the writer was in Bethlehem, and some years later was still at the same work.

Being the first piece work started in the works, it excited considerable opposition, both on the part of the workmen and of several of the leading men in the town, their opposition being based mainly on the old fallacy that if piece work proved successful a great many men would be thrown out of work, and that thereby not only the workmen but the whole town would suffer.

One after another of the new men who were started singly on this job were either persuaded or intimidated into giving it up. In many cases they were given other work by those interested in preventing piece work, at wages higher than the ruling wages. In the meantime, however, the first man who started on the work earned steadily $1.85 per day, and this object lesson gradually wore out the concerted opposition, which ceased rather suddenly after about two months. From this time on there was no difficulty in getting plenty of good men who were anxious to start on piece work, and the difficulty lay in making with sufficient rapidity the accurate time study of the elementary operations or "unit times" which forms the foundation of this kind of piece work.

Throughout the introduction of piece work, when after a thorough time study a new section of the work was started, one man only was put on each new job, and not more than one man was allowed to work at it until he had demonstrated that the task set was a fair one by earning an average of $1.85 per day. After a few sections of the work had been started in this way, the complaint on the part of the better workmen was that they were not allowed to go on to piece work fast enough.

It required about two years to transfer practically all of the yard labor from day to piece work. And the larger part of the transfer was made during the last six months of this time.

As stated above, the greater part of the time was taken up in studying "unit times," and this time study was greatly delayed by having successively the two leading men who had been trained to the work leave because they were offered much larger salaries elsewhere. The study of "unit times" for the yard labor took practically the time of two trained men for two years. Throughout this time the day and piece workers were under entirely separate and distinct management. The original foremen continued to manage the day work, and day and piece workers were never allowed to work together. Gradually the day work gang was diminished and the piece workers were increased as one section of work after another was transformed from the former to the latter.

Two elements which were important to the success of this work should be noted:

First, on the morning following each day's work, each workman was given a slip of paper informing him in detail just how much work he had done the day before, and the amount he had earned. This enabled him to measure his performance against his earnings while the details were fresh in his mind. Without this there would have been great dissatisfaction among those who failed to climb up to the task asked of them, and many would have gradually fallen off in their performance.

Second, whenever it was practicable, each man's work was measured by itself. Only when absolutely necessary was the work of two men measured up together and the price divided between them, and then care was taken to select two men of as nearly as possible the same capacity. Only on few occasions, and then upon special permission, signed by the writer, were more than two men allowed to work on gang work, dividing their earnings between them. Gang work almost invariably results in a falling off in earnings and consequent dissatisfaction.

An interesting illustration of the desirability of individual piece work instead of gang work came to our attention at Bethlehem. Several of the best piece workers among the Bethlehem yard laborers were informed by their friends that a much higher price per ton was paid for shoveling ore in another works than the rate given at Bethlehem. After talking the matter over with the writer he advised them to go to the other works, which they accordingly did. In about a month they were all back at work in Bethlehem again, having found that at the other works they were obliged to work with a gang of men instead of on individual piece work, and that the rest of the gang worked so slowly that in spite of the high price paid per ton they earned much less than at Bethlehem.

[The table] gives a summary of the work done by the piece-work laborers in handling raw materials, such as ores, anthracite and bituminous coal, coke, pig-iron, sand, limestone, cinder, scale, ashes, etc., in the works of the Bethlehem Steel Company, during the year ending April 30, 1900. This work consisted mainly in loading and unloading cars on arrival or departure from the works, and for local transportation, and was done entirely by hand, *i.e.*, without the use of cranes or other machinery.

The greater part of the credit for making the accurate time study and actually managing the men on this work should be given to Mr. A. B. Wadleigh, the writer's assistant in this section at that time.

When the writer left the steel works, the Bethlehem piece workers were the finest body of picked laborers that he has ever seen together. They were practically all first-class men, because in each case the task which they were called upon to perform was such that only a first-class man could do it. The tasks were all purposely made so severe that not more than one out of five laborers (perhaps even a smaller percentage than this) could keep up.

It was clearly understood by each newcomer as he went to work that unless he was able to average at least $1.85 per day he would have to make way for another man who could do so. As a result, first-class men from all over that part of the country, who were in most cases earning from $1.05 to $1.15 per day, were anxious to try their hands at earning $1.85 per day. If they succeeded they were naturally contented, and if they failed they left, sorry that they were unable to maintain the proper pace, but with no hard feelings either toward the system or the management. Throughout the time that the writer was there, labor was as scarce and as difficult to get as it ever has been in the history of this country, and yet there was always a surplus of first-class men ready to leave other jobs and try their hand at Bethlehem piece work.

Perhaps the most notable difference between these men and ordinary piece workers lay in their changed mental attitude toward their employers and their work, and in the total absence of soldiering on their part. The ordinary piece worker would have spent a considerable part of his time in deciding just how much his employer would allow him to earn without cutting prices and in then trying to come as close as possible to this figure, while carefully guarding each job so as to keep the management from finding out how fast it really could be done. These men,

Relative Cost of Yard Labor Under Task Piece Work and Old Style Day Work

	Piece Work	Day Work
Number of tons (2,240 lbs. per ton) handled on piece work during the year ending April 30, 1901	924,040 13/100	
Total cost of handling 924,040 13/100 tons including the piece work wages paid the men, and in addition all incidental day labor used	$30,797.78	
Former cost of handling the same number of tons of similar materials on day work		$67,215.47
Net saving in handling 924,04013/100 tons of materials, effected in one year through substituting piece work for day work	$36,417.69	
Average cost for handling a ton (2,240 lbs.) on piece and day work	$0.033	$0.072
Average earnings per day, per man	[1]$1.88	$1.15
Average number of tons handled per day per man	[2]57	16

[1]It was our intention to fix piece work rates which should enable first-class workmen to average about 60 percent more than they had been earning on day work, namely $1.85 per day. A year's average shows them to have earned $1.88 per day, or three cents per man per day more than we expected—an error of 1 6/10 percent.
[2]The piece workers handled on an average 3 56/100 times as many tons per day as the day workers.

SOURCE: Table 1 from Taylor, Frederick Winslow. *Shop Management.* New York: Harper & Brothers, 1911 however, were faced with a new but very simple and straightforward proposition, namely, am I a first-class laborer or not? Each man felt that if he belonged in the first class all he had to do was to work at his best and he would be paid sixty per cent. more than he had been paid in the past. Each piece work price was accepted by the men without question. They never bargained over nor complained about rates, and there was no occasion to do so, since they were all equally fair, and called for almost exactly the same amount of work and fatigue per dollar of wages.

Further Resources

BOOKS

Kanigel, Robert. *The One Best Way: Frederick Winslow Taylor and the Enigma of Efficiency.* New York: Viking, 1997.

WEBSITES

Accel-Team.com. "Frederick Winslow Taylor." Available online at http://www.accel-team.com/scientific/scientific_02.html; website home page http://www.accel-team.com/ (accessed December 27, 2002).

Papesh, Mary Ellen. "Frederick Winslow Taylor." Available online at http://www.stfrancis.edu/ba/ghkickul/stuwebs/bbios/biograph/fwtaylor.htm; website home page http://www.stfrancis.edu (accessed December 27, 2002).

Taylor, Frederick Winslow. *The Principles of Scientific Management,* 1911. Available online at http://melbecon.unimelb.edu.au/het/taylor/sciman.htm; website home page http://melbecon.unimelb.edu.au (accessed December 27, 2002).

Thirteenth Census of the United States Taken in the Year 1910, Volume VIII, Manufactures: 1909

Tables

By: U.S. Bureau of the Census

Date: 1913

Source: United States Bureau of the Census. *Thirteenth Census of the United States Taken in the Year 1910. Volume VIII, Manufactures: 1909.* Washington, D.C.: Government Printing Office, 1913, Tables 4 and 6, pp. 50, 63–65.

About the Census Bureau: The Constitution mandates the taking of a census every ten years as a means of determining representation in the House of Representatives and taxation. The first census in 1790 simply counted the population. The census of 1850 marked a dramatic expansion in the breadth of the data collected to include economic and other relevant social topics. Thereafter, the census steadily expanded its scope, becoming an increasingly valuable tool for contemporaries and historians in understanding American life. ■

Men work in the tool room of the National Cash Register Company in Dayton, Ohio, 1904. THE LIBRARY OF CONGRESS.

Introduction

The first decade of the twentieth century was a period of tremendous economic growth. By 1890, the United States had surpassed Great Britain and Germany to become the world's leading industrial nation. Although economic progress had been slowed by a severe and prolonged depression in the 1890s, the country resumed its remarkable expansion following the Spanish-American War (1898). Technological development, business consolidation, cheap labor, a sophisticated transportation network, and the availability of abundant natural resources all helped create an economic boom that lasted, with only a brief interlude in 1907, from the late 1890s to 1920.

The data in the tables from the 1909 Census of Manufactures provides an interesting perspective on that industrial expansion. Table 4 indicates an exceptional eighty percent growth in the value of manufactured products between 1899 and 1909. This growth rate is, in itself, significant in understanding the era. It was a prosperous time for most segments of the economy and, as a result, a period of relative confidence. There were significant national problems, but most Americans had faith in the country's ability to address those problems.

In addition to the big picture, however, a review of the industry-by-industry growth rates reveals, or at least hints at, the changes occurring in society. For example, the figures for "Automobile, including bodies and parts" and "Carriages and wagons" make evident that the change that was to dramatically alter life in America was already taking place. Another trend is indicated in the difference between the growth of "Flour-mill and gristmill products" and that of "Bread and other bakery products." The increasing importance of prepared foods can also be seen in the growth rates shown for "Butter, cheese and

Increase in Wage Earners, Value of Products and Value Added by Manufacture for Leading Industries: 1899 and 1909

Note—The figures for the following industries given in this table do not agree with those in other tables, because a combination of industries and other adjustments were necessary in order to make the totals for the two censuses more exactly comparable:

Chemicals.—The totals for 1909 include the figures for "sulphuric, nitric, and mixed acids" and "wood distillation, not including turpentine and rosin," which are shown as separate industries in other tables. These industries were included with "chemicals" in 1899.

Coffee and spice, roasting and grinding.—The totals for 1909 include the figures for "peanuts, grading, roasting, cleaning, and shelling," which is shown as a separate industry in other tables. This industry was included with "coffee and spice, roasting and grinding," in 1899.

Foundry and machine-shop products.—The totals for 1909 include the figures for "stoves and furnaces, including gas and oil stoves" and "locomotives, not made by railroad companies," which are shown as separate industries in other tables. These industries were included with "foundary and machine-shop products" in 1899.

Marble and stone work.—The totals for 1909 include the figures for "artificial stone," which is shown as a separate industry in other tables. This industry was included with "marble and stone work" in 1899.

Soap.—The totals for 1909 include the figures for "candles," which is shown as a separate industry in other tables. This industry was included with "soap" in 1899.

Sugar and molasses, not including beet sugar.—The totals for 1909 include the figures for "sugar, refining, not including beet sugar" and "sugar and molasses," which are shown as separate industries in most of the other tables. These industries were not reported separately in 1899.

Industry	Wage Earmers (Average Number)				Value of Products				Value Added by Manufacture			
			Increase[1]				Increase[1]				Increase[1]	
	1909	1899	Number	Per cent	1909	1899	Amount	Per cent	1909	1899	Amount	Per cent
All industries	6,615,046	4,712,763	1,902,283	40.4	$20,672,051,870	$11,406,926,701	$9,265,125,169	81.2	$8,529,260,992	$4,831,075,210	$3,698,185,782	76.5
Agricultural implements	50,551	46,582	3,969	8.5	146.329,268	101,207,428	45,121,840	44.6	86.022,749	57,262,800	28,759,949	50.2
Automobiles, including bodies and parts	75,721	2,241	73,480	3,278.9	249,202,075	4,748,011	244,454,064	5,148.6	117,556,339	2,943,724	114,612,615	3,893.1
Boots and shoes, including cut stock and findings	198,297	151,231	47,066	31.1	512,797,642	290,047.087	222,750,555	76.8	180,059,429	98,591,560	81,467,969	82.6
Brass and bronze products	40,618	27,166	13,452	49.5	149,989,058	88,653,987	61,335,071	69.2	50,760,646	27,464,663	23,295,983	84.8
Bread and other bakery products	100,216	60,192	40,024	66.5	396,864,844	175,368,682	221,496,162	126.3	158,831,181	80,316,730	78,514,451	97.8
Butter, cheese, and condensed milk	18,431	12,799	5,632	44.0	274,557,718	130,783,349	143,774,369	109.9	39,011,654	21,942,149	17,069,505	77.8
Canning and preserving	59,968	57,012	2,956	5.2	157,101,201	99,335,464	57,765,737	58.2	55,278,142	35,667,896	19,610,246	55.0
Carriages and wagons and materials	69,928	73,812	−3,884	−5.3	159,892,547	138,261,763	21,630,784	15.6	77,941,259	71,489,844	6,451,415	9.0
Cars and general shop construction and repairs by steam-railroad companies	282,174	173,595	108,579	62.5	405,600,727	218,113,658	187,487,069	86.0	206,187,315	108,641,305	97,546,010	89.8
Cars, steam-railroad, not including operations of railroad companies	43,086	33,453	9,633	28.8	123,729,627	90,510,180	33,219,447	36.7	44,976,766	28,767,433	16,209,333	56.3
Chemicals	28,687	19,020	9,667	50 8	137,309,942	62,637,008	74,672,834	119.2	61,926,727	28,091,146	33,835,581	120.4
Clothing, men's, including shirts	239,696	157,549	82,147	52.1	568,076,635	323,838,887	244,237,748	75.4	270,561,189	155,669,525	114,891,664	73.8
Clothing, women's	153,743	83,739	70,004	83.6	384,751,649	159,339,539	225,412,110	141.5	175,963,423	74,634,947	101,328,476	135.8
[continued]												

Primary Source

SYNOPSIS: Table 4 from the 1910 U.S. Census describes the state of American manufacturing in 1909 and compares it to 1899. It shows that almost all industries grew during the decade, many by very large percentages. The rise in value of products is greater than the increase in the number of employees, demonstrating that industry was becoming more efficient. The automobile industry, tiny in 1899, enjoyed particularly noteworthy growth.

Increase in Wage Earners, Value of Products and Value Added by Manufacture for Leading Industries: 1899 and 1909 [CONTINUED]

Industry	Wage Earners (Average Number)				Value of Products				Value Added by Manufacture			
			Increase[1]				Increase[1]				Increase[1]	
	1909	1899	Number	Per cent	1909	1899	Amount	Per cent	1909	1899	Amount	Per cent
Coffee and spice, roasting and grinding	9,439	6,387	3,052	47.8	120,269,338	69,527,108	50,742,230	73.0	28,452,176	14,414,905	14,037,271	97.4
Confectionery	44,638	26,866	17.772	66.1	134,795,913	60,643,946	74,151,967	122.3	53,645,140	25,289,738	28,355,402	112.1
Copper, tin, and sheet-iron products[2]	73,615	38,317	35,298	92.1	199,824,218	78,359,069	121,465,149	155.0	87,241,945	35,757,319	51,484,626	144.0
Cotton goods, including cotton small wares	378,880	302,861	76,019	25.1	628,391,813	339,200,320	289,191,493	85.3	257,382,343	162,648,793	94,733,550	58.2
Electrical machinery, apparatus, and supplies	87,256	42,013	45,243	107.7	221,308,563	92,434,435	128,874,128	139.4	112,742,159	42,976,163	69,765,996	162.3
Fertilizers	18,310	11,581	6,729	58.1	103,960,213	44,657,385	59,302,828	132.8	34,438,293	15,698,912	18,739,381	119.4
Flour-mill and gristmill products	39,453	32,226	7,227	22.4	883,594,405	501,396,304	382,188,101	76.2	116,007,926	73,279,547	42,728,379	58.3
Food preparations[3]	14,968	8,214	6,754	82.2	125,331,181	39,836,882	85,494,299	214.6	41,389,032	15,060,257	26,328,775	174.8
Foundry and machine-shop products	583,050	426,985	156,065	36.6	1,338,910,773	798,454,071	540,456,702	67.7	754,501,390	435,418,012	319,083,378	73.3
Furniture and refrigerators	128,452	90,591	37,861	41.8	239,886,506	130,633,872	109,252,634	83.6	131,111,664	73,227,723	57,883,941	79.0
Gas, illuminating and heating	37,215	22,459	14,756	65.7	166,814,371	75,716,693	91,097,678	120.3	114,386,527	55,111,337	59,275,190	107.6
Hosiery and knit goods	129,275	83,691	45,584	54.5	200,143,527	95,833,692	104,309,835	108.8	89,902,474	44,638,362	45,264,112	101.4
Iron and steel, blast furnaces	38,429	39,241	−812	−2.1	391,429,283	206,756,557	184,672,726	89.3	70,791,394	75,252,902	−4,461,508	−5.9
Iron and steel, steel works and rolling mills	240,076	183,249	56,827	31.0	985,722,534	597,211,716	388,510,818	65.1	328,221,678	206,316,439	121,905,239	59.1
Leather goods	34,907	29,274	5,633	19.2	104,719,008	60,414,008	44,305,000	73.3	44,692,240	27,219,432	17,472,808	64.2
Leather, tanned, curried, and finished	62,202	52,109	10,093	19.4	327,874,187	204,038,127	123,836,060	60.7	79,595,254	49,038,123	30,557,131	62.3
Liquors, distilled	6,430	3,720	2,710	72.8	204,699,412	96,793,681	107,905,731	111.5	168,722,519	81,648,318	87,074,201	106.6
Liquors, malt	54,579	39,459	15,120	38.3	374,730,096	236,914,914	137,815,182	58.2	278,134,460	185,316,667	92,817,793	50.1
Lumber and timber products	695,019	508,766	186,253	36.6	1,156,128,747	760,992,360	395,136,387	51.9	648,011,168	396,028,519	251,982,649	63.6
Marble and stone work	75,560	41,686	33,874	81.3	131,688,655	63,667,234	68,021,421	106.8	87,248,579	42,121,424	45,127,155	107.1
Oil, cottonseed, and cake	17,071	11,007	6,064	55.1	147,867,894	58,726,632	89,141,262	151.8	28,034,419	13,560,809	14,473,610	106.7
Paint and varnish	14,240	9,697	4.543	46.8	124,889,422	69,562,235	55,327,187	79.5	45,873,867	24,823,718	21,050,149	84.8
Paper and wood pulp	75,978	49,646	26,332	53.0	267,656,964	127,326,162	140,330,802	110.2	102,214,623	56,795,926	45,418,697	80.0

[continued]

Primary Source

Part two of the 1910 U.S. Census table on American manufacturers. Slaughtering and meat packing was the single largest U.S. industry by value in 1909.

Increase in Wage Earners, Value of Products and Value Added by Manufacture for Leading Industries: 1899 and 1909 [CONTINUED]

Industry	Wage Earners (AverageNumber)				Value of Products				Value Added by Manufacture			
			Increase[1]				Increase[1]				Increase[1]	
	1909	1899	Number	Per cent	1909	1899	Amount	Per cent	1909	1899	Amount	Per cent
Patent medicines and and druggists' preparations compounds	22,895	19,028	3,867	20.3	141,941,602	88,790,774	53,150,828	59.9	91,565,937	56,840,884	34,725,053	61.1
Petroleum, refining	13,929	12,199	1,730	14.2	236,997,659	123,929,384	113,068,275	91.2	37,724,257	21,070,043	16,654,214	79.0
Printing and publishing	258,434	195,260	63,174	32.4	737,876,087	395,186,629	342,689,458	86.7	536,101,497	291,532,345	244,569,152	83.9
Rubber goods, not elsewhere specified[4]	26,521	20,404	6,117	30.0	128,435,747	52,621,830	75,813,917	144.1	46,243,926	19,139,516	27,104,410	141.6
Silk and silk goods, including throwsters	99,037	65,416	33,621	51.4	196,911,667	107,256,258	89,655,409	83.6	89,144,751	44,849,593	44,295,158	98.8
Slaughtering and meat packing	89,728	69,264	20,464	29.5	1,370,568,101	788,367,647	582,200,454	73.8	167,740,317	103,057,548	64,682,769	62.8
Smelting and refining, copper	15,628	11,324	4,304	38.0	378,805,974	165,131,670	213,674,304	129.4	45,274,336	42,957,541	2,316,795	5.4
Smelting and refining, lead	7,424	8,319	−895	−10.8	167,405,650	175,466,304	−8,060,654	−4.6	15,442,628	31,271,141	−15,828,513	−50.6
Soap	13,538	9,487	4,051	42.7	114,488,298	53,231,017	61,257,281	115.1	40,132,778	20,087,787	20,044,991	99.8
Sugar and molasses, not including beet sugar	13,526	14,129	−603	−4.3	279,249,397	239,711,011	39,538,386	16.5	31,666,593	18,326,242	18,340,351	72.8
Tobacco manufactures	166,810	132,526	34,284	25.9	416,695,104	263,713,173	152,981,931	58.0	239,509,483	170,846,631	68,662,852	40.2
Woolen, worsted, and felt goods, and wool hats	168,722	130,697	38,025	29.1	435,978,558	248,798,133	187,180,425	75.2	153,100,519	94,867,725	58,232,794	61.4
All other industries	1,498,696	1,066,274	432,422	40.6	3,819,868,070	2,012,780,425	1,807,087,645	89.8	1,807,795,891	973,101,147	834,694,734	85.8

[1]A minus sign (−) denotes decrease.
[2]Includes for 1909 some establishments which were included under "enameling and japanning" in 1899.
[3]Includes for 1909 establishments compounding table sirups which were included under "sugar and molasses" in 1899.
[4]Includes for 1899 some establishments included under "furnishing goods, men's," in 1909.

SOURCE: Table 4 from *Thirteenth Census of the United States Taken in the Year 1910,* Volume VIII, *Manufactures: 1909.* Washington: U.S. Government Printing Office, 1913.

Primary Source

Part three of the 1910 U.S. Census table of American manufacturers.

Five Leading Industries of Each State as Measured by Value of Products: 1909

State and Industry	Value of products	Percent of Total for All Industries in the State		Percent of Total for the Industry in the United States	
		Value of products	Wage earners (average number)	Value of products	Wage earners (average number)
ALABAMA					
Lumber and timber products	$26,057,662	17.9	31.1	2.3	3.2
Cotton goods, including cotton small wares	22,211,748	15.2	17.6	3.5	3.4
Iron and steel, blast furnaces	21,235,984	14.5	5.2	5.4	9.8
Foundry and machine-shop products	11,550,217	7.9	8.2	0.9	1.1
Oil, cottonseed, and cake	9,178,016	6.3	2.2	6.2	9.5
ARIZONA					
Smelting and refining, copper	41,059,240	81.7	48.6	10.8	20.0
Cars and general shop construction and repairs by steam-railroad companies	2,393,930	4.8	16.9	0.6	0.4
Lumber and timber products	1,419,114	2.8	13.0	0.1	0.1
Flour-mill and gristmill products	1,316,757	2.6	0.8	0.1	0.1
Printing and publishing	784,487	1.6	4.2	0.1	0.1
ARKANSAS					
Lumber and timber products	40,640,327	54.2	73.2	3.5	4.7
Oil, cottonseed, and cake	7,788,885	10.4	2.4	5.3	6.4
Flour-mill and gristmill products	5,615,486	7.5	0.7	0.6	0.8
Cars and general shop construction and repairs by steam-railroad companies	4,153,926	5.5	7.2	1.0	1.2
Printing and publishing	2,082,865	2.8	2.2	0.3	0.4
CALIFORNIA					
Lumber and timber products	45,000,276	8.5	19.9	3.9	3.3
Smelting and refining, lead	—	—	—	—	—
Slaughtering and meat packing	34,280,003	6.5	1.4	2.5	1.8
Canning and preserving	32,914,829	6.2	6.7	21.0	12.9
Foundry and machine-shop products	26,730,891	5.1	7.3	2.2	1.6
COLORADO					
Smelting and refining, lead	—	—	—	—	—
Beet sugar	—	—	—	—	—
Iron and steel, steel works and rolling mills	—	—	—	—	—
Slaughtering and meat packing	9,656,810	7.4	2.3	0.7	0.7
Flour-mill and gristmill products	7,867,706	6.1	1.0	0.9	0.7
CONNECTICUT					
Brass and bronze products	66,932,969	13.7	8.0	44.6	41.4
Foundry and machine-shop products	65,535,155	13.4	17.9	5.3	7.1
Cotton goods, including cotton small wares	24,231,881	4.9	6.8	3.9	3.8
Silk and silk goods, including throwsters	21,062,687	4.3	4.1	10.7	8.8
Firearms and ammunition	19,948,235	4.1	4.0	58.5	58.0
DELAWARE					
Leather, tanned, curried, and finished	12,079,225	22.9	14.3	3.7	4.9
Foundry and machine-shop products	4,781,195	9.0	10.4	0.4	0.4
Cars, steam-railroad, not including operations of railroad companies	3,628,093	6.9	7.9	2.9	3.9
Cars and general shop construction and repairs by steam-railroad companies	3,251,201	6.2	7.2	0.8	0.5
Dyeing and finishing textiles	—	—	—	—	—
DISTRICT OF COLUMBIA					
Printing and publishing	$4,899,492	19.4	20.3	0.7	0.6
Bread and other bakery products	3,589,554	14.2	12.7	0.9	1.0
Gas, illuminating and heating	2,305,340	9.1	8.0	1.4	1.7
Slaughtering and meat packing	1,889,575	7.5	1.8	0.1	0.2
Liquors, malt	1,804,791	7.1	3.2	0.5	0.5
FLORIDA					
Tobacco manufactures	21,575,021	29.6	21.4	5.2	7.4
Lumber and timber products	20,863,016	28.6	33.5	1.8	2.8
Turpentine and rosin	11,937,518	16.4	31.6	47.2	45.9
Fertilizers	3,878,296	5.3	1.0	3.7	3.2
Printing and publishing	1,865,848	2.6	1.6	0.3	0.4
GEORGIA					
Cotton goods, including cotton small wares	48,036,817	23.7	26.6	7.6	7.3
Lumber and timber products	24,632,093	12.1	21.3	2.1	3.2
Oil, cottonseed, and cake	23,640,779	11.7	2.8	16.0	16.9
Fertilizers	16,800,301	8.3	2.6	16.2	15.1
Flour-mill and gristmill products	7,999,912	3.9	0.4	0.9	1.0
IDAHO					
Lumber and timber products	10,689,310	47.7	63.4	0.9	0.7
Flour-mill and gristmill products	2,479,719	11.1	1.5	0.3	0.3
Beet sugar	—	—	—	—	—
Cars and general shop construction and repairs by steam-railroad companies	1,366,408	6.1	10.3	0.3	0.3
Printing and publishing	1,148,033	5.1	5.7	0.2	0.2
ILLINOIS					
Slaughtering and meat packing	389,594,906	20.3	5.7	28.4	29.8
Foundry and machine-shop products	138,578,993	7.2	11.2	11.3	9.8
Clothing, men's, including shirts	89,472,755	4.7	7.8	15.8	15.1
Printing and publishing	87,247,090	4.5	6.1	11.8	11.1
Iron and steel, steel works and rolling mills	86,608,137	4.5	3.8	8.8	7.3
INDIANA					
Slaughtering and meat packing	47,289,469	8.2	2.4	3.5	4.9
Flour-mill and gristmill products	40,541,422	7.0	1.2	4.6	5.8
Foundry and machine shop products	39,883,774	6.9	8.5	3.2	3.0
Iron and steel, steel works and rolling mills	38,651,848	6.7	6.6	3.9	5.1
Liquors, distilled	31,610,468	5.5	0.2	15.4	6.7
IOWA					
Slaughtering and meat-packing	59,045,232	22.8	6.7	4.3	4.6
Butter, cheese, and condensed milk	25,849,866	10.0	2.0	9.4	6.7
Foundry and machine-shop products	14,064,382	5.4	8.3	1.1	1.0
Flour-mill and gristmill products	12,870,603	5.0	1.0	1.5	1.6
Lumber and timber products	12,659,259	4.9	7.6	1.1	0.7
KANSAS					
Slaughtering and meat packing	165,360,516	50.9	24.0	12.1	11.8
Flour-mill and gristmill products	68,476,410	21.1	5.3	7.7	6.0
Cars and general shop construction and repairs by steam-railroad companies	11,193,106	3.4	17.4	2.8	2.7
Smelting and refining, zinc	10,857,250	3.3	4.1	31.7	27.4
Printing and publishing	7,008,865	2.2	7.3	0.9	1.3

[continued]

Primary Source

SYNOPSIS: This table from the 1910 U.S. Census describes the major industries of each state and the District of Columbia.

Five Leading Industries of Each State as Measured by Value of Products: 1909 [CONTINUED]

State and Industry	Value of products	Percent of Total for All Industries in the State		Percent of Total for the Industry in the United States	
		Value of products	Wage earners (average number)	Value of products	Wage earners (average number)
KENTUCKY					
Liquors, distilled	$44,360,104	19.8	3.9	21.7	39.5
Flour-mill and gristmill products	22,364,950	10.0	2.1	2.5	3.6
Lumber and timber products	21,380,564	9.6	19.9	1.8	1.9
Tobacco manufactures	18,597,786	8.3	6.1	4.5	2.4
Foundry and machine-shop products	9,626,686	4.3	6.9	0.8	0.8
LOUISIANA					
Lumber and timber products	62,837,912	28.1	60.5	5.4	6.6
Sugar, refining, not including beet sugar	34,774,173	15.5	1.5	14.0	12.4
Sugar and molasses	29,001,027	12.9	5.2	94.7	95.2
Oil, cottonseed, and cake	13,084,586	5.8	1.2	8.8	5.2
Rice, cleaning and polishing	12,528,656	5.6	0.9	56.0	55.9
MAINE					
Paper and wood pulp	33,950,230	19.3	10.8	12.7	11.4
Lumber and timber products	26,124,640	14.8	18.9	2.3	2.2
Cotton goods, including cotton small wares	21,932,225	12.5	18.3	3.5	3.9
Woolen, worsted, and felt goods, and wool hats	18,490,120	10.5	10.9	4.2	5.2
Boots and shoes, including cut stock and findings	15,508,771	8.8	8.3	3.0	3.3
MARYLAND					
Clothing, men's, including shirts	36,921,294	11.7	18.3	6.5	8.3
Smelting and refining, copper	—	—	—	—	—
Copper, tin, and sheet-iron products	16,909,447	5.4	4.9	8.5	7.2
Canning and preserving	13,709,449	4.3	8.0	8.7	14.4
Slaughtering and meat packing	13,682,951	4.3	1.0	1.0	1.2
MASSACHUSETTS					
Boots and shoes, including cut stock and findings	236,342,915	15.9	14.2	46.1	41.9
Cotton goods, including cotton small wares	186,462,313	12.5	18.6	29.7	28.7
Woolen, worsted, and felt goods, and wool hats	141,966,882	9.5	9.2	32.6	31.9
Foundry and machine-shop products	86,925,671	5.8	7.6	7.1	8.3
Printing and publishing	47,445,006	3.2	3.0	6.4	6.8
MICHIGAN					
Automobiles, including bodies and parts	96,651,451	14.1	11.0	38.8	33.6
Lumber and timber products	61,513,560	9.0	15.4	5.3	5.1
Foundry and machine-shop products	45,399,023	6.6	9.4	3.7	4.1
Flour-mill and gristmill products	34,860,803	5.1	0.7	3.9	3.9
Furniture and refrigerators	28,641,684	4.2	7.2	11.9	12.9
MINNESOTA					
Flour-mill and gristmill products	139,136,129	34.0	5.1	15.7	11.0
Lumber and timber products	42,352,507	10.3	24.4	3.7	3.0
Slaughtering and meat packing	25,753,697	6.3	2.3	1.9	2.1
Butter, cheese, and condensed milk	25,287,462	6.2	1.4	9.2	6.4
Printing and publishing	15,982,212	3.9	6.7	2.2	2.2
MISSISSIPPI					
Lumber and timber products	42,792,844	53.1	66.3	3.7	4.8
Oil, cottonseed, and cake	$15,965,543	19.8	5.0	10.8	14.7
Cars and general shop construction and repairs by steam-railroad companies	3,233,288	4.0	5.1	0.8	0.9
Cotton goods, including cotton small wares	3,102,398	3.8	5.2	0.5	0.7
Fertilizers	2,125,029	2.6	0.9	2.0	2.5
MISSOURI					
Slaughtering and meat packing	79,581,294	13.9	3.1	5.8	5.2
Boots and shoes, including cut stock and findings	48,751,235	8.5	11.4	9.5	8.8
Flour-mill and gristmill products	44,508,106	7.8	1.4	5.0	5.6
Tobacco manufactures	30,950,638	5.4	2.9	7.4	2.7
Printing and publishing	29,651,153	5.2	7.1	4.0	4.2
MONTANA					
Smelting and refining, copper	—	—	—	—	—
Lumber and timber products	6,333,778	8.6	26.6	0.5	0.4
Smelting and refining, lead	—	—	—	—	—
Cars and general shop construction and repairs by steam-railroad companies	2,810,521	3.8	16.4	0.7	0.7
Liquors, malt	2,439,832	3.3	2.1	0.7	0.4
NEBRASKA					
Slaughtering and meat packing	92,305,484	46.4	24.7	6.7	6.7
Smelting and refining, lead	—	—	—	—	—
Flour-mill and gristmill products	17,835,596	9.0	3.4	2.0	2.1
Butter, cheese, and condensed milk	7,681,272	3.9	1.6	2.8	2.1
Printing and publishing	6,667,290	3.3	9.6	0.9	0.9
NEVADA					
Smelting and refining, copper	—	—	—	—	—
Cars and general shop construction and repairs by steam-railroad companies	1,032,707	8.7	36.2	0.3	0.3
Slaughtering and meat packing	—	—	—	—	—
Flour-mill and gristmill products	597,929	5.0	1.1	0.1	0.1
Printing and publishing	519,243	4.4	8.0	0.1	0.1
NEW HAMPSHIRE					
Boots and shoes, including cut stock and findings	39,439,544	24.0	18.1	7.7	7.2
Cotton goods, including cotton small wares	33,601,830	20.4	28.3	5.3	58.8
Woolen, worsted, and felt goods, and wool hats	16,730,652	10.2	12.1	3.8	5.6
Lumber and timber products	15,284,357	9.3	10.8	1.3	1.2
Paper and wood pulp	13,994,251	8.5	4.3	5.2	4.5
NEW JERSEY					
Smelting and refining, copper	125,651,087	11.0	0.7	33.2	14.9
Petroleum, refining	—	—	—	—	—
Silk and silk goods, including throwsters	65,429,550	5.7	9.3	33.2	30.6
Foundry and machine-shop products	65,398,437	5.7	8.5	5.3	5.2
Slaughtering and meat packing	37,583,395	3.3	0.6	2.7	2.0

[continued]

Primary Source

Part two of the 1910 U.S. Census table of the major manufacturing industries of each state.

Five Leading Industries of Each State as Measured by Value of Products: 1909 [CONTINUED]

State and Industry	Value of products	Percent of Total for All Industries in the State: Value of products	Percent of Total for All Industries in the State: Wage earners (average number)	Percent of Total for the Industry in the United States: Value of products	Percent of Total for the Industry in the United States: Wage earners (average number)
NEW MEXICO					
Cars and general shop construction and repairs by steam-railroad companies	$2,250,920	28.5	35.9	0.6	0.5
Lumber and timber products	2,162,396	27.4	35.6	0.2	0.2
Coke	—	—	—	—	—
Printing and publishing	588,782	7.5	6.8	0.1	0.1
Flour-mill and gristmill products	461,621	5.8	0.7	0.1	0.1
NEW YORK					
Clothing, women's	272,517,792	8.1	9.8	70.8	63.8
Clothing, men's, including shirts	266,075,427	7.9	9.1	46.8	38.1
Printing and publishing	216,946,482	6.4	6.3	29.4	24.4
Foundry and machine-shop products	154,370,346	4.6	6.4	12.6	12.1
Slaughtering and meat packing	127,130,051	3.8	0.6	9.3	6.8
NORTH CAROLINA					
Cotton goods, including cotton small wares	72,680,385	33.5	38.9	11.6	12.5
Tobacco manufactures	35,986,639	16.6	6.8	8.6	4.9
Lumber and timber products	33,524,653	15.5	28.0	2.9	4.9
Oil, cottonseed, and cake	8,504,477	3.9	1.0	5.8	6.8
Flour-mill and gristmill products	8,501,219	3.9	0.4	1.0	1.3
NORTH DAKOTA					
Flour-mill and gristmill products	11,685,116	61.1	15.6	1.3	1.1
Printing and publishing	1,909,514	10.0	28.3	0.3	0.3
Butter, cheese, and condensed milk	1,029,135	5.4	2.2	0.4	0.3
Leather goods	683,273	3.6	3.5	0.7	0.3
Cars and general shop construction and repairs by steam-railroad companies	679,612	3.6	16.6	0.2	0.2
OHIO					
Iron and steel, steel works and rolling mills	197,780,043	13.8	8.6	20.1	16.1
Foundry and machine-shop products	145,836,648	10.1	14.5	11.9	12.2
Iron and steel, blast furnaces	83,699,238	5.8	1.6	21.4	19.0
Rubber goods, not elsewhere specified	53,910,531	3.7	2.3	42.0	39.1
Slaughtering and meat packing	50,804,100	3.5	0.7	3.7	3.4
OKLAHOMA					
Flour-mill and gristmill products	19,144,475	35.7	6.4	2.2	2.1
Oil, cotton seed, and cake	5,186,605	9.7	4.4	3.5	3.4
Lumber and timber products	4,438,563	8.3	24.2	0.4	0.5
Printing and publishing	3,988,542	7.4	12.9	0.5	0.7
Smelting and refining, zinc	3,002,233	5.6	4.3	8.8	8.5
OREGON					
Lumber and timber products	30,199,857	32.5	52.4	2.6	2.2
Flour-mill and gristmill products	8,891,001	9.6	1.4	1.0	1.0
Slaughtering and meat packing	5,879,615	6.3	1.3	0.4	0.4
Printing and publishing	5,040,523	5.4	5.1	0.7	0.6
Butter, cheese, and condensed milk	4,920,462	5.3	1.5	1.8	2.3
PENNSYLVANIA					
Iron and steel, steel works and rolling mills	500,343,995	19.0	14.5	50.8	52.9
PENNSYLVANIA					
Foundry and machine-shop products	$210,746,257	8.0	9.9	17.2	16.4
Iron and steel, blast furnaces	168,578,413	6.4	1.7	43.1	37.8
Leather, tanned, curried, and finished	77,926,321	3.0	1.6	23.8	22.5
Woolen, worsted, and felt goods, and wool hats	77,446,996	2.9	3.1	17.8	16.2
RHODE ISLAND					
Woolen, worsted, and felt goods, and wool hats	74,600,240	26.6	22.0	17.1	14.8
Cotton goods, including cotton small wares	50,312,597	17.9	25.4	8.0	7.6
Jewelry	20,685,100	7.4	8.4	25.7	31.3
Foundry and machine-shop products	20,611,693	7.4	9.6	1.7	2.1
Dyeing and finishing textiles	13,955,700	5.0	6.9	16.7	17.7
SOUTH CAROLINA					
Cotton goods, including cotton small wares	65,929,585	58.2	62.2	10.5	12.0
Lumber and timber products	13,140,885	11.6	20.0	1.1	2.1
Oil, cottonseed, and cake	10,902,935	9.6	2.4	7.4	10.3
Fertilizers	9,024,900	8.0	2.5	8.7	10.1
Printing and publishing	1,600,691	1.4	1.1	0.2	0.3
SOUTH DAKOTA					
Flour-mill and gristmill products	6,208,216	34.7	7.9	0.7	0.7
Butter, cheese, and condensed milk	2,685,511	15.0	3.9	1.0	0.8
Printing and publishing	1,975,976	11.1	22.9	0.3	0.3
Bread and other bakery products	1,160,536	6.5	7.9	0.3	0.3
Lumber and timber products	944,777	5.3	12.5	0.1	0.1
TENNESSEE					
Lumber and timber products	30,456,807	16.9	30.3	2.6	3.2
Flour-mill and gristmill products	29,070,019	16.1	2.1	3.3	4.0
Foundry and machine-shop products	9,189,791	5.1	5.5	0.7	0.8
Printing and publishing	7,173,230	4.0	3.9	1.0	1.1
Cars and general shop construction and repairs by steam-railroad companies	6,776,511	3.8	7.5	1.7	2.0
TEXAS					
Slaughtering and meat packing	42,529,746	15.6	5.2	3.1	4.1
Flour-mill and gristmill products	32,484,612	11.9	1.7	3.7	3.1
Lumber and timber products	32,201,440	11.8	33.5	2.8	3.4
Oil, cottonseed, and cake	29,915,772	11.0	4.4	20.2	18.0
Petroleum, refining	—	—	—	—	—
UTAH					
Smelting and refining, copper	—	—	—	—	—
Smelting and refining, lead	—	—	—	—	—
Beet sugar	—	—	—	—	—
Flour-mill and gristmill products	3,130,895	5.1	1.6	0.4	0.5
Cars and general shop construction and repairs by steam-railroad companies	2,740,463	4.4	14.7	0.7	0.6
VERMONT					
Marble and stone work	12,395,379	18.1	30.8	11.0	15.9
Lumber and timber products	8,598,084	12.6	14.2	0.7	0.7

[continued]

Primary Source

Part three of the 1910 U.S. Census table of the major manufacturing industries of each state.

Five Leading Industries of Each State as Measured by Value of Products: 1909 [CONTINUED]

State and Industry	Value of products	Percent of Total for All Industries in the State		Percent of Total for the Industry in the United States	
		Value of products	Wage earners (average number)	Value of products	Wage earners (average number)
VERMONT					
Butter, cheese, and condensed milk	$8,112,239	11.9	1.5	3.0	2.8
Woolen, worsted, and felt goods, and wool hats	4,496,903	6.6	6.8	1.0	1.4
Flour-mill and gristmill products	4,133,337	6.0	0.5	0.5	0.4
VIRGINIA					
Lumber and timber products	35,855,310	16.3	31.5	3.1	4.8
Tobacco manufactures	25,385,414	11.5	7.5	6.1	4.7
Flour-mill and gristmill products	17,598,045	8.0	1.0	2.0	2.6
Cars and general shop construction and repairs by steam-railroad companies	9,955,501	4.5	7.2	2.5	2.7
Leather, tanned, curried, and finished	8,266,850	3.8	1.5	2.5	2.6
WASHINGTON					
Lumber and timber products	89,154,820	40.4	63.3	7.7	6.3
Flour-mill and gristmill products	17,852,944	8.1	0.9	2.0	1.6
Slaughtering and meat packing	15,653,998	7.1	1.2	1.1	0.9
Canning and preserving	9,595,387	4.3	2.9	6.1	3.4
Printing and publishing	9,286,188	4.2	3.8	1.3	1.0
WEST VIRGINIA					
Lumber and timber products	28,758,481	17.8	29.2	2.5	2.7
Iron and steel, steel works and rolling mills	22,435,411	13.9	7.9	2.3	2.1
WEST VIRGINIA					
Leather, tanned, curried, and finished	$12,450,592	7.7	2.5	3.8	2.5
Tin plate and terneplate	9,257,524	5.7	2.1	19.3	24.9
Glass	7,779,483	4.8	9.7	8.4	9.0
WISCONSIN					
Lumber and timber products	57,969,170	9.8	18.7	5.0	4.9
Foundry and machine-shop products	54,124,000	9.2	13.3	4.4	4.6
Butter, cheese, and condensed milk	53,843,249	9.1	1.6	19.6	15.6
Leather, tanned, curried, and finished	44,667,676	7.6	4.1	13.6	12.1
Liquors, malt	32,125,919	5.4	2.8	8.6	9.3
WYOMING					
Cars and general shop construction and repairs by steam-railroad companies	2,336,678	37.4	58.9	0.6	0.6
Lumber and timber products	751,249	12.0	22.6	0.1	0.1
Flour-mill and gristmill products	746,299	11.9	1.0	0.1	0.1
Printing and publishing	489,544	7.8	5.6	0.1	0.1
Iron and steel, steel works and rolling mills	—	—	—	—	—

SOURCE: Table 6 from *Thirteenth Census of the United States Taken in the Year 1910,* Volume VIII, *Manufactures: 1909.* Washington: U.S. Government Printing Office, 1913.

Primary Source

Part four of the 1910 U.S. Census table of the major manufacturing industries of each state.

condensed milk," "Confectionery," and "Food preparations."

Significance

Table 6 gives a different look at industrial growth. It lists the top five industries in each state and the significance of each industry for total U.S. production. As one might predict, automobile manufacturing was the leading industry in Michigan in 1909, generating nearly forty percent of the country's auto production. The importance of "Butter, cheese and condensed milk" in Wisconsin makes it clear why Wisconsin is known as "the Dairy State." Oddly, though, in 1909 "Printing and publishing" was the third largest industry in South Dakota—just as it was in the nation's publishing capital, New York.

Few certain conclusions can be drawn from this data, though many hypotheses can be formed. These tables can stimulate numerous questions about life in America at the turn of the last century. Examining them provides a snapshot of America in 1909 and perhaps can lead to insights about modern-day America.

Further Resources

BOOKS

Wattenburg, Ben J., ed. *The Statistical History of the United States from Colonial Times to the Present.* New York: Basic Books, 1976.

WEBSITES

Bureau of the Census. *200 Years of Census Taking: Population and Housing Questions, 1790–1990.* Washington, D.C.: Bureau of the Census, 1989. Available online as "Historical Background" at http://fisher.lib.virginia.edu/census/background/; website home page: http://fisher.lib.virginia.edu (accessed December 27, 2002).

Bill Haywood's Book

Autobiography

By: William D. Haywood

Date: 1929

Source: Haywood, William D. *Bill Haywood's Book: The Autobiography of William D. Haywood.* New York: International Publishers, 1929, 207–216.

About the Author: Big Bill Haywood (1869–1928) led two of America's most successful radical labor unions, the Western Federation of Miners (WFM) and the Industrial Workers of the World (IWW). Haywood—big, burly, and gruff—detested capitalism and represented the revolutionary socialist worker feared by big business and political conservatives and moderates. An outspoken opponent of World War I (1914–1918), Haywood was arrested in 1917 on charges of treason. Released on bail, he fled to Russia, where he died. ■

Introduction

On the evening of December 20, 1905, Idaho governor Frank Steunenberg was killed in a bomb explosion. A former miner, Steunenberg had broken with the Western Federation of Miners during strikes in Coeur d'Alenes, Idaho, several years earlier. Suspicion immediately fell on the WFM, who regarded Stuenenberg as a traitor. Within days, Harry Orchard, a Canadian-born drifter and apparent associate of several union leaders, was arrested. After several days of questioning by Pinkerton detective, John McParland, Orchard confessed. He claimed that four WFM leaders, including Haywood, had hired him to murder Steunenberg. The four union men were living in Colorado, so Idaho sought extradition. Unwilling to wait for the legal process to work, Colorado officials cooperated with Idaho agents to virtually kidnap Haywood and two others; the fourth disappeared and was never found. The three "arrested" miners were taken to Idaho to stand trial in 1907. The volatile situation in the western mining camps, the radical nature of the WFM, Haywood's reputation, and the dubious testimony of the scurrilous Harry Orchard combined to make the trials a national attraction.

Significance

For union sympathizers, the trial was a sham. It was, they felt, based solely on the testimony of the disreputable Harry Orchard. The real motive, workers believed, was the destruction of the WFM. Standing boldly for radical change and willing to challenge powerful mining interests—including the Guggenheim and Rockefeller empires—the WFM was a threat to the established order.

There was considerable truth in the miners' position. The mining interests ran roughshod over the miners' rights and made every effort to condemn the WFM and Haywood. Even President Theodore Roosevelt (served 1901–1909) called the defendants "undesirable citizens." In such a climate, the Haywood trial became a celebrated case for workers, and supporters were able to raise the considerable sum of $250,000 for the defense of the three accused labor leaders.

Leading the defense was noted liberal attorney, Clarence Darrow. Darrow, who had appeared for the defense in many celebrated labor and civil rights cases for over thirty years, was aggressive, unapologetic, and a spellbinding orator. His scathing cross-examination of Orchard and a summation that struck at both the weakness of the prosecution's case and the broader issue of labor's struggle for justice won a quick acquittal from the jury. Harry Orchard was later convicted and spent the rest of his life—he died in 1954—in the Idaho State Penitentiary.

Primary Source

Bill Haywood's Book [excerpt]

SYNOPSIS: Haywood's autobiography, published after his death in the Soviet Union, lacks the depth and balance hoped for in the narrative of such an important figure in American labor history. It does, however, devote several chapters to the events surrounding the Steunenberg murder trial. The excerpt describing the trial includes portions of Darrow's closing argument.

The Boise Trial

My trial began on the ninth of May, 1907. William E. Borah, who had been elected United States Senator by the previous legislature, the man who had prosecuted Paul Corcoran, was a special prosecutor in this case. James Hawley, a one-time miner who had been the lawyer for the Cœur d'Alenes prisoners when they had occupied the jail we now lived in, was also a special prosecutor. Hawley was the man who had suggested to the imprisoned miners that an organization should be formed comprising all the miners of the West. The Caldwell County attorney was one of the assistant prosecutors. . . .

The regular jury when finally selected was composed almost entirely of farmers. The bankers and business men had been challenged by the defense; the few union men or Socialists called had been challenged by the prosecution. Another thing had happened to lower still further my estimation of the law; the legislature had enacted an ex-post-facto law which added to the number of jury challenges of the state.

The prosecution laid their foundation for the trial with the testimony of several minor witnesses. Then Harry Orchard was called to the stand. He was neatly dressed in a gray suit of the warden's, was clean

George Pettibone, Bill Haywood and Charles Moyer, leaders of the Western Federation of Miners, were acquitted on conspiracy to commit murder charges in the assassination of Idaho governor, Frank Steunenberg. © CORBIS. REPRODUCED BY PERMISSION.

shaven, with his hair combed smoothly over a head as round as a billiard-ball. I remarked his resemblance to MacParland the detective. Far from being the furtive weasel of a man that his story would lead one to expect, Orchard was well-set-up, bluff, with an apparently open manner. I kept my eyes on that man while he was on the stand, but he never met my gaze.

He was not questioned much by Borah, but was told to tell his story in narrative form. He related a blood-curdling tale, commencing with his life in Canada. He had left a wife and child in Ontario after burning down a cheese-factory there. He said his real name was Albert Horseley. The next exploit that he claimed to his credit was the lighting of one of the fuses that had caused the explosion that destroyed the Bunker Hill and Sullivan Mill in the Cœur d'Alenes. At that time he claimed to have been one of the owners of the Headlight group of mines near Burke, Idaho.

As a gambler and rounder he had made his way to the Cripple Creek district. There he seemed to have taken an active part in the union work for a time, in order to gain the confidence of the miners, and was at the same time the associate and employee of the Citizens' Alliance. It was at about this time that he had first come to the headquarters of the Federation, at the request, as we later discovered, of Detective Scott, by whom he was paid and to whom he reported. His next visit to headquarters was when he went to Ouray with Moyer. Beckmann and McKinley were his coworkers. These men, it will be remembered, had tried to wreck a train in Cripple Creek, which they said they were willing to do for five hundred dollars, though it might cost the lives of two hundred and fifty or more people. For this they had been employed by Scott and Sterling, both of whom now sat in the Boise courtroom listening to Orchard's story. Neither of them took the stand as witnesses in this case.

Orchard told of his connection with the Vindicator explosion, the Independence Depot explosion, and of many attempts on the lives of Governor Peabody, Judges Gabbert and Goddard, and McNeil,

Hearn, Bradley and others. It was a revolting story of a callous degenerate, and no one will ever know how much of it was true and how much fabrication. He concluded his tale by telling how he had caused the death of ex-governor Frank Steunenberg.

From beginning to end he mentioned the names of Pettibone, Moyer and myself as having been the instigators of his murders; saying that either one or the other of us had instructed him in the commission of the work that he had engaged in. He varied little in his story under cross-examination, having been well drilled by his mentor, James MacParland, head of the Denver agency of the Pinkerton Detectives. This was the same man who had started his career long before by swearing away the lives of the Molly Maguires in Pennsylvania.

After the testimony of Orchard, the prosecution introduced old numbers of the Anarchist paper, the *Alarm,* which had been edited by Albert Parsons in 1886. Many articles were read to prove the theory and practice of the Western Federation of Miners twenty years later. Then they introduced copies of the *Miners' Magazine.* O'Neill had written an editorial describing the explosion which killed Governor Steunenberg, which was supposed to show the animus of the Federation. Perhaps the prosecution had expected us to mourn the governor's death. . . .

As soon as Orchard's testimony was heralded over the country, telegrams began coming in from people he had mentioned, offering to come as witnesses to repudiate what he had said. Bill Davis and others came and demolished that part of Orchard's testimony that referred to them. Two men came from Mullan, Idaho, and testified that Orchard was playing poker with them in the rear of a cigar store in Mullan at the time of the explosion that destroyed the Bunker Hill and Sullivan mill. A contractor and builder from San Francisco testified that the building from the roof of which Orchard claimed to have stepped to the Bradley home, had not yet been built when Orchard said he had been in San Francisco. A woman from Cripple Creek gave evidence about the many times that Orchard had visited the rooms of Stirling and Scott in her rooming house. Charles Moyer was a creditable witness, but to my surprise, when we returned to the cell where Pettibone was, he blurted out, "I hope that will please the Goddam revolutionists!"

Ed Boyce, former president of the Western Federation, was also a witness. He was severely cross-examined by Borah, but he never flinched. He stated that he had said in his report in 1896 that he "hoped to hear the martial tread of twenty-five thousand armed miners before the next convention," and that he was in earnest in this desire because of what had happened in the Cœur d'Alenes, Cripple Creek and Leadville. It gave me a thrill of the old days to hear Boyce testify.

Darrow, in this case as in others that he has defended, picked out a "goat" among the prosecution lawyers. In this instance it was Jim Hawley upon whom he concentrated his sarcasm. He was at times so venomous that Hawley's son threatened him with personal violence. Darrow was not always the smiling, suave, persuasive individual that he is sometimes described. His grandest moments were when he was in the attitude of attack. Some of the witnesses suffered severely. He tore the degenerate Orchard to fragments, and said, "It is this arch criminal that the prosecution is protecting!" to which Senator Borah took exception, saying with uplifted hand, "May my right hand wither if this man is not prosecuted!" . . .

When I went on the witness stand the examination was conducted by Darrow. I went over the history of my life, my connection with the Western Federation, my knowledge of Orchard, and everything that had happened with which I had anything to do, down to that hour. Borah in his cross-examination did not have things all his own way. He faced me with his bulldog expression and the deep dimple in his chin, and asked about the resolution that I had written in Silver City. He said:

"You felt very bitter against Governor Steunenberg?"

"Yes," I answered, "I felt toward him much as I did toward you and others who were responsible for martial law and the bull-pen in the Cœur d'Alenes."

"So I have understood," the senator remarked. Just what he meant I could not make out.

During his cross-examination the sun was sinking and shining through a window toward which I was facing. I said to the judge, "If your Honor please, will you kindly have the shutters closed on that window? The sun is shining in my face and I cannot see the senator's eyes."

It was not my intention to disconcert the senator, but I was told afterward that he said he had never heard of a man on trial for his life who was so anxious to see the prosecutor's eyes. He said, "It doubled me up like a jack-knife!"

One day when I was on the stand being cross-examined, the judge announced that there would probably be a night session. The senator protested, saying that he felt as if he had already done two days' work in one.

I was examined and cross-examined about Stewart's testimony that I had said Governor Steunenberg should be exterminated. I said that, to the best of my remembrance, I had said he should be eliminated. . . .

The concluding address to the jury in my behalf was made by Clarence Darrow, who is not only a great lawyer but a keen psychologist.

When Darrow rose to address the jury he stood big and broad-shouldered, dressed in a slouchy gray suit, a wisp of hair down across his forehead, his glasses in his hand, clasped by the nose-piece. He began by tracing the history of the Western Federation of Miners, from the jail that had been our home for the past eighteen months, where the organization had been conceived. He pictured the isolated assemblies of the Knights of Labor and the efforts of these organizations to maintain a decent standard of living. He told of the Cœur d'Alenes strike of 1892 and the strike of 1899 which had been called an insurrection. He told about the calling of the Federal soldiers into the Cœur D'Alenes district at the time of these strikes, of martial law, of bull-pens, special prosecutions and imprisonments.

He went over in detail the many strikes that the W.F.M. had conducted in Colorado, showing that when the eight-hour law for which the organization had fought was passed, the unions were compelled to strike in order to enforce the law. He spoke of the effect of martial law on the people of a state or district where it prevailed, and of the suffering and worry that it entailed upon all who lived under such conditions.

He went over the testimony of the various witnesses for the state and then drew a comparison between them and the people who had given testimony for me. He told again of the illegal arrest, the kidnaping, the special train and military guard, showed that the prosecution would have shrunk from nothing in order to implicate me in this murder.

> To kill him, gentlemen! I want to speak to you plainly. Mr. Haywood is not my greatest concern. Other men have died before him. Other men have been martyrs to a holy cause since the world began. Wherever men have looked upward and onward, forgotten their selfishness, struggled for humanity, worked for the poor and the weak, they have been sacrificed. They have been sacrificed in the prison, on the scaffold, in the flame. They have met their death, and he can meet his if you twelve men say he must. But, gentlemen, you short-sighted men of the prosecution, you men of the Mine Owners' Association, you people who would cure hatred with hate, you who think you can crush out the feelings and the hopes and the aspirations of men by tying a noose around his neck, you who are seeking to kill him, not because it is Haywood, but because he represents a class, don't be so blind, be so foolish as to believe you can strangle the Western Federation of Miners when you tie a rope around his neck. Don't be so blind in your madness as to believe that if you make three fresh, new graves you will kill the labor movement of the world. I want to say to you, gentlemen, Bill Haywood can't die unless you kill him. You have got to tie the rope. You twelve men of Idaho, the burden will be on you. If, at the behest of this mob, you should kill Bill Haywood, he is mortal, he will die, and I want to say that a million men will take up the banner of labor at the open grave where Haywood lays it down, and in spite of prisons or scaffolds or fire, in spite of prosecution or jury, these men of willing hands will carry it on to victory in the end. . . .
>
> If you kill him your act will be applauded by many; if you should decree Haywood's death, in the great railroad offices of our great cities men will sing your praises. If you decree his death, amongst the spiders and vultures of Wall Street will go up paeans of praise for those twelve good men and true who killed Bill Haywood. . . .
>
> In almost every bank in the world, where men wish to get rid of agitators and disturbers, where men put in prison one who fights for the poor and against the accursed system upon which they live and grow fat, from all these you will receive blessings and praise that you have killed him.
>
> But if you free him there are still those who will reverently bow their heads and thank these twelve men for the character they have saved. Out on our broad prairies, where men toil with their hands: out on the broad ocean, where men are sailing the ships: through our mills and factories: down deep under the earth, thousands of men, of women, of children, men who labor, men who suffer, women and children weary with care and toil, these men and these women and these children will kneel tonight and ask their God to guide your judgment. These men and these women and these little children, the poor and the weak and the suffering of the world, will stretch out their hands to this jury and implore you to save Haywood's life. . . .

He had spoken eleven hours. While he spoke he was sometimes intense, his great voice rumbling, his left hand shoved deep in his coat pocket, his right arm uplifted. Again he would take a pleading attitude, his voice would become gentle and very quiet. At times he would approach the jury almost on tiptoe. This speech was, I think, one of Clarence Darrow's greatest.

A part of the instructions that were read to the jury by Judge Woods was written by John Murphy in his sick-bed at the hospital. The case went to the jury on the night of June twenty-seventh.

That night I went to bed at about the usual time, and slept undisturbed until they aroused me in the morning with the news that the verdict had been brought in. There was no hint as to what the verdict might be.

When I came into the court the room was filled with people. The jury was called and the judge asked if they had come to a verdict. The foreman answered that they had and briefly added, "Not guilty."

There was some commotion as the jurymen began to step from their places. At the request of Richardson they were called back and polled, each one answering formally as he was called upon, "Not guilty."

Further Resources

BOOKS

Archer, Jules. *Strikes, Bombs & Bullets: Big Bill Haywood and the IWW.* New York: J. Messner, 1972.

Foner, Philip S. *History of the Labor Movement in the United States: Vol. 4. The Industrial Workers of the World, 1905–1917.* New York: International Publishers, 1987.

Weinberg, Arthur, ed. *Attorney for the Damned.* New York: Simon and Schuster, 1957.

WEBSITES

Linder, Douglas. "Famous American Trials: Bill Haywood Trial, 1907." Available online at www.law.umkc.edu/faculty/projects/ftrials/haywood/HAYWOOD.htm; website home page: http://www.law.umkc.edu (accessed December 26, 2002).

3

Education

KRISTINA PETERSON

Entries are arranged in chronological order by date of primary source. For entries with one primary source, the entry title is the same as the primary source title. Entries with more than one primary source have an overall entry title, followed by the titles of the primary sources.

CHRONOLOGY

PRIMARY SOURCES

Important Events in Education, 1900–1909

1900

- In January, 250,000 U.S. children under age fifteen did not attend school. Instead they worked in mines and factories.
- In March, the New York City Board of Education plans to allow students to bathe in some schools.
- On May 12, representatives from thirteen colleges and preparatory schools establish the College Entrance Examination Board.
- On July 11, renowned progressive educator Francis W. Parker pleads for the centrality of art in education, asserting in a speech to the National Education Association that there is "art in everything."
- In September, forty-eight students enroll in the new Department of School Administration at Teachers' College, Columbia University.
- On September 15, the Atlanta school system turns away four hundred students because of a lack of space in city schools.
- On November 12, Stanford University President David Starr Jordan ignites a national debate on academic freedom when he dismisses Professor Edward A. Ross for making "radical" political statements.
- On November 15, steel magnate Andrew Carnegie founds the Carnegie Institute of Technology in Pittsburgh, Pennsylvania. It will become Carnegie-Mellon University, a center for education and research in engineering and science.

1901

- Bryn Mawr College President M. Carey Thomas declares in *Educational Review* that higher education for women should be the same as that for men.
- In January, Daniel Coit Gilman, president of Johns Hopkins University since its founding, announces his impending retirement.
- In June, high school students take the College Board's college entrance examination for the first time.
- On June 12, pupils at Bunsen School in Belleville, Illinois, petition for a shorter school day.
- On June 25, advocates of the "elective system" in high schools win a victory when the Boston School Committee adopts an elective system for all of its high schools. The only requirements are courses in hygiene, gymnastics or military drill, and music.
- In September, an international congress of nurses meeting in Buffalo, New York, passes a resolution in favor of the registration and certification of all nurses and the standardization of educational requirements for prospective nurses.
- In September, John D. Rockefeller establishes the Rockefeller Institute for Medical Research in New York City. Today it is Rockefeller University.
- On November 4, the reform-minded Southern Education Board convenes its first meeting.
- In December, Andrew Carnegie announces a gift of $10 million to endow a science research center, the Carnegie Institution of Washington.

1902

- John Dewey, in the book, *The Child and the Curriculum,* gives the clearest and best-known explanation of his theory of curriculum.
- Walter Hines Page galvanizes support for southern public-school reform with the publication of *The Rebuilding of Old Commonwealth.*
- Baltimore public schools institute special classrooms for "unmanageable" boys after the Maryland legislature passed a compulsory school attendance law the previous year.
- On March 26, A bequest from Cecil John Rhodes establishes Rhodes Scholarships.
- On April 5, a federal judge in Illinois rules on a Chicago Teachers' Federation suit, ordering five major utility and street railway companies in Chicago to pay $598,000 in back taxes to the Chicago City Council.
- On June 9, the Board of Trustees appoints Woodrow Wilson president of Princeton University. Wilson had been a political science professor at Princeton before serving as president.
- In July, Emory University Professor Andrew Sledd attacks lynching and supports racial moderation in an article in the July issue of *Atlantic Monthly.* University officials ask for his resignation after conservative whites throughout the U.S. condemn the article.
- In November, James K. Vardaman wins the Mississippi gubernatorial race. During the campaign he had pledged to increase funding for white schools by taking money from African American schools.
- On November 8, the Chicago Teachers' Federation joins the American Federation of Labor, becoming the first teachers' union in the United States.

1903

- Chicago's Englewood High School establishes a school lunchroom, the first in the city.
- On January 12, the General Education Board receives its charter and becomes a clearinghouse for the educational philanthropy of John D. Rockefeller.
- In March, philosopher William James complains of the abuses of graduate study in his article "The Ph.D Octopus," published in *Harvard Monthly.*

- On April 18, W.E.B. Du Bois, in his book *The Souls of Black Folk,* breaks with Booker T. Washington's racial-accommodationist approach to social and educational matters. DuBois advocates the "talented tenth," who through their education and professional achievements, will open higher education and thus access to the professions to African Americans.
- In July, Liberty Hyde Bailey becomes Dean of the College of Agriculture at Cornell University in Ithaca, New York. Bailey will use his position to advocate teaching and research in agricultural science as the solutions to the problems of American agriculture.
- On October 19, Judge William T. Gary of Augusta, Georgia, draws national attention by stating his opposition to schools for African Americans, claiming that education makes African American workers "unfit for the walks of life open to [them]."

1904

- Educational psychologist Granville Stanley Hall publishes his pivotal work, *Adolescence: Its Psychology and Its Relations to Physiology, Anthropology, Sociology, Sex, Crime, Religion, and Education.* Hall asserts that adolescents require an education different from that of children and adults.
- The newly formed National Child Labor Committee advocates the passage of laws restricting child labor and mandating compulsory school attendance.
- In April, John Dewey accepts a professorship at Columbia University, where he will remain until his retirement twenty-six years later.
- On June 7, University of Wisconsin President Charles Van Hise states in his inaugural address the rationale for the "Wisconsin Idea" of university service. That is, professors should do more than teach and publish; they should serve the common good by sharing their expertise with the public through volunteer service.
- On July 1, labor leader Margaret Haley implores teachers to unionize in a speech at the annual meeting of the National Education Association.
- On August 22, University of California President Benjamin Wheeler tells women students that they are to prepare for marriage and motherhood and should not use a college education, as men do, to prepare for a career.
- In October, Mary McLeod Bethune founds in Florida the Daytona Literary and Industrial Institute for the Training of Negro Girls. It later becomes Bethune College.

1905

- On February 27, Edwin Dexter reports to colleagues in the National Society for the Scientific Study of Education that 70 percent of male high school teachers and 53 percent of female high school teachers are college graduates.
- On April 16, Andrew Carnegie endows the Carnegie Foundation for the Advancement of Teaching with $10 million.
- In June, Lumina Cotton Riddle is the first woman to receive a Ph.D., in botany, from Ohio State University in Columbus. Since its inception in 1870, the university had enrolled both men and women.
- In July, a National Education Association study of urban public schools finds that 100 percent of district superintendents and 94 percent of all high school principals are men.

1906

- William T. Harris resigns as commissioner of education in his seventeenth year on the job.
- In April, the Massachusetts Commission on Industrial and Technical Education recommends teaching vocational skills to students in the state's public schools.
- In June, John Hope becomes president of Morehouse College, then named Atlanta Baptist College. He is the first African American president of this historically African American college.
- In September, George Pierce Baker teaches the first drama workshop in the country, English 47, at Harvard University.
- On November 16, the National Society for the Promotion of Industrial Education holds its first meeting in New York City. The society urges the development and full funding of a comprehensive program of vocational education in the schools.

1907

- William C. Bagley calls for a business approach to education in his widely used textbook *Classroom Management.*
- On February 8, Cleveland, Ohio mayor Tom Johnson denounces John D. Rockefeller's gift of $32 million to the General Education Board, charging that the donation perpetuates the privileges of the Standard Oil Company.
- On March 12, Alain Locke becomes the first African American to receive the prestigious Rhodes Scholarship. There will be no other African American recipient for half a century.
- On May 6, the American School Hygiene Association is organized.
- On June 13, the New York City Board of Education votes to provide free eyeglasses for needy students.
- On July 20, the National Education Association condemns the "deteriorating" behavior of students.
- On October 16, in Hattiesburg, Mississippi, school officials ask the city council to create a separate school for children of immigrants.
- On November 20, the New York City school board bans Christmas carols from its schools in an attempt to eliminate "sectarianism."

1908

- Schools in Gary, Indiana, begin operating under William Wirt's "platoon system" of schooling, also known as the "Gary Plan."
- In February, at the Lowell Institute Lectures in Boston, historian Albert Bushnell Hart laments the neglect of African American public schools in the South. The lectures are published in 1910 as *The Southern South.*

- On February 29, the Anna T. Jeanes Foundation is created to improve schools for African American students in the rural South.
- On March 4, 174 children perish in a fire caused by faulty steam pipes in a school in Collinwood, Ohio.
- In April, in his article "Why Teaching Repels Men" in *Educational Review* C.W. Bardeen writes that few men enter teaching, because it is a "hireling" profession that "belittles men."
- In June, the first issue of *School Hygiene* is published.
- In September, fifty-six students enroll as candidates for Harvard University's new Master's in Business Administration (MBA) program in the Graduate School of Business Administration.
- On September 12, the Chicago school board suspends fifty-two students for joining a fraternity. Three days later the fraternity sues the board.
- On November 9, the U.S. Supreme Court, in *Berea College* v. *Kentucky,* upholds a Kentucky law prohibiting racial integration in private schools by a 7-2 vote.
- In December, the U.S. Immigration Commission releases a study that 72 percent of New York City schoolchildren are either immigrants or children of immigrants.
- On December 31, the American Home Economics Association is founded. The organization seeks "to improve the conditions of living in the home, the institutional household, and the community." It aims to advance its purposes "by securing recognition of subjects related to the home in the curricula of existing schools and colleges."

1909

- On January 23, the Federal Commission on Country Life reports to the president that schools fail to provide "good training for country life" and are "largely responsible for ineffective farming, lack of ideals, and the drift to town."
- From February 22 to February 24, the National Society for the Scientific Study of Education focuses on sex education at its annual meeting in Chicago.
- On March 15, Harvard University President Charles W. Eliot announces his plan to create a "five-foot shelf of books" to provide someone with little formal schooling the knowledge necessary to be deemed well-educated.
- On April 3, in Sayville, New York, a youth is expelled for bringing a revolver to school.
- From May 11 to May 13, the American Federation of Arts is founded. Organizers support the study of art in public schools and the creation of art societies, art schools, and galleries.
- On May 19, A. Lawrence Lowell succeeds Charles W. Eliot as president of Harvard University.
- On July 29, Ella Flagg Young becomes the first female superintendent of an urban school system when the Chicago Board of Education appoints her to the post.
- In September, the Cincinnati public-school system establishes the country's first continuation school, a part-time school for employed children and youth.
- In September, in his only visit to the United States, Sigmund Freud lectures at Clark University in Worcester, Massachusetts.
- On September 13, Public School 100, the first public vocational school in the city of New York, opens.
- In November, the College Entrance Examination Board approves the use of the "Carnegie unit" by its member schools.
- On November 18, the New York City public-school system abolishes its football program.

In 1897, journalist Walter Hines Page called for improved public schooling in the southern United States. He praised North Carolina's fledgling public school program for its focus on the "forgotten" men and women of the South. **THE LIBRARY OF CONGRESS.**

"The Forgotten Man"

Speech

By: Walter H. Page

Date: June 1897

Source: Page, Walter H. "The Forgotten Man" speech. Reprinted in Page, Walter H. *The Rebuilding of Old Commonwealths: Being Essays Towards the Training of the Forgotten Man in the Southern States.* New York: Doubleday, Page, 1902, 1–3, 22–35, 47.

About the Author: Walter Hines Page (1855–1918), journalist, author, and diplomat, was born in North Carolina and graduated from Randolph-Macon College. He ran the *Raleigh State Chronicle* from 1883 to 1887. He left to join *The Forum,* a New York monthly magazine that he made a great success. In 1899, Page became a partner in the Doubleday, Page and Company publishing house and founded the *World's Work* magazine in 1900. He was appointed U.S. Ambassador to Great Britain in 1913. ■

Introduction

Historically, educational development in the South had lagged behind that in the North for several reasons. Strongly individualist in outlook, many southerners resisted taxation, especially for schools. Schooling was not commonly regarded as a function of the state; rather, it was viewed as a luxury to be paid for by individuals who could afford it. Another contributing factor was the rural character of much of the South; sparsely settled areas made schools impractical. Some progress had been made by the time of the Civil War (1861–1865). By the 1860s, most southern states had established funding for the minimal provision of education of the very poor, supplemented by efforts of churches and philanthropists. While few communities chose to support a school—North Carolina, especially, had made great strides—public school systems did not exist in the South prior to the Civil War.

After the Civil War, the South was physically and economically devastated. What advances had been made prior to the war were erased. The collapse of the economic system, the burden of rebuilding, and the persistence of prewar beliefs greatly hindered the growth of schools. Northern philanthropy and federal government efforts during Reconstruction were responsible for much progress, especially regarding education for newly freed slaves. However, Reconstruction efforts toward public schools were widely resented by southerners as yet another unwelcome instance of Yankee interference. While publicly funded education made gradual progress during the remainder of the nineteenth century, the end of Reconstruction brought the establishment of Jim Crow laws, the "separate but equal" doctrine, and a general backlash against African Americans. All did not benefit equally from educational advances.

By the turn of the twentieth century, the South was experiencing an economic revival and the concept of education for all was gaining wider acceptance. The South was ready for an "educational awakening."

Significance

Since the start of his journalism career in the early 1880s, Walter Page wrote numerous articles advocating the development of universal education in the South. His 1897 speech, "The Forgotten Man," stimulated public support for southern education reform while at the same time infuriating some southerners who saw this "southern yankee" as criticizing the traditions of his native region and trying to impose northern ideas. However, Page's speech was especially successful in galvanizing support among northerners in a position to help. The Conference for Education in the South held its first meeting in 1898. In 1901, with the help of wealthy philanthropists such as Robert C. Ogden and John D. Rockefeller, the conference founded the Southern Education Board (SEB) to operate a "campaign of education for free schools for all the people." Page was active in both of these organizations.

The SEB was responsible, through public campaigns and funding, for an improvement in almost every aspect of education—school budgets increased, enrollment and attendance went up, school terms were longer, and more schools were built. However, the improvements did not benefit all groups equally. While the SEB and Page himself upheld ideals of equal education for "all the people," these ideals were compromised in order to gain support and funding from whites: Black education received far less funding than white education while, at the same time, the needs of black education were greater. There were also racial inequities in the type of education the SEB was willing to support. The SEB hired prominent African American leader Booker T. Washington as its agent for African Americans and, though he was never allowed to attend meetings, his programs of industrial and agricultural education for African Americans received support while whites received funds for higher education.

Primary Source

"The Forgotten Man" [excerpt]

SYNOPSIS: Page discusses the high rate of illiteracy and lack of education for the poor, especially women, in the South. Page encourages education as the most beneficial focus of philanthropy, for educating the common people will uplift the entire society.

[*An Address delivered at the State Normal and Industrial School for Women at Greensboro, North Carolina, June, 1897.*] . . .

We have often reminded ourselves and informed other people that we have incalculable undeveloped resources in North Carolina, in our streams, our forests, our mines, our quarries, our soil—that Nature has been most bountiful; so that our undeveloped resources invite men under the pleasantest conditions to productive industry. And so they do. But there is one undeveloped resource more valuable than all these, and that is the people themselves. It is about the development of men that I shall speak, more particularly about the development of forgotten and neglected men. . . .

In 1890, twenty-six per cent of the white persons of the State were unable even to read and write. One in every four was wholly forgotten. But illiteracy was not the worst of it; the worst of it was that the stationary social condition indicated by generations of illiteracy had long been the general condition. The forgotten man was content to be forgotten. He became not only a dead weight, but a definite opponent of social progress. . . .

I have thus far spoken only of the forgotten man. I have done so to show the social and educational structure in proper perspective. But what I have come to speak about is the forgotten woman. Both the aristocratic and the ecclesiastical systems made provision for the women of special classes—the fortunately born and the religious well-to-do. But all the other women were forgotten. Let any man whose mind is not hardened by some worn-out theory of politics or of ecclesiasticism go to the country in almost any part of the State and make a study of life there, especially of the life of the women. He will see them thin and wrinkled in youth from ill prepared food, clad without warmth or grace, living in untidy houses, working from daylight till bed-time at the dull round of weary duties, the slaves of men of equal slovenliness, the mothers of joyless children—all uneducated if not illiterate. Yet even their condition were endurable if there were any hope, but this type of woman is encrusted in a shell of dull content with her lot; she knows no better and can never learn better, nor point her children to a higher life. . . .

Now one of the two things is true—either these forgotten men and women are incapable of development, and belong to a lower order of intelligence than any other people of Anglo-Saxon stock; or our civilization, so far as they are concerned, has been a failure. Of course there is no doubt which of these suppositions is true; for these people are capable of development, capable of unlimited growth and elevation. But, if they be capable of development, then both the aristocratic and the ecclesiastical systems of society have failed to develop them.

Since both the politician and the preacher have failed to lift this life after a century of unobstructed opportunities, it is time for a wiser statesmanship and a more certain means of grace. . . .

But now the story brightens. These old educational systems having failed here, as they have failed in other States, the public-spirited, far-sighted and energetic young men, chief among them your own President and the President of the University, who came into activity ten years or more ago, began seriously to develop a public school system, first of course in the towns. . . .

In my judgment there has been no other event in North Carolina since the formation of the American Union that is comparable in importance to this new educational progress. The movement now has such momentum that nothing can hinder the complete development of the public school system till every child is reached. . . .

As the movement to establish public schools everywhere gathers force, men of wealth will find that they can do no public service with their money so sure to bring lasting results as to build schoolhouses. The history of philanthropy shows that no public benefaction brings the same sure and permanent results as provision for the free education of the masses. The battle will be practically won when the whole State shall stand on this platform:

> A public school system generously supported by public sentiment, and generously maintained by both State and local taxation, is the only effective means to develop the forgotten man, and even more surely the only means to develop the forgotten woman. . . .

Too poor to maintain schools? The man who says it is the perpetuator of poverty. It is the doctrine that has kept us poor. It smells of the almshouse and the hovel. It has driven more men and more wealth from the State and kept more away than any other political doctrine ever cost us—more even than the doctrine of Secession. Such a man is the victim of an ancient and harmful falsehood. . . .

The most sacred thing in the Commonwealth and to the Commonwealth is the child, whether it be your child or the child of the dull-faced mother of the hovel. The child of the dull-faced mother may, for all you know, be the most capable child in the State. At its worst, it is capable of good citizenship and a useful life, if its intelligence be quickened and trained. . . .

This institution and your presence is proof that the State has remembered the forgotten woman. You in turn will remember the forgotten child; and in this remembrance is laid the foundation of a new social order. The neglected people will rise and with them will rise all the people.

Further Resources

BOOKS

Bremner, Robert H. *American Philanthropy.* Chicago: University of Chicago Press, 1960.

Butts, R. Freeman, and Lawrence Cremin. *A History of Education in American Culture.* New York: Henry Holt, 1953.

Cooper, John Milton. *Walter Hines Page: The Southerner as American, 1855–1918.* Chapel Hill, N.C.: University of North Carolina Press, 1977.

Dabney, Charles William. *Universal Education in the South.* New York: Arno Press, 1969.

Fosdick, Raymond. *The Story of the Rockefeller Foundation.* New Brunswick, N.J.: Transaction Publishers, 1989.

Goodenow, Ronald K., and Arthur O. White, eds. *Education and the Rise of the New South.* Boston: G.K. Hall, 1981.

Harlan, Louis R. *Separate and Unequal: Public School Campaigns and Racism in the Southern Seaboard States, 1901–1915.* Chapel Hill, N.C.: University of North Carolina Press, 1958.

"The Little Schoolboy"

Textbook

By: William Holmes McGuffey

Date: 1901

Source: McGuffey, William Holmes. "The Little Schoolboy." In *The New McGuffey Second Reader.* New York: American Book Company, 1901, 29–31.

About the Author: William Holmes McGuffey (1800–1873) graduated from Washington College, having worked his way through as a schoolmaster. He taught ancient languages and mental philosophy at Miami University in Ohio and later taught at Woodward College and the University of Virginia. McGuffey was also the president of Cincinnati College and Ohio University. He successfully worked to pass the general school law in Ohio. McGuffey is best known as the original author of the McGuffey Reader series and has been called "Schoolmaster to the Nation." ■

Introduction

During the first half of the nineteenth century, leaders in the common school movement worked toward a system of schools that was publicly funded and controlled and universally attended. Such schools, common school reformers argued, would unify a diverse population and train loyal citizens with strong American values. Yet education for most people at the time meant character and moral development taught within the context of religion. If the common schools were to be truly "common" to all, the problem of religious diversity had to be addressed. Some school reformers, such as Thomas Mann in Massachusetts, argued that nonsectarian moral values common to all religions could be taught in schools without offending any group. "Nonsectarian" referred, at the time, to material common to all *Christian* religions, specifically Protestant Christian. Therefore, Bible readings,

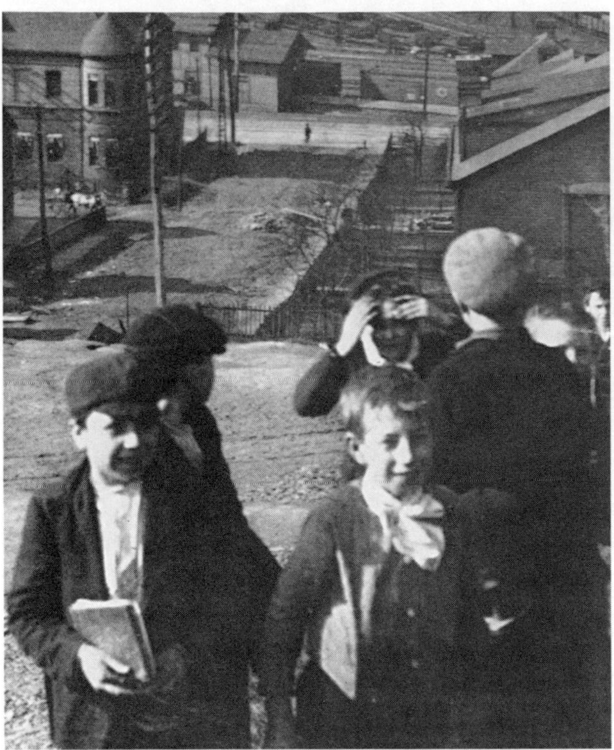

Schoolboys carry their books as they make their way to school in Homestead, Pennsylvania, c. 1900. © CORBIS. REPRODUCED BY PERMISSION.

without comment by the teacher, could be considered nonsectarian instruction. Other religious groups such as Catholics and Jews protested that the reading of the Protestant Bible constituted sectarianism, but nevertheless the common school agenda moved forward on this premise.

The rapid growth of the common schools created a demand for schoolbooks that would instill moral values, patriotism, and general Christian beliefs. In this context, the McGuffey's First and Second Readers were published in 1836 and the Third and Fourth Readers in 1837. In 1841, a higher reader was introduced, and in 1853, the revised series was issued as a six-volume set called the "New Readers." The books were revised several more times throughout the nineteenth and early twentieth centuries. The McGuffey First Reader began with the alphabet and simple stories of mostly one-syllable words. Reading was taught through lessons relying on phonics and the division of words into syllables. The later readers introduced selections from great writers such as Shakespeare, Milton, and Bacon. An emphasis was placed on the skills of reading aloud and effectively conveying the meaning of an author to an audience.

Through stories and poems, the McGuffey Readers taught values such as industry, thrift, punctuality, self-denial, sobriety, economy, kindness, generosity, honesty, courage, and duty. They instilled patriotism and American nationalism in addition to the values of capitalism, including economic individualism and competition. While the books had much Protestant Christian content, including Bible stories, in the earlier editions, this type of material had been largely eliminated by the end of the nineteenth century. The McGuffey Readers both influenced and reflected the moral values of the time.

Significance

The McGuffey Readers were widely used; some have claimed they were nearly universal except in New England. Over 122 million copies were sold between 1836 and 1920. These books were not only widely read but often remained in the memory of many students well into adulthood. According to historian Henry Steele Commager, the McGuffey Readers gave nineteenth century children "a common body of allusions, a sense of common experience, and of common possession." When President Theodore Roosevelt (served 1901–1909) stated that he did not want to be a "Meddlesome Matty," his reference to a McGuffey Reader story was easily understood by the American public.

Many credit the McGuffey series with introducing great literature and moral values to generations of American children. Critics of textbooks today lament the bland fare, limited vocabularies, moral relativism, and lack of literary merit of current "basal readers" compared with the McGuffey Readers. Yet others fault the McGuffey Readers for their exclusively middle-class Protestant values, lack of diverse portrayals, and overly moralistic tone.

Though their popularity declined after the 1930s, the McGuffey Readers have never gone out of print since their original publication. Sales of over 200,000 annually were recorded as recently in the 1990s. They are occasionally adopted for use by some schools today.

Primary Source

"The Little Schoolboy"

SYNOPSIS: In this story excerpted from *The New McGuffey Second Reader,* a boy skips school in order to play outside. He discovers that the bee, the dog, and the bird are all too busy working to play with him. He concludes that everyone must work and so returns to school. This story is representative of the type of material included in the McGuffey readers intended to instill morals such as the value of hard work.

One day our teacher told us of a little boy who did not like his books or his school. "I do not want to go to school," he said. "I want to play all day.

"The sun is shining, and the birds are singing, and I cannot bear to be shut up in school on this fine day. Why is it that boys have to work? I think I will go and have some fun in the fields."

So off he ran into the green fields. He saw a bee flying about from flower to flower. "Please, little bee," he said, "please come and play with me."

But the pretty bee said: "Oh no, no; I have no time to play. I have so much work to do that I must not be idle. I must get all the honey I can;" and away went the bee, buzzing among the flowers.

Then the boy saw a dog. "Come here, my pretty dog," he said, "come and have some fun with me."

But the dog said: "I cannot come. I must take care of all the sheep that you see in this field;" and he ran to drive back some lambs that were too near the road.

Then the boy saw a bird picking up a straw from the ground, and he said: "My sweet little bird, will you come and play with me? Will you sing me a pretty song?"

But the bird said: "No, no, I cannot be idle. I must get straw and sticks, and build my nest. So good morning;" and away it flew with the straw in its mouth.

Then the little boy began to think. "I see," said he, "that even the birds, the bees, and the dogs are busy. There is work for all to do, and I must not be idle."

So he ran to school as fast as he could, and never again wished that he might play all the time.

Further Resources

BOOKS

Lindberg, Stanley W. *The Annotated McGuffey.* New York: Van Nostrand Reinhold, 1976.

Mosier, Richard D. *Making the American Mind: Social and Moral Ideas in the McGuffey Readers.* New York: King's Crown Press, 1947.

Sullivan, Dolores P. *William Holmes McGuffey: Schoolmaster to the Nation.* Cranbury, N.J.: Associated University Presses, 1994.

Vail, Henry H. *A History of the McGuffey Readers.* Cleveland, Ohio: Burrows Brothers, 1910.

Westerhoff, John H. *McGuffey and His Readers: Piety, Morality, and Education in Nineteenth-Century America.* Nashville, Tenn.: Abingdon, 1978.

PERIODICALS

Commager, Henry Steele. "McGuffey and His Readers." *Saturday Review of Literature,* June 16, 1962.

Murphy, Anna Marie, and Cullen Murphy. "Onward, Upward with McGuffey and Those Readers." *Smithsonian,* November 1984, 182–208.

"The Ideal School as Based on Child Study"

Journal article

By: G. Stanley Hall

Date: 1901

Source: Hall, G. Stanley. "The Ideal School as Based on Child Study." *National Education Association Journal of Proceedings and Addresses,* 1901, 474–483. Reprinted in Calhoun, Daniel, ed. *The Educating of Americans.* Boston: Houghton Mifflin, 1969, 374–378.

About the Author: Granville Stanley Hall (1844–1924) graduated from Williams College and earned the first Ph.D. in psychology from Harvard in 1878. He taught at Johns Hopkins University and then became the president of Clark University in 1889. Under Hall's leadership, Clark became a center of research in child development and child study. Hall founded the Child Study Association of America in 1888 and became the first president of the American Psychological Association in 1889. ■

Introduction

Charles Darwin's *On the Origin of Species,* published in 1859, presented an alternative to the traditionally held belief that humans were created by God at a particular point in time and have not changed significantly since. Rather, Darwin asserted that humans have evolved through a natural process from lower animals. This revolutionary idea led many to view humans as part of the natural, not the supernatural, world and therefore a proper subject of science. American philosopher and psychologist William James and others began to think about the possibility that human behavior and learning could be objectively studied using the scientific method. The result was the "New Psychology."

One of James' students, G. Stanley Hall, basing his ideas partially on those of Herbert Spencer, applied the idea of evolution to human psychological development. Hall's "general psychonomic law" stated that each child develops through the same stages as humankind in its progress from a primitive stage to civilization. Very young children in the primitive stage of development are unable to reason and should not be placed under any unnecessary constraints or be exposed to formal education. The focus should be on the development of the body rather than the mind. After age eight, according to Hall, the child is able to benefit from formal learning, yet abstract reasoning skills are not fully developed. During the stage of adolescence, the child is rapidly developing emotionally and morally. Adolescents need more freedom because of their need to express their individuality. Able to absorb much, the adolescent is yet unable to express thoughts and ideas in a polished manner.

In 1901 G. Stanley Hall presented a paper to the National Education Association advocating designing educational programs around the needs of the students. © BETTMANN/CORBIS. REPRODUCED BY PERMISSION.

For Hall, these stages are natural and, therefore, desirable. Since the process will unfold on its own, the main duty of the educator is to avoid interfering and, ideally, to promote natural development. Whereas in the past, the child was forced to adapt to the school, Hall's view indicates that the school should adapt to the child. In the past, a child's failure to learn was the fault of the child alone. Hall proposed that teachers and schools are responsible for creating the conditions under which the child can learn.

Significance

Hall is the founder of the child study movement dedicated to promoting a fuller understanding of the stages of growth and the creation of methods and curricula appropriate to each stage. If the school is to provide conditions conducive to the child's development, Hall believed, then it is of primary importance that educators know and understand this development. Child study takes a scientific approach to collecting data about the growth and development of children and using the findings to create appropriate school settings.

Along with philosopher and educator John Dewey, Hall was an early advocate of the child-centered school, popularized by the progressive education movement. The child-centered school is one that uses methods, materials, and curricula suited to the needs of the child as opposed to the traditional approach of forcing the child to fit the structure of the school. The child study movement and child-centered education were key elements of the agenda of the progressive education movement. Progressive educators sought to develop an "objective" science of education and welcomed enthusiastically Hall's pioneering studies of child development and child psychology.

Hall's ideas influenced later prominent theorists such as Jean Piaget and continue to impact education today. In contemporary schools, "developmentally appropriate" and "learner-centered" instruction are commonplace approaches. Yet some educators are critical of Hall's developmentalism because of the assumption that the natural stages are "good" and therefore should not be interfered with, encouraging parents and teachers to passively accept whatever a child seems willing to do—adult attempts to promote development are considered harmful.

Primary Source

"The Ideal School as Based on Child Study" [excerpt]

SYNOPSIS: In this excerpt, G. Stanley Hall describes the characteristics of adolescence and the optimal educational environment adapted to this stage of development. He argues that high schools should end their reliance on the requirements of colleges in determining how they operate. Rather, schools should base their approach to adolescents on the needs of the adolescents themselves. He calls for more study of adolescents in order to determine what these needs are.

Adolescence is a term now applied to a pretty well-marked stage, beginning at about thirteen with girls and a year later with boys, and lasting about ten years, to the period of complete sexual maturity. It is subdivided into pubescence, the first two years; youth proper, from sixteen to twenty in boys and perhaps fifteen to nineteen in girls; and a finishing stage thru the early twenties. The first stage is marked by a great increase in the rate of growth in both height and weight. It is a period of greater susceptibility to sickness for both sexes; but this vulnerability is due to the great changes, and the death-rate Is lower in the early teens than at any other age. It is the time when there is the most rapid development of the heart and all the feelings and emotions. Fear, anger, love, pity, jealousy, emulation, ambition, and sympathy are either now born or springing into their most intense life. Now young people are interested in adults, and one of their strong passions is to be treated as if they were mature. They desire to know, do, and be all that becomes a man or woman. Childhood is ending, and plans for future vocations now spring into existence, and slowly grow definite and controlling.

There is often a new and exquisite sensitiveness to every breath of criticism, praise, or blame. All are anxious to know whether they are inferior or superior to others. There may be observed both a new diffidence and a new self-assertion. The largest percentage of criminals is found in the later teens, and at this time most conversions occur also. Both pleasure and pain are vastly intensified. Pugnacity becomes very strong, as does the instinct for showing off. The large muscles and then the small develop rapidly, but are at first unenduring and clumsy. The heart and arteries are suddenly enlarged, and the blood pressure is increased. Blushing is greatly developed. Nature puts body and soul on their mettle. Heredity chiefly, and environment next, determine whether the individual can cross this *pons* successfully; whether he can molt into maturity completely without loss or arrest. New friendships and new secrets are formed; the imagination blossoms; the soul is never so sensitive to all the aspects of nature; music, which may have been studied before, is now felt; the excelsior motive or the developmental push upward makes this the very best and richest season of life. New curiosities, amounting to intellectual hungers, are felt.

Thus again a few years or even months give us a new kind of being, which demands a new environment, new methods, and new matter. Instinct, now so much wiser than reason, feels this break of continuity. It is the age when the majority leave school forever and begin life for themselves. The apex of the runaway and truancy curve is here. It is the age of spring fever, when previous life seems dead, and the soul would molt it and be done with it. It is the most vulnerable and difficult of all periods after infancy, the severest test of parent, teacher, and pedagogical methods. It is the point where, in the sequential history of the race, education has begun in every indigenous race and from which it widens up toward the university and down toward the kindergarten, just in proportion as civilization advances and the mass of culture material grows. What we shall do with the hobbledehoys, *Backfische,* larrikins, is the oldest problem of education, and one answer is plain: We must first study them. This process has been begun, and has yielded a few results, some very clear and some still uncertain.

First of all, the drill and mechanism of the previous period must be gradually relaxed, and an appeal must be made to freedom and interest. Individuality must have a far longer tether. We must, and can, really teach nothing that does not appeal to interests deep enough to make it seem of almost supreme value in the world. We can no longer coerce and break, but must lead and inspire. To drill merely is now to arrest. Each individual must be studied and made a special problem, if his personality is to come to full maturity. Hence, there must be a wide range of elective study for those who continue at school. Boys can hereafter rarely do their best work under female teachers, however well equipped these may be mentally. They feel their manhood, and need the dominance of male influences.

In the ideal school system the sexes will now, for a time at least, pretty much part company. They are beginning to differ in every cell and tissue, and girls for a time need some exemption from competition. They have more power than boys to draw upon their capital of physical energy and to take out of their system more than it can afford to lose, for the individuals of one generation can consume more than their share of vigor at the expense of posterity. In soul and body girls are more conservative; males vary, differentiate, and are more radical. Reproduction requires a far larger proportion of body and function in females. Now the leaders of the new education for girls recommend training them for self-support, assuming that, if wifehood and motherhood come, those who have received such a training can best take care of themselves. This assumption is radically wrong and vicious, and should be reversed. Every girl should be educated primarily to become a wife and mother, and, if this is done wisely and broadly, the small minority who remain single will, with this training, be best able to care for themselves.

A third conclusive and far-reaching principle is that at no stage of life is the power to appreciate and apprehend so very far ahead of the power to express. Hence we should let up on examinations; we should cast our bread upon the waters, knowing that it will be found after many days, because so sensitized is the soul now that nothing is lost. Mental and

Teachers and students in a high school science class, 1900. The idea that educators needed to study students to develop the best instructional methods was a new idea in the 1900s.

moral teaching and influences sink at once too deep to be reproduced in examinations of the present type, without injury to both mind and will. There is nothing in the whole environment to which the adolescent nature does not keenly respond. Neither you nor I, however specialized our knowledge, know anything really worth knowing, the substance of which cannot be taught now if we have pedagogical tact; but, if we wait for its reproduction in the pupil, we starve and retard his soul. Hence facts, ideas, laws, and principles should be in the very atmosphere, for they are now the ingenuous youth's native breath, his vital air. He is all insight and receptivity; he has just entered the stage of apprenticeship to life; he has awakened to it as at a second birth, and has found all things new and glorious.

Yet another change is well defined. Whereas previously the pupil could work with some skill and accuracy, now body and mind are both again so plastic and unformed that they are clumsy, and precision and finish cannot be bought except at too great a price. The teacher's cue is now to graft the soul all over with buds and scions, and not to try to gather a harvest. The mind has laid aside its power to finish and elaborate. It can rudely assimilate everything by turns, but nothing well. The fundamental system of the body, which consists of the large muscles and not the small, and which therefore makes coarse, massive movements and not exact ones, has now its innings; and the fundamentals of the soul, which are instinct and intuition, and not pure intellect, are now in season. We must lay new and larger foundations.

But, more specifically, what do these changes involve in the ideal school of the future? The transition from the grammar to the high school in this country corresponds far better than the European system to the need of changed environment at the age of fourteen; and this constitutes a rare opportunity, which has, however, been thrown away. Altho education, as we have seen, begins here, and many races have no other than a brief training at the dawn of the ephebic period, by a strange irony of fate secondary education has more or less lapsed to a mere link. Its functions are partly those of preparation for college, and are partly shaped by the mere momentum of the lower grades. The high school has lost its independence, and of all stages and grades has least interest in the large problems of education, namely, what to teach and how, in order to develop the nascent periods during the teens and to save powers now new-born in most profusion, but sure to be atrophied or perverted if not studied with tact and federated with individual adaptation.

For all these problems as a class, high-school teachers care less than those of any other grade, if, indeed, they suspect their existence. For them adolescence is just a stage when children are so much farther along than in the grammar school, and know so much less than they must to enter college. For such teachers the task is simply to convert their pupils into freshmen, and they await with hope or fear the assignment of their stint in the form of college requirements. They have abandoned all initiative; have renounced their birthright of interpreting, and ministering to, the needs of one stage of life; have had little professional training; have little interest in education in the large meaning of that term; and care little for work of the lower grades. Their motto almost seems to be, *Non vitae sed scholae discimus.* The result is that boys, who insist more on their own individuality, leave the high school: in the country at large about 60 per cent of its pupils are now girls. Noble ideals are gone; the independent function of the secondary stage of education is almost abandoned; and the pupil and teacher devote themselves to a routine of tasks in an artificial program imposed by the will of others, and fitting, not for the world, but for college. The pupils do not regard their work as set on a basis which gives it a value and meaning in itself to which each day contributes. Nothing can be done then until the high school takes a stronger hold on the interests and affections of the pupil.

At the sessions of the representatives of New England high schools and colleges, all the discussions and interests center more and more in the details of how to fit in this and that study, and whether a little more or less should be required or methods tinkered. College requirements, and suggestions how they may be best met, have ceased to be educational themes in any large sense. It is high time to reverse this relation. The college depends on the high school, and not *vice versa.* The latter should declare its independence, and proceed to solve its own problems in its own way; it should strive to fit for life those whose education stops here, and should bring the college to meet its own demands. It should ask again how best to feed the interests and capacities peculiar to this age; how to fill and develop mind, heart, will, and body, rather than how to distill a budget of prepared knowledge decreed by professors who know no more of the needs of this age than teachers of other grades. The current "link" theory and practice interfere, moreover, with the natural selective functions; favor uniformity and inflexibility; and ignore the needs of the majority of high-school pupils who go no farther.

Under this condition it is idle to study adolescence or to plan for it, because nothing worth while can be done; altho the inverse relation I plead for would be vastly to the interests of the colleges, and would in a few years greatly increase their classes and the efficacy of the whole system. Few institutions of modern civilization so distrust human nature as does the modern American high school, when under college domination. For lower grades the law of compulsory attendance is analogous to a high protective tariff, which removes the stimulus to better methods of manufacture, and interferes with the law of competition which is the mainspring of evolution. The high school is no less effectively protected against the currents of new ideas, and is left to be a victim of tradition, routine, the iron law of mechanism. It takes the easiest way by working under the shelter and dictation of the college above and on the momentum of the grammar school below. This, I believe, accounts for the rapidly decreasing numbers as we go up the high-school classes; for the decreasing proportion of high-school boys who go to college; for the preponderance of girls in the high school; and for the educational apathy of the high-school teacher, who is prone to all the narrowness and affectation of the specialist, without his redeeming virtue of productiveness in research.

The teacher must teach more, and know more; he must be a living fountain, not a stagnant pool. He should not be a dealer in desiccated, second-hand knowledge, a mere giver-out and hearer of lessons. That is the chief and humiliating difference between our secondary teachers and those abroad, who are mostly doctors of philosophy, as they should be. If we could move many university profesors to the college, many college professors to the high school, many high-school teachers to the grammar school, and some grammar-school teachers, with at least a sprinkling of college graduates, into the kindergarten, it would do much. In the German and French schools the teacher is one who knows a great deal about his subject and is nearer to original sources; who tells the great truths of the sciences almost like stories; and who does not affect the airs and methods of the university professor. Very many secondary teachers are masters and authorities. Here, most of our university pedagogy is a mere device for so influencing high-school principals and teachers as to correlate curricula, in order to corral in students, and little interest is taken in the grammar grades, and none in the kindergarten.

I have spoken frankly, and have dealt only with general principles over a vast field, far too large to be adequately discussed here. I have carefully avoided all details, altho I have fully worked them out on paper at great length, for each topic to the close of the high-school period or the age of nineteen when physical growth is essentially completed. This material will soon appear in a volume. The chief petition in my daily prayer now is for a millionaire. With the means at hand, I have no shadow of doubt or fear but that in five years from the date of any adequate gift we shall be able to invite all interested to a system of education, covering this ground, which will be a practical realization of much present prophecy, and which will commend itself even to the most conservative defenders of things as they are and have been, because the best things established will be in it. But it will be essentially pedocentric rather than scholiocentric; it may be a little like the Reformation, which insisted that the sabbath, the Bible, and the church were made for man and not he for them; it will fit both the practices and the results of modern science and psychological study; it will make religion and morals more effective; and, perhaps above all, it will give individuality in the school its full rights as befits a republican form of government, and will contribute something to bring the race to the higher maturity of the superman that is to be, effectiveness in developing which is the highest and final test of art, science, religion, home, state, literature, and every human institution.

Further Resources

BOOKS

Hall, G. Stanley. *Adolescence: Its Psychology and Its Relations to Physiology, Anthropology, Sociology, Sex, Crime, Religion, and Education.* New York: Appleton, 1904.

———. *The Content of Children's Minds on Entering School.* New York: E.L. Kellogg, 1893.

———. *The Life and Confessions of a Psychologist.* New York: Appleton, 1923.

Ross, Dorothy. *G. Stanley Hall: The Psychologist as Prophet.* Chicago: University of Chicago Press, 1972.

WEBSITES

"G. Stanley Hall." The PSI Cafe: A Psychology Research Site. Available online at http://www.psy.pdx.edu/PsiCafe/KeyTheorists/Hall.htm; website home page: http://www.psy.pdx.edu/ (accessed April 2, 2003).

"The G. Stanley Hall School." Marquardt School District 15. Available online at http://www.d15.dupage.k12.il.us/Schools/Hall/HallWeb.html; website home page: http://www.d15.dupage.k12.il.us/ (accessed April 2, 2003).

"The Child and the Curriculum"

Nonfiction work

By: John Dewey

Date: 1902

Source: Dewey, John. *The Child and the Curriculum.* Chicago: University of Chicago Press, 1902. Reprinted in Dworkin, Martin S., ed. *Dewey on Education.* New York: Teachers College Press, 1959, 92, 94, 101–102, 105–108, 110–111.

About the Author: John Dewey (1859–1952), philosopher and educator, had an enormous impact on education as well as other fields of knowledge. Often considered the leader of the progressive education movement, he established the famous "Laboratory School" while a professor at the University of Chicago. In 1904, he accepted an appointment at Columbia University, where he taught philosophy and education until his retirement in 1939. He continued to speak and publish prolifically until the end of his life. ■

Introduction

Dewey's philosophy of education emphasized the motivations and interests of the child, freedom and self-expression, socialization, hands-on activities, useful curriculum, and learning how to think rather than what to think. He developed his philosophy in the context of nineteenth and early twentieth century educational norms, emphasizing memorization and rigid methods. Dewey criticized the method of imposing organized subject matter on young children with no regard to the meaning, if any, the child derived from this process. Many educators interpreted Dewey to mean that the child, with the interests and motivations he or she brings to school, is "good" and the organized curriculum is "bad." In *The Child and the Curriculum,* Dewey clarifies his meaning on this subject.

Dewey describes an apparent conflict between the two main factors in education: the child, knowing only his or her own little world of personal experience, and the curriculum, the wide world of cultural knowledge. Educators have broken into opposing camps: one group "sides with" the child and his or her current interests and abilities, viewing these as the beginning and end of education: The child is wonderfully complete as is. Their "method" is to leave the child to do as he or she pleases. The other camp "sides with" the curriculum and views the child as ignorant, an empty container needing to be filled with knowledge that will broaden the child's narrow world. The method for this camp is to present the material in abstract form and compel the child to memorize it.

In reality, the child and the curriculum are just two ends of the education continuum, not enemy forces. The child has abilities and interests that can, with the "appropriate stimuli," be used as a starting point to guide the child toward the eventual goal of organized subject matter. Organized subject matter is a desirable goal, but it must be "psychologized," in other words, connected to the child's own experience: The child has a true motivation to learn a particular piece of knowledge because it solves some real problem that the child is experiencing.

Without this connection to real problems and motivations in the child's life, problems result. First, the subject matter is a collection of mere symbols to the child without the meaning that is symbolized. Second, without a real need to know, the child must somehow be motivated through "tricks" or an "artificial bribe." Much energy is wasted trying to make the child pay attention. Third, ready-made subject matter is missing evidence of the logical activity that produced it (that is, the thinking and experimentation a scientist does to create new knowledge), nor does the child gain the knowledge through his or her own logical processes. It is just something to memorize, "non-science" as Dewey refers to it.

Dewey concludes that what appears to be a necessary choice between letting the child do whatever he or she wants or stuffing children's heads with "truth" is not a choice at all. Children do what they do, not in a vacuum of self-activity but in an environment. On the other hand, "truths" cannot be inserted in a child's head. Rather, the role of the teacher is to arrange the environment of the child so that he or she is directed, through interaction with that environment, toward the goal. The value of organized subject matter, then, is not as a body of facts to be presented to the child but as a guide for the teacher, a description of the goal toward which children are to be guided.

Significance

Dewey is often considered the leader of the progressive education movement that began in the 1870s and continued through the 1950s. Nonetheless, he often found himself at odds with those who considered themselves "progressive educators." Many educational innovations of the progressive era were supposedly based on Dewey's philosophy. Yet some were not at all in line with his ideas, such as the extreme examples of "child-centered" schools where students were left to do entirely as they pleased in the name of "freedom" and "self-expression." In *The Child and the Curriculum,* Dewey is critical of those who, having found previous educational methods wanting, swing to the other extreme.

Philosopher and educator John Dewey, around 1900. Dewey made influential arguments for school reforms to form a closer connection between schoolwork and the day-to-day lives of children. SPECIAL COLLECTIONS RESEARCH CENTER, MORRIS LIBRARY, SOUTHERN ILLINOIS UNIVERSITY, CARBONDALE, IL. REPRODUCED BY PERMISSION.

Primary Source

"The Child and the Curriculum" [excerpt]

SYNOPSIS: Dewey addresses the apparent conflict between freedom for the child and the need to learn content. He asserts that no conflict exists. Children should gradually come to understand content through their own activities under the guidance of the teacher. It is the process of imposing content as something to be memorized that is harmful.

The fundamental factors in the educative process are an immature, undeveloped being; and certain social aims, meanings, values incarnate in the matured experience of the adult. The educative process is the due interaction of these forces. Such a conception of each in relation to the other as facilitates completest and freest interaction is the essence of educational theory. . . .

These apparent deviations and differences between child and curriculum might be almost indefinitely widened. But we have here sufficiently fundamental divergences: first, the narrow but personal world of the child against the impersonal but infinitely extended world of space and time; second, the unity, the single whole-heartedness of the child's life, and the specializations and divisions of the curriculum; third, an abstract principle of logical classification and arrangement, and the practical and emotional bonds of child life. . . .

There are those who see no alternative between forcing the child from without, or leaving him entirely alone. Seeing no alternative, some choose one mode, some another. Both fall into the same fundamental error. Both fail to see that development is a definite process, having its own law which can be fulfilled only when adequate and normal conditions are provided. . . .

If, once more, the "old education" tended to ignore the dynamic quality, the developing force inherent in the child's present experience, and therefore to assume that direction and control were just matters of arbitrarily putting the child in a given path and compelling him to walk there, the "new education" is in danger of taking the idea of development in altogether too formal and empty a way. The child is expected to "develop" this or that fact or truth out of his own mind. He is told to think things out, or work things out for himself, without being supplied any of the environing conditions which are requisite to start and guide thought. Nothing can be developed from nothing; nothing but the crude can be developed out of the crude—and this is what surely happens when we throw the child back upon his achieved self as a finality, and invite him to spin new truths of nature or of conduct out of that. It is certainly as futile to expect a child to evolve a universe out of his own mere mind as it is for a philosopher to attempt that task. Development does not mean just getting something out of the mind. It is a development of experience and into experience that is really wanted. And this is impossible save as just that educative medium is provided which will enable the powers and interests that have been selected as valuable to function. They must operate, and how they operate will depend almost entirely upon the stimuli which surround them, and the material upon which they exercise themselves. The problem of direction is thus the problem of selecting appropriate stimuli for instincts and impulses which it is desired to employ in the gaining of new experience. What new experiences are desirable, and thus what stimuli are needed, it is impossible to tell except as there is some comprehension of the development which is aimed at; except, in a word, as the adult knowledge is drawn upon as revealing the possible career open to the child. . . .

It is the failure to keep in mind the double aspect of subject-matter which causes the curriculum and child to be set over against each other as described in our early pages. The subject-matter, just as it is for the scientist, has no direct relationship to the child's present experience. It stands outside of it. The danger here is not a merely theoretical one. We are practically threatened on all sides. Textbook and teacher vie with each other in presenting to the child the subject-matter as it stands to the specialist. Such modification and revision as it undergoes are a mere elimination of certain scientific difficulties, and the general reduction to a lower intellectual level. The material is not translated into life-terms, but is directly offered as a substitute for, or an external annex to, the child's present life.

Three typical evils result: In the first place, the lack of any organic connection with what the child has already seen and felt and loved makes the material purely formal and symbolic. There is a sense in which it is impossible to value too highly the formal and the symbolic. The genuine form, the real symbol, serve as methods in the holding and discovery of truth. They are tools by which the individual pushes out most surely and widely into unexplored areas. They are means by which he brings to bear whatever of reality he has succeeded in gaining in past searchings. But this happens only when the symbol really symbolizes—when it stands for and sums up in shorthand actual experiences which the individual has already gone through. A symbol which is induced from without, which has not been led up to in preliminary activities, is, as we say, a *bare* or *mere* symbol; it is dead and barren. Now, any fact, whether of arithmetic, or geography, or grammar, which is not led up to and into out of something which has previously occupied a significant position in the child's life for its own sake, is forced into this position. It is not a reality, but just the sign of a reality which *might* be experienced if certain conditions were fulfilled. But the abrupt presentation of the fact as something known by others, and requiring only to be studied and learned by the child, rules out such conditions of fulfilment. It condemns the fact to be hieroglyph: it would mean something if one only had the key. The clue being lacking, it remains an idle curiosity, to fret and obstruct the mind, a dead weight to burden it.

The second evil in this external presentation is lack of motivation. There are not only no facts or truths which have been previously felt as such with which to appropriate and assimilate the new, but there is no craving, no need, no demand. When the subject-matter has been psychologized, that is, viewed as an outgrowth of present tendencies and activities, it is easy to locate in the present some obstacle, intellectual, practical, or ethical, which can be handled more adequately if the truth in question be mastered. This need supplies motive for the learning. An end which is the child's own carries him on to possess the means of its accomplishment. But when material is directly supplied in the form of a lesson to be learned as a lesson, the connecting links of need and aim are conspicuous for their absence. What we mean by the mechanical and dead in instruction is a result of this lack of motivation. The organic and vital mean interaction—they mean play of mental demand and material supply.

The third evil is that even the most scientific matter, arranged in most logical fashion, loses this quality, when presented in external, ready-made fashion, by the time it gets to the child. It has to undergo some modification in order to shut out some phases too hard to grasp, and to reduce some of the attendant difficulties. What happens? Those things which are most significant to the scientific man, and most valuable in the logic of actual inquiry and classification, drop out. The really thought-provoking character is obscured, and the organizing function disappears. Or, as we commonly say, the child's reasoning powers, the faculty of abstraction and generalization, are not adequately developed. So the subject-matter is evacuated of its logical value, and, though it is what it is only from the logical standpoint, is presented as stuff only for "memory." This is the contradiction: the child gets the advantage neither of the adult logical formulation, nor of his own native competencies of apprehension and response. Hence the logic of the child is hampered and mortified, and we are almost fortunate if he does not get actual non-science, flat and commonplace residua of what was gaining scientific vitality a generation or two ago—degenerate reminiscence of what someone else once formulated on the basis of the experience that some further person had, once upon a time, experienced.

The train of evils does not cease. It is all too common for opposed erroneous theories to play straight into each other's hands. Psychological considerations may be slurred or shoved one side; they cannot be crowded out. Put out of the door, they come back through the window. Somehow and somewhere motive must be appealed to, connection must be established between the mind and its material. There is no question of getting along without this bond of connection; the only question is whether it be such as grows out of the material itself in relation to the mind, or be imported and hitched on from some outside source. If the subject-matter of the lessons be such as to have an appropriate place within the expanding consciousness of the child, if it grows out of his own past doings, thinkings, and sufferings, and grows into application in further achievements and receptivities, then no device or trick of method has to be resorted to in order to enlist "interest." The psychologized *is* of interest—that is, it is placed in the whole of conscious life so that it shares the worth of that life. But the externally presented material, that, conceived and generated in standpoints and attitudes remote from the child, and developed in motives alien to him, has no such place of its own. Hence the recourse to adventitious leverage to push it in, to factitious drill to drive it in, to artificial bribe to lure it in. . . .

How, then, stands the case of Child *vs.* Curriculum? What shall the verdict be? The radical fallacy in the original pleadings with which we set out is the supposition that we have no choice save either to leave the child to his own unguided spontaneity or to inspire direction upon him from without. Action is response; it is adaptation, adjustment. There is no such thing as sheer self-activity possible—because all activity takes place in a medium, in a situation, and with reference to its conditions. But, again, no such thing as imposition of truth from without, as insertion of truth from without, is possible. All depends upon the activity which the mind itself undergoes in responding to what is presented from without. Now, the value of the formulated wealth of knowledge that makes up the course of study is that it may enable the educator *to determine the environment of the child,* and thus by indirection to direct. Its primary value, its primary indication, is for the teacher, not for the child. It says to the teacher: Such and such are the capacities, the fulfilments, in truth and beauty and behavior, open to these children. Now see to it that day by day the conditions are such that *their own activities* move inevitably in this direction, toward such culmination of themselves. Let the child's nature fulfil its own destiny, revealed to you in whatever of science and art and industry the world now holds as its own.

The case is of Child. It is his present powers which are to assert themselves; his present capacities which are to be exercised; his present attitudes which are to be realized. But save as the teacher knows, knows wisely and thoroughly, the race-experience which is embodied in that thing we call the Curriculum, the teacher knows neither what the present power, capacity, or attitude is, nor yet how it is to be asserted, exercised, and realized.

Further Resources

BOOKS

Cremin, Lawrence A. *The Transformation of The School: Progressivism in American Education, 1876–1957.* New York: Knopf, 1961.

Dewey, John. *Dewey on Education: Selections.* Martin S. Dworkin, ed. New York: Teachers College Press, 1959.

———. *Experience and Education.* New York: Macmillan, 1938.

———. *Schools of To-morrow.* New York: Dutton, 1915.

Dykhuizen, George. *The Life and Mind of John Dewey.* Carbondale, Ill.: Southern Illinois University Press, 1973.

WEBSITES

"The Center for Dewey Studies, Southern Illinois University." Available online at http://www.siu.edu/~deweyctr/; website home page: http://www.siu.edu (accessed January 24, 2003).

"The John Dewey Society for the Study of Education and Culture, University of Chicago." Available online at http://cuip.uchicago.edu/jds/; website home page: http://cuip.uchicago.edu (accessed January 24, 2003).

AUDIO AND VISUAL MEDIA

John Dewey: His Life and Work Directed by Frances W. Davidson. Davidson Films. Videocassette, 2001.

The Elective System in Higher Education

"The Elective System at Harvard"

Magazine article

By: Charles S. Moore
Date: June 1903

Source: Moore, Charles S. "The Elective System at Harvard." *Harvard Graduates Magazine,* June 11, 1903, 530–534. Reprinted in *American Higher Education: A Documentary History.* Chicago: The University of Chicago Press, 1961, 737–741.

About the Author: Charles Moore (1855–1942), journalist and city planner, was born in Ypsilanti, Michigan. He attended the Kenmore School in Pennsylvania, Phillips Andover Academy, and Harvard College, studying history, political science, and philosophy. In school he edited the student newspaper, and after graduating he worked for various Detroit-area newspapers, purchasing several. In 1888, he became involved in city planning as Senator James McMillan's political secretary. From 1912 to 1919, he was president of the Detroit City Plan and Improvement Commission. In 1910, Moore was appointed by President Taft to the new federal Fine Arts Commission, and worked as its chairman from 1915 until his retirement in 1937.

"Report of the Committee on Improving Instruction in Harvard College"

Report

By: Harvard College Faculty of Arts and Sciences Committee
Date: June 1904

Source: "Report of the Committee on Improving Instruction in Harvard College." *Harvard Graduates Magazine,* June 12, 1904, 611–614, 616–619. Reprinted in *American Higher Education: A Documentary History.* Chicago: The University of Chicago Press, 1961, 745–747. ■

Introduction

Traditionally, higher education in the United States offered little freedom of choice—all students took identical courses in a prescribed order. The college curriculum consisted of a program devoted to classical Greek and Latin, as well as literature, mathematics, philosophy, and theology. The prevailing theory of learning in the nineteenth century, "mental discipline," held that people were endowed with God-given "faculties" that are developed through serious study of particular subjects such as classical languages and mathematics. These faculties, trained through study in much the same way that muscles are strengthened through exercise, could then be successfully applied to whatever field or profession the student later entered.

However, in considering the purpose of higher education in a democracy, Thomas Jefferson proposed that students should be free to choose a course of study in accordance with their interests and abilities. In his plan for the University of Virginia, implemented in 1825, he proposed that the university be composed of separate "schools" representing broad subject areas. Although students chose which school to attend, they followed a

Harvard seniors enter Sander's Theatre, Cambridge, Massachusetts, c. 1906. In the early 1900s, a committee was appointed to research and improve the instruction at Harvard to ensure that the standard of work required of students remained high. THE LIBRARY OF CONGRESS.

prescribed course of study within that school. Harvard also experimented with the elective system, allowing students limited freedom of choice.

A number of factors contributed to an increasing demand for the elective system in colleges and universities after the Civil War (1861–1865). Knowledge, especially in the sciences, was growing at an astounding rate. As new subjects were added to course catalogs, it became clear that no student could master everything—some specialization was necessary. In addition, the popularity of the theory of mental discipline was eroding as scholars of the "new psychology" asserted that there are no "faculties" but that the mind is a function or process. Therefore, no particular type of study is needed; students should study the areas of knowledge they will need in the future. Also, more students were attending college, resulting in a greater diversity of interests, ability, and goals. A single program could not meet the needs of all students.

Significance

The Harvard elective program under president Charles W. Eliot (served 1869–1909) was a focal point for a significant debate in the late nineteenth and early twentieth centuries between proponents of freedom of choice for students and advocates of a classical, prescribed curriculum. Eliot expanded the curriculum to include new and more utilitarian subjects and allowed students wide latitude in choosing a program of study. Critics, including Andrew F. West, charged that students would respond by taking easier courses, drop the traditional liberal arts, specialize excessively, or adopt an unfocused program leading to superficial knowledge in many areas but a mastery of none. In addition, elective-system foes continued to support the theory of mental discipline and advocated a return to a prescribed course of classical studies. Elective courses in social science, technical or vocational subjects, and science could not train the mental faculties or teach moral thinking. A liberal arts course of study should be pursued for its own sake, not evaluated for its practical use. Nonetheless, the liberal arts, these critics asserted, are the most useful preparation for any specific profession or vocation.

By the early twentieth century, colleges in the United States varied widely in terms of student choice. Most allowed some choice within an otherwise structured program. While many of the dire predictions of elective-system critics did not materialize, many educators became concerned about a lack of a common body of knowledge among students. Most colleges adopted a system, common today, that allows the student the choice of a major and minor concentration within the framework of a required course of liberal studies.

Primary Source

"The Elective System at Harvard" [excerpt]

SYNOPSIS: In this article Charles S. Moore notes the principal objections to Harvard's elective system, that it can lead to either overspecialization or an overly broad and easy course of study. In order to demonstrate the extent to which this might be occuring, he then presents statistics on Harvard's 1901 graduating class.

The following facts (with many others) were obtained from a detailed examination of the programs of study of 448 members of the Class of 1901. ...

Some objections to the Elective System at Harvard imply that the choice of studies thereunder is practically unrestricted. It should, however, be understood that the choice of the Freshmen is practically limited to certain specified elementary courses, comprising only about 20 per cent of all the courses offered to undergraduates, and that a Freshman cannot take more than two courses in any one subject. Besides, English, and either French or German, must be taken by almost all Freshmen. Freshmen and Special Students must secure the approval of their choices by specially appointed advisers. Elementary courses must, of course, be taken prior to more advanced courses in the same subject, and a large number of the courses offered may be taken only in case the applicants satisfy the instructors in those courses of their fitness to take them. Furthermore, the whole body of courses offered is divided into about 14 examination groups, and no two courses in the same group may be taken at the same time. No more than six courses may be taken at a time, the requirement being five courses for a Freshman, and four for upper classmen with an extra half course in English Composition for those whose work in Freshman English was not satisfactory.

Let us now see what general lines of choice are followed at Harvard, the facts being obtained from an examination of the programs of study of 448 members of the Class of 1901. Of 33 subjects offered for choice, the first 14 that were chosen (the order being based upon the number of students making the choice and also substantially, upon the number of courses taken in each subject) were as follows:—

English (facile princeps)

History

Economics

German

French

Philosophy

Fine Arts

Chemistry

Latin

Geology

Government

Greek

Mathematics

Physics

Arranged according to the average number of courses taken by each student, the first 14 are English, History, Music, Economics, Engineering, Chemistry, Philosophy, German, French, Architecture, Greek, Fine Arts, Latin, and Spanish. Mathematics drops to the 19th place, Geology and Government to the 22nd, Physics to the 26th. While relatively few students chose Music, Engineering, and Architecture, each of those students took a large number of courses, and while relatively many took Geology, Government, and Physics, each one took but little in each subject. . . .

Examining the 448 programs for evidence of evasion of hard work, we find 20 that show from six to eight choices (out of a total of about 20 choices) among courses having the reputation to a greater or less degree of being "snap" courses. Several of these are the programs of men of high rank who graduated with a *magna cum.* Fewer than one eighth of the choices of the entire class were made from such courses, and but a few programs (only five indisputably) show a preponderance of "snap" and elementary, *i.e.* introductory, courses.

It is to be recognized that the term "snap" is a very inexact term, and also that a number of lecture courses of an introductory character are essential both for later work, and also for general culture. It would be unfortunate should the Elective System, through its marked tendency to increase the standard of work, change the character of such courses.

Let us consider next the extent to which the Elective System has led to specialization.

■ ■ ■

... [O]f the four-year men 6 per cent have specialized throughout the four years; 12 per cent more for three years; and 19 per cent failed to specialize even for one year.

It is interesting to note that of the men who completed the four years' work in three years, but 4 per cent specialized throughout the three years, while on the other hand but 12 per cent failed to specialize even for one year. Three fourths of the men who, coming from other colleges, were admitted to the senior class, specialized during their one year.

Nearly one half of the men who specialized during three and four years, did so in English, one sixth in Modern Languages (except English), and less than one eighth in the Classics, and also in History and Government.

If we seek out the programs that show such specialization every year, or for some part of the time that the work was confined to a narrow field, we find that there are 29 which appear open to the charge of showing undue specialization. This is 7.8 per cent of the 372 who did the full work for a diploma at Harvard. Of these 29, 14 specialized in History and Political Science, and nine of the 14 are now studying Law. Ten specialized in History and Modern Languages, of whom two are studying Law, and two are teaching Modern Languages. Three specialized in the Classics, two now being candidates for the doctor's degree, and one studying for the Ministry. Of the remaining two, one specialized in Engineering and is now studying Engineering, and one in Psychology, and is now studying Medicine. Nine of the 29 were three-year men.

If we examine the data to see to what extent there was a lack of proper concentration of energy, we find 17 students (or 4½ per cent of the 372 who did full work at Harvard) whose programs show a small amount of work in any one subject or group together with a wide range of subjects or groups. The work of these 17 is so scattered that thoroughness seems impossible; yet three of them received the A.B. *magna cum laude,* one of them being a Phi Beta Kappa man, and one received the A.B. *cum laude.*

There is another point of view which should be taken in studying the actual working of the Elective System. A program should be well-balanced, that is, should include some work in each of, say, three groups of subjects, Languages, Social Studies, and Science. It seems a reasonable requirement that each of these groups should be represented by at least 15 per cent of the total work of the student. This would leave 55 per cent for distribution according to interest, aptitude, or future needs. It might be stated in this way, that the presence of this minimum of 15 per cent would save a program from condemnation as ill-balanced. Turning now to the actual programs of the three hundred and seventy-two who completed their work at Harvard, we find that there was no one who failed to take some work in the Linguistic group, but two who failed to take some work in the Sociological group, and sixteen who failed to take some work in the Scientific group, while three failed to take the minimum of 15 per cent in the Linguistic group, twenty-one in the sociological, and one hundred and ninety in the Scientific.

Taking into consideration individual subjects, we find that of the 372 who completed at Harvard all the requirements for the degree of A.B. 254 (68%) took no Physics; 250 (67%) took no Mathematics; 247 (66%) took no Greek; 215 (58%) took no Chemistry; 178 (48%) took no Latin; 147 (39%) took no Fine Arts; 140 (37%) took no Philosophy; 137 (36%) took neither Greek nor Latin; 87 (23%) took neither Latin nor Mathematics; 29 (8%) took no science of any kind; 8 (2%) took neither Physics nor Chemistry; 60 (16%) took neither Botany, Zoölogy, Mineralogy, nor Hygiene.

These facts are interesting, and are given without comment as evidence of the actual working of the Elective System as at present administered at Harvard. The writer has at his command similar sets of statistics from Wellesley, Dartmouth, and Radcliffe, which may be made public at a later date. . . .

Primary Source

"Report of the Committee on Improving Instruction in Harvard College" [excerpt]

SYNOPSIS: In this report, the committee recommends raising standards and making courses more uniform in amount of work required. All courses offered should be taught as "liberal" courses. Large lecture courses are necessary, but standards should be raised, and these courses should not be required as prerequisites for other courses.

The replies received by the Committee leave no reasonable doubt that there is a place, and an important place, for large lecture courses in Harvard College, and that they are not destined to pass away with the further development of the elective system.

In 1882–83 there were only 5 courses with more than 100 members, and none with more than 200; in 1892–93 there were 18 with between 100 and 200 members, and 10 with more than 200; in 1901–02 there were 25 with between 100 and 200 members, and 14 with more than 200. Moreover, the very large courses containing two fifths or more of a whole class have increased from three in 1882–83 to eight and a half in 1901–02; and in 1901–02 there were two elective courses each of which contained more than four fifths as many students as could be found in the whole Freshman class. The larger courses grow, the more evident it becomes that the object of the lectures in them is not so much to impart concrete information as to stimulate thought and interest in the subject; and since the stimulus depends in part on the attitude in which the audience stands towards the lecturer, it is important that these courses should be conducted by the men who have already achieved a reputation. Indeed, the replies of the students make it clear that to be effective the lecture courses must be conducted by the best lecturers in the University. . . .

The Committee believes that the lectures in the large courses should treat general principles rather than details which may be readily obtained from books, and that in these and all other courses much which instructors now dictate or put upon the board should be printed or mimeographed. Furthermore, it believes that, though large lecture courses which maintain the proper standard of work are both valuable and necessary, it is a misfortune when they are required as preliminary to all further study of the subjects that they treat. Such a requirement in some Departments amounts to little less than the reëstablishment of prescribed courses.

An interesting problem was brought to the attention of the Committee by the students' answers to the question why they had chosen this or that elective course. Among both students and members of the Faculty there appears to be a growing tendency to regard certain subjects as designed peculiarly for general culture, and certain others as designed for the scholastic training of specialists. That a student's opinion of the motives which induced him to elect a certain course is often far from correct is shown by the fact that the motive of general fashion was recognized by only two persons. . . . It is noticeable that the students regard English and other modern languages, philosophy, history, geology, and some other studies, as culture subjects in a higher sense than mathematics, the classics, and most of the sciences. The Committee believes that such a distinction is unfortunate, and that, so far as possible, every Department ought to provide courses for students who are not to be specialists in it, and that such courses should require as much systematic work as other courses in the Department. . . .

In connection with this subject, the Committee would point out the importance of encouraging a greater number of men to take honors at graduation, and of making honors something more than a purely scholastic distinction for young specialists; for the Committee believes that students in pursuit of general culture should be encouraged in a thorough and somewhat advanced study of subjects to which they do not intend to devote their lives. The fact that ambitious students find little incentive to take honors is one of the glaring failures of our system. . . .

The Committee proposes no formal vote, but summarizes its conclusions as follows:

1. The relation between the instructors and the students is good, and the students are in general satisfied with their elective studies.
2. The average amount of study, however, is discreditably small.
3. The difficulty of raising the standard is seriously increased by students taking six courses each.
4. The requirements of time and study in the various courses should be as nearly equivalent as possible. Certainly there should not be such discrepancies as exist at present.
5. Large lecture courses have come to stay.
6. Yet in the large lecture courses a special effort should be made to increase the amount and the thoroughness of the work.
7. For this purpose the number of assistants should be increased.
8. Every effort should be made to secure such a number and such an appointment of lecture rooms as shall enable the instructor to use his lecture room before and after the hour of his lecture.

9. It is a mistake to prescribe introductory lecture courses as a preliminary to all further study of the subjects that they treat.
10. Every subject in the College should be taught on the principle that a thorough knowledge of it is a valuable part of a liberal education.
11. Every serious man with health and ability should be encouraged to take honors in some subject.

L. B. R. Briggs
W. E. Byerly
A. L. Lowell
M. H. Morgan
B. S. Hurlbut
J. B. Woodworth
R. Cobb
O. M. W. Sprague
C. H. Grandgent

Further Resources

BOOKS

Butts, R. Freeman, and Lawrence Cremin. *A History of Education in American Culture.* New York: Henry Holt, 1953.

Cohen, Arthur M. *The Shaping of American Higher Education: Emergence and Growth of the Contemporary System.* San Francisco: Jossey-Bass, 1998.

West, Andrew F. *American General Education: A Short Study of Its Present Condition and Needs.* Princeton, N.J.: Princeton University Press, 1932.

———. *Short Papers on American Liberal Education.* New York: Scribner's, 1907.

"Industrial Education for the Negro"

Nonfiction work

By: Booker T. Washington

Date: September 1903

Source: Washington, Booker T. "Industrial Education for the Negro." In *The Negro Problem: A Series of Articles by Representative American Negroes of Today.* New York: J. Pott, 1903, 9–19, 28–29. Available online at http://douglass.speech.nwu.edu/wash_b04.htm; website home page: http://douglass.speech.nwu.edu (accessed April 5, 2003).

About the Author: Booker Taliaferro Washington (1856–1915), educator, speaker, author, and prominent black leader, was born a slave in Virginia. He worked his way through the Hampton Institute and later taught there before, in 1881, founding the Tuskegee Institute, which became one of the leading schools for African Americans. Washington's autobiography, *Up From Slavery,* was influential worldwide. ■

Introduction

During the twelve-year period of Reconstruction following the Civil War (1861–1865), large social, economic, and political gains were made for southern blacks. Afterwards, though, they faced steadily worsening conditions, including Jim Crow laws supporting segregation and the rise of white supremacist groups such as the Ku Klux Klan. Black leaders looked for a way to improve conditions and secure full civil rights for their people. Some leaders viewed education as an important solution, but differences emerged regarding the type of education to be advocated.

Following his famous "Atlanta Compromise" speech in 1895, Booker T. Washington emerged as the most prominent black leader of the time. Addressing a mostly white audience at the Cotton States and International Exposition in Atlanta, he expressed acceptance of segregation: "In all things that are purely social we can be as separate as the fingers, yet one as the hand in all things essential to mutual progress." Washington was proposing a mutually beneficial relationship between blacks and whites: blacks would accept current social conditions and contribute to the economic development of the South, and in exchange, whites would provide employment and trades education for blacks. Washington believed that blacks, as a race, should begin their progress at the bottom. The majority of blacks should learn trades and become reliable workers or buy land and become farmers. Once basic economic security had been gained and blacks had shown themselves to be responsible citizens and valuable to the development of the South, white acceptance and the granting of full political rights would be automatic: "No race that has anything to contribute to the markets of the world is long in any degree ostracized."

Ultimately, Washington sought the full inclusion of blacks in mainstream social, economic, and political life, along with the option of obtaining a college education. However, he believed that, for the time being, blacks should learn to do jobs that they will be "permitted to do in the community in which they reside." In this way, blacks would amass wealth and gain the acceptance of whites, on which opportunities for the enjoyment of higher learning and culture would be built.

Significance

The views of Booker T. Washington represent an important school of thought regarding the education of African Americans during the early twentieth century. Because he encouraged blacks to accept segregation and discrimination and aspire to lower-level jobs, his proposal was embraced by many whites and his preeminence as a black leader was due largely to white support. His advice was sought by presidents and powerful businessmen, and white philanthropists enthusiastically funded Tuskegee

Booker Taliaferro Washington, April 12, 1902. Washington established and headed the Tuskegee Institute, a trade school for young African Americans. © CORBIS. REPRODUCED BY PERMISSION.

and his other projects. Because he controlled such a large portion of available funds, Washington was able to funnel money toward industrial and agricultural education for blacks and away from institutions offering blacks a liberal college education, such as Atlanta University. As a result, Washington was the most influential shaper of black education up to the time of his death in 1915.

Washington's article includes references to the opinions of important black leaders such as W.E.B. Du Bois who opposed his agenda and disagreed with the assertion that blacks should "earn" their rights as American citizens. Du Bois encouraged blacks to work for immediate civil rights and believed that the hope of the African American people was to be found in a college-educated leadership. Both Du Bois and Washington spoke of the "foundation" of black progress. However, for Washington, the foundation was economic self-sufficiency; for Du Bois, the foundation was a broad and liberal education for life, not just for work.

Washington's views receive little sympathy today. The Civil Rights movement of the 1960s reflected the conviction that blacks should not have to wait for or earn rights already guaranteed in the Constitution. Although Washington's goal was full equality for blacks, the approach he advocated is unacceptable to most people, white or black, today.

Primary Source

"Industrial Education for the Negro" [excerpt]

SYNOPSIS: Booker T. Washington makes his case for industrial education for blacks. Most blacks should learn a trade or agriculture and in this way create the economic foundation that will lead to the attainment of civil rights and white acceptance. The belief in the inferiority of blacks, he asserts, can only be countered through proof—demonstrating that blacks can be responsible and productive members of society.

One of the most fundamental and far-reaching deeds that has been accomplished during the last quarter of a century has been that by which the Negro has been helped to find himself and to learn the secrets of civilization—to learn that there are a few simple, cardinal principles upon which a race must start its upward course, unless it would fail, and its last estate be worse than its first.

It has been necessary for the Negro to learn the difference between being worked and working—to learn that being worked meant degradation, while working means civilization; that all forms of labor are honorable, and all forms of idleness disgraceful. It has been necessary for him to learn that all races that have got upon their feet have done so largely by laying an economic foundation, and, in general, by beginning in a proper cultivation and ownership of the soil.

Forty years ago my race emerged from slavery into freedom. If, in too many cases, the Negro race began development at the wrong end, it was largely because neither white nor black properly understood the case. Nor is it any wonder that this was so, for never before in the history of the world had just such a problem been presented as that of the two races at the coming of freedom in this country.

For two hundred and fifty years, I believe the way for the redemption of the Negro was being prepared through industrial development. Through all those years the Southern white man did business with the Negro in a way that no one else has done business with him. In most cases if a Southern white man wanted a house built he consulted a Negro mechanic about the plan and about the actual building of the structure. If he wanted a suit of clothes made he went to a Negro tailor, and for shoes he went to a shoemaker of the same race. In a certain way every slave plantation in the South was an industrial school. On these plantations young colored men and women were constantly being trained not only as farmers but as carpenters, blacksmiths, wheelwrights, brick masons, engineers, cooks, laundresses, sewing women and housekeepers.

I do not mean in any way to apologize for the curse of slavery, which was a curse to both races, but in what I say about industrial training in slavery I am simply stating facts. This training was crude, and was given for selfish purposes. It did not answer the highest ends, because there was an absence of mental training in connection with the training of the hand. To a large degree, though, this business contact with the Southern white man, and the industrial training on the plantations, left the Negro at the close of the war in possession of nearly all the common and skilled labor in the South. The industries that gave the South its power, prominence and wealth prior to the Civil War were mainly the raising of cotton, sugar cane, rice and tobacco. Before the way could be prepared for the proper growing and marketing of these crops forests had to be cleared, houses to be built, public roads and railroads constructed. In all these works the Negro did most of the heavy work. In the planting, cultivating and marketing of the crops not only was the Negro the chief dependence, but in the manufacture of tobacco he became a skilled and proficient workman, and in this, up to the present time, in the South, holds the lead in the large tobacco manufactories.

In most of the industries, though, what happened? For nearly twenty years after the war, except in a few instances, the value of the industrial training given by the plantations was overlooked. Negro men and women were educated in literature, in mathematics and in the sciences, with little thought of what had been taking place during the preceding two hundred and fifty years, except, perhaps, as something to be escaped, to be got as far away from as possible. As a generation began to pass, those who had been trained as mechanics in slavery began to disappear by death, and gradually it began to be realized that there were few to take their places. There were young men educated in foreign tongues, but few in carpentry or in mechanical or architectural drawing. Many were trained in Latin, but few as engineers and blacksmiths. Too many were taken from the farm and educated, but educated in everything but farming. For this reason they had no interest in farming and did not return to it. And yet eighty-five per cent. of the Negro population of the Southern states lives and for a considerable time will continue to live in the country districts. The charge is often brought against the members of my race—and too often justly, I confess—that they are found leaving the country districts and flocking into the great cities where temptations are more frequent and harder to resist, and where the Negro people too often become demoralized. Think, though, how frequently it is the case that from the first day that a pupil begins to go to school his books teach him much about the cities of the world and city life, and almost nothing about the country. How natural it is, then, that when he has the ordering of his life he wants to live it in the city. . . .

Some years ago, when we decided to make tailoring a part of our training at the Tuskegee Institute, I was amazed to find that it was almost impossible to find in the whole country an educated colored man who could teach the making of clothing. We could find numbers of them who could teach astronomy, theology, Latin or grammar, but almost none who could instruct in the making of clothing, something that has to be used by every one of us every day in the year. How often have I been discouraged as I have gone through the South, and into the homes of the people of my race, and have found women who could converse intelligently upon abstruse subjects, and yet could not tell how to improve the condition of the poorly cooked and still more poorly served bread and meat which they and their families were eating three times a day. It is discouraging to find a girl who can tell you the geographical location of any country on the globe and who does not know where to place the dishes upon a common dinner table. It is discouraging to find a woman who knows much about theoretical chemistry, and who cannot properly wash and iron a shirt.

In what I say here I would not by any means have it understood that I would limit or circumscribe the mental development of the Negro student. No race can be lifted until its mind is awakened and strengthened. By the side of industrial training should always go mental and moral training, but the pushing of mere abstract knowledge into the head means little. We want more than the mere performance of mental gymnastics. Our knowledge must be harnessed to the things of real life. I would encourage the Negro to secure all the mental strength, all the mental culture—whether gleaned from science, mathematics, history, language or literature that his circumstances will allow, but I believe most earnestly that for years to come the education of the people of my race should be so directed that the greatest proportion of the mental strength of the masses will

Students work in the wheelwright shop at Tuskegee Institute, Alabama. The famed Negro college was founded by Booker T. Washington to teach trades, professions, and practical skills, which Washington saw were missing from other educational institutes. © BETTMANN/CORBIS. REPRODUCED BY PERMISSION.

be brought to bear upon the every-day practical things of life, upon something that is needed to be done, and something which they will be permitted to do in the community in which they reside. And just the same with the professional class which the race needs and must have, I would say give the men and women of that class, too, the training which will best fit them to perform in the most successful manner the service which the race demands.

I would not confine the race to industrial life, not even to agriculture, for example, although I believe that by far the greater part of the Negro race is best off in the country districts and must and should continue to live there, but I would teach the race that in industry the foundation must be laid—that the very best service which any one can render to what is called the higher education is to teach the present generation to provide a material or industrial foundation. On such a foundation as this will grow habits of thrift, a love of work, economy, ownership of property, bank accounts. Out of it in the future will grow practical education, professional education, positions of public responsibility. Out of it will grow moral and religious strength. Out of it will grow wealth from which alone can come leisure and the opportunity for the enjoyment of literature and the fine arts.

In the words of the late beloved Frederick Douglass:

> Every blow of the sledge hammer wielded by a sable arm is a powerful blow in support of our cause. Every colored mechanic is by virtue of circumstances an elevator of his race. Every house built by a black man is a strong tower against the allied hosts of prejudice. It is impossible for us to attach too much importance to this aspect of the subject. Without industrial development there can be no wealth; without wealth there can be no leisure; without leisure no opportunity for thoughtful reflection and the cultivation of the higher arts.

I would set no limits to the attainments of the Negro in arts, in letters or statesmanship, but I believe the surest way to reach those ends is by laying the foundation in the little things of life that lie immediately about one's door. I plead for industrial education and development for the Negro not because I want to cramp him, but because I want to free him. I want to see him enter the all-powerful business and commercial world. . . .

I close, then, as I began, by saying that as a slave the Negro was worked, and that as a freeman he must learn to work. There is still doubt in many quarters as to the ability of the Negro unguided, unsupported, to hew his own path and put into visible, tangible, indisputable form, products and signs of civilization. This doubt cannot be much affected by abstract arguments, no matter how delicately and convincingly woven together. Patiently, quietly, doggedly, persistently, through summer and winter, sunshine and shadow, by self-sacrifice, by foresight, by honesty and industry, we must re-enforce argument with results. One farm bought, one house built, one home sweetly and intelligently kept, one man who is the largest tax payer or has the largest bank account, one school or church maintained, one factory running successfully, one truck garden profitably cultivated, one patient cured by a Negro doctor, one sermon well preached, one office well filled, one life cleanly lived—these will tell more in our favor than all the abstract eloquence that can be summoned to plead our cause. Our pathway must be up through the soil, up through swamps, up through forests, up through the streams, the rocks, up through commerce, education and religion!

Further Resources

BOOKS

Harlan, Louis R. *Booker T. Washington: The Making of a Black Leader, 1856–1901.* New York: Oxford University Press, 1972.

———. *Booker T. Washington: The Wizard of Tuskegee, 1901–1915.* New York: Oxford University Press, 1983.

———. *Booker T. Washington in Perspective: Essays of Louis R. Harlan.* Raymond W. Smock, ed. Jackson, Miss.: University Press of Mississippi, 1988.

Harris, Thomas E. *Analysis of the Clash Over the Issues Between Booker T. Washington and W.E.B. Du Bois.* New York: Garland, 1993.

Moore, Jacqueline M. *Booker T. Washington, W.E.B. Du Bois, and the Struggle for Racial Uplift.* Wilmington, Del.: Scholarly Resources, 2003.

Verney, Kevern. *The Art of the Possible: Booker T. Washington and Black Leadership in the United States, 1881–1925.* New York: Routledge, 2001.

Washington, Booker T. *Up From Slavery: An Autobiography.* New York: Doubleday, Page, 1901.

Wintz, Cary D. *African American Political Thought, 1890–1930: Washington, Du Bois, Garvey, and Randolph.* Armonk, N.Y.: M.E. Sharpe, 1996.

WEBSITES

"African American Education." Available online at http://www.theatlantic.com/unbound/flashbks/blacked/aaedintr.htm; website home page: http://www.theatlantic.com/ (accessed March 10, 2003).

"Tuskegee University." Available online at http://www.tusk.edu/ (accessed March 13, 2003).

"The Two Nations of Black America." Available online at http://www.pbs.org/wgbh/pages/frontline/shows/race/etc/road.html; website home page: http://www.pbs.org/ (accessed March 10, 2003).

AUDIO AND VISUAL MEDIA

Black Paths of Leadership. Directed by Pam Hughes. Churchill Films. Videocassette, 1984.

Booker T. Washington: The Life and Legacy. Pathways to Greatness Series. Directed by William Greaves. Academic Industries Video Division. Videocassette, 1993.

"The True Character of the New York Public Schools"

Magazine article

By: Adele Marie Shaw

Date: December 1903

Source: Shaw, Adele Marie. "The True Character of the New York Public Schools." *The World's Work* 7, no. 2, December 1903, 4204–4221.

About the Author: Adele Marie Shaw (1865?–1941) graduated from Smith College and taught in a girls' high school in Brooklyn, New York. She was hired as a special correspondent from 1903 to 1904 by *The World's Work* magazine to study conditions in public schools. Shaw was also the author of many articles in a variety of popular magazines. ■

Introduction

Although Americans had put great faith in the public schools, by 1890 serious problems had emerged. Rural schools were largely underequipped, dilapidated, and taught by underprepared teachers. Urban schools were crowded, poorly maintained, and struggling to cope with problems presented by large numbers of immigrant students. It was in this context that Joseph Mayer Rice undertook a study of American public schools and published his findings in a series of articles in *The Forum* from October 1892 to June 1893. The articles resulted in a public uproar and a stream of angry denials on the part of the education profession. While visiting schools

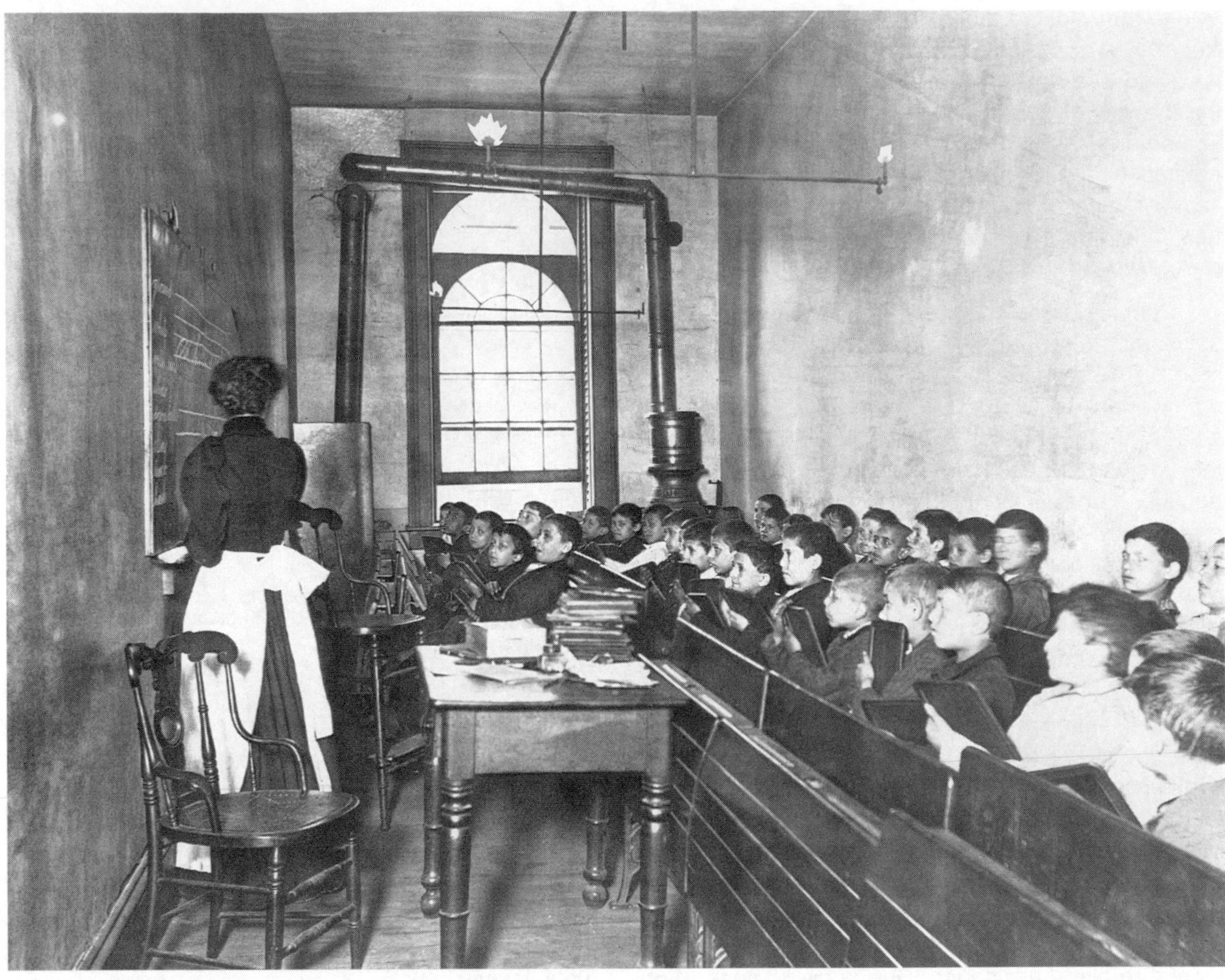

Students in a crowded public school classroom in a condemned school building, with gas-burning stoves and lights, New York, 1902. At the time students endured very poor conditions in the New York school system. © CORBIS. REPRODUCED BY PERMISSION.

in thirty-six cities, Rice found numerous instances of incompetent teachers, methods relying on rote memory and drill, corruption, and political meddling in the schools. Yet some schools were experimenting with new methods, broadening the curriculum, and maintained an encouraging and positive atmosphere. Rice held up these "progressive" schools as an attainable ideal for the rest of the nation.

Rice was the first to apply the so-called muckraking approach to the subject of education. The time period from the late 1890s to 1920 saw the rise of this method of investigative journalism, as muckrakers such as Upton Sinclair, Lincoln Steffens, and Ida Tarbell studied and reported on a variety of subjects from corporate and political corruption to the atrocious conditions in meat-processing plants. Popular magazines, such as *McClure's* and *Everybody's,* found that these articles sold magazines, but the work of these journalists also led to important reforms such as the passage of state child labor laws and the Meat Inspection Act of 1906.

When Shaw undertook her study of the American public schools for *The World's Work* ten years after Rice, she found that conditions had not changed significantly. Shaw spent a year visiting schools in urban, suburban, and rural areas throughout the country. She found that in many urban districts, schools were run more for the benefit of politicians than students. The physical condition of many schools was dreadful: poorly ventilated, dark, filthy, lice-infested, and crowded buildings contributed to the spread of disease including tuberculosis. Teachers were frequently cruel and inflexible and lacked sympathy for immigrant children. Unavoidably in classrooms housing more than sixty children, memorization and recitation were often the only methods employed. Most schools failed to take into account the needs of the population of students they served, whether urban, rural, or immigrant.

Significance

Shaw's work was part of, and contributed to, the growth of the progressive education movement. Her criticism and praise followed along the general lines of progressive education: Schools should concern themselves with the whole child, including physical, psychological, and social growth. The focus in the curriculum should be on the practical and useful and should be tailored to the individual student. Students should be approached within the context of home, family, and community. For progressives, education is largely an experimental endeavor requiring teachers to continuously test and improve their approach.

Shaw's articles did not galvanize quite as much controversy and discussion as Rice's did; to a degree, the public had become accustomed to, and somewhat weary of, the muckrakers' steady stream of appalling revelations and calls to action. Yet she contributed significantly to the growing public awareness of problems in the schools and the desire, on the part of many, to bring about change.

While, in true muckraking style, Shaw's articles focused on the most shocking aspects of schools, her reports also served to draw attention to positive examples. Her description of the innovative and successful schools of Menomonie, Wisconsin, for example, provided a model on which reform efforts could be based.

Primary Source

"The True Character of the New York Public Schools" [excerpt]

SYNOPSIS: In this excerpt from one of a series of articles based on her investigation of U.S. public schools, Shaw describes the deplorable conditions she observed in the New York public schools, including dark, dirty, crowded, and poorly ventilated buildings. She also found abusive teachers and rigid, mechanical teaching techniques. Shaw recommends restricting immigration and drastically increasing school budgets.

The Dark Side of the Picture

New York children do not have equal chances, physically, in the New York schools. Yet the custom of seating two children (and in crowded classrooms I frequently saw *three*) at the same desk cannot be done away with till money can be spared for new furniture and space allowed for single desks. A New York physician has said that ninety-nine out of a hundred girls are deformed by the schoolroom postures before they reach the high school; curvature of the spine is one of the commonest effects of schoolroom chairs. Yet the new course of study, which insists upon a sensible change of position, with calisthenics and deep breathing at frequent intervals, is condemned by old-fashioned teachers as "wasting time." At present the attention given in the lower schools to keeping children straight and well developed varies with the caprices of the individual instructor.

The conditions of public education should provide for the right growth of body, mind, and character; and proper physical training demands good air, cleanliness, and freedom from degrading surroundings. Good air in the months of September and October is not hard to obtain, yet in nearly every classroom that I entered the atmosphere was foul. Sometimes even the assembly hall and the corridors were distinctly offensive. A room in which forty-six little girls live and work five hours in the day contained only one outside window. The miserably flickering gas over their heads consumed the oxygen needed by starved lungs, and yet on the three warm days during which I visited this class I did not once see the window opened more than a few inches. The scourge of New York is consumption; the preventive of consumption is fresh air; and these children say "Draught" as they might cry "Tiger!"

A Murderous Hole of Darkness

The darkness would be less oppressive in such cases if the gas that burns on cloudy days in certain rooms of half the schools I saw, and on all days in some, was good gas, but its feeble uncertainty adds a melancholy to the gloom. In one dim assembly hall I groped my way to a platform on either side of which was drawn a cloth curtain. Behind the curtains two classes went on in simultaneous confusion, and I talked with the principal in a kind of cloth-bound cave, with grammar on one side, arithmetic on the other, and a "bad boy" awaiting discipline down in front.

The gas jets that eked out the scanty daylight in the curtained recesses had in one instance been replaced by Welsbach burners, and as one of the teachers said, "They're always breaking, and then they're worse than nothing."

The windows of this building opened on two sides into tenement back yards, whose washings were strung within a few feet of the children's desks, and whose sheds and water-closets just below were close to the schoolhouse wall.

Because of the stench that had floated in the windows, complaint had been made of the yard closets, and I was told that they had been closed and the air purified. I was not conscious of any unpleasant odor, but the closets were not entirely out of use.

In this building both principal and teachers appeared to take great pains with ventilation, but the conditions of their labors were more than difficult. The playground space was a small dark basement divided so as to give the girls the larger share. Sunken between the tenements and the school building was a narrow court not so large as a good city back yard, where 500 boys "went out to play." On rainy days they are often crowded so close in the hopeless darkness of the basement that there is barely standing-room. The teacher in charge of the playground must stay in this cell, though to see what is going on is impossible, and although on winter days the place is miserably cold for her and for the boys. . . .

The Wrong Kind of Teaching

Nor is there any greater equality in the conditions in which the New York public-school child develops mind and character.

The well-to-do, who furnish the principal support of the public schools, send their children elsewhere. Three-fourths of New York's elementary teachers could not get positions in private schools.

"Who told you to speak out?" "*You've* paid attention!" scolded or sneered at a boy who is struggling to express an independent thought, will not make him a ready user of the gifts with which he is endowed.

The tone of continual exasperation in which more than one class is addressed would blight the forth-putting powers of a Macaulay. Truancy from some of these classes should be imputed to a child for righteousness. In one room, where a geography recitation was in lumbering progress, I volunteered the beaming comment: "These seem like nice boys." "I haven't found them so," answered the teacher sourly, and a sudden animation and general straightening lapsed into stodginess. . . .

In one school in which I spent the better part of two days I did not once hear any child express a thought in his own words. Attention was perfect. No pupil could escape from any grade without knowing the questions and answers of that grade. Every child could add, subtract, multiply, and divide with accuracy; every child could and did pronounce his reading words with unusual distinctness. The chant in which recitations were delivered was as uniform as everything else. "*Wren: w* is silent. The only sound of *r;* the second sound of *e;* the only sound of *n,*" was as near the heavy accentuation as I can get. It was the best and the worst school I ever saw. The best, because no pains, no time, *nothing* had been spared to bring it up to the principal's ideal; and the effort had been crowned with entire success. The worst, because it ignored absolutely any individuality in the pupils and rewarded them for nothing more than a mechanical obedience to another's thinking. . . .

No School Better than this School

In this school there exists a rigidity that is like a *rigor mortis;* it forbids such a natural outgiving of the natural teacher as the syllabus suggests. Here the subordinate must be forever on the jump to accomplish the set end of her day's labor, and while the principal is calm, pleasant in manner, and God-fearing in her life, most of the teachers who carry out her conscientiously relentless will are harassed, visibly worn, harsh, and unkind.

The children are apparently callous and happy in their indifference toward their environments. I saw a small boy whose elbow was suddenly jerked and shaken sneak a little mischievous grin toward the back of the room.

In one class the very way in which the teacher intoned "You—are—not—still" gave me a sensation of quick fright that brought back the awful moment of my childhood when I saw a boy arrested and haled away by a policeman. "Somebody—foot!" the same teacher shouted suddenly, and my circulation stopped. My own foot, I felt sure, had moved.

No child in this school ever "raises his hand" above the level of the shoulder excepting during the arithmetic recitation, when pencils that are not in actual use are held in the clenched fingers of the right hand, the right elbow resting on the desk, the left hand laid flat on the other side.

"My answer is—" began an infant arithmetician.

"Don't say that in my class" . . .

"Don't stand in my class with pencil, pen, or book in hand," snapped the teacher.

"Indeed! But you'll please sit down," was the sneer that greeted a wrong answer.

Neither the principal nor her first assistant, who was both sweet and gentle, "snapped," but the manner of one of the younger teachers who seemed a "kind of right-hand man" gave me an overwhelming desire to rescue the class committed to her, and to do it, if necessary, by physical violence.

In this school, probably the only one of its kind in the world, there is at least no indirection, no flabbiness. The apparent cruelty that kept me "on edge" is not half so fatal as the actual cruelty of methods known elsewhere.

"You dirty little Russian Jew, what are you doing?" seems even more ruinous to a child's spirit and temper.

The school most unrelieved in badness had no principal in evidence. Opposite the name of the "head" in charge I wrote in my notebook: "Coarse, fat woman, sensual look, youngish, diamond earrings, talks dialect." This woman's methods are summary, but according to her lights. If a child gets in her way she throws him out, lifting him by any portion of his person that "comes handy." From such a school graduate the brutal truck-drivers, the amateur criminals who, having little better in their minds, devise much mischief.

That the imitative powers of childhood are startling; that the teacher's thoughts, feelings, aspirations even, transfer themselves on invisible wings to the members of her class, proves itself every instant of the day. Yet in a majority of the schools I was continually embarrassed by the discourtesy with which the children were addressed—or ignored. There is sentimentalism that forgets the teacher's difficulties and there is "plain good sense." It is not sentimentality to recognize rudeness as rudeness even when its object is a child. What possible end but a common misery is to be attained by pointing out the "bad boy" to a stranger? What sort of example is the taste that discusses quickeared children even in lowered tones when they are present? "Get on to those eyes!" brought me a glance quite uncomfortable but already self-conscious. "*He* is a degenerate!" procured a sullen look of blank defiance that changed to sullen watchfulness as the talk went on. . . .

General Conclusions

Four conclusions stand out in my mind as the result of these weeks of visiting New York public schools and of study of the huge problem.

1. New York City has the most difficult educational problem in the country. It stands in a class by itself and has difficulties that no other city presents.
2. Under the present school administration it is doing wonderful work toward solving that problem.
3. But conditions still exist that put the complete solution of the problem beyond the reach of any normal effort and expense.
4. The only remedies for such conditions are the restriction of immigration and a vast increase in expenditure—larger than has yet been dreamed of.

Further Resources

BOOKS

Colburn, David R., and George E. Pozzetta. *Reform and Reformers in the Progressive Era.* Westport, Conn.: Greenwood, 1983.

Cremin, Lawrence A. *The Transformation of the School: Progressivism in American Education, 1876–1957.* New York: Knopf, 1961.

Filler, Louis. *Progressivism and Muckraking.* New York: R.R. Bowker, 1976.

Rice, Joseph Mayer. *The Public School System of the United States.* New York: Arno Press, 1969. (Book version of Rice's series in *The Forum.*)

Serrin, Judith, and William Serrin. *Muckraking!: The Journalism That Changed America.* New York: New Press, 2002.

Charter and By-Laws

Charter

By: General Education Board

Date: 1903

Source: General Education Board. *Charter and By-Laws.* New York, 1938, 1–5. Reprinted in *Readings In American Educational History.* New York: Appleton-Century-Crofts, 1951, 569–571.

About the Author: John D. Rockefeller (1839–1937), founder of the General Education Board, began his career as a bookkeeper after taking a short business course. In 1863, he started an oil refinery business with two partners but bought out the other partners in 1865. He organized the Standard Oil Company in 1870 and, by buying out other companies, came to control most of the oil refining in the United States. In 1896, Rockefeller turned his attention to giving away the bulk of his enormous fortune. ■

Introduction

By the end of the nineteenth century, education in the South was much in need of development and reform, though this was far from being a new state of affairs. Education in the South had for more than a century lagged behind that in the North for a number of reasons. Taxation for the public support of schools was a difficult idea to sell to southerners steeped in a tradition of individualism and a belief that schooling was for those who could pay for it out of their own pockets. The destruction wrought by the Civil War (1861–1865) and the economic collapse of the South reversed previous advances and

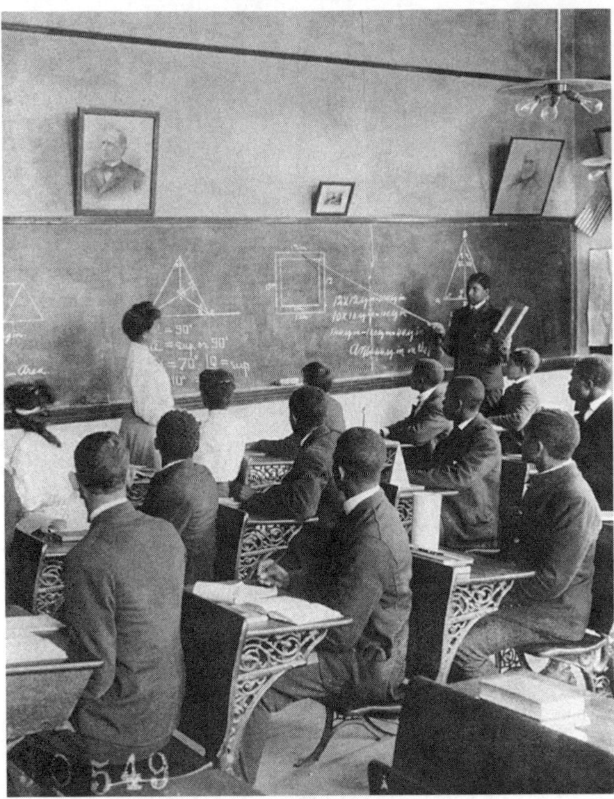

An African American teaches class in a southern school, April 11, 1906. The General Education Board helped build schools and train teachers to provide educational opportunities for African Americans. © CORBIS. REPRODUCED BY PERMISSION.

obstructed further progress. Spurred by the advocacy of Walter Hines Page, and financed by John D. Rockefeller and other wealthy northern businessmen, the Southern Education Board was founded in 1901 for the purpose of promoting the development of a system of free public education in the South.

In 1902, *McClure's* magazine published an exposé of the business practices of Standard Oil by journalist Ida Tarbell. The public was outraged, and Rockefeller found himself constantly plagued by negative press. Seeking to improve his public image through philanthropy and perplexed by this enormous task, Rockefeller hired Frederick T. Gates, a Baptist minister, as his financial advisor. Gates's approach to philanthropy was to target the roots of social problems. It was Gates and Rockefeller's son, John D. Rockefeller, Jr., who directed the elder Rockefeller's attention to the southern education problem.

Rockefeller established the General Education Board (GEB) in 1903 for "the promotion of education within the United States without distinction of race, sex or creed." Six of the first ten members of the board of the new organization were selected by Rockefeller from the Southern Education Board. At first, the two organizations had very similar agendas, with the GEB focusing efforts on assisting the SEB with issues of southern education. The GEB then broadened its scope to include all levels of education nationwide.

Significance

The GEB had a significant impact on education in the United States at all levels. Colleges and universities received general support as well as funding for special projects and scholarships. Hundreds of high schools were built, and the GEB supported the development of public schools for whites and blacks, especially in the South. It promoted agricultural education in the form of assistance to demonstration projects in the South. The board also supported projects to promote the development of economic resources that would in turn encourage the improvement of schools.

While the GEB supported education for all races, funding tended to be directed to industrial education for blacks and higher education for whites. In addition, a motivation of social control is apparent in the statements of board members. Frederick T. Gates, in discussing the goals of the GEB, stated: "We shall not try to make these people or any of their children into philosophers or men of learning, or men of science. . . . [Rather we will] teach them to do in a perfect way the things their fathers and mothers are doing in an imperfect way, in the homes, in the shops and on the farm." The GEB aimed not to promote economic mobility or equal opportunity but, rather, a more stable social order.

Over the years of its existence from 1903 to the final appropriation in 1964, the GEB distributed a total of $325 million in charitable gifts. Later, the organization focused on assisting higher education and medical schools. The GEB provided a powerful stimulus for the development of a system of public education in the South and assisted in the economic development of the region.

Primary Source

Charter and By-Laws

SYNOPSIS: The charter of the General Education Board sets forth the aims and scope of its activities, the members of the board, the procedure for the selection of new board members, and logistical issues involving property, the creation of by-laws, tax-exempt status, and the general administration of the organization.

Be it enacted by the Senate and House of Representatives of the United States of America in Congress assembled, That William H. Baldwin, Junior, Jabez L. M. Curry, Frederick T. Gates, Daniel C. Gilman, Morris K. Jesup, Robert C. Ogden, Walter H. Page,

George Foster Peabody, and Albert Shaw, and their successors, be, and they hereby are, constituted a body corporate of the District of Columbia; that the name of such body corporate shall be General Education Board, and that by such name the said persons and their successors shall have perpetual succession.

Sec. 2. That the object of the said corporation shall be the promotion of education within the United States of America, without distinction of race, sex, or creed.

Sec. 3. That for the promotion of such object the said corporation shall have power to build, improve, enlarge, or equip, or to aid others to build, improve, enlarge, or equip, buildings for elementary or primary schools, industrial schools, technical schools, normal schools, training schools for teachers, or schools of any grade, or for higher institutions of learning, or, in connection therewith, libraries, workshops, gardens, kitchens, or other educational accessories; to establish, maintain, or endow, or aid others to establish, maintain, or endow, elementary or primary schools, industrial schools, technical schools, normal schools, training schools for teachers, or schools of any grade, or higher institutions of learning; to employ or aid others to employ teachers and lecturers; to aid, coöperate with, or endow associations or other corporations engaged in educational work within the United States of America, or to donate to any such association or corporation any property or moneys which shall at any time be held by the said corporation hereby constituted; to collect educational statistics and information, and to publish and distribute documents and reports containing the same, and in general to do and perform all things necessary or convenient for the promotion of the object of the corporation.

Sec. 4. That the said corporation shall further have power to have and use a common seal and to alter and change the same at its pleasure; to sue or be sued in any court of the United States or other court of competent jurisdiction; to make by-laws for the admission or exclusion of its members, for the election of its trustees, officers, and agents, and otherwise; for the casting of votes by its members or trustees by proxy; for the purchase, management, sale, or transfer of its property, the investment and control of its funds, and the general transaction of its business; to take or receive, whether by gift, grant, devise, bequest, or purchase, any real or personal estate, or to hold, grant, convey, hire, or lease the same for the purposes of its incorporation; to accept and administer any trust of money or of real

Frederick Taylor Gates was instrumental in the foundation of the General Education Board and was its first chairman. UNIVERSITY OF CHICAGO LIBRARY. REPRODUCED BY PERMISSION.

or personal estate for any educational purpose within the object of the corporation as aforesaid; to prescribe by by-laws or otherwise the terms and conditions upon which money, real estate, or personal estate shall be acquired, or received by the said corporation, and for the grant, transfer, assignment, or donation of any or all property of the said corporation, real or personal, to any society or corporation for any of the said purposes for which the said corporation is hereby incorporated, and otherwise generally for the management of the property and the transaction of the business of the corporation.

Sec. 5. That the members of the corporation shall be not less than nine in number and not more than seventeen, as may be prescribed by the by-laws of the corporation: Provided, however, That if and when the number of members shall be less than nine, the members remaining shall have power to add and shall add to their number until the number shall be not less than nine: And provided, That no act of the corporation shall be void because at the time such act shall be done the number of the members of the corporation shall be less than nine; that all the members of the corporation shall be its trustees; that no member of the said association shall, by reason of such membership or his trusteeship, be personally liable for any of its debts or obligations; that each member of the corporation shall hold his membership for a term of three years and until his successor shall be chosen; Provided, however, That the members shall be at all times divided into three classes numerically, as nearly as may be, and that the original members shall, at their first meeting, or as soon thereafter as shall be convenient, be divided into three classes, the members of the first class to hold their membership and office until the expiration of one year from the first day of January next after the enactment of this law, the members of the second class until the expiration of two years thereafter, and the members of the third class until the expiration of three years thereafter, and that in every case the member shall hold office after the expiration of his term until his successor shall be chosen: And provided, further, That in case any member shall, by death, resignation, incapacity to act, or otherwise, cease to be a member during his term, his successor shall be chosen to serve for the remainder of such term and until his successor shall be chosen; and that the principal office of the said corporation shall be in the City of Washington, District of Columbia: Provided, That meetings may be held elsewhere within the United States as may be determined by the members or provided by the by-laws.

Sec. 6. That all real property of the corporation within the District of Columbia which shall be used by the corporation for the educational or other purposes of the corporation as aforesaid, other than the purpose of producing income, and all personal property and funds of the corporation held, used, or invested for educational purposes as aforesaid, or to produce income to be used for such purposes, shall be exempt from taxation: Provided, however, That this exemption shall not apply to any property of the corporation which shall not be used for, or the income of which shall not be applied to, the educational purposes of the corporation: And provided further, That the corporation shall annually file with the Secretary of the Interior of the United States a report in writing stating in detail the property, real and personal, held by the corporation, and the expenditure or other use or disposition of the same or the income thereof during the preceding year.

Sec. 7. That this charter shall be subject to alteration, amendment, or repeal at the pleasure of the Congress of the United States.

Approved, January 12, 1903.

Further Resources

BOOKS

Bremner, Robert H. *American Philanthropy.* Chicago: University of Chicago Press, 1960.

Butts, R. Freeman, and Lawrence Cremin. *A History of Education in American Culture.* New York: Henry Holt, 1953.

Dabney, Charles William. *Universal Education in the South.* New York: Arno Press, 1969.

Fosdick, Raymond. *The Story of the Rockefeller Foundation.* New Brunswick, N.J.: Transaction Publishers, 1989.

Goodenow, Ronald K., and Arthur O. White, eds. *Education and the Rise of the New South.* Boston: G.K. Hall, 1981.

"The Talented Tenth"

Nonfiction work

By: W.E.B. Du Bois

Date: 1903

Source: Du Bois, W.E.B. "The Talented Tenth." In *The Negro Problem: A Series of Articles by Representative American Negroes of Today.* New York: J. Pott, 1903, 33–34, 45–48, 51–55, 73–75. Available online at http://douglassarchives.org/dubo_b05.htm; website home page: http://douglassarchives.org (accessed April 5, 2003).

About the Author: William Edward Burghardt Du Bois (1868–1963), the first African American to earn a Ph.D. from Harvard, taught at Atlanta University, Wilberforce, and the University of Pennsylvania. He helped found the NAACP and was editor of the organization's magazine, *Crisis,* from 1910 to 1934. Du Bois was an influential black leader and educator, and the author of many books and articles. ■

Introduction

After the Civil War (1861–1865), the Reconstruction period resulted in federal legislation aimed at ensuring equal rights for blacks and assisting them to make the transition from slavery to citizenship. Part of this effort was the 1865 act establishing the Bureau of Refugees, Freedmen and Abandoned Lands, commonly known as the Freedmen's Bureau, for the purpose of administrating relief and educational services for the newly freed slaves. The bureau opened schools for blacks throughout the South and founded colleges for blacks such as Howard University and Fisk University. Through educational opportunities such as these, federal legislation conferring equal rights, and the protective presence of federal troops, many blacks attained prominent positions of leadership, including seats in the U.S. House and Senate.

The close of Reconstruction and the withdrawal of federal troops spelled the end for many of the reforms benefiting southern blacks. States began passing Jim Crow laws to enforce racial segregation, and the Ku Klux

Klan and other white supremacist groups used intimidation and violence to prevent blacks from exercising their newly won citizenship rights. Northern white sympathy for Reconstruction efforts was waning, and funding for southern black colleges from the federal government and northern white philanthropists was drying up.

In this context of deteriorating conditions for southern blacks, W.E.B. Du Bois and other black leaders near the end of the twentieth century looked for a solution. Du Bois advocated maintaining the educational progress begun by Reconstruction by continuing to provide the most talented members of the black community with a liberal college education. This group, the "talented tenth," would provide leadership to the black community in its struggle to recover from slavery and join the larger culture as equal members. A liberal education, in the sense of an education appropriate for a free person, provides a broad knowledge of the world and culture, including history, philosophy, literature, languages, and science. For Du Bois, this type of education, an education for "life," would give the black leader the vision to understand the factors that led to the current situation and chart a course for the future. Such vision cannot, Du Bois believed, be gained through the narrow study of a particular trade or profession.

Significance

Du Bois' views in this article are stated in opposition to the opinions of Booker T. Washington, the most prominent black leader of the time. The conflict between these two leaders defined the debate over black education at the time. Initially a supporter of Washington, Du Bois came to believe that Washington's focus on industrial and agricultural education for blacks was an obstacle to black progress. Du Bois emerged as an upstart leader, challenging the established viewpoint. His reference to "the mole with his eyes in the earth" refers to Washington. While Washington and Du Bois shared the goal of complete black equality, they differed in their focus and approach.

Du Bois' vision of the mass of blacks, the majority of the population in the South, led by a college-educated group willing to agitate for black civil rights, was a threatening one for whites. Because Washington exhorted blacks to accept segregation and low-level jobs, he received greater support from whites, and his projects, such as the Tuskegee Institute, received more funding.

While Washington's views dominated in the first two decades of the twentieth century, Du Bois and his supporters provided an important alternative. By the late 1950s, and the beginnings of the Civil Rights movement, Du Bois' view came to predominate. Blacks, no longer willing to "begin at the bottom" and earn the equality already guaranteed them in the Constitution, began to demand their rights as U.S. citizens.

William Edward Burghardt Du Bois, c. 1904. Du Bois argued that sending the most talented African Americans to colleges and universities was the best way for blacks to rise to social and economic equality with white Americans.

Primary Source

"The Talented Tenth" [excerpt]

SYNOPSIS: In "The Talented Tenth," Du Bois argues that the goal of education is not just to produce workers but rather to prepare "men" for life. He points to those blacks who received a college education during Reconstruction, especially teachers, and who were serving as leaders and role models for the black community. A select group must receive a broad, liberal college education in order to gain the necessary knowledge and perspective for leadership.

The Negro race, like all races, is going to be saved by its exceptional men. The problem of education, then, among Negroes must first of all deal with the Talented Tenth; it is the problem of developing the Best of this race that they may guide the Mass away from the contamination and death of the Worst, in their own and other races. Now the training of men is a difficult and intricate task. Its technique is a matter for educational experts, but its object is for the vision of seers. If we make money the object of man-training, we shall develop money-makers but not necessarily men; if we make technical skill the object of education, we may possess artisans but not, in nature, men. Men we shall have only as we make manhood the object of the work of the schools—intelligence, broad sympathy, knowledge of the world that was and is, and of the relation of men to it—this is the curriculum of that Higher Education which must underlie true life. On this foundation we may build bread winning, skill of hand and quickness of brain, with never a fear lest the child and man mistake the means of living for the object of life. . . .

How then shall the leaders of a struggling people be trained and the hands of the risen few strengthened? There can be but one answer: The best and most capable of their youth must be schooled in the colleges and universities of the land. We will not quarrel as to just what the university of the Negro should teach or how it should teach it—I willingly admit that each soul and each race-soul needs its own peculiar curriculum. But this is true: A university is a human invention for the transmission of knowledge and culture from generation to generation, through the training of quick minds and pure hearts, and for this work no other human invention will suffice, not even trade and industrial schools.

All men cannot go to college but some men must; every isolated group or nation must have its yeast, must have for the talented few centers of training where men are not so mystified and befuddled by the hard and necessary toil of earning a living, as to have no aims higher than their bellies, and no God greater than Gold. This is true training, and thus in the beginning were the favored sons of the freedmen trained. Out of tile colleges of the North came, after the blood of war, Ware, Cravath, Chase, Andrews, Bumstead and Spence to build the foundations of knowledge and civilization in the black South. Where ought they to have begun to build? At the bottom, of course, quibbles the mole with his eyes in the earth. Aye! truly at the bottom, at the very bottom; at the bottom of knowledge, down in the very depths of knowledge there where the roots of justice strike into the lowest soil of Truth. And so they did begin; they founded colleges, and up from the colleges shot normal schools, and out from the normal schools went teachers, and around the normal teachers clustered other teachers to teach the public schools; the college trained in Greek and Latin and mathematics, 2,000 men; and these men trained full 50,000 others in morals and manners, and they in turn taught thrift and the alphabet to nine millions of men, who to-day hold $300,000,000 of property. It was a miracle—the most wonderful peace-battle of the 19th century, and yet to-day men smile at it, and in fine superiority tell us that it was all a strange mistake; that a proper way to found a system of education is first to gather the children and buy them spelling books and hoes; afterward men may look about for teachers, if haply they may find them; or again they would teach men Work, but as for Life—why, what has Work to do with Life, they ask vacantly. . . .

The most interesting question, and in many respects the crucial question, to be asked concerning college-bred Negroes, is: Do they earn a living? It has been intimated more than once that the higher training of Negroes has resulted in sending into the world of work, men who could find nothing to do suitable to their talents. Now and then there comes a rumor of a colored college man working at menial service, etc. Fortunately, returns as to occupations of college-bred Negroes, gathered by the Atlanta conference, are quite full—nearly sixty per cent. of the total number of graduates.

This enables us to reach fairly certain conclusions as to the occupations of all college-bred Negroes. Of 1,312 persons reported, there were:

Teachers	53.4%
Clergymen	16.8%
Physicians, etc.	6.3%
Students	5.6%
Lawyers	4.7%
In Govt. Service	4.0%
In Business	3.6%
Farmers and Artisans	2.7%
Editors, Secretaries and Clerks	2.4%
Miscellaneous	.5%

Over half are teachers, a sixth are preachers, another sixth are students and professional men; over 6 per cent. are farmers, artisans and merchants, and 4 per cent. are in government service. In detail the occupations are as follows:

Occupations of College-Bred Men

701 Teachers:

- Presidents and Deans, 19
- Teacher of Music, 7
- Professors, Principals and Teachers, 675

221 Clergymen:

- Bishop, 1
- Chaplains U. S. Army, 2

Missionaries, 9
Presiding Elders, 12
Preachers, 197

83 Physicians:
Doctors of Medicine, 76
Druggists, 4
Dentists, 3

74 Students

62 Lawyers

53 in Civil Service:
U. S. Minister Plenipotentiary, 1
U. S. Consul, 1
U. S. Deputy Collector, 1
U. S. Gauger, 1
U. S. Postmasters, 2
U. S. Clerks, 44
State Civil Service, 2
City Civil Service, 1

47 Business Men:
Merchants, etc., 30
Managers, 13
Real Estate Dealers, 4

26 Farmers

22 Clerks and Secretaries:
Secretary of National Societies, 7
Clerks, etc., 15

9 Artisans

9 Editors

5 Miscellaneous

These figures illustrate vividly the function of the college-bred Negro. He is, as he ought to be, the group leader, the man who sets the ideals of the community where he lives, directs its thoughts and heads its social movements. It need hardly be argued that the Negro people need social leadership more than most groups; that they have no traditions to fall back upon, no long established customs, no strong family ties, no well defined social classes. All these things must be slowly and painfully evolved. The preacher was, even before the war, the group leader of the Negroes, and the church their greatest social institution. Naturally this preacher was ignorant and often immoral, and the problem of replacing the older type by better educated men has been a difficult one. Both by direct work and by direct influence on other preachers, and on congregations, the college-bred preacher has an opportunity for reformatory work and moral inspiration, the value of which cannot be overestimated.

It has, however, been in the furnishing of teachers that the Negro college has found its peculiar function. Few persons realize how vast a work, how mighty a revolution has been thus accomplished. To furnish five millions and more of ignorant people with teachers of their own race and blood, in one generation, was not only a very difficult undertaking, but very important one, in that, it placed before the eyes of almost every Negro child an attainable ideal. It brought the masses of the blacks in contact with modern civilization, made black men the leaders of their communities and trainers of the new generation. In this work college-bred Negroes were first teachers, and then teachers of teachers. And here it is that the broad culture of college work has been of peculiar value. Knowledge of life and its wider meaning, has been the point of the Negro's deepest ignorance, and the sending out of teachers whose training has not been simply for bread winning, but also for human culture, has been of inestimable value in the training of these men. . . .

Thus, again, in the manning of trade schools and manual training schools we are thrown back upon the higher training as its source and chief support. There was a time when any aged and wornout carpenter could teach in a trade school. But not so today. Indeed the demand for college-bred men by a school like Tuskegee, ought to make Mr. Booker T. Washington the firmest friend of higher training. Here he has as helpers the son of a Negro senator, trained in Greek and the humanities, and graduated at Harvard; the son of a Negro congressman and lawyer, trained in Latin and mathematics, and graduated at Oberlin; he has as his wife, a woman who read Virgil and Homer in the same class room with me; he has as college chaplain, a classical graduate of Atlanta University; as teacher of science, a graduate of Fisk; as teacher of history, a graduate of Smith,—indeed some thirty of his chief teachers are college graduates, and instead of studying French grammars in the midst of weeds, or buying pianos for dirty cabins, they are at Mr. Washington's right hand helping him in a noble work. And yet one of the effects of Mr. Washington's propaganda has been to throw doubt upon the expediency of such training for Negroes, as these persons have had.

■ ■ ■

Men of America, the problem is plain before you. Here is a race transplanted through the criminal foolishness of your fathers. Whether you like it or not the millions are here, and here they will remain. If you do not lift them up, they will pull you down. Education and work are the levers to uplift a people. Work alone will not do it unless inspired by the right ideals and guided by intelligence. Education must not simply teach work—it must teach Life. The Talented Tenth of the Negro race must be made leaders of thought and missionaries of culture among their people. No others can do this work and Negro colleges must train men for it. The Negro race, like all other races, is going to be saved by its exceptional men.

Further Resources

BOOKS

Du Bois, W.E.B. *Dusk of Dawn.* New York: Harcourt, Brace, 1940.

———. *Souls of Black Folk.* New York: Knopf, 1993.

Harris, Thomas E. *Analysis of the Clash over the Issues Between Booker T. Washington and W.E.B. Du Bois.* New York: Garland, 1993.

Horne, Gerald, and Mary Young, eds. *W.E.B. Du Bois: An Encyclopedia.* Westport, Conn.: Greenwood, 2001.

Lewis, David L. *W.E.B. Du Bois: Biography of a Race, 1868–1919.* New York: Henry Holt, 1993.

Moore, Jacqueline M. *Booker T. Washington, W.E.B. Du Bois, and the Struggle for Racial Uplift.* Wilmington, Del.: Scholarly Resources, 2003.

Rudwick, Elliott M. *W.E.B. Du Bois, Voice of the Black Protest Movement.* Urbana, Ill.: University of Illinois Press, 1982.

Wintz, Cary D. *African American Political Thought, 1890–1930: Washington, Du Bois, Garvey, and Randolph.* Armonk, N.Y.: M.E. Sharpe, 1996.

Wolters, Raymond. *Du Bois and His Rivals.* Columbia, Mo.: University of Missouri Press, 2002.

Zamir, Shamoon. *Dark Voices: W.E.B. Du Bois and American Thought, 1888–1903.* Chicago: University of Chicago Press, 1995.

WEBSITES

"African American Education." Available online at http://www.theatlantic.com/unbound/flashbks/blacked/aaedintr.htm; website home page: http://www.theatlantic.com/ (accessed March 10, 2003).

"The Two Nations of Black America." Available online at http://www.pbs.org/wgbh/pages/frontline/shows/race/etc/road.html; website home page: http://www.pbs.org/ (accessed March 10, 2003).

AUDIO AND VISUAL MEDIA

Black Paths of Leadership. Directed by Pam Hughes. Churchill Films. Videocassette, 1984.

W.E.B. Du Bois: A Biography in Four Voices. Directed by Louis Massiah. Videocassette, 1995.

W.E.B. Du Bois of Great Barrington. Produced by Lillian Baulding. PBS Video. Videocassette, 1992.

Farmington

Autobiography

By: Clarence S. Darrow

Date: 1904

Source: Darrow, Clarence S. *Farmington.* Chicago: A.C. McClurg, 1904. Reprinted in Fuess, Claude M. and Emory S. Basford, eds. *Unseen Harvests.* New York: Macmillan, 1947, 43–45, 47.

About the Author: Clarence Seward Darrow (1857–1938) was well known for his defense of labor organizations and for his skill as a criminal lawyer. He became famous in the "Scopes Monkey Trial," when he defended high school teacher John T. Scopes, who had violated Tennessee's ban on teaching Darwin's theory of evolution. Darrow was born in Kinsman, Ohio, in 1857 and died in Chicago in 1938. ■

Introduction

First published in 1904, *Farmington* is Darrow's autobiography and recounts his youth in Ohio. In "The School Readers," Darrow provides an example of what generations of schoolchildren experienced as they learned to read.

Ever since the colonial schoolroom, American children had their reading lessons mixed with moral precepts. At first these lessons were based on the Bible. *The New England Primer* of the eighteenth and nineteenth centuries began with "In Adam's Fall/We Sinned All." By Darrow's time they had moved on to teach general moral values such as thrift and honesty, represented by the story "The Contented Boy."

Significance

The problem with these stories, as Darrow's autobiography recalls, was that they were so obvious in their intention to teach a lesson, and yet their situations were so unlike what children were likely to experience in real life. Progressive educators believed that readers should focus more on the "how" of reading instead of the "what." In the 1930s, these reformers developed their own reading primers, resulting in the popular *Dick and Jane* series.

Primary Source

Farmington [excerpt]

SYNOPSIS: In this excerpt, Darrow questions whether old-fashioned school readers like those he

The *Dick and Jane* Reading Experience

By the 1930s, progressive educators had already attacked character education programs that emphasized morality codes or teaching specific virtues, such as Darrow's school reader tried to do. In the 1932 report of the Character Education Committee of the National Education Association's Department of Superintendence, educators called for moral education that didn't consist of simple, abstract, and absolute rules, but instead taught the complex application of values to particular situations. Following the lead of John Dewey's pragmatism in the social sciences, where the value of experience, experimentation, and results counted for more than dogma, the report declared, "relativity must replace absolutism in the realm of morals as well as in the spheres of physics and biology. This of course does not involve the denial of the principle of continuity in human affairs. Nor does it mean that each generation must repudiate the system of values of its predecessors. It does mean, however, that no such system is permanent; that it will have to change and grow in response to experience."

For the school reader, this meant a significant change in approach as well. To teach the value of cooperation and other virtues, schools could now rely more on extracurricular clubs and other character-building groups like the Boy Scouts and Girl Scouts. The school reader could go from being a tool of moral education to one that focused on the process of reading.

The best way to learn how to read is still hotly debated. In the phonics method, a student learns by recognizing letters and their sounds and decodes words this way. In the whole word method, children are taught to understand the meaning of entire words in their context, not by sounding out individual letters.

In the nineteenth century, McGuffey Readers were predominant, with 122 million copies reaching school classrooms. These readers taught by having students read aloud, and included the kind of moral lessons Darrow's autobiography recounts.

By the turn of the century, new printing technology enabled school readers to include color pictures such as illustrations of children and animals. But by the 1930s, progressive educators who had surveyed the schools discovered that many schoolchildren still could not read properly, and had not benefited from the rote memorization of earlier techniques.

It was William S. Gray, an editor of the Elson Readers published by Scott Foresman, who conducted many of these reading studies. Working with supervising editor Zerna Sharp and illustrator Eleanor Campbell, the *Dick and Jane* readers were created, emphasizing seeing and doing over abstract virtues and moral lessons. Gray developed a whole word reading method that *showed* instead of described stories from a family's life with a brother, Dick, his sister, Jane, and their dog, Spot.

Dick and Jane first appeared in the 1930 *Elson Basic Reader* pre-primer. They were a huge success. During the Great Depression, children were a symbol of hope of better things to come for adults, and the happy world of Dick and Jane was an escape for schoolchildren. From the 1930s to the 1960s Scott Foresman's New Basic Reading program would teach millions of children how to read and would become a lasting part of America's cultural landscape.

SOURCE: Kismaric, Carole, and Marvin Heiferman. *Growing up with Dick and Jane: Learning and Living the American Dream.* San Francisco: Collins, 1996.

was taught with, with their abstract generalizations about contented boys, could really have the effect of teaching the moral lessons they intended.

If we scholars did not grow up to be exemplary men and women, it surely was not the fault of our teachers or our parents,—or of the school-book publishers.

When I look back to those lessons that we learned, I marvel that I ever wandered from the straight path in the smallest possible degree. Whether we were learning to read or write, studying grammar or composition, in whatever book we chanced to take, there was the moral precept plain on every page. Our many transgressions could have come only from the fact that we really did not know what these lessons meant; and doubtless our teachers also never thought they had any sort of relation to our lives.

How these books were crammed with noble thoughts! In them every virtue was extolled and every vice condemned. I wonder now how the book publishers could ever have printed such tales, or how they reconciled themselves to the hypocrisy they must have felt when they sold the books.

This moral instruction concerned certain general themes. First of all, temperance was the great lesson taught. I well remember that we children believed that the first taste of liquor was the fatal one; and we never even considered that one drop could be taken without leading us to everlasting ruin and despair. There were the alms-house, the jail, and the

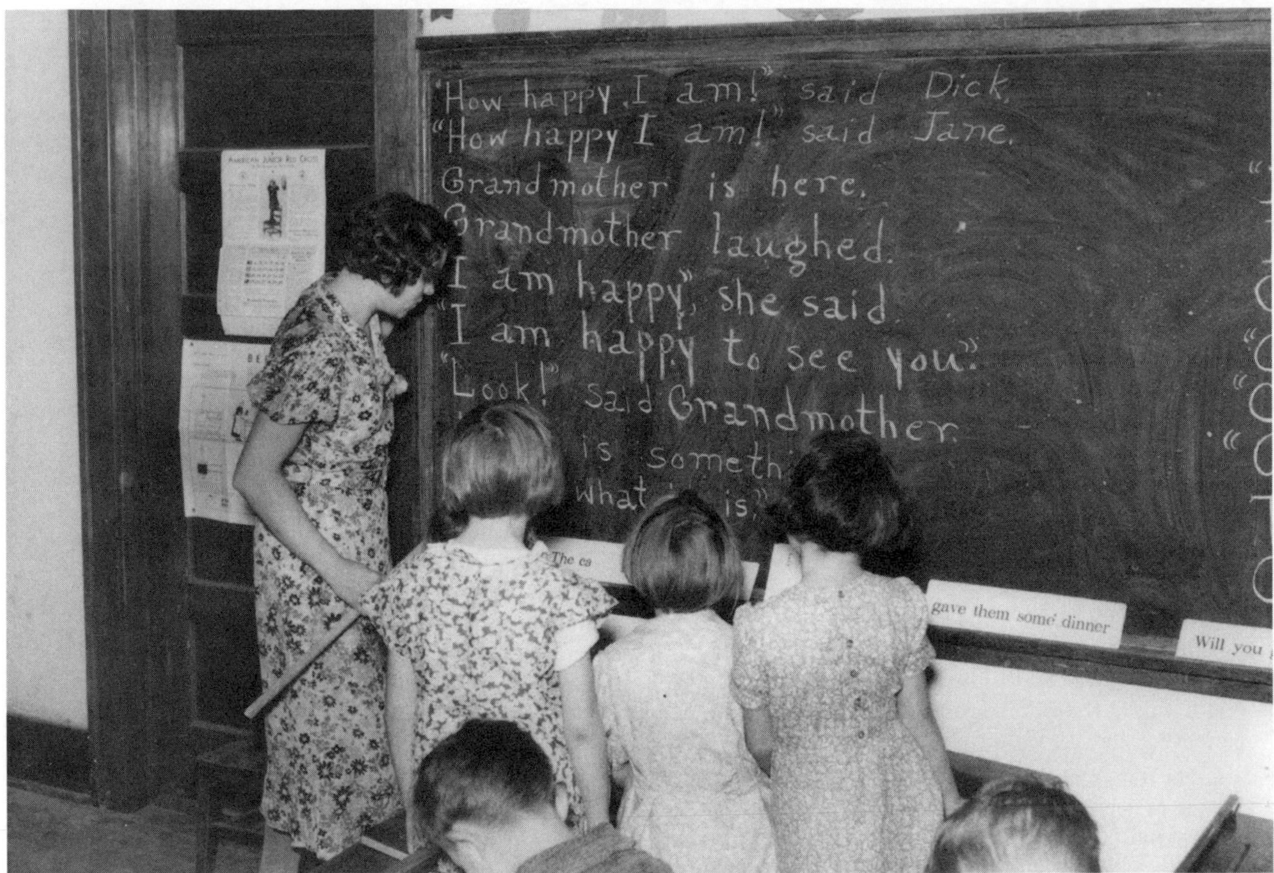

An outgrowth of the attack on character education programs that emphasized morality codes or teaching specific values, as Darrow's school reader tried to do, were the *Dick and Jane* readers. Here, a teacher uses "Dick and Jane" study tools to teach reading at a rural North Dakota school in 1937. **THE LIBRARY OF CONGRESS.**

penitentiary square, in front of every child who even considered taking the first drink; while all the rewards of this world and the next were freely promised to the noble lad who should resist.

As I look back to-day, it seems as if every moral lesson in the universe must have grown into my being from those books. How could I have ever wandered from the narrow path? I look back to those little freckled, trifling boys and girls, and I hear them read their lessons in their books so long ago. The stories were all the same, from the beginning to the end. We began in the primer, and our instruction in reading and good conduct did not end until the covers of the last book were closed.

It seems to me today that I can hear those little urchins reading about the idle lazy boy who tried to get the bee and the cow and the horse to play with him,—though what he wanted of the bee I could never understand,—but they were all too busy with their work, and so he ran away from school and had a most miserable day alone. How could we children ever stay away from school after we had read this lesson? And yet, I cannot now recall that it made us love our books, or think one whit less of the free breeze, the waving grass and trees, or the alluring coaxing sun.

We were taught by our books that we must on all accounts speak the truth; that we must learn our lessons; that we must love our parents and our teachers; must enjoy work; must be generous and kind; must despise riches; must avoid ambition; and then, if we did all these things, some fairy godmother would come along at just the darkest hour and give us everything our hearts desired. Not one story in the book told how any good could ever come from wilfulness, or selfishness, or greed, or that any possible evil ever grew from thrift, or diligence, or generosity, or kindness. And yet, in spite of all these precepts, we were young savages, always grasping for the best, ever fighting and scheming to get the advantage of our playmates, our teachers, and our tasks.

A quarter of a century seems not to have wrought much change; we still believe in the old moral precepts, and teach them to others, but we still strive to get the best of everything for ourselves.

I wonder if the old school-readers have been changed since I was a boy at school. Are the same lessons there to-day? We were such striking examples of what the books would not do that one would almost think the publishers would drop the lessons out.

I try to recall the feelings of one child who read those stories in the little white schoolhouse by the country road. What did they mean to me? Did I laugh at them, as I do to-day? Or did I really think that they were true, and try and try, and then fail in all I tried, as I do now? I presume the latter was the case; yet for my life I cannot recall the thoughts and feelings that these stories brought to me. But I can still recall the stories.

I remember, as if it were yesterday, the story about the poor widow of Pine Cottage, in the winter, with her five ragged children hovering around her little table. Widows usually had large families then, and most of their boys were lame. This poor widow had at last reached the point where starvation faced her little brood. She had tasted no food for twenty-four hours. Her one small herring was roasting on the dying coals. The prospect was certainly very dark; but she had faith, and somehow felt that in the end she would come out all right. A knock is heard at the back door. A ragged stranger enters and asks for food; the poor widow looks at her five starving children, and then she gives the visitor the one last herring; he eats it, and lo and behold! the stranger is her long-lost son,—probably one that was left over from the time when she was a widow before. The long-lost son came in this disguise to find out whether or not his mother really loved him. He was, in fact, rich; but he had borrowed the rags at the tavern, and had just arrived from India with a shipload of gold, which he at once divided among his mother and brothers and sisters. How could any child fail to be generous after this? And yet I venture to say that if any of us took a herring to school for dinner the day that we read this story in our class, we clung to it as tenaciously as a miser to his gold.

Then there was the widow with her one lame son, who asks the rich merchant for a little charity. He listens to her pathetic story, and believes she tells the truth. He asks her how much she needs. She tells him that five dollars will be enough. He writes a check, and tells her to go across the street to the bank. She takes it over without reading it. The banker counts out fifty dollars. She says, "There is a mistake; I only asked for five dollars." The banker goes across the street to find out the truth, and the merchant says: "Yes, there was a mistake, I should have made it five hundred,"—which he straightway does. Thus honesty and virtue are rewarded once again. I have lived many years and travelled in many lands, and have seen more or less of human nature and of suffering and greed; I have seen many poor widows,—but have never yet come across the generous merchant.

There was no end to the good diligent boys and girls of whom the readers told; they were on every page we turned, and every one of them received his or her reward and received it right away in cash. There never was the slightest excuse or need for us to be anything but diligent and kind,—and still our young hearts were so perverse and hard that we let the lessons pass unheeded, and clutched at the smallest piece of pie or cake, or the slightest opportunity to deceive some good kind teacher, although we must have known that we missed a golden chance to become President of the United States and have money in the bank besides. . . .

One great beauty of the lessons which our school readers taught was the directness and certainty and promptness of the payment that came as a reward of good conduct. Then, too, the recompense was in no way uncertain or ethereal, but was always paid in cash, or something just as material and good. Neither was any combination of circumstances too remote or troublesome or impossible to be brought about. Everything in the universe seemed always ready to conspire to reward virtue and punish vice.

Further Resources

BOOKS

Elliott, David L., and Arthur Woodward, eds. *Textbooks and Schooling in the United States: Eighty-ninth Yearbook of the National Society for the Study of Education, Part I.* Chicago: University of Chicago Press, 1990.

Kismaric, Carole, and Marvin Heiferman. *Growing up with Dick and Jane: Learning and Living the American Dream.* San Francisco: Collins Publishers, 1996.

McClellan, B. Edward. *Moral Education in America: Schools and the Shaping of Character from Colonial Times to the Present.* New York: Teachers College Press, 1999.

Urban, Wayne, and Jennings Wagoner. *American Education: A History.* Boston: McGraw-Hill, 2000.

WEBSITES

"Clarence Darrow is Dead in Chicago." Obituary of Clarence Darrow. *The New York Times,* March 14, 1938. Available online at http://www.nytimes.com/learning/general/onthisday/bday/0418.html; website home page: http://www.nytimes.com (accessed April 20, 2002).

AUDIO AND VISUAL MEDIA

Inherit the Wind. MGM Home Entertainment. Directed by Daniel Petrie. VHS, 1999.

Letter of Gift to the Trustees of the Carnegie Foundation for the Advancement of Teaching

Letter

By: Andrew Carnegie

Date: April 16, 1905

Source: Carnegie, Andrew. Letter of Gift to the Trustees of the Carnegie Foundation for the Advancement of Teaching. April 16, 1905. Reprinted in The Carnegie Foundation for the Advancement of Teaching. *First Annual Report of the President and Treasurer*, 1906, 7–8.

About the Author: Andrew Carnegie (1835–1919) was born into a poor family in Scotland and received no formal schooling. He emigrated to the United States in 1848 and later was a telegrapher during the Civil War (1861–1865). A shrewd businessman, Carnegie started the Carnegie Steel Company and amassed an immense fortune. After his retirement in the early 1900s, he began to engage in large-scale philanthropy. ■

Introduction

When Andrew Carnegie became a Cornell University trustee in 1890, he found to his surprise that professors were paid very little, about as much as a low-level office worker, and certainly not enough to save for retirement. After his retirement, when he began the process of giving away most of his enormous fortune, much of it for education and libraries, he wanted to do something to assist college professors. He reasoned that the low pay and lack of pension would persuade many talented people to avoid teaching as a career. Consequently, in 1905, Carnegie created the Carnegie Foundation for the Advancement of Teaching with a $10,000,000 endowment to provide free pensions for college and university professors, excluding state universities and those controlled by a particular religious group. He appointed Henry S. Pritchett, then president of The Massachusetts Institute of Technology, as president of the foundation.

Problems arose immediately. Pritchett found that the definitions of *college, university,* and *denominational* were not as clear as originally thought. State universities argued that their exclusion was unfair. In 1908, Carnegie allowed for state universities to be included and gave $5,000,000 in additional funds for this purpose.

But by 1909, it was clear that no endowment would be sufficient to provide free pensions for all eligible professors at the nation's rapidly expanding colleges and universities. Therefore, with an initial grant of $1,000,000 from the Carnegie Foundation, the Teachers Insurance and Annuity Association (TIAA) was created in 1918 as a separate entity to provide pensions and life insurance for college professors at reduced rates and on a contractual basis.

The Carnegie Foundation gradually transformed from an administrator of pensions into a policy and research center independent of any educational institution. The phrase in the original letter of gift allowing the board to "apply the revenue in a different manner and for a different though similar purpose" provided this flexibility. The foundation had already produced six bulletins, including one on the financial status of professors (1908) and another on medical education (1910), when the Carnegie Foundation gave an additional $1,250,000 for the Division of Educational Enquiry. The foundation went on to produce influential reports on education in Vermont, legal education, college sports, and teacher training in Missouri.

Significance

The creation of the Carnegie Foundation drew attention to the financial problems of professors and their negative effects on the quality of higher education. Although it was unable to fulfill the original mission to provide free pensions, the resulting creation of the TIAA was an important gain for professors. Increasing awareness of the problem led colleges, universities, and legislatures to take steps toward improvement.

Over the years, the Carnegie Foundation for the Advancement of Teaching has produced an enormous number of bulletins on educational topics. Many, such as the reports on medical education and college sports, have resulted in widespread changes. The foundation's studies have often served as models for studies conducted by other institutions. In addition, the foundation created the Educational Testing Service and played a significant role in the effort toward federal aid for higher education. The foundation's presidents have been influential leaders in education.

In 1979, the foundation officially separated from the Carnegie Corporation and is now independent. Today, its mission is "to do and perform all things necessary to encourage, uphold, and dignify the profession of the teacher and the cause of higher education." Because the foundation views all parts of the educational system as interdependent, studies are conducted pertaining to all levels of education from preschool through professional schools.

Primary Source

Letter of Gift to the Trustees of the Carnegie Foundation for the Advancement of Teaching

SYNOPSIS: In this letter to the trustees of the new Carnegie Foundation for the Advancement of Teaching, Andrew Carnegie expresses his concern that college professors are not compensated well enough and do not receive pensions. Higher education and the professors themselves consequently suffer. He announces an endowment of $10,000,000 to provide revenue for pensions for teachers of private, nonsectarian colleges and universities.

New York, April 16, 1905

Gentlemen:

I have reached the conclusion that the least rewarded of all the professions is that of the teacher in our higher educational institutions. New York City generously, and very wisely, provides retiring pensions for teachers in her public schools and also for her policemen. Very few indeed of our colleges are able to do so. The consequences are grievous. Able men hesitate to adopt teaching as a career, and many old professors whose places should be occupied by younger men, cannot be retired.

I have, therefore, transferred to you and your successors, as Trustees, $10,000,000.00, 5% First Mortgage Bonds of the United States Steel Corporation, the revenue from which is to provide retiring pensions for the teachers of Universities, Colleges, and Technical Schools in our country, Canada and Newfoundland under such conditions as you may adopt from time to time. Expert calculation shows that the revenue will be ample for the purpose.

The fund applies to the three classes of institutions named, without regard to race, sex, creed or color. We have, however, to recognize that State and Colonial Governments which have established or mainly supported Universities, Colleges or Schools may prefer that their relations shall remain exclusively with the State. I cannot, therefore, presume to include them.

There is another class which states do not aid, their constitution in some cases even forbidding it, viz., Sectarian Institutions. Many of these established long ago, were truly sectarian, but today are free to all men of all creeds or of none—such are not to be considered sectarian now. Only such as are under the control of a sect or require Trustees (or a majority thereof), Officers, Faculty or Students, to belong to any specified sect, or which impose any theological test, are to be excluded.

Andrew Carnegie in 1905, the year he established the Carnegie Foundation for the Advancement of Teaching, donating money to provide for the retirement of teachers. THE LIBRARY OF CONGRESS.

Trustees shall hold office for five years and be eligible for re-election. The first Trustees shall draw lots for one, two, three, four or five year terms, so that one-fifth shall retire each year. Each institution participating in the Fund shall cast one vote for Trustees.

The trustees are hereby given full powers to manage the Trust in every respect, to fill vacancies of non-ex-officio members; appoint executive committees; employ agents; change securities, and, generally speaking, to do all things necessary, in their judgment, to secure the most beneficial administration of the Funds.

By a two-thirds vote they may from time to time apply the revenue in a different manner and for a different, though similar purpose to that specified, should coming days bring such changes as to render this necessary in their judgment to produce the best results possible for the teachers and for education.

No Trustee shall incur any legal liability flowing from his Trusteeship. All travelling and hotel expenses incurred by Trustees in the performance of their duties shall be paid from the Fund. The expenses of a wife or daughter accompanying the Trustees to the Annual meeting are included.

I hope this Fund may do much for the cause of higher education and to remove a source of deep and constant anxiety to the poorest paid and yet one of the highest of all professions.

Gratefully yours,
Andrew Carnegie

Further Resources

BOOKS

Flexner, Abraham. *Henry S. Pritchett: A Biography.* New York: Columbia University Press, 1943.

Krass, Peter. *Carnegie.* New York: Wiley, 2002.

Lagemann, Ellen Condliffe. *Private Power for the Public Good: A History of the Carnegie Foundation for the Advancement of Teaching.* Middletown, Conn.: Wesleyan University Press, 1983.

Schlabach, Theron F. *Pensions for Professors.* Madison, Wisc.: State Historical Society of Wisconsin for the Department of History, University of Wisconsin, 1963.

Swetnam, George. *Andrew Carnegie.* Boston: Twayne, 1980.

WEBSITES

Carnegie Foundation for the Advancement of Teaching. Available online at http://www.carnegiefoundation.org/ (accessed March 22, 2003).

"The Certification of Teachers"

Journal article

By: Ellwood P. Cubberley

Date: 1906

Source: Cubberley, Ellwood P. "The Certification of Teachers." *The Fifth Yearbook of the National Society for the Scientific Study of Education,* Part II, 1906, 73–77.

About the Author: Ellwood Patterson Cubberley (1868–1941) graduated from Indiana University and earned an M.A. and a Ph.D from Columbia University. He taught at Vincennes University before serving as its president from 1893 to 1896. Cubberley was a superintendent of schools before accepting a position at Stanford University, where he taught education. He served as dean of the Stanford School of Education from 1917 until his retirement in 1933. Cubberley was a speaker and an author of many books. ■

Introduction

Historically, schoolteachers have enjoyed little status and prestige in the United States. In the eighteenth and nineteenth centuries, expectations were low and teachers were paid accordingly. Initially, most teachers were men who often regarded teaching as a mere steppingstone on the way to better professions. On the other hand, men considered unfit for other jobs could find work as schoolmasters. For women, who made up the majority of the profession by 1870, teaching was frequently a temporary situation before marriage.

Most nineteenth-century Americans lived in rural areas, often on farms. Children could, and did, learn most of what they needed to know in life working alongside their parents. In this context, the need for schooling was limited, and expectations for the teacher were low. If students learned the rudiments of reading, writing, and basic math, the teacher was successful. Methods were simple—students memorized the material and then demonstrated mastery through recitation. Consequently, teachers needed to know only as much as they had to teach. It was not unheard of for a girl as young as fourteen to complete the limited curriculum and immediately be employed as a teacher.

The industrialization and urbanization of America resulted in new demands on education. The need for a trained labor force necessitated an expansion of the curriculum. Child labor laws and compulsory attendance meant that students who might otherwise have stayed away took their seats in the classroom. Teachers were called upon to assimilate the immigrant children pouring into urban schools. The old curriculum was not enough; teachers had to find a way to provide an appropriate education for a new population of students in a rapidly changing environment.

At the same time that the larger society was changing, the field of education was experiencing a revolution. New philosophies and the development of fields such as educational psychology and child development meant a broader concept of teaching. Methods became more complex and less mechanical, requiring content knowledge far beyond what the teacher was expected to teach. Schools, called upon to fulfill many more functions, broadened the curriculum. Under these conditions, teachers needed far more professional training than in years past.

Significance

Ellwood Cubberley addresses the problems of teacher certification at a crucial time. The need for better-prepared teachers was evident, yet the system of teacher training lagged behind the demand. For Cubberley, the root of the problem was financial. High standards of teacher preparation required higher salaries. Yet the pattern of hiring poorly prepared individuals for meager pay continued. In addition, the strong American tradition

Young women study in the library of a normal school, Washington, D.C., 1899. The turn of the century brought many improvements in teacher preparation programs. **THE LIBRARY OF CONGRESS.**

of local control of schools had resulted in a hodgepodge of requirements for teachers. Diplomas from normal schools, indicating a relatively high level of preparation, were not recognized in many localities. Although higher standards depended on a more uniform system, the requirements for teachers were still, at this time, very much locally determined.

Calls for change from prominent educators such as Cubberley, combined with increasing demands on schools from the larger society, led to major changes in expectations for future teachers. Whereas previously a high school diploma or completion of a two-year normal school course was more than sufficient, teachers were increasingly expected to earn a four-year degree from a normal school or university. In addition to longer courses of study, the content of teacher-training programs was also broadening to include courses such as history and philosophy of education alongside traditional offerings in content and methods. The move was on to transform teaching into a profession.

Primary Source

"The Certification of Teachers" [excerpt]

SYNOPSIS: Ellwood P. Cubberley argues that the main problems involved in the certification of teachers could be solved by high standards, uniformity of training, uniformity from place to place in requirements for employment, separate certificates for high school and elementary school teachers, training for educational leaders, and the acceptance of education and experience in lieu of written tests. Underlying the problems of teacher certification is inadequate funding of schools.

Defects and Remedies in the Certification of Teachers, 1906

In the study we have made of present conditions, perhaps the two most significant weaknesses revealed in our systems of certification were the low standards and the great lack of uniformity. To raise and to standardize our certification requirements ought to be the main lines of future progress.

The amount of common knowledge which we as a people have is increasing so rapidly, our elementary-school curriculum is being enriched so fast, and the general intelligence of our people is becoming of such a standard that the teacher with a meagre intellectual equipment should no longer have a place in our educational system. Yet [a study] shows clearly that, for the twenty-eight states tabulated, it is possible to secure a third-grade teacher's certificate in 90 per cent of the number with no educational test beyond the common-school branches; and for the thirty-seven states tabulated it is possible to secure a first-grade certificate, in two-thirds of these states, without giving evidence of knowing anything about a single high-school subject except algebra, and in two-fifths of the states without knowing even this. These low-standard certificates are wholly out of place to-day, and ought to be eliminated at the earliest possible moment.

The great diversity in our requirements and our unwillingness to recognize equivalents are two of our marked educational characteristics. So great is the diversity that a good teacher today is unnecessarily hampered in his ability to move about, not only from state to state, but also from county to county, and often from county to city and from one city to another. Many of these restrictions are not warranted by any educational standards, but are more of the nature of a protective tariff levied on foreign capacity and in favor of home production. This makes the local examination system, with its accompanying barriers, in the nature of a protected industry, and this is not in the interests of good education. The strict county system too often perpetuates the rule of the weak by shielding them from the competition of the strong. All barriers to competency are wrong.

That these barriers exist has been pointed out frequently in previous chapters, and need only be summarized here. In fourteen states there is no admission to the teaching profession except on examination. In eleven of these states forty or more subjects are required to secure the highest certificate granted, and all must be secured on examination. In fourteen states no recognition is given to diplomas from normal schools or other institutions of learning within the state. The graduates of such institutions are placed on a par with the "graduates" of the country school. In nineteen states absolutely no recognition is given to any form of credential from another state. Only eleven states recognize normal-school diplomas from other states; seventeen recognize college or university diplomas from outside the state; and eighteen recognize a life-diploma or state professional certificate from elsewhere. In a number of our states there is no recognition of certificates from one county to another within the state. Many of these barriers are indefensible, while the defense of others can be eliminated with ease by raising and standardizing requirements. . . .

Each state must, of course, be allowed to set its own standards, and it cannot be expected to accept certificates or diplomas from states having a distinctly lower standard. This should be recognized and accepted, and reciprocity should not be expected. Instead of being "uppish" about it and striking back by way or retaliation, as certain states do because their credentials are not accredited by some more progressive state, they should on the contrary welcome a teacher from such a state because of his better training and what he may bring. . . .

In almost every state, too, these low-standard certificates are good for teaching in any part of the school system in which the holder can secure employment. This should not be allowed to continue, but separate certificates should be erected for special fields of work. In the case of high-school teachers this is especially important. Teachers in all branches of the service should be required to know more than they are expected to teach, and the importance of this for high-school teachers cannot be overemphasized.

In the field of supervision we have scarcely made a beginning in the preparation and selection of a body of educational leaders, and we are tied to present practices by a political string. In our lack of leadership we partake of a common weakness of democracy—that of emphasizing the importance of the masses and forgetting the leader who must lead and direct them. The soldier, the lawyer, the doctor, and the engineer have cast aside the apprenticeship and the successful-practitioner methods, but the educator has not as yet evolved that far in his thinking. Our pedagogical departments and the organized body of our pedagogical knowledge are too recent to have reached the point of general use and application. We are in education where the army and the navy were before the establishment of West Point and Annapolis, and where the engineer, the doctor, and the lawyer were a generation ago, before the development of modern professional schools for the training of leaders in these fields. Yet leaders must be trained for work in education, as in these other professional fields, if we are to make any great and worthy progress in the future.

In the matter of examinations there is great need of our decreasing the emphasis we now place on the written test. We could greatly improve our certificating systems by erecting certain educational prerequisites and accepting evidence of education in lieu of at least part of the examinations. As fast as can be done, the periodical written examination ought to be diminished in importance as a means of recruiting our teaching force. We ought to insist more and more on securing the educated and trained teacher instead of the new recruit. Not only should the number of examinations be decreased, but teachers of training or of long and satisfactory experience ought to be relieved of the necessity of frequent tests. There is no valid excuse, for example, for compelling a graduate of a state normal school to pass a county examination before she can teach. If her normal-school diploma does not stand for better education and better professional preparation than the county examination represents, and if she is not superior to the untrained product of the county examination method, then it is time either to renovate the normal schools of the state and put in a corps of teachers who can produce a better output, or to abolish them entirely and save an unnecessary expense.

The securing of the educated and trained teacher instead of the raw recruit is, however, an economic problem as well as an educational one, though this economic problem has an educational aspect as well. There never can be high educational standards for teachers in states which are organized on the district system, and which apportion their money on the very objectionable census basis and which raise but a small general tax, until there is a radical reform in the methods of raising school revenue and of apportioning funds after they have been raised. In the ultimate analysis there are but three primary problems in education. The first is how properly to finance a school system. The second is how to secure a trained teaching force for it. The third is how to supervise it and to produce leaders for its management and improvement. The financial problem always underlies the other two.

Further Resources

BOOKS

Butts, R. Freeman, and Lawrence Cremin. *A History of Education in American Culture.* New York: Henry Holt, 1953.

Cremin, Lawrence A. *The Transformation of the School: Progressivism in American Education, 1876–1957.* New York: Knopf, 1961.

The Move to Transform Normal Schools into Colleges, Seventh Annual Report of the Carnegie Foundation for the Advancement of Teaching. New York: Carnegie Foundation, 1912.

"The Public School and the Immigrant Child"

Speech

By: Jane Addams

Date: 1908

Source: Addams, Jane. "The Public School and the Immigrant Child." *National Education Association, Journal of Proceedings and Addresses,* 1908.

About the Author: Jane Addams (1860–1935), an advocate of progressive education, founded Hull House, the most famous of the American settlement houses aimed at improving the lives of urban immigrants. She worked toward the reform of the public schools, ending child labor, and international peace. She was the first American woman to receive the Nobel Peace Prize in 1931. Addams was the author of many books and articles and was a popular speaker. ■

Introduction

Immigrants arriving in the United States prior to the 1880s were likely to be from northern Europe and therefore similar in appearance, culture, language, and religion to the majority group. Beginning in the 1880s, new waves of immigrants from southern and eastern Europe left their homelands for the United States. These newcomers were more likely to be Catholic, illiterate, and non-English-speaking. Also, whereas the German, Irish, and Scandinavian immigrants of years past had moved inland to start farms, the new immigrants clustered in insular urban ghettos made up of residents from the same European country or even the same region or town. This pattern allowed immigrants to avoid assimilation and to retain their own culture and language. At the same time, the majority group, northern European Protestants, were wary of these new immigrants and perceived them to be a threat to "true" American culture.

The hope of a better life in America prompted many of these immigrants to leave home. Yet most soon found themselves packed into squalid tenement houses and working long hours for low pay under miserable conditions. Helping to improve the lot of low-income urban immigrants was a chief aim of progressive educators during this time. The classical college-preparatory curriculum was no longer adequate. Schools, progressives asserted, should strive to be meaningful for students in the context of their homes, families, and communities. The curriculum should be practical and useful, focusing on solutions to everyday problems. In addition, schools

A child of Italian immigrants stands with his industrial coworkers, Lawrence, Massachusetts. The immigrant child's public school experience often did not prepare him for life in America. © CORBIS. REPRODUCED BY PERMISSION.

should prepare urban immigrants for their likely future in industrial jobs. For progressives, like Jane Addams, that meant more than technical skills. Students should learn about the wider context in which they would work, rendering their labor more meaningful and humane.

Significance

Addams' approach to education for immigrants represented an important departure from the prevailing view of the time. Many Americans felt that the new immigrants were too different to fit in and feared that northern European Protestant culture was in danger of being engulfed by Italians, Russians, and other immigrant groups. Public schools were called upon to assimilate the immigrant children by removing all vestiges of the old country and replacing them with "American" language, beliefs, and culture. Addams spoke out against this approach, calling for teachers to learn about their students' cultures, communities, and families and to incorporate this knowledge into the curriculum. Rather than cutting students off from family and origins, teachers should help students to appreciate the value and beauty of the Old World while learning the skills and knowledge they would need in their new home. Children should be cultural ambassadors and assist their parents in adjusting to their new circumstances, while retaining respect for parental experience and authority.

While Addams was concerned with school reform, she felt that educational programs in the community, as in the settlement houses, could do more to effect widespread social change. The program at Hull House, serving all ages, was similar to the approach she recommends for public schools. Some activities were aimed at helping immigrants learn what they needed to know to survive in America, including classes and clubs designed to teach nutrition, child rearing, and sanitation practices. Others, such as discussion and book groups, helped participants to understand the wider context in which they worked. At the same time, immigrants were encouraged to keep ties with their original culture through activities such as artistic and musical presentations.

Addams' views prefigure the approach, common today, called multiculturalism. Students learn what they need to know to succeed in this country while learning to value and preserve their original culture and respect those who are different.

Primary Source

"The Public School and the Immigrant Child"

SYNOPSIS: Jane Addams presents three areas in which she perceives the public schools to be lacking in regard to the education of the immigrant child. Schools tend to alienate children from their parents, fail to prepare students for their future work in industry, and fail to prepare them to run a household. Schools should lead students to know and appreciate the culture of the old country and understand what it has to contribute to American life.

I am always diffident when I come before a professional body of teachers, realizing as I do that it is very easy for those of us who look on to bring indictments against results; and realizing also that one of the most difficult situations you have to meet is the care and instruction of the immigrant child, especially as he is found where I see him, in the midst of crowded city conditions.

And yet in spite of the fact that the public school is the great savior of the immigrant district, and the one agency which inducts the children into the changed conditions of American life, there is a certain indictment which may justly be brought, in that the public school too often separates the child from his parents and widens that old gulf between fathers and sons which is never so cruel and so wide as it is between the immigrants who come to this country and their children who have gone to the public school and feel that they have there learned it all. The parents are thereafter subjected to certain judgment, the judgment of the young which is always harsh and in this instance founded upon the most superficial standard of Americanism. And yet there is a notion of culture which we would define as a knowledge of those things which have been long cherished by men, the things which men have loved because thru [sic] generations they have softened and interpreted life, and have endowed it with value and meaning. Could this standard have been given rather than the things which they see about them as the test of so-called success, then we might feel that the public school has given at least the beginnings of culture which the child ought to have. At present the Italian child goes back to its Italian home more or less disturbed and distracted by the contrast between the school and the home. If he throws off the control of the home because it does not represent the things which he has been taught to value he takes the first step toward the Juvenile Court and all the other operations of the law, because he has prematurely asserted himself long before he is ready to take care of his own affairs.

We find in the carefully prepared figures which Mr. Commons and other sociologists have published that while the number of arrests of immigrants is smaller than the arrests of native born Americans, the number of arrests among children of immigrants is twice as large as the number of arrests among the children of native born Americans. It would seem that in spite of the enormous advantages which the public school gives to these children it in some way loosens them from the authority and control of their parents, and tends to send them, without a sufficient rudder and power of self-direction, into the perilous business of living. Can we not say, perhaps, that the schools ought to do more to connect these children with the best things of the past, to make them realize something of the beauty and charm of the language, the history, and the traditions which their parents represent. It is easy to cut them loose from their parents, it requires cultivation to tie them up in sympathy and understanding. The ignorant teacher cuts them off because he himself cannot understand the situation, the cultivated teacher fastens them because his own mind is open to the charm and beauty of that old-country life. In short, it is the business of the school to give to each child the beginnings of a culture so wide and deep and universal that he can interpret his own parents and countrymen by a standard which is world-wide and not provincial.

The second indictment which may be brought is the failure to place the children into proper relation toward the industry which they will later enter. . . . I believe that the figures of the United States census show the term to be something like six years for the women in industry as over against twenty-four years for men, in regard to continuity of service. Yet you cannot disregard the six years of the girls nor the twenty-four years of the boys, because they are the immediate occupation into which they enter after they leave the school—even the girls are bound to go thru that period—that is, the average immigrant girls are—before they enter the second serious business of life and maintain homes of their own. Therefore, if they enter industry unintelligently, without some notion of what it means, they find themselves totally unprepared for their first experience with American life, they are thrown out without the proper guide or clue which the public school might and ought to have given to them. Our industry has become so international, that it ought to be easy to use the materials it offers for immigrant children. The very processes and general principles which industry represents give a chance to prepare these immigrant children in a way which the most elaborated curriculum could not present. Ordinary material does not give the same international suggestion as industrial material does.

Third, I do not believe that the children who have been cut off from their own parents are going to be those who, when they become parents themselves, will know how to hold the family together and to connect it with the state. I should begin to teach the girls to be good mothers by teaching them to be good daughters. Take a girl whose mother has come from South Italy. The mother cannot adjust herself to the changed condition of housekeeping, does not know how to wash and bake here, and do the other things which she has always done well in Italy, because she has suddenly been transported from a village to a tenement house. If that girl studies these household conditions in relation to the past and to the present needs of the family, she is under-taking the very best possible preparation for her future obligations to a household of her own. And to my mind she can undertake it in no better way. Her own children are mythical and far away, but the little brothers and sisters pull upon her affections and her loyalty, and she longs to have their needs recognized in the school so that the school may give her some help. Her mother complains that the baby is sick in America because she cannot milk her own goat; she insists if she had her own goat's milk the baby would be quite well and flourishing, as the children were in Italy. If that girl can be taught that the milk makes the baby ill because it is not clean and be provided with a simple test that she may know when milk is clean, it may take her into the study not only of the milk within the four walls of the tenement house, but into the inspection of the milk of her district. The milk, however, remains good educational ma-

Jane Addams, c. 1907. Addams addressed the National Education Association with concerns about the public schools not serving the needs of the immigrant children. **THE LIBRARY OF CONGRESS.**

terial, it makes even more concrete the connection which you would be glad to use between the household and the affairs of the American city. Let her not follow the mother's example of complaining about changed conditions; let her rather make the adjustment for her mother's entire household. We cannot tell what adjustments the girl herself will be called upon to make ten years from now; but we can give her the clue and the aptitude to adjust the family with which she is identified to the constantly changing conditions of city life. Many of us feel that, splendid as the public schools are in their relation to the immigrant child, they do not understand all of the difficulties which surround that child—all of the moral and emotional perplexities which constantly harass him. The children long that the school teacher should know something about the lives their parents lead and should be able to reprove the hooting children who make fun of the Italian mother because she wears a kerchief on her head, not only because they are rude but also because they are stupid. We send young people to Europe to see Italy, but we do not utilize Italy when it lies about the schoolhouse. If the body of teachers in our great cities could take hold of the immigrant colonies, could bring out of them their handicrafts and occupations, their traditions, their folk songs and folk lore, the beautiful stories which every immigrant colony is ready to tell and translate; could get the children to bring these things into school as the material from which culture is made and the material upon which culture is based, they would discover that by comparison that which they give them now is a poor meretricious and vulgar thing. Give these children a chance to utilize the historic and industrial material which they see about them and they will begin to have a sense of ease in America, a first consciousness of being at home. I believe if these people are welcomed upon the basis of the resources which they represent and the contributions which they bring, it may come to pass that these schools which deal with immigrants will find that they have a wealth of cultural and industrial material which will make the schools in other neighborhoods positively envious. A girl living in a tenement household, helping along this tremendous adjustment, healing over this great moral upheaval which the parents have suffered and which leaves them bleeding and sensitive—such a girl has a richer experience and a finer material than any girl from a more fortunate household can have at the present moment.

I wish I had the power to place before you what it seems to me is the opportunity that the immigrant colonies present to the public school: the most endearing occupation of leading the little child, who will in turn lead his family, and bring them with him into the brotherhood for which they are longing. The immigrant child cannot make this demand upon the school because he does not know how to formulate it; it is for the teacher both to perceive it and to fulfil it.

Further Resources

BOOKS

Addams, Jane. *Jane Addams: A Centennial Reader.* New York: Macmillan, 1960.

———. *Jane Addams on Education.* Ellen Condliffe Lagemann, ed. New York: Teachers College Press, 1985.

———. *Twenty Years at Hull House: With Autobiographical Notes.* New York: New American Library, 1981.

Cremin, Lawrence A. *The Transformation of the School: Progressivism in American Education, 1876–1957.* New York: Knopf, 1961.

Elshtain, Jean Bethke. *Jane Addams and the Dream of American Democracy.* New York: Basic Books, 2002.

Lintelman, J. *The Go-betweens: The Lives of Immigrant Children.* Minneapolis: University Art Museum, University of Minnesota, 1986.

WEBSITES

"Immigration History Research Center, University of Minnesota." Available online at http://www1.umn.edu/ihrc/; website home page: http://www1.umn.edu (accessed May 15, 2003).

"Jane Addams." Available online at http://nlu.nl.edu/ace/Resources/Addams.html; website home page: http://nlu.nl.edu/ (accessed May 15, 2003).

Stubborn Fool: A Narrative

Memoir

By: Estelle Aubrey Brown

Date: 1952

Source: Brown, Estelle Aubrey. *Stubborn Fool: A Narrative.* Caldwell, Idaho: Caxton, 1952.

About the Author: Estelle Aubrey Brown (1877–1958) began her teaching career in a one-room schoolhouse at the age of sixteen. She saved her earnings in order to further her education during vacations. After passing a civil service exam in 1902, she accepted the offer of a position at the Crow Creek Indian school in South Dakota. She went on to work at various Indian schools for the next sixteen years. ■

Introduction

The U.S. Congress began allocating funds to build schools for Native Americans in 1877, and in 1891, school attendance for American Indians was made compulsory. By 1907, over half of Native American children were enrolled in schools run by the Bureau of Indian Affairs (BIA).

The assumption of many white Americans during the 1900s was that Native American culture was "savage," "uncivilized," and generally inferior to white culture. Schools were an important tool used to assimilate Native Americans and help the "benighted children of the red men . . . speedily emerge from the ignorance of centuries." According to a former Commissioner of Indian Affairs in 1881, Native Americans had two choices: "extermination or civilization."

Consequently, a major aim of BIA schools was the assimilation of Native American children into Protestant European-American culture. The language, clothing, hairstyles, habits, beliefs, and even names that children brought with them were replaced with those of the dominant American culture. When children returned to their homes, they often found themselves estranged from their cultures and families. Attendance was not always voluntary. Parents were often pressured or coerced into enrolling their children, and children were also taken by force. Students were sometimes kept in locked dormitories.

By the late 1870s, day schools located on reservations began to be replaced by boarding schools. Day schools were found to be unsatisfactory for the full assimilation of Native American children because of the daily contact that children had with family and tribe. Indeed, one complaint of boarding school staff was that children often returned to their "bad Indian habits" during vacations at home.

Aside from cultural issues and homesickness, boarding school students also suffered from widespread malnutrition, corporal punishment, overwork, and disease resulting from unsanitary and overcrowded conditions. Tuberculosis, scrofula, and trachoma were common among students.

Native Americans were sometimes successful in resisting the boarding school agenda. Parents might refuse to send children, hide them, or encourage them to run away. Students disrupted classes, ran away, burned buildings, and engaged in passive resistance, illustrated by this poem written by a group of Navajo students about their school:

If I do not believe you
The things you say,
Maybe I will not tell you
That is my way.

Maybe you think I believe you
That thing you say,
But always my thoughts stay with me
My own way.

Significance

Estelle Brown was fairly typical of teachers working in BIA schools during this time period. Most of these teachers, Brown included, were single, white Christian women who found that teaching was one of the few employment opportunities available to them. Brown also encountered many of the problems commonly found in BIA schools at the time. She documents the disease, overwork, and malnutrition suffered by her students.

Her memoir is significant in that she discusses some of the misgivings she had about the boarding school system. She questions the program of assimilation for several reasons. Students were forced to learn, and become accustomed to, a lifestyle that most would not be able to maintain outside of school. Few opportunities existed at the time for Native Americans to obtain high-level employment. She wonders what use students would make of their education when they returned to the reservation. She notes the irony of students learning the "Christian" values of a culture that had so often dealt dishonestly and unfairly with them. She questions the right of the government to take children away from their parents and to destroy families.

Brown's memoir illustrates the dilemma of many BIA teachers: Wanting to help, these teachers found instead that they had become part of a system that was doing more harm than good.

Primary Source

Stubborn Fool: A Narrative [excerpt]

SYNOPSIS: In the following passages, Estelle Brown documents the conditions under which students were living at the Crow Creek and Navajo schools. She discusses her initial impressions upon arriving at Crow Creek and reflects upon some of her later misgivings regarding the aims and methods of the schools in which she worked.

I expected Indian children to be shining with health. The faces in that circle shone, but with mercuric ointment generously spread over their scrofula sores. Mrs. Hillyard had given me a list of their names. But how attach the correct name to its owner when he refused to acknowledge ownership? The sores helped. I separated the children with visible sores and so came to identify Sophia Ghost Bear by the running sore on the right side of her neck. Elaine Medicine Blanket had her sore on the left. Genevieve Big Buck's finger joints were badly inflamed, as were Roland Little Elk's.

Tribal names had been too literally translated. As these children entered school with no Christian names, these were arbitrarily assigned them. Someone's fancy roamed not fitly but too far. There was a Rose, a Violet, and an Eloise. An Eloise with a dirty nose was somehow irritating. I resented the perversity of nature that made the noses of those pitiful children run freely but denied their tongues the same facility. If an Indian child ever has a handkerchief, only omniscience knows where it blows to. . . .

The work called for unlimited patience and I was naturally impatient. It called for a belief in the necessity for recreating primitive children in my own image. In sixteen years I did not acquire that belief. I had a vague sense of incongruity in the routine and purposes of the school but was too ignorant to trace it to a reliable source. Yet I instinctively felt that, in teaching Indian children to like and want the things we liked and wanted, we were headed in the wrong direction. Had nature fitted these children to like and want these things? Could they make use of these things on the reservation? Were we doing anything to make it possible for them to live there as we were teaching them to want to live? I did not know. During my time at Crow Creek the subject of improving reservation conditions was not mentioned in my hearing. . . .

As time passed and I learned how that school was conducted, I was indignant for the first time, but by no means for the last. Crow Creek was an isolated Federal institution that had to maintain itself. There were only a few white people. Who did the work? The children. . . .

In a corner of the sewing room the small girls from the kindergarten darned stockings four hours daily except on Sunday. We had set their feet on the long, hard road to civilization. On it they wore their first stockings, their first hated shoes. The size of holes in toes, heels, and knees mutely testified to the difficulties of that road. The little pioneers sat patiently darning with their inflamed finger joints, with no outcry for hands pricked at unaccustomed tasks. Poor little pioneers. . . .

Who kept the shabby, desolate buildings in a semblance of cleanliness? The children.

Children were forever scrubbing. Under their matron's watchful eyes, boys scrubbed their own building daily. I wished I might know their thoughts as, on hands and knees, they wielded brush and soap before the white man's goddess of sanitation. I felt certain that for this or any other goddess they felt not the slightest need. Their own tribal deities were male and did not require them to perform tasks fit only for women. I was never able to visualize those boys scrubbing a tepee. . . .

At the foot of my table in the mess hall sat a plainly dressed, smiling woman of sixty, Miss Blanchard. She was a woman whose garment other women would be honored to touch. She was girls' matron and sister of Mrs. Burt, whose evangelism she shared. She had mothered many Indian girls through the years, had labored to give them her own faith in a prayer-hearing and prayer-answering God. She had watched them leave the school to go back to the poverty and squalor of the reservation. Did she expect her teaching to serve as a leaven in their own and in their parents' lives? Against that teaching was opposed centuries of a primitive way of life, with its own beliefs adapted to its racial development. Of a certainty, Crow Creek was the substance of things hoped for.

Miss Blanchard's girls loved and respected her. Never behind her back did they put brown, contemptuous thumbs to brown, contemptuous noses, as they did to many of us. Her girls seemed to know that she was there because she wanted to help them, just as they knew all the rest of us were there to make a living. . . .

They taught and lived a way of life that embraced a Christian faith in love and selflessness and fair dealing. Yet they appeared before the Sioux Indians as members of a race that had broken every early treaty with them in the interests of its own greed. Again I wondered. Could these Indians add the Burts' teaching to their broken treaties that despoiled them of their lands and obtain a sum that, to them, would be a better guide than their own gods and beliefs? . . .

The dining room was long and narrow, with twenty tables, each seating ten boys and girls. At the far end the coal stove was drawing merrily, but it could make no appreciable impression on the frigidity of the barracks-like room. Overhead burned three large oil lamps, the ceiling black above them.

In the kitchen beyond the girls were dishing up the oatmeal, breaking loaves of bread into chunks, filling pitchers with coffee. I had seen the coarse, grayish flour supplied the school and was not surprised that bread made from it was heavy and unappetizing. Sacks of low-grade coffee beans came in over the same route. The cook had to roast each day's supply in the oven, grind it in a hand mill. These children drank coffee three times daily. For it there was neither sugar nor milk. Butter, cheese, fresh fruit, and vegetables were never seen in that dining room. The daily diet of bread and molasses, coffee, meat and gravy was as unalterable as the law of the Medes and Persians. The small school herd supplied milk for the oatmeal only. That morning there was no milk. . . .

I heard the girls coming downstairs from their dormitory. That dormitory was unheated. I knew routine required the girls to fold their garments neatly at night, to stand beside their beds to dress in the morning. I also knew that Miss Blanchard's kind heart led her to break routine on mornings such as this, that she permitted her girls to warm their cold clothes beneath their bed blankets and to dress there as best they could.

The long lines of girls entered. They were wearing their small head shawls, again due to Miss Blanchard's kindness. They took their places at table, standing half frozen to await the arrival of the boys. . . .

The boys were late. On the tables oatmeal and coffee were cold by the time the door burst open and one hundred young Indians crowded through with much brushing of snow and blowing on fingers. They had neither overcoats nor mittens. They were wearing their everyday clothes, far less warm than their wool uniforms for Sunday. Routine took no cognizance of blizzards. Those boys looked, and were, half frozen. And at the end of the room was that invitingly warm stove.

I took my place on the dais in center of the room; I waited longer than usual for the boys to take their places, for silence—or for what passed for silence in a Sioux dining room. Most of those miserable boys went obediently to their tables, but at the far end of the room several of the larger boys remained beside the stove. I did not blame them, but routine reared its ugly head.

"Please take your places, boys." Two boys did so. Three remained by the stove.

"Please go to your tables." They did not obey.

Leaving the dais, I went down to the stove amid a dead silence as the eyes of two hundred Indians watched with interest the outcome of this unusual event. Shaking with cold, I said as pleasantly as chattering teeth permitted:

"I know you are cold, boys. We are all cold, and your breakfast is getting cold, too. You must go to your tables."

Two boys did so. The largest, a head taller than I, glared at me with hatred and did not move. I did not blame him for hating me. Why shouldn't he? Rebellion in every fiber of his half-frozen body, he said insolently:

"I do not mind a woman. I stand here."

The blow I landed on that young Indian's chin may not have hurt him much, but it surprised him as much as it surprised me. It had not been premeditated. I expected a blow in return but was too mad to retreat.

"Go to your table!" A reluctant image of hatred, he did so.

As I went back to the dais, every joint in my armor, every hook and eye and button and safety pin, even the tie strings, creaked with rage. Not at that boy, but at the intolerable conditions at that Federal institution. From my vantage point, I looked at those cold, miserable children. There they stood, every one of them oozing ingratitude, waiting for me to be grateful for them.

It was too much. I bowed my stiff neck.

"Lord, we are not thankful for cold oatmeal without any sugar and milk. We are not thankful for this

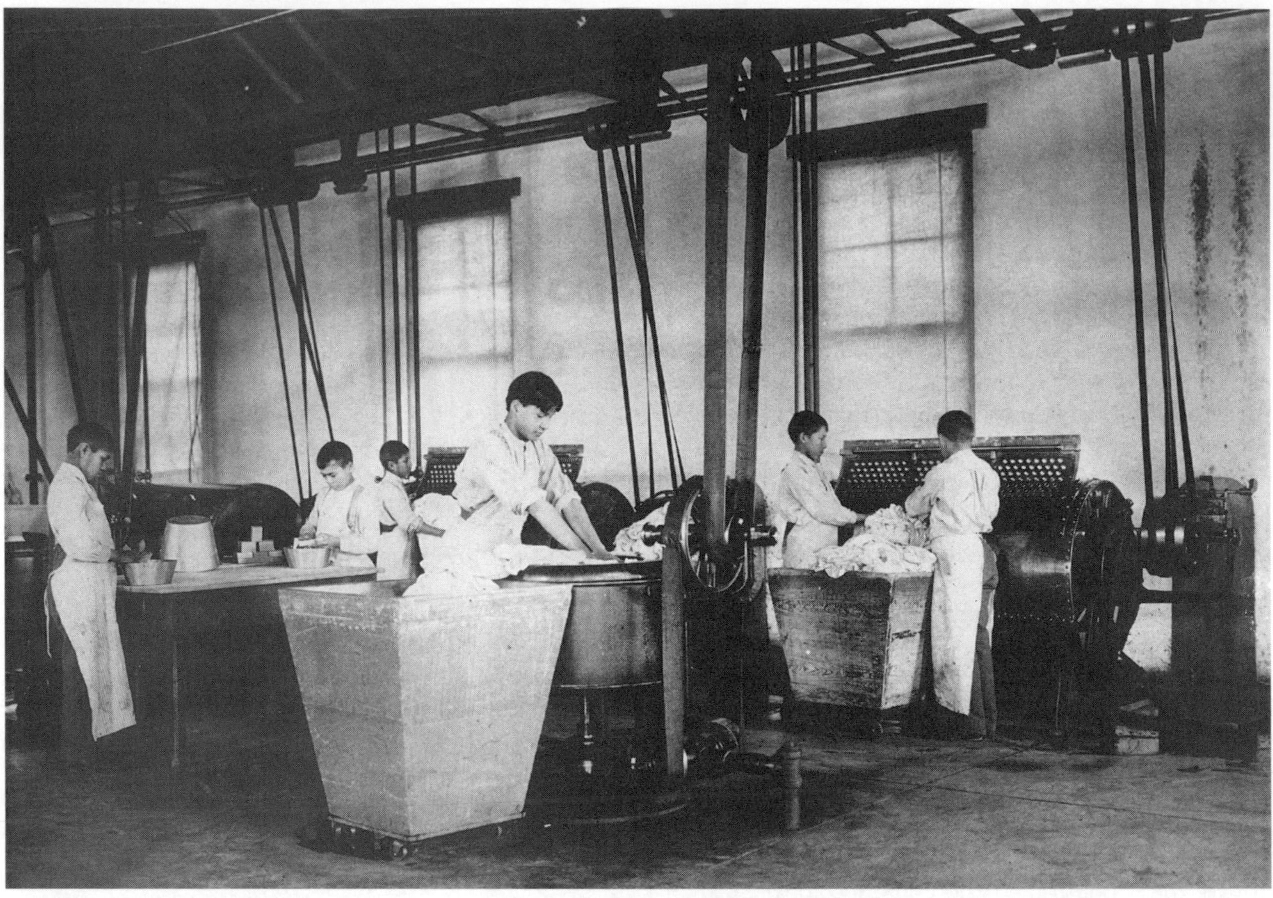

Students wash clothes at the U.S. Indian School, Carlisle, Pennsylvania, c. 1902. Early schools for Native Americans were criticized for a variety of shortcomings, including not doing anything to help improve conditions on reservations. **THE LIBRARY OF CONGRESS.**

poor bread and molasses. We are not thankful for anything in this horrible place. Amen." . . .

From the first I had been surprised by the tender years of the Navajo children in the school. When it was opened, few parents brought their children in. Employees had been sent out to search the hogans, to scour the reservation for children. Few girls as old as thirteen were found who were not married. Navajo tribal custom permitted marriage at puberty. There were few older girls here to do the heavy work of laundry and sewing room and kitchen. Girls of ten years had to do this work. Many of the children were only five years old. They had known only the free nomadic life of the desert. They had never sat on chairs, slept in a bed, used knives and forks. They did not know how to wear their new clothes. Many of them were seeing white people for the first time and discovering little in us to admire. They were in school against their own will and, in most cases, the will of their parents.

For the first time in this work I asked myself: What right have we to take these children from their parents? What right have we to break up Indian homes? Why do we deny Indians the rights we claim for ourselves?

Further Resources

BOOKS

Adams, David Wallace. *Education for Extinction: American Indians and the Boarding School Experience, 1875–1928.* Lawrence, Kans.: University Press of Kansas, 1995.

Archuleta, Margaret L., Brenda J. Child, and K. Tsianina Lomawaima. *Away From Home: American Indian Boarding School Experiences, 1879–2000.* Phoenix, Ariz.: Heard Museum, 2000.

Coleman, Michael C. *American Indian Children at School, 1850–1930.* Jackson, Miss.: University Press of Mississippi, 1993.

Ellis, Clyde. *To Change Them Forever: Indian Education at the Rainy Mountain Boarding School, 1893–1920.* Norman, Okla.: University of Oklahoma Press, 1996.

Golden, Gertrude. *Red Moon Called Me: Memoirs of a School Teacher in the Government Indian Service.* San Antonio, Tex.: Naylor, 1954.

Johnston, Basil H. *Indian School Days.* Norman, Okla.: University of Oklahoma Press, 1988.

WEBSITES

"Assimilation Through Education: Indian Boarding Schools in the Pacific Northwest." University of Washington Libraries Digital Collection. Available online at http://content.lib.washington.edu/aipnw/marr/index.html; website home page: http://www.washington.edu (accessed December 23, 2002).

"Carlisle Indian Industrial School (1879–1918)." Available online at http://home.epix.net/~landis/; website home page: http://home.expix.net (accessed December 23, 2002).

"The Reservation Boarding School System in the United States, 1870–1928." Available online at http://www.twofrog.com/rezsch.html; website home page: http://www.twofrog.com (accessed December 23, 2002).

AUDIO AND VISUAL MEDIA

In the White Man's Image. The American Experience Series. Produced by Christine Lesiak and Mathew Jones. PBS Home Video. Videocassette, 1991.

Where the Spirit Lives. Directed by Bruce Pittman. Studio Entertainment. Videocassette, 1989.

4

Fashion and Design

Anita Miller Stamper

Entries are arranged in chronological order by date of primary source. For entries with one primary source, the entry title is the same as the primary source title. Entries with more than one primary source have an overall entry title, followed by the titles of the primary sources.

CHRONOLOGY

PRIMARY SOURCES

Important Events in Fashion and Design, 1900–1909

1900

- The S-curve silhouette is the dominant look in women's fashion.
- Rollin H. White of the White Sewing Machine Company of Cleveland, Ohio, begins marketing a steam-engine automobile, which he calls "The Incomparable White." Stately and powerful, the White becomes the first official presidential car when it is adopted by the William Howard Taft administration.
- The Franklin, Peerless, Stearns, Packard, and Auburn gasoline-powered automobiles are introduced.
- Woods Electrical Car, with enclosed passenger compartment and elevated seat for a footman, sells for three thousand dollars.
- The influence of American architect Louis Sullivan on Finnish architect Eliel Saarinen is displayed in his designs for the Finnish Pavilion at the Paris Exposition.
- From November 3 to November 10, the first U.S. automobile show, featuring a wide array of steam-, electric-, and gasoline-powered models, opens in Madison Square Garden in New York City.

1901

- A *New York Times* want ad for a dressmaker offers $2.50 per day. An advertisement for women's shirtwaist suits carries prices of $2.25 to $4.50.
- Architects Charles and Henry Greene build one of their first bungalows in Pasadena, California, for David B. Gamble.
- Architect Frank Lloyd Wright delivers his influential lecture "The Art and Craft of the Machine" at Chicago's Hull House.
- Gustav Stickley begins publishing *The Craftsman,* a magazine that promotes the Arts and Crafts Movement, and the ideology that finely crafted, handmade objects should be used in daily life.
- Architect Horace Trumbauer completes The Elms, the Newport, Rhode Island, mansion of Philadelphia coal magnate Edward Julius Berwind that is modeled on a French chateau.
- The architectural firm of Babb, Cook, and Willard completes the neo-Georgian mansion of steel magnate Andrew Carnegie on New York City's Fifth Avenue at 92nd Street.
- Francis E. and Freelan O. Stanley, forty-seven-year-old identical twins, return to the steam-car business after selling their original designs for a quarter of a million dollars in 1899.
- Ransom E. Olds introduces the Oldsmobile Curved Dash Runabout.
- The Apperson motorcar and the Pierce Motorette are introduced.
- On January 22, Britain's Queen Victoria dies and is succeeded by her son, Edward VII, inaugurating the Edwardian Age in fashion.
- From late October to early November, Ransom Olds has Roy Chapin drive his Curved Dash Runabout 820 miles to New York, an unheard-of distance. It takes Chapin seven and a half days and generates fame for the Olds Motor Works.

1902

- The twenty-story, steel-frame Fuller Building, nicknamed the "Flatiron Building" because of its shape, is completed in New York City by Chicago architect Daniel H. Burnham. At two hundred and eighty-five feet, and one of the first buildings with a steel frame, it is the tallest building in New York City. Supposedly, its shape creates eddies of wind that lift the skirts of passing women. As a result, men stand on the corner of 23rd Street trying to catch a glimpse of ankle. Policemen shoo away the oglers with "23 skidoo," a phrase which becomes the parent of "scram."
- New York architect Stanford White completes Rosecliff, the Newport, Rhode Island, mansion of Mrs. Hermann Oelrichs.
- The architectural firm of Carrère and Hastings completes Whitehall, the seventy-three-room, $2.5 million Spanish-inspired Palm Beach, Florida, mansion of Florida East Coast Railway magnate Henry M. Flagler.
- The Stanley brothers switch their Locomobile from steam to gasoline.
- The Studebaker electric car and the Marmon and Overland gasoline-powered cars are introduced.
- On March 4, the American Automobile Association is formed to give a national voice to the growing number of local auto clubs. By the end of the decade AAA will have twenty-five thousand members in more than thirty states.

1903

- American women swim in black sleeveless dresses and long, full-length leggings. Men swim in tank tops and knee-length shorts.
- An advertisement in the Columbia, S.C., *State* newspaper offers a "sack business suit; worn by most business men of your acquaintance" for $8.50.
- The Olds Motor Works turns out 4,000 Curved Dash Runabouts, up from 450 in 1901, and shows a profit of six hundred thousand dollars.
- Frank Lloyd Wright modernizes Chicago's Rookery. The Larkin Building, his innovative office building—created with simplified masses, few windows, and a large central open court that allowed light—is also completed in 1903.

- Ninety-three percent of America's 2.3 million miles of roads are little better than plain dirt paths.
- Architect Louis Sullivan completes the Holy Trinity Cathedral in Chicago.
- The Greene brothers build their most famous bungalow, the Bandini bungalow, in Pasadena, California.
- The Chadwick gasoline-powered car is introduced by engineer Lee Sherman Chadwick; it can reach a speed of sixty miles per hour and sells for four thousand dollars.
- The sixteen-story Ingalls Building, the first skyscraper with a reinforced-concrete skeleton, is completed in Cincinnati. It will be renamed the Transit Building in 1959.
- The Model A Ford is introduced.
- In January, Henry Martyn Leland unveils the first Cadillac.
- On May 23, Dr. Horatio Nelson Jackson and mechanic Sewall K. Crocker leave San Francisco in a twenty-horsepower Winton Touring Car; they arrive in New York sixty-four days later, having completed the first coast-to-coast automobile trip. On his return home Jackson is fined for exceeding a six-mile-an-hour speed limit. Within a few weeks a Packard and an Oldsmobile make the same trip.
- On September 1, Massachusetts issues the first automobile license plate.

1904

- Ford sells fourteen hundred Model A's, calling the car "positively the most perfect machine on the market."
- Millionaire sportsman William Vanderbilt inaugurates the Vanderbilt Cup, a four-hour automobile race on the back roads of Long Island. The race is run every year until 1910, sometimes attracting more than 250,000 spectators.
- The George N. Pierce Company introduces the Pierce Arrow and the luxury Great Arrow; the latter sells for four thousand dollars.
- Ransom E. Olds, having left the Olds Motor Works, founds the R.E. Olds Company; when the Olds Motor Works threatens a lawsuit over the name, Olds changes his company's name to his initials, forming the Reo Motor Car Company. The first Reo car is introduced; it has a steering wheel instead of a tiller.
- Architect Frank Lloyd Wright begins the Darwin D. Martin Complex in Buffalo, New York. It is Wright's most extensive "Prairie House," a multi-structure composition integrated into a richly designed landscape.
- English-born architect Ernest Coxhead completes the Andrew Carrigan House in San Anselmo, CA. In the shingle style, it is an artful, understated collage with a Tuscan portico, a Tudor bay, and medieval buttresses.
- Architect Daniel Burnham completes Orchestra Hall and the Railway Exchange Building in Chicago.
- On August 13, the first Buick is delivered to Dr. Herbert Hills of Flint, Michigan.

1905

- An advertisement in the *Chicago Tribune* offers women's tailor-made suits for $35.
- U.S. automobile production reaches twenty-five thousand units.
- The electric car's share of the automobile market drops to less than 7 percent from its height of 38 percent in 1900.
- William C. Durant takes over the Buick Motor Company; within a year he sells fourteen hundred Buicks to the growing millionaire market.

1906

- Paris designers introduce the Empire dress, a narrower-cut, high-waisted dress that does away with the tight curves, luxurious bosoms, and narrow waists of the S-shaped dresses that had dominated women's fashion.
- The Ford Motor Company begins twenty-four consecutive years of industry sales leadership.
- Ford introduces the Model N, a two-passenger runabout with an efficient four-cylinder engine priced at six hundred dollars. *Cycle and Automobile* magazine proclaims it "distinctively the most important technical event of 1906."
- The Chadwick Six, a six-cylinder car, is introduced by Lee Sherman Chadwick.
- At Ormond Beach, Florida, a Stanley race car captures the world's land speed record at 127 MPH.

1907

- Australian long-distance swimmer Annette Kellerman is arrested for indecent exposure at Revere Beach in Boston for wearing a one-piece bathing suit without a skirt.
- Paris causes a stir by introducing a "short" skirt that ends at the top of the fashionable woman's boot.
- Feather boas are the rage.
- A man's raccoon-fur automobile coat is advertised in *The New York Times* for $47.50, a derby hat for $2.75.
- Architect Daniel Burnham completes the Marshall Field and Company building in Chicago and Union Station in Washington, D.C.
- U.S. automobile production reaches forty-three thousand units.
- Alanson Partridge Brush introduces the Brush Runabout automobile, priced at five hundred dollars; a Cadillac sells for eight hundred dollars.

1908

- The *San Francisco Examiner* advertises women's "pretty hats for Easter with ribbon" for $6.50.
- U.S. automobile production reaches 63,500 units; there are 200,000 cars on the road.
- Automaker Charles Duryea estimates for *Motor Magazine* that as many as half of the 515 companies that were producing cars in 1900 have gone bankrupt.
- The Hupp Motor Car Company of Detroit introduces the Hupmobile.
- William Durant sells 8,800 Buicks, second only to Ford in market share.

- Architect Louis Sullivan completes the National Farmers Bank Building in Owatonna, Minnesota.
- Upon completion, the forty-seven story Singer Tower, designed by Ernest Flagg, is the tallest building in the world.
- On February 12, the New York-to-Paris auto race begins; it will proceed through Detroit, Cleveland, Chicago, Salt Lake City, and San Francisco, then via sea to Tokyo, through Vladivostok, Irkutsk, Moscow, Berlin, Bonn, and Brussels. After 169 days and 13,341 miles, the lone American entry, a Thomas Flyer driven by George Schuster, is the winner.
- On August 12, the Model T Ford is introduced, priced at $850.

1909

- The Empire line is incorporated into the S-curve silhouette in women's dresses, which are still one piece but now have slightly raised waistlines and long, sweeping trains.
- Women's hats keep getting bigger, with wider brims; these large hats require the longest hatpins in history.
- U.S. automobile production reaches 127,731. The ratio of Americans to automobiles drops from one car for every ninety-five hundred people to one for every two hundred people.
- The Hudson Fulton Exhibition of American furniture opens in the Metropolitan Museum of Art in New York City.
- Charles and Henry Greene establish a trend in American architectural regionalism with the Gamble House in Pasadena, California.
- The world's tallest building (until 1913), the forty-two-story, seven hundred foot Metropolitan Life Insurance Tower, is completed in New York City by Napoleon Le Brun and Sons.
- Frank Lloyd Wright completes the Frederick G. Robie House, for which he even designs the furniture, in Chicago. Its powerful horizontals mirror the terrain of the prairie, blending with its environment. Its cantilevered forms, low pitched roof, and extended eave become components of Wright's work. Wright closes his studio in the Chicago suburb of Oak Park and departs for Europe, initiating a flurry of activity for Prairie School architects who had long been dominated by his presence.
- On June 1, six cars—two Model T Fords, an Acme, an Itala, a Shawmut, and a Stearns—leave New York in the first transcontinental automobile race; one of the Model T's wins, arriving in Seattle on 22 June.
- In October, the American Ladies Tailors Association exhibition in New York highlights the "suffragette suit," designed in protest against heavy, impractical skirts. It features a jacket with many pockets and a separated skirt with creases and cuffs like those of men's trousers.

Louis Sullivan, Architect

"Architecture and the People"

Journal article

By: Louis H. Gibson

Date: 1898

Source: Gibson, Louis H. "Architecture and the People." *The New England Magazine* 24, no. 1, March 1898, 21–26. Available online at http://library5.library.cornell.edu/moa (accessed February 22, 2003).

About the Author: Louis H. Gibson was an architect, author, and architectural critic. His work appeared in journals of the time, and he wrote two books on residential architecture.

"Gage Building, Exterior, Chicago, IL"; "Babson House, Exterior, Riverside, IL"

Photographs

By: Louis H. Sullivan

Date: 1902; 1910

Source: Sullivan, Louis H. "Gage Building Exterior, Chicago, IL"; "Babson House, Exterior, Riverside, IL." *American Landscape and Architectural Design, 1850–1920.* American Memory digital primary source collection, Library of Congress. Available online at http://memory.loc.gov /ammem/award97/mhsdhtml/aladhome.html; website home page: http://memory.loc.gov (accessed February 22, 2003).

About the Author: Louis H. Sullivan (1856–1924) was born in Boston and studied at both the Massachusetts Institute of Technology and the École des Beaux-Arts before settling in Chicago in 1875. Sullivan's influence can be seen in the work of his most famous pupil, Frank Lloyd Wright. Sullivan coined the popular maxim "form follows function." ■

Introduction

In his 1898 journal article "Architecture and the People," Louis H. Gibson provided a scathing overview of most contemporary architecture—both commercial and residential—for its mindless copying of foreign and historical styles. He specified major public buildings of his time that failed to reflect in any way the spirit, culture, and unique attributes of their places. The architects of both the Library of Congress Building and the Boston Library came in for equal rebuke for failing to express anything characteristic of "the history of the times of those who built it." He called for an American architecture that was both rational and local and named Louis Sullivan specifically as exemplifying the type of architect capable of forging this new ideal. Gibson lauded Sullivan's melding of form and function in creating a building that reflected a modern spirit of domestic architecture.

A later structure than the one to which Gibson made reference, The Gage Building, completed in 1902 in Chicago by architects Holabird & Roche with façade by Sullivan, answers Gibson's plea for a modern and uniquely American style. As seen in the lantern slide (first produced in the mid-1900s, a lantern slide is a plate of glass on which an image has been made and which can be viewed on a wall or screen using a lantern-like projector), the Gage Building obviously relied on no previous historical period or foreign country for its design inspiration. The simplicity of the overall form, the multiple stories, and the extensive use of glass were all in keeping with the functional requirements of an urban commercial building and demonstrated a form that evolved directly from intended function. The Babson House, a residential design by Sullivan, likewise reflected a uniquely American approach to designing spaces for family life, spaces that nestled into their surroundings and reflected the geography as well as the needs of modern families. The contemporary lantern slide captured the external appearance as Sullivan envisioned it, with spacious grounds and landscaping for privacy.

Significance

Writing just at the turn of the century, Gibson's words seem prophetic in calling for the development of a unique American style, one which was even then developing in the work of Sullivan and the Chicago School of architects which he founded. Gibson was not alone in his aversion to copying other times and countries rather than creating fresh designs that honored but did not imitate design heritage. Sullivan and other architects of the Chicago School answered Gibson's call for change. One of Sullivan's major contributions to the development of a new style was in perfecting the use of steel in the skeletal infrastructure of his commercial buildings. This structural innovation led to two major design possibilities noted in the Gage Building: greater height and increased exterior surface that could be glassed. The skyscrapers of the future would be built on the design foundations of Sullivan's work because his work was so functional. Stacking multiple floors to make high-rise structures was an economic use of limited urban space, and the exten-

Primary Source

Gage Building, exterior, Chicago, IL, 1902

SYNOPSIS: This photo shows a commercial building in downtown Chicago, Illinois, completed between the years 1898 and 1902, with façade designed by Louis H. Sullivan.

sive use of windows provided increased illumination for the day work conducted inside.

Ornamentation was used by Sullivan, extensively in some designs, but the overall structural design quality did not depend upon ornamentation to make its statement, and this is clear when viewing the Gage Building. The details of ornamentation in the Sullivan-designed façade are not even clearly visible in the old photo, but the quality of the lines is very evident. In the Babson House, as well, the ornamentation is hardly visible, but the clean, functional lines of the home and its marriage to the natural setting are emphasized. Many architectural details of the Babson House, including the use of the setting as part of the overall design, are obvious precursors to what one of Sullivan's students, Frank Lloyd Wright, would take to an entirely new level of excellence.

Primary Source

"Architecture and the People" [excerpt]

SYNOPSIS: In this excerpt from a journal article, Louis H. Gibson decries the prevailing dependence upon historical and foreign models for modern American architecture and calls for the development of a uniquely modern American architecture.

There is nothing so encouraging as good example. Mere destructive criticism is useless. We find encouragement for the future in some of our commercial structures and in the modern spirit of domestic architecture. There is a tall building in Buffalo, the Guaranty Building, by Mr. Louis Sullivan. There are others, taller and larger, elsewhere: but one does not have to count the number of stories in this building

Primary Source

Babson House, exterior, Riverside, IL, 1910

This photo shows a Louis H. Sullivan residential design, a home for the Babson family, completed in 1910 in Riverside, Illinois. COURTESY OF THE FRANCES LOEB LIBRARY, HARVARD DESIGN SCHOOL. REPRODUCED BY PERMISSION.

to appreciate its greatness. It is a natural development of a commercial structure. It is the simple application of form to function. The hand, guided by the heart and mind of a great artist, touches this simple mass, and we have great art. The entire surface of the great structure is profusely ornamented, but without a square inch of ornament this building is easily the greatest piece of commercial architecture in America. There is a nobility and simplicity in it which reach the heart and mind. It is sad to state that a building such as this, or the Schiller Theatre, or the Stock Exchange, in Chicago, does not come as a public expression. They are the personal expression of an individual—its architect. The people will grow to an appreciation of them. This work will educate them. They will not express themselves in terms of the architect, but, like him, they will be thoughtful, simple and rational. Mr. Sullivan's detail, his ornament, is the least important part of his work. Its keynote is the spirit of reasonableness and seriousness.

The spirit of domesticity is a dominant force in our time. The love of home is a sentiment high enough to form the nucleus of great art. The emotion which originates in family attachments and home life develops a seriousness and delicacy which might belong to a Greek, and emotion as powerful as that which found expression in the mediaeval architecture of the thirteenth century. Great architecture has always been the expression of high sentiment. It must come from a new and original impulse. We have an opportunity in home life. It may spring from the family and express all that is beautiful, tender and ennobling in family life. It must relate the love of men, women and children, youth and old age. The world has never had a worthier motive for great art. There has never before been possible the opportunity for a general public expression of this universal sentiment. With opportunity, knowledge and desire, the architecture must come. Art is not resuscitation; it is creation. We should remember that our hearts beat in the nineteenth century.

Architecture has always been the frankest and most permanent expression of a people. Art must now be democratic, individual, as never before. Hence the people should have a knowledge which will enable them knowingly to demand a worthy expression. Ultimately the architect must express the people. If they have the knowledge to demand the best, we shall once more have a live, modern architecture. Then this democratic art will be moved by the spirit that now moves painting and sculpture, music and literature.

Further Resources

BOOKS

Eaton, Leonard K. *American Architecture Comes of Age: European Reaction to H.H. Richardson and Louis Sullivan.* Cambridge, Mass.: MIT Press, 1972.

Elia, Mario M. *Louis Henry Sullivan.* New York: Princeton Architectural Press, 1996.

Sullivan, Louis H. *Autobiography of an Idea.* New York: Dover, 1980.

Van Zanton, David. *Sullivan's City: The Meaning of Ornamentation for Louis Sullivan.* New York: W.W. Norton, 2000.

WEBSITES

"Architect Louis H. Sullivan." Greatbuildings.com. Available online at http://www.greatbuildings.com/architects/Louis_H._Sullivan.html; website home page: http://www.greatbuildings.com/gbc.html (accessed February 23, 2003).

"Leiber-Meister Louis Sullivan The Architect and His Work." Available online at http://www.geocities.com/SoHo/1469/sullivan.html (accessed February 23, 2003).

"Louis H. Sullivan." Vitruvio.ch. Available online at http://www.vitruvio.ch/arc/masters/sullivan.htm; website homepage: http://www.vitruvio.ch/index.html (accessed February 23, 2003).

"Up-to-Date Bathing Requisites"

Advertisement

By: Butterick Publishing Company
Date: 1900
Source: Butterick Publishing Company. "Up-to-Date Bathing Requisites." *The Delineator,* May 1900, 727–728.

About the Author: The Butterick Publishing Company was founded by Ebeneezer Butterick as a means of marketing the paper garment patterns he had begun producing in 1863. He introduced the company's first fashion magazine, *Ladies Quarterly of Broadway Fashions,* in 1867, and *The Delineator* in 1873. The latter continued in production until 1937, rapidly moving beyond a pattern marketing device to providing instruction, advice, advertisements, and, of course, paper patterns to order. ■

Introduction

It required most of a century, from the early 1800s, before swimming became an acceptable diversion and exercise for women. During much of that time, women, men, and children increasingly spent time in what many regarded as a healthful occupation—taking in the sea air. But for the majority of seaside visitors, this meant little more than walking along the beach. When women did actually come in direct contact with water, it was usually just by wading, and attire was designed to keep the body completely covered and untouched by sun. Bathing attire recommended by fashion magazines in 1810 and 1864, for example, showed women in essentially the same kinds of clothing they would have worn on the street. In later issues, bloomers—a version of pants—were worn, but the entire costume was made of heavy flannel and not meant for swimming. For women who wished to immerse themselves, little horse-drawn bath houses could be rented. The woman entered, put on her bathing attire, was drawn out into deeper water to take a dip, and then pulled back to shore. Concepts of modesty and appropriate behavior for women prevented the design of more functional garments.

By the end of the century, women were insisting on more active participation in all sports, including swimming, and this demanded more efficient bathing garments than the ones meant for dipping alone. The garments pictured in *The Delineator* show the extent of adaptation, which left a lot yet to be accomplished in terms of functionality. But the change was significant. The bathing costumes pictured in the pattern supplement and in the photograph show much shorter skirts, garments made of fabric that appears to be lighter and less absorbent than wool flannel, and short sleeves that left the arm bare. All of these features were helpful, but the excessive trimming and fullness gathered into the skirts continued to insure that the woman who tried to swim would be hampered by the sheer weight of her waterlogged clothing. The public was moving toward acceptance of more body-revealing styles, but the arrest of the Australian swimmer Annette Kellerman in 1909 for wearing a one-piece swimsuit showed they weren't quite ready. Within barely a year, styles similar to Kellerman's would begin to be the norm, paving the way for women to swim for health, for recreation, and competitively.

THE DELINEATOR. 727

A good idea of UP-TO-DATE BATHING REQUISITES is given in the following illustrations. The Patterns are to be obtained from THE BUTTERICK PUBLISHING CO. (Limited), and their agencies everywhere.

Ladies' Bathing Costume (Closed at the Left Side): consisting of a Blouse, a 1-Piece Circular Skirt without Fulness at the Back, and Knickerbockers (To have the Skirt Sewed to the Blouse for wear with the Knickerbockers or with Tights, or the Knickerbockers Sewed to the Blouse and the Skirt Finished with a Belt.) 32 to 40 inches bust, 5 sizes. Price, 1s. or 25 cts.

Ladies' Bathing Costume: consisting of a Straight, Full Skirt and a Combination Blouse and Drawers. (To be made with Full-Length Bishop or Short Puff Sleeves.) 30 to 46 inches bust, 9 sizes. Price, 1s. or 25 cents.

Ladies' Bathing Costume: consisting of a Straight, Full Skirt and a Combination Blouse and Drawers. (To be made with a High or Slightly Low Neck and with Full-Length Bishop or Short Puff Sleeves.) 30 to 46 inches bust, 9 sizes. Price, 1s. or 25 cents.

Ladies' Bathing Costume: consisting of a 4-Gored Skirt and a Combination Blouse and Drawers. (To be made with Open or High Neck and with Full-Length Bishop or Short Puff Sleeves.) 30 to 46 inches bust, 9 sizes. Price, 1s. or 25 cents.

Ladies' Bathing Costume: consisting of a Circular or Gathered Skirt, and a Combination Drawers and Double-Breasted Blouse. 30 to 44 inches bust, 8 sizes. Price, 1s. or 25 cents.

Ladies' Bathing Costume, having Knickerbockers and a Gathered Skirt. Known as the Ostend Bathing Suit. 30 to 46 inches bust, 9 sizes. Price, 1s. or 25 cents.

Ladies' Bathing Costume. Known as the Trouville Bathing Suit. 30 to 46 inches bust, 9 sizes. Price, 1s. or 25 cents.

Ladies' Knickerbocker Costume, having the Blouse and Bloomers in One. 30 to 42 inches bust, 7 sizes. Price, 1s. or 25 cents.

Ladies' and Girls' Swimming Suit. (To be made with a High or Square Neck.) 24 to 44 inches bust, 11 sizes. Price, 1s. or 25 cents.

728 THE DELINEATOR.

Ladies' Bathing Corset. 28 to 46 inches bust, 10 sizes. Price, 10d. or 20 cents.

Ladies' and Misses' Bathing Cap. 2 sizes, ladies' and misses.' Price, 5d. or 10 cents.

Misses' and Girls' Bathing Costume: consisting of a Four-Gored Skirt and a Combination Blouse and Drawers. (To be made with Open or High Neck and with Bishop or Short Puff Sleeves.) Ages, 6 to 16 years, 6 sizes. Price, 10d. or 20 cents.

Misses' and Girls' Bathing Costume: consisting of a Straight, Full Skirt and a Combination Blouse and Drawers. (To be made with Full-Length Bishop or Short Puff Sleeves.) Ages, 6 to 16 years, 6 sizes. Price, 10d. or 20 cents.

Misses' and Girls' Bathing Costume: consisting of a Circular or Gathered Skirt and a Combination Drawers and Double-Breasted Blouse. (To be made with High or Open Neck, Leg-o'-Mutton Sleeves or Short Puff Sleeves.) Ages, 6 to 16 years, 6 sizes. Price, 10d. or 20 cts.

Misses' and Girls' Sailor Bathing Costume: consisting of a Shield Body and Drawers in One and a Full Skirt. (To be made with a High or Open Neck and with Sailor Sleeves or Short Puff Sleeves.) Ages, 6 to 16 years, 6 sizes. Price, 10d. or 20 cents.

Misses' and Girls' French Bathing Costume: consisting of a Yoke Body and Drawers in One, and a Four-Gored Skirt. (To be made with a High or Round Neck and with Bishop Sleeves or Short Puff Sleeves.) Ages, 6 to 16 years, 6 sizes. Price, 10d. or 20 cents.

Misses' and Girls' Bathing Costume, having Knickerbockers and a Gathered Skirt. (To be made with a High or Square Neck.) Known as the Ostend Bathing Suit. Ages, 4 to 16 years, 7 sizes. Price, 10d. or 20 cents.

Misses' and Girls' Knickerbocker Costume, for Swimming, Gymnastic and Other Exercises. Ages, 6 to 16 years, 6 sizes. Price, 1s. or 25 cents.

Girls' Bathing Costume: consisting of a Straight, Full Skirt and a Combination Blouse and Drawers. Ages, 4 to 12 years, 5 sizes. Price, 10d. or 20 cents.

Child's Paddling Drawers. (Desirable for Waterproof Cloth, Cravenette, etc.) Ages, 2 to 10 years, 5 sizes. Price, 5d. or 10 cents.

Ladies' and Misses' Bathing Wrap. 26 to 46 inches bust, 6 sizes. Price, 1s. 6d. or 35 cents.

Child's Yoke Bathing Suit, Buttoned on the Shoulders and having the Body and Drawers in One. (To be made with a High or Low Neck.) Ages, 2 to 8 years, 4 sizes. Price, 10d. or 20 cents.

Child's Bathing Suit. Ages, 2 to 8 years, 4 sizes. Price, 7d. or 15 cents.

Primary Source

"Up-to-Date Bathing Requisites" (1 OF 2)

SYNOPSIS: Paper pattern advertisements from Butterick Publishing Company in *The Delineator* show a variety of acceptable styles for the day, the extent to which bathing and physical activity were becoming acceptable to the American public, and the beginning of the end of the corset. THE DELINEATOR, MAY 1900, P. 727.

Primary Source

"Up-to-Date Bathing Requisites" (2 OF 2)

Several bathing suit illustrations from an advertisement for patterns from Butterick Publishing Co., May 1900. THE DELINEATOR, MAY 1900, P. 728.

Women and children walk the beach at Coney Island, New York in fashionable bathing suits, circa 1900. THE LIBRARY OF CONGRESS.

Significance

The large number of stylistic variations shown in the advertisement and the informality of the bathing scene on the beach speak to the change in public attitudes toward women's participation in physical activity and toward what was considered proper attire for that activity. This obviously was not a first issue of bathing suit patterns, and contemporary photographs indicate bathing attire was common on pubic beaches. The idea of swimming in any of the costumes pictured in this 1900 advertisement may seem nearly impossible today, but at the time the garments were revolutionary in the amount of freedom they afforded women to engage in physical activity and in the amount of the woman's body allowed to be unfettered. All of the costumes would probably have been worn with stockings and shoes, as period photographs show, but an observer could still see the shape of the human form underneath, a concept that would have been anathema just a few years earlier. For nearly the last half of the nineteenth century, even women's shoes were covered. The clothing shown here and the indication that it could be worn for swimming, gymnastics, or other exercise is indicative of the change in attitude toward women's health and how that related to physical activity.

Also significant in the movement to functional swimwear is the concurrent decline in body shape formed by tightly laced corsets. Swimming and many other of the sports then becoming popular would have been impossible for women in the restrictive, long corsets of that time period. They obviously were not worn, as the silhouette of the bodies shown in the drawings have the waistline at the waist. The drawings show a beginning of the rapid decline of the corset altogether.

Further Resources

BOOKS

Gerber, Ellen W. *The American Woman in Sport.* Reading, Massachusetts: Addison-Wesley Publishing Company, 1974.

Kidwell, Claudia. *Women's Bathing and Swimming Costume in the United States.* Washington, D.C.: Smithsonian Institution Press, 1968.

Schreier, Barbara A. "Sporting Wear." In *Men and Women Dressing the Part.* Washington, D.C.: Smithsonian Institution Press, 1989, 92–123.

PERIODICALS

Warner, Patricia Campbell. "Clothing as Barrier: American Women in the Olympics, 1900–1920." *Dress* 24, 1997, 55–68.

———. "Public and Private: Men's Influence on American Women's Dress for Sport and Physical Education." *Dress* 14, 1988, 49–55.

WEBSITES

Thomas, Pauline Weston. "Early Swimwear." Available online at http://www.fashion-era.com/early_swimwear.htm; website home page: http://www.fashion-era.com/ (accessed February 22, 2003).

Works of Frank Lloyd Wright

"Hickox House Plans, Elevations, Kankakee, IL"; "Hickox House, Exterior, Kankakee, IL"

Architectural designs

By: Frank Lloyd Wright

Date: 1900

Source: Wright, Frank Lloyd. "Hickox House Plans, Elevations, Kankakee, IL"; "Hickox House, Exterior, Kankakee, IL." *American Landscape and Architectural Design, 1850–1920.* American Memory digital primary source collection, Library of Congress. Available online at http://memory.loc.gov/ammem/award97/mhsdhtml/aladhome.html; website home page: http://memory.loc.gov (accessed April 8, 2003).

Easy chair

Furniture design

By: Frank Lloyd Wright

Date: c. 1903

Source: Wright, Frank Lloyd. Easy chair. c. 1903. In the Unified Vision collection, Minneapolis Institute of Arts. Available online at http://www.artsmia.org/unified-vision/collection/object-detail.cfm?start=8&art;_id=3347&artist;_id=258; website home page: http://www.artsmia.org (accessed April 8, 2003).

"Stained Glass Dining Room Ceiling Light From Ward Willits House"

Architectural design

By: Frank Lloyd Wright

Date: 1901

Source: Wright, Frank Lloyd. "Stained Glass Dining Room Ceiling Light From Ward Willits House, by Studio of Frank Lloyd Wright." Corbis. Image no. AACZ001158. Available online at http://pro.corbis.com (accessed April 10, 2003).

About the Artist: Frank Lloyd Wright (1867–1959) was born and raised in Wisconsin. He is known as one of the greatest architects of the twentieth century, and he adhered to the principles of what he called organic architecture to create flexible, flowing spaces integrated into their surroundings. He was much more than an architect, however. His work includes the design of fabrics, furniture, stained glass, molded glass tiles, and complete interiors. He was also a teacher, writer, and lecturer. ■

Introduction

Following a period of experimentation with architectural style in the last years of the nineteenth century, Wright embarked on a new concept at the beginning of the twentieth century, the Prairie Style. Beginning with the Ward Willits residence and including the Frederick C. Robie House, completed in 1909, the Prairie Style would become the foremost influence in residential architecture in the United States. Houses built in the style were characterized by a long, low form closely connected to the earth from which they rose, with overhanging rooflines further compressing the sense of space from the buildings' exterior views. Inside, the houses seemed much larger because of the open quality of the existing space. The Hickox House shows the grid system of spatial organization and Wright's growing use of open space, a direct departure from traditional Victorian plans that tended to divide and compartmentalize space, thereby restricting the possibilities of its use. The huge fireplace and chimney form a central focus to the ground floor, another characteristic of the style.

His buildings were by far the largest investment his clients would make, but Wright's work and his vision of space did not stop with the structure. He frequently designed furniture specifically for his buildings, both for his own homes and those of clients. The 1903 easy chair in the collections of the Minneapolis Institute of Arts is such an example. Wright created the chair for the Francis W. Little home of his design in Peoria, Illinois. The linear, clean lines in both the wood structure and the upholstered cushions follow the same design themes as his architecture.

Wright also designed extensively with glass and used stained glass for both decorative and functional purposes. The ceiling light shown here combines exclusively linear elements to create a pattern of incredible intricacy, but with an overall presentation of elegant simplicity perfectly suited to Wright's buildings.

Significance

The pair of lantern slides provides a perspective on Wright's work that is difficult to achieve from pho-

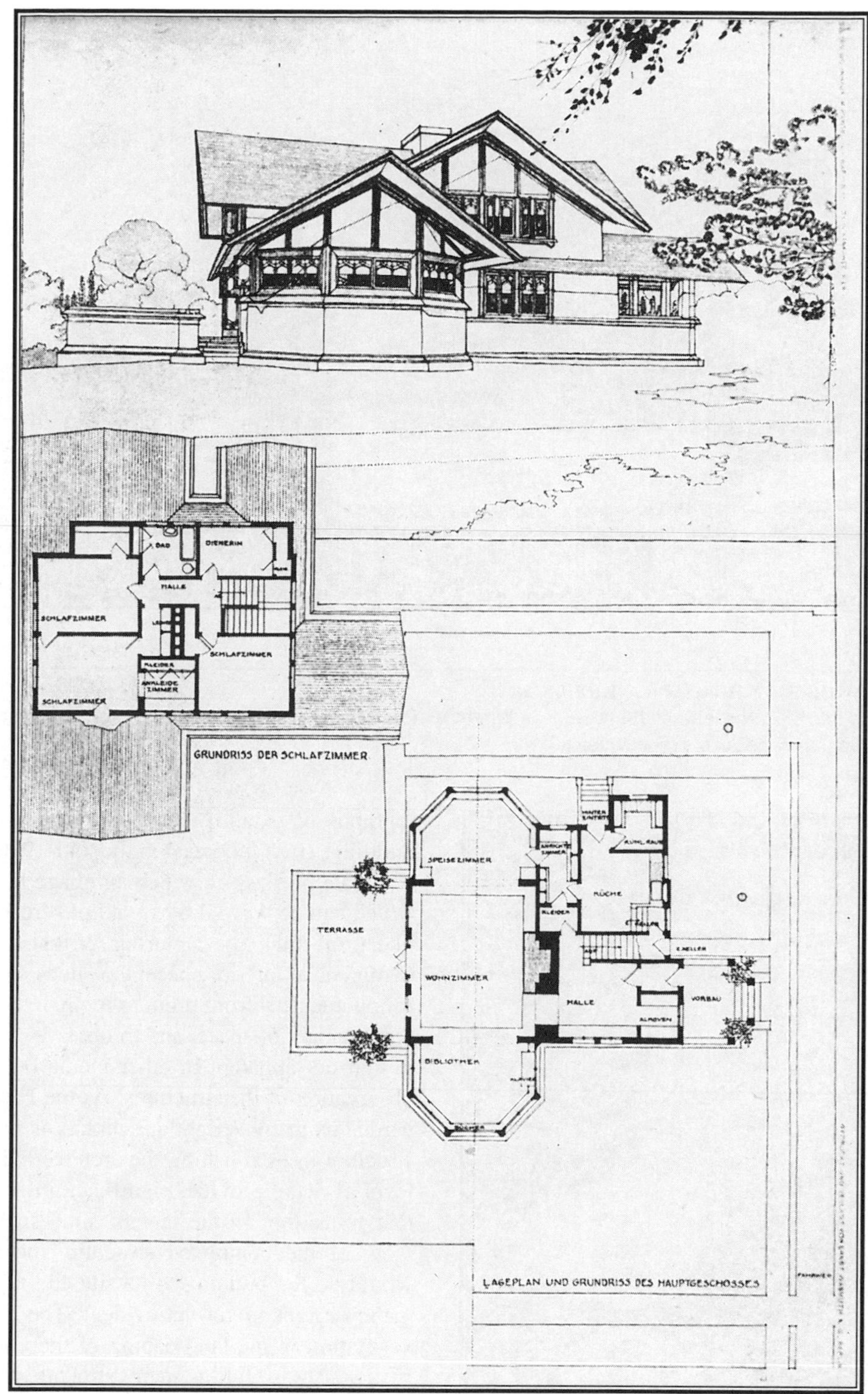

Primary Source

"Hickox House, Plans, Elevations, Kankakee, IL" (1 OF 2)

SYNOPSIS: Architectural plans and elevation drawings for the Hickox House designed by Frank Lloyd Wright in 1900. Wright's plans were first published in Berlin, Germany in 1910. The portfolio contained one hundred plates of his drawings. They had a profound influence on European architects, particularly two young Germans, Mies van der Rohe and Walter Gropins COURTESY OF THE FRANCES LOEB LIBRARY, HARVARD DESIGN SCHOOL. REPRODUCED BY PERMISSION.

Primary Source

Hickox House, exterior, Kankakee, IL (2 OF 2)

The Hickox House is seen as the establishing work of Wright's "Prairie Style," 1900. COURTESY OF THE FRANCES LOEB LIBRARY, HARVARD DESIGN SCHOOL. REPRODUCED BY PERMISSION.

Primary Source

Easy Chair

This prairie style easy chair was designed for Francis W. Little of Peoria, IL by architect Frank Lloyd Wright. THE MINNEAPOLIS INSTITUTE OF ARTS, GIFT OF RUTH L. AND WALTER SWARDENSKI. REPRODUCED BY PERMISSION.

tographs of extant buildings or even of tours of those buildings (first produced in the mid-1900s, a lantern slide is a plate of glass on which an image has been made and which can be viewed on a wall or screen using a lantern-like projector). By capturing Wright's two-dimensional treatment of interior space, the slides allow the viewer to follow the flow from room to room, to note allocation and arrangement of space, and to observe details of structural design not apparent in other media or even from actual observation of the structures. As the Hickox House is regarded by many Wrightian scholars as a major transitional structure in establishing the architect's Prairie Style, this level of detail provides significant information in tracing that transition. In the lantern slide showing an exterior view of the completed structure, the landscaping that would tie the building to its site and typify Wright's organic designs is not yet evident. The absence of mature vegetation in the landscaping of the completed house is particularly useful, as many structures were built within a construction envelope that preserved mature growth and resulted in a building that seemed to have grown up with the landscape. While such a presentation was exactly what Wright intended with organic architecture, it makes careful observation of architectural nuances very difficult.

Compared to a typical Victorian stuffed and tufted and carved and trussed chair, Wright's easy chair for the Francis W. Little home shows the radical departure in both style and materials. Like his contemporaries Gustav

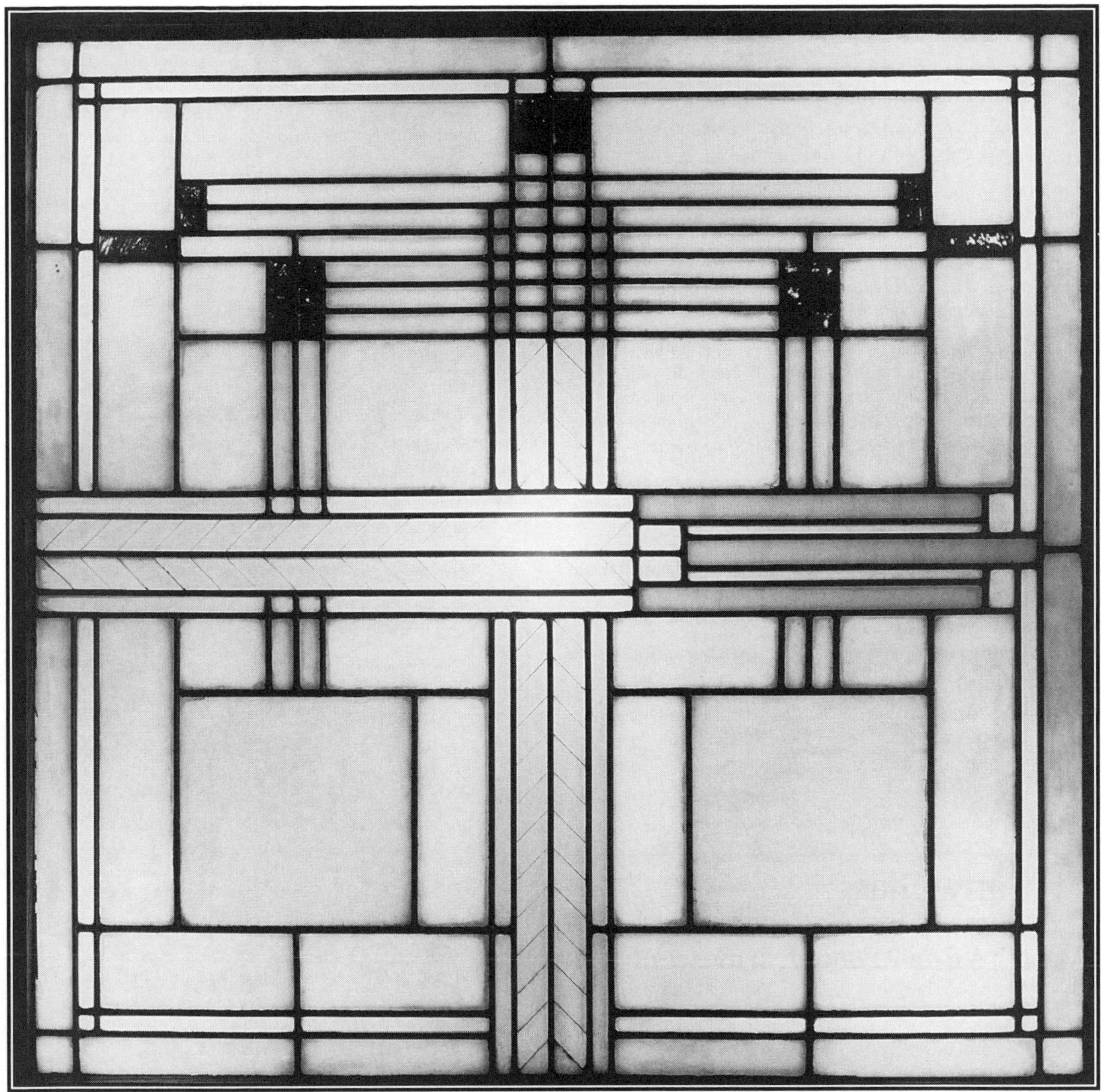

Primary Source

"Stained Glass Dining Room Ceiling Light From Ward Willits House"

Designed by Frank Lloyd Wright in 1901, this stained glass dining room ceiling light is from the Ward Willits House.

Stickley, Greene & Greene, Harvey Ellis, Elbert Hubbard (Roycroft), William Morris, and others, Wright favored lighter woods without carved ornamentation, as well as straight lines, simple but elegant materials, superior craftsmanship, and comfort. These same qualities are apparent in Wright's stained glass designs. They complemented the overall environment stylistically and functioned to admit light and decrease the separation of interior from exterior. They supplanted heavy drapes in many instances, as they blocked direct view even as they permitted the flow of sunlight.

Further Resources

BOOKS

Heinz, Thomas A. *The Vision of Frank Lloyd Wright.* Edison, N.J.: Chartwell, 2000.

Lind, Carla. *Frank Lloyd Wright's Furnishings.* Rohnert Park, Calif.: Pomegranate, 1995.

Storrer, William Allin. *A Frank Lloyd Wright Companion.* Chicago: University of Chicago Press, 1994.

———. *The Architecture of Frank Lloyd Wright: A Complete Catalogue.* Chicago: University of Chicago Press, 2002.

WEBSITES

"All Wright Site: Frank Lloyd Wright Building Guide." Available online at http://www.geocities.com/SoHo/1469/flwbuild.html (accessed January 3, 2003). *Contains information on more than 420 Frank Lloyd Wright buildings in more than 37 states/locations and indexes several hundred websites.*

"Frank Lloyd Wright." Artcyclopedia. Available online at http://www.artcyclopedia.com/artists/wright_frank_lloyd.html; website home page: http://www.artcyclopedia.com (accessed February 22, 2003). *This site provides numerous links to Wright artifacts in museums across the country.*

The Frank Lloyd Wright Building Conservancy. Available online at http://www.savewright.org (accessed February 22, 2003).

"The Hickox House." Available online at http://hubcap.clemson.edu/~tcline/Hickox.html (accessed February 22, 2003).

AUDIO AND VISUAL MEDIA

Frank Lloyd Wright. Directed by Lynn Novick and Ken Burns. PBS Home Video, 2001, DVD.

Frank Lloyd Wright: The Mike Wallace Interviews. Directed by Bob Eisenhardt. PBS Home Video, 2001, DVD.

Tiffany Glass

"Vase"; "Bowl Footed, Iridescent Blue"

Works of art

By: Louis Comfort Tiffany

Date: 1900–1902

Source: Tiffany, Louis Comfort. "Vase, circa 1902." Number 1989.36.16; "Bowl Footed, Iridescent Blue, circa 1901." Number 1989.36.12. Fine Arts Museums of San Francisco. Available online at http://www.thinker.org (accessed February 22, 2003).

"Tiffany Mansion Living Room"

Photograph

By: Louis Comfort Tiffany

Date: c. 1924

Source: Tiffany, Louis Comfort. "Tiffany Mansion Living Room." *Built in America: Historic American Buildings Survey/Historic American Engineering Record, 1933–Present.* American Memory digital primary source collection, Library of Congress. Available online at http://memory.loc.gov/ammem/hhhtml/hhhome.html; website home page: http://memory.loc.gov (accessed February 22, 2003).

About the Artist: Louis Comfort Tiffany (1848–1933) is best remembered for his invention of stunning iridescent decorative glass objects in the Art Nouveau style and for stained glass lamps and windows in that same style. Tiffany headed a design firm—Associated Artists—that engaged in complete interior decoration, including textile designs and the specification of decorative objects. Tiffany also painted, dabbled in architecture, and presided over the jewelry store (Tiffany and Company) founded by his father. ■

Introduction

Tiffany was one of the leading proponents of the Art Nouveau style in America, and his work was highly successful both at home and abroad. He was one of the first American designers to be accepted in Europe, and he exhibited in Siegfried Bing's gallery, L'Art Nouveau, the year it opened in 1895. Tiffany's aesthetic style

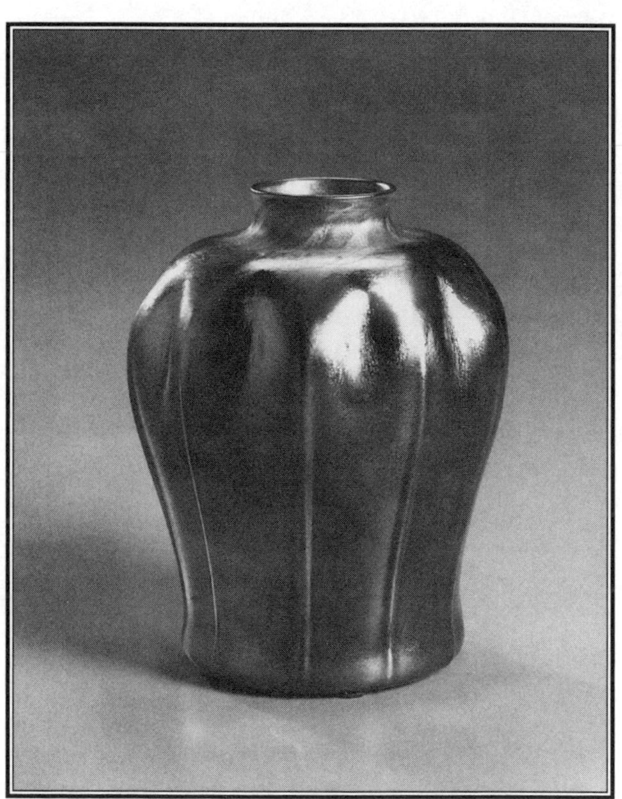

Primary Source

"Vase" (1 OF 2)

SYNOPSIS: These two examples of Tiffany's blown and molded glass represent the apex of his expertise in producing favrile glass; they illustrate the simple elegance of the Art Nouveau style; and they mark a sharp break with the excessive, often applied rather than integral, ornamentation of the previous century. FINE ARTS MUSEUM OF SAN FRANCISCO, THE LILLIAN AND DONALD JOHNS COLLECTION, 1989.36.12.

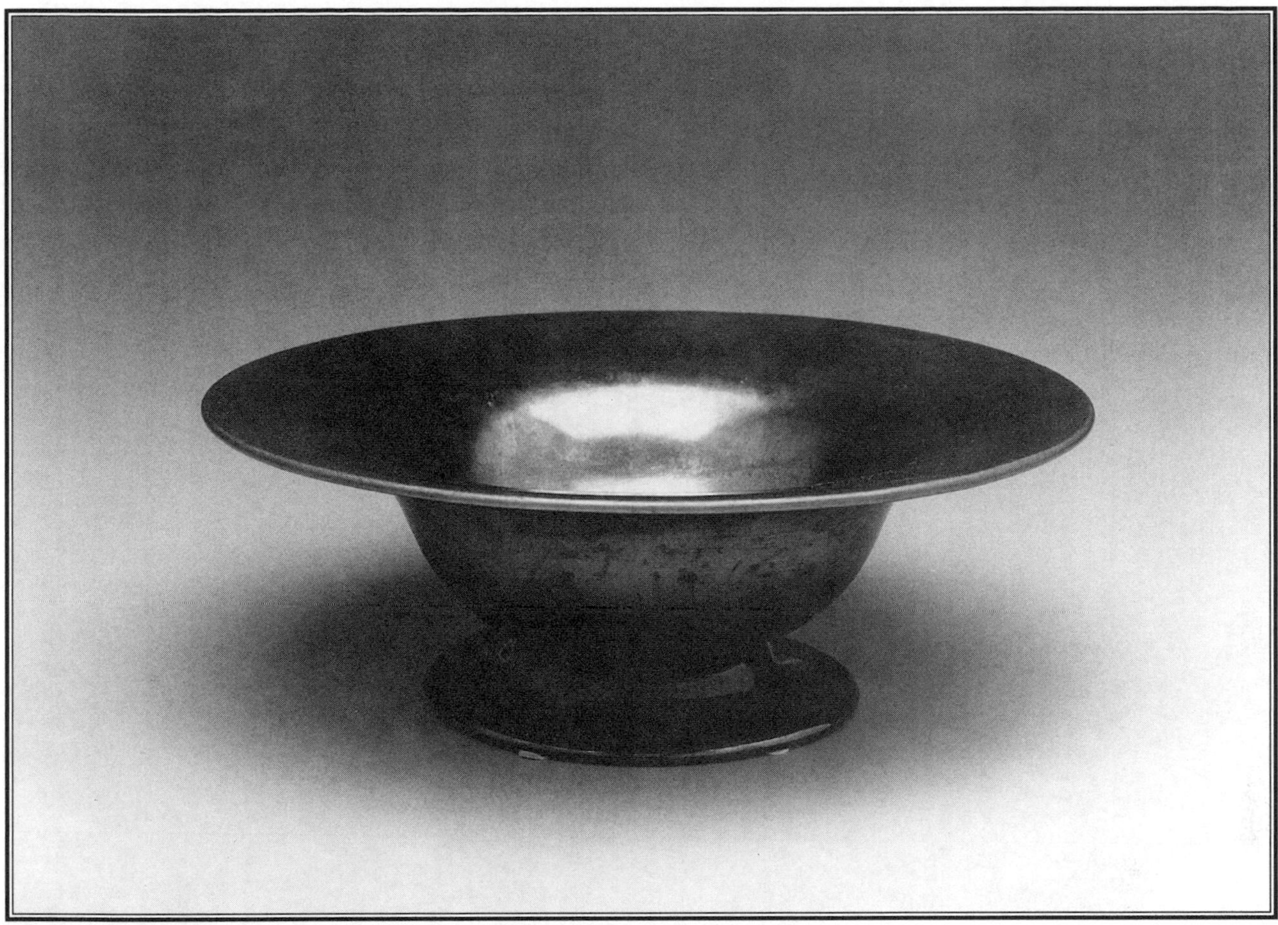

Primary Source

"Bowl Footed, Iridescent Blue" (2 OF 2)
An iridescent blue blown Favrile glass footed bowl created by Louis Comfort Tiffany's studio, circa 1901. FINE ARTS MUSEUM OF SAN FRANCISCO, THE LILLIAN AND DONALD JOHNS COLLECTION, 1989.36.12.

showed a strong connection to nature and to natural, usually plant, forms with their lush colors and sensuous forms. Tiffany founded his own firm in 1885 and focused on new methods of glass manufacture. His work in glass at the turn of the century shows the swirling, organic shapes typical of Art Nouveau and his particular specialty, favrile glass—the iridescent, multicolored, shimmering finish heretofore unknown. The subtle coloration and shapes and simple lines of his glass are in stark contrast to the heavy, extremely ornate Victorian designs against which the artists of the Art Nouveau style rebelled.

While many proponents of the Arts and Crafts movement were unable to sustain commercial success combined with the philosophical demands of handcrafted work, Tiffany flourished. His large personal fortune allowed him to make aesthetic decisions that a less financially healthy business could not. Tiffany is reported to have once said his life was dedicated to the pursuit of beauty, and in his life and work he demonstrated the ultimate of that pursuit. Like many followers of the Arts and Crafts and Art Nouveau aesthetic and philosophy, he extended his creative endeavors to all aspects of the near environment, designing whole interiors, his own home on Long Island, jewelry, pottery, and a myriad of other objects. But it was in glass that he truly achieved excellence. The two examples of his famous favrile glass shown here are some of his best work in his favorite medium, each showing a slightly different aspect of his genius.

Significance

The footed blue bowl exemplifies some of the finest examples of favrile glass extant. The intense cobalt blue color permeates the entire piece and is remarkably consistent in coloration, while maintaining the opalescence of favrile, shown to excellent advantage in the unornamented shape. In the second example, a 1902

Primary Source

"Tiffany Mansion Living Room"

SYNOPSIS: Laurelton Hall's living room is decorated with Tiffany lamps and vases on the shelves behind the lighting fixtures. THE LIBRARY OF CONGRESS.

rib-molded and blown favrile vase, the ornamentation is subtle and organic. The peacock blue-green iridescence of the main vase body merges into a much lighter patterned swirl design forming a collar and short neck of the vase. The subtle multi-colored design picks up the tones of the iridescence and creates a perfect finial to the piece.

Taken together, the two pieces of blown and molded glass afford an excellent representation of the similarity yet unique aspects of Tiffany glass. The iridescence which Tiffany was able to repeatedly achieve in his pieces, whether large or small, whether red or blue or multicolored, had previously only been hinted at by the rich patina of ancient glass excavated from ruins. Tiffany's achievement in integral iridescence was especially significant. He was able to incorporate multiple colors within the molten glass as it was blown, thereby fixing the design permanently, as shown in the 1902 vase neck and collar. Additionally, his combination of minerals in the original mixture as well as his method of producing the finished piece yielded a patina that was richer by far than those occurring naturally.

Further Resources

BOOKS

Duncan, Alastair. *Louis Comfort Tiffany.* New York: Harry Abrams, 1992.

Greenhalgh, Charles. *Art Nouveau, 1890–1914.* New York: Harry N. Abrams, 2000.

Koch, Robert. *Louis C. Tiffany's Glass-Bronzes-Lamps.* New York: Crown Publishers, 1971.

WEBSITES

"The Lamps of Tiffany." The Knoxville Museum of Art. Available online at http://www.knoxart.org/html/exhibits/bio.html;

Louis Comfort Tiffany, founder of Tiffany Studios, which created glass vases and lamps that were considered to be art as well as functional pieces, 1908. THE LIBRARY OF CONGRESS.

website home page: http://www.knoxart.org/body.htm (accessed February 22, 2003).

"Louis Comfort Tiffany." Artcyclopedia.com. Available online at http://www.artcyclopedia.com/artists/tiffany_louis_comfort.html?noframe; website home page: http://www.artcyclopedia.com/ (accessed February 22, 2003).

"Louis Comfort Tiffany." The Charles Hosmer Morse Foundation. Available online at http://www.morsemuseum.org/louis.html (accessed February 22, 2003).

AUDIO AND VISUAL MEDIA

Art Nouveau, 1890–1914. Home Vision Entertainment, 2000.

Clothing the American Woman

"Effective Street Gowns"; "Women's Gowns"

Illustrations

By: Butterick Publishing Company

Date: 1900; 1906

Source: *The Delineator,* May 1900, 591; April 1906, 623.

About the Organization: Butterick Publishing Company grew out of Ebeneezer Butterick's success in creating paper dress patterns that women could order by mail as well as buy in some mercantile stores. Inspired by his wife's difficulty in creating patterns in a variety of sizes, he undertook the task of making a pattern in multiple sizes, eventually extending the concept to include men's and children's clothing. The company published *The Delineator* between the years 1873–1937.

"Singer Bros. Winter Catalogue 1905–1906"

Catalog

By: Singer Brothers Company

Date: 1905

Source: Singer Brothers Company. "Singer Bros. Winter Catalogue 1905–1906." St. Louis: Singer Brothers Company, 1905, 11. Reproduced in John W. Hartman Center for Sales, Advertising & Marketing History. *Emergence of Advertising in America: Advertising Ephemera.* Available online at http://scriptorium.lib.duke.edu/cgi-bin/nph-dweb/dynaweb/eaa/databases/ephemera; website home page: http://scriptorium.lib.duke.edu/eaa (accessed February 22, 2003).

About the Organization: The Singer Brothers in St. Louis, Missouri, was one of several clothing manufacturers and distributors to offer ready-made apparel through mail order. ■

Introduction

In the shift from home to commercial production of clothing, three major events provided the demand to fuel the required marketplace changes. Other events and situations provided the means to meet that demand. Both the Civil War and the gold rush created a need for men's clothing manufacture, and measurements taken for military uniforms formed a data base for some standardization of sizes. The huge movement of men moving west needed replacement and new clothing which they were not skilled at providing for themselves, thus creating another segment of market demand. The third factor was the increased employment of women outside the home as well as an increase in leisure activities for women—both with their accompanying specialized garment needs.

Coincidental with these demand factors were changes in production equipment and techniques. The invention of the sewing machine in the 1850s had a tremendous impact on the speed and durability of sewing, whether at home or in mass production. Hand sewing of all clothing prior to this invention had required major allocations of domestic labor, whether slaves, servants, or family members. Most women without household help and without the means to hire tailors or milliners spent at least a portion of nearly every day producing apparel and home furnishings for themselves and their families. Until Butterick invented the graded paper pattern and

Primary Source

"Effective Street Gowns"

SYNOPSIS: For the middle and lower classes in particular, magazines such as *The Delineator* and catalogues such as the ones available from Singer Brothers provided fashion advice and instruction as well as materials and actual garments, allowing fashion innovation to spread at a rapid rate. This illustration shows gowns designed for walking and outdoor activity. THE DELINEATOR, MAY 1900, P. 591.

9159, BLOUSE BODICE, *with Short Sleeves.*
SKIRT 9133.

9177, BOLERO JACKET, *with Girdle.*
SKIRT 9169.

623

for April, 1906

Primary Source

"Women's Gowns"

This illustration of women's fashions provides descriptions of the outfits and pattern numbers for ordering sewing patterns.

THE DELINEATOR, APRIL 1906, P. 623.

SINGER BROS., ST. LOUIS, MO.
11
No. 490. Ladies' Rain Coat of good quality Covert Cloth, cravenetted, Empire style with box plaited back and front, neatly tailor stitched around neck and button trimmed. Colors, Oxford, Olive, Tan.
No. 493. Ladies' Rain Coat of Cravenette Mixture with belt and buckle ornaments. Colors, Oxford and Brown.
No. 497. Ladies' Rain Coat of good quality Cravenette Mixture, neatly shirred at waist, self strap trimmed with belt and buckle ornaments. Colors, Oxford, Castor, Olive.
No. 499. Ladies' Rain Coat of Cravenette Mixture, neatly shirred at waist with belt and buckle ornaments. Colors, Oxford, Brown.
490
497
493
499
FOR PRICE, SEE LAST PAGE.

Primary Source

"Singer Bros. Winter Catalogue 1905–1906" (1 OF 2)

This page from the 1905–06 Singer Bros. Winter Catalog illustrates stylish raincoats for women. "WINTER CATALOG 1905–1906" ITEM #: A0181-12. EMERGENCE OF ADVERTISING IN AMERICA. 2000. RARE BOOK, MANUSCRIPT, AND SPECIAL COLLECTIONS LIBRARY, DUKE UNIVERSITY. [HTTP://SCRIPTORIUM.LIB.DUKE.EDU/EAA/].

made it available for women's fashions in the 1860s, women's only recourse for creating fashion was to draw out the patterns themselves, often using their own clothing or borrowed fashions that were taken apart and used as a basis for sizing and some design features.

Style also played a part in the growth of the fashion manufacturing industry. When the tightly fitted, boned garments of the Victorian era gave way to more loosely fitting styles, it became practical to manufacture clothing without individual measurements. Adoption of separate skirts and blouses (or waists), made fitting by waist and bust measurements a real possibility. With huge pools of cheap immigrant labor available on the East Coast, the revolution of fashion production was well underway by 1900.

Significance

By the twentieth century, fashion was truly available to the masses, as illustrated in these advertisements. Although manufactured clothing had been available since the founding of the country, it was limited to unfitted outerwear—such as capes and cloaks—and undergarments, socks, shoes, and similar items. Clothing for children, particularly layette garments, also required less exacting standards of fitting. But for women's fashionable clothing in the early years of the twentieth century, there were basically three main sources: for the well-to-do, personal dressmakers or expensive milliners and tailors provided the clothing in consultation with the women being dressed. For the rest of the country, women primarily made their own clothing or they bought some items in department stores and from mail order catalogues. In addition to mail order companies such as Sears Roebuck, many department stores—such as Singers in Missouri and Bloomingdales in New York—were involved in the mail order business. Improved postal service, affordable goods at reasonable quality, a fairly good chance at adequate fit, and convenience led

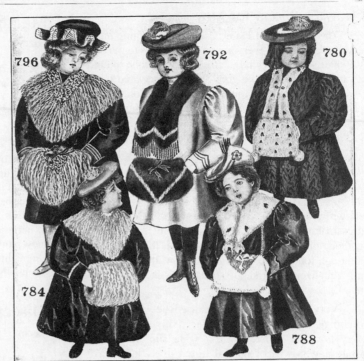

SINGER BROS., ST. LOUIS, MO.

No. 780. Child's combination Fur Set of Ermine.

No. 784. Child's Fur Set of White Angora, Muff and Scarf.

No. 788. Child's Fur Set of Ermine and Chinchilla, Muff and Scarf.

No. 792. Misses' Fur Set of Brown Coney Hare with Combination of Ermine, Muff and Scarf.

No. 796. Child's Fur Set of White Angora and Astrachan.

Full line of Misses' and Children's Fur Sets, ranging in price from 50c to $3.75.

796 792 780 784 788

FOR PRICE, SEE LAST PAGE.

Primary Source

"Singer Bros. Winter Catalogue 1905–1906" (2 OF 2)

Winter outerwear styles are illustrated in this page from the 1905–06 Singer Bros. Winter Catalog. "WINTER CATALOG 1905–1906" ITEM #: A0181-22. EMERGENCE OF ADVERTISING IN AMERICA. 2000. RARE BOOK, MANUSCRIPT, AND SPECIAL COLLECTIONS LIBRARY, DUKE UNIVERSITY. [HTTP://SCRIPTORIUM.LIB.DUKE.EDU/EAA/].

to widespread consumer acceptance of ordering clothing. Even when women and family members sewed a portion of their fashionable clothing, the catalogues for rural populations and department stores in cities helped make up the difference.

For the thousands of women still actively involved in the production of their own and their family members' fashions, paper patterns and fashion magazines gave them both design ideas and detailed instructions. *The Delineator* was one such magazine, and it established a dialogue with its public about what was fashionable in every season of the year and how, exactly, the women were to create these fashions. Even details of trim and fabric choice and color were prescribed. Taken together, the two publications show the very early stages of what would be, by the 1950s, a complete revolution in how fashion was acquired in America.

Further Resources

BOOKS

Bradfield, Nancy Margetts. *Costume in Detail: Women's Dress 1730–1930.* Boston: Plays, Inc., 1968.

Gordon, S.S. *Turn-of-the-Century Fashion Patterns and Tailoring Techniques.* New York: Dover Publications, 2000.

Hall, Lee. *Common Threads: A Parade of American Clothing.* Boston: Bulfinch Press, 1992.

Kidwell, Claudia B. *Cutting a Fashionable Fit.* Washington, D.C.: Smithsonian Institution Press, 1979.

Schroeder, Joseph J. Jr., ed. *The Wonderful World of Ladies' Fashion 1850–1920.* Northfield, Illinois: Digest Books, 1971.

Tortora, Phyllis G., and Keith Eubank. *Survey of Historic Costume.* New York: Fairchild Publications, 1998.

PERIODICALS

Bates, Christina. "Women's Hats and the Millinery Trade, 1840–1940." *Dress* 27, 2000, 49–58.

"New Fashions for May"

The demands of Dame Fashion are getting more and more exacting every year, and it seems to me that we shall want a very large closet or wardrobe to hold all the toilettes that the good lady has declared to be absolutely necessary for the coming season. Never probably has there been a time when an entirely new outfit was more compulsory that it is today, for collars and sleeves have changed their shape and our skirts bear very little relation to those of twelve months ago.

The most delightful gowns of voile, as well as all sorts of fine silk and wool veilings, are being shown at the openings of some of the fashionable dressmaking houses. The skirts are much fuller, and gathers, pin-tucks and pleats appear at the back, and, although long, there is no actual train, the length being equalized so gradually that the back hangs quite level.

Very wide insertions are used between bands, ruchings, tucks and motifs of lace, velvet or embroidery are laid at intervals on wide filet insertions. Charming gowns of natural tinted grass lawn have large medallions of lace or broad insertions and several frills of the material at the edge.

All the new gowns are made of soft materials to best display the fashionable fullness, flounces, gathers, pleats, tucks, ruchings and ruffles that the styles call for. Crêpe de chine, mousseline, chiffon, voile, batiste besides other dainty wash goods show this increasing tendency to soft fabrics. Even the French taffetas take on a totally novel aspect with their lighter and softer finish.

SOURCE: Modish, Betty. "New Fashions for May." *McCall's,* May 1904, 631.

Belleau, Bonnie D. "Cyclical Fashion Movement: Women's Day Dresses: 1860–1980." *Dress* 5, no. 2, Winter 1987, 15–20.

WEBSITES

"Fashion-Era." Available online at www.fashion-era.com (accessed February 22, 2003). This site gives a capsule course in fashion history. Chronological overviews included.

Seneca, Tracy. "The History of Women's Magazines: Magazines as Virtual Communities." Available online at http://is.gseis.ucla.edu/impact/f93/students/tracy/tracy_hist.html (accessed February 22, 2003).

"The Costume Gallery." Available online at http://www.costumegallery.com (accessed February 22, 2003). Information on male and female attire as well as hairstyles and accessories, beginning in the 1800s.

Middle-class Housework

Martha Jane Mixon Hearn Diaries

Diary

By: Martha Jane Mixon Hearn

Date: 1900–1909

Source: Hearn, Martha. *Martha Jane Mixon Hearn Diaries 1873-1909* in David Russell Hearn and Family Papers. Jackson, Mississippi: Mississippi Department of Archives and History. Z/1839.000/S, Box 4.

About the Author: Martha Jane Mixon Hearn (1837–1915) was an upper middle class southern woman who lived an unremarkable life typical of many in her social class. Martha, her husband, and their four children lived and farmed near Madison Station in Madison County, Mississippi. In addition to farming, the family owned and operated a mill. Unlike most women in her social class, Martha kept a detailed diary, chronicling the work involved in producing and maintaining the family's clothing and household textiles.

Directions for Making Soap

Recipe

By: Mary Ann Zahm

Date: c. 1905

Source: Zahm, Mary Ann. Directions for Making Soap. c. 1905. *An American Time Capsule: Three Centuries of Broadsides and Other Printed Ephemera,* American Memory digital primary source collection, Library of Congress. Available online at http://memory.loc.gov/ammem/rbpehtml/pehome.html; website homepage: http://memory.loc.gov (accessed May 15, 2003). ■

Introduction

The division of labor by gender varied according to socioeconomic level during this decade as in many others. The upper classes showed the greatest division and the greatest access to, and influence on, fashion. The male head of the household was responsible for providing, the female for consuming. The beautiful confections that graced the society pages of urban newspapers required the hand labor of hundreds of poor women who earned barely enough to subsist.

The growing middle classes aspired to the fashions they saw pictured, but most often they were more directly involved in their production at home. Women traded assistance in sewing clothing, as they did in quilting and many other textile production methods, but they were still responsible for the majority of production within the home. There, depending upon the level of wealth, these woman might also be restricted to household and social activity.

As income level declined, the distinction faded in terms of what women could do; they did whatever work

DIRECTIONS

Take 5½ pounds of left-over fat. Keep 3 gallons of soft (or rain) water in a tub near the kettle for convenience. Add about 2 quarts of water to the fat in the kettle to keep from scorching; cover closely; let simmer till the mass is dissolved. While the fat is simmering take a one-pound can of concentrated lye, put in a separate vessel, pour 2 quarts of boiling water on slowly; stir till the lye is dissolved; fill up the vessel till you have about 6 quarts; then add 2 quarts of this strong liquid lye to the simmering grease. Stir, mix quickly, keep on adding about 1 quart of the liquid lye at a time, till the 6 quarts have been filled in. A brisk fire under the kettle must keep the mixture boiling till the remaining 6 quarts of soft water have been added. Slacken the fire while you are adding the last four quarts of water.

It is better to keep back 1 quart of cold water to pour in the boiling soap to check its boiling over. Have ready half-pint of kerosene, stir in with three-fourths pint of coarse salt. Boil slowly ten minutes; dip out into a tub, or let stand in the kettle till soap is hard.

If you do not have soft water get 2 ounces of lump borax, crush it, then dissolve in water to make it soft—the soap will get lighter in color.

When the soap has hardened, cut in bars, scrape off the lye from the under part.

This soap will wash in soft or hard water.

Machinists' clothes put in a kettle with about 6 quarts of cold rain-water to half-pint of this lye and boiled slowly half an hour, will take out the dirt and grease finely.

Original by

Mrs. MARY ANN ZAHM.

Primary Source

Directions for Making Soap

SYNOPSIS: This 1905 document by Mrs. Mary Ann Zahm gives the steps necessary for making soap. THE LIBRARY OF CONGRESS.

An advertisement from the May 1900 *The Delineator* magazine for a sewing machine. THE DELINEATOR, MAY 1900, P. 740.

had to be done, inside and out. Men did not share that flexibility, and tended not to involve themselves in household production of any sort, regardless of income. In this diary of a farm woman of fairly decent income level, we see the typical daily life events which defined her role: she cooked, cleaned, sewed, cared for farm animals, grew food, seeded and carded cotton, quilted, cut patterns, made soap, boiled starch, mended, ironed, thanked God for their health and His goodness, went to bed, and got up to another day of the same.

There is no reference to purchasing ready-to-wear clothing other than socks, although there are Butterick and Delineator commercial dress patterns in the Hearn family artifacts maintained by the Old Capitol Museum of Mississippi History. The Hearns owned a sewing machine which was used for some, but not all of the sewing, and they owned at least two washing machines, a steam washer in 1890, and a new Sears "Syclone washer & wringer" in 1900.

Significance

The diary entries of Martha Jane Mixon Hearn provide a remarkably consistent account of the daily life of a family in the upper-middle class of southern society from 1900 through 1909. The Hearns exemplified home production at a time when a consumer class was just beginning to be an economic force. Virtually every garment and item of household textiles was made by Martha, her two daughters, other relatives, and family friends. If the pages of fashion magazines and newspaper society columns portrayed the fashionable life of the upper classes—and they did—then private manuscripts such as Martha Hearn's diary provide a glimpse of another, larger segment of society.

The diary also shows the actual division of household labor typical of many farm families during this period. The women were responsible for the production and maintenance of clothing, food, and shelter. The men worked outside, logging, hoeing corn, planting commercial crops. There were areas of overlap, such as some of the gardening, but for the most part, the division of labor was clear. In Martha's diary, there was never any questioning of what must have seemed the natural order of such things.

The diary is also useful as an insight into how women viewed their roles. Through the act of keeping a daily record and by the nature of the entries, diarists indicated what they viewed as important events in their lives. In a society that accorded no economic value to women's work—even though the work was critical to the maintenance of that very society—women often found other ways to document their contributions. By the almost daily listing of her work, Martha Jane Mixon Hearn affirmed to herself that her work had value in the context of her family's economic health.

Primary Source

Martha Jane Mixon Hearn Diary [excerpt]

SYNOPSIS: This series of excerpts from diaries that Martha kept over a period of thirty-six years chronicles the extraordinary amount of time and effort required for ordinary women to produce and care for the clothing and textiles required for fashionable middle class families.

January 17, 1900: I worked on my quilt.

January 18, 1900: I worked all day on my quilt.

February 8, 1900: I finished the blocks of my Old Maid quilt.

February 9, 1900: I sewed some on my quilt & ironed some.

February 13, 1900: I peiced on my quilt for little bed.

February 15, 1900: I helped cook & cut some quilt peices.

February 22, 1900: Alice & I worked on patchwork.

February 24, 1900: I ironed & worked some on my patchwork.

February 27, 1900: I got my quilt ready to put together.

February 28, 1900: I finished another quilt.

March 1, 1900: I cut quilt peices & sewed some on Alices quilt.

March 2, 1900: I washed & cut some quilt peices.

March 5, 1900: I pieced on Alices quilt.

March 6, 1900: Alice did the cooking. I pieced on her quilt.

March 12, 1900: I sewed on Alices quilt some.

March 15, 1900: Alice did the cooking & finished her Economy quilt. I helped her & sewed some on Mauds Mosaic quilt.

April 6, 1900: I helped cook & sewed some on Mauds quilt.

April 7, 1900: I mended some & sewed some on quilt.

May 9, 1900: I helped cook & worked on a quilt, the morning star.

May 10, 1900: Alice & I did the housework & peiced on quilt.

May 11, 1900: I peiced on my morning star quilt & helped do the housework.

May 14, 1900: Alice run the sewing machine. I did the cooking & peiced on my quilt.

May 15, 1900: I did the cooking & peiced on my quilt. Alice finished her Mother hubbard.

May 16, 1900: I did the cooking & worked some on my quilt.

May 17, 1900: I did the cooking & worked some on my quilt.

May 18, 1900: I washed & cut some quilt peices.

May 22, 1900: I helped cook & worked on my quilt.

May 23, 1900: I helped cook & made a border for my quilt.

May 24, 1900: I helped cook & cut peices for my quilt.

May 25, 1900: I washed & sewed some on my quilt

May 26, 1900: I did the kitchen work & put my quilt together.

May 28, 1900: I helped cook & finished my morning star quilt.

May 30, 1900: Alice crocheted all day. I cooked & worked some on my log cabbin quilt.

June 4, 1900: I helped cook & worked on my quilt.

June 5, 1900: I worked on my quilt.

June 23, 1900: I did the cooking & finished my dress that dear Jim gave me & made 2 block for my log cabbin quilt. Alice finished a skirt for Georgia & a shirt for Mr. Hearn.

The IMPROVED Acme Washer

is built on the only correct principle for a washing machine. It cleans the clothes by driving the water with great force through every fold and fibre, instead of merely churning them around in the water, as in many machines, or rubbing them, as in others. It will wash thoroughly and perfectly clean anything, from the finest piece of lace to the heaviest blanket, without tearing a thread or breaking a button. Even a heavy rug or carpet can be washed in the **IMPROVED ACME** as easily and thoroughly as a bed sheet. In fact, there is nothing in the way of washing which can be done by hand or with any other machine which cannot be done better, more easily and more rapidly with the **IMPROVED ACME** Washer.

As a time saver the **IMPROVED ACME** is unsurpassed by any machine made. Do not stand over a steaming tub, with your hands almost continually in hot, strong suds, rubbing away your health and strength, during four or five long, weary hours. Let the **ACME** do your work. It will do it in a third of the time, and do it better, saving you many valuable hours.

Now, it is true there are other machines which, it is claimed, do the same things in almost the same way, but if you will read the following you will find that the **IMPROVED ACME** is

The Most Practical Washer Made

In addition to being made of the very best materials throughout, handsomely finished in natural wood, it has a number of *special features* which are not found on any other machine. There is no other washer like it: there is *no other washer* "just as good" as the **IMPROVED ACME.**

1. **THE MOVABLE WRINGER STAND** is made of two strong angle-steel uprights, between the upper ends of which is bolted a piece of hard maple board, to which the wringer is to be fastened. The lower ends of these uprights are attached to the framework of the machine. They are movable, forward and back, and are firmly held in any position by handscrews. When the wringer is to be used, loosen the hand-screws, push the stand toward the tub until the angle-steel uprights rest against it on either side, and tighten the screws. (No tools needed.) The position of the wringer is then directly over the tub, where it is rigidly held, and every single drop of water falls back into the tub instead of on the floor. (See illustration below.) When through wringing, push the stand back into place. The wringer, once attached, need never be taken off again.

2. **THE HINGED LID.** This consists of two parts. The inner, with cleats attached and holes bored through it, technically called the "rubber," serves to hold the clothes in place, adjusting itself to their height. The outer, or actual cover, fits the tub snugly all around, being practically steam-tight and preventing the water from splashing over. When ready to do the wringing or otherwise wanting access to the tub you merely raise this double cover and rest it back against the handle, which allows all suds to drain back into the tub.

3. **EXTENSION STAND.** This is another of the many advantages of the **IMPROVED ACME.** When the machine is not in use, or when washing only, this stand is folded up out of the way. (See illustration above.) When ready to wring the clothes into a tub of rinsing water or into the clothes basket, let down the extension stand—just two motions required—and it will hold tub or basket close to and on a level with the machine tub. There is no danger of clothes falling on the floor, no need of an overturned chair or box, and no necessity of continually stooping over.

There are many other points about the **IMPROVED ACME** which prove it to be in every way superior to any other washer made. For instance, there is no iron post running through our machine, to rust and stain, or possibly tear the clothes. We cannot enumerate all these points here, but have fully set them forth in a booklet entitled "Wash-Day Comfort." This is **FREE** for the asking. May we send you a copy?

Is This a Fair Offer?

We want to prove to you the superiority of the IMPROVED ACME WASHER, and there is no better way than to let you try it out fully in your own home, right where you'll use it if you buy it—and you will buy it if you give it half a chance to prove its value.

(1) The movable wringer stand brings the wringer over the tub so that no water falls on the floor; (2) the extension stand holds the clothes basket on a level with the machine tub; (3) the hinged lid and "rubber" leans back on the handle, so that all suds drain into the tub.

If you will write us that you are interested, we will give you the name of the dealer in your town who handles the **IMPROVED ACME WASHER.** You can see the machine at his store and learn all about it before you buy it. If you buy it, it is with the understanding that any time within 30 days, if the machine is not in every way satisfactory, he will take it away and give you back your money. He will do this cheerfully and readily, because our guarantee to him protects him against loss. You risk nothing but a two-cent postage stamp to mail us your letter.

WRITE TO-DAY—to-morrow it may be forgotten! **WRITE TO-DAY**—even if you are not just ready to buy or even try a machine; in that case let us send the little booklet—remember, it's **FREE—WRITE TO-DAY!**

ACME WASHING MACHINE COMPANY
2512 S. HIGH ST., COLUMBUS, OHIO., U. S. A.

728

An advertisement for a hand-cranked washing machine from Acme Washing Machine Company, from *The Delineator* magazine, April 1906. THE DELINEATOR, APRIL 1906, P. 728.

September 24, 1900: Alice did the kitchen work & cut & made a gown for Hearn. I sewed on my log cabbin quilt.

September 25, 1900: I finished my log cabbin quilt.

December 20, 1900: Lida finished picking seeds out of 2 ½ lbs of cotton & carded some bats.

March 20, 1901: I mended some & cut some quilt pieces.

June 18, 1901: Lida got her quilt out of frames.

September 2, 1901: I helped cook put a quilt in frames quilted some & mended some.

September 3, 1901: Lida & I did the cooking & quilted 2 rows of shells.

September 4, 1901: Lida quilted one row of shells on my quilt.

September 9, 1901: Lida & I did the cooking & quilted some on Mauds quilt.

September 13, 1901: Lida finished Mauds quilt & took it out of frames.

October 7, 1901: I cooked & cleaned up the house & carded some bats for a quilt.

October 8, 1901: I did the cooking & put up a quilt.

October 10, 1901: I did the cooking and cleaning up & quilted some. Lida quilted some for me.

October 14, 1901: I did all the housework & quilted some. Mr. Hearn run the mill. Lida quilted some.

October 16, 1901: I did the housework & quilted some. Lida quilted some too.

March 27, 1902: I peiced on Alices quilt. Alice did the kitchenwork.

April 4, 1902: I cooked dinner & cut some quilt peices & boiled soap all afternoon.

April 7, 1902: I cut quilt peices all day.

April 8, 1902: I cooked my soap little more & sewed some on quilt.

October 2, 1902: I helped cook starched the clothes mended some & made 2 aprons for myself.

February 24, 1903: I helped clean up & sewed some on quilt.

March 2, 1903: I cut peices & sewed on quilt.

March 3, 1903: I sewed on a quilt.

March 4, 1903: I worked on a quilt.

March 5, 1903: I sewed some on quilt & mended some.

March 6, 1903: Alice cooked & cut a garment for herself. Puss sewed on her quilt. I sewed some.

March 11, 1903: I cleaned up house & made a union suit for Alice.

March 24, 1903: I cleaned out big room, suned bed & quilts washed bedstead & oiled it.

April 6, 1903: I help cook cleaned up house went after milk and cut a bonnet & made it.

April 7, 1903: I helped cook made a border for a quilt & set it.

April 14, 1903: I sewed some on my quilt.

April 15, 1903: I cleaned up house suned beds, set out 20 cabbage plants, cut some quilt peices.

April 17, 1903: I cleaned up house cut some quilt peices & mended some.

April 23, 1903: I helped clean up & mended some & cut some quilt peices.

May 28, 1903: I worked some in garden helped cook breakfast cut 2 aprons for Power and an apron pattern made one apron & nearly another.

June 1, 1903: I cooked dinner cleaned up & worked all day on Alices dress. Alice cut her white waist & made it.

March 7, 1904: Mr. Hearn went to Canton & back got pr shoes for him self 3.50 pr pants 1.50 socks 1.00 & drawing knife got me a dress pattern & muslin.

March 25, 1904: I carried 7 Doz eggs to Mr. Gough got 16 yds of cloth (unbleached) & a calf rope. Mr. Hearn sawed. I made 4 pillowcases & partly made a hen coop. Alice cooked & milked.

September 16, 1904: Lida put quilt in frames & ironed some.

September 17, 1904: Lida ironed some & quilted some.

September 19, 1904: Lida quilted.

September 20, 1904: I helped cook & quilted some on Lida's quilt.

September 21, 1904: I helped cook & quilted some.

May 15, 1906: I cleaned up after breakfast & dinner, cut a bonnet & commenced to cut a wrapper for myself & tended the chickens.

May 18, 1906: Mr. Hearn hoed corn I helped do the housework & basted on my wrapper.

January 31, 1907: I made three pillow slips & a pillow tick & fixed my undervest. My Eyes are very bad.

April 4, 1907: I did the housework & washed 20 peices. Mr Hearn fixed the sewing machine on a stand.

June 4, 1907: I cleaned up 2 rooms churned & sewed some on Kitties quilt.

August 20, 1907: I did the cooking & made two quilt linings.

August 30, 1907: I did the cooking, hemed a quilt & mended some & cut & made myself an apron.

September 7, 1907: I did the cooking & finished heming my quilt.

November 7, 1907: I cooked dinner & put water on ash leach & finished hemming a quilt & mended some.

October 19, 1908: I cooked churned & cut some quilt peices.

October 20, 1908: I churned cooked dinner & cut some quilt peices.

October 21, 1908: I cooked dinner cleaned up one room & cut some quilt peices.

October 26, 1908: I cooked, cleaned up, and cut quilt peices.

October 27, 1908: I cooked churned & cut quilt peices.

October 28, 1908: I sewed some on my quilt.

November 2, 1908: I did the cooking mended some & sewed some on my quilt.

December 2, 1909: I cleaned up my room tended the Poultry & worked on Loulies quilt.

December 3, 1909: I sewed on my quilt.

December 7, 1909: I sewed on Loulies quilt.

December 13, 1909: I cleaned up my room & cut quilt peices & churned.

December 14, 1909: I cleaned up my room & worked some on quilt.

Further Resources

BOOKS

Bryk, Nancy Villa. *American Dress Pattern Catalogue 1873–1909.* New York: Dover Publications, 1988.

Harris, Kristina. *Authentic Victorian Dressmaking Techniques.* New York: Dover Publications, 1999.

Harris, Kristina (ed.). *Authentic Victorian Fashion Patterns: Complete Lady's Wardrobe.* New York: Dover Publications, 2000.

Lohrenz, Mary, and Anita Stamper. *Mississippi Homespun: Nineteenth-Century Textiles and the Women Who Made Them.* Jackson, Mississippi: Mississippi Department of Archives and History, 1989.

Oliver, Valerie B. and M. Thomas Inge. *Fashion and Costume in American Popular Culture: A Reference Guide.* Westport, Connecticut: Greenwood Press, 1996.

Scott, Anne Firor. *The Southern Lady: From Pedestal to Politics, 1830–1930.* Charlottesville: University Press of Virginia, 1995.

PERIODICALS

Farrell-Beck, Jane, and Joyce Starr Johnson. "Remodeling and Renovating Clothes." *Dress* 19, 1992.

Feather, Betty L., and Joann Gregory Ritter. "Practices, Procedures and Attitudes Toward Clothing Maintenance: 1850–1860 and 1900–1910." *Dress* 17, 1990.

Milspaw, Yvonne J. "Regional Style in Quilt Design." *Journal of American Folklore* 110, no. 438, Fall 1997, 363–390.

Art Pottery in the New Century

"Rookwood Is the Best Gift"

Advertisement

By: Rookwood Pottery Company

Date: 1906

Source: "Rookwood Is the Best Gift." In *Emergence of Advertising in America: J. Walter Thompson House Ads,* Duke University Digital Scriptorium. Available online at http://scriptorium.lib.duke.edu/cgi-bin/nph-dweb/dynaweb/eaa/databases/jwt/; website home page: http://scriptorium.lib.duke.edu/eaa/index.html (accessed February 14, 2003).

About the Artist: The Rookwood Pottery Company (1880–1967) was established by Maria Longworth Nichols in Cincinnati, Ohio, and would become the leader in the American art pottery movement before a decline in quality and subsequent bankruptcy in 1941.

"Van Briggle Art Pottery"

Work of art

By: Van Briggle Art Pottery; H.S. Poley

Date: 1902

Source: Van Briggle Art Pottery; H.S. Poley. "Van Briggle Art Pottery." *History of the American West, 1860–1920: Photographs from the Collection of the Denver Public Library.* American Memory digital primary source collection, Library of Congress. Available online at http://memory.loc.gov/ammem/award97/codhtml/hawphome.html; website home page: http://memory.loc.gov (accessed February 14, 2003).

About the Artist: Artus Van Briggle (1869–1904) worked in the Rookwood Pottery from 1887 until he left in 1899 for

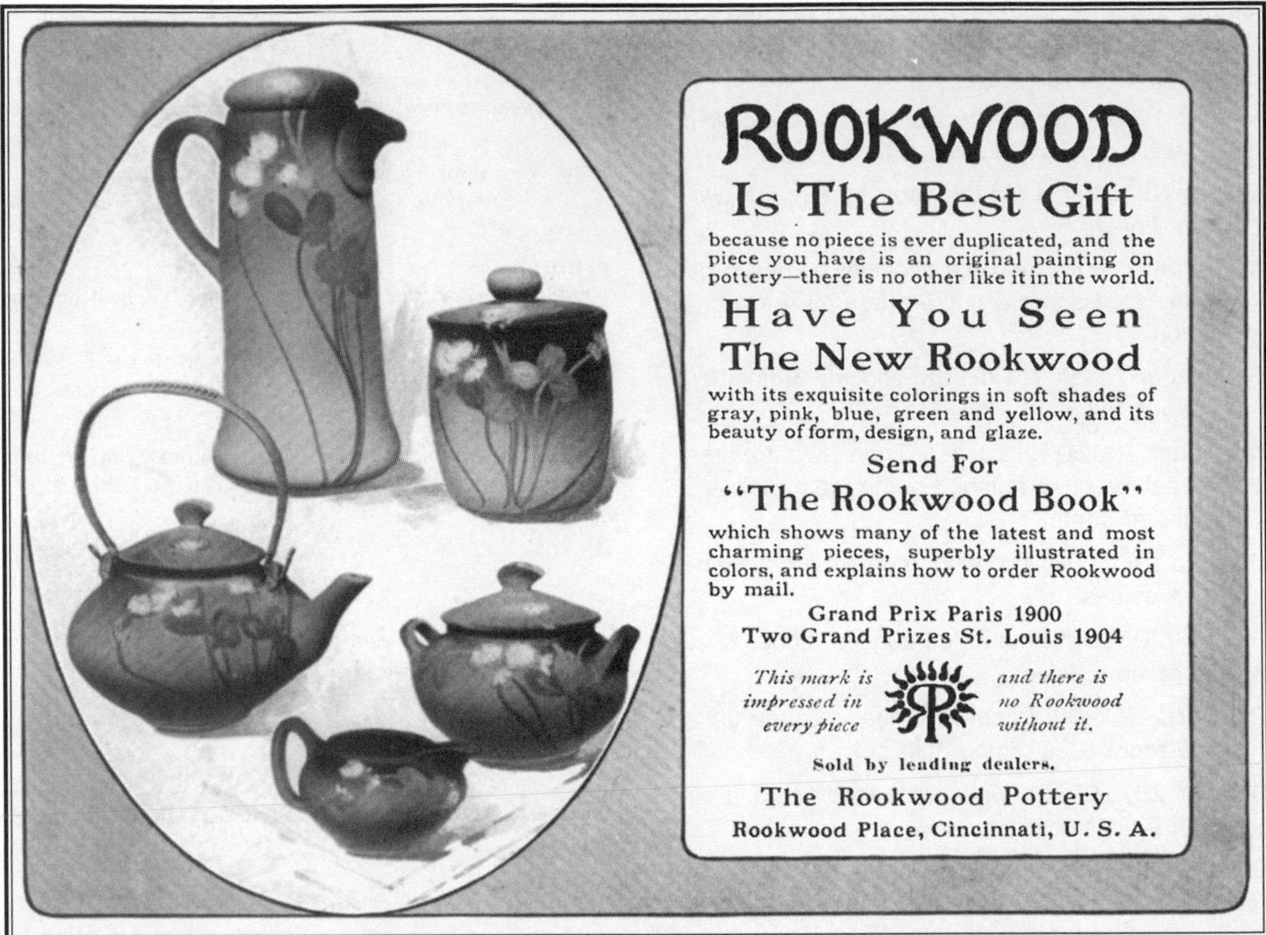

ROOKWOOD
Is The Best Gift
because no piece is ever duplicated, and the piece you have is an original painting on pottery—there is no other like it in the world.
Have You Seen
The New Rookwood
with its exquisite colorings in soft shades of gray, pink, blue, green and yellow, and its beauty of form, design, and glaze.
Send For
"The Rookwood Book"
which shows many of the latest and most charming pieces, superbly illustrated in colors, and explains how to order Rookwood by mail.
Grand Prix Paris 1900
Two Grand Prizes St. Louis 1904
This mark is impressed in every piece
and there is no Rookwood without it.
Sold by leading dealers.
The Rookwood Pottery
Rookwood Place, Cincinnati, U. S. A.

Primary Source

"Rookwood Is the Best Gift"

SYNOPSIS: The pieces featured in the Rookwood ad are clearly reflective of the Art Nouveau movement which had dominated decorative arts since shortly before the turn of the century. "ROOKWOOD IS THE BEST GIFT." ITEM #:J0034. EMERGENCE OF ADVERTISING IN AMERICA. 2000. RARE BOOK, MANUSCRIPT, AND SPECIAL COLLECTIONS LIBRARY, DUKE UNIVERSITY. [HTTP://SCRIPTORIUM.LIB.DUKE.EDU/EAA/] COURTESY OF ROOKWOOD POTTERY CO., BROOKLYN, MICHIGAN.

Colorado because of health reasons. He established his own pottery workshop there, practicing until his death. ■

Introduction

The Arts and Crafts movement that had begun in England with the teaching and work of William Morris spread to the United States. By the 1870s, schools such as the Cincinnati School of Design and the Rhode Island School of Design offered art education programs of study based on the principles of the Arts and Crafts movement. National and international fairs and expositions displayed products of the movement, adding impetus to its adoption in America. Often seen as a reaction to the proliferation of machine-based and executed design as well as the mindless copying or adaptation of styles from other historical periods, the movement espoused a return to hand craftsmanship, a state of production in which the maker was a craftsman, not a mere anonymous laborer. In all aspects of the decorative arts, the Arts and Crafts style was influential, as exemplified by the infusion of art pottery into the marketplace. By the end of the 1890s, there were hundreds of small pottery works, concentrated primarily in Ohio and the northeastern states. Rookwood and Van Briggle are but two of numerous art pottery manufacturers that were able to sustain successful production in response to the changing public aesthetic.

Rookwood Pottery was begun in 1871 by Maria Longworth Nichols, initially as an outgrowth of her own interest in china painting. By 1900, she had transferred ownership to her business manager. With wares that had developed a significant style and quality, it was both an aesthetically and a financially successful venture. Artus

Primary Source

"Van Briggle Art Pottery"

SYNOPSIS: The Van Briggle Art Pottery selection reflects the artist's finer pottery, created more for the collector than the middle-class consumer. WESTERN HISTORY/GENEALOGY DEPARTMENT, DENVER PUBLIC LIBRARY.

Van Briggle was one of Rookwood's most successful decorators and showed a particular interest in and aptitude for glazes. Nichols recognized his talent and sent Van Briggle to Europe for two years to study glaze techniques. It was a business move that would pay off for Rookwood Pottery as its reputation for excellence grew.

Significance

In its heyday, Rookwood produced some of the finest pottery in the country, a reputation to which the advertisement alludes. Although Rookwood pottery won prizes in both the 1900 and the 1904 international expositions, it is highly unlikely that the pieces shown in the advertisement for Rookwood Pottery represent their prize winners at either expositions. The five pieces of what appears to be painted stoneware exhibit a return to the commercialization which would have been anathema to the original company's designers. This was also the beginning of a slow but inevitable decline in both the overall quality of Rookwood production and its financial stability as a company. The utilitarian nature of the objects offered by Rookwood and the inclusion of only hand painted pieces marked the advertisement for a growing middle class market. These pieces exemplify a less than optimum quality in the company's products and signify its drift from the philosophy of the Art Nouveau and Arts and Crafts movements with their emphasis on individual craftsmanship.

The photograph of Van Briggle's work shows the actual nine pieces that took first prize at both the Paris and St. Louis expositions of 1900 and 1904, respectively. Van Briggle's pottery remained true to its Art Nouveau origins in both design and quality of design and workmanship. The Van Briggle Pottery never achieved the size or production capacity of some of the larger firms, such as Rookwood, and Van Briggle himself along with his wife, Anna, remained directly involved in both design and production. Some molded pieces were made at his pottery, and these increased in number after his death, but the majority of work attributed directly to Artus Van Briggle shows the beautiful glazes and organic, sculptural motifs that seemed to grow directly out of the pottery itself.

Further Resources

BOOKS

Ellis, Anita J. *Rookwood Pottery: The Glorious Gamble.* Cincinnati: Cincinnati Art Museum, 1992.

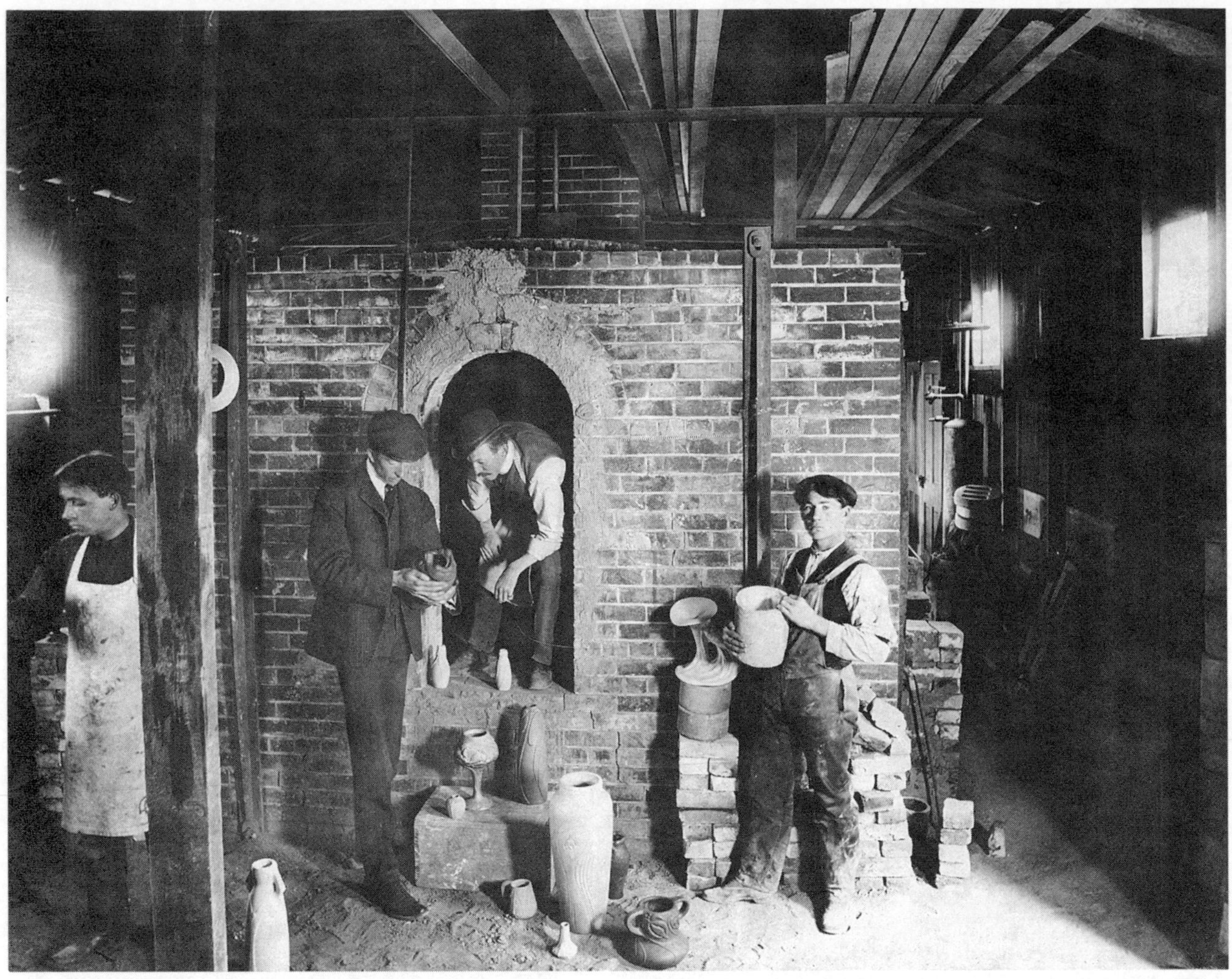

Artus Van Briggle inspects the first Van Briggle Art Pottery to be fired as it comes out of the kiln at the Van Briggle Pottery Factory in Colorado Springs, 1902. **WESTERN HISTORY/GENEALOGY DEPARTMENT, DENVER PUBLIC LIBRARY.**

Nelson, Scott H. *A Collector's Guide to Van Briggle Pottery.* Indiana, Pa.: A.G. Halldin Publishing Company, 1986.

Perry, Barbara A. *American Art Pottery: From the Collection of Everson Museum of Art.* New York: Harry N. Abrams, 1997.

WEBSITES

"Artus Van Briggle (1869–1904)—USA." Available online at http://www.ceramique1900.com/vanbriggle.html; website home page: http://www.ceramique1900.com (accessed February 14, 2003).

"Arts & Crafts Movement." Available online at http://www.morsemuseum.org/artscrafts.html; website home page: http://www.morsemuseum.org/ (accessed February 14, 2003).

Girello, Christine. "Rookwood Pottery." In *Antiques & Art Around Florida, Summer/Fall 1997.* Available online at http://www.aarf.com/ferook97.htm (accessed February 14, 2003).

"Newcomb Pottery and the Arts and Crafts Movement in Louisiana." Available online at http://lsm.crt.state.la.us/newcomb/newcomb1.htm#Early; website home page http://lsm.crt.state.la.us/ (accessed May 16, 2003).

The Gibson Girl

"The Weaker Sex II" and "Studies in Expression at a Fashionable Funeral"

Drawings

By: Charles Dana Gibson

Date: 1903

Source: Gibson, Charles Dana. "The Weaker Sex II." *Collier's Weekly,* July 4, 1903, 12–13; "Studies in Expression at a Fashionable Funeral." *Life,* October 22, 1903, 388–389.

About the Artist: Charles Dana Gibson (1867–1944) was born in Roxbury, Massachusetts. He attended the Arts Students League in Manhattan for two years and then began the initially slow process of achieving commercial success. He sold his first pen and ink drawing in 1886 to the editor of *Life* magazine. By 1890, Gibson was working for all the major publications in New York. He remains famous today for his creation of the fashionable Gibson Girl. ■

Primary Source

"The Weaker Sex II"

SYNOPSIS: One of a series of illustrations satirizing the concept of women as the weaker sex, this depiction of beautiful women leisurely studying a microscopic male as if he were a laboratory specimen appeared in *Collier's Weekly* in 1903. THE LIBRARY OF CONGRESS.

Introduction

The unique Gibson style seemed to develop following an extended trip to Paris and England, where he met the satirist George du Maurier. When he returned to America, Gibson turned to the same source of inspiration that characterized du Maurier's work—society women. Gibson's satiric eye for social nuance, his evocative and highly recognizable rendering of the American female, and a transitional time for women's roles in America set the stage for the popularity of his images. In particular, his images of young, upwardly mobile American women of fashion became the hallmark of his career, even though he illustrated many other types of subject matter. Despite the popularization of this one aspect of his work—the Gibson Girl phenomenon—Gibson was never considered a fashion illustrator, but a social commentator.

Women's roles were changing dramatically in the 1900s. Previously, women had been regarded as the weaker sex, unable to fend for themselves, dependent upon men for protection, supervision, and financial support. But sports and the emergence of possible employment were beginning to change those traditional social constructs. Gibson observed those changes and used his art to share his observations with his audience. In a series called "The Weaker Sex," for example, Gibson turned the title into a satirical comment, as the women he drew were clearly in charge of the situations in which they were portrayed.

The identity of any one female who served as Gibson's inspiration is still debated. Jobyna Howland, an actress and comedienne, is sometimes credited with being the original "Gibson Girl." After Gibson married Irene Langhorne, she often served as his model. In actuality, the Gibson Girl could be all women and every woman. She represented possibilities and change, hence her appeal to men and women alike.

Significance

Gibson's rendition of what he perceived as the American girl became famous, and his name became forever

Primary Source

"Studies in Expression at a Fashionable Funeral"

SYNOPSIS: Here is one example in another illustration series offering commentary on typical social attitudes and activities of the day. Others of the series include "When Women are Jurors" and "In the Monkey House." "Studies in Expression at a Fashionable Funeral" appeared in the October 1903 issue of *Life* magazine. THE LIBRARY OF CONGRESS.

linked with that image. In these two illustrations, both the visual aspects that have been extrapolated from his drawings into a composite of the New American Woman and the underlying sense of what Gibson was really about are both evident. "The Weaker Sex II" is one of a series of satirical drawings in which Gibson portrayed women and men interacting, with the women clearly the stronger of the two. The hairstyles and mannerisms are typical of Gibson's relaxed style of presentation, one that would be imitated by other illustrators and reproduced endlessly.

In "Studies in Expression at a Fashionable Funeral," the people attending the funeral appear more interested in each other and in their appearance than in the purpose of the funeral itself. In both illustrations, the fashions of men and women are carefully shown and consistent with Gibson's fashion images, but the underlying social comment is the real message. The Gibson Girl was not a bystander to life. She was in charge of herself and of the men around her. In creating her, Gibson created a role model for the twentieth-century American woman.

Gibson's work gained familiarity to the American audience through periodicals such as *Scribner's, Harpers, Collier's,* and *The Century.* As his popularity grew, the familiar images were soon showing up on wallpaper and matchboxes, Royal Doulton china and Rookwood Pottery. In 1904 *The Delineator* offered a catalogue of Gibson designs for wood and leather burning, and the work of other illustrators showed definite similarity to his style. Gibson's image of American womanhood came to symbolize the first decade of the twentieth century and is still relevant at the start of the twenty-first century.

Further Resources

BOOKS

Gibson, Charles Dana. *The Gibson Girl and Her America.* New York: Dover Publications, 1969.

"Gibson, Charles Dana." In *The Columbia Encyclopedia,* 6th ed. New York: Columbia University Press, 2000.

Gibson, Langhorne, Jr. *The Gibson Girl: Portrait of a Southern Belle.* Richmond, Virginia: Commodore Press, 1997.

Actress Jobyna Howland, one of the many women who claimed to be the original "Gibson Girl," posing for Charles Dana Gibson, the creator of the famous image, circa 1900. WESTERN HISTORY/GENEALOGY DEPARTMENT, DENVER PUBLIC LIBRARY.

WEBSITES

"Charles Dana Gibson." Available at http://www.heraldsquarehotel.com/CDGibson.htm: website home page: http://www.heraldsquarehotel.com (accessed February 23, 2003).

Freeman, Kevin. "Charles Dana Gibson." Mutoworld.com. Available online at http://www.mutoworld.com/Gibson.htm; website home page: http://www.mutoworld.com/home.htm (accessed February 23, 2003).

"The Gibson Girl." Available online at http://www.ibiscom.com/gibson.htm; website home page: http://www.ibiscom.com (accessed February 23, 2003).

Photographs of Poor Miners

"A Young Apprentice and His Papa," "Some of Our Future Citizens," and "Economy in a Mining Town"

Photographs

By: Peter Roberts

Date: 1904

Source: Roberts, Peter. Originally published in *Anthracite Coal Communities.* New York: MacMillan Company, 1904. Available online at *Coal Mining in the Gilded Age and Progressive Era,* http://home.earthlink.net/~scheppg/UnionHistory.html; website home page: http://www.history.ohio-state.edu/web.htm (accessed February 22, 2003).

About the Photographer: Peter Roberts (1859–1932) studied the anthracite coal community from the standpoint of both economics and social welfare. Considered an expert, he was often quoted and referred to in discussions of coal mining, particularly as related to the outcomes of mining practices and the impact on workers. An Episcopalian minister, Roberts firmly believed that many immigrants were mentally inferior to Americans and posed a potential threat to a unified citizenry. ■

Introduction

The opening years of the twentieth century saw immense industrial and economic growth, but with a gravely disproportionate division of that wealth. At the upper ends of the social and economic strata, practical buying power was essentially unlimited. A middle class, composed of industrial and trading families, was growing and

Primary Source

"A Young Apprentice and His Papa" (1 OF 3)

SYNOPSIS: Images of coal miners and their families show how their appearance compares to that of other classes and also provide insight into their meager living conditions. Photos like these forced society to become aware of class struggles and the exploitation of the poor. REPRINTED FROM PETER ROBERTS, ED., *ANTHRACITE COAL COMMUNITIES,* ARNO PRESS, 1970.

Primary Source

"Some of Our Future Citizens" (2 OF 3)

Immigrants pose for a photograph in a mining town. REPRINTED FROM PETER ROBERTS, ED., *ANTHRACITE COAL COMM* PRESS, 1970.

represented another market segment, but there remained millions who lived on the very brink of starvation. Both immigrants and native-born Americans swelled this huge lower class that fueled industrial growth. The rural poor could provide their own food. But in the cities and mining towns across America, the plight of the laborers was almost always one of endless work, low pay, and severe deprivation in basic living conditions.

These laborers fueled the apparel manufacturing industry; they worked in cotton and wool mills, in steel and copper; they worked in the mines. In the older industrial settings, immigrants made up large portions of the work force, with more highly skilled, experienced workers following higher wages and better opportunities in the middle, western, and southern states. Local populations and internal immigrants from rural America were also significant members of these work forces. The lucky ones had employment and housing, albeit of substandard quality. Many immigrants and native-born Americans in the cities were homeless, including thousands of children. For them, the new century's promises of economic well-being seemed distant.

These three photographs give an overview of the clothing, appearance, and housing of those Americans at the lower end of the socioeconomic strat as well as in housing, there was stark contr ions of the upper or even middle classes shown in these pictures is reduced to so basic function: protection and modesty.

Significance

Considered along with the images of fas icans seen in the newspapers and fashion m day, these images help to complete a full-s of clothing and appearance in America decade of the new century. But the stratific seen so clearly in these diverse images wa considerable concern to social commentator cial critics used images such as these fron dustry to speak out against the inhumane class by members of another. The upp women had beautiful dresses made and broidered or embellished by textile worke to-wear shirts and suits were sewn in factori welfare was not taken into consideration. isted and expanded actually grew out of th the very lowest social class. Their labor cre mered in fashion, but they did not bask in th

"Twenty-sixth Anniversary of the Standard Underwear of the World"

Catalog (text and images)

By: Gustave Jaeger

Date: 1905

Source: Jaeger, Gustave. "Twenty-sixth Anniversary of the Standard Underwear of the World." New York: Dr. Jaeger's Sanitary Woolen System Co., 1909. *Emergence of Advertising: Advertising Ephemera.* Available online at http://scriptorium.lib.duke.edu/cgi-bin/nphdweb/dynaweb/eaa/databases/ephemera/@Generic__BookTextView/15727;nh=1?DwebQuery=jaeger; website home page: http://scriptorium.lib.duke.edu/(accessed February 22, 2003).

About the Author: Dr. Gustav Jaeger was born in Germany, then immigrated to the United States. Emigration records from Germany show a Gustav Ludwig Jaeger, born in 1835, applying for passage to North America in 1855. Jaeger eventually founded a company for his products and marketed them worldwide. He exhibited knitted undergarments as early as 1884 at the International Health Exhibition in Kensington, England, and published a book called *Rational Clothing* in 1880. ■

Introduction

Dress reform in the United States began as part of the feminist movement and only later acquired aspects that related more to health than to equality. By the twentieth century, both causes were powerful proponents of changing the way Americans—particularly women—dressed. Clothing manufacturers had less social and political controversy to overcome, and were thus able to gain inroads that the feminist reformers were not. They were also able to manipulate the fear factor in a country where infant mortality was still a major problem. In fact, wool had long been a customary fabric for winter undergarments, and it was accepted as an excellent choice for providing warmth during cold seasons. Wool varies greatly in softness and fineness, however, so less expensive wool often was scratchy and uncomfortable next to the skin. For this reason, many people preferred cotton to wool, and used multiple layers for warmth. The Jaeger advertisements attempted to overcome this preference by touting the qualities of his products, and the dangers of imitations obviously being produced by his competitors. He offered garments "incapable of causing the skin irritation often associated with wool." This claim could, in fact, have been supported by scientific evidence, although he offered none.

The woolen undergarments were knitted, and that structure was considerably different from woven cottons which tended to be very rigid in their construction. Women's boned corsets were made to constrict the body, often to the point that organs were displaced. By com-

parison panded

Signifi

Dr. the lack were ty forming nineteen claims f reform Many o of the m and som used tha their cla planatio ative inf interest dation p claimed claims—

Som bloomers Fashions allowing employm children other pur much of were heal 1930s an eral Trade tercede b advertisin health clai if unsuppo

Primary

"Twenty-s Underwea

SYNOP was a two de the tw riety o duced are tex

Guaran

DR. JAEGER'S

Men's Normal Sanatory Combination Suits.

IN NATURAL COLOR ONLY.

DOUBLE-BREASTED.

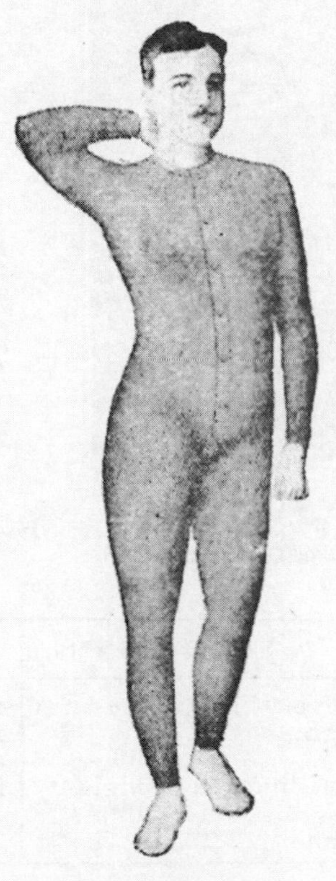

SINGLE-BREASTED.

Sizes (Chest)—Inches:	34	36	38	40	42	44	46
Inseam:	28	30 or 32	30 or 32	30 or 32	31	31	31
Gauze (Very Light), Single-Breasted..............	$4 20	$4 45	$4 70	$5 00	$5 30	$5 60	$5 90
K, Light- Single-Breasted.	4 20	4 45	4 70	5 00	5 30	5 60	5 90
K, Wgt., Double- "	4 55	4 80	5 05	5 35	5 65	5 95	6 25
KK, " "	5 40	5 65	5 90	6 20	6 50	6 80	7 10
B, " "	5 55	5 80	6 05	6 35	6 65	6 95	7 25
A, " "	6 45	6 75	7 05	7 40	7 75	8 10	8 45
F, " "	6 80	7 20	7 60	8 00	8 40	8 80	9 20

Primary Source

"Twenty-sixth Anniversary of the Standard Underwear of the World" (1 OF 2)

A page from Dr. Jaeger's Woolen System Co. catalog illustrates men's undergarments. "TWENTY-SIXTH ANNIVERSARY OF THE STANDARD UNDERWEAR. . ." ITEM #: A0175-04. EMERGENCE OF ADVERTISING IN AMERICA. 2000. RARE BOOK, MANUSCRIPT, AND SPECIAL COLLECTIONS LIBRARY, DUKE UNIVERSITY. [HTTP://SCRIPTORIUM.LIB.DUKE.EDU/EAA/].

DR. JAEGER'S
LADIES' NORMAL SANATORY UNDERVESTS.

Style 2—
"O. F."—Open Front.
Single or Double Breasted.

Style 3—
High Neck, Short Sleeves.
Single-Breasted.

Style 4—
Low-Neck, No Sleeves.

Style 2

Sizes (Bust), Inches:	30	32	34	36	38	40	42	44
Gauze, very light, single-br's'd	$2 15	$2 35	$2 55	$2 75	$2 95	$3 15	$3 35	$3 60
K—Light, " "	2 15	2 35	2 55	2 75	2 95	3 15	3 35	3 60
K— " double- "	2 40	2 60	2 80	3 00	3 20	3 40	3 65	3 90
KK—Medium Q'l'y, single-"	2 75	2 95	3 15	3 35	3 55	3 75	4 00	4 25
KK— " " double- "	3 00	3 20	3 40	3 60	3 80	4 00	4 25	4 50
B—Winter " " "	3 10	3 30	3 50	3 70	3 90	4 10	4 35	4 60

Style 3

Sizes (Bust), Inches:	30	32	34	36	38	40	42	44
Gauze (very light)...........	$1 90	$2 10	$2 30	$2 50	$2 70	$2 90	$3 10	$3 35
K—Light	1 90	2 10	2 30	2 50	2 70	2 90	3 10	3 35

Style 4

Sizes (Bust), Inches:	30	32	34	36	38	40	42	44
Gauze (very light)...........	$2 00	$2 20	$2 40	$2 60	$2 80	$3 00	$3 25	$3 50
K—Light....................	2 00	2 20	2 40	2 60	2 80	3 00	3 25	3 50

The Natural Wool is doubtless preferable to the White, but Qualities Gauze, K and KK can also be had in the *latter at 30c. more than the Natural, but single-breasted only.*

Primary Source

"Twenty-sixth Anniversary of the Standard Underwear of the World" (2 OF 2)

SYNOPSIS: This page from Dr. Jaeger's Woolen System Co. catalog shows women's undergarments. "TWENTY-SIXTH ANNIVERSARY OF THE STANDARD UNDERWEAR. . ." ITEM #: A0175-09. EMERGENCE OF ADVERTISING IN AMERICA. 2000. RARE BOOK, MANUSCRIPT, AND SPECIAL COLLECTIONS LIBRARY, DUKE UNIVERSITY. [HTTP://SCRIPTORIUM.LIB.DUKE.EDU/EAA/].

Actress Jobyna Howland, one of the many women who claimed to be the original "Gibson Girl," posing for Charles Dana Gibson, the creator of the famous image, circa 1900. WESTERN HISTORY/GENEALOGY DEPARTMENT, DENVER PUBLIC LIBRARY.

WEBSITES

"Charles Dana Gibson." Available at http://www.heraldsquarehotel.com/CDGibson.htm: website home page: http://www.heraldsquarehotel.com (accessed February 23, 2003).

Freeman, Kevin. "Charles Dana Gibson." Mutoworld.com. Available online at http://www.mutoworld.com/Gibson.htm; website home page: http://www.mutoworld.com/home.htm (accessed February 23, 2003).

"The Gibson Girl." Available online at http://www.ibiscom.com/gibson.htm; website home page: http://www.ibiscom.com (accessed February 23, 2003).

Photographs of Poor Miners

"A Young Apprentice and His Papa," "Some of Our Future Citizens," and "Economy in a Mining Town"

Photographs

By: Peter Roberts
Date: 1904

Source: Roberts, Peter. Originally published in *Anthracite Coal Communities.* New York: MacMillan Company, 1904. Available online at *Coal Mining in the Gilded Age and Progressive Era,* http://home.earthlink.net/~scheppg/UnionHistory.html; website home page: http://www.history.ohio-state.edu/web.htm (accessed February 22, 2003).

About the Photographer: Peter Roberts (1859–1932) studied the anthracite coal community from the standpoint of both economics and social welfare. Considered an expert, he was often quoted and referred to in discussions of coal mining, particularly as related to the outcomes of mining practices and the impact on workers. An Episcopalian minister, Roberts firmly believed that many immigrants were mentally inferior to Americans and posed a potential threat to a unified citizenry. ■

Introduction

The opening years of the twentieth century saw immense industrial and economic growth, but with a gravely disproportionate division of that wealth. At the upper ends of the social and economic strata, practical buying power was essentially unlimited. A middle class, composed of industrial and trading families, was growing and

Primary Source

"A Young Apprentice and His Papa" (1 OF 3)
SYNOPSIS: Images of coal miners and their families show how their appearance compares to that of other classes and also provide insight into their meager living conditions. Photos like these forced society to become aware of class struggles and the exploitation of the poor. REPRINTED FROM PETER ROBERTS, ED., *ANTHRACITE COAL COMMUNITIES,* ARNO PRESS, 1970.

Primary Source

"Some of Our Future Citizens" (2 OF 3)

Immigrants pose for a photograph in a mining town. REPRINTED FROM PETER ROBERTS, ED., *ANTHRACITE COAL COMMUNITIES*, ARNO PRESS, 1970.

represented another market segment, but there remained millions who lived on the very brink of starvation. Both immigrants and native-born Americans swelled this huge lower class that fueled industrial growth. The rural poor could provide their own food. But in the cities and mining towns across America, the plight of the laborers was almost always one of endless work, low pay, and severe deprivation in basic living conditions.

These laborers fueled the apparel manufacturing industry; they worked in cotton and wool mills, in steel and copper; they worked in the mines. In the older industrial settings, immigrants made up large portions of the work force, with more highly skilled, experienced workers following higher wages and better opportunities in the middle, western, and southern states. Local populations and internal immigrants from rural America were also significant members of these work forces. The lucky ones had employment and housing, albeit of substandard quality. Many immigrants and native-born Americans in the cities were homeless, including thousands of children. For them, the new century's promises of economic well-being seemed distant.

These three photographs give an overview of the clothing, appearance, and housing of those Americans at the lower end of the socioeconomic strata. In clothing, as well as in housing, there was stark contrast to the fashions of the upper or even middle classes. The clothing shown in these pictures is reduced to some of its most basic function: protection and modesty.

Significance

Considered along with the images of fashionable Americans seen in the newspapers and fashion magazines of the day, these images help to complete a full-spectrum picture of clothing and appearance in America during the first decade of the new century. But the stratification of society seen so clearly in these diverse images was the subject of considerable concern to social commentators of the day. Social critics used images such as these from the mining industry to speak out against the inhumane treatment of one class by members of another. The upper-middle class women had beautiful dresses made and extensively embroidered or embellished by textile workers. Men's ready-to-wear shirts and suits were sewn in factories where worker welfare was not taken into consideration. Fashion as it existed and expanded actually grew out of the exploitation of the very lowest social class. Their labor created all that glimmered in fashion, but they did not bask in the reflected glow.

Primary Source

"Economy in a Mining Town" (3 OF 3)

Women use a hydrant to gather water in a mining town. The hydrant supplies water for twenty-five families. REPRINTED FROM PETER ROBERTS, ED., *ANTHRACITE COAL COMMUNITIES*, ARNO PRESS, 1970.

The first decade of the twentieth century was a time of tremendous activity in organizing the labor force into a unified voice that could have the strength in numbers to be heard above the din of cash registers ringing up profits. As images of the laboring class were made available through the press, the public began to respond with support. Moving accounts of personal tragedies or inhumane treatment were printed alongside the images even in some fashion magazines. The press, and the public to which they connected, thus proved a powerful force when combined with the labor movement itself. While unionization of workers had its roots in this decade, it would be 1938 before the federal government would pass the Fair Labor Standards Act, the first piece of lasting legislation to regulate labor conditions for all ages, including children.

Further Resources

BOOKS

Bae, Youngsoo. *Labor in Retreat: Class and Community Among Men's Clothing Workers of Chicago, 1871–1929.* Albany, New York: State University of New York Press, 2001.

Bigott, Joseph C. *From Cottage to Bungalow: Houses and the Working Class in Metropolitan Chicago, 1869–1929.* Chicago: University of Chicago Press, 2001.

Fishback, Price V. *Soft Coal, Hard Choices: The Economic Welfare of Bituminous Coal Miners, 1890–1930.* New York: Oxford University Press, 1992.

Greene, Nancy L. *Ready-To-Wear and Ready-To-Work: A Century of Industry and Immigrants in Paris and New York.* Durham, North Carolina: Duke University Press, 1997.

Hourwich, Isaac A. *Immigration and Labor: The Economic Aspects of European Immigration to the United States.* New York: G. P. Putnam's Sons, 1912.

McDonald, David J. *Coal and Unionism: A History of the American Coal Miners' Unions.* Silver Spring, Maryland: Cornelius Printing Company, 1939.

Steele, Valerie. "Dressing for Work." In *Men and Women Dressing the Part.* Washington, D.C.: Smithsonian Institution Press, 1989, 64–91.

West, Elliott. *Growing up in Twentieth-Century America: A History and Reference Guide.* Westport, Connecticut: Greenwood Press, 1996.

WEBSITES

"Labor Union History." Available online at http://home.earthlink.net/~scheppg/UnionHistory.html (accessed February 22, 2003). Includes images and information about miners and textile workers.

"Twenty-sixth Anniversary of the Standard Underwear of the World"

Catalog (text and images)

By: Gustave Jaeger

Date: 1905

Source: Jaeger, Gustave. "Twenty-sixth Anniversary of the Standard Underwear of the World." New York: Dr. Jaeger's Sanitary Woolen System Co., 1909. *Emergence of Advertising: Advertising Ephemera.* Available online at http://scriptorium.lib.duke.edu/cgi-bin/nphdweb/dynaweb/eaa/databases/ephemera/@Generic__BookTextView/15727;nh=1?DwebQuery=jaeger; website home page: http://scriptorium.lib.duke.edu/(accessed February 22, 2003).

About the Author: Dr. Gustav Jaeger was born in Germany, then immigrated to the United States. Emigration records from Germany show a Gustav Ludwig Jaeger, born in 1835, applying for passage to North America in 1855. Jaeger eventually founded a company for his products and marketed them worldwide. He exhibited knitted undergarments as early as 1884 at the International Health Exhibition in Kensington, England, and published a book called *Rational Clothing* in 1880. ■

Introduction

Dress reform in the United States began as part of the feminist movement and only later acquired aspects that related more to health than to equality. By the twentieth century, both causes were powerful proponents of changing the way Americans—particularly women—dressed. Clothing manufacturers had less social and political controversy to overcome, and were thus able to gain inroads that the feminist reformers were not. They were also able to manipulate the fear factor in a country where infant mortality was still a major problem. In fact, wool had long been a customary fabric for winter undergarments, and it was accepted as an excellent choice for providing warmth during cold seasons. Wool varies greatly in softness and fineness, however, so less expensive wool often was scratchy and uncomfortable next to the skin. For this reason, many people preferred cotton to wool, and used multiple layers for warmth. The Jaeger advertisements attempted to overcome this preference by touting the qualities of his products, and the dangers of imitations obviously being produced by his competitors. He offered garments "incapable of causing the skin irritation often associated with wool." This claim could, in fact, have been supported by scientific evidence, although he offered none.

The woolen undergarments were knitted, and that structure was considerably different from woven cottons which tended to be very rigid in their construction. Women's boned corsets were made to constrict the body, often to the point that organs were displaced. By comparison, a stretchy fabric that fitted smoothly yet expanded during activity offered many comfort advantages.

Significance

Dr. Jaeger's claims for his woolen underwear and the lack of scientific evidence presented with those claims were typical of the extended and diverse attempts at reforming fashion that started around the middle of the nineteenth century. The use of scientific terminology and claims for health benefits are also very typical of the dress reform movement that lasted for nearly seventy years. Many of the leading spokespersons for various threads of the movement actually had some scientific education, and some were physicians. Most of them, like Dr. Jaeger, used that background to lend the weight of expertise to their claims, but they did not provide true scientific explanations. The field of scientific inquiry was still in relative infancy, lacking the funding, the expertise, and the interest to pursue theoretical positions through the validation process. The majority of the health benefits claimed for a variety of dress reforms were just that—claims—with no validation offered.

Some aspects of dress reform, like Amelia's bloomers, never made much impact on the fashion scene. Fashions changed with the social atmosphere of the times, allowing women more freedom for physical activity and employment outside the home. Much to the chagrin of children across the country, however, Dr. Jaeger and other purveyors of wool were successful in convincing much of the consuming public that wool undergarments were healthier; they continued to be popular well into the 1930s and 40s. It would not be until 1914 that the Federal Trade Commission would come into being and intercede between business and consumer for truth in advertising. In the meantime, dress reform based on health claims provided manufacturers with a competitive, if unsupported, edge.

Primary Source

"Twenty-sixth Anniversary of the Standard Underwear of the World" [text excerpt]

SYNOPSIS: The Dr. Jaeger woolen underwear system was a major player in dress reform from the last two decades of the nineteenth century until well into the twentieth. His products were available in a variety of weights for year-round wear, and were produced for men, women, and children. Included here are text and images of Jaeger's woolen underwear.

Dr. Jaeger's

Normal Sanatory Underclothing

Guaranteed to be of Absolutely Pure Undyed Wool.

Manufactured by the Renowned Firm of WILH. BENGER SOEHNE, of Stuttgart, UNDER THE SUPERVISION OF DR. G. JAEGER.

No better goods were ever offered to the American Public. They excel in every textile quality; in fineness of wool; in softness and delicacy of texture in various weights, from the lightest summer to the heaviest winter wear; while the peculiar mode of weaving the "Stockinet," of which they are all constructed, imparts an elasticity and freshness not to be found in any other brand.

In the manufacture of this underwear only the natural gray or white wool is used. This being undyed, and of the finest quality, it makes a garment so soft and pliable as to be not only non-irritating, but positively pleasurable to the most delicate skin.

The structure and influence of the fabric are such as to produce a glow of health on the body's surface, while the anatomical and physiological adaptation of the garments practically averts the danger of taking cold from the sudden changes so peculiar to our climate.

Moreover, as the garments can be had Double over the Chest and Abdomen, they afford protection at all times to the vital organs. Not only does the *Jaeger Sanatory Woolen Underwear* thus conduce to the general health, but it is admittedly the best all-around security yet devised against attacks of pneumonia.

We advise all who are not yet prepared to adopt the System in its entirety to make a beginning with this Jaeger Sanatory Woolen Underwear.

It is a STRIKING AND SIGNIFICANT FACT that CHILDREN reared under this system of clothing are far more robust and free from disease than members of the same family who wear the ordinary clothing. All persons who have the least tendency to neuralgia, rheumatism, rheumatic gout, gouty deposits in the joints, or who are debilitated from any cause, will find that the benefits derived from the use of these goods, both day and night, will be immediately apparent, and generally permanent.

Our large and complete Catalogue furnished free on request. Please write for same to our agents in your city or to 85 Fifth Avenue, New York.

The Value of the Jaeger Trade-Mark

Caution!

The prompt recognition by the public of the superiority of the Dr. Jaeger Woolen Underclothing to the flannel and other so called woolen underwear generally made has induced much unscrupulous imitation of the Genuine Dr. Jaeger Goods, which, however, remain unique in their high quality, durability and absolute freedom from adulteration.

The JAEGER Trade-mark guarantees Pure Wool, in place of Wool frequently mixed with from 25 to 75 per cent. of Cotton or other cheap and inferior adulterants: it also guarantees that the stockinet underwear is made of undyed "Natural" yarns, in place of yarns dyed to look like "Natural" color.

It makes a successful stand against the Dishonesty of Adulteration, and is accepted by the general public as a guarantee against adulteration—a proof that Honesty is the Best Policy.

Adulterated and otherwise inferior Imitations of the garments designed and popularized by Dr. JAEGER are offered by unscrupulous traders as "JAEGER" goods; and as Cotton is much less costly than Wool, the mixture can be sold more cheaply than the pare material, which, however, is far more healthy, comfortable and economical in the end.

The penalties for imitating a Trade-mark are so severe that the Public may rely on the genuineness of underwear which bears the above Brand; and the JAEGER Company venture to appeal to consumers, in their own interest and in that of commercial honesty, to note and make use of this certain means of detecting and rejecting, Spurious so-called "JAEGER" underwear.

■ ■ ■

The Genuine Dr. Jaeger Underwear is manufactured by the Renowned Firm of Wilh. Benger Soehne, of Stuttgart, under the Supervision of Dr. G. Jaeger.

Further Resources

BOOKS

Crane, Diana. *Fashion and Its Social Agendas: Class, Gender, and Identity in Clothing.* Chicago: University of Chicago Press, 2000.

Cunnington, C. Willett, and Phillis Cunnington. *The History of Underclothes.* New York: Dover, 1992.

Waugh, Norah. *Corsets and Crinolines.* New York: Routledge Press, 1954.

PERIODICALS

Kesselman, Amy. "The 'Freedom Suit': Feminism and Dress Reform in the United States, 1848–1975." *Gender and Society* 5, 1991, 495–510.

WEBSITES

Cunningham, Patricia. "Reforming Fashion, 1850–1914." The Historic Costume & Textile Collection, The Ohio State University. Available online at http://costume.osu.edu/Reforming_Fashion/reformdress.htm; website home page: http://costume.osu.edu/ (accessed February 22, 2003).

Doak, Melissa and Melissa Karetny. "How Did Diverse Activists Shape the Nineteenth-Century Dress Reform Movement?" In *Women and Social Movements in the United States, 1775–2000.* State University of New York at Binghamton. Available online at http://womhist.binghamton.edu/dress/intro.htm; website home page: http://womhist.binghamton.edu/index.html (accessed February, 2003). This site contains a collection of primary documents pertaining to women and social movements.

Thomas, Pauline Weston. "Rational Dress Reform." Available online at http://www.fashion-era.com/rational_dress.htm; website home page: http://www.fashion-era.com/ (accessed February 22, 2003).

"Houses Unique in Interest"

Magazine article

By: Alice M. Kellogg

Date: 1906

Source: Kellogg, Alice M. "Houses Unique in Interest." *The Delineator,* April 1906, 696–697.

About the Author: Alice M. Kellogg (1862–1911) was an author of occasional pieces such as this one in *The Delineator.* She wrote about matters of household decoration and taste, giving advice to women on fashion in the home, much as other writers advised about clothing. ■

Introduction

Women's magazines of the day provided advice on every aspect of living, from what to wear to parenting and home decorating advice. Kellogg's article is similar to many that filled these magazines. Their audience could be found in the rising middle classes—those who could afford to purchase or build new homes and decorate them as well. The heavy, ornately decorated, often stuffy Victorian interiors were going out of style, to be replaced by simpler styles that could be more easily mass-produced and yet retain a reasonable quality of workmanship and materials. The bungalows represented a move away from crowded city interiors to somewhat more spacious urban or even suburban lots. In their style and details, they also represent numerous socio-demographic changes as well as an alteration in the national aesthetic.

Prior to 1907, fewer than 10 percent of American homes had electrical power, a figure that would grow to 35 percent by 1920. The interior shown here is thus on the cutting edge of what middle class housing would resemble in the years to come. Increasingly, writers for popular magazines were calling for increased consideration of children's roles, both in society and in families. Instead of relegating children to distant rooms of the house where they were cared for by hired professionals out of sight and earshot of their parents, the new philosophy of parenting called for them to be more closely integrated into the family. Interior decorating was now taking into consideration the activities and needs of children, even including special rooms for their play whenever possible. There were many Americans who could afford the new bungalow styles and they followed the advice of columnists such as Kellogg in decorating their new living spaces. There were also still tens of thousands in the cities and countryside for whom such a home would forever remain an impossible dream.

Significance

"Birdcliff," the house described and pictured in this detailed article, was an excellent example of the Arts and Crafts style, a derivative from the low, broad houses initiated by Louis Sullivan and perfected by Frank Lloyd Wright. The details of this article show the extent to which those original ideas had been modified for a broader market, that of the growing middle class, the clientele for whom articles such as Kellogg's were written and who might have built and furnished such homes. The article also shows the full interpretation of the Arts and Crafts style in the interior. Often called Mission Style or Craftsman Style, the related strains reflected the common element of the leading architects, which was to develop a style that was unique to America, modern in the sense that it was not a repetition of earlier stylistic periods. The new style required excellent craftsmanship using high quality materials, and was made available to a broad spectrum of the population.

Kellogg does not identify the furniture manufacturers, but the styles are clearly in the manner of Elbert Hubbard (founder of the popular Roycroft furniture) and Gustav Stickley. The linear, often rustic designs emphasized value and durability with their smooth, heavy expanses of wood. Rather than applied ornamentation, the pieces relied on the richness of the wood grain and the form of the piece for its beauty. Details of the joinery were frequently visible in these pieces, adding interest to the design. Drawer pulls, door handles, and hinges of hammered metal provided another source of ornamentation that still met the requirement of function. By the time of Kellogg's article in 1906, Mission style furniture was widely available for both private and public buildings, and the popular press played a significant role in showing how it could be used to complete the aesthetic statement of the new democratic architecture.

Further Resources

BOOKS

Duchscherer, Paul, and Douglas Keister. *Inside the Bungalow: America's Arts & Crafts Interior.* Toronto: Penguin Canada, 1997.

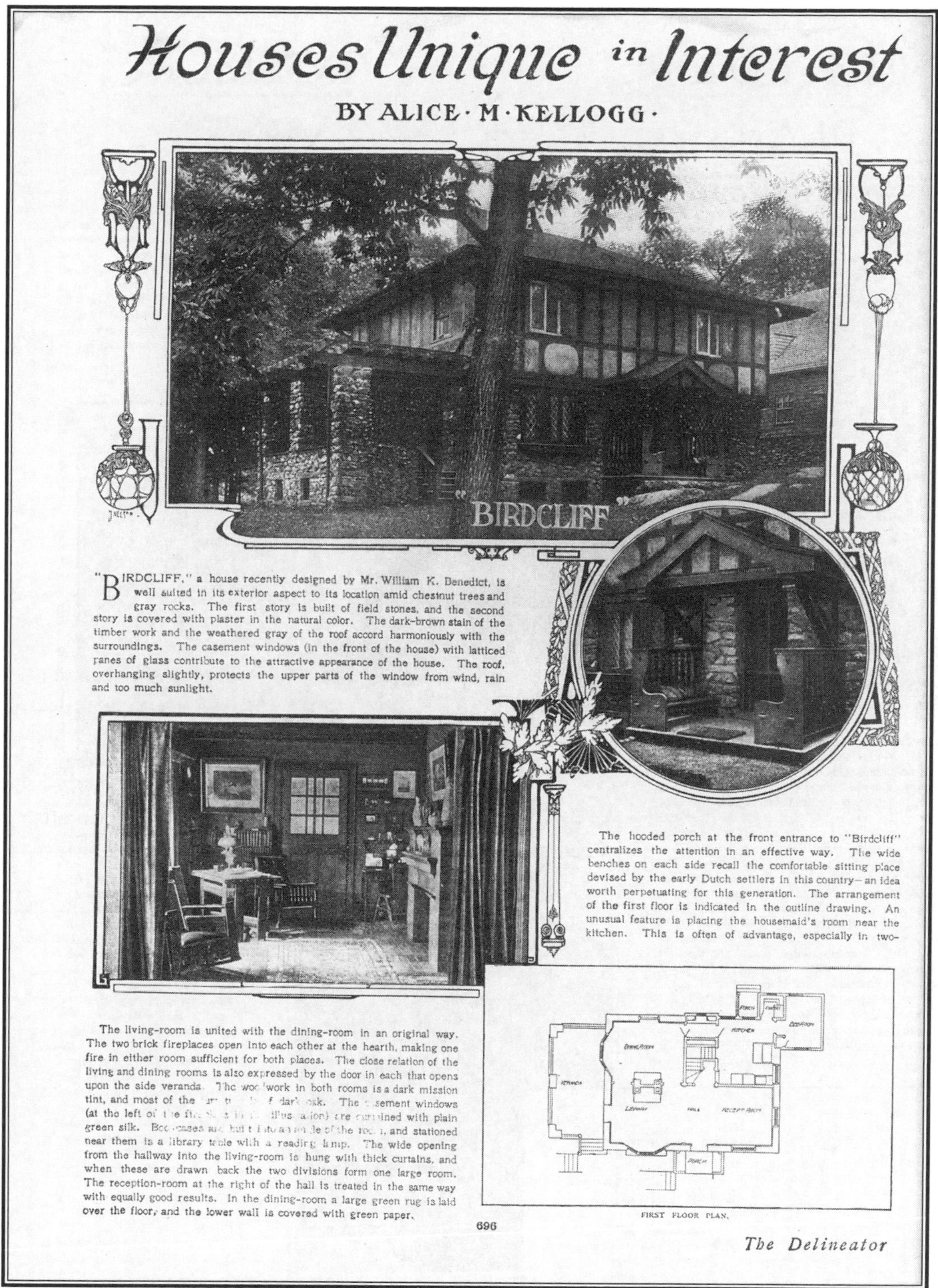

Houses Unique in Interest

BY ALICE · M · KELLOGG ·

"BIRDCLIFF"

"BIRDCLIFF," a house recently designed by Mr. William K. Benedict, is well suited in its exterior aspect to its location amid chestnut trees and gray rocks. The first story is built of field stones, and the second story is covered with plaster in the natural color. The dark-brown stain of the timber work and the weathered gray of the roof accord harmoniously with the surroundings. The casement windows (in the front of the house) with latticed panes of glass contribute to the attractive appearance of the house. The roof, overhanging slightly, protects the upper parts of the window from wind, rain and too much sunlight.

The hooded porch at the front entrance to "Birdcliff" centralizes the attention in an effective way. The wide benches on each side recall the comfortable sitting place devised by the early Dutch settlers in this country—an idea worth perpetuating for this generation. The arrangement of the first floor is indicated in the outline drawing. An unusual feature is placing the housemaid's room near the kitchen. This is often of advantage, especially in two-

The living-room is united with the dining-room in an original way. The two brick fireplaces open into each other at the hearth, making one fire in either room sufficient for both places. The close relation of the living and dining rooms is also expressed by the door in each that opens upon the side veranda. The woodwork in both rooms is a dark mission tint, and most of the [illegible] dark oak. The [illegible]sement windows (at the left of [illegible] illustration) are [illegible]ined with plain green silk. Boo[illegible] of the roo[illegible], and stationed near them is a library table with a reading lamp. The wide opening from the hallway into the living-room is hung with thick curtains, and when these are drawn back the two divisions form one large room. The reception-room at the right of the hall is treated in the same way with equally good results. In the dining-room a large green rug is laid over the floor, and the lower wall is covered with green paper.

FIRST FLOOR PLAN.

696

The Delineator

Primary Source

"Houses Unique in Interest" (1 OF 2)

SYNOPSIS: This article in a popular women's magazine shows the extent to which the architectural vision of Louis Sullivan and Frank Lloyd Wright, and the interior furnishing styles of Elbert Hubbard and Gustav Stickley, were being realized in a broad segment of American life. THE DELINEATOR, APRIL 1906, P. 696.

WITH FLOOR PLANS AND INTERIOR VIEWS

The living piazza in any home has requirements on quite a different scale from those of the entrance porch. In "Birdcliff," distinction is given to the latter by its architectural conception. The solidity of the out-door sitting place is expressed by the rugged stone work of the supports for the roof and the open beams of the ceiling. The projection of the beams gives an opportunity for vines to add their graceful decoration in Summer time to the stone and wood of the piazza. The wide ledges of the stone work around the piazza are available for plant boxes, and they take the place of seats. Steps to the front yard are not overlooked in planning the living porch, and in their introduction the simplicity of line that characterizes the main part of "Birdcliff" is followed.

story houses, where all of the second floor is required for members of the family. The light, well-ventilated cellar in "Birdcliff," divided into laundry, furnace, storage and workroom, yields almost the space of a third floor. The architectural lines of the interior of "Birdcliff" are illustrative of the healthful reaction from an earlier and popular style of over-ornamented woodwork in which stair rails and hall pillars played a conspicuous part. The charm of simple lines so evident here can never be thoroughly appreciated until compared with others ornate, cheap and showy. The wood finish in the hall is a shade of green that shows well on the open grain of the chestnut. The panels are filled with Japanese leather paper, and the floor is partially covered with foreign rugs. The electric lighting is artistically carried out in small square lanterns of dull-colored brass filled with amber glass. On the second floor the four chambers are assured a full measure of length and breadth from the almost square outlines of the plan.

A glimpse of "Birdcliff" through the unique gateway, designed by Mr. Wilson Eyre for an adjacent dwelling, gives an idea of the pictorial possibilities for moderate-priced houses that are being achieved in the present day. We have much to glean from the past in domestic architecture, and with the raising of the standard of art in all its useful and decorative lines, the modern home stands for a much more subtle, interesting type than that of even a few years back. The inflammable character of shingled and straight-boarded houses has drawn attention to other materials for construction, and whenever the locality will provide stones or brick, the increase in expense is not so great as when these materials must be brought from a distance. The growing interest in the use of cement, stucco and concrete is not only satisfactory as a precaution against fire but as a m[illegible] for securing [illegible] effe[illegible] [illegible]ut are not [illegible] woo[illegible] buildings. [illegible] than those sho[illegible]n in [illegible] illustr[illegible]tions "Birdcliff" has some radi[illegible] departures from the ordinary suburban or country house. These are evidence of the appreciation of a more simple disposition of the home interior.

SECOND FLOOR PLAN.

697

for April, 1906

Primary Source

"Houses Unique in Interest" (2 OF 2)

Second page of "Houses Unique in Interest," by Alice M. Kellogg from *The Delineator,* April 1906. THE DELINEATOR, APRIL 1906, P. 697.

Craftsman style furniture decorates the lounging room of the Nast Hotel in Nast, Colorado, circa 1900. **WESTERN HISTORY/GENEALOGY DEPARTMENT, DENVER PUBLIC LIBRARY.**

Ewald, Chase Reynolds. *Arts & Crafts Style & Spirit: Craftspeople of the Revival.* Salt Lake City: Gibbs Smith Publisher, 1999.

Mayer, Barbara, Rob Gray, and Elaine Hirschl Ellis. *In the Arts & Crafts Style.* San Francisco: Chronicle Books, 1992.

Via, Maria, and Marjorie Searl, eds. *Head, Heart, and Hand: Elbert Hubbard and the Roycrofters.* New York: University of Rochester Press, 1994.

Wallace, Ann. *Arts & Crafts Textiles.* Salt Lake City: Gibbs Smith Publisher, 1999.

WEBSITES

American Bungalow. Available online at www.ambungalow.com/ (accessed May 16, 2003.)

"The Arts & Crafts Society." Available online at http://www.arts-crafts.com/ (accessed February 22, 2003). This website has excellent sources for information on all aspects of bungalow life, including furniture and findings.

"Arts & Crafts, Craftsman or Mission Antiques." Available online at http://www.ragtime.org/miss/index.html; website home page: http://www.ragtime.org/ (accessed February 22, 2003).

"The Webpage of the Roycrofters." Available online at http://www.roycrofter.com (accessed February 22, 2003).

Changes in Textiles and Advertising

"Heatherbloom Petticoats"

Advertisement

By: A.G. Hyde & Sons

Date: 1908

Source: A.G. Hyde & Sons. "Heatherbloom Petticoats." *The Delineator,* April 1908, 631. ■

"Here Is the Truth About Dyes"

Advertisement

By: Wells & Richardson Co.
Date: 1906
Source: Wells & Richardson Co. "Here Is the Truth About Dyes." *The Delineator,* April 1906, 740.

Introduction

The advertisement for Diamond dyes shows the extent to which the synthetic dyeing industry had progressed from the first dye introduction in 1856. Up until that point, all textile colorants were derived from natural products (plant, animal, or mineral sources) and required fairly extensive preparations to achieve inconsistent results. By the time of this ad's publication in 1906, the entire process of making and using textile dyes had changed, with the result that the consuming public required some education in the use of the new products. The use of natural dyes had a long cultural and technical history, with specific colors, natural sources, and processes associated with specific fibers among the limited number then available. The Wells & Richardson Company of Burlington, Vermont, wanted the users of their products to be successful in their dyeing attempts so that they would become repeat customers. Their instructional advertisement contains not only print samples of the full spectrum of their dye colors, but also an elementary lesson in textile science.

The advertisement for Heatherbloom petticoats, by contrast, is a study in lack of technical information. The fabric from which the petticoats are made is compared to silk (just as beautiful, less expensive, and three times more durable), but there is never a clear statement about just what this new fabric is. In fact, the only possibility at this time would have been rayon, the first manufactured fiber. The vague but laudatory language in this ad for A.G. Hyde & Sons, the makers of Hydegrade fabrics, was not necessarily an advertising ploy to keep consumers from knowing the true content, but probably a result of some confusion about just what this new fiber was to be called. The industry of manufacturing fibers was yet so young there were no standards governing the nomenclature and no legal constraints about truth in advertising. Like many other manufacturers of fabric and clothing, Hyde was pushing a fashion product and trying to be economically successful.

Significance

These advertisements illustrate what was to be a dramatic revolution in the technology required to produce and finish textile products, and a corresponding shift in how textile products were consumed. During the 1900s, the public was still primarily consuming familiar prod-

Primary Source

"Heatherbloom Petticoats" (1 OF 2)

SYNOPSIS: This April 1908 advertisement for Heatherbloom Petticoats claims that the material in Heatherbloom Petticoats feels just like silk, but without identifying the fabric. In contrast, the Diamond Dyes ad attempts to educate consumers with detailed information. THE DELINEATOR, APRIL 1908.

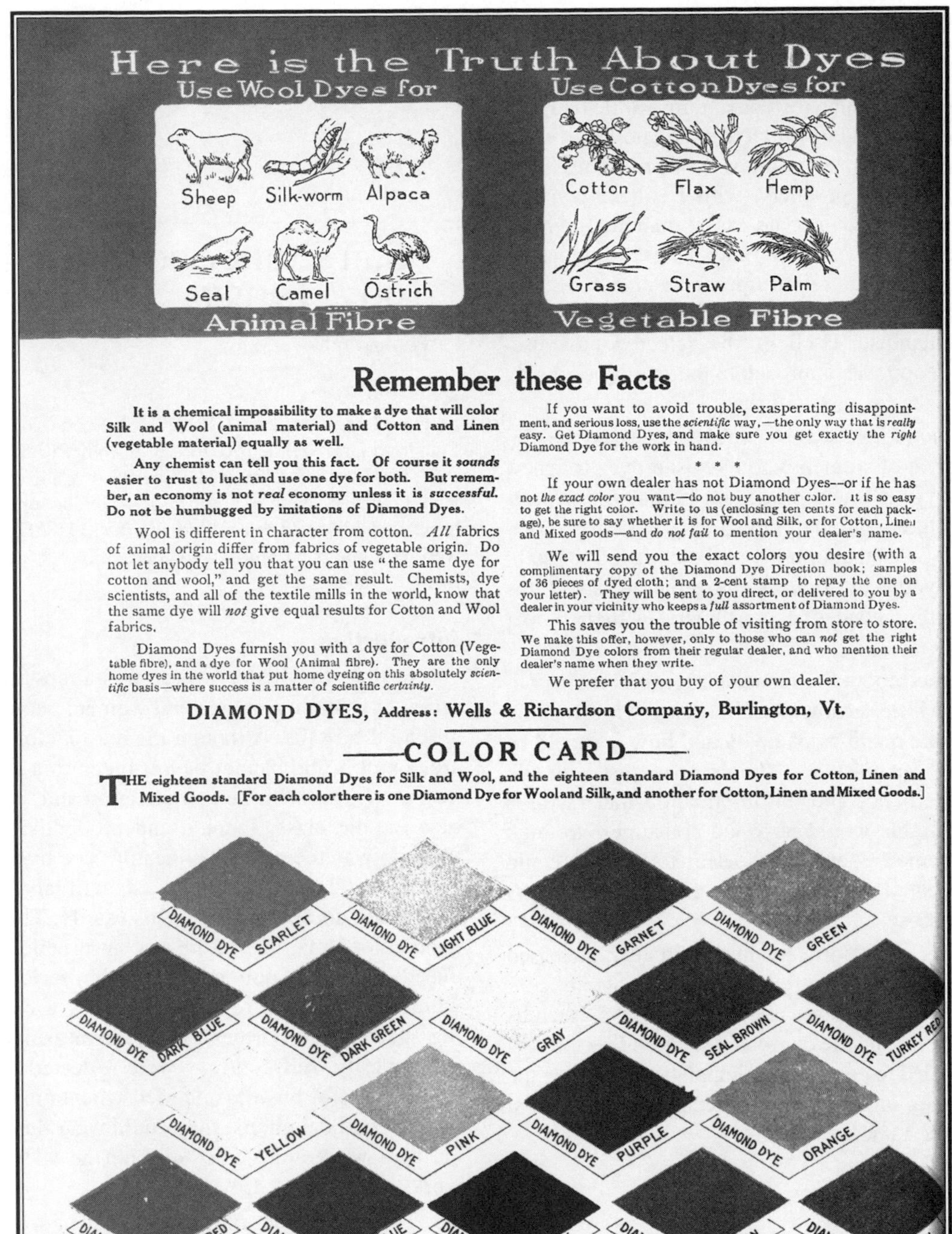

Primary Source

"Here Is the Truth About Dyes" (2 OF 2)

Advertisement for Diamond Dyes produced by the Wells & Richardson Company. THE DELINEATOR, APRIL 1906, P. 732.

ucts and using them to satisfy their household needs. But this picture would rapidly change as the new technologies multiplied exponentially and created a plethora of new products about which the consuming public had very little information and with which they had no experience. Advertising thus assumed a dual role of providing information and hawking products, with frequent conflicts between the two roles. In some cases, manufacturers attempted to educate consumers about these changes; in other cases, advertisers relied upon consumers' lack of clear information to make dubious claims about the unfamiliar merchandise. Each of the selected advertisements takes an opposite approach to the rapidly changing technology in the fashion industry.

The Diamond Dye advertisement appeals to the previous experience of women who had used dyes to renew old textiles or finish new ones, and perhaps represents the germ of today's infomercials. Such marketing strategies—and the firms that employed them—tried to establish brand loyalty by sharing information about the products and thus educating consumers in their proper use.

The Heatherbloom Petticoats advertisement, in contrast, provides little technical and no useful information about the unique qualities of rayon and how it should be cared for most successfully. The comparisons with silk in terms of aesthetics and the implication that rayon is much more durable would have led consumers to think this new, unnamed fiber was superior to silk but could probably be treated in the same way. In fact, both claims were patently false.

Both types of advertisements ultimately increased the amount of product information available to consumers, albeit with questionable strategies. Ads such as Heatherbloom's—and the confusion surrounding the new textile fibers—led to government legislation requiring the accurate labeling of all textile products with the natural or generic fiber name.

Further Resources

BOOKS

Kadolph, Sara, and Anna Langford. *Textiles,* 9th ed. Englewood Cliffs, N.J.: Prentice Hall, 2001.

Tortora, Phyllis G., Robert S. Merkel, and Phyllis B. Tortora, eds. *Fairchild's Dictionary of Textiles,* 7th ed. New York: Fairchild, 1996.

WEBSITES

"A Short History of Manufactured Fibers." Fibersource.com. Available online at http://www.fibersource.com/f-tutor/history.htm; website home page: http://www.fibersource.com/fiber.html (accessed February 23, 2003).

"A Short History of Microfiber." Googalies.com. Available online at http://www.googalies.com/microfsa.html; website home page: http://www.googalies.com (accessed December 8, 2002).

"Timeline." *Emergence of Advertising in America: 1850–1920.* Available online at http://scriptorium.lib.duke.edu/eaa/timeline.html; website home page: http://scriptorium.lib.duke.edu (accessed February 23, 2003).

"San Francisco Graft Trial, 1907–1908"

Photographs

Date: 1907–1908

Source: Image numbers 02613, 02614, and 02617. "San Francisco Graft Trial, 1907–1908. BANK PIC 1905.0261-PIC, The Bancroft Library, University of California, Berkeley." Online Archive of California. Available online at http://findaid.oac.cdlib.org/findaid/ark:/13030/tf7p30102q; website home page: http://www.oac.cdlib.org/ (accessed February 22, 2003). ■

Introduction

For most of history, there was almost equal elaboration of costume for men and women, but that changed around the 1840s. Although the reasons for this change are complex and cannot be attributed to a single event, they coincided with industrialization and the expansion of a middle class. Income and productivity, not aristocracy, was the social delineator. The businessman of the industrial society was not a man of land and leisure; he worked and provided for his family. The more subdued colors, plainer and more comfortable cut, and reduced ornamentation spoke of the seriousness with which businessmen regarded this new way of organizing society. The virtues of the businessman—reliability, integrity, self-control—were reflected in his attire. The successful businessman left ostentation in dress to his wife and daughters; they could wear the evidence of his hard work and dedication, but he was too hard at work to be bothered.

The new basic silhouette for men's business and most social attire has never changed. Tailors were influential, acting as personal fashion advisors to men who could afford their services. Menswear manufacturers were obviously influenced by what the tailors made, just as the men who purchased their goods were influenced by the attire of businessmen who patronized those tailors. Theirs was a subtle influence, but no less important than the fashion magazines that decreed what women would wear season by season and hour by hour.

There were, of course, many variations in the clothing that was worn by men, and these variations reflected their income and social levels. Quality of fabric was one important distinction, with the best wool and silks made

Primary Source

San Francisco Graft Trial, 1907–1908 (1 OF 3)

SYNOPSIS: Photographs of the prosecuted and the prosecuting during one of the most famous corruption trials of the century show an amazing consistency of appearance and a clothing style that would last virtually unchanged for the next hundred years. The "Big Four" Graft trial prosecutors illustrate fashions worn by professional men, circa 1907. COURTESY OF THE BANCROFT LIBRARY, UNIVERSITY OF CALIFORNIA, BERKELEY. REPRODUCED BY PERMISSION.

to measure by either private or commercial tailors. The cut and fit of these suits was impeccable and contrasted with the lower middle class businessmen's suits that were bought off the rack (ready made) and made of poorer quality cloth. Those same distinctions applied to the minor wardrobe components as well. Not all businessmen could afford whole shirts, regardless of cloth quality, and used detachable collars and cuffs or partial shirt fronts to give the illusion of a dress shirt. Only upon close inspection could some of these minor differences in quality—and class—be differentiated.

Significance

The series of photographs show the similarity of men's dress during this decade. The photograph "Curly Boss" is an image of Abraham Reuf, who was one of the key figures in an extensive and famous graft trial of city officials and a host of agents from utility and transportation companies. Reuf, believed to have been one of the key players, if not the mastermind, in the complicated series of schemes, is shown here on the courthouse steps during the trial. He could have been posing for a fashion photograph, given his demeanor and his carefully groomed appearance, but instead he was caught leaving the scene of his own criminal trial. The remaining photographs show some of the prosecutors in the trial. Only the captions identify the differences between the lawyers and the criminals. Regardless of which side of law and order the men could be found, they were well dressed in nearly identical clothing.

Primary Source

San Francisco Graft Trial, 1907–1908 (2 OF 3)

Men wearing hats and suits typical of the decade and professional status gather outside of the courthouse during the Graft Trial, circa 1907. COURTESY OF THE BANCROFT LIBRARY, UNIVERSITY OF CALIFORNIA, BERKELEY. REPRODUCED BY PERMISSION.

Many members of the rising business and professional classes of the early 1900s had to work their way up to their current class standing. For the men, in particular, competing successfully in business or in politics required that one look as well as play the part. The business suit became the uniform for identifying the members of this group. It set them apart from laborers and signified to the world that they were men of substance and importance, hence deserving of trust and respect. Corrupt officials, inhumane manufacturers, unethical businessmen, or unscrupulous clergy were able to blend, chameleon-like, with their respectable associates. They were thus able to win the trust of an uneducated public using appearance as the sole means of communication. That aspect of clothing, like the men's business suit, has been a stable component of fashionable clothing and behavior over time.

Further Resources

BOOKS

DeMarly, Diana. *Fashion for Men: An Illustrated History.* New York: Holmes & Meier, 1985.

Martin, Richard and Harold Koda. *Jocks and Nerds: Men's Style in the Twentieth Century.* New York: Rizzoli, 1989.

Smith, Barbara C. and Kathy Peiss. *Men and Women: A History of Costume, Gender, and Power.* Washington, D.C.:

Primary Source

San Francisco Graft Trial, 1907–1908 (3 OF 3)
A typical men's business suit of the 1900s as worn by Abe Ruef during the San Francisco Graft Trials, 1907. COURTESY OF THE BANCROFT LIBRARY, UNIVERSITY OF CALIFORNIA, BERKELEY. REPRODUCED BY PERMISSION.

National Museum of American History;Smithsonian Institution, 1989.

Steel, Valerie. "Appearance and Identity." In *Men and Women: Dressing the Part.* Washington, D.C.: Smithsonian Institution Press, 1989.

WEBSITES

"Arrow." Available online at http://www.arrowshirt.com/about_us.cfm?CFID=690877&CFTOKEN;=11073012 (accessed February 22, 2003). The site has a history of the Arrow shirt with images of details by decades.

"Men's Togs Catalogue: 1910 Menswear Fashion Trends." Available online at http://www.costumegallery.com/1910/Men/Suits/ (accessed February 22, 2003).

Sears Modern Homes Catalogues

"Modern Home No. 125"; "Modern Home No. 144"

Architectural designs

By: Sears, Roebuck and Company

Date: 1908; 1909

Source: Sears, Roebuck and Company. *1908 Modern Homes Catalogue.* Chicago: 1908; 54. Sears, Roebuck and Company. *1909 Modern Homes Catalogue.* Chicago: 1909, 26.

About the Company: Sears, Roebuck and Company was founded in 1893, a partnership between Richard Sears and Alvah Roebuck. The firm quickly became a household name, delivering goods at lower prices than local stores and making a consistent style and quality of goods available across America. When the new Sears, Roebuck and Company building opened on Chicago's south side in 1906, it was the largest business building at that time in the world. ■

Introduction

During the decade that Sears and other purveyors introduced houses from kits, ownership of automobiles increased from about eight thousand to over four hundred sixty thousand, ushering in the birth of the suburb. Calls for a new American architecture had been answered by Louis Sullivan, Frank Lloyd Wright, and many of their followers, and were now being reinterpreted on a more frugal and simplified scale to meet the needs of urban and rural members of the growing middle class. The members of this class were less likely than in previous times to have the time and skills needed to design, draw up the plans, and construct their own homes. Indoor plumbing and electricity required more skilled labor for installation than many amateur carpenters or home builders had, as well. The kits filled a growing need for providing expertise in

$945.00 Builds This $1,500.00 to $1,800.00 Eight-Room Bungalow Style House

AN IDEAL COTTAGE FOR A SUMMER HOME OR WATERING RESORT.

This extremely low price is made possible by the very plain and economical arrangement of this house, our building plans as explained on page 2, and the extremely low prices we ask for the material which we furnish at half regular prices.

MODERN HOME No. 125

By referring to the floor plan you will note that the side bedrooms consist of large rooms 25 feet in length by 10 feet in width, which are divided into three fair size, well lighted and ventilated bedrooms. This bungalow has a large living room with brick mantel and open fireplace which is built in the rustic style. Large and spacious porch 33 feet in length by 8 feet in width.

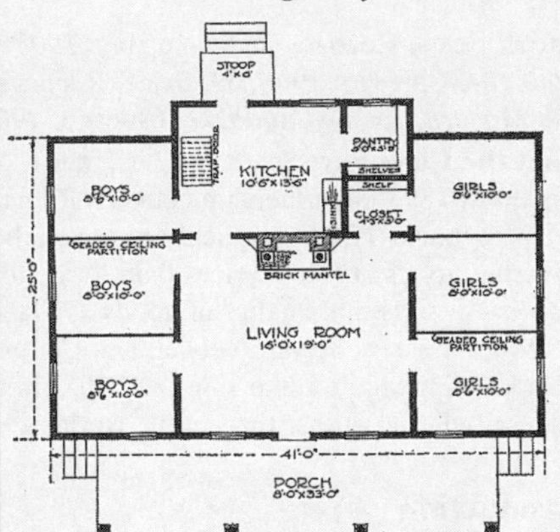

The arrangement of this house is as follows:

Living Room	16 feet by 19 feet
Four Bedrooms	8 feet 6 inches by 10 feet
Two Bedrooms	8 feet by 10 feet
Kitchen	13 feet 6 inches by 10 feet 6 inches
Pantry	5 feet by 5 feet 9 inches
Closet	4 feet 3 inches by 5 feet
Front Porch	33 feet by 8 feet
Height of Ceiling	10 feet 4 inches

Cellar, 10 feet by 18 feet, 6 feet deep, with frame foundation

IF YOU ARE CONTEMPLATING BUILDING A COUNTRY COTTAGE

do not overlook the fact that this is the finest cottage ever constructed at a price less than $1,500.00, and if built according to our plans, specifications and bill of materials can be built for $945.00. These plans cost you nothing, as fully explained on page 2. The deposit of $1.00 to be sent with your request, is applied as cash on your order for mill work amounting to $10.00 or more.

Sears, Roebuck & Co., Chicago, Ill. —54— **BOOK OF MODERN HOMES**

Primary Source

Modern Home No. 125 (1 OF 2)

SYNOPSIS: Two catalog offerings for Sears, Roebuck and Company mail-order houses show the floor plans, dimensions, and intended uses for a new type of housing for middle-class Americans and reflect the changing demographics of the country in the new century. FROM THE COLLECTION OF ROBERT SCHWEITZER, DIRECTOR OF RESEARCH FOR THE ARTS & CRAFTS SOCIETY (WWW.ARTS-CRAFTS.COM)

$882.00 PAYS FOR ALL THE MATERIAL

FOR THIS FANCY NINE-ROOM TWO-STORY BUNGALOW WITH BATHROOM.

This price includes the Mill Work, Ceiling, Siding, Flooring and Finishing Lumber, Building Paper, Pipe, Gutter, Sash Weights, Mantel, Hardware, Painting Materials and Lumber. By allowing a fair price for labor this house can be built for $1,850.00.

ON PAGE 2 WE EXPLAIN HOW YOU CAN GET PLANS, SPECIFICATIONS AND BILL OF MATERIALS FOR THIS HOUSE FOR NOTHING.

MODERN HOME No. 144

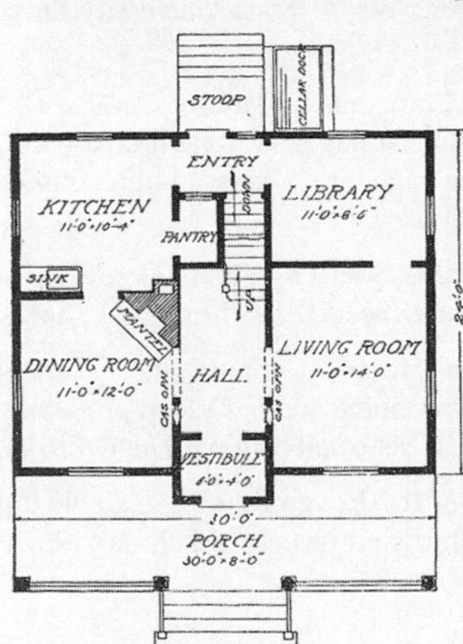

For the above price we will furnish a high grade of material, as you will note by some of the following items: Windsor front door, glazed with leaded glass; clear five-cross panel inside doors; solid yellow pine trim throughout the house; clear gum or hazelwood floor; mantel for living room; clear yellow pine stair material for open stairway.

Measurement of house, 30 feet wide by 24 feet long. Porch, 8 feet wide by 30 feet long. Basement under entire building, 6 feet 6 inches from floor to joists. First story, 9 feet from floor to ceiling. Second story, 8 feet from floor to ceiling.

This house would ordinarily cost $2,800.00 to $3,000.00 if you purchased from your local dealer a high grade of material equal to what we furnish, and obtained your plans from your local architect; but by furnishing you a set of plans more complete than 95 per cent of the plans furnished by ordinary architects and supplying our strictly high grade of material at least 35 to 50 per cent cheaper than you could buy it from other sources, we make it possible for you to build this house for $1,850.00. The first story of this house is sided with narrow beveled siding and the second story with shingles, which produces a very rich effect.

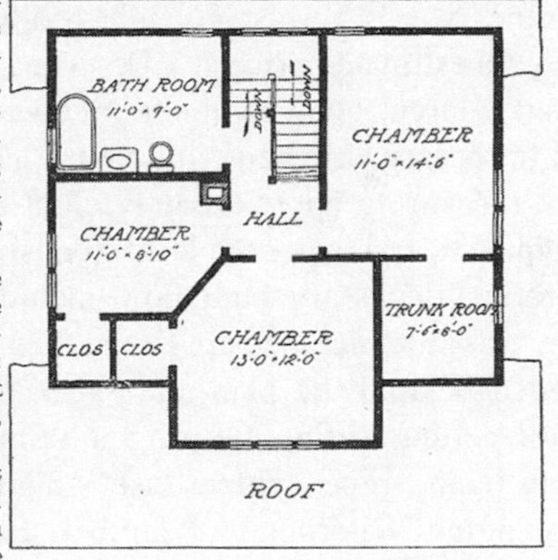

Complete Hot Air Heating Plant, for soft coal, extra	$ 84.34
Complete Hot Air Heating Plant, for hard coal, extra	86.60
Complete Steam Heating Plant, extra	162.65
Complete Hot Water Heating Plant, extra	193.30
Complete Plumbing Outfit, extra	108.39

Sears, Roebuck & Co., Chicago, Ill. —26— BOOK OF MODERN HOMES

Primary Source

Modern Home No. 144 (2 OF 2)

This page from the 1909 Sears, Roebuck & Co. catalog offers plans and materials for a typical two-story bungalow. FROM THE COLLECTION OF ROBERT SCHWEITZER, DIRECTOR OF RESEARCH FOR THE ARTS & CRAFTS SOCIETY (WWW.ARTS-CRAFTS.COM)

design, materials, and construction details all in one handy, economical package. During the years that Sears offered the homes catalogs (1908–1940), the company is reported to have sold over ten thousand homes.

This new way of housing the populace was offered by other companies as well, including Ye Planry and Aladdin (purported to be the first to offer kit houses), among others. The total estimated output of homes sold through catalogs is estimated to have approached half a million between 1900 and World War II (1939–1945). Originally advertised as summer or vacation cottages, the ready-made houses captured a growing share of the housing market with their innovative way to build affordable housing. The styles became familiar in small towns across America, as the simplified interpretations of Prairie Style architecture dispersed throughout all levels of society. The similarity between the first "prefab" housing and locally designed and built bungalows is so great that restoration experts have to use catalog images and text to identify extant houses.

Significance

Considered together, the floor plans and building information give an excellent means of comparison to the Prairie Style homes which began the movement. Consistent with their prices, the catalog homes were much simpler, smaller, and less ornamented. Only the basic external lines are suggestive of their aesthetic origins. Modern Home No. 125 was an eight-room bungalow style house with estimated price at $945. The simple floor plan featured a large, open living room focused on the fireplace, a fairly large kitchen with pantry, and six bedrooms, each measuring approximately eight by ten feet. Modern Home No. 144 was even less expensive, at $882. That nine-room, two story bungalow included a bathroom. (One was not included in Home 125.) A list of items included beyond the plan and specifications was for mill work, ceiling, siding, flooring and finishing lumber, building paper, pipe, gutter, sash weights, mantel, hardware, painting materials and lumber. Heating systems and plumbing were extra—indicative of a time when many rural and urban homes were heated by fireplaces or small stoves alone. The provision for including a centralized heating system places these houses in a transitional period with regard to heat sources. Both houses included a basement or cellar for placement of the heating system.

Omission of a bathroom in the earlier plan helps identify the time period and the socioeconomic level of the intended client more closely. Many rural houses did not have indoor plumbing until much later in the twentieth century. One other omission in both sets of plans also speaks to market niche and changing demographics of the consuming public. While all of the grander houses in the first emergence of the Prairie or Arts and Crafts style had designated space for a servant or servants, the houses shown here do not, and they are reflective of how the majority of middle class people lived and would continue to live in America.

Further Resources

BOOKS

Cathers, David M. *Stickley Style: Arts and Crafts Home in the Craftsman Tradition.* New York: Simon and Schuster, 1999.

Mayer, Barbara, Rob Gray, and Elaine Hirschl Ellis. *In the Arts & Crafts Style.* San Francisto: Chronicle Books, 1992.

Schweitzer, Robert, and Michael Davis. *America's Favorite Homes.* Detroit: Wayne State University Press, 1990.

WEBSITES

"Arts & Crafts, Craftsman or Mission Antiques." Ragtime.org. Available online at http://www.ragtime.org/miss/index.html; website home page: http://www.ragtime.org/ (accessed February 23, 2003).

"The Arts & Crafts Society." Available online at http://www.arts-crafts.com/ (accessed February 23, 2003).

"The Craftsman Homes Connection." Available online at http://www.crafthome.com/. Offers products for sale, including a 2-CD set of all original *The Craftsman Magazine.*

"The Webpage of the Roycrofters." Available online at http://www.roycrofter.com (accessed February 23, 2003).

5

Government and Politics

James N. Craft

Entries are arranged in chronological order by date of primary source. For entries with one primary source, the entry title is the same as the primary source title. Entries with more than one primary source have an overall entry title, followed by the titles of the primary sources.

CHRONOLOGY

PRIMARY SOURCES

Important Events in Government and Politics, 1900–1909

1900

- On January 2, Secretary of State John Hay announces that he has completed negotiations for the "Open Door" policy in China.
- On February 6, President William McKinley appoints William Howard Taft, a federal circuit judge, to head the Philippine Commission to establish a civil government in the islands.
- On March 9, the Social Democratic Party meeting in Indianapolis, Indiana nominates the Socialist Eugene V. Debs of Indiana for President and Job Harrison of California as Vice-President.
- On March 24, the new Carnegie Steel Company is incorporated in New Jersey in violation of the Sherman Antitrust Law of 1890. The law has proven ineffective in preventing the establishment of industrial monopolies. Capitalized at $160 million, Carnegie Steel is the largest incorporation to date.
- On April 4, Admiral George Dewey, naval hero of the Spanish-American War, announces his willingness to be a candidate for the presidency.
- On April 12, the Organic Act for Civil Government extends American navigation laws and federal statutes to Puerto Rico. Island residents are Puerto Rican citizens, except those Spaniards who elect to remain Spaniards.
- On April 13, for the fourth time in eight years, the House of Representatives adopts a resolution favoring a constitutional amendment for the election of United States Senators by direct vote of the people instead of by state legislatures. The Senate concurs in 1911.
- On April 30, Congress grants the Hawaii Islands territorial status, joining Alaska, Oklahoma, New Mexico, and Arizona as American territories. Sanford B. Dole is appointed governor of the new territory.
- On May 9, a splinter group of the Populist Party, meeting in Cincinnati, Ohio, nominates Wharton Barker of Pennsylvania for President and Ignatius Donnelly of Minnesota for Vice-President. On the same day, the main branch of the Populist Party, meeting in Sioux Falls, South Dakota, nominates William Jennings Bryan for President and Charles A. Towne for Vice-President.
- On May 14, the United States Supreme Court rules that the inheritance tax, levied for the first time under the War Revenue Act of 1898, is constitutional.
- On June 2, the Socialist Labor Party meeting in New York City nominates Joseph P. Maloney of Massachusetts for President and Valentine Remmel of Pennsylvania for Vice-President.
- From June 19 to June 21, the Republican National Convention meeting in Philadelphia nominates President William McKinley for a second term. The convention nominates the "Rough Rider," Theodore Roosevelt, for Vice-President. The platform endorses the gold standard, an aggressive foreign policy, and an isthmian canal to be constructed, owned, and controlled by the United States.
- On June 27, the National Prohibition Party nominates John G. Wooley of Illinois for President and Henry B. Metcalf of Rhode Island for Vice-President.
- On July 3, Chinese revolutionaries are prevented from killing the diplomats trapped in the British legation by the timely arrival of American, British, Japanese, and French troops. In the aftermath of the revolt, Secretary of State Hay issues a second "Open Door" note reiterating the need to protect Chinese territorial integrity and to leave all parts of China open to equal and impartial trade.
- From July 4 to July 6, the Democratic National Convention nominates William Jennings Bryan of Nebraska, already the Populist Party presidential candidate, for President and Adlai E. Stevenson of Illinois for Vice-President. The platform denounces imperialism and the gold standard, while supporting bimetallism.
- On August 8, Wisconsin Republicans nominate the Progressive reformer Robert M. La Follette for governor. The platform calls for political party nominations by direct popular vote and the abolition of party caucuses and conventions.
- On September 8, a devastating hurricane kills six thousand people in Galveston, Texas, causing property damage in excess of $15 million. The subsequent municipal confusion leads to the establishment of a commission form of city government, which becomes a model for municipal-government reforms nationwide.
- From September 17 to October 25, 112,000 anthracite-coal miners in the Northeast go on strike, causing the price of coal in New York to rise from $1.00 to $6.50 a ton. Acting on behalf of President McKinley, Senator Mark Hanna mediates a quick settlement.
- On September 18, the first direct primary election in the United States is held in Hennepin County, Minnesota. This is an important Progressive reform.
- On November 6, Republican William McKinley easily defeats his Democratic opponent William Jennings Bryan in the presidential election. The Republicans hold majorities in both houses of Congress.

1901

- On March 2, Congress passes an Army Appropriations Act that includes the Platt Amendment, which establishes American control of Cuban foreign affairs. The amendment is abrogated on May 29, 1934.
- On March 4, William McKinley is inaugurated for a second term as President. Theodore Roosevelt is sworn in as Vice-President.

- On March 23, Emilio Aguinaldo, leader of the Filipino rebellion against the United States, is captured by American forces in Luzon.
- On April 19, Aguinaldo issues a proclamation ending the Filipino revolt against the United States. One thousand prisoners are released after taking an oath of allegiance to the United States.
- On May 27, the United States Supreme Court issues opinions on the first of what are known as the Insular Cases, some fourteen decisions rendered during 1901–1904 that define the application of the Constitution and the Bill of Rights to overseas territories. The court declares that territories acquired as a result of the Spanish-American War are neither foreign countries nor part of the United States.
- On June 12, Cubans adopt the Platt Amendment as part of their Constitution.
- On July 25, against the protests of American commercial interests, President McKinley issues a proclamation establishing free trade between Puerto Rico and the United States.
- On September 6, President McKinley, while visiting the Pan-American Exhibition in Buffalo, New York, is shot by the anarchist Leon Czolgosz.
- On September 14, following the death of McKinley, Theodore Roosevelt takes the oath as President.
- On October 17, President Roosevelt invites prominent African American leader Booker T. Washington to the White House for dinner, outraging southern Democrats.
- On November 11, Alabama adopts a new constitution that contains a "grandfather clause," which effectively disenfranchises African Americans by allowing illiterate whites, whose grandfathers had voted prior to the Civil War, to vote. It further disenfranchises sharecropping African Americans by granting suffrage to those who pay taxes on three hundred dollars worth of land.
- On November 18, Great Britain and the United States sign the Hay-Pauncefote Treaty, which authorizes the United States to build, operate, and fortify a canal across the Central American isthmus.
- On December 3, in his first address to Congress, President Roosevelt outlines a Progressive agenda, which includes regulation of business trusts "within reasonable limits," civil service reform, and extending the powers of the Interstate Commerce Commission. In addition, he is the first president to advocate the conservation of natural resources on public land.
- On December 16, the Senate ratifies the Hay-Pauncefote Canal Treaty on a vote of 72-6.

1902

- On January 3, the French-owned Panama Canal Company makes a formal offer to sell its property and franchises to the United States for $40 million.
- On January 24, the United States signs a treaty with Denmark to purchase the Virgin Islands for $5 million. However, the Danish Parliament rejects it.
- On March 6, Congress creates the United States Bureau of the Census.
- On March 8, Congress passes the Philippines Tariff Act, which allows Filipino exports to enter the United States at a lower tariff rate than that of other nations.
- On March 10, on President Roosevelt's orders, Attorney General Philander C. Knox files a lawsuit to dissolve the Northern Securities Company, the largest company in the United States, under the Sherman Antitrust Act.
- On May 20, the United States formally transfers authority over Cuba to President Tomas Estrada Palma, the first president of the newly independent nation.
- On June 17 Congress passes the Newlands Reclamation Act, which devotes almost the entire amount of proceeds of public land sales in sixteen western states to fund the construction and maintenance of Western irrigation works.
- On June 28, Congress passes the Isthmian Canal Act, which appropriates $40 million for the purchase of the French Canal Company and provides for the construction of a canal across the Isthmus of Panama.
- On July 1, Congress passes the Philippine Government Act, which authorizes President Roosevelt, with the advice and consent of the United States Senate, to appoint a commission to govern the islands. The act also declares that the inhabitants of the 7,000-island archipelago are citizens of the Philippines, but are entitled to American protection.
- On July 1, Congress passes an act to prevent false branding and marketing of foods and dairy products.
- On August 16, President Roosevelt issues a proclamation creating the Little Belt Mountains Reserve and the Madison Forest Reserve in Montana, and the Alexander Archipelago Forest Reserve in Alaska.
- On October 2, Elizabeth Cady Stanton, one of the leading figures of the Women's Rights Movement, dies.
- On October 14, the World Court of Arbitration at The Hague, in its first decision, rules that Mexico must pay $1,420,682 and successive annual installments of $43,050 to the United States in lieu of past debts and interest payments.
- On October 21, the United Mine Workers anthracite-coal strike, which began on 12 May, ends after the direct intervention of President Roosevelt. This is the first time that a president directly intervenes into a labor dispute as an independent arbitrator. The miners and the owners agree to abide by the decision of the President's Anthracite Coal Commission.
- On December 29, Standard Oil Company establishes a pension system for its employees.

1903

- On January 1, United States Steel offers its employees a profit sharing plan and the option to buy company stock.
- On January 18, President Roosevelt talks to Great Britain's King Edward by telephone.
- On January 22, Colombia and the United States sign the Hay-Herran Treaty, granting the United States a ninety-nine-year lease on a 6-mile-wide zone in which to construct the Panama Canal. The Colombian Senate rejects the treaty on August 12.

- On February 11, Congress passes the Expedition Act, which gives priority to the attorney general's antitrust cases in federal court.
- On February 14, President Roosevelt creates the Department of Commerce and Labor, appointing George B. Cortelyou to head the new department. President Roosevelt also creates the Bureau of Corporations, appointing James R. Garfield as commissioner.
- On February 19, Congress passes the Elkins Act, which prohibits shippers from providing monopolies with rebates on railroad freight rates. This act allows smaller companies, who did not receive rebates, to better compete with their larger competitors.
- On February 16 and February 23, President Roosevelt signs agreements with Cuba, allowing the United States to acquire coaling and naval stations on the southern island.
- On March 21, the President's Anthracite Coal Commission increases the miner's wages 10 percent and shortens the number of hours of work per week. However, the commission rules that mine owners do not have to recognize the worker's union.
- On April 27, the United States Supreme Court upholds the clause in the Alabama constitution that disenfranchises African Americans.
- On May 1, a South Carolina law prohibiting children under the age of ten from working in cotton mills goes into effect.
- On May 23, Wisconsin becomes the first state to adopt the Progressive direct primary election law.
- On July 4, a Pacific cable stretching from San Francisco via Hawaii and Guam to the Philippines is completed. President Roosevelt sends the first message to the Philippines, along with a second message that circles the world in 12 seconds.
- On November 2, President Roosevelt orders three United States Navy warships to the Colombian province of Panama to prevent Colombian troops from landing within 50 miles of Panama.
- On November 3, Panamanian forces rebel and Colombia dispatches its navy to suppress the revolt. However, the Columbians are prevented from landing by the U.S.S. *Nashville* at Colón.
- On November 6, the United States recognizes the independence of Panama.
- On November 10, Joseph G. Cannon becomes Speaker of the House of Representatives. He becomes one of the most powerful speakers in United States history.
- On November 18, the United States and Panama sign the Hay-Varilla Treaty giving the United States full sovereignty to a 10-mile-wide strip of land across the Isthmus. In return, Panama receives a cash payment of $10 million and an annual payment of $250,000.
- On December 2, Panama ratifies the Hay-Bunau-Varilla Treaty.
- On December 10, United States Marines occupy the Guantanamo naval station ceded to the United States by Cuba.
- On December 30, a fire at the Iroquois Theater in Chicago kills 588 persons, mostly women and children. Public reaction forces state governments to enact new theater codes, including more fire walls and exits.
- On December 31, the federal government announces that 857,046 immigrants have entered the country within the past year, a new record.

1904

- On January 4, the United States Supreme Court rules in *Gonzalez* v. *Williams* that Puerto Ricans are not aliens and may not be refused admission to the continental United States. The decision does not, however, grant Puerto Ricans the additional privileges of American citizenship.
- On February 29, President Roosevelt appoints a seven-man Panama Canal Commission to oversee completion of the canal.
- On March 14, in *Northern Securities Company* v. *United States,* the first case in Roosevelt's campaign to rein in abusive trusts, the United States Supreme Court rules that the company violates the Sherman Antitrust Act and orders its dissolution.
- On May 5, the Socialist Party Convention meeting in Chicago nominates Eugene V. Debs for President and Benjamin Hanford of New York for Vice-President.
- From June 21 to June 23, the Republican National Convention meeting in Chicago nominates Theodore Roosevelt for President and Charles W. Fairbanks of Indiana for Vice-President.
- On June 29, the Prohibition Party Convention meeting in Indianapolis, Indiana nominates Silas C. Swallow of Pennsylvania for President and George W. Carroll of Texas for Vice-President.
- On July 4, the Populist Party Convention meeting at Springfield, Illinois nominates Thomas E. Watson of Georgia for President and Thomas H. Tibbles of Nebraska for Vice-President.
- From July 6 to July 9, the Democratic National Convention meeting at St. Louis, Missouri nominates Alton B. Parker of New York for President and Henry G. Davis of West Virginia for Vice-President. Parker agrees to accept the nomination on the condition that the Democratic Party agrees to denounce bimetallism and accept the gold standard
- On November 8, Theodore Roosevelt is elected President of the United States, defeating his Democratic opponent by more than 2.5 million votes. Roosevelt wins the Electoral College vote 336 to 140. Afterward, Roosevelt announces that under no circumstances will he run for reelection. He regrets this statement in 1912.
- On December 6, in his annual message to Congress, President Roosevelt announces the Roosevelt Corollary to the Monroe Doctrine. The corollary states that the United States has the responsibility to insist on proper redress for wrongs inflicted on a foreign state by any Western Hemisphere nation within the American sphere of influence.

1905

- On January 21, President Roosevelt invokes the Roosevelt Corollary for the first time. As a result, the United States takes over the republic's custom house and supervises its national and international debt payments.

- On January 30, in *Swift & Co.* v. *United States* the United States Supreme Court rules unanimously in favor of the government in its attempt to regulate the "Beef Trust." However, the ruling fails to dissolve the National Packing Company.
- On March 4, Theodore Roosevelt is inaugurated as President. He is the youngest person elected president to date.
- On April 17, in *Lochner* v. *New York* the United States Supreme Court rules that a state law limiting work hours for bakers to ten per day or sixty per week is unconstitutional. The Court holds that such a law interferes with the right to free contract and is an improper use of police powers. In his dissenting opinion, Justice Oliver Wendell Holmes Jr. argues that the Constitution "is not intended to embody a particular economic theory, whether of paternalism . . . or of *laissez-faire*."
- On June 8, President Roosevelt urges Japan and Russia to negotiate an end to their war that erupted in February 1904. The two countries accept Roosevelt's request.
- From August 9 to September 5, at the invitation of President Roosevelt, Japan and Russia negotiate in Portsmouth, New Hampshire. The final agreement makes Korea a Japanese protectorate and gives Japan the South Manchurian Railway and the southern Liaodong Peninsula. The two countries divide Sakhalin Island in half, and Japan gives up its demand for Russian economic restitution. President Roosevelt receives the Nobel Peace Prize for his role as mediator.

1906

- On March 12, the United States Supreme Court rules in *Hale* v. *Henkel* that employees can be compelled to give testimony against their corporations and to produce papers and documents that might prove pertinent to the case. The ruling has a large impact on testimony in antitrust hearings.
- On May 21, the United States and Mexico reach an agreement over water distribution of the Rio Grande River. The United States is diverting more and more water to farmers for irrigation.
- On June 29, Congress passes the Hepburn Act, which puts teeth in the Interstate Commerce Act by giving it the authority to fix railroad rates.
- On June 30, Congress passes the Meat Inspection Act, which gives the federal government the authority to inspect meat shipped over state lines. Congress also passed the Pure Food and Drug Act, which prohibits interstate commerce in adulterated or mislabeled food and drugs.
- On September 12, President Roosevelt orders war ships to Cuba to prevent revolution.
- On September 22, sparked by rumors of African American men attacking white women, whites riot in the African American section of Atlanta, leaving twelve African Americans dead. The city is placed under martial law.
- On September 29, responding to Secretary of War William H. Taft's call for military intervention, the United States invokes the Platt Amendment and assumes military control of Cuba. Taft serves as provisional governor until October 12, when he is replaced by Charles E. Magoon. The United States continues to govern Cuba until January 1909.
- On October 11, the San Francisco Board of Education orders segregated schooling for children of Asian ancestry. Worried about the international consequences of the law, President Roosevelt persuades the board to rescind the order, with the understanding that the White House will attempt to discourage Japanese immigration to the United States.
- From November 9 to November 26, President Roosevelt visits the Panama Canal. He is the first acting President to take a trip abroad.

1907

- On January 26, Congress passes an act forbidding corporations from contributing money to political candidates running for federal office.
- On February 25, the United States Senate ratifies the agreement between President Roosevelt and the Dominican Republic, which authorizes the United States to supervise the nation's custom house until foreign creditors have been repaid.
- On March 14, President Roosevelt issues an executive order excluding all Japanese laborers from Mexico, Canada, or Hawaii from entering the country.
- On March 14, President Roosevelt appoints the Inland Waterways Commission to study and report on various problems associated with waterways and forest preservation.
- On March 21, under the Roosevelt Corollary, United States Marines land in Honduras to protect lives and property put in jeopardy by revolution.
- On June 30, the federal government reports that immigration for the year reached 1,285,349, a new record.
- On October 1, a downturn in the stock market touches off the Panic of 1907. At the request of the federal government, J. Pierpont Morgan arranges for the transfer of $100 million in gold from Europe to restore confidence in the economy and to end the currency panic that is causing depositors to remove their savings from banks.
- On November 16, Oklahoma becomes the forty-sixth state. Its constitution bans the sale and consumption of alcoholic beverages, reflecting the influence of Progressive reformers and conservative Protestant religious leaders.
- From December 16 to February 21, President Roosevelt sends the "Great White Fleet" consisting of sixteen battleships and about twelve thousand men on a world cruise. Roosevelt wants to demonstrate to the world that the United States is an international power.

1908

- On February 3, in *Loewe* v. *Lawlor* the United States Supreme Court rules that antitrust laws apply to labor unions as well as capital combinations and declares union boycotting illegal.
- On February 18, Japan and the United States announce the "Gentlemen's Agreement," a plan that restricts Japanese emigration to America.

- On February 24, in *Muller* v. *Oregon* the United States Supreme Court rules that an Oregon law setting ten hours as the maximum workday for women in factories and laundries is constitutional and denies that it curtails the liberty of contract guaranteed by the Fourteenth Amendment.
- On April 2, the Populist Party Convention meeting at St. Louis, Missouri nominates Thomas E. Watson of Georgia for President and Samuel W. Williams of Indiana for Vice-President.
- On April 12, federal troops are ordered to Pensacola, Florida to stop striking street car employees from rioting.
- On May 10, the National Convention of the Socialist Party meeting in Chicago once again nominates Eugene V. Debs of Indiana for President and Benjamin Hanford of New York for Vice-President.
- From May 13 to May 15, President Roosevelt invites the Conference of Governors of the States and Territories and prominent citizens, including former President Grover Cleveland, William Jennings Bryan, and Andrew Carnegie, to the White House to discuss conservation of natural resources.
- On May 28, Congress enacts a model law regulating the employment of children in the District of Columbia. Congress hopes that the states will adopt similar measures.
- On June 6, President Roosevelt appoints a fifty-seven-member National Commission for the Conservation of Natural Resources. Roosevelt names Gifford Pinchot, the head of the United States Forestry Service, to chair the commission.
- From June 16 to June 19, the Republican National Convention meeting in Chicago nominates Secretary of War William Howard Taft of Ohio for President and Congressman James S. Sherman of New York for Vice-President.
- On July 2, the Socialist Labor Convention meeting in New York City nominates Martin R. Preston of Nevada for President. Preston is in prison for killing a man while on picket duty. After Preston is ruled ineligible for political office, the party nominates August Gilhaus of New York for President and Donald L. Munro for Vice-President.
- From July 7 to July 10, the National Democratic Convention meeting in Denver, Colorado again nominates William Jennings Bryan of Nebraska for President and John W. Kern of Indiana for Vice-President.
- On July 15, the Prohibition Party Convention meeting at Columbus, Ohio nominates Eugene W. Chafin for President and Aaron S. Watkins of Ohio for Vice-President.
- On July 27, the Independence Party Convention (Hearst's Party) nominates Thomas L. Hisgen of Massachusetts for President and John Temple Graves of Georgia for Vice-President.
- On August 14, race riots break out in Springfield, Illinois. Governor Charles S. Deneen declares martial law, but to little effect when several African Americans are lynched.
- On November 3, Republican William Howard Taft wins the Presidential election with 1,269,900 more votes than William Jennings Bryan. The Republicans maintain their majorities in both houses of Congress.

1909

- On January 28, the military occupation of Cuba ends with the withdrawal of American troops.
- On March 4, William Howard Taft is inaugurated as the twenty-seventh President of the United States.
- On March 23, former President Roosevelt undertakes a scientific expedition to Africa for the Smithsonian Institution, followed by a triumphant tour of European capitals.
- On April 9, the House passes the Payne Tariff Act, which places coal, iron, ore, and wood pulp on the free list, and reduces tariff duties on iron, steel, lumber, chemicals, and refined sugar.
- On May 22, President Taft opens 700,000 acres of public land to settlers in the states of Washington, Montana, and Idaho.
- On July 8, the Senate passes the Aldrich Tariff Act, which restores iron ore to the dutiable list, increases tariffs on iron and steel goods, and, in comparison to the House version passed on April 9, increases tariffs on over six hundred other products.
- On July 13, the Sixteenth Amendment, which authorizes the federal income tax, is submitted to the states for ratification.
- On August 5, Congress passed the Payne-Aldrich Act, which increases tariff duties on over 200 products and reduces tariffs on over 584 goods. In addition, the act imposes a one percent tax on corporations with net earnings in excess of five thousand dollars.
- On September 13, President Taft releases a letter exonerating Secretary of the Interior Richard Ballinger of any wrongdoing in his handling of Alaskan coal claims. Taft feels compelled to act after Gifford Pinchot, head of the United States Forest Service, disobeyed his orders and publicly accused Ballinger of illegal involvement in the case. Taft fires Pinchot in January 1910. This controversy, along with the opening of seven hundred thousand acres of public land to western settlers, diminishes Taft's popularity among conservationists and angers former President Roosevelt.
- On September 27, President Taft withdraws three million acres of oil-rich public land in California and Wyoming for future governmental needs.
- On November 10, Present Taft sends two United States warships to Nicaragua following reports that five hundred revolutionaries, including two Americans, have been executed by Nicaraguan dictator José Santos Zelaya.
- On November 29, President Taft serves formal notice to President Zelaya that he holds the Nicaraguan government responsible for the execution of the two Americans.

Golden Rule Jones Reforms Toledo

Samuel M. Jones was mayor of Toledo from 1897 through 1904. A Progressive reformer, he believed in applying the Golden Rule to government, and worked to make municipal government more effective and responsive to the public.

"Fifth Annual Message of Samuel M. Jones for the Year 1901" and "The Golden Rule"

Speeches

By: Samuel M. Jones

Date: February 24, 1902; April 1900

Source: Jones, Samuel M. Speeches "Fifth Annual Message of Samuel M. Jones for the Year 1901"; "The Golden Rule." Reprinted in *Papers of Samuel M. Jones.* Toledo Public Library, Reel 12.

About the Author: Samuel Milton Jones' (1846–1904) employment philosophy, based on a practical application of the Golden Rule, gained him a local reputation as a liberal, and the popular nickname of Golden Rule Jones. His reputation, combined with his community activities, led to his nomination as the compromise mayoral candidate of the Republican Party in 1897. Once elected, Jones applied his unique ideas to the running of the city government and became popular with the working class. Although he was regarded as a dangerous radical by Toledo's traditional power structure, he was re-elected three times. An advocate of fundamental urban reforms, the eccentric Jones was widely recognized as one of the country's leading reform mayors. ■

Introduction

The reform impulse known as Progressivism began in response to a newly emerging industrial society in the United States. The infrastructure of the nation's cities—housing, road construction, water, sewage, gas, electricity, and public transportation—could not keep pace with unparalleled expansion. Consequently, the physical challenges of creating a habitable environment in rapidly growing urban areas were staggering. Americans were appalled by wretched living conditions among the poor, especially in cities faced with the problem of absorbing millions of immigrants from southern and eastern Europe. Out of this environment came the evils of political corruption and bossism, creating a national scandal.

Although urban problems and efforts to correct them did not originate in the 1890s, previous reform efforts had been unsuccessful. The main reason was that reform measures did not systematically deal with root problems, but instead were simply aimed at replacing corrupt local officials with honest ones. Progressives moved beyond driving out corrupt officials to focusing on more fundamental reforms. They wanted to create a system that ensured the appointment of responsive public servants. For some Progressives, the establishment of democratic systems that gave the people control over the elective process was sufficient. Most, however, were convinced that structural changes in society were necessary to address the specific problems of the new urban, industrial, and multicultural society that was the obvious future of America.

Common objectives of urban Progressives included:

- improvement of public services ranging from garbage collection to police protection;
- public control of municipal facilities, primarily utilities and transportation systems;
- elimination of the corrupting influence of big business in local government;

- equitable distribution of taxes to provide comparable tax rates for individuals and corporations;
- expansion of social services;
- election of responsive local governments by the people;
- greater autonomy for city governments, whose freedom of action—particularly in the areas of taxation, sale of public bonds, public ownership of services, and civil service reform—was severely limited by state laws.

Significance

Although a bit eccentric, Golden Rule Jones is representative of urban political reformers. Heavily influenced by his business experience and his Christian upbringing, Jones was also inspired by such reform writers and philosophers as Henry Lloyd, author of *Wealth Against Commonwealth,* and single-tax advocate, Henry George. As mayor, Jones was an outspoken advocate of public ownership of municipal utilities and services, including street railways, and non-partisan local politics. Like other reform mayors, Jones concluded that cities, whose political existence and powers were strictly controlled by state legislatures, required expanded powers to address the numerous issues resulting from urban growth.

Jones died in office in 1904, when the outcome of Progressive reform battles was still in doubt. Ultimately, the resulting reforms laid the basis for much of the modern political system in the United States. Various election practices we take for granted today originated with urban Progressives. These include the secret ballot, recall, referendum and initiative, the primary system of selecting candidates, and non-partisan elections. Another major Progressive achievement was public ownership and regulation of utilities and local transportation.

Even the basic structure of local government changed as Progressives sought ways to maintain popular control, prevent corruption, and apply professional management techniques to the administration of a city. The ward system was widely abandoned and replaced by streamlined mayor-council systems, city commissions, and city-manager forms of local government. Cities also obtained from state legislatures much-needed revisions of charters to grant home rule, which expanded the power of local authorities to manage their affairs without the approval of state governments.

Primary Source

"Fifth Annual Message of Samuel M. Jones for the Year 1901" [excerpt]

SYNOPSIS: The following two documents reflect both the character of Sam Jones' activities as well as the views of urban reformers at the turn of the twentieth century. The excerpts from Jones' annual mayoral address describe the achievements of his administration in 1901 and his objectives for 1902. Although Jones was speaking about the conditions in Toledo, his message describes the issues confronted by urban reformers across the country.

Former Recommendations Again Urged

Among the measures of improvement in our municipal affairs that I have recommended to your body in former messages have been: A new charter providing for home rule free from state interference; a new city building with central plaza on the plot of ground bounded by Ontario, Michigan, Adams and Madison streets; a commission on a new charter; municipal ownership of all public utilities. Riper experience has served to emphasize and confirm the convictions expressed in all of these recommendations.

Municipal Ownership

In my first and every succeeding message, I have been a persistent advocate of municipal ownership of all public utilities. I stand to-day more ardently for that policy than ever before, and I see no hope of improvement in our political relation except we shall develop a love and patriotism that will lead us to trust each other and to find pleasure in doing the business of the city that is now carried on by private companies ourselves, for the good of all of the people, with *private profit* eliminated.

Distrust of Municipal Ownership is distrust of Government. To distrust the ability of the city to manage water works, electric and gas lighting, telephones, schools, street paving, cleaning and repair, sewer building, heating plants, parks, public baths, play-grounds, etc., and to say that the city can run some of these and furnish the service to the people at cost, but that it cannot so manage others, and that they must be run by private persons for the sake of *private profit* is distrusting ourselves, distrusting humanity itself, and, indeed we can never successfully manage any public service or any branch of it until we first learn to believe that we are able to do so; learn, indeed, to believe in each other.

Unbelief the Only Obstacle

Infidelity then is the only obstacle in the way of successful city government. The man who stands with his face to the wall and decries all effort to awaken the social instinct, constantly distrusting his fellowmen and the government that they have built, he is the infidel that more than all others hinders the progress of the race toward Equality, Liberty and Fraternity.

Patriotism and the National Government

With singular inconsistency, we hear many of the opponents of collective ownership declaiming loudly of their love and patriotism for the national government, but ever decrying what they call "our corrupt municipal governments." This is equivalent to saying that the people are competent to select their national officials, few of whom they ever see or know, but they are not competent to select their neighbors to administer the affairs of the local government. Or it is equal to saying that a million gallons of water taken from a lake is purer than a pint taken from the million gallons. It is clear that if there are corruption and poison germs in the pint, the million gallons are affected with the same poison in the same proportion. The best way to get pure water, then, is to go to a pure source of supply, and pure government can only be had by the same slow and painful processes.

Poison in Our Government

The poison in our government; municipal, state and national, is partyism, or the spirit that seeks to run every department of government for the benefit of the party or the few, instead of seeking to carry it on for the good of all. The poison of partyism is rapidly disappearing from our municipal politics and will disappear last from national politics, for this reason—the best and purest example of government that we have to-day is in our municipalities; for, imperfect as they are, there is less of the poison of separateness than in the state and national government.

Government Not of Force, But of Service

The only justification that can be offered for the right of a government to exist and to levy taxes upon the people to pay its expenses is that it makes conditions of life easier and better for the people than they could possibly be without it. Its mission then is to *serve* rather than to rule by force, and it is valuable only in proportion as it is the servant of the people to help them to better living. . . .

The License System

The system of raising revenue by license or direct tax upon industry, that is now in vogue in our city, is an outrageous injustice, in the first place, and much of it is very probably without even the backing of a law to sustain it, but owing to the fact that the people who are mainly oppressed by it are poor, it has stood for some years without question. Nevertheless, we ought to be ready to put a stop to injustice whenever we have the ability to do so, and I sincerely hope that the Common Council will repeal all of these laws which levy a direct tax upon the poor, without forcing them to fight expensive law suits through the courts. The constitution of the state provides that "All property in Ohio shall be returned for taxation at its true value in money." This indicates clearly the source from which the various branches of government should derive revenue, and our license system is in direct violation of this principle as well as of the plainest principle of common justice.

The Wheel Tax

I regard the wheel tax as little short of infamy. The idea that thousands of men and women, boys and girls, who work for small wages and strive to economize by using bicycles to go to and from their work, many of them making great sacrifices to get possession of even a cheap wheel, and that these must yet be subjected to a tax for the privilege of riding their wheels is a wrong and a shame. Let us make amends, as far as we can, by repealing the law. Of course, bicycles and wagons and vehicles of all kinds are "property," and when they have once been returned for taxation according to the provision of the constitution, that should end the matter. If they have not been returned, that is the fault of the assessor presumably, or is due to the delinquency of the tax inquisitor.

The Huckster License

Is a direct tax on the poor. Only the poorer classes of people patronize hucksters; the rich and well-to-do mainly go to the telephone and "order" their supplies from the grocer. The tax of fifty dollars that is levied upon each huckster must be added to the price of his vegetables and fruits, and this becomes another method of shifting the expense of government on to the backs of those least able to bear it.

The Second-Hand Store License

Can any one give any righteous reason why a man should pay a special tax for the privilege of selling old clothes, old furniture, old books, old trunks and old stoves? I know of no reason, and I believe the main one that makes this tax collectable at all is the fact that the people who pay it are poor and cannot resist it.

Street Signs

Our city is shamefully neglected in the matter of street signs, and if I had the same liberty as mayor that I have as manager of a private business, I would buy the material, have the street-signs made and put up, doing all the work by the day labor plan. The Council can authorize the street committee or the city civil engineer or the mayor or any other official to do this. It is the way any of us would do it if we were working for ourselves. Why not do it that way?

The Garbage

The garbage ought to be collected and burned, the city doing the work on the day labor plan. This is the position I took when I vetoed the present contract. Our experience with the contract is all the argument needed against further trifling with the city's comfort and health by inviting a repetition of the experience through another contract. Let us take care of our own garbage by *the day labor plan, then we can be just to ourselves,* and, in some measure, just to the men who do the work.

Primary Source

"The Golden Rule"

SYNOPSIS: To Jones, the Golden Rule—"Whatsoever ye would that men should do unto you, do ye even unto them"—was the guiding principle of his personal life. In this speech, he illustrates the practical incorporation of the Golden Rule into his business and political philosophies. A strong religious underpinning was typical of the Progressives. Rigorous adherence to religious doctrine had declined in the late nineteenth century, but Progressive reform was firmly rooted in the traditional Christian values of Protestant America. Jones reflected that characteristic.

One of the most promising signs that I see today is the awakening interest in the simple philosophy of the Golden rule, this simple philosophy of our childhood is conclusive evidence that the very soul of art, which is simplicity, is stirring within the hearts of the people at this time as it has never yet been stirred since the world began.

With a sort of sense of shame I confess that in the adolescent period of my life, and indeed until I was past fourty, I was rather inclined to look upon the Golden Rule as something that would do very well for children, something that it was well and proper to talk about in the Sunday school, sing in the day school and preach in the pulpit, but quite impracticable to think of applying to the affairs of everyday life. The riper judgement of more mature years have convinced me that I, in common with the world about me, was at fault; that instead of being impracticable, the Golden Rule is really the only practicable rule by which we may hope to persue a continuously positive, affirmative, constructive life policy.

Not long since I was talking on this subject with a young business man, a member of an orthodox church and one who aspires according to the light that he has to be a Christian. In my effort to lead him to see the possibility of living according to the Golden Rule, I quoted some of the details of such a life directly from the words of Jesus, as recorded in the Sermon on the Mount, one of the most revolutionary documents that has come down to us from the ages of the past. I said, "You know Jesus gave his followers some simple rules of living, quite contrary to our practice nowadays; for example, he said to them, 'Love your enemies', 'Do good to them that hate you', 'Give to every one that asketh of thee', 'Pray for them that despitefully use you'. He also told them with very great emphasis that his mission was to teach them that the purpose of life, was Life itself. He said, 'I am come that you might have life', and he used impressive parables to teach them that Life does not consist in things, in property, in possession or position. To lead their thoughts away from such vulgarities to the Life Beautiful, the artistic life of simplicity; and for their true ideals of life and beauty, he turns to the "lilies of the field," to the flowers, the free life of the birds of the air, and the simple ethics and freedom that guide the little children in their association. Finally He summed the whole of His philosophy up in the propositions that we should love God supremely and our neighbor as ourself. He did not leave them in darkness as to how they could manifest their love for God. We all know very well that we cannot simply sit down and love Him straight up in the air; we must *do* something; we must give expression to this love in association with our fellows according to those simple and artistic rules of Equality that this great teacher gave us. Now, our practice is even yet quite contrary to the formulas I have quoted. Instead of loving our enemies we kill and destroy them as nations, and I am sure that as long as nations continue to kill their enemies, individuals will believe that it is right to kill theirs. Instead of giving to every one that asks us, we send for a policeman to arrest people for begging. Having used the superior ability with which God has endowed us to practically make slaves of our fellows, who are born equals, we proceed according to the "laws" and rules which are made by those of us possessing the superior ability, to parcel *off* the earth by meets and bounds, and then order those who have less ability than we, to keep off from our possession. "Now," I said, "this great teacher expected us to live according to these rules, to actually *do* these things, for His most impressive and pathetic utterance, save His last expiring cry on the cross, was this, spoken to His disciples who were evidently given to manifestations of adoration and worship, much after the manner of our hero worshipers of the present day—'Why call ye me Lord, Lord, and *do* not the things that I say?' "Well" said this successful young business man, "you don't suppose that Jesus intended that we should actually live according to those rules now?" I said, "He most certainly intended that those who call themselves Christians should so live," and this practical young man replied with great earnestness, "Why, you could not do that, it would ruin business."

Now, I quite agree that the adoption of such a pronounced socialistic programme as is outlined in the Sermon on the Mount, the recognition of Equality as an absolutely fundamental principle in human affairs would be very disasterous to present day business methods; and it is because present day business methods have failed and are giving way to better methods, to more human methods, that we now see this awakening interest in the study of the Golden Rule. . . .

The practical result of this effort has been to raise the standard of the common life of the people about our factory several degrees, and the best evidence of this is found in the absence of servile appreciation that so many people look for among employees wherever a little extra effort is made to do justice to them. In our factory we work the eight hour day or the straight forty-eight hour week with a Saturday half holiday; that is, we work 8 ¾ hours for five days and 4 ½ hours on Saturday. Our wage is fully up to, if not higher, than the average of similar shops where ten hours work or the sixty hour week is expected. For the past five years we have had an annual dividend of profits among the employees amounting to five per cent (5%) of the wage paid, and last year every man in the employ had a week's vacation with full pay. . . .

My study has convinced me that we are now in a period of peaceful revolution. Social and political idols are being cast down and destroyed. There is a revival of faith now going on that is to sweep this country from ocean to ocean. We are to be the greatest nation that the world has yet seen. Whitman, with prophetic vision, has given us a glimpse in these lines:

Come, I will make a continent indissoluble
I will make divine magnetic lands,
by the love of Comrades
By the manly love of Comrades.

You and I can make our contribution to this cause best only by living up to the very best that there is in us. Do not be afraid to step out from old traditions or old faiths. Let us learn to believe in men, believe in one another, and learning this lesson, we shall learn to believe in and live according to, the Golden Rule; and so living, we shall demonstrate here and now that we are truly "Sons of God."

Further Resources

BOOKS

Buenker, John D. *Urban Liberalism and Progressive Reform.* New York: Norton, 1978.

Ebner, Michael H., and Eugene M. Tobin, eds. *The Age of Urban Reform: New Perspectives on the Progressive Era.* Port Washington, N.Y.: Kennikat Press, 1977.

Jones, Marnie. *Holy Toledo: Religion and Politics in the Life of "Golden Rule" Jones.* Lexington: University Press of Kentucky, 1998.

WEBSITES

"Golden Rule Jones, Mayor of Toledo." Available online at http://www.cyberspacei.com/jesusi/authors/crosby/goldenrule/goldenrule.html; website home page http://www.cyberspacei.com (accessed December 14, 2002).

"The Writings of Samuel 'Golden Rule' Jones." Available online at http://www.attic.utoledo.edu/att/jones/jones.html; website home page http://www.attic.utoledo.edu (accessed December 14, 2002).

"To the Person Sitting in Darkness"

Magazine article

By: Mark Twain

Date: February 1901

Source: Twain, Mark. "To the Person Sitting in Darkness." *North American Review.* February 1901, 2–5, 7–9, 14–15.

About the Author: Even today, Mark Twain (1834–1910) is one of America's best known and most distinctive authors. Born in the Mississippi River town of Hannibal, Missouri, he was a humorist, lecturer, and author. While Twain is best known for such novels as *Tom Sawyer* and *Huckleberry Finn,* he was capable of biting satire in his works. He did not hesitate to use this skill to take a stand on social and political issues. ■

Introduction

In the century and more following the creation of the United States in 1783, the most consistent themes of

Mark Twain (Samuel Langhorne Clemens) at work at his desk in the 1900s. Twain was one of many Americans to object to the U.S. occupation of the Philippines. THE LIBRARY OF CONGRESS.

American foreign policy were avoiding "entangling alliances" with foreign powers, defending the territorial integrity of the homeland from external threat, and promoting American commercial and trading interests.

For much of this time, most Americans also supported expansion. Faced with a nearly empty continent, an energetic population, and a supreme confidence in U.S. democracy as the model for the future of mankind, Americans were certain that it was their destiny to expand across the continent.

Territorial acquisitions in the 1840s—Texas, Oregon, and the Mexican Cession—made the United States a continental power. While expansion into largely unclaimed and sparsely settled areas had now been completed within the United States, ambitions for new territories did not come to an end. In the 1850s, some Americans turned their attention to the Caribbean, northern Mexico, and Central America. Still others began to cast an eye toward islands in the Pacific, particularly Hawaii. Although some efforts were made in these directions, growing national divisions that led to the Civil War (1861–1865) stopped serious consideration of additional expansion.

Following the Civil War, the United States briefly resumed pre-war expansion, purchasing Alaska and occupying Midway Island in the central Pacific. The American public, however, showed little interest in such adventures. Instead, the country turned its attention to encouraging more settlement of the Great Plains and promoting industrial growth within the United States. For a variety of reasons, however, the pendulum began to swing back toward expansionist sympathies in the 1890s. The increasingly global nature of the economy and the empire-building tendency of European nations left Americans concerned that they were being shut out of markets that were needed to absorb their surplus industrial and agricultural production. The need for markets became particularly relevant in the 1890s, as the country plunged into a deep depression.

An additional factor was the influence of Social Darwinism, which applied Charles Darwin's concepts of natural selection to the broader context of society. This theory led many to believe that Teutonic peoples, particularly Anglo-Saxons, were destined for world leadership. Americans had, from the beginning of their national existence, considered the political and economic systems of the United States to be the model for future generations around the world. Social Darwinism provided "scientific" evidence to support that belief.

It was in this setting that American opposition to Spanish rule in Cuba led to the Spanish-American War (1898), during the administration of President William McKinley (served 1897–1901). Entering the war for allegedly altruistic motives, the United States surprised other nations by actually withdrawing from Cuba and leaving the Cubans to establish their own government. The same could not be said, however, of the other great prize taken from Spain in 1898—the Philippine Islands.

Significance

Once the Spanish-American War broke out, the Spanish fleet in Manila was a legitimate target of the United States. In early 1898, Assistant Secretary of War, Theodore Roosevelt, posted Admiral George Dewey to the Pacific as head of the U.S. naval squadron, with instructions to destroy the Spanish fleet. Dewey's navy was victorious against the Spanish, leaving the United States in control of the Philippines.

The decision to withdraw from Cuba shortly after the war's end was consistent with the purpose for war in the first place—that is, Cuban independence. The Philippines were a different story. Right or wrong, President McKinley concluded that the Philippines could not be given independence. Although the islands could not be left under Spanish rule, he argued, the Filipinos were not ready to govern themselves. If the United States Navy steamed out of the Philippines, a French or, more likely, German fleet would steam in. After much apparent anxiety, McKinley concluded that there was no alternative but to take control of the islands.

McKinley's decision raised a storm of protest among Americans who accused him of empire-building: Not only was the United States now in control of the Philippines, but Puerto Rico had also been captured from Spain during the war, and Hawaii had been annexed to the United States in the same year. This became an issue of great importance in February 1899, when Filipinos, led by Emilio Aguinaldo, revolted against their newly arrived American rulers. The ensuing war to suppress the insurgents was far more costly than the Spanish-American War itself. And the conflict placed the United States in the awkward position of battling against a people who were fighting for their freedom.

Primary Source

"To the Person Sitting in Darkness" [excerpt]

SYNOPSIS: At the time of the Filipino uprising, Great Britain was engaged in defeating the Boer Republic in South Africa. The Boer War (1899–1902), like the Filipino insurrection, was particularly brutal. It pitted a large, powerful nation against people who sought only their freedom. In "To the Person Sitting in Darkness," Mark Twain satirizes American control of the Philippines, comparing President McKinley to British Colonial Secretary Joseph Chamberlain, the chief architect of British policy against the Boers.

Extending the Blessings of Civilization to our Brother who Sits in Darkness has been a good trade and has paid well, on the whole; and there is money in it yet, if carefully worked—but not enough, in my judgment, to make any considerable risk advisable. The People that Sit in Darkness are getting to be too scarce—too scarce and too shy. And such darkness as is now left is really of but an indifferent quality, and not dark enough for the game. The most of those People that Sit in Darkness have been furnished with more light than was good for them or profitable for us. We have been injudicious.

The Blessings-of-Civilization Trust, wisely and cautiously administered, is a Daisy. There is more money in it, more territory, more sovereignty and other kinds of emolument, than there is in any other game that is played. But Christendom has been playing it badly of late years, and must certainly suffer by it, in my opinion. She has been so eager to get every stake that appeared on the green cloth, that the People who Sit in Darkness have noticed it—they have noticed it, and have begun to show alarm. They have become suspicious of the Blessings of Civilization. More—they have begun to examine them. This is not well. The Blessings of Civilization are all right, and a good commercial property; there could not be a better, in a dim light. In the right kind of a light, and at a proper distance, with the goods a little out of focus, they furnish this desirable exhibit to the Gentlemen who Sit in Darkness:

LOVE,

JUSTICE,

GENTLENESS,

CHRISTIANITY,

PROTECTION TO THE WEAK,

TEMPERANCE,

LAW AND ORDER,

LIBERTY

EQUALITY,

HONORABLE DEALING,

MERCY,

EDUCATION,

—and so on.

There. Is it good? Sir, it is pie. It will bring into camp any idiot that sits in darkness anywhere. But not if we adulterate it. It is proper to be emphatic upon that point. This brand is strictly for Export—apparently. *Apparently.* Privately and confidentially, it is nothing of the kind. Privately and confidentially, it is merely an outside cover, gay and pretty and attractive, displaying the special patterns of our Civilization which we reserve for Home Consumption, while *inside* the bale is the Actual Thing that the Customer Sitting in Darkness buys with his blood and tears and land and liberty. That Actual Thing is, indeed, Civilization, but it is only for Export. Is there a difference between the two brands? In some of the details, yes.

We all know that the Business is being ruined. The reason is not far to seek. It is because our Mr. McKinley, and Mr. Chamberlain, and the Kaiser, and the Czar and the French have been exporting the Actual Thing *with the outside cover left off.* This is bad for the Game. It shows that these new players of it are not sufficiently acquainted with it.

It is a distress to look on and note the mismoves, they are so strange and so awkward. Mr. Chamberlain manufactures a war out of materials so inadequate and so fanciful that they make the boxes grieve and the gallery laugh, and he tries hard to persuade himself that it isn't purely a private raid for cash, but has a sort of dim, vague respectability about it somewhere, if he could only find the spot; and that, by and by, he can scour the flag clean again after he has finished dragging it through the mud, and make it shine and flash in the vault of heaven once more as it had shone and flashed there a thousand years in the world's respect until he laid his unfaithful hand upon it. It is bad play—bad. For it exposes the Actual Thing to Them that Sit in Darkness, and they say: "What! Christian against Christian? And only for money? Is *this* a case of magnanimity, forbearance, love, gentleness, mercy, protection of the weak—this strange and over-showy onslaught of an elephant upon a nest of field-mice, on the pretext that the mice had squeaked an insolence at him—conduct which 'no self-respecting government could allow to pass unavenged?' as Mr. Chamberlain said. Was that a good pretext in a small case, when it had not been a good pretext in a large one?—for only recently Russia had affronted the elephant three times and survived alive and unsmitten. Is this Civilization and Progress? Is it something better than we already possess? These harryings and burnings and desert-makings in the Transvaal—is this an improvement on our darkness? Is it, perhaps, possible that there are two kinds of Civilization—one for home consumption and one for the heathen market?"

Then They that Sit in Darkness are troubled, and shake their heads; and they read this extract from a letter of a British private, recounting his exploits in one of Methuen's victories, some days before the affair of Magersfontein, and they are troubled again:

> We tore up the hill and into the intrenchments, and the Boers saw we had them; so they dropped their guns and went down on their knees and put up their hands clasped, and begged for mercy. And we gave it them—*with the long spoon.*

The long spoon is the bayonet. See *Lloyd's Weekly,* London, of those days. The same number—and the same column—contains some quite unconscious satire in the form of shocked and bitter upbraidings of the Boers for their brutalities and inhumanities! . . .

And by and by comes America, and our Master of the Game plays it badly—plays it as Mr. Chamberlain was playing it in South Africa. It was a mistake to do that; also, it was one which was quite

The United States captured the Philippines from Spain in the Spanish-American War (1898). When the United States refused to grant the Philippines indepedence, the Filipinos rebelled, leading to a bloody, four-year war won by the United States. **THE LIBRARY OF CONGRESS.**

unlooked for in a Master who was playing it so well in Cuba. In Cuba, he was playing the usual and regular *American* game, and it was winning, for there is no way to beat it. The Master, contemplating Cuba, said: "Here is an oppressed and friendless little nation which is willing to fight to be free; we go partners, and put up the strength of seventy million sympathizers, and the resources of the United States: play!" Nothing but Europe combined could call that hand: and Europe cannot combine on anything. There, in Cuba, he was following our great traditions in a way which made us very proud of him, and proud of the deep dissatisfaction which his play was provoking in Continental Europe. Moved by a high inspiration, he threw out those stirring words which proclaimed that forcible annexation would be "criminal aggression;" and in that utterance fired another "shot heard round the world." The memory of that fine saying will be outlived by the remembrance of no act of his but one—that he forgot it within the twelvemonth, and its honorable gospel along with it.

For, presently, came the Philippine temptation. It was strong; it was too strong, and he made that bad mistake: he played the European game, the Chamberlain game. It was a pity; it was a great pity, that error; that one grievous error, that irrevocable error. For it was the very place and time to play the American game again. And at no cost. Rich winnings to be gathered in, too; rich and permanent; indestructible; a fortune transmissible forever to the children of the flag. Not land, not money, not dominion—no, something worth many times more than that dross: our share, the spectacle of a nation of long harassed and persecuted slaves set free through our influence; our posterity's share, the golden memory of that fair deed. The game was in our hands. If it had been played according to the American rules, Dewey would have sailed away from Manila as soon as he had destroyed the Spanish fleet—after putting up a sign on shore guaranteeing foreign property and life against damage by the Filipinos, and warning the Powers that interference with the emancipated patriots would be regarded as an act unfriendly to the United States. The Powers cannot combine, in even a bad cause, and the sign would not have been molested.

Dewey could have gone about his affairs elsewhere, and left the competent Filipino army to starve out the little Spanish garrison and send it home, and the Filipino citizens to set up the form of government they might prefer, and deal with the friars and their doubtful acquisitions according to Filipino ideas of fairness and justice—ideas which have since been tested and found to be of as high an order as any that prevail in Europe or America.

But we played the Chamberlain game, and lost the chance to add another Cuba and another honorable deed to our good record.

The more we examine the mistake, the more clearly we perceive that it is going to be bad for the Business. The Person Sitting in Darkness is almost sure to say: "There is something curious about this—curious and unaccountable. There must be two Americas: one that sets the captive free, and one that takes a once-captive's new freedom away from him, and picks a quarrel with him with nothing to found it on; then kills him to get his land."

The truth is, the Person Sitting in Darkness *is* saying things like that; and for the sake of the Business we must persuade him to look at the Philippine matter in another and healthier way. We must arrange his opinions for him. I believe it can be done; for Mr. Chamberlain has arranged England's opinion of the South African matter, and done it most cleverly and successfully. He presented the facts—some of the facts—and showed those confiding people what the facts meant. He did it statistically, which is a good way. He used the formula: "Twice 2 are 14, and 2 from 9 leaves 35." Figures are effective; figures will convince the elect. . . .

Having now laid all the historical facts before the Person Sitting in Darkness, we should bring him to again, and explain them to him. We should say to him:

"They look doubtful, but in reality they are not. There have been lies; yes, but they were told in a good cause. We have been treacherous; but that was only in order that real good might come out of apparent evil. True, we have crushed a deceived and confiding people; we have turned against the weak and the friendless who trusted us; we have stamped out a just and intelligent and well-ordered republic; we have stabbed an ally in the back and slapped the face of a guest: we have bought a Shadow from an enemy that hadn't it to sell; we have robbed a trusting friend of his land and his liberty; we have invited our clean young men to shoulder a discredited musket and do bandit's work under a flag which bandits have been accustomed to fear, not to follow; we have debauched America's honor and blackened her face before the world; but each detail was for the best. We know this. The Head of every State and Sovereignty in Christendom and ninety per cent of every legislative body in Christendom, including our Congress and our fifty State Legislatures, are members not only of the church, but also of the Blessings-of-Civilization Trust. This world-girdling accumulation of trained morals, high principles, and justice, cannot do an unright thing, an unfair thing, an ungenerous thing, an unclean thing. It knows what it is about. Give yourself no uneasiness; it is all right."

Now then, that will convince the Person. You will see. It will restore the Business. Also, it will elect the Master of the Game to the vacant place in the Trinity of our national gods; and there on their high thrones the Three will sit, age after age, in the people's sight, each bearing the Emblem of his service: Washington, the Sword of the Liberator; Lincoln, the Slave's Broken Chains; the Master, the Chains Repaired.

It will give the Business a splendid new start. You will see.

Further Resources

BOOKS

Stanley, Peter W. *A Nation in the Making: The Philippines and the United States, 1899–1921.* Cambridge, Mass.: Harvard University Press, 1974.

Young, Marilyn Blatt *American Expansionism; The Critical Issues.* Boston: Little, Brown, 1973.

Zwick, Jim, ed. *Mark Twain's Weapons of Satire: Anti-Imperialist Writings on the Philippine-American War.* Syracuse, N.Y.: Syracuse University Press, 1992.

WEBSITES

"The Debate over the Philippines, 1898–1900." Available online at http://home.att.net/~betsynewmark2/DebatePhilippines.htm website home page http://home.att.net (accessed March 14, 2003).

McKinley, William. "Decision on the Philippines" (1900). Available online at http://occawlonline.pearsoned.com /bookbind/pubbooks/nash5e_awl/medialib/timeline/docs /sources/theme_primarysources_Military_2_6.html; website home page http://occawlonline.pearsoned.com (accessed March 14, 2003).

Translation of the Proposed Constitution for Cuba, the Official Acceptance of the Platt Amendment, and the Electoral Law

Constitutional amendment

By: Elihu Root

Date: November 1901

Source: *Translation of the Proposed Constitution for Cuba, the Official Acceptance of the Platt Amendment, and the Electoral Law.* Elihu Root, trans. Washington, D.C.: Government Printing Office, 1901.

About the Author: Elihu Root (1845–1937) was a corporate lawyer and U.S. attorney who served as secretary of war from 1899 to 1903 under presidents William McKinley (served 1897–1901) and Theodore Roosevelt (served 1901–1909) and as secretary of state from 1905 to 1909 under Roosevelt. Awarded the Nobel Peace Prize in 1912, Root was one of the few Republican supporters of the League of Nations. Although he was the architect and negotiator of the Platt Amendment, it bears the name of Orville H. Platt (1827–1905), Republican senator from Connecticut, who sponsored the measure in the U.S. Senate. ■

5000
Pub^d & for Sale by J L Magee 34 Mott S^t NY
GEN^L LOPEZ THE CUBAN PATRIOT GETTING HIS CASH
LOPEZ. Well! we have not Revolutionized Cuba, but then we have Got what we came for, my Comrades came for Glory, I came for Cash, I've Got the Cash, they've Got the Glory, & I suppose we're all satisfied.
I'm O. P. H. for the United States again. Cant Live under a Millitary Despotism

This 1899 political cartoon implies that the revolution in Cuba that helped trigger the Spanish-American War (1898) was sponsored by America in a successful attempt to gain control of the island. © **BETTMANN/CORBIS. REPRODUCED BY PERMISSION.**

Introduction

For at least sixty years prior to the turn of the twentieth century, the United States pursued a special relationship with Cuba, then governed by Spain. The main reason was Cuba's strategic location near approaches to the Mississippi River, the Gulf of Mexico, the Caribbean Sea, and the Isthmus of Panama. During the 1840s and 1850s, American expansionists had made several failed attempts to purchase Cuba from Spain. The lengths to which the United States was prepared to go in acquiring the island can be seen in the Ostend Manifesto (1854), a confidential government report recommending the seizure of Cuba. Illegal, privately financed military raids had also been made in an attempt to gain control of Cuba.

The possibility of acquiring Cuba, a slave-holding province, diminished during the 1850s. By this time the United States had become more embroiled in the slavery issue, which would become one of the principal causes of the Civil War (1861–1865). Nonetheless, interest in Cuba remained high for the rest of the century, and the American military quickly liberated the island from Spain in the Spanish-American War (1898). Upon achieving victory, the United States declared its intention of establishing Cuba as an independent country.

Maintaining Cuba's independence proved to be a complex challenge. Of primary importance was the strategic position of the island. The United States had previously tolerated control of Cuba by a weak and impoverished Spain, yet the country could still be taken over by a more aggressive foreign power. In addition, Cuba offered the potential for military bases that would allow the United States to extend its influence into the Caribbean basin. Secondly, the inevitable political and economic fragility of an independent Cuba opened up the possibility of internal chaos, which could be harmful to U.S. economic interests, and risk intervention by another country.

Third, most Americans felt an obligation to help Cubans establish a stable, democratic government. The United States had, after all, gone to war to promote a free and independent Cuba. They felt it would not be appropriate to let Cuba fall into anarchy, if such an outcome was preventable. Although the United States had no interest in exercising direct control, Americans did not want to leave Cubans at the mercy of internal or external predators. Secretary of War, Elihu Root, therefore, developed proposals that Senator Orville H. Platt attached to the Army Appropriations Bill on March 2, 1901, outlining necessary additions to the emerging Cuban constitution. The adoption of these provisions was a prerequisite to the withdrawal of the U.S. Army from Cuba.

Significance

Convened by order of General Leonard Wood, the U.S. military governor of Cuba, the Cuban Constitutional Convention completed a constitution on February 21, 1901. The Cuban Constitutional Convention initially rejected the so-called Platt Amendment. Root assured the Cubans, however, that the U.S. intention was merely to protect the country from foreign intervention and domestic insurrection. Confronted with few options, the convention added the provisions to the constitution. The Platt Amendment was approved reluctantly by the convention on June 12, 1901, and formalized in a treaty between the United States and Cuba the following year.

Under the authority granted by the Platt Amendment, the United States intervened in Cuban affairs on several occasions before the treaty provisions were repudiated by the United States in 1934. The most notable intervention took place in 1906, when the Cuban government virtually collapsed. The United States established—and still maintains—a naval base on Guantánamo Bay, at the southeast end of the island.

Primary Source

Translation of the Proposed Constitution for Cuba, the Official Acceptance of the Platt Amendment, and the Electoral Law [excerpt]

SYNOPSIS: The main provisions of the Platt Amendment forbade Cuba to allow foreign occupation of any part of the island, limited the amount foreign debt to the country's capacity to repay any debt, and required the sale or lease of territory to the United States for a naval base. The amendment also left open the status of the Isle of Pines, a small island off the southwest coast of Cuba, and required the implementation of sanitation programs initiated by the U.S. Army to eradicate yellow fever. Most importantly, the amendment authorized U.S. intervention to enforce these provisions.

June 13, 1901

Havana

Honorable Military Governor of Cuba

Honorable Sir:

Replying to your official letter dated on the eighth (8th), whereby you forward to the undersigned the report of the Honorable the Secretary of War, dated May 31st last, I have the honor to advise you that at the session held yesterday, June 12th, by the Constitutional Convention, there was taken the following

Resolution

The Constitutional Convention, in conformity with the order from the military governor of the island, dated July 25th, 1900, whereby said convention was convened, has determined to add, and hereby does add, to the Constitution of the Republic of Cuba, adopted on the 21st of February ultimo, the following:

Appendix

Article I. The Government of Cuba shall never enter into any treaty or other compact with any foreign power or powers which will impair or tend to impair the independence of Cuba, nor in any way authorize or permit any foreign power or powers to obtain by colonization or for naval or military purposes, or otherwise, lodgement or control over any portion of said island.

Art. II. That said Government shall not assume or contract any public debt to pay the interest upon which, and to make reasonable sinking-fund provision for the ultimate discharge of which the ordinary revenues of the Island of Cuba, after defraying the current expenses of the Government, shall be indequate.

Art. III. That the Government of Cuba consents that the United States may exercise the right to intervene for the preservation of Cuban independence, the maintenance of a government adequate for the protection of life, property, and individual liberty, and for discharging the obligations with respect to Cuba imposed by the Treaty of Paris on the United States, now to be assumed and undertaken by the Government of Cuba.

Art. IV. That all the acts of the United States in Cuba during the military occupancy of said island shall be ratified and held as valid, and all rights legally acquired by virtue of said acts shall be maintained and protected.

Art. V. That the Government of Cuba will execute, and, as far as necessary, extend the plans already devised, or other plans to be mutually agreed upon, for the sanitation of the cities of the island, to the end that a recurrence of epidemic and infectious diseases may be prevented, thereby assuring protection to the people and commerce of Cuba, as well as to the commerce of the Southern ports of the United States and the people residing therein.

Art. VI. The island of Pines shall be omitted from the boundaries of Cuba specified in the Constitution, the title of ownership thereof being left to future adjustment by treaty.

Art. VII. To enable the United States to maintain the independence of Cuba, and to protect the people thereof, as well as for its own defence, the Cuban Government will sell or lease to the United States the lands necessary for coaling or naval stations, at certain specified points, to be agreed upon with the President of the United States.

Art. VIII. The Government of Cuba will embody the foregoing provisions in a permanent treaty with the United States.

With the testimony of our greatest consideration, very respectfully, the President,

Domingo Méndez Capote.

Further Resources

BOOKS

Dulles, Foster Rhea. *America's Rise to World Power, 1898–1954.* New York: Harper, 1955.

Pratt, Julius W. *A History of United States Foreign Policy.* Englewood Cliffs, N.J.: 1965.

WEBSITES

"Spanish American War." Available online at http://www.loc.gov/rr/hispanic/1898/index.html; website home page http://www.loc.gov (accessed December 24, 2002).

"United States Occupation and the Platt Amendment." Available online at http://www.cubafacts.com/History/history_of_cuba5.htm; website home page http://www.cubafacts.com (accessed December 24, 2002).

Robert M. La Follette was a leader of the Progressive movement. One of its most prominent and successful politicians, he served as a U.S. representative, senator, and governor of Wisconsin. **THE LIBRARY OF CONGRESS.**

"Equal Voice Essential"

Speech

By: Robert M. La Follette

Date: 1901

Source: La Follette, Robert M. "Equal Voice Essential" Speech to Wisconsin legislature, 1901. Reprinted in Torelle, Ellen, ed. *The Political Philosophy of Robert M. La Follette.* Madison, Wis.: Robert M. La Follette Co., 1920, 30–40.

About the Author: Robert Marion La Follette (1855–1925) was one of the most influential leaders of the Progressive movement. The son of a prosperous Wisconsin farmer, La Follette served as a U.S. congressman from 1885 to 1891. He campaigned against corrupt political practices in unsuccessful bids for the Republican nomination for governor of Wisconsin in 1896 and 1898. After running successfully a third time, he was elected governor in 1900 and launched a thorough reform of Wisconsin politics. La Follette went on to make that state a model of Progressivism for the entire country. Elected to the Senate in 1905, he quickly became a leader of Progressive elements in Congress. In 1924, La Follette gathered a credible five million votes as the Progressive Party candidate for U.S. president. ■

Introduction

A fundamental difference over the meaning of the American Revolution became evident at the outset of the founding of the republic. One faction, represented by Alexander Hamilton, known as the Hamiltonians or federalists, wanted a government run by the best elements of society. While their objective was liberty, they feared direct democracy, which, they believed, pandered to the base and selfish interests of the worst elements of society. In their minds, it was a short step from democracy to mob rule. Hamiltonians were in the ascendancy at the writing of the Constitution of the United States, and tangible results of their philosophy included the indirect election of the Senate, the president, and federal judges. Only in the House of Representatives did the people select their representatives directly.

Thomas Jefferson (served 1801–1809) personified early opposition to application of the conservative, Hamiltonian theory at the national level. Under the leadership of the Jeffersonian party, the drift toward a more popularly based government began almost immediately. By the time Andrew Jackson (served 1829–1837) became president in 1829, the conservative ideas of Hamilton and the federalists had been thoroughly discredited. The "people" had become king. In the years following the Civil War (1861–1865), the rise of the Progressive movement resulted from the emergence of corrupt bossism in local government and the simultaneous growth of powerful business interests that controlled the political process at all levels.

Progressive reformers believed the will of the people was being subverted by a corrupt political system that excluded citizens from effective participation. For many Progressives, the solution was implementation of democratic reforms to re-establish a political system that was responsive to the people who, in their collective wisdom, would address the many problems plaguing society. Armed with a great faith in the judgment of the average person, Progressives pushed for a variety of democratic reforms. These included the secret ballot, the direct primary, the direct election of senators, the elimination of the ward system in cities, and the triad of direct democracy reforms: initiative, referendum, and recall.

Significance

The Progressive movement reached its fullest flowering in Wisconsin. Under the leadership of Robert M. La Follette, Progressives dominated state politics, initiating a variety of political and economic reforms that became known collectively as the Wisconsin Idea. Passage of a direct primary law was one of La Follette's major campaign issues in 1900. The law was intended to eliminate the caucus and convention systems used by political parties to select candidates. Reformers argued that candidates selected by caucus or convention were beholden to the political bosses who had engineered their nomination, rather than to the people who had elected them.

Despite overwhelming support for a direct primary law in Wisconsin, through flagrant bribery conservatives were initially able to prevent La Follette's Progressive wing from achieving its objective. Unwilling to accept a compromise, La Follette vetoed a watered-down bill and campaigned hard for a primary law in the subsequent session. This time, conservative forces were held in check and the primary bill was passed, subject to a popular referendum. The referendum also passed, creating the country's first primary for statewide elections. Almost immediately, other states began to fall into line, and, by 1917, all but four states had adopted some form of direct primary for statewide elections.

Primary Source

"Equal Voice Essential" [excerpt]

SYNOPSIS: The following speech was given by La Follette to the Wisconsin legislature in 1901. Supporting the use of direct primaries in the nomination of candidates for political office, La Follette argued that the caucus and convention systems formed the basis of machine politics. So long as this corrupt system controlled the nomination process, he believed, democracy was an illusion.

Commissioned by the suffrages of the citizens of this state to represent them, you will have neither in the session before you nor in any official responsibility which you may assume, a more important duty than that of perfecting and writing upon the statute books of Wisconsin a primary election law.

It is a fundamental principle of this republic that each citizen shall have equal voice in government. This is recognized and guaranteed to him through the ballot. In a representative democracy, where a citizen cannot act for himself for any reason, he must delegate his authority to the public official who acts for him. Since government, with us, is conducted by the representatives of some political party, the citizen's voice in making and administering the laws is expressed through his party ballot. This privilege is vital. This is the initial point of all administration. It is here government begins, and if there be failure here, there will be failure throughout. Control lost at this point is never regained; rights surrendered here are never restored. The naming of the men upon the party ticket is the naming of the men who will make and enforce the laws. It not only settles the policy of the party, it determines the character of the government.

For many years the evils of the caucus and convention system have multiplied and baffled all attempts at legislative control or correction. The reason for this is elementary. The evils come not from without but from within. The system in all its details is inherently bad. It not only favors, but, logically and inevitably, produces manipulation, scheming, trickery, fraud and corruption. The delegate elected in caucus is nominally the agent of the voter to act for him in convention. Too frequently he has his own interests alone at heart, and, for this reason, has secured his selection as a delegate. As a consequence, he acts not for the voter, but serves his own purpose instead. This fact in itself taints the trust from the outset, and poisons the system at its very source. No legitimate business could survive under a system where authority to transact its vital matters were delegated and re-delegated to agents and sub-agents, who controlled their own selection, construed their own obligations, and were responsible to nobody.

The officials nominated by the machine become its faithful servants and surrender judgment to its will. This they must do in self-preservation or they are retired to private life. Wielding a power substantially independent of the voter, it is quite unnecessary to regard him as an important factor in government. He can usually be depended upon in the elections, because campaigns are so managed as to make strong appeal to party feeling, and he has to vote his party ticket or support that of the opposition nominated by the same method. Under our system of party government the selection of the candidate is the vital question.

A political convention is never a deliberative body. It is impossible from the brevity of its life, the confusion of its proceedings, the intangible character of its records, to fix or attach any abiding sense of responsibility in its membership. Its business is rushed through under pressure for time. Excitement and impatience control, rather than reason and judgment. Noisy enthusiasm outweighs the strongest argument. Misstatements and misunderstandings will defeat the best candidate. The plain truth can hardly keep pace with hurrying events. It is rare, indeed, that the results of a convention are satisfactory to anybody excepting the few who secure some personal advantage or benefit from it.

It is the essence of republican government that the citizen should act for himself directly wherever possible. In the exercise of no other right is this so important as in the nomination of candidates for office. It is of primary importance that the public official should hold himself directly accountable to the citizen. This he will do only when he owes his nomination directly to the citizen. If between the citizen and the official there is a complicated system of caucuses and conventions, by the easy manipulation of which the selection of candidates is controlled by some other agency or power, then the official will so render his services as to have the approval of such agency or power. The overwhelming demand of the people of this state, whom you represent, is that such intervening power and authority, and the complicated system which sustains it, shall be torn down and cast aside. This is your duty, and high privilege as well, to accomplish it in the session before you. This, it is well understood, cannot be accomplished by any temporizing measure or so-called caucus reforms. The defects of the caucus, convention and delegate system are fatal because organic. It cannot be amended, reconstructed or reorganized, and its perpetuation secured. Its end is decreed by the enlightened moral sentiment of the entire country. It can no more resist the development which is sweeping it aside than could the adoption of the Australian ballot be successfully opposed a short ten years ago. It may secure trifling delays by temporary expedients. Its advocates may insist on making it a fetich and being sacrificed with it. But its knell has been sounded in Wisconsin, where it is already defeated, and a decade will leave scarcely a trace of its complicated machinery in existence in any State of the Union.

Further Resources

BOOKS

La Follette, Robert M. *La Follette's Autobiography; A Personal Narrative of Political Experiences.* Madison, Wis.: Robert M. La Follette Co., 1913.

Unger, Nancy C. *Fighting Bob La Follette: The Righteous Reformer.* Chapel Hill: University of North Carolina Press, 2000.

Weisberger, Bernard A. *The La Follettes of Wisconsin: Love and Politics in Progressive America.* Madison: University of Wisconsin Press, 1994.

WEBSITES

"Fighting Bob La Follette." Available online at http://www.sustainingwisconsin.org/about/fighting_bob.asp; website home page http://www.sustainingwisconsin.org (accessed May 19, 2003).

"Primary Election." Available online at http://gi.grolier.com/presidents/ea/side/primary.html; website home page http://gi.grolier.com (accessed March 14, 2003).

"Progressive Era, 1900–1920." Available online at http://www.iupui.edu/~history/fall01/progressiveera.htm; (accessed May 19, 2003).

"At Music Hall, Cincinnati, Ohio, on the Evening of September 20, 1902"

Speech

By: Theodore Roosevelt

Date: September 20, 1902

Source: Roosevelt, Theodore. "At Music Hall, Cincinnati, Ohio, on the Evening of September 20, 1902." Reprinted in *Presidential Addresses and State Papers of Thesodore Roosevelt, Part One.* New York: Klaus Reprint, 1970.

About the Author: Theodore Roosevelt (1858–1919) became president of the United States (served 1901–1909) in 1901, following the assassination of President William McKinley (served 1897–1901). Born into a New York patrician family, Roosevelt was part of America's upper class. When he entered politics, he was taking an unusual step for men of his social standing. During his formative years as a politician, he generally avoided taking a position on increasing corporate abuse of economic power. As president he

President Theodore Roosevelt gives a speech in Evanston, Illinois, in the early 1900s. ARCHIVE PHOTOS. REPRODUCED BY PERMISSION.

could not ignore the issue, however, so he was almost immediately drawn into the fray. Despite his popular reputation as a "trust buster," Roosevelt was actually ambivalent toward large corporations. ■

Introduction

William McKinley was elected president as a strong supporter of business. Upon McKinley's death on September 14, 1901, Vice President Theodore Roosevelt took over the presidency. He entered the White House as a young, popular, and energetic leader whose attitudes regarding business were generally unknown. Around Roosevelt swirled intense popular anxiety about the economic and political power that had been acquired by powerful capitalists like Andrew Carnegie, J.P. Morgan, John D. Rockefeller, and the Guggenheim and Du Pont families. The giant trusts that were increasingly dominating the economy and influencing government policy were widely regarded as a threat to American democracy and the economic traditions of free enterprise.

In the months before McKinley was murdered, the country had witnessed the creation of two new trusts, both engineered by J.P. Morgan. The first was the United States Steel Corporation, which gained control of eighty to ninety percent of the steel making capacity in the country. The second was the Northern Securities Company, the result of a compromise between the competing forces of James J. Hill and Edward H. Harriman. To stop a destructive raid by Harriman on the stock of Hill's Northern Pacific, Morgan brokered a deal that combined the competing railroads, giving the newly formed entity a virtual monopoly on all railroad shipping west of the Mississippi River.

Under McKinley, big business was left to operate with little regulation. His death brought a new philosophy to the White House. Although not a radical by any means, Roosevelt was uncomfortable with the seemingly unchecked power of big business. As president, he was determined to take action.

Significance

Roosevelt initially assured the country that he would adhere to McKinley's policies—and McKinley's chief policy was support of big business. Although Roosevelt's own attitudes toward trusts and large corporations were generally unknown, it became immediately clear that he was unlike any previous president. A fearless, tireless man of strong beliefs, he gave Wall Street a reason to be concerned. Still, his public pronouncements, particularly his annual address delivered in December 1901, created a sense of security among the giants of American finance. This comfort soon proved illusory. On February 18, 1902, Attorney General Philander Knox announced that, on the president's request, he had examined the Northern Securities merger and had determined that it violated the Sherman Anti-Trust Act. He was, therefore, filing suit asking for dissolution of the corporation.

Despite Roosevelt's aggressive actions, he was careful to distinguish between good and bad trusts. Unlike some reformers who felt size was a sufficient reason to break up trusts, Roosevelt applied more subjective standards. Before he would take action, he needed to be convinced that the targeted company was using its economic power contrary to the country's interests. In truth, his successor, William Howard Taft (served 1909–1913) was more aggressive in attacking the trusts. Nonetheless, Roosevelt established the federal government as an arbiter of the national economy and fully deserves the sobriquet of "Trust Buster."

Primary Source

"At Music Hall, Cincinnati, Ohio, on the Evening of September 20, 1902" [excerpt]

SYNOPSIS: The following speech was delivered by Theodore Roosevelt on September 20, 1902, in Cincinnati, Ohio. With the trust issue of primary importance to the nation and the Northern Securities Case underway, Roosevelt took this opportunity to explain his views on trusts and government regulation of big business.

The whole subject of the trusts is of vital concern to us, because it presents one and perhaps the most conspicuous, of the many problems forced upon our attention by the tremendous industrial development which has taken place during the last century, a development which is occurring in all civilized countries, notably in our own. There have been many factors responsible for bringing about these changed conditions. Of these, steam and electricity are the chief. The extraordinary changes in the methods of transportation of merchandise and of transmission of news have rendered not only possible, but inevitable, the immense increase in the rate of growth of our great industrial centres—that is, of our great cities. I want you to bring home to yourselves that fact. When Cincinnati was founded news could be transmitted and merchandise carried exactly as had been the case in the days of the Roman Empire. You had here on your river the flat-boat, you had on the ocean the sailing-ship, you had the pack-train, you had the wagon, and every one of the four was known when Babylon fell. The change in the last hundred years has been greater by far than the changes in all the preceding three thousand. Those are the facts. Because of them have resulted the specialization of industries, and the unexampled opportunities offered for the employment of huge amounts of capital, and therefore for the rise in the business world of those master-minds through whom alone it is possible for such vast amounts of capital to be employed with profit. It matters very little whether we like these new conditions or whether we dislike them; whether we like the creation of these new opportunities or not. Many admirable qualities which were developed in the older, simpler, less progressive life have tended to atrophy under our rather feverish, high-pressure, complex life of to-day. But our likes and dislikes have nothing to do with the matter. The new conditions are here. You can't bring back the old days of the canalboat and stagecoach if you wish. The steamboat and the railroad are here. The new forces have produced both good and evil. We can not get rid of them—even if it were not undesirable to get rid of them; and our instant duty is to try to accommodate our social, economic and legislative life to them, and to frame a system of law and conduct under which we shall get out of them the utmost possible benefit and the least possible amount of harm. It is foolish to pride ourselves upon our progress and prosperity, upon our commanding position in the international industrial world, and at the same time have nothing but denunciation for the men to whose commanding position we in part owe this very progress and prosperity, this commanding position.

Whenever great social or industrial changes take place, no matter how much good there may be to them, there is sure to be some evil; and it usually takes mankind a number of years and a good deal of experimenting before they find the right ways in which so far as possible to control the new evil, without at the same time nullifying the new good. I am stating facts so obvious that if each one of you will think them over you will think them trite, but if you read or listen to some of the arguments advanced, you will come to the conclusion that there is need of learning these trite truths. In these circumstances the effort to bring the new tendencies to a standstill is always futile and generally mischievous; but it is possible somewhat to develop them aright. Law can to a degree guide, protect and control industrial development, but it can never cause it, or play more than a subordinate part in its healthy development—unfortunately it is easy enough by bad laws to bring it to an almost complete stop.

In dealing with the big corporations which we call trusts, we must resolutely purpose to proceed by evolution and not revolution. We wish to face the facts, declining to have our vision blinded either by the folly of those who say there are no evils, or by the more dangerous folly of those who either see, or make believe that they see, nothing but evil in all the existing system, and who if given their way would destroy the evil by the simple process of bringing ruin and disaster to the entire country. The evils attendant upon over-capitalization alone are, in my judgment, sufficient to warrant a far closer supervision and control than now exists over the great corporations. Wherever a substantial monopoly can be shown to exist we should certainly try our utmost to devise an expedient by which it can be controlled. Doubtless some of the evils existing in or because of the great corporations can not be cured by any legislation which has yet been proposed, and doubtless others, which have really been incident to the sudden development in the formation of corporations of all kinds, will in the end cure themselves. But there will remain a certain number which can be cured if we decide that by the power of the Government they are to be cured. The surest way to prevent the possibility of curing any of them is to approach the subject in a spirit of violent rancor, complicated with total ignorance of business interests and fundamental incapacity or unwillingness to understand the limitations upon all lawmaking bodies. No problem, and least of all so difficult a problem as this, can be solved if the qualities brought to its solution are panic, fear, envy, hatred, and ignorance. There can exist in a free republic no man more wicked, no man more dangerous to the people, than he who would arouse these feelings in the hope that they would redound to his own political advantage. Corporations that are handled honestly and fairly, so far from being an evil, are a natural business evolution and make for the general prosperity of our land. We do not wish to destroy corporations, but we do wish to make them subserve the public good. All individuals, rich or poor, private or corporate, must be subject to the law of the land; and the government will hold them to a rigid obedience thereof. The biggest corporation, like the humblest private citizen, must be held to strict compliance with the will of the people as expressed in the fundamental law. The rich man who does not see that this is in his interest is indeed short-sighted. When we make him obey the law we ensure for him the absolute protection of the law. . . .

Before speaking, however, of what can be done by way of remedy let me say a word or two as to certain proposed remedies which, in my judgment, would be ineffective or mischievous. The first thing to remember is that if we are to accomplish any good at all it must be by resolutely keeping in mind the intention to do away with any evils in the conduct of big corporations, while steadfastly refusing to assent to indiscriminate assault upon all forms of corporate capital as such. The line of demarcation we draw must always be on conduct, not upon wealth; our objection to any given corporation must be, not that it is big, but that it behaves badly. Perfectly simple again, my friends, but not always heeded by some of those who would strive to teach us how to act toward big corporations. Treat the head of the corporation as you would treat all other men. If he does well stand by him. You will occasionally find the head of a big corporation who objects to that treatment; very good, apply it all the more carefully. Remember, after all, that he who objects because he is the head of a big corporation to being treated like any one else is only guilty of the same sin as the man who wishes him treated worse than any one else because he is the head of a big corporation. Demagogic denunciation of wealth is never wholesome and is generally dangerous; and not a few of the proposed methods of curbing the trusts are dangerous chiefly because all insincere advocacy of the impossible is dangerous. It is an unhealthy thing for a community when the appeal is made to follow a course which those who make the appeal either do know, or ought to know, can not be followed; and which, if followed, would result in disaster to everybody. Loose talk about destroying monopoly out of hand without a hint as to how the monopoly should even be defined offers a case in point.

Nor can we afford to tolerate any proposal which will strike at the so-called trusts only by striking at the general well-being. We are now enjoying a period of great prosperity. The prosperity is generally diffused through all sections and through all classes. Doubtless there are some individuals who do not get enough of it, and there are others who get too much. That is simply another way of saying that the wisdom of mankind is finite; and that even the best human system does not work perfectly. You don't have to take my word for that. Look back just nine years. In 1893 nobody was concerned in downing the trusts. Everybody was concerned in trying to get up himself. The men who propose to get rid of the evils of the trusts by measures which would do away with the general well-being, advocate a policy which would not only be a damage to the community as a whole, but which would defeat its own professed object. If we are forced to the alternative of choosing either a system under which most of us prosper somewhat, though a few of us prosper too much, or else a system under which no one prospers enough, of course we will choose the former. If the policy advocated is so revolutionary and destructive as to involve the whole community in the crash of common disaster, it is as certain as anything can be that when the disaster has occurred all efforts to regulate the trusts will cease, and that the one aim will be to restore prosperity. . . .

You must face the fact that only harm will come from a proposition to attack the so-called trusts in a vindictive spirit by measures conceived solely with a desire of hurting them, without regard as to whether or not discrimination should be made between the good and evil in them, and without even any regard as to whether a necessary sequence of the action would be the hurting of other interests. The adoption of such a policy would mean temporary damage to the trusts, because it would mean temporary damage to all of our business interests; but the effect would be only temporary, for exactly as the damage affected all alike, good and bad, so the reaction would affect all alike, good and bad. The necessary supervision and control, in which I firmly believe as the only method of eliminating the real evils of the trusts, must come through wisely and cautiously framed legislation, which shall aim in the first place to give definite control to some sovereign over the great corporations, and which shall be followed, when once this power has been conferred, by a system giving to the Government the full knowledge which is the essential for satisfactory action. Then when this knowledge—one of the essential features of which is proper publicity—has been gained, what further steps of any kind are necessary can be taken with the confidence born of the possession of power to deal with the subject, and of a thorough knowledge of what should and can be done in the matter.

We need additional power; and we need knowledge. Our Constitution was framed when the economic conditions were so different that each State could wisely be left to handle the corporations within its limits as it saw fit. Nowadays all the corporations which I am considering do what is really an inter-state business, and as the States have proceeded on very different lines in regulating them, at present a corporation will be organized in one State, not because it intends to do business in that State, but because it does not, and therefore that State can give it better privileges, and then it will do business in some other States, and will claim not to be under the control of the States in which it does business; and of course it is not the object of the State creating it to exercise any control over it, as it does not do any business in that State. Such a system can not obtain. There must be some sovereign. It might be better if all the States could agree along the same lines in dealing with these corporations, but I see not the slightest prospect of such an agreement. Therefore, I personally feel that ultimately the nation will have to assume the responsibility of regulating these very large corporations which do an interstate business. The States must combine to meet the way in which capital has combined; and the way in which the States can combine is through the National Government. But I firmly believe that all these obstacles can be met if only we face them, both with the determination to overcome them, and with the further determination to overcome them in ways which shall not do damage to the country as a whole; which on the contrary shall further our industrial development, and shall help instead of hindering all corporations which work out their success by means that are just and fair toward all men. . . .

I wish to repeat with all emphasis that desirable though it is that the nation should have the power I suggest, it is equally desirable that it should be used with wisdom and self-restraint. The mechanism of modern business is tremendous in its size and complexity, and ignorant intermeddling with it would be disastrous. We should not be made timid or daunted by the size of the problem; we should not fear to undertake it; but we should undertake it with ever present in our minds dread of the sinister spirits of rancor, ignorance, and vanity. . . . The marvelous prosperity we have been enjoying for the past few years has been due primarily to the high average of honesty, thrift, and business capacity among our people as a whole; but some of it has also been due to the ability of the men who are the industrial leaders of the nation. In securing just and fair dealing by these men let us remember to do them justice in return, and this not only because it is our duty, but because it is our interest; not only for their sakes, but for ours. We are neither the friend of the rich man as such, nor the friend of the poor man as such; we are the friend of the honest man, rich or poor; and we intend that all men, rich and poor alike, shall obey the law alike and receive its protection alike.

Further Resources

BOOKS

Ekirch, Arthur Alphonse. *Progressivism in America; A Study of the Era from Theodore Roosevelt to Woodrow Wilson.* New York: New Viewpoints, 1974.

Mowry, George Edwin. *The Era of Theodore Roosevelt, 1900–1912.* New York: Harper, 1958.

Roosevelt, Theodore. *Theodore Roosevelt, An Autobiography.* New York: Scribner's, 1926.

WEBSITES

"Roosevelt and the Trusts." Available online at http://1912.history.ohio-state.edu/Trusts/roosevel.htm; website home page http://1912.history.ohio-state.edu (accessed May 15, 2003).

"Teddy Roosevelt & Trusts." Hyperlinked text with political cartoons. Available online at http://www.westirondequoit.org/ihs/library/Indrevprogera.htm; website home page http://www.westirondequoit.org (accessed May 15, 2003).

"Tweed Days in St. Louis"

Magazine article

By: Lincoln Steffens

Date: 1902

Source: Steffens, Lincoln. "Tweed Days in St. Louis." 1902. Reprinted in *The Shame of the Cities.* New York: P. Smith, 1948, 132–136.

About the Author: Lincoln Steffens (1866–1936) was a leading journalist and Progressive reformer who captured the attention of the American public with a series of articles describing misgovernment and corruption in cities. Originally published in *McClure's Magazine* and later collected in a

A proponent of the muckraking style of journalism, Lincoln Steffens wrote to expose local government corruption in some of his publications

book titled *The Shame of the Cities.* Steffens' articles are some of the best-known "muckraking" publications of the Progressive era. Steffens left *McClure's* in 1906 to become a freelance writer. He published his *Autobiography* in 1931. ■

Introduction

A major catalyst for Progressive reforms was the appalling condition of American cities in the late nineteenth century. While the physical and social problems of urban areas were enormous, the most troubling was pervasive corruption among politicians. Money raised for improvements was being squandered through graft, bribery, misallocation of resources, and outright theft. Setting out to combat corruption, middle-class reformers crusaded for good government. One of the most powerful tools of reform was investigative reporting done by such writers as Lincoln Steffens, Ida Tarbell, and Ray Stannard Baker.

Derisively labeled "muckrakers" by President Theodore Roosevelt (served 1903–1909) in 1906, these journalists exposed the American public to the misdeeds of corrupt and inept leaders. They revealed terrible conditions in Pennsylvania coalmines, among child workers in southern textile factories, and in the Chicago meatpacking industry. They exposed corruption in the U.S. Senate and in the great corporations. Confronted with a multitude of social ills, citizens were challenged to do something about the deplorable situation.

Lincoln Steffens' series on city governments began almost by accident. In his *Autobiography,* he recounts a conversation with S.S. McClure, his employer, when McClure told Steffens: "You may be an editor. But you don't know how to edit a magazine. You must learn to." "How can I learn?" Steffens asked. "Not here," McClure said. "You can't learn to edit a magazine here in this office. . . . Get out of here, travel, go—somewhere. . . . Buy a railroad ticket, get on a train, and there, where it lands you, there you will learn to edit a magazine."

So Steffens left. The result was the collection of articles on urban corruption known as *The Shame of the Cities.* Steffens' eye-opening articles forced Americans to come face-to-face with the startling degree to which corruption ruled in the cities. Steffens' main thesis was summed up in his analogy with the expulsion of Adam and Eve from the Garden of Eden. While some blamed Adam, others blamed Eve, and still others blamed the serpent. Steffens blamed the apple—in other words, the wealth that was there for the taking. And he held the American people responsible for their collective inability to resist the temptation. It was, like the best of the muckraker articles, a powerful catalyst for change.

Significance

The first of Steffens' articles on urban corruption was "Tweed Days in St. Louis." In St. Louis, he found one of the most flagrantly corrupt cities in the country: "It isn't our worst governed city; Philadelphia is that. But St. Louis is worth examining," Steffens wrote. And examine it he did. He was drawn to St. Louis by the chance to meet the energetic and moralistic district attorney, Joseph W. Folk, who was struggling to bring bribery cases to justice. St. Louis, like other cities, was undergoing fantastic growth. In the late nineteenth century, cities were letting huge contracts for construction of the infrastructure to support a burgeoning population. Cities were also selling monopolistic, long-term charters to companies to operate public utilities—water, electricity, gas (for lighting and heating), and public transportation (street cars).

Millions of dollars were at stake, and owners of the companies saw an opportunity for acquiring great wealth from these contracts. Even the most respected businessmen were not above using illegal means to get a piece of the action. By 1900, corruption and bribery had become the norm. This was the situation Steffens found in St. Louis. Working with a local newspaperman, Claude H.

Wetmore, and with the support of "Holy Joe" Folk, Steffens exposed the "boodling" (graft) system that was the "Shame" of St. Louis.

"Tweed Days in St. Louis" appeared in October, 1902. As a result of the publicity, Folk was able to generate popular support for indictments against some of the leading grafters in St. Louis. The influence of an interlocking network of "boodlers" was sufficient to make actual convictions very difficult. It was not, however, sufficient to stop Folk, who followed the thread of corruption to the state government. Based on the reputation he earned as a reformer in St. Louis, Folk was elected governor of Missouri in 1904. During his four years in office, he launched major reforms, including a statewide primary system, initiative and referendum laws, child labor and factory inspection laws, and regulation of utilities. He also initiated antitrust suits, including prosecution of Standard Oil Company for monopolistic business practices.

Primary Source

"Tweed Days in St. Louis"

SYNOPSIS: The excerpt below describes one of many incidents of corruption Steffens uncovered during his investigations in St. Louis. As was often the case in large cities, the controversy involved St. Louis's street railway system. To build such rail systems, cities granted franchises to companies to operate specific lines or, in some cases, city-wide networks. The franchises were typically sold for ten- to twenty-five-year periods and ensured the fortunate company a virtual monopoly over public transportation. Such was the situation when Steffens arrived in St. Louis.

Early in 1898 a "promoter" rented a bridal suite at the Planters' Hotel, and having stocked the rooms with wines, liquors and cigars until they resembled a candidate's headquarters during a convention, sought introduction to members of the Assembly and to such political bosses as had influence with the city fathers. Two weeks after his arrival the Central Traction bill was introduced "by request" in the Council. The measure was a blanket franchise, granting rights of way which had not been given to old-established companies, and permitting the beneficiaries to parallel any track in the city. It passed both houses despite the protests of every newspaper in the city, save one, and was vetoed by the mayor. The cost to the promoter was $145,000.

Preparations were made to pass the bill over the executive's veto. The bridal suite was restocked, larger sums of money were placed on deposit in the banks, and the services of three legislative agents were engaged. Evidence now in the possession of the St. Louis courts tells in detail the disposition of $250,000 of bribe money. Sworn statements prove that $75,000 was spent in the House of Delegates. The remainder of the $250,000 was distributed in the Council, whose members, though few in number, appraised their honor at a higher figure on account of their higher positions in the business and social world. Finally, but one vote was needed to complete the necessary two-thirds in the upper Chamber. To secure this a councilman of reputed integrity was paid $50,000 in consideration that he vote aye when the ordinance should come up for final passage. But the promoter did not dare risk all upon the vote of one man, and he made this novel proposition to another honored member, who accepted it:

"You will vote on roll call after Mr.—. I will place $45,000 in the hands of your son, which amount will become yours, if you have to vote for the measure because of Mr.—'s not keeping his promise. But if he stands out for it you can vote against it, and the money shall revert to me."

On the evening when the bill was read for final passage the City Hall was crowded with ward heelers and lesser politicians. These men had been engaged by the promoter, at five and ten dollars a head, to cheer on the boodling assemblymen. The bill passed the House with a rush, and all crowded into the Council Chamber. While the roll was being called the silence was profound, for all knew that some men in the Chamber whose reputations had been free from blemish were under promise and pay to part with honor that night. When the clerk was two-thirds down the list those who had kept count knew that but one vote was needed. One more name was called. The man addressed turned red, then white, and after a moment's hesitation he whispered "Aye"! The silence was so deathlike that his vote was heard throughout the room, and those near enough heard also the sigh of relief that escaped from the member who could now vote "No" and save his reputation.

The Central Franchise bill was a law, passed over the mayor's veto. The promoter had expended nearly $300,000 in securing the legislation, but within a week he sold his rights of way to "eastern capitalists" for $1,250,000. The United Railways Company was formed, and without owning an inch of steel rail, or a plank in a car, was able to compel every street railroad in St. Louis, with the exception of the Suburban, to part with stock and right of way and agree to a merger. Out of this grew the St. Louis Transit Company of today.

Several incidents followed this legislative session. After the Assembly had adjourned, a promoter entertained the $50,000 councilman at a downtown restaurant. During the supper the host remarked to his guest, "I wish you would lend me that $50,000 until tomorrow. There are some of the boys outside whom I haven't paid." The money changed hands. The next day, having waited in vain for the promoter, Mr. Councilman armed himself with a revolver and began a search of the hotels. The hunt in St. Louis proved fruitless, but the irate legislator kept on the trail until he came face to face with the lobbyist in the corridor of the Waldorf-Astoria. The New Yorker, seeing the danger, seized the St. Louisan by the arm and said soothingly, "There, there; don't take on so. I was called away suddenly. Come to supper with me; I will give you the money."

The invitation was accepted, and champagne soon was flowing. When the man from the West had become sufficiently maudlin the promoter passed over to him a letter, which he had dictated to a typewriter while away from the table for a few minutes. The statement denied all knowledge of bribery.

"You sign that and I will pay you $5,000. Refuse, and you don't get a cent," said the promoter. The St. Louisan returned home carrying the $5,000, and that was all.

Meanwhile the promoter had not fared so well with other spoilsmen. By the terms of the ante-legislation agreement referred to above, the son of one councilman was pledged to return $45,000 if his father was saved the necessity of voting for the bill. The next day the New Yorker sought out this young man and asked for the money.

"I am not going to give it to you," was the cool rejoinder. "My mamma says that it is bribe money and that it would be wrong to give it to either you or father, so I shall keep it myself." And he did. When summoned before the grand jury this young man asked to be relieved from answering questions. "I am afraid I might commit perjury," he said. He was advised to "Tell the truth and there will be no risk."

"It would be all right," said the son, "if Mr. Folk would tell me what the other fellows have testified to. Please have him do that."

Two indictments were found as the result of this Central Traction bill, and bench warrants were served on Robert M. Snyder and George J. Kobusch. The state charged the former with being one of the promoters of the bill, the definite allegation being bribery. Mr. Kobusch, who is president of a street-car manufacturing company, was charged with perjury.

The first case tried was that of Emil Meysenburg, the millionaire who compelled the Suburban people to purchase his worthless stock. He was defended by three attorneys of high repute in criminal jurisprudence, but the young Circuit Attorney proved equal to the emergency, and a conviction was secured. Three years in the penitentiary was the sentence. Charles Kratz, the Congressional candidate, forfeited $40,000 by flight, and John K. Murrell also disappeared. Mr. Folk traced Murrell to Mexico, caused his arrest in Guadalajara, negotiated with the authorities for his surrender, and when this failed, arranged for his return home to confess, and his evidence brought about the indictment, on September 8, of eighteen members of the municipal legislature. The second case was that of Julius Lehmann. Two years at hard labor was the sentence, and the man who had led the jokers in the grand jury anteroom would have fallen when he heard it, had not a friend been standing near.

Besides the convictions of these and other men of good standing in the community, and the flight of many more, partnerships were dissolved, companies had to be reorganized, business houses were closed because their proprietors were absent, but Mr. Folk, deterred as little by success as by failure, moved right on; he was not elated; he was not sorrowful. The man proceeded with his work quickly, surely, smilingly, without fear or pity. The terror spread, and the rout was complete.

When another grand jury was sworn and proceeded to take testimony there were scores of men who threw up their hands and crying "Mea culpa!" begged to be permitted to tell all they knew and not be prosecuted. The inquiry broadened. The son of a former mayor was indicted for misconduct in office while serving as his father's private secretary, and the grand jury recommended that the ex-mayor be sued in the civil courts, to recover interests on public money which he had placed in his own pocket. A true bill fell on a former City Register, and more assemblymen were arrested, charged with making illegal contracts with the city. At last the ax struck upon the trunk of the greatest oak of the forest. Colonel Butler, the boss who has controlled elections in St. Louis for many years, the millionaire who had risen from bellows-boy in a blacksmith's shop to be the maker and guide of the governors of Missouri, one of the men who helped nominate and elect

Folk—he also was indicted on two counts charged with attempted bribery. That Butler has controlled legislation in St. Louis had long been known. It was generally understood that he owned assemblymen before they ever took the oath of office, and that he did not have to pay for votes. And yet open bribery was the allegation now. Two members of the Board of Health stood ready to swear that he offered them $2,500 for their approval of a garbage contract.

Pitiful? Yes, but typical. Other cities are today in the same condition as St. Louis before Mr. Folk was invited in to see its rottenness. Chicago is cleaning itself up just now, so is Minneapolis, and Pittsburgh recently had a bribery scandal; Boston is at peace, Cincinnati and St. Louis are satisfied, while Philadelphia is happy with the worst government in the world. As for the small towns and the villages, many of these are busy as bees at the loot.

St. Louis, indeed, in its disgrace, has a great advantage. It was exposed late; it has not been reformed and caught again and again, until its citizens are reconciled to corruption. But, best of all, the man who has turned St. Louis inside out, turned it, as it were, upside down, too. In all cities, the better classes—the businessmen—are the sources of corruption; but they are so rarely pursued and caught that we do not fully realize whence the trouble comes. Thus most cities blame the politicians and the ignorant and vicious poor.

Mr. Folk has shown St. Louis that its bankers, brokers, corporation officers—its businessmen—are the sources of evil, so that from the start it will know the municipal problem in its true light. With a tradition for public spirit, it may drop Butler and its runaway bankers, brokers and brewers, and pushing aside the scruples of the hundreds of men down in blue book, and red book, and church register, who are lying hidden behind the statutes of limitations, the city may restore good government. Otherwise the exposures by Mr. Folk will result only in the perfection of the corrupt system. For the corrupt can learn a lesson when the good citizens cannot. The Tweed regime in New York taught Tammany to organize its boodle business: the police exposure taught it to improve its method of collecting blackmail. And both now are almost perfect and safe. The rascals of St. Louis will learn in like manner; they will concentrate the control of their bribery system, excluding from the profit-sharing the great mass of weak rascals, and carrying on the business as a business in the interest of a trustworthy few. District Attorney Jerome cannot catch the Tammany men, and Circuit Attorney Folk will not be able another time to break the St. Louis ring. This is St. Louis' one great chance.

But, for the rest of us, it does not matter about St. Louis any more than it matters about Colonel Butler et al. The point is, that what went on in St. Louis is going on in most of our cities, towns and villages. The problem of municipal government in America has not been solved. The people may be tired of it, but they cannot give it up—not yet.

Further Resources

BOOKS

Smith, Page. *America Enters the World.* New York: McGraw-Hill, 1985.

Steffens, Lincoln. *The Autobiography of Lincoln Steffens.* New York: Harcourt, Brace, 1931.

Weinberg, Arthur, and Lila Weinberg, eds. *The Muckrakers; The Era in Journalism that Moved America to Reform—The Most Significant Magazine Articles of 1902–1912.* New York: Simon and Schuster, 1961.

WEBSITES

"Lincoln Steffens." Available online at http://www.american.edu/kdurr/steffens.html; website home page http://www.american.edu (accessed March 14, 2003).

"Lincoln Steffens, from *The Shame of the Cities.*" Available online at http://mohawk.k12.ny.us/progressive/Steffens1.htm; website home page http://mohawk.k12.ny.us (accessed March 14, 2003).

Speeches Before the National American Woman Suffrage Association Conventions, 1903–1906

Speeches

By: Henry Dixon Bruns, Belle Kearney, Helen Loring Grenfell, Anna Howard Shaw, and Jane Addams

Date: 1903, 1903, 1904, 1905, 1906

Source: Harper, Ida Husted, ed. *The History of Woman Suffrage.* Volume V. New York: Little & Ives, 1922, 66–67, 82–83, 102–103, 125, 169–170, 178–179.

About the Author: Dr. Henry Dixon Bruns (1859–1933) was born in Charleston, South Carolina, on the eve of the Civil War (1861–1865). He graduated from the medical college of the University of Louisiana and spent most of his professional career in New Orleans. Belle Kearney (1863–1939) was a Mississippi-born advocate of woman suffrage. Widely traveled, Kearney was a prominent speaker who addressed audiences across the country on suffrage and temperance issues. Helen Grenfell was one of the first women in the United States elected to statewide public office. She was chosen as

Colorado's superintendent of instruction in 1899. Dr. Anna Howard Shaw (1847–1919), along with Susan B. Anthony, was a leader of the National American Woman Suffrage Association, founded in 1890. The British-born Shaw was also a leading temperance activist, a licensed physician, and the first woman ordained as minister in the Methodist Protestant Church. Jane Addams (1860–1935) was an active social reformer best know as the founder of Hull House Settlement in Chicago. Addams's interests and influence in various social movements were extensive, including her prominent role in the woman suffrage campaign. Her involvement in international pacifism led to her being awarded the Nobel Peace Prize in 1931. ■

Introduction

The woman suffrage movement began with the Seneca Falls Convention of 1848. Organized by Lucretia Coffin Mott and Elizabeth Cady Stanton, the Seneca Falls Convention passed twelve resolutions outlining inequities affecting women, ranging from limitations on property and parental rights to disenfranchisement. An element of a much broader reform movement, the Seneca Falls agenda, like other reform initiatives of the period, overlapped with and was eventually subsumed by anti-slavery agitation. It was not until after that controversy was resolved that there was any hope of focusing popular attention on woman suffrage.

Leaders of the woman suffrage movement viewed the Union victory in the Civil War and the beginning of reconstruction after the war as a unique opportunity to achieve voting rights for women. Women had battled for abolition and had made significant contributions to the Union cause on the home front. Many expected their (male) anti-slavery allies to fight for universal suffrage, rather than merely gaining voting rights for freed black men. This did not happen. When the Fourteenth and Fifteenth Amendments were enacted to enfranchise former male slaves, women were totally ignored.

One outcome of the struggle over the amendments was the emergence of stronger woman suffrage organizations. In May1869, Stanton and Susan B. Anthony led a splinter group at the annual meeting of the Equal Rights Association to form the National Woman Suffrage Association. Limited only to women, this organization reflected the frustration Stanton and Anthony felt over insufficient interest shown by the male leadership of the Equal Rights Association in regard to women's issues.

The competing American Woman Suffrage Association was established in November 1869. Led by former allies in the Equal Rights Association, including Lucy Stone and Julia Ward Howe, the American Association was more conservative in its approach. This rift in the woman suffrage movement, centered less on objectives than on tactics, lasted until 1890. Unification was made possible primarily because the entire movement became more legitimized. The confrontational approach the National Association used in their early years diminished. The suffrage movement, in fact, had become a socially acceptable activity dominated by middle-class and upper-class women.

At the same time, women were finding themselves drawn into the workforce out of necessity. The highly industrialized, urban world regularly thrust women into situations in which they had to work to support themselves and their families. They confronted overwhelming obstacles, since cities lacked the support network traditionally available in rural communities. With the influx of immigrants and rural Americans into the cities, women played an increasingly critical role in the new economy. In addition to more traditional roles as teachers and house servants, woman workers dominated much of the textile industry, clerked in the growing retail trade, and began to take on clerical roles (using the catalyst for female independence—the typewriter) in the growing corporate and governmental bureaucracies.

Significance

The emerging role of women in public and economic life made the lack of voting rights increasingly anachronistic. Nonetheless, resistance continued to come from various segments of society. Social conservatives, often using religious or biblical rationalizations, clung to traditional male and female roles. The South, hard at work creating a society that systematically excluded black males from voting, was not interested in raising the issue of an expanded franchise. Some business leaders were often concerned that an enfranchised female population would support labor legislation. Most active in the fight against woman suffrage, however, were the liquor interests. Their fear, probably correct, was that women voters would tip the scale in favor of prohibition. As a result, progress was very slow. By 1900, women could vote only in Wyoming, Utah, Colorado, and Idaho, and in the occasional school-board election in less liberal states. At the dawn of the new century, the suffrage movement was in the doldrums.

After 1900, the suffrage movement was reinvigorated by Progressives. They agitated for a more democratic political system, and the adoption by some suffrage groups movement of a more visible and confrontational style, in imitation of British suffragists. Gradually, the pace of activity increased, and, after 1910, a number of victories had been achieved at the state level.

Primary Source

Speeches Before the National American Woman Suffrage Association Conventions, 1903–1906

SYNOPSIS: The National American Woman Suffrage Association held annual conventions, meeting on alternate years in a different location around the country; otherwise the convention was held in Washington, D.C. Below are brief excerpts from speeches given at National American Woman Suffrage Association conventions between 1900 and 1909. These speeches touch on various arguments used to support woman suffrage.

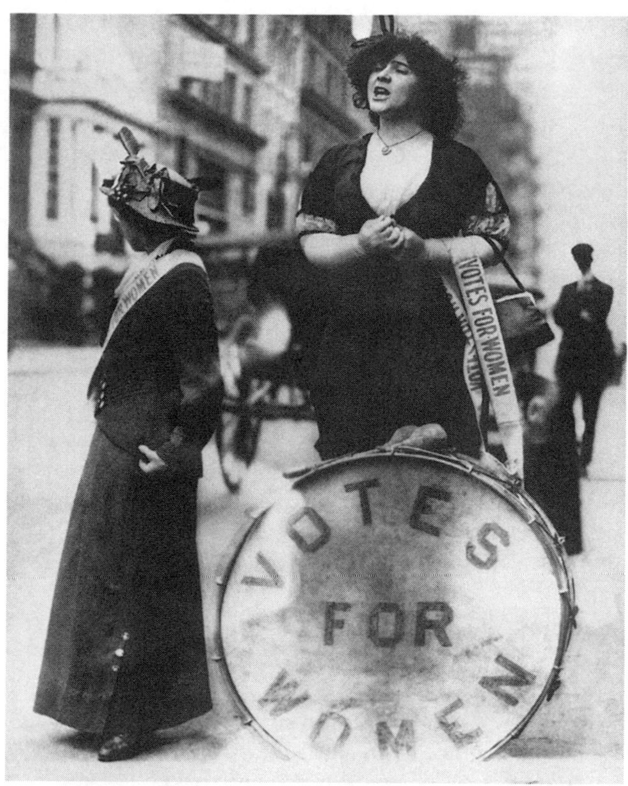

Two women stand on a city street in 1905, beating a drum and singing songs to attract attention to the cause of women's suffrage. © HULTON-DEUTSCH COLLECTION/CORBIS. REPRODUCED BY PERMISSION.

One of the notable addresses of the convention was that of the eminent physician, Dr. Henry Dixon Bruns—a lifelong advocate of woman suffrage—on Liberty, Male and Female, a part of which was as follows:

> I can conceive of but one watchword for a free people. It is written between the lines of our own constitution and underlies the institutions of every liberal government: "Equal rights and opportunities for all; special privileges to none," understanding by this that the Government shall protect all in the enjoyment of their natural rights—life, liberty, and the pursuit of happiness—and that all who measure up to a certain standard shall have a voice in shaping the policy and choosing the agents of the government under which they live. I can imagine none better than that now accepted by a majority, I believe, of the American people, namely, evidence of intelligence and the possession of a certain degree of education and of character evidenced by the acquirement of a modicum of property and the payment of a minimum tax. It was for regulation of the full suffrage in this manner that I contended in our constitutional convention of 1898, to wit: the admission to the franchise of all women possessing these qualifications. I still believe that this would have afforded the best solution of our peculiar difficulties and have spared us the un-American subterfuge of "mother tongue" and "grandfather" clause. If a vote could have been taken immediately after the notable address made by your distinguished president before the convention, I feel confident that women would have been admitted to the suffrage in this State. . . .
>
> Keep ever in your mind that the professional politician is your implacable enemy. To him an election is not a process for ascertaining the will of the majority but a battle to be won by any strategy whose maneuvers do not end within the walls of a penitentiary. He knows that yours would be an uninfluenceable vote, that you do not loaf on street corners or spend your time in barrooms and he could not "get at" you; therefore he will never consent to your enfranchisement until compelled by the gathering force of public opinion; then, as usual, he will probably undergo a sudden change of heart and be found in the forefront of your line of battle. . . . Do not rely upon wise and eloquent appeals to Legislatures and conventions. It is in the campaigns for the election of the legislative bodies that you should marshal your forces and use to the full the all-sufficient influence with which your antagonists credit you. Secure the election of men who do not give up to party all that was meant for mankind and your pleas are not so likely to be heard in vain.

■ ■ ■

The address of Miss Belle Kearney, Mississippi's famous orator, was a leading feature of the last evening's program—The South and Woman Suffrage. It began with a comprehensive review of the part the South had had in the development of the nation from its earliest days. "During the seventy-one years reaching from Washington's administration to that of Lincoln," she said, "the United States was practically under the domination of southern thought and leadership." She showed the record southern leaders had made in the wars; she traced the progress of slavery, which began alike in the North and South but proved unnecessary in the former, and told of the enormous struggle for white supremacy which had been placed on the South by the enfranchisement of the negro. "The present suffrage laws in the southern States are only temporary measures for protection," she said. "The enfranchisement of women will have to be effected and an educational and property qualification for the ballot be made to apply without discrimination to both sexes and both races." The address closed as follows:

> The enfranchisement of women would insure immediate and durable white supremacy, honestly attained, for upon unquestioned authority it is stated that in every southern State but one there are more educated women than all the illiterate voters, white and black, native and foreign, combined. As you probably know, of all the women in the South who can read and write, ten out of every eleven are white. When it comes to the proportion of property between the races, that of the white outweighs that of the black immeasurably. The South is slow to grasp the great fact that the enfranchisement of women would settle the race question in politics. The civilization of the North is threatened by the influx of foreigners with their imported customs; by the greed of monopolistic wealth and the unrest among the working class; by the strength of the liquor traffic and encroachments upon religious belief. Some day the North will be compelled to look to the South for redemption from those evils on account of the purity of its Anglo-Saxon blood, the simplicity of its social and economic structure, the great advance in prohibitory law and the maintenance of the sanctity of its faith, which has been kept inviolate. Just as surely as the North will be forced to turn to the South for the nation's salvation, just so surely will the South be compelled to look to its Anglo-Saxon women as the medium through which to retain the supremacy of the white race over the African.

■ ■ ■

Mrs. Helen Loring Grenfell, as State Superintendent of Education, spoke with high authority and by her dignified and beautiful presence no less than by her ability made a deep impression on all who heard her. She pointed out that Colorado came into the Union in 1876 with School suffrage for women and through this they had always been able to keep the schools on a nonpartisan basis. She showed that it paid more per capita for public schools than any other State, leaving even New York and Massachusetts behind; described its advanced position from kindergartens to training schools and colleges, with especial care in guarding the welfare of children, and continued:

> In the East we hear of "the question of co-education." It is not a question west of the Mississippi River, it never has been, it never will be. The eastern arrangement seems to us merely a curious survival of antiquated ideas, a kind of sex-consciousness which we have lost sight of in our care for the human being. . . . The place of State Superintendent has always been held by a woman since women became eligible. The first superintendent elected was a Republican, the second a Democrat, each holding the place for one term; the third, who is now serving her third term, was nominated as a Silver Republican but has really been elected and twice re-elected without regard to politics—an example of the independence of the vote where school affairs are concerned. There are 59 counties in Colorado and 33 of them, including most of those with the largest population, have women county superintendents. . . .
>
> I have found Colorado women much like their sisters elsewhere save that they have a broader view of public affairs and they take naturally a more active interest in the world's work. They have learned to think and to say what they think simply and freely in gatherings where men and women meet to discuss the vital concerns of life. They have not forgotten that they are women but they have come to know that they are also human beings, and, like Terence, they find nothing that concerns humanity foreign to them. Surely had we not been faithful in the smaller things, we should not have had these large opportunities given to us. . . . I can not help thinking that my sisters elsewhere have lost something rare and precious from their lives through the lack of that complete citizenship which has been bestowed upon the women of Colorado, and I hope the day may be near when those sisters may be made man's equal under the law of the land as they have always been under the law of God.

■ ■ ■

[Dr. Anna Howard Shaw] The recent attacks of Cardinal Gibbons and former President Cleveland, who had protested against women taking part in the Government lest it interfere with the home, she answered with keen analysis, saying in part:

> The great fear that the participation of women in public affairs will impair the quality and character of home service is irrational and contrary to the tests of experience. Does an intelligent interest in the education of a child render a woman less a mother? Does the housekeeping instinct of woman, manifested in a desire for clean streets, pure water and unadulterated food, destroy her efficiency as a home-maker? Does a desire for an environment of moral and civic purity show neglect of

the highest good of the family? It is the "men must fight and women must weep" theory of life which makes men fear that the larger service of women will impair the high ideal of home. The newer ideal that men must cease fighting and thus remove one prolific cause for women's weeping, and that they shall together build up a more perfect home and a more ideal government, is infinitely more sane and desirable. Participation in the larger and broader concerns of the State will increase instead of decrease the efficiency of government and tend to development that self-control, that more perfect judgment which are wanting in much of the home training of today.

■ ■ ■

It was at this meeting that Miss Jane Addams of Hull House, Chicago, made the address on The Modern City and the Municipal Franchise for Women, which was thenceforth a part of the standard suffrage literature. Quotations are wholly inadequate.

It has been well said that the modern city is a stronghold of industrialism quite as the feudal city was a stronghold of militarism, but the modern cites fear no enemies and rivals from without and their problems of government are solely internal. Affairs for the most part are going badly in these great new centres, in which the quickly-congregated population has not yet learned to arrange its affairs satisfactorily. Unsanitary housing, poisonous sewage, contaminated water, infant mortality, the spread of contagion, adulterated food, impure milk, smoke-laden air, ill-ventilated factories, dangerous occupations, juvenile crime, unwholesome crowding, prostitution and drunkenness are the enemies which the modern cities must face and overcome, would they survive. Logically their electorate should be made up of those who can bear a valiant part in this arduous contest, those who in the past have at least attempted to care for children, to clean houses, to prepare foods, to isolate the family from moral dangers; those who have traditionally taken care of that side of life which inevitably becomes the subject of municipal consideration and control as soon as the population is congested. To test the elector's fitness to deal with this situation by his ability to bear arms is absurd. These problems must be solved, if they are solved at all, not from the military point of view, not even from the industrial point of view, but from a third, which is rapidly developing in all the great cities of the world—the human-welfare point of view. . . .

City housekeeping has failed partly because women, the traditional housekeepers, have not been consulted as to its multiform activities. The men have been carelessly indifferent to much of this civic housekeeping, as they have always been indifferent to the detail of the household. . . . The very multifariousness and complexity of a city government demand the help of minds accustomed to detail and variety of work, to a sense of obligation for the health and welfare of young children and to a responsibility for the cleanliness and comfort of other people. Because all these things have traditionally been in the hands of women, if they take no part in them now they are not only missing the education which the natural participation in civic life would bring to them but they are losing what they have always had.

Further Resources

BOOKS

Evans, Sara M. *Born for Liberty: A History of Women in America.* New York: Free Press, 1989.

Flexner, Eleanor, and Ellen Fitzpatrick. *Century of Struggle, The Woman's Rights Movement in the United States.* Cambridge, Mass.: Harvard University Press, 1975.

WEBSITES

"Conflict in the United States: Woman Suffrage Movement between 1904–1912." Available online at http://www.geocities.com/emilyc_25/; website home page http://www.geocities.com (accessed May 19, 2003).

"History of Woman Suffrage in the United States." Available online at http://www.dpsinfo.com/women/history/timeline.html; website home page http://www.dpsinfo.com (accessed May 19, 2003).

"Woman Suffrage Timeline—Winning the Vote." Available online at http://www.womenshistory.about.com/library/weekly/aa031600a.htm; website home page http://www.womenshistory.about.com (accessed May 19, 2003).

Acquiring the Panama Canal

A Statement of Action in Executing the Act Entitled "An Act to Provide for the Construction of a Canal Connecting the Waters of the Atlantic and Pacific Oceans," Approved June 28, 1903

Message

By: Theodore Roosevelt

Date: January 4, 1904

Source: Roosevelt, Theodore. *A Statement of Action in Executing the Act Entitled "An Act to Provide for the Construction of a Canal Connecting the Waters of the Atlantic and*

Pacific Oceans," Approved June 28, 1903. Washington, D.C.: Government Printing Office, 1904, 4–9.

About the Author: Theodore Roosevelt (1858–1919) succeeded to the U.S. presidency (served 1901–1909) following the assassination of President William McKinley (served 1897–1901) in 1901. He was far ahead of most of the country's leaders in recognizing that the United States must play an active, engaged role in international affairs. Roosevelt sincerely believed this role to be not only in the interests of the United States, but also the nation's responsibility.

"An Open Letter to John Hay"

Letter

By: Daniel Henry Chamberlain

Date: October 2, 1904

Source: Chamberlain, Daniel Henry. "An Open Letter to John Hay." *The New York Times.* October 2, 1904.

About the Author: Daniel Henry Chamberlain (1835–1907) was president of the Anti-Imperialist League from 1904 until 1907. After serving as captain of the Fifth Massachusetts Colored Regiment in the Civil War (1861–1865), he became governor of South Carolina during reconstruction. Following the withdrawal of federal troops from the South in 1877, Chamberlain moved to New York City, where he practiced law. ■

Introduction

American interest in a water passage through Central America dates back to the 1840s. The United States had become a transcontinental nation with the acquisition of California and the Oregon Territory, and a connection between the Atlantic and the Pacific oceans was now a matter of national importance. As early as 1850, American businessman, Cornelius Vanderbilt, operated a coach and steamship route through Nicaragua. Soon a railroad was constructed across the Isthmus of Panama. Meanwhile, the United States and Great Britain signed the Clayton-Bulwar Treaty, in which both countries agreed never to obtain control of a Central American canal connecting the Atlantic and the Pacific, but instead to encourage private efforts and to ensure the neutrality of any such crossing.

Despite the obvious value of a canal through Panama or Nicaragua, such a waterway remained only a dream for most of the nineteenth century. It was not until 1881 that the French Panama Canal Company obtained a charter from Colombia, whose boundaries included the Isthmus of Panama, and began building a canal. Directed by Ferdinand de Lesseps, the builder of the Suez Canal, French efforts created a furor in the United States. Nevertheless, the U.S. government did nothing to intervene, even though the United States had obvious strategic interests in the region and had declared the French to be in violation of the Monroe Doctrine. Congress did, however, charter an American company to build a canal across the longer but easier route through Nicaragua. The requisite treaty was then negotiated with Nicaragua, but nothing came of the effort. Meanwhile, the French Panama Canal Company was in the process of going bankrupt. Defeated by the terrain and disease, the French gave up the project in the early 1890s.

Significance

American interests in a Central American canal were revived with the Spanish-American War (1898). Compelled to fight a two-ocean war, the Unites States recognized the need for more rapid movement of naval vessels between the Atlantic and Pacific oceans. Following the war, construction of a canal became an important object of American foreign policy. To accomplish this goal, three major obstacles needed to be addressed. First, the Clayton-Bulwar Treaty, which prohibited Britain or the United States from controlling a canal, had to be abrogated. Second, a route—through the Isthmus of Panama or Nicaragua—needed to be selected. Third, authorization from the host country was required and, in the case of Panama, the French Panama Canal Company's access rights had to be acquired.

The first obstacle was removed by the Hay-Pauncefote Treaty, which the United States and Britain signed in 1901. Britain was then engaged in the Boer War (1899–1902) and had become increasingly concerned about growing German military power. The British government was, therefore, willing to concede American pre-eminence in the Caribbean basin in exchange for strengthening its relationship with the United States. Selection of the route was the subject of considerable debate. Eventually, however, the French Panama Canal Company dropped the price for its transit rights to $40 million. Following an earthquake and volcanic eruption in the area of the Nicaraguan route, the U.S. Congress passed the Isthmian Canal Act on June 28, 1902. The act authorized the president to acquire the transit rights, as well as the necessary canal zone to protect the canal, from Colombia.

Negotiations between Secretary of State John Hay and Colombian Chargés d'Affairs Dr. Tomas Herran resulted in a preliminary agreement in January 1903. The Colombian senate rejected the treaty, however, arguing that the $10-million price tag was too low and the proposed American authority in the canal zone was too extensive.

A furious President Roosevelt refused to negotiate further with the Colombians. In fact, he made known in "private" conversations that he would find it understandable if the people of the Panama province revolted against Colombia. Whether the United States had any direct involvement in subsequent events remains unclear; nonetheless, on November 3, 1903, a revolt is exactly what took place. Coincidentally, a U.S. warship, the

A bird's eye view of a portion of the Panama Canal under construction. Massive locks had to be built to enable the raising and lowering of ships through Panama's mountains. **THE LIBRARY OF CONGRESS.**

U.S.S. *Nashville,* happened to be in the region at the time. Under the provisions of a treaty between the United States and Colombia, the United States was authorized to ensure that crossing Panama by rail was protected from hostile forces. Using this dubious piece of logic, the President ordered the *Nashville* to prevent Colombia from reenforcing its small garrison in Panama.

Under the circumstances, the Panamanian revolt quickly succeeded. On November 6, 1903, the United States recognized the independent nation of Panama. On November 18, the United States and Panama signed an agreement, identical to the one rejected by Colombia. It gave the United States the right to build a canal and to occupy a protective canal zone "in perpetuity." A few months later, the official transfer of the French property took place.

The majority of Americans, and certainly Congress, accepted acquisition of the territory because the United States now had the required strip of land to build the long-awaited canal. Nevertheless, opponents at home and abroad attacked Roosevelt's actions. Historians have questioned not only his unwillingness to continue negotiations with Colombia, but also his failure to more seriously consider the alternate route through Nicaragua. Roosevelt brushed aside any opposition. He was confident he had acted in the best interests of the country and knew that the value of a canal to all nations was well recognized.

Primary Source

A Statement of Action in Executing the Act Entitled "An Act to Provide for the Construction of a Canal Connecting the Waters of the Atlantic and Pacific Oceans," Approved June 28, 1903 [excerpt]

SYNOPSIS: On January 4, 1904, Theodore Roosevelt forwarded a message to the U.S. Congress, explaining American recognition of an independent Panama. The president's message summarized the events leading up to the rebellion and American actions in response to those of Colombia and Panama. It also included a number of relevant letters and notes from participants. The message is a forceful assertion that American actions were entirely above board. Several years later Roosevelt was more candid in describing his role in taking the canal zone. Short excerpts from this message follow.

The United States has taken the position that no other Government is to build the canal. In 1889, when France proposed to come to the aid of the

In this cartoon a giant President Theodore Roosevelt shovels dirt onto the Colombian captial as he digs the Panama Canal. Roosevelt encouraged Panama to revolt from Colombia and recognized it as an independent country to overcome Colombian objections to an American canal there. **COURTESY OF BOONDOCKSNET.COM. REPRODUCED BY PERMISSION.**

French Panama Company by guaranteeing their bonds, the Senate of the United States in executive session, with only some three votes dissenting, passed a resolution as follows:

> That the Government of the United States will look with serious concern and disapproval upon any connection of any European government with the construction or control of any ship canal across the Isthmus of Darien or across Central America, and must regard any such connection or control as injurious to the just rights and interests of the United States and as a menace to their welfare.

Under the Hay-Pauncefote treaty it was explicitly provided that the United States should control, police, and protect the canal which was to be built, keeping it open for the vessels of all nations on equal terms. The United States thus assumed the position of guarantor of the canal and of its peaceful use by all the world. The guarantee included as a matter of course the building of the canal. The enterprise was recognized as responding to an international need; and it would be the veriest travesty on right and justice to treat the governments in possession of the Isthmus as having the right, in the language of Mr. Cass, "to close the gates of intercourse on the great highways of the world, and justify the act by the pretension that these avenues of trade and travel belong to them and that they choose to shut them." . . .

When in August it began to appear probable that the Colombian Legislature would not ratify the treaty it became incumbent upon me to consider well what the situation was and to be ready to advise the Congress as to what were the various alternatives of action open to us. There were several possibilities. One was that Colombia would at the last moment see the unwisdom of her position. That there might be nothing omitted, Secretary Hay, through the minister at Bogota, repeatedly warned Colombia that grave consequences might follow from her rejection of the treaty. Although it was a constantly diminishing chance, yet the possibility of ratification did not wholly pass away until the close of the session of the Colombian Congress.

A second alternative was that by the close of the session on the last day of October, without the ratification of the treaty by Colombia and without any steps taken by Panama, the American Congress on assembling early in November would be confronted with a situation in which there had been a failure to come to terms as to building the canal along the Panama route, and yet there had not been a lapse of a reasonable time—using the word reasonable in any proper sense—such as would justify the Administration going to the Nicaragua route. This situation seemed on the whole the most likely, and as a matter of fact I had made the original draft of my Message to the Congress with a view to its existence.

It was the opinion of eminent international jurists that in view of the fact that the great design of our guarantee under the treaty of 1846 was to dedicate the Isthmus to the purposes of interoceanic transit, and above all to secure the construction of an interoceanic canal, Colombia could not under existing conditions refuse to enter into a proper arrangement with the United States to that end, without violating the spirit and substantially repudiating the obligations of a treaty the full benefits of which she had enjoyed for over fifty years. My intention was to consult the Congress as to whether under such circumstances it would not be proper to announce that the canal was to be dug forthwith; that we would give the terms that we had offered and no others; and that if such terms were not agreed to we would enter into an arrangement with Panama direct, or take what other steps were needful in order to begin the enterprise.

A third possibility was that the people of the Isthmus, who had formerly constituted an independent state, and who until recently were united to Colombia only by a loose tie of federal relationship, might take the protection of their own vital interests into their own hands, reassert their former rights, declare their independence upon just grounds, and establish a government competent and willing to do its share in this great work for civilization. This third possibility is what actually occurred. Everyone knew that it was a possibility, but it was not until towards the end of October that it appeared to be an imminent probability. Although the Administration, of course, had special means of knowledge, no such means were necessary in order to appreciate the possibility, and toward the end the likelihood, of such a revolutionary outbreak and of its success. It was a matter of common notoriety. Quotations from the daily papers could be indefinitely multiplied to show this state of affairs; a very few will suffice. . . .

I hesitate to refer to the injurious insinuations which have been made of complicity by this Government in the revolutionary movement in Panama. They are as destitute of foundation as of propriety. The only excuse for my mentioning them is the fear lest unthinking persons might mistake for acquiescence the silence of mere self-respect. I think proper to say, therefore, that no one connected with this Government had any part in preparing, inciting, or encouraging the late revolution on the Isthmus of Panama, and that save from the reports of our military and naval officers, given above, no one connected with this Government had any previous knowledge of the revolution except such as was accessible to any person of ordinary intelligence who read the newspapers and kept up a current acquaintance with public affairs.

By the unanimous action of its people, without the firing of a shot—with a unanimity hardly before recorded in any similar case—the people of Panama declared themselves an independent Republic. Their recognition by this Government was based upon a state of facts in no way dependent for its justification upon our action in ordinary cases. I have not denied, nor do I wish to deny, either the validity or the propriety of the general rule that a new state should not be recognized as independent till it has shown its ability to maintain its independence. This rule is derived from the principle of nonintervention, and as a corollary of that principle has generally been observed by the United States. But, like the principle from which it is deduced, the rule is subject to exceptions; and there are in my opinion clear and imperative reasons why a departure from it was justified and even required in the present instance. These reasons embrace, first, our treaty rights; second, our national interests and safety; and, third, the interests of collective civilization. . . .

In view of the manifold considerations of treaty right and obligation, of national interest and safety, and of collective civilization, by which our Government was constrained to act, I am at a loss to comprehend the attitude of those who can discern in the recognition of the Republic of Panama only a general approval of the principle of "revolution" by which a given government is overturned or one portion of a country separated from another. Only the amplest justification can warrant a revolutionary movement of either kind. But there is no fixed rule which can be applied to all such movements. Each case must be judged on its own merits. There have been many revolutionary movements, many movements for the dismemberment of countries, which were evil, tried by any standard. But in my opinion no disinterested and fair-minded observer acquainted with the circumstances can fail to feel that Panama had the amplest justification for separation from Colombia under the conditions existing, and, moreover, that its action was in the highest degree beneficial to the interests of the entire civilized world by securing the immediate opportunity for the building of the interoceanic canal. . . . I firmly believe of the adjacent parts of Central and South America, will be greatly benefited by the building of the canal and the guarantee of peace and order along its line; and hand in hand with the benefit to them will go the benefit to us and to mankind. By our prompt and decisive action, not only have our interests and those of the world at large been conserved, but we have forestalled complications which were likely to be fruitful in loss to ourselves, and in bloodshed and suffering to the people of the Isthmus.

Primary Source

"An Open Letter to John Hay" [excerpt]

SYNOPSIS: In the following excerpt from an open letter to Secretary of State John Hay, published in *The New York Times,* Daniel Henry Chamberlain criticizes the Panama policy of the Roosevelt administration. Chamberlain is particularly critical of Hay, in part, because of the higher standard expected of Hay due to his association with President Abraham Lincoln. As a young Illinois lawyer, Hay had come to Lincoln's attention and served as the president's private secretary. Hay held a variety of diplomatic positions before being appointed secretary of state by President McKinley. He continued in this post under President Roosevelt, until 1905.

The Honorable John Hay,
Secretary of State, Washington, D.C.

Dear Sir:

. . . The foregoing facts are all beyond dispute, and are not disputed, so far as I know. In fine, they establish that the Republic of Colombia, in the last year of grace, had been for full fifty years a recognized, well-established, respectable, and fairly prosperous republic—respectable in size, in population, in history, and in character. It was, of course, in the eye of international law, on a footing with any government in the world in respect of public political rights and privileges.

It seems hardly necessary to allude to the peculiar claims which this sister republic had upon our own. Our greatness should have been her shield against all oppression. Colombia's comparative feebleness should have made it impossible for us to treat her with less than chivalrous and generous kindness. The fact of her helplessness against our power should have been her safety from all injury or questionable action on our part toward her.

It seems necessary, in view of your treatment of the Panama affair, as well as the President's treatment of it—if I am at liberty to make any distinction between the two—to recur at the outset to one or two of the most elementary principles or rules of morals and of international law. They are: (1) That international law is founded upon morality; upon the agreed or common notions of the civilized nations of the world regarding the duties reciprocally due by each and all the nations to each and all the other nations. Nothing is more perfectly conceded, as nothing can be more fundamental than this concept. (2) That all nations, great and small, feeble and powerful, in the forum of international law have perfect equality of rights. This is finely stated by the great elder Woolsey, thus:

> All nations stand on an equality, meaning equality of rights—the old and the new, the large and the small, monarchies and republics.

Such, as now set forth, was the situation of the Republic of Colombia, and such was her standing toward all who were in the comity of the nations,—all the nations owing allegiance to international law,—in October, 1903, when the drama now called the Panama affair began publicly to open. The President in his apology, called message, to Congress of January 4, 1904, distinctly and with repetition states that revolution in the Province of Panama was apprehended by our Government as early as August 31, 1903—that such was the information gathered and published by the newspapers, and officially reported by our naval officers in those waters. In view of this the President states that orders were given between October 19 and 30, 1903, for three ships of our navy to proceed to the immediate vicinity, or within quick reach, of Panama—the Nashville being ordered to Colon, a port of Colombia on the north side of the Isthmus. He continues that, hearing that both sides—that is, Colombia and Panama—were making ready forces, orders were sent November 2, 1903, to the commanders of the three designated ships to prevent the landing of any armed forces, either government or insurgent, at any point within fifty miles of Panama, meaning the town of Panama on the Gulf of Panama, and a part of the Province of Panama, and of the Republic of Colombia. This order the President professes to rest upon certain orders issued one and two years previously, which in turn were based upon the claim of the guarantee of neutrality of the Isthmus of Panama, and "of transit from sea to sea," as Secretary Moody's order of September, 1902, phrased it. All this is claimed to have been our right and duty under the treaty of 1846.

This large claim must be carefully examined.

The treaty in question is entitled, "Treaty of Peace, Amity, Navigation, and Commerce." It was concluded December 12, 1846, and was proclaimed June 12, 1848. It consists of thirty-six articles, with an additional article, and the contracting parties are the United States of North America and the Republic of New Granada, the latter being the predecessor of the present Republic of Colombia. As its title imports, all its articles deal exclusively with matters of commerce and navigation, or matters strictly relating thereto. The last article but one, the thirty-fifth, declares the desire of the contracting parties "to make as durable as possible the relations established by virtue of this treaty," and to that end adds six additional "points," which together make up Article 35. In the first of these points "the Government of New Granada guarantees to the Government of the United States that the right of way or transit across the Isthmus of Panama upon any modes of communication that now exist or that may be hereafter constructed, shall be open and free to the Government and citizens of the United States;" and reciprocally it is declared that "in order to secure to themselves the tranquil and constant enjoyment of these advantages the United States guarantee positively and efficaciously to New Granada, by the present stipulation, the perfect neutrality of the before-mentioned Isthmus;" "and in consequence, the United States also guarantee, in the same manner, the rights of sovereignty and property which New Granada has and possesses over the said territory."

Here are mutual guarantees, or a guarantee and counter guarantees; or, first, a guarantee, on the part of New Granada, of open and free transit across the Isthmus to the United States Government and citizens; and, second, a guarantee on the part of the United States of the perfect neutrality of the Isthmus, the United States further, in consequence of the privilege or right of free transit as aforesaid, guaranteeing "the rights of sovereignty and property which New Granada has and possesses over the said territory." . . .

Such are the provisions, and all the provisions, of the much vaunted treaty of 1846, so far as they enter into the late Panama affair, conducted by you as our Secretary of State. Put in brief form, we have here (1) a guarantee by New Granada to the United States of free transit across the Isthmus; (2) a guarantee by the United States to New Granada, to guarantee positively and efficaciously the perfect neutrality of the said Isthmus; and (3) a further guarantee by the United States to New Granada of New Granada's rights of sovereignty and property which she has and possesses over the said territory—that is, the Isthmus.

The President's claim is that under the provisions now stated, he alone, without Congressional or other authorization, as President, had the right to order the prevention of armed forces of Colombia from landing "at any point within fifty miles of (the town of) Panama," this limit being sufficient to exclude Colombia from landing troops on the Isthmus at all, or, at any rate, at any available port or point on the Isthmus.

The question which now arises is perfectly obvious. It is: Did the treaty of 1846 give such a right as was claimed and exercised by the President? No man will maintain that, except under the treaty of 1846, the United States had the right to issue any order touching Panama in August or October, 1903, or at any other times while Panama remained *de jure* a part of the territory of the Republic of Colombia; or if any one has so maintained, or should so maintain, the position is, and would be, too palpably wrong to call for discussion.

Answering the question just above stated, I forbear from detailed discussion, because certain conclusions are clear without discussion. First, that no valid or reasonable or admissible interpretation and construction of the provisions of the treaty of 1846 can evolve, from its terms or its history, such a right as the President, presumably on your advice, claimed and exercised in the premises. Second, that no such, nor any similar, interpretation or construction had, in fact, ever been put on the treaty of 1846, prior to the events of the Panama affair of 1903, by either of the parties thereto.

How, it is still well to ask, out of a guarantee of free transit on the one part, and of maintenance of neutrality on the other part, and in addition a guarantee of the sovereign rights of the first party, can be derived a right to prevent the last named party from asserting and enforcing its sovereign rights? In other words, with New Granada guaranteeing free transit across the Isthmus, the United States guaranteeing the neutrality of the Isthmus, and guaranteeing also the sovereign rights of New Granada, by what hocus-pocus of argumentation can the right be drawn of the United States to close absolutely the transit by New Granada of her troops destined to any point or for any use to which New Granada may choose to put them? This is to exclude New Granada from the exercise of the very sovereign rights which it was one plain object of the treaty of 1846 to secure to New Granada. Substituting only Colombia for New Granada, her successor in rights under the treaty, we have the whole case as it stood when, with your advice and sanction, and doubtless on your draft, the fifty-miles order of November 2, 1903, was issued.

Antecedently to any search for precedents on this point, one who felt anything of respect for simple justice, for the integrity and function of human language, or the spirit of American diplomacy in its prior dealings with our South American neighbor republics, could have had no doubt how the precedents must stand in such a case. And so they do stand. Till 1901, 1902 and 1903, when President Roosevelt's ruthless and oppressive policy, under your responsible auspices, was begun, no American Secretary of State, no responsible American statesman or public man, ever dreamed of putting upon the thirty-fifth article of the treaty of 1846 the meaning which you and the President have put upon it. Upon this point your position and his position—which are strictly identical, except that you were undoubtedly the chief sinner, being the adviser of a President notoriously destitute of knowledge of such a question—are grossly wrong, according to the words of the treaty and the precedents of both Governments acting under it.

Further Resources

BOOKS

Burton, David Henry. *Theodore Roosevelt: Confident Imperialist.* Philadelphia: University of Pennsylvania Press, 1968.

McCullough, David. *The Path Between the Seas: The Creation of the Panama Canal, 1870–1914.* New York: Simon and Schuster, 1977.

Snapp, Jeremy Sherman. *Destiny by Design: The Construction of the Panama Canal.* Lopez Island, Wash.: Pacific Heritage Press, 2000.

WEBSITES

"History: Panama Canal." Available online at http://www.purl.oclc.org/corc/system/Pathfinder/2180:xid=LCP; website home page http://www.purl.oclc.org (accessed December 24, 2002).

"Panama Canal." Available online at http://www.panamaliving.com/locks.html; website home page http://www.panamaliving.com (accessed December 24, 2002).

Panama Canal History Museum. Available online at http://www.canalmuseum.com/ (accessed December 24, 2002).

Theodore Roosevelt to Elihu Root, May 20, 1904

Letter

By: Theodore Roosevelt

Date: May 20, 1904

Source: Roosevelt, Theodore. "Theodore Roosevelt to Elihu Root, May 20, 1904." Reprinted in *The Writings of Theodore Roosevelt.* William H. Harbaugh, ed. New York: Bobbs-Merrill, 1967, 72–73.

About the Author: Theodore Roosevelt (1858–1919) was a president (served 1901–1909) who believed intensely in the greatness and destiny of the United States. Although he was actively engaged in supporting and sometimes leading progressive domestic reforms, his real passion was international affairs. Roosevelt took the country onto the world stage, extending American influence in the Caribbean basin, and engaging in European and Asian affairs. ■

Introduction

The Monroe Doctrine has been a cornerstone of American foreign policy since it was announced in 1823. The concept was initially proposed by British Foreign Secretary, George Canning, as a joint United States-British pronouncement intended to dissuade European nations from intervening in colonies that had recently gained their independence from Spain. Recognizing British opposition to such intervention and reluctant to appear to be unduly swayed by Britain, President James Monroe (served 1817–1825) took a different tack, at the urging of Secretary of State, John Quincy Adams. Monroe unilaterally declared European involvement in the affairs of the Western Hemisphere to be "dangerous to our peace and safety" and a "manifestation of unfriendly disposition toward the United States."

In reality, general disinterest and the British fleet, not the U.S. military or American moral superiority, prevented a European presence in former Spanish colonies throughout most of the nineteenth century. It was not until the latter part of the 1800s that events compelled the United States to invoke and re-evaluate the Monroe Doctrine.

Incidents in the 1890s brought home to Americans a potential European menace in the affairs of Latin America. The situation was beginning to change at the turn of the twentieth century. This was an age of steamships, aggressive imperialism, and the emergence of a powerful Germany, which longed for a "place in the sun" comparable to that of Great Britain. The relative isolation of the Western Hemisphere was no longer sufficient to protect Latin American states from European intervention. While there is little indication that Europeans intended to seize territory, as was happening in Africa, there is ample evidence that they hoped to gain an advantage by aggressively managing commercial relations in Latin America.

In large part, Latin American countries created their own problems. Leaders who incurred debt they could not afford headed the frequently unstable governments. When the debts went unpaid, European creditors sought redress, often with the support of their own governments. Europeans saw this situation as an excuse for intervention. Although the need for aggressive debt collection was possibly justified, the United States considered such action to be a threat to the Western Hemisphere. The paradox was that while the United States was prepared to invoke the Monroe Doctrine to prohibit European intervention, it did little to eliminate the circumstances that made intervention necessary.

Significance

Theodore Roosevelt recognized the obligation of the United States to play an active and constructive role in international affairs. Whereas most Americans favored isolation from world politics, Roosevelt knew this was impossible. For complex reasons—including national security, economic interest, moral commitment, national pride, and personal ego—he wanted the United States to play a greater role on the international stage.

Although Roosevelt was a staunch supporter of the Monroe Doctrine, he recognized its primary deficiency: if the United States could not compel Latin American countries to adhere to accepted standards of behavior, it had little right to prevent other countries from doing so. Faced with this logic, a man of Roosevelt's temperament reached an inevitable conclusion—a European presence in the Western Hemisphere was contrary to the best interests of the United States and other countries of the New World. Still, Latin American nations must abide by international law and custom. If the United States would not allow Europeans to compel Latin American compliance with those standards, it was obligated to enforce them itself.

The crisis, in Roosevelt's mind, came in 1902, when Venezuela defaulted on its foreign loans. To put pressure on Cipriano Castro, the Venezuelan dictator, Germany and Great Britain had blockaded Venezuelan ports. This dispute was eventually settled through negotiation, but it did not occur without the possibility of conflict with Germany. The president needed a permanent solution to the continuing threat of European intervention in the hemisphere. His answer was the Roosevelt Corollary to the Monroe Doctrine. Under the Roosevelt Corollary, the United States claimed for itself the right to intervene in the Western Hemisphere to prevent flagrant disregard of accepted standards of international behavior. The United States would, Roosevelt declared, reluctantly assume the role of policeman to ensure that European countries would not step in.

Primary Source

Theodore Roosevelt to Elihu Root, May 20, 1904

SYNOPSIS: The Roosevelt Corollary was announced in a letter from President Roosevelt that was read by Secretary of War, Elihu Root, on May 20, 1904, at a dinner celebrating the anniversary of Cuban independence. Roosevelt repeated, almost word for word, the same message at his State of the Union address in December 1904.

Washington, May 20, 1904

My dear Mr. Root:

Through you I want to send my heartiest greetings to those gathered to celebrate the second anniversary of the Republic of Cuba. I wish that it were possible to be present with you in person. I rejoice in what Cuba has done and especially in the way in which for the last two years her people have shown their desire and ability to accept in a serious spirit the responsibilities that accompany freedom. Such determination is vital, for those unable or unwilling to shoulder the responsibility of using their liberty aright can never in the long run preserve such liberty.

As for the United States, it must ever be a source of joy and gratification to good American citizens that they were enabled to play the part they did as regards Cuba. We freed Cuba from tyranny; we then stayed in the island until we had established civil order and laid the foundations for self-government and prosperity; we then made the island independent, and have since benefited her inhabitants by making closer the commercial relations between us. I hail what had been done in Cuba not merely for its own sake, but as showing the purpose and desire of this nation toward all the nations south of us. It is not true that the United States has any land hunger or entertains any projects as regards other nations, save such as are for their welfare.

All that we desire is to see all neighboring countries stable, orderly and prosperous. Any country whose people conduct themselves well can

This political cartoon shows a giant President Theodore Roosevelt splashing through the Caribbean Sea, carrying a big stick and towing a line of warships. In his corollary to the Monroe Doctrine, Roosevelt called for the use of American power, including military force, to make Latin American countries meet their international obligations. © CORBIS. REPRODUCED BY PERMISSION.

count upon our hearty friendliness. If a nation shows that it knows how to act with decency in industrial and political matters, if it keeps order and pays its obligations, then it need fear no interference from the United States. Brutal wrongdoing, or an impotence which results in a general loosening of the ties of civilized society, may finally require intervention by some civilized nation, and in the Western Hemisphere the United States cannot ignore this duty; but it remains true that our interests, and those of our southern neighbors, are in reality identical. All that we ask is that they shall govern themselves well, and be prosperous and orderly. Where this is the case they will find only helpfulness from us.

To-night you are gathered together to greet a young nation which has shown hitherto just these needed qualities; and I congratulate not only Cuba but also the United States upon the showing which Cuba has made.

Further Resources

BOOKS

Burton, David Henry. *Theodore Roosevelt: Confident Imperialist.* Philadelphia: University of Pennsylvania Press, 1968.

Pratt, Julius W. *A History of United States Foreign Policy.* Englewood Cliffs, N.J.: 1965.

Roosevelt, Theodore. *Theodore Roosevelt, An Autobiography.* New York: Scribner's, 1926.

WEBSITES

"The Roosevelt Corollary to the Monroe Doctrine." Available online at http://www.uiowa.edu/~c030162/Common/Handouts/POTUS/TRoos.html; website home page http://www.uiowa.edu (accessed March 17, 2003).

"U.S. Policy in Central America, 1898–1970." Available online at http://www.icomm.ca/carecen/page74.html; website home page http://www.icomm.ca (accessed March 17, 2003).

"Problems of Immigration"

Journal article

By: Frank P. Sargent

Date: 1904

Source: Sargent, Frank P. "Problems of Immigration." *The Annals of the American Academy of Political and Social Science.* Philadelphia: American Academy of Political and Social Science, 1904, 153–158.

About the Author: Frank Pierce Sargent (1854–1908) served in the U.S. Cavalry and participated in the campaign to capture the Apache chieftain, Geronimo. He later gained prominence working for the American Federal of Labor and was twice appointed to positions in the administration of President William McKinley (served 1897–1901). President Theodore Roosevelt (served 1901–1909) later named him commissioner general of immigration. As commissioner, he attempted to represent the interests of laborers, who generally opposed unrestricted immigration. ■

Introduction

The United States has always been a nation of immigrants. Until the late 1800s, the preponderance of immigrants came from countries in northern and western Europe—England, Scotland, Ireland, Germany, and Scandinavia. Beginning around 1880, the immigrant tide began to swell, and a shift occurred in the countries of origin. The so-called "New Immigrants" came from southern and eastern Europe, and they were generally poorer and less well-educated than their predecessors. They were also invariably Catholic or Jewish, whereas the earlier immigrants, except for the Irish, had been predominantly Protestant.

A staggering number of immigrants came to the United States between 1900 and 1914. In 1900, the population of the United States was seventy-six million; between 1900 and 1909, nearly eight million people migrated to the United States. Over the next five years, an additional five million people arrived; nearly eighty percent were from eastern and southern Europe. By contrast, in the 1870s, approximately 2.7 million immigrants arrived; fewer than seven percent came from eastern and southern Europe.

Whether digging coal and iron from the ground or manning the steel mills of Pittsburgh or plying needle and thread in New York's garment industry, immigrants played a critical role in the growth of the American industrial empire. Indeed, industry required the plentiful, cheap, and relatively docile labor force provided by the waves of immigrants who came to the United States after the Civil War (1861–1865). The concentration of new immigrants in cities, and their large presence among industrial laborers, put them in an unfavorable position. It led millions of "Old Stock," or native-born, Americans to conclude that the new immigrants were the root of urban problems and the cause of revolutionary ideas promoted by the labor movement.

Immigrants, who often lived in squalid conditions in urban slums, were seen as the creators of the slums. Those who received subsistence support from political bosses in cities in exchange for votes were blamed for corruption in city governments. Many Americans attributed strikes and labor unrest to radical foreign workers, rather than to low pay, unsteady employment, and dangerous working conditions. Meanwhile, native-born workers accused immigrants of driving down wages and working as strikebreakers. Worse, perhaps, were the racial overtones often used to describe the new immigrants. All too often, critics ascribed immigrant-related problems to what they considered to be the inherently inferior characteristics of the Russian or Pole or Italian or Jew—inferior, that is, to the Anglo-Saxon or Teutonic peoples.

Despite the fact that the United States was a nation of immigrants and that immigrants were valuable to the economy, foreign-born people were increasingly seen as a threat to American society. The threat came not only in the form of more slums or radical politics, but also in the risk of polluting the Anglo-Saxon stock that had built America. In an age when Darwin's theory of evolution had been widely accepted, notions of a continuous struggle, not only of individuals but of species, drove many to conclude that it was appropriate for the "superior" Anglo-Saxon peoples to defend themselves from the "lesser races."

Significance

By 1900, the concern over immigration was having an impact on public policy. Two primary issues were at stake. Foremost was the question of Americanization of the immigrant. It was important, many Americans felt, to encourage foreign-born people to leave behind the customs and mores of their native lands and to adopt those of the United States. Language and political philosophy were paramount issues; also important was the adoption of American cultural and social habits, such as dress, food, and other norms. As a result, various Americanization programs were established, ranging from settlement houses to business-sponsored initiatives for foreign-born employees and their families.

The second issue was the limitation of immigration. As early as 1882, Chinese immigrants were barred from entry into the United States. In subsequent years, minor restrictions were passed to keep out various categories of people, such as criminals, the insane, anarchists, and polygamists. These restrictions, however, were very specific and did not, nor were they intended to, have an impact on the number of immigrants admitted to the country. Increasingly, however, a combination of factors began to

Orchard Street, an immigrant neighborhood on the Lower East Side of New York City, in 1912. ARCHIVE PHOTOS. INC. REPRODUCED BY PERMISSION.

generate support for serious restriction. Despite growing concerns, the open door for immigrants remained in effect until 1921. That year, and again in 1924, prohibitive and discriminatory immigration laws were passed, reducing immigration to a trickle. While restricting all immigration, the laws established quotas that specifically favored immigrants from northwestern Europe—Great Britain, Ireland, Scandinavia, and Germany.

Primary Source

"Problems of Immigration"

SYNOPSIS: In the following article, which appeared in the bi-monthly publication of the American Academy of Political and Social Science, Commissioner Frank P. Sargent describes the changing character of immigration into the United States. For twenty years, the shift toward immigrants from southern and eastern European countries had become increasingly evident. In pointing out the problems caused by the large number of immigrants and their concentration in urban ghettos, Sargent presents a case for expanded government regulation of immigration.

No question of public policy is of greater importance or affects so closely the interests of the people of this country for the time present and to come as that of immigration. It presents both a practical and a sentimental side. It cannot be dealt with as other public issues. It does not deal with the question of revenue. Its subjects are not inanimate like merchandise; they are human beings. They have aspirations, hopes, fears and frailties. The methods by which other laws are administered cannot, with regard to such a subject, be resorted to in the enforcement of the immigration laws. These laws, be it remembered, with one exception, are not laws of exclusion, but laws of selection. They do not shut out the able-bodied, law-abiding and thrifty alien who seeks to make a home among us, and to help at once his individual condition and the welfare of his adopted country. To such it is the part both of policy and good government, as well as of justice and fair play, to extend the hand of welcome. But it has long since been learned in the school of practical experience that the universal welcome which should be extended by a free people to those of oppressed nations, should be restrained by considerations of prudence and a regard for the safety and well-being of the country itself. Hence it has become an established principle of this Government to frown upon the efforts of foreign countries and of interested individuals and corporations to bring to the United States, to become burdens thereupon, the indigent, the morally depraved, the physically and mentally diseased, the shiftless, and all those who are induced to leave their own country, not by their own independent volition and their own natural ambition to seek a larger and more promising field of individual enterprise, but by some selfish scheme, devised either to take undue advantage of some classes of our own people, or for other improper purpose. That such a policy is a wise one, as well as obligatory upon the Government of this great country, is too obvious to require elaborate argument.

The total estimated alien immigration to the United States from 1776 to 1820 was 250,000. The arrivals, tabulated by years, from 1820 to 1903, aggregate 21,092,614, distributed among the foreign countries as follows:

Netherlands	138,298
France	409,320
Switzerland	211,007
Scandinavia, which includes Denmark, Norway and Sweden	1,610,001
Italy	1,585,477
Germany	5,100,138
Austria-Hungary	1,518,582
United Kingdom (Great Britain and Ireland)	7,061,710
Russia	1,122,591
Japan	64,313
China	288,398
Other countries such as Roumania, Greece, Turkey, Portugal and Poland	1,984,779

The total number of arrivals for the fiscal year ending June 30th, 1903, was 857,046, divided as follows:

Netherlands	3,998
France	5,578
Switzerland	3,983
Scandinavia	77,647
Italy	230,622
Germany	40,086
Austria-Hungary	206,011
United Kingdom (Great Britain and Ireland)	68,947
Russia	136,093
Japan	19,988
Other countries, such as Roumania, Greece, Turkey, Portugal and Poland	64,113

This is the greatest number that ever applied for admission in a single year. The nearest approach to this was in 1882, when 789,000 were admitted.

The character of the arriving aliens, however, during the past years differs greatly from that of 1882 and the years previous. Since the foundation of our Government until within the past fifteen years practically all of the immigrants came from Great Britain and Ireland, Germany and the Scandinavian countries and were very largely of Teutonic stock, with a large percentage of Celtic. Fifteen millions of them have made their homes with us. In fact, they have been the pathfinders in the West and Northwest. They are an intelligent, industrious and sturdy people. They have contributed largely to the development of our country and its resources, and to them is due, in a great measure, the high standard of American citizenship.

The character of our immigration has now changed. During the past fifteen years we have been receiving a very undesirable class from Southern and Eastern Europe, which has taken the place of the Teutons and Celts. During the past fiscal year nearly 600,000 of these have been landed on our shores, constituting nearly 70 per cent of the entire immigration for that year. Instead of going to those sections where there is a sore need for farm labor, they congregate in the larger cities mostly along the Atlantic seaboard, where they constitute a dangerous and unwholesome element of our population.

About 50 per cent of the 196,000 aliens who came from Southern Italy during the past year were unable to read or write any language, and the rate of illiteracy among the rest of these Mediterranean and Slavic immigrants ranges from 20 per cent to 70 per cent, while among the Teutonic and Celtic races the rate of illiteracy is less than 1 per cent to 4 per cent. This change which has taken place during the past fifteen years has resulted in raising the average of illiteracy of all aliens from about 5 per cent in former years to 25 per cent at the present time.

What I desire, however, to call attention to, I have already indicated, and that is that in the enforcement of the immigration laws, since the subjects thereof are human beings, the treatment is two-sided. One-half of the work incumbent upon the Government has been done when those whose presence would militate against the interests of the people of this country have been detected and returned to their homes. Under the direction of the Bureau of

Early twentieth century immigrants to the United States sit with their luggage, waiting to be processed, on Ellis Island, New York. **THE LIBRARY OF CONGRESS.**

Immigration all aliens are carefully examined by immigrant inspectors and surgeons of the Marine Hospital Service at the ports of entry for the purpose of rejecting those not admissible under the provisions of the immigration laws. During the past year more than 1 per cent of those who applied for admission were rejected and returned to the countries whence they came. The total number thus debarred during the year was 8,769, for the following causes, viz.:

Paupers 5,812

Afflicted with a loathsome or a dangerous contagious disease 1,773

Contract laborers 1,086

Convicts 51

For all other causes 47

In addition thereto 547 were deported who were found to be in the United States in violation of law.

There still remains the larger question, the question that more individually and vitally affects the interests of our people. What shall we do with the thousands that are admitted? Shall they be allowed to form alien colonies in our great cities, there to maintain the false ideals and to propagate the lawless views born thereof as the result of their experience—foreign not alone from their origin geographically, but foreign as well to this country in their ideals of human liberty and individual rights? To answer this question affirmatively is simply to transfer the evils which may be admitted to exist in foreign countries to our own shores. Immigration left thus is a menace to the peace, good order and stability of American institutions, a menace which will grow and increase with the generations and finally burst forth in anarchy and disorder. It is thus necessary, as a measure of public security, to devise and put in force some means by which alien arrivals may be distributed throughout this country and thus afforded the opportunities by honest industry of securing homes for themselves and their children, the possession of which transforms radical thinkers into conservative workers and makes all that which threatens the welfare of the commonwealth a means to preserve its security and permanency.

The Department of Commerce and Labor, through the Bureau of Immigration, should, in my judgment, furnish information to all desirable aliens as to the best localities for the profitable means of earning a livelihood, either as settlers, tradesmen or laborers. The States and Territories which need immigration should file with the Department such evidence of the advantages offered to aliens to settle in localities where conditions are favorable, so that the tide of immigration will be directed to the open and sparsely settled country. That the Bureau of Immigration should be the medium of distributing the aliens is to my mind as much of a duty as it is to decide to whom the right to enter shall be given.

There are confined in the penal, reformatory and charitable institutions of the eleven States from Maine to Maryland, including Delaware, 28,135 aliens. The Irish, Slavs, Germans, Italians and English make up 85 per cent of the total. There are 9,390 Irish; 5,372 Slavic; 4,426 Germans; 2,623 Italians, and 2,622 English. In the State of Pennsylvania there are 5,601 aliens confined in these institutions, 90 per cent of whom are of the same five races in the following numbers: 1,772 Slavic; 1,218 Irish; 1,078 Germans; 673 Italians, and 423 English.

As I have already stated, the question has two sides. The other side is the humanitarian. It refers to the claims upon our consideration of alien arrivals as fellow beings. This side equally demands of a just and humane government the adoption of practical methods for such a distribution of these people as I have already indicated. On their own account, and in consideration of their ignorance and helplessness, they should be taken out of the great centers of population, where restricted space compels them to live together in a very unhealthful and unsanitary condition, and where competition for the means of existence forces them to prey upon each other and upon American citizens engaged in the same pursuits by a system of underbidding for work, a condition which reduces the cost of labor and lowers the standard of living. Such colonization, furthermore, by its consequent disregard of sanitary laws, threatens the physical health of the communities affected.

I cannot, in the brief space at my disposal, do more than merely advert to the principal features of this great governmental policy regulating immigration, a policy whose administration, to some extent, has been confided to my hands. I feel with every day of added experience the gravity of the interests involved, and that it calls for all that is best and highest in ability and moral stamina to accomplish the best results. It would be impossible for any right-minded man—it certainly has been to me—to undertake such a task without soon learning how much it exacts. In every moment of doubt or uncertainty, however, I have endeavored to be governed by that fundamental principle of our Government which recognizes the sacredness of right and individual opportunity, whether the person affected has fortunately been born under the shadow of the stars and stripes, or whether, when the opportunity comes to him to exercise his own volition in selecting a home for himself and his children, he seeks that protection. Exact justice to all, irrespective of present or previous condition, is the rule by which I have endeavored to enforce the immigration laws, bearing in mind always that in any conflict of interests between my own people and those of other countries my primary duty is so to act that the balance will incline in favor of the citizens of this country, in whose service I am employed.

Further Resources

BOOKS

Clarke, Duncan. *A New World: The History of Immigration into the United States.* San Diego, Cal.: Thunder Bay, 2000.

Daniels, Roger. *Not Like Us: Immigrants and Minorities in America, 1890–1924.* Chicago: Ivan R. Dee, 1997.

Handlin, Oscar. *The Uprooted: The Epic Story of the Great Migrations that Made the American People.* Boston: Little, Brown, 1951.

WEBSITES

American Family Immigration History Center. Available online at http://www.ellisisland.org/EIinfo/aboutAFIHC.asp; website home page http://www.ellisisland.org (accessed March 14, 2003).

"Immigration and the United States—Four Periods of Immigration." Available online at http.//www.americanhistory.about.com/cs/immigration/; website home page http://www.americanhistory.about.com (accessed March 14, 2003).

Sin and Society: An Analysis of Latter-Day Iniquity

Nonfiction work

By: Edward Alsworth Ross

Date: 1907

Source: Ross, Edward Alsworth. *Sin and Society: An Analysis of Latter-Day Iniquity.* Gloucester, Mass.: Peter Smith, 1965, 3–19.

About the Author: Edward Alsworth Ross (1866–1951) was a founder of American sociology and a leading intellectual

Sociologist Edward A. Ross, an influential Progressive reformer from early twentieth century America. **THE LIBRARY OF CONGRESS.**

proponent of Progressive ideology. A widely published and influential professor who served on the faculties of Stanford University, the University of Nebraska, and the University of Wisconsin, Ross rejected the prevalent social and political philosophies of late nineteenth century America. ■

Introduction

In the years following the Civil War (1861–1865), conservative ideas dominated American political, economic, and social philosophy. Conservative thinkers attributed personal success and failure to the Darwinist theory of "survival of the fittest," and the playing out of immutable natural social and economic laws. The results were thought to be the inevitable unfolding God's plan. While charity might be extended to the needy, efforts to intervene to alter the working of the natural order were deemed, at best, futile. Reformers, among them Edward Alsworth Ross, increasingly saw the concentration of wealth and power into the hands of a relatively few Americans as a threat to the continued existence of a democratic society. They began to recognize that the individualistic philosophy of a self-sufficient, agrarian American society were inappropriate in the far more complex urban, industrial society that emerged in the post-war years.

Rejection of conservative ideologies gained momentum in the 1870s, as labor and agricultural movements found increasing support from intellectuals. The various reform-minded groups coalesced into the Populist movement of the 1880s and 1890s. By the late 1890s, disenchantment had evolved into one of America's most important reform movements, known as progressivism. Led primarily by urban, middle-class, old-stock Protestants, the Progressive movement resulted in fundamental changes in American political and economic life.

Significance

Sin and Society was a short, but influential, book that offered a succinct explanation of the changing character of American society. It also provided justification for an active government in correcting the inequities of modern society. Ross's ideas played an important role in explaining the changed character of American society and in rationalizing the need for a more active government to correct social imbalances.

In *Sin and Society,* Ross contrasted the personal "sins" that characterized the relatively simple society of pre-industrial America with the more impersonal "sins" of the complex society that predominated at the turn of the century. The sins of the earlier period included assault, robbery, and drunkenness. The perpetrator was clear, as was the direct harm to specific individuals and to society as a whole. In the modern world, however, the consequences of "sin" were more far-reaching in their impact, but responsibility was obscure. These sins were often the result of impersonal business decisions, resulting from the inevitable working out of natural laws.

In this new age, identification of the "sinner" was all the more difficult because often the responsible parties were generous and honorable people. They started charities, founded innumerable worthy causes, and were models of impeccable integrity. It was ironic that the same person who might build a children's hospital would also own a coal mine where nine-year-old breaker boys worked twelve hours a day separating coal from slag. Or that owners of wretched slum housing would fund working men's libraries and shelters for the homeless. Or that tax-evading millionaires would regularly make personal contributions to the care of the needy.

To Ross, part of the solution was intervention by the state. The absence, in modern society, of personal accountability for many of society's evils required a neutral third party to adjust the rules and protect the helpless. It was this advocacy of a collective responsibility—in contrast to "rugged individualism"—that appealed to Theodore Roosevelt (served 1901–1909) and the Progressives.

Primary Source

Sin and Society: An Analysis of Latter-Day Iniquity [excerpt]

SYNOPSIS: The following excerpt is the opening chapter of Edward Alsworth Ross's short, but influential, book, *Sin and Society: An Analysis of Latter-Day Iniquity.* First published in 1907, it contained an introductory letter from President Theodore Roosevelt. The president praised Ross for bringing to the public's attention a "wholesome and sane" argument urging "that our moral judgment may be recast in order more effectively to hold to account the really dangerous foes of our present civilization."

New Varieties of Sin

The sinful heart is ever the same, but sin changes its quality as society develops. Modern sin takes its character from the mutualism of our time. Under our present manner of living, how many of my vital interests I must intrust to others! Nowadays the water main is my well, the trolley car my carriage, the banker's safe my old stocking, the policeman's billy my fist. My own eyes and nose and judgment defer to the inspector of food, or drugs, or gas, or factories, or tenements, or insurance companies. I rely upon others to look after my drains, invest my savings, nurse my sick, and teach my children. I let the meat trust butcher my pig, the oil trust mould my candles, the sugar trust boil my sorghum, the coal trust chop my wood, the barb wire company split my rails.

But this spread-out manner of life lays snares for the weak and opens doors to the wicked. Interdependence puts us, as it were, at one another's mercy, and so ushers in a multitude of new forms of wrong-doing. The practice of mutualism has always worked this way. Most sin is preying, and every new social relation begets its cannibalism. No one will "make the ephah small" or "falsify the balances" until there is buying and selling, "withhold the pledge" until there is loaning, "keep back the hire of the laborers" until there is a wage system, "justify the wicked for a reward" until men submit their disputes to a judge. The rise of the state makes possible counterfeiting, smuggling, peculation, and treason. Commerce tempts the pirate, the forger, and the embezzler. Every new fiduciary relation is a fresh opportunity for breach of trust. Today the factory system makes it possible to work children to death on the double-quick, speculative building gives the jerry-builder his chance, long-range investment spawns the get-rich-quick concern, and the trust movement opens the door to the bubble promoter.

The springs of the older sin seem to be drying up. Our forced-draught pace relieves us of the superabundance of energy that demands an explosive outlet. Spasms of violent feeling go with a sluggish habit of life, and are as out of place to-day as are the hard-drinking habits of our Saxon ancestors. We are too busy to give rein to spite. The stresses and lures of civilized life leave slender margin for the gratification of animosities. In quiet, side-tracked communities there is still much old-fashioned hatred, leading to personal clash, but elsewhere the cherishing of malice is felt to be an expensive luxury. Moreover, brutality, lust, and cruelty are on the wane. In this country, it is true, statistics show a widening torrent of bloody crime, but the cause is the weakening of law rather than an excess of bile. Other civilized peoples seem to be turning away from the sins of passion.

The darling sins that are blackening the face of our time are incidental to the ruthless pursuit of private ends, and hence quite "without prejudice." The victims are used or sacrificed not at all from personal ill-will, but because they can serve as pawns in somebody's little game. Like the way-farers run down by the automobilist, they are offered up to the God of Speed. The essence of the wrongs that infest our articulated society is betrayal rather than aggression. Having perforce to build men of willow into a social fabric that calls for oak, we see on all hands monstrous treacheries,—adulterators, peculators, boodlers, grafters, violating the trust others have placed in them. The little finger of Chicane has come to be thicker than the loins of Violence.

The sinister opportunities presented in this webbed social life have been seized unhesitatingly, because such treasons have not yet become infamous. The man who picks pockets with a railway rebate, murders with an adulterant instead of a bludgeon, burglarizes with a "rake-off" instead of a jimmy, cheats with a company prospectus instead of a deck of cards, or scuttles his town instead of his ship, does not feel on his brow the brand of a malefactor. The shedder of blood, the oppressor of the widow and the fatherless, long ago became odious, but latter-day treacheries fly no skull-and-crossbones flag at the mast-head. The qualities which differentiate them from primitive sin and procure them such indulgence may be clearly defined.

Modern Sin is not Superficially Repulsive

To-day the sacrifice of life incidental to quick success rarely calls for the actual spilling of blood. How decent are the pale slayings of the quack, the adulterator, and the purveyor of polluted water, compared with the red slayings of the vulgar bandit or assassin!

Even if there is blood-letting, the long-range, tentacular nature of modern homicide eliminates all personal collision. What an abyss between the knife-play of brawlers and the law-defying neglect to fence dangerous machinery in a mill, or to furnish cars with safety couplers! The providing of unsuspecting passengers with "cork" life-preservers secretly loaded with bars of iron to make up for their deficiency in weight of cork, is spiritually akin to the treachery of Joab, who, taking Amasa by the beard "to kiss him," smote Amasa "in the fifth rib;" but it wears a very different aspect. The current methods of annexing the property of others are characterized by a pleasing indirectness and refinement. The furtive, apprehensive manner of the till-tapper or the porch-climber would jar disagreeably upon the tax-dodger "swearing off" his property, or the city official concealing a "rake-off" in his specifications for a public building. The work of the card-sharp and the thimblerigger shocks a type of man that will not stick at the massive "artistic swindling" of the contemporary promoter. A taint of unworthiness, indeed, always attaches to transactions that force the person into humiliating postures. Your petty parasite or your minor delinquent inspires the contempt that used to be felt for the retailer. The confidence man is to the promoter what the small shopkeeper was to the merchant prince.

Modern Sin Lacks the Familiar Tokens of Guilt

The stealings and slayings that lurk in the complexities of our social relations are not deeds of the dive, the dark alley, the lonely road, and the midnight hour. They require no nocturnal prowling with muffled step and bated breath, no weapon or offer of violence. Unlike the old-time villain, the latter-day malefactor does not wear a slouch hat and a comforter, breathe forth curses and an odor of gin, go about his nefarious work with clenched teeth and an evil scowl. In the supreme moment his lineaments are not distorted with rage, or lust, or malevolence. One misses the dramatic setting, the time-honored insignia of turpitude. Fagin and Bill Sykes and Simon Legree are vanishing types. Gamester, murderer, body-snatcher, and kidnapper may appeal to a Hogarth, but what challenge finds his pencil in the countenance of the boodler, the savings-bank wrecker, or the ballot-box stuffer? Among our criminals of greed, one begins to meet the "grand style" of the great criminals of ambition, Macbeth or Richard III. The modern high-power dealer of woe wears immaculate linen, carries a silk hat and a lighted cigar, sins with a calm countenance and a serene soul, leagues or months from the evil he causes. Upon his gentlemanly presence the eventual blood and tears do not obtrude themselves.

This is why good, kindly men let the wheels of commerce and of industry redden and redden, rather than pare or lose their dividend. This is why our railroads yearly injure one employee in twenty-six, and we look in vain for that promised "day of the Lord" that "will make a man more precious than fine gold."

Modern Sins are Impersonal

The covenant breaker, the suborned witness, the corrupt judge, the oppressor of the fatherless,—the old-fashioned sinner, in short,—knows his victim, must hearken, perhaps, to bitter upbraidings. But the tropical belt of sin we are sweeping into is largely impersonal. Our iniquity is wireless, and we know not whose withers are wrung by it. The hurt passes into that vague mass, the "public," and is there lost to view. Hence it does not take a Borgia to knead "chalk and alum and plaster" into the loaf, seeing one cannot know just who will eat that loaf, or what gripe it will give him. The purveyor of spurious life-preservers need not be a Cain. The owner of rotten tenement houses, whose "pull" enables him to ignore the orders of the health department, foredooms babies, it is true, but for all that he is no Herod.

Often there are no victims. If the crazy hulk sent out for "just one more trip" meets with fair weather, all is well. If no fire breaks out in the theatre, the sham "emergency exits" are blameless. The corrupt inspector who O.K.'s low-grade kerosene is chancing it, that is all. Many sins, in fact, simply augment risk. Evil does not dog their footsteps with relentless and heart-shaking certainty. When the catastrophe does come, the sinner salves his conscience by blasphemously calling it an "accident" or an "act of God."

Still more impersonal is sin when the immediate harm touches beneficent institutions rather than individuals, when, following his vein of private profit, the sinner drives a gallery under some pillar upholding our civilization. The blackguarding editor is really undermining the freedom of the press. The policy kings and saloon keepers, who get out to the polls the last vote of the vicious and criminal classes, are sapping manhood suffrage. Striking engineers who spitefully desert passenger trains in mid-career are jeopardizing the right of a man to work only when he pleases. The real victim of a lynching mob is not the malefactor, but the law-abiding spirit. School-board grafters who blackmail applicants for a teacher's position are stabbing the free public school. The corrupt bosses and "combines" are murdering representative government. The perpetrators of election frauds unwittingly assail the institution of the ballot. Rarely, however, are such transgressions abominated as are offenses against persons.

Because of the special qualities of the Newer Unrighteousness, because these devastating latter-day wrongs, being comely of look, do not advertise their vileness, and are without the ulcerous hag-visage of the primitive sins, it is possible for iniquity to flourish greatly, even while men are getting better. Briber and boodler and grafter are often "good men," judged by the old tests, and would have passed for virtuous in the American community of seventy years ago. Among the chiefest sinners are now enrolled men who are pure and kind-hearted, loving in their families, faithful to their friends, and generous to the needy.

One might suppose that an exasperated public would sternly castigate these modern sins. But the fact is, the very qualities that lull the conscience of the sinner blind the eyes of the onlookers. People are sentimental, and bastinado wrong-doing not according to its harmfulness, but according to the infamy that has come to attach to it. Undiscerning, they chastise with scorpions the old authentic sins, but spare the new. They do not see that boodling is treason, that blackmail is piracy, that embezzlement is theft, that speculation is gambling, that tax-dodging is larceny, that railroad discrimination is treachery, that the factory labor of children is slavery, that deleterious adulteration is murder. It has not come home to them that the fraudulent promoter "devours widows' houses," that the monopolist "grinds the faces of the poor," that mercenary editors and spellbinders "put bitter for sweet and sweet for bitter." The cloven hoof hides in patent leather; and to-day, as in Hosea's time, the people "are destroyed for lack of knowledge." The mob lynches the red-handed slayer, when it ought to keep a gallows Haman-high for the venal mine inspector, the seller of infected milk, the maintainer of a fire-trap theatre. The child-beater is forever blasted in reputation, but the exploiter of infant toil, or the concocter of a soothing syrup for the drugging of babies, stands a pillar of society. The petty shoplifter is more abhorred than the stealer of a franchise, and the wife-whipper is outcast long before the man who sends his over-insured ship to founder with its crew.

There is a special cause for the condoning of sins committed in the way of business and without personal malice. Business men, as a rule, insist upon a free hand in their dealings, and, since they are conspicuous and influential in the community, they carry with them a considerable part of the non-business world. The leisured, the non-industrial employees, the bulk of professional men, and many public servants, hold to the unmitigated maxim of *caveat emptor,* and accept the chicane of trade as reasonable and legitimate. In England till 1487 any one who knew how to read might commit murder with impunity by claiming "benefit of clergy." There is something like this in the way we have granted quack and fakir and mine operator and railroad company indulgence to commit manslaughter in the name of business.

On the other hand, the active producers, such as farmers and workingmen, think in terms of livelihood rather than of profit, and tend therefore to consider the social bearings of conduct. Intent on well-being rather than on pecuniary success, they are shocked at the lenient judgment of the commercial world. Although they have hitherto deferred to the traders, the producers are losing faith in business men's standards, and may yet pluck up the courage to validate their own ethics against the individualist, anti-social ethics of commerce.

Still, even if the mass turns vehement, it is not certain the lash of its censure can reach the cuticle of the sinner. A differentiated society abounds in closed doors and curtained recesses. The murmurs of the alley do not penetrate to the boulevard. The shrieks from the blazing excursion steamer do not invade the distant yacht of her owners. If the curses of tricked depositors never rise to the circles of "high finance" that keep the conscience of the savings-bank wrecker, why should the popular hiss stay the commercial buccaneer? All turns on the power of the greater public to astringe the flaccid conscience of business men until they become stern judges of one another. If we have really entered upon the era of jangling classes, it is, of course, idle to hope for a truly public sentiment upon such matters. Nevertheless, in the past, antiseptic currents of opinion have mounted from the healthy base to the yellowing top of the social tree, and they may do so again.

While idealists are dipping their brushes into the sunset for colors bright enough to paint the Utopias that might be if society were quite made over, one may be pardoned for dreaming of what would be possible, even on the plane of existing institutions, if only in this highly articulated society of ours every one were required to act in good faith, and to do what he had deliberately led others to expect of him.

Further Resources

BOOKS

Buenker, John D. *Urban Liberalism and Progressive Reform.* New York: Norton, 1978.

Crunden, Robert Morse. *Ministers of Reform: the Progressives' Achievement in American Civilization, 1889–1920.* New York: Basic Books, 1982.

Resek, Carl. *The Progressives.* Indianapolis: Bobbs-Merrill, 1967.

WEBSITES

"Edward Alsworth Ross: Social Psychology: Table of Contents." Available online at http://spartan.ac.brocku.ca/~lward/Ross/Ross_1919/Ross_1919_toc.html; website home page http://spartan.ac.brocku.ca (accessed May 15, 2003).

"Sentinel of Social Control: An Intellectual Biography of Edward Alsworth Ross." Available online at http://www.fsu.edu/gradstudies/thesis/1996/Spring96/mcmahon.html ; website home page: http://www.fsu.edu (accessed May 19, 2003).

Declaration of Governors for Conservation of Natural Resources

Report

By: Governors Conference on Conservation

Date: December 6, 1908

Source: Governors Conference on Conservation. *Declaration of Governors for Conservation of Natural Resources.* Farmers' Bulletin 340. Washington, D.C.: Government Printing Office, 1908.

About the Organization: The Governors Conference on Conservation was convened by President Theodore Roosevelt (served 1901–1909) at the White House in May 1908. Governors of the forty-four states, their advisors, and scores of experts attended the three-day meeting. At the conclusion of the conference, the governors unanimously adopted a report titled *Declaration of Governors for Conservation of Natural Resources,* drafted by Governors Newton C. Blanchard (Louisiana), John Franklin Fort (New Jersey), J.O. Davidson (Wisconsin), John C. Cutler (Utah), and Martin F. Ansel (South Carolina). ■

Introduction

When settlers arrived on the eastern shores of the present-day United States in the early seventeenth century, they found seemingly limitless natural resources—farmland, timber, waterways, wildlife, minerals, and ores. Over the next two hundred years, waves of immigrants expanded the thriving country as they moved steadily westward in search of new land and more resources. By the nineteenth century, the United States had broken the bounds of the Appalachian Mountains and spanned the continent, from the Atlantic Ocean to the Pacific Ocean. During this time, a few forward-looking thinkers became concerned about the eventual exhaustion of the nation's natural resources.

In 1890, the United States Census Bureau published the declaration that the entire transcontinental nation was now officially settled. Seeing this as a potentially threatening situation, conservationists issued a warning: Since the frontier had ceased to exist, resources were no longer limitless. Without careful management, they argued, the rich natural inheritance of future American generations would be squandered within only a few years. It was, perhaps, providential that as the conservation issue emerged on the national scene, President Theodore Roosevelt was himself a skilled naturalist and outdoorsman. His personal interests coincided with the national need for strong leadership in the use of still-abundant, though limited, resources.

Beginning with the passage of the Reclamation Act in 1902, the Roosevelt administration pressed an aggressive conservation policy upon a reluctant nation. Roosevelt and his allies thus met increasingly stiff resistance to their plans. The main reason was that, throughout the nation's history, many wealthy and influential people had become prosperous through wasteful exploitation of land, forests, and other vital resources. Although the West was no longer a "frontier" at the turn of the twentieth century, "men on the make" sought their fortune by continuing the tradition of exploiting this vast, thinly populated region. A politically powerful group with considerable congressional support, they viewed conservationists as a threat. By 1907, Roosevelt's resource management program had run into serious obstacles.

Significance

A coordinated conservation program was one of the major achievements of the Roosevelt administration, as it required the United States to confront the need for resource management. While only a beginning, Roosevelt's policies established a new direction for the country.

The first major piece of legislation was the 1902 Reclamation Act, initiating irrigation and hydroelectric projects in western states. In 1905, the United States Forestry Service was organized under Gifford Pinchot. The 1906 Antiquities Act protected historic property on federal lands and granted the president the authority to establish national monuments. During Roosevelt's administration, forest reserves were increased from approximately forty-three million acres to over 190 million acres. The president was instrumental in establishing twenty reclamation projects, eighteen national monuments, five national parks, four wildlife preserves, and fifty-one bird sanctuaries.

These efforts were not universally appreciated. Near the end of his second administration, Roosevelt began to have serious difficulties with Congress over conservation policy. He made many enemies by aggressively setting aside forest lands, and, in 1908, congressional opposition killed two Roosevelt conservation initiatives: the National Country Life Commission and the Inland Waterways Commission.

A third initiative, the Governor's Conference on Conservation, was successful, however, and had far-reaching effects. Meeting at the White House for three days in May 1908, the forty-four state governors, their advisors, and a variety of experts heard reports and discussed conservation and resource management. The result of the conference was the *Declaration of Governors for Conservation of Natural Resources,* establishing a broad consensus for a committed program of federal and state resource management. Within eighteen months, the meeting had inspired the establishment of forty-one state conservation commissions; it also inaugurated an annual governor's conference, which has taken place ever since.

PROCEEDINGS OF A
CONFERENCE OF GOVERNORS

IN THE WHITE HOUSE
WASHINGTON, D. C.
MAY 13–15, 1908

EDITED UNDER THE DIRECTION OF
NEWTON C. BLANCHARD, CHAIRMAN
JOHN FRANKLIN FORT JAMES O. DAVIDSON
JOHN C. CUTLER MARTIN F. ANSEL
THE COMMITTEE OF GOVERNORS

BY W J McGEE
RECORDING SECRETARY OF THE CONFERENCE

PUBLISHED BY AUTHORITY OF CONGRESS

Washington
Government Printing Office
1909

The title page of the official proceedings of the historic conference on environmental and resource conservation held at the White House, May 13–15, 1908. **THE LIBRARY OF CONGRESS.**

Primary Source

Declaration of Governors for Conservation of Natural Resources

SYNOPSIS: The *Declaration of Governors for Conservation of Natural Resources* is a brief but broad-ranging report that urged a concerted effort on the part of the federal and state governments to preserve and protect natural resources for future American generations. The declaration addressed the need for conserving mineral, timber, and water resources; halting soil erosion; and developing irrigation and other land reclamation projects. It also asserted that these "sources of national wealth exist for the benefit of the people, and that monopoly thereof should not be tolerated."

Introduction

The Declaration of Governors contained in this bulletin was adopted by the conference of governors of the States and Territories called by the President to consider the conservation of our natural resources, and which met at the White House May 13, 14, and 15, 1908. Besides the governors there were invited to the conference the members of the Cabinet, the justices of the Supreme Court, the members of both Houses of Congress, representatives of the great national organizations, the Inland Waterways Commission, and, as special guests, Hon. William Jennings Bryan, Mr. James J. Hill, Mr. Andrew Carnegie, and Mr. John Mitchell. The late ex-President Grover Cleveland was also invited as a special guest, but illness prevented him from attending. At the request of the President each governor brought with him to the conference three citizens from his State or Territory to act as assistants or advisers.

The object of the conference was stated by the President in his letter of invitation to the governors, in which he said:

> It seems to me time for the country to take account of its natural resources, and to inquire how long they are likely to last. We are

prosperous now; we should not forget that it will be just as important to our descendants to be prosperous in their time.

Papers which discussed the present state of our various natural resources were read by experts and specialists in each respective line, and these were followed by an open discussion among the governors of the points brought out.

The conference then appointed a committee to draft a declaration, consisting of the following: Governor Newton C. Blanchard, of Louisiana; Governor John Franklin Fort, of New Jersey; Governor J. O. Davidson, of Wisconsin, Governor John C. Cutler, of Utah; and Governor Martin F. Ansel, of South Carolina.

This committee prepared and submitted the declaration which follows, and it was unanimously adopted by the conference of governors as embodying their conclusions on the question of conservation.

Declaration

We, the governors of the States and Territories of the United States of America, in conference assembled, do hereby declare the conviction that the great prosperity of our country rests upon the abundant resources of the land chosen by our forefathers for their homes, and where they laid the foundation of this great nation.

We look upon these resources as a heritage to be made use of in establishing and promoting the comfort, prosperity, and happiness of the American people, but not to be wasted, deteriorated, or needlessly destroyed.

We agree that our country's future is involved in this; that the great natural resources supply the material basis upon which our civilization must continue to depend, and upon which the perpetuity of the nation itself rests.

We agree, in the light of the facts brought to our knowledge and from information received from sources which we can not doubt, that this material basis is threatened with exhaustion. Even as each succeeding generation from the birth of the nation has performed its part in promoting the progress and development of the Republic, so do we in this generation recognize it as a high duty to perform our part; and this duty in large degree lies in the adoption of measures for the conservation of the natural wealth of the country.

We declare our firm conviction that this conservation of our natural resources is a subject of transcendent importance, which should engage unremittingly the attention of the nation, the States, and the people in earnest cooperation. These natural resources include the land on which we live and which yields our food; the living waters which fertilize the soil, supply power, and form great avenues of commerce; the forests which yield the materials for our homes, prevent erosion of the soil, and conserve the navigation and other uses of the streams; and the minerals which form the basis of our industrial life, and supply us with heat, light, and power.

We agree that the land should be so used that erosion and soil wash shall cease; and that there should be reclamation of arid and semiarid regions by means of irrigation, and of swamp and overflowed regions by means of drainage; that the waters should be so conserved and used as to promote navigation, to enable the arid regions to be reclaimed by irrigation, and to develop power in the interests of the people; that the forests which regulate our rivers, support our industries, and promote the fertility and productiveness of the soil should be preserved and perpetuated; that the minerals found so abundantly beneath the surface should be so used as to prolong their utility; that the beauty, healthfulness, and habitability of our country should be preserved and increased; that sources of national wealth exist for the benefit of the people, and that monopoly thereof should not be tolerated.

We commend the wise forethought of the President in sounding note of warning as to the waste and exhaustion of the natural resources of the country, and signify our high appreciation of his action in calling this conference to consider the same and to seek remedies therefor through cooperation of the Nation and the States.

We agree that this cooperation should find expression in suitable action by the Congress within the limits of and coextensive with the national jurisdiction of the subject, and, complementary thereto, by the legislatures of the several States within the limits of and coextensive with their jurisdiction.

We declare the conviction that in the use of the national resources our independent States are interdependent and bound together by ties of mutual benefits, responsibilities, and duties.

We agree in the wisdom of future conferences between the President, Members of Congress, and the governors of States on the conservation of our natural resources with a view of continued cooperation and action on the lines suggested; and to this end we advise that from time to time, as in his judgment may seem wise, the President call the governors of States and Members of Congress and others into conference.

We agree that further action is advisable to ascertain the present condition of our natural resources and to promote the conservation of the same; and to that end we recommend the appointment by each State of a commission on the conservation of natural resources, to cooperate with each other and with any similar commission of the Federal Government.

We urge the continuation and extension of forest policies adapted to secure the husbanding and renewal of our diminishing timber supply, the prevention of soil erosion, the protection of headwaters, and the maintenance of the purity and navigability of our streams. We recognize that the private ownership of forest lands entails responsibilities in the interests of all the people, and we favor the enactment of laws looking to the protection and replacement of privately owned forests.

We recognize in our waters a most valuable asset of the people of the United States, and we recommend the enactment of laws looking to the conservation of water resources for irrigation, water supply, power, and navigation, to the end that navigable and source streams may be brought under complete control and fully utilized for every purpose. We especially urge on the Federal Congress the immediate adoption of a wise, active, and thorough waterway policy, providing for the prompt improvement of our streams and the conservation of their watersheds required for the uses of commerce and the protection of the interests of our people.

We recommend the enactment of laws looking to the prevention of waste in the mining and extraction of coal, oil, gas, and other minerals with a view to their wise conservation for the use of the people, and to the protection of human life in the mines.

Let us conserve the foundations of our prosperity.

Further Resources

BOOKS

Cutright, Paul. *Theodore Roosevelt the Naturalist.* New York: Harper, 1956.

Miller, Char. *Gifford Pinchot and the Making of Modern Environmentalism.* Washington, D.C.: Island/Shearwater, 2001.

Petulla, Joseph M. *American Environmental History: The Exploitation and Conservation of Natural Resources.* San Francisco: Boyd & Fraser, 1977.

WEBSITES

"Almanac of Theodore Roosevelt Conservation." Available online at http://www.theodore-roosevelt.com/trenv.html; website home page http://www.theodore-roosevelt.com (acessed October 25, 2002).

"Theodore Roosevelt & Conservation." U.S. National Park Service. Available online at http://www.nps.gov/thro/tr_cons.htm; website home page http://www.nps.gov (accessed October 25, 2002).

My Story

Autobiography

By: Tom Loftin Johnson

Date: 1911

Source: Johnson, Tom Loftin. *My Story.* Kent, Ohio: Kent State University Press, 1993, 121–130.

About the Author: Tom Loftin Johnson (1854–1911) was one of the great mayors in American history. The son of a Confederate Army officer, Johnson began his career in Louisville in the street railway business. He eventually settled in Cleveland, Ohio, and became wealthy from his interests in street railways and steel. In 1891, Johnson abandoned business for the life of a reform-minded politician. He served two terms in the U.S. House of Representatives (served 1891–1895) and was elected to four terms as mayor of Cleveland (served 1901–1909). ■

Introduction

Numerous critiques of the American economic and political system evolved during the two decades after the Civil War (1861–1865). One of the most influential was *Progress and Poverty* by Henry George, first published in 1879. In the book, George pointed out the failure of the existing system to develop into one that ensured a more equitable distribution of wealth. Despite tremendous technological advances and increases in the productive capacity of the nation, he noted, poverty was on the rise instead of being eradicated by this new wealth.

An important part of George's solution was a "single tax" levied on the value of unproductive land. He argued that such a measure would reduce or eliminate taxes on value-added activities, encourage productive use of land, force land redistribution, and stimulate full employment. He convincingly argued that gross inequities in wealth distribution could be substantially addressed "by taxing nothing but the values of land, natural resources, and monopolies."

According to Tom Johnson's autobiography, Johnson became aware of George's theories after a conductor on one of Johnson's streetcars gave him a copy of *Progress*

As mayor of Cleveland from 1901 through 1909, the Progressive politician Tom L. Johnson dramatically reformed city government. **THE LIBRARY OF CONGRESS.**

and Poverty. Johnson concluded that if George was correct, he (Johnson) had been guided by incorrect principles in living his life. He then asked his attorney and other wealthy business associates to disprove George's thesis. Unable to find fault in George's arguments, Johnson devoted the rest of his life to correcting the fundamental errors in society. After being elected mayor of Cleveland in 1901, Johnson was determined to make the city a model for the United States. Three major objectives of his administration were public ownership of utilities, including the street railway system, home rule for Ohio's cities, and the implementation of George's single-tax program.

Soon after taking office, Johnson ordered a detailed review of taxes paid on each parcel of land in the city. Once this laborious task was completed, he took the results to the people, giving lectures called the "Tax School" in a large circus tent. He hoped this "Tax School" would educate the people on the inequities of the tax system and show how the greatest corporations and property holders paid a much lower tax rate than ordinary citizens. It was a standard article of faith among Progressives that public knowledge would drive change.

When Johnson was nominated to run for governor in 1902, he took the "Tax School" on the road. Putting up his tent in towns throughout Ohio, he delivered rousing speeches in support of his campaign and tax reform. Although conservative forces led by the powerful Mark Hanna defeated Johnson, he nevertheless focused popular attention on the need for tax reform. Similar efforts across the country soon resulted in tax reform at all levels. Of most immediate impact to citizens were new laws that created more equitable taxation of the property holdings of large corporations. This same reform spirit led to the passage of the Sixteenth Amendment (1913), which authorized a national income tax.

Significance

Lincoln Steffens wrote in *The Shame of the Cities* that, under Tom Loftin Johnson's leadership, Cleveland became the best-run city in America. Johnson upgraded services, built parks and public bathhouses, improved streets, reformed the police department, and made changes in the penal system. Most importantly, he launched battles to reduce fares on streetcars, sought to bring public transportation and other utilities under public control, supported home rule, and led a statewide campaign for an equitable tax system. During his years as mayor, Johnson waged a continuous battle against entrenched interests in Cleveland and Ohio. Repeatedly, Johnson forces won local battles, only to have wealthy interest groups and corrupt officials overturn those successes through the intervention of the state government and court injunctions.

Johnson fought on, but in the end he was defeated. He finally retired after losing a close re-election bid in 1910. Suffering ill health and having lost much of his wealth, he wondered if he had done any good at the time of his death in 1911. He had. Johnson had left Cleveland a far better city in which to live, one that had made considerable progress in meeting the needs of the poor. Moreover, within a few years, states across the country enacted home-rule bills, utilities and public transportation came under public ownership or regulation, and the tax structure underwent major reform. While the results did not go so far as Johnson had wished, his record of accomplishments was matched by few other mayors in all of American history.

Primary Source

My Story [excerpt]

SYNOPSIS: In the following excerpts from *My Story,* Johnson describes some of the early progress he made in addressing Cleveland's problems. He also gives an account of his initial efforts to reform the tax system.

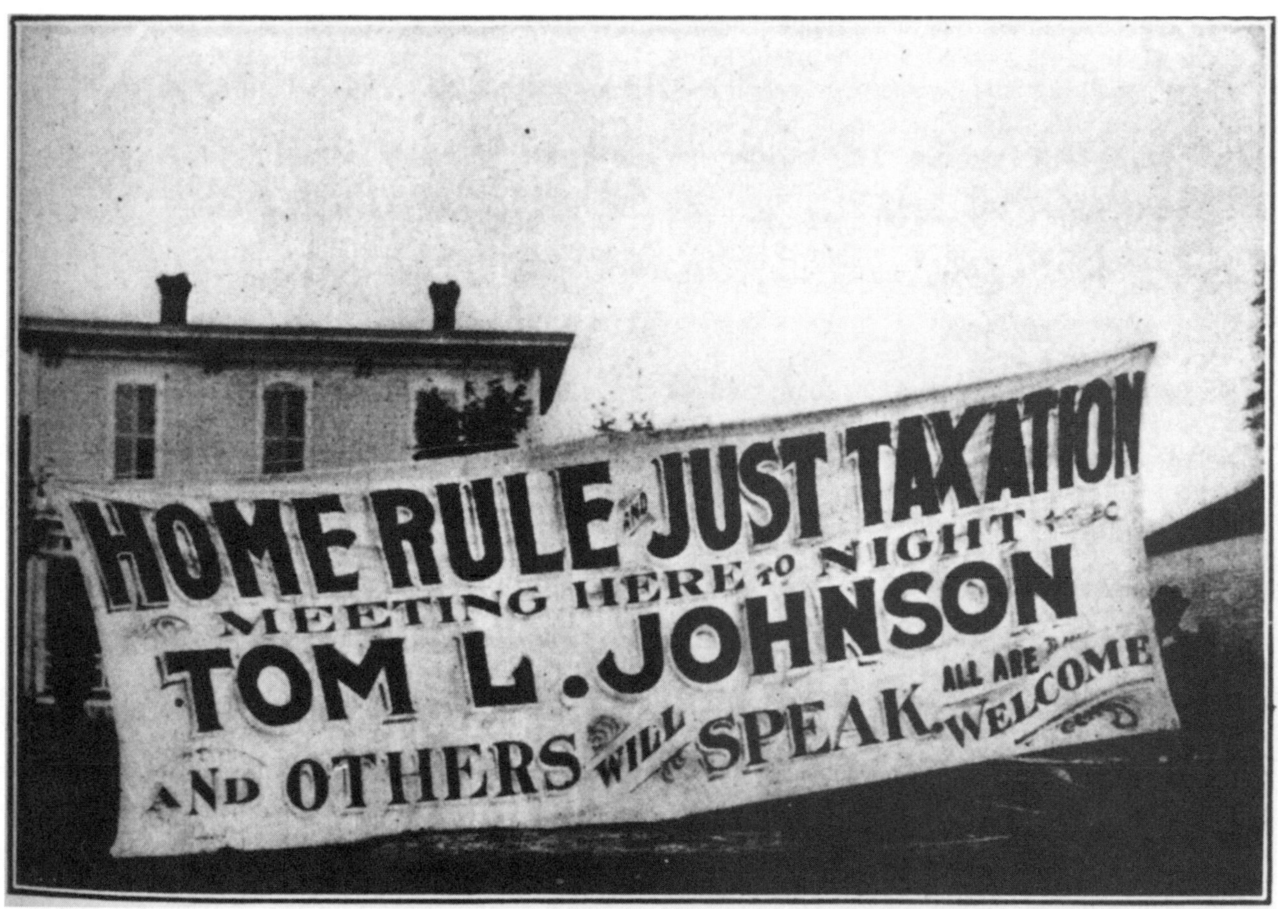

In the early twentieth century cities were generally under tight control from their state governments. It was also common for taxes on businesses to be much lower than those on individuals. These were just two of the many issues that Progressives like Tom L. Johnson sought to reform. **PHOTO BY L. VAN OEYEN FOR TOM L. JOHNSON, *MY STORY*, KENT, OHIO: KENT STATE UNIVERSITY PRESS, 1993.**

The City Government and the Tax School

There were innumerable matters calling for immediate consideration and I acted as quickly as possible in as many directions as I could. The secret of a good executive is this—one who always acts quickly and is sometimes right.

In less than a week after taking office I ordered uniformed policemen stationed at the doors of gambling houses and houses of prostitution having saloons in connection, and instructed them to take the names and addresses of all persons who entered. It makes a man mighty uncomfortable to go on record in this way, even if he gives a fictitious name and address. This method proved so successful as to the gambling houses that in a short time public gambling in Cleveland was practically abolished. I knew that we couldn't rid the city of the social evil any more than we could rid it of private gambling, but I was determined to permit no saloons in connection with houses of prostitution and to destroy the pernicious practice of the police of levying fines upon unfortunate women. It had long been the custom in Cleveland, as in other large cities, for the police to raid these houses and collect a lot of fines whenever the funds of the police court got low. This simply amounted to blackmail and hadn't the slightest effect in checking the evil, but rather stimulated it and gave rise to a horrible system of favoritism and extortion. I called my policemen together and told them that not a cent was to come into the city's hands by this method, that if the police court had to depend for revenue upon fines imposed in this manner, it would have to go without pay. Street soliciting by either sex was strictly prohibited. . . .

I ordered a strict inspection of theatres and other public buildings, made immediate war on billboards and ordered old frame structures torn down, put a force of "white wings" to work cleaning up the down town streets, inaugurated steps looking towards a better lighting system, set the law department to hunting up expiring street railway franchises, moved to reduce water rents, had a contest with the Pennsylvania Railroad over the ownership of twenty-nine streets, looked after some city cases pending in the federal court, established a department examiner to keep an eye on all departments of the city government, took down the "Keep Off the Grass" signs in the parks, commenced to institute people's amusements in the parks and pardoned eleven out of fifteen applicants for pardon in the city workhouse. . . .

Of course all these activities cost money and as there wasn't sufficient available money in sight, the usual howl of "extravagance" was raised. But I knew these things had to be done if we were to keep our promise to give good government and I went ahead and did them, trusting to devise a way to get the funds afterwards.

Under what is called economy in city government there is much foolish holding back of necessary public improvements. If fraud and graft are kept out there is not apt to be much unwisdom in public expenditures; and from the business man's standpoint the return for the original outlay is very large—even where debt is created within reasonable limits.

With anything like an equitable system of collecting the just revenues of a city, the cost of these improvements, if paid in the first instance by tax levy, would be wise. Good sanitary conditions, public parks, pure water, playgrounds for children and well paved streets are the best kind of investments, while the absence of them entails not only heavy pecuniary loss, but operates to the moral and physical deterioration of the city's inhabitants. . . .

But to give "good government" in the ordinarily accepted sense of the term, wasn't the thing I was in public life for. It was a part of our policy from the beginning of our work in Cleveland, it is true, but as a side issue, merely. While we tried to give the people clean and well lighted streets, pure water, free access to their parks, public baths and comfort stations, a good police department, careful market inspection, a rigid system of weights and measures, and to make the charitable and correctional institutions aid rather than punish wrongdoers, and to do the hundred and one other things that a municipality ought to do for its inhabitants—while we tried to do all these things, and even to outstrip other cities in the doing of them, we never lost sight of the fact that they were not fundamental. However desirable good government, or government by good men may be, nothing worth while will be accomplished unless we have sufficient wisdom to search for the causes that really corrupt government. I agree with those who say that it is big business and the kind of big business that deals in and profits from public service grants and taxation injustices that is the real evil in our cities and the country to-day. This big business furnishes the sinews of war to corrupt bosses regardless of party affiliations. This big business which profits by *bad government* must stand against all movements that seek to abolish its scheme of advantage.

It was these fundamental wrongs that I wished to attack and one of my first acts as mayor was to establish a Tax School designed to show the inequalities in taxation. Peter Witt was put in charge with Newton D. Baker (who afterwards became city solicitor) as legal adviser and with numerous assistants.

The constitution of Ohio says that all property shall be appraised at its true value in money and the statute carrying this provision into effect uses the same words.

Land and buildings were appraised once in ten years by appraisers elected in the wards of cities and the townships of counties. These appraisers were expected to complete their work in a ninety-day period of time. New buildings as they were erected were added to the tax duplicate by the city annual board of equalization appointed by the mayor, which board also took care of the personal property returns, and was clothed with power to change gross inequalities in appraisals of land made by the decennial appraisers.

Steam railroad property, both realty and personal, was appraised annually by the county auditors in the counties through which the railroads ran. These auditors sat as a board and convened in the largest city of the various counties which the railroads traversed. Auditors were elected by popular vote.

Outside of cities there were assessors appointed by the county auditors whose duty it was to appraise personal property annually.

This, briefly, was the system of taxation in operation when we started our Tax School.

The local taxing board, or board of equalization, appointed by previous mayors, was in the control of tax-dodgers. While it was really vested with great power this board had exercised that power principally in correcting clerical errors or in adding to the tax duplicate the value of additions to small property like painting houses or putting in bathtubs.

The steam railroads, as has been stated, were assessed by boards of county auditors in the counties traversed by the railroads.

Small taxpayers generally were paying full rates, while the public service corporations, steam railroads and large land-owning interests were paying between ten and twenty per cent only of the amount required by law. More than half the personal property and nearly all the valuable privileges were escaping taxation.

At first our Tax School was maintained by private funds and had no legal connection with the city government, but those in charge of it were granted the use of city maps and were permitted to call upon employés of the civil engineer's department for help in connection with the maps. Witt was the first man I appointed and he objected to taking the position, but I would not take "no" for an answer.

The clerks employed first copied the records in the county auditor's office showing the assessed value of all lots and buildings in the city. From these records, on a map sixteen feet square and comprising one whole ward, we showed the inequalities in assessed values. Citizens in general and taxpayers in particular were invited to a large room in the City Hall, at one end of which this map was suspended. Pursuing this method by multiplying the number of maps the assessment of real estate block by block and ward by ward was shown. Discussion was invited, criticisms and suggestions asked for, and by means of this discussion, together with a searching investigation of the records of real estate transfers and leases, we ascertained the real value of one foot front of land by one hundred feet in depth, which method is known as the Somers unit system of taxation and without which no fair and accurate appraisal of land can be made.

When the unit values were finally agreed to they were written into the center of each block on the various maps. The members of the city board of equalization then signed the map making it thereby a public record showing the date on which the values had been agreed upon. Then a photographer made a picture of the map and negatives of this photograph were furnished the clerks who were at work in another room, and they, having the small maps before them showing the individual ownerships and the photographic record of the unit values, worked out and wrote into each space provided on these small maps, the actual cash value of each particular piece of land and the assessed value as well. The total number of subdivisions of land in Cleveland was one hundred and one thousand and the assessed values varied from two per cent of to sixty-eight per cent above the actual or market value.

We were not satisfied with getting this information to the persons who visited the Tax School. We wanted to reach every tax-payer in the city with it. So the Tax School issued a circular letter to the people of each ward, which letter set forth the cash value of all land in Cleveland, the appraised value of all land in Cleveland, the cash value of all land in that particular ward, likewise its appraised value, then the number of parcels assessed at *less* than the average value in the ward, citing the best known pieces as a concrete illustration; then the number of parcels assessed at *more* than the average value and again using the best known piece as the illustration of this point.

The city board of equalization, already referred to, was a municipal institution of long standing. Its members were appointed by the mayor. It was these members who signed the map in the Tax School and it was this board which would have corrected the inequalities in taxation *had not the State legislature wiped it out by legislative enactment,* and provided in its stead a board of review appointed by State officials.

This board of review was paid from county funds for a purely municipal service. To this board we sent the names of all owners and the description of their property which was under assessed. To the people we sent the letter already mentioned and requested all those whose property was over assessed to seek their remedy from the board of review.

So far as I know this was the first intelligent and concerted effort to relieve the people of Ohio of the injustice of the privilege in taxation which had been a decennial bone of contention in the State for eighty years.

By this time the Tax School was operating as a part of the city machinery, council having made an appropriation for its maintenance. The greatest of all privileges is the privilege of having another man pay your taxes and the beneficiaries of this unjust taxation could not stand our agitation, so on October 8, 1902, W. J. Crawford, the Republican boss, and a large property owner, brought suit to enjoin the expenditure of city money in this manner.

The case was carried through the courts, the temporary injunction was made permanent and the Tax School was eventually forced to suspend. However, it had now been in operation twenty months and its work could not be undone. Not only was it instrumental in making public service corporations pay sixty thousand dollars a year more in taxes, but, fearing the result of a tax fight, these same corporations made a secret settlement of back taxes at the end of his term with county auditor Craig who was their friend, by paying into the county treasury more than one hundred thousand dollars of back taxes.

The following year in my campaign for Governor of Ohio we dug out the inequalities in taxation in every city in which my tent was pitched and by the use of a stereopticon we showed not only the inequalities existing in Cleveland but gave many local illustrations as well.

Further Resources

BOOKS

Adams, Charles. *Those Dirty Rotten Taxes: The Tax Revolts that Built America.* New York: Free Press, 1998.

Buenker, John D. *Urban Liberalism and Progressive Reform.* New York: Norton, 1978.

Ebner, Michael H., and Eugene M. Tobin, eds. *The Age of Urban Reform: New Perspectives on the Progressive Era.* Port Washington, N.Y.: Kennikat Press, 1977.

WEBSITES

"*My Story,* by Tom Johnson." Cleveland Memory Project. Available online at http://clevelandmemory.org/ebooks/johnson/; website home page: http://clevelandmemory.org (accessed March 15, 2003).

6

Law and Justice

Scott A. Merriman

Entries are arranged in chronological order by date of primary source. For entries with one primary source, the entry title is the same as the primary source title. Entries with more than one primary source have an overall entry title, followed by the titles of the primary sources.

CHRONOLOGY

PRIMARY SOURCES

Important Events in Law and Justice, 1900–1909

1900

- Twenty-five law schools form the Association of American Law Schools; law students must have high school diplomas, take a two-year course of instruction, and have access to a law library.
- On December 27, Prohibitionist Carry Nation begins raiding saloons in Kansas.

1901

- On May 27, the Supreme Court decides the first of the "Insular Cases," which declare that some, but not all, provisions of the U.S. Constitution and laws apply in former Spanish colonies that are now American territories (Puerto Rico, the Philippines, Guam).
- On September 6, President McKinley is shot in Buffalo, New York, by Leon Czolgosz, an anarchist. McKinley dies on September 14. Theodore Roosevelt becomes president.
- On September 23, Leon Czolgosz goes on trial for murdering President McKinley. He is convicted.
- On October 29, Czolgosz is electrocuted.

1902

- During the first two years of the twentieth century, 214 people are lynched in the United States.
- On March 10, the United States charges the Northern Securities Company with violating the Sherman Antitrust Act.
- On September 15, Horace Gray, associate justice of the Supreme Court, dies.
- On December 8, Oliver Wendell Holmes, Jr., is sworn in as an associate justice of the Supreme Court. He will serve on the high court until his retirement in 1932, just shy of his ninety-first birthday.

1903

- On January 5, in *Lone Wolf v. Hitchcock* the Supreme Court rules that Congress has absolute control over Indian land, even through Congress is abrogating a prior treaty by taking it.
- On February 23, in *Champion v. Ames* the Supreme Court rules that Congress has the authority to prohibit lottery tickets being sent through the mail.
- On March 2, William R. Day is sworn in as an associate justice on the Supreme Court. He replaces George Shiras, who has retired.
- On March 9, in *Brownfield v. South Carolina* the Supreme Court upholds the murder conviction of John Brownfield, an African American defendant, despite the fact that African Americans, who make up 80 percent of the population in the county, were excluded from the jury.
- On April 9, Federal circuit court judge Amos Thayer rules that Northern Securities Company violates the Sherman Antitrust Act. J. P. Morgan and James J. Hill appeal the case to the U.S. Supreme Court.
- On April 27, the Supreme Court, in *Giles v. Harris,* rules that Alabama's state constitution, which requires a literacy test for voters, does not discriminate on the basis of race.

1904

- On January 4, the Supreme Court rules that citizens of Puerto Rico are neither aliens nor citizens of the United States; they cannot be refused admission to the United States, but neither are they guaranteed all civil rights of American citizens.
- On March 14, in the *Northern Securities* case the Supreme Court rules that Northern Securities Corporation violates the Sherman Antitrust Act and orders the company dissolved.
- In August, race riots break out in Statesboro, Georgia.
- In September, race riots break out in Springfield, Ohio.
- On September 9, New York City employs its first unit of mounted police.
- On September 21, a woman is arrested for smoking in an open automobile on Fifth Avenue in New York City.
- On October 24, in *McCray v. United States* the Supreme Court rules that Congress may tax oleomargarine. The tax, passed under pressure from the dairy industry, was not designed for revenue but to make margarine nearly as expensive as butter.

1905

- Pennsylvania forms a state constabulary, a special unit also called the coal and iron police, to fight unions.
- The Association of American Law Schools requires that member schools have a three-year course of instruction.
- On January 30, in *Swift & Co. v. United States* the Supreme Court rules that the beef trust violates the Sherman Antitrust Act; Justice Holmes introduces the idea that interstate commerce is a stream involving different actions, including manufacturing and processing.
- On February 20, in *Jacobsen v. Massachusetts* the Supreme Court rules that states may require vaccinations.
- On April 17, in *Lochner v. New York* the Supreme Court rules that a New York law restricting bakers to a sixty-hour workweek interferes with their liberty to make contracts.
- On July 9, facing a rising tide of racism and lynchings, African American leaders including Ida B. Wells Barnett, Monroe Trotter, and W.E.B. Du Bois meet at Niagara Falls, Canada, to discuss strategy. This "Niagara Movement" op-

poses the policies of Booker T. Washington and pushes for full political and civil rights.

- In August, Nashville, Tennessee, imposes Jim Crow laws requiring African Americans to ride on the outside platform of streetcars. African Americans boycott the streetcar lines but do not succeed in forcing the city to rescind the ordinance.
- On December 30, Former Idaho governor Frank Steunenberg is killed by a bomb; it is suspected that members of the Industrial Workers of the World (IWW) killed him in retaliation for his crushing of an 1899 strike.

1906

- On January 31, the Niagara Movement is incorporated in Washington, D.C.
- On February 15, Idaho authorities arrest IWW leader William "Big Bill" Haywood in Colorado and charge him with the murder of former governor Steunenberg.
- On March 12, in *Hale v. Henkel* the Supreme Court rules that witnesses can be compelled to testify and to produce evidence against their corporations.
- On March 19, African American Ed Johnson is lynched by a mob in Chatanooga. Johnson was convicted of raping a white woman. Before his appeal is heard, he is lynched. The Secret Service investigates, and discover evidence that the Sheriff Joseph F. Shipp is involved. In an unprecedented action, the Supreme Court contends that Shipp and others committed contempt of court, and orders their trial before the Supreme Court. The decision is handed down in 1909.
- On May 28, associate justice of the Supreme Court Henry B. Brown resigns from the Supreme Court.
- In August, race riots erupt in Brownsville, Texas; President Roosevelt suspends a battalion of African American soldiers from Fort Brown after the riot.
- On September 22, race riots in Atlanta kill twenty-one people, eighteen of whom are African American. The city is placed under martial law.
- On December 17, William H. Moody is sworn in as an associate justice of the Supreme Court.

1907

- On April 15, in *Patterson v. Colorado* the U.S. Supreme Court upholds the conviction of a publisher whose newspaper carried cartoons criticizing the state supreme court.
- On July 28, an Idaho jury acquits Bill Haywood.
- In December, Samuel Gompers defies a court order and encourages a boycott against Buck's Stove and Range Company.

1908

- The Boston Watch and Ward Society prosecutes book salesmen for distributing the racy novel *Three Weeks* by Elinor Glyn.
- On January 27, the Supreme Court, in *Adair v. United States,* strikes down the Federal Employers' Liability Act and holds that making "yellow dog" contracts illegal interferes with due process rights under the Fifth Amendment.
- On February 3, in *Loewe v. Lawlor* the Supreme Court rules that striking workers violated the Sherman Antitrust Act by calling for a boycott against a Danbury hat manufacturer.
- On February 20, the Illinois Supreme Court rules that picketing is illegal.
- On February 24, in *Muller v. Oregon* the U.S Supreme Court upholds Oregon's ten-hour workday law for women.
- On August 14, race riots break out in Springfield, Illinois.
- In October, the New York State Court of Appeals upholds an eight-hour workday.
- In November, New York district attorney William T. Jerome investigates lawyers who extort property from poor clients.
- On November 9, in *Twining v. New Jersey,* the U.S. Supreme Court rules that states are not required to guarantee a right against self-incrimination.
- In December, in *Gompers v. Buck's Stove and Range Company* a federal district court in Washington, D.C., finds a boycott organized by the American Federation of Labor violated the Sherman Antitrust Act and holds Samuel Gompers and other labor leaders in contempt of court for supporting the boycott.

1909

- On April 30, Learned Hand is appointed to the federal district court for southern New York, the beginning of a half century of distinguished service as a federal judge.
- On May 24, the Supreme Court hands down its decision in *U.S. v. Shipp,* relating to the 1906 lynching of Ed Johnson. The court finds Shipp, a jailer, and four others guilty, ruling that Shipp at the very least acquiesced in the lynching. Shipp is sentenced to 90 days. When he returns to Chatanooga, a hero's welcome greets him.
- On May 30, in response to increasing racial tensions, white liberals, including Oswald Garrison Villard, Mary White Ovington, and Florence Kelley, convene a National Conference on the Negro; it merges with the Niagara Movement in 1911 to form the National Association for the Advancement of Colored People (NAACP).
- On September 4, the Tennessee chancery court upholds the state Prohibition law.
- On October 24, Rufus Peckham, associate justice of the Supreme Court, dies.
- On November 4, in an Oklahoma case, a federal district court rules that the state cannot seize interstate shipments of liquor.
- On December 16, the Indiana Supreme Court upholds the local option law.

Champion v. Ames

Supreme Court decision

By: John Marshall Harlan

Date: February 23, 1903

Source: Harlan, John Marshall. *Champion v. Ames.* 188 U.S. 161 (1908). Available online at http://www.caselaw.lp.findlaw.com (accessed November 22, 2002).

About the Author: John Marshall Harlan (1833–1911), "the Great Dissenter," was born in Kentucky. After pursuing a career as a lawyer and politician, he served on the U.S. Supreme Court from 1877 until his death. Harlan was famous for his dissenting opinions, including his lone dissents in *Plessy v. Ferguson* and *Berea College v. Kentucky.* Before becoming a Supreme Court justice, he was attorney general of Kentucky and the Republican gubernatorial candidate in Kentucky in 1871 and in 1875. ■

Introduction

In 1895, the U.S. Congress passed a law forbidding people from shipping lottery tickets between states, justifying the act as part of its commerce power under the Constitution of the United States. Above and beyond the lottery issue, the act was one of the first times Congress had attempted to forbid a mostly noncommercial item from being passed through interstate commerce. The commerce clause in the Constitution allows Congress to "regulate" interstate commerce, but it was not at all clear that banning something from interstate commerce was not stepping beyond the bounds of merely "regulating." The lottery act, therefore, raised several questions: Could Congress regulate a noncommercial item? Could Congress enact social policy through the commerce clause? Finally, could Congress ban an item from being shipped in interstate commerce? All of these questions were presented by the *Champion v. Ames* case, which was decided by the Supreme Court in 1908.

Significance

In *Champion v. Ames,* the Supreme Court ruled in favor of the federal government, thereby allowing it to prohibit commerce as part of the process of regulation. This decision opened the way for future rulings on interstate commerce. In a later case, the Supreme Court allowed Congress to tax "yellow oleo," now called margarine, as a part of its taxing power. The oleo law had clearly been passed to help butter manufacturers fight off competition from margarine makers, but the Court upheld the legislation. The Supreme Court also allowed Congress to ban impure foods, impure drugs, and impure meats from interstate commerce. The only items not allowed to be banned were products of child labor. The Supreme Court was less generous in other areas of the commerce clause in the early twentieth century, as it struck down congressional attempts to regulate railroad labor.

In the 1930s, the Supreme Court broadened its view of the commerce clause again by allowing Congress to regulate labor conditions. However, the Court began to take a more narrow view of "immoral" products that were subject to being banned. Magazines, for instance, could be viewed as a function of the press, and they began to be protected under a wider view of the freedom of the press by the Warren Court. During the last third of the twentieth century, the Burger and Rhenquist Courts narrowed this protection while allowing Congress latitude under the commerce clause.

Primary Source

Champion v. Ames [excerpt]

SYNOPSIS: John Marshall Harlan presented the Court's ruling on *Champion v. Ames.* He first holds that lottery tickets, being part of interstate traffic, are part of interstate commerce. He then states that a ban on such tickets is an allowable regulation. Harlan closes by arguing that the regulation is a reasonable one, and that it is not invalidated by potential abuses of the commerce clause. The Harlan dissent takes the position that regulation is an exercise of police power, which resides solely with the states; therefore, since *Champion v. Ames* would give such power to the federal government, it should be declared unconstitutional.

Mr. Justice Harlan delivered the opinion of the court:

The appellant [Charles F. Champion] insists that the carrying of lottery tickets from one state to another state by an express company engaged in carrying freight and packages from state to state, although such tickets may be contained in a box or package, does not constitute, and cannot by any act of Congress be legally made to constitute, commerce among the states within the meaning of the clause of the Constitution of the United States providing that Congress shall have power "to regulate commerce with foreign nations, and among the several states, and with the Indian tribes;" consequently, that Congress cannot make it an offense to cause such tickets to be carried from one state to another.

The government insists that express companies, when engaged, for hire, in the business of transportation from one state to another, are instrumentalities of commerce among the states; that the carrying of lottery tickets from one state to another is commerce which Congress may regulate; and that as a means of executing the power to regulate interstate commerce Congress may make it an offense against the United States to cause lottery tickets to be carried from one state to another.

The questions presented by these opposing contentions are of great moment, and are entitled to receive, as they have received, the most careful consideration. . . .

It was said in argument that lottery tickets are not of any real or substantial value in themselves, and therefore are not subjects of commerce. If that were conceded to be the only legal test as to what are to be deemed subjects of the commerce that may be regulated by Congress, we cannot accept as accurate the broad statement that such tickets are of no value. Upon their face they showed that the lottery company offered a large capital prize, to be paid to the holder of the ticket winning the prize at the drawing advertised to be held at Asuncion, Paraguay. Money was placed on deposit in different banks in the United States to be applied by the agents representing the lottery company to the prompt payment of prizes. These tickets were the subject of traffic; they could have been sold; and the holder was assured that the company would pay to him the amount of the prize drawn. . . .

We are of opinion that lottery tickets are subjects of traffic, and therefore are subjects of commerce, and the regulation of the carriage of such tickets from state to state, at least by independent carriers, is a regulation of commerce among the several states.

But it is said that the statute in question does not regulate the carrying of lottery tickets from state to state, but by punishing those who cause them to be so carried Congress in effect prohibits such carrying; that in respect of the carrying from one state to another of articles or things that are, in fact, or according to usage in business, the subjects of commerce, the authority given Congress was not to prohibit, but only to regulate. This view was earnestly pressed at the bar by learned counsel, and must be examined. . . .

We have said that the carrying from state to state of lottery tickets constitutes interstate commerce, and that the regulation of such commerce is within the power of Congress under the Constitution. Are we prepared to say that a provision which is, in effect, a prohibition of the carriage of such articles from state to state is not a fit or appropriate mode for the regulation of that particular kind of commerce? If lottery traffic, carried on through interstate commerce, is a matter of which Congress may take cognizance and over which its power may be exerted, can it be possible that it must tolerate the traffic, and simply regulate the manner in which it may be carried on? Or may not Congress, for the protection of the people of all the states, and under the power to regulate interstate commerce, devise such means, within the scope of the Constitution, and not prohibited by it, as will drive that traffic out of commerce among the states?

Supreme Court Justice John Marshall Harlan (1877–1911). He held that the commerce clause of the Fourteenth Amendment could apply in banning the sale of lottery tickets. THE LIBRARY OF CONGRESS.

In determining whether regulation may not under some circumstances properly take the form or have the effect of prohibition, the nature of the interstate traffic which it was sought by the act of May 2d, 1895, to suppress cannot be overlooked. . . . In other cases we have adjudged that authority given by legislative enactment to carry on a lottery, although based upon a consideration in money, was not protected by the contract clause of the Constitution; this, for the reason that no state may bargain away its power to protect the public morals, nor excuse its failure to perform a public duty by saying that it had agreed, by legislative enactment, not to do so. . . .

If a state, when considering legislation for the suppression of lotteries within its own limits, may properly take into view the evils that inhere in the raising of money, in that mode, why may not Congress, invested with the power to regulate commerce among the several states, provide that such commerce shall not be polluted by the carrying of lottery tickets from one state to another? . . .

It is said, however, that if, in order to suppress lotteries carried on through interstate commerce, Congress may exclude lottery tickets from such commerce, that principle leads necessarily to the conclusion that Congress may arbitrarily exclude from commerce among the states any article, commodity, or thing, of whatever kind or nature, or however useful or valuable, which it may choose, no matter with what motive, to declare shall not be carried from one state to another. It will be time enough to consider the constitutionality of such legislation when we must do so. The present case does not require the court to declare the full extent of the power that Congress may exercise in the regulation of commerce among the states. We may, however, repeat, in this connection, what the court has heretofore said, that the power of Congress to regulate commerce among the states, although plenary, cannot be deemed arbitrary, since it is subject to such limitations or restrictions as are prescribed by the Constitution. This power, therefore, may not be exercised so as to infringe rights secured or protected by that instrument. It would not be difficult to imagine legislation that would be justly liable to such an objection as that stated, and be hostile to the objects for the accomplishment of which Congress was invested with the general power to regulate commerce among the several states. But, as often said, the possible abuse of a power is not an argument against its existence. There is probably no governmental power that may not be exerted to the injury of the public. If what is done by Congress is manifestly in excess of the powers granted to it, then upon the courts will rest the duty of adjudging that its action is neither legal nor binding upon the people. But if what Congress does is within the limits of its power, and is simply unwise or injurious, the remedy is that suggested by Chief Justice Marshall in Gibbons v. Ogden, when he said: "The wisdom and the discretion of Congress, their identity with the people, and the influence which their constituents possess at elections, are, in this, as in many other instances, as that, for example, of declaring war, the sole restraints on which they have relied, to secure them from its abuse. They are the restraints on which the people must often rely solely, in all representative governments."

The whole subject is too important, and the questions suggested by its consideration are too difficult of solution, to justify any attempt to lay down a rule for determining in advance the validity of every statute that may be enacted under the commerce clause. We decide nothing more in the present case than that lottery tickets are subjects of traffic among those who choose to sell or buy them; that the carriage of such tickets by independent carriers from one state to another is therefore interstate commerce; that under its power to regulate commerce among the several states Congress—subject to the limitations imposed by the Constitution upon the exercise of the powers granted—has plenary authority over such commerce, and may prohibit the carriage of such tickets from state to state; and that legislation to that end, and of that character, is not inconsistent with any limitation or restriction imposed upon the exercise of the powers granted to Congress.

The judgment is affirmed.

Mr. Chief Justice Fuller, with whom concur Mr. Justice Brewer, Mr. Justice Shiras, and Mr. Justice Peckham, dissenting: . . .

The maked [sic] question is whether the prohibition by Congress of the carriage of lottery tickets from one state to another by means other than the mails is within the powers vested in that body by the Constitution of the United States. That the purpose of Congress in this enactment was the suppression of lotteries cannot reasonably be denied. That purpose is avowed in the title of the act, and is its natural and reasonable effect, and by that its validity must be tested. . . .

The power of the state to impose restraints and burdens on persons and property in conservation and promotion of the public health, good order, and prosperity is a power originally and always belonging to the states, not surrendered by them to the general government, nor directly restrained by the Constitution of the United States, and essentially exclusive, and the suppression of lotteries as a harmful business falls within this power, commonly called, of police. . . .

Thus it is seen that the right of passage of persons and property from one state to another cannot be prohibited by Congress. But that does not challenge the legislative power of a sovereign nation to exclude foreign persons or commodities, or place an embargo, perhaps not permanent, upon foreign ships or manufactures. . . .

I regard this decision as inconsistent with the views of the framers of the Constitution, and of Marshall, its great expounder. Our form of government may remain notwithstanding legislation or decision, but, as long ago observed, it is with governments, as with religions: the form may survive the substance of the faith.

In my opinion the act in question in the particular under consideration is invalid, and the judgments below ought to be reversed, and my brothers Brewer, Shiras and Peckham concur in this dissent.

Further Resources

BOOKS

Barker, Thomas, and Marjie Britz. *Jokers Wild: Legalized Gambling in the Twenty-First Century.* Westport, Conn.: Praeger, 2000.

———. *Select Federal Gaming, Horseracing, and Lottery Laws.* United States: Trace Publications, 1994.

Clotfelter, Charles T., and Philip J. Cook. *Selling Hope: State Lotteries in America.* Cambridge, Mass.: Harvard University Press, 1989.

Furer, Howard B. *The Fuller Court, 1888-1910.* Danbury, Conn.: Grolier Educational Corp, 1995.

Mason, John Lyman, and Michael Nelson. *Governing Gambling.* New York: Century Foundation Press. 2001.

Shorter, Gary W. *Should the Federal Government Sponsor a National Lottery? Some Preliminary Considerations.* Washington, D.C.: Congressional Research Service, 1985.

Weiss, Ann E. *Lotteries: Who Wins, Who Loses?* Hillside, N.J.: Enslow, 1991.

WEBSITES

Champion v. Ames. Available online at http://www.tltc.ttu.edu/Cochran/Cases%20&%20Readings/Gaming/champion.htm; website home page: http://www.tltc.ttu.edu/content/asp/main/start.asp (accessed January 9, 2003).

Federal Trade Commission. "Catch the Bandit in Your Mailbox." Available online at http://www.ftc.gov/bcp/conline/pubs/tmarkg/bandit.pdf; website home page: http://www.ftc.gov (accessed January 9, 2003).

Northern Securities Co. v. U.S.

Supreme Court decision

By: John Marshall Harlan

Date: March 14, 1904

Source: Harlan, John Marshall. *Northern Securities Co. v. U.S.* 193 U.S. 197 (1904). Available online at http://www.caselaw.lp.findlaw.com (accessed November 22, 2002).

About the Author: John Marshall Harlan (1833–1911), "the Great Dissenter," was born in Kentucky. After pursuing a career as a lawyer and politician, he served on the U.S. Supreme Court from 1877 until his death. Harlan was famous for his dissenting opinions, including lone dissents in *Plessy v. Ferguson* and *Berea College v. Kentucky.* Before being appointed a Supreme Court justice, he was attorney general of Kentucky and the Republican gubernatorial candidate in Kentucky in 1871 and in 1875. ■

Introduction

In the late 1880s, American industry rapidly expanded into the production of coal, steel, iron, and oil. With the rise of heavy industry came large, dominating conglomerates such as John D. Rockefeller's Standard Oil and Andrew Carnegie's Carnegie Steel, which grew into monopolies. These huge companies drove competitors out of business, often in ruthless ways, and their owners were known as either robber barons or captains of industry (or possibly both). Frequently, the public was not served by the lack of competition, so pressure was put upon the U.S. Congress to do something to combat monopolies. In response, Congress passed the Sherman Anti-Trust Act (1890), which outlawed all business combinations that restrain interstate commerce. Monopolies and monopolistic devices would seem to fall under this ban, yet the power of Congress reached only to interstate commerce. The reason was that the Constitution of the United States grants Congress sole power in that area. (Intrastate commerce, or commerce within a state, is regulated by the state).

The exact limitations of the Sherman Anti-Trust Act quickly became a subject of litigation. One of the first prosecutions under the Sherman Act was brought against the E.C. Knight Company, which controlled production of 98 percent of the nation's sugar. Nevertheless, the Supreme Court ruled in *U.S. v. E.C. Knight Company* (1895) that the Sherman Act could not be used to regulate Knight's activities. The Court held that manufacturing was different from interstate commerce, and that Knight's manufacturing operations took place in a single state. The Sherman Act was quite limited by this ruling, thereby making the act ineffective against monopolies. The situation changed in 1901, when Theodore Roosevelt became president and vowed to be a "trust-buster."

James Hill is buried under the wreck of the Northern Securities Company merger that is blocked by the Sherman Act. Levers under the boulder read "United States Circuit Court of Appeals Decree" as that court found the Sherman Act applicable in blocking the merger, before the case was appealed to the Supreme Court. COURTESY OF BOONDOCKSNET.COM. REPRODUCED BY PERMISSION.

Roosevelt publicly went after trusts and monopolies, choosing the Northern Securities Company as one of his first targets.

Significance

Northern Securities was a holding company—that is, a company created to "hold" the stock and assets of other companies. Organized to control railroads owned by James Hill and E.H. Harriman, Northern Securities was clearly a railroad monopoly. When confronted with this charge, the company responded with the lawsuit *Northern Securities Co. v. U.S.* Northern Securities argued that it had been created by the buying and selling of securities and therefore did not engage in any commerce covered by the Sherman Act. The Supreme Court rejected this argument, ruling that if a company acted to abridge interstate commerce, it could be regulated by the Sherman Act.

Two years later, the Court followed up the *Northern Securities* decision with a ruling in *Swift v. United States.* In this case, the justices held that manufactured products could be regulated as long as the products were part of a "stream of commerce." At that time, laborers' hours and working conditions had not yet been placed under federal regulation, and a ban on child labor had been held unconstitutional. Congress had tried to ban child labor, but the Court ruled that child labor was part of production and thus came under the control of the state. Then Congress tried to tax the products of child labor, and that law was struck down as well. Congress also made halting attempts to allow workers to form unions and to prevent those unions from being hindered by anti-trust laws. These efforts were struck down as being controls over production. It was not until the 1930s that federal laws were enacted to help unions, ban child labor, and establish a maximum work week and a minimum wage. Since the 1940s, the Supreme Court has generally allowed Congress to regulate any activity that has a "substantial effect" on interstate commerce, as long as there is a "rational relationship" between the law's ends and means.

Primary Source

Northern Securities Co. v. U.S. [excerpt]

SYNOPSIS: John Marshall Harlan delivered the opinion of the Court. He first notes that the main question is whether or not the Sherman Act applies to all combinations in restraint of trade, or just the unreasonable ones. He holds that it applies to all combinations. Harlan then describes the Sherman Act as a reasonable regulation and holds that it extends to railroads. Oliver Wendell Holmes Jr. read his dissent, arguing that the Sherman Act does not apply to trusts and combinations, but only to practices that restrain trade.

Mr. Justice Harlan announced the affirmance of the decree of the circuit court, and delivered the following opinion: . . .

The government charges that if the combination was held not to be in violation of the act of Congress, then all efforts of the national government to preserve to the people the benefits of free competition among carriers engaged in interstate commerce will be wholly unavailing, and all transcontinental lines, indeed, the entire railway systems of the country, may be absorbed, merged, and consolidated, thus placing the public at the absolute mercy of the holding corporation. . . .

In our judgment, the evidence fully sustains the material allegations of the bill, and shows a violation of the act of Congress, in so far as it declares illegal every combination or conspiracy in restraint of commerce among the several states and with foreign nations, and forbids attempts to monopolize such commerce or any part of it. . . .

Is the act to be construed as forbidding every combination or conspiracy in restraint of trade or commerce among the states or with foreign nations? Or, does it embrace only such restraints as are unreasonable in their nature? Is the motive with which a forbidden combination or conspiracy was formed at all material when it appears that the necessary tendency of the particular combination or conspiracy in question is to restrict or suppress free competition between competing railroads engaged in commerce among the states? Does the act of Congress prescribe, as a rule for interstate or international commerce, that the operation of the natural laws of competition between those engaged in such commerce shall not be restricted or interfered with by any contract, combination, or conspiracy? . . .

We will not encumber this opinion by extended extracts from the former opinions of this court. It is sufficient to say that from the decisions . . . certain propositions are plainly deducible and embrace the present case. Those propositions are:

That although the act of Congress known as the anti-trust act has no reference to the mere manufacture or production of articles or commodities within the limits of the several states, it does embrace and declare to be illegal every contract, combination, or conspiracy, in whatever form, of whatever nature, and whoever may be parties to it, which directly or necessarily operates in restraint of trade or commerce among the several states or with foreign nations;

That the act is not limited to restraints of interstate and international trade or commerce that are unreasonable in their nature, but embraces all direct restraints imposed by any combination, conspiracy, or monopoly upon such trade or commerce;

That railroad carriers engaged in interstate or international trade or commerce are embraced by the act;

That combinations, even among private manufacturers or dealers, whereby interstate or international commerce is restrained, are equally embraced by the act;

That Congress has the power to establish rules by which interstate and international commerce shall be governed, and, by the anti-trust act, has prescribed the rule of free competition among those engaged in such commerce:

That every combination or conspiracy which would extinguish competition between otherwise competing railroads engaged in interstate trade or commerce, and which would in that way restrain such trade or commerce, is made illegal by the act;

That the natural effect of competition is to increase commerce, and an agreement whose direct effect is to prevent this play of competition restrains instead of promoting trade and commerce; That to vitiate a combination such as the act of Congress condemns, it need not be shown that the combination, in fact, results or will result, in a total suppression of trade or in a complete monopoly, but it is only essential to show that, by its necessary operation, it tends to restrain interstate or international trade or commerce or tends to create a monopoly in such trade or commerce and to deprive the public of the advantages that flow from free competition;

That the constitutional guaranty of liberty of contract does not prevent Congress from prescribing the rule of free competition for those engaged in interstate and international commerce; and,

That under its power to regulate commerce among the several states and with foreign nations, Congress had authority to enact the statute in question. . . .

The means employed in respect of the combinations forbidden by the anti-trust act, and which Congress deemed germane to the end to be accomplished, was to prescribe as a rule for interstate and international commerce (not for domestic commerce) that it should not be vexed by combinations, conspiracies, or monopolies which restrain commerce by destroying or restricting competition. We say that Congress has prescribed such a rule, because, in all the prior cases in this court, the anti-trust act has been construed as forbidding any combination which, by its necessary operation, destroys or restricts free competition among those engaged in interstate commerce; in other words, that to destroy or restrict free competition in interstate commerce was to restrain such commerce. Now, can this court say that such a rule is prohibited by the Constitution or is not one that Congress could appropriately prescribe when exerting its power under the commerce clause of the Constitution? Whether the free operation of the normal laws of competition is a wise and wholesome rule for trade and commerce is an economic question which this court need not consider or determine. Undoubtedly, there are those who think that the general business interests and prosperity of the country will be best promoted if the rule of competition is not applied. But there are others who believe that such a rule is more necessary in these days of enormous wealth than it ever was in any former period of our history. Be all this as it may, Congress has, in effect, recognized the rule of free competition by declaring illegal every combination or conspiracy in restraint of interstate and international commerce. . . .

We cannot agree that Congress may strike down combinations among manufacturers and dealers in iron pipe, tiles, grates, and mantels that restrain commerce among the states in such articles, but may not strike down combinations among stockholders of competing railroad carriers, which restrain commerce as involved in the transportation of passengers and property among the several states. If private parties may not, by combination among themselves, restrain interstate and international commerce in violation of an act of Congress, much less can such restraint be tolerated when imposed or attempted to be imposed, upon commerce as carried on over public highways. Indeed, if the contentions of the defendants are sound, why may not all the railway companies in the United States, that are engaged, under state charters, in interstate and international commerce, enter into a combination such as the one here in question, and, by the device of a holding corporation, obtain the absolute control throughout the entire country of rates for passengers and freight, beyond the power of Congress to protect the public against their exactions? The argument in behalf of the defendants necessarily leads to such results, and places Congress, although invested by the people of the United States with full authority to regulate interstate and international commerce, in a condition of utter helplessness, so far as the protection of the public against such combinations is concerned. . . .

Many suggestions were made in argument based upon the thought that the anti-trust act would, in the end, prove to be mischievous in its consequences. Disaster to business and widespread financial ruin, it has been intimated, will follow the execution of its provisions. Such predictions were made in all the cases heretofore arising under that act. But they have not been verified. It is the history of monopolies in this country and in England that predictions of ruin are habitually made by them when it is attempted, by legislation, to restrain their operations and to protect the public against their exactions. In this, as in former cases, they seek shelter behind the reserved rights of the states and even behind the constitutional guaranty of liberty of contract. But this court has heretofore adjudged that the act of Congress did not touch the rights of the states, and that liberty of contract did not involve a right to deprive the public of the advantages of free competition in trade and commerce. Liberty of contract does not imply liberty in a corporation or individuals to defy the national will, when legally expressed. Nor does the enforcement of a legal enactment of Congress infringe, in any proper sense, the general inherent right of every one to acquire and hold property. That right, like all other rights, must be exercised in subordination to the law. . . .

It was said in argument that the circumstances under which the Northern Securities Company obtained the stock of the constituent companies imported simply an investment in the stock of other corporations, a purchase of that stock; which investment or purchase, it is contended, was not forbidden by the charter of the company, and could not be made illegal by any act of Congress. This view is wholly fallacious, and does not comport with the actual transaction. There was no actual investment, in any substantial sense, by the Northern Securities Company in the stock of the two constituent companies. If it was, in form, such a Transaction, it was not, in fact, one of that kind. However that company may have acquired for itself any stock in the Great Northern and Northern Pacific Railway Companies, no matter how it obtained the means to do so, all the stock it held or acquired in the constituent companies was acquired and held to be used in suppressing competition between those companies. It came into existence only for that purpose. . . .

We will now inquire as to the nature and extent of the relief granted to the government by the decree below. . . .

Guided by these long-established rules of construction, it is manifest that if the antitrust act is held not to embrace a case such as is now before us, the plain intention of the legislative branch of the government will be defeated. If Congress has not, by the words used in the act, described this and like cases, it would, we apprehend, be impossible to find words that would describe them. . . .

AFFIRMED.

Mr. Justice Holmes, with whom concurred the Chief Justice, Mr. Justice White, and Mr. Justice Peckham, dissenting: . . .

Great cases, like hard cases, make bad law. For great cases are called great, not by reason of their real importance in shaping the law of the future, but because of some accident of immediate overwhelming interest which appeals to the feelings and distorts the judgment. . . .

A partnership is not a contract or combination in restraint of trade between the partners unless the well known words are to be given a new meaning, invented for the purposes of this act. It is true that the suppression of competition was referred to in *United States v. Trans–Missouri Freight* . . . but, as I have said, that was in connection with a contract with a stranger to the defendant's business,—a true contract in restraint of trade. To suppress competition in that way in [sic] one thing; to suppress it by fusion is another. The law, I repeat, says nothing about competition, and only prevents its suppression by contracts or combinations in restraint of trade, and such contracts or combinations derive their character as restraining trade from other features than the suppression of competition alone. . . . For, again I repeat, if the restraint on the freedom of the members of a combination, caused by their entering into partnership, is a restraint of trade, every such combination, as well the small as the great, is within the act.

In view of my interpretation of the statute I do not go further into the question of the power of Congress. That has been dealt with by my brother White and I concur, in the main, with his views. I am happy to know that only a minority of my brethren adopt an interpretation of the law which, in my opinion, would make eternal the bellum omnium contra omnes and disintegrate society so far as it could into individual atoms. If that were its intent I should regard calling such a law a regulation of commerce as a mere pretense. It would be an attempt to reconstruct society. I am not concerned with the wisdom of such an attempt, but I believe that Congress was not intrusted by the Constitution with the power to make it, and I am deeply persuaded that it has not tried.

I am authorized to say that the Chief Justice, Mr. Justice White, and Mr. Justice Peckham concur in this dissent.

Further Resources

BOOKS

Apple, R.W. "The Case of the Monopolistic Railroadmen: *Northern Securities Co. et al. v. U.S.,* 193 U.S. 197." In *Quarrels that Have Shaped the Constitution.* John Arthur Garraty, ed. New York: Harper & Row, 1987, 175–192.

Mercer, Lloyd J. *E.H. Harriman, Master Railroader.* Boston: Twayne, 1985.

Meyer, Balthasar Henry. *A History of the Northern Securities Case.* New York, Da Capo Press, 1976.

Rosenberry, Walter. *The Political and Economic Significance of the Northern Securities Company.* Undergraduate thesis, Harvard College, 1953.

Spence, James A. *A History of the Northern Securities Company.* Master's Thesis, University of Missouri-Kansas City, 1969.

White, G. Edward. *Justice Oliver Wendell Holmes: Law and the Inner Self.* New York: Oxford University Press, 1993.

Yarbrough, Tinsley E. *Judicial Enigma: The First Justice Harlan.* New York: Oxford University Press, 1995.

WEBSITES

"The Northern Securities Case." Available online at http://www.1912.history.ohio-state.edu/Trusts/NorthernSecurities.htm; website home page: http://www.1912.history.ohio-state.edu (accessed January 9, 2003).

Swift & Co. v. U.S.

Supreme Court decision

By: Oliver Wendell Holmes Jr.

Date: January 30, 1905

Source: Holmes, Oliver Wendell, Jr. *Swift & Co. v. United States.* 196 U.S. 375 (1905). Available online at http://www.caselaw.lp.findlaw.com (accessed November 22, 2002).

About the Author: Oliver Wendell Holmes Jr. (1841–1935) served for three years in the Union Army during the Civil War (1861–1865). He joined the Massachusetts Supreme Court as an associate justice in 1883, and sixteen years later he became chief justice of that court. In 1902, when Holmes was sixty-one, President Theodore Roosevelt appointed him associate justice to the U.S. Supreme Court, where he served for 30 years. ■

Introduction

During the rapid growth of the U.S. economy in the late 1800s, companies became more national in scope. In the process, companies such as Standard Oil and Carnegie Steel mushroomed into monopolies that stifled competition within their respective industries. States frequently had difficulty regulating these gigantic businesses, which were often chartered out of state or were too large to be overseen by one state. Some state regulations were also struck down by courts as violating the sole power of the U.S. Congress to regulate interstate commerce. The public clamored for action, vigorously speaking out against monopolies. In response, Congress used its power over interstate commerce to pass the Sherman Anti-Trust Act (1890), which, on its face, banned all trusts and monopolies.

The U.S. Supreme Court struck a blow against this legislation in 1895 in the case of *United States v. E.C. Knight.* The administration of President Grover Cleveland initiated prosecution of the E.C. Knight Company because it controlled 98 percent of the nation's sugar production. The Court, however, ruled that commerce was separate from manufacturing and that the Sherman Act, therefore, could not be used against Knight. For the next five years, presidents did little to go after trusts and monopolies. The situation changed, especially in the eyes of the public, with the ascension of Theodore Roosevelt to the presidency. Although Roosevelt personally favored going after only "unreasonable" trusts, he knew the public wanted action. Taking a highly publicized anti-trust position, Roosevelt went after a number of trusts, including Swift & Company, which controlled much of the meat production in the country.

Significance

Under the terms of the ruling in *E.C. Knight,* which defined interstate commerce as being separate from production, the Sherman Act could not be applied to Swift. In *Swift & Co. v. U.S.,* the case that resulted from the government's action, the Supreme Court redefined interstate commerce. The Court determined that the definition must include all transactions of the company, because those transactions had an effect on the "current of commerce." Taking a much broader view of interstate commerce, the Court held that since a meatpacking operation had regional significance, it was part of interstate commerce. This interpretation, which allows regulation of production, and especially of a company that produces items, has generally held sway since that time.

Monopolies still won some victories. An example is the Standard Oil case (1911), in which the Supreme Court held that only "unreasonable" monopolies are affected by the Sherman Act. That view was later repudiated. Labor conditions and the number of hours put in by a worker, while considered part of production, generally did not pertain to "current of commerce" or "stream of commerce." Instead, they were held to be part of individual liberty, since a worker has a right to contract for any desired number of hours, for whatever wages. Child labor was also held to be outside of interstate commerce. Thus, for about thirty years, Congress could regulate monopolies, but not workplace practices.

Workplace laws were implemented under the National Labor Relations Act (known as the Wagner Act, 1935), which protected workers' right to unionize, and the First Labor Standards Act (1938), which established controls over child labor and set minimum wages and maximum hours for workers. The legislation was upheld when the Supreme Court ruled that Congress could regulate any activity that had a "substantial effect on interstate commerce." This view has generally prevailed up to the present, even though recent courts have somewhat narrowed the power of Congress.

Primary Source

Swift & Co. v. U.S. [excerpt]

SYNOPSIS: In delivering the opinion of the Supreme Court in the Swift case, Oliver Wendell Holmes Jr. first states that the activities of Swift & Company were different from manufacturing, thereby distinguishing it from the E.C. Knight case. Next, he argues that there was an attempt to interfere with commerce. Finally, Holmes concludes that the commerce in question is part of the "current of commerce" between several different states, and so is part of interstate commerce.

Meat inspectors at Swift and Co., Chicago, circa 1900. THE LIBRARY OF CONGRESS.

Mr. Justice Holmes delivered the opinion of the court: . . .

The scheme as a whole seems to us to be within reach of the law. The constituent elements, as we have stated them, are enough to give to the scheme a body and, for all that we can say, to accomplish it. Moreover, whatever we may think of them separately, when we take them up as distinct charges, they are alleged sufficiently as elements of the scheme. It is suggested that the several acts charged are lawful, and that intent can make no difference. But they are bound together as parts of a single plan. The plan may make the parts unlawful. . . . The statute gives this proceeding against combinations in restraint of commerce among the states and against attempts to monopolize the same. Intent is almost essential to such a combination, and is essential to such an attempt. Where acts are not sufficient in themselves to produce a result which the law seeks to prevent—for instance, the monopoly—but require further acts in addition to the mere forces of nature to bring that result to pass, an intent to bring it to pass is necessary in order to produce a dangerous probability that it will happen. . . . But when that intent and the consequent dangerous probability exist, this statute, like many others, and like the common law in some cases, directs itself against that dangerous probability as well as against the completed result. What we have said disposes incidentally of the objection to the bill as multifarious. The unity of the plan embraces all the parts. . . .

Therefore the case is not like *United States v. E. C. Knight Co.,* . . . where the subject-matter of the combination was manufacture, and the direct object monopoly of manufacture within a state. However likely monopoly of commerce among the states in the article manufactured was to follow from the agreement, it was not a necessary consequence nor a primary end. Here the subject-matter is sales, and the very point of the combination is to restrain and monopolize commerce among the states in respect to such sales. The two cases are near to each other, as sooner or later always must happen where lines are to be drawn, but the line between them is distinct. . . .

For the foregoing reasons we are of opinion that the carrying out of the scheme alleged, by the means set forth, properly may be enjoined, and that the bill cannot be dismissed.

So far it has not been necessary to consider whether the facts charged in any single paragraph constitute commerce among the states or show an interference with it. There can be no doubt, we apprehend, as to the collective effect of all the facts, if true, and if the defendants entertain the intent alleged. We pass now to the particulars, and will consider the corresponding parts of the injunction at the same time. The first question arises on the 6th section. That charges a combination of independent dealers to restrict the competition of their agents when purchasing stock for them in the stock yards. The purchasers and their slaughtering establishments are largely in different states from those of the stock yards, and the sellers of the cattle, perhaps it is not too much to assume, largely in different states from either. The intent of the combination is not merely to restrict competition among the parties, but, as we have said, by force of the general allegation at the end of the bill, to aid in an attempt to monopolize commerce among the states.

It is said that this charge is too vague and that it does not set forth a case of commerce among the states. Taking up the latter objection first, commerce among the states is not a technical legal conception, but a practical one, drawn from the course of business. When cattle are sent for sale from a place in one state, with the expectation that they will end their transit, after purchase, in another, and when in effect they do so, with only the interruption necessary to find a purchaser at the stock yards, and when this is a typical, constantly recurring course, the current thus existing is a current of commerce among the states, and the purchase of the cattle is a part and incident of such commerce. What we say is true at least of such a purchase by residents in another state from that of the seller and of the cattle. And we need not trouble ourselves at this time as to whether the statute could be escaped by any arrangement as to the place where the sale in point of law is consummated. . . .

Decree modified and affirmed.

Further Resources

BOOKS

Baker, Liva. *The Justice from Beacon Hill: The Life and Times of Oliver Wendell Holmes.* New York: HarperCollins, 1991.

Comanor, William S., and F. M. Scherer. *Rewriting History: The Early Sherman Act Monopolization Cases.* Cambridge, Mass.: Research Programs, John F. Kennedy School of Government, Harvard University, 1993.

Hervey, John G. *The Anti-Trust Laws of the United States.* Philadelphia: The American Academy of Political and Social Science, 1930.

Hadlick, Paul E. *Criminal Prosecutions under the Sherman Anti-Trust Act.* Washington, D.C.: Ransdell, 1939.

Novick, Sheldon M. *Honorable Justice: The Life of Oliver Wendell Holmes.* Boston: Little, Brown, 1989.

White, G. Edward. *Justice Oliver Wendell Holmes: Law and the Inner Self.* New York: Oxford University Press, 1993.

WEBSITES

Major Supreme Court Decisions. Available online at http:// www.simonmagus.org/eb/study_guide/Supreme-Court-Decisions.html; website home page: http://www.simonmagus.org (accessed January 9, 2003).

Lochner v. New York

Supreme Court decision

By: Rufus W. Peckham; John Marshall Harlan; Oliver Wendell Holmes Jr.

Date: April 17, 1905

Source: Peckham, Rufus W., John Marshall Harlan and Oliver Wendell Holmes Jr. *Lochner v. State of New York* 198 U.S. 45 (1905). Available online at http://www.caselaw.lp.findlaw.com (accessed November 22, 2002).

About the Authors: Rufus W. Peckham (1838–1909) was appointed to the U.S. Supreme Court in 1896 and served until his death. He previously sat for nearly ten years on the New York Court of Appeals.

John Marshall Harlan (1833–1911), known as "The Great Dissenter," was famous for his dissents in such cases as *Plessy v. Ferguson.* He served on the U.S. Supreme Court for thirty-four years.

Oliver Wendell Holmes Jr. (1841–1935), a Union Army veteran, served on the Massachusetts Supreme Court for sixteen years. At age sixty-one he was appointed to the Supreme Court, where he served for thirty years. ■

Introduction

With the rise of industrialization came the fall of the worker's status. In the late nineteenth century, workers were often abused by their employers, who were generally quite distant from them. Employers were much more concerned with making money than with laborers' health and working conditions. They could afford to take this attitude, because there was a steady stream of immigrants into the country throughout the latter half of the century. Efforts to unionize workers were met with stiff resistance by company owners, who employed strikebreakers and spies to destroy unions. Owners also made workers sign "yellow dog contracts," which stated that if a worker joined a union the employment contract was void and the worker was automatically fired. The government was also on the side of the owners, taking the view that unions were radical and dangerous.

Legislation also harmed workers by creating a legal fiction called "liberty of contract." According to this concept, each person had the liberty to enter into a contract, and any attempt to limit that liberty would violate individual protection guaranteed by the Fourteenth Amendment. The doctrine assumed that owners and workers had equal bargaining power, which of course was fallacious. At the beginning of the twentieth century, some states began to make halting moves to protect workers. These efforts were motivated by a number of concerns, including health considerations. It was believed that an employer would have safer workers and better products if hours were limited. Consequently, a number of states passed laws limiting the work week. Among them was New York, which passed a measure prohibiting bakers from working over ten hours a day, six days a week, or a total of sixty hours per week.

Significance

In *Lochner v. State of New York,* the U.S. Supreme Court struck down the New York law. By prohibiting

A young girl stands in front of Lochner's Home Bakery in Utica, New York, circa 1900. **ONEIDA COUNTY HISTORICAL DISTRICT.**

states from placing limitations on the work week, the Court had incorporated the concept of "liberty of contract" into the Constitution of the United States. The *Lochner* decision left open the opportunity for hourly regulation, but it required that states demonstrate a clear connection between the law and benefits to the health of workers. Dissenting justices, led by John Marshall Harlan, pointed out those benefits, while Oliver Wendell Holmes Jr. argued that a state should be allowed to regulate hours, unless such regulation violated the Constitution.

The next case to come before the Supreme Court concerning the regulation of hours in the workplace was a maximum hours law for women, which the court upheld in *Muller v. Oregon.* Louis Brandeis presented a detailed brief arguing that women were weaker than men and needed protection lest their child-bearing capacities be damaged. Protections for men and women received a generally positive reaction over the next two decades. However, a federal minimum wage law for women was struck down in 1923. It was not until the 1930s that maximum hour and minimum wage legislation would be passed at the federal level for most jobs. In 1941, the Court upheld this legislation in *U.S. v. Darby Lumber Company,* thus bringing to an end the concept of "liberty of contract." Since *Darby,* the validity of a maximum work week has remained unchallenged.

Primary Source

Lochner v. State of New York [excerpt]

SYNOPSIS: The following excerpts from *Lochner v. State of New York* open with Rufus W. Peckham noting how the statute interferes with the right of the employee to contract, and how the state may regulate contracts but only within limits. The Court opinion holds that the state exceeds these limits and so cannot be allowed. John Marshall Harlan argues that baking work is indeed dangerous, that the state has the power to regulate dangerous things, and that baking can therefore be regulated. Oliver Wendell Holmes dissents because he sees the opinion as promoting a specific economic view.

Mr. Justice Peckham . . . delivered the opinion of the court: . . .

The statute necessarily interferes with the right of contract between the employer and employees, concerning the number of hours in which the latter may labor in the bakery of the employer. The general right to make a contract in relation to his business is part of the liberty of the individual protected by the 14th Amendment of the Federal Constitution. . . . Under that provision no state can deprive any person of life, liberty, or property without due process of law.

Supreme Court Justice Rufus Wheeler Peckham (served 1895–1909). In *Lochner v. New York,* he held that limiting the hours an employee could work interfered with rights to liberty ensured by the Fourteenth Amendment **THE LIBRARY OF CONGRESS/CORBIS. REPRODUCED BY PERMISSION.**

The right to purchase or to sell labor is part of the liberty protected by this amendment, unless there are circumstances which exclude the right. There are, however, certain powers, existing in the sovereignty of each state in the Union, somewhat vaguely termed police powers, the exact description and limitation of which have not been attempted by the courts. Those powers, broadly stated, and without, at present, any attempt at a more specific limitation, relate to the safety, health, morals, and general welfare of the public. Both property and liberty are held on such reasonable conditions as may be imposed by the governing power of the state in the exercise of those powers, and with such conditions the 14th Amendment was not designed to interfere. . . .

The question whether this act is valid as a labor law, pure and simple, may be dismissed in a few words. There is no reasonable ground for interfering with the liberty of person or the right of free contract, by determining the hours of labor, in the occupation of a baker. . . .

It is a question of which of two powers or rights shall prevail, the power of the state to legislate or the right of the individual to liberty of person and freedom of contract. . . .

We think the limit of the police power has been reached and passed in this case. There is, in our judgment, no reasonable foundation for holding this to be necessary or appropriate as a health law to safeguard the public health, or the health of the individuals who are following the trade of a baker. . . . Some occupations are more healthy than others, but we think there are none which might not come under the power of the legislature to supervise and control the hours of working therein, if the mere fact that the occupation is not absolutely and perfectly healthy is to confer that right upon the legislative department of the government. It might be safely affirmed that almost all occupations more or less affect the health. . . .

Statutes of the nature of that under review, limiting the hours in which grown and intelligent men may labor to earn their living, are mere meddlesome interferences with the rights of the individual, and they are not saved from condemnation by the claim that they are passed in the exercise of the police power and upon the subject of the health of the individual whose rights are interfered with, unless there be some fair ground, reasonable in and of itself, to say that there is material danger to the public health, or to the health of the employees, if the hours of labor are not curtailed. If this be not clearly the case, the individuals whose rights are thus made the subject of legislative interference are under the protection of the Federal Constitution regarding their liberty of contract as well as of person; and the legislature of the state has no power to limit their right as proposed in this statute. . . .

It is manifest to us that the limitation of the hours of labor as provided for in this section of the statute under which the indictment was found, and the plaintiff in error convicted, has no such direct relation to, and no such substantial effect upon, the health of the employee, as to justify us in regarding the section as really a health law. It seems to us that the real object and purpose were simply to regulate the hours of labor between the master and his employees (all being men, Sui juris), in a private business, not dangerous in any degree to morals, or in any real and substantial degree to the health of the employees. Under such circumstances the freedom of master and employee to contract with each other in relation to their employment, and in defining the same, cannot be prohibited or interfered with, without violating the Federal Constitution. . . .

REVERSED.

Mr. Justice Harlan (with whom Mr. Justice White and Mr. Justice Day concurred) dissenting:

While this court has not attempted to mark the precise boundaries of what is called the police power of the state, the existence of the power has been uniformly recognized, equally by the Federal and State courts.

All the cases agree that this power extends at least to the protection of the lives, the health, and the safety of the public against the injurious exercise by any citizen of his own rights. . . .

The authorities on the same line are so numerous that further citations are unnecessary.

I take it to be firmly established that what is called the liberty of contract may, within certain limits, be subjected to regulations designed and calculated to promote the general welfare, or to guard the public health, the public morals, or the public safety. . . .

It is plain that this statute was enacted in order to protect the physical well-being of those who work in bakery and confectionery establishments. It may be that the statute had its origin, in part, in the belief that employers and employees in such establishments were not upon an equal footing, and that the necessities of the latter often compelled them to submit to such exactions as unduly taxed their strength. Be this as it may, the statute must be taken as expressing the belief of the people of New York that, as a general rule, and in the case of the average man, labor in excess of sixty hours during a week in such establishments may endanger the health of those who thus labor. Whether or not this be wise legislation it is not the province of the court to inquire. Under our systems of government the courts are not concerned with the wisdom or policy of legislation. So that, in determining the question of power to interfere with liberty of contract, the court may inquire whether the means devised by the state are germane to an end which may be lawfully accomplished and have a real or substantial relation to the protection of health, as involved in the daily work of the persons, male and female, engaged in bakery and confectionery establishments. . . .

Let the state alone in the management of its purely domestic affairs, so long as it does not appear beyond all question that it has violated the Federal Constitution. This view necessarily results from the principle that the health and safety of the people of a state are primarily for the state to guard and protect.

I take leave to say that the New York statute, in the particulars here involved, cannot be held to be in conflict with the 14th Amendment, without enlarging the scope of the amendment far beyond its original purpose, and without bringing under the supervision of this court matters which have been supposed to belong exclusively to the legislative departments of the several states when exerting their conceded power to guard the health and safety of their citizens by such regulations as they in their wisdom deem best. . . .

[According to *Atkin v. Kansas*] " . . . We are reminded by counsel that it is the solemn duty of the courts in cases before them to guard the constitutional rights of the citizen against merely arbitrary power. That is unquestionably true. But it is equally true—indeed, the public interests imperatively demand—that legislative enactments should be recognized and enforced by the courts as embodying the will of the people, unless they are plainly and palpably beyond all question in violation of the fundamental law of the Constitution." . . .

The judgment, in my opinion, should be affirmed.

Mr. Justice Holmes dissenting:

. . . The 14th Amendment does not enact Mr. Herbert Spencer's Social Statistics. . . . Some of these laws embody convictions or prejudices which judges are likely to share. Some may not. But a Constitution is not intended to embody a particular economic theory, whether of paternalism and the organic relation of the citizen to the state or of laissez faire. It is made for people of fundamentally differing views, and the accident of our finding certain opinions natural and familiar, or novel, and even shocking, ought not to conclude our judgment upon the question whether statutes embodying them conflict with the Constitution of the United States.

General propositions do not decide concrete cases. The decision will depend on a judgment or intuition more subtle than any articulate major premise. But I think that the proposition just stated, if it is accepted, will carry us far toward the end. Every opinion tends to become a law. I think that the word "liberty," in the 14th Amendment, is perverted when it is held to prevent the natural outcome of a dominant opinion, unless it can be said that a rational and fair man necessarily would admit that the statute proposed would infringe fundamental principles as they have been understood by the traditions of our people and our law. It does not need research to show that no such sweeping condemnation can be passed upon the statute before us. A reasonable man might think it a proper measure on the score of health. Men whom I certainly could not pronounce unreasonable would uphold it as a first installment of a general regulation of the hours of work. Whether in the latter aspect it would be open to the charge of inequality I think it unnecessary to discuss.

Further Resources

BOOKS

Kens, Paul. *"Lochner" v. "New York": Economic Regulation on Trial.* Lawrence, Kans.: University Press of Kansas, 1998.

Parker, Alton B. *Address of Alton B. Parker. Memorial Exercises of the Late Mr. Justice Peckham, Washington, December 18, 1909.* 1910.

Riley, James Andrew. *The Influence of Frontier Theories of National Development on Constitutional Jurisprudence: A Comparative Study of Stephen J. Field and Oliver Wendell Holmes.* Master's thesis, University of Kentucky, 1997.

United States Supreme Court. *Proceedings of the Bar and Officers of the Supreme Court of the United States in Memory of Rufus Wheeler Peckham, December 18, 1909.* Washington, D.C., 1910.

WEBSITES

"Liberty of Contract." Available online at http://www.law.umkc.edu/faculty/projects/ftrials/conlaw/libertyofk.htm; website home page: http://www.law.umkc.edu (accessed January 8, 2003).

AUDIO AND VISUAL MEDIA

Kens, Paul, Jerome H. Supple, and Leonardo Cardenas. *The Presidential Seminar.* Video recording. Southwest Texas State University. Media Services, 1992.

An Act for the Preservation of American Antiquities

Law

By: U.S. Congress and Theodore Roosevelt

Date: June 8, 1906

Source: U.S. Congress and Theodore Roosevelt. *An Act for the Preservation of American Antiquities* S. 4698. Public, No. 209. June 8, 1906.

About the Author: Theodore Roosevelt (1858–1919) was the youngest man to serve as president of the United States (served 1901–1909). He was the vice president when he ascended to the presidency in 1901, at age forty-two, after the assassination of President William McKinley. Known for his boundless energy, Roosevelt had already been a rancher, assistant secretary of the navy, governor of New York, assemblyman, and sheriff. He had also written over forty books and had organized his own cavalry regiment in the Spanish-American War (1898). During his presidency, he promoted conservation and publicly fought against trusts. ■

Introduction

Prior to the late nineteenth century, Americans were not especially concerned about preserving the natural environment. One reason was the seemingly endless supply of resources such as vast forests, rich gold streams, and huge buffalo herds. It soon became obvious that these resources were not endless. Many gold streams were tapped out, buffalo herds had been greatly reduced in numbers, and many forests had disappeared. Wildlife species were also becoming extinct, as had, for instance, the passenger pigeon in 1912.

People finally showed interest in preserving rural green space and planning for urban parks. New York City's Central Park was created in the 1860s, and a variety of conservation movements sprang up throughout the country. Some called for preservation of natural resources by setting aside areas for little or no use in order to save them. Others promoted planned development through a judicious process of preserving resources for future use. Theodore Roosevelt, who had been a rancher and sheriff in the West, belonged to the second group. At the turn of the twentieth century, the United States had few national parks; the first was Yellowstone, which had been established as recently as 1872. In an effort to create more national parks and forests, the president pushed for legislation that would allow him to set aside territory for preservation. This did not come without opposition, and Congress passed a bill restricting Roosevelt's power. So Roosevelt moved quickly to add more forests and water areas before the bill went into effect.

Significance

The result of Roosevelt's efforts was An Act for the Preservation of American Antiquities, which went into effect in June 1906 and allowed the president to protect many of America's natural treasures. It was one of the weapons Roosevelt used to greatly increase the size of national parks and forests, adding more land than all of the previous presidents combined. He also issued executive orders to add land to national forests, thus limiting development. Even today, the federal government owns much of the western part of the United States.

The debate over "proper" use of America's natural resources has continued, and management has become a complex issue. In the 1930s, many dams were built, turning land into lakes, creating waterfront areas, and providing a cheap form of electrical power. Over time, though, rivers that had been dammed to build lakes often filled up with silt and did not function well. Questions also arose about the right to use water, particularly in the water-starved West. Since the 1930s, people have

President Roosevelt (center), his friend, naturalist John Burroughs (left front), and companions set up camp during their 1903 expedition to Yellowstone National Park. NEG. NO. 333914. COURTESY DEPARTMENT OF LIBRARY SERVICES, AMERICAN MUSEUM OF NATURAL HISTORY

tried to clean up rivers and to balance the benefits of a dam against damage to a river. In addition, overuse of national parks and forests has caused damage, as resorts built in many of the western parks have encroached on forests and killed many old trees. Efforts to prevent forest fires have prevented the birth of new redwoods, since existing redwoods need flames to open seeds. The battle over use of resources continues as some interest groups promote oil drilling in the Arctic National Forest. So while An Act for the Preservation of American Antiquities and similar legislation represented significant advances, the issue is not dead.

Primary Source

An Act for the Preservation of American Antiquities

SYNOPSIS: Section 1 of the act establishes penalties for misuse or destruction of federal lands; Section 2 gives the president power to designate national lands, historic landmarks, and historic structures; Section 3 allows for the preservation of ancient sites for educational and scientific purposes; and Section 4 specifies publication of provisions of the act.

Be it enacted by the Senate and House of Representatives of the United States of America in Congress assembled, That any person who shall appropriate, excavate, injure, or destroy any historic or prehistoric ruin or monument, or any object of antiquity, situated on lands owned or controlled by the Government of the United States, without the permission of the Secretary of the Department of the Government having jurisdiction over the lands on which said antiquities are situated, shall, upon conviction, be fined in a sum of not more than five hundred dollars or be imprisoned for a period of not more than ninety days, or shall suffer both fine and imprisonment, in the discretion of the court.

A woman enjoys the view of the Grand Canyon. The canyon was designated as a national preserve area in 1906. REPRODUCED FROM THE COLLECTIONS OF THE LIBRARY OF CONGRESS.

Sec. 2. That the President of the United States is hereby authorized, in his discretion, to declare by public proclamation historic landmarks, historic and prehistoric structures, and other objects of historic or scientific interest that are situated upon the lands owned or controlled by the Government of the United States to be national monuments, and may reserve as a part thereof parcels of land, the limits of which in all cases shall be confined to the smallest area compatible with the proper care and management of the objects to be protected: *Provided,* That when such objects are situated upon a tract covered by a bona fide unperfected claim or held in private ownership, the tract, or so much thereof as may be necessary for the proper care and management of the object, may be relinquished to the Government, and the Secretary of the Interior is hereby authorized to accept the relinquishment of such tracts in behalf of the Government of the United States.

Sec. 3. That permits for the examination of ruins, the excavation of archaeological sites, and the gathering of objects of antiquity upon the lands under their respective jurisdictions may be granted by the Secretaries of the Interior, Agriculture, and War to institutions which they may deem properly qualified to conduct such examination, excavation, or gathering, subject to such rules and regulations as they may prescribe: *Provided,* That the examinations, excavations, and gatherings are undertaken for the benefit of reputable museums, universities, colleges, or other recognized scientific or educational institutions, with a view to increasing the knowledge of such objects, and that the gathering shall be made for permanent preservation in public museums.

Sec. 4. That the Secretaries of the Departments aforesaid shall make and publish from time to time uniform rules and regulations for the purpose of carrying out the provisions of this Act.

Approved, June 8, 1906.

Further Resources

BOOKS

Brands, H.W. *T. R.: The Last Romantic.* New York: Basic Books, 1997.

Grover, Barbara L. *The Antiquities Act of 1906: The Public Response to the Use of Presidential Power in Managing Public Lands.* Master's thesis, 1998.

McCullough, David G. *Mornings on Horseback.* New York: Simon and Schuster, 1981.

Morris, Edmund. *Theodore Rex.* New York: Random House, 2001.

United States General Accounting Office. *Federal Land Management Information on Usage of the Antiquities Act.* General Accounting Office: Washington, D. C., 1999.

Whithorn, Doris, and Aubrey L Haines. *Twice Told on the Upper Yellowstone.* Livingston, Mo: D. Whithorn, 1994.

PERIODICALS

Thompson, Raymond H., and Ronald F. Lee. "An Old and Reliable Authority: An Act for the Preservation of American Antiquities." *Journal of the Southwest* vol. 42, No. 2, Summer 2000, 191–381.

WEBSITES

"Theodore Roosevelt and the National Park System." Available online at http://www.cr.nps.gov/history/hisnps/NPSH/TEDDY.HTM; website home page: http://www.cr.nps.gov (accessed January 9, 2003).

The Jungle

Novel

By: Upton Sinclair

Date: 1906

Source: Sinclair, Upton. *The Jungle.* New York, 1906.

About the Author: Upton Sinclair (1878–1968) was a short story writer, essayist, novelist, and playwright. Author of more than 100 books, Sinclair put himself through Columbia College by writing. He also ran for governor of California in 1934 on a socialist ticket, receiving 900,000 votes. He is best known for his book, *The Jungle,* which had the most profound social impact of any novel since *Uncle Tom's Cabin. The Jungle* is still widely read today. ■

Introduction

Prior to the beginning of the nineteenth century, most meat processing in the United States was done on a local level. The reasons were that an inadequate transportation network and limited preservation methods prevented large-scale operations. By the late nineteenth century, significant advances were made possible through development of a national railroad system and use of refrigerated railroad cars. Large quantities of animals could now be moved to a central location, where meat was processed and then shipped out again on the same railroads. The result of these advances, however, was the growth of huge meatpacking monopolies, which states were frequently too weak to fight against. When states did enact legislation to regulate monopolies, it was struck down as being an interference with interstate commerce, which was controlled by the U.S. Congress.

For most of the nineteenth century, the general public and Congress were not aware of the serious social and labor problems caused by large corporations. Therefore, Congress was not especially interested in regulating monopolies, nor was it concerned about regulating the workplace. With the start of the Progressive movement in the early 1900s, however, journalists known as "muckrakers" began reporting on the corrupt practices of giant industries. Ida B. Tarbell, for instance, exposed the abuses of the Standard Oil Company, triggering calls for reform. Upton Sinclair wanted to do the same for workers. In *The Jungle,* he dramatized the problems in the meatpacking industry, hoping to spur workers into campaigning for broad-based change through establishment of a socialist state.

Significance

The Jungle created a sensation by drawing attention to a nationwide scandal in the meatpacking industry. It was said that President Theodore Roosevelt became sick at breakfast after reading the novel. Roosevelt appointed committees to investigate the situation, and meatpackers tried to suppress the reports. However, the president believed it was time for action. Amid increasing public alarm, he pushed through the Meat Inspection Act, which provided for federal inspection. This act ultimately resulted in safer meat products and helped to bring about better working conditions. Nevertheless, Sinclair did not succeed in gaining popular support for a socialist government. He bemoaned this fact, reportedly stating, "I aimed at the nation's heart and hit its stomach." The federal system of meat inspection largely remains in place today, as the United States Department of Agriculture plays a large role in keeping foods safe. Theodore Roosevelt also broke up some of the abusive monopolies and trusts that sparked Sinclair's novel.

Sinclair remained in the public eye, running unsuccessfully for governor of California on a Socialist ticket in 1934. Around this time, changes he had been hoping to spark with his depiction of working conditions came about. A federal work week and federal minimum wage were both instituted in 1938 as part of the New Deal, a series of government programs enacted by President Franklin D. Roosevelt (served 1933–1945). Franklin Roosevelt also helped to bring about the National Labor Relations Act (NLRA), which protected workers who wanted to organize unions. These measures resulted in a better and safer workplace. Since that time, reforms have largely stayed in place, although later Republican administrations did weaken the NLRA. Even though this was not the socialism desired by Sinclair, life was still better for the average worker, meatpacker or otherwise, and for the average meat eater in America.

Primary Source

The Jungle [excerpt]

SYNOPSIS: In the following excerpt from *The Jungle,* Upton Sinclair describes the working conditions in a meatpacking factory. He depicts hard-working men who are faced with overwhelming difficulties, such as physical debilitation, infectious disease, and other dangers. In one scene, he describes men falling into a steam vat and being sent out as lard.

So Jurgis learned a few things about the great and only Durham canned goods, which had become a national institution. They were regular alchemists at Durham's; they advertised a mushroom catsup, and the men who made it did not know what a mushroom looked like. They advertised "potted chicken,"—and it was like the boarding-house soup of the comic papers, through which a chicken had walked with rubbers on. Perhaps they had a secret process for making chickens chemically—who knows? Said Jurgis's friends; the things that went into the mixture were tripe, and the fat of pork, and beef suet, and hearts of beef, and finally the waste ends of veal, when they had any. They put these up in several grades, and sold them at several prices; but the contents of the cans all came out of the same hopper. And then there was "potted game" and "potted grouse," "potted ham" and "devilled ham"—de-vyled, as the men called it. "De-vyled" ham was made out of the waste ends of smoked beef that were too small to be sliced by the machines; and also tripe, dyed with chemicals so that it would not show white; and trimmings of hams and corned beef; and potatoes, skins and all; and finally the

Making link sausages—machines stuff ten feet per second at Swift & Co.'s packing house in Chicago, c. 1905. THE LIBRARY OF CONGRESS.

hard cartilaginous ingenious mixture was ground up and flavoured with spices to make it taste like something. Anybody who could invent a new imitation had been sure of a fortune from old Durham. . . .

There was another interesting set of statistics that a person might have gathered in Packingtown—those of the various afflictions of the workers. When Jurgis had first inspected the packing plants with Szedvilas, he had marvelled while he listened to the tale of all the things that were made out of the carcasses of animals, and of all the lesser industries that were maintained there; now he found that each one of these lesser industries was a separate little inferno, in its way as horrible as the killing beds, the source and fountain of them all. The workers in each of them had their own peculiar diseases. And the wandering visitor might be sceptical about all the swindles, but he could not be sceptical about these, for the worker bore the evidence of them about on his own person—generally he had only to hold out his hand.

There were the men in the pickle rooms, for instance, where old Antanas had gotten his death; scarce a one of these that had not some spot of horror on his person. Let a man so much as scrape his finger pushing a truck in the pickle rooms, and he might have a sore that would put him out of the world; all the joints in his fingers might be eaten by the acid, one by one. Of the butchers and floorsmen, the beef-goners and trimmers, and all those who used knives, you could scarcely find a person who had the use of his thumb; time and time again the base of it had been slashed, till it was a mere lump of flesh against which the man pressed the knife to hold it. The hands of these men would be criss-crossed with cuts, until you could no longer pretend to count them or to trace them. They would have no nails—they had worn them off pulling hides; their knuckles were swollen so that their fingers spread out like a fan. There were men who worked in the cooking rooms, in the midst of steam and sickening odours, by artificial light; in these rooms the germs of tuberculosis might live for two years, but the supply was renewed every hour. There were the beef-luggers, who carried two-hundred-pound quarters into the refrigerator cars—a fearful kind of work, that began at four o'clock in the morning, and that wore out the most powerful men in a few years. There were those who worked in the chilling rooms, and whose special disease was rheumatism; the time limit that a man could work in the chilling rooms was said to be five years. There were the wool-pluckers, whose hands went to pieces even sooner than the hands of the pickle men; for the pelts of the sheep had to be painted with acid to loosen the wool, and then the pluckers had to pull out this wool with their bare hands, till the acid had eaten their fingers off. There were those who made the tins for the canned meat; and their hands, too, were a maze of cuts, and each cut represented a chance for blood poisoning. Some worked at the stamping machines, and it was seldom that one could work long there at the pace that was set, and not give out and forget himself, and have a part of his hand chopped off. There were the "hoisters," as they were called, whose task it was to press the lever which lifted the dead cattle off the floor. They ran along upon a rafter, peering down through the damp and the steam; and as old Durham's architects had not built the killing room for the convenience of the hoisters, at every few feet they would have to stoop under a beam, say four feet above the one they ran on; which got them into the habit of stooping, so that in a few years they would be walking like chimpanzees. Worst of any, however, were the fertilizer-men, and those who served in the cooking rooms. These people could not be shown to the visitor, for the odour of a fertilizer-man would scare any ordinary visitor at a hundred yards; and as for the other men, who worked in tank rooms full of steams, and in some of which there were open vats near the level of the floor, their peculiar trouble was that they fell into the vats; and when they were fished out, there was never enough of them left to be worth exhibiting—sometimes they would be overlooked for days, till all but the bones of them had gone out to the world as Durham's Pure Leaf Lard!

Further Resources

BOOKS

Bloodworth, William A. *Upton Sinclair.* Boston: Twayne, 1977.

Goodwin, Lorine Swainston. *The Pure Food, Drink, and Drug Crusaders, 1879–1914.* Jefferson, N.C.: McFarland, 1999.

Herms, Dieter *Upton Sinclair: Literature and Social Reform.* New York: Lang, 1990.

McCullough, David G. *Mornings on Horseback.* New York: Simon and Schuster, 1981.

Morris, Edmund. *Theodore Rex.* New York: Random House, 2001.

Sinclair, Upton. *Autobiography.* New York: Harcourt, Brace, 1962.

Suh, Suk Bong. *Upton Sinclair and "The Jungle": A Study of American Literature, Society, and Culture.* Seoul: American Studies Institute, 1997.

Young, James Harvey. *Pure Food: Securing the Federal Food and Drugs Act of 1906.* Princeton, N.J.: Princeton University Press, 1989.

WEBSITES

Collier's Weekly. Available online at http://www.spartacus.schoolnet.co.uk/USAcolliers.htm; website home page: http://www.spartacus.schoolnet.co.uk (accessed January 9, 2003).

A Guide to Resources on the History of the Food and Drug Administration. Available online at http://www.fda.gov/oc/history/resourceguide/background.html; website home page: http://www.fda.gov (accessed January 9, 2003).

Patterson v. Colorado

Supreme Court decision

By: Oliver Wendell Holmes Jr.; John Marshall Harlan; David J. Brewer

Date: April 5, 1907

Source: Holmes, Oliver Wendell, Jr., John Marshall Harlan, David J. Brewer *Patterson v. Colorado.* 205 U.S. 454 (1907). Available online at http://www.caselaw.lp.findlaw.com (accessed November 6, 2002).

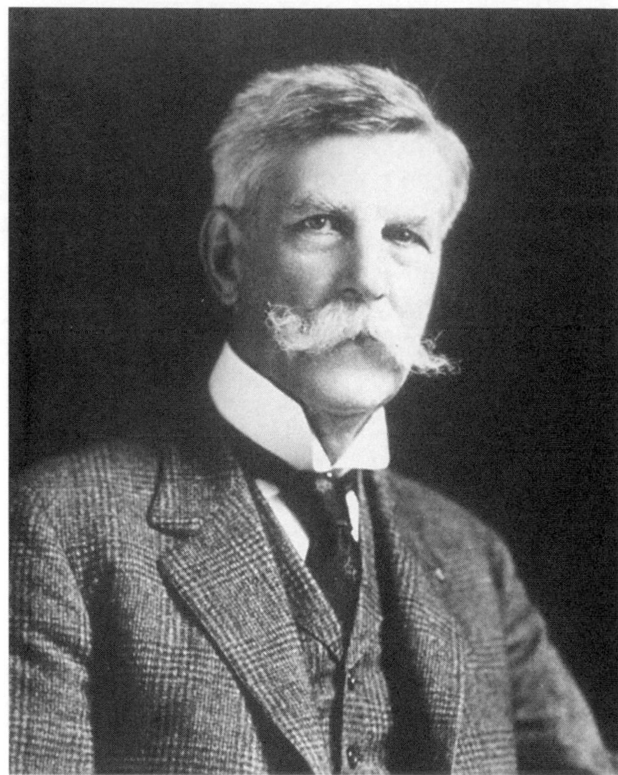

Supreme Court Justice Oliver Wendell Holmes (served 1902–1932). In *Patterson v. Colorado* he held that the First Amendment did not protect those sued or arrested for libel or slander. **THE LIBRARY OF CONGRESS.**

About the Authors: Oliver Wendell Holmes Jr. (1841–1935), a Union Army veteran, served on the Massachusetts Supreme Court for sixteen years. At age sixty-one he was appointed to the Supreme Court, where he served for thirty years.

John Marshall Harlan (1841–1935) served on the Court for thirty-four years, becoming known as "the Great Dissenter" because of his dissents in such cases as *Plessy v. Ferguson.*

David Brewer (1837–1910) served on the Supreme Court from 1889 until 1910. He was a graduate of Yale University and attended Albany Law School. ■

Introduction

The First Amendment was added to the Constitution of the United States in 1789, as part of the Bill of Rights. However, the exact meaning of the amendment, especially in the areas of freedom of speech and freedom of the press, has never been clear. Some have argued that it should operate only to ban prior restraints on publishing and speaking, while others have posited that it works to prohibit all governmental interference. One factor limiting the debate, particularly in the nineteenth and early twentieth centuries, was that the U.S. Supreme Court did not hear many cases dealing with the First Amendment. The first governmental intrusion into freedom of speech and the press were the *Alien and Sedition Acts,* which banned criticism of the government in 1798. These acts were never tested by the Court, and many historians have considered them a mistake. The next time the freedoms of speech and the press became a major issue was during the Civil War (1861–1865), when President Abraham Lincoln imprisoned people who spoke out against the war. He also revoked the writ of habeas corpus (the right of the accused to be informed of the nature of his or her crime). Once again, the constitutionality of these restrictions was never directly ruled on by the Court.

By 1900, the Supreme Court had made few rulings on these issues, even though they had been touched on by lower federal courts. States and the federal government were also acting to control speech and the press during this period. The federal government had passed the *Comstock Act* (1873), which regulated items transmitted by mail and included a ban on birth-control information. States generally had passed anti-libel and anti-slander ordinances as well. The Court directly addressed the First Amendment in *Patterson v. Colorado.* The case resulted when Thomas M. Patterson, a Colorado newspaper publisher, was arrested for contempt of court—meaning he had treated a court with disrespect—for publishing cartoons and other matter critical of the Colorado Supreme Court. Patterson claimed that his actions were protected under the First Amendment.

Significance

Patterson was found guilty of contempt, and his conviction was upheld by the Supreme Court in its decision on *Patterson v. Colorado.* Oliver Wendell Holmes Jr. took a narrow view of the First Amendment in this case, holding that only when a government prohibited publication of an item, a process called prior restraint, was the First Amendment violated. In Holmes' view, the First Amendment offers no protection when one publishes something and then is sued for libel or arrested for contempt. This narrow interpretation continued to be held throughout World War I (1914–1918), when the government imposed censorship upon the press. During the war, Holmes and Justice Louis Brandeis began to offer a wider view of the First Amendment, arguing that only those items that presented a "clear and present danger" could be criminalized or punished. These two justices were, however, in the minority.

Another problem for those who wished to publish freely is that the First Amendment, on its face, restrains only the federal government. The Fourteenth Amendment prohibits a state from denying an individual "liberty" without "due process of law," but the meanings of "liberty" and "due process" are unclear. In the nineteenth century, the Supreme Court had held that not all of the Bill of Rights was applied to the states through the Fourteenth Amendment. In 1925, however, the Supreme Court remarked, in passing, that First Amendment protections limit a state's power. In 1931, the First Amendment was used for the first time to strike down a statute as being in violation of First Amendment rights. More due process guarantees have been added as being applicable against states by succeeding courts, even though recent courts have begun to narrow individual rights again.

Primary Source

Patterson v. Colorado [excerpt]

SYNOPSIS: Oliver Wendell Holmes Jr. comments that the Supreme Court can reverse a contempt conviction only if a constitutional violation has occurred. He next argues that the First Amendment, via the Fourteenth, may apply, but that it does not prevent a contempt citation, and that, on the whole, the court has no jurisdiction. In presenting the dissent, John Marshall Harlan argues that the Fourteenth Amendment does apply and prevents a conviction. David J. Brewer, in another dissent, argues that the court does have jurisdiction.

Mr. Justice Holmes delivered the opinion of the court:

This is a writ of error to review a judgment upon an information for contempt. . . . The contempt alleged was the publication of certain articles and a cartoon, which, it was charged, reflected upon the motives and conduct of the supreme court of Colorado in cases still pending, and were intended to embarrass the court in the impartial administration of justice. There was a motion to quash on grounds of local law and the state Constitution and also of the 14th Amendment to the Constitution of the United States. This was overruled and thereupon an answer was filed, . . . Upon this answer the court, on motion, ordered judgment fining the plaintiff in error for contempt.

The foregoing proceedings are set forth in a bill of exceptions, and several errors are alleged. . . . The only question for this court is the power of the state. . . .

It is argued that the decisions criticized, and in some degree that in the present case, were contrary to well-settled previous adjudications of the same court, and this allegation is regarded as giving some sort of constitutional right to the plaintiff in error. But while it is true that the United States courts do not always hold themselves bound by state decisions in cases arising before them, that principle has but a limited application to cases brought from the state courts here on writs of error. Except in exceptional cases the grounds on which the circuit courts are held authorized to follow an earlier state decision rather than a later one, or to apply the rules of commercial law as understood by this court rather than those laid down by the local tribunals, are not grounds of constitutional right, but considerations of justice or expediency. There is no constitutional right to have all general propositions of law once adopted remain unchanged. Even if it be true, as the plaintiff in error says, that the supreme court of Colorado departed from earlier and well-established precedents to meet the exigencies of this case, whatever might be thought of the justice or wisdom of such a step, the Constitution of the United States is not infringed. It is unnecessary to lay down an absolute rule beyond the possibility of exception. Exceptions have been held to exist. But, in general, the decision of a court upon a question of law, however wrong and however contrary to previous decisions, is not an infraction of the 14th Amendment merely because it is wrong or because earlier decisions are reversed.

It is argued that the articles did not constitute a contempt. In view of the answer, which sets out more plainly and in fuller detail what the articles insinuate and suggest, and in view of the position of the plaintiff in error that he was performing a public duty, the argument for a favorable interpretation of the printed words loses some of its force. However, it is enough for us to say that they are far from showing that innocent conduct has been laid hold of as an arbitrary pretense for an arbitrary punishment. Supposing that such a case would give the plaintiff in error a standing here, anything short of that is for the state court to decide. What constitutes contempt, as well as the time during which it may be committed, is a matter of local law.

The defense upon which the plaintiff in error most relies is raised by the allegation that the articles complained of are true, and the claim of the right to prove the truth. He claimed this right under the Constitutions both of the state and of the United States, but the latter ground alone comes into consideration here, for reasons already stated. . . . We do not pause to consider whether the claim was sufficient in point of form, although it is easier to refer to the Constitution generally for the supposed right than to point to the clause from which it springs. We leave undecided the question whether there is to be found in the 14th Amendment a prohibition similar to that in the 1st. But even if we were to assume that freedom of speech and freedom of the press were protected from abridgments on the part not only of the United States but also of the states, still we should be far from the conclusion that the plaintiff in error would have us reach. In the first place, the main purpose of such constitutional provisions is "to prevent all such previous restraints upon publications as had been practiced by other governments," and they do not prevent the subsequent punishment of such as may be deemed contrary to the public welfare. . . . The preliminary freedom extends as well to the false as to the true; the subsequent punishment may extend as well to the true as to the false. This was the law of criminal libel apart from statute in most cases, if not in all. . . .

In the next place, the rule applied to criminal libels applies yet more clearly to contempts. A publication likely to reach the eyes of a jury, declaring a witness in a pending cause a perjurer, would be none the less a contempt that it was true. It would tend to obstruct the administration of justice, because even a correct conclusion is not to be reached or helped in that way, if our system of trials is to be maintained. The theory of our system is that the conclusions to be reached in a case will be induced only by evidence and argument in open court, and not by any outside influence, whether of private talk or public print.

What is true with reference to a jury is true also with reference to a court. Cases like the present are more likely to arise, no doubt, when there is a jury, and the publication may affect their judgment. Judges generally perhaps are less apprehensive that publications impugning their own reasoning or motives will interfere with their administration of the law. But if a court regards, as it may, a publication concerning a matter of law pending before it, as tending toward such an interference, it may punish it as in the instance put. When a case is finished courts are subject to the same criticism as other people; but the propriety and necessity of preventing interference with the course of justice by premature statement, argument, or intimidation hardly can be denied. . . . It is objected that the judges were sitting in their own case. But the grounds upon which contempts are punished are impersonal. . . . No doubt judges naturally would be slower to punish when the contempt carried with it a personal dishonoring charge, but a man cannot expect to secure immunity from punishment by the proper tribunal, by adding to illegal conduct a personal attack. It only remains to add that the plaintiff in error had his day in court and opportunity to be heard. We have scrutinized the case, but cannot say that it shows an infraction of rights under the Constitution of the United States, or discloses more than the formal appeal to that instrument in the answer to found the jurisdiction of this court.

Writ of error dismissed.

Mr. Justice Harlan, dissenting:

I cannot agree that this writ of error should be dismissed.

By the 1st Amendment of the Constitution of the United States, it is provided that "Congress shall make no law respecting an establishment of religion, or abridging the freedom of speech, or of the press, or of the right of the people peaceably to assemble and to petition the government for redress." In the civil Rights Cases . . . it was adjudged that the 13th Amendment, although in form prohibitory, had a reflex character, in that it established and decreed universal civil and political freedom throughout the United States. In *United States v. Cruikshank* . . . we held that the right of the people peaceably to assemble and to petition the government for a redress of grievances—one of the rights recognized in and protected by the 1st Amendment against hostile legislation by Congress—was an attribute of "national citizenship." So the 1st Amendment, although in form prohibitory, is to be regarded as having a reflex character, and as affirmatively recognizing freedom of speech and freedom of the press as rights belonging to citizens of the United States; that is, those rights are to be deemed attributes of national citizenship or citizenship of the United States. No one, I take it, will hesitate to say that a judgment of a Federal court, prior to the adoption of the 14th Amendment, impairing or abridging freedom of speech or of the press, would have been in violation of the rights of "citizens of the United States" as guaranteed by the 1st Amendment; this, for the reason that the rights of free speech and a free press were, as already said, attributes of national citizenship before the 14th Amendment was made a part of the Constitution.

Now, the 14th Amendment declares, in express words, that "no state shall make or enforce any law which shall abridge the privileges or immunities of citizens of the United States." As the 1st Amendment guaranteed the rights of free speech and of a free press against hostile action by the United States, it would seem clear that, when the 14th Amendment prohibited the states from impairing or abridging the privileges of citizens of the United States, it necessarily prohibited the states from impairing or abridging the constitutional rights of such citizens to free speech and a free press. But the court announces that it leaves undecided the specific question whether there is to be found in the 14th Amendment a prohibition as to the rights of free speech and a free press similar to that in the 1st. It yet proceeds to say that the main purpose of such constitutional provisions was to prevent all such "previous restraints" upon publications as had been practised by other governments, but not to prevent the subsequent punishment of such as may be deemed contrary to the public welfare. I cannot assent to that view, if it be meant that the legislature may impair or abridge the rights of a free press and of free speech whenever it thinks that the public welfare requires that to be done. The public welfare cannot override constitutional privileges, and if the rights of free speech and of a free press are, in their essence, attributes of national citizenship, as I think they are, then neither Congress nor any state, since the adoption of the 14th Amendment, can, by legislative enactments or by judicial action, impair or abridge them. In my judgment the action of the court below was in violation of the rights of free speech and a free press as guaranteed by the Constitution.

I go further and hold that the privileges of free speech and of a free press, belonging to every citizen of the United States, constitute essential parts of every man's liberty, and are protected against violation by that clause of the 14th Amendment forbidding a state to deprive any person of his liberty without due process of law. It is, I think, impossible to conceive of liberty, as secured by the Constitution against hostile action, whether by the nation or by the states, which does not embrace the right to enjoy free speech and the right to have a free press.

Mr. Justice Brewer, dissenting:

While not concurring in the views expressed by Mr. Justice Harlan, I also dissent from the opinion and judgment of the court. The plaintiff in error made a distinct claim that he was denied that which he asserted to be a right guaranteed by the Federal Constitution. His claim cannot be regarded as a frivolous one, nor can the proceedings for contempt be entirely disassociated from the general proceedings of the case in which the contempt is charged to have been committed. I think, therefore, that this court has jurisdiction and ought to inquire and determine the alleged rights of the plaintiff in error. As, however, the court decides that it does not have jurisdiction, and has dismissed the writ of error, it would not be fit for me to express any opinion on the merits of the case.

Further Resources

BOOKS

Beth, Loren P. *John Marshall Harlan: The Last Whig Justice.* Lexington, Ky.: University Press of Kentucky, 1992.

Brodhead, Michael J. *David J. Brewer: The Life of a Supreme Court Justice, 1837–1910.* Carbondale, Ill.: Southern Illinois University Press, 1994.

Eitzen, D. Stanley. *David J. Brewer, 1837–1910, a Kansan on the United States Supreme Court.* Emporia, Kans.: Graduate Division, Kansas State Teachers College, 1964.

Novick, Sheldon M. *Honorable Justice: The Life of Oliver Wendell Holmes.* Boston: Little, Brown, 1989.

Rabban, David. *Free Speech in its Forgotten Years.* Cambridge, Mass.: Cambridge University Press, 1997.

White, G. Edward *Justice Oliver Wendell Holmes: Law and the Inner Self.* New York: Oxford University Press, 1993.

Yarbrough, Tinsley E. *Judicial Enigma: The First Justice Harlan.* New York: Oxford University Press, 1995.

WEBSITES

"Development of the Clear and Present Danger Test." Available online at http://www.law.umkc.edu/faculty/projects/ftrials/conlaw/clear&pdanger; website home page: http://www.law.umkc.edu (accessed January 9, 2003).

"Summation in the Haywood Trial"

Speech

By: Clarence Darrow

Date: 1907

Source: Darrow, Clarence. "Summation in the Haywood Trial." In Lindner, Doug, ed. *Famous Trials in American History: The Trial of Bill Haywood.* Available online at http://www.law.umkc.edu/faculty/projects/ftrials/haywood/HAY_SUMD.HTM; website home page: http://www.law.umkc.edu (accessed May 15, 2003)

About the Author: Clarence Darrow (1857–1938) was one of the most famous criminal defense and civil liberties lawyers in the twentieth century. He represented miners in a coal strike in Pennsylvania in 1903, but his most famous case was his defense in the Scopes Monkey Trial in 1925. Among his other clients were Nathan Leopold and Richard Loeb, defendants in the "thrill" murder trial (1924), and Eugene Debs, the Socialist leader. Darrow defended over 100 people accused of murder, none of whom were given the death penalty. ■

Introduction

American industry started out as small enterprises based in homes or in small shops. With the rise of the Industrial Revolution in the mid-1800s, workers began taking jobs in larger factories. This obviously removed direct contact between the owner and the worker, and

Clarence Darrow. Darrow's successful defense of Bill Haywood gave him great fame. Years later in 1925 he was defense attorney in the infamous Scopes monkey trial. NATIONAL ARCHIVES AND RECORDS ADMINISTRATION

competitive pressures led to longer working hours, poor working conditions, and low pay. Conditions worsened after the Civil War (1861–1865). Workers continued to be abused, as many lived in poverty, and most were expected to work six days a week for at least ten hours a day. Workers' attempts at unionization were violently opposed by owners, who used spies and other measures to oppose them. Laborers who worked in the mining or the lumber industry and railroad construction had many of the same problems.

As a response, in the early 1900s, some Socialists and other radicals, including William Haywood, founded the Industrial Workers of the World. Their goal was to form "One Big Union." A former miner, Haywood was secretary-treasurer of the Western Federation of Miners (WFM), a union that had organized workers in several western mines. In 1905, Frank Steunenberg, a former governor of Idaho, was murdered by Harry Orchard, an odd drifter. Orchard, at the urging of the state, admitted that he committed the crime but claimed that WFM leaders, including Haywood, had put him up to it.

Even though Haywood and two other men had been in Colorado at the time, and even though Colorado law did not allow them to be extradited to Idaho, they were seized by Colorado authorities. The men were then taken to Idaho, and the courts of the nation upheld the illegal extradition. They remained in prison for a year, while the state tried to strong-arm witnesses to corroborate Orchard's story. In 1907, Haywood was finally tried, with Clarence Darrow defending him and future U.S. Senator William Borah appearing for the prosecution. At the end of the trial, Darrow gave his summation.

Significance

Haywood was acquitted, and Darrow gained great fame for his defense skills in the trial. The other two men indicted with Haywood were also spared, with one being acquitted and charges dropped against the second. However, testimony at the trial established the WFM as a violent organization and damaged its reputation. The IWW remained alive but weak, and continued to try to create one comprehensive union in America. The IWW had some success and appeared to be gaining strength prior to World War I (1914–1918). With the outbreak of war, however, the IWW was crushed, as the U.S. government used the wartime Espionage and Sedition Acts to imprison hundreds of IWW members. Haywood was convicted and sentenced to twenty years in prison. The IWW eventually raised bond for Haywood and, while out on bail, he fled to the Soviet Union, where he remained until his death in 1928.

Darrow remained famous as a defense attorney, appearing in the 1925 "Scopes monkey trial" in Tennessee, among others. The Haywood case demonstrated the lengths the state would go to in order to convict radical labor leaders. It was, ironically, only after the death of Haywood that America's unions flourished. With the passage of the *National Labor Relations Act* in 1935, unions gained legitimacy, even though they fought for higher wages and shorter hours, rather than social change, which had been the original goal of the IWW. Unions are weaker today than in the past, but are still much stronger and more respected than they were in Idaho in 1907.

Primary Source

"Darrow's Summation in the Haywood Trial" [excerpt]

SYNOPSIS: Clarence Darrow opens his summation in the Haywood trial by arguing that Harry Orchard, key witness for the prosecution, cannot be believed. He then asks the jury to be skeptical of Hawley, the prosecutor, and his weak case, rather than blindly trusting him. Defending the accused, Darrow argues that if Haywood is unjustly convicted, hundreds more will take his place. Finally, Darrow passionately expresses his belief in Haywood, proclaiming that if the jury acquits him, working men will forever love them.

On the Credibility of Harry Orchard

Gentlemen, I sometimes think I am dreaming in this case. I sometimes wonder whether this is a case, whether here in Idaho or anywhere in the country, broad and free, a man can be placed on trial and lawyers seriously ask to take away the life of a human being upon the testimony of Harry Orchard. We have the lawyers come here and ask you upon the word of that sort of a man to send this man to the gallows, to make his wife a widow, and his children orphans—on his word. For God's sake, what sort of an honesty exists up here in the state of Idaho that sane men should ask it? Need I come here from Chicago to defend the honor of your state? A juror who would take away the life of a human being upon testimony like that would place a stain upon the state of his nativity—a stain that all the waters of the great seas could never wash away. And yet they ask it. You had better let a thousand men go unwhipped of justice, you had better let all the criminals that come to Idaho escape scot free than to have it said that twelve men of Idaho would take away the life of a human being upon testimony like that.

Why, gentlemen, if Harry Orchard were George Washington who had come into a court of justice with his great name behind him, and if he was impeached and contradicted by as many as Harry Orchard has been, George Washington would go out of it disgraced and counted the Ananias of the age. . . .

I don't believe that this man [Orchard] was ever really in the employ of anybody. I don't believe he ever had any allegiance to the Mine Owners Association, to the Pinkertons, to the Western Federation of Miners, to his family, to his kindred, to his God, or to anything human or divine. I don't believe he bears any relation to anything that a mysterious and inscrutable Providence has ever created. . . . He was a soldier of fortune, ready to pick up a penny or a dollar or any other sum in any way that was easy . . . to serve the mine owners, to serve the Western Federation, to serve the devil if he got his price, and his price was cheap. . . .

Attacks on Hawley and the Prosecutor's Case

He said to you, gentlemen of the jury, that he would not prosecute this case unless he believed this defendant guilty. Now, why? Is he prosecuting it because he believes him guilty, is that it? Or is he prosecuting it because he may want to put another "ell" on his house and wants some more deficiency warrants with which to do it? Which is it? Has any man a right to make a statement like that? I hope there is not anybody here who cares a fig about what Mr. Hawley thinks about this case. He may be bughouse, and he is if all of his statements are true. Or he is worse. Let me show you what he said and then judge for yourself. We are trying Mr. Hawley. We will try him on an inquest of lunacy. He said to these twelve men, men of fair intelligence and fair learning, that you would be warranted in convicting Bill Haywood if you took Harry Orchard's evidence out of this case. And still he says he is honest. Maybe he is, but if he is honest he is bughouse, and he can have his choice. . . .

On Bill Haywood and His Possible Execution

He has fought many a fight, many a fight with the persecutors who are hounding him into this court. He has met them in many a battle in the open field, and he is not a coward. If he is to die, he will die as he has lived, with his face to the foe.

To kill him, gentlemen? I want to speak to you plainly. Mr. Haywood is not my greatest concern. Other men have died before him, other men have been martyrs to a holy cause since the world began. Wherever men have looked upward and onward, forgotten their selfishness, struggled for humanity, worked for the poor and the weak, they have been sacrificed. They have been sacrificed in the prison, on the scaffold, in the flame. They have met their death, and he can meet his if you twelve men say he must. Gentlemen, you short-sighted men of the prosecution, you men of the Mine Owners' Association, you people who would cure hatred with hate, you who think you can crush out the feelings and the hopes and the aspirations of men by tying a noose around his neck, you who are seeking to kill him not because it is Haywood but because he represents a class, don't be so blind, don't be so foolish as to believe you can strangle the Western Federation of Miners when you tie a rope around his neck. Don't be so blind in your madness as to believe that if you make three fresh new graves you will kill the labor movement of the world. I want to say to you, gentlemen, Bill Haywood can't die unless you kill him. You have got to tie the rope. You twelve men of Idaho, the burden will be on you. If at the behest of this mob you should kill Bill Haywood, he is mortal. He will die. But I want to say that a hundred will grab up the banner of labor at the open grave where Haywood lays it down, and in spite of prisons, or scaffolds, or fire, in spite of prosecution or jury, these men of willing hands will carry it on to victory in the end.

Labor leader Bill Haywood was arrested for the murder of a former Idaho governor in 1906. THE LIBRARY OF CONGRESS.

Darrow's Belief in His Case

Gentlemen, Mr. Hawley has told you that he believes in this case, that he would not ask you to convict unless he believes Haywood was guilty. I tell you, I believe in my case. I believe in it as I believe in my very life, and my belief does not amount, nor his belief does not amount to anything or count. I am not an unprejudiced witness in this case. Nobody knows it better than I. My mind is not unbiased in this great struggle. I am a partisan and a strong partisan at that. For thirty years I have been working to the best of my ability in the cause in which these men have given their toil and risked their lives. For thirty years I have given the best ability that the God has given me. I have given my time, my reputation, my chances—all this to the cause which is the cause of the poor. I may have been unwise, I may have been extravagant in my statements, but this cause has been the strongest devotion of my life, and I want to say to you that never in my life did I feel about a case as I feel about this. Never in my life did I wish anything as I wish the verdict of this jury. And if I live to be a hundred years old, never again in my life will I feel that I am pleading a case like this.

Darrow's Final Appeal:

I have known Haywood. I have known him well and I believe in him. I do believe in him. God knows it would be a sore day to me if he should ascend the scaffold; the sun would not shine or the birds would not sing on that day for me. It would be a sad day indeed if any calamity should befall him. I would think of him, I would think of his mother, I would think of his babes, I would think of the great cause that he represents. It would be a sore day for me.

But, gentlemen, he and his mother, his wife and his children are not my chief concern in this case. If you should decree that he must die, ten thousand men will work down in the mines to send a portion of the proceeds of their labor to take care of that widow and those orphan children, and a million people throughout the length and the breadth of the civilized world will send their messages of kindness and good cheer to comfort them in their bereavement. It is not for them I plead.

Other men have died, other men have died in the same cause in which Bill Haywood has risked his life, men strong with devotion, men who love liberty, men who love their fellow men have raised their voices in defense of the poor, in defense of justice, have made their good fight and have met death on the scaffold, on the rack, in the flame and they will meet it again until the world grows old and gray. Bill Haywood is no better than the rest. He can die if die he needs, he can die if this jury decrees it; but, oh, gentlemen, don't think for a moment that if you hang him you will crucify the labor movement of the world.

Don't think that you will kill the hopes and the aspirations and the desires of the weak and the poor, you men, unless you people who are anxious for this blood—are you so blind as to believe that liberty will die when he is dead? Do you think there are no brave hearts and no other strong arms, no other devoted souls who will risk their life in that great cause which has demanded martyrs in every age of this world? There are others, and these others will come to take his place, will come to carry the banner where he could not carry it.

Gentlemen, it is not for him alone that I speak. I speak for the poor, for the weak, for the weary, for that long line of men who in darkness and despair have borne the labors of the human race. The eyes of the world are upon you, upon you twelve men of Idaho tonight. Wherever the English language is spoken, or wherever any foreign tongue known to the civilized world is spoken, men are talking and wondering and dreaming about the verdict of these twelve men that I see before me now. If you kill him your act will be applauded by many. If you should decree Bill Haywood's death, in the great railroad offices of our great cities men will applaud your names. If you decree his death, amongst the spiders of Wall Street will go up paeans of praise for those twelve good men and true who killed Bill Haywood. In every bank in the world, where men hate Haywood because he fights for the poor and against the accursed system upon which the favored live and grow rich and fat—from all those you will receive blessings and unstinted praise.

But if your verdict should be "Not Guilty," there are still those who will reverently bow their heads and thank these twelve men for the life and the character they have saved. Out on the broad prairies where men toil with their hands, out on the wide ocean where men are are tossed and buffeted on the waves, through our mills and factories, and down deep under the earth, thousands of men and of women and children, men who labor, men to suffer, women and children weary with care and toil, these men and these women and these children will kneel tonight and ask their God to guide your judgment. These men and these women and these little children, the poor, the weak, and the suffering of the world will stretch out their hands to this jury, and implore you to save Haywood's life.

Further Resources

BOOKS

Borah, William E., William D. Haywood, Albert E. Horsley, Harry Orchard, and Frank Steunenberg. *State of Idaho v. William D. Haywood.* Manuscript collection. Microfilmed Transcript of Trial in Possession of the Colorado Historical Society.

Darrow, Clarence. *Crimes, Causes and the Courtroom.* Cary, N.C.: North Carolina Bar Association Foundation, 1999.

———. *The Moyer-Haywood Outrage.* New York: Moyer-Haywood Labor Conference, 1908.

Darrow, Clarence. *The Story of My Life.* New York: Da Capo Press, 1996.

Dubofsky, Melvyn. *"Big Bill" Haywood.* Manchester: Manchester University Press, 1987.

———, and Joseph Anthony McCartin. *We Shall Be All: A History of the Industrial Workers of the World.* Abridged ed.. Urbana, Ill.: University of Illinois Press, 2000.

Weinberg, Arthur, and Lila Shaffer Weinberg. *Clarence Darrow, a Sentimental Rebel.* New York: Putman, 1980.

WEBSITES

"William Haywood." Available online at http://www.spartacus.schoolnet.co.uk/USAhaywood.htm; website home page: http://www.spartacus.schoolnet.co.uk (accessed January 9, 2003).

Adair v. U.S.

Supreme Court decision

By: John Marshall Harlan

Date: January 27, 1908

Source: Harlan, John Marshall. *Adair v. U.S.* 208 U.S. 161 (1908). Available online at http://www.caselaw.lp.findlaw.com (accessed November 22, 2002).

About the Author: John Marshall Harlan (1833–1911) was born in Kentucky and pursued a career as a lawyer and politician. He served on the Supreme Court from 1877 until his death. Known as "the Great Dissenter," Harlan was famous for his dissenting opinions in such cases as *Plessy v. Ferguson* and *Berea College v. Kentucky.* Before being appointed Supreme Court justice, he was attorney general of Kentucky and the Republican gubernatorial candidate in Kentucky in 1871 and in 1875. ■

Introduction

The Industrial Revolution of the mid-nineteenth century had a devastating impact on workers, in America and around the globe. Rapid mechanization and mass production destroyed the shop-based industry that had developed over several centuries. As a result, jobs for skilled workers were eliminated, connections between shop owner and worker were broken, and workers lost their bargaining power. By the late 1800s, most laborers worked over sixty hours a week, frequently putting in twelve-hour days, six days a week. In the steel industry, employees worked twelve hours a day, seven days a week. Every two weeks, steel workers would switch shifts, working a full twenty-four hours to transfer from one shift to the next, in what was called the "long turn."

Workers tried to respond to these conditions by organizing unions, but many barriers were in their way. One such barrier was the ethnic divisions among the workers themselves. Another was hostility from the government, which would often use military troops to break strikes. A third, and by far the most important, was opposition from industry owners. They generally obstructed unions in any way possible, firing workers who joined unions, using spies, and bringing in strikebreakers. One method was the "yellow-dog" contract, which stipulated that the worker signing the contract would not join a union and that the company could fire the worker for doing so. Such contracts were banned in 1898 by the U.S. government as a response to the bloody Pullman strike.

Workers lay the first rails of the new U.S. railroad at Ship Creek in Alaska. Workers at the turn of the twentieth century tried to respond to long work hours by organizing unions. **THE LIBRARY OF CONGRESS.**

Ten years later, the law was challenged in the *Adair v. U.S.* case.

Significance

In *Adair v. U.S.,* William Adair, an agent for the Louisville & Nashville Railroad Company, was charged with discriminating against O.B. Coppage, a railroad employee whom he had fired in 1906 for being a member of a union. In its ruling, the Supreme Court struck down the law banning yellow-dog contracts, holding that it violated a worker's "liberty of contract." That doctrine held that, under the concept of individual liberty "protected by the Fourteenth Amendment," each worker had the right to enter into a contract freely, without interference from the federal government. However, this limited the ability of a state or the federal government to pass protective legislation for workers. In 1908, the same year as the *Adair* case, the Court allowed states to pass protective legislation for women, but that was justified by what the Court considered women's special condition.

The "liberty of contract" doctrine was finally phased out in the 1930s. By that time, the states and the federal government had been given more power to protect and help workers. Nevertheless, in 1908, the Court decision on *Adair* took a narrow view of the idea of commerce, holding that Congress' constitutional power to regulate commerce does not reach to labor regulations. Thus, even if the idea of liberty of contract did not apply, Congress probably would not have been able to pass legislation banning yellow-dog contracts, as it was outside its power in 1908. This narrow view limited Congress' power, and it was not changed until the 1940s. At that time, the Supreme Court took a broad view of commerce, holding that activities only had to have a substantial effect on interstate commerce for regulation to be allowed. Succeeding courts have largely continued this line of reasoning, rather than returning to the view of the commerce clause held at the time *Adair* was decided.

Primary Source

Adair v. U.S. [excerpt]

SYNOPSIS: In presenting the ruling of the Court, John Marshall Harlan first examines the congressional statute. He argues that outlawing "yellow-dog" contracts violates the Fifth Amendment's prohibition against denying one's liberty without due process of law. Harlan also argues that Congress does have the power to regulate interstate commerce, but that labor unions are not part of commerce. Holmes' dissent argues that unions and labor are closely enough connected with interstate commerce for Congress to pass this law.

Mr. Justice Harlan delivered the opinion of the court: . . .

May Congress make it a criminal offense against the United States—as, by the 10th section of the act of 1898, it does—for an agent or officer of an interstate carrier, having full authority in the premises from the carrier, to discharge an employee from service simply because of his membership in a labor organization?

This question is admittedly one of importance, and has been examined with care and deliberation. And the court has reached a conclusion which, in its judgment, is consistent with both the words and spirit of the Constitution, and is sustained as well by sound reason.

The first inquiry is whether the part of the 10th section of the act of 1898 upon which the first count of the indictment was based is repugnant to the 5th Amendment of the Constitution, declaring that no person shall be deprived of liberty or property without due process of law. In our opinion that section, in the particular mentioned, is an invasion of the personal liberty, as well as of the right of property, guaranteed by that Amendment. Such liberty and right embrace the right to make contracts for the purchase of the labor of others, and equally the right to make contracts for the sale of one's own labor; each right, however, being subject to the fundamental condition that no contract, whatever its subject-matter, can be sustained which the law, upon reasonable grounds, forbids as inconsistent with the public interests, or as hurtful to the public order, or as detrimental to the common good. . . . Without stopping to consider what would have been the rights of the railroad company under the 5th Amendment, had it been indicted under the act of Congress, it is sufficient in this case to say that, as agent of the railroad company, and, as such, responsible for the conduct of the business of one of its departments, it was the defendant Adair's right—and that right inhered in his personal liberty, and was also a right of property—to serve his employer as best he could, so long as he did nothing that was reasonably forbidden by law as injurious to the public interests. It was the right of the defendant to prescribe the terms upon which the services of Coppage would be accepted, and it was the right of Coppage to become or not, as he chose, an employee of the railroad company upon the terms offered to him. . . .

In *Lochner v. New York* . . . the court said: "The general right to make a contract in relation to his business is part of the liberty of the individual protected by the 14th Amendment of the Federal Constitution. . . ."

While, as already suggested, the right of liberty and property guaranteed by the Constitution against deprivation without due process of law is subject to such reasonable restraints as the common good or the general welfare may require, it is not within the functions of government—at least, in the absence of contract between the parties—to compel any person, in the course of his business and against his will, to accept or retain the personal services of another, or to compel any person, against his will, to perform personal services for another. The right of a person to sell his labor upon such terms as he deems proper is, in its essence, the same as the right of the purchaser of labor to prescribe the conditions upon which he will accept such labor from the person offering to sell it. So the right of the employee to quit the service of the employer, for whatever reason, is the same as the right of the employer, for whatever reason, to dispense with the services of such employee. It was the legal right of the defendant, Adair,—however unwise such a course might have been,—to discharge Coppage because of his being a member of a labor organization, as it was the legal right of Coppage, if he saw fit to do so,—however unwise such a course on his part might have been,—to quit the service in which he was engaged, because the defendant employed some persons who were not members of a labor organization. In all such particulars the employer and the employee have equality of right, and any legislation that disturbs that equality is an arbitrary interference with the liberty of contract which no government can legally justify in a free land. . . .

But it is suggested that the authority to make it a crime for an agent or officer of an interstate carrier, having authority in the premises from his principal, to discharge an employee from service to such carrier, simply because of his membership in a labor organization, can be referred to the power of Congress to regulate interstate commerce, without regard to any question of personal liberty or right of property arising under the 5th Amendment. This suggestion can have no bearing in the present discussion unless the statute, in the particular just stated, is, within the meaning of the Constitution, a regulation of commerce among the states. If it be not, then clearly the government cannot invoke the commerce clause of the Constitution as sustaining the indictment against Adair.

Let us inquire what is commerce, the power to regulate which is given to Congress?

This question has been frequently propounded in this court, and the answer has been—and no more specific answer could well have been given—that commerce among the several states comprehends traffic, intercourse, trade, navigation, communication, the transit of persons, and the transmission of messages by telegraph,—indeed, every species of commercial intercourse among the several states,—but not that commerce "completely internal, which is carried on between man and man, in a state, or between different parts of the same state, and which does not extend to or affect other states." . . .

. . . Manifestly, any rule prescribed for the conduct of interstate commerce, in order to be within the competency of Congress under its power to regulate commerce among the states, must have some real or substantial relation to or connection with the commerce regulated. But what possible legal or logical connection is there between an employee's membership in a labor organization and the carrying on of interstate commerce? Such relation to a labor organization cannot have, in itself and in the eye of the law, any bearing upon the commerce with which the employee is connected by his labor and services. Labor associations, we assume, are organized for the general purpose of improving or bettering the conditions and conserving the interests of its members as wage-earners,—an object entirely legitimate and to be commended rather than condemned. But surely those associations, as labor organizations, have nothing to do with interstate commerce, as such. One who engages in the service of an interstate carrier will, it must be assumed, faithfully perform his duty, whether he be a member or not a member of a labor organization. His fitness for the position in which he labors and his diligence in the discharge of his duties cannot, in law or sound reason, depend in any degree upon his being or not being a member of a labor organization. It cannot be assumed that his fitness is assured, or his diligence increased, by such membership, or that he is less fit or less diligent because of his not being a member of such an organization. It is the employee as a man, and not as a member of a labor organization, who labors in the service of an interstate carrier. . . .

It results, on the whole case, that the provision of the statute under which the defendant was convicted must be held to be repugnant to the 5th Amendment, and as not embraced by nor within the power of Congress to regulate interstate commerce, but, under the guise of regulating interstate commerce, and as applied to this case, it arbitrarily sanctions an illegal invasion of the personal liberty as well as the right of property of the defendant, Adair.

. . . The judgment must be reversed, with directions to set aside the verdict and judgment of conviction, sustain the demurrer to the indictment, and dismiss the case.

It is so ordered. . . .

■ ■ ■

Mr. Justice Holmes, dissenting:

I also think that the statute is constitutional, and, but for the decision of my brethren, I should have felt pretty clear about it.

As we all know, there are special labor unions of men engaged in the service of carriers. These unions exercise a direct influence upon the employment of labor in that business, upon the terms of such employment, and upon the business itself. Their very existence is directed specifically to the business, and their connection with it is, at least, as intimate and important as that of safety couplers, and, I should think, as the liability of master to servant,—matters which, it is admitted, Congress might regulate, so far as they concern commerce among the states. I suppose that it hardly would be denied that some of the relations of railroads with unions of railroad employees are closely enough connected with commerce to justify legislation by Congress. If so, legislation to prevent the exclusion of such unions from employment is sufficiently near. The ground on which this particular law is held bad is not so much that it deals with matters remote from commerce among the states, as that it interferes with the paramount individual rights secured by the 5th Amendment. The section is, in substance, a very limited interference with freedom of contract, no more. It does not require the carriers to employ anyone. It does not forbid them to refuse to employ anyone, for any reason they deem good, even where the notion of a choice of persons is a fiction and wholesale employment is necessary upon general principles that it might be proper to control. The section simply prohibits the more powerful party to exact certain undertakings, or to threaten dismissal or unjustly discriminate on certain grounds against those already employed. I hardly can suppose that the grounds on which a contract lawfully may be made to end are less open to regulation than other terms. So I turn to the general question whether the employment can be regulated at all. I confess that I think that the right to make contracts at will that has been derived from the work "liberty" in the Amendments has been stretched to its extreme by the decisions; but they agree that sometimes the right may be restrained. Where there is, or generally is believed to be, an important ground of public policy for restraint, the Constitution does not forbid it, whether this court agrees or disagrees with the policy pursued. It cannot be doubted that to prevent strikes, and, so far as possible, to foster its scheme of arbitration, might be deemed by Congress an important point of policy, and I think it impossible to say that Congress might not reasonably think that the provision in question would help a good deal to carry its policy along. But suppose the only effect really were to tend to bring about the complete unionizing of such railroad laborers as Congress can deal with, I think that object alone would justify the act. I quite agree that the question what and how much good labor unions do, is one on which intelligent people may differ; I think that laboring men sometimes attribute to them advantages, as many attribute to combinations of capital disadvantages, that really are due to economic conditions of a far wider and deeper kind; but I could not pronounce it unwarranted if Congress should decide that to foster a strong union was for the best interest, not only of the men, but of the railroads and the country at large.

Further Resources

BOOKS

Brotherhood of Railroad Trainmen. *The Railroad Trainman Serial Publication.* Monthly, 1883–1948.

Foner, Philip Sheldon, and Ronald L. Lewis. *The Black Worker During the Era of the American Federation of Labor and the Railroad Brotherhoods.* Philadelphia: Temple University Press, 1979.

Foster, William Z. *The Railroaders' Next Step—Amalgamation.* Chicago: The Trade Union Educational League, 1922.

Howell, David. *Aldershot.* Hants, U.K.: Ashgate, 1999.

Middleton, P. Harvey. *Railways and Organized Labor.* Chicago: Railway Business Association, 1941.

Stewart, Debra and Phil Headley, *Railroads and Unions in the 1930's.* Oral Interview. East Peoria, Ill.: Illinois Central College, 1975.

Wood, Louis Aubrey. *Union-Management Coöperation on the Railroads.* New York: AMS Press, 1976.

PERIODICALS

Wilner, Frank N. "Income Protection Sets Carriers, Unions Apart: What the Pittsburgh & Lake Erie Battle was All About." *Trains* vol. 51, no. 5, March 1991, 23–24.

WEBSITES

"Employment at Will." Available online at http://alumnus.caltech.edu/~rbell/atwill.htm; website home page: http://www.alumnus.caltech.edu (accessed January 9, 2003).

Loewe v. Lawlor

Supreme Court decision

By: Melville W. Fuller

Date: February 3, 1908

Source: Fuller, Melville W. *Loewe v. Lawlor.* 208 U.S. 412 (1908). Available online at http://www.caselaw.lp.findlaw.com (accessed November 22, 2002).

About the Author: Melville Fuller (1833–1910) was chief justice of the U.S. Supreme Court from 1888 until his death. Prior to beginning his career, he read law and attended Yale Law School for six months. The Maine native was the manager for Stephen Douglas' presidential campaign in 1860 and later became active in real estate law. Fuller's appointment as chief justice met opposition from those who questioned his loyalty to the Union during the Civil War (1861–1865). He started the custom of Supreme Court justices shaking hands before their conferences. ■

Introduction

In the early 1800s, most industry took place in small shops or in the home. There was little or no need for unions, as there was direct contact between workers and owners, and often the owner was a worker in the factory as well. However, with the rise of the modern large corporation, this direct contact was lost. Workers began to try to form unions to protect themselves. These early attempts at unionization foundered for several reasons, including ethnic divisions among workers, opposition from factory owners, and indifference, if not opposition, from government. Several early attempts, including those by the Knights of Labor, at organizing one mass union for all workers failed miserably. Unions that attempted to organize workers in one industry did somewhat better. The American Federation of Labor (AFL) followed this approach, aiming at only organizing skilled workers.

Once unions had gained a foothold, employers did not give up their attempts to break the unions. One tactic used by employers was to persuade the government to obtain injunctions against union activities. In response to popular pressure against monopolies, the government passed the Sherman Anti-Trust Act (1890), which held that any restraint of trade was illegal. The stated purpose of this law was to prevent monopolies similar to John D. Rockefeller's Standard Oil Company. However, owners soon were clamoring for use of the law against unions, arguing that unions restrained trade. The United Hatters Union called for a boycott against people who sold hats made by a Danbury, Connecticut, manufacturer that would not recognize the union. In *Loewe v. Lawlor,* the company sued the union in turn, arguing that the union had violated the Sherman Act.

Women model hats at a millinery. The United Hatters Union called for a boycott against people who sold hats made by a Connecticut manufacturer that would not recognize the union. **THE LIBRARY OF CONGRESS.**

Significance

In the decision on *Loewe v. Lawlor,* the Supreme Court ruled that the Sherman Act does apply against unions, but not against manufacturers, because a 1895 case had held that manufacturing is not part of commerce. From this decision came another weapon for manufacturers and the government to use against unions. Union pressure forced Congress to exempt unions from the *Clayton Act* (1914), an anti-trust measure. However, the Supreme Court later upheld an injunction against a union's attempt to organize a coal company and ruled that "yellow-dog contracts," which swore that the worker would not join a union and allowed the worker to be fired if he did, were legitimate. In 1921, the Supreme Court again upheld an injunction against labor, again ruling secondary boycotts illegal, even after the Clayton Act. The next year, the Court again ruled that the Sherman Act could be used against labor.

It was not until the 1930s that the government began to put the weight of its power behind labor. The National Industrial Recovery Act (NIRA) and the National Labor Relations Act (NLRA) both declared unions to be legitimate and forced companies to bargain with unions. The first law was struck down by the Supreme Court in 1935, but the Supreme Court upheld the NLRA in 1937. This upholding of the right of workers to unionize and of the government's ability to force companies to bargain with unions greatly increased unions' power and made it possible for unions to survive. The founding of the Congress of Industrial Organizations (CIO) in 1936 also helped unions to organize both skilled and unskilled workers, unlike the AFL. Unions had their heyday in the 1940s and 1950s, and with the subsequent decline of heavy industry, unions have declined as well. However, the very existence of unions will probably never be in doubt, as it was at the time of *Loewe v. Lawlor.*

Primary Source

Loewe v. Lawlor [excerpt]

SYNOPSIS: In presenting the Court's ruling, Chief Justice Fuller first notes that cases such as *E.C. Knight* are inapplicable. He then comments that interstate traffic existed between hatmakers and their customers and the union here aimed to destroy that commerce. He then notes that it is irrelevant that the union was not in interstate commerce, since the commerce the union wanted to control was in interstate commerce. Fuller closes by noting that a case under the Sherman Act had been proven.

Mr. Chief Justice Fuller delivered the opinion of the court: . . .

We do not pause to comment on cases such as *United States v. E. C. Knight Co.* . . . in which the undisputed facts showed that the purpose of the agreement was not to obstruct or restrain interstate commerce. The object and intention of the combination determined its legality. . . .

The averments here are that there was an existing interstate traffic between plaintiffs and citizens of other states, and that, for the direct purpose of destroying such interstate traffic, defendants combined not merely to prevent plaintiffs from manufacturing articles then and there intended for transportation beyond the state, but also to prevent the vendees from reselling that hats which they had imported from Connecticut, or from further negotiating with plaintiffs for the purchase and intertransportation of such hats from Connecticut to the various places of destination. So that, although some of the means whereby the interstate traffic was to be destroyed were acts within a state, and some of them were, in themselves, as a part of their obvious purpose and effect, beyond the scope of Federal authority, still, as we have seen, the acts must be considered as a whole, and the plan is open to condemnation, notwithstanding a negligible amount of intrastate business might be affected in carrying it out. If the purposes of the combination were, as alleged, to prevent any interstate transportation at all, the fact that the means operated at one end before physical transportation commenced, and, at the other end, after the physical transportation ended, was immaterial.

Nor can the act in question be held inapplicable because defendants were not themselves engaged in interstate commerce. The act made no distinction between classes. It provided that "every" contract, combination, or conspiracy in restraint of trade was illegal. The records of Congress show that several efforts were made to exempt, by legislation, organizations of farmers and laborers from the operation of the act, and that all these efforts failed, so that the act remained as we have it before us. . . .

At the risk of tediousness, we repeat that the complaint averred that plaintiffs were manufacturers of hats in Danbury, Connecticut, having a factory there, and were then and there engaged in an interstate trade in some twenty states other than the state of Connecticut; that they were practically dependent upon such interstate trade to consume the product of their factory, only a small percentage of their entire output being consumed in the state of Connecticut; that, at the time the alleged combination was formed, they were in the process of manufacturing a large number of hats for the purpose of

Cartoon depicts the Sherman Anti-Trust Law being resurrected by President Roosevelt. **PUBLIC DOMAIN.**

fulfilling engagements then actually made with consignees and wholesale dealers in states other than Connecticut, and that, if prevented from carrying on the work of manufacturing these hats, they would be unable to complete their engagements.

That defendants were members of a vast combination called The United Hatters of North America, comprising about 9,000 members, and including a large number of subordinate unions, and that they were combined with some 1,400,000 others into another association known as The American Federation of Labor, of which they were members, whose members resided in all the places in the several states where the wholesale dealers in hats and their customers resided and did business; that defendants were "engaged in a combined scheme and effort to force all manufacturers of fur hats in the United States, including the plaintiffs, against their will and their previous policy of carrying on their business, to organize their workmen in the departments of making and finishing, in each of their factories, into an organization, to be part and parcel of the said combination known as the United Hatters of North America, or, as the defendants and their confederates term it, to unionize their shops, with the intent thereby to control the employment of labor in and the operation of said factories, and to subject the same to the direction and control of persons other than the owners of the same, in a manner extremely onerous and distasteful to such owners, and to carry out such scheme, effort, and purpose by restraining and destroying the interstate trade and commerce of such manufacturers, by means of intimidation of and threats made to such manufacturers and their customers in the several states, of boycotting them, their product, and their customers, using therefor all the powerful means at their command as aforesaid, until such time as, from the damage and loss of business resulting therefrom, the said manufacturers should yield to the said demand to unionize their factories."

That the conspiracy or combination was so far progressed that out of eighty-two manufacturers of this country engaged in the production of fur hats, seventy had accepted the terms and acceded to the demand that the shop should be conducted in accordance, so far as conditions of employment were concerned, with the will of the American Federation of Labor; that the local union demanded of plaintiffs that they should unionize their shop under peril of being boycotted by this combination, which demand plaintiffs declined to comply with; that thereupon the American Federation of Labor, acting through its official organ and through its organizers, declared a boycott. . . .

And then followed the averments that the defendants proceeded to carry out their combination to restrain and destroy interstate trade and commerce between plaintiffs and their customers in other states by employing the identical means contrived for that purpose; and that, by reason of those acts, plaintiffs were damaged in their business and property in some $80,000.

We think a case within the statute was set up.

Further Resources

BOOKS

Ely, James W. *The Chief Justiceship of Melville W. Fuller, 1888–1910.* Columbia, S.C.: University of South Carolina Press, 1995.

Furer, Howard B. *The Fuller Court, 1888–1910.* Millwood, N.Y: Associated Faculty Press, 1986.

King, Willard L. *Melville Weston Fuller, Chief Justice of the United States, 1888–1910.* New York: Macmillan, 1950.

Lichtenstein, Nelson. *The Most Dangerous Man in Detroit: Walter Reuther and the Fate of American Labor.* New York: Basic Books, 1995.

Montgomery, David. *The Fall of the House of Labor: The Workplace, the State, and American Labor Activism, 1865–1925.* Cambridge: Cambridge University Press, 1987.

United States Supreme Court. *Proceedings of the Bar and Officers of the Supreme Court of the United States in Memory of Melville Weston Fuller, December 10, 1910.* Washington, D.C., 1911.

PERIODICALS

Fournie, Judith A. "Melville W. Fuller: A Sketch of his Life in Chicago and his Career as Chief Justice of the Supreme Court." *Illinois Bar Journal* vol. 65, no.5, January 1977, 329–335, 354.

WEBSITES

Loewe v. Lawlor. Available online at http://www2.law.cornell.edu/cgi-bin/foliocgi.exe/historic/query=3D%5Bgroup+f_labor!3A%5D/doc/%7Bt11539%7D/hit_headings/words=3D4/pageitems=3D%7Bbody%7D; website home page: http://www.law.cornell.edu (accessed January 8, 2003).

Muller v. Oregon

Supreme Court decision

By: David J. Brewer

Date: February 24, 1908

Source: Brewer, David J. *Muller v. Oregon.* 208 U.S. 274 (1908). Available online at http://www.caselaw.lp.findlaw.com (accessed November 22, 2002).

About the Author: David J. Brewer (1837–1910) served on the U.S. Supreme Court from 1889 until his death. Born in what is now Turkey, he was the son of U.S. missionaries. Brewer graduated from Yale University, read law for one year, and attended Albany Law School. He served on the Kansas Supreme Court for over a decade before being nominated for the Eighth Circuit Court of Appeals. Brewer was appointed to the Supreme Court by President Benjamin Harrison (served 1889–1893). ■

Introduction

Sexism has, unfortunately, long been a part of American history. Only a few states allowed women the right to vote just after the American Revolution (1775–1783), and some of those soon revoked that privilege. In 1848, American middle-class women, led by activists such as Susan B. Anthony and Elizabeth Cady Stanton, issued the Seneca Falls Declaration and started a campaign for the right to vote. Lower-class women were less involved in the women's rights movement because they frequently had to work outside the home and did not have time for political activities. Lower-class men generally did not earn enough money to support their families, so women and children worked alongside husbands and fathers in factories and mines. At the same time women were demanding the right to vote, there also arose a concern about women's ability to bear children. "Research studies" concluded that women who worked too long could not bear healthy children, so reformers started to argue that the way to a healthier race was to limit the working hours of women.

In keeping with social expectations of the day, the studies assumed that a woman's duty (and preference) was to grow up, get married, and bear children. Therefore, the only real choice for a woman was whether or not to work outside the home. On the basis of this research, many reform agencies pressured states to limit the length of time women could work. Oregon was one of the more responsive states, adopting a law that barred women from working over ten hours a day, unless overtime rates were paid beyond ten hours, with a limit of thirteen. This law was the basis of *Muller v. Oregon.* In 1905, Curt Muller, owner of a laundry in Portland, Oregon, was convicted of requiring Mrs. E. Gotcher, a female employee, to work more than ten hours. Muller then sued the State of Oregon, challenging the constitutionality of the law. The case was ultimately appealed to the Supreme Court.

Significance

In previous cases, the Supreme Court had struck down state attempts to regulate workers' hours. The Court had held that each employee had an inalienable right, protected by the Fourteenth Amendment, to contract for any desired number of hours. In rendering the *Muller v. Oregon* decision in 1908, the Court ruled women to be different, justifying "special legislation" for that sex and concluding that "woman has always been dependent upon man." Nearly a decade later, in *Bunting v. Oregon,* the Supreme Court upheld a provision limiting workers, both male and female, to a ten-hour day in many industrial occupations. The provision also forced employers to pay overtime if employees worked more than ten hours (thirteen was the absolute maximum). In addition, a minimum wage law for women was held to be constitutional. However, in 1923, a federal minimum wage law for women was struck down, seemingly creating a contradiction between that case and *Muller.* It was not until the 1930s, during the Great Depression, that a nationwide minimum wage and maximum hour law was passed for the vast majority of workers. The law was held to be constitutional in 1941. The idea of a maximum hour limit (with overtime pay for extra hours worked) has never been challenged, politically or constitutionally, since that time.

Not all gender-specific legislation passed during this period was beneficial to women. Some states established laws forbidding women to be bartenders while allowing them to be waitresses; the only real difference between the two positions was that bartenders had more responsibility and were better paid. Similar discrepancies existed in other legislation.

Primary Source

Muller v. Oregon [excerpt]

SYNOPSIS: In presenting the ruling of the Court, David J. Brewer first states that the only question is whether the statute is constitutional. He then notes that *Lochner* would seem to be controlling, but the difference between men and women does play a role. The opinion discusses the distinctions between men and women and reviews evidence offered in favor of the law. It closes by noting that since men and women are different, an hours law is allowable for the latter group.

Supreme Court Justice Louis D. Brandeis prepared a special brief for *Muller v. Oregon* in favor of legislation setting maximum work hours for women.

Mr. Justice Brewer delivered the opinion of the court: . . .

The single question is the constitutionality of the statute under which the defendant was convicted, so far as it affects the work of a female in a laundry. That it does not conflict with any provisions of the state Constitution is settled by the decision of the supreme court of the state. . . .

It is the law of Oregon that women, whether married or single, have equal contractual and personal rights with men. . . .

It thus appears that, putting to one side the elective franchise, in the matter of personal and contractual rights they stand on the same plane as the other sex. Their rights in these respects can no more be infringed than the equal rights of their brothers.

Proprietor Curt Muller (center) and workers stand outside the Lace House Laundry in 1903. **MRS. FRAN WHISNANT, PORTLAND, OREGON. REPRODUCED BY PERMISSION.**

We held in *Lochner v. New York* . . . that a law providing that no laborer shall be required or permitted to work in bakeries more than sixty hours in a week or ten hours in a day was not as to men a legitimate exercise of the police power of the state, but an unreasonable, unnecessary, and arbitrary interference with the right and liberty of the individual to contract in relation to his labor, and as such was in conflict with, and void under, the Federal Constitution. That decision is invoked by plaintiff in error as decisive of the question before us. But this assumes that the difference between the sexes does not justify a different rule respecting a restriction of the hours of labor.

In patent cases counsel are apt to open the argument with a discussion of the state of the art. It may not be amiss, in the present case, before examining the constitutional question, to notice the course of legislation, as well as expressions of opinion from other than judicial sources. In the brief filed by Mr. Louis D. Brandeis for the defendant in error is a very copious collection of all these matters . . .

The legislation and opinions referred to . . . may not be, technically speaking, authorities, and in them is little or no discussion of the constitutional question presented to us for determination, yet they are significant of a widespread belief that woman's physical structure, and the functions she performs in consequence thereof, justify special legislation restricting or qualifying the conditions under which she should be permitted to toil. Constitutional questions, it is true, are not settled by even a consensus of present public opinion, for it is the peculiar value of a written constitution that it places in unchanging form limitations upon legislative action, and thus gives a permanence and stability to popular government which otherwise would be lacking. At the same time, when a question of fact is debated and debatable, and the extent to which a special constitutional limitation goes is affected by the truth in respect to that fact, a widespread and long continued belief concerning it is worthy of consideration. We take judicial cognizance of all matters of general knowledge.

It is undoubtedly true, as more than once declared by this court, that the general right to contract in relation to one's business is part of the liberty of the individual, protected by the 14th Amendment to the Federal Constitution; yet it is equally well settled that this liberty is not absolute and extending to all contracts, and that a state may, without conflicting with the provisions of the 14th Amendment, restrict in many respects the individual's power of contract. . . .

That woman's physical structure and the performance of maternal functions place her at a disadvantage in the struggle for subsistence is obvious. This is especially true when the burdens of motherhood are upon her. Even when they are not, by abundant testimony of the medical fraternity continuance for a long time on her feet at work, repeating this from day to day, tends to injurious effects upon the body, and, as healthy mothers are essential to vigorous offspring, the physical well-being of woman becomes an object of public interest and care in order to preserve the strength and vigor of the race.

Still again, history discloses the fact that woman has always been dependent upon man. He established his control at the outset by superior physical strength, may, without conflicting with the provisions and this control in various forms, with diminishing intensity, has continued to the present. As minors, though not to the same extent, she has been looked upon in the courts as needing especial care that her rights may be preserved. Education was long denied her, and while now the doors of the schoolroom are opened and her opportunities for acquiring knowledge are great, yet even with that and the consequent increase of capacity for business affairs it is still true that in the struggle for subsistence she is not an equal competitor with her brother. Though limitations upon personal and contractual rights may be removed by legislation, there is that in her disposition and habits of life which will operate against a full assertion of those rights. She will still be where some legislation to protect her seems necessary to secure a real equality of right. Doubtless there are individual exceptions, and there are many respects in which she has an advantage over him; but looking at it from the viewpoint of the effort to maintain an independent position in life, she is not upon an equality. Differentiated by these matters from the other sex, she is properly placed in a class by herself, and legislation designed for her protection may be sustained, even when like legislation is not necessary for men, and could not be sustained. It is impossible to close one's eyes to the fact that she still looks to her brother and depends upon him. Even though all restrictions on political, personal, and contractual rights were taken away, and she stood, so far as statutes are concerned, upon an absolutely equal plane with him, it would still be true that she is so constituted that she will rest upon and look to him for protection; that her physical structure and a proper discharge of her maternal functions—having in view not merely her own health, but the well-being of the race—justify legislation to protect her from the greed as well as the passion of man. The limitations which this statute places upon her contractual powers, upon her right to agree with her employer as to the time she shall labor, are not imposed solely for her benefit, but also largely for the benefit of all. Many words cannot make this plainer. The two sexes differ in structure of body, in the functions to be performed by each, in the amount of physical strength, in the capacity for long continued labor, particularly when done standing, the influence of vigorous health upon the future well-being of the race, the self-reliance which enables one to assert full rights, and in the capacity to maintain the struggle for subsistence. This difference justifies a difference in legislation, and upholds that which is designed to compensate for some of the burdens which rest upon her.

We have not referred in this discussion to the denial of the elective franchise in the state of Oregon, for while that may disclose a lack of political equality in all things with her brother, that is not of itself decisive. The reason runs deeper, and rests in the inherent difference between the two sexes, and in the different functions in life which they perform.

For these reasons, and without questioning in any respect the decision in Lochner v. New York, we are of the opinion that it cannot be adjudged that the act in question is in conflict with the Federal Constitution, so far as it respects the work of a female in a laundry, and the judgment of the Supreme Court of Oregon is affirmed.

Further Resources

BOOKS

Brodhead, Michael J. *David J. Brewer: The Life of a Supreme Court Justice, 1837–1910.* Carbondale, Ill.: Southern Illinois University Press, 1994.

Eitzen, D. Stanley. *David J. Brewer, 1837–1910, a Kansan on the United States Supreme Court.* Emporia, Kans.: Graduate Division, Kansas State Teachers College, 1964.

Muller, Curt, and Louis Dembitz Brandeis. *Curt Muller. Plaintiff in Error v. State of Oregon. Brief for Defendant in Error. Louis D. Brandeis, Counsel for State of Oregon.* Boston, 1907.

Woloch, Nancy. *"Muller" v. "Oregon": A Brief History with Documents.* Boston: Bedford Books, 1996.

PERIODICALS

Gamer, Robert E. "Justice Brewer and Substantive Due Process: a Conservative Court Revisted." *Vanderbilt Law Review* vol. 18, no. 2, March 1965, 615–641.

Hylton, J. Gordon. "The Judge Who Abstained in *Plessy v. Ferguson*: Justice David Brewer and The Problem of Race." *Mississippi Law Journal* vol. 61, no. 2, Fall 1991, 315–364.

WEBSITES

"Backgrounder on the Court Opinion on the *Muller v. Oregon* case." Available online at http://usinfo.state.gov/usa/infousa/facts/democrac/30.htm; website home page: http://www.usinfo.state.gov (accessed January 8, 2003).

Twining v. New Jersey

Supreme Court decision

By: William H. Moody; John Marshall Harlan

Date: November 9, 1908

Source: Moody, William H. and John Marshall Harlan. *Twining v. State of New Jersey.* 211 U.S. 78 (1908). Available online at http://www.caselaw.lp.findlaw.com (accessed November 6, 2002).

About the Authors: William H. Moody (1853–1917) graduated from Harvard and went into the practice of law, gaining fame for his unsuccessful prosecution of Lizzie Borden. He served first as secretary of the navy and then as attorney general under President Theodore Roosevelt, who nominated him for the U.S. Supreme Court in 1906.

John Marshall Harlan (1833–1911), called "the Great Dissenter," was born in Kentucky and pursued a career as a lawyer and politician. Serving on the U.S. Supreme Court from 1877 to 1911, he was famous for his dissenting opinions in such cases as *Plessy v. Ferguson* and *Berea College v. Kentucky.* ■

Introduction

The first ten amendments to the Constitution of the United States are collectively known as Bill of Rights. By 1790, two years after ratification of the Constitution, the U.S. Congress had adopted the Bill of Rights in answer to the claims of many anti-federalists. They feared that the federal government was being given too much power. However, the Bill of Rights, like the Constitution itself, was not a self-executing document, and its provisions were unclear. One question was whether the Bill of Rights applied to the states or solely to the federal government. This question was answered in 1833 in the case of *Barron v. Baltimore,* wherein the Bill of Rights was held to apply only to the federal government. After the Civil War (1861–1865), the Fourteenth Amendment prohibited state governments from denying "due process of law" to all citizens. It was not immediately clear, though, what the phrase "due process of law" actually meant.

In the case of *Hurtado v. California* (1884), the Supreme Court held that the "due process" clause did not require an indictment by a grand jury in a capital crime, that is, one that could result in the death penalty. Thus, indictment by a grand jury, which was required in a federal court, was not required in a state court. In another case, the Supreme Court upheld a conviction by an eight-person jury, which is smaller than the traditional twelve-member jury. The question remained, however, as to which of the other provisions of the Fifth Amendment a state must follow in implementing the Fourteenth Amendment. The Supreme Court addressed this matter in *Twining v. New Jersey.* Specifically, the court considered whether a state was required to observe the privilege against self-incrimination, as required in the Fifth Amendment, or whether it could assume that a defendant's refusal to testify in court was a sign of guilt.

Significance

In *Twining v. New Jersey,* the Supreme Court ultimately determined that the privilege against self-incrimination is not protected by the due process clause. The court held that this privilege was not necessary for due process and, further, that it was not a fundamental right. However, by using the latter consideration of a fundamental right, the court did create the possibility that courts at a later date could apply some parts of the Bill of Rights against the states. Before *Twining,* the Supreme Court had stricken down some laws as denying liberty without due process of law, stating that there was interference with a person's freedom of contract. The court reached a similar decision after this case.

It was not until *Gitlow v. New York* (1925) that the court would incorporate the First Amendment into the Fourteenth Amendment. It noted in passing that a state cannot violate freedom of speech or freedom of the press, as both were protected as part of the "liberty" mentioned in the Fourteenth Amendment. In 1931, the Supreme Court struck down a state law because it violated the First Amendment as protected through the Fourteenth

Amendment. Thus, some aspects of the Bill of Rights were protected from state infringement. It would not be until the Warren Court that most of the criminal due process guarantees were protected against state interference. In 1963, one's right to an attorney was guaranteed and, in 1964, the Court held that one had to be read one's rights after arrest. That same year, the Supreme Court overruled *Twining* and held that states were not allowed to violate the privilege against self-incrimination, stating that this Fifth Amendment privilege was the same, regardless of whether a defendant was in state or federal court. These rulings have been somewhat eroded by the Burger and Rhenquist courts, but on the whole they still hold true.

Primary Source

Twining v. New Jersey [excerpt]

SYNOPSIS: William H. Moody read the court's decision, first noting that the privilege against self-incrimination limits the federal government. He then holds that the right not to incriminate oneself has not been an "immutable principle of justice," and therefore is not part of "due process," as that term is used in the Fourteenth Amendment. Consequently, states are not required to respect that privilege. Holmes dissents, arguing that the privilege against self-incrimination was one of the privileges and immunities guaranteed by the Fourteenth Amendment.

Mr. Justice Moody, . . . delivered the opinion of the court:

. . . The general question, therefore, is, whether such a law violates the 14th Amendment, either by abridging the privileges or immunities of citizens of the United States, or by depriving persons of their life, liberty, or property without due process of law. . . .

The exemption from testimonial compulsion, that is, from disclosure as a witness of evidence against oneself, forced by any form of legal process, is universal in American law, though there may be differences as to its exact scope and limits. . . . The privilege was not included in the Federal Constitution as originally adopted, but was placed in one of the ten amendments which were recommended to the states by the first Congress, and by them adopted. . . . It is obvious from this short statement that it has been supposed by the states that, so far as the state courts are concerned, the privilege had its origin in the Constitutions and laws of the states, and that persons appealing to it must look to the state for their protection. . . .

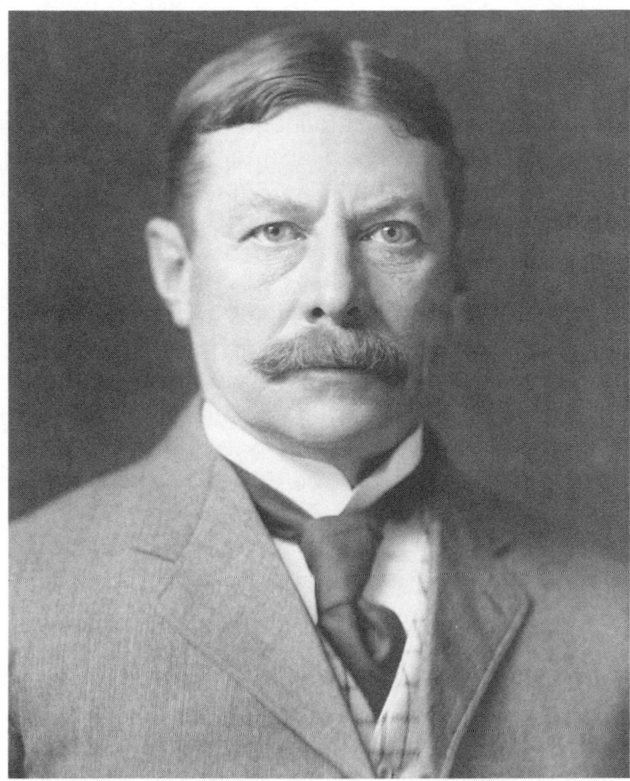

Supreme Court Justice William Henry Moody (served 1906–1910).

The defendants, however, do not stop here. They appeal to another clause of the 14th Amendment, and insist that the self-incrimination which they allege the instruction to the jury compelled was a denial of due process of law. . . . If this is so, it is not because they are of such a nature that they are included in the conception of due process of law. . . .

The question under consideration may first be tested by the application of these settled doctrines of this court. . . . For nothing is more certain, in point of historical fact, than that the practice of compulsory self-incrimination in the courts and elsewhere existed for four hundred years after the granting of Magna Charta, continued throughout the reign of Charles I. (though then beginning to be seriously questioned), gained at least some foothold among the early colonists of this country, and was not entirely omitted at trials in England until the eighteenth century. . . .

But, . . . we prefer to rest our decision on broader grounds, and inquire whether the exemption from self-incrimination is of such a nature that it must be included in the conception of due process. Is it a fundamental principle of liberty and justice which inheres in the very idea of free government and is the inalienable right of a citizen of such a government?

If it is, and if it is of a nature that pertains to process of law, this court has declared it to be essential to due process of law. . . .

Thus it appears that four only of the thirteen original states insisted upon incorporating the privilege in the Constitution, and they separately and simultaneously with the requirement of due process of law, and that three states proposing amendments were silent upon this subject. . . . This survey does not tend to show that it was then in this country the universal or even general belief that the privilege ranked among the fundamental and inalienable rights of mankind; and what is more important here, it affirmatively shows that the privilege was not conceived to be inherent in due process of law, but, on the other hand, a right separate, independent, and outside of due process. Congress, in submitting the Amendments to the several states, treated the two rights as exclusive of each other. . . .

Even if the historical meaning of due process of law and the decisions of this court did not exclude the privilege from it, it would be going far to rate it as an immutable principle of justice which is the inalienable possession of every citizen of a free government. . . . It has no place in the jurisprudence of civilized and free countries outside the domain of the common law, and it is nowhere observed among our own people in the search for truth outside the administration of the law. It should, must, and will be rigidly observed where it is secured by specific constitutional safeguards, but there is nothing in it which gives it a sanctity above and before constitutions themselves. . . . There seems to be no reason whatever, however, for straining the meaning of due process of law to include this privilege within it, because, perhaps, we may think it of great value. The states had guarded the privilege to the satisfaction of their own people up to the adoption of the 14th Amendment. No reason is perceived why they cannot continue to do so. The power of their people ought not to be fettered, their sense of responsibility lessened, and their capacity for sober and restrained self- government weakened, by forced construction of the Federal Constitution. If the people of New Jersey are not content with the law as declared in repeated decisions of their courts, the remedy is in their own hands. . . .

Judgment affirmed.

■ ■ ■

Mr. Justice Harlan, dissenting: . . .

. . . Certain it is, that when the present government of the United States was established it was the belief of all liberty-loving men in America that real, genuine freedom could not exist in any country that recognized the power of government to compel persons accused of crime to be witnesses against themselves. And it is not too much to say that the wise men who laid the foundations of our constitutional government would have stood aghast at the suggestion that immunity from self-incrimination was not among the essential, fundamental principles of English law. . . .

Can there be any doubt that, at the opening of the War of Independence, the people of the colonies claimed as one of their birthrights the privilege of immunity from self-incrimination? This question can be answered in but one way. If, at the beginning of the Revolutionary War, any lawyer had claimed that one accused of crime could lawfully be compelled to testify against himself, he would have been laughed at by his brethren of the bar, both in England and America. . . .

So, when the first Congress met, there was entire unanimity among statesmen of that day as to the necessity and wisdom of having a national Bill of Rights. . . . By the 5th Amendment, as already stated, it was expressly declared that no one should be compelled, in a criminal case, to be a witness against himself. Those Amendments being adopted by the nation, the people no longer feared that the United States or any Federal agency could exert power that was inconsistent with the fundamental rights recognized in those Amendments. It is observed that the Amendments introduced no principle not already familiar to liberty-loving people. They only put in the form or constitutional sanction, as barriers against oppression, the principles which the people of the colonies, with entire unanimity, deemed vital to their safety and freedom. . . .

The 14th Amendment would have been disapproved by every state in the Union if it had saved or recognized the right of a state to compel one accused of crime, in its courts, to be a witness against himself. We state the matter in this way because it is common knowledge that the compelling of a person to incriminate himself shocks or ought to shock the sense of right and justice to everyone who loves liberty. . . .

I am of opinion that, as immunity from self-incrimination was recognized in the 5th Amendment of the Constitution, and placed beyond violation by any Federal agency, it should be deemed one of the immunities of citizens of the United States which the 14th Amendment, in express terms, forbids any state from abridging, . . . Even if I were anxious or willing to cripple the operation of the 14th Amendment by strained or narrow interpretations, I should feel obliged to hold that, when that Amendment was adopted, all these last-mentioned exemptions were among the immunities belonging to citizens of the United States, which, after the adoption of the 14th Amendment, no state could impair or destroy. But, as I read the opinion of the court, it will follow from the general principles underlying it, or from the reasoning pursued therein, that the 14th Amendment would be no obstacle whatever in the way of a state law or practice under which, for instance, cruel or unusual punishments (such as the thumbscrew, or the rack, or burning at the stake) might be inflicted. . . .

It is my opinion, also, that the right to immunity from self-incrimination cannot be taken away by any state consistently with the clause of the 14th Amendment that relates to the deprivation by the state of life or liberty without due process of law. . . .

I cannot support any judgment declaring that immunity from self-incrimination is not one of the privileges or immunities of national citizenship, nor a part of the liberty guaranteed by the 14th Amendment against hostile state action. The declaration of the court, in the opinion just delivered that immunity from self-incrimination is of great value, a protection to the innocent, and a safeguard against unfounded and tyrannical prosecutions, meets my cordial approval. And the court having heretofore, upon the fullest consideration, declared that the compelling of a citizen of the United States, charged with crime, to be a witness against himself, was a rule abhorrent to the instincts of Americans, was in violation of universal American law, was contrary to the principles of free government, and a weapon of despotic power which could not abide the pure atmosphere of political liberty and personal freedom, I cannot agree that a state may make that rule a part of its law and binding on citizens, despite the Constitution of the United States. No former decision of this court requires that we should now so interpret the Constitution.

Further Resources

BOOKS

Allen, Ronald J., and Richard B Kuhns. *Constitutional Criminal Procedure: An Examination of the Fourth, Fifth, and Sixth Amendments and Related areas.* Supplement. Boston: Little, Brown, 1986.

Bosmajian, Haig A. *The Freedom Not to Speak.* New York: New York University Press, 1999.

Fifth Amendment Rights. Sanford, N.C.: Microfilming Corporation of America, 1981.

Helmholz, R.H. *The Privilege Against Self-Incrimination: Its Origins and Development.* Chicago: University of Chicago Press, 1997.

Levy, Leonard Williams. *Origins of the Fifth Amendment; the Right Against Self-Incrimination.* New York: Oxford University Press, 1968.

Meltzer, Milton. *The Right to Remain Silent.* New York: Harcourt Brace Jovanovich, 1972.

Nevins, Winfield S. *Proceedings at the Meeting of the Essex Bar in the Supreme Judicial Court: In Memory of Hon. William Henry Moody.* 1919.

Yarbrough, Tinsley E. *Judicial Enigma: The First Justice Harlan.* New York: Oxford University Press, 1995.

WEBSITES

Twining v. New Jersey. Available online at http://www.arapaho.nsuok.edu/~halpernj/twining.htm; website home page: http://www.arapaho.nsuok.edu (accessed January 9, 2003).

Berea College v. Kentucky

Supreme Court decision

By: David J. Brewer; John Marshall Harlan

Date: November 9, 1908

Source: Brewer, David J., and John Marshall Harlan. *Berea College v. Kentucky.* 211 U.S. 45 (1908). Available online at http://www.caselaw.lp.findlaw.com (accessed November 6, 2002).

About the Authors: David Brewer (1837–1910) served on the U.S. Supreme Court from 1889 until his death. A graduate of Yale University, he attended Albany Law School. Brewer served on the Kansas Supreme Court and the Eighth Circuit Court of Appeals before being appointed to the U.S. Supreme Court.

John Marshall Harlan (1833–1911) was born in Kentucky and pursued a career as a lawyer and politician. He served on the Supreme Court for thirty-four years, becoming famous for his dissents in such cases as *Plessy v. Ferguson.* He became known as "the Great Dissenter." ■

Introduction

The Civil War (1861–1865) in the United States resulted in the abolition of slavery, but the post-war status of freed slaves was not settled. During Reconstruction, the U.S. Congress passed the Civil Rights Act of 1866, partially in response to Black Codes, which many southern states had passed after the end of the war. These acts basically reimposed slavery upon the freedmen in all but name, prohibiting them from owning property and allowing heavy fines for vagrancy, among other things. President Andrew Johnson vetoed the Civil Rights Act, and Congress overrode the veto. Congress also wanted

A group shot of students at racially-integrated Berea College, taken around 1899. THE LIBRARY OF CONGRESS.

to protect the civil rights of African Americans permanently and passed the Fourteenth Amendment in order to do so. This amendment guaranteed equal protection and due process to all citizens, and gave citizenship to all the former slaves.

The U.S. Supreme Court soon weakened the Fourteenth Amendment, holding that the states were the main guarantors of the rights granted, and that segregation could not be banned by Congress. As a response to these rulings, and as a way to increase control over former slaves, many states passed "Jim Crow" laws, which segregated public facilities such as railroad cars and theaters. The Supreme Court upheld segregation in the infamous *Plessy v. Ferguson* case (1895), ruling that "separate but equal" facilities were allowable. Many states took this ruling as license to deny facilities to African Americans, generally not building high schools for African American students, among other measures. Kentucky went a step further and passed a law prohibiting the education of African Americans and whites at the same facility at the same time. This law was aimed at Berea College, the only integrated private school in Kentucky. The law came before the Supreme Court in *Berea College v. Kentucky.*

Significance

The Supreme Court upheld Kentucky's law, avoiding the issue of equality and segregation. Addressing only the matter of contracts, the Court dealt with the school's state-issued charter. The Court held that the state had reserved the right to alter the charter and therefore could ban integrated education. John Marshall Harlan, however, confronted the issue, holding that "the capacity to impart instructions to others is given by the Almighty for beneficent purposes; and its use may not be forbidden or interfered with by government. . . ." His view was not supported by any other members of the Court. (Justice Day dissented without giving a reason.) Segregated education would remain the law of the land for the next forty-six years. In *Gong Lum v. Rice* (1927), the Supreme Court upheld the right of the State of Mississippi to send a Chinese student to a segregated school for African Americans. In 1938, the National Association for the Advancement of Colored People (NAACP) challenged segregated education, winning a case in which Missouri refused to allow an African American to attend law school but offered to pay his tuition to go out of state. The court held that states had to offer equal opportunities within their boundaries, meaning a state could still practice segregation, but it had to provide comparable facilities.

The Supreme Court continued to chip away at segregation in education until 1954, when, in *Brown v. Board of Education of Topeka, Kansas,* the Court held that "separate educational facilities are inherently unequal." This decision overruled *Plessy* in education, but it was slow in being implemented. Many southern states maintained segregated facilities until the 1964 Civil Rights Act prohibited segregation. The federal government also passed several aid programs for education, refusing aid to discriminatory facilities. These laws proved to be the death knell for both *Plessy v. Ferguson* and *Berea College v. Kentucky.*

Primary Source

Berea College v. Kentucky [excerpt]

SYNOPSIS: Justice David Brewer states that the only issue to be considered is whether or not the charter granted to Berea College can be altered. He concludes that since Kentucky, in its most recent constitution, reserved the right to change contracts, the law passed is constitutional. John Marshall Harlan's dissent argues that the purpose of the law is to ban integrated education, and therefore must be considered in that light. Harlan closes by arguing that such a law violates the Fourteenth Amendment.

Mr. Justice Brewer delivered the opinion of the court: . . .

Again, the decision by a state court of the extent and limitation of the powers conferred by the state upon one of its own corporations is of a purely local nature. In creating a corporation a state may withhold powers which may be exercised by and cannot be denied to an individual. It is under no obligation to treat both alike. . . .

But it is unnecessary for us to consider anything more than the question of its validity as applied to corporation. . . .

While the terms of the present charter are not given in the record, yet it was admitted on the trial that the defendant was a corporation organized and incorporated under the general statutes of the state of Kentucky, and of course the state courts, as well as this court on appeal, take judicial notice of those statutes. . . . The Constitution of 1891 provided in 3 of the Bill of Rights that "every grant of a franchise, privilege, or exemption shall remain, subject to revocation, alteration, or amendment." Carroll, Stat. (Ky.) 1903, p. 86. So that the full power of amendment was reserved to the legislature.

It is undoubtedly true that the reserved power to alter or amend is subject to some limitations, and that, under the guise of an amendment, a new contract may not always be enforceable upon the corporation or the stockholders; but it is settled "that a power reserved to the legislature to alter, amend, or repeal a charter authorizes it to make any alteration or amendment of a charter granted subject to it, which will not defeat or substantially impair the object of the grant, or any rights vested under it, and which the legislature may deem necessary to secure either that object or any public right." . . .

Construing the statute, the court of appeals held that "if the same school taught the different races at different times, though at the same place, or at different times at the same place, it would not be unlawful." Now, an amendment to the original charter, which does not destroy the power of the college to furnish education to all persons, but which simply separates them by time or place of instruction, cannot be said to "defeat or substantially impair the object of the grant." . . .

Supreme Court Justice David Josiah Brewer (served 1889–1910). **THE LIBRARY OF CONGRESS.**

We are of opinion, for reasons stated, that it does come within that power, and, on this ground, the judgment of the Court of Appeals of Kentucky is affirmed.

Mr. Justice Holmes and Mr. Justice Moody concur in the judgment.

■ ■ ■

Mr. Justice Harlan, dissenting:

. . . It was the teaching of pupils of the two races together, or in the same school, no matter by whom or under whose authority, which the legislature sought to prevent. The manifest purpose was to prevent the association of white and colored persons in the same school. That such was its intention is evident from the title of the act, which, as we have seen, was "to prohibit white and colored persons from attending the same school." Even if the words in the body of the act were doubtful or obscure, the title may be looked to in aid of construction. . . .

In my judgment the court should directly meet and decide the broad question presented by the statute. It should adjudge whether the statute, as a whole, is or is not unconstitutional, in that it makes

A School Ahead of Its Time

Berea was originally founded in Kentucky in 1855 as an elementary school by abolitionist John G. Fee for the purpose of providing integrated education for black and white students. He envisioned the school becoming an institution similar to Oberlin College in Ohio, an antislavery college and a stop on the "Underground Railroad." Berea was closed in 1859 when threats forced Fee and his teaching staff to leave the state. The school reopened in 1867 and was incorporated as a college in 1869. In 1904, the "Day Law" was passed by the Kentucky legislature specifically to end integrated education at Berea College. The law stated that black and white students could not be taught at the same school unless the two races were taught at separate facilities at least twenty-five miles apart.

In this context of increasing segregation in the southern states, Berea faculty and students fought a four-year legal battle to maintain the school as a racially integrated institution as established in its charter. The struggle ended in defeat for Berea when the Supreme Court found the Day Law to be constitutional and blacks students were forced to leave the campus. The Court reasoned that states have the right to regulate corporations, including, as in this case, determining whether and under what conditions a college may teach. In addition, the Court stated that the defendant was the college, not the black students; corporations are not individual people and therefore do not have rights as citizens.

The decision in *Berea* was significant because it established the right of states not only to maintain segregated public schools systems but also to prohibit private schools from providing integrated education.

Thirty years after *Berea,* the Supreme Court ruled in *Missouri ex rel. Gaines v. Canada* (1938) that blacks could attend the University of Missouri Law School because there were no public law schools for blacks in the state. Then in 1950, the Court held in *Sweatt v. Painter* that a black student could attend the University of Texas Law School since the law school for blacks was clearly inferior. The same day the Court ruled in *McLaurin v. Oklahoma State Regents* that schools could not segregate blacks in designated areas within a white school.

As the legal basis for segregation crumbled, the Kentucky legislature passed a law in 1950 allowing black students to attend Berea as long as similar courses were not available at the Kentucky State College for Negroes. Finally, in 1954, *Berea* was overturned by the decision in *Brown v. Board of Education* making segregated schools illegal. Black students were again admitted to Berea. Today, Berea College continues to operate with conscious integration as an essential part of its mission.

—By Kristina Peterson

it a crime against the state to maintain or operate a private institution of learning where white and black pupils are received, at the same time, for instruction. In the view which I have as to my duty I feel obliged to express my opinion as to the validity of the act as a whole. I am of opinion that, in its essential parts, the statute is an arbitrary invasion of the rights of liberty and property guaranteed by the 14th Amendment against hostile state action, and is, therefore, void. . . .

This court has more than once said that the liberty guaranteed by the 14th Amendment embraces "the right of the citizen to be free in the enjoyment of all his faculties," and "to be free to use them in all lawful ways." . . . If pupils, of whatever race,—certainly, if they be citizens,—choose, with the consent of their parents, or voluntarily, to sit together in a private institution of learning while receiving instruction which is not in its nature harmful or dangerous to the public, no government, whether Federal or state, can legally forbid their coming together, or being together temporarily, for such an innocent purpose. If the common-wealth of Kentucky can make it a crime to teach white and colored children together at the same time, in a private institution of learning, it is difficult to perceive why it may not forbid the assembling of white and colored children in the same Sabbath school, for the purpose of being instructed in the Word of God, although such teaching may be done under the authority of the church to which the school is attached as well as with the consent of the parents of the children. . . . Again, if the views of the highest court of Kentucky be sound, that commonwealth may, without infringing the Constitution of the United States, forbid the association in the same private school of pupils of the Anglo-Saxon and Latin races respectively, or pupils of the Christian and Jewish faiths, respectively. Have we become so inoculated with prejudice of race than an American government, professedly based on the principles of freedom, and charged with the protection of all citizens alike, can make distinctions between such citizens in the matter of their voluntary meeting for innocent purposes, simply because of their respective races? Further, if the lower court be right, then a state may make it a crime for white and colored persons to frequent the same market places at the same time, or appear in an assemblage of citizens convened to consider questions of a public or political nature, in which all citizens, without regard to race, are equally interested. Many other illustrations might be given to show the mischievous, not to say cruel, character of the statute in question, and how inconsistent such legislation is with the great principle of the equality of citizens before the law. . . .

Mr. Justice Day also dissents.

Further Resources

BOOKS

Brodhead, Michael J. *David J. Brewer: The Life of a Supreme Court Justice, 1837–1910.* Carbondale, Ill.: Southern Illinois University Press, 1994.

Eitzen, D. Stanley. *David J. Brewer, 1837–1910, a Kansan on the United States Supreme Court.* Emporia, Kans.: Graduate Division, Kansas State Teachers College, 1964.

Gamer, Robert E. "Justice Brewer and Substantive Due Process: a Conservative Court Revisited." *Vanderbilt Law Review* vol. 18, no. 2, March 1965, 615–641.

Peck, Elisabeth Sinclair. *Emily Ann Smith, Berea's First 125 Years, 1855–1980.* Lexington, Ken.: University Press of Kentucky, 1982.

Sears, Richard D. *A Utopian Experiment in Kentucky: Integration and Social Equality at Berea, 1866–1904.* Westport, Conn.: Greenwood Press, 1996.

Yarbrough, Tinsley E. *Judicial Enigma: The First Justice Harlan.* New York: Oxford University Press, 1995.

WEBSITES

"*Plessy v. Lochner,* the Berea College Case." Available online at http://www.gmu.edu/departments/law/faculty/papers/docs/00-13.pdf; website home page: http://www.gmu.edu (accessed January 9, 2003).

U.S. v. Shipp

Supreme Court decision

By: Melville W. Fuller

Date: May 24, 1909

Source: Fuller, Melville W. *U.S. v. Shipp.* 214 U.S. 386 (1909). Available online at http://www.caselaw.lp.findlaw.com (accessed November 22, 2002).

About the Author: Melvin W. Fuller (1833–1910) was chief justice of the U.S. Supreme Court from 1888 until 1910. A native of Maine, he read law and attended Yale Law School. Fuller was the manager for Stephen Douglas' presidential campaign in 1860 and later became active in real estate law. There was some opposition to Fuller's appointment as Chief Justice due to concerns about his loyalty to the Union during the Civil War (1861–1865). Fuller started the custom, which continues to this day, of Supreme Court justices shaking hands before their conferences. ■

Introduction

Slavery was officially abolished in the United States in 1865, after the Civil War (1861–1865), but discrimination toward African Americans lingered long past that point. Efforts were made to help freed slaves during Reconstruction, the rehabilitation program established by the U.S. government in the South after the war. Northern politicians soon grew tired of assisting ex-slaves, however, and prejudice persisted in the North. Since discrimination remained entrenched in the South, treatment of African Americans worsened when northerners were less involved in rehabilitation efforts. White domination was once again absolute, and any resistance by blacks led to arrests and beatings. Many African Americans were lynched or murdered in a ritualistic way (often hanged with much violence and mutilation) for a variety of alleged crimes, ranging from rape to merely looking at a white woman. Lynchings reached a peak in the 1890s, when 187 men, mostly southern blacks, were hung. If a black man was not lynched when he was suspected of committing a crime against a white person, he would be taken into a court of law, indicted in front of an all-white grand jury, and tried before an all-white jury. The result was almost always conviction and a harsh sentence, usually death. Protests against this system of justice were few in the nineteenth century.

The tide turned in 1906, with the decision of the U.S. Supreme Court in *U.S. v. Shipp.* The case began when Ed Johnson, a black man, was accused of raping a white woman in Hamilton County, Tennessee. After Johnson was arrested, a lynch mob formed around the jail, but he had already been moved to another town. A quick trial was held in Chattanooga, on February 11, 1906, and Johnson was convicted, even though he had an alibi and thirteen alibi witnesses. Court-appointed attorneys decided against an appeal, fearing that doing so would lead to a lynching. Other attorneys appealed to the Supreme Court, which issued a brief stay of execution on March 10 in order to consider the issues. When townspeople heard about the stay, a mob broke into the jail and lynched Johnson on the evening of March 19 or the morning of March 20. Upon learning this news, the Court decided to try the Hamilton County sheriff, Joseph F. Shipp, and eight others—whose last names were Galloway, Gibson, Ward, Williams, Nolan, Justice, Padgett, and Mayse—for defying the Court.

Significance

This decision resulted in the convictions of six of the men—Shipp, Gibson, Williams, Nolan, Padgett, and Mayse—who served ninety days in prison. Upon returning to Chattanooga, they were greeted as heroes by a mob of 10,000 people. Abuse of African Americans continued throughout much of the twentieth century, particularly in the South. African Americans were prohibited from voting and were arrested on specious charges if they dared to protest. The nation did not focus greatly on the plight of African Americans until the civil rights movements of the 1950s and 1960s. Court decisions during both decades, along with political victories in the 1960s, slowly began to eradicate much of this discrimination.

The *U.S. v. Shipp* ruling met heavy opposition. Some have argued that this decision brought about a rebirth of federalism, and the Supreme Court then lessened its oversight of state courts. In part because of the reaction to *U.S. v. Shipp,* other authorities continued to flout the Supreme Court throughout the nation. In the 1950s, during the desegregation battles, the Supreme Court had to rely on the executive branch to enforce judicial branch decisions. The Supreme Court is generally respected today, and local and state officials are expected to follow its decisions. Nevertheless, there is still little, if any, mechanism for direct enforcement. The *Shipp* decision remains the only time the Supreme Court has directly heard a criminal case, and one of the few times that the Court has issued a penalty for defying its ruling.

Primary Source

U.S. v. Shipp [excerpt]

SYNOPSIS: In presenting the ruling of the Supreme Court, Chief Justice Fuller notes the feeling of the townspeople at the time of the lynching. He argues that Shipp should have expected an attempt to lynch Johnson. The Court determined that the sheriff did nothing, either before the lynching or during it, to hinder the mob. In fact, he may even have facilitated the lynching through this inaction (if not pro-lynching action), and therefore was guilty of contempt of court. Fuller then discusses the other defendants and their level of guilt.

Mr. Chief Justice Fuller delivered the opinion of the court: . . .

In this instance an appeal was granted by this court, and proceedings specifically ordered to be stayed. The persons who hung and shot this man were so impatient for his blood that they utterly disregarded the act of Congress as well as the order of this court.

As heretofore stated, the defendants to the information remaining to be dealt with on the facts are Shipp, Galloway, Gibson, Nolan, Williams, Justice, Padgett, Mayse, and Ward. Of these, Shipp was the sheriff, and Galloway and Gibson two of his deputies. The others are charged with active participation in the lynching. . . .

It must be admitted that intense feeling against Johnson existed from the time of the commission of the crime until after his conviction, and that this feeling frequently manifested itself, although Johnson was not in Chattanooga from the time of his arrest until his trial began. The intensity of this feeling, and the great apprehension of the officers of mob violence, is shown in the testimony of defendants' own witnesses, describing the precautions and secrecy exercised by them in the way they took Johnson in and out of Chattanooga, as well as by the fact that they kept him away from Chattanooga from the day of his arrest until March 11, two days before the time set for his execution, with the exception of the three days he was there attending his trial. Undoubtedly the public believed that Johnson would be executed on March 13, until the reprieve to March 20 was granted on March 11; and, after the petition for habeas corpus was denied by the circuit court, believed that Johnson would then be executed on the 20th.

Sheriff Shipp testifies that inflammatory reports of the habeas corpus proceedings and efforts to appeal the case to the Supreme Court were sent out by the newspapers on March 11, and because of that he had fear of mob violence to Johnson. The efforts made by Johnson's attorneys to obtain an appeal were kept before the public by the newspapers. . . .

The assertions that mob violence was not expected, and that there was no occasion for providing more than the usual guard of one man for the jail in Chattanooga, are quite unreasonable and inconsistent with statements made by Sheriff Shipp and his deputies, that they were looking for a mob on the next day. Officers and others were heard to say that they expected a mob would attempt to lynch Johnson on the 20th. There does not seem to be any foundation for the belief that the mob would be considerate enough to wait until the 20th. If the officers expected a mob at all, as they say that they did, they cannot shield themselves behind the statement that they expected it on the 20th, the day that had been appointed for Johnson to die, and did not expect it the night before. But no orders had been given and nothing had been done up to half-past 8 o'clock on the night of the 19th to protect Johnson from the mob which was, according to their present statements, expected the next day. . . .

The testimony of the reporter that Shipp made these statements was corroborated by the evidence of another reporter who interviewed Shipp on the following day regarding them, and is not denied by

Shipp except in an immaterial particular. From this it appears that defendant Shipp looked for trouble on the 20th, but, as he says, not that night; that he did not attempt to hurt any of the mob, "and would not have made such an attempt if I could."

He evidently resented the necessary order of this court as an alien intrusion, and declared that the court was responsible for the lynching. . . . In other words, his view was that because this court, in the discharge of its duty, entered the order which it did, that therefore the people of Hamilton county would not submit to its mandate, and hence the court became responsible for the mob. He took the view expressed by several members of the mob on the afternoon of the 19th and before the lynching, when they said, referring to the Supreme Court, that "they had no business interfering with our business at all." His reference to the "people" was significant, for he was a candidate for re-election, and had been told that his saving the prisoner from the first attempt to mob him would cost him his place, and he had answered that he wished the mob had got him before he did.

It seems to us that to say that the sheriff and his deputies did not anticipate that the mob would attempt to lynch Johnson on the night of the 19th is to charge them with gross neglect of duty and with an ignorance of conditions in a matter which vitally concerned them all as officers, and is directly contrary to their own testimony. It is absurd to contend that officers of the law who have been through the experiences these defendants had passed through two months prior to the actual lynching did not know that a lynching probably would be attempted on the 19th. Under the facts shown, when the sheriff and his deputies assert that they expected a mob on the 20th, they practically concede the allegation of the information that they were informed and had every reason to believe that an attempt would be made on the evening of the 19th or early on the morning of the 20th.

In view of this, Shipp's failure to make the slightest preparation to resist the mob, the absence of all of the deputies, except Gibson, from the jail during the mob's proceedings, occupying a period of some hours in the early evening, the action of Shipp in not resisting the mob, and his failure to make any reasonable effort to save Johnson or identify the members of the mob, justify the inference of a disposition upon his part to render it easy for the mob to lynch Johnson, and to acquiesce in the lynching. After Shipp was informed that a mob was at the jail, and he could not do otherwise than go there, he did not and in fact at no time hindered the mob or caused it to be interfered with, or helped in the slightest degree to protect Johnson. And this in utter disregard of this court's mandate, and in defiance of this court's orders. . . .

Supreme Court Justice Melville Weston Fuller (served 1888–1910).

It is testified that some time after the mob had left the jail for the bridge, Shipp sent Galloway and Clark down to the bridge, but he made no effort to go himself.

There was in the crowd around the jail and at the scene of the lynching a substantial number of law-abiding men of good character.

That assistance in suppressing the mob might have been easily obtained if effort had been made is shown by the testimony of the chairman of the board of safety, who testifies that, at the time of the first lynching, in going four or five blocks to the jail, he gathered about 16 men to help put down the mob.

The militia was drilling on the night of the 19th between 8 and 10:30 in the armory, a well-known place, three blocks from the jail. It was not called upon to assist in suppressing the mob, although it

Sheriff Joseph Shipp was found guilty of criminal contempt by the Supreme Court after consideration that he and his deputies allowed the lynching of Ed Johnson. **PHOTO BY THE CHATTANOOGA TIMES, APRIL 19, 1923. REPRINTED FROM MARK CURRIDEN, *CONTEMPT OF COURT: THE TURN OF THE CENTURY LYNCHING THAT LAUNCHED 100 YEARS OF FEDERALISM*, FABER AND FABER: NEW YORK, 1999.**

had been called out twice before by the governor, and was bound to respond to another call by him. . . .

From the time he reached there, about 6 o'clock, until the mob came, Gibson was the only officer in charge of the jail. But there was much evidence that customarily many deputies were there nightly, and that several were present on the night of the 19th until just before the irruption of the mob.

Heavy iron chains were sometimes used as additional guards upon circular doors in the jail, such as that leading to Johnson's corridor. These were locked by the prisoners on the inside. During the trial of Johnson these chains were used on the circular doors. But none were on the circular door leading to Johnson's cell on the 19th. It also appears that Johnson's cell door was not locked.

Winchester rifles which were kept to defend the jail against mob violence were, at the time the mob attacked the jail on the 19th, in a show case in the office. These were taken out of the show case by the mob and unloaded.

Although Shipp was in the midst or near the members of the mob for about an hour when they were in the jail, he did not seek to obtain information so that he could identify any of them, and he testifies that he does not know any member of the mob.

Only one conclusion can be drawn from these facts, all of which are clearly established by the evidence,—Shipp not only made the work of the mob easy, but in effect aided and abetted it.

Gibson is involved in the same condemnation though under less responsibility. We think belief on his part that a mob would attempt to enter the jail and lynch Johnson on the night of the 19th must be presumed. . . .

This brings us to a consideration of the case in respect of the six defendants who are charged as members of the mob and participants in its action.

As to Williams and Nolan, there is direct testimony to their participation in the lynching, and we do not think that the evidence relied on to weaken that conclusion is sufficient to do so.

As to Padgett and Mayse, there is testimony of statements on their part on the afternoon of the 19th and the morning of the 20th, which, if believed, demonstrates their guilt. We have carefully examined and analyzed the evidence to impeach the principal witness to these conversations, and also to make out alibis, but we cannot accept it as convincing.

We hold that the case as to Justice and Ward fails on the evidence.

In our opinion it does not admit of question on this record that this lamentable riot was the direct result of opposition to the administration of the law by this court. It was not only in defiance of our mandate, but was understood to be such. The Supreme Court of the United States was called upon to abdicate its functions and decline to enter such orders as the occasion, in its judgment, demanded, because of the danger of their defeat by an outbreak of lawless violence. It is plain that what created this mob and led to this lynching was the unwillingness of its members to submit to the delay required for the appeal. The intent to prevent that delay by defeating the hearing of the appeal necessarily follows from the defendants' acts, and, if the life of anyone in the custody of the law is at the mercy of a mob, the administration of justice becomes a mockery.

When this court granted a stay of execution on Johnson's application it became its duty to protect him until his case should be disposed of. And when its mandate, issued for his protection, was defied, punishment of those guilty of such attempt must be awarded.

Further Resources

BOOKS

Curriden, Mark, and Leroy Phillips. *Contempt of Court: The Turn-of-the-Century Lynching that Launched 100 years of Federalism.* New York: Faber and Faber, 1999.

Dray, Philip. *At the Hands of Persons Unknown: The Lynching of Black America.* New York: Random House, 2002.

Ely, James W. *The Chief Justiceship of Melville W. Fuller, 1888–1910.* Columbia: University of South Carolina Press, 1995.

Furer, Howard B. *The Fuller Court, 1888–1910.* Millwood, N.Y.: Associated Faculty Press, 1986.

King, Willard L. *Melville Weston Fuller, Chief Justice of the United States, 1888–1910.* New York: Macmillan, 1950.

Smead, Howard. *Blood Justice: The Lynching of Mack Charles Parker.* New York: Oxford University Press, 1986.

Wexler, Laura. *Fire in a Canebrake: The Last Mass Lynching in America.* New York: Scribner, 2003.

WEBSITES

"Lynching in America: Carnival of Death." Available online at http://www.crimelibrary.com/classics2/carnival/5.htm; website home page: http://www.crimelibrary.com (accessed January 9, 2003).

"Lynching on the Walnut Street Bridge." Available online at http://www.timesfreepress.com/2000/FEB/29FEB00/OPITI0129FEB.html; website home page: http://www.timesfreepress.com (accessed January 9, 2003).

7

LIFESTYLES AND SOCIAL TRENDS

JAMES N. CRAFT

Entries are arranged in chronological order by date of primary source. For entries with one primary source, the entry title is the same as the primary source title. Entries with more than one primary source have an overall entry title, followed by the titles of the primary sources.

CHRONOLOGY

PRIMARY SOURCES

Important Events in Lifestyles and Social Trends, 1900–1909

1900

- The census reports a population of 75,994,575.
- The divorce rate reaches one in twelve marriages.
- Illiteracy in the United States is reduced to a new low of 10.7 percent of the population.
- Excavation begins on the New York City subway system, which will become the most extensive system in the United States.
- The tobacco industry produces four billion cigarettes, which remain less popular than cigars, pipes, and chewing tobacco.
- Eight thousand passenger automobiles are registered in the United States. Of these, half are of European manufacture.
- The International Ladies Garments Workers Union is founded in New York City. Its membership is composed primarily of Jewish and Italian immigrants. Reformer Jacob Riis reports that women laboring in their homes for the garment industry make at most thirty cents a day.
- The number of telephones in use reaches 1,335,911.
- Short moving pictures become popular in vaudeville theaters across the nation. Generally under five minutes in length, they allow theater managers to sell candy between the live acts.
- Not wanting to waste the scraps of meat from his steak sandwiches, Louis Lassen grinds them up and sells the first hamburgers from his New Haven, Connecticut, lunch wagon. Other new products available this year include roast coffee in vacuum cans and paperclips.
- In March, the Good Roads Campaign begins, in an effort to macadamize the dirt roads that prevail in rural areas and make them safe for automobiles. There are approximately ten miles of paved roads in the United States at the beginning of the decade.
- On January 20, African American Representative G.H. White of North Carolina introduces a bill into Congress to make lynching a federal crime. The proposal fails to pass.
- On April 30, railroad engineer Casey Jones dies at the controls of his runaway locomotive. The passengers' lives are saved and a ballad about Jones' heroic act becomes popular across the nation.
- On May 14, Carry Nation throws rocks at saloons in Kiowa, Kansas, thus marking the start of her militant and well-publicized campaign against liquor.
- On September 18, the first direct primary election is held in Minneapolis. The idea of voters getting to pick the candidates who will run in the general election gains appeal and rapidly spreads across the nation. Wisconsin is first to adopt the system statewide in 1903.
- On October 16, the Automobile Club of America gathers for the first time. From November 3 to November 10, it holds the first auto show in the United States, in Madison Square Garden.

1901

- The Socialist Party of America is formed. The socialist movement draws significant support from the growing immigrant population.
- The National Bureau of Standards is established to make weights and measures of consumer products more consistent.
- Jessie Field founds the predecessors of the 4-H Club, the Boys Corn Club and Girls Home Club, in Shenandoah, Iowa.
- Booker T. Washington founds the National Negro Business League, dedicated to creating a prosperous, autonomous African American economic sector.
- King Camp Gillette begins manufacturing the modern safety razor. Other new products introduced to consumers during this year include Jergens lotion, Quaker oats, and electric hearing aids.
- The Scholastic Aptitude Test (SAT) is given for the first time.
- On March 12, a $5.2 million gift from Andrew Carnegie endows the New York City public library system. Carnegie's gift provided for the construction of thirty-nine branch libraries.
- On June 1, newspapers in Springfield, Massachusetts, announce that a motorized bicycle is now available to the public.
- On September 5, the Pan-American Exposition, a celebration of the United States' global economic power, opens in Buffalo, New York. President William McKinley is shot at the Exposition on September 6 by immigrant anarchist Leon Czolgosz and dies September 14.
- On October 16, new president Theodore Roosevelt causes a national controversy when he dines with African American leader Booker T. Washington at the White House.
- On November 28, Alabama adopts a new constitution that deprives African Americans of the right to vote. It establishes literacy tests, property requirements, and ancestry as qualifications for voting in the state.

1902

- The first public-school nursing system is organized by Lillian Wald and Lina Rogers.
- Ragtime music, particularly that of composer and pianist Scott Joplin, is all the rage.
- New products available to Americans this year include Jello, Crayola crayons, and Barnum's animal crackers. Polygraph ("lie detector") machines are also introduced into use.

- On April 29, the Chinese Exclusion Act, originally adopted in 1882, is extended to ban the immigration of Chinese laborers from the Philippines. The measure is strongly supported by politicians and trade unions on the West Coast.
- On May 12, a bitter and violent anthracite coal strike begins in Pennsylvania, affecting 140,000 miners. Miners demand an eight-hour workday and a 20 percent pay increase. President Theodore Roosevelt appoints a commission to arbitrate the dispute on October 16, and on October 21, John Mitchell, the United Mine Workers' president, declares the strike at an end.
- On June 2, Oregon adopts the statewide initiative and referendum system, extending direct popular rule for the first time, at the instigation of Gov. William S. U'Ren. It becomes known as the Oregon System.
- On June 15, the New York Central Railroad makes the trip from New York to Chicago in twenty hours.

1903

- Edwin S. Porter's *The Great Train Robbery* is screened. It is the first American film with a plot and features the first movie close-ups. Shot in New Jersey, the 12-minute film draws long lines of moviegoers.
- The National Women's Trade Union League is founded by both women trade unionists and middle-class settlement-house women to encourage female workers to join unions and to carry out a campaign of public information. Its ranks are open to anyone "who will declare himself or herself willing to assist those trade unions already existing, which have some women workers, and to aid in the formation of new unions of women wage earners."
- Theodore Roosevelt makes Pelican Island off the Florida coast the first federal wildlife sanctuary.
- Massachusetts becomes the first state to require license plates on motor vehicles.
- In Chicago, James Lewis Kraft begins buying cheese from wholesalers and, using a rented horse and wagon, resells it direct to area grocers, saving them a trip to buy it themselves. Kraft's initial sixty-five dollar investment soon produces a thriving business.
- On May 1, New Hampshire creates a licensing system for the sale of liquor, ending a forty-eight-year ban on alcohol.
- On July 4, labor leader Mother Jones, age 73, leads a large group of children on a march from Philadelphia. Many of them are disfigured from industrial accidents. Jones hopes to call Roosevelt's attention to the plight of child workers in the United States. The president, at his summer home in Oyster Bay, New York, says that he will not receive the marchers.
- On July 23, Henry Ford announces that a gasoline-powered vehicle, which he calls the Model A, will sell for $850. The first Model A is purchased by a Detroit physician.
- On July 26, Dr. Horatio Nelson Jackson and Sewall K. Crocker complete the first cross-country automobile trip when they arrive in New York City. Their trip had begun on May 23 in San Francisco.
- On December 30, a fire in the Iroquois Theatre in Chicago kills 602 patrons and leads to the adoption of new safety codes for theaters in cities across the country.

1904

- Phonograph rolls, a new use of one of Thomas Edison's inventions for sound recording, become a popular form of entertainment in American homes.
- The first automobile road maps are published, essential in an age before highways are numbered and towns marked with signs.
- The first automobile speed limits are adopted in New York State, establishing top speeds of ten miles per hour in densely populated areas and twenty miles per hour in rural areas.
- African American blackface vaudevillians Bert Williams and George Walker teach the popular cakewalk dance to the Prince of Wales.
- Syrian immigrant pastry maker Ernest Hamwi introduces the ice cream cone at the St. Louis World's Fair. When a neighboring ice cream stand runs out of dishes, Hamwi rolls some of his pastries into cones, lets them cool, and sells them to the ice cream vendor. The fair also introduces iced tea to the public. The year's other notable new products include Campbell's Pork and Beans and Colgate "ribbon dental cream."
- Montgomery Ward mails out three million product catalogs and Sears & Roebuck mails one million. The free catalogs are popular shopping guides for families across rural America.
- Southern whites increasingly turn to Jim Crow laws to enforce racial segregation. African Americans protest such laws by boycotting segregated streetcars in Atlanta, New Orleans, Houston, and several other southern cities.
- Some 3.2 million immigrants have arrived in the United States since 1900.
- On January 4, the Supreme Court rules that although Puerto Ricans are not citizens, they also are not aliens and thus cannot be denied entry to the United States.
- On April 15, Andrew Carnegie gives $5 million to establish a hero fund to honor those who put themselves at risk to save others.
- On May 23, steerage rates on transatlantic steamships are cut to ten dollars per person as shipping lines from Belgium, France, Germany, and the Netherlands intensify their competition with British ships for the lucrative business of ferrying immigrants to the United States. For passengers who can afford it, private cabins are available for fifty-two dollars and up.
- On June 15, the *General Slocum,* a pleasure steamboat, burns in the Hell Gate passage of New York City's East River, killing more than one thousand of the eighteen hundred picnickers aboard, mostly immigrant women and children.
- On July 25, a long and bitter strike by some twenty-five thousand Massachusetts textile mill workers begins in Fall River. The strike brings working conditions in the mills to national attention. As a result, the National Child Labor Committee is founded in New York City by social workers Florence Kelley and Lillian Wald. It will agitate for stronger child-labor laws at the state level and for national legislation covering industries engaged in interstate commerce.

- On September 28, New York City police arrest a woman for smoking in an open automobile. There is no law against women smoking in public, but custom defines smoking as a male practice.
- In October, the New York City Young Men's Christian Association opens a training school for chauffeurs.
- On October 8, it is reported that more than twenty-two thousand automobiles have been manufactured and sold in 1904. Electric and steam-powered cars are still most common, but gasoline-powered cars are becoming more common.
- On November 2, Evangeline Booth becomes the first commander of the Salvation Army in the United States.

1905

- Population density in the worst New York City slums climbs to one thousand people per acre.
- Seventy-eight thousand passenger automobiles are registered in the United States.
- Novocaine, a nonaddictive relative of cocaine, is produced for the first time as a painkilling medicine.
- Comedians Fatty Arbuckle and Harry Bulger, along with actor John Mason, become the first popular entertainers to appear in cigarette advertisements.
- Designer Elsie de Wolfe gets her first interior decorating commission. She revolutionizes interiors, freeing them from Victorian darkness.
- Madame C. J. Walker (Sarah Breedlove) perfects and markets a hair straightener for African American women. The success of the product makes Walker a prominent businesswoman in the African American community.
- Thomas Dixon publishes *The Clansman,* which romanticizes the origins of the Ku Klux Klan and is later made into a controversial 1915 film, *Birth of a Nation,* by D. W. Griffith.
- The first nickelodeons open in cities around the nation. Showing films on a white curtain accompanied by a tinny piano, their five-cent admission offers affordable entertainment to even the poor.
- Cellophane, Vicks VapoRub, and double-sided gramophone records are among the year's popular new products.
- On April 23, the Rotary Club begins in Chicago as a volunteer community-service organization. The club is founded by a Chicago attorney, Paul Percy Harris, and takes its name from the practice of gathering in the offices of individual members on a rotating basis.
- In June, Wallace Nutting opens a Southbury, Connecticut, workshop specializing in colonial reproduction furniture and "colonial" photographs, signaling the growing popularity of a colonial revival in interior decoration.
- On June 18, the Twentieth Century Limited begins train service between Chicago and New York, boasting a travel time of only eighteen hours between the two cities.
- On July 13, W. E. B. Du Bois and William Monroe Trotter found the Niagara Movement, forerunner of the National Association for the Advancement of Colored People (NAACP).
- On November 8, the Union Pacific Railroad introduces electric lighting on the Overland Limited, its Chicago to San Francisco luxury train. Passengers no longer have to rely on gas lamps. They now have only to flip a switch in their compartments.
- On December 5, President Theodore Roosevelt tells Congress in his annual message that "there is no danger in having too many immigrants of the right kind." He welcomes the arrival of immigrants willing to learn English, be law abiding, adopt middle class values, and work hard in their jobs or professions.

1906

- Cocaine, a small but vital ingredient of Coca-Cola (to which the soft drink owes its name), is removed from the formula. Coca-Cola continues to advertise itself as a stimulant, although caffeine is now the agent of wakefulness.
- W.K. Kellogg launches the production of his corn flakes breakfast cereal in Battle Creek, Michigan. The cereal is the result of an accident at his brother's nearby health spa, when workers let all the water boil away from the grain they were cooking, leaving crispy flakes of toasted grain at the bottom of the pot.
- Home delivery of the daily and Sunday *Washington Post* costs seventy cents per month.
- On June 30, the Pure Food and Drug Act is signed into law, along with the Meat Inspection Act, to prevent what had been rampant adulteration of food and medicines and lax quality control. Manufacturers now also have to list accurately the ingredients of their products, though enforcement remains inadequate.
- In July, New Jersey passes the first law requiring the licensing of automobile operators.
- On August 14, African American soldiers stationed outside Brownsville, Texas, are involved in a riot in which one person is killed and one is wounded. The entire regiment is court-martialed and dishonorably discharged by President Theodore Roosevelt despite conflicting testimony and slender evidence. In 1972 Congress restores members of the regiment, most of whom had died by then, to good standing.
- On September 24, Theodore Roosevelt dedicates Devils Tower in Wyoming as the first national monument in the United States.
- On October 11, San Francisco officials order that "Oriental" children be segregated from non-Asian children in the city's schools.
- On November 23, world-famous opera singer Enrico Caruso is convicted of molestation in New York City for touching a woman's left forearm with his right elbow.
- On December 12, Theodore Roosevelt appoints Oscar S. Straus as secretary of commerce and labor. Straus is the first Jewish American to hold a cabinet position.

1907

- Florenz Ziegfeld's musical stage extravaganzas, the Follies, begin in New York City.

- "Animal dances" such as the Turkey Trot, Kangaroo Hop, and Grizzly Bear have their heyday.
- Suffragist Harriet Stanton Blatch founds the Equality League of Self-Supporting Women to organize working-class support for women's suffrage.
- Canada Dry Ginger Ale is first produced. Other new products include the electric washing machine and the Hoover electric vacuum cleaner.
- The Pittsburgh Survey, the first large social-science survey of urban living conditions, is sponsored by the new Russell Sage Foundation.
- Studies show that many slum dwellers move each year because landlords often offer a month's free rent to attract new tenants.
- "Diamond Jim" Brady's tastes in showgirl companions and good food are legendary. His dinner parties for fifty or more guests can last for five hours and cost as much as one hundred thousand dollars.
- On February 26, Congress authorizes six hundred thousand dollars for a presidential panel on immigration. Labor groups have been at the front of those calling for reform. Immigrants are only 14 percent of the population but 50 percent of the workforce. "Cheap labor, ignorant labor, takes our jobs and cuts our wages," complains American Federation of Labor president Samuel Gompers. Nearly 1.3 million more immigrants will arrive in the United States in 1907.
- On March 13, the San Francisco school board rescinds its order of the previous October to segregate Asian students.
- On March 14, Theodore Roosevelt issues an executive order restricting the immigration of laborers from Korea and Japan.
- In May, the first taxicabs with meters in the United States arrive in New York City from Paris.
- Miss Anna M. Jarvis holds the first Mother's Day observance in Grafton, West Virginia.
- On September 12, the world's largest steamship, the *Lusitania,* completes its initial voyage, having set a new speed record of five days from Ireland to New York.
- On September 17, Oklahoma, which will become the forty-sixth state on November 16, adopts a constitution that includes prohibition of alcohol.

1908

- Airplane advertising is used for the first time, to promote a Broadway play.
- For twelve dollars, emigrants can travel in steerage from Genoa, Italy, to New York City.
- General Electric patents the electric iron and toaster.
- Construction begins on the Owens Valley Aqueduct that will supply the water Los Angeles needs to sustain growth.
- Magician Harry Houdini is thrilling crowds in America and Europe by walking though solid walls and escaping from locked boxes underwater.
- On January 21, New York City passes the Sullivan Ordinance, which prohibits females from smoking cigarettes.
- On April 30, Worcester, Massachusetts, becomes the largest "dry" city in the country when it passes a Prohibition ordinance. It is joined by seventeen other cities and 249 towns in Massachusetts. Worcester's action resulted in the closing of seventy-six saloons and the unemployment of two thousand.
- On May 28, child-labor legislation is adopted for the District of Columbia. Advocates of the measure work to make it a model for similar legislation in the states.
- On June 8, President Theodore Roosevelt establishes the National Conservation Commission to devise policies to conserve the nation's national resources and protect its natural treasures.
- On August 14, race riots break out in Springfield, Illinois. The governor declares martial law, but the city's African American community is attacked and several African Americans are lynched.
- On September 17, the first airplane fatality occurs when Lt. Thomas W. Selfridge dies after a plane piloted by Orville Wright (who is seriously injured) crashes.
- On October 1, a two-cent postage rate goes into effect to send a letter from the United States to Great Britain.
- In December, in its first Christmas Seals campaign, the American Red Cross sells $135,000 worth of the stamps to raise money to fight tuberculosis.
- On December 24, the licenses of 550 nickelodeons are revoked on the grounds of being open on Sundays and showing "immoral films."

1909

- Only eleven states require automobile operators to have licenses, but thirty-four have a twenty-five miles per hour speed limit for their vehicles.
- The invention of Bakelite plastic is announced by Leo H. Baekeland, a Belgian-born American inventor. The new product will lead to affordable plastic containers and appliances.
- Congress bans the importation of opium except for medical use.
- Immigration from 1905 through 1909 is 4.9 million and for the first decade of the century totals over 8 million, or nearly 9 percent of the nation's population.
- On February 12, William English Walling, Mary White Ovington, and Oswald Garrison Villard found the National Association for the Advancement of Colored People (NAACP) in Ovington's New York City apartment. W. E. B. Du Bois signs the organizing document, as do Jane Addams, John Dewey, and William Dean Howells.
- On March 7, this day is designated as Arbor Day by the state of California in honor of its native son, the botanist Luther Burbank.
- From June 9 to August 6, Alice Huyler Ramsey, with three women companions, becomes the first woman to drive cross-country, from New York to San Francisco.
- On July 17, Congress proposes the Sixteenth Amendment to the Constitution, which will allow the federal government to tax the incomes of workers.

- On August 2, the Philadelphia mint issues the Lincoln penny to replace the Indian head penny, which had been in circulation for half a century.
- On September 10, noted Austrian neurologist Dr. Sigmund Freud and his devoted disciple Dr. Carl Jung begin a month-long speaking tour of the eastern United States.
- On September 27, President Taft sets aside three million western acres for national park land.
- On October 1, Henry Ford introduces the Model T automobile, which costs about $850, cruises at twenty-five miles per hour, and comes in one color, black. "Stronger than a horse—and easier to maintain," says a Ford ad for the new "flivver." Nearly 20,000 are sold in 1909, among the 128,000 autos produced during the year.
- On November 12, statistics released by the federal government show that prices have risen about 10 percent in the past three years. At the same time, however, family size is going down. Many families now have only two or three children.
- On November 24, the "Uprising of the Thirty Thousand," a garment workers' strike, erupts in New York City. It is the first female-dominated (more than 80 percent of strikers are women) mass action. After fourteen weeks the workers win. The victory establishes the International Ladies Garment Workers Union as a force with which to be reckoned.

Theodore Roosevelt and Booker T. Washington

Letters to Lucius L. Littauer, Curtis Guild, and Albion W. Tourgée, 1901

Letters

By: Theodore Roosevelt

Date: October 24, October 28, and November 8, 1901

Source: Roosevelt, Theodore. *The Selected Letters of Theodore Roosevelt.* H.W. Brands, ed. New York: Cooper Square, 2001, 273–274.

About the Author: Theodore Roosevelt (1858–1919) entered politics at age 23. Famously energetic, he held numerous positions. In 1898, he fought in the Spanish-American War with the "Rough Riders" volunteer cavalry regiment that he had formed. He was elected governor of New York that same year. In 1900, he was elected vice president of the United States. When President McKinley (served 1897–1901) was assassinated in 1901, Roosevelt became president. Serving until 1909, President Roosevelt is famous for his efforts to regulate business, break up monoplies, and conserve the nation's natural spaces. His strong foreign policy included interventions in Latin America, beginning the Panama Canal, and negotiating peace between Japan and Russia. Roosevelt ran for president in 1912 as the Progressive candidate but was defeated. Out of office, he continued to be an influential national figure and an author. ■

Introduction

Theodore Roosevelt (served 1901–1909) assumed the presidency of the United States on September 14, 1901. On that same day, he telegraphed Booker T. Washington, president of Tuskegee Institute and the country's leading spokesman for African American affairs. They exchanged telegrams several times over the next few weeks, primarily concerning presidential appointments.

Roosevelt invited Washington to dinner at the White House, as he would invite any other prominent figure. There is no indication Roosevelt gave the matter much thought, and on October 16, 1901, Washington dined with the president and his family. It was the first time such an honor had been given to an African American.

The response from the South was immediate and scathing. Roosevelt was castigated in the vilest and most racist terms for inviting an African American to the White House. Washington, too, was viciously attacked for having the insolence to accept such an invitation.

Roosevelt's reaction to the furor was one of shock and disgust. He did not invite Washington to set a precedent or to make a statement about his administration's racial policies. For Roosevelt, inviting a prominent educator and political personage to dinner was perfectly natural. Despite the uproar, Roosevelt continued to consult regularly with Washington on appointments and other matters that impacted African Americans.

Significance

The black community was overjoyed with Roosevelt's dinner with, and continued recognition of, Booker T. Washington. Already firmly in the Republican camp, most blacks warmed quickly to Roosevelt and became some of his staunchest supporters.

Roosevelt's relationship with the African American community suffered a severe blow, however, as a result of an incident involving members of the all-black 25th Infantry Regiment. Stationed in Brownsville, Texas, the 25th Regiment, which had fought in Cuba with Roosevelt's Rough Riders, was extremely unpopular with local whites, who requested the regiment be withdrawn. This was not done, and on the night of August 3, 1906, a group of men dressed as soldiers opened fire on the town. One man was killed and a police officer wounded.

Although the evidence was inconclusive—it has been suggested that the perpetrators were townspeople dressed in discarded uniforms and armed with government-issue rifles—the official investigation concluded that the shooters were men from the 25th Regiment. Because no one from the regiment would testify, Roosevelt ordered 160 men from the regiment's three companies discharged from the Army.

Washington notified Vice President William Howard Taft (Roosevelt was in Central America at the time, observing construction of the Panama Canal) that the African American community was very upset over the treatment of a heretofore highly regarded regiment of the United States Army. However, despite the caution subsequently urged by Taft, Washington, and other prominent Republicans, Roosevelt refused to change his order.

While this incident permanently damaged Roosevelt's standing in the black community, African Americans had little choice but to continue to support the Republican Party. Washington continued to advise Roosevelt and his successor, Taft (served 1909–1913), on appointments and other matters affecting African Americans.

Theodore Roosevelt and Booker T. Washington continued their association despite the criticism Roosevelt received. Here President Roosevelt stands next to Washington as they watch a parade in the president's honor at the Tuskegee Institute, in 1905. © CORBIS. REPRODUCED BY PERMISSION.

Primary Source

Letters to Lucius L. Littauer, Curtis Guild, and Albion W. Tourgée, 1901

SYNOPSIS: In the following letters, Roosevelt responds to his friends' observations of the reaction to Booker T. Washington's visit to the White House. Lucius Littauer, a New York congressman, and Curtis Guild, future governor of Massachusetts, were old friends and advisers of Roosevelt's. Albion Tourgée, a northern judge in the post-Reconstruction South, was a prominent lawyer who had argued against segregation in *Plessy v. Ferguson,* the 1896 Supreme Court case that legalized "separate but equal" public facilities.

To Lucius L. Littauer

October 24, 1901

Washington
Personal

Dear Lucius:

I cannot write that message, though I should like to.

As to the Booker T. Washington incident, I had no thought whatever of anything save of having a chance of showing some little respect to a man whom I cordially esteem as a good citizen and good American. The outburst of feeling in the South about it is to me literally inexplicable. It does not anger me. As far as I am personally concerned I regard their attacks with the most contemptuous indifference, but I am very melancholy that such feeling should exist in such bitterly aggravated form in any part of our country.

There are certain points where I would not swerve from my views if the entire people was a unit against me, and this is one of them. I would not lose my self-respect by fearing to have a man like Booker T. Washington to dinner if it cost me every political friend I have got. Nevertheless it is very gratifying to have you write as you do.

By the way, I want Odell to tell you all about our meeting the other day. It was most satisfactory and I don't think there is the least chance of any future misunderstanding.

Faithfully yours
—Theodore Roosevelt

To Curtis Guild

October 28, 1901

Washington
Personal

Dear Curtis:

I would rather have you do that than anyone. I would not have the faintest idea what reminiscences to dictate. I have not seen Wister's article, but I have seen unfavorable comments on it.

I am confident I am all right in my Southern policy, which is to insist upon good men and take the best man white or black. The negroes and Republicans all were fearful when this policy seemed to imply that a great majority of the present negro appointees would be cut out; and now I am sorry to say that the idiot or vicious Bourbon element of the South is crazy because I have had Booker T. Washington to dine. I shall have him to dine just as often as I please, exactly as I should have Eliot or Hadley.

Faithfully yours
—Theodore Roosevelt

To Albion W. Tourgée

November 8, 1901

Washington
Personal & Private

My dear Mr. Tourgée:

Your letter pleases and touches me. I too have been at my wits' ends in dealing with the black man. In this incident I deserve no particular credit. When I asked Booker T. Washington to dinner I did not devote very much thought to the matter one way or the other. I respect him greatly and believe in the work he has done. I have consulted so much with him it seemed to me that it was natural to ask him to dinner to talk over this work, and the very fact that I felt a moment's qualm on inviting him because of his color made me ashamed of myself and made me hasten to send the invitation. I did not think of its bearing one way or the other, either on my own future or on anything else. As things have turned out, I am very glad that I asked him, for the clamor aroused by the act makes me feel as if the act was necessary.

I have not been able to think out any solution of the terrible problem offered by the presence of the negro on this continent, but of one thing I am sure, and that is that inasmuch as he is here and can neither be killed nor driven away, the only wise and honorable and Christian thing to do is to treat each black man and each white man strictly on his merits as a man, giving him no more and no less than he shows himself worthy to have. I say I am "sure" that this is the right solution. Of course I know that we see through a glass dimly, and, after all, it may be that I am wrong; but if I am, then all my thoughts and beliefs are wrong, and my whole way of looking at life is wrong. At any rate, while I am in public life, however short a time that may be, I am in honor bound to act up to my beliefs and convictions. I do not intend to offend the prejudices of anyone else, but neither do I intend to allow their prejudices to make me false to my principles.

Faithfully yours
—Theodore Roosevelt

Further Resources

BOOKS

Hawkins, Hugh, ed. *Booker T. Washington and His Critics: Black Leadership in Crisis.* Lexington, Mass.: Heath, 1974.

Miller, Kelly. "Booker T. Washington as Ambassador and Spokesman." In *Roosevelt and the Negro.* Washington, D.C.: Hayworth, 1907. Available online at http://douglass.speech.nwu.edu/mill_a66.htm; website home page: http://douglassarchives.org (accessed January 15, 2003).

Mowry, George Edwin. *The Era of Theodore Roosevelt, 1900–1912.* New York: Harper and Brothers, 1958.

Washington, Booker T. Letter to Theodore Roosevelt, October 31, 1901. In *The Booker T. Washington Papers, Volume 6: 1901–1902.* Louis R. Harlan and Raymond W. Smock, eds. Champaign, Ill.: University of Illinois Press, 1977, 283. Available online at http://stills.nap.edu/btw/Vol.6/html/283.html; website home page: http://www.historycoop.org/btw (accessed January 15, 2003).

———. *Up From Slavery: An Autobiography.* New York: Doubleday, Page, 1901.

"The Road Problem"

Speech

By: William Jennings Bryan

Date: 1903

Source: Bryan, William Jennings. "The Road Problem." In *Proceedings of the National Good Roads Convention, Held at St. Louis, Mo., April 27 to 29, 1903.* Washington, D.C.: Government Printing Office, 1903.

About the Author: William Jennings Bryan (1860–1925), a leading Democratic and Populist reformer, was the Democratic presidential nominee in 1896, 1900, and 1908. Most closely associated with the movement for the free coinage of silver (an inflationary strategy to ease the debt pressure on farmers), Bryan was a gifted orator, able to rouse his supporters to great passion. With the prosperity that followed the Spanish-American War (1898), Bryan's association with free silver and Midwestern agricultural interests hurt his political prestige. Nonetheless, he remained a popular and powerful Democratic leader up to his death. ■

Introduction

In 1900, the United States had a transportation system that was the envy of the modern world. The country had nearly 200,000 miles of railroad track and plenty of rolling stock and locomotives. It was blessed with outstanding water transportation, as well. An extensive network of navigable rivers and critical canals covered much of the country. The Great Lakes opened up the rich interior, and a long coastline was open to seaborne traffic year round. Combined, these waterways and railroads enabled goods and people to move cheaply and efficiently across the country.

The great weakness of the American transportation system was the country's abysmal road system. Only a handful of roads spanned long distances, and these were poorly maintained and, in some cases, privately owned. Worse was the sorry state of the short-haul roads that connected farm to town and town to city. During part of the year, they were impassable because of rain and flooding. In truth, there was no road "system" in the United States; there was, for the most part, a collection of dirt tracks that offered minimal improvement over traveling across open ground.

While the need for better roads was obvious, opposition was surprisingly strong. The United States was vast and decentralized and had a long tradition of states' rights and opposition to taxation in all forms. In addition, the country was still smarting from its disastrous expenditures on internal improvements in the 1830s. It is little wonder, then, that "good roads" advocates struggled to win support.

Significance

The bleak state of American roads began to change in the 1890s. A major reason was the safety bicycle. Unlike the high-wheeled contraptions it replaced, the safety bicycle was efficient, reasonably affordable, and easy to ride. In the decade before the automobile, the bicycle was considered the future of personal transportation.

To be useful, however, bicycles needed reasonably smooth, dry roads. As the number of riders grew—annual bicycle production exceeded one million units by the end of the 1890s—the various wheelmen associations took the lead in the good-roads movement. Urban, middle-class, and forward-thinking, these associations launched aggressive local, state, and national campaigns to improve the country's roads. While they found ready allies in rural America, resistance to the increased taxes required to fund road construction remained, and progress was slow.

As the twentieth century dawned, there were few automobiles in the country—and these were generally regarded as rich people's toys. By 1910, however, Henry Ford had begun production of the mass-assembled Model T, a development that made it clear that the automobile represented the future of transportation. Just as clear, however, was the need for improved roads if the automobile was to end the isolation most farmers experienced and give urban dwellers the freedom to escape the confines of the city.

The enormous impact that good roads and the automobile had on the country is suggested by the amount of state and federal investment in roads between 1900 and 1920. In 1900, the total state debt for road construction was $13 million, and only a few hundred miles of improved roads existed in the country. By 1920, state investment in road construction had risen to $360 million, resulting in more than 300,000 miles of improved roads. The federal government also committed itself to road-building. By 1923, it was spending in excess of $200 million per year on road construction, with 170,000 miles of roads designated as part of the newly created federal highway system.

In less than a generation, improved roads and the Model T had completely reshaped the landscape of the United States. Americans had fallen in love with the automobile, in the process becoming the most mobile population in human history. The physical, social, and economic impact was unprecedented.

Primary Source

"The Road Problem" [excerpt]

SYNOPSIS: The National Good Roads Convention met April 27–29, 1903, in St. Louis, Missouri. Attendees included President Theodore Roosevelt (served 1901–1909) and two-time Democratic presidential nominee William Jennings Bryan. Bryan, more than any other political leader of the time, represented rural America. He saw good roads as economically beneficial and liberating for farmers. Farmers were, in Bryan's view, the lifeblood of the country. They were entitled to better roads as their share of the government's bounty, which, in Bryan's opinion, usually went to benefit the cities.

I want to acknowledge my obligation to your president, Mr. Moore, for his efforts to enlighten me. He came out to Nebraska some three or four weeks ago and urged upon me the importance of attending this

An automobile stuck in the mud of a rural American road around 1908. THE LIBRARY OF CONGRESS.

meeting. I have learned more about good roads from him and from the literature that he has brought to my attention than I ever knew before. I want to thank him for the effort he made to turn my attention to this subject.

I hardly know in what capacity I speak to you this afternoon—whether I come as one of the officials of the Jefferson Memorial Road Association, which is interested in rearing a monument to Jefferson, as a citizen of a State carved out of the Louisiana purchase, as the editor of a paper, or as a farmer. I hardly know what my real position is. But I am here, and I am glad the spring has been backward, so I do not lose much time from corn plowing while I am here. [Laughter.]

I have become exceedingly interested in this subject of transportation as I have studied it. They tell us about the wonderful improvement in shipping. I was interested this morning when I heard of the launching of a great boat that would carry more than any other boat ever built. Thus we get some idea of the magnitude of our foreign commerce. In this country we have an amazing railroad development. But nothing to which I have turned my attention in the last few years has seemed to come nearer to the people than this question of good roads. [Applause.] I find there is a new field here, and I have got so far along that I have made up my mind to build a little sample road out on my farm; and not only that, but to do what I can to get my county and my State to do something in the matter of roads. [Applause.]

The expenditure of money for the permanent improvement of the common roads can be defended (1) as a matter of justice to the people who live in the country, (2) as a matter of advantage to the people who do not live in the country, and (3) on the ground that the welfare of the Nation demands that the comforts of country life shall, as far as possible, keep pace with the comforts of city life.

It is a well-known fact, or a fact easily ascertained, that the people in the country, while paying their full share of county, State, and Federal taxes, receive as a rule only the general benefits of government, while the people in the cities have, in addition to the protection afforded by the Government, the advantage arising from the expenditure of public moneys in their midst. The county seat of a county, as a rule, enjoys the refreshing influence of an expenditure of county money out of proportion to its population. The capital of a State and the city where the State institutions are located, likewise receive the benefit of an expenditure of public money out of proportion to their population. When we come to consider the distribution of the moneys collected by the Federal Government, we find that the cities, even in

Bedford Road in Pleasantville, New York, is an example of a well-built and maintained road from the 1900s. **THE LIBRARY OF CONGRESS.**

a larger measure, monopolize the incidental benefits that arise from the expenditure of public moneys. . . .

I emphasize this because it is a fact I have not heard referred to. The point is that the farmer not only pays his share of the taxes, but more than his share, yet very little of what he pays gets back to the farmer. . . .

The improvement of the country roads can be justified also on the ground that the farmer, the first and most important of the producers of wealth, ought to be in position to hold his crop and market it at the most favorable opportunity, whereas at present he is virtually under compulsion to sell it as soon as it is matured, because the roads may become impassable at any time during the fall, winter, or spring. Instead of being his own warehouseman the farmer is compelled to employ middlemen, and share with them the profits upon his labor.

I believe, as a matter of justice to the farmer, he ought to have roads that will enable him to keep his crop and take it to the market at the best time, and not place him in a position where they can run down the price of what he has to sell during the months he must sell, and then, when he has disposed of it, run the price up and give the speculator what the farmer ought to have.

The farmer has a right to insist upon roads that will enable him to go to town, to church, to the schoolhouse, and to the homes of his neighbors, as occasion may require; and, with the extension of rural mail delivery, he has additional need for good roads in order that he may be kept in communication with the outside world.

A great deal has been said, and properly so, in regard to the influence of good roads upon education. In the convention held at Raleigh, N.C., the account of which I had the pleasure of reading, great emphasis was placed upon the fact that you can not have a school system such as you ought to have unless the roads are in condition for the children to go to school.

While we are building great libraries in the great cities we do not have libraries in the country; and there ought to be a library in every community. Instead of laying upon the farmer the burden of buying his own books, we ought to make it possible for the farmer to have the same opportunity as the people in the city to use the same books, and thus economize on the expense of a library. I agree with Professor Jesse in regard to the consolidation of schoolhouses in such a way as to give the child in the country the same advantages which the child in the city has. We have our country schools, but it is impossible in any community to have a well-graded school with only a few pupils, unless you go to great expense. In cities, when a child gets through the graded school he can remain at home, and, without expense to himself or his parents, go on through the high school. But if the country boy or girl desires to go from the graded school to the high school, as a rule it is necessary to go to the county seat and there board with some one; so the expense to the country child is much greater than to the child in the city. I was glad, therefore, to hear Professor Jesse speak of such a consolidation of schools as will give to the children in the country advantages equal to those enjoyed by the children of the city.

And as you study this subject, you find it reaches out in every direction; it touches us at every vital point. What can be of more interest to us than the schooling of our children? What can be of more interest to every parent than bringing the opportunity of educational instruction within the reach of every child? It does not matter whether a man has children himself or not. He may have the kind of family that they say the graduates of Yale and Harvard have, averaging about three. Or, he may have one large enough to excite the admiration of the President. [Laughter and applause.] No matter whether he is guilty of race suicide or race flood, no matter whether he has few children or many, every citizen of a community is interested in the intellectural life of that community. Sometimes I have heard people complain that they were overburdened with taxes for the education of other people's children. My friends, the man who has no children can not afford to live in a community where there are children growing up in ignorance; the man with none has the same duty as the man with many, barring the personal pride of the parent.

I say, therefore, that anything that contributes to the general diffusion of knowledge, anything that makes more educated boys and girls throughout our country, is a matter of intense interest to every citizen, whether he be the father of a family or not; whether he lives in the country or in the town.

And ought not the people have the opportunity to attend church? I am coming to believe that what we need in this country, even more than education of the intellect, is the education of the moral side of our nature. I believe, with Jefferson, that the church and the state should be separate. I believe in religious freedom, and I would not have any man's conscience fettered by act of law; but I do believe that the welfare of this Nation demands that man's moral nature shall be educated in keeping with his brain and with his body. In fact, I have come to measure civilization by the harmonious development of the body, the mind, and the heart. We make a mistake if we believe that this Nation can fulfill its high destiny and mission either with mere athletes or mere scholars. We need the education of the moral sense; and if these good roads will enable men, women, and children to go more frequently to church, and there hear expounded the gospel and receive inspiration therefrom, that alone is reason enough for good roads. [Applause.]

The people of the towns, especially the rural towns, are interested in making it possible for the people in the country to reach their local market or trading place during all times of the year, for, throughout the agricultural portion of the country at least, the villages and the cities rest upon and derive their support from the farms. The farm is the life of the city, and the people in the cities are intensely and vitally interested in enabling the country people to get to the towns to do their trading. Sometimes I have heard country merchants express dissatisfaction because the people of the country would buy of the mail-order house. If the country merchant wants to keep his trade at home, let him make the roads good between his patron and his store. That is the best way. [Applause.]

There is a broader view of this question, however, that deserves consideration. The farm is, and always has been, conspicuous because of the physical development it produces, the intellectual strength it furnishes, and the morality it encourages. The young people in the country find health and vigor in the open air and in the exercise which farm life gives; they acquire habits of industry and economy; their work gives them opportunity for thought and reflection; their contact with nature teaches them reverence, and their environment promotes good habits. The farms supply our colleges with their best students and they also supply our cities with leaders in business and professional life. In the country there is neither great wealth nor great poverty—"the rich and the poor meet together" and recognize that "the Lord is the father of them all." There is a fellowship and, to use the word in its broadest sense, a democracy, in the country that is much needed to-day to temper public opinion and protect the foundations of free government. A larger percentage of the people in the country than in the city study public questions, and a smaller percentage are either corrupt or are corrupted. It is important, therefore, for the welfare of our Government and for the advancement of our civilization that we make life upon the farm as attractive as possible. Statistics have shown the constant increase in the urban population and the constant decrease in the rural population from decade to decade. Without treading upon controversial ground or considering whether this trend has been increased by legislation hostile to the farm, it will be admitted that the Government is in duty bound to jealously guard the interests of the rural population, and, as far as it can, make farm life inviting. In the employment of modern conveniences the city has considerably outstripped the country, and naturally so, for in a densely populated community the people can by cooperation supply themselves with water, light, and rapid transit at much smaller cost than they can in a sparsely settled country. But it is evident that during the last few years much has been done to increase the comforts of the farm. In the first place, the rural mail delivery has placed millions of farmers in daily communication with the world. It has brought not only the letter but the newspaper to the door. Its promised enlargement and extension will make it possible for the wife to order from the village store and have her purchases delivered by the mail carrier.

The telephone has also been a great boon to the farmer. It lessens by one-half the time required to secure a physician in case of accident or illness—an invention which every mother can appreciate.

The extension of the electric-car line also deserves notice. It is destined to extend the borders of the city and to increase the number of small farms at the expense of flats and tenement houses. The suburban home will bring light and hope to millions of children.

But after all this, there still remains a pressing need for better country roads. As long as mud placed an embargo upon city traffic the farmer could bear his mud-made isolation with less complaint, but with the improvement of city streets and with the establishment of parks and boulevards, the farmers' just demands for better roads finds increasing expression.

Just to what extent action should be taken by the Federal Government, the State government, the county, and the precinct, or in what proportion the burden should be borne is a question for discussion; but that country roads should be constructed with a view to permanent and continuous use is scarcely open to debate. There must be a recognition of disease before there can be an intelligent discussion of a remedy, but when the disease is once located the people may be depended upon to find not only a remedy, but the right remedy. The people now realize that bad roads are indefensible, and are prepared to consider the remedy.

Further Resources

BOOKS

Arizona Good Roads Association. *Illustrated Road Maps and Tour Book.* 1913. Reprint, Phoenix: Arizona Highways Magazine, 1987.

WEBSITES

"Roads, Highways, and Ecosystems: Links to Online Resources." National Humanities Center. Available online at http://www.nhc.rtp.nc.us:8080/tserve/nattrans/ntuseland/uselinksroads.htm; website home page: http://www.nhc.rtp.nc.us:8080 (accessed January 17, 2003).

"U.S. 231—Indiana to Florida: How a Highway Grew." Federal Highway Administration. Available online at http://www.fhwa.dot.gov/infrastructure/us231.htm; website home page: http://www.fhwa.dot.gov (accessed January 16, 2003).

Weingroff, Richard F. "Good Roads Everywhere: Charles Henry Davis and the National Highways Association." Federal Highway Administration. Available online at www.fhwa.dot.gov/infrastructure/davis.htm; website home page: http://www.fhwa.dot.gov (accessed January 16, 2003).

"What Is a Lynching?"

Magazine article

By: Ray Stannard Baker

Date: February 1905

Source: Baker, Ray Stannard. "What Is a Lynching? A Study of Mob Justice, South and North." *McClure's Magazine* 24, no. 4, February 1905, 430.

About the Author: Ray Stannard Baker (1870–1946) was a muckraking journalist, noted for his investigative articles for *McClure's Magazine.* He began his literary career in Chicago, joining *McClure's* in 1898. In 1906, Baker, along with Lincoln Steffens, Ida Tarbell, and William Allen White, left *McClure's* and founded *American Magazine,* with which Baker remained until 1915, when he obtained a position in the administration of Woodrow Wilson (served 1913–1921). An active supporter of Wilson, Baker produced several major works on the president, including the eight-volume authorized biography *Woodrow Wilson: Life and Letters,* and coedited (with William Dodd) the six-volume *The Public Papers of Woodrow Wilson.* ■

A huge lynch mob looks on as their African American victim is burned to death in Waco, Texas, in 1917. © CORBIS. REPRODUCED BY PERMISSION.

Introduction

Slavery was outlawed as a result of the Civil War (1861–1865), and for nearly a generation thereafter there appeared to be some progress toward racial equality. By the 1880s, however, after years of stiff Southern resistance, Northerners began to tire of intervening on behalf of freedmen in the South. With little to stop them, Southern whites began to eliminate the limited political power that blacks had acquired during Reconstruction. One of the heinous developments of this period was the use of "lynching" to coerce African Americans into submission.

Lynching, as the term was then used, applied to the execution of suspected criminals by an extralegal (not sanctioned by law) group called a mob. The typical victim of lynching was an African American male who had been accused, and sometimes convicted, of a crime, usually rape or murder, and was in the custody of the local sheriff. For various reasons, a mob would form, seize the defendant, and hang him. Sometimes the lynching was accompanied by other barbaric acts, including dismemberment and burning.

Lynching was, perhaps, an extension of frontier justice, in which communities, usually rural and without adequate police protection, took the law into their own hands to punish perceived threats. The pervasiveness of racial hatred and fear, the relative isolation of many Southern and Northern communities, and the urge of whites to maintain control over blacks created a period of terror in the decades after 1880 during which African Americans lived in constant fear for their lives.

Significance

In 1904, with lynching a national scandal, journalist Ray Stannard Baker began investigating the practice for *McClure's Magazine.* His meticulous reporting exposed the country's deep racist undercurrents. In the late-nineteenth and early-twentieth centuries, racism, historically directed at blacks, took on broader significance. There were several reasons for this:

First, for more than a generation, the country had been exposed to the pseudo-scientific claims of radical

Social Darwinists, who used this theory to demonstrate the racial superiority of the Germanic people. Adherents argued that, in the struggle for survival, some races, notably the Anglo-Saxons, had proved their superiority and that it was part of a divine plan in which individuals and species competed for survival. The most fit would dominate, while the less fit would assume a subordinate role or perish.

Second, the United States had recently become an imperial power, occupying areas populated by nonwhites. It was an essential part of the justification for this imperial policy that, by some higher law, superior races were obliged to rule and bring inferior races as far down the path of civilization as possible.

Third, the country was in the midst of an enormous influx of non-Germanic immigrants. The issue of Anglo-Saxon dominance in America had become more relevant and now affected the North, where the majority of these new immigrants settled. This tended to make Northerners far more sympathetic to the racist attitudes of Southern whites than had previously been the case.

Baker's articles on lynching, therefore, were indicative of the broadly racist attitudes of the time. While he regarded lynching as barbaric and evil, Baker—as was typical of Progressives of the time—was not necessarily opposed to the act because he felt the need for racial equality. Although far more enlightened than most white Americans on the subject of race, he was most concerned with the effect lynching had on the breakdown of the legal system and the associated toleration of violence. It was the negative impact on the country's legal institutions he held in such high regard that troubled Baker the most.

Primary Source

"What Is a Lynching?" [excerpt]

SYNOPSIS: Ray Stannard Baker's articles on lynching appeared in the January and February 1905 issues of *McClure's Magazine*. The January article described lynching in the South, while the February one focused its attention on incidents in the North. His conclusions stressed the breakdown of the law. He argued that this breakdown was not peculiar to the South and that it paralleled the political corruption of American cities.

I—Lynching in the South

All the stored-up racial animosity came seething to the surface; all the personal grudges and spite. As I have already related, two negro women were whipped on the Sunday night before the lynching. On the day following the lynching the father of the women was found seeking legal punishment for the men who whipped his daughters, and he himself was taken out and frightfully beaten. On the same day two other young negroes, of the especially hated "smart nigger" type, were caught and whipped—one for riding a bicycle on the sidewalk, the other, as several citizens told me, "on general principles." But this was not the worst. On Wednesday night an old negro man and his son—negroes of the better class—were sitting in their cabin some miles from Statesboro, when they were both shot at through the window and badly wounded. Another respectable negro, named McBride, was visited in his home by a white mob, which first whipped his wife, who was confined with a baby three days old, and then beat, kicked, and shot McBride himself so horribly that he died the next day. The better class of citizens, the same men who would perhaps, condone the burning of Reed and Cato, had no sympathy with this sort of thing. Some of them took McBride's dying statement, and four white men are now under arrest, charged with the murder. But, as a prominent citizen told me, "They will prove alibis."

Indeed, the mob led directly to a general increase of crime in Bulloch County. As Judge Daley said in his charge to a subsequent grand jury:

> Mob violence begets crime. Crime has been more prevalent since this lynching than ever before. In the middle circuit the courts have been so badly crowded with murder trials that it has been almost impossible to attend to civil business.

Another evil result of the lynching was that it destroyed valuable evidence. The prosecutors had hoped to learn from the convicted Reed and Cato the details of the assassination society of which I have already spoken, and thereby bring to justice all the other negroes suspected of complicity in the murder of the Hodges'. This is now impossible, and if the Before Day Club ever existed, most of the criminals who composed it are still at large, awaiting the next opportunity to rob and murder.

Mob Justice and the Cotton Crop

Mob-law has not only represented a moral collapse in this community, but it struck, also, at the sensitive pocket of the business interests of the county. Frightened by the threatening attitude of the whites, the negroes began to leave the county. It was just at the beginning of the cotton-picking season, when labor of every sort was much needed, negro labor especially. It would not do to frighten away all the negroes. On Thursday some of the officials and citizens of Statesboro got together, appointed extra marshals, and gave notice that there were to be no more whippings, and the mob spirit disappeared—until next time.

II—Lynching in the North

. . . Yet several states, notably Ohio, have passed laws to prevent lynching—which have not stopped mob violence, and never will stop it.

The only remedy is a strict enforcement of all the laws, all along the line, all the time, so that no man, rich or poor, white or black, can escape. That is the remedy, and the only remedy; and, like most real remedies, not patent nostrums, it is simplicity itself—if lived up to. It gets back, after all, like every one of these great questions, to us, personally. We, the people, are the government, we execute the law, and if we are too bad or too lazy to do our work properly, let us in all honesty take the blame—and not shoulder it on the irresponsible negro.

Further Resources

BOOKS

Dray, Philip. *At the Hands of Persons Unknown: The Lynching of Black America.* New York: Random House, 2002.

Levine, Michael L. *African-Americans and Civil Rights: From 1619 to the Present.* Phoenix: Oryx, 1996.

PERIODICALS

"Georgia Lynching Victims." *The Atlanta Journal-Constitution,* April 28, 2002.

Page, Thomas Nelson. "The Lynching of Negroes—Its Cause and Prevention." *The North American Review* 178, 1904, 33–48.

Wells-Barnett, Ida B. "Lynch Law in America." *The Arena* 23, no. 1, January 1900, 15–24.

"The Niagara Movement"

Speech

By: W.E.B. Du Bois

Date: September 1905

Source: DuBois, W.E.B. "The Niagara Movement." *The Voice of the Negro* 2, no. 9, September 1905, 619–622. Reprinted in Foner, Philip S., ed. *W.E.B. Du Bois Speaks: Speeches and Addresses 1890–1919.* New York: Pathfinder Press, 1970, 144–149.

About the Author: William Edward Burghardt Du Bois (1868–1963) was a leading intellectual activist for black rights in the United States and worldwide. After receiving a doctorate from Harvard, Du Bois authored *The Souls of Black Folk: Essays and Sketches* (1903), which established him as a leader in the struggle for black equality. His positions were in sharp contrast to those of Booker T. Washington, the most prominent African American of the time. Du Bois was a founding member of the National Association for the Advancement of Colored People (NAACP) and editor of its publication, *The Crisis,* from 1910 until his resignation in 1934. Increasingly radical and global in perspective, and active in African affairs for many years, Du Bois became gradually estranged from the civil rights movement in America. He renounced his U.S. citizenship and become a citizen of Ghana shortly before his death. ■

Introduction

The hope that came with the ending of slavery and the initially noble efforts of Reconstruction gradually faded in the last quarter of the nineteenth century. As the attention of the nation shifted to other matters, resolving the difficult questions relating to race in America ceased to be important. Northerners, more concerned with bringing the South back into the mainstream than with continuing the policies of Reconstruction, increasingly neglected Southern African Americans, leaving the fate of the freed slaves in the hands of the region's white majority.

By 1900, the strict segregationist and discriminatory system known as Jim Crow had been implemented in the South and would expand, over the next two decades, to the point that African Americans in all walks of life were relegated to a permanent second class role. It was a system held in place by law, social pressure, and, in the end, violence. Though less formalized, segregation and discrimination were also the norms outside of the South.

African Americans, of whom 90 percent resided in the South in 1900, were restricted to menial jobs. They could not vote. They were forced into segregated public spaces. Their children were required to attend segregated schools that offered a fraction of the resources made available to white children. They endured the constant humiliation of being treated as subhuman by whites in every interaction. Racially motivated murders and beatings were employed to keep African Americans "in their place."

Booker T. Washington, founder of the Tuskegee Institute, was the leading spokesperson for African Americans for a generation. Although opposed to the racist practices blacks experienced on a daily basis, Washington believed that it was in the best interests of blacks to improve their economic position, and, for the time being, defer the struggle for full equality. Washington's leadership was widely accepted in the black community, and he was regarded by influential whites as representative of African American interests, likely because of his patient approach to the race issue. However, not all African Americans shared his patience.

Chief among the dissenters was W.E.B. Du Bois. An outspoken critic of Washington's policies, Du Bois demanded full equality for African Americans immediately. He joined with another Washington critic, William Trotter, editor of *The Guardian* (a militant African American newspaper), in calling for a meeting of like-minded blacks in Niagara Falls, New York, in July 1905. Unable to find accommodations on the American side of the falls, the 29 delegates crossed over to Canada to hold the initial meeting of what came to be known as the Niagara Movement.

Significance

The time was not right, however, for the social changes proposed by the Niagara Movement, which began to stumble almost immediately. Washington, a powerful and influential leader, opposed the Niagara Movement from the beginning. The somewhat unsteady Trotter broke from the group in 1907 to form his own organization. In 1909, in response to a violent riot in Springfield, Illinois, that left three African Americans dead, Du Bois joined with a group of prominent white liberals to call for the formation of a biracial organization to address the race issue in America. Distrustful of whites, Trotter would not participate, but Du Bois invited the remaining members of the Niagara Movement to a preliminary meeting in New York City. The result of this gathering was the formation of the NAACP, which would become a prominent organization representing African American interests.

Primary Source

"The Niagara Movement"

SYNOPSIS: Du Bois was the leading spokesman of the Niagara Movement. During its brief existence he delivered numerous addresses stating its objectives and organization and refuted the criticism that the goals were unattainable. The essential objective was full equality, and the movement was to be a loosely organized association of local groups committed to this principle. Du Bois recognized the difficulty of the path he proposed but argued simply that blacks must try.

What is the Niagara Movement?

The Niagara Movement is an organization composed at present of fifty-four men resident in eighteen states of the United States. These men having common aspirations have banded themselves together into an organization. This organization was perfected at a meeting held at Buffalo, N.Y., July 11, 12 and 13, 1905, and was called "The Niagara Movement." The present membership, which of course we hope to enlarge as we find others of like thought and ideal, consists of ministers, lawyers, editors, businessmen and teachers. The honor of founding the organization belongs to F.L. McGhee, who first suggested it; C.C. Bentley, who planned the method of organization and W.M. Trotter, who put the backbone into the platform.

The organization is extremely simple and is designed for effective work. Its officers are a general secretary and treasurer, a series of state secretaries and a number of secretaries of specific committees. Its membership in each state constitutes the state organization under the state secretary.

Why this organization is needed

The first exclamation of any one hearing of this new movement will naturally be: "Another!" Why, we may legitimately be asked, should men attempt another organization after the failures of the past? We answer soberly but earnestly, "For that very reason." Failure to organize Negro-Americans for specific objects in the past makes it all the more imperative that we should keep trying until we succeed. Today we have no organization devoted to the general interests of the African race in America. The Afro-American Council, while still in existence, has done practically nothing for three years, and is today, so far as effective membership and work is concerned, little more than a name. For specific objects we have two organizations, the New England Suffrage League and the Negro Business League. There is, therefore, without the slightest doubt room for a larger national organization. What now is needed for the success of such an organization? If the lessons of the past are read aright there is demanded:

1. Simplicity of organization.
2. Definiteness of aim.

The country is too large, the race too scattered and the rank and file too unused to organized effort to attempt to impose a vast machine-like organization upon a wavering, uncertain constituency. This has been the mistake of several efforts at united work among us. Effective organization must be simple—a banding together of men on lines essentially as simple as those of a village debating club. What is the essential thing in such organization. Manifestly it is like-mindedness. Agreement in the object to be worked for, or in other words, *definiteness of aim.*

Among ten million people enduring the stress under which we are striving there must of necessity be great and far-reaching differences of opinions. It is idle, even nonsensical, to suppose that a people just beginning self-mastery and self-guidance should be able from the start to be in perfect accord as to the wisdom or expediency of certain policies. And some universal agreement is impossible. The best step is for those who agree to unite for the realization of those things on which they have reached agreement. This is what the Niagara Movement has done. It has simply organized and its members agree as to certain great ideals and lines of policy. Such people as are in agreement with them it invites to co-operation and membership. Other persons its seeks to convert to its way of thinking; it respects their opinion, but believes thoroughly in its own. This the world teaches us is the way of progress.

What the Niagara Movement proposes to do

What now are the principles upon which the membership of the Niagara Movement are agreed? As set forth briefly in the constitution, they are as follows:

a. Freedom of speech and criticism.
b. An unfettered and unsubsidized press.
c. Manhood suffrage.
d. The abolition of all caste distinctions based simply on race and color.
e. The recognition of the principle of human brotherhood as a practical present creed.
f. The recognition of the highest and best training as the monopoly of no class or race.
g. A belief in the dignity of labor.
h. United effort to realize these ideals under wise and courageous leadership.

All these things we believe are of great and instant importance; there has been a determined effort in this country to stop the free expression of opinion among black men; money has been and is being distributed in considerable sums to influence the attitude of certain Negro papers; the principles of democratic government *are* losing ground, and caste distinctions are growing in all directions. Human brotherhood is spoken of today with a smile and a sneer; effort is being made to curtail the educational opportunities of the colored children; and while much is said about money-making, not enough is said about efficient, self-sacrificing toil of head and hand. Are not all these things worth striving for? *The Niagara Movement* proposes to gain these ends.

All this is very well, answers the objector, but the ideals are impossible of realization. We can never gain our freedom in this land. To which we reply: We certainly cannot unless we try. If we expect to gain our rights by nerveless acquiescence in wrong, then we expect to do what no other nation ever did. What must we do then? We must complain. Yes, plain, blunt complaint, ceaseless agitation, unfailing exposure of dishonesty and wrong—this is the ancient, unerring way to liberty, and we must follow it. I know the ears of the American people have become very sensitive to Negro complaints of late and profess to dislike whining. Let that worry none. No

W.E.B. Du Bois sits with other members of the Niagara Movement during their 1906 meeting at Harpers Ferry, West Virginia. NIAGARA MOVEMENT MEETING, 1906, HARPERS FERRY, WEST VIRGINIA, PHOTOGRAPH.

nation on earth ever complained and whined so much as this nation has, and we propose to follow the example. Next we propose to work. These are the things that we as black men must try to do:

To press the matter of stopping the curtailment of our political rights.

To urge Negroes to vote intelligently and effectively.

To push the matter of civil rights.

To organize business cooperation.

To build schoolhouses and increase the interest in education.

To open up new avenues of employment and strengthen our hold on the old.

To distribute tracts and information in regard to the laws of health.

To bring Negroes and labor unions into mutual understanding.

To study Negro history.

To increase the circulation of honest, unsubsidized newspapers and periodicals.

To attack crime among us by all civilized agencies. In fact to do all in our power by word or deed to increase the efficiency of our race, the enjoyment of its manhood, rights and the performance of its just duties.

This is a large program. It cannot be realized in a short time. But something can be done and we are going to do something. It is interesting to see how the platform and program has been received by the country. In not a single instance has the justice of our demands been denied. The *Law Register* of Chicago acknowledges openly that "the student of legal and political history is aware that every right secured by men either individually or as a nation has been won only after asserting the right and sometimes fighting for it. And when a people begin to voice their demand for a right and keep it up, they ultimately obtain the right as a rule." The *Mail and Express* says that this idea is "that upon which the American white man has founded his success." All this *but*—and then have come the excuses: *The Outlook* thinks that "A child should use other language." It is all right for the white men says the *Mail and Express,* but black men—well they had better "work." Complaint has a horrible and almost a treasonable sound to the *Tribune* while the *Chicago Record-Herald* of course makes the inevitable discovery of "social equality." Is not this significant? Is justice in the world to be finally and definitely labeled white and that with your apathetic consent? Are we not men enough to protest, or shall the sneer of the *Outlook* and its kind be proven true that out of ten millions there are only a baker's dozen who will follow these fifty Negro-Americans and dare to stand up and be counted as demanding every single right that belongs to free American citizens? This is the critical time, black men of America; the staggering days of Emancipation, of childhood, are gone.

"God give us men! A time like this demands
Strong minds, great hearts, true faith, and ready hands;
Men whom lust of office does not kill;
Men whom the spoils of office cannot buy;
Men who possess opinions and a will;
Men who have honor, men who will not lie;
Men who can stand before a demagogue,
And damn his treacherous flatterers without winking.
Tall men, sun-crowned, who live above the fog
In public duty and private thinking.
For when the rabble, with their thumb-worn creeds,
Their large professions and their little deeds,
Mingle in selfish strife—lo, Freedom weeps,
Wrong rules the land, and waiting Justice sleeps."

Further Resources

BOOKS

Du Bois, W.E.B. *The Autobiography of W.E.B. Du Bois: A Soliloquy on Viewing My Life From the Last Decade of Its First Century.* New York: International Publishers, 1968.

———. *The Souls of Black Folk.* New York: Dover, 1994.

———. "The Talented Tenth." In *The Negro Problem: A Series of Articles by Representative American Negroes of Today: Contributions by Booker T. Washington, W.E. Burghardt Du Bois, Paul Laurence Dunbar, Charles W. Chesnutt, and others.* New York: J Pott & Company, 1903, 33–75.

Kellogg, Charles Flint. *NAACP: A History of the National Association for the Advancement of Colored People.* Baltimore: Johns Hopkins, 1967.

Marable, Manning. *W.E.B. Du Bois, Black Radical Democrat.* Boston: Twayne, 1986.

WEBSITES

Hynes, Gerald C. "A Biographical Sketch of W.E.B. Du Bois." Available online at http://www.duboislc.org/html/DuBoisBio.html; website home page: http://www.duboislc.org/html/Intro.html (accessed January 29, 2003).

Emporia and New York

Nonfiction work

By: William Allen White

Date: 1906

Source: White, William Allen. *Emporia and New York.* New York: Phillips, 1906.

About the Author: William Allen White (1868–1944) was born in Kansas, where he spent most of his life. He became nationally known as editor of the *Emporia Gazette* and as an author and contributor to national magazines and newspapers. White wrote of the virtues of small-town America while taking an active role in national Progressive politics. A close friend and supporter of President Theodore Roosevelt (served 1901–1909), White was in many ways a prototypical Progressive. An old-stock Protestant of the solid middle class, he was optimistic about the country's future and cognizant of the need for reform to ensure that the American promise was available to all citizens. ■

Introduction

The beginning of the twentieth century was a pivotal period in American history. The country was becoming increasingly urbanized, and its prosperity was becoming more dependent on the industrial sector and less on agriculture. Nonetheless, the majority of Americans continued to live on farms and in small towns. According to the 1900 census, the population was 76 million, of which nearly 40 million lived in rural areas, while an additional 9 million lived in communities with fewer than 5,000 inhabitants. They were farmers or part of the infrastructure that directly served those farmers on a daily basis.

Thus, although urban America had become the center of economic and cultural life, the population remained

Downtown Emporia, Kansas, in 1909. THE LIBRARY OF CONGRESS.

much the same as it had been the previous 50 years. For most small-town folk, the pace of life was that of nature. People rose with the sun. They lived in homogeneous communities and moved at a pace no faster than a horse could walk. The values and the bustle of the city were of an entirely different world.

In the city, technology had taken over: electricity, telephones, electric street cars, automobiles, electrical appliances, department stores, prepared foods, and a dizzying array of products were pouring out of the nation's factories. Rural America knew of these things and occasionally enjoyed some of these new luxuries—they did, after all, have newspapers, magazines, and the ever-present Sears catalog to keep abreast of world affairs and new products.

Still, the countryside changed little, and rural and small-town residents became known as "hicks" or "bumpkins" or "hayseeds." The youth of the farms and hamlets was drawn to the cities—toward the bright lights and away from the rustic, isolated life of farm and village. That migration would become a flood during World War I (1914–1918) and continue until the Great Depression made cities less attractive.

Significance

Despite the pronounced urban shift, the country remained predominantly rural and its values essentially the values of the country. It was a lifestyle that placed great emphasis on community, family, and religion. Personal independence and self-reliance were prized. Outside the South, though not devoid of class distinction, there were few great disparities of wealth. All children went to the same school. Community celebrations or tragedies affected everyone. The most prosperous residents were not far above the norm, nor did they live a life isolated from the less fortunate. It was the America of myth and, to some degree, that myth was reality.

The democratic reforms associated with Progressive reform—primaries, direct election of senators, recall, referendum, initiative—were attempts to keep "the people" in control of their government. "Trust busting" was the economic equivalent of those reforms. Progressives desired a competitive economic environment of small merchants and industrialists; the economic power of the great industrialists and financiers was anathema to them. For most Progressives, it was irrelevant if the power was used for good or ill—it was simply too much power in the hands of a few.

Primary Source

Emporia and New York [excerpt]

SYNOPSIS: William Allen White was a Midwestern Progressive who played a critical role in the reform efforts of the first quarter of the twentieth century. From his perch in Emporia, Kansas, White commented on society from the view of the small town, extolling the virtues of middle America that represented the best traditions. The following extract is from White's short book *Emporia and New York,* written in 1906. While speaking of the virtues of small-town America, he also describes the common threads binding city and country together as parts of the same American whole.

. . . At the annual dinners of the Christian Union, given at the Campbellite Church—which, of course, no one joins to get into society, as sometimes people are suspected of joining the Episcopal Church or the Congregational Church or the Presbyterian Church—about two hundred people from all the churches, and the Big Church, to which many of the men belong, sit down for an evening's social communion and good-fellowship. At this table are bankers and grocery clerks and lawyers and railroad men and farmers and mechanics, two-percent. money lenders and all classes and conditions of men. But the important consideration is that their wives and sisters and mothers are there also. It is no trouble to get men to fraternize. Indeed, it is hard to keep them from it. There isn't a man in Emporia who could refrain from talking politics and business with his footman if he had one. But, on the other hand, there are few women in town who wouldn't be grand ladies in ten minutes if they had maids. But

The corner of Fifth Avenue and Forty-sixth Street, New York City. The streets are crowded with well-to-do families heading to and from church on a Sunday morning in 1902. **THE LIBRARY OF CONGRESS.**

no woman in town has a maid. The prospect of a bride coming to town with a maid once set the town to wondering what the standing of this prospective maid would be with the other girls in town who do general housework, and when it turned out that the bride really had no maid, and was a good cook herself, the town was greatly relieved. Therefore, one may know that for Mrs. Butcher to sit down beside Mrs. Banker, and Mrs. Baker and Mrs. Lawyer to be *vis-a-vis,* and for the haughty Merchant girls and the pretty Mrs. Barber to sit amicably at the same table, the town is essentially democratic, in spite of the social formaldehyde that the Whist Club uses in preserving its exclusiveness. Excepting the score of children whose parents send them to the Catholic school, through a sense of religious duty, every child in town goes to the public schools. And in the public schools money does not make for leadership. So the boys and girls of one generation, whose high school amalgamations often form the lines of social cleavage in the next, break up any disposition to a hereditary nobility in the town.

Thus, broadly speaking, one may say that in Emporia there is that equality of opportunity for the youth—equality of education, of financial backing, of social standing—which guarantees a democratic community. Not long ago there was a gathering of women from all over Kansas in Emporia, and the leading hotel was a-flutter with silk petticoats. Emporia clubwomen gathered up all the solid silver in town and borrowed both of the cut-glass punch-bowls and gave a reception that easily discounted any previous social celebration that we ever held. The hotel glowed with splendor that night. And one of the most prominent guests on that occasion had once been head waitress at the hotel. The town knew it, and respected her for it as much as it would respect a man whose proud boast was that he had once been a bell-boy and had risen in the world. Stronger proof of our real democratic spirit may not be found.

Yet this same degree of democratic enthusiasm is found in nearly every country town of the east and north and west. Emporia is rather typical than exceptional. Country-dwelling American men and most of the women are instinctively democratic. And being democratic, the cities sadden us country people. For the city—and New York is typical of urban America—fosters too much of the sham relation between men that one finds where class lines are set. The eternal presence of a serving class, whose manners may some day petrify into servility, the continual discovery that the man who brings the food, or sweeps the street, or drives the cab, considers wholesome conversation with him from his patrons as a sign of low breeding, the presence of the man who fawns for a quarter, all these make the countryman in New York desire to rush home and organize Sitting Bull Lodge of Ancient and Amiable Anarchists! It is not the extravagances of the rich, but the limber knees of too many of the poor, that disgust the countryman in New York. The saddest thing in that great city, to one who comes from the frank, wholesome, clean, happy faces of the country, is not the painted lady's face, with its glassy eyes, not the overfed, puffy-necked figures of the lazy, respectable hotel-dwelling women, who get no more exercise that stuffed geese, not the besotted faces of the men about the barrel houses—though a merciful God knows they are sad enough; but sadder than they are the loathsome, wooden faces of the men who stand decked out like human manikins in purples and greens and what-not of modish silliness and, for a price, surrender themselves to be made part of the landscape. For years Mickle the painter was the lowest form of humanity we had in Emporia. He was the town drunkard, and once they fined him for beating his wife; drink made him a loafer and a brute. But some way one felt that down in Mickle there was the soul of a man; some way one knew that he would not do certain things for money; some way one always understood that Mickle could still look into depths of personal degradation below him, and tell whoever tempted him there to go to hell! . . .

We are of one blood—city and country—in America; our differences are superficial; it is our likeness that is fundamental. We even have the same folk tales. In New York, for instance, they will tell you, with bated breath, that a man named Straus finances the big department stores and controls the policies of the newspapers, and that they do not dare to breathe without consulting him. In Emporia, they say the same thing of George Newman, our leading drygoods merchant. . . .

But it would be interesting to inquire who gets the most out of life for the money invested—Mr. Straus, the pillar of finance in New York, or George Newman and Major Hood, pillars of finance in Emporia. We who know Emporia well and love her best are inclined to think that a dollar will buy about as much of the comforts that make for happiness here as it will any place in the world. To begin with, the Newman home and the Hood home in Emporia stand on great, wide lawns, and around them are beautiful gardens. Civilization has brought to Emporia every comfort that electricity and gas can afford a man in New York, and after a hard day at the store—a day just as hard as Mr. Straus has at his office—Mr. Newman gets into his automobile and goes to his farm, two miles from town, where he kicks around until dinner time. It is a great, broad, beautiful field, lying in a rich valley; on the farm are blooded cattle and hogs, and pottering with them is a lot of fun—and the fun is enhanced by the fact that they pay well. But an hour or two a day on that farm is making George Newman hale and hearty, and the sweep of the fields and the close, first-hand relations with men who have not learned the primary lessons in servility will make him a better, braver, kinder man than life in the store or shop can make any man. Every year the Newmans can go to New York and see all that Mr. Straus sees. They have the best of Emporia and New York. But has New York anything to offer Mr. Straus every day in the year as compensation for not living in Emporia? New York can offer more money. Yet the house of Newman in Emporia will endure to the second or the third generation. It will be a respectable house. It will have peace and plenty, in so much as it really cares for peace and plenty. The house of Straus cannot ask more—and if it does ask it, probably that's all it will get. We shall all lie down beside George Newman out in Maplewood on the hill when our time comes, and others will come after us who will forget this generation and how it strived. Perhaps it is provincial, perhaps it is merely a countryman's view, but one is constrained to think that he who lives his life honorably and kindly among real neighbors will take more with him on his long journey, after leaving all his money here, than he who lives, perhaps just as honorably, in an environment full of men who must needs be strangers, and whose hearts he can never hope to know.

For there is something in touching elbows with men at work—men who are your equals and make you acknowledge it a thousand times a day—that gives a man a philosophy worth more than millions. And we are philosophers in Emporia—if nothing else. None of us is too busy, none of us is too poor, nor of too low an estate to have his opinion about things. . . .

. . . It is a curious thing about human nature that when men live closely together, a score or two in a building on a twenty-five-foot lot, they are impelled to hold one another at arm's length; but when they live as we live here in Emporia, every family on its fifty-foot lot, with many families living on much larger lots, they feel the need of drawing one another together. And so no one ever starves to death in Emporia, even though we have no more food to give than New Yorkers; but we have what is more essential than food in the human partnership—we have a strong social sympathy.

And that social sympathy is the basis of whatever real difference there is between New York and Emporia, between the city and the country. Not that there is more in one town than in the other—for New Yorkers are most sympathetic when they see suffering. But we in Emporia see the suffering. We are so close to one another that we almost anticipate the need of our friends. Therefore, in computing what the man at the bottom of the industrial ladder gets out of life, in our town, and in comparing it with wages in New York, the element of social sympathy existing in the country should be considered as a real factor in the calculation. . . .

Further Resources

BOOKS

Immell, Myra H., ed. *The 1900s.* San Diego, Calif.: Greenhaven, 2000.

Smith, Page. *America Enters the World: A People's History of the Progressive Era and World War I.* New York: McGraw-Hill, 1985.

Sullivan, Mark. *Our Times: The United States 1900–1925,* Vols. 1 and 2. New York and London: Charles Scribner's Sons, 1928–1935.

White, William Allen. *The Real Issue: A Book of Kansas Stories.* Chicago: Way and Williams, 1897. Reprint, Freeport, N.Y.: Books for Libraries, 1969.

PERIODICALS

White, William Allen. "What's the Matter with Kansas?" *Emporia Gazette,* August 15, 1896.

The Courtesies

Guidebook

By: Eleanor B. Clapp

Date: 1906

Source: Clapp, Eleanor B. *The Courtesies: A Book of Etiquette for Every Day.* New York: A.S. Barnes, 1906, 115; 119–127.

About the Author: Eleanor Bassett Clapp was born in Pawtucket, Rhode Island. From 1896 to 1911 she was an editor of *McCall's Magazine.* She was a frequent contributor to newspapers and magazines. ■

Introduction

Domestic servants have existed since the beginning of civilization and have been in America since the establishment of the first settlements. In an age before electricity and the many home conveniences it made possible, before permanent press clothes and prepared foods, it is difficult to imagine the effort required to run even a modest home. Whenever possible—that is, when finances would allow—help was brought in to cook, clean, launder, iron, and tend the children. No self-respecting middle-class husband would subject his spouse to the drudgery of domestic chores if he could afford to hire help.

The demand for domestic help grew rapidly after the Civil War (1861–1865) as the growing urban and suburban middle class required assistance to manage their substantial households. Women became increasingly involved in community affairs. Volunteer workers were often the leaders and always the foot soldiers in attending to the civic and social needs of every community. These women dealt with the various forms of charitable aid to the needy. They built and maintained the local educational and healthcare institutions. They directed the various cultural activities as small as the Independence Day parades in towns and villages across the country and as large as fund raising for orchestras of the great cities. And they played critical roles in the various social reforms ranging from the temperance crusade to the playground movement.

If women benefited from domestic help, it was also women who performed it. In 1870, 48 percent of female workers were engaged in domestic service. By 1910, however, women were entering other occupations, including factory jobs, retail sales, and clerical and professional positions (primarily teaching), with the result that in that year only 24 percent of female workers worked as domestics. According to the census of 1870 there were one million domestic workers making up 7.7 percent of the workforce; in 1910 there were more than two million domestic workers. Nonetheless, supply could not keep up with demand.

In 1900, the servant population was fairly evenly divided among native-born whites, recent immigrants, and, especially in the South, African Americans. For most, domestic service was a temporary occupation. It was only as live-out domestics, the norm in the South since the Civil War, became more widespread that it became possible for women to have a family and continue in domestic work.

Significance

Throughout the nineteenth century and up to World War II (1939–1945), the "servant problem" was a constant issue for middle- and upper-class Americans. The fundamental issues to employers were: 1) the lack of sufficient qualified help; 2) the frequency with which they left positions; 3) their insolence; 4) the intrusive nature of live-in help; and 5) the cost.

The employed saw things differently. To them the problems were primarily the disrespect with which the employer treated them, the lack of personal time and, for many, the simple fact that the days were filled with long hours of hard work.

There was a steady stream of advice books for women on managing the household, including managing the help. The subject received steady coverage in newspapers and magazines. *Ladies Home Journal* and *Good Housekeeping,* for example, were two of the many popular magazines that began in the late nineteenth century and that devoted a steady stream of articles to the "servant problem."

By 1900, the "servant problem" came to be seen through the Progressive perspective and was addressed as part of a much larger movement aimed at bringing scientific management to the home. A major product of this movement was a new field of study known today as home economics. The 1897 book, *Domestic Service,* by Lucy Maynard Salmon, was a notable example of the efforts to improve home management and address the mutual concerns of employer and employee in the domestic arena.

Salmon proposed four main remedies. First was to eliminate the social stigma associated with being in domestic service. Domestics needed to be treated with appropriate respect—as employees, not servants. Second, technology and capabilities outside of the home should be used to meet the household needs. Prepared foods and professional laundry businesses, for example, reduced the need for domestic staff. Third was the need for educating staff and employer on managing a home. The goal was to professionalize the workforce, resulting in better employees and making the career more desirable. Finally, Salmon hoped to see the development of financial incentives (she suggested some form of profit sharing) to motivate and reward household staff.

For their part, household workers did not seem to have had much interest in the reforms advocated by Salmon and others. Although there were surprisingly frequent attempts at unionization, the goals were usually too ambiguous and the workers too isolated for the efforts to have much chance of success, particularly in a world hostile to unions.

The real solution to the "servant problem" came with technology. As significant labor-saving devices became available to the homemaker, the need for full-time, live-in domestic staff diminished. While domestic assistance remained in great demand, it was increasingly delivered by outside help and on a strictly professional basis.

A domestic servant tends to her employer's hair. © **CORBIS. REPRODUCED BY PERMISSION.**

Primary Source

The Courtesies [excerpt]

SYNOPSIS: Chapter Ten of Clapp's self-help book offers advice on how, with only a single general housekeeping servant, a proper (although simple) dinner may be prepared and served. Clapp suggests that patient training of the servant, skillful planning, and a non-complex menu will win the day. *The Courtesies* was one book in a six-part series that provided domestic advice to women.

For the Woman With One Servant

The mistresses of some households seem to imagine that because they are only able to afford "a girl for general housework" it is impossible for her to wait on the table properly, no matter how light her duties may otherwise be.

Now, when the family is small and the work not too heavy, one domestic, with a little assistance from the lady of the house, can easily do it all and yet find time to pass the viands correctly at dinner. . . .

Serving the Dinner

The inexperienced maid should be instructed that everything should be passed at the left side of the person who is being served. Before announcing dinner she should see that all she can possibly want during the meal is on the sideboard; for instance, the requisite number of spoons and forks for the different dishes, and in addition to these a few spoons and forks, both large and small, and a knife or two, in case they should be needed, and also an ample supply of bread.

As soon as the family are seated at dinner, the cover from the soup-tureen should be removed, and the maid should be in attendance on the left of the master to take each plate of soup, as he helps it, to the various persons at table. As soon as the soup is finished, the plates should be removed, and the tureen should be replaced as quickly as possible by the fish; if this is served from the table, the maid will proceed in just the same way as for the soup, but if it is a "made-up" dish of fish, hot plates should be distributed round the table, and then the dish containing the fish handed to each person to help himself. She should pass all plates of soup, fish, meat, etc., on a small tray. Before the dessert is served, the crumbs should all be removed from the tablecloth, using for this purpose a crumb tray and scraper or small brush. The coffee should be served last in a course by itself.

The maid should try and anticipate the requirements of those who are dining by offering bread, vegetables, etc., and filling up the glasses, without being requested to do so.

Now let us suppose that you want to invite a few friends to dinner and are anxious to have everything go off as well with your one maid as if you had a retinue of servants. Six people are about all that one servant can attend to comfortably unless she has a helper in the kitchen, so restrict your invitations to four, or at most six, if your family numbers two. Then after you have received your acceptances, sit down quietly and plan your menu carefully, choosing dishes that are not too rich or too elaborate and that go well together. A few well-cooked and well-served dishes are a thousand times more acceptable than a too-pretentious meal. Quality, not quantity, should be your motto when entertaining with only one maid. The following is rather a nice little menu:

Noodle Soup

Deviled Clams

Celery

Roast Chicken with Chestnut Dressing

Mashed Potatoes

French Peas

Tomato Jelly Salad

Olives

Salted Almonds

Frozen Fruit Compote

Cocoanut Bonbons

Coffee

This reads as if it were rather elaborate, but the dishes are really all very simple and can easily be prepared by the maid-of-all-work with a little assistance from her mistress. The soup should always be made the day before it is needed, so that it can stand over night and every particle of fat can be taken from it in the morning. The salad should be prepared on the morning of the little dinner party. It can be made as follows:

Tomato Jelly Salad—Take the contents of a quart can of prime tomatoes and add one small sliced onion, six cloves (if preferred the cloves can be omitted), one-half a cupful of finely chopped celery and boil for half an hour; then strain, season to taste with salt and a dash of paprika, and then add one-third of a box of gelatine dissolved in a little of the boiling liquid; pour into small cups (after-dinner coffee cups are a good size); and set away to cool. When ready to use turn out of the cups onto a bed of lettuce leaves and serve with thick mayonnaise poured around.

The cocoanut bonbons should be made the day before, so as not to take valuable time on the day of the entertainment. For these, take two cups of sugar, one-half cup of desiccated cocoanut, one-half cup of milk and boil all together for five minutes. Pour out part of this onto a buttered plate to harden. Divide the remainder into two portions, leave one in the kettle and pour the other into another saucepan, add to this a few drops of cochineal or a little strained cranberry to turn it a pretty pink, stir just long enough to get the coloring to take evenly, and turn out to harden. To the last portion add two tablespoonfuls of melted chocolate. Cook for two minutes, and turn out to cool. If you have any difficulty in managing the recipe in this way, the three different flavorings can be made separately.

The chicken should be prepared in the morning with the dressing ready to put in, so that when the time arrives there will be no delay, and directly the luncheon is out of the way the frozen fruit compote can be prepared and packed in ice and salt and set away to freeze while other duties are attended to.

Frozen Fruit Compote—Take a can of preserved pineapple and shred the pieces very fine with a silver fork, then take the same quantity of cut-up oranges and pour over the whole enough rich cream to entirely cover. Put this in a mold and pack in salt and chopped ice for three hours.

The clams should be left until just before dinner, as they are easy to prepare and would be spoiled if cooked too soon.

Deviled Clams—Chop up a dozen soft clams rather fine. Then add half a saltspoonful of cayenne or paprika, one and a half tablespoonfuls of lemon juice, the beaten yolk of an egg and enough cracker crumbs to make a soft paste; spread this over thin square crackers. Put in a pan and place in the oven until the batter is quite stiff. This will take about ten minutes. Serve at once.

The whole secret of giving a successful dinner or luncheon party with one maid is in having everything possible down to its minutest detail prepared beforehand, so that the servant is able to give her whole mind to the duties of serving the guests. If she has to stop to fix the salad, to hunt for the dessert dishes, or do any of the hundred and one little things that both she and her mistress forgot to arrange beforehand, there are embarrassing delays in the service of the meal and, as likely as not, the poor girl loses her head and the result is a fiasco.

In serving the simple little dinner described, place the salad with its plates piled up beside it upon the sideboard or serving table, put the ice-cream plates there also, and the proper utensils for serving them, as well as an extra supply of tablespoons and a carafe filled with cold water for refilling the glasses. After she has put the chicken in the oven to roast and prepared the vegetables, the maid should set the table as described. If guests are expected it is well for the mistress to give her some assistance, as one pair of hands, however willing, cannot do the work of cook and waitress for half a dozen people.

When everything is well under way the maid should change her gingham morning gown for a simple black dress with white apron, collar, and cuffs, and a waitress' cap if she will wear it, but most general servants object to this last touch, so it is not well to insist. When everything is ready, and the hour for dinner has arrived, the maid goes to the drawing-room door and quietly announces to her mistress that "Dinner is served." When the guests are seated she brings in the soup in a tureen which she places before her mistress; a pile of hot soup plates are then brought in and placed beside the tureen. She then stands at the left side of her mistress with a small tray, covered with a doily, in her left hand, and takes the plates of soup as soon as they are filled and passes them at the left side of each guest, taking the soup off the tray with her right hand and placing it in front of each person.

After the soup plates have been removed the roast is brought in with its hot plates. This is carved and served in the same manner as the soup, after which the maid immediately begins to pass the vegetables that accompany it. These vegetables are not put on the table, but brought from the kitchen, where they have been kept warm, and passed on the tray to each guest, who helps himself from the dish. At the salad course the plates, cold this time naturally, are placed before each person and the salad passed on the tray. The salted almonds are passed between the courses by those at the table. After the salad the crumbs are brushed from the table, and then the dessert is served. This, with its pile of plates, is set in front of the hostess, who dishes it out, and the maid passes each person's portion upon her tray. The bonbons can be passed with the dessert or can accompany the coffee, as one desires. The dessert plates are removed and the maid then brings in the black coffee, direct from the kitchen, carrying several cups upon her tray at once and passing one to each guest. She then retires from the dining room.

The guests should be served in turn as they sit, first a gentleman and then a lady, as this is the quickest and most correct way to manage it. The host or hostess, whichever is serving, appropriately takes the last plate.

The manner of serving a luncheon is in the main the same as the dinner. Full details of setting the table, etc., for this will be found in Chapter IX.

In small cities or country places where it is customary to dine in the middle of the day, a dinner party, unless it is a Sunday dinner, is rarely given, but supper parties are the correct form of entertainment. These are very easy to manage, as they are customarily served in but two or at most three courses, so the duties of the waitress are greatly lessened.

Further Resources

BOOKS

Sutherland, Donald E. *Americans and Their Servants: Domestic Service in the United States from 1800 to 1920.* Baton Rouge: Louisiana State University Press, 1981.

Van Raaphorst, Donna L. *Union Maids Not Wanted: Organizing Domestic Workers, 1870–1940.* New York: Praeger, 1988.

WEBSITES

"The 1900 House—The Scullery—Servants." Available online at http://www.pbs.org/wnet/1900house/house/scullery/servants.html; website home page: http://www.pbs.org/wnet/1900house/ (accessed January 31, 2003).

"The Corner Stone Laid"

Newspaper article

By: *Miamisburg News*
Date: July 15, 1909
Source: *Miamisburg News,* Miamisburg, Ohio, July 15, 1909.
About the Publication: The *Miamisburg News* issued its first paper on April 1, 1880. One of four early newspapers reporting on the small town of Miamisburg in southwestern Ohio, the *News* covered all significant local events. The publisher and editor, Charles Kinder, was a descendant of one of the city's oldest families, and he followed in the footsteps of his uncle, also a newspaper publisher in Ottawa, Ohio. Kinder, in addition to publishing the newspaper, was mayor and postmaster, and his motto was that "Every small city needs good streets, good libraries, first-class schools, good citizenship, in the securing of which the local newspaper can and does aid more than any other agency." Though currently owned by a different publisher, the *Miamisburg News* continues to report on the local events for the citizens of Miamisburg. ■

Introduction

Andrew Carnegie is one of America's great rags-to-riches stories. The son of a handloom weaver from Scotland, Carnegie came to Allegheny, Pennsylvania, with his family in 1848 at the age of seven. Starting work at 12, Carnegie was successful in the railroad industry and as an investor before turning his attention to the manufacture of steel in the early 1870s. Carnegie was an early user of the Bessemer process for making steel, and under his talented leadership Carnegie Steel became the dominant steel producer in the country.

Already committed to returning to society the vast wealth he had accumulated, Carnegie sold his company in 1901 to a syndicate formed by J.P. Morgan to form United States Steel Corporation. He then devoted all of his energies and resources to philanthropic activities. Before he died, Carnegie distributed virtually his entire fortune of $350 million to various organizations and institutions for the purpose of bettering society.

Carnegie was not an almsgiver; he did not intend to "save" individuals or organizations. He intended to provide such assistance as would allow people to help themselves. In a famous article entitled "Wealth" (later republished as "The Gospel of Wealth"), published in 1889, Carnegie wrote:

> In bestowing charity, the main consideration should be to help those who will help themselves; to provide part of the means by which those who desire to improve may do so; to give those who desire to rise the aids by which they may rise; to assist, but rarely or never to do all.

Carnegie believed that one of the best means whereby he could aid a great number of people and remain consistent to his philosophy of giving was through the establishment of free public libraries, a rare commodity in Carnegie's youth. His personal interest was explained in "Wealth":

> When I was a working-boy in Pittsburgh, Colonel Anderson of Allegheny—a name I can never speak without a feeling of devotional gratitude—opened his little library of four hundred books to boys. Every Saturday afternoon he was in attendance at his house to exchange books. No one but he who has felt it can ever know the intense longing with which the arrival of Saturday was awaited, that a new book might be had. . . . It was when reveling in the treasures which he opened to us that I resolved, if ever wealth came to me, that it should be used to establish free libraries, that other poor boys might receive opportunities similar to those for which we were indebted to that noble man.

Significance

Carnegie began making his library grants in 1889, the first in Allegheny, Pennsylvania. The gifting of libraries by wealthy benefactors was not new, and Carnegie's initial grants followed fairly traditional forms. The libraries tended to be large, attractive public spaces that were relatively inefficient in their primary purpose. The cynic could label them as monumental works to the greatness of Andrew Carnegie.

By 1900, however, Carnegie's approach began to change. First, he was stung by criticism of wealthy philanthropists who made "charitable" donations with "tainted money" that had been earned off the back of oppressed workers. Second, Carnegie, and his chief aid James Bertram, became increasingly committed to building libraries compatible with the needs of librarians rather than architects anxious to build great works of art. Third, Carnegie began to realize that his initial grants had not been consistent with the gifting ideas expressed in "Wealth." He came to believe that it was critical for the communities to play a more active role in the process. Fourth, due to the sale of Carnegie Steel, more resources and time were available for this noble work. Carnegie felt it was necessary to put the process on a more systematic and businesslike basis. This would ensure grants were made and distributed based on an established formula rather than on the whim of the benefactor. It would also result in more efficient use of his funds and, at the same time, undercut some of the criticism of his well-intentioned philanthropies.

The basic formula that developed required the following:

1. Local governments would have to make formal requests for aid;

2. Detailed reports would be completed providing such information as population, condition of the existing library, collection size, prior year circulation, and financial condition;
3. The local government must acquire the land and commit to raising annual tax revenue equal to 10 percent of the gift to cover operating expenses and buy books.

If all was in order, Carnegie committed to gifting at the rate of (typically) two dollars per person to communities of more than 1,000 people for the purposes of building a library. Carnegie himself established the basic criteria and then left actual approvals to James Bertram, his secretary. Bertram and Carnegie later encouraged designs favored by the American Library Association, but the final architectural decisions were left to the local community.

Before the program ended in 1917, ostensibly because of World War I (1914–1918), Carnegie funds had built 1,679 libraries in 1,412 cities and towns across the United States at a cost of $41 million. When buildings outside the U.S. are included, the number approaches 3,000 libraries. The contribution and impact was incalculable. While libraries were being constructed in any event, it would certainly not have happened as rapidly without Carnegie's assistance. Furthermore, Carnegie helped bring about a consistent high standard in the design and purpose of local libraries.

Primary Source

"The Corner Stone Laid"

SYNOPSIS: The cornerstone for the Miamisburg Public Library was laid on July 9, 1908. As was often the case in small towns, the idea for a library originated with the local literary clubs. The proposal obtained support from the school, and it was suggested the town approach Carnegie. The response—probably from James Bertram and not Andrew Carnegie—was quick and favorable. In less than a year, the idea of a Miamisburg Free Library had become a reality.

The Cornerstone of the New Carnegie Library building was laid Friday afternoon with most impressive ceremonies, under the auspices of Minerva Lodge No. 98, and the Grand Lodge of Ohio, F. & A. M.

At 4 o'clock the Masons met at the Masonic Temple and proceeded to the scene of the ceremony, marching south to Linden avenue, west to Main, north on Main to City Hall, where the city officials fell in line, and thence east on Central avenue to the park.

A typical early 20th-century Carnegie library. This one was located in Sheldon, Iowa, around 1909. **THE LIBRARY OF CONGRESS.**

The Masonic procession was composed of the following:

Grand Master, Horace A. Irvin

Grand Marshall, Geo. L. Marshall

Dep. G. M., L. H. Zehring

Gr. S. W., D. H. Allen

Gr. J. W., A. C. Schell

Gr. Treas., C. F. Eck

Gr. Sec., C. A. Schuster

Master, Robert Plocher

Gr. Orator, Chas. E. Kinder

Gr. Chaplain, Dr. H. M. Herman

Light Bearers, C. W. Grove, M. G. Bohn, J. T. Brown

Architect, John Plocher

Gr. Deacons, Joel Willis, Henry Schuberth

Gr. Tyler, Otto Buehner

Gr. Stewards, John Schoenfeld, C. F. Young

Tyler, John A. Hall

Stewards, Walter Britton, Andrew Sneller

Choir, S. S. Sutherland, C. W. Bechtol, C. E. Kinder, C. A. Schuster, H. W. Wantz, E. J. Rogers, Robert Brough, Carl Shuler, C. L. Mitchell

At the park the officers were seated in the building, while the Masonic brethren formed a hollow square.

Mayor Reiter and the city officials, Councilmen, Board of Education, Park Commissioners, Board of Affairs, Board of Health were all represented.

Mayor W. A. Reiter, in behalf of the village of Miamisburg, presented Grand Master Irvin a trowel and

The Carnegie library of Guthrie, Oklahoma. Opened in 1902, it is now on the National Register of Historic Places. **THE LIBRARY OF CONGRESS.**

requested that he lay the cornerstone in due and ancient form. After proclamation by Grand Marshall Geo. L. Marshall, the Grand Master proceeded with the ceremonial.

The Grand Treasurer, C. F. Eck, appeared with the copper box (contributed by Miss Caroline Cade) and read a list of the contents.

The box contained the following:

List of Officers of the Village of Miamisburg for the year 1909.

Annual Report of Village Clerk for year 1908.

List showing names of Officers and Teachers of Public Schools, and the number of pupils enrolled.

List of employees of the Miamisburg Postoffice, and full set of U.S. Postage Stamps.

Roster of Minerva Lodge and Trinity Chapter, F. & A. M.

Roster of Marion Lodge, I. O. O. F.

Year Books of Literary and Musical Societies:—

The Monday Night Club.

The Research Club.

The Chopin Club.

Letter Heads from various Manufacturers, Business Men and Merchants.

Illustrated Views of the Principal Buildings of Miamisburg.

Souvenirs and Papers giving description of the Wright Brothers Celebration at Dayton, Ohio.

Copies of The Miamisburg News, and Miamisburg News History of the Town.

Several pieces of Coin.

Names of Contractors and Sub-contractors of Library Building.

List of Masonic Brethren officiating at the Laying of Stone.

Copy of this list.

The box was then deposited, and corn, wine and oil were poured upon and over the stone by L. H. Zehring, D. H. Allen, and A. C. Schell, repeating the ritual.

The choir then sang the Masonic hymn.

The Grand Master then delivered the tools and plans of the building to Architecht John Plocher. (Plocher & Son are the contractors and builders of the Library.) This was the second time Mr. Plocher officiated on occasions of this time, having been the builder of the Masonic Temple.

Grand Master Irvin then delivered the concluding address, and Grand Chaplain Rev. H. M. Herman, D. D., pronounced the benediction.

After the ceremonies Mayor W. A. Reiter made an interesting address, referring to the action of the Monday Night Club and other literary clubs in beginning the agitation for a public library, and stated that in just twelve days from the time he as mayor wrote to Mr. Carnegie asking for a library building, a letter was received, granting the request. Mayor Reiter referred to the importance of the occasion, and the benefits that would accrue from the Library to all our people, particularly the younger generation. He then introduced Supt. Of Schools W. T. Trump. Mr. Trump said in part,

> Very few men and women in Miamisburg past forty years of age will become readers because of the founding of this library, or because they have better access to books. It is not primarily for men and women that this library is being built, but for boys and girls and generations yet unborn.
>
> Last fall the subject of a public library seemed to be in the air. The literary clubs in town were discussing it, one of the papers before the School and Home Association was on the value of a public library, one of the ministers in the town preached a sermon in which he dwelt largely on the development of the mind through the use of a public library
>
> At last the literary clubs appointed a general committee to wait on the school board to ask for the use of the school library. The plan of the committee was to rent a room and hire a librarian.
>
> One of the School Board suggested to the committee it ask for a Carnegie library. The other members of the Board also urged the same with the result that we are today laying the cornerstone of a public library.
>
> Boys and girls now running the streets of Miamisburg will some day bless the name of the good people who are responsible for this work.
>
> Nor should we forget Mr. Carnegie who in his adopted country has made a fortune and is giving the money to build this library.
>
> Possibly no other thing has such power to lift the poor out of his poverty; the wretched out of his misery; to make the burden-bearer forget his burden; the sick his pain; the downtrodden his degradation, as has books.
>
> They are the friends of the lonely, the companions of the deserted; a joy to the joyless, a hope to the hopeless.
>
> Look if you will down into the soul of a little child. On the tablet thereof you will find written ambition, eloquence, poetry, purity, love and confidence. Feed the soul of that child on the right kind of mental food and you will make of him one of God's noblemen who will be a blessing to humanity.
>
> Many a boy has passed his life in mediocrity because his soul was starved in childhood. He longed for mental food and found it not.
>
> All about us we see people who are children mentally because they were not nourished on the thoughts that ennoble and give life.
>
> In this library the boy that runs our streets barefooted may sit down so to speak in the palace of a king and for the time being wear the royal robes of a prince.
>
> I am for the boys and girls of Miamisburg. Nothing is too good for them. Let us give them the best we possibly can.
>
> Here is a chance for some of our good citizens to make their names famous, by giving to this library a fund to endow it and thereby insure its future. It costs but seventy cents tax per thousand dollars.
>
> Is there a man in Miamisburg who has property to the amount of one thousand dollars who is not willing to pay seventy cents for the support of this library?

Further Resources

BOOKS

Jones, Theodore. *Carnegie Libraries Across America: A Public Legacy.* Washington: Preservation Press; New York: Wiley, 1997.

Judson, Clara. *Andrew Carnegie.* Chicago: Follett, 1964.

Simon, Charnan. *Andrew Carnegie: Builder of Libraries.* New York: Children's Press, 1997.

Van Slyck, Abigail A. *Free to All: Carnegie Libraries and American Culture, 1890–1920.* Chicago: University of Chicago Press, 1995.

PERIODICALS

Carnegie, Andrew. "Wealth." *North American Review* 148, no. 391, June 1889, 653, 657–662.

WEBSITES

"Carnegie Corporation of New York." Available online at http://www.carnegie.org/ (accessed February 2, 2003).

"Carnegie Libraries: The Future Made Bright." Teaching with Historic Places, National Register of Historic Places, National Park Service. Available online at http://www.cr.nps.gov/nr

/twhp/wwwlps/lessons/50carnegie/50carnegie.htm; website home page: http://www.cr.nps.gov/nr/twhp (accessed February 2, 2003).

Lorenzen, Michael. "Deconstructing the Philanthropic Library: The Sociological Reasons Behind Andrew Carnegie's Millions to Libraries." Available online at http://www.lib.msu.edu/lorenze1/carnegie.htm; website home page: http://www.lib.msu.edu/ (accessed February 2, 2003).

Walsh, Glenn A. "History of Andrew Carnegie and Carnegie Libraries." Available online at http://andrewcarnegie.tripod.com (accessed February 3, 2003).

The Chautauqua Movement

"Miami Valley Chautauqua Opens Friday, July 16th"; "Chautauqua"

Newspaper articles

By: *Miamisburg News*

Date: July 1909; July 22, 1909

Source: "Miami Valley Chautauqua Opens Friday, July 16th"; "Chautauqua." *Miamisburg News,* July 1909; July 22, 1909.

About the Publication: The *Miamisburg News* issued its first paper on April 1, 1880. One of four early newspapers reporting on the small town of Miamisburg in southwest Ohio, the *News* covered all significant local events. Its publisher, Charles Kinder, was a descendant of one of the city's oldest families, and he followed in the footsteps of his uncle, also a newspaper publisher in Ottawa, Ohio. Though currently owned by a different publisher, the *Miamisburg News* continues to report the local events for the citizens of Miamisburg. ■

Introduction

Chautauqua is the name of a lake and county in southwest New York that became the original site of a cultural and educational phenomenon called the Chautauqua movement. The movement has three distinct components: the original site at Lake Chautauqua in New York; other Chautauqua sites located across the country, and traveling Chautauquas that first appeared in the early 1900s. All of these played a significant part in what is today collectively referred to as "Chautauqua."

The original Chautauqua in New York was founded by Bishop John H. Vincent, of New Jersey, and Lewis Miller, an inventor and manufacturer from Ohio. They wanted to build a summer camp to train Sunday school teachers in a relaxing and uplifting educational environment. The camp soon evolved into an expanded summer-long program that featured lectures, concerts, roundtable discussions, and wholesome recreation and entertainment. The Chautauqua Institution became an accredited University, and it continues to provide intellectual and spiritual programs much as it did at the beginning of the twentieth century.

Significance

The popularity of New York's Chautauqua led to other permanent summer encampments, usually in resort settings, that to a greater or lesser degree copied the very successful cultural, educational, and recreational format used at the original location. The first off-site Chautauqua was established in 1876 at Lakeside, Ohio, along the south shore of Lake Erie. Modeled closely after the program in New York, although not technically affiliated, it was called Chautauqua II.

Chautauqua programs soon spread to Iowa and Michigan, and by 1900 there were 200 permanent sites in 31 states. Each program followed the pattern of Vincent's New York program as closely as possible, but each took on its own characteristics. A typical program, like one held in Battle Creek, Michigan, in 1909, lasted 10 days, with special days devoted to ladies, children, farmers, businessmen, working men, and teachers. The program included entertainment by quartets and orchestras, a magician, a humorist, and lectures by such distinguished guests as a senator, a governor, a doctor, a teacher, a member of a religious ministry, and other accomplished orators.

Procuring speakers, musicians, and other paid talent for the management of various Chautauquas was a difficult and time-consuming task for the largely volunteer local Chautauquas. In 1903, Keith Vawter, a booking agent with experience in the Lyceum circuit (an adult education movement), saw this need as an opportunity to use Lyceum expertise and contacts to organize entire Chautauqua shows, essentially selling the entire program to the local Chautauqua association.

Although he lost money the first year, new arrangements that required hosting towns to absorb all of the financial risk helped the Chautauqua traveling circuit survive. Downplaying the financial aspect, Vawter instead worked from the principle that it was each hosting town's civic duty to provide cultural activities and education for its citizens. Very soon, competing programs patterned on Vawter's Redpath Chautauqua appeared. For the next twenty years, traveling Chautauquas with talent provided by any one of dozens of Chautauqua organizations brought education, culture, and entertainment to several thousand small towns each summer.

In 1924, the Chautauqua phenomenon celebrated its 50th anniversary. That year Chautauquas were held in an estimated 12,000 cities and were attended by 30 million people (one quarter of the population at that time). That year, however, was the program's peak. Just one year later, most circuits were gone. Local interest had diminished, and the quickly ascending popularity of radio, phonographs, and movies, as well as the mobility afforded by the automobile, provided regular access to formal educational programs, cultural activities, entertainment, and recreation. A few traveling programs lasted until as late as 1932, and some of the better-established permanent Chautauquas continue to operate today.

Primary Source

"Miami Valley Chautauqua Opens Friday, July 16th"

SYNOPSIS: Miamisburg, Ohio, held its annual Chautauqua on its permanent grounds in 1909. The *Miamisburg News* advertised the upcoming program. The Miamisburg site remains in use as a church-run family camp and retreat center.

The Miami Valley Chautauqua, July 16th to August 13th, 1909, will be the best of the several remarkable assemblies held by this Chautauqua, which now has a national reputation for giving the very best program that genius can devise or money can procure. Men whose superior ability as orators and preachers is world-wide, will appear from day to day. The various courses of lectures, each under the personal direction of a most scholarly and skillful director, make this Chautauqua a real summer university for the people. The athletic and aquatic sports are most satisfactory. The advantages of summer cottages and tent life with abounding fresh air, pure water and proper sanitation at this place have been commended by thousands of patrons.

The superiority of the Miami Valley Chautauqua is not questioned by persons familiar with places appealing to the public for support. Its equal is to be found at but few places in the whole country and then at a marked increase in expense. The claim has long been to furnish the best program given in at less expense than can be found elsewhere. As is well known, these are the only grounds in the State bought, owned and operated solely for Chautauqua purposes. The management assures the growing number of friends and guests that it is deeply appreciative of the permanent and increasing success of its efforts to furnish programs and helpful vacations.

The amusements and entertainments are wholesome. The moral, intellectual and religious instruction is given by acknowledged leaders.

A glance at the rich program will reveal the fact that no expense has been spared in securing the very best orators and lecturers which the country affords.

Part of the crowd of spectators at the 1907 Chautauqua at Charles City, Iowa. THE LIBRARY OF CONGRESS.

There is also the best music, with the finest readers, singers, moving pictures, novelties, and all that goes to the building of an unique and delightful program.

For those who attend there is an assurance that the days that follow will bring pleasant memories of a vacation worth while.

Primary Source

"Chautauqua"

SYNOPSIS: The *Miamisburg News* reported on the Chautauqua. William Jennings Bryan, Democratic presidential candidate in 1908 and friend of the farmer, was one of the featured speakers at Miamisburg's Chautauqua and was a common speaker for Chautauqua programs throughout the country.

Splendid Program. Fine Attractions. Large Attendance.

Without a doubt this has been and will be throughout the most successful and entertaining assembly ever held on the Miami Valley Chautauqua grounds. The 550 tents are all occupied, and more are pitched every day. The hotels and cottages are accommodating those who do not care for camp life. From the first day the services have been well attended and are much enjoyed.

Col. George Bain of Kentucky, who gave the opening address, was in best form and gave a splendid lecture. Dr. F. W. Gunsaulus of Chicago gave two excellent talks Saturday to immense crowds. Senator Bob Taylor spoke Tuesday afternoon. Sen. Taylor is a word painter, a humorist, and a story teller without a peer on the lecture platform. His fun is sandwiched in when least expected, and he kept his

Robert M. LaFollette, Wisconsin governor and a progressive, at an Illinois Chautauqua around 1905. Chautauquas often featured famous political orators among their attractions. THE LIBRARY OF CONGRESS.

audience in a continual uproar. His jokes are bright and he reached the hearts of all who heard him.

Temperance Day was observed Tuesday by the W. C. T. U., and hundreds were present to hear a splendid talk by Mrs. Florence Richards, national lecturer and organizer of the Union.

Rounds Orchestra furnished entertainment for several days.

The Hinshaw Grand Opera Quartette and the Ferguson Glee Club gave splendid concerts during the week. They are without exception the best in their respective classes ever heard at Chautauqua.

Nicola, magician and handcuff king, will give an entertainment Friday evening, and another on Saturday evening. Nicola is the youngest magician on the stage and has many new and wonderful tricks. Dobski and Princess La Yiyia, his assistants, are more than able, and the Nicola company win the hearts of their audience from the very first.

Dr. Byron W. King is a master of eloquence and is capable of moving his audience to laughter or tears as best subserves the point he is trying to bring out. His smile is contagious, and his hearers are with him throughout his address. He will conduct a series of Shakespearian lectures, and give a number of afternoon addresses.

Dr. D. F. Fox, one of Chicago's most successful ministers, speaks Sunday. He has enlisted in the forces fighting against evil and has been a real power in the work. To hear him is to realize the splendor, the witchery, and the power of perfect speech.

Religious services will be held in the morning Sunday with a sermon by Rev. H. T. Sell of Ft. Wayne, Ind., and another in the afternoon by Dr. Fox.

A sacred concert by the Rounds will be given in the evening.

Hon. William Jennings Bryan will speak Tuesday afternoon, July 27, and doubtless thousands will hear him.

Col. Robt. Glenn, Governor of North Carolina, one of the best known men in the United States, will give an address Thursday afternoon.

There are many interesting lectures and entertainments which cannot fail to please.

Further Resources

BOOKS

Harrison, Harry P. *Culture Under Canvas: The Story of Tent Chautauqua.* New York: Hastings House, 1958.

Simpson, Jeffrey. *Chautauqua: An American Utopia.* New York: Harry N. Abrams in association with Chautauqua Institution, 1999.

Vincent, John Heyl. *The Chautauqua Movement.* Boston: Chautauqua Press, 1886.

WEBSITES

"Chautauqua Institution." Available online at http://www.Chautauqua-inst.org (accessed February 1, 2003).

Maxwell, Jeffrey Scott. "The Complete Chautauquan: Chautauqua Talent Bureaus." Available online at http://members.aol.com/AlphaChautauquan/bureaus.html; website home page: http://members.aol.com/AlphaChautauquan/ (accessed February 1, 2003).

"Traveling Culture: Circuit Chautauqua in the Twentieth Century." American Memory, Library of Congress. Available online at http://memory.loc.gov/ammem/award98/iauhtml/tccchome.html; website home page: http://lcweb2.loc.gov/ammem/ (accessed February 1, 2003).

"What was Chautauqua?" Available online at http://sdrc.lib.uiowa.edu/traveling-culture/essay.htm; website home page: http://memory.loc.gov/ammem/award98/iauhtml/ (accessed February 1, 2003).

The Anti-Saloon League Year Book

Handbook

By: Anti-Saloon League
Date: 1909

Source: Cherrington, Ernest Hurst, ed. *The Anti-Saloon League Year Book: An Encyclopedia of Facts and Figures Dealing with the Liquor Traffic and the Temperance Reform.* Columbus, Ohio: The Anti-Saloon League, 1909, 31, 79–80, 125–128, 135.

About the Organization: The Anti-Saloon League was established in 1893 in Oberlin, Ohio, as a prohibition organization. It became a national association in 1895 and, along with the Women's Christian Temperance Union, led the crusade against drink that resulted in the Eighteenth Amendment to the U.S. Constitution banning the sale and manufacture of alcoholic beverages in the United States. The Anti-Saloon League continued after the repeal of the Eighteenth Amendment in 1933, merging with other temperance societies in 1950 to form the National Temperance League. ■

Introduction

The Temperance Movement began early in the nineteenth century, but did not begin to achieve national prominence until after 1825. Initially centered in New England and upstate New York, temperance was one of several major reform movements that emerged from the revivalist urge that swept that area in the 1820s and 1830s. Others included abolitionism and women's rights. The Temperance Movement was one of the longest lasting and most influential reform impulses in American history.

The Temperance Movement was an attempt to reduce or eliminate the negative impact associated with the consumption of alcoholic beverages. Although slowed by the Civil War (1861–1865), temperance showed remarkable resilience. In the post–Civil War years, the Women's Christian Temperance Union (est. 1874), the Temperance Society of the Methodist Church, and the Anti-Saloon League were the leading temperance organizations.

The initial impulse for temperance was in response to the perceived excesses in the consumption of alcoholic beverages, particularly distilled spirits (whiskey). Temperance advocates felt that the personal tragedies and the broader social consequences associated with drink required intervention. The degree of that intervention varied considerably among advocates. Initially, avoidance of hard liquor or moderation in its use was sufficient for most reformers.

By 1900, the concept of temperance had tightened into prohibition. Temperance had become firmly established as an important element of the broader reform impulse and was now primarily focused on total abstinence. While the essential argument remained the harmful effects of alcohol, opponents of alcohol increasingly blamed alcohol-induced intoxication for the urban problems confronting the country.

Prohibition appealed to old-stock, rural, Protestant values. Its advocates saw cities as corrupt and filled with "new immigrants." Cities were, not coincidentally, also the centers of alcohol abuse. Eliminating alcohol would, in the minds of prohibitionists, achieve several goals. First, it would be an important step toward reducing poverty—wages spent on drink and lost due to alcohol-related absenteeism would benefit wives and children and remain in the family. Also, prohibition would provide employers with more reliable employees, and employees would be more likely to keep their jobs.

Second, the saloon and alcohol industries were considered to be a central source of urban corruption. They were seen as the backdrop for prostitution, usury, gambling, petty crime, and other social ills associated with urban life. The political bosses, reformers felt, ran their corrupt businesses in this environment and from it generated the revenue necessary to bribe police and other officials.

Third, alcoholic consumption was believed to be an integral part of southern and eastern European cultures that were being transplanted by immigrants to America. If these people were to become Americanized, they must adopt American customs. Rural, evangelical Protestants felt that alcohol prevented that transition.

For a variety of reasons, therefore, prohibition became an important part of the reform movement sweeping the country in the early years of the twentieth century, particularly among those from non-urban areas. While Progressives, particularly those from small-town and rural America, often embraced prohibition, it included social conservatives whose interests did not extend to other reforms associated with Progressivism.

Significance

The appeal that temperance and prohibition had to the broader reform effort resulted in a significant spread of anti-alcoholic drink legislation in the years prior to World War I (1914–1918). A wide array of state and local laws was passed, making approximately half the country "dry" by 1909. Success at state and local levels built the momentum for action at the national level. What the consequences would have been without the arrival of war are debatable. The coming of World War I, however, smoothed the way for federal legislation.

Once war was declared, the need for total national commitment was paramount. The country could neither afford to divert grain supplies to alcohol production, nor risk lost productivity due to alcohol-induced absenteeism or on-the-job accidents. As a result of the war, Congress passed the Lever Act early in 1917 to regulate food production and distribution during the emergency. It also banned the use of grain for distilling whiskey. In December, Congress, spurred by wartime needs and the steady pressure of the anti-drink forces, passed the Eighteenth Amendment prohibiting the manufacture and sale of all alcoholic beverages. The requisite number of states ratified it by January 1919. The country had gone dry.

The failure of prohibition became clear to most observers within a few years. It was the last gasp of a pre-urbanized society imbued with strong and absolute moral values that had been rapidly overtaken by a twentieth-century urban society whose moral precepts were more flexible and cosmopolitan. Unwilling to abandon the "noble experiment," however, successive Republican administrations, steeped in the traditions of that older world, continued to cling to prohibition. It was not until the Depression and the election of Franklin Roosevelt (served 1933–1945), a Democrat with strong support in the cities and among the first- and second-generation immigrants, that the Eighteenth Amendment was finally repealed in 1933.

Primary Source

The Anti-Saloon League Year Book [excerpt]

SYNOPSIS: *The Anti-Saloon League Yearbook* for 1909 provided a report of the crusade against alcohol. In addition to state updates on the progress of legislation, it presented an overview of the various types of measures being considered. In the excerpt below, some of the specific arguments in support of prohibition are presented.

Indiana

There are over 700 fewer saloons in Indiana as a result of the remonstrance campaigns of 1908. Of 36,350 square miles in the state, 26,172 compose the dry area. 1,640,000 people in the Hoosier State are now living in dry territory. Between September, 1907 and September, 1908, 16 cities, 20 counties, and 22 county seats have abolished the saloon. There are now in the license areas of the state about 4,500 saloons, but the county local option law, passed at the special session of the legislature in September, 1908, under which the counties are just now beginning to vote, will in all probability make great inroads on the license territory of the state during the next six months. The first elections were held under this law, on December 29, when the two counties voting gave decisive "dry" majorities. On December 31, a third county election resulted in victory against the saloons. Brewery and liquor forces are concentrating all their efforts to secure a repeal of this county local option law at the coming session of the legislature, and while it is expected that the fight will be hot, the strong public sentiment against the saloon throughout the state, indicates that in all probability no backward step in the matter of temperance legislation will be taken. 839 of the 1,016 townships are now dry under the remonstrance law. . . .

The Family Income and the Drink Bill

It has been fairly well determined that the average man who drinks spends 50 cents a day for liquor. These figures are for this country. I believe he spends a little less in Germany and more in England. This takes from his income $182.50 a year. A man who is a steady drinker requires more medical attendance in a year than a man who is not. This has been demonstrated by physicians. More men are rejected by life insurance companies because they are drinkers than men who are weak otherwise. We have, therefore, less financial protection for the family of a drinker than for the family of a temperance person. A man who drinks creates more debts, as a rule, than a man who does not drink. Summing up all these things against the annual earnings of such a man, we find that he costs his family, through his habit, about $250 a year, which includes his liquor bill, his debts, his medical attendance and loss of profit in an insurance policy.

Now in the United States there are 2,352,000 farm families whose annual income is less than $400; 3,422,000 city families whose income is less than $400; 1,447,000 farm families whose income is less than $600; 2,230,000 city families whose income is less than $600; 274,000 farm families whose income is between $1,200 and $1,800; and 1,413,000 city families whose income is from $1,200 to $1,800.

You deduct from the farm and city families having annual incomes less than $400, $250 for liquor, sickness, debts and loss of insurance, and you are steadily driving that family into bankruptcy or crime. The condition is a little better for those families whose incomes are $600 a year, and who have net for their necessities but $350 a year, if the father is a drinking man. The loss is not so severe on the families with the larger income, but it, nevertheless, is a steady financial drain.

The diversion of so much money into a single habit and its attendant evils affects the purse of the breadwinner, the comforts of the home, and the schooling of the children; and the comforts and physical character of the head of the family himself are attacked.

The average factory worker of the United States receives $490 per year in wages, and there are 6,152,000 of such workers. Deduct from this $250 a year for liquor and its miseries, and half of the family's income is taken away. The average wage-earnings per year in the North Atlantic states of this Union are $479; in the South Atlantic states, $335; in the North Central states, $503; in the Western states, where mining is profitable, $670; or an average per year per man for the whole United States of $477. Take from this the $250 put into a habit and the blow which is dealt the individual and the family is too palpable to be ignored.

Figures of this character cannot be disputed. They are having extraordinary weight in this progressive day with thinking people, and in some ways they are doing more for the cause of temperance than a hundred other arguments that might be advanced—Franz V. Feldman. . . .

Pauperism Under License and No-License

A Comparison in New England

Of the six states that compose the New England group, Maine is under prohibition; Vermont and New Hampshire are over three-fourths dry under the local option laws; more than one-half of the territory of Massachusetts is dry under the local option law of that state, while in Connecticut and Rhode Island, the larger part of the area is under license, and the great majority of the people live in saloon territory. The two states of Connecticut and Rhode Island are the best representatives of license states in New England, while Maine is the only prohibition state in the group.

The latest comparative official figures (January 1, 1905) disclose some most interesting comparisons between Maine and these two license states.

On January 1, 1905, there were in the state of Maine 1,124 paupers in almshouses, or 163 paupers for every 100,000 of the population. In the State of Connecticut on the same date there were 2,330 paupers in almshouses, or 256 for every 100,000 of the population, while in Rhode Island there were 829 paupers in almshouses, or 196 for every 100,000 of the population.

These figures are based on the population of the states according to the 1900 census, and speak for themselves.

The other states of the New England group tell practically the same story in proportion to the condition of license or no license.

Pauperism in Two Cities

From August, 1907, to August, 1908, the township trustees paid for the support of the poor of East Liverpool, O., a city of 20,000, $1,041.44; Wellsville, O., also without saloons, a city of 11,000, paid $354; while Steubenville, O., a city of 17,000, with saloons galore, spent $8,765.42, and during July and August the treasury was so depleted that citizens had to subscribe $2,000 in addition to help the starving and clothe them. The amount spent for the poor in the two places, Steubenville and East Liverpool, are in the ratio of $10.76 to $1.00.

Pauperism In "Wet" And "Dry" Ohio Counties.

County	Population	No. Saloons	No. Paupers
Van Wert	30,394	22	614
Huron	32,330	50	355
Hancock	41,934	41	354
Williams	24,953	22	264
Tuscarawas	53,751	97	466
Mahoning	70,134	299	912
Highland	30,982	0	64
Morgan	17,905	0	39
Fayette	21,715	1	53
Clinton	24,202	0	86
Harrison	20,486	0	78
Ashland	21,284	1	94

From reports of Ohio Secretary of State and Ohio Auditor of 1907.

Part IV. Liquor Traffic and Insanity

Alcohol was a cause of insanity in 21.66 per cent of the cases admitted to public insane hospitals in Massachusetts in 1906, according to the report of the state board of insanity. If the same percentage holds true for other inmates of the hospitals, there were in Massachusetts, in 1906, 2,190 insane persons whose insanity was due in part, at least, to drink. Their support cost the state not far from $600,000. Among the insane criminals, alcohol was given as a cause of insanity in 47.22 per cent.

Massachusetts Bureau Report

As a result of the investigation of the Bureau of Statistics of Labor, in Massachusetts, we have the following for the years in which the investigation was made.

Total number of insane	1,836
Number where cause could not be ascertained	330
Total number considered in investigation	1506
Number where insanity was caused by personal use of liquor	383
Number where insanity was caused by use of liquor by parents	20
Number where insanity was caused by use of liquor by others	123

Thus it will be seen that of the 1506 cases investigated, 526, or 35 per cent, were due directly or indirectly to the use of liquors.

Alcohol and Insanity

Considering the United States as a whole, it is variously estimated that from 25 to 30 per cent of all the insane patients admitted to the asylums year by year owe their misfortune, directly or indirectly to the abuse of alcohol. The statistics of other countries are closely similar. In England and Wales, according to the estimate of Dr. Robert Jones, alcohol claims 17,000 victims among an asylum population of 116,000.

The testimony of Continental alienists is no less unequivocal, and the statistics upon which their opinions are based are no less suggestive as to the alarming increase in the ravages of alcohol in recent years. Thus the official returns from the asylum of St. Anne, in Paris, for the period 1872–1885 show that of 31,733 insane patients, 28 percent of the men and less than 6 percent of the women owed their condition to alcoholism. But of the patients in the same institution in 1900, according to Dr. Legrain, no fewer than 51 percent of the men and 22 percent of the women were alcoholics.

Altogether similar are the returns from the asylums of Vienna. According to Tilkowski, 14,391 insane patients were under treatment there during the period 1871–1882; and of these 25 percent of the men were victims of alcohol. At the International Congress Against Alcohol, held in Vienna in 1901, it was shown that the corresponding percentages for these institutions had grown to over 31 percent for the period 1885–1896. For the years 1894 and 1895, the figures rose to just over 40 percent. . . .

Drs. Baer and Laquer report that in the asylums for the insane in Prussia, in the years 1880–1883, the proportion of alcoholics among the male patients was 30 to 32 percent. In 1886 the proportion had risen to 35 percent; in 1887 to 37 percent; in 1888 to 40 percent. If cases of congenital idiocy were included in the estimate, the power of alcohol made itself felt, in the last named year, to the extent of 45.5 percent. The reports of individual asylums of Prussia are not altogether confirmatory. Thus Dr. Nasse, at Sieburg, found alcohol a factor in the causation of insanity among 27 percent of the male patients in the institution; Dr. Jung, in Lebus, places the figures at 25 percent of all admissions; and Dr. Pelham, at Grafenberg, reports 22 percent of male patients in the same category.—*Henry Smith Williams, M. D., L. L. D. . . .*

Liquor Manufacturers and the Workingman

(According to the Last Government Census Report.)

How some of the industries gave employment to working people according to the money invested in the various industries:

The boot and shoe manufacturers employed one person to each $675 invested in the industry.

The hoisery and knit goods manufacturers employed one person to each $950 invested in the industry.

The cotton goods manufacturers employed one person to each $1,522 invested in the industry.

The woolen goods manufacturers employed one person to each $1,749 invested in the industry.

The slaughter and packing industry employed one person to each $2,402 invested in the industry.

The flour and grist mills employed one person to each $5,102 invested in the industry.

The manufacturers of liquor employed one person to each $8,688 invested inthe industry.

The Case of Rochester, N.Y.

Capital invested in breweries	$6,455,000
Capital invested in clothing manufactories	6,150,000
Capital invested in boot and shoe manufactories	3,281,000

From these industries the following table is taken:

	Amount invested.	Men employed.	Wages paid.
Brewers	$6,455,000	434	$ 381,000
Clothing	6,150,000	3,132	1,561,000
Boots and shoes	3,281,000	4,868	2,031,000

From *The Anti-Saloon League Year Book*, 1909.

Further Resources

BOOKS

Blocker, Jack S. Jr., ed. *Alcohol, Reform, and Society: The Liquor Issue In Social Context.* Westport, Conn.: Greenwood Press, 1979.

———, ed. *American Temperance Movements: Cycles of Reform.* Boston: Twayne Publishers, 1989.

Timberlake, James H. *Prohibition and the Progressive Movement.* Cambridge, Mass: Harvard University Press, 1963.

WEBSITES

"Anti-Saloon League." Ohio State University Department of History. Available online at http://prohibition.history.ohio-state.edu/asl/; website home page: http://prohibition.history.ohio-state.edu/ (accessed February 2, 2003).

"Anti-Saloon League 1893–1933." Westernville Public Library. Available online at http://www.wpl.lib.oh.us/AntiSaloon; website home page: http://www.wpl.lib.oh.us/ (accessed February 2, 2003).

From the Old Country

Oral history

By: Walter Mrozowski

Date: c. 1909

Source: Stave, Bruce M., John F. Sutherland, and Aldo Salerno, eds. *From the Old Country: An Oral History of European Migration to America.* New York: Twayne, 1994, 22–23, 26–28.

About the Author: Walter Mrozowski was born in Poland in the late nineteenth century. He immigrated to Germany while in his teens, fought in the Russo-Japanese War (1904–1905), then came to the United States a few years later, seeking, like many other immigrants, a better life in a new land. ■

Introduction

Prior to the passage of laws restricting immigration to the United States in 1924, America had a virtual open door for European immigrants. The underlying motive of the immigrants was usually economic. If America was not actually viewed as a land where the streets were paved with gold, it was, nonetheless, perceived by most immigrants to be a land of economic opportunity.

The economic motivation varied. In some cases, immigrants were reasonably well off—middle-class professionals, solid working-class people, and independent farmers. Their goal was not to escape poverty but to better themselves. They were ambitious and considered the United States to be a place where they could rise up the economic scale and achieve far more financially than they could at home.

At the other end of the spectrum were the "wretched poor" who fled abject poverty. These sought not wealth, but survival. The Irish who left their country during the famine years in the mid-1840s are an example. So, too, were many peasant farmers who fled Poland, Italy, Russia and other eastern and southern European countries. Overpopulation, consolidation of farms into ever larger land holdings, foreign competition, and increasing mechanization were factors that made remaining in the ancient villages of their ancestors untenable.

In addition to the economic forces, a variety of other factors came into play. Religious oppression drove Jews from Russia. Swedes fed up with the influence of the Lutheran Church or Italians tired of the overbearing Catholic Church left for America. Poles, their country divided since the 1790s between the Russian, German, and Austrian Empires, were treated as second-class citizens, particularly by the Germans and the Russians. Faced with universal conscription throughout Europe, young men often left to avoid being drafted.

There were also those who left for adventure. Bored with the monotony of small village life and hating the drudgery of farming, they saw America as a land of new experiences.

So they left. Attracted by steamship lines selling cheap passage or American railroads promising cheap land along their rail lines, or lured by agents of factories or industrial associations—desperate, bored and/or ambitious Europeans boarded ships in Bremen or Liverpool or Genoa confident of high wages. Convinced by the letters of relatives who had already left that there was at least hope in America, they saved to buy a ticket to the promised land.

Significance

There was an ebb and flow to the migration to America. It was impacted by events in Europe, such as the Irish potato famine and the European revolutions of 1848, Bismarck's Kulturkampf that forced out thousands of German Catholics in the 1880s, and, beginning in the 1880s, Russian pogroms that attempted to make Jews the scapegoats for the various ills confronting the Czar's government.

On the American side of the Atlantic, depressions (1837, 1857, 1873, and 1893) and the Civil War (1861–1865) brought immigration to temporary standstills. In good times, Europeans came by the tens of thousands, then by the hundreds of thousands. From 1907 to 1914, more than 1 million people entered the country each year.

Landing at Ellis Island, many immigrants remained in New York, entering the garment trade. But many others moved on. They went to the coal fields of Pennsylvania or West Virginia. They went to Pittsburgh and made steel or to Detroit and made automobiles. They worked in the copper mines in Calumet, Michigan, and the iron mines of Hibbing, Minnesota. They slaughtered hogs and cattle in the Chicago meat packing plants of the Swift Company. They worked as farm hands in the wheat and corn fields of the Midwest and the copper and silver mines of the Rocky Mountains.

They often settled in neighborhoods occupied by others of their nationality. Irish, Poles, Italians, and Jews established communities within the great cities. Poor and often unwelcome in the mainstream community, many first- and second-generation immigrants remained within these enclaves their entire lives. There they clung to some of the traditions of the homeland, while their children, wishing to be accepted in America, often resented the old ways.

Primary Source

From the Old Country [excerpt]

SYNOPSIS: Walter Mrozowski's parents were relatively prosperous Polish farmers. His primary goal

Immigrants to the United States from around the world stand in line at Ellis Island, New York, waiting to begin immigration proceedings. STATUE OF LIBERTY NATIONAL MONUMENT / AP/WIDE WORLD PHOTOS. REPRODUCED BY PERMISSION.

in immigrating to America seems to have been to escape the drudgery of farm life. At 16 he left home for Germany. Later he volunteered in the Russian Army during the Russo-Japanese War (1904–1905). His story, while uniquely individual, also reflects the experience of thousands of immigrants who attempted to establish a better life in an unfamiliar country and culture.

I was born in Poland on a farm near Ludz. It was about like Fairfield and Bridgeport, four or five miles apart. My parents had eight children, five boys and three daughters. I was the fifth child. There were two kinds of people in Poland, poor people and rich people. My parents happened to be what you would call "rich." My father had a good business and made money. He had farms and raised vegetables which he sold in the markets of the city. He was also a butcher and he ran a restaurant. He used to make trips into Russia to buy wild horses. He would bring them back to his farm and train them and then sell them.

All children in the family got good educations. My father could afford it. Public schools were few and some of them were miles away from the farms. I did not go to a public school. My parents decided I should go to a private school and I did. I had to live at the school, but went home on holidays. Also the professor used to take us on trips and show us the fields and forests and tell us how they grew.

I liked to go on these trips. I learned a lot that helped me later on when I left home. The professor was kind to every child. My parents were glad when I got through with school. I went right back to the farms and helped out along with the other children. When I left school I had not made up my mind what I would like to do. But I knew I did not want to stay on the farms all of my life. I wanted to see the world.

I stayed on the farms about two years. Then I made up my mind to leave. I went to Germany. I was 16 years old at the time. I was only a boy. I had some luck when I got to Germany, more than I looked for. I met a man who was a major in the army. He asked me what I was doing and I told him I had just come from Poland. He took a liking to me. He asked me if I knew anything about forests and I told him I did. We had a long talk and it wound up with him hiring me.

He sent me to his farm and told me I was to have charge of 13 persons, 7 girls and 6 boys. I thought I was pretty young for such a job, but I was out to make a living and took it. We were to plant a forest. The man agreed to pay me one penny for every section we planted. I paid each of the workers one-half a penny each. They were satisfied and I made some money. The work for me was not hard. I used a string and measured the distance from one hole to another, where shrubs should be planted. I liked the work and remained in the farm about two and one-half years. That experience proved I could make money, good money, if I tried hard.

Russia went to war with Japan and I got an idea I would like to fight, so I joined the Russian army. I went as a volunteer and I was with the army for more than a year. Then I got out. It was the kind of work I did not like. I felt when I joined it would be good fun, but I did not have much fun while I carried a gun and wore a uniform. I got all I wanted of war. I don't know how many Japs I shot. All I know was I kept shooting and never got shot myself.

After I got out of the Russian army I went back to Germany. I went to the man for whom I had worked before the war and asked him for a job. He liked my work when I was with him before, so he hired me again. I was glad to get back to the forests and away from gunfire. I worked for the man about a year. I was 21 years old at the time, still a young man. After leaving the job I went back to my father's farm and stayed there about two years. But I had lost interest in farm life and wanted to get away from it. The longer I stayed on the farm, the more I wanted to get away. And I did. I decided I would go to America. . . .

I decided I would go to America. I had heard about the United States and what a grand country it was. I had enough money to pay my way over, so I went to Hamburg and got passage. I went on board the *President Lincoln.* I was leaving my homeland and relatives, but I had made up my mind. Nothing could stop me from seeing the United States. Anyway, after the boat headed for this country, I knew I had to go along with it.

As I could speak German, I met a man on the boat who spoke that language. He asked me if I had an address of someone in the United States. I told him "No." He said I would have to have one when I landed or I couldn't get off the boat. I did not know what to do. I did not know anyone in the United States. So he helped me out. He gave me an address of a woman. I found out later it was the address of his sister in New York. I did not go to her. She did not know me.

So when the boat landed in New York I found there were two classes of people: the poor ones and the ones who looked like they had some money and were dressed that way. I was among those who looked like I had money, so I had no trouble getting off the boat.

Do you know when I left the boat I had only $10 in my pocket. I was in a new world with but a few dollars. But I said to myself, "Walter, you have got to get a job, you are far away from home." I kept my courage up. I had to. There was no one to help me. I was a young fellow with no relatives or friends I could call on. It was a tough spot I was in, but I made up my mind I would make the best of it. I could not go back to Poland as I did not have the money to buy my ticket. So I walked around New York for the rest of the day. As night came on, I felt tired and sleepy but I knew I could not spend any money for a hotel room.

I thought things over again. I said, "Walter, you have got to hang on to that $10 or the best part of it—it's all you have." So I kept walking and finally found myself where there were some freight cars. I walked along and saw one with the door open. I looked in and saw it was empty. I said to myself, "This is where I sleep tonight and save my money." So I got in and went over in the corner and lay down. I was soon asleep. I don't know how long I slept, but I woke up and found the train was moving. And it was going at a fast clip. So I decided to stay in the car and wait until the train stopped. I stayed awake for an hour or so and then went back to sleep. No one bothered me. I got a good rest and in the morning I was all ready to leave my hotel.

The train did stop and I left the car. I went into the town. I still had the best part of my $10 in my pocket. I did not know anyone. I saw a man who looked like a foreigner and I went up to him and spoke in German. He understood me. I told him I had just gotten off a freight train and did not know where I was. "You're in Torrington, Connecticut," he said. That did not mean anything to me. I told the man I wanted a job. He could not help me. So I sat around for about two weeks, that is when I was not going to some factory looking for work. I found my money was getting low and knew I had to do something pretty quick. I went to one factory every day, and I guess the man got tired seeing me every day and he decided to put me to work. I asked him what kind of work I would do and he said I was to sweep the floor and make myself useful in anything they wanted me to do.

Before I went to work, my boss sent me downtown with a man to get some overalls, shoes, and other things I would need in the work. I tell you, I felt like a fellow who had come into some money. I had heard about a Santa Claus and now I knew that there was one. But still I had very little money, not enough to get a room, so I slept on the floor of the factory. And I was glad to get such a place. I went along at the sweeping business for a while, and one day the boss said he was going to put me in the machine shop. He said he liked me and wanted to help me. So I went into the machine shop and helped around the machines.

The boss told the men in the shop to help me all they could, and they did. I stayed with the factory for about five years, and when I got through I was a toolmaker. But I did not know much about the English language, and while working in the factory I made up my mind to go to school. I went to night school for three winter sessions. I learned something about reading, writing, and arithmetic, and I want to tell you it did me a lot of good.

Further Resources

BOOKS

Clarke, Duncan. *A New World: The History of Immigration into the United States.* San Diego, Calif.: Thunder Bay, 2000.

Coan, Peter Morton. *Ellis Island Interviews: In Their Own Words.* New York: Facts on File, 1997.

Daniels, Roger. *Not Like Us: Immigrants and Minorities in America, 1890–1924.* Chicago: Ivan R. Dee, 1997.

Handlin, Oscar. *The Uprooted: The Epic Story of the Great Migrations That Made the American People.* Boston: Little, Brown, 1951.

WEBSITES

"American Family Immigration History Center Passenger Records Fact Sheet." The Statue of Liberty-Ellis Island Foundation, Inc. Available online at http://www.ellisisland.org/Eiinfo/Press_PASSENGER.asp; website home page: http://www.ellisisland.org/ (accessed January 29, 2003).

"Immigration and the United States—Four Periods of Immigration to America." Available online at http://americanhistory.about.com/cs/immigration/; website home page: http://americanhistory.about.com/mbody.htm (accessed January 29, 2003).

Ohio Electric Railway "The Way to Go"

Pamphlet

By: The Ohio Electric Railway Company

Date: February 1910

Source: The Ohio Electric Railway Company. *Ohio Electric Railway "The Way to Go."* Cincinnati: Roessler Brothers, 1910.

About the Organization: The Ohio Electric Railway Company, formed in 1907 with the consolidation of 14 smaller interurban railways, was one of Ohio's largest interurban systems. It connected Toledo, Lima, Dayton, Columbus, and Cincinnati, providing efficient passenger service to scores of small towns in western Ohio. The line evolved into the Cincinnati and Lake Erie Railroad and expanded its services. However, business conditions of the 1930s led to the complete replacement of interurbans with buses by 1939. The company changed its name to Cincinnati & Lake Erie Transportation, and it was absorbed by the Greyhound system in 1947. ■

Introduction

Interurbans were electric-powered trains. From the early 1890s until the 1950s, they provided fast, efficient, middle-distance transportation (usually less than 40 miles) for millions of riders each year. Although some were pulled by freight engines, most interurbans were self-propelled passenger cars, the largest of which were comparable to standard railroad passenger cars both in design and (nearly) in size. Initially, however, they were simply somewhat larger and more powerful versions of their ancestor, the electric streetcar.

The first streetcars were horse-drawn cars on rails in the 1830s. In the mid-1880s, electric motor technology developed sufficiently to enable motors to replace the horse. The transition to electric power was rapid and completed within a decade.

Eventually, streetcar companies began to extend beyond city limits, connecting nearby cities by electric trolley. In 1896, another technological breakthrough made the required low-voltage electric current available over long distances. With this innovation, the interurban age began.

Although the United States had an outstanding railroad system, railroads were designed for moving freight over long distances. Passenger service, while similarly effective for transporting people over long distances, was inefficient for shorter trips.

Built for hauling large loads of freight, powerful and heavy steam locomotives required expensive track systems. Locomotives were slow to start and required a long distance to stop. They were most effective when they were able to get up to speed and maintain that speed for hours on end. Because of their pulling capacity and cost, it was impractical to run a large number of trains carrying small loads. Even the busiest lines ran passenger trains relatively infrequently. This setup was efficient for freight but hardly convenient for passengers.

The interurban cars overcame many of these impediments. Built primarily for passenger service, they did not haul great loads nor were they nearly as heavy. This meant that the track bed did not need to be as elaborate, and track could be built quickly and at much less expense. The interurbans could stop in relatively short distances, load/unload, and be back up to speed (often 50–60 miles per hour) very quickly. As the interurbans were self-propelled, even lines with only a few cars could run service far more frequently than traditional railroads. In addition, given the relatively modest cost of construction and operation, lines could be built providing smaller population centers with access to rapid transportation.

Significance

By 1918, more than 18,000 miles of interurban track had been laid across the country. Reflecting the modest investment required, there were more than 500 interurban companies serving primarily local needs. Despite the decentralized ownership, the interurbans overlapped and, at least in the northeast, provided a fairly continuous service. It was possible, for example, to ride interurbans from New York to St. Louis, except for a brief gap in western Pennsylvania.

Nearly 40 percent of the interurban track was laid in the five Great Lakes states of Ohio, Indiana, Illinois, Wisconsin, and Michigan. The relatively flat terrain, combined with a mixed economy of industry and agriculture and a large number of small, medium, and large urban centers, made the interurban ideally suited to the region and an excellent solution to the problem of moving people quickly, cheaply, and efficiently.

Despite these advantages, the interurbans had a relatively brief existence. By 1920, the interurban had passed its peak. Automobiles and buses had become the transportation method of choice for Americans, providing even greater flexibility to travelers. Interurban track was cut nearly in half by 1930, and the Great Depression proved fatal for most of the remaining lines. A few well-positioned lines continued to operate until the 1950s, usually as commuter routes serving large cities or as local freight carriers.

Further Resources

BOOKS

Blake, Henry Williams, and Walter Jackson. *Electric Railway Transportation.* New York: McGraw-Hill, 1917.

Harwood, Herbert H., and Robert S. Korach. *The Lake Shore Electric Railway Story.* Bloomington: Indiana University Press, 2000.

Yepsen, Roger. *City Trains: Moving Through America's Cities by Rail.* New York: Macmillan, 1993.

WEBSITES

Bell, Jon. "The Last Interurbans." Available online at http://web.presby.edu/~jtbell/transit/last-interurbans.html; website home page: http://web.presby.edu/~jtbell/transit/ (accessed February 3, 2003).

Calvert, J.B. "Interurbans." Available online at http://www.du.edu/~jcalvert/railway/trolley.htm; website home page: http://www.du.edu/~jcalvert/railway/railhom.htm#elec (accessed February 3, 2003).

Vandervoot, Bill. "Chicago Interurbans." Available online at http://hometown.aol.com/metrafan/interurb.html (accessed February 3, 2003).

Primary Source

Ohio Electric Railway Schedule, Front Cover

(1 OF 4)

SYNOPSIS: Ohio had more miles of interurban track than any other state in the country. The Ohio Electric Rail Company provided interurban transportation for much of western Ohio. Operating out of two main hubs, Lima and Dayton, the main routes paralleled I-75 and I-70. (I-70 follows the route of the old National Road.) In addition to a map and general operating information, the brochure provides schedule information for the Cincinnati–Dayton run. This is the front cover of the train schedule. TOLEDO-LUCAS COUNTY PUBLIC LIBRARY. REPRODUCED BY PERMISSION.

MAP OF THE OHIO ELECTRIC RY.

AND CONNECTIONS

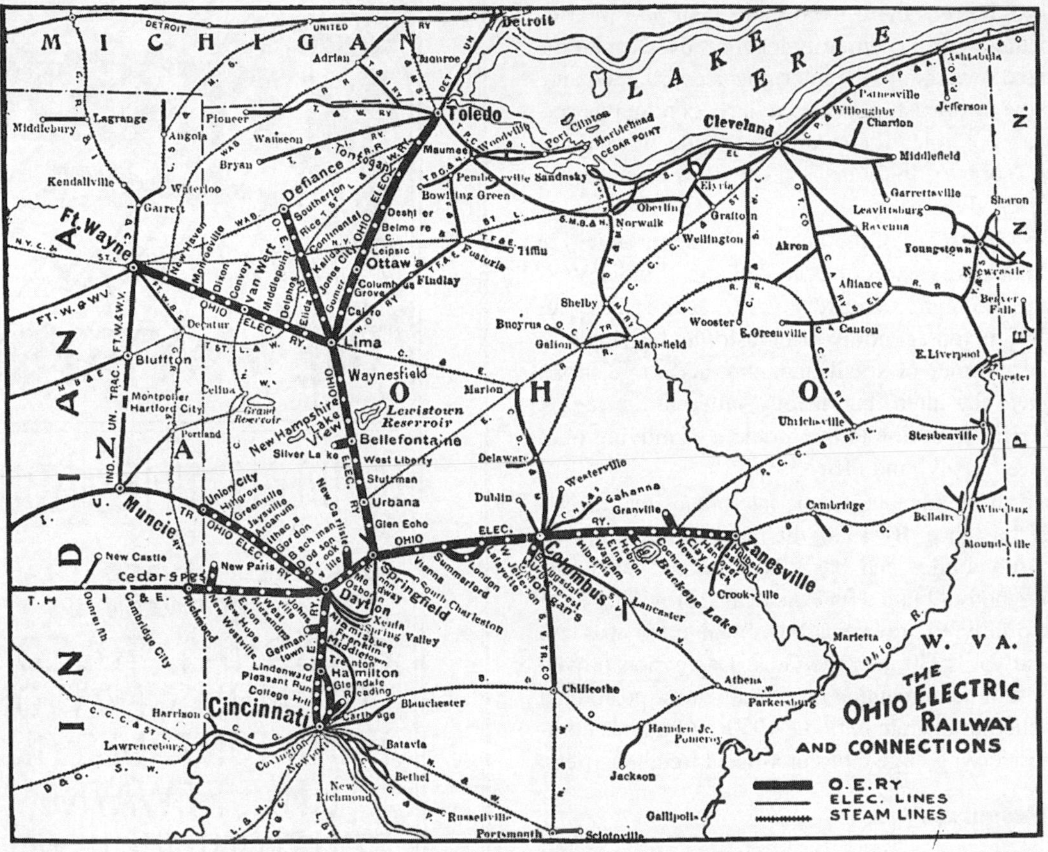

NEW THROUGH LIMITED

DAILY BETWEEN

LIMA and COLUMBUS

Leave Lima	7:10 A. M.	Leave Columbus . . .	4:40 P. M.
Arrive Columbus . . .	10:40 A. M.	Arrive Lima	8:10 P. M.

THE ONLY LINE WITH THROUGH SERVICE BETWEEN THESE POINTS.

THE OHIO ELECTRIC RAILWAY COMPANY E

ROESSLER BROS., 528 WALNUT ST., CINCINNATI

Primary Source

Ohio Electric Railway Schedule, Page Two (2 OF 4)

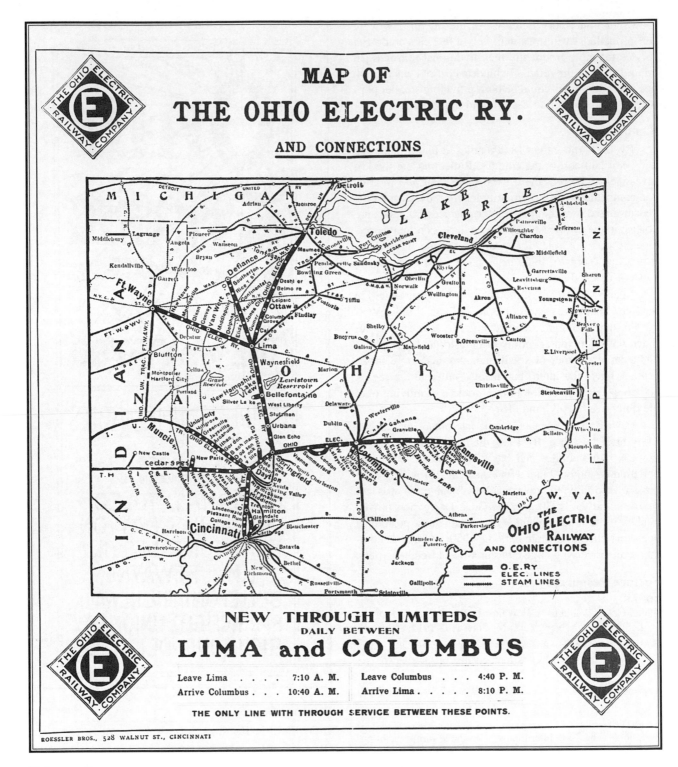

Page two of an Ohio Electric Railway schedule from February 1910. This route map shows the Ohio Electric's many lines and stations, as well as junctions with other railroads.

Connections

Connections are made with other traction lines as shown below:

COLUMBUS, O.

COLUMBUS, DELAWARE & MARION RY.

Trains leave for Marion 6:30 a. m. and hourly until 7:30 p. m.; 8:40 p. m.; for Delaware 9:30, 10:30, 11:30 p. m.

Trains arrive from Marion 8:25 a. m. and hourly until 11:25 p. m.; from Delaware 7:25 a. m.

SCIOTO VALLEY TRACTION CO.

Trains leave for Lancaster 6:00 a. m. and hourly until 7:00 p. m.; 9:00 and 11:25 p. m. For Chillicothe 6:30 a. m. and hourly until 9:30 p. m.; 11:30 p. m.

Trains arrive from Lancaster 6:35, 7:40, 8:50 a. m. and hourly until 10:50 p. m.; 12:15 a. m. From Chillicothe 8:20 a. m. and hourly until 11:20 p. m.; 12:15 a. m.

DAYTON, O.

DAYTON & TROY ELECTRIC RY.

Trains leave for Troy and Piqua 6:30 a. m. and hourly until 11:30 p. m. Limited trains 7:10 a. m. and every two hours until 9:10 p. m.

Trains arrive 7:22 a. m. and hourly until 11:22 p. m.; 12:10 a. m. Limited trains 9:25 a. m. and every two hours until 11:25 p. m.

DAYTON, COVINGTON & PIQUA TRACTION CO.

Trains leave for Piqua 6:00 a. m. and hourly until 9:00 p. m.; 10:00 and 11:00 p. m. to West Milton.

Trains arrive 7:45 a. m. and hourly until 10:45 p. m.

DAYTON & XENIA TRACTION CO.

Trains leave for Xenia 6:00 a. m. and hourly until 11:00 p. m.

Trains arrive 6:55 a. m. and hourly until 11:55 p. m.

FRANKLIN, O.

LEBANON & FRANKLIN TRACTION CO.

FT. WAYNE, IND.

FT. W. & W. V. TRACTION CO.

Trains leave for Wabash, Peru, Logansport and Lafayette 6:00 a. m. and every two hours until 2:00 p. m.; 4:30, 6:00 7:30, 9:00 p. m. to Logansport. Limiteds 7:20 a. m., 1:20 and 3:30 p. m. Limiteds for Wabash, Peru, Kokomo and Indianapolis leave 7:20, 9:20 a. m., 1:20, 5:40 p. m.

Trains arrive 10:45 a. m., 1:15, 3:15, 5:45, 7:15, 8:45, 10:45 p. m.; 7:45 a. m. from Wabash; 9:15 a. m. from Logansport. Indianapolis limiteds arrive 11:40 a. m., 3:40, 11:30 p. m.

Trains leave for Bluffton 7:15 a. m. and every two hours until 7:15 p. m.; 11:15 p. m. Limiteds for Hartford City, Muncie, Anderson and Indianapolis leave 6:20, 8:20, 10:20 a. m., 2:20, 6:20, 8:20 p. m.; 10:20 p. m. to Muncie.

Trains arrive 6:50, 7:03, 9:05 a. m. and every two hours until 9:05 p. m. Indianapolis limiteds arrive 9:30 a. m., 1:30, 5:30, 7:30, 9:30, 11:30 p. m.

FT. WAYNE & SPRINGFIELD RY.

Trains leave for Decatur 7:00 a. m. and every 1½ hours until 8:30 p. m., 11:00 p. m.

Trains arrive 6:55, 8:15 a. m. and every 1½ hours until 8:15 p. m., 10:45 p. m.

TOLEDO & CHICAGO INT. RY.

Trains leave for Kendallville and Waterloo 6:08 a. m. and every hour until 11:08 p. m.

Trains arrive 6:52 a. m. and every hour until 11:52 p. m.

HAMILTON, O.

OHIO TRACTION CO.

LIMA, O.

WESTERN OHIO RY.

Trains arrive from Wapakoneta, St. Marys and Celina and leave for Bluffton and Findlay 6:35 a. m., 9:22 a. m. and every two hours until 7:22 p. m.; 12:00 night to Bluffton.

Trains arrive from Findlay and Bluffton and leave for Wapakoneta, St. Marys and Celina 7:34 a. m. and every two hours until 5:34 p. m., 7:34 to Wapakoneta, 10:35 p. m. to St. Marys.

RICHMOND, IND.

T. H., I. & E. TR. CO.

Trains leave for Indianapolis 6:00, 8:00, 10:00, 11:00 a. m., 12:00 noon, 1:00, 3:00, 4:00, 7:30 p. m. Limiteds leave 7:25, 9:25 a. m., 2:25, 5:25, 8:40 p. m.

Trains arrive 9:30, 11:30 a. m., 1:30, 2:30, 3:30, 4:30, 6:30, 7:30, 10:50 p. m. Limiteds arrive 9:55, 11:55 a. m.; 4:55, 7:55, 11:15 p. m. See schedule for Dayton-Indianapolis through limited trains.

SPRINGFIELD, O.

S. T. & P. TR. CO.

Trains leave 5:00, 5:45, 6:40 a. m. and hourly until 10:40 p. m.

Trains arrive 6:00, 7:20 a. m. and hourly until 12:20 a. m.

SPRINGFIELD & XENIA RY.

Trains leave Springfield and Xenia 6:00 a. m. and hourly until 7:00 p. m.; 9:00, 11:00 p. m. Saturdays 5:00 a. m. until 11:00 p. m. Sundays 6:00 a. m. until 11:00 p. m.

TOLEDO, O.

DET., MON. & TOL. RY.; L. S. ELEC. RY.; TOL. & IND. RY.; TOL. & WEST. R. R.; T. P. C. & L. RY., TOL. U. & I. RY.

UNION CITY, IND.

INDIANA UNION TR. CO.

Trains leave 5:00, 6:35, 7:35, 8:35, 9:35, 10:35, 11:35 a. m., 12:35, 1:35, 2:35, 3:35, 4:35, 5:35, 6:35, 7:45, 9:48, 11:00 p. m.

Trains arrive 6:20, 7:25, 8:05, 9:05, 10:05, 11:05 a. m., 12:05, 1:05, 2:05, 3:05, 4:05, 5:05, 6:05, 7:30, 9:15, 10:35 p. m., 12:35 a. m.

THE OHIO ELECTRIC RY.

General Information

TIME.

The time herein is subject to change without notice and is not guaranteed, nor does The Ohio Electric Railway hold itself responsible for omissions or errors in time given herein.

RATES FOR CHILDREN.

Children under five years of age, in charge of a competent person, will be carried free. Children over five and under twelve years of age, will be charged half rates; over twelve, full rates.

BAGGAGE.

Baggage not exceeding 150 pounds in weight checked free on one full ticket and 75 pounds on one half ticket. No baggage will be checked free where the one way fare is less than 25 cents.

Where the fare is less than 25 cents, agents will check baggage under the rule by collecting the difference between the ticket fare and 25 cents.

No single piece of baggage weighing over 250 pounds will be checked.

Baggage consists of wearing apparel or personal effects necessary for use and comfort of passengers, and may be checked in trunks, valises, satchels, suit cases, boxes roped, with handles.

Sample cases, tool chests, pack and whip cases are not baggage, and when checked it is done as a matter of courtesy, and this Company will not be responsible for any loss or damage to contents, reserving the right to refer such passengers to the Express Department.

EXCESS BAGGAGE.

Excess weight will be charged for at regular tariff rates, which are about sixteen percent of ticket rates per 100 pounds.

BICYCLES—Bicycles will be checked free under the rules governing Free Baggage to points wholly within the State of Ohio, where fare is 25 cents or more. To other points charge will be made same as for 100 pounds of excess baggage.

GO-CARTS—Go-carts, folded, in charge of owner, will be carried free.

DOGS—Dogs, when accompanied by owner or caretaker, and provided with strong collar and chain, will be transported in baggage compartment of cars at owner's risk only. Charge will be the full, regular fare with minimum charge of 25 cents and maximum charge of 50 cents between any two points on this line. To obtain the benefit of this rate over two or more divisions, tickets must be purchased at ticket office.

PARTY AND EXCURSION RATES—Rates for parties of ten or more, or for excursions, will be made on application to nearest Ticket Agent.

CHARTERED CARS—Cars for special parties furnished on short notice at reasonable rates.

MILEAGE AND COUPON BOOKS—C. E. T. A. Interchangeable 1,000-Mile Book, $17.50. This book is now on sale. It is good over all divisions of this Company, and also twenty-four lines in Ohio and Indiana, for bearer, or two or more persons traveling together.

350-MILE BOOK—Good over division for which sold, for bearer, or two or more persons traveling together.

COUPON BOOK, $1.00—22 five-cent coupons, good anywhere on the line.

The above are on sale at all ticket offices.

INTERLINE TICKETS—Through tickets to all Ohio and Indiana Interurban points may be purchased at ticket offices and baggage checked thereon to destination.

Through tickets to Western Points via Wabash Railroad on sale at stations on The Lima-Fort Wayne Division.

DISPUTES.

Agents and conductors are governed by the rules of this Company. In cases of disputes with them, it is always best to pay the fare requested and refer the matter to the General Passenger Agent, who will promptly investigate and adjust any differences.

Full information in regard to tickets, rates, routes and connections will be given and folders furnished on application to nearest Ticket Agent, or by addressing

ALFRED KOCH, Dis. Pass. and Frt. Agent,
111 East Third street, Dayton, Ohio.
'Phones, Bell 1796. Home 6798.

F. A. BURKHARDT, Dis. Pass. and Frt. Agent,
16 Public Square, Lima, Ohio.
Both 'Phones 39.

A. G. H. JENSSEN, Dis. Pass. and Frt. Agent,
619 Madison avenue, Toledo, Ohio
'Phones, Bell, Main 4091. Home, Main 1171.

B. B. BELL, Dis. Pass. and Frt. Agent,
39 East Rich Street, Columbus, Ohio.
'Phones, Bell, Main 4041. Home 2265.

W. S. WHITNEY, Gen'l Pass. and Frt. Agent,
Springfield, Ohio.
'Phone, Bell, Main 552.

Primary Source

Ohio Electric Railway Schedule, Page Three (3 OF 4)

Page three of an Ohio Electric Railway schedule from February 1910. This page lists connections with other railroads and the general rules and regulations of the Ohio Electric.

4

THE OHIO ELECTRIC RY.

TABLE No. 1. CINCINNATI-DAYTON DIVISION--Northbound

Mil		*am	*am	*am	*am	*am	*am	*am	*am	*am	*am	*am	*am	*am	*am	*am	*am	
0	Cincinnati ..Lv	....	....	....	....	....	....	==	6 00	....	7 00	....	8 00	8 30	9 00	9 30	10 00	And HALF HOURLY thereafter until
4	College Hill....	....	....	....	....	....	....	5 47	6 17	....	7 17	....	8 17	8 47	9 17	9 47	10 17	
6	Mt. Healthy....	....	....	....	....	....	==	5 52	6 22	....	7 22	==	8 22	8 52	9 22	9 52	10 22	
16	Lindenwald ...	....	....	....	....	....	5 50	6 20	6 50	....	7 50	8 20	8 50	9 20	9 50	10 20	10 50	
18	Hamilton	==	==	==	==	==	6 00	6 30	7 00	==	8 00	8 30	9 00	9 30	10 00	10 30	11 00	
27	Trenton	4 30	4 45	5 00	5 30	6 00	6 30	7 00	7 30	8 00	8 30	9 00	9 30	10 00	10 30	11 00	11 30	
32	Middletown ...	4 45	4 57	5 15	5 45	6 15	6 45	7 15	7 45	8 15	8 45	9 15	9 45	10 15	10 45	11 15	11 45	
38	Franklin	5 05	5 15	5 35	6 05	6 35	7 05	7 35	8 05	8 35	9 05	9 35	10 05	10 35	11 05	11 35	12 05	
40	Chautauqua	5 13	==	5 43	6 13	6 43	7 13	7 43	8 13	8 43	9 13	9 43	10 13	10 43	11 13	11 43	12 13	
44	Miamisburg ...	5 25	....	5 55	6 25	6 55	7 25	7 55	8 25	8 55	9 25	9 55	10 25	10 55	11 25	11 55	12 25	
47	W. Carrollton..	5 34	....	6 04	6 34	7 04	7 34	8 04	8 34	9 04	9 34	10 04	10 34	11 04	11 34	12 04	12 34	
48	Alexandersville	5 35	....	6 05	6 35	7 05	7 35	8 05	8 35	9 05	9 35	10 05	10 35	11 05	11 35	12 05	12 35	
55	Dayton ......Ar	5 58	....	6 28	6 58	7 28	7 58	8 28	8 58	9 28	9 58	10 28	10 58	11 28	11 58	12 28	12 58	
		am	am	am	am	am	am	am	am	am	am	am	am	am	am	pm	pm	

Mil		*pm	*pm	*pm	*pm	*pm	*pm	*pm	*pm	*pm	*pm	*pm	*pm	*pm	*am
0	Cincinnati ..Lv	3 30	4 00	4 30	5 00	5 30	6 00	6 30	7 00	7 30	8 00	9 00	10 00	11 00	12 20
4	College Hill....	3 47	4 17	4 47	5 17	5 47	6 17	6 47	7 17	7 47	8 17	9 17	10 17	11 17	12 34
6	Mt. Healthy....	3 52	4 22	4 52	5 22	5 52	6 22	6 52	7 22	7 52	8 22	9 22	10 22	11 22	12 39
16	Lindenwald ...	4 20	4 50	5 20	5 50	6 20	6 50	7 20	7 50	8 20	8 50	9 50	10 50	11 50	1 02
18	Hamilton	4 30	5 00	5 30	6 00	6 30	7 00	7 30	8 00	8 30	9 00	10 00	11 00	12 00	1 10
27	Trenton	5 00	5 30	6 00	6 30	7 00	7 30	8 00	8 30	==	9 30	10 30	11 30	12 30	==
32	Middletown ...	5 15	5 45	6 15	6 45	7 15	7 45	8 15	8 45	....	9 45	10 45	11 45	12 45	....
38	Franklin	5 35	6 05	6 35	7 05	7 35	8 05	==	9 05	....	10 05	11 05	12 05	==	....
40	Chautauqua	5 43	6 13	6 43	7 13	7 43	8 13	....	9 13	....	10 13	11 13	==	....	....
44	Miamisburg ...	5 55	6 25	6 55	7 25	7 55	8 25	....	9 25	....	10 25	11 25	....	....	....
47	W. Carrollton..	6 04	6 34	7 04	7 34	8 04	8 34	....	9 34	....	10 34	11 34	....	....	....
48	Alexandersville	6 05	6 35	7 05	7 35	8 05	8 35	....	9 35	....	10 35	11 35	....	....	....
55	Dayton ......Ar	6 28	6 58	7 28	7 58	8 28	8 58	....	9 58	....	10 58	11 58	....	....	....
		pm	pm	pm	pm	pm	pm	pm	pm	pm	pm	pm	am	am	am

SOUTHBOUND

Mil		*am	*am	*am	*am	*am	*am	*am	*am	*am	*am	*am	*am	*am	*am	
0	Dayton Lv	....	....	....	....	6 00	6 30	7 00	7 30	8 00	8 30	9 00	9 30	10 00	10 30	And HALF HOURLY thereafter until
7	Alexandersville	....	....	....	....	6 24	6 54	7 24	7 54	8 24	8 54	9 24	9 54	10 24	10 54	
8	W. Carrollton..	....	....	....	....	6 25	6 55	7 25	7 55	8 25	8 55	9 25	9 55	10 25	10 55	
11	Miamisburg ...	....	....	....	....	6 35	7 05	7 35	8 05	8 35	9 05	9 35	10 05	10 35	11 05	
15	Chautauqua ...	....	....	==	==	6 46	7 16	7 46	8 16	8 46	9 16	9 46	10 16	10 46	11 16	
17	Franklin	....	==	5 25	5 55	6 55	7 25	7 55	8 25	8 55	9 25	9 55	10 25	10 55	11 25	
23	Middletown ...	....	5 15	5 45	6 30	7 15	7 45	8 15	8 45	9 15	9 45	10 15	10 45	11 15	11 45	
28	Trenton	==	5 30	6 00	6 45	7 30	8 00	8 30	9 00	9 30	10 00	10 30	11 00	11 30	12 00	
37	Hamilton	5 00	6 00	6 30	7 15	8 00	8 30	9 00	9 30	10 00	10 30	11 00	11 30	12 00	12 30	
39	Lindenwald ...	5 10	6 10	6 40	7 25	8 10	8 40	9 10	9 40	10 10	10 40	11 10	11 40	12 10	12 40	
49	Mt. Healthy....	5 35	6 37	7 07	7 52	8 37	9 07	9 37	10 07	10 37	11 07	11 37	12 07	12 37	1 07	
51	College Hill....	5 40	6 42	7 12	7 57	8 42	9 12	9 42	10 12	10 42	11 12	11 42	12 12	12 42	1 12	
55	Cincinnati ..Ar	5 55	6 55	7 25	8 10	8 55	9 25	9 55	10 25	10 55	11 25	11 55	12 25	12 55	1 25	
		am	am	am	am	am	am	am	am	am	am	am	pm	pm	pm	

Mil		*pm	*pm	*pm	*pm	*pm	*pm	*pm	*pm	*pm	*pm	*pm	*pm	*pm	*pm	*am	*pm
0	Dayton Lv	3 30	4 00	4 30	5 00	5 30	6 00	6 30	7 00	7 30	8 00	8 30	9 00	10 00	11 00	....	12 00
7	Alexandersville	3 54	4 24	4 54	5 24	5 54	6 24	6 54	7 24	7 54	8 24	8 54	9 24	10 24	11 24	....	12 24
8	W. Carrollton..	3 55	4 25	4 55	5 25	5 55	6 25	6 55	7 25	7 55	8 25	8 55	9 25	10 25	11 25	....	12 25
11	Miamisburg ...	4 05	4 35	5 05	5 35	6 05	6 35	7 05	7 35	8 05	8 35	9 05	9 35	10 35	11 35	....	12 35
15	Chautauqua ...	4 16	4 46	5 16	5 46	6 16	6 46	7 16	7 46	8 16	8 46	9 16	9 46	10 46	11 46	==	12 46
17	Franklin	4 25	4 55	5 25	5 55	6 25	6 55	7 25	7 55	8 25	8 55	9 25	9 55	10 55	11 55	12 21	12 55
23	Middletown ...	4 45	5 15	5 45	6 15	6 45	7 15	7 45	8 15	8 45	9 15	9 45	10 15	11 15	12 15	12 45	1 15
28	Trenton	5 00	5 30	6 00	6 30	7 00	7 30	8 00	8 30	9 00	9 30	10 00	10 30	11 30	12 30	1 00	1 30
37	Hamilton	5 30	6 00	6 30	7 00	7 30	8 00	==	9 00	==	10 00	==	11 00	12 00	==	==	==
39	Lindenwald ...	5 40	6 10	6 40	7 10	7 40	8 10	....	9 10	....	10 10	....	11 10	12 10	....	....	....
49	Mt. Healthy....	6 07	6 37	7 07	7 37	==	8 37	....	9 37	....	10 37	....	11 37	==	....	....	....
51	College Hill....	6 12	6 42	7 12	7 42	....	8 42	....	9 42	....	10 42	....	11 42	....	....	....	....
55	Cincinnati ..Ar	6 25	6 55	7 25	7 55	....	8 55	....	9 55	....	10 55	....	11 55	....	....	....	....
		pm	pm	pm	pm	pm	pm	pm	pm	pm	pm	pm	pm	am	am	am	am

Connections at Franklin for Red Lion and Lebanon.
Germantown Trains—Leave Miamisburg 6 05 am, and hourly until 8 05 pm, 9 35, 10 35, 11 35 pm, 12 35 am.
Leave Germantown 5 30 am, and hourly until 7 30 pm, 9 00, 10 00, 11 00 and 12 00 pm. Running Time Twenty-three minutes.

TABLE No. 2. DAYTON-COLUMBUS DIVISION--Eastbound

Mil		†am	*am	*am	*pm	*pm	*am	*am	*am	*am	*am	*am	*am	*am
0	Dayton Lv	7 00		10 00	1 00	4 00	....	....	5 10	6 00	7 30	8 30	9 30	10 30
11	Fairfield	....	LIMA LIMITED	....	....	....	....	....	5 36	6 24	8 04	9 04	10 04	11 04
12	Osborn	....		....	....	....	....	....	5 38	6 26	8 06	9 06	10 06	11 06
15	§Carlisle Jct..............	....		....	....	....	....	....	5 45	6 34	8 13	9 13	10 13	11 13
16	Medway	....		....	....	....	....	....	5 47	6 37	8 15	9 15	10 15	11 15
18	Donnelsville	....		....	....	....	....	....	5 52	6 43	8 21	9 21	10 21	11 21
20	Enon	....		....	....	....	....	....	5 56	6 47	8 25	9 25	10 25	11 25
23	Durbin	....		....	....	....	....	....	6 01	6 53	8 32	9 32	10 32	11 32
27	Springfield ....Ar	7 52	==	10 52	1 52	4 52	....	==	6 15	7 10	8 50	9 50	10 50	11 50
	" Lv	7 55	9 15	10 55	1 55	4 55	....	5 55	6 55	7 55	8 55	9 55	10 55	11 55
33	Harmony	....	....	....	....	....	....	6 10	7 10	8 10	9 10	10 10	11 10	12 10
38	Vienna	....	....	....	....	....	....	6 18	7 18	8 18	9 18	10 18	11 18	12 18
41	Brighton	....	....	....	....	....	....	6 23	7 23	8 23	9 23	10 23	11 23	12 23
44	Summerford	....	....	....	....	....	....	6 30	7 30	8 30	9 30	10 30	11 30	12 30
48	London	....	....	....	....	....	....	6 40	7 40	8 40	9 40	10 40	11 40	12 40
53	Lafayette	....	....	....	....	....	==	6 51	7 51	8 51	9 51	10 51	11 51	12 51
60	▼West Jefferson..........	8f38	10f06	11f38	2f38	5f38	5 35	7 08	8 08	9 08	10 08	11 08	12 08	1 08
65	Alton	....	....	....	....	....	5 46	7 17	8 17	9 17	10 17	11 17	12 17	1 17
67	Rome	....	....	....	....	....	5 51	7 23	8 23	9 23	10 23	11 23	12 23	1 23
76	Columbus ....Ar	9 10	10 40	12 10	3 10	6 10	6 20	7 55	8 55	9 55	10 55	11 55	12 55	1 55
		am	am	pm	pm	pm	am	am	am	am	am	am	pm	pm

Mil		*am	*pm	*pm	*pm	*pm	*pm	*pm	*pm	*pm	*pm	*pm	*pm	*pm
0	Dayton Lv	11 30	12 30	1 30	2 30	3 30	4 30	5 30	6 30	7 30	8 30	9 30	10 30	11 30
11	Fairfield	12 04	1 04	2 04	3 04	4 04	5 04	6 04	7 04	8 04	9 04	10 04	11 04	12 03
12	Osborn	12 06	1 06	2 06	3 06	4 06	5 06	6 06	7 06	8 06	9 06	10 06	11 06	12 05
15	§Carlisle Jct..............	12 13	1 13	2 13	3 13	4 13	5 13	6 13	7 13	8 13	9 13	10 13	11 13	12 11
16	Medway	12 15	1 15	2 15	3 15	4 15	5 15	6 15	7 15	8 15	9 15	10 15	11 15	12 13
18	Donnelsville	12 21	1 21	2 21	3 21	4 21	5 21	6 21	7 21	8 21	9 21	10 21	11 21	12 17
20	Enon	12 25	1 25	2 25	3 25	4 25	5 25	6 25	7 25	8 25	9 25	10 25	11 25	12 20
23	Durbin	12 32	1 32	2 32	3 32	4 32	5 32	6 32	7 32	8 32	9 32	10 32	11 32	12 25
27	Springfield ....Ar	12 50	1 50	2 50	3 50	4 50	5 50	6 50	7 50	8 50	9 50	10 50	11 50	12 40
	" Lv	12 55	1 55	2 55	3 55	4 55	5 55	6 55	7 55	8 55	9 55	10 55	11 55	==
33	Harmony	1 10	2 10	3 10	4 10	5 10	6 10	7 10	8 10	9 10	10 10	11 10	12 10	....
38	Vienna	1 18	2 18	3 18	4 18	5 18	6 18	7 18	8 18	9 18	10 18	11 18	12 18	....
41	Brighton	1 23	2 23	3 23	4 23	5 23	6 23	7 23	8 23	9 23	10 23	11 23	12 23	....
44	Summerford	1 30	2 30	3 30	4 30	5 30	6 30	7 30	8 30	9 30	10 30	11 30	12 30	....
48	London	1 40	2 40	3 40	4 40	5 40	6 40	7 40	8 40	9 40	10 40	11 40	12 40	....
53	Lafayette	1 51	2 51	3 51	4 51	5 51	6 51	7 51	8 51	9 51	10 51	11 51	12 49	....
60	▼West Jefferson..........	2 08	3 08	4 08	5 08	6 08	7 08	8 08	9 08	10 08	11 08	12 07	1 00	....
65	Alton	2 17	3 17	4 17	5 17	6 17	7 17	8 17	9 17	10 17	11 17	12 15	==	....
67	Rome	2 23	3 23	4 23	5 23	6 23	7 23	8 23	9 23	10 23	11 21	12 19	....	....
76	Columbus ....Ar	2 55	3 55	4 55	5 55	6 55	7 55	8 55	9 55	10 55	11 45	12 45	....	....
		pm	pm	pm	pm	pm	pm	pm	pm	pm	pm	am	am	am

WESTBOUND

Mil		†am	*am	*pm	*pm	*pm	*am	*am	*am	*am	*am	*am	*am	*am
0	Columbus Lv	6 40	9 40	12 40	3 40	4 40	....	....	5 00	6 00	7 00	3 00	9 00	10 00
9	Rome	....	....	....	....	....	....	....	5 36	6 36	7 36	3 36	9 36	10 36
11	Alton	....	....	....	....	....	....	....	5 43	6 43	7 43	3 43	9 43	10 43
16	▼West Jefferson..........	7f21	10f21	f1 21	4f21	5f21	....	....	5 53	6 53	7 53	8 53	9 53	10 53
23	Lafayette	....	....	....	....	....	....	....	6 07	7 07	8 07	9 07	10 07	11 07
28	London	....	....	....	....	....	....	....	6 19	7 19	8 19	9 19	10 19	11 19
32	Summerford	....	....	....	....	....	....	==	6 30	7 30	8 30	9 30	10 30	11 30
35	Brighton	....	....	....	....	....	....	5 38	6 37	7 37	8 37	9 37	10 37	11 37
38	Vienna	....	....	....	....	....	....	5 41	6 41	7 41	8 41	9 41	10 41	11 41
43	Harmony	....	....	....	....	....	....	5 49	6 49	7 49	8 49	9 49	10 49	11 49
49	Springfield ....Ar	8 06	11 06	2 06	5 06	6 06	==	6 05	7 05	8 05	9 05	10 05	11 05	12 05
	" Lv	8 10	11 10	2 10	5 10	==	4 55	6 10	7 10	8 10	9 10	10 10	11 10	12 10
53	Durbin	....	....	....	....	LIMA LIMITED	5 07	6 27	7 27	8 27	9 27	10 27	11 27	12 27
56	Enon	....	....	....	....		5 12	6 35	7 35	8 35	9 35	10 35	11 35	12 35
58	Donnelsville	....	....	....	....		5 15	6 39	7 39	8 39	9 39	10 39	11 39	12 39
60	Medway	....	....	....	....		5 19	6 45	7 45	8 45	9 45	10 45	11 45	12 45
61	§Carlisle Jct..............	....	....	....	....		5 20	6 47	7 47	8 47	9 47	10 47	11 47	12 47
64	Osborn	....	....	....	....		5 26	6 53	7 53	8 53	9 53	10 53	11 53	12 53
65	Fairfield	....	....	....	....		5 28	6 56	7 56	8 56	9 56	10 56	11 56	12 56
76	Dayton ....Ar	9 00	12 00	3 00	6 00	....	5 55	7 25	8 25	9 25	10 25	11 25	12 25	1 25
		am	M	pm	pm	pm	am	am	am	am	am	am	pm	pm

Mil		*am	*M	*pm	*pm	*pm	*pm	*pm	*pm	*pm	*pm	*pm	*pm	*pm
0	Columbus Lv	11 00	12 00	1 00	2 00	3 00	4 00	5 00	6 00	7 00	8 00	9 00	10 00	11 15
9	Rome	11 36	12 36	1 36	2 36	3 36	4 36	5 36	6 36	7 36	8 36	9 36	10 36	11 45
11	Alton	11 43	12 43	1 43	2 43	3 43	4 43	5 43	6 43	7 43	8 43	9 43	10 43	11 50
16	▼West Jefferson..........	11 53	12 53	1 53	2 53	3 53	4 53	5 53	6 53	7 53	8 53	9 53	10 53	11 59
23	Lafayette	12 07	1 07	2 07	3 07	4 07	5 07	6 07	7 07	8 07	9 07	10 07	11 07	12 12
28	London	12 19	1 19	2 19	3 19	4 19	5 19	6 19	7 19	8 19	9 19	10 19	11 19	12 22
32	Summerford	12 30	1 30	2 30	3 30	4 30	5 30	6 30	7 30	8 30	9 30	10 30	11 30	12 30
35	Brighton	12 37	1 37	2 37	3 37	4 37	5 37	6 37	7 37	8 37	9 37	10 37	11 37	12 37
38	Vienna	12 41	1 41	2 41	3 41	4 41	5 41	6 41	7 41	8 41	9 41	10 41	11 41	12 41
43	Harmony	12 49	1 49	2 49	3 49	4 49	5 49	6 49	7 49	8 49	9 49	10 49	11 49	12 48
49	Springfield ....Ar	1 05	2 05	3 05	4 05	5 05	6 05	7 05	8 05	9 05	10 05	11 05	12 00	1 00
	" Lv	1 10	2 10	3 10	4 10	5 10	6 10	7 10	8 10	9 10	10 10	11 10	==	==
53	Durbin	1 27	2 27	3 27	4 27	5 27	6 27	7 27	8 27	9 27	10 27	11 27	....	....
56	Enon	1 35	2 35	3 35	4 35	5 35	6 35	7 35	8 35	9 35	10 35	11 35	....	....
58	Donnelsville	1 39	2 39	3 39	4 39	5 39	6 39	7 39	8 39	9 39	10 39	11 39	....	....
60	Medway	1 45	2 45	3 45	4 45	5 45	6 45	7 45	8 45	9 45	10 45	11 45	....	....
61	§Carlisle Jct..............	1 47	2 47	3 47	4 47	5 47	6 47	7 47	8 47	9 47	10 47	11 47	....	....
64	Osborn	1 53	2 53	3 53	4 53	5 53	6 53	7 53	8 53	9 53	10 53	11 53	....	....
65	Fairfield	1 56	2 56	3 56	4 56	5 56	6 56	7 56	8 56	9 56	10 56	11 56	....	....
76	Dayton ....Ar	2 25	3 25	4 25	5 25	6 25	7 25	8 25	9 25	10 25	11 25	12 25	....	....
		pm	pm	pm	pm	pm	pm	pm	pm	pm	pm	am	pm	am

* Daily. † Daily except Sunday. ‡ Saturday only. f Stop on signal. § Close connections at Carlisle Jct. for New Carlisle. ▼ Limited will stop at West Jefferson for passengers to or from Springfield, or points beyond.

Primary Source

Ohio Electric Railway Schedule, Page Four (4 OF 4)

Page four of an Ohio Electric Railway schedule from February 1910. These are the routes and departure times for the Ohio Electric's trains.

Sears, Roebuck Home Builder's Catalog

Architectural designs

By: Sears, Roebuck and Co.

Date: 1910

Source: Sears, Roebuck and Co. *Sears, Roebuck Home Builder's Catalog: The Complete Illustrated 1910 Edition.* New York: Dover Publications, 1990.

About the Organization: Richard W. Sears (1863–1914) founded the R.W. Sears Watch Company, a mail-order business based in Minneapolis, in 1886. Sears moved to Chicago and hired watchmaker Alvah C. Roebuck (1864–1948) in 1887. After selling the watch business, Sears and Roebuck formed a mail-order business selling general merchandise. Their famous catalog carried a broad array of modestly priced goods conveniently available to the country's farmers and villagers for the first time. The automobile, which gave rural customers much greater mobility, caused the company to rethink its sales strategy, and in 1925 Sears opened its first retail store. Within a few years the retail business passed mail-order revenues, and for most of the next fifty years Sears was the nation's largest retailer. ■

Introduction

Housing shortages have been common throughout most of America's history. From the time the first Europeans arrived in the New World and for the next 300 years thereafter, Americans were continually moving west into unsettled territory. Each move required new housing. In a country with a rapidly growing population, housing availability rarely met local needs, even in relatively settled areas.

By the end of the nineteenth century, westward expansion had ended. No longer were Americans and newly arrived immigrants moving into unsettled lands. They were, however, moving into cities and suburbs, creating a new set of housing problems. As industry brought about rapid growth of urban areas, concentrations of people in unprecedented numbers spurred massive housing construction. Between 1900 and 1910, 3.6 million non-farm housing units were built, two-thirds of which were single family homes. Still, construction could not keep pace with demand. Population increased from 76 million to 92 million in the same 10 years while urban population went from 30 million to 42 million people.

One of the innovations to meet the housing need was the development of a prefabricated home industry. The need for moderately priced, quality housing was evident, and by the turn of the century several factors combined to create a new industry that helped meet that need.

First, there was a sophisticated manufacturing infrastructure capable of producing the consistent pre-cut lumber and the other housing components necessary to meet the requirements of a standardized, mass-marketing approach. Second, an extensive railroad network allowed the relatively inexpensive shipping of home building kits to most of the country. Third, by the late nineteenth century, Americans had become accustomed to shopping by catalog. It was an effective advertising system that helped niche manufactures to produce items in large enough quantities to develop significant efficiencies of scale.

By the early 1900s, Sears, Roebuck and Company and other large catalog retailers were selling every product imaginable for the home. Soon they would be selling the home, as well.

Significance

Since the 1820s, home building plans and ideas had been published in a variety of books and magazines. After the Civil War (1861–1865), catalogs of house plans became widely available. They typically displayed exterior drawings and floor plans along with estimated costs of construction. Builders or potential homeowners could acquire general plans for these homes for a relatively modest sum.

The first complete home packages were sold by the Aladdin Company of Bay City, Michigan, in 1906. Inspired by two companies that built prefabricated boats in Bay City, W.J. and Otto E. Sovereign gambled that buildings could be similarly built. Their first success was a modest summer cottage sold in 1906. The next year, strapped for cash, they invested in a single advertisement in the *Saturday Home Journal.* Fortunately, this advertisement landed additional orders, and a new industry was born. By 1911, the Aladdin catalog included 47 house plans and two garages.

It was not long before other packaged home manufacturers entered the market. Sears, Roebuck and Company soon became the largest producer of prefabricated, catalog homes. Sears had been selling a full range of home building materials since 1895, so the expansion to the complete home was easily accomplished. Beginning in 1908 and lasting until 1940, the Sears Modern Homes Department sold approximately 70,000 catalog homes. In addition, Sears built another 30,000–50,000 homes, primarily in the Chicago area, as a traditional contractor.

The homes sold by Sears and others through their catalogs were complete structures, although plumbing, electrical fixtures, and heating components were sometimes extra. Full-size homes were built using pre-cut lumber that could be assembled with little more than a hammer and nails. High volume and sophisticated milling techniques helped control the costs of materials. The prefabricated components kept construction expenses down

4 SEARS, ROEBUCK AND CO., CHICAGO, ILLINOIS.

No. 102

FOR $861.00 we will furnish all the material to build this ten-room house. This price includes mill work, lumber, building paper, eaves troughs, hardware and painting material. By allowing a fair price for labor this house can be built for $1,995.00.

No. 131

FOR $1,420.00 we will furnish all the material to build this thirteen-room, two-family house. This price includes mill work, lumber, building paper, eaves troughs, mantels, hardware, and painting material. By allowing a fair price for labor this house can be built for $3,167.00.

No. 123

FOR $1,073.00 we will furnish all the material to build this nine-room house. This price includes mill work, lumber, building paper, eaves troughs, mantels, hardware and painting material. By allowing a fair price for labor this house can be built for $2,578.00.

No. 111

FOR $879.00 we will furnish all the material to build this nine-room house. This price includes mill work, lumber, building paper, eaves troughs hardware and painting material. By allowing a fair price for labor this house can be built for $2,130.00.

First Floor Plan for No. 102 Modern Home shown above

OUR $100.00 BUILDING PLANS COST YOU NOTHING

AS EXPLAINED ON THE OPPOSITE PAGE.

IN OUR BOOK OF MODERN HOMES we illustrate eighty different styles of houses adapted for city dwellings, suburban homes, country and farm houses; ranging in cost for building from $500.00 to $5,000.00. A few of these are illustrated on this and the opposite page.

OUR PLANS are the work of the best known licensed architects specially engaged by us for this service. They fully investigated the requirements of home builders everywhere in the United States and have embodied in our plans the very latest ideas of the best posted contractors and builders in this country, as well as the very best architects, giving us a variety of houses specially adapted for city, town or farm homes. Ideas and suggestions impossible for you to secure elsewhere at any price.

OUR BUILDING PLANS, specifications and bill of materials, which cost you nothing, as explained on opposite page, include the following:

1—A complete set of working drawings, blue prints, with all details and dimensions plainly marked, drawn to the scale of ¼ inch to the foot, a most convenient scale. They are so accurately drawn and so complete that any mechanic can understand and follow them easily.

FRONT ELEVATION, showing the front view of the house.
RIGHT SIDE ELEVATION, showing the right side view of the house.
LEFT ELEVATION, showing the left side view of the house.
REAR ELEVATION, giving a back view of the house.
LONGITUDINAL PLANS, showing cross section.
FOUNDATION PLANS, giving information with reference to excavation, foundation, etc.
FIRST FLOOR PLANS, with sizes of rooms, partitions, doorways, windows, etc., given in detail.
SECOND FLOOR PLANS (if a two-story structure) giving size of rooms, partitions, location of windows, doors, etc., in detail.

DETAILED DRAWINGS OF MATERIALS, showing stair finish, balusters, style of window trimmings, hardware, porch finish, cornice finish, and all the material necessary to give style and character to the structure inside and out.

2—Complete specifications of material and labor required, outlining all the conditions under which a contract may be let, enabling you to protect your interests perfectly if house is to be built by contract.

3—Complete bill of materials, explaining the cost, quantity and dimensions of timbers required, also the quantity and kind of exterior finishing lumber, porch work, roofing, flooring, window and door frames, doors and windows, inside finishing lumber including all molding, stairwork, etc., building hardware, such as door locks, hinges, cupboard catches, drawer pulls, sash locks, gutters and eaves troughs, glass, paints, varnishes and fillers for outside and inside painting.

COMPARE THE COST ESTIMATES of the houses illustrated on this and the opposite page with the cost of houses erected in your neighborhood during the past five years. Our plans and building material prices enable you to save fully one-third or more.

OUR PLANS AND SPECIFICATIONS CALL FOR THE HIGHEST GRADE MATERIALS AND LABOR.

We specify the best grade of mill work, dimension lumber, hardware and paint, as well as the highest grade workmanship throughout. Our estimates are accurate. We prove them by giving you exact figures on every item. We send you a typewritten bill of materials with our blue print and specifications. We guarantee our prices on lumber, mill work, such as windows, doors, interior trim, flooring, siding, hardware, paint, mantels, plumbing and heating. On these we save you nearly one-half. Write and get our Book of Modern Homes at once.

Second Floor Plan for No. 102 Modern Home shown above

FOR $744.00 we will furnish all the material to build this nine-room concrete block house. This price includes mill work, lumber, hardware and painting material. By allowing a fair price for labor this house can be built for $1,998 00.

No. 52

FOR $873.00 we will furnish all the material to build this eight-room house. This price includes mill work, lumber, building paper, eaves troughs, hardware and painting material. By allowing a fair price for labor this house can be built for $1,790.00.

No. 34

FOR $532.00 we will furnish all the material to build this six-room house. This price includes mill work, lumber, building paper, eaves troughs, hardware and painting material. By allowing a fair price for labor this house can be built for $1,278.00.

No. 103

Primary Source

Sears, Roebuck Home Builder's Catalog

SYNOPSIS: This page is from Sears' third home catalog. Starting with a catalog of 22 home designs in 1908, Sears eventually developed more than 400 home designs ranging from simple two-room cottages to expansive ten-room homes. Designs changed annually, reflecting customer demand. Most catalogs contained 50–70 options for homes, cottages, and other buildings. The designs were not innovative—Sears' strategy was to provide proven styles to the buying public, rather than attempting to be a trendsetter. The average cost for a new home in 1900–1910 was approximately $2,400. REPRINTED FROM SEARS, ROEBUCK AND CO. *SEARS, ROEBUCK HOME BUILDER'S CATALOG: THE COMPLETE ILLUSTRATED 1910 EDITION.* NEW YORK: DOVER PUBLICATIONS, 1990.

whether the work was performed by an outside builder or the actual homeowner. Catalog homes could be completed in approximately 60 percent of the time required for a comparable home built using traditional methods—a significant labor savings.

Although concentrated in the Midwest, Sears and other catalog homes can be found throughout the country. Indicative of the quality, many of these homes, probably a significant majority, are still in use, although there is no complete inventory. In Carlinville, Illinois, for example, 152 of the 156 homes ordered by the Standard Oil Company for its employees in 1919 are currently occupied.

The boom years for the catalog home industry lasted until 1930, when the Depression brought home construction to a virtual standstill. During that time Sears and Aladdin alone produced nearly 100,000 mail-order homes. While Sears dropped out of the home business in 1940, Aladdin delivered homes until 1983. The prefabricated home industry continues to flourish in various forms. Trailer homes are a direct descendent of catalog homes, and currently the country's largest homebuilder is a manufacturer of prefabricated homes.

Further Resources

BOOKS

Schweitzer, Robert, and Michael W.R. Davis. *America's Favorite Homes: Mail-Order Catalogues as a Guide to Popular Early 20th-Century Houses.* Detroit: Wayne State University Press, 1990.

Stevenson, Katherine Cole, and H. Ward Jandl. *Houses by Mail: A Guide to Houses by Sears Roebuck and Company.* Washington: Preservation Press, 1986.

WEBSITES

Roth, Ronica. "Built in a Day." Available online at http://www.wethepeople.gov/neh/articles/aladdin.html; website home page: http://www.wethepeople.gov/ (accessed February 2, 2003).

"Sears Homes." Carlinville Community School District. Available online at www.carlinville.macoupin.k12.il.us/middle/cyber2002/mywebs/sears.htm; website home page: http://www.carlinville.macoupin.k12.il.us/ (accessed February 2, 2003).

Thornton, Rosemary. "A Significant Bunch of Sears Homes." *Old House Chronicle,* 3, 18, May/June 2001. Available online at http://www.oldhousechronicle.com/archives/vol03/issue18/articles/sears2.html; website home page: http://www.oldhousechronicle.com/ (accessed February 2, 2003). *Old House Chronicle* is a free online magazine covering old houses and the people who live in them.

"Seven Years of Child Labor Reform"

Report

By: Owen R. Lovejoy

Date: 1911

Source: National Child Labor Committee. "Seven Years of Child Labor Reform." *Uniform Child Labor Laws: Proceedings of the Seventh Annual Conference, Birmingham, Alabama, March 9–12, 1911.* New York: National Child Labor Committee 1911, 31–38.

About the Author: Owen R. Lovejoy (1866–1961), minister and social worker, was one of the leading spokespersons in the opposition to child labor. Born near Grand Rapids, Michigan, Lovejoy was educated at Albion College and became a minister in 1891. He was asked to report on the conditions in the anthracite fields of eastern Pennsylvania during the 1902 coal strike, and in doing so he observed children working in the mines. In 1904, the newly formed National Child Labor Committee (NCLC) asked him to return to the area to study the conditions of child labor. As a result of that report, Lovejoy joined the NCLC and in 1907 became the organization's general secretary, a position he held until 1926. Lovejoy remained active in child labor and welfare issues until his retirement in 1937. ■

Introduction

Child labor was a part of life in pre-industrial society. On farms children were assigned chores as soon as they were able and were expected to contribute to the well being of the family. In the villages, children entered the workforce as helpers to their craftsmen fathers and as apprentices. While there were certainly abuses, the pace of life was relatively easy and the children were generally under the care of parents or another relative.

As large-scale industry evolved, first in Britain and later in the United States, the employment of children initially did not seem unusual. Alexander Hamilton, for example, thought that the ability for simplified factory tasks to be performed by unskilled children was a virtue of industrialization. By the 1830s, however, Britain began to pass restrictive child labor laws following the investigations of the Earl of Shaftesbury. Early laws were not very effective, but Britain had made a start.

In the United States, labor unions led the opposition to child labor even before the Civil War (1861–1865). Given the heavily rural population and the laissez-faire attitude of government, however, opposition to child labor did not generate much non-union support until decades later. It was the census of 1900 that seemed to crystallize the opposition. That census showed that 1.7 million children between the ages of 10 and 14, nearly 20 percent of that age group, were employed. While this statistic understated the problem, it was sufficient to spur concerned citizens to act.

Another catalyst for action was a number of books and articles that reported on child workers. Among others, John Spargo's *The Bitter Cry of the Children* (1906) and Edwin Markham's series in *Cosmopolitan* entitled "The Hoe-Man in the Making" (1906–1907) vividly described child labor in the United States. Even more graphic was Lewis Hine's photographic series commissioned by the National Child Labor Committee, which visually documented children working in coal mines, textile mills, sweatshops, and food processing plants.

While Progressives were fairly ambivalent about the working conditions of adult males, they adopted a far more protective posture with regard to women and children in the workforce. They sought state and federal legislation to limit hours, ensure safe working conditions, and, in the case of school-age children, severely restrict or outlaw employment.

Significance

The National Child Labor Committee was a leading advocate of child labor reform. Established in 1904, the NCLC had an extensive network of state and local chapters, often composed primarily of leaders of local women's clubs. While they favored federal legislation, the NCLC was most effective at the state level.

Resistance to child labor laws came from various sources, especially the affected business owners. In the South, the standard cry was that without child labor, the mills could not compete and would be forced to close or go where the laws were more amenable to business realities. Often the children themselves had parents who were opposed to reform. The parents needed the small

The National Child Labor Committee photographed these boys in 1908. They work as doffers at the Trenton Mills in Gastonia, North Carolina. **THE LIBRARY OF CONGRESS.**

amounts their children earned in order to make ends meet.

Within a fairly short period of time, the NCLC and other organizations succeeded in effecting the passage of state laws restricting child labor. These, combined with stricter truancy laws, caused child labor to decline. At the federal level, however, success was limited. Two pieces of legislation restricting child labor, demanded in part to offset the relatively poor enforcement record of early state laws, were declared unconstitutional in 1918 and 1922. A constitutional amendment that would have enabled federal child labor legislation passed Congress in 1924 but failed to win ratification from the required number of states. It was not until the passage of the Fair Labor Standards Act in 1938 that the federal government began regulating child labor.

Primary Source

"Seven Years of Child Labor Reform" [excerpt]

SYNOPSIS: The following report was delivered at the Seventh Annual Conference of the National Child Labor Committee held in Birmingham, Alabama, in March 1911. In it, Owen R. Lovejoy describes the success of the NCLC through its first seven years of operation. He outlines the general history of the recent opposition to child labor, provides a summary of state-by-state legislation, and highlights some problems facing the anti-child-labor movement.

At the completion of seven years of work for the improvement of child labor conditions in America, it is fitting that the National Child Labor Committee should present a concrete statement of its record. This is important, not so much in justification of the policies and expenditures of the committee, in order that the public may judge whether we are worthy [of] further support and co-operation, but especially that we may estimate the extent to which the American people have awakened in opposition to this national vice, in order more accurately to judge the possibilities that lie ahead.

When this Committee was formed seven years ago, there was no accepted national standard of protection against the abuses of child exploitation. The trade unions were committed to an eight-hour-day;

some of the woman's clubs, to the general abolition of child labor; and the Socialist Party to the elimination of all children under sixteen from wage-earning industries. But the trade union was accused of selfishness; the woman's clubs were charged with feminine sentiment, and the Socialist Party was ignored as without power and influence. The general public, indeed, had not awakened to a realization that such an evil existed, and except for the Consumers' League and a respectable number of enlightened individuals, child labor in America may be said to have been without an enemy. We were chiefly interested in the subject as an academic theme, enabling the eloquent portrayal of the greed and cruelty of European civiliations.

Then rapidly, as public intelligence and interest are wont to grow, there swept over the face of the country the exciting news that child labor existed in America, that the coal mines, glass factories, cotton and silk mills, cigar and cigarette factories, and even our public streets were the scenes of hardship, danger and oppression to the tender bodies and souls of little boys and girls. At this point a group of the more calm and discerning of those who were horrified by the evil decided to band themselves together for the purpose of conserving this public interest and seeking to direct it into definite channels of activity, in order that the sentiment against child labor should not spend its force in futile denunciation, but should realize improvement through definite results.

And it is to the credit of the South, a tribute which we gladly pay, that the initial suggestion of such a militant band on a national scale originated with a citizen of your own commonwealth. After a struggle with the mercenary elements of Alabama to wrest from their control the lives of hundreds of little children and to secure to them the opportunities which childhood may fairly claim, it seemed to Mr. Edgar Gardner Murphy, who led the fight, that an interchange of thought and experience among citizens of the various commonwealths would so unite and direct the work of reform as to hasten the day of child freedom.

From a membership of less than fifty people, the Committee has grown, in seven years, to a contributing membership of more than 5,000, who cover an annual budget of nearly $60,000. Twenty-seven state and local committees are affiliated and the Committee is in definite co-operation with educators, medical experts, jurists, reform agencies, relief societies, woman's clubs, trade unions, manufacturers' organizations, churches, and all agencies working for the protection of child life.

While we do not look upon the enactment of child labor laws as more important than their enforcement, or than the constructive policies which seek to provide the child, excluded from prohibited industries, the physical, mental and moral opportunities needed to develop efficient citizenship, yet the changes secured in child labor laws within the past seven years will perhaps measure more accurately than anything else the extent to which the public is awake to the importance of safeguarding the child.

Standards of Protection

Before recording these specific results, however, we need to state briefly the standards aimed at—the principles upon which adequate laws for such protection seem to us to be based. The word "child" covers so wide a span in human life, we recognize that some children should not be employed at all, while others may wisely contribute to their own support and to social wealth. Obviously no child should be subjected to industrial burdens too heavy, either because of youth or because of physical or mental weakness; also, obviously, in seeking legislation to protect such children, some arbitrary line must be drawn. Without entering into detail, we may note that the recognized standard of all civilized nations excludes the child under fourteen years from the field of competitive industry. This we have adopted as a minimum standard, below which no community, alert to its larger interest, can afford to fall. We recognize that such an age test is arbitrary; that some children are more advanced than others, and we welcome all results of physiological investigations which may fix more accurate and scientific standards. But for the present we are safe, since this point in age is intended to apply to the most advanced, while those who fall below, either as to physical or mental growth, are to be still further safeguarded, until sufficiently developed to venture upon the minimum industrial hazard.

The other classes of children for whose employment regulation rather than prohibition is sought are those between fourteen and twenty-one years of age. The state is the natural guardian and protector of all minor children, and it is our contention that the labor of all minors should be regulated in harmony with principles that conserve individual and social interests.

To illustrate: our Federal Government is on record in favor of a maximum eight-hour day for men in government contracts and many other lines of

A girl at work on a power loom in a Cherryville, North Carolina, textile mill, 1908. **THE LIBRARY OF CONGRESS.**

Federal activity. Similarly, many states have established the eight-hour day, both in relation to state contracts and the treatment of convicts in penitentiaries and reformatories. Recent utterances from high medical authority testify to the danger, especially to women, from the toxin of fatigue. Obviously a day long enough for adult men and women is not too short for undeveloped children. We therefore seek to establish as rapidly as possible a maximum of eight hours in the daily labor of children in manufacturing and mercantile pursuits.

It is also the prevailing testimony of medical authorities that hard work is more injurious by night than by day. Practically every physician will unhesitatingly affirm that during youth and adolescence the human life should be protected through regular hours of rest, recreation and feeding, and we therefore contend that children under sixteen years of age should be prohibited from such occupations as demand their service at night.

Industrial Hazards

Statisticians everywhere recognize a certain hazard in industry, and a body of legislation is being created in this country for the purpose of laying upon society and upon the industries involved, a larger share of the burden which now falls so heavily upon those injured in mines, factories, workshops and transportation operations. The principle of social responsibility, already fairly recognized, is especially applicable to children. Not only are children less intelligent, less cautious and less able to defend their own rights, but their physical inferiority subjects them to dangers which do not threaten the adult. Reports from the few states which have taken the matter of child exposure in industry seriously enough to report upon it, indicate that children sixteen years of age and under are injured or killed at a ratio startlingly higher than are adults in the same industries. The percentages run from 250 in one state, to 450 in another. We acknowledge that statistical reports are meager, and that many sections of the country are entirely devoid of this information. However, we have considered it important that a committee formed to protect the interests of working children should not wait until a complete body of statistics had been gathered, but should at once attempt to correct an abuse which obviously threatens the safety of the young. Therefore, leaving to statistical experts and medical scientists the more satisfying work of determining the exact extent of accidents to working children, we have set ourselves to the humbler task of arousing public interest and securing legislation against this sacrifice, on the assumption that children are unsafe industrial risks, and that child labor in certain specific dangerous occupations may without injury to society be suspended to the age of sixteen, eighteen or even twenty-one.

We shall not enter into the more distinctly technical phases of the problem of child labor legislation, but it should not be overlooked that laws which seek to establish protection for children must provide methods and machinery for administration so as to dignify the legislation by serious attention to its operation. Factory inspection departments, birth registration, a system of certification which shall prove beyond question the age and development of the child in question, are all matters claiming serious attention.

Summary of Legislation

Measured by the foregoing, the outline of achievements of the American people in developing legislation to protect the working child may be seen at a glance by the following schedules:

1. During seven years five states passed their first law upon this subject: Delaware, Florida, Georgia, Mississippi, Oklahoma, and the District of Columbia.

2. The eight-hour day has been established in Ohio, Illinois, Indiana, Nebraska, New York, Wis-

consin, Colorado, Oklahoma, North Dakota, Kansas, and the District of Columbia.

3. Night work under sixteen years has been made illegal in Alabama, California, Delaware, Idaho, Indiana, Iowa, Kansas, Kentucky, Louisiana, Mississippi, Missouri, Nebraska, New Jersey, North Dakota, Oklahoma, Rhode Island, South Carolina, Vermont, Washington, and the District of Columbia.

4. A fourteen-year-age limit as the minimum for employment in industry has been established in the following states: California, Colorado, Delaware, Idaho, Iowa, Kentucky, Louisiana, Maine, Missouri, Nebraska, Pennsylvania, North Dakota, New Jersey, Tennessee, West Virginia, Rhode Island, Kansas, and the District of Columbia.

5. Departments of factory inspection have been established in Alabama, Colorado, Delaware, Kansas, Louisiana, Maryland, North Dakota, Oklahoma, South Carolina, Texas, Tennessee, Virginia, and the District of Columbia.

6. Methods of proving the age of children seeking employment have been provided in the following: California, Iowa, Kansas, Kentucky, Louisiana, Maine, Maryland, Michigan, Missouri, Nebraska, North Dakota, Oklahoma, Oregon, Pennsylvania, Rhode Island, Washington, Wisconsin, and the District of Columbia.

Meantime, compulsory education laws have been enacted or improved in a large number of states.

Serious Defects

It might appear from this record that so much has been accomplished the public could reasonably rest. We are apt to forget how large a country we have. There are still seven of our states which have not reached the fourteen-year-age limit, even for employment in factories. These states are: North Carolina, Maryland, Alabama, Florida, Georgia, Mississippi, South Carolina.

Alabama, Florida, Maryland, North Carolina, North Dakota, Pennsylvania, South Carolina, Virginia permit the employment of boys of twelve years in mines.

Children under sixteen are still permitted to work at night in Arizona, Colorado, Connecticut, Delaware, Maine, Maryland, Montana, Nevada, New Hampshire, South Dakota, Tennessee, Utah, West Virginia and Wyoming.

There are thirty-five states in the Union in which children under sixteen years of age may work more than eight hours a day. . . .

In twenty-three of our states there is up to the present time no method of determining how old the children are who seek work in our industries. Our agents have frequently found eight, nine and ten-year-old boys applying for work in glass factories or coal mines, upon affidavits certifying them to be fourteen or sixteen years of age. In all these efforts at reform we must keep in mind the honor and dignity of our social institutions, and nothing is more fatal to the integrity of the American people than contempt for its own laws. When, by the very nature of the problem we lay upon the ignorant, impoverished or greedy parent the temptation to deceive in order to secure employment for a child, we are guilty of placing the burden on the weak, where it does not belong, and promoting perjury by process of law.

The states in which we do not require any proof of the child's age, or at least any proof worthy the name, are Colorado, Florida, Louisiana, Nevada, South Dakota, Texas, Utah, Vermont, Virginia, Wyoming, Alabama, Arkansas, Delaware, Georgia, Idaho, Indiana, Missouri, Mississippi, New Hampshire, North Carolina, South Carolina, and Tennessee. . . .

We believe the record of the past seven years gives promise that the American people are ready to rally to the establishment of laws which, throughout the nation, shall guarantee to every child an adequate opportunity to play and grow and learn, and that we shall soon permit ourselves to be brought among those nations truly civilized that recognize in their child-life the most valuable asset among all their treasures. To the realization of this high standard the National Child Labor Committee is committed, and confidently solicits the co-operation of all who believe in lifting from the bent shoulders of the little child the burdens that now crush him.

Further Resources

BOOKS

Goldberg, Vicki. *Lewis W. Hine: Children at Work.* New York: Prestel, 1999.

Hindman, Hugh D. *Child Labor: An American History.* Armonk, N.Y.: M.E. Sharpe, 2002.

Lovejoy, Owen R. "Child Labor in the United States." In Bliss, William D.P., and Rudolph M. Binder, eds., *The New Encyclopedia of Social Reform, Including All Social-Reform Movements and Activities, and the Economic, Industrial, and Sociological Facts and Statistics of All Countries and All Social Subjects.* New York: Funk and Wagnalls, 1908.

Spargo, John. *The Bitter Cry of the Children.* New York and London: Macmillan, 1906.

WEBSITES

"Photographs of Lewis Hine: The Documentation of Child Labor." Illinois Labor History Society. Available online at http://www.kentlaw.edu/ilhs/hine.htm; website home page: http://www.kentlaw.edu/ilhs/ (accessed February 1, 2003).

The House on Henry Street

Nonfiction work, Photograph

By: Lillian Wald

Date: 1915

Source: Wald, Lillian. *The House on Henry Street.* New York: Holt, Rinehart and Winston, 1915. Reprint, New York: Dover Publications, 1971, 57–62.

About the Author: Lillian Wald (1867–1940) was a nurse and social worker who started her career serving the downtrodden of New York's Lower East Side, establishing the Henry Street Settlement in 1895. She later became a public health official, teacher, author, editor, women's rights activist, and founder of the Visiting Nurse Society. Wald persuaded President Theodore Roosevelt (served 1901–1909) to create a Federal Children's Bureau to protect the rights of children, helped form the Women's Trade Union to protect the rights of women, and lobbied for workplace health inspections to protect the rights of workers. Her visionary social service programs have been a model for similar programs worldwide. ■

Introduction

Urban population at the beginning of the twentieth century was increasing at an astounding rate. In the fifty years between 1870 and 1920, the population of America's towns and cities grew from ten million to fifty million. People came from America's farm communities to find work where factories were springing up rapidly. Immigrants came in search of employment and a better life. They were motivated by the promise of the "American Dream" and envisioned running their own shops and providing a comfortable living for their families.

While some first-generation immigrants realized this dream, most lived in very harsh conditions in America's burgeoning cities. Overcrowding resulted in inadequate housing and sanitation. Garbage and sewage piled up in the streets and attracted rats, insects, and germs. Disease ran rampant. Entire families lived in one room. Wages were too low to purchase even the basic necessities.

These were the conditions Lillian Wald found in her first home nursing visit in 1893. When Wald was studying at Medical College, she developed a class in home nursing that was adapted to the patients she had been treating as part of her practical training. She conducted the class in an old building on Henry Street, in the center of a dense industrial population. A little girl who happened to be at the class one morning asked Wald to come help her mother, who had just had a baby. The child led Wald over piles of trash and through squalid neighborhoods into the family sickroom. The family of seven shared two rooms with boarders. The sick woman lay on an unclean bed. Wald called that morning a "baptism of fire." It drew her immediately into the task of caring for these people, never to return to the laboratories and academia of her college studies again.

Significance

Wald shared her ideas about how to educate and care for families like the one she had seen that morning with Mary Brewster, a fellow nurse and good friend. The plans that followed became the basis for two long-standing service establishments. Wald and Brewster founded the Visiting Nurse Service in 1893 and, with the help of friends and philanthropists, began the Henry Street Settlement House in 1895.

Wald believed that educating and providing a social outlet for people was just as important as tending to their physical ailments, so the Settlement House provided a wide range of services including healthcare, dramatic activities, vocational training, a library, a savings bank, and a social hall. In the early 1900s, branches of the Henry Street Settlement opened in Manhattan and the Bronx, catering specifically to Italian, Hungarian, and African American communities. By 1903, Henry House's Visiting Nursing Service was caring for 4,500 patients per year, and the numbers kept growing.

The Henry Street Settlement was part of a much larger settlement house movement that had started in 1889 with Jane Addams' Hull House in Chicago. Other reformers and social activists recognized the need to address the concerns of the overcrowded urban centers, and hundreds of settlement houses were established. Like the Henry Street Settlement, they met more than just physical needs. Typically a settlement house was a combination boarding house, dispensary, nursery, school, and social and cultural center for the neighborhood.

Primary Source

The House on Henry Street: Nonfiction work [excerpt]

SYNOPSIS: Many public health and education initiatives resulted from the Henry Street Settlement House and its Visiting Nurse Service. In this excerpt from Wald's memoirs of the Henry Street Settlement, she recalls her efforts to promote training and standards for midwives. She also writes of the importance of establishing a system of visiting nurses for home and workplace, particularly in outlying areas, to be under the administration of the Red Cross. She envisions a time when trained graduate nurses will provide in-home care and instruction from coast to coast. A photograph from Wald's book is also here.

Primary Source

The House on Henry Hill: Photograph

SYNOPSIS: This image appeared in Lillian Wald's *The House on Henry Hill.* Besides providing urban children with health care and their parents with advice, Lillian Wald and the Henry Street Settlement tried to give the children a safe place to play, like this playground in the backyard of one of the organization's branch offices. REPRINTED FROM LILLIAN WALD, *THE HOUSE ON HENRY STREET,* NEW YORK: HENRY HOLT AND COMPANY, INC., 1915.

Perhaps nothing indicates more impressively our contempt for alien customs than the general attitude taken toward the midwife. In other lands she holds a place of respect, but in this country there seems to be a general determination on the part of physicians and departments of health to ignore her existence and leave her free to practice without fit preparation, despite the fact that her services are extensively used in humble homes. In New York City the midwife brings into the world over forty per cent. of all the babies born there, and ninety-eight per cent. of those among the Italians.

We had many experiences with them, beginning with poor Ida, the carpenter's wife, and some that had the salt of humor. Before our first year had passed I wrote to the superintendent of a large relief society operating in our neighborhood, advising that the society discontinue its employment of midwives as a branch of relief, because of their entire lack of standards and their exemption from restraining influence.

To force attention to the harmful effect of leaving the midwife without training in midwifery and asepsis free to attend women in childbirth, the Union Settlement in 1905 financed an investigation under the auspices of a committee of which I was chairman.

A trained nurse was selected to inquire into and report upon the practice of the midwives. The inquiry disclosed the extent to which habit, tradition, and economic necessity made the midwife practically indispensable, and gave ample proof of the neglect, ignorance, and criminality that prevailed; logical consequences of the policy that had been

Lillian Wald, founder of the Henry Street Settlement and author of *The House on Henry Street.* PHOTOGRAPH BY UNDERWOOD & UNDERWOOD. LIBRARY OF CONGRESS

pursued. The Commissioner of Health and eminent obstetricians now co-operated to improve matters, and legislation was secured making it mandatory for the Department of Health to regulate the practice of midwifery. Five years later the first school for midwives in America was established in connection with Bellevue Hospital.

Part of the duty assigned to nurses of the Bureau of Child Hygiene is to inspect the bags of the midwives licensed to practice, and to visit the new-born in the campaign to wipe out *ophthalmia neonatorum,* that tragically frequent and preventable cause of blindness among the new-born.

These are a few of the manifestations of the new era in the development of the nurse's work. She is enlisted in the crusade against disease and for the promotion of right living, beginning even before life itself is brought forth, through infancy into school life, on through adolescence, with its appeal to repair the omissions of the past. Her duties take her into factory and workshop, and she has identified herself with the movement against the premature employment of children, and for the protection of men and women who work that they may not risk health and life itself while earning their living. The nurse is being socialized, made part of a community plan for the communal health. Her contribution to human welfare, unified and harmonized with those powers which aim at care and prevention, rather than at police power and punishment, forms part of the great policy of bringing human beings to a higher level.

With the incorporation of the nurse's service in municipal and state departments for the preservation of health, other agencies, under private and semi-public auspices, have expanded their functions to the sick.

I had felt that the American Red Cross Society held a unique position among its sister societies of other nations, and that in time it might be an agency that could consciously provide valuable "moral equivalents for war." The whole subject, in these trouble times, is revived in my memory, and I find that in 1908 I began to urge that in a country dedicated to peace it would be fitting for the American Red Cross to consecrate its efforts to the upbuilding of life and the prevention of disaster, rather than to emphasize its identification with the ravages of war.

The concrete recommendation made was that the Red Cross should develop a system of visiting nursing in the vast, neglected country areas. The suggestion has been adopted and an excellent beginning made with a Department of Town and Country Nursing directed by a special committee. A generous gift started an endowment for its administration. Many communities not in the registered area and remote from the centers of active social propaganda will be given stimulus to organize for nursing service, and from this other medical and social measures will inevitably grow. It requires no far reach of the imagination to visualize the time when our country will be districted from the northernmost to the southernmost point, with the trained graduate nurse entering the home wherever there is illness, caring for the patient, preaching the gospel of health, and teaching in simplest form the essentials of hygiene. Such an organization of national scope, its powers directed toward raising the standard in the homes without sacrifice of independence, is bound to promote the social progress of the nation.

Further Resources

BOOKS

Angle, Ann. *America in the 20th Century, Vol. 1: 1900–1909.* North Bellmore, N.Y.: Marshall Cavendish, 1995.

Duffus, R.L. *Lillian Wald, Neighbor and Crusader.* New York: Macmillan, 1938.

Hall, Helen. *Unfinished Business in Neighborhood and Nation.* New York: Macmillan, 1971.

Wald, Lillian. *Windows on Henry Street.* Boston: Little, Brown, 1934.

WEBSITES

"About Henry Street." Available online at http://www.henrystreet.org/site/PageServer?pagename=abt_home; website home page: http://www.henrystreet.org/ (accessed February 3, 2003).

"Henry Street Settlement." New York University Office of Community Service. Available online at http://www.nyu.edu/community.service/c-team/HENRY.html; website home page: http://www.nyu.edu/community.service/ (accessed February 3, 2003).

"Lillian Wald." Jewish Women's Archive. Available online at http://jwa.mit.edu/exhibits/wald/lwbio.htm; website home page: http://www.jwa.org/ (accessed February 3, 2003).

"Bring Playgrounds to Detroit"

Speech

By: Clara B. Arthur

Date: 1926

Source: Arthur, Clara B. "Bring Playgrounds to Detroit."*Clara B. Arthur Papers.* Detroit, Mich.: Burton Historical Collection, Detroit Public Library.

About the Author: Clara B. Arthur (1858–1929) was a prominent social activist in Detroit. Her deep concern for the welfare of women and children led to the development of visionary public programs and changes in the city's political system. An important leader of the Woman's Suffrage Movement, Arthur served as president or vice president of the Michigan Equal Suffrage Association from 1896 to 1913. She used her superior organizational skills and patient tenacity to persevere despite many early defeats. Her efforts paid off as she eventually brought playgrounds and public bath houses to Detroit, helped effect changes in labor conditions for women and children, and improved conditions for tuberculosis victims. In her retirement, she saw full suffrage for women become a reality with the passage of the Nineteenth Amendment in 1920. ■

Introduction

The Playground Movement grew out of a concern, beginning in the middle 1800s, for children to have wholesome alternatives for their leisure time. Until the industrial boom following the Civil War (1861–1865), most American children grew up on farms or in small towns, where there was ample open space to play. By 1900, however, nearly 14 million people lived in cities of more than 100,000 people. As population densities in these places grew, children lost access to their natural play areas—woods and fields, the fishing spot by the creek, and the old swimming hole. In addition, the Industrial Revolution drew many children into factories and sweatshops.

Cities were overcrowded with scarcely enough room for families to live comfortably. Often entire families lived in one or two rooms, and there wasn't adequate space for children to play. About the same time, however, urban middle-class Americans began to adopt a new view of childhood that included education and the opportunity to play as an important part of maturing.

Slowly, conditions began to change. Schools were made available to children, and attendance gradually became mandatory. Legislation prohibited underage children from working. These factors, combined with the unhealthy environment in which many urban children were dwelling, focused increasing attention on child welfare.

Children were often without acceptable outlets for youthful energy and curiosity. There was little for children to do in the cities that was not meant for adults. Boys learned to smoke and gamble and tell obscene stories. There were accidents resulting from children playing in the streets. Poolrooms and dance halls were crowded with children spending money and being lured by sexual temptation and alcohol. Parents, psychologists studying child development, supporters of civil order and moral standards, and activists for children's rights began to take a collective interest in what children were doing with their leisure time.

Significance

This interest became action in the late 1800s, when Joseph Lee started one of America's first public playgrounds in Boston. Inspired by the play movement in Germany, Lee is considered the father of the Playground Movement in America and was the first American to write a book on the subject. Following Lee's early efforts in Boston, playgrounds began to emerge in Chicago and in New York. In 1898, New York City opened 31 playgrounds under the auspices of the Board of Education.

In 1906, the Playground Association of America was founded in Washington, D.C. President Theodore Roosevelt (served 1901–1909) was elected honorary president, and Joseph Lee took the helm in 1909 at the Association's fourth congress. The Association's earliest goals were to conduct studies of playground sites and to prepare a historical account of the play movement. Another goal was to develop a college course in play, which inspired similar courses in teacher colleges across the country. The Playground Association also developed a Committee on State Laws, aimed at securing laws in each state requiring every city of 10,000 or more to vote whether or not it would maintain playgrounds.

The main work of the Association, however, was to provide survey results and expert information to help guide

Children play on a teeter-totter in a playground on Belle Isle, Detroit, Michigan, around 1905. **THE LIBRARY OF CONGRESS.**

cities in the development of playgrounds. In this effort, they were remarkably successful. At the time of the 1909 congress of the Playground Association, 20 cities were maintaining playgrounds. By 1917, that number exceeded 500 cities, and by the early 1920s, parks and recreation departments had become a regular feature of most state and city governments, and structured play activities had found their way into school curriculums across the country.

Primary Source

"Bring Playgrounds to Detroit" [excerpt]

SYNOPSIS: The following excerpt from a speech given by Clara Arthur to a Detroit women's group relates how she became involved in the playground movement beginning in her own Detroit neighborhood when her children and their friends had no proper place to play outdoors. Her interest and efforts in the movement grew to a much wider scope and were eventually successful in winning citywide support for playgrounds, swimming pools, and organized recreation for children. It started, however, as a very personal endeavor.

On a bright warm day in June twenty-five years ago, a little group of women sat in the garden of Mrs. E.C. Skinner, 150 Bagg Street, formulating plans to demonstrate the playground idea in Detroit. Mrs. Skinner's spacious home in its beautiful garden was long the center of hospitality for new civic enterprises; especially was it the meeting place of club women. Its site is now occupied by the Ansonia Apartments, Temple Avenue.

Those in the garden this June day were Mrs. Skinner, her sister Helen P. Jenkins, Dr. Mary A. Willard, Dr. Gertrude S. Banks, Mrs. Sexton, Mrs. Mildred I. Bolt and Mrs. Clara B. Arthur, all now deceased but Mrs. Arthur.

They were a volunteer committee of the Local Council of Women then recently organized in Detroit by Miss Octavia Bates at the suggestion of Miss Susan B. Anthony who with Mrs. Stanton in 1889 organized the National Council.

This local council was comprised largely of organizations not eligible for membership in the Federation of Woman's Clubs whose platform then was "Literary." The Societies making up the Council were: Woman's Independent Voter's Association, Detroit Sorosis, Woman's Christian Temperance Union, Sara J. LaTour Hive of Maccabees, the unpopular Equal Suffrage Club, Woman's Protective Agency and Per Gradis Club.

A year or more before this time, on another June day, the writer heard under her window boys who lived on Jerry and Henrie Avenues planning an important baseball match, and lamenting the lack of a proper "lot," where the bogey of window breaking would not dampen their joy. A quick swing on a bicycle revealed the rapid contraction of play space in this location of good homes, and it was noted that within walking distance of most Detroit children this was fast becoming increasingly so.

The writer had visited some of the playgrounds of Boston and had written of them in the Detroit press, had, as a member, appealed to the newly-organized Twentieth Century Club, to finance and supervise a demonstrating public playground. But for a long time the people of Detroit refused to believe that their beloved and beautiful city needed playgrounds for its children. Detroit was so tree-shaded, so wide-streeted, so clean, so American. Above and beyond all this Detroit had Belle Isle, and the river.

It seems incredible now that Detroit's school yards were then such small, gravel, wildernesses. Not one had a swing, teeter, or other play appliance. No child could linger either before or after school. No efforts were made to organize games or promote "teams." In vacation time children were rigidly excluded. When the writer would talk to friends and neighbors of the development of the play ideas of eastern cities or of Chicago and the spread of the belief that there was a sure salvation for "the gang" in supervised play incredulity and a firm stand against raising taxes met any plea.

■ ■ ■

(rewritten) A belief in other cities, that supervised play or even place and space to play was a correction for the gang spirit was slow to find advocates in Detroit. A principal of one of the schools publicly declared it was unwise and unsafe to draw children from their homes to playgrounds.

■ ■ ■

But now in Mrs. Skinner's garden the decision was made to conduct a playground in a section of the city most in need of what playgrounds could provide using the site of the old reservoir in the Seventh ward at Erskine and Riopelle Streets if the city fathers would permit.

■ ■ ■

The reservoir site, among a congested population, was a forlorn spot, two city blocks in extent, a nightmare of civic neglect. Goats, geese and children swarmed over its hummocks and dumps and puddles. For twenty five years the writer has experienced recurring shocks of surprise at the temerity and optimism of herself and other committee members. Had they realized the mental obstacles to be met and overcome they might have faltered before the added burden of the physical difficulties of the reservoir ground.

Mrs. Arthur was made the chairman. A few days later the Committee, now numbering ten, a member from each cooperating society, went to the City Hall to request permission to operate a public playground on this worse than idle city property, or a portion of it.

The City Hall was unfamiliar and the Committee felt exceedingly de trop. For the Council Chamber was closed, and the aldermen were not to be disturbed. The police officer on guard explained that among other business preparations were in progress for meeting the body of Ex-Mayor and Governor Pingree due to arrive soon from Europe, and the council was selecting some of its members to send on this errand.

The Committee waited perhaps an hour in the stifling corridor. Mrs. Bolt remarking that we were a standing committee all right. It was a boiling hot summer night, and presently the wilted women accepted the suggestion of the distressed officer to write the substance of the errand and send the message in. Ten minutes later an alderman in whose ward the reservoir was located came from the Council Chamber and asked for details. Mrs. Arthur explained that if the use of the land was allowed for one year the local Council would clear it off, partially level it, erect a shelter pavilion, equip a playground with vacation school features, supervise it all day and every evening, except Sundays, and all without cost to the city.

Leveling a finger at the speaker, the alderman exclaimed "What you women know about boys play!—No," and at once withdrew to the Council Chamber.

At that time women, even direct, tax-paying women, were nobody's constituents, but the short sighted alderman refusing so preemptively a request made by an organization of women in behalf of children showed the committee the magnitude of the problem.

Obtaining the ready promise of Dr. E.S. Sherril of the Board of Education to champion the request, the Playground Committee wrote the Board asking the use of the large yard, the basement and corridor of the Russell School on Russell Street, near

Benton not far from the old reservoir site, carefully explaining its plans. Inspector Bourke of the seventh ward claimed the right in the Board meeting to move that the request be granted and with no dissenting word the motion carried.

The committee at once appealed to its friends for funds. The first gift, aside from those of the committee members was a check from the late Schyler Grant, second a dozen large balls and other play material from Mayor Maybury, the third a generous assortment of small iron toys from the Ideal Manufacturing Company whose invoice is one of the treasures of the voluminous playground scrapbooks of the Committee Chairman.

The ground was liberally supplied with all kinds of play apparatus then procurable in the stores, the late J. L. Hudson insisting on sending at least one sample of all the games and toys his store handled. Miss Mary Hulbert, a very young, very enthusiastic, and beloved by the children, had charge of the playground, assisted by two young men. At first supervision was very arduous, but it was soon impressed upon the children that to enjoy themselves they must permit others to do so too and all must observe the rights of all. A member of the Council of Women was present every day the playground operated to assist the supervisors. If she desired to make the day a musical one she brought friends who sang, played the violin or school piano in the corridor. Or they taught the children songs, and often hundreds of adults stood outside the school yard to enjoy the music, or watch the games. Or if a lady so wished she made her day a story-telling or reading day, or a sewing, or a millinery or a book-binding day, accordingly bringing her helpers while the daily play went on among children too young or too wild to care for specializing. Many knew nothing of games or the delights of group play and fights were at first frequent. A short expulsion soon remedied this, and such discipling as the committee furnished diverted aimless mischief makers into eager learners and helpers.

The playground was open and carefully supervised every week day for nine weeks from 8 a.m. to 8 p.m. and for the first time in Detroit the people's school property was used when its need was greatest.

Further Resources

BOOKS

Curtis, Henry Stodard. *The Play Movement and Its Significance.* New York: Macmillan, 1917.

National Recreation Association. *Park Recreation Areas in the United States.* Washington: U.S. Government Printing Office, 1928.

National Recreation Association. *Play Space in New Neighborhoods: A Committee Report on Standards of Outdoor Recreation Areas in Housing Developments.* New York: National Recreation Association, 1939.

WEBSITES

"History of Playgrounds." Charlottesville, Virginia. Available online at http://www.cstone.net/~stowek/CityParks/WashingtonPark/ed6.html; website home page: http://www.charlottesville.org/ (accessed February 3, 2003).

O'Brien, Ellen. "Chicago Parks in the Early Twentieth Century." Available online at http://www.chipublib.org/003cpl/hf/obrien.html; website home page: http://www.chipublib.org/cpl.html (accessed February 3, 2003).

Connecticut Clockmaker

Memoir

By: Francis Donovan

Date: January 5, 1939

Source: Donovan, Francis. *Connecticut Clockmaker.* Living Lore in New England series, Works Progress Administration. Reproduced in *American Life Histories: Manuscripts From the Federal Writers' Project, 1936–1940.* American Memory digital primary source collection, Library of Congress. Available online at http://memory.loc.gov/ammem/wpaintro/wpahome.html; website home page: http://memory.loc.gov (accessed March 11, 2003).

About the Author: Little is known about Francis Donovan, other than his participation in the Federal Writer's Project. An outgrowth of the Works Progress Administration (WPA), the Federal Writer's Project was an attempt to shift government subsidy of private labor to utilize skilled professionals. The other two projects supported theater and the arts. The WPA was the brainchild of its director, Harry Hopkins, and President Franklin D. Roosevelt, who envisioned it as a means of administering federal relief funds to the unemployed by giving them meaningful work. ■

Introduction

The very first automobile was released in 1893, an internal-combustion vehicle introduced by brothers Charles and Frank Duryea. Ford's competitor was introduced shortly thereafter. Other methods of powering the automobile followed shortly, and included both electric and steam motors. By 1908, automobiles had been transformed from little more than engine-powered wagons or buckboards to comfortable cars that could accelerate to as much as sixty miles per hour. Some early reactions to the automobile had been to call it an expensive toy for the well-to-do, but those early doubts were soon dispelled by rapid developments in performance and affordability. Just as the bicycle had revolutionized transportation and its associated fashions in the previous decade, so did the au-

Early automobiles used a variety of different engines. The steam-powered Stanley Steamer, like this one from 1906, is one of the most famous early automobiles. AMERICAN AUTOMOBILE MANUFACTURERS ASSOCIATION. REPRODUCED BY PERMISSION.

tomobile very quickly change many aspects of American life. Despite the expense and inconsistent performance of early models, the public immediately recognized the possibilities inherent in this new mode of transportation, and those who could afford to do so embraced it immediately. For the multitudes who could not afford the automobile, the bicycle remained a primary mode of transportation.

Although the transition from bicycle to automobile was protracted, the latter was a significant force in commerce, leisure, communications, and fashion from the first years of the twentieth century. Special clothing to resist the dust and dirt of open-road traffic, goggles to protect the eyes, and special hats and veils were being widely advertised by the middle of the century. Songs were written about the automobile; advertisements lauded the various makes and models; whole parts of the country suddenly became more accessible, spurring a new concept of tourism in out-of-the-way places. Entire new industries sprang up to service this new transportation form, and governmental investment in road and highway building became a major consideration.

Significance

The Works Progress Administration (WPA) was begun in the 1930s as a national effort to stimulate the economy and reduce the hardships of unemployment by putting people to work. Initially, the work projects required and utilized unskilled labor, mostly in construction and road maintenance. In an attempt to engage more highly skilled workers, special programs were created by President Roosevelt and WPA Director Hopkins. These were the Federal Writer's, Theatre, and Art projects. When the WPA was terminated in 1939, over nine million workers had earned at least part-time income, thus providing a stimulus to the depressed economy. Perhaps more importantly, the country was left with a wealth of documentation about life in this country that would never have existed otherwise. The Donovan transcription of an interview with a New Englander identified only as Mr. Botsford is just one example of the thousands of similar interview transcriptions that record a rich local history with a very personal perspective from Americans across the country. The document is significant in capturing the

A GOOD KIND OF AUTOMOBILE GLASSES.

An illustration from *The Delineator* magazine, March 1904, showing a woman wearing automobile glasses. Since most early cars were open air, driving glasses were often used. **THE DELINEATOR, MARCH 1904, P. 445.**

joys and dangers of bicycling, the extent to which bicycles were still being used for transportation in the early years of the twentieth century, the slow transition to automobile travel, the makes of vehicles available, and the method by which they were tested for power and durability. Mr. Botsford's friends tested these automobiles, told him about their features and shortcomings, gave him fast rides, and bragged about the performance of their personal favorites.

Advertisements, company records, photographs, and actual automotive artifacts present a unique perspective and contribute invaluable information about an invention that changed the way Americans worked, played, and lived. From those sources, we can see how the automobile looked, what fashions were associated with its use, the economics and logistics of production, and the speed of proliferation. Personal recollections such as Mr. Botsford's, however, give readers a more intimate view of how ordinary people perceived the innovations that would change an entire nation and world.

Primary Source

Connecticut Clockmaker [excerpt]

SYNOPSIS: In this 1930s reminiscence, a New Englander identified only as Mr. Botsford recalls for a Federal Writer's Project worker the early years of automobile transportation, as it gradually began to replace the bicycle as a means of travel for fun and for business.

Great times, great times, on the bicycles. Then the automobiles come along. Of course it was a long time before everybody got to ownin' them too. Most any one could have a bicycle. I remember when they was seventy-five of them over in the sheds by the Marine shop every day.

But automobiles was a different proposition. Jack Coates used to have a job testin' em for the Pope Hartford Company. He used to ride 'em all over the state. They'd tell him how many miles to go and they didn't care where he went. He'd just rig up an old seat on the chassis and start out, no windshield or or nothin', and come back when he got the mileage made up.

That's how I got my first and fastest auto ride. I was goin' to Springfield and I was hikin' along over towards Terryville to get the trolley and Jack come along and I flagged him. I was late. I says, "Jack, can we make the trolley," and he says, "Sure," and how we did fly. We made it all right.

The different cars they used to be. I used to keep a list of 'em. There was the Pope Hartford, and the Stevens Duryea, and the Locomobile, and the Peerless and the National, and the Saxon, and the Metz—I can't remember them all.

Billy Gilbert, that used to live next to me here, he had a Stanley Steamer. He was an engineer. He's out in Califony now. Spent all his life on the railroads and he swore by steam. Wouldn't have a gasoline engine.

After he moved to Califony he wrote me a letter. Said there was a big hill out there beyond San Francisco nine miles long. Said ten tow cars was kept busy on that hill all the time. But that steamer of his just ate it up.

You'd ought to be able to remember when they used Plymouth Hill for testin' cars. It was quite a trick for a car to go over there in high. Good many of 'em would start off in high, then shift to second, then low, then they'd get stuck. But it's a damn poor car that won't go over in high these days. Man wouldn't buy a car that wouldn't make it in high.

Well, I got to go down town, but I ain't goin' to give you no lift today. I'm not goin' to take the car out, I feel as though the walk will do me good. So you just wait till I put the cat out and fix my fires and we'll walk down together.

Further Resources

BOOKS

Rae, John B. *American Automobile Manufacturers: The First Forty Years.* Philadelphia: Chilton, 1959.

PERIODICALS

Palmer, Alexandra. "Form Follows Fashion: A Motorcoat Considered." *Dress* 12, 1986, 4–10.

WEBSITES

"Automobile History." About.com. Available online at http://f.about.com/z/js/spr04.htm; website home page: http://inventors.about.com/mbody.htm (accessed February 22, 2003).

"Automotive History." Michigan.gov. Available online at http://mel.lib.mi.us/business/autos-history.html (accessed February 22, 2003).

"Early Adventures With the Automobile." Available online at http://www.ibiscom.com/auto.htm; website home page: http://www.ibiscom.com (accessed February 22, 2003).

8

THE MEDIA

DAN PROSTERMAN

Entries are arranged in chronological order by date of primary source. For entries with one primary source, the entry title is the same as the primary source title. Entries with more than one primary source have an overall entry title, followed by the titles of the primary sources.

CHRONOLOGY

PRIMARY SOURCES

Important Events in the Media, 1900–1909

1900

- Lincoln Steffens joins *McClure's* as managing editor.
- Arthur Brisbane, editor, launches William Randolph Hearst's *Chicago American* newspaper.
- Herbert Croly founds the *Architectural Record.*
- Frank Munsey changes title of *Puritan Magazine* to *Junior Munsey.*
- The first volume of *Who's Who in America* is published.
- McClure Phillips, book publisher, is founded.
- C. M. Clark, the only turn-of-the-century Boston publishing house owned by a woman, is launched.
- The Supreme Court of Illinois rules that the Associated Press wire service is a public utility and must not discriminate among subscribers. The AP declares bankruptcy in Illinois and reincorporates in New York.
- In November, Walter Hines Page founds the public-affairs monthly *World's Work* to promote business and good labor relations.

1901

- *House and Garden* is founded.
- *Appeal to Reason,* a socialist paper, is founded by J. A. Wayland in Girard, Kansas.
- Irvin S. Cobb becomes editor of the *Paducah* (Ky.) *News-Democrat.*
- Upton Sinclair founds Sinclair Press to publish his own books.
- Frank Munsey buys the *New York Daily News* and the *Washington Times*; a year later he buys the *Boston Journal* and, in 1908, the *Baltimore Evening Times.*
- *The Guardian,* a militant African American paper, is founded in Boston by William Monroe Trotter with George Forbes.
- Albert Paine's play *The Great White Way* is published, giving the new Times Square theater district its nickname.
- *The Octopus,* Frank Norris's explosive exposé of economic abuses by the nation's railroads, is published.
- *Up from Slavery,* the autobiography of Booker T. Washington, is published.
- The new "panoramic" technique of the film *New York in a Blizzard* sweeps or "pans" the camera across a scene in order to record a greater amount of information.
- On June 29, the trade journal *Editor and Publisher* is founded in New York by James B. Shale, publisher of the *McKeesport* (Pa.) *News,* to crusade against the abuses of press agentry, bad advertising, and fraudulent information.
- On July 1, Aldoph S. Ochs becomes majority stockholder of *The New York Times.*
- On September 5, Leon Czolgosz shoots President William McKinley at Buffalo, New York. The rumor circulates that the assassin carried a copy of Hearst's virulently anti-McKinley *New York Journal* in his pocket.
- On October 24, Eastman Kodak incorporates in Trenton, New Jersey. George Eastman consolidates most British and U.S. manufacturers of photographic equipment. His big seller is the Brownie Box Camera, which sells for one dollar.
- In November, *The New York Times* marks its fiftieth anniversary.
- On December 12, Guglielmo Marconi sends the letter *S* two thousand miles across the Atlantic from Cornwall, England, to Saint John's, Newfoundland.

1902

- The B. W. Huebsch publishing company is launched.
- Norman Hapgood becomes editor of *Collier's Weekly,* a position he will hold until 1912.
- E. W. Scripps founds the Newspaper Enterprise Association, a news syndicate for his papers.
- The first installment of Ida Tarbell's exposé, "The History of the Standard Oil Company" appears in *McClure's.*
- The *South Atlantic Quarterly* is founded.
- In September, *McClure's* publishes Lincoln Steffens's "The Tweed Days in St. Louis."
- In October, *Junior Munsey* is merged into *Argosy Magazine.*

1903

- *Redbook* is founded.
- The Bobbs-Merrill publishing company is founded in Indianapolis.
- Abraham Cahan assumes complete control of the *Jewish Daily Forward.*
- Jampes Palmer Knapp founds *Associated Sunday Magazine,* the first newspaper magazine supplement.
- Gilbert Grosvenor becomes editor of *National Geographic,* a position he holds until 1954.
- The "Nantucket Limerick" comes into vogue in newspapers. (There once was a man from Nantucket / Who kept all his cash in a bucket; / But his daughter, named Nan, / Ran away with a man, / And as for the bucket, Nantucket.)
- *Everybody's Magazine,* founded as an adjunct to Wanamaker's Department Store in 1899, is purchased by Erman Jesse Ridgway and becomes a leading muckraking journal.

- In January, the groundbreaking issue of *McClure's* magazine publishes articles by Ida Tarbell, Ray Stannard Baker, and Lincoln Steffens and establishes the substance, form, and style of muckraking.
- In February, the *Ladies' Home Journal* becomes the first American magazine to reach one million paid subscriptions.
- On February 22, Marconi publishes a newspaper on the Cunard liner *Etruria,* the first printed at sea.
- On March 29, Regular telegraph service begins between New York and London on Marconi's wireless.
- On July 4, President Roosevelt inaugurates the first Pacific communication cable by sending a message around the world and receiving it twelve minutes later.
- On August 15, Joseph Pulitzer gives $2 million to Columbia University to begin a school of journalism.

1904

- Lincoln Steffens publishes *The Shame of the Cities,* a collection of his articles on municipal corruption.
- The University of Illinois institutes the first four-year journalism curriculum, directed by Frank W. Scott.
- In May, Edward Bok of the *Ladies' Home Journal* declares editorial war on patent medicines.
- In December, the first radio transmission by Reginald Fessenden of music (from Brant Rock, Massachusetts) takes place.
- The new *New York Times* building opens on Longacre Square in midtown Manhattan, which becomes known as Times Square.

1905

- W. D. Moffat leaves Charles Scribner's Sons to form the publishing company Moffat Yard with Robert Yard.
- Chicago's *Defender* is founded by Robert S. Abbott to decry racial injustice.
- Sime Silverman founds *Variety* as a weekly theatrical trade journal.
- Thomas Dixon publishes *The Clansman,* which romanticizes the origins of the Ku Klux Klan. D. W. Griffith later turns the book into the controversial 1915 film, *Birth of a Nation.*
- In January, *National Geographic* magazine publishes eleven pages of photographs of the Tibetan capital, Lhasa.
- On May 15, Charles Alexander launches the monthly *Alexander's Magazine* for African American readers.
- In October, Samuel Hopkins Adams's series on patent medicines, "The Great American Fraud," begins appearing in *Collier's.*
- On November 25, Alfred Stieglitz opens a photo gallery in the attic of his Fifth Avenue brownstone in New York. Editor of several photographic journals, Stieglitz is a leading proponent of photography as more than an information medium. His gallery will bring it one step closer to recognition as an art form as well.

1906

- W. E. B. Du Bois publishes *Moon Illustrated Weekly* from a small print shop in Memphis.
- *Little Nemo in Slumberland,* Winsor McCay's popular comic strip, is first published in syndication.
- In February, Upton Sinclair publishes *The Jungle,* a novel depicting horrifying conditions in the meatpacking industry and spurring the passage of the Meat Inspection Act. Also in 1906, Congress passes the Pure Food and Drug Act and the Hepburn Act, enlarging regulation over the railroads. Muckraking journalists are given credit for creating public demand for all of this legislation.
- On April 7, Lee De Forest announces the first successful wireless transmission across the Atlantic. A 40,000-watt transmitter sends the signal from Manhattan Beach in New York City to a receiver in Ireland. During this year De Forest also invents the triode vacuum tube, a critical development in broadcasting, amplification, high-fidelity music systems, public address systems, and sound film.
- On March 17, President Theodore Roosevelt makes a speech in Washington, D.C., condemning those journalists who, by consistently exposing corruption and abuse, miss the larger social picture. He introduces the term "muckraking."
- On April 18, a major earthquake and fire destroy much of San Francisco, but the following day the city's three newspapers join forces and print a single edition across the bay in Oakland.
- In April, Mitchell Kennerley announces his book publishing imprint of American authors and English imports.
- In July, *National Geographic* publishes a unique set of photos of animals in nature at night.
- On September 22, a violent race riot begins in Atlanta, Georgia, when newspapers publish dubious reports of assaults on white women by African American men. Four African Americans are killed and many more are injured.
- In October, Ida Tarbell, Lincoln Steffens, and Ray Stannard Baker leave the staff of *McClure's* to take over the *American Magazine.* They are joined by John S. Phillips, Finley Peter Dunne, and William Allen White. The magazine soon fails.
- On November 21, Reginald Fessenden, using a high-frequency alternator built by Ernst F. W. Alexanderson, sends the first voice radio transmissions, covering the eleven miles between Plymouth and Brant Rock, Massachusetts.
- On December 24, Fessenden broadcasts both words and music on the radio for the first time from Brant Rock, Massachusetts. His only listeners are radio operators on fishing and military boats at sea.

1907

- W. E. B. Du Bois establishes *Horizon* magazine, intended to spread the views of the Niagara Movement of African American intellectuals.
- The George H. Doran publishing company is launched.
- E. W. Scripps founds the United Press Association, a commercial wire service, by combining two regional news services in the Midwest. The UP soon has bureaus in many

foreign capitals and news exchanges with leading foreign newspapers.

- The publication of philosopher William James' book *Pragmatism* introduces the American public to this new way of thinking and problem solving.
- The novel *Three Weeks* by British author Elinor Glyn uses the term *It* as a euphemism for sex. Nevertheless, the book is banned in Boston. However, her American tour still draws huge, adoring crowds.
- The first showing of a color motion picture with sound is held in Cleveland, Ohio. The footage includes a bull fight with natural sounds and a political speech with sounds of derision.
- Lee De Forest begins regular radio broadcasts from lower Manhattan.
- On January 23, the "Trial of the Century" begins in New York, where millionaire Harry K. Thaw is charged with the murder of world-famous architect Stanford White over the honor of Thaw's wife, showgirl Evelyn Nesbit. Irvin S. Cobb labels Hearst reporter Annie Laurie (Winifred Black) and her associates "Sob Sisters" for their melodramatic coverage.
- In April, Ray Stannard Baker's pathbreaking series on race, "Following the Color Line," begins appearing in the *Atlantic Monthly.*
- On November 15, Bud Fisher's comic strip about the unlikely sidekicks *Mutt and Jeff* becomes a daily addition to the *San Francisco Chronicle.* It is inspired by the success of other recent comic strips such as *Little Nemo in Slumberland* in the *New York Herald* and Rudolph Dirk's *The Katzenjammer Kids* in the *New York Journal.*

1908

- P. F. Volland Company is founded in Chicago to publish greeting cards; later they begin publishing children's books.
- Mary Baker Eddy founds the *Christian Science Monitor* to "injure no man, but to bless all mankind" and achieves a national circulation of more than 150,000 with no sensationalism of any kind.
- The University of Missouri founds the first separate School of Journalism, with Walter Williams as dean.

1909

- Sigma Delta Chi is founded at DePauw University as a professional fraternity for journalists.
- William Randolph Hearst founds the International News Service, the third major U.S. press association after the Associated Press and the United Press.
- James H. Anderson founds the New York *Amsterdam News* in Harlem, which would become one of the nation's largest and most influential African American newspapers.
- *La Follette's Weekly* is founded by Robert La Follette in Madison, Wisconsin, to further progressive reform.
- Rube Goldberg's "Foolish Questions" in the *New York Evening Mail* is popular. Goldberg is best known for drawing nonsensical machines that solve a problem in an unnecessarily elaborate way.
- The first significant animated cartoon shown in the United States is *Gertie the Dinosaur.* It is produced from ten thousand drawings done by Winsor McCay.
- The National Board of Censors worries about the role models being provided by the movies. *Motion Picture Weekly* asserts that movies are now providing the public with more information than newspapers.
- The first radio talk broadcast is given by Harriot Stanton Blanch, Lee De Forest's mother-in-law. Her topic is "Woman Suffrage."
- The first radio station with a regular series of programs is begun by Charles D. "Doc" Herrold of San Jose, who powers his station by illegally tapping into the streetcar lines of the Santa Fe Railway.
- On March 23, Former president Theodore Roosevelt leaves for a hunting trip in Africa. *Scribner's* pays him five hundred thousand dollars for his account of the trip.
- On April 9, Enrico Caruso broadcasts from the Metropolitan Opera House in Manhattan to the house of Lee De Forest.
- On May 3, the first wireless press message is sent from New York City to Chicago.
- In September, during the first week of the month, both Frederick Cook and Robert E. Peary make claims to have reached the North Pole the preceding April. Most scientists come to believe that Peary was the actual winner, and his account of his journey appears in *The New York Times* from September 8 to September 11.
- On November 15, Herbert Bayard Swope takes a job as a reporter for the *New York World.*

Ida B. Wells-Barnett achieved nationwide attention as the leader of the antilynching crusade. ARCHIVE PHOTOS/R. GATES. REPRODUCED BY PERMISSION.

"Lynch Law in America"

Journal article

By: Ida B. Wells-Barnett

Date: January 1900

Source: Wells-Barnett, Ida B. "Lynch Law in America." *The Arena* 23, no. 1, January 1900, 15–24. Available online at http://courses.washington.edu/spcmu/speeches/idabwells.htm (accessed May 23, 2003).

About the Author: Ida B. Wells-Barnett (1862–1931) was born to slave parents in Holly Springs, Mississippi, just six months before the Emancipation Proclamation took effect. As editor of the *Memphis Free Speech and Headlight* after 1889, she became the most influential black female activist in the country and perhaps the world. Her antilynching writings included "Southern Horrors: Lynch Law in All Its Phases" (1892). Wells-Barnett helped found the NAACP in 1909 and criticized racial accommodationists such as Booker T. Washington. ■

Introduction

The American news media of the 1900s strove to expose inequity in all facets of public life. While the most famous journalists of the period, so-called muckrakers such as Lincoln Steffens, investigated malfeasance in industry and government in the hopes of engendering reform, Ida B. Wells-Barnett and other African Americans created activist reports for civil rights laws in the United States. The end of federal reconstruction policies in 1877 spelled the beginning of a long nadir in the struggle for black equality following emancipation. By the turn of the nineteenth century, legalized racial discrimination existed throughout all regions of the country. The U.S. Supreme Court decision in *Plessy v. Ferguson* (1896) exemplified the federal government's attitude toward race relations during this period. This ruling held that segregation and other policies claiming separate but equal treatment for blacks and whites was constitutional and could be instituted in every state of the union. As the nation's highest court encouraged racism in Washington, D.C., hundreds of lynchings, or the organized murder of African Americans for alleged crimes, occurred every year in the 1890s and 1900s. Wells' activist reporting emphasized that while most of these assaults took place in the states of the former Confederacy, many also transpired in areas outside of the South.

Wells first petitioned President William McKinley (served 1897–1901) in 1898 following the lynching of an African American postmaster in South Carolina: "Nowhere in the civilized world save the United States of America do men, possessing all civil and political power, go out in bands of 50 and 5,000 to hunt down, shoot, hang or burn to death a single individual, unarmed and absolutely powerless" (*Cleveland Gazette,* April 9, 1898. Reprinted in Herbert Aptheker, ed., *A Documentary History of the Negro People in the United States,* 2 [1970], 798). Her argument conveyed the horrors of racial violence and reflected her passionate writing that would become even more strident in the 1900s.

Significance

Ida B. Wells-Barnett's powerful exposé of lynching in the United States provided the statistical evidence reformers needed to campaign for a national antilynching law. From the opening sentence, "Our country's national crime is lynching," Wells-Barnett argued that lynching was a nationwide problem caused by deep-rooted legal, social, and racial prejudice against African Americans. Directly countering the stereotype that race violence occurred only in the South, she presented statistics that depicted the national scope of lynching in the United States. She emphasized how many, if not most, of the attacks were founded upon baseless charges and accusations. She also showed that despite claims that lynchings were a response to sexual assaults on white women, these claims were misplaced and did not account for the bulk of the murders, which were cold and calculated attacks intended to maintain white superiority in economic, political, and social relations. In the face of hundreds, if not thousands, of lynchings perpetrated every year, she turned the ideology of manifest destiny, an imperialist ideology that characterized expansion as a duty thrust upon white Americans because of their racial superiority, on its head. Rather than challenging this racist vision, Wells-Barnett manipulated it into a damning indictment of this nation's wholly uncivilized "hanging, shooting, and burning" of African Americans.

Primary Source

"Lynch Law in America" [excerpt]

SYNOPSIS: The following excerpt from Ida B. Wells-Barnett's article "Lynch Law in America" reveals the author's interweaving of legal and statistical evidence with impassioned pleas for social change. Appearing in January 1900, this article provides a fitting beginning to a decade that media historians remember chiefly for muckraking exposés that challenged government officials and the public to rebel against the status quo.

Our country's national crime is *lynching*. It is not the creature of an hour, the sudden outburst of uncontrolled fury, or the unspeakable brutality of an insane mob. It represents the cool, calculating deliberation of intelligent people who openly avow that there is an "unwritten law" that justifies them in putting human beings to death without complaint under oath, without trial by jury, without opportunity to make defense, and without right of appeal. . . .

. . . These advocates of the "unwritten law" boldly avowed their purpose to intimidate, suppress, and nullify the negro's right to vote. In support of its plans the Ku-Klux Klans, the "red-shirt" and similar organizations proceeded to beat, exile, and kill negroes until the purpose of their organization was accomplished and the supremacy of the "unwritten law" was effected. Thus lynchings began in the South, rapidly spreading into the various States until the national law was nullified and the reign of the "unwritten law" was supreme. Men were taken from their homes by "red-shirt" bands and stripped, beaten, and exiled; others were assassinated when their political prominence made them obnoxious to their political opponents; while the Ku-Klux barbarism of election days, reveling in the butchery of thousands of colored voters, furnished records in Congressional investigations that are a disgrace to civilization.

The alleged menace of universal suffrage having been avoided by the absolute suppression of the negro vote, the spirit of mob murder should have been satisfied and the butchery of negroes should have ceased. But men, women, and children were the victims of murder by individuals and murder by mobs, just as they had been when killed at the demands of the "unwritten law" to prevent "negro domination." Negroes were killed for disputing over terms of contracts with their employers. If a few barns were burned some colored man was killed to stop it. If a colored man resented the imposition of a white man and the two came to blows, the colored man had to die, either at the hands of the white man then and there or later at the hands of a mob that speedily gathered. If he showed a spirit of courageous manhood he was hanged for his pains, and the killing was justified by the declaration that he was a "saucy nigger." Colored women have been murdered because they refused to tell the mobs where relatives could be found for "lynching bees." Boys of fourteen years have been lynched by white representatives of American civilization. In fact, for all kinds of offenses—and, for no offenses—from murders to misdemeanors, men and women are put to death without judge or jury; so that, although the political excuse was no longer necessary, the wholesale murder of human beings went on just the same. A new name was given to the killings and a new excuse was invented for so doing.

Again the aid of the "unwritten law" is invoked, and again it comes to the rescue. During the last ten years a new statute has been added to the "unwritten law." This statute proclaims that for certain crimes or alleged crimes no negro shall be allowed a trial; that no white woman shall be compelled to charge an assault under oath or to submit any such charge to the investigation of a court of law. The result is that many men have been put to death whose innocence was afterward established; and to-day, under this reign of the "unwritten law," no colored man, no matter what his reputation, is safe from lynching if a white woman, no matter what her standing or motive, cares to charge him with insult or assault.

It is considered a sufficient excuse and reasonable justification to put a prisoner to death under this "unwritten law" for the frequently repeated charge that these lynching horrors are necessary to prevent crimes against women. The sentiment of the country has been appealed to, in describing the isolated condition of white families in thickly populated negro districts; and the charge is made that these homes are in as great danger as if they were surrounded by wild beasts. And the world has accepted this theory without let or hindrance. In many cases there has been open expression that the fate meted out to the victim was only what he deserved. In many other instances there has been a silence that says more forcibly than words can proclaim it that it is right and proper that a human being should be seized by a mob and burned to death upon the unsworn and the uncorroborated charge of his accuser. No matter that our laws presume every man innocent until he is proved guilty; no matter that it leaves a certain class of individuals completely at the mercy of another class; no matter that it encourages those criminally disposed to blacken their faces and commit any crime in the calendar so long as they can throw suspicion on some negro, as is frequently done, and then lead a mob to take his life; no matter that mobs make a farce of the law and a mockery of justice; no matter that hundreds of boys are being hardened in crime and schooled in vice by the repetition of such scenes before their eyes—if a white woman declares herself insulted or assaulted, some life must pay the penalty, with all the horrors of the Spanish Inquisition and all the barbarism of the Middle Ages. The world looks on and says it is well.

Not only are two hundred men and women put to death annually, on the average, in this country by mobs, but these lives are taken with the greatest publicity. In many instances the leading citizens aid and abet by their presence when they do not participate, and the leading journals inflame the public mind to the lynching point with scare-head articles and offers of rewards. Whenever a burning is advertised to take place, the railroads run excursions, photographs are taken, and the same jubilee is indulged in that characterized the public hangings of one hundred years ago. There is, however, this difference: in those old days the multitude that stood by was permitted only to guy or jeer. The nineteenth century lynching mob cuts off ears, toes, and fingers, strips off flesh, and distributes portions of the body as souvenirs among the crowd. If the leaders of the mob are so minded, coal-oil is poured over the body and the victim is then roasted to death. This has been done in Texarkana and Paris, Tex., in Bardswell, Ky., and in Newman, Ga. In Paris the officers of the law delivered the prisoner to the mob. The mayor gave the school children a holiday and the railroads ran excursion trains so that the people might see a human being burned to death. In Texarkana, the year before, men and boys amused themselves by cutting off strips of flesh and thrusting knives into their helpless victim. At Newman, Ga., of the present year, the mob tried every conceivable torture to compel the victim to cry out and confess, before they set fire to the faggots that burned him. But their trouble was all in vain—he never uttered a cry, and they could not make him confess.

This condition of affairs were brutal enough and horrible enough if it were true that lynchings occurred only because of the commission of crimes against women—as is constantly declared by ministers, editors, lawyers, teachers, statesmen, and even by women themselves. It has been to the interest of those who did the lynching to blacken the good name of the helpless and defenseless victims of their hate. For this reason they publish at every possible opportunity this excuse for lynching, hoping thereby not only to palliate their own crime but at the same time to prove the negro a moral monster and unworthy of the respect and sympathy of the civilized world. But this alleged reason adds to the deliberate injustice of the mob's work. Instead of lynchings being caused by assaults upon women, the statistics show that not one-third of the victims of lynchings are even charged with such crimes. The Chicago *Tribune,* which publishes annually lynching statistics, is authority for the following:

In 1892, when lynching reached high-water mark, there were 241 persons lynched. . . .

Of this number, 160 were of negro descent. Four of them were lynched in New York, Ohio, and Kansas; the remainder were murdered in the South. Five of this number were females. The charges for which they were lynched cover a wide range. They are as follows:

Rape	46
Murder	58
Rioting	3
Race Prejudice	6
No cause given	4
Incendiarism	6
Robbery	6
Assault and battery	1

Attempted rape 11
Suspected robbery 4
Larceny 1
Self-defense 1
Insulting women 2
Desperadoes 6
Fraud 1
Attempted murder 2
No offense stated, boy and girl 2

In the case of the boy and girl above referred to, their father, named Hastings, was accused of the murder of a white man. His fourteen-year-old daughter and sixteen-year-old son were hanged and their bodies filled with bullets; then the father was also lynched. This occurred in November, 1892, at Jonesville, La.

Indeed, the record for the last twenty years shows exactly the same or a smaller proportion who have been charged with this horrible crime. Quite a number of the one-third alleged cases of assault that have been personally investigated by the writer have shown that there was no foundation in fact for the charges; yet the claim is not made that there were no real culprits among them. The negro has been too long associated with the white man not to have copied his vices as well as his virtues. But the negro resents and utterly repudiates the efforts to blacken his good name by asserting that assaults upon women are peculiar to his race. The negro has suffered far more from the commission of this crime against the women of his race by white men than the white race has ever suffered through *his* crimes. Very scant notice is taken of the matter when this is the condition of affairs. What becomes a crime deserving capital punishment when the tables are turned is a matter of small moment when the negro woman is the accusing party.

But since the world has accepted this false and unjust statement, and the burden of proof has been placed upon the negro to vindicate his race, he is taking steps to do so. The Anti-Lynching Bureau of the National Afro-American Council is arranging to have every lynching investigated and publish the facts to the world, as has been done in the case of Sam Hose, who was burned alive last April at Newman, Ga. The detective's report showed that Hose killed Cranford, his employer, in self-defense, and that, while a mob was organizing to hunt Hose to punish him for killing a white man, not till twenty-four hours after the murder was the charge of rape, embellished with psychological and physical impossibilities, circulated. That gave an impetus to the hunt, and the Atlanta *Constitution*'s reward of $500 keyed the mob to the necessary burning and roasting pitch. Of five hundred newspaper clippings of that horrible affair, nine-tenths of them assumed Hose's guilt—simply because his murderers said so, and because it is the fashion to believe the negro peculiarly addicted to this species of crime. All the negro asks is justice—a fair and impartial trial in the courts of the country. That given, he will abide the result.

But this question affects the entire American nation, and from several points of view: First, on the ground of consistency. Our watchword has been "the land of the free and the home of the brave." Brave men do not gather by thousands to torture and murder a single individual, so gagged and bound he cannot make even feeble resistance or defense. Neither do brave men or women stand by and see such things done without compunction of conscience, nor read of them without protest. Our nation has been active and outspoken in its endeavors to right the wrongs of the Armenian Christian, the Russian Jew, the Irish Home Ruler, the native women of India, the Siberian exile, and the Cuban patriot. Surely it should be the nation's duty to correct its own evils!

Second, on the ground of economy. To those who fail to be convinced from any other point of view touching this momentous question, a consideration of the economic phase might not be amiss. It is generally known that mobs in Louisiana, Colorado, Wyoming, and other States have lynched subjects of other countries. When their different governments demanded satisfaction, our country was forced to confess her inability to protect said subjects in the several States because of our State-rights doctrines, or in turn demand punishment of the lynchers. This confession, while humiliating in the extreme, was not satisfactory; and, while the United States cannot protect, she can pay. This she has done, and it is certain will have to do again in the case of the recent lynching of Italians in Louisiana. The United States already has paid in indemnities for lynching nearly a half million dollars. . . .

Third, for the honor of Anglo-Saxon civilization. No scoffer at our boasted American civilization could say anything more harsh of it than does the American white man himself who says he is unable to protect the honor of his women without resort to such brutal, inhuman, and degrading exhibitions as characterize "lynching bees." The cannibals of the South

Sea Islands roast human beings alive to satisfy hunger. The red Indian of the Western plains tied his prisoner to the stake, tortured him, and danced in fiendish glee while his victim writhed in the flames. His savage, untutored mind suggested no better way than that of wreaking vengeance upon those who had wronged him. These people knew nothing about Christianity and did not profess to follow its teachings; but such primary laws as they had they lived up to. No nation, savage or civilized, save only the United States of America, has confessed its inability to protect its women save by hanging, shooting, and burning alleged offenders.

Finally, for love of country. No American travels abroad without blushing for shame for his country on this subject. And whatever the excuse that passes current in the United States, it avails nothing abroad. With all the powers of government in control; with all laws made by white men, administered by white judges, jurors, prosecuting attorneys, and sheriffs; with every office of the executive department filled by white men—no excuse can be offered for exchanging the orderly administration of justice for barbarous lynchings and "unwritten laws." Our country should be placed speedily above the plane of confessing herself a failure at self-government. This cannot be until Americans of every section, of broadest patriotism and best and wisest citizenship, not only see the defect in our country's armor but take the necessary steps to remedy it.

Further Resources

BOOKS

Harris, Trudier, ed. *Selected Works of Ida B. Wells-Barnett.* New York: Oxford University Press, 1991.

McMurry, Linda O. *To Keep the Waters Troubled: The Life of Ida B. Wells.* New York: Oxford University Press, 1998.

Thompson, Mildred. *Ida B. Wells-Barnett: An Exploratory Study of an American Black Woman, 1893–1930.* Brooklyn, N.Y.: Carlson, 1990.

Schlipp, Madelon Golden, and Sharon M. Murphy. *Great Women of the Press.* Carbondale, Ill.: Southern Illinois Press, 1983.

Woodward, C. Vann. *The Strange Career of Jim Crow,* 3rd ed. New York: Oxford University Press, 1974.

WEBSITES

"How Did Black and White Southern Women Campaign to End Lynching, 1890–1942?" *Women and Social Movements in the United States, 1775–2000.* Available online at http://womhist.binghamton.edu/aswpl/intro.htm; website home page: http://womhist.binghamton.edu/ (accessed May 27, 2003).

News Coverage of Natural Disasters

The Galveston Hurricane and Flood

Illustration

Date: 1900

Source: The Galveston Hurricane and Flood. 1900. Corbis, Image no. BE057194. Available online at http://pro.corbis.com (accessed June 18, 2003).

"Earthquake and Fire: San Francisco in Ruins"

Newspaper articles

By: *The Call-Chronicle-Examiner*

Date: April 19, 1906

Source: "Earthquake and Fire: San Francisco in Ruins." *The Call-Chronicle-Examiner.* April 19, 1906. Available online at http://www.loc.gov/exhibits/treasures/images/uc005119.jpg; website home page: http://www.loc.gov (accessed June 18, 2003).

"San Francisco, April 18, 1906"

Photograph

By: Arnold Genthe

Date: April 18, 1906

Source: "San Francisco, April 18, 1906." Library of Congress, Arnold Genthe collection, Image no. LC-G403-0271-D. Available online at http://lcweb.loc.gov (accessed May 28, 2003). ■

Introduction

Covering the natural disasters of the 1900s suited yellow journalists perfectly. Yellow journalism developed from the ongoing competition between William Randolph Hearst's *New York Journal* and Joseph Pulitzer's *New York World* at the turn of the century. Critics argued that these papers degraded the status of journalism by resorting to the lowest denominator to attract readership. Reporters emphasized the most melodramatic, sensational aspect of a story, real or fabricated, to increase circulation as much as possible. This brand of journalism influenced American entrance into the Spanish-American War in 1898, making plain the power of the yellow press. Using many of the editorial techniques developed to encourage and then cover the war, the press entered the twentieth century with an ardent desire to sustain booming circulation figures spawned by the foreign conflict. With technological improvements, newspapers became capable of running millions of copies every day

Primary Source

The Galveston Hurricane and Flood

SYNOPSIS: This lithograph illustrates the tidal wade that devastated Galveston, Texas, on September 8, 1900. People are shown being washed away by the tide, along with homes and rubble. On-the-spot news photography was often impossible in the early twentieth century so newspapers relied heavily on illustrations like these based on eyewitness accounts or sometimes on pure speculation.

of the year, each featuring intricately designed lithographs, photographs, and drawings to attract readers with striking visuals.

Significance

The lithograph reprinted here depicted the human trauma of the Galveston Flood of 1900. About five thousand Galveston residents, one-eighth of the city's population, died from a hurricane that smashed into Galveston Island on September 7, 1900. The storm destroyed many of the city's buildings and all of the bridges connecting it to the mainland. The loss of the bridges, railroad, and telegraph lines prevented escape and also hampered relief efforts. Into this horrible situation stepped Winifred Sweet Black, who wrote under the name Annie Laurie. Black was the first reporter to report from the scene and provided William Randolph Hearst's papers with startling commentaries on the damage inflicted in Galveston. Hearst and Black went so far as to organize a fund-raising drive to provide support for the victims of the flood, eventually collecting $350,000 in donations. Black's harrowing reporting reflected much of the press's reporting of the Galveston disaster. The lithograph offered readers an urgent, violent representation of the storm's impact. For virtually every person in the United States who could not see the devastation firsthand, illustrations such as this provided a critical instrument to communicate the nature of the disaster to readers nationwide.

The San Francisco earthquake of April 18, 1906, and the fires that erupted following the quake destroyed many of the city's downtown buildings and killed hundreds of

The Call-Chronicle-Examiner

SAN FRANCISCO, THURSDAY, APRIL 19, 1906.

EARTHQUAKE AND FIRE: SAN FRANCISCO IN RUINS

DEATH AND DESTRUCTION HAVE BEEN THE FATE OF SAN FRANCISCO. SHAKEN BY A TEMBLOR AT 5:13 O'CLOCK YESTERDAY MORNING, THE SHOCK LASTING 48 SECONDS, AND SCOURGED BY FLAMES THAT RAGED DIAMETRICALLY IN ALL DIRECTIONS, THE CITY IS A MASS OF SMOULDERING RUINS. AT SIX O'CLOCK LAST EVENING THE FLAMES SEEMINGLY PLAYING WITH INCREASED VIGOR, THREATENED TO DESTROY SUCH SECTIONS AS THEIR FURY HAD SPARED DURING THE EARLIER PORTION OF THE DAY. BUILDING THEIR PATH IN A TRIANGUAR CIRCUIT FROM THE START IN THE EARLY MORNING, THEY JOCKEYED AS THE DAY WANED, LEFT THE BUSINESS SECTION, WHICH THEY HAD ENTIRELY DEVASTATED, AND SKIPPED IN A DOZEN DIRECTIONS TO THE RESIDENCE PORTIONS. AS NIGHT FELL THEY HAD MADE THEIR WAY OVER INTO THE NORTH BEACH SECTION AND SPRINGING ANEW TO THE SOUTH THEY REACHED OUT ALONG THE SHIPPING SECTION DOWN THE BAY SHORE, OVER THE HILLS AND ACROSS TOWARD THIRD AND TOWNSEND STREETS. WAREHOUSES, WHOLESALE HOUSES AND MANUFACTURING CONCERNS FELL IN THEIR PATH. THIS COMPLETED THE DESTRUCTION OF THE ENTIRE DISTRICT KNOWN AS THE "SOUTH OF MARKET STREET." HOW FAR THEY ARE REACHING TO THE SOUTH ACROSS THE CHANNEL CANNOT BE TOLD AS THIS PART OF THE CITY IS SHUT OFF FROM SAN FRANCISCO PAPERS.

AFTER DARKNESS, THOUSANDS OF THE HOMELESS WERE MAKING THEIR WAY WITH THEIR BLANKETS AND SCANT PROVISIONS TO GOLDEN GATE PARK AND THE BEACH TO FIND SHELTER. THOSE IN THE HOMES ON THE HILLS JUST NORTH OF THE HAYES VALLEY WRECKED SECTION PILED THEIR BELONGINGS IN THE STREETS AND EXPRESS WAGONS AND AUTOMOBILES WERE HAULING THE THINGS AWAY TO THE SPARSELY SETTLED REGIONS. EVERYBODY IN SAN FRANCISCO IS PREPARED TO LEAVE THE CITY, FOR THE BELIEF IS FIRM THAT SAN FRANCISCO WILL BE TOTALLY DESTROYED.

DOWNTOWN EVERYTHING IS RUIN. NOT A BUSINESS HOUSE STANDS. THEATRES ARE CRUMBLED INTO HEAPS. FACTORIES AND COMMISSION HOUSES LIE SMOULDERING ON THEIR FORMER SITES. ALL OF THE NEWSPAPER PLANTS HAVE BEEN RENDERED USELESS, THE "CALL" AND THE "EXAMINER" BUILDINGS, EXCLUDING THE "CALL'S" EDITORIAL ROOMS ON STEVENSON STREET BEING ENTIRELY DESTROYED.

IT IS ESTIMATED THAT THE LOSS IN SAN FRANCISCO WILL REACH FROM $150,000,000 TO $200,000,000. THESE FIGURES ARE IN THE ROUGH AND NOTHING CAN BE TOLD UNTIL PARTIAL ACCOUNTING IS TAKEN.

ON EVERY SIDE THERE WAS DEATH AND SUFFERING YESTERDAY. HUNDREDS WERE INJURED, EITHR BURNED, CRUSHED OR STRUCK BY FALLING PIECES FROM THE BUILDINGS AND ONE OF TEN DIED WHILE ON THE OPOPERATING TABLE AT MECHANICS' PAVILION, IMPROVISED AS A HOSPITAL FOR THE COMFORT AND CARE OF 300 OF THE INJURED. THE NUMBER OF DEAD IS NOT KNOWN BUT IT IS ESTIMATED THAT AT LEAST 500 MET THEIR DEATH IN THE HORROR.

AT NINE O'CLOCK, UNDER A SPECIAL MESSAGE FROM PRESIDENT ROOSEVELT, THE CITY WAS PLACED UNDER MARTIAL LAW. HUNDREDS OF TROOPS PATROLLED THE STREETS AND DROVE THE CROWDS BACK, WHILE HUNDREDS MORE WERE SET AT WORK ASSISTING THE FIRE AND POLICE DEPARTMENTS. THE STRICTEST ORDERS WERE ISSUED, AND IN TRUE MILITARY SPIRIT THE SOLDIERS OBEYED. DURING THE AFTERNOON THREE THIEVES MET THEIR DEATH BY RIFLE BULLETS WHILE AT WORK IN THE RUINS. THE CURIOUS WERE DRIVEN BACK AT THE BREASTS OF THE HORSES THAT THE CAVALRYMEN RODE AND ALL THE CROWDS WERE FORCED FROM THE LEVEL DISTRICT TO THE HILLY SECTION BEYOND TO THE NORTH.

THE WATER SUPPLY WAS ENTIRELY CUT OFF, AND MAY BE IT WAS JUST AS WELL, FOR THE LINES OF FIRE DEPARTMENT WOULD HAVE BEEN ABSOLUTELY USELESS AT ANY STAGE. ASSISTANT CHIEF DOUGHERTY SUPERVISED THE WORK OF HIS MEN AND EARLY IN THE MORNING IT WAS SEEN THAT THE ONLY POSSIBLE CHANCE TO SAVE THE CITY LAY IN EFFORT TO CHECK THE FLAMES BY THE USE OF DYNAMITE. DURING THE DAY A BLAST COULD BE HEARD IN ANY SECTION AT INTERVALS OF ONLY A FEW MINUTES, AND BUILDINGS NOT DESTROYED BY FIRE WERE BLOWN TO ATOMS. BUT THROUGH THE GAPS MADE THE FLAMES JUMPED AND ALTHOUGH THE FAILURES OF THE HEROIC EFFORTS OF THE POLICE, FIREMEN AND SOLDIERS WERE AT TIMES SICKENING, THE WORK WAS CONTINUED WITH A DESPERATION THAT WILL LIVE AS ONE OF THE FEATURES OF THE TERRIBLE DISASTER. MEN WORKED LIKE FIENDS TO COMBAT THE LAUGHING, ROARING, ONRUSHING FIRE DEMON.

NO HOPE LEFT FOR SAFETY OF ANY BUILDINGS

San Francisco seems doomed to entire destruction. With a lapse in the raging of the flames just before dark, the hope was raised that with the use of the tons of dynamite the course of the fire might be checked and confined to the triangular sections it had cut out for its path. But on the Barbary Coast the fire broke out anew and as night closed in the flames were eating their way into parts untouched in their ravages during the day. To the south and the north they spread; down to the docks and out into the resident section, in and to the north of Hayes Valley. By six o'clock practically all of St. Ignatius' great buildings were no more. They had been leveled to the fiery heap that marked what was once the metropolis of the West.

The first of the big structures to go to ruin was the Call Building, the famous skyscraper. At eleven o'clock the big 18-story building was a furnace. Flames leaped from every window and shot skyward from the circular windows in the dome. In less than two hours nothing remained but the tall skeleton.

By five o'clock the Palace Hotel was in ruins. The old hostelry, famous the world over, withstood the seige until the last and although dynamite was used in frequent blasts to drive

Continued on Page Two

BLOW BUILDINGS UP TO CHECK FLAMES

The dynamiting of buildings in the track of the fire, to stay the progress of the flames, was in charge of John Bermingham, Jr., superintendent of the California Powder Works. Several experienced men from the powder works, assisted by policemen and members of the fire department, did the hazardous work of blowing up the buildings. They were razed in sets of threes, but the open spaces where the shattered buildings fell were quickly turned into holocausts of flame. The work was most effective in the business blocks east of Kearny street.

WHOLE CITY IS ABLAZE

At 10 o'clock last night the Occidental Hotel was destroyed by the flames which swept unchecked across Montgomery street and attacked the block bounded by Montgomery, Sutter, Bush and Kearny. The new Merchants' Exchange building was a mass of flames from basement to tower.

The Union Trust building and Crocker-Woolworth Bank were both ablaze and the Chronicle building and other buildings in that block were threatened by the flames.

Shortly after 10 o'clock the fire had eaten its way southward from Portsmouth Square to Kearny and California streets. The entire section fronting on the west side of Kearny street seemed doomed.

All the building adjoining the Hall of Justice were ablaze and the firemen were striving to save the structure by using dynamite. It is almost a certainty that every building contained in the section bounded by Clay, Kearny, Market and East streets will be consumed.

The flames had eaten their way westward in the residence section as far as Gough street. There, by dynamiting blocks after blocks, the firemen succeeded in checking the devouring element.

CHURCH OF SAINT IGNATIUS IS DESTROYED

The magnificent church and College of St. Ignatius, on the northwest corner of Van Ness avenue and Hayes street represents in its destruction a material loss of over $1,000,000. The actual cost of the great building was over $800,000, but during the years which have elapsed since its erection the church has been enriched by paintings and frescoes, which were priceless. Some of them were works of art which can never be replaced, however willing those interested in the church might be to meet any expense in the effort.

MAYOR CONFERS WITH MILITARY AND CITIZENS

At 1 o'clock yesterday afternoon 50 representative citizens of San Francisco met the Mayor, the Chief of Police and the United States Military authorities in the police office in the basement of the Hall of Justice. They had been summoned thither by Mayor Schmitz early in the forenoon, the fearful possibilities of the situation having forced themselves upon him immediately after the shock of earthquake in the morning, and the news which at once reached him of the completeness of the disaster. He lost no time in making out a list of citizens from whom to seek advice and assistance, and in summoning them to the conference. It was called at the Hall of Justice, as virtually the first news which reached the Mayor regarding the extent of the disaster was that of the ruin of the City Hall. He did not realize that even while the conference was to be going on cornices would be crashing down and windows falling in fragments in the Hall of Justice also, and that before sunset desperate efforts would be made to blow the structure up in the vain endeavor by this means to check the advance of the flames in the northern section of the downtown district.

All, or nearly all of the citizens summoned to the conference

Continued on Page Two

Primary Source

"Earthquake and Fire: San Francisco in Ruins"

SYNOPSIS: A powerful earthquake struck San Francisco on April 18, 1906. It and the resulting fires destroyed much of the city. The three major daily newspapers in San Francisco teamed up on April 19th to produce a joint issue on the disaster. The front page of *The Call-Chronicle-Examiner* issue is shown here. THE LIBRARY OF CONGRESS.

Primary Source

"San Francisco, April 18, 1906"

SYNOPSIS: This photograph, taken by Arnold Genthe in San Francisco's old Chinatown, captures smoke rising from the fires caused by the April 18, 1906, earthquake. THE LIBRARY OF CONGRESS, PRINTS & PHOTOGRAPHS DIVISION, ARNOLD GENTHE COLLECTION.

residents. In an unprecedented display of editorial solidarity, the editors of the city's three major papers, the *Call,* the *Chronicle,* and the *Examiner,* united to produce an issue the day after the quake as people continued to fight blazes throughout the city. Under the headline "Earthquake and Fire: San Fransisco in Ruins," the first edition described the massive shock and suffering being endured. The lead sentence read like an emergency telegraph: "Death and destruction have been the fate of San Francisco." The report ended with a scene seemingly out of war: "During the day a blast could be heard in any section at intervals of only a few minutes, and buildings not destroyed by fire were blown to atoms. But through the gaps made the flames jumped and although the failures of the heroic efforts of the police firemen and soldiers were at times sickening, the work was continued with a desperation that will live as one of the features of the terrible disaster. Men worked like fiends to combat the laughing, roaring, onrushing fire demon."

While journalists struggled to report from San Francisco, other national papers attempted to manage as best they could without reporters at the scene. Hearst's *New York American* attempted to stay ahead of the competition by using a doctored photograph from the Baltimore fire of 1904. Other writers simply created harrowing descriptions of the fires by use of the imagination, contriving details, and sometimes entire stories out of thin air. Despite the obvious differences in the techniques used to depict natural disasters displayed below, it may be helpful to consider which provided the most informative or most dramatic presentation of the event in question—the lithograph, the headlines and text, or the photograph.

Further Resources

BOOKS

Emery, Michael, and Edwin Emery. *The Press and America: An Interpretive History of the Mass Media,* 7th ed. Englewood Cliffs, N.J.: Prentice Hall, 1992.

"'Tabloid Journalism': Its Causes and Effects"

Journal article

By: A. Maurice Low

Date: March 1901

Source: Low, A. Maurice. "'Tabloid Journalism': Its Causes and Effects." *The Forum* 31, March 1901, 56–61.

About the Author: British by birth, Sir A. Maurice Low (1860–1929) wrote extensively about America, where he earned his master's degree. Low reported for the *Boston Globe,* performed policy research for the U.S. and British governments, and wrote dozens of articles and books, including the two-volume *The American People: A Study in National Psychology.* When Low died, he was the chief U.S. correspondent for the *London Post* in Washington, D.C., where he had lived for fifteen years. He was knighted after his death. ■

Introduction

Today, *tabloid journalism* possesses a purely pejorative connotation. The term conveys substandard, biased, or salacious reporting. The public views tabloids purely as entertainment rather than as a source for well-researched coverage and insightful commentary. Originally, though, the term *tabloid* referred primarily to the newspaper's smaller-than-average size rather than its content. Tabloids appeared early in American history, but they exploded in the early decades of the twentieth century, as new printing methods permitted greater circulation, more illustrations and intricate designs, and lower costs. In 1901, tabloids had begun in England, and A. Maurice Low, a commentator on British and American affairs, wrote the article "'Tabloid Journalism': Its Causes and Effects" to examine the American media environment and the possible ramifications of tabloids in the United States.

Significance

In light of the growing movement toward investigative journalism later known as muckraking, Low viewed the tabloid as simplistic, striving to avoid trouble in order to curry favor with the widest possible readership. The tabloid sought to provide the urban masses with short, concise news reports that neither incited nor bored but always strived to avoid controversy. Low's critique reflected a broader debate within journalism during the 1900s between the so-called yellow journalism and muckraking. Yellow journalism enticed readers with entertaining stories and pictures, while muckrakers investigated public and private corruption in the hopes of creating public support for reform.

Low saw a different course for newspapers in the United States. He saw the future of American journalism in the growing popularity of tabloids in England. Considering the growing influence of tabloid papers in England, Low believed that daily papers in the United States were beginning to inform readers with a more concise news presentation. Mirroring the objectives that led to the creation of *USA Today* in the 1980s, Low contended that papers were attempting to reach the greatest audience by providing readers with neutral, brief articles of only a few hundred words. Publications such as Alfred Harmsworth's *Daily Mail* offered news that, according to Low's article, "was neither vicious nor virtuous; it did not elevate, neither did it demoralize; it was not witty or

Newspaper magnate Alfred Harmsworth on a visit to Washington, D.C., in 1917. HULTON ARCHIVE. REPRODUCED BY PERMISSION.

enlightening; it was simply commonplace, dull, trivial, and exactly suited to the mental requirements of its readers." By decreasing cost and tailoring papers to the reading levels of the urban masses, Low believed that American news outlets would further increase their circulations in the twentieth century. Daily papers would be just that: daily—relevant to only a single day and, in Low's words, ready "to spoil twelve hours after manufacture." Many of the core strategies described by Low would shape the evolution of mass media through the twentieth century. A tabloid news story hooked readers with a sharp yet imaginative lead sentence, grabbing the reader's attention before some distraction or boredom led him or her to turn the page—or, in a later period, change the channel.

Low recognized that American journalism already seemed guided by many of the practices then new to English journalists and readers, and he decried the impact of tabloid news. He declared, "As it seems to me, the effect of tabloid journalism is distinctly bad in that it destroys the taste for more serious reading." At the same time, Low concluded that newspapers could not strive to be tools of intellectual advancement, as their primary focus should be on presenting the news in a brief, digestible format. He recognized the jarring combination of news included in any given daily paper—murder, graft, and natural disasters amid lighter fare, such as sports, fashion, and comics. Foreshadowing ongoing debates on the media's role in society, Low worried about the impact of this phenomenon, where serious news coverage appears to become just another form of entertainment.

Low nonetheless found hope for American journalism. He saw a reading public that desired concise but thorough reporting and information both interesting and useful. Despite this fairly optimistic conclusion, Low's commentary mirrored that of contemporary critics who characterized the journalism profession as overly concerned with circulation and inept at providing readers with nuanced, complex investigations of difficult subjects.

Primary Source

"'Tabloid Journalism': Its Causes and Effects"

SYNOPSIS: Low's primary subject, Alfred Harmsworth, pioneered the advent of tabloid journalism in Great Britain before influencing publishers in the United States. Harmsworth had founded the *Daily Mail* of London in 1896 and would eventually create the *Daily Mirror* in 1903. The latter paper, the first tabloid in London, soon had a daily circulation of over one million. Harmsworth was very influential in encouraging Joseph Pulitzer to begin a tabloid paper in the United States. Pulitzer allowed Harmsworth to begin editing *The World* on January 1, 1901, two months before the publication of the following article. Harmsworth, also known as Lord Northcliffe, eventually urged Joseph Medill Patterson to begin his own tabloid, the *New York Illustrated Daily News,* which began in 1919 and gained a circulation of 750,000 within five years, cementing the power, if not the stature, of the tabloid in American journalism.

Recently, we have been treated to an experiment in daily journalism. Mr. Alfred Harmsworth has given us his idea of what the twentieth century newspaper should be. He calls it "tabloid journalism." Like everything new, it has been talked about, condemned, and approved.

This is an age of tabloids, which is only another name for concentration. We take our medicines in the form of pills and capsules and tabloids; we take our nourishment in the form of an ox boiled down to a tea cup; even our intellectual *pabulum* must come in a similar form. It is all characteristic of the rush, hurry, superficiality, and the desire to avoid trouble, which were the distinguishing traits of the century just closed. If a man is sick he takes his capsule because he can absorb it anywhere; it does not cause him to lose even a minute from his business; it is so delightfully simple; and so, in the same way, he can snatch a meal out of a spoonful of beef tea. He can also read the history of the world in one sitting in Somebody's "The Universe at a Glance in Pointed Paragraphs."

Mr. Alfred Harmsworth is a genius. He possesses the three great gifts which make for success wherever they may be employed. He has tremendous vitality; he has the power intuitively to divine what the world wants, and he has the ability to execute. Such a man would make his mark in any line of endeavor. He would be as successful in finance or statesmanship or war as he has been in journalism; and what he has accomplished in journalism the world knows.

A man of unusually keen perceptions and with the audacity which is spelled genius when it wins, Mr. Harmsworth saw in London a mine so rich and so easily to be worked that its golden possibilities were staggering. Education in England had succeeded admirably in turning out every year an ever-increasing host of half-baked sciolists of both sexes. The board schools, the Acts of Parliament, and the ever-zealous educational officers had enabled them to get hold of a smattering; and with the "Three Rs" they acquired something which had not been provided for by Parliament or boards of education. Crude, immature, raw, and unable to assimilate the little knowledge which had been tabloidly furnished to them, the result of education, in nine cases out of ten, was to give them a vague longing for something which they could not define or express. It had given them aspiration for what they knew not; it had stirred passions and aroused desires which had shadowed across their minds, but never assumed substance. The "work'us kid," whose past was a grim recollection of starvation and torture, and whose anticipation of the future was equally joyless, gave way to the "board school boy," who quickly forgot his multiplication table and his grammar, but who never forgot that not everybody worked. In a word, he wanted to be amused.

Here was a constituency ready made. Mr. Harmsworth gave the world—his world of London, a city, remember, with a population greater than that of any State of the American Union, with three exceptions—"Answers." It was exactly what had been demanded; it was the answer to the unexpressed desire. It was neither vicious nor virtuous; it did not elevate, neither did it demoralize; it was not witty or enlightening; it was simply commonplace, dull, trivial, and exactly suited to the mental requirements of its readers. And that, after all, was the secret of nineteenth century commercial success—to give the people precisely what they wanted. Errand boys and factory hands invested their coppers in "Answers." They read it at their lunch, and it was the Attic salt to their hunk of dry bread and rancid bacon. The errand boy took a tabloid, one of Mr. Harmsworth's paragraphs, as he went loitering between the bank and Lombard street; the young clerk in the interval between measuring half a yard of ribbon, furtively snatched a tabloid under the counter when the floorwalker's back was turned. Mr. Harmsworth was the P. T. Barnum of England. He furnished a "refined entertainment." He gave his readers amusement; he provided them with "jokes." Some of his tabloids were so deftly sugar-coated that "the useful information" which they contained could be taken by even the most sensitive stomachs.

One of the phenomena of the nineteenth century—one wonders if the same thing will continue during the present—was the fecundity created by a demand. When a demand existed and an attempt was made to satisfy it, instead of the public being satiated, a new appetite was born. In nothing has this been so marked as in cheap literature, including in the term newspapers and magazines as well as books. The circulation of newspapers and magazines has enormously increased since their reduction in price. One "Answers" could not supply the ever-increasing demand. Mr. Harmsworth's rivals, who were without his creative force, but intelligent enough to follow where he led, saw their opportunity and threw into the insatiable maw "Answers" under other names.

Nor did Mr. Harmsworth propose to suffer the fate of most pioneers and, after having cleared the ground, see others garner the crops. He duplicated and reduplicated his original production, the prototype of the whole family, until to-day the news stands of London are covered with "Answers," "Tit-Bits," "Smith's Scraps," "Jones' Sayings," "Brown's Hash," and so on through a couple of score more until one wonders who reads them and how they manage to exist. But the question who reads them is quickly answered. Go into any bus or train or lunch room at any hour of the day or night and you see men and boys and women and girls taking and enjoying their tabloids.

The curious thing is that the reading is no longer confined to the class for whom it was originally intended, as the people of greater intelligence are not ashamed to acknowledge that they are addicted to tabloidism. Last summer, while going from London to Glasgow, I fell in with a middle-aged Englishman, whom I later learned was the executive of a large corporation. He had a bundle of papers and magazines, among them half a dozen brands of tabloids. We engaged in conversation, and he courteously handed me a tabloid. When I expressed a preference for nutriment in another form, he explained that he found in tabloids a mental diversion. "I get tired of 'The Saturday Review' and 'The Spectator,'" he said, "and I read these things because they keep me from thinking."

They are all the same. They are all stamped from one die. Mr. Harmsworth knows his readers better than they know themselves. He knows that they are incapable of sustained thought, and that with them language is direct. Consequently, you must talk to them in as few words as possible; you must hold their attention in a sentence and not in a paragraph. In a story they want situations, not incidents. Occasionally, the proprietor originates a prize—a life insurance policy, a catchpenny scheme of some kind—and immediately his rivals take it for their own. Having assimilated one tabloid you have taken all; and, like the modern patent medicine, these tabloids have a variety of uses—from wrapping up the errand boy's lunch to lining the pantry shelves.

From the weekly "Answers" to the "Daily Mail" is a short step. Until the advent of Mr. Harmsworth into daily journalism, the London newspapers were the dullest, the heaviest, the most unattractive, and the least intelligent press in the world. This last assertion, I suppose, will be questioned. It is a fact, however, that in their gathering and treatment of news, which includes the editorial comment upon it, the London newspapers have always displayed antiquated methods and an unintelligent grasp of events. I am quite aware of the fact that the editorial writers on the leading London papers are men of wide and thorough knowledge, and that it is popularly supposed that the important editorials are written by specialists—men who, in addition to their literary ability, have a professional and intimate knowledge of their subject; and yet, despite their knowledge and their professional attainments, the ignorance and glaring inaccuracies are astounding.

No one can know everything; and when I am given a ponderous column and a half on the latest archæological discovery I am quite willing to accept the writer's dictum for the correctness of his conclusions; but when I glanced over a review of a session of Congress just closed, as I did in London last summer, and in a column editorial discovered by actual count fourteen misstatements of facts and confusion of men and things, I wondered what had happened to the American "specialist." The old motto, "False in one, false in all," might be justly applied. If these writers are so ignorant of America, a country which has been brought so close to them, and whose people speak their own tongue, is it not a fair presumption that their ignorance must be much greater of countries more remote, whose peoples are alien to them in language and thought?

The editorial page of a London newspaper is ponderous, and the news pages are unsatisfactory, dull, and monotonous. The English reporter or correspondent is not trained to write, but simply to record facts. The well written account of an important event—the opening of Parliament, the departure of troops, the return of a popular hero, a yacht race—which is such a marked feature of an American newspaper is unknown in England. The London editor shows his appreciation of the value of news by space. He gives to it several columns; but we find nothing but words, words, words. The descriptive, the photographic reproduction, the light and shade, the touch of wit, the playful fancy of the writer, the human interest—all this we know in the American newspaper; but one never sees it in the London reporter's "story." In fact, if I were asked to present the distinction between American and English reporting in a few words, I should say that in America we aim to give photographs, while in England they content themselves with working drawings made to exact scale.

If the people wanted tabloids once a week, was it not reasonable to suppose, Mr. Harmsworth argued, that they would swallow them every morning before breakfast? Again Mr. Harmsworth gave them just what they wanted. There are no heavy editorials in the "Mail"; there are no long and dull articles in its news columns. It is not well written, but it is not disreputable. It has none of the spice of the devil about it. It has no shrinking modesty. If it sends a special correspondent to Timbuctoo you are apt to know it; and you will be probably told of the *enormous* expense, the *wonderful* enterprise, and the *gigantic* labor involved. The dispatches from Timbuctoo appear in large type, and illustrated with maps and pictures. The correspondent is lurid and so graphically exact that one wonders how *he* can know so much when no one else knows anything. Perhaps later you find out that he has been a trifle imaginative, but no one cares for yesterday's tabloid.

Tabloids are warranted not to keep in any climate and to spoil twelve hours after manufacture. They are like yesterday's snowstorm.

All this is an old story in the United States, although it was very new in London. To a certain extent Mr. Harmsworth has revolutionized English journalism, and he has revolutionized it by applying methods which have long been in vogue on this side of the Atlantic. The "Mail" furnishes no new suggestion to an American newspaper manager.

Thus far, the causes of what Mr. Harmsworth has ingeniously called "tabloid journalism." Now, what are its effects? As it seems to me, the effect of tabloid journalism is distinctly bad in that it destroys the taste for more serious reading. The ordinary daily newspaper is unquestionably an educational medium; and the majority, the great majority, of editors are to be found on the side of morality and decent living and civic virtue. Yet newspaper reading is not an intellectual training, and the man who devotes much time to the newspapers finds it difficult to concentrate his thoughts on books, which are not to be assimilated at a glance. In the nature of things it must be so. No newspaper writer dares to be deep or exhibit his knowledge. That would be fatal. He must be light, even flippant, and always interesting. Nor will the reader waste much time over what does not interest him in the first few lines. If it does not hold his attention he skips to something else; and after his spirits have been depressed by reading an editorial on the state of trade in South America, he can recover his vitality by perusing the "Humorous Side of Life."

Mr. Harmsworth would make the condition even worse than this. He would offer everything to his reader in concentrated form and would still further discourage his necessity to think. And that is the psychological explanation of tabloidism. The editor of one of the most successful magazines of the day said recently to a writer: "Your article is excellent and most interesting; but, unfortunately, it makes the reader think, and our aim is to amuse and not to instruct the readers of our magazine." Remembering what my English acquaintance said, it looks as if the whole world at this day were trying not to think, but simply to amuse itself.

Fortunately, the American newspaper reader has not yet reached the tabloid state. He wants his news presented as concisely as possible; he does not want long disquisitions on recondite subjects which have no possible interest for him; he cares more for news than views; but he does not care for a diet of scraps. If a story is to be told he wants it told in full; and if it is well written and has intrinsic importance, he does not find two or three columns any too much. He does not want essays served with his breakfast coffee, but he is prepared to read a not too abstruse article which may instruct him. In other words, his appetite is too healthy to be satisfied with tabloids.

Further Resources

BOOKS

Chalmers, David Mark. *The Muckrake Years.* New York: Van Nostrand, 1974.

Emery, Michael, and Edwin Emery. *The Press and America: An Interpretive History of the Mass Media,* 7th ed. Englewood Cliffs, N.J.: Prentice Hall, 1992.

Filler, Louis. *The Muckrakers.* University Park, Pa.: Pennsylvania State University Press, 1976.

PERIODICALS

McClure, S.S. "Concerning Three Articles in this Number of McClure's, and a Coincidence that May Set Us Thinking." *McClure's,* January 1903, 336.

WEBSITES

Historic Congressional Cemetery. A. Maurice Low obituary. Available online at http://www.congressionalcemetery.org/PDF/Obits/L/Obits_Low.PDF; website home page: http://www.congressionalcemetery.org/ (accessed May 26, 2003).

Political Cartoons Critical of U.S. Imperialism

"The Powers Celebrating the Fall of Pekin;" "Performing His Duty;" "Alligator Bait"

Political cartoons

Date: August 1901; January 1902; January 1909

Source: Mayfield, R.B. "The Powers Celebrating the Fall of Pekin." *The Bookman,* August 1901.; "Performing His Duty." *Brooklyn Eagle,* January 1902.; "Alligator Bait." *Detroit Journal,* January 1909. Available online at http://www.boondocksnet.com/gallery/us_000600.html; http://www.boondocksnet.com/gallery us_020100a.html; http://www.boondocksnet.com/gallery/us_090100a.html; website home page: Zwick, Jim, ed. Political Cartoons and Cartoonists. http://www.boondocksnet.com/gallery/pc_intro.htm (accessed May 27, 2003). ■

Introduction

The so-called American century began with the United States establishing its own empire to rival that of

Primary Source

"The Powers Celebrating the Fall of Pekin" (1 OF 3)

SYNOPSIS: With growing press and public criticism of American intervention in foreign affairs, journalists fashioned strident critiques of American empire throughout the 1900s. These political cartoons appeared in the midst of enormous American territorial expansion, and they examine the arguments behind this advancement and convey the ways in which both critics and supporters of American foreign policy often portrayed the subject peoples as unequal to Americans in terms of culture and power. The cartoon above, "The Powers Celebrating the Fall of Pekin," by R.B. Mayfield, was originally published in *The Bookman* in August 1901. It portrays the United States as one of several powerful nations trampelling over the native Chinese in celebration after putting down the Boxer Rebellion in that country.

Europe in the eastern and western hemispheres. Publisher William Randolph Hearst led the campaign for war and eagerly printed inflammatory, often unsubstantiated headlines concerning atrocities committed by the Spanish in Cuba and the Philippines. Following the explosion of the USS *Maine* in Havana harbor on February 15, 1898, Hearst and his competitors increased their competition by attempting to one-up the other in patriotic calls for glory, war, and American expansion. President William McKinley (served 1897–1901), who had considered entering into war with Spain for months, eventually called for such a conflict in a speech before Congress

Primary Source

"Performing His Duty" (2 OF 3)

"Performing His Duty" was originally published in the *Brooklyn Eagle,* reprinted in *American Review of Reviews* in January 1902. The cartoon appeared during the crisis that led to Panama's indepedence from Colombia, during which the United States intervened to serve its own interests.

Primary Source

"Alligator Bait" (3 OF 3)

"Alligator Bait," by Mayfield, was originally published in the *Detroit Journal,* and reprinted in *American Review of Reviews* in January 1909. The Haitian government is portrayed as childlike and weak in the face of revolution in this cartoon, as the United States looks on, contemplating intervention.

on April 11, 1898. He justified the war "to secure in the island the establishment of a stable government, capable of maintaining order and observing its international obligations, insuring peace and tranquility and the security of its citizens as well as our own." (http://www.mtholyoke.edu/acad/intrel/mkinly2.htm). Thus, according to McKinley, the "dictates of humanity" required American intervention. The president echoed the press's argument that "manifest destiny" obliged the United States to enter the conflict in order to aid the development of liberty and civilization throughout the world. The Spanish-American War, fought in less than four months from April 21, 1898, until August 12, 1898, witnessed 379 American troops dying in combat. The war ended with American occupation of formerly Spanish colonies such as Cuba, Puerto Rico, Guam, and the Philippines. The United States also formally annexed the Hawaiian Islands in July 1898.

In the 1900s, the United States continued to serve as an occupation force in the territories acquired during the Spanish-American War. In 1904, President Theodore Roosevelt (served 1901–1909) further expanded the nation's power in world affairs with his Corollary to the Monroe Doctrine of 1904. Theodore Roosevelt's policy declared that the United States possessed the inherent right to serve as an international police force in Latin America if deemed necessary to preserve stability in the region. At the same time, from its new base of operations in the Philippines, the United States strengthened its presence in Asia.

Political cartooning has a long history in American journalism. Colonial revolutionaries distributed caricatures of King George and the British Empire during their campaign for independence. But due to production technology constraints, newspapers offered cartoons infrequently until after the Civil War (1861–1865). The 1870s and 1880s saw an explosion of illustrations with sharp editorial slants. Cartoonist Thomas Nast offered the most influential and memorable series of the period in drawings for *Harper's Weekly.* Nast's vitriolic depictions of the corrupt Tammany Hall political machine in New York City helped bring down Tammany head William Marcy Tweed. In the process, Nast's drawings illustrated the massive power political cartooning could wield in American society.

Throughout this period, the mass media did far more than simply report the news. In many respects, the press became an active participant in debates over the extent to which the United States should become an international power. Hearst's influence in the decision to go to war with Spain increased the stakes of reporting, as journalists recognized the significant power they wielded from the newsroom. As the news media boomed following America's victory in the Spanish-American War, the *American Review of Reviews* reprinted hundreds of cartoons and articles on a monthly basis at the turn of the century. The following cartoons represent the anti-imperialist critiques levied by political cartoonists during the 1900s.

Significance

R. B. Mayfield's "The Powers Celebrating the Fall of Pekin" appeared in *The Bookman* in August 1901, shortly after a coalition of Western imperialists defeated the Boxer Rebellion in Beijing (Peking), China. The artist portrayed Uncle Sam as bloated, jolly, and ultimately naive, prancing along with the other world powers as they carelessly prepared to stomp over the Chinese. The cartoon reflected a theme common to anti-imperialist illustrations of the period: the United States was simply joining a crowd of selfish nations bent on destroying rather than uplifting colonized peoples.

"Battle Hymn of the Republic (Brought Down to Date)": Mark Twain

Mine eyes have seen the orgy of the launching of the Sword;
He is searching out the hoardings where the stranger's wealth is stored;
He hath loosed his fateful lightnings, and with woe and death has scored;
His lust is marching on.

I have seen him in the watch-fires of a hundred circling camps;
They have builded him an altar in the Eastern dews and damps;
I have read his doomful mission by the dim and flaring lamps—
His night is marching on.

I have read his bandit gospel writ in burnished rows of steel:
"As ye deal with my pretensions, so with you my wrath shall deal;
Let the faithless son of Freedom crush the patriot with his heel;
Lo, Greed is marching on!"

We have legalized the strumpet and are guarding her retreat;*
Greed is seeking out commercial souls before his judgement seat;
O, be swift, ye clods, to answer him! be jubilant my feet!
Our god is marching on!

In a sordid slime harmonious Greed was born in yonder ditch,
With a longing in his bosom—and for others' goods an itch.
As Christ died to make men holy, let men die to make us rich—
Our god is marching on.

* NOTE: In Manila the Government has placed a certain industry under the protection of our flag. (M.T.)

SOURCE: Twain, Mark. *Collected Tales, Sketches, Speeches, & Essays, 1891–1910.* New York: The Library of America, 1992. Available online at http://www.atheist-community.org/library/library_battle_hymn_of_the_republic.htm; website home page: http://www.atheist-community.org/index.htm (accessed June 2, 2003).

The *Brooklyn Eagle,* the daily paper for New York's most populous borough, printed "Performing His Duty" in January 1902, as President Theodore Roosevelt directed American forces to prevent battles between Columbian soldiers and Panamanian revolutionaries from disrupting the creation of the Panama Canal. This typically prejudicial cartoon depicted the U.S. "policeman" as upright, fair, and powerful. The indigenous population, on the other hand, appeared wild and uncivilized. While this cartoon would seem to support the American intervention and use of "Monroe Doctrine" to stabilize the region, the drawing also implicitly criticized the government argument of benevolent intervention in Latin America. This illustration displayed American military force being used solely for the purpose of expanding American economic power through control over the Isthmus of Panama.

May's "Alligator Bait," printed in the *Detroit Journal* in January 1909, further conveyed the idea that critiques of American imperialism need not present positive depictions of indigenous populations. This depiction of Haitian government officials resorted to popular racist drawings of people of African descent as infantile, uneducated, and unable to care for themselves. As revolutionaries threatened the American-allied government, U.S. officials debated whether to counter the insurrection (shown here as Uncle Sam peering from the American coast at the coming attack). While the caption appeared to encourage U.S. action to save the "helpless child," the cartoon reflected a prevalent criticism of American intervention. Critics often argued that the outcome might not be worth the effort. The victim displayed in this cartoon almost certainly would not have appeared sympathetic to the contemporary reader. Instead, the argument implied in this drawing was that the United States should probably avoid the conflict altogether.

Further Resources

BOOKS

Emery, Michael, and Edwin Emery. *The Press and America: An Interpretive History of the Mass Media,* 7th ed. Englewood Cliffs, N.J.: Prentice Hall, 1992.

Stephanson, Anders. *Manifest Destiny: American Expansionism and the Empire of Right.* New York: Hill and Wang, 1995.

Did the *New York Journal* Kill President McKinley?

"Assassination a Good Thing!"

Newspaper editorial

By: *New York Sun*

Date: September 8, 1901

Source: "Assassination a Good Thing!" *New York Sun,* September 8, 1901, 6.

"A Menace to Our Civilization"

Newspaper editorial

By: *New York Sun*

Date: September 12, 1901

Source: "A Menace to Our Civilization." *New York Sun,* September 12, 1901, 6.

"Responsibility for Yellow Journalism"

Newspaper editorial

By: *New York Evening Post*

Date: September 21, 1901

Source: "Responsibility for Yellow Journalism." *New York Evening Post,* September 21, 1901, 4. ■

Introduction

The term *yellow journalism* arose from a cartoon character, the "Yellow Kid," which first appeared in the *New York World,* only to be transferred to the *New York Journal* once its owner, William Randolph Hearst, hired its author away from Pulitzer's paper. Yellow journalism, though, symbolized something far graver than the cheery "Yellow Kid." Critics developed the term in response to what they saw as the degradation of journalism standards in the increasingly brutal conflict between Hearst and rival publisher Joseph Pulitzer. In battling to win the circulation war in New York City, the two publishers attempted to attract the largest number of readers by creating a new breed of popular journalism. The papers offered their audience sensational news coverage, along with new sections devoted to fashion, arts, culture, business, sports, and comics. This brand of popular journalism enraged some commentators, who decried a shift toward news as entertainment rather than public service.

The most famous examples of yellow journalism run amok appeared during the onset of the Spanish-American War in 1898. With President McKinley vacillating over whether to commit American troops against the Spanish empire in Cuba and the Philippines, Hearst vowed to create the war if only his reporters would send him suitable copy. Hearst used the campaign for war as a means of boosting his paper's popularity and influence. Once under way, the conflict brought an explosion in circulation figures for Hearst-run publications, especially the *Journal.*

The quick victory in the conflict did not end the publisher's antagonism toward the president. Hearst campaigned for the Democrat William Jennings Bryan and continued his criticism of McKinley after Bryan's defeat in 1900. Ambrose Bierce, one of Hearst's most famous and notorious writers, wrote the following quatrain run in the *Journal* following the assassination of Kentucky governor-elect William Goebel on February 4, 1900:

The bullet that pierced Goebel's breast
Can not be found in all the West;
Good reason, it is speeding here
To lay McKinley on his bier.

The poem brought immediate public rebuke, and the insinuation that Hearst supported the assassination of the president led him to temporarily suspend the most violent barbs directed at McKinley. On April 10, 1901, the *Journal* ran an editorial that closed with the statement, "If bad institutions and bad men must be got rid of only by killing, then killing must be done." When a mentally ill anarchist shot President McKinley on September 5, 1901, in Buffalo, New York, the public and Hearst's media enemies leapt at the opportunity to attack the publisher. In the interim between the shooting and McKinley's death on September 14, mobs burned Hearst in effigy throughout the country, and newspapers ran hundreds of editorials excoriating yellow journalism as cause for the assassination.

Significance

Three days after the shooting, the *New York Sun,* a bitter rival of Hearst's *Journal,* reprinted a *Journal* editorial from June 1, 1901, entitled "Assassination a Good Thing!" The *Journal* column did not mention McKinley by name, but it asserted that assassinations of political leaders throughout human history have sometimes caused positive change. Even the murder of Abraham Lincoln, according to the *Journal*'s editorial staff, fostered sectional reconciliation after the Civil War by "uniting in sympathy and regret all good people in the North and South." In the context of the Bierce poem and the *Journal*'s other previous criticisms of McKinley, "Assassination a Good Thing!" appeared to many in the press and in the public as a not-so-subtle prodding for a direct assault upon the President of the United States.

The *Sun,* among many other anti-Hearst newspapers in New York City and across the nation, eagerly reminded their audiences of previous anti-McKinley pieces in Hearst papers. These publications spread the unsubstantiated rumor that assassin Leon Czolgosz was carrying a copy of the *Journal* when he shot the president. The papers printed hundreds of letters to the editor that attacked Hearst and his staff with unflinching charges that focused on the power of the press at the turn of the century.

Publishing magnate William Randolph Hearst put sensational reporting into the pages of the most widely read newspapers in the U.S. THE LIBRARY OF CONGRESS.

The *Sun* seemed to relish the scores of letters it received from angry readers who charged that the *Journal*'s editorials directly led to the shooting of President McKinley. As displayed in "A Menace to Our Civilization," from September 12, 1901, the *Sun* further kindled readers' emotions with characterizations of the *Journal* as dangerous, evil, and even "satanic." As one reader wrote, in a letter printed on September 13, 1901, "The responsibility for the dreadful blow to the Nation rests upon the journalistic stinkweed that pollutes New York." A separate letter run in the same edition read: "The New York Journal is a rag which has no place in civilized society, no mission except to preach anarchy and beget discontent on the part of the ignorant with their condition in life. Shame or decency has it none, not a vestige. In short, the Journal is a mortal offence to the city of New York, a pestilential offence, a menace to society." Yet many of the attacks proved broader in focus, waging a battle against the freedom of the press itself. "The Crime

The assassination of President William McKinley by Leon Czolgosz on September 6, 1901, is depicted in this illustration by T. Dart Walker. Controversy surrounded publisher Hearst as, several months before this, he had advocated political assassinations in an editorial. **THE LIBRARY OF CONGRESS.**

Against the State: Disgust and Anger of an Indignant People," raged the headline of a collection of letters printed by the *Sun* on September 11, 1901, that charged media organizations, the *New York Journal* in particular, with too much freedom and too little oversight. One author, a "professor of logic and mental philosophy" at Rutgers College, directed a characteristic assault at the *Journal:* "Behind the much-abused license of printing you have for years been uttering, both by word and by picture, that which you knew to be lies of the most damnable blackness. . . . This constant hell-broth of vituperation and lies, spewed all over the land, has done its legitimate work. It has incited weak men like this ignorant and fanatical Polish Anarchist to do a deed in which you, the real assassin, gloat in your immortal soul, but from which in your craven terror you crouch like a frightened hare!"

The *New York Evening Post* proposed an alternative critique of the assassination a week after the president's death. In its editorial page, the *Post* argued that sensational reporting did not develop against popular will. Instead, the editorial emphasized the culpability of the buying public in the popularity of yellow journalism. The *Post* argued that the public, government officials, religious leaders, and business executives who patronized the news media prior to the shooting appeared hypocritical in then damning the press after the assault. The "Responsibility for Yellow Journalism" resided in the community at large. Thus, the *Post* concluded, this community must lead by example and refuse to sponsor such journalism if they truly expected it to cease.

Primary Source

"Assassination a Good Thing!"

SYNOPSIS: On September 5, 1901, President McKinley was shot. He would die nine days later. On September 8th, the *New York Sun* reprinted an editorial from its competitor, the *New York Journal* that claimed that assassination was sometimes a good thing. This editorial took on sinister implications now that the president had been shot, especially considering that the *Journal* had long been critical of McKinley.

From the *New York Journal,* June 1, 1901.

Has assassination ever changed the world's history? If so, which one?

The question will perhaps interest our readers who devote themselves to the philosophical consideration of history. It may bring us some interesting letters. . . .

Was not the history of the world changed when Philip, the father of Alexander the Great, was murdered in the midst of his festivals and rejoicings? Left unmurdered he might have reigned until long past the day that Alexander the Great died and went under ground. . . .

If Cromwell had not resolved to remove the head of Charles I from his lace collar, would England be what she is to-day—a really free nation and a genuine republic?

Did not the murder of Lincoln, uniting in sympathy and regret all good people in the North and South, hasten the era of American good feeling and perhaps prevent the renewal of fighting between brothers?

The murder of Cæsar certainly changed the history of Europe, besides preventing that great man from ultimately displaying vanity as great as his ability.

When wise old sayings, such as that of Disraeli about assassination, are taken up it is worth while, instead of swallowing them whole, to analyze them. We invite our readers to think over this question. The time devoted to it will not be wasted. Any kind of harmless thinking is as good for the brain as any kind of harmless exercise is good for the muscles.

In expressing the belief that certain murders have changed the "history of the world," we do not mean that any assassination has ever changed radically the history of the *human race.* That history is mapped out for us ahead and is not left to our direction. In the progress of the whole race the coming and going of this or that drop of humanity—common felon or greatest emperor—counts not at all.

A "great" man murdered may mean some slight change in what we call history—the petty transactions of a few hundred years. But real history spreads over periods so vast that we cannot comprehend them, and nothing that happens to one man can have permanent effect.

Primary Source

"A Menace to Our Civilization"

SYNOPSIS: This September 12, 1901, editorial from the *New York Sun* decries "yellow journalism" as a threat to America, and the root cause of the recent assassination of President McKinley. This was one of a series of articles subsequent to the assassination that attempted to lay the blame for McKinley's death on the rival newspaper the *New York Journal.* Although the *Journal* is not mentioned by name, the *Sun* had already pointed out to its readers that the *Journal* supposedly supported assassination as a political tool and opposed McKinley.

We are receiving by every post and from all parts of the Union great numbers of letters urging and exhorting us to advocate and formulate measures for the extirpation of the variety of journalism which has come to be known as "yellow." So many are these letters that the limitations of our space permit us to print only a selected few of them, though in their literary character and because of their high moral and intellectual level, they all invite publication.

This school of journalism began with vulgarity and indecency, and for that reason it was soon excluded from the homes of refined and self-respecting families as a corrupting influence, and by formal action from all reputable clubs. Gradually, however, it has been able to appeal to the consideration of certain uncritical minds who have been induced to use it as a vehicle of communication with a supposedly large part of the public, to which its very coarseness gives it peculiar access. Even Christian ministers have consented to become conspicuous contributors to one of the journals of this school. . . .

Now that an atrocious Anarchistic assault on the President has been provoked by the teachings of this journalistic school, perhaps these Bishops and other clergy will begin to see that their alliance was only courted in order that incendiary journalism might seem to have the sanction of priests of religion. For such journalism, from its original ribaldry and coarseness, adopted at first in order to attract the vulgar crowd, has now graduated into a serious and studied propaganda of social revolution. . . .

Never before in the history of civilization anywhere was an instrument of disorder and sedition used so effectually and none ever had so great opportunities for its malign propaganda.

Now, this is something we say with great reluctance concerning any American newspaper, for it is our wish and our habit rather to discover and applaud the merit and ability and honorable purpose which so generally distinguish American journalism. In this country there are many thousands of newspapers, relatively to the population far more than in any other part of civilization, and as an educating force among our people they are of the first importance. . . . [T]he exceptions are so few and rare that the forbidden school of journalism to which we are referring stands out the more flagrantly in its loathsome distinction.

Nor is this journalist offal reprobated by the rest because it competes with decent examples of journalism; it monopolizes a field by itself, into which it has no fear of intrusion. Simply because it tends to the degradation of the whole body of newspapers in the public estimation, and is likely to bring, if it has not already brought, a noble profession into reproach and suspicion, its prosperity is resented by all decent newspapers. It has tainted the whole business in the minds of very many people and awakened distrust of the motives and contempt for the authority of the newspaper generally.

Another matter, also, we refer to with reluctance; but we must speak of it frankly. The existence of this forbidden journalism would be impossible except for the substantial subsidy it receives from the reputable business community in the way of advertising. . . . The evil association does far more damage to the decent advertiser than the vile publicity secured can benefit him. Even readers attracted by its satanic cynicism have no respect for it or anything printed in it, if they are of an intelligent discrimination which makes profitable or desirable the appeal of an advertiser to them. Even the unintelligent who are dazzled by its flash are not foolish enough to go to it for business guidance. All the same, this school of journalism seems to be prospering because of the financial support it receives from mercantile houses otherwise jealous of their reputation. They are feeding a monster which is using the strength they are giving nutrition to in an effort to strike down the civilization upon which they depend.

The great flood of letters now pouring in upon *The Sun* bears witness, however, that the intelligent public are more alive to the danger.

Primary Source

"Responsibility for Yellow Journalism"

SYNOPSIS: This *New York Evening Post* editorial defends the *New York Journal* against claims that the *Journal's* editorial and reporting were what drove Leon Czolgosz to fatally shoot President McKinley on September 5, 1901. The editorial goes on to denounce the "yellow journalism" practiced by the *Journal,* however.

Ever since President McKinley was shot, a fortnight ago, there has been a tremendous manifestation of popular indignation against yellow journalism, and particularly against its worst exemplar in New York City. Like all sudden outbursts of rage, this has been largely undiscriminating, and much of it has been quite beside the mark.

The theory, which has been seriously advanced, that Czolgosz was led to assassinate President McKinley by reading a certain daily newspaper, is without a particle of evidence, and is an affront to common sense. One might with as much reason have argued that Guiteau was impelled to kill President Garfield in 1881 by reading the bitter diatribes in Republican newspapers during that period of heated factional controversy in the Republican party which preceded the assassination. Hardly less justifiable have been the more extreme complaints regarding the treatment of the late President by yellow journals, going as they often have virtually to the length of declaring that public men must be relieved from criticism by the writer or the cartoonist.

Freedom of legitimate discussion must be maintained. If any editor or any public man feels persuaded that a President is working harm to the republic, he must have the right to say so plainly and emphatically. . . . So, too, we must render it possible always for a Nast to expose a Tweed, or a Keppler a Blaine, in a cartoon which puts a whole argument in a single picture.

The real offense of yellow journalism is not so much that it holds a public man up to undeserved ridicule, or visits upon him censure which he does not deserve, as that its pervading spirit is one of vulgarity, indecency, and reckless sensationalism; that it steadily violates the canons alike of good taste and sound morals; that it cultivates false standards of life, and demoralizes its readers; that it recklessly uses language which may incite the crack-brained to lawlessness; that its net influence makes the world worse. A force working to such ends surely ought to be restrained, and public opinion ought to be brought to bear against it in the most effective possible ways.

There has been much discussion as to the responsibility for this sort of journalism, but the real blame surely rests upon the community which sustains it. Fortunately, too, this responsibility can be narrowed down. Those most to blame for the existence of any evil are the people who could do most to suppress it, by giving the force of their example, as well as their words, against it. One can, and should, "have nothing to do with him" in the case of any private citizen who has forfeited public respect by gross misconduct; refuse to go to his house, to recognize him on the street, to endorse his course in any way. Precisely the same thing can and should be done in the case of a newspaper.

It is a disagreeable truth, but one which ought to be told, that yellow journalism, in its worst New York exemplar, stood upon a higher plane of respectability on the day Mr. McKinley was shot than ever before, because it had just secured the endorsement of a number of the most prominent men in the community. . . . [I]t was thus enabled, with apparent truth, to boast that it was not only a most reputable publication, but that it was of all newspapers in New York the one which offered the best medium for public teachers to employ. The dead walls of this city two weeks ago were placarded with great posters displaying this certificate of good character.

The *Journal* was just the same newspaper when it was given this certificate that it had always been; it became no different when it published communications on labor and capital by these highly respectable and influential men. They knew its character well when they agreed to furnish such articles. They ought to have known, too, that it wanted simply the endorsement of their names in order to convince doubters that it was a fit paper for the home. They ought also to have known that the readers would turn from their articles to pages of scandal, vulgarity, indecency, and sensationalism. They sinned against light.

"Why will people buy such a newspaper?" has been the most common question. Why should they not buy it, when our best men write for it? Why should we expect people not to patronize a paper which can advertise that it is vouched for by leaders in the church, in law, in finance? With what force can we condemn a newspaper for its vulgarity, indecency, and general demoralization, with what force can we criticize the ignorant and the untrained for reading such a paper, when our very teachers of morality pronounce it a fit instructor for them? These are the questions we must now ask.

Further Resources

BOOKS

Emery, Michael, and Edwin Emery. *The Press and America: An Interpretive History of the Mass Media,* 7th ed. Englewood Cliffs, N.J.: Prentice Hall, 1992.

Swanberg, W.A. *Citizen Hearst.* New York: Scribner's, 1961.

WEBSITES

Leonard, Thomas C. "Hearst, William Randolph." Available online at http://www.anb.org/articles/16/16-00738.html; website home page: http://www.anb.org/ (accessed May 26, 2003).

Our National Parks

Nonfiction work

By: John Muir

Date: 1901

Source: Muir, John. *Our National Parks.* Boston: Houghton Mifflin, 1901. Available online at http://memory.loc.gov/cgi-bin/query/r?ammem/consrv:@field(DOCID+@lit(vg305)); website home page: http://memory.loc.gov/ammem/ammemhome.html (accessed May 23, 2003).

About the Author: Born in Scotland, conservation pioneer John Muir (1838–1914) contributed to the founding of the U.S. National Park System and the modern environmental movement. Immigrating to Wisconsin in 1849, Muir studied at the University of Wisconsin then conducted various field studies of the natural world. His meticulous journals led to many books and articles detailing the need for nature preservation. Muir successfully campaigned for the creation of Yosemite National Park in 1890 and helped establish the Sierra Club in 1892, heading the organization until his death. ■

Introduction

The turn-of-the-century American press concerned itself with selling publications and with social reform. So-called muckrakers revealed corruption in business and government in the hopes of bringing change through public and private action. This activist news media was based in the densely populated, industrial cities, primarily in the Northeast and Midwest. In a surprising and interesting way, this foundation in urban America fueled one of the fundamental principles behind the era's growing conservation movement.

Significance

John Muir and other naturalists called for conservation as a means of improving the lives of city dwellers. In his opening chapter to *Our National Parks,* he championed nature's ability "to get rid of rust and disease." Much as many civil engineers designed parks to improve the quality of life in increasingly overpopulated cities, Muir urged the protection of the wilderness. He saw beauty but also the prospect of danger as westward expansion threatened to destroy forever the nation's wildlife.

Muir used the mass media to engender popular support for conservation efforts and to save the few remaining unspoiled sections of land. Toward the east, he saw the annihilation of nature from human settlement and industrial development. But in the west, Muir found the possibility to save broad sections of territory for future generations if only Americans would act. These pleas might have fallen on deaf ears if not for Muir's exquisite writing skills. He conjured the grandeur of the natural world by blending scientific categorization with lush descriptions of scenery that bordered on fantasy. For

Ecologist and conservationist John Muir was cofounder of the Sierra Club. **THE LIBRARY OF CONGRESS.**

millions of Americans unable to travel to the Rocky Mountains or to the Pacific Coast, Muir communicated the spectacle of the nation's varied terrain, with its countless species of plant and animal life and millennia of geologic development.

Primary Source

Our National Parks [excerpt]

SYNOPSIS: The following excerpts appeared in *Our National Parks,* published in 1901. The chapters of this book first gained public attention in the 1890s as articles for the *Atlantic Monthly.* The first section from Chapter 1, "The Wild Parks and Forest Reservations of the West," was printed in January 1898. The concluding portion from Chapter 10, "The American Forests," hit newsstands in August 1897. Muir's ability to collect these stories into a single volume for publication in 1901 reveals the popularity of his writings at the time.

The tendency nowadays to wander in wildernesses is delightful to see. Thousands of tired, nerve-shaken, over-civilized people are beginning to find out that going to the mountains is going home; that wildness is a necessity; and that mountain parks and reservations are useful not only as fountains of timber and irrigating rivers, but as fountains of life. Awakening from the stupefying effects of the vice of over-industry and the deadly apathy of luxury, they are trying as best they can to mix and enrich their own little ongoings with those of Nature, and to get rid of rust and disease. Briskly venturing and roaming, some are washing off sins and cobweb cares of the devil's spinning in all-day storms on mountains; sauntering in rosiny pinewoods or in gentian meadows, brushing through chaparral, bending down and parting sweet, flowery sprays; tracing rivers to their sources, getting in touch with the nerves of Mother Earth; jumping from rock to rock, feeling the life of them, learning the songs of them, panting in whole-souled exercise, and rejoicing in deep, long-drawn breaths of pure wildness. This is fine and natural and full of promise. So also is the growing interest in the care and preservation of forests and wild places in general, and in the half wild parks and gardens of towns. Even the scenery habit in its most artificial forms, mixed with spectacles, silliness, and kodaks; its devotees arrayed more gorgeously than scarlet tanagers, frightening the wild game with red umbrellas,—even this is encouraging, and may well be regarded as a hopeful sign of the times.

All the Western mountains are still rich in wildness, and by means of good roads are being brought nearer civilization every year. To the sane and free it will hardly seem necessary to cross the continent in search of wild beauty, however easy the way, for they find it in abundance wherever they chance to be. Like Thoreau they see forests in orchards and patches of huckleberry brush, and oceans in ponds and drops of dew. Few in these hot, dim, strenuous times are quite sane or free; choked with care like clocks full of dust, laboriously doing so much good and making so much money,—or so little,—they are no longer good for themselves.

When, like a merchant taking a list of his goods, we take stock of our wildness, we are glad to see how much of even the most destructible kind is still unspoiled. Looking at our continent as scenery when it was all wild, lying between beautiful seas, the starry sky above it, the starry rocks beneath it, to compare its sides, the East and the West, would be like comparing the sides of a rainbow. But it is no longer equally beautiful. The rainbows of to-day are, I suppose, as bright as those that first spanned the sky; and some of our landscapes are growing more beautiful from year to year, notwithstanding the clearing, trampling work of civilization. New plants and animals are enriching woods and gardens, and many landscapes wholly new, with divine sculpture and architecture, are just now coming to the light of day as the mantling folds of creative glaciers are being withdrawn, and life in a thousand cheerful, beautiful forms is pushing into them, and new-born rivers are beginning to sing and shine in them. The old rivers, too, are growing longer, like healthy trees, gaining new branches and lakes as the residual glaciers at their highest sources on the mountains recede, while the rootlike branches in the flat deltas are at same time spreading farther and wider into the seas and making new lands.

Under the control of the vast mysterious forces of the interior of the earth all the continents and islands are slowly rising or sinking. Most of the mountains are diminishing in size under the wearing action of the weather, though a few are increasing in height and girth, especially the volcanic ones, as fresh floods of molten rocks are piled on their summits and spread in successive layers, like the wood-rings of trees, on their sides. New mountains, also, are being created from time to time as islands in lakes and seas, or as subordinate cones on the slopes of old ones, thus in some measure balancing the waste of old beauty with new. Man, too, is making many far-reaching changes. This most influential half animal, half angel is rapidly multiplying and spreading, covering the seas and lakes with ships, the land with huts, hotels, cathedrals, and clustered city shops and homes, so that soon, it would seem, we may have to go farther than Nansen to find a good sound solitude. None of Nature's landscape are ugly so long as they are wild; and much, we can say comfortingly, must always be in great part wild, particularly the sea and the sky, the floods of light from the stars, and the warm, unspoilable heart of the earth, infinitely beautiful, though only dimly visible to the eye of imagination. The geysers, too, spouting from the hot underworld; the steady, long-lasting glaciers on the mountains, obedient only to the sun; Yosemite domes and the tremendous grandeur of rocky cañons and mountains in general,—these must always be wild, for man can change them and mar them hardly more than can the butterflies that hover above them. But the continent's outer beauty is fast passing away, especially the plant part of it, the most destructible and most universally charming of all.

Only thirty years ago, the great Central Valley of California, five hundred miles long and fifty miles wide, was one bed of golden and purple flowers. Now it is ploughed and pastured out of existence, gone forever,—scarce a memory of it left in fence corners and along the bluffs of the streams. The gardens of the Sierra, also, and the noble forests in both the reserved and unreserved portions are sadly hacked and trampled, notwithstanding, the ruggedness of the topography,—all excepting those of the parks guarded by a few soldiers. In the noblest forests of the world, the ground, once divinely beautiful, is desolate and repulsive, like a face ravaged by disease. This is true also of many other Pacific Coast and Rocky Mountain valleys and forests. The same fate, sooner or later, is awaiting them all, unless awakening public opinion comes forward to stop it. Even the great deserts in Arizona, Nevada, Utah, and New Mexico, which offer so little to attract settlers, and which a few years ago pioneers were afraid of, as places of desolation and death, are now taken as pastures at the rate of one or two square miles per cow, and of course their plant treasures are passing away,—the delicate abronias, phloxes, gilias, etc. Only a few of the bitter, thorny, unbitable shrubs are left, and the sturdy cactuses that defend themselves with bayonets and spears.

Most of the wild plant wealth of the East also has vanished,—gone into dusty history. Only vestiges of its glorious prairie and woodland wealth remain to bless humanity in boggy, rocky, unploughable places. Fortunately, some of these are purely wild, and go far to keep Nature's love visible. . . .

The most extensive, least spoiled, and most unspoilable of the gardens of the continent are the vast tundras of Alaska. . . .

This is Nature's own reservation, and every lover of wildness will rejoice with me that by kindly frost it is so well defended. The discovery lately made that it is sprinkled with gold may cause some alarm; for the strangely exciting stuff makes the timid bold enough for anything, and the lazy destructively industrious. . . . In spite of frowning hardships and the frozen ground, the Klondike gold will increase the crusading crowds for years to come, but comparatively little harm will be done. Holes will be burned and dug into the hard ground here and there, and into the quartz-ribbed mountains and hills; ragged towns like beaver and muskrat villages will be built, and mills and locomotives will make rumbling, screeching, disenchanting noises; but the miner's pick will not be followed far by the plough, at least not until Nature is ready to unlock the frozen soil-beds with her slow-turning climate key. On the other hand, the roads of the pioneer miners will lead many a lover of wildness into the heart of the reserve, who without them would never see it.

In the meantime, the wildest health and pleasure grounds accessible and available to tourists seeking escape from care and dust and early death are the parks and reservations of the West. There are four national parks,—the Yellowstone, Yosemite,

President Theodore Roosevelt and his party at Inspiration Point, Yosemite Valley, California, 1903. **THE LIBRARY OF CONGRESS.**

General Grant, and Sequoia,—all within easy reach, and thirty forest reservations, a magnificent realm of woods, most of which, by railroads and trails and open ridges, is also fairly accessible, not only to the determined traveler rejoicing in difficulties, but to those (may their tribe increase) who, not tired, not sick, just naturally take wing every summer in search of wildness. The forty million acres of these reserves are in the main unspoiled as yet, though sadly wasted and threatened on their more open margins by the axe and fire of the lumberman and prospector, and by hoofed locusts, which, like the winged ones, devour every leaf within reach, while the shepherds and owners set fires with the intention of making a blade of grass grow in the place of every tree, but with the result of killing both the grass and the trees. . . .

The Grand Cañon Reserve of Arizona, of nearly two million acres, or the most interesting part of it, as well as the Rainier region, should be made into a national park, on account of their supreme grandeur and beauty. Setting out from Flagstaff, a station on the Atchison, Topeka, and Santa Fé Railroad, on the way to the cañon you pass through beautiful forests of yellow pine,—like those of the Black Hills, but more extensive,—and curious dwarf forests of nut pine and juniper, the spaces between the miniature trees planted with many interesting species of eriogonum, yucca, and cactus. After riding or walking seventy-five miles through these pleasure-grounds, the San Francisco and other mountains, abounding in flowery parklike openings and smooth shallow valleys with long vistas which in fineness of finish and arrangement suggest the work of a consummate landscape artist, watching you all the way, you come to the most tremendous cañon in the world. It is abruptly countersunk in the forest plateau, so that you see nothing of it until you are suddenly stopped on its brink, with its immeasurable wealth of divinely colored and sculptured buildings before you and beneath you. No matter how far you have wandered hitherto, or how many famous gorges and valleys you have seen, this one, the Grand Cañon of the Colorado, will seem as novel to you, as unearthly in the color and grandeur and quantity of its architecture, as if you had found it after death, on some other star; so incomparably lovely and grand and supreme is it above all the other cañons in our fire-moulded, earthquake-shaken, rain-washed, wave-washed, river and glacier sculptured world. It is about six thousand feet deep where you first see it, and from rim to rim ten to fifteen miles wide. Instead of being dependent for interest upon waterfalls, depth, wall sculpture, and beauty of parklike floor, like most other great cañons, it has not waterfalls in sight, and no appreciable floor spaces. The big river has just room enough to flow and roar obscurely, here and there groping its way as best it can, like a weary, murmuring, overladen traveler trying to escape from the tremendous, bewildering labyrinthic abyss, while its roar serves only to deepen the silence. Instead of being filled with air, the vast space between the walls is crowded with Nature's grandest buildings,—a sublime city of them, painted in every color, and adorned with richly fretted cornice and battlement spire and tower in endless variety of style and architecture. Every architectural invention of man has been anticipated, and far more, in this grandest of God's terrestrial cities.

Further Resources

BOOKS

Fox, Stephen R. *John Muir and His Legacy: The American Conservation Movement.* Boston: Little, Brown, 1981.

"American Progress in Habana"

Magazine article, Photographs

By: *National Geographic*

Date: March 1902

Source: "American Progress in Habana," *National Geographic* 13, March 1902, 97–108.

About the Publication: The National Geographic Society formed in January 1888 to encourage exploration and the dissemination of geographical knowledge. The first edition of the organization's magazine was published later that year. The publication later expanded on its original plan, documenting exploration of remote regions of the globe to the outer reaches of the solar system and the universe. *National Geographic* offered dramatic photographic essays that brought the different peoples and places of the planet into the sight of ordinary Americans. ■

Introduction

Improvements in printing and photographic technology enabled newspapers and magazines to publish more and more images at the turn of the century. Editors responded with countless drawings, illustrations, and photographs that gave readers an entirely new way of seeing the world. Ready to find any means possible of increasing circulation, the news media leapt at the opportunity to depict growing tensions between the United States and Spain as dramatically as possible. In certain instances, newspapers did more than simply convey international discord; the *New York Journal,* for instance, actively campaigned for war. Publisher William Randolph Hearst ordered the fabrication of stories and pictures that inflamed popular sentiment and influenced President William McKinley's (served 1897–1901) ultimate call for war in April 1898.

Victorious in the four-month Spanish-American War (1898), the United States took over Spanish colonies such as the Philippines, Guam, and Cuba and formally annexed the territory of Hawaii. Most daily papers and current-interest magazines gloried in the patriotic fervor of America's emergence as a global power, while a few publications countered the dominant euphoria with criticism of expansion. Yet, the vast majority of Americans had no firsthand knowledge of the peoples, cultures, and lands acquired from Spain.

As the publication of the National Geographic Society, *National Geographic* magazine's coverage centered on revealing the nature of the land and the people acquired in the war. Reporters often came from the ranks of military and occupation personnel responsible for governing these territories. Then secretary of war and future president, William Howard Taft (served 1909–1913), contributed "The Philippines" in August 1905. Also in that year, *National Geographic* printed "Our Smallest Possession—Guam," by a former lieutenant in the U.S. Navy.

Significance

When *National Geographic* ran "American Progress in Habana" in March 1902, U.S. forces still occupied the island, along with other territory acquired during the 1898 war. Imperialists argued that the United States possessed a solemn duty to bring civilization to the former Spanish colonies, such as the Philippines and Cuba. Anti-imperialists argued vociferously that such occupations caused more harm than good. In this context, *National*

Primary Source

Cuba Before American Occupation

A photograph from page 100 of *National Geographic* illustrates a Cuban street before the American occupation in 1900–1901. FROM NATIONAL GEOGRAPHIC MAGAZINE. REPRODUCED BY PERMISSION.

Geographic provided readers with a fascinating photo essay detailing the social and economic changes created by American intervention in Cuba.

The following excerpts reveal the publication's adherence to core imperialist assumptions about the occupation and the Cuban people. The article included several so-called before and after pictures of streets and parks in the city of Habana (Havana). The photographs depicted American imperialism as a humanitarian policy that materially improved Cuban society. The accompanying text incorporated stereotypes of the island's population prevalent in the period's press coverage. The magazine subtly, and sometimes not so subtly, portrayed the Cuban people as lazy, backward children unable and unwilling to improve their lives without American direction. Yet the concluding paragraphs concerning dissent toward the imperialists expressed the ongoing animosity between Cubans and American occupiers. Battles between Cuban nationalists and American troops flared throughout the decade, as the United States continued to dominate economic and political developments in Cuba.

Primary Source

"American Progress in Habana" [excerpt]

SYNOPSIS: In the 1900s *National Geographic* published dozens of articles and photographs similar to those presented here. As the United States expanded abroad, the magazine brought these new areas into the view of common Americans. In this context, it would be important to consider how readers in 1902 would have gauged the depiction of American imperialism. How would the article affect someone who had never seen Cuba or a Cuban? Would it encourage support for American occupation policies or further U.S. conquest?

The city of Habana has so long been considered as a sort of nursery of diseases for the United

Primary Source

Cuba After American Occupation

A photograph from page 101 of *National Geographic* illustrates the same Cuban street after the American occupation in 1900–1901. FROM NATIONAL GEOGRAPHIC MAGAZINE. REPRODUCED BY PERMISSION.

States that the average American citizen finds it hard to realize that today Habana is clear and pure, more healthy than Washington and many cities on the American continent. Unenviable has been the record of the Cuban capital; yellow fever, typhoid fever, and filth diseases have found a luxurious home there for one hundred years. In 1896 1,262 deaths from yellow fever alone were reported by the city government. In 1899, the year of least yellow fever during eleven years, 1889–1899, 101 persons died in Habana with the dreaded pest. The average for the eleven years was 440 fatal cases. In 1901, for the first time in the history of the city, the yellow fever season—April 1 to January 1—has passed with only five fatal cases of the disease occurring. October, November, and December, 1901, the months during which the fever was wont to play the fastest, each came and went without a single case.

The wise, conscientious, persistent measures which for three years the United States officers have been enforcing throughout Habana, despite the opposition and dislike of the Cubans, have delivered the city of its old foes—filth and filth diseases.

The illustrations that accompany this brief paper show strikingly the contrast between Habana of the past and Habana of today. The pictures were loaned to this Magazine by Major Wm. M. Black, of the Engineer Corps of the U. S. Army. On the United States occupation of Habana, January, 1899, to Major Black was given charge of the engineering work of the city, and to him are due in large measure the splendid results that have been achieved. His courageous and broad-minded enthusiasm overcame prejudice and opposition and found inexpensive methods of accomplishing tasks which were thought impracticable because of their supposed cost. . . .

The hovels on the left, in picture No. 3, were formerly breeding dens of disease. They had been built on public parking by some investor who had bribed the Spanish officials to overlook his appropriation of public property. The miserable huts were crowded with the refuse of humanity, and the investor and disease had reaped equally rich harvests. One of the first things the new administration did was to tear down the row. Picture No. 4 shows the transformation. The high wall on the left is a part of the old city wall, of which only this small section remains. The parking inside the wall belongs to the people. . . .

It should be remembered that every dollar spent for the improvements of the capital and elsewhere in the island of Cuba has come from the pockets of the Cubans, and not one cent from the United States.

The Cubans have not liked the process which has made them cleaner and healthier. If they could have voted on it, probably they would have vetoed to a man the house and street cleaning proposition. What was good enough for their fathers and grandfathers was quite good enough for them. But now that the parks have been made enjoyable and sea promenades built where they can loaf at ease and in safety, they begin to take pride in the improvements to their capital.

The reputation of the city of Habana is rapidly changing for the better. The beautiful surroundings which Nature has given it and the mildness of its climate in winter make the city a Paradise to northerners during the harsh season of the year. There are many who believe that Palm Beach and the winter resorts of Florida are many times eclipsed by the charms of the Cuban capital, and that in the near future it will rightly become the most popular of American winter resorts.

Further Resources

BOOKS

Paterson, Thomas G., J. Garry Clifford, and Kenneth J. Hagan. *American Foreign Relations: A History, Since 1895,* Volume II, 5th ed. Boston: Houghton Mifflin, 2000.

Stephanson, Anders. *Manifest Destiny: American Expansionism and the Empire of Right.* New York: Hill and Wang, 1995.

WEBSITES

National Geographic Magazine. Available online at http://www.nationalgeographic.com (accessed May 26, 2003).

Zwick, Jim. *Anti-Imperialism in the United States, 1898–1935.* Available at http://www.boondocksnet.com/ai/index.html (accessed May 26, 2003).

The Great Train Robbery

Movie stills

By: Edwin S. Porter

Date: 1903

Source: *The Great Train Robbery* (1903). Description and screen stills at The Library of Congress: American Memory, http://memory.loc.gov/ammem/edhtml/gtr.html; website home page: http://memory.loc.gov (accessed May 26, 2003).

About the Author: Edwin Stanton Porter (1870–1941) worked odd jobs for much of his youth. After U.S. Navy service, he worked with famed inventor Thomas A. Edison and began directing his own motion pictures. *The Great Train Robbery,* produced in 1903, placed Porter in the pantheon of American filmmaking and cemented the national popularity of motion pictures. Porter invented and developed critical techniques in filmmaking, but he never produced another movie comparable to *The Great Train Robbery* and eventually left directing to head a projector manufacturing company. ■

Introduction

Thomas A. Edison and his associates produced the first motion pictures in the 1890s. Yet, public interest grew so rapidly that companies devoted to filmmaking began operating at the turn of the century. As technology advanced during the 1900s, audiences moved from single-person viewers to theaters capable of displaying motion pictures in primarily urban settings. Most films from this period showed single, brief scenes, without a narrative or plot structure, such as comedies, magic acts, or news footage. In this context, J. Stuart Blackton produced *The Great Train Robbery* in 1903. Blackton based the film on actual events that were fresh in the public's mind. In 1900, the famed Hole in the Wall Gang held up a locomotive in Wyoming, captured the mail car, and escaped with thousands of dollars in cash. A posse soon caught and killed the bandits in a shootout that inspired the 1960s film *Butch Cassidy and the Sundance Kid,* starring Paul Newman and Robert Redford.

Significance

The Great Train Robbery is credited with being the first narrative motion picture. Basically, the film told a story through a scene-by-scene presentation of characters and events within a coherent plot structure. While the final version lasted a mere twelve minutes, paltry by today's standards, *The Great Train Robbery* constituted an epic for this period. Rather than the usual single-scene setting, this production featured a total of fourteen scenes, with indoor and outdoor sets. Shot in New Jersey rather than on location, the film ran a budget of about $150 and included about forty actors.

The film offered a plethora of filmmaking innovations, including stunts where one character jumped out

Primary Source

The Great Train Robbery (1 OF 2)

SYNOPSIS: Crime dramas at the beginning of the twentieth century received enormous play in the news, and the exploits of the Hole in the Wall Gang became the stuff of legend. Capitalizing on the public's fascination, J. Stuart Blackton and his crew devoted unprecedented resources to *The Great Train Robbery* in 1903. The following screen stills display the sets, costumes, and cinematography used in the most popular film of the decade and one of the most pioneering films ever made. © BETTMANN/CORBIS. REPRODUCED BY PERMISSION.

of a moving train, and jump cuts, used to depict action occurring at the same time but in different places. *The Great Train Robbery* established many of the core themes and clichés of action movies that would be repeated throughout the next century of filmmaking. The climax, for instance, showed a massive shootout where the heroic armed posse attacks the bandits and kills them. The final scene presented one of the bandits pointing a gun at the camera/the audience and firing. The eerie finale riveted audiences unaccustomed to motion pictures that directly addressed viewers.

Early news coverage afforded motion pictures the status of low-brow, vaudeville productions. While publications such as *The New York Times* marveled at the technological prowess of filmmaking, journals mostly avoided any substantive criticism of the actual stories depicted in the movies. This began to change by the end of the decade. Covering the film industry exclusively, *The Film Index* began publishing motion picture reviews in August 1909 on a weekly basis. *The New York Times* soon followed suit with a review of the D.W. Griffith movie *Pippa Passes* published on October 10, 1909.

Further Resources

BOOKS

Gunning, Tom. *D.W. Griffith and the Origins of American Narrative Film: The Early Years at Biograph.* Urbana, Ill.: University of Illinois Press, 1991.

"Browning Now Given In Moving Pictures: 'Pippa Passes' the Latest Play Without Words to be Seen in the Nickelodeons"

[As in a poem by Robert Browning, Pippa spends her yearly single-day holiday from the mills walking through her town singing, unaware of her calming effect on others. Although the film's plot did not break much ground, the lighting effects used to convey the passage of time caught reviewers' attention.]

"Pippa Passes" is being given in the nickelodeons and Browning is being presented to the average motion picture audience, which has received it with applause and is asking for more. This achievement is the present nearest-Boston record of the reformed moving picture play producing, but from all accounts there seems to be no reason why one may not expect to see soon the intellectual aristocracy of the nickelodeons demanding Kant's "Prolegomena to Metaphysic" with the Kritek of Pure Reason for a curtain raiser.

Since popular opinion has been expressing itself through the Board of Censors of the People's Institute, such material as "The Odyssey," the Old Testament, Tolstoy, George Eliot, De Maupassant, and Hugo has been drawn upon to furnish the films, in place of the sensational blood-and-thunder variety which brought down public indignation upon the manufacturers six months ago. Browning, however, seems to be the most rarified dramatic stuff up to date.

As for the "Pippa" without words, the first films show the sunlight waking Pippa for her holiday, with light and shade effects like those obtained by the "Secessionist" photographers. Then Pippa goes on her way, dancing and singing; the quarreling family hears her, and forgets its dissension; the taproom brawlers cease their carouse, and so on, with the pictures alternately showing Pippa on her way, and then the effect of her "passing" on the various groups in the Browning poem. The contrast between the "tired business man" at a roof garden and the sweatshop worker applauding Pippa is certainly striking.

That this demand for the classics is genuine is indicated by the fact that the adventurous producers who inaugurated these expensive departures from cheap melodrama are being overwhelmed by orders from the renting agents. Not only the nickelodeons of New York but those of many less pretentious cities and towns are demanding Browning and the other "high-brow effects." The clergymen who denounced the cheap moving picture plays of the past would be surprised and enlightened to find the Biblical teaching, eliminated from the public schools, being taken up in motion pictures. Impressive nativity plays have been given with excellent scenic effects, while Mounet-Sully played Judas in an Easter play prepared by a French firm. An American firm is now specializing on the Old Testament. "Jeptha's daughter and "The Judgment of Solomon" have already been given in excellent form, and have proved very popular. A play of Joseph and his brethren is being prepared.

A series of historical plays have been done, and more will follow. An experimental afternoon was given in a public school on Fifth Street, with a programme of instructional plays for history and English courses. . . .

It would be absurd to pretend that the manufacturers had voluntarily turned from cheap to expensive productions. The change has been brought about indirectly through the establishment of the Board of Censorship at the request of the "show men." They were tired of being arrested for questionable plays, which they had only rented from the manufacturers, and were individually powerless to control. They presented their case to the People's Institute, which evolved the censorship plan. Any manufacturer who refused to submit his films to the board was to be blacklisted.

In the very first month the board destroyed $12,000 worth of films. Then the manufacturers began to fall in line and sent orders to their playwrights forbidding "murders, burglaries," and other questionable themes as subject for plays. The board now censors all the films used in New York and 55 per cent. of the output for National use, for the censorship is now maintained at the request of the censored. The European producers proved a trifle obdurate . . . but now have settled things by sending only plays for Puritans to their American agents.

In some ways the manufacturers have gone further than the censors in forbidding their authors to construct plots involving battle, murder, and sudden death. The law of the board is not the decalogue, according to John Collier, the General Secretary, but the rules of good taste. "To eliminate all murders would be to eliminate Shakespeare and nearly all the classic drama, which would be absurd. But we object to laboratory displays of crime. We won't have a burglar demonstrate exactly how one picks a lock or jimmies open a door. You must remember our audience consists largely of impressionable children and young people. It is not a Broadway audience. We have Miss Evangeline Whitney and Gustave Straubenmuller of the Board of Education to guide the decisions on what is harmful for children, but the rules of good taste for humor as well as plot are insisted on."

In Chicago, a Police Lieutenant has charge of the censoring, and certain acts of violence are on a proscribed list. Some films are expurgated by merely cutting out the portion of the picture in which the proscribed act occurs. A duel is censored, for instance, by omitting the precise moment at which one of the men is killed. This, the National Board believes, is a typical example of the workings of hard-and-fast censorship rules.

SOURCE: *The New York Times*, October 10, 1909, 8.

Primary Source

The Great Train Robbery (2 OF 2)

A film still from the final scene of *The Great Train Robbery.* The leader of the outlaw bandits takes aim at the screen and shoots at the audience. THE KOBAL COLLECTION/EDISON. REPRODUCED BY PERMISSION.

Niver, Kemp R. *D.W. Griffith: His Biograph Films in Perspective,* Bebe Bergsten, ed. Los Angeles: John D. Roche, 1974.

Schickel, Richard. *D.W. Griffith: An American Life.* New York: Simon and Schuster, 1984.

WEBSITES

McDonald, Archie P. "Porter, Edwin Stanton." Available online at http://www.anb.org/articles/18/18-00947.html; website home page: http://www.anb.org/ (accessed May 26, 2003).

"The College of Journalism"

Journal article

By: Joseph Pulitzer

Date: May 1904

Source: Pulitzer, Joseph. "The College of Journalism." *North American Review,* May 1904, 641, 678–680.

About the Author: Born in Hungary, Joseph Pulitzer (1847–1911) remains the most influential journalist in American history. His brand of newspaper publishing, dubbed "yellow journalism," offered readers titillating accounts of trials, trysts, and tragedy, but its foundation was investigative reporting and sharp editorials. Pulitzer's $2 million contribution to Columbia University helped create a graduate school for journalism and establish the Pulitzer Prizes. First awarded in 1917, the prizes soon became the most prestigious awards in journalism, while also honoring excellence in other creative fields. ■

Introduction

A battle for the soul of journalism raged through the first decade of the twentieth century as journalists and the public wrestled with a number of questions: What is the purpose of the press? Should journalists strive for a seemingly impossible objective perspective on the world's events? Should popular taste dictate content, or must publishers tailor their news to suit the larger number of consumers?

Tensions between substance and sensationalism drove some in the news media to urge for a standardized education for journalists. Rather than simply running stories to sell more papers, publishers and editors asserted the fundamental requirement of professionalism in the field of journalism. Reporters were not simply born but needed to be trained and educated in the techniques of investigative reporting. By connecting journalism with academic instruction, journalists such as Joseph Pulitzer attempted to elevate the entire profession. When Pulitzer decided to donate $2 million to Columbia University to create a school devoted to journalism, he laid the groundwork for one of the most respected academic programs of the next century.

Significance

Pulitzer wrote "The College of Journalism" for the *North American Review* to justify his decision to help establish the School of Journalism at Columbia University in 1903. In addition to those who argued that journalism did not possess the stature to qualify for a separate academic school, much less a department or major, many journalists argued that good reporting skills simply could not be taught. They contended that adept reporters possessed news instincts that develop only in the newsroom and on the beat. Pulitzer argued that the stakes were too high to let journalism training occur by happenstance.

While agreeing that reporters improved with on-the-job training, Pulitzer saw the necessity of a journalism curriculum to further advance the level of news coverage in the United States. His ultimate objective, though, did not rest with bettering news coverage. He saw excellence in journalism as absolutely essential to national development. This explained Pulitzer's decision to open his article with a quotation from President Theodore Roosevelt (served 1901–1909), at times an intense critic of the press and of Pulitzer in particular. Roosevelt declared on April 7, 1904, "The man who writes, the man who month in and month out, week in and week out, day in and day out, furnishes the material which is to shape the thoughts of our people, is essentially the man who more than any other determines the character of the people and the kind of government this people shall possess." Likewise, Pulitzer viewed the establishment of professional training in journalism as critical to the social reform he encouraged as editor of the *New York World.*

Primary Source

"The College of Journalism" [excerpt]

SYNOPSIS: The article excerpted below arrived at a time of dramatic change in American journalism education. The year before, Pulitzer endowed a graduate School of Journalism at Columbia University. The school would offer a two-year program in journalism culminating in the awarding of a master's degree. In 1904, the same year as this article, the University of Illinois instituted the first four-year program in journalism.

The editor of the *North American Review* has asked me to reply to an article recently printed in its pages criticising the College of Journalism which it has been my pleasure to found and permanently to endow in Columbia University. In complying with his request I have enlarged the scope of the reply to include all other criticisms and misgivings, many honest, some shallow, some based on misunderstanding, but the most representing only prejudice and ignorance. If my comment upon these criticisms shall seem to be diffuse and perhaps repetitious, my apology is that—alas!—I am compelled to write by voice, not by pen, and to revise the proofs by ear, not by eye—a somewhat difficult task. . . .

Public Service the Supreme End

> *"What are great gifts but the correlative of great work? We are not born for ourselves but for our kind, for our neighbors, for our country."*
>
> —*Cardinal Newman.*

It has been said by some that my object in founding the College of Journalism was to help young men who wish to make this their vocation. Others have commended it as an effort to raise journalism to its real rank as one of the learned professions. This is true. But while it is a great pleasure to feel that a large number of young men will be helped to a better start in life by means of this college, this is not my primary object. Neither is the elevation of the profession which I love so much and regard so highly. In all my planning the chief end I had in view was the welfare of the Republic. It will be the object of the college to make better journalists, who will make better newspapers, which will better serve the public. It will impart knowledge—not for its own sake, but to be used for the public service. It will try to develop character, but even that will be only a means to the one supreme end—the public good. We are facing that hitherto-unheard-of portent—an innumerable, world-wide, educated, and self-conscious democracy. The little revolutions of the past have been effected by a few leaders working upon an ignorant populace, conscious only of vague feelings of discontent. Now the masses read. They know their grievances and their power. They discuss in New York the position of labor in Berlin and in Sydney. Capital, too, is developing a world-wide class feeling. It likewise has learned the power of cooperation.

What will be the state of society and of politics in this Republic seventy years hence, when some of the children now in school will be still living? Shall we preserve the government of the Constitution, the equality of all citizens before the law and the purity of justice—or shall we have the government of either money or the mob?

The answers to these questions will depend largely upon the kind of instruction the people of that day draw from their newspapers—the text-books, the orators, the preachers of the masses.

I have said so much of the need for improvement in journalism that to avoid misconception I must put on record my appreciation of the really admirable work so many newspaper men are doing already. The competent editorial writer, for instance—how much sound information he furnishes every day! How generally just his judgments are, and how prompt his decisions! Unknown to the people he serves, he is in close sympathy with their feelings and aspirations, and, when left to himself and unhampered by party prejudices, he generally interprets their thought as they would wish to express it themselves.

It is not too much to say that the press is the only great organized force which is actively and as a body upholding the standard of civic righteousness. There are many political reformers among the clergy, but the pulpit as an institution is concerned with the Kingdom of Heaven, not with the Republic of America. There are many public-spirited lawyers, but the bar as a profession works for its retainers, and no law-defying trust ever came to grief from a dearth of legal talent to serve it. Physicians work for their patients and architects for their patrons. The press alone makes the public interests its own. "What is everybody's business is nobody's business"—except the journalist's; it is his by adoption. But for his care almost every reform would fall stillborn. He holds officials to their duty. He exposes secret schemes of plunder. He promotes every hopeful plan of progress. Without him public opinion would be shapeless and dumb. He brings all classes, all professions together, and teaches them to act in concert on the basis of their common citizenship.

The Greeks thought that no republic could be successfully governed if it were too large for all the citizens to come together in one place. The Athenian democracy could all meet in the popular assembly. There public opinion was made, and accordingly as the people listened to a Pericles or to a Cleon the state flourished or declined. The orator that reaches the American democracy is the newspaper. It alone makes it possible to keep the political blood in healthful circulation in the veins of a continental republic. We have—it is unfortunately true—a few newspapers which advocate dangerous fallacies and falsehoods, appealing to ignorance, to partisanship, to passion, to popular prejudice, to poverty, to hatred of the rich, to socialism, sowing the seeds of discontent—eventually sure, if unchecked, to produce lawlessness and bloodshed. Virtue, said Montesquieu, is the principle of a republic, and therefore a republic, which in its purity is the most desirable of all forms of government, is the hardest of all to preserve. For there is nothing more subject to decay than virtue.

Our Republic and its press will rise or fall together. An able, disinterested, public-spirited press, with trained intelligence to know the right and courage to do it, can preserve that public virtue without which popular government is a sham and a mockery. A cynical, mercenary, demagogic press will produce in time a people as base as itself. The power to mould the future of the Republic will be in the hands of the journalists of future generations. This is why I urge my colleagues to aid the important experiment which I have ventured to endow. Upon their generous aid and cooperation the ultimate success of the project must depend.

Further Resources

BOOKS

Emery, Michael, and Edwin Emery. *The Press and America: An Interpretive History of the Mass Media,* 7th ed. Englewood Cliffs, N.J.: Prentice Hall, 1992.

WEBSITES

Pfaff, Daniel W. "Pulitzer, Joseph." Available online at http://www.anb.org/articles/16/16-01333.html; website home page: http://www.anb.org/ (accessed May 26, 2003).

The Shame of the Cities

Nonfcition work

By: Lincoln Steffens

Date: 1904

Source: Steffens, Lincoln. *The Shame of the Cities.* New York: Hill and Wang, 1904. Available online at http://historymatters.gmu.edu/d/5732/; website home page: http://historymatters.gmu.edu/ (accessed May 23, 2003).

About the Author: Lincoln Steffens (1866–1936) pioneered the 1900s journalism movement known as muckraking. Born in San Francisco, California, Steffens studied at the University of California at Berkeley, then in Germany and France. He worked for several New York newspapers before becoming managing editor of the muckraking journal *McClure's.* His articles on government corruption led to his groundbreaking and most significant work, *The Shame of the Cities.* Steffens' crowning achievement was his two-volume *Autobiography* (1931). ■

Introduction

Lincoln Steffens began his research into municipal government and corruption as a police reporter in the 1890s. While covering the police beat, he befriended Jacob Riis, then a reporter for the *New York Evening Sun* and author of *How the Other Half Lives* (1890). This study of conditions endured by the city's poor stood as the most influential piece of reform-minded journalism of the era. Steffens also met the reform-minded police commissioner Theodore Roosevelt, who served in the position from 1895 until 1897. Roosevelt worked in the good government administration of Mayor William L. Strong, who campaigned against the nation's symbol of municipal corruption, the Tammany Hall Democratic political machine. Steffens wrote dozens of articles about the robust commissioner's crusade to reform the police department. While Roosevelt rose quickly to the White House by 1901 (served 1901–1909), Steffens continued to hone his investigative reporting style into what became known as muckraking, a term coined by Roosevelt himself in 1906. Just as good government politicians sought to root out malfeasance from within government, muckraking journalists such as Steffens focused their newswriting on exposing such corruption to the public in hopes of arousing them to reform the system.

Significance

Lincoln Steffens' *The Shame of the Cities* was a collection of seven articles written for *McClure's* in 1902 and 1903 on municipal corruption in St. Louis, Minneapolis, Pittsburgh, Philadelphia, Chicago, and New York City. With colorful interviews and in-depth portraits of each city and its residents, Steffens detailed the methods by which political machines controlled large cities at the turn of the century. These organizations used graft, patronage, and other corrupt schemes to buy voters, enrich political leaders at the public's expense, and, at times, provide basic services to the burgeoning cities. While good government advocates alerted citizens to the problems fostered by the machines, muckraking would not have been muckraking if everyone agreed on the issue. George Washington Plunkitt, the colorful defender of Tammany Hall, justified the machine and even certain forms of corruption as the only means of providing for New Yorkers:

> I've been readin' a book by Lincoln Steffens on The Shame of the Cities. Steffens means well but, like all reformers, he don't know how to make distinctions. He can't see no difference between honest graft and dishonest graft and, consequent, he gets things all mixed up. There's the biggest kind of a difference between political looters and politicians who make a fortune out of politics by keepin' their eyes wide open. The looter goes in for himself alone without considerin' his organization or his city. The politician looks after his own interests, the organization's interests, and the city's interests all at the same time. See the distinction? For instance, I ain't no looter. The looter hogs it. I never hogged. I made my pile in politics, but, at the same time, I served the organization and got more big improvements for New York City than any other livin' man.
>
> *(From Riordan, William L. "On the Shame of the Cities." Plunkitt of Tammany Hall. New York: 1903; cited at the Gilder Lehrman Center. "On the Shame of the Cities." Available online at http://www.yale.edu/glc/archive/992.htm.)*

In the Introduction to *The Shame of the Cities* excerpted below, Steffens characterized his investigations as a call to arms. He targeted not only the bosses and government officials who expanded their wallets through municipal corruption but also the public. He chastised the citizenry for ignoring the corruption rampant throughout the country and, in terms similar to those of S.S. McClure presented in the sidebar, warned that Americans would face only further urban disintegration if they did not act immediately. This combination of investigative reporting and a call for reform provided the clearest example of muckraking in the 1900s.

Primary Source

The Shame of the Cities [excerpt]

SYNOPSIS: The first article reprinted in *The Shame of the Cities* appeared in *McClure's* in October 1902. This article, along with others published in 1902 and 1903, was extremely popular, spurring *McClure's* to publish a single volume that reprinted them in their entirety. This excerpt from the Introduction expounded the core muckraking ideals: investigative reporting to arouse popular support/action for reform.

Introduction and Some Conclusions

This is not a book. It is a collection of articles reprinted from *McClure's Magazine.* Done as journalism, they are journalism still, and no further pretensions are set up for them in their new dress. This classification may seem pretentious enough; certainly it would if I should confess what claims I make for my profession. . . .

They were written with a purpose, they were, published serially with a purpose, and they are reprinted now together to further that same purpose, which was and is—to sound for the civic pride of an apparently shameless citizenship.

There must be such a thing, we reasoned. All our big boasting could not be empty vanity, nor our pious pretensions hollow sham. American achievements in science, art, and business mean sound abilities at bottom, and our hypocrisy a race sense of fundamental ethics. Even in government we have given proofs of potential greatness, and our political failures are not complete; they are simply ridiculous. But they are ours. Not alone the triumphs and the statesmen, the defeats and the grafters also represent us, and just as truly. Why not see it so and say it?

Because, I heard, the American people won't "stand for" it. You may blame the politicians, or, indeed, any one class, but not all classes, not the people. Or you may put it on the ignorant foreign immigrant, or any one nationality, but not on all nationalities, not on the American people. But no one class is at fault, nor any one breed, nor any particular interest or group of interests. The misgovernment of the American people is misgovernment by the American people.

When I set out on my travels, an honest New Yorker told me honestly that I would find that the Irish, the Catholic Irish, were at the bottom of it all everywhere. The first city I went to was St. Louis, a German city. The next was Minneapolis, a Scandinavian city, with a leadership of New Englanders.

Cover of January 1903 issue of *McClure's* magazine. MCCLURE'S MAGAZINE.

Then came Pittsburgh, Scotch Presbyterian, and that was what my New York friend was. "Ah, but they are all foreign populations," I heard. The next city was Philadelphia, the purest American community of all, and the most hopeless. And after that came Chicago and New York, both mongrel-bred, but the one a triumph of reform, the other the best example of good government that I had seen. The "foreign element" excuse is one of the hypocritical lies that save us from the clear sight of ourselves.

Another such conceit of our egotism is that which deplores our politics and lauds our business. This is the wail of the typical American citizen. Now, the typical American citizen is the business man. The typical business man is a bad citizen; he is busy. If he is a "big business man" and very busy, he does not neglect, he is busy with politics, oh, very busy and very businesslike. I found him buying boodlers in St. Louis, defending grafters in Minneapolis, originating corruption in Pittsburgh, sharing with bosses in Philadelphia, deploring reform in Chicago, and beating good government with corruption funds in New York. He is a self-righteous fraud, this big business man. He is the chief source of corruption, and it were a boon if he would neglect politics. But he is not the business man that neglects politics; that worthy is the good citizen, the typical business man. He too is busy, he is the one that has no use and therefore no time for politics. When his neglect has permitted bad government to go so far that he can be stirred to action, he is unhappy, and he looks around for a cure that shall be quick, so that he may hurry back to the shop. Naturally, too, when he talks politics, he talks shop. His patent remedy is quack; it is business. . . .

The commercial spirit is the spirit of profit, not patriotism; of credit, not honor; of individual gain, not national prosperity; of trade and dickering, not principle. "My business is sacred," says the business man in his heart. "Whatever prospers my business, is good; it must be. Whatever hinders it, is wrong; it must be. A bribe is bad, that is, it is a bad thing to take; but it is not so bad to give one, not if it is necessary to my business." "Business is business" is not a political sentiment, but our politician has caught it. He takes essentially the same view of the bribe, only he saves his self-respect by piling all his contempt upon the bribe-giver, and he has the great advantage of candor. "It is wrong, maybe," he says, "but if a rich merchant can afford to do business with me for the sake of a convenience or to increase his already great wealth, I can afford, for the sake of a living, to meet him half way. I make no pretensions to virtue, not even on Sunday." And as for giving bad government or good, how about the merchant who gives bad goods or good goods, according to the demand? . . .

But do the people want good government? Tammany says they don't. Are the people honest? Are the people better than Tammany? Are they better than the merchant and the politician? Isn't our corrupt government, after all, representative?

. . . We are pathetically proud of our democratic institutions and our republican form of government, of our grand Constitution and our just laws. We are a free and sovereign people, we govern ourselves and the government is ours. But that is the point. We are responsible, not our leaders, since we follow them. We let them divert our loyalty from the United States to some "party"; we let them boss the party and turn our municipal democracies into autocracies and our republican nation into a plutocracy. We cheat our government and we let our leaders loot it, and we let them wheedle and bribe our sovereignty from us. True, they pass for us strict laws, but we are content to let them pass also bad laws, giving away public property in exchange; and our good, and often impossible, laws we allow to be used for oppression and blackmail. And what can we say? We break our own laws and rob our own government, the lady at the customhouse, the lyncher with his rope, and the captain of industry with his bribe and his rebate.

The spirit of graft and of lawlessness is the American spirit. . . .

The people are not innocent. That is the only "news" in all the journalism of these articles, and no doubt that was not new to many observers. It was to me.

When I set out to describe the corrupt systems of certain typical cities, I meant to show simply how the people were deceived and betrayed. But in the very first study—St. Louis—the startling truth lay bare that corruption was not merely political; it was financial, commercial, social; the ramifications of boodle were so complex, various, and far-reaching, that one mind could hardly grasp them, and not even Joseph W. Folk, the tireless prosecutor, could follow them all. This state of things was indicated in the first article which Claude H. Wetmore and I compiled together, but it was not shown plainly enough. Mr. Wetmore lived in St. Louis, and he had respect for names which meant little to me, but when I went next to Minneapolis alone, I could see more independently, without respect for persons, and there were traces of the same phenomenon. The first St. Louis article was called "Tweed Days in St. Louis," and though the "better citizen" received attention the Tweeds were the center of interest. In "The Shame of Minneapolis," the truth was put into the title; it was the Shame of Minneapolis; not of the Ames administration, not of the Tweeds, but of the city and its citizens. And yet Minneapolis was not nearly so bad as St. Louis; police graft is never so universal as boodle. It is more shocking, but it is so filthy that it cannot involve so large a part of society. So I returned to St. Louis, and I went over the whole ground again, with the people in mind, not alone the caught and convicted boodlers. And this time the true meaning of "Tweed Days in St. Louis" was made plain. The article was called "The Shamelessness of St. Louis," and that was the burden of the story. In Pittsburgh also the people was the subject, and though the civic spirit there was better, the extent of the corruption throughout the social organization of the community was indicated. But it was not till I got to Philadelphia that the possibilities

"Concerning Three Articles in this Number of McClure's, and a Coincidence that May Set Us Thinking"

[S. S. McClure began *McClure's* in 1893 to provide a cheaper alternative to the dominant current events journals of the day. The three central articles in the famed January 1903 edition—by Steffens, Ida Tarbell, and Ray Stannard Baker—now stand as the birth of muckraking in American journalism. McClure succinctly outlined the danger of ignoring crime and moral disintegration in the United States. For McClure, and perhaps most muckrakers, the ultimate cost of popular apathy would be liberty itself.]

How many of those who have read through this number of the magazine noticed that it contains three articles on one subject? We did not plan it so; it is a coincidence that the January *McClure's* is such an arraignment of American character as should make every one of us stop and think. How many noticed that?

The leading article, "The Shame of Minneapolis," might have been called "The American Contempt of Law." That title could well have served for the current chapter of Miss Tarbell's History of Standard Oil. And it would have fitted perfectly Mr. Baker's "The Right to Work." All together, these articles come pretty near showing how universal is this dangerous trait of ours. Miss Tarbell has our capitalists conspiring among themselves, deliberately, shrewdly, upon legal advice, to break the law so far as it restrained them, and to misuse it to restrain others who were in their way. Mr. Baker shows labor, the ancient enemy of capital, and the chief complainant of the trusts' unlawful acts, itself committing and excusing crimes. And in "The Shame of Minneapolis" we see the administration of a city employing criminals to commit crimes for the profit of the elected officials, while the citizens—Americans of good stock and more than average culture, and honest, healthy Scandinavians—stood by complacent and not alarmed.

Capitalists, workingmen, politicians, citizens—all breaking the law, or letting it be broken. Who is left to uphold it? The lawyers? Some of the best lawyers in this country are hired, not to go into court to defend cases, but to advise corporations and business firms how they can get around the law without too great a risk of punishment. The judges? Too many of them so respect the laws that for some "error" or quibble they restore to office and liberty men convicted on evidence overwhelmingly convincing to common sense. The churches? We know of one, an ancient and wealthy establishment, which had to be compelled by a Tammany hold-over health officer to put its tenements in sanitary condition. The colleges? They do not understand.

There is no one left; none but all of us. Capital is learning (with indignation at labor's unlawful acts) that its rival's contempt of law is a menace to property. Labor has shrieked the belief that the illegal power of capital is a menace to the worker. These two are drawing together. Last November when a strike was threatened by the yard-men on all the railroads centering in Chicago, the men got together and settled by raising wages, and raising freight rates too. They made the public pay. We all are doing our worst and making the public pay. The public is the people. We forget that we all are the people; that while each of us in his group can shove off on the rest the bill of to-day, the debt is only postponed; the rest are passing it on back to us. We have to pay in the end, every one of us. And in the end the sum total of the debt will be our liberty.

SOURCE: McClure, S.S. "Concerning Three Articles in this Number of McClure's, and a Coincidence that May Set Us Thinking." *McClure's,* January 1903, 336.

of popular corruption were worked out to the limit of humiliating confession. That was the place for such a study. There is nothing like it in the country, except possibly, in Cincinnati. Philadelphia certainly is not merely corrupt, but corrupted, and this was made clear. Philadelphia was charged up to—the American citizen. . . .

This is all very unscientific, but then, I am not a scientist. I am a journalist. I did not gather with indifference all the facts and arrange them patiently for permanent preservation and laboratory analysis. I did not want to preserve, I wanted to destroy the facts. My purpose was no more scientific than the spirit of my investigation and reports; it was, as I said above, to see if the shameful facts, spread out in all their shame, would not burn through our civic shamelessness and set fire to American pride. That was the journalism of it. I wanted to move and to convince. . . .

■ ■ ■

. . . The real triumph of the year's work was the complete demonstration it has given, in a thousand little ways, that our shamelessness is superficial, that beneath it lies a pride which, being real, may save us yet. And it is real. The grafters who said you may put the blame anywhere but on the people, where it belongs, and that Americans can be moved only by flattery—they lied. They lied about themselves. They, too, are American citizens; they too, are of the people; and some of them also were reached by shame. . . .

We Americans may have failed. We may be mercenary and selfish. Democracy with us may be impossible and corruption inevitable, but these articles, if they have proved nothing else, have demonstrated beyond doubt that we can stand the truth; that there is pride in the character of American citizenship; and that this pride may be a power in the land. So this little volume, a record of shame and yet of self-respect.

Further Resources

BOOKS

Emery, Michael, and Edwin Emery. *The Press and America: An Interpretive History of the Mass Media,* 7th ed. Englewood Cliffs, N.J.: Prentice Hall, 1992.

Riordon, William L. *Plunkitt of Tammany Hall.* 1905. Reprint, New York: E.P. Dutton and Company, 1963.

WEBSITES

CJR Online. "What a Century!" *CJR 21st Century Project.* Available online at http://www.cjr.org/year/99/1/century.asp; website home page: http://www.cjr.org/ (accessed May 30, 2003).

Gale, Robert L. "McClure, Samuel Sidney." Available online at http://www.anb.org/articles/16/16-01087.html; website home page: http://www.anb.org/ (accessed May 26, 2003).

Mooney-Melvin, Patricia. "Steffens, Lincoln." Available online at http://www.anb.org/articles/15/15-00644.html; website home page: http://www.anb.org/ (accessed May 26, 2003).

"Humorous Phases of Funny Faces"

Cartoon

By: J. Stuart Blackton

Date: April 6, 1906

Source: Blackton, J. Stuart, producer and animator. "Humorous Phases of Funny Faces." Vitagraph, 1906. Available online at Origins of American Animation, Library of Congress; http://www.americaslibrary.gov/sh/animation/sh_animation_blcktn_3.html; website home page: http://www.americaslibrary.gov (accessed May 27, 2003).

About the Author: Born in Sheffield, England, James Stuart Blackton (1875–1941) moved to the United States in 1886, where Thomas Edison's invitation to participate in a film, "Blackton, the Evening World Cartoonist" (1896), changed his life. By the end of the next year, Blackton had formed the Vitagraph Company for producing his own motion pictures. "The Enchanted Drawing" (1900) and "Humorous Phases of Funny Faces" (1906) featured the first uses of animation techniques. Blackton lost a fortune in the stock market crash of 1929, and at the time of his death he was working as a carpenter in Los Angeles. ■

James Stuart Blackton is known as the father of American animation. THE LIBRARY OF CONGRESS.

Introduction

Developed at the turn of the century, the first motion pictures would probably appear as just that to modern viewers: moving pictures. The film camera quickly shot a series of photographs, exposing one after the other in rapid succession. Inventor Thomas Edison developed many of the technologies used in these earlier productions, such as roll film, the kinetograph camera, and a kinetoscope viewer. When run through the kinetoscope, still pictures appeared to come alive, having recorded actors moving about the field of view. Early special effects made use of stop-motion photography, where the camera operator turned off the machine, changed the scene or set design, and turned the camera back on to make it seem as if time had passed or to display events occurring at the same time in different places. Edison's viewers provided peep-hole viewing and allowed for only a single viewer at a time. Advances in projection technology in the 1900s increased the popularity of motion pictures, as film displays in theaters provided dozens of people access at a single showing.

Significance

Working primarily with Edison-made equipment, J. Stuart Blackton and Edison produced "The Enchanted

Primary Source

"Humorous Phases of Funny Faces"

SYNOPSIS: About a decade after the production of the first motion pictures, J. Stuart Blackton created the rudimentary structure of modern cartoons. His animated pictures used the rapid projection of images like those presented in these stills to create the illusion of movement. "Humorous Phases of Funny Faces," despite its jerky movement and simplistic drawings, represented a new phenomenon in motion pictures. The unnamed, fairly uncharismatic characters displayed in this film set the stage for Mickey, Bugs, and the rise of the American cartoon industry. THE LIBRARY OF CONGRESS.

Drawing" in 1900. This ninety-second film featured one of the earliest uses of motion pictures to animate hand-drawn illustrations. The film presented one of the Blackton's "lightning sketches" vaudeville acts, with so-called magic filmmaking effects. The film showed a human artist standing before a large white board, on which he quickly drew a man's face along with a top hat, wine bottle, glass, and cigar. After each drawing, unbeknownst to later viewers, the camera was stopped, producing an edit certainly not seamless by modern standards. The next frame, or picture, brought a seemingly magical change in the scene. With a quick edit, the artist grasped the bottle and glass, poured himself a drink, and took a swig. After he appeared to pour some of the drink into the drawing's mouth, the face brightened with a large grin. This stop-motion technique created the illusion of movement in the drawing and the apparent transformation of illustrations into real objects.

"Humorous Phases of Funny Faces," produced in 1906, used a similar filming method to show drawings seemingly moving on their own, becoming animated in the film. With a full three minutes devoted to motion-picture animation, this film is usually credited as the first of its kind. After a human hand enters the picture to draw a character with chalk on a blackboard, the drawing appears to come to life. The film featured different scenes with a variety of characters performing simple movements. A stout man flips his umbrella and lowers his hat. A man blows cigar smoke into a woman's face. One scene, played in reverse, begins with a partially erased drawing of male and female heads. As the scene progresses, the erasures disappear, revealing the finished drawings. Then, the illustrations steadily lose their features as they become "undrawn," as if by an invisible hand. The technique mirrored a far older, and still popular, form of entertainment—the flip book, which included a stack of papers with subtly different drawings on each sheet. By swiftly flipping through the pages, the viewer enjoyed the illusion that the drawings were moving.

The images presented here helped form the final film, "Humorous Phases of Funny Faces," where in one scene a simply drawn clown plays several tricks. First, it juggles a hat, then a dog, and then throws each through a hoop. The final product resulted from hundreds of images such as these, each representing a separate drawing or moment in time, displayed in rapid succession to produce the world's first animated film.

Further Resources

BOOKS

Musser, Charles. *The Emergence of Cinema.* Berkeley, Calif.: University of California Press, 1990.

Trimble, Marian Blackton. *J. Stuart Blackton.* Metuchen, N.J.: Scarecrow Press, 1985.

"The Man with the Muck Rake"

Speech

By: Theodore Roosevelt

Date: April 15, 1906

Source: Roosevelt, Theodore. "The Man With the Muck Rake." April 15, 1906. Available online at Texas A&M University, The Program in Presidential Rhetoric. http://www

.tamu.edu/scom/pres/speeches/trmuck.html (accessed May 23, 2003).

About the Author: Theodore Roosevelt (1858–1919) shaped the modern chief executive's relationship with the press. The youngest U.S. president, he ascended to the office in 1901, at age forty-two, after the assassination of President William McKinley (served 1897–1901). Known for his boundless energy, Roosevelt had already been a rancher, assistant secretary of the navy, governor of New York, assemblyman, and sheriff. He had also written over forty books and had organized his own cavalry regiment in the Spanish-American War (1898). During his presidency (1901–1909), he promoted conservation and publicly fought against trusts. He also used American power to intervene in Latin America and its prestige to help negotiate peace between other major countries. Out of office, he continued to be a prominent voice in public affairs. He ran for a third term in 1912 as the Progressive Party candidate but was defeated by Woodrow Wilson. ■

Introduction

President Theodore Roosevelt's "New Nationalism" characterized the president as the "steward of the public welfare." To strengthen popular support for his policy reforms, Roosevelt restructured the relationship between the White House and the press. TR developed the concept of the "bully pulpit," which emphasized the president's power to shape public opinion through rhetoric and the news media. He sought to create substantial connections between him and reporters, even going so far as to invite his favorites to join him for his morning shave. The president used these private sessions to gauge popular support for various programs under consideration, a process known as the "trial balloon." His recognition of the press's role in the creation of public policy was cemented with the installation of permanent press offices in the new West Wing to the White House in 1902. Roosevelt kept a close eye on media investigations that seemed relevant to his own goals of industrial reform and regulation. In 1906, Roosevelt successfully called for the passage of the Pure Food and Drug and Meat Inspection Acts following the publication of Upton Sinclair's *The Jungle* earlier that year.

There also existed a tempestuous side to the new president-press relationship. Roosevelt became so enraged with criticisms from publisher Joseph Pulitzer in the *New York World* that he sued Pulitzer (unsuccessfully) for libel. In 1906, he coined the term "muckraking" to decry what he saw as careless, harmful investigative practices of the press.

Significance

The speech excerpted below expressed many of the central dilemmas in the history of American journalism. At what point does investigative journalism become an invasion of privacy? Where does public interest end and a person's right to privacy begin? Roosevelt began his address with a reference to the seventeenth-century allegorical tale *Pilgrim's Progress* by John Bunyan. The president characterized the most soulless, uncaring journalist of the 1900s as akin to "the Man with the Muck Rake, the man who could look no way but downward, with the muck rake in his hand; who was offered a celestial crown for his muck rake, but who would neither look up nor regard the crown he was offered, but continued to rake to himself the filth of the floor."

According to Roosevelt, the muckraking journalist represented one of the many evils in American society at the dawn of the twentieth century. Just as corrupt business and government leaders threatened the public welfare, so too did reporters whose only concern centered on tearing down all public and private officials without a care for the social impact. As Roosevelt declared, "But the man who never does anything else, who never thinks or speaks or writes, save of his feats with the muck rake, speedily becomes, not a help but one of the most potent forces for evil."

Although Roosevelt levied these attacks upon journalists of the early 1900s, many of his criticisms remain relevant more than a century later. Journalists and public officials in the twenty-first century argue, just as Roosevelt did, that the media's desire for salacious private details discourages able individuals from seeking to aid society by working in the public sphere. At the same time, critics worry about the enduring ramifications sensational reporting has on the public, in particular whether such news stories increase apathy and reduce civic consciousness. Interestingly, Samuel S. McClure offered a similar assessment in his editor's statement of the famous January 1903 edition of *McClure's* magazine. He argued that the public must avoid complacency and the reform-minded journalist must accept as part of his or her responsibility to spur the audience to action. Roosevelt's argument that journalists must expose corruption in wealthy and nonwealthy sectors alike also found an ally in McClure, who built his famous issue around articles that investigated corruption in city government, corporations, and labor unions.

It is not surprising that Roosevelt's chastising characterization of so-called muckrakers came to be worn as a badge of honor by many contemporary journalists. Muckraking soon came to represent an entire era of reporting designed to expose corruption and engender popular support for reform. "The Man with the Muck Rake," though, seemed to spell a turning point in the muckraking movement of the 1900s. Ironically, the new wave of journalism that shaped news coverage in the 1910s and 1920s saw a rejuvenation in the kind of press abhorred by both muckrakers and Roosevelt himself: sensational coverage of trials, murders, and sex scandals that ignored, for the most part, the continuing problems in American society.

A NAUSEATING JOB, BUT IT MUST BE DONE
(President Roosevelt takes hold of the investigating muck-rake himself in the packing-house scandal.)
From the *Saturday Globe* (Utica)

President Theodore Roosevelt takes hold of the investigating muck-rake in the meat packing-house scandal in this political cartoon from the *Utica Saturday Globe.*

Primary Source

"The Man with the Muck Rake"

SYNOPSIS: President Roosevelt delivered "The Man with the Muck Rake" on Sunday, April 15, 1906, at the laying of the cornerstone of the Cannon Office Building in Washington, D.C. He spoke about the need for reform in journalism in the immediate aftermath of a series of articles critical of the president's congressional allies. Famed muckraker Lincoln Steffens reportedly said to Roosevelt the day after this speech, "Well, you have put an end to all these journalistic investigations that have made you" (from http://www.spartacus.schoolnet.co.uk /Jmuckraking.htm).

Over a century ago Washington laid the corner stone of the Capitol in what was then little more than a tract of wooded wilderness here beside the Potomac. We now find it necessary to provide by great additional buildings for the business of the government.

This growth in the need for the housing of the government is but a proof and example of the way in which the nation has grown and the sphere of action of the national government has grown. We now administer the affairs of a nation in which the extraordinary growth of population has been outstripped by the growth of wealth in complex interests. The material problems that face us today are not such as they were in Washington's time, but the underlying facts of human nature are the same now as they were then. Under altered external form we war with the same tendencies toward evil that were evident in Washington's time, and are helped by the same tendencies for good. It is about some of these that I wish to say a word today.

In Bunyan's "Pilgrim's Progress" you may recall the description of the Man with the Muck Rake, the man who could look no way but downward, with the muck rake in his hand; who was offered a celestial crown for his muck rake, but who would neither look up nor regard the crown he was offered, but continued to rake to himself the filth of the floor.

In "Pilgrim's Progress" the Man with the Muck Rake is set forth as the example of him whose vision is fixed on carnal instead of spiritual things. Yet he also typifies the man who in this life consistently refuses to see aught that is lofty, and fixes his eyes with solemn intentness only on that which is vile and debasing.

Now, it is very necessary that we should not flinch from seeing what is vile and debasing. There is filth on the floor, and it must be scraped up with the muck rake; and there are times and places where this service is the most needed of all the services that can be performed. But the man who never does anything else, who never thinks or speaks or writes, save of his feats with the muck rake, speedily becomes, not a help but one of the most potent forces for evil.

There are in the body politic, economic and social, many and grave evils, and there is urgent necessity for the sternest war upon them. There should be relentless exposure of and attack upon every evil man, whether politician or business man, every evil practice, whether in politics, business, or social life. I hail as a benefactor every writer or speaker, every man who, on the platform or in a book, magazine, or newspaper, with merciless severity makes such attack, provided always that he in his turn remembers that the attack is of use only if it is absolutely truthful.

The liar is no whit better than the thief, and if his mendacity takes the form of slander he may be worse than most thieves. It puts a premium upon knavery untruthfully to attack an honest man, or even with hysterical exaggeration to assail a bad man with untruth.

An epidemic of indiscriminate assault upon character does no good, but very great harm. The soul of every scoundrel is gladdened whenever an honest man is assailed, or even when a scoundrel is untruthfully assailed.

Now, it is easy to twist out of shape what I have just said, easy to affect to misunderstand it, and if it is slurred over in repetition not difficult really to misunderstand it. Some persons are sincerely incapable of understanding that to denounce mud slinging does not mean the endorsement of whitewashing; and both the interested individuals who need whitewashing and those others who practice mud slinging like to encourage such confusion of ideas.

One of the chief counts against those who make indiscriminate assault upon men in business or men in public life is that they invite a reaction which is sure to tell powerfully in favor of the unscrupulous scoundrel who really ought to be attacked, who ought to be exposed, who ought, if possible, to be put in the penitentiary. If Aristides is praised overmuch as just, people get tired of hearing it; and overcensure of the unjust finally and from similar reasons results in their favor.

Any excess is almost sure to invite a reaction; and, unfortunately, the reactions instead of taking the form of punishment of those guilty of the excess, is apt to take the form either of punishment of the unoffending or of giving immunity, and even strength, to offenders. The effort to make financial or political profit out of the destruction of character can only result in public calamity. Gross and reckless assaults on character, whether on the stump or in newspaper, magazine, or book, create a morbid and vicious public sentiment, and at the same time act as a profound deterrent to able men of normal sensitiveness and tend to prevent them from entering the public service at any price.

As an instance in point, I may mention that one serious difficulty encountered in getting the right type of men to dig the Panama canal is the certainty that they will be exposed, both without, and, I am sorry to say, sometimes within, Congress, to utterly reckless assaults on their character and capacity. . . .

It is because I feel that there should be no rest in the endless war against the forces of evil that I ask the war be conducted with sanity as well as with resolution. The men with the muck rakes are often indispensable to the well being of society; but only if they know when to stop raking the muck, and to look upward to the celestial crown above them, to the crown of worthy endeavor. There are beautiful things above and round about them; and if they gradually grow to feel that the whole world is nothing but muck, their power of usefulness is gone.

If the whole picture is painted black there remains no hue whereby to single out the rascals for distinction from their fellows. Such painting finally induces a kind of moral color blindness; and people affected by it come to the conclusion that no man is really black, and no man really white, but they are all gray.

In other words, they neither believe in the truth of the attack, nor in the honesty of the man who is attacked; they grow as suspicious of the accusation as of the offense; it becomes well nigh hopeless to stir them either to wrath against wrongdoing or to enthusiasm for what is right; and such a mental attitude in the public gives hope to every knave, and is the despair of honest men. To assail the great and admitted evils of our political and industrial life with such crude and sweeping generalizations as to include decent men in the general condemnation means the searing of the public conscience. There results a general attitude either of cynical belief in and indifference to public corruption or else of a distrustful inability to discriminate between the good and the bad. Either attitude is fraught with untold damage to the country as a whole.

The fool who has not sense to discriminate between what is good and what is bad is well nigh as dangerous as the man who does discriminate and yet chooses the bad. There is nothing more distressing to every good patriot, to every good American, than the hard, scoffing spirit which treats the allegation of dishonesty in a public man as a cause for laughter. Such laughter is worse than the crackling of thorns under a pot, for it denotes not merely the vacant mind, but the heart in which high emotions have been choked before they could grow to fruition. There is any amount of good in the world, and there never was a time when loftier and more disinterested work for the betterment of mankind was being done than now. The forces that tend for evil are great and terrible, but the forces of truth and love and courage and honesty and generosity and sympathy are also stronger than ever before. It is a foolish and timid, no less than a wicked thing, to blink the fact that the forces of evil are strong, but it is even worse to fail to take into account the strength of the forces that tell for good. . . .

At this moment we are passing through a period of great unrest—social, political, and industrial unrest. It is of the utmost importance for our future that this should prove to be not the unrest of mere rebelliousness against life, of mere dissatisfaction with the inevitable inequality of conditions, but the unrest of a resolute and eager ambition to secure the betterment of the individual and the nation.

So far as this movement of agitation throughout the country takes the form of a fierce discontent with evil, of a determination to punish the authors of evil, whether in industry or politics, the feeling is to be heartily welcomed as a sign of healthy life.

If, on the other hand, it turns into a mere crusade of appetite against appetite, of a contest between the brutal greed of the "have nots" and the brutal greed of the "haves," then it has no significance for good, but only for evil. If it seeks to establish a line of cleavage, not along the line which divides good men from bad, but along that other line, running at right angles thereto, which divides those who are well off from those who are less well off, then it will be fraught with immeasurable harm to the body politic. . . .

More important than aught else is the development of the broadest sympathy of man for man. The welfare of the wage worker, the welfare of the tiller of the soil, upon these depend the welfare of the entire country; their good is not to be sought in pulling down others; but their good must be the prime object of all our statesmanship.

Materially we must strive to secure a broader economic opportunity for all men, so that each shall have a better chance to show the stuff of which he is made. Spiritually and ethically we must strive to bring about clean living and right thinking. We appreciate that the things of the body are important; but we appreciate also that the things of the soul are immeasurably more important.

The foundation stone of national life is, and ever must be, the high individual character of the average citizen.

Further Resources

BOOKS

Chalmer, David Mark. *The Muckrake Years.* New York: Van Nostrand, 1974.

Morris, Edmund. *Theodore Rex.* New York: Random House, 2001.

PERIODICALS

McClure, S.S. "Concerning Three Articles in This Number of *McClure's,* and a Coincidence that May Set Us Thinking." *McClure's,* January 1903, 336.

WEBSITES

Harbaugh, William H. "Roosevelt, Theodore." Available online at http://www.anb.org/articles/06/06-00569.html; website home page: http://www.anb.org (accessed May 27, 2003).

"Muckraking." Available online at http://www.spartacus.schoolnet.co.uk/Jmuckraking.htm.

The Outlook and the Civil Rights Movement

"The Platform of the Niagara Movement;" "The Platform of The Outlook;" "The Negro Problem: Booker Washington's Platform"

Journal articles

By: *The Outlook*

Date: September 1, 1906; September 1, 1906; September 8, 1906

Source: "The Platform of the Niagara Movement" and "The Platform of The Outlook." *The Outlook* 84, September 1, 1906, 3–4; "The Negro Problem: Booker Washington's Platform." *The Outlook* 84, September 8, 1906, 54–55.

About the Publication: *The Outlook* developed from *Christian Union,* a religious journal created by noted evangelical leader Henry Ward Beecher in 1870 and edited by clergyman Lyman Abbott after 1881. Desiring to expand the journal's audience and reflect its support of progressive reform, Abbott renamed it *The Outlook* in 1893. Under Abbott, the weekly greatly expanded its circulation to more than 100,000 copies at the turn of the century. The journal's liberalism and desire to disavow any association with religious causes gradually reduced its popularity in the 1910s and 1920s, and it ceased publication in 1935. ■

Introduction

Born to an enslaved mother in 1856, Booker Taliaferro Washington devoted his life to improving his family's condition in the midst of wrenching poverty. In 1872, he enrolled at the Hampton Institution, a school devoted to vocational training with a strong Christian emphasis. The philosophy of mind and body that Washington learned at Hampton would shape his entire adult life. His belief in the need for racial uplift guided by a strong work ethic and Christian virtues became the driving force behind his establishment of the Tuskegee Institute in Alabama in the early 1880s.

Washington's famous "Atlanta Compromise" address of 1895 set forth a strategy of accommodation with whites in the hopes of curing racial tensions without radical change in the American legal or political structure. He argued that "agitation of questions of social equality is the extremest folly" and that change must come from "constant struggle rather than of artificial forcing." This notion of "mutual progress" linked the destinies of whites and African Americans and encouraged alliances between the races. Many viewed this platform as accommodationist to whites, meaning that Washington hoped to foment change by appealing to whites rather than challenging them. Moreover, Washington argued that improvement in the lives of blacks must come from within, by uplifting the race through work, religion, and civic pride.

Washington's strategies succeeded in currying favor, if not much substantive support, from white political leaders and the press. He participated in well-publicized, and controversial, meetings with Presidents William McKinley (served 1897–1901) in 1898 and Theodore Roosevelt (served 1901–1909) in 1901, further strengthening his stature as perhaps the most powerful black leader of his era. Washington's notoriety increased through the 1900s, with the publication of several works concerning his philosophy of racial uplift, the most famous of which was his autobiography, *Up From Slavery* (1901). In the face of lynchings and anti-black violence throughout the period, though, many saw Washington's argument as acquiescence rather than leadership.

Born in 1868, William Edward Burghardt Du Bois grew up far from the slave plantations of the South, in Great Barrington, Massachusetts. He attended a racially integrated high school and became its first black graduate in 1884. Du Bois's pursuit of advanced academic studies led him to Fisk University in Nashville, Tennessee. His undergraduate career at Fisk exposed Du Bois for the first time to the racial tensions of life in the South. He continued his intellectual training at Harvard, receiving a master's degree and a Ph.D. (1895) at the prestigious university. Similar to Washington's experience at Hampton, Du Bois's academic career helped him structure an important critique of race relations and conceptualize reforms to empower to African Americans. With the publication of *The Philadelphia Negro* (1899) and *The Souls of Black Folk* (1903), Du Bois defined his own ideology of the need for radical change within the American economic, political, and legal landscape. Du Bois argued that such change and the ultimate equality of African Americans required the establishment and protection of civil rights in the United States. Only through massive campaigns and social struggle could blacks hope to gain power in the twentieth century. In *The Souls of Black Folk,* Du Bois scathingly criticized Booker T. Washington for, according to Du Bois, allying with the perpetrators of racism and denying rather than enabling progress. In 1905, Du Bois helped form the Niagara Movement, which called for federal government intervention in race relations. The group's core objectives, which included black suffrage and the abolition of segregation, would continue to be struggled for until the Civil Rights Act of 1964 and the Voting Rights Act of 1965.

Significance

The debate between Booker T. Washington and W.E.B. Du Bois over the strategy and objectives for

African American progress shaped the news media's coverage of civil rights issues throughout the 1900s. As displayed by even the moderately progressive journal *The Outlook,* much of the era's press appeared ambivalent toward civil rights, especially the more strident protests of Du Bois. The articles reprinted below emphasize the journal's support of segregation, opposition to equal voting rights for African Americans, and the general denunciation of political activism for civil rights. Instead, the journal favored Washington's perspective, which seemed to blame problems within African American communities on the residents themselves rather than on entrenched racism. In a decade known for reform-minded, muckraking journalism, the prevailing sentiment of the majority of publications remained against progressive strides for racial equality.

With the white press predominantly against civil rights, Du Bois and other African American writers began to organize their own publications. Between 1890 and 1910, activists founded some of most influential journals in the history of the black press, including the *New York Age* (1890), Baltimore's *Afro-American* (1892), the *Chicago Defender* (1905), and the *Amsterdam News of Harlem* (1909). The period culminated with the creation of the National Association for the Advancement of Colored People in 1909 and Du Bois's managing of the NAACP's journal, *The Crisis,* which began in 1910 and reached a circulation of one hundred thousand by 1918.

W.E.B. Du Bois was the corresponding secretary of the Eighth Conference for the Study of the Negro Problems and editor of a report done of the Black Church which was presented there on May 26, 1903.

Primary Source

"The Platform of the Niagara Movement;" "The Platform of The Outlook;" "The Negro Problem: Booker Washington's Platform"

SYNOPSIS: The columns reprinted below appeared in the midst of growing tensions over race relations in the United States. The first summarizes the official position of the Niagara Movement, then recently formed by W.E.B. Du Bois, which called for massive reforms to improve the position of African Americans in the United States. The second article, which appeared next to the first, demonstrates that mainstream White Americans, even reformers like the editors of *The Outlook,* did not support this view. The final article summarizes Booker T. Washington's less confrontational and gradual approach to racial equality, a position which *The Outlook* and many other liberal White Americans considered to be the best approach.

"The Platform of the Niagara Movement"

The second annual meeting of the so-called Niagara Movement was held recently at Harper's Ferry. This is a movement of negroes for negro rights. It represents the more political and the more assertive spirit in the negro race, under the leadership of Dr. Du Bois, as the Tuskegee Movement under the leadership of Dr. Washington represents the more industrial and the more pacific spirit. It is probably not unjust to say that something of the quality of the Niagara Movement is indicated by the fact that its leaders chose this year Harper's Ferry for its place of assemblage, and in its closing utterance the assembly declared, "Here, on the scene of John Brown's Martyrdom, we reconsecrate ourselves, our honor, our property, to the final emancipation of the race which John Brown died to make free." Its adopted platform comprises five principles: (1) The right to vote: "We want full manhood suffrage, and we want it now, henceforth, and forever." (2) Condemnation of all race discrimination in public accommodations: "Separation in railway and street cars, based simply on race and color, is un-American, undemocratic, and silly." (3) Freedom of social intercourse: "We claim the right of freemen to walk, talk, and be with them that wish to be with us. No man has a right to choose another man's friends, and to attempt to do so is an impudent interference with the most fundamental human privilege." (4) Equality in the enforcement of laws: "Justice even for criminals and outlaws;" "Congress to take charge of Congressional elections;" "the Fourteenth and Fifteenth Amendments enforced." (5) "The National Government to step in and wipe out illiteracy in the South;" an undying hostility to "any proposal to educate black boys and girls simply as servants and underlings, or simply for the use of other people."

■ ■ ■

"The Platform of The Outlook"

We can best state our views respecting these demands by putting with them what appear to us to be the just and reasonable bases for the settlement of the so-called race issue. Those bases we should state somewhat as follows: (1) Manhood suffrage, provided the manhood comes first and the suffrage afterwards. The ballot is not a natural right, like the right to the protection of person and property; it is a prerogative to be given only to those, black or white, who have furnished some evidence that they possess the intellectual and moral qualifications to use the ballot for the benefit of the community. But it should be based on personal qualifications, not on race or color. (2) It is better for both races that they have their separate schools and separate churches. It is no more an injustice to the black race than to the white race to provide separate cars for them, if the accommodations are equally good for both races. (3) Social fellowship cannot be restrained by law, neither can it be claimed as a right. In general, the way to secure social recognition is not to demand it. (4) The demand for the equality of law enforcement is wholly just. The demand for Congressional charge of Congressional elections is wholly unnecessary. Congress has already charge of Congressional elections. It has the right to reject any Representative on evidence that his election has been accomplished by corruption, fraud, violence, or threatening of any description, and it ought to exercise this right far more vigorously than it has been accustomed to do. (5) We want the National Government to "wipe out illiteracy in the South," and we protest against any "proposal to educate black boys and girls simply as servants and underlings;" but we also affirm as a truth of universal applicability that the end of all education should be to fit the pupil for the work which it is probable he will have to do, for the service which he will probably have to render. We add the demand for the open door of industrial opportunity to all men, black and white, and insistence upon the principle that every man shall fit himself, as his first duty to the community, to render the best service of which, taking account of his training and his inheritance, he is capable. On the whole, we think the Niagara Movement would be more useful if it demanded more of the negro race and put less emphasis on its demands for the negro race.

■ ■ ■

"The Negro Problem: Booker Washington's Platform"

In The Outlook of last week we gave a summary of the platform adopted at the second annual meeting of the so-called Niagara Movement held at Harper's Ferry under the special leadership of Dr. Du Bois. It is instructive to compare with this platform the address by Dr. Booker Washington before the meeting of the National Negro Business League, of which he is President, held last week at Atlanta, Georgia. This address may fairly be regarded as embodying the platform of this League; and just as the Niagara Movement stands for the more political and assertive spirit in the negro race, so the National Business League, as represented in Dr. Washington's address, stands for the industrial and pacific spirit. Dr. Washington expressed this tersely when he said, "Let constructive progress be the dominant note among us in every section of America; an inch of progress is worth more than a yard of faultfinding." He declared that "while the world may pity a crying, whining race, it seldom respects it." As to the progress actually made, he pointed out that in Georgia alone the negroes own $20,000,000 worth of taxable property, and that in the whole country, at a conservative estimate, the negro is now paying taxes upon over $300,000,000 worth of property, while in the Southern States negroes are conducting thirty-three banks. In fact, Dr. Washington believes that there is practically no section of the South where encouragement cannot be found for the negro farmer, mechanic, merchant, and even banker, with reasonable opportunity for prosperity, and he reaffirms his formerly expressed opinion that the Southern States offer the best permanent abode for the negro. He would welcome immigration, for he believes that healthy competition is much needed in the South, and that the salvation of his race is to be found "not in our ability to keep another race out of the territory, but in our learning to get as much out of the soil, out of our occupations or business, as any other race can get out of theirs." Dr. Washington spoke strongly and plainly as to crime on the part of the negro; he admitted the seriousness of the problem, did not hesitate to say that the large number of crimes committed by members of his race was deplorable, but challenged his hearers to show instances of crime committed by graduates of the educational institutions, or, with rare exceptions, by negroes who own their homes, are taxpayers, have regular occupation, and have received education. From these facts he argued that "ignorance will always mean crime, and crime will mean an unwieldy burden fastened about the neck of the South." The crime of lynching was equally denounced. Dr. Washington said: "Let us bear in mind that every man, white or black, who takes the law into his hands to lynch or burn or shoot human beings supposed to be or guilty of crime is insulting the executive, judicial, and lawmaking bodies of the State in which he resides. Lawlessness in one direction will inevitably lead to lawlessness in other directions. This is the experience of the whole civilized world." The trend and force of Dr. Washington's address might almost be summed up in this sentence: "The more I study our conditions and needs, the more I am convinced that there is no surer road by which we can reach civic, moral, educational, and religious development than by laying the foundation in the ownership and cultivation of the soil, the saving of money, commercial growth, and the skillful and conscientious performance of any duty with which we are intrusted." Comparing this utterance with the platform quoted last week, it will be seen that they are not antagonistic, but that they differ in spirit. One makes demands for the negroes, the other lays its demands upon the negro; one emphasizes his rights, the other his duties; one complains of the wrongs the white inflicts upon the negro, the other asks for co-operation between the white and the negro. We see far more hope for the negro in the spirit of the Business Men's League than in that of the Niagara Movement.

Further Resources

BOOKS

Du Bois, W.E.B. *The Souls of Black Folk.* Chicago: A.C. McClurg, 1903.

Emery, Michael, and Edwin Emery. *The Press and America: An Interpretive History of the Mass Media,* 7th ed. Englewood Cliffs, N.J.: Prentice Hall, 1992.

WEBSITES

Du Bois, W.E. Burghardt. *The Souls of Black Folk.* Electronic Text Center, University of Virginia Library. Available online at http://etext.lib.virginia.edu/toc/modeng/public/DubSoul.html; website home page: http://etext.lib.virginia.edu/ (accessed June 2, 2003).

Washington, Booker T. *Up from Slavery: An Autobiography.* Garden City, N.Y.: Doubleday, 1901. Available online at Documenting the American South Collection, University of North Carolina at Chapel Hill Libraries, http://metalab.unc.edu/docsouth/washington/menu.html; website home page: http://docsouth.unc.edu/ (accessed June 2, 2003).

The Jungle

Novel

By: Upton Sinclair

Date: 1906

Source: Sinclair, Upton. *The Jungle.* New York: Doubleday, Page, 1906. Available online at http://sunsite.berkeley.edu/Literature/Sinclair/TheJungle/ (accessed May 23, 2003).

About the Author: Upton Sinclair (1878–1968) campaigned for social reform for most of his ninety-year lifetime. He excelled in studies at an early age and entered City College of New York in 1892. After joining the Socialist Party a decade later, he embarked upon a distinguished, controversial career in muckraking. His most famous exposé, *The Jungle* (1906), investigated the Chicago meatpacking industry and led to passage of the Meat-Inspection Act and Pure Food and Drug Act of 1906. Sinclair wrote more than two thousand published works and established himself as the quintessential radical activist/journalist. ■

Introduction

Industrialization created great turmoil in American society. Fueled by massive European immigration, advances in machinery technology, and the move toward assembly-line production, enormous business corporations devoted more and more resources to heavy industry. The population of cities such as Chicago, the setting for *The Jungle,* swelled to unprecedented levels. Immigrant families settled in overcrowded tenements, working and living in grossly unsanitary conditions. Reform-minded reporters and photographers visited the burgeoning slums of urban America to detail the horrors encountered by immigrants. In 1890, Jacob Riis wrote the most famous example of this new brand of journalism, *How the Other Half Lives.* Through page after page of wrenching photographs and text, Riis revealed the squalor of tenement life to middle- and upper-class readers. The book prompted several regulations to improve tenement housing and emboldened activists to use the press as a means of urging reform. By the 1900s, this interest in reporting for social betterment led to the rise of the so-called muckraking press, with newspapers, magazines, journals, and entire books devoted to exposing the underside of industrialization and to improving life in the United States.

Social reformer and author of *The Jungle,* Upton Sinclair, around 1905.

Significance

Upton Sinclair traveled to the stockyards of Chicago in 1904 expressly for the purpose of producing a series of articles detailing the filth, disease, and human loss of immigrant America. Writing for the socialist journal *Appeal to Reason,* the twenty-five-year-old Sinclair decided to produce a fictional account of a Lithuanian family based upon his observations. His writing left nothing to the imagination, detailing in page after page the wretched working conditions faced by poor laborers who spent their lives mired in the waste and blood flowing through the factory floors. After Doubleday, Page published the articles as a single volume in February 1906, *The Jungle* soon became an international best-seller. President Theodore Roosevelt (served 1901–1909) invited Sinclair to the White House and urged Congress to pass immediate legislation to improve working conditions and institute sanitation standards in the nation's food industry. As a direct result of Sinclair's investigation and impassioned writing, Congress passed the Pure Food and Drug Act and the Meat-Inspection Act in June 1906. *The Jungle*'s dramatic impact on national policy buttressed muckraking in journalism and spurred generations of reform-minded journalists to report for the amelioration of society's ills.

Primary Source

The Jungle [excerpt]

SYNOPSIS: The following excerpt from *The Jungle* dramatically depicts the deplorable conditions faced by Lithuanian immigrants working in Chicago's meatpacking district, Packingtown. The blunt descriptions of rancid food, deplorable working conditions, and the ghastly existence endured by poor urban laborers spurred passage of federal legislation aimed at establishing safety standards for food production in the United States.

Chapter 13

During this time that Jurgis was looking for work occurred the death of little Kristoforas, one of the children of Teta Elzbieta. Both Kristoforas and his brother, Juozapas, were cripples, the latter having lost one leg by having it run over, and Kristoforas having congenital dislocation of the hip, which made it impossible for him ever to walk. He was the last of Teta Elzbieta's children, and perhaps he had been intended by nature to let her know that she had had enough. At any rate he was wretchedly sick and undersized; he had the rickets, and though he was over three years old, he was no bigger than an ordinary child of one. All day long he would crawl around the floor in a filthy little dress, whining and fretting; because the floor was full of drafts he was always catching cold, and snuffling because his nose ran. This made him a nuisance, and a source of endless trouble in the family. For his mother, with unnatural perversity, loved him best of all her children, and made a perpetual fuss over him—would let him do anything undisturbed, and would burst into tears when his fretting drove Jurgis wild.

And now he died. Perhaps it was the smoked sausage he had eaten that morning—which may have been made out of some of the tubercular pork that was condemned as unfit for export. At any rate, an hour after eating it, the child had begun to cry with pain, and in another hour he was rolling about on the floor in convulsions. Little Kotrina, who was all alone with him, ran out screaming for help, and after a while a doctor came, but not until Kristoforas had howled his last howl. No one was really sorry about this except poor Elzbieta, who was inconsolable. Jurgis announced that so far as he was concerned the child would have to be buried by the city, since they had no money for a funeral; and at this the poor woman almost went out of her senses, wringing her hands and screaming with grief and despair. Her child to be buried in a pauper's grave! And her stepdaughter to stand by and hear it said without protesting! It was enough to make Ona's father rise up out of his grave to rebuke her! If it had come to this, they might as well give up at once, and be buried all of them together! . . . In the end Marija said that she would help with ten dollars; and Jurgis being still obdurate, Elzbieta went in tears and begged the money from the neighbors, and so little Kristoforas had a mass and a hearse with white plumes on it, and a tiny plot in a graveyard with a wooden cross to mark the place. The poor mother was not the same for months after that; the mere sight of the floor where little Kristoforas had crawled about would make her weep. He had never had a fair chance, poor little fellow, she would say. He had been handicapped from his birth. If only she had heard about it in time, so that she might have had that great doctor to cure him of his lameness! . . . Some time ago, Elzbieta was told, a Chicago billionaire had paid a fortune to bring a great European surgeon over to cure his little daughter of the same disease from which Kristoforas had suffered. And because this surgeon had to have bodies to demonstrate upon, he announced that he would treat the children of the poor, a piece of magnanimity over which the papers became quite eloquent. Elzbieta, alas, did not read the papers, and no one had told her; but perhaps it was as well, for just then they would not have had the carfare to spare to go every day to wait upon the surgeon, nor for that matter anybody with the time to take the child.

■ ■ ■

All this while that he was seeking for work, there was a dark shadow hanging over Jurgis; as if a savage beast were lurking somewhere in the pathway of his life, and he knew it, and yet could not help approaching the place. There are all stages of being out of work in Packingtown, and he faced in dread the prospect of reaching the lowest. There is a place that waits for the lowest man—the fertilizer plant!

The men would talk about it in awe-stricken whispers. Not more than one in ten had ever really tried it; the other nine had contented themselves with hearsay evidence and a peep through the door. There were some things worse than even starving to death. They would ask Jurgis if he had worked there yet, and if he meant to; and Jurgis would debate the matter with himself. As poor as they were, and making all the sacrifices that they were, would he dare to refuse any sort of work that was offered to him, be it as horrible as ever it could? Would he dare to go home and eat bread that had been earned by Ona, weak and complaining as she was, knowing that he had been given a chance, and had not had the nerve to take it?—And yet he might argue that way with himself all day, and one glimpse into the fertilizer works would send him away again shuddering. He was a man, and he would do his duty; he went and made application—but surely he was not also required to hope for success!

The fertilizer works of Durham's lay away from the rest of the plant. Few visitors ever saw them, and the few who did would come out looking like Dante, of whom the peasants declared that he had been into hell. To this part of the yards came all the "tankage" and the waste products of all sorts; here they dried out the bones,—and in suffocating cellars where the daylight never came you might see men and women and children bending over whirling machines and sawing bits of bone into all sorts of shapes, breathing their lungs full of the fine dust, and doomed to die, every one of them, within a certain definite time. Here they made the blood into albumen, and made other foul-smelling things into things still more foul-smelling. In the corridors and caverns where it was done you might lose yourself as in the great caves of Kentucky. In the dust and the steam the electric lights would shine like far-off twinkling stars—red and blue-green and purple stars, according to the color of the mist and the brew from which it came. For the odors of these ghastly charnel houses there may be words in Lithuanian, but there are none in English. The person entering would have to summon his courage as for a cold-water plunge. He would go in like a man swimming under water; he would put his handkerchief over his face, and begin to cough and choke; and then, if he were still obstinate, he would find his head beginning to ring, and the veins in his forehead to throb, until finally he would be assailed by an overpowering blast of ammonia fumes, and would turn and run for his life, and come out half-dazed.

On top of this were the rooms where they dried the "tankage," the mass of brown stringy stuff that was left after the waste portions of the carcasses had had the lard and tallow dried out of them. This dried material they would then grind to a fine powder, and after they had mixed it up well with a mysterious but inoffensive brown rock which they brought

Packing-house workers inspect hog carcasses at Swift & Company in 1906. THE LIBRARY OF CONGRESS/CORBIS. REPRODUCED BY PERMISSION.

in and ground up by the hundreds of carloads for that purpose, the substance was ready to be put into bags and sent out to the world as any one of a hundred different brands of standard bone phosphate. And then the farmer in Maine or California or Texas would buy this, at say twenty-five dollars a ton, and plant it with his corn; and for several days after the operation the fields would have a strong odor, and the farmer and his wagon and the very horses that had hauled it would all have it too. In Packingtown the fertilizer is pure, instead of being a flavoring, and instead of a ton or so spread out on several acres under the open sky, there are hundreds and thousands of tons of it in one building, heaped here and there in haystack piles, covering the floor several inches deep, and filling the air with a choking dust that becomes a blinding sandstorm when the wind stirs.

It was to this building that Jurgis came daily, as if dragged by an unseen hand. The month of May was an exceptionally cool one, and his secret prayers were granted; but early in June there came a record-breaking hot spell, and after that there were men wanted in the fertilizer mill.

Further Resources

BOOKS

Harris, Leon. *Upton Sinclair: American Rebel.* New York: Crowell, 1975.

Sinclair, Upton. *The Autobiography of Upton Sinclair.* New York: Harcourt, Brace & World, 1962.

The Christian Science Monitor

Newspaper

By: Mary Baker Eddy

Date: 1908

Source: *The Christian Science Monitor,* Issue 1, 1908. Available online at Library of Congress Prints and Photographs Division, http://lcweb2.loc.gov (accessed May 27, 2003).

About the Author: Mary Baker Eddy (1821–1910) overcame various personal trials to become the founder of one of the longest enduring American churches. In 1866, a healing event led her to reconsider the nature of God and the relationships among spirituality, the mind, and health. Devoting the rest of her life to her new theology, Christian Science, she wrote *Science and Health* (1875), which remained in print into the twenty-first century, and formed the Church of Christ, Scientist, in 1879. ■

Introduction

As Eddy's religious teachings grew in popularity at the beginning of the twentieth century, so too did criticism from within her organization, the press, and the public at large. Muckraking journalists and social commentators, most notably Joseph Pulitzer and Mark Twain, investigated the Church of Christ, Scientist, and wrote scathing reports on the group's internal dissension and Eddy's own mental stability. Perhaps partially in response to these media attacks, Eddy created *The Christian Science Monitor,* a newspaper devoted to so-called objective reporting of current events, in 1908.

Significance

According to Eddy, *The Christian Science Monitor* would serve as an antidote to the more inflammatory reporting she associated with the muckrakers. She established the paper, in her words, to "injure no man, but to bless all mankind" (http://www.csmonitor.com/aboutus/about_the_monitor.html). Although founded as part of the Church of Christ, Scientist, the paper was not designed as a religious publication, except for a single column, "The Home Forum," that has appeared in every edition at Eddy's request.

THE CHRISTIAN SCIENCE MONITOR

CITY EDITION. BOSTON, MASS., WEDNESDAY, NOVEMBER 25, 1908.—VOL. I., NO. 1. PRICE TWO CENTS.

CARNEGIE DOES NOT WANT TO BE TARIFF WITNESS

Steel Magnate Says He Has Served His Time in Matters and Views Are Well Known.

71 YEARS OLD TODAY

Chairman Payne of Ways and Ceans Committee Make Public His Correspondence With Multi-Millionaire.

CONSTRUCTION WORK RAPIDLY PROGRESSES ON GREAT DAM ACROSS THE CHARLES RIVER BASIN

Lock and Sluices Completed and Machinery Installed in New Lock-House on Boston Side of Stream.

LOCK IN OPERATION

LOCKS AND SLUICES IN CHARLES RIVER DAM.

SHIP RELIEF IS SAFE AT LUZON

SARDINIA BEACHED BECAUSE OF FIRE

Liner Burned Just Outside Malta While on Her Way From Liverpool—Many Lives Lost.

CALL TROOPS TO QUELL STUDENTS

THANKSGIVING SERVICE.

BOSTON LIBRARY IS GIVEN A RARE BOOK COLLECTION

Mrs. Louise Chandler Moulton and Philip Bourke Marston Volumes Include Many Autograph Copies.

TURKEY IS SENT TO PRESIDENT

Chestnut-Fed Bird Specially Raised in Westerly, R. I., by Horace Vose and Tips Scales at 26 Pounds.

EXPERT REVIEWS CONDITIONS IN THE DISTURBED BALKAN COUNTRIES

Interesting Phase of Economic Duel Between England and Germany Discussed.

LANDMARK HISTORY

Installment Stories of Situation in Near-Far East Presented for Readers of The Christian Science Monitor.

The Christian Science Monitor has arranged to have a comprehensive review of the past and present conditions existing in the Balkan peninsula and a discussion of the future prospects presented to its readers in installments from the pen of a close student of the situation in this near Eastern country. The first installment is given below.

DEALER CORNERS ALL WHALE BONE

Edgar R. Lewis Has $1,000,000 Worth of Bone in His Storehouse in New Bedford, Mass.

TAX REFORMERS WILL BANQUET

VOTE DECISIVELY FOR NO LICENSE

37,000 TURKEYS FOR HOME MARKET

CONTINUED ON PAGE TWO.

PLANNING HOMES FOR LOVED ONES

Knights of Pythias and Odd Fellows Spending Thousands of Dollars for This Work.

BROCKTON CHURCH DEDICATION NEAR

SPEAKER'S CLUB FOR HARVARD MEN

DOG SLEDS WILL TAKE MAIL NORTH

SAILS TO SEE DAUGHTER WED

WAYS AND MEANS LISTENING TO TARIFF TALK

Maximum and Minimum Schedule Likely to Be Submitted by the Committee at Coming Session.

GIVE AND TAKE PLAN

NIGHT SCHOOLS FOR DES MOINES

Success of Plan Last Year Causes Educational Board to Resume Sessions This Season.

OPPOSE UNIFORM BILL OF LADING

WEATHER FORECAST

For New England: Fair in the north, generally cloudy in south portion tonight; Thursday, cloudy, probably occasional rain; light easterly to southerly winds.

NEW FACTORY SOON TO START

SALVED WOOL SOLD FOR $75,000.

Primary Source

The Christian Science Monitor

SYNOPSIS: The cover of the first issue of Mary Baker Eddy's *Christian Science Monitor,* 1908. Two years after President Theodore Roosevelt coined the term *muckraking* to decry the lack of proper standards in journalism, Mary Baker Eddy created a newspaper designed to counter the period's more sensational press. Many initially balked at the idea of a daily journal published by her church. But *The Christian Science Monitor* thrived as a consistent source of balanced, substantive reporting, eventually winning seven of the most prestigious awards in journalism, including the Pulitzer Prize. PHOTO COURTESY OF THE MARY BAKER EDDY LIBRARY FOR THE BETTERMENT OF HUMANITY. AN IMAGE OF THE MONITOR COVER IS ALSO CURRENTLY BEING DISPLAYED AS PART OF AN INTERACTIVE EXHIBIT IN THE MONITOR GALLERY OF THE MARY BAKER EDDY LIBRARY FOR THE BETTERMENT OF HUMANITY, BOSTON, MASSACHUSETTS.

Mary Baker Eddy was founder of Christian Science. **THE LIBRARY OF CONGRESS.**

Critics used the terms *muckraking* and *yellow journalism* to criticize the news media of the 1890s and 1900s. Public figures such as Mary Baker Eddy and President Theodore Roosevelt (served 1901–1909) seemed to blend these terms in their denunciations of the press, reflecting the hazy differences between the two editorial strategies. S.S. McClure, the publisher of *McClure's* magazine, the leading muckraking journal of the period, defined this sort of investigative reporting as geared to bring about public awareness of public and private corruption in the hope of reforming American society. In his 1906 address "The Man With the Muck Rake," Roosevelt argued that journalists who sought only to criticize and protest ultimately damaged the cause of reform by preventing progressive leadership from establishing itself. Yellow journalism developed from a so-called lowering of journalism standards to popularize news and thus increase circulation. But by the very nature of McClure's and the muckrakers' goals, these journalists often designed their stories to attract as large an audience as possible. This desire resulted in the sort of exploitative investigations criticized by Eddy and Roosevelt. Yet by refusing to acknowledge the diversity of quality and perspective in American journalism, media critics damaged the stability of muckrakers whom reformers such as Roosevelt himself relied upon to promote progressive public policy.

Aside from Eddy's creation of *The Monitor* as a response to what she saw as the evils of turn-of-the-century editorial standards, her media influence reflected the increased influence of women in journalism in the early twentieth century. Ironically, the most influential women in the press were muckrakers and yellow journalists, such as civil rights activist Ida B. Wells and Ida Tarbell. Both of these women exemplified the core of the muckraking movement—vibrant, passionate depictions of wrongdoing in American society (lynching and corporate malfeasance) for the purpose of spurring reform. The famous "Sob Sisters," including Dorothy Dix, Ada Patterson, Nixola Greeley-Smith, and Annie Laurie (Winifred Sweet Black), offered melodramatic reports of popular court cases involving divorce cases, marital infidelity, murder, sex, and other sensationalized events for an increasingly hungry audience.

Further Resources

BOOKS

Emery, Michael, and Edwin Emery. *The Press and America: An Interpretive History of the Mass Media,* 7th ed. Englewood Cliffs, N.J.: Prentice Hall, 1992.

Peel, Robert. *Mary Baker Eddy: The Years of Discovery.* New York: Holt, Rinehart and Winston, 1966. Volume one of three-volume biography.

———. *Mary Baker Eddy: The Years of Trial.* New York: Holt, Rinehart and Winston, 1971. Volume two of three-volume biography.

———. *Mary Baker Eddy: The Years of Authority.* New York: Holt, Rinehart and Winston, 1977. Volume three of three-volume biography.

Schlipp, Madelon Golden, and Sharon M. Murphy. *Great Women of the Press.* Carbondale, Ill.: Southern Illinois Press, 1983.

WEBSITES

The Christian Science Monitor. Available online at http://www.csmonitor.com (accessed May 27, 2003).

The Mary Baker Eddy Library for the Betterment of Humanity. Available online at http://www.marybakereddylibrary.org.

9

MEDICINE AND HEALTH

CHRISTOPHER CUMO

Entries are arranged in chronological order by date of primary source. For entries with one primary source, the entry title is the same as the primary source title. Entries with more than one primary source have an overall entry title, followed by the titles of the primary sources.

CHRONOLOGY

PRIMARY SOURCES

Important Events in Medicine and Health, 1900–1909

1900

- Dr. Ludvig Hektoen creates one of the earliest experimental disease models, for cirrhosis of the liver.
- Dr. Ernest Amory Codman begins his work on diseases and injuries of the shoulder.
- On January 1, more than 7,000 women physicians practice medicine in the U.S.
- In February, Dr. George Blumer demonstrates that trichinosis, a disease caused by a worm infecting undercooked pork, is more widespread in the United States than previously believed.
- In February, Sen. Jacob H. Gallinger introduces a bill to regulate medical research on humans in the District of Columbia. Congress does not enact the bill.
- On March 6, the body of a Chinese laborer is discovered in the Globe Hotel's basement in the Chinese district of San Francisco. Local officials find that he died of bubonic plague. The outbreak of the disease will last for four years and kill more than one hundred people.
- On March 16, Wyoming physician C. Dana Carter performs the first caesarean section.
- In May, Dr. Eugene Lindsay Opie discovers the relationship between degeneration of the islets of Langerhans (the special cells of the pancreas that secrete insulin) and diabetes.
- On May 2, Colonel Theodore Roosevelt of the Rough Riders makes headlines by testifying before Congress that he would rather eat his hat than another tin of meat, because of its filth. His testimony raises public concern over the wholesomeness and quality of U.S. meat.
- In June, the American Medical Association appoints a Committee on Organization and a Special Committee on Reorganization. The committees recommend that the AMA enlarge its membership and strengthen connections with state and local medical societies.
- In June, biochemist Otto Knut Olof Folin begins work on the chemistry of urine; his methods will be adapted in a decade to study blood and tissues.
- In June, Dr. Carlos Finlay urges the U.S. Army Yellow Fever Commission to focus its attention on the *Aedes aegypti* mosquito as the carrier of Yellow Fever.
- In September, Dr. Walter B. Cannon persuades Harvard Medical School to use the case method of teaching.
- On September 25, U.S. Army major, physician, and head of the Yellow Fever Commission, Walter Reed, writes in a letter of his suspicion that the *Aedes aegypti* mosquito transmits the Yellow Fever microbe to humans.

1901

- African American physician Aaron M. Moore opens Lincoln Hospital in Durham, North Carolina.
- Dr. Jay Frank Schamberg describes a progressive noninflammatory skin disease that later will be named after him.
- Dr. Arthur Robertson Cushny begins work on the chemistry of kidney secretion.
- The American Medical Association's House of Delegates approves a reorganization plan.
- Dr. Dorothy R. Mendenhall disproves the prevailing belief that Hodgkin's disease is a type of tuberculosis. Rather it is type of cancer.
- In February, the Rockefeller Institute for Medical Research is organized.
- In March, the U.S. Commission to Investigate Plague, headed by Dr. Simon Flexner, confirms the disease in San Francisco.
- On March 3, Congress passes the Sundry Civil Appropriation Act, which includes a thirty-five thousand dollar budget for the Hygienic Laboratory, a part of the U.S. Marine Hospital Service. The laboratory is the forerunner of the National Institutes of Health.
- On July 8, Congress gives permanent status to the U.S. Army Nurse Corps.
- On September 14, President William McKinley dies from gangrene from improperly dressed wounds after being shot twice by a deranged anarchist.
- In November, physician-dentist Dr. William Herbert Rollins announces that his research on guinea pigs shows that X-rays can cause death.

1902

- Sen. Jacob H. Gallinger reintroduces his bill to regulate medical research on humans in the District of Columbia. Congress again does not enact the bill.
- Dr. Hugh Hampton Young performs the first perineal prostatectomy at Johns Hopkins Hospital in Baltimore, Maryland.
- Dr. John Miller Turpin Finney performs the first standard surgical procedure for duodenal ulcer relief.
- Dr. Isaac Arthur Abt begins almost forty years as editor of the *Yearbook of Pediatrics.*
- In March, the McCormack Institute for Infectious Diseases is founded in Chicago.
- In May, at the Pan-American Sanitary Congress, Dr. Charles Wardell Stiles of the U.S. Public Health Service identifies the hookworm parasite devastating the South.
- In June, Dr. H. F. Harris reports on his diagnosis of pellagra in a poor farmer at the annual medical association meeting in Georgia. The disease results from a diet deficient in

the B vitamin niacin or the amino acid tryptophan. During the first decade of the twentieth century, physicians would identify pellagra as endemic to the American South.

- On August 17, Congress passes the Biologics Control Act to regulate vaccines and antitoxins.

1903

- Dr. Arnold Schwyzer performs the first surgical removal of a foreign body from the lung.
- Homer Folks conducts the first survey in New York City on tuberculosis, a disease endemic to cities. Its high mortality leads people to call it "the white plague."
- The research of chemist Edwin Freemont Ladd leads the North Dakota legislature to pass a Pure Food and Drug Law, a forerunner of the Pure Food and Drug Act.
- In January, California governor Henry Gage denies that plague has infected anyone in the state in an effort to lessen public fears of an outbreak.
- In July, Dr. Frederick George Novy establishes the first unit to fight rabies in the United States in Ann Arbor, Michigan.

1904

- Dr. Hugh Hampton Young performs the first operation on a cancerous prostate.
- Dr. Joseph Erlanger studies kidney output in persons suffering from albuminuria, the failure of kidneys to process protein for excretion from the body.
- African American physician Daniel H. Williams develops a technique of closing a ruptured spleen with stitches.
- On February 19, health officials in San Francisco, California confirm the decade's last case of plague.
- In March, Homer Folks and Dr. Lawrence Flick found the National Association for the Study and Prevention of Tuberculosis in Philadelphia. It becomes a model for subsequent private health associations.
- In April, the Rockefeller Institute for Medical Research opens.
- In September, Dr. John LaRue Robinson founds the first general hospital in Nevada—People's Hospital.

1905

- The American Medical Association, the Association of American Medical Colleges, and the Southern Medical College Association form the Council on Medical Education to reform the nation's medical schools.
- Dr. Louis Blanchard Wilson develops a method for quick and accurate laboratory analysis of surgical tissue specimens.
- Dr. Arthur Douglass Hirschfelder becomes director of the physiological laboratory at Johns Hopkins Medical School. Two other clinical research facilities are also established—the first such divisions in the United States.
- The last yellow fever epidemic in the United States hits New Orleans.
- In March, Dr. Ludvig Hektoen demonstrates that measles transmits from one human to another. Measles, therefore, is a contagious disease.
- On April 1, Standard diphtheria antitoxin is introduced.
- In August, the Long Island Society of Anesthetists, forerunner of the American Society of Anesthesiologists, is founded in New York.
- In August, the *Appeal to Reason*, a socialist newspaper, begins publishing in serial form.
- Upton Sinclair's novel *The Jungle* is published. Describing the unsanitary condition under which U.S. meatpackers process meat, the novel ignites public indignation and will lead Congress to pass the Meat Inspection Act.

1906

- Yale University economist J. Pease Norton recommends a federal department of health to examine the high costs of illness and premature death to the U.S. economy.
- Medical societies in Oklahoma and Indian Territory are merged into a single society.
- Dr. James Hall Mason Knox Jr. organizes in Baltimore the Babies' Milk Fund Association to give milk to infants in low-income families.
- In January, physiological chemist Russell Henry Chittenden and others establish the American Society of Biological Chemists.
- In January, Dr. Emanuel Libman begins work on use of blood cultures to diagnose subacute bacterial endocarditis, a disease attacking heart valves and previously identifiable only at autopsy.
- On June 30, Congress passes the Meat Inspection Act after public outrage over unsanitary conditions in the meatpacking industry. The Act empowers the U.S. Department of Agriculture to certify the wholesomeness of meat.
- On June 30, Congress passes the Pure Food and Drug Act, empowering the U.S. Department of Agriculture to test food and medicines for safety and truth in labelling.
- In July, University of Chicago pathologist Dr. Howard Taylor Ricketts begins work that will identify ticks as the carrier of Rocky Mountain spotted fever.
- In October, Johns Hopkins Medical School establishes the first biochemical research facility in the United States. Dr. Carl Voegtlin directs the facility.
- In November, Drs. Milton Joseph Rosenau and John F. Anderson publish the first of their studies on anaphylaxis, or hypersensitivity.

1907

- Police arrest Bernarr Macfadden for mail distribution of obscene materials—a magazine issue explaining to men how venereal disease is contracted.
- Dr. E.I. McKesson promotes using a blood pressure test in conjunction with surgical anesthesia.
- Drs. C.C. Guthrie and F. H. Pike use plasma and serum to replace blood during surgery.
- The Council on Medical Education asks the Carnegie Foundation to study medical education in the United States. Carnegie hires Abraham Flexner, a layman, to conduct the study, which is completed two years later and published in 1910.

- Dr. S. Josephine Baker begins a hygiene program for children at the New York City Department of Health.
- Dr. Ross G. Harrison performs pioneering work in the exploration of the relationship between nerve cells and nerve fibers.
- African American physicians Eugene T. Hinson and Algernon Brashear found Mercy Hospital, the second oldest African American hospital in Philadelphia, Pennsylvania.
- Dr. Charles Solomon Caverly and others found the Vermont Tuberculosis Sanitarium.
- African American physician Mathilde A. Evans opens the first hospital for African Americans in Columbia, South Carolina.
- Drs. Martha Wollstein and Simon Flexner conduct the first experiments on cause and treatment of polio.
- On March 15, the Indiana legislature grants state courts the power to authorize surgeons to sterilize criminals, idiots and the insane.
- In May, Dr. Robert Tait McKenzie of the University of Pennsylvania becomes the first professor of physical therapy at an American university.
- In September, Dr. Simon Flexner develops serum treatment for spinal meningitis, a bacterial infection.
- In October, Dr. James Ewing and others found the American Association for Cancer Research.
- In November, the Rockefeller Institute for Medical Research opens a facility in New Jersey to breed animals for laboratory research. Arsonists will destroy it two years later.
- On November 15, American Indian physician Susan La Flesche Picotte advises Commissioner of Indian Affairs Francis E. Leupp of a tuberculosis outbreak on a Nebraska reservation. She asks Leupp for an additional nurse to help her treat patients.
- In December, Dr. Ross G. Harrison of Johns Hopkins Medical School performs the first successful tissue culture using frog embryos.

1908

- Drs. E. Zeh Hawkes and Edward Wharton Sprague perform the first blood transfusion in New Jersey.
- African American physicians found the *Journal of the National Medical Association.*
- Dr. Yandell Henderson of Yale University publishes his landmark paper on the relationship of carbon dioxide, shock, and heart rate.
- Dr. David Linn Edsall gives the first description of "heat cramps," a severe reaction in workers exposed to intense heat.
- The American Society for Clinical Investigation, the first organization devoted to patient research, is founded.
- In February, Clifford Whittingham Beers and Drs. Adolph Meyer and William H. Welch found the Connecticut Society for Mental Hygiene, the world's first mental health organization.
- In April, the American Medical Association creates the Council on the Defense of Medical Research. Harvard physiologist Walter B. Cannon is director.
- In June, the first National Conference on Pellagra is held in Columbia, South Carolina.
- In October, Dr. David Marine publishes his first paper on the role of iodine in thyroid function. The thyroid regulates body growth.

1909

- The Committee of One Hundred on National Health issues a report recommending a federal department of health.
- Philanthropist Nathan Straus establishes the first tuberculosis prevention facility for children, in Lakewood, New Jersey.
- Dr. Frederick Parker Gay publishes the first English translation of Jules Bordet's classic *Studies in Immunity.*
- Dr. James Grassick founds the North Dakota Tuberculosis Association.
- Dr. John Howland demonstrates that the anesthetic gas chloroform can poison the liver. His research leads physicians to decrease its use during surgery.
- The College of Medical Evangelists is founded by Seventh-Day Adventists in Loma Linda, California.
- Walter B. Cannon, chair of the American Medical Association's Council on the Defense of Medical Research, circulates a set of guidelines to all U.S. laboratories and medical schools using animals in research.
- In June, the National Association for the Study of Pellagra is founded. South Carolina physician James Babcock is president.
- In September, Dr. William Snow Miller teaches a seminar on medical history at the University of Wisconsin. The seminar becomes a model for other universities.
- In October, the Rockefeller Foundation creates the Rockefeller Sanitary Commission to educate southerners about the dangers of hookworm.

Letter to Jefferson Randolph Kean

Letter

By: Walter Reed

Date: September 25, 1900

Source: Reed, Walter. Letter to Jefferson Randolph Kean, September 25, 1900. University of Virginia Library. Available online at http://etext.lib.virginia.edu/etcbin/fever-browseprint?id=02125001; website home page: http://etext.lib.virginia.edu (accessed March 14, 2003)

About the Author: Walter Reed (1851–1902) was born in Belroi, Virginia, and received two doctorates of medicine, the first from the University of Virginia in 1869 and the second from Bellevue Hospital Medical College in New York City in 1870. He preferred research to the routine of private practice. His books and articles on typhoid and yellow fever established his reputation and led the U.S. Army to appoint him head of a team of researchers in Cuba. There, Reed eventually isolated the mosquito *Aedes aegypti* as the carrier of yellow fever. ■

Army Surgeon, Major Walter Reed led studies in Cuba on yellow fever.

Introduction

A flavivirus causes yellow fever. A flavivirus is a type of virus that infects both arthropods (insects) and vertebrates (mammals). Unlike a bacterium, which is a complete cell, capable of multiplying in a host, a virus is just a sequence of nucleotide bases (large carbon-based molecules that build deoxyribonucleic acid [DNA]) encased in a protein coat. Outside a host, a virus is inactive. Inside a host, a virus invades and instructs cells to make additional copies of itself. Once inside a cell, then, a virus becomes active.

Yellow fever symptoms include fever, bleeding through the mouth and nose, and vomiting black discharge, all of which are similar to symptoms of plague. In addition, yellow fever damages the liver, causing jaundice and death within two weeks. Between the 1600s and 1905, yellow fever repeatedly struck the southeastern United States during the summer months and abated in cold weather. In densely populated cities, yellow fever killed as many as one hundred thousand people in a single summer.

Yellow fever commanded attention from the federal government during the Spanish-American War (1898), which by 1900 gave the United States control of Cuba in the Caribbean and the Philippines in the Pacific Ocean. Yellow fever was endemic to Cuba, and the U.S. Army was determined to eradicate it. To accomplish this goal, the army had to discover how the disease spread, a task it assigned to a team of soldiers and physicians led by Major Walter Reed.

Significance

Reed prided himself on being a cautious physician who would go no further than where evidence led. This caution led him to be suspicious of hypotheses. Thus, the fact that two American physicians in the nineteenth century had fingered a mosquito as the carrier of yellow fever did not immediately impress him. Nor was he completely convinced when in 1897, physician Ronald Ross discovered that a particular species of mosquito is the carrier of malaria. What was true of malaria might not be true of yellow fever. Yet, when two members of his team contracted yellow fever after being bitten by mosquitoes, Reed edged toward the mosquito hypothesis.

Eventually, his convictions hardened. He understood that the only link between those who had yellow fever was that all had been bitten by mosquitoes. He isolated the mosquito *Aedes aegypti* as the carrier, and early in 1901 U.S. Army chief sanitation officer and physician

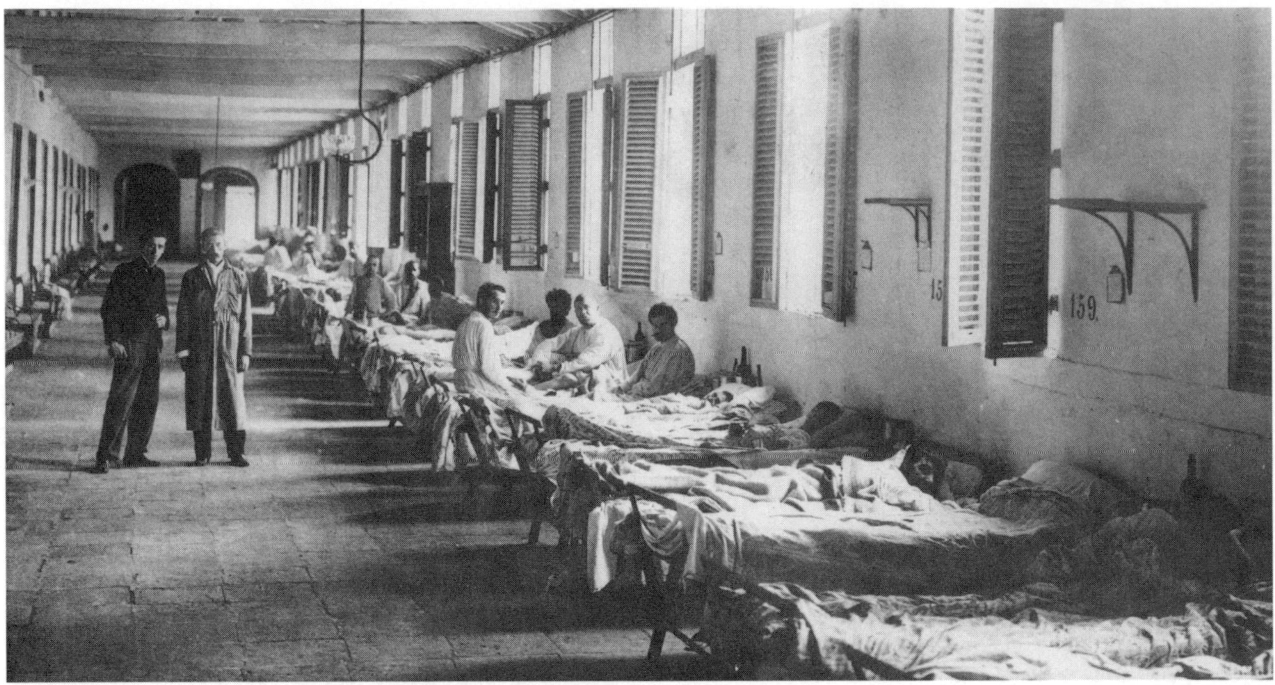

A ward of a hospital for yellow fever patients in Havana, Cuba. **THE LIBRARY OF CONGRESS.**

William Gorgas ordered all standing water in Cuba drained or coated with oil, depriving female mosquitoes of places to lay their eggs. Cases of yellow fever plummeted, and, with the introduction of these measures in the United States, yellow fever ceased to plague Americans by the end of the decade.

Primary Source

Letter to Jefferson Randolph Kean

SYNOPSIS: In this letter, Reed reveals his willingness to consider alternatives to the hypothesis that a species of mosquito carries yellow fever. Early in the letter, he suggests that he had always suspected a mosquito, but at the letter's end he acknowledges the possibility that his two colleagues who had yellow fever "may have contracted the disease in some other way than by the mosquito."

Confidential.
War Department,
Surgeon General's Office,
Army Medical Museum and Library,
Washington.

Sept. 25, 1900

My dear Dr. Kean:

You must pardon my delay in answering your letter. When it came, I was so immersed in the finishing touches to the typhoid Report that I put it aside to answer later. I have now only just returned from my outing in the hills of Pa, and am so distressed to hear that Lazear is down with yellow fever. The General handed me your cable yesterday afternoon, as soon as I entered his office. I shall await your next with much anxiety. Still I somehow feel that Lazear will pull through, as he is such a good, brave fellow. I have been so ashamed of myself for being here in a safe country, while my associates have been coming down with yellow Jack. The General has suggested that I do not return, but somehow I feel that, as the Senior member of a Bd-investigating yellow Fever, my place is in Cuba, as long as the work goes on. I shall, of course, take every precaution that I can against contracting the disease, and I certainly shall not, with the facts that we now have allow a "*loaded*" mosquito to bite me! That would be fool-hardy in the extreme. You know that from the . . . beginning of our work, I have insisted upon the commonsense theory of an intermediate host, such as the mosquito, being the carrier of the parasite of y. fever, but have said that *human* experimentation *alone* could determine the question. Just how far Carroll's & Lazear's cases go to support that supposition, I don't know, but hope to find out when I get there. Personally, I think that we are on the eve of an important "find" & hence I am writing all of this to you in strictest confidence.

Perhaps I owe my life to my departure from Cuba, for I had agreed to be bitte[n] along with the others. Being an old man, I might have been quickly carried off. I only wish that Dr Pinto might have had a *mild* attack! Do pray, don't talk to anyone about this line of work of our Board, as I know that you will not, as we shall hope soon to publish a Preliminary note on the etiology of yellow fever. I have engaged passage on the Crook which sails next Friday 28th, & should reach Havana on Octr 2nd or 3rd.

A matter of some importance. I shall expect to take up my old quarters next to Dr Pinto, provided you think that there is no probability of that being in an infected area—that is, on the supposition that Carroll & Lazear may have contracted the disease in some other way than by the mosquito. If so, I would ask you to engage me a couple of rooms somewhere in the vacant sets along the officer's line at Camp Columbia. I should *prefer* to be in my old quarters [however]. Hoping to gaze into your honest face once more very soon, believe me,

Sincerely, your friend,
Walter Reed

Further Resources

BOOKS

Dolan, Edward. *Walter Reed, Vanquishing Yellow Fever.* Chicago: Britannica, 1962.

Hallock, Grace T. *Walter Reed and the Conquest of Yellow Fever.* New York: School Health Bureau, 1958.

Hill, Ralph N. *The Doctors Who Conquered Yellow Fever.* New York: Random House, 1957.

Kelly, Howard A. *Walter Reed and Yellow Fever.* Baltimore, Md.: Medical Standard Book Company, 1906.

Professional Guide to Diseases. 6th ed. Springhouse, Penn.: Springhouse, 1998.

PERIODICALS

Tone, John L. "How the Mosquito (Men) Liberated Cuba." *History and Technology,* December 2002, 277–309.

"Walter Reed—Soldier-Surgeon." *Arizona Highways,* January 2003, 5.

WEBSITES

"Walter Reed." Garden of Praise. Available online at http://www.gardenofpraise.com/ibdreed.htm; website home page: http://www.gardenofpraise.com (accessed March 14, 2003).

"Walter Reed and James Carroll." University of Virginia Health Sciences Library. Available online at http://www.med.virginia.edu/hs-library/historical/yelfev/pan6.html; website home page: http://www.med.virginia.edu/hs-library (accessed March 14, 2003).

"Yellow Fever and Dr. Walter Reed." The Fight for Life: Medical Innovation During War. Available online at http://www.mcatmaster.com/medicine&war;/yellowfever.htm; website home page: http://www.mcatmaster.com/medicine&war; (accessed March 14, 2003).

"Yellow Fever/Reed Commission Exhibit." University of Virginia Health Sciences Library. Available online at http://hsc.virginia.edu/hs-library/historical/yelfev/tabcon.html; website home page: http://hcs.virginia.edu (accessed March 14, 2003).

1900 Rambler and 1900 Pierce-Arrow

Photographs

By: The Bicycle Museum of America

Date: 1900

Source: 1900 Rambler and 1900 Pierce-Arrow. The Bicycle Museum of America. Available online at http://www.bicyclemuseum.com/Html/bike6.html; website home page: http://www.bicyclemuseum.com (accessed March 14, 2003).

About the Organization: The Bicycle Museum of America opened on July 23, 1997, in New Bremen, Ohio. Among its collection are nineteenth-century antiques, balloon-tire classics from the 1940s, and the banana seat bikes of the 1960s. Its oldest bicycle is an 1816 German model and its most recent a 1998 Huffy touring bike, the last model manufactured in Ohio. ■

Introduction

Between roughly 1890 and 1910, an interest in bicycling for health and recreation swept the United States. Physicians touted the cardiovascular benefits of cycling, and physicists explored its mechanics. The activity was so popular that *Scientific American* featured an issue on cycling in 1896. By then, the United States had more than 150 bicycle manufacturers who built a thousand models for men, women, and children. The bicycle for two had by then come into its own, though the first models featured cyclists beside one another rather than one behind the other. The side-by-side arrangement made conversation between cyclists easier and more natural and illustrated that bicycling had become a mass activity, one that brought Americans together socially as well as recreationally.

But cycling was more than a social event. Physician Henry J. Garrigus of Chicago made his reputation as a cycling enthusiast. "From a medical standpoint bicycling is valuable both as a prophylactic and as a curative agent," he said. Cycling stimulated one to take in fresh air outdoors, a practice that had unanimous endorsement from physicians around 1900 as protection against tuberculosis. Garrigus championed cycling as an activity that strengthened all the muscles in the body as well as "the whole nervous system." This endorsement was perhaps

Primary Source

1900 Rambler Bicycle

SYNOPSIS: The photographs display two bicycles from 1900. Both models are no-frills road bikes built for durability. Each bike has one gear, the frame is iron, and the tires are thicker than those on a modern road bike. REPRODUCED BY PERMISSION OF THE BICYCLE MUSEUM OF AMERICA.

an exaggeration. True, cycling strengthens the quadriceps muscles, which do the pedaling, but it does little to strengthen the muscles of the torso and arms. Cycling, Garrigus concluded, "is a wholesome and inspiring exercise, and has provided of practical value as a means of rapid locomotion." Again, Garrigus exaggerated. Even on modern bicycles, cyclists seldom cover more than fifteen miles an hour, much slower than the locomotive and the car, which though not in mass production in 1900, had been invented some twenty years earlier.

Significance

Many of those who took up cycling did so with one of the popular models from 1900. One was a 1900 Rambler manufactured by Gormully and Jeffery Manufacturing Company in Chicago. The other was a 1900 Pierce-Arrow manufactured by George N. Pierce Company in Buffalo, New York. Both were no-frills road bikes (the mountain bike did not then exist) built for durability. Each bike had one gear, obviating the need for a mechanism to shift gears, which was then expensive and confined to racing bikes. The frame of each was iron, heavy but durable. At that time in history, aluminum was seldom used except on racing bikes. Road and racing bikes differed, as they do today, because they served different clienteles. Road bikes served people interested in cycling for health and recreation, whereas racing bikes served athletes who sought victory. For them, health was a by-product of competition, not a goal to pursue for its own sake.

An important aspect of bicycling in 1900 was its appeal to women. They derived the same health benefits as men, physicians stressed, and cycling was a socially respectable activity for women. Moderate rather than strenuous activity benefited women, physicians held, and bicycle manufacturers took care to display illustrations of women in proper attire and without a drop of perspiration on them. Intentional or not, the appeal of bicycling was its democratizing influence: women's health issues were as important as those of men. Moreover, cycling gave women a proactive way of improving their health. No longer were they to wait passively for the intervention of a physician. Bicycle ads also included illustrations of children cycling, implying that the health benefits of cycling extended throughout a person's life, from childhood to maturity.

Primary Source

1900 Pierce Arrow Bicycle

The 1900 Pierce-Arrow bicycle was a road bike used mainly for health and recreation. REPRODUCED BY PERMISSION OF THE BICYCLE MUSEUM OF AMERICA.

Further Resources

BOOKS

Burke, Ed. *Benefits of Bicycling and Walking to Health.* Washington, D.C.: Federal Highway Administration, 1992.

Palmer, Arthur J. *Riding High: The Story of the Bicycle.* New York: Putnam, 1956.

Sloane, Eugene A. *The Complete Book of Bicycling.* New York: Trident, 1970.

PERIODICALS

Bandrapalli, Suman. "Pivotal Dates in Bicycle History." *Christian Science Monitor,* February 13, 2001, 19.

Hunt, Kenneth. "Ups and Downs of Bicycles." *Colonial Homes,* August 1996, 44–46.

Ledes, Allison E. "The Bicycle, 1817–1920." *Magazine Antiques,* June 1997, 790–792.

WEBSITES

"1896: The Bicycle Craze." Vassar College Library. Available online at http://iberia.vassar.edu/1896/bicycle.html; website home page: http://iberia.vassar.edu (accessed March 14, 2003).

"Bicycle History: United States of America." International Bicycle Fund. Available online at http://www.ibike.org/historyusa.htm; website home page: http://www.ibike.org (accessed March 14, 2003).

The History of the Bicycling Craze. Available online at http://www.cruzio.com/~bedard/bike/history/bikehist.html; website home page: http://www.cruzio.com (accessed February 5, 2003).

"Online Archives: Bicycling Craze." Portage County Historical Society of Wisconsin. Available online at http://www.pchswi.org/archives/sports/bicyclingcraze.html; website home page: http://www.pchswi.org (accessed March 14, 2003).

"How to Prevent Consumption (Tuberculosis) and Other Germ Diseases"

Pamphlet

By: Gardner Association for the Prevention and Relief of Tuberculosis

Date: 1900

Source: Gardner Association for the Prevention and Relief of Tuberculosis. "How to Prevent Consumption (Tuberculosis) and Other Germ Diseases." U.S. National Library of Medicine. Available online at http://www.nlm.nih.gov/exhibition/ephemera/images/tb17.gif; website home page: http://www.nlm.nih.gov (accessed March 14, 2003).

About the Organization: The Gardner Association for the Prevention and Relief of Tuberculosis was organized in 1884 as a nonprofit organization in Rhode Island for the eradication of tuberculosis. Its leaflets offered commonsense advice in helping people avoid contracting tuberculosis and other infectious diseases. ■

Introduction

The bacterium *Mycobacterium tuberculosis* causes tuberculosis, a disease that was also called "consumption" because it consumed or wasted away its victims. When airborne, the bacterium infects the lungs in humans. Humans may also contract tuberculosis by eating meat or drinking milk infected by the bacterium. In 1908, the U.S. Department of Agriculture issued a report in its *Yearbook of Agriculture* warning Americans against the danger of drinking milk infected by the bacterium and warning that infected milk was present in grocery stores. People who lived and worked in crowded, poorly ventilated buildings, a circumstance common in U.S. cities, were also at risk of contracting tuberculosis.

Symptoms include fever, night sweats, weight loss, coughing, chest pain, and fatigue. The bacterium can also scar the lungs. Poor nutrition and a weak immune system make a person susceptible to tuberculosis, as was the case when an exhausted Eugene O'Neill, the only playwright to win a Nobel Prize in literature, contracted tuberculosis. Tuberculosis is the silent killer that circulates throughout his play *Long Day's Journey Into Night* (1956). O'Neill captured Americans' fear of tuberculosis, which they saw as a death sentence because it killed roughly half its victims before the development of antibiotics.

Local governments and wealthy benefactors founded sanitoriums as early as the 1880s, though many Americans feared them as places where families sent the ill to die. Sanitoriums encouraged patients to take in the fresh air of the countryside, eat a nutritious diet, and exercise.

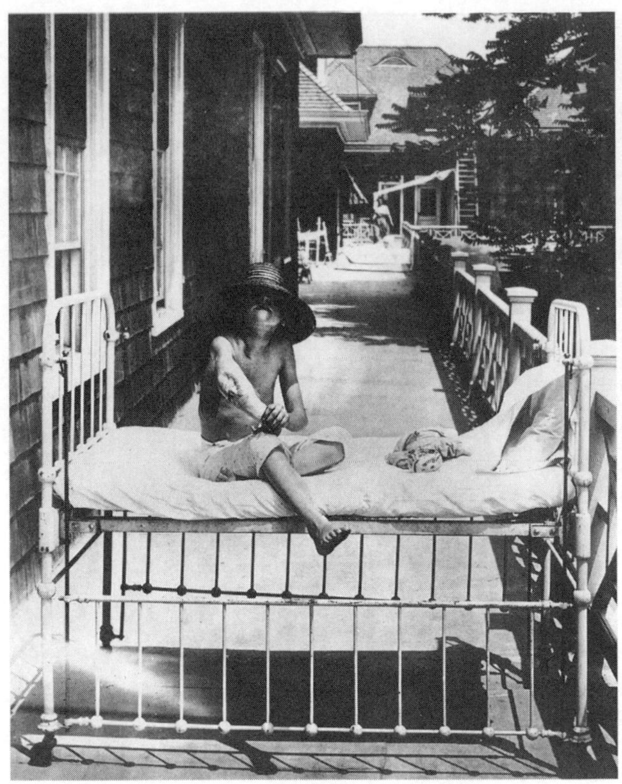

Tubercular child at Sea Breeze Hospital, Coney Island, New York. THE LIBRARY OF CONGRESS.

Significance

Around 1900, the Gardner Association for the Prevention and Relief of Tuberculosis issued a leaflet listing the measures people should take to prevent tuberculosis and other contagious diseases. It urged Americans to cover their mouth when coughing, to keep their hands and homes clean, to eat nutritious foods, to spend time outdoors breathing in fresh air, and to visit their physician when ill. It also urged that people not cough or sneeze toward someone, not drink from another's cup, not spit on the floor, and not kiss a sick friend.

The association leaflet was part of a campaign by private agencies and government in the first decade of the twentieth century to educate Americans about the dangers of tuberculosis and the measures to take to protect themselves from it. As early as 1892, physician Lawrence Flick had led a group of doctors and public health officials to form the Pennsylvania Society for the Prevention of Tuberculosis. Others organizations followed, and in 1904 Flick and a hundred other physicians formed the National Association for the Study and Prevention of Tuberculosis. These organizations sponsored public lectures and wrote newspaper articles in hopes of raising awareness about tuberculosis and its treatment.

HOW TO PREVENT CONSUMPTION (TUBERCULOSIS) AND OTHER GERM DISEASES

For School Children to Take Home and to Read Every Day.

DON'T FORGET THESE FACTS.

Germs are very small microscopic plants. Germs are found in all *Dust* and *Dirt*. Some germs are harmless, others cause disease. *Germs cause Consumption.* Avoid germs and Prevent Consumption.

TRY TO	TRY NOT TO
TRY to breathe through the nose rather than through the mouth.	Try NOT to take a full breath in a cloud of dust.
TRY to fill the lungs with pure air, free from dust.	Try NOT to cough or sneeze in another's face.
TRY to turn the head away from a person when coughing or sneezing, or hold a handkerchief or your hand over your mouth.	Try NOT to swallow what you raise in coughing.
TRY to spit out material coughed up from the lungs.	Try NOT to spit upon the floor or sidewalk.
TRY to spit into a piece of paper or cloth and burn as soon as possible.	Try NOT to cough long without seeing a physician.
TRY to gargle your throat with salt water or some other mild mouth wash after being exposed to any contagious disease.	Try NOT to kiss a sick friend.
TRY to clean the nose with a handkerchief.	Try NOT to pick your nose with your fingers.
TRY to keep the hands clean.	Try NOT to eat with dirty hands.
TRY to keep your finger nails cut short.	Try NOT to eat things made dirty by the handling of other persons.
TRY to brush your teeth night and morning.	Try NOT to eat a piece of candy or apple picked up from the sidewalk or street.
TRY to eat clean food and drink pure water.	Try NOT to have long and dirty finger nails.
TRY to eat slowly and chew your food well.	Try NOT to go about with unclean teeth.
TRY to keep moving about when heated from play.	Try NOT to drink out of a cup that has been used unless you wash it first.
TRY to keep your feet dry.	Try NOT to eat when heated or tired.
TRY to sleep in a room with partly-opened windows.	Try NOT to eat fast.
TRY to live in the sunshine.	Try NOT, when heated, to sit down where it is cold.
TRY to be out of doors as much as possible.	Try NOT to play in wet shoes and stockings.
	Try NOT to sleep in a warm or hot room.
	Try NOT to shut out the sunshine.
	Try NOT to form the habit of living around a stove.

Gardner Association for the Prevention and Relief of Tuberculosis.

Primary Source

"How to Prevent Consumption (Tuberculosis) and other Germ Diseases"

SYNOPSIS: In this leaflet, the Gardner Association for the Prevention and Relief of Tuberculosis lists measures people should take to avoid contracting tuberculosis and other contagious diseases. The commonsense directives include actions to take and others to avoid. COURTESY OF THE NATIONAL LIBRARY OF MEDICINE.

These efforts could not eradicate tuberculosis. Only the manufacture of penicillin in large quantities during the 1940s gave Americans a weapon against tuberculosis. That decade microbiologist Selman A. Waksman at Rutgers University and the New Jersey Agricultural Experiment Station discovered the antibiotic Streptomycin, produced by a soil microbe. Streptomycin was more effective against tuberculosis than any other antibiotic and won Waksman the 1952 Nobel Prize in physiology or medicine. Despite the work of scientists and physicians, antibiotic-resistant strains of tuberculosis arose during the 1980s. These strains, combined with the spread of HIV, have again made tuberculosis lethal, particularly among the homeless and poor.

Further Resources

BOOKS

Caldwell, Mark. *The Last Crusade: The War on Consumption, 1862–1954.* New York: Atheneum, 1988.

Dormandy, Thomas. *The White Death: A History of Tuberculosis.* New York: New York University Press, 2000.

Dublin, Louis I. *A Forty Year Campaign Against Tuberculosis.* New York: Metropolitan Life Insurance Company, 1952.

Professional Guide to Diseases. 6th ed. Springhouse, Penn.: Springhouse, 1998.

Sava, George. *The Conquest of Tuberculosis.* London: MacDonald, 1946.

U.S. Department of Agriculture. *Yearbook of Agriculture, 1908.* Washington, D.C.: U.S. Government Printing Office, 1909.

PERIODICALS

Britton, Warwick J., and Umaimainthan Palendira. "Improving Vaccines Against Tuberculosis." *Immunology and Cell Biology,* February 2003, 34–46.

WEBSITES

The Nobel Prize in Physiology or Medicine, 1952. Nobel e-Museum. Available online at http://www.nobel.se/medicine/laureates/1952/press.html; website home page: http://www.nobel.se (accessed March 14, 2003).

Tuberculosis Resources. Available online at http://www.cpmc.columbia.edu/tbcpp/ (accessed March 14, 2003).

Tuberculosis: Strategy and Operations, Monitoring and Evaluation. Available online at http://www.who.int/gtb (accessed March 14, 2003).

Waksman, Selman A. "Streptomycin: Background, Isolation, Properties and Utilization." Nobel e-Museum. Available online at http://www.nobel.se/medicine/laureates/1952/waksman-lecture.html; website home page: http://www.nobel.se (accessed March 14, 2003).

"Preliminary Report of the Committee on Organization"

Journal article

By: Joseph N. McCormack, P. Maxwell Foshay; George H. Simmons

Date: May 25, 1901

Source: McCormack, Joseph N., P. Maxwell Foshay, and George H. Simmons. "Preliminary Report of the Committee on Organization." *Journal of the American Medical Association,* May 25, 1901, 1435–1451.

About the Authors: Joseph N. McCormack (1847–1922) was born in Kentucky and graduated from the Miami University at Cincinnati with a doctorate in medicine in 1870. From 1883 to 1913, he served as secretary of Kentucky's state medical board. He chaired the committee on organization of the American Medical Association (AMA) from 1899 to 1913.

P. Maxwell Foshay held a doctorate in medicine and served as the editor of the *Cleveland Journal of Medicine.*

George H. Simmons (1852–1937) was born in England and attended Hahnemann Medical College, Chicago, where he received his doctorate in medicine in 1882. He then returned to Lincoln, Nebraska, to practice medicine until 1899. He was editor of the *Journal of the American Medical Association* from 1899 to 1924. ■

Introduction

American physicians were very factionalized in the mid-nineteenth century. Organizing efforts had failed, and medical colleges were not overly interested in being involved in this process. Sectional issues also divided the country. Differences in training divided physicians—some had been trained by apprenticeship while others were trained in medical colleges. There were also battles between types of physicians—homeopaths and eclectics battled with traditional practitioners.

After organizing in 1848, the AMA limited its membership to traditional, white, male practitioners. Those who did not fit these classifications had to establish their own societies. Besides struggling to keep itself together, it faced a number of issues. One major problem was with medical education, as over one hundred medical colleges were in existence, most of which did not require a bachelor's degree for admission. Another problem was attracting members. Very often the only permanent members were those who came to every convention, and, as its annual convention moved around the country, this was difficult to do. Others were "invited" to be members, but often they maintained their membership for only one year. The way that the AMA allowed representation from other organizations also had significant flaws. It was also very regional, as there were more members from the northeast than from other regions. Finally, only a small percentage of physicians were members.

Something needed to be done, and, in 1901, the Special Committee on Reorganization set forth its proposal, which eventually led to the AMA reorganizing itself.

Significance

Following the AMA's reorganization, its membership increased tenfold between 1900 and 1920. This increase solved one of its main problems: that it had previously possessed a very limited membership. Now, people who wanted to join the AMA did so simply by joining their local medical society. The AMA also became a national organization, instead of just reflecting the desires of the northeastern part of the Untied States. Furthermore, it created a House of Delegates, which allowed the delegates, elected by each state, and from several other societies, to make policy. This both eliminated the shifting number of voting members at each convention and provided a stable way to make policy.

With a larger member base, the AMA became actively involved in supporting and fighting a number of issues. It backed Abraham Flexner's report on medical schools, which greatly changed medical education by eliminating a large number of the substandard medical colleges and forcing premedical students to get a bachelor's degree before entering medical school.

In the second decade of the twentieth century, the AMA undertook a strong effort against medical quackery and patent medicines, mostly by educating the public. In the 1920s, it successfully fought against federal health insurance. During the 1930s, it opposed Social Security and loudly decried any thoughts of national health insurance similar to that in most European countries.

After World War II (1939–1945), the AMA successfully opposed President Harry S. Truman's (served

1945–1953) attempts to establish a national health plan. In the 1960s, it unsuccessfully opposed President Lyndon B. Johnson's (served 1963–1969) Medicare and Medicaid programs. From the 1970s to 1990s, it opposed more attempts by the federal government to create a national health insurance program.

Throughout the last half of the twentieth century, the AMA has been relatively successful at maintaining control over the medical industry, but difficulties remain, including skyrocketing medical costs and lack of health insurance for many. How the AMA will deal with these difficulties remains to be seen.

Primary Source

"Preliminary Report of the Committee on Organization" [excerpt]

SYNOPSIS: The proposal begins with a list of twelve recommended changes for the AMA, both in terms of how members are chosen and how the ruling body shall be constituted. It then outlines the current problems with the AMA, other advantages gained by these changes, and how the annual meeting will be altered. It concludes by discussing the financial benefits to the changes, and how the reorganization solves all of the difficulties outlined.

Your Committee expected at this time to submit a Constitution and By-Laws revised in accordance with its recommendations; these are not yet complete. They will be printed in time for distribution at the St. Paul meeting. The following embody the recommendations which will be incorporated in the Constitution and By-Laws to be submitted:

1. The delegate body shall hereafter be known as the "House of Delegates of the American Medical Association."
2. The House of Delegates shall consist of not more than 150 members and shall be created as follows: a, one delegate for every 500 members or fraction thereof of the state and territorial societies recognized by the American Medical Association; b, one delegate from each of the Sections of the American Medical Association, to be elected as are other officers of the Section; c, one representative each from the U. S. Army, the U. S. Navy, and the U. S. Marine-Hospital Service.
3. Delegates representing the state societies shall serve for two years, one-half, or as near as may be, of such delegates to be elected the first year for one year only.
4. Whenever the number of delegates exceeds 150 there shall be such a reapportionment among the affiliated state societies as will bring the total membership of the House of Delegates below that number.
5. The House of Delegates—as the Sections—shall hold its sessions daily, from 9 A. M. to 12 M. and from 2 P. M. to 5 P. M., or so much of such time as may be necessary, provided that it shall hold no session on the morning of the first day of the annual meeting, nor during the time of the General Sessions.
6. The General Sessions of the American Medical Association shall be composed of members and delegates who may be in attendance at the annual meeting, and the time of meeting shall be 11 A. M. on the first day of the annual meeting, 7:30 P. M. on the first three days of the annual meeting, and 12 noon (or such other hour as may be agreed upon) on the last day of the meeting, which session shall be for the installation of the officers for the ensuing year and other concluding exercises.
7. All the officers of the Association shall be elected by the House of Delegates, but no member of the House of Delegates shall be eligible to any office whose incumbent is elected by that body.
8. No one shall be elected a member of the House of Delegates who has not been a permanent member of the American Medical Association for at least two years.
9. The election shall take place on the morning of the fourth day of each annual meeting.
10. No one shall be elected to any office who is not present at the annual meeting at which the election occurs.
11. The officers elected shall be installed at 12 o'clock on the last day of the annual meeting.
12. The membership of the Association, in addition to the delegates, shall be composed of permanent members, honorary members, and associate members. . . .

Objections to Present Conditions

No Present Restrictions of Delegate Representation

As the right to vote in the general sessions is limited to delegates who are presumed to represent others, this right should be carefully guarded. In all great representative bodies every precaution is taken to restrict the right of voting to those who are entitled to it. But at the annual meetings of the Association this restriction has become an impossibility. Registration of all who attend as delegates is such an enormous task that its accomplishment in a satisfactory manner is out of the question if there is the slightest attempt made to scrutinize the credentials. While the right of a society to send delegates is verified, attempt to limit each society to the number to which it is entitled would be fruitless. This could be done if there were a system of reporting membership, but not otherwise. As this system exists in but few states, any attempt at scrutiny in this regard is useless.

A large majority of those who attend the annual meetings do so without any authority to represent others. Nominally, delegates are supposed to be elected; practically, certificates are granted by secretaries of societies on request of those who desire to attend the annual meeting. While this may not be true in a few instances, the exceptions are so few that the rule is as stated.

Correct Registration of Delegates Now Practically Impossible

The By-Laws of the American Medical Association call for the preparation of the list of delegates for accuracy in calling the ayes and nays. At the last meeting over 1600 delegates were registered, and to get such a number in any uniformity for roll-call would be impossible in the time, and the calling of such a long roll as the list of delegates makes would take so long that this is now out of the question. In *viva voce* voting in the general body it is impossible to tell who are and who are not delegates.

Difficulties Increasing Yearly

The above difficulties are becoming more noticeable each succeeding year. The number of affiliated societies is rapidly increasing, and with this also the number of delegates increases. In brief, the number of delegates has become so great that a verification of the credentials is impracticable, and the separation of the delegates from the few who have not the right to vote is so difficult that the question resolves itself into this: Shall the delegates be reduced in number so that they shall make a body that is manageable, or shall the pretense of delegates be done away with and allow all to vote who attend the meetings? The Committee believes that the latter would be preferable to the present conditions. . . .

Other Objects of Organization

There are other evils to be met besides those enumerated, such as that which our confrères in England are meeting under what they call the "battle of the clubs." Lodge and club practice is only just beginning to be felt here and the only way in which to meet these is by counter-organization. Most of the quackery and fraud in its protean aspects against the people and much of the evils with which the profession of this country is afflicted are the result of apathy and lack of organization. Organization will give confidence to make effort, and with this confidence apathy will vanish.

There are medicosocial questions that may be worthy of consideration in a national representative body of medical men. Among these is the advisability of creating a department of insurance for the superannuated, for the establishment of a home for those among us who, through misfortune, have become incapacitated, for mutual protection in malpractice suits, etc. Medicoethical questions are continually arising, such as that now prominently before the profession, namely, the giving of commissions. Such questions as these should be met fairly and squarely by a representative body qualified to consider them.

The American Medical Association's Annual Meeting

The annual meeting, under the proposed reorganization, will consist of General Sessions, meetings of the House of Delegates, and meetings of the various Sections. The House of Delegates will meet at the same hours as the Sections, and in effect the House of Delegates will be the legislative and business Section of the Association. . . .

Functions of the House of Delegates

The House of Delegates, to all intents and purposes, will be the legislative and executive body of the Association and will take the place of the delegate body as it now exists. The only change from present conditions will be that the delegate body will be reduced in number and its members elected by the state societies only. It will elect all the officers; it will have control of all the affairs of the Association; it will be the mouth-piece to give expression to the desires of the profession of the country in regard to business and legislative affairs; and it will consider other problems affecting the profession from time to time as they arise. It will be a confederation of the state societies of the country, which in turn must be a confederation of the local societies in the state. Being created by the state societies, it must be responsible to them for its actions.

In the revised Constitution, the Committee recommends that the following be incorporated:

No member of the House of Delegates shall be eligible to any office in the Association.

By adopting this proposition, it is believed that "medical politics" will be reduced to a minimum.

The Board of Trustees shall have control of the finances of the American Medical Association as at present, and be considered officers of the Association, and therefore can not be elected from among the delegates.

The object of this is that there may be thrown around all financial matters as much protection as possible. While the Board of Trustees will be created by the House of Delegates, its term of office will extend as now for three years, one-third going out each year. Two-thirds of the Board of Trustees will always be independent of the existing House of Delegates and will be in a position to act independently as a protection should that body any year recommend some extravagant expenditure. As now the Board of Trustees could expend no money unless so ordered by the House of Delegates, except in the management of The Journal. . . .

Financial Reasons

As will be seen, the most important result of enlarging the scope of the state society will be the increased revenue. This is an important consideration, as now the lack of money prevents the execution of important measures. Only a few now contribute to the expenses, whereas these should be divided among the many, for all are benefited.

Referring again to the four states above, we find that the annual dues of the California State Society are $5.00, and that with the present membership this brings in $1310. With the county society members added, with dues $1, this would amount to $1162, not as much as at present, of course, but how much easier these dollars would be paid, compared to the $5.00 now. Illinois claims a membership of about 800, and the annual dues are $3, making a total income of $2400. If the members of the county societies should be included, and a per capita assessment of $1 were made, there would be an income to the state society of $3800, and yet the assessment on each member would be so small that certainly no one could object to it. The annual dues of Iowa are $2, which nets that body $1468 annually, whereas a $1 assessment on the members when membership of the county societies is admitted, will bring in $2734. In Ohio the claimed membership is 940, the annual dues are $2, making the total income to the state society $1880. Admit the members of the county societies and make the assessment $1, and the state society will have an income of $3940.

It might not be amiss here to refer to another phase of this question. The annual transactions of many of the state societies record the fact that the most discouraging feature is the collection of dues. In many societies this is an annual and a very vexed question. It is not an uncommon thing for a physician to join a state society, pay his annual fee, and then through non-attendance let his dues lapse for one, two or three years. These will then amount to such a sum that it has a great tendency to keep him away from the annual meeting and from becoming an active member again. Many societies adopt resolutions every few years remitting past dues, for the purpose of getting such men to come in and renew their membership.

The transactions of many state societies show that anywhere from 25 per cent to 50 per cent of the members are in arrears. In a circular now before us is an announcement by the secretary of one society to the effect that, while the membership is given as about 725, only 420 have paid their dues and are entitled to the transactions for the year. Under the proposed method, the county societies will collect the annual dues, adding to the sum necessary for local expenses $1 for the state society, and this will be paid direct to the state by the county society, as is done by other bodies. . . .

The Remedy for the Above Conditions

The only remedy for these evils is a systematic, all-pervasive organization, beginning with the county society as the broad foundation, and extending through the state societies to the American Medical Association, conferring, so far as may be possible, equal privileges and blessings on the members in New York and Chicago, and on those located in the remote hamlets of Maine and California. With such organization all things reasonably desired become possible to us, and through us to the people, for whom, as regards all protective sanitary and medical legislation, our profession must think and labor. What the Committee suggests will require time, much patient effort and no little expense. . . .

Each state society must insist (1) that there must be a society in every county where there are ten regular physicians; (2) that physicians must belong to their own county society, (an exception should be made where one lives much nearer to the place of meeting of an adjoining county society than to his own. In such cases his own society should have the privilege of granting him the right to associate with the other); (3) that where the population is scattered and physicians few, two or more counties may unite and form a district society.

Some of the recommendations in this report are not applicable to certain thinly-settled parts of our country. For instance, Arizona has only about 125 regular physicians, with about 62 members of the state society. Idaho has probably 190 regular physicians in the Territory and only about 48 are members of the state society. Montana has probably 275 regular physicians and probably 90 are members of the state society. Nevada has probably 55 regular physicians and about 25 are members of the state society. New Mexico has probably 130 regular physicians and about 30 are members of the state society. North Dakota has probably 275 regular physicians and about 125 are members of the state societv. Utah has probably 275 regular physicians and about 84 are members of the state society. Wyoming has less than 100 regular physicians and about 33 are members of the state society. It will, of course, be impossible to organize county societies in much of this territory, but the information for a complete enrollment of the whole profession of this country can be had in this territory with very little expense on the part of the representative bodies in them. These should be asked to co-operate to make our plan complete, although they should not be asked to go into the details as suggested, neither is it possible for them to do so. There may be other states not mentioned in which the same difficulty will arise. The Committee only suggests the above where it is applicable.

In conclusion, the Committee believes that the recommendations above made are in no way Utopian or impractical, but that they are such as can be carried out in every part of our great country and that they will result in a scientific, social, and material benefit to the individual and to the profession as a whole, as well as to the well-being of the people.

Further Resources

BOOKS

American Medical Association. *Caring for the Country: A History and Celebration of the First 150 years of the American Medical Association.* Chicago: American Medical Association, 1997.

Burrow, James Gordon. *AMA: Voice of American Medicine.* Baltimore, Md.: Johns Hopkins University Press, 1963.

Campion, Frank D. *The AMA and U.S. Health Policy Since 1940.* Chicago: Chicago Review, 1984.

Cooper, Melvin Wayne. *The Adoption of a Code of Medical Ethics by the American Medical Association.* Beaumont, Tex.: Lamar University, 1999.

Johnson, James A., and Walter J. Jones. *The American Medical Association and Organized Medicine: A Commentary and Annotated Bibliography.* New York: Garland, 1993.

Prabhu, Maya Gopika. "Bitter Medicine: The Role of the Canadian and American Medical Associations in Obstructing National Health Insurance Legislation, 1945–1962." Master's thesis, Harvard University, 1994.

WEBSITES

"A Guide to Resources on the History of the Food and Drug Administration." Office of the Commissioner. Available online at http://www.fda.gov/oc/history/resourceguide/background.html; website home page: http://www.fda.gov (accessed March 14, 2003).

The Jungle

Novel

By: Upton Sinclair

Date: 1906

Source: Sinclair, Upton. *The Jungle.* New York: Doubleday, Page, 1906. Reprinted in New York: Penguin, 1990, 39–44. Available online at http://www.roggeman.com/jungle (accessed March 15, 2003).

About the Author: Upton Sinclair (1878–1968) was born in Baltimore, Maryland, and studied at the City College of New York and Columbia University. While at Columbia, he wrote six novels. Of these, *The Jungle* (1906) won him celebrity. Not content as a novelist, he unsuccessfully ran four times for political office in California. His closest bid came in 1934 when he narrowly lost the gubernatorial race. ■

Introduction

Like the rest of the U.S. economy, the meatpacking industry grew rapidly during the nineteenth century. Its success stemmed from the expansion of hog raising from western Ohio through Indiana, Illinois, Missouri, and Iowa. In the west and south lay the grasslands on which cattle fed. The cattle range spread from Texas in the south to the Dakotas and Montana in the north.

Chicago, sitting astride the hog and cattle empires and blessed with a network of railroads running both east and west, emerged as the center of the meatpacking industry. Demand for pork and beef in the United States and overseas led meatpackers to process thousands of hogs and cattle every day.

Aside from workers in the industry, few Americans knew the unsanitary conditions under which carcasses were processed. Workers had to maintain a frenetic pace that invited sloppy and unsanitary practices. Workers added dead and putrid rats and feces to the vats into which they put the carcasses of cattle and hogs. Hair, some of it human, and animal hides and bones also found their way into the vats. Supervisors did nothing to stop these practices. They cared only for profit, which could only be earned by processing carcasses as rapidly as possible.

That Americans sometimes became ill from eating pork and beef did not attract national attention in the nineteenth century. In 1900, however, Theodore Roosevelt, who had been colonel of the Rough Riders during the Spanish-American War (1989) and had fashioned himself into a national hero, testified before Congress that he and his troops became ill eating the canned meat the U.S. Army served as rations. The climax of his testimony came when Roosevelt declared he would rather eat his hat than another tin of meat. His declaration made newspaper headlines, and although some Americans dismissed his words as typical Roosevelt bluster, others were alarmed. Newspapers began to report on the quality of pork and beef.

Significance

In 1905, the *Appeal to Reason,* a socialist newspaper, hired Sinclair to investigate the meatpackers. Posing as a worker, Sinclair spent seven weeks in the plants, observing conditions and talking with workers. He saw workers fill vats with rats' corpses, feces, hair, hide, and bones. These abuses filled his fictionalized account of the meatpacking industry, *The Jungle,* which the *Appeal to Reason* serialized. Meanwhile, Sinclair sought a publisher for the novel in complete form. Several rejected it for fear that meatpackers would attack them. In 1906, Doubleday, Page, and Company agreed to publish the novel, gambling that profits would offset condemnation from meatpackers. Before publishing the novel, Doubleday dispatched editor Isaac F. Marcosson to Chicago to confirm Sinclair's observations. Marcosson returned to report that conditions were worse than Sinclair had written.

The novel was an immediate sensation. Newspapers carried reports that news of its contents had prompted Roosevelt, by now president (served 1901–1909), to throw his breakfast sausages out a White House window. Sinclair received additional publicity when Roosevelt summoned him to the White House.

At the same time, Roosevelt dispatched U.S. labor commissioner Charles P. Neill and prominent New York attorney James B. Reynolds to investigate the meatpackers. Like Marcosson before them, they reported that conditions were even worse than what Sinclair had written. For a time, Roosevelt did nothing with Neill and Reynolds's report for fear that his popularity might suffer in a confrontation with meatpackers. When Sinclair leaked the report to the *New York Times,* Roosevelt had no choice but to release it.

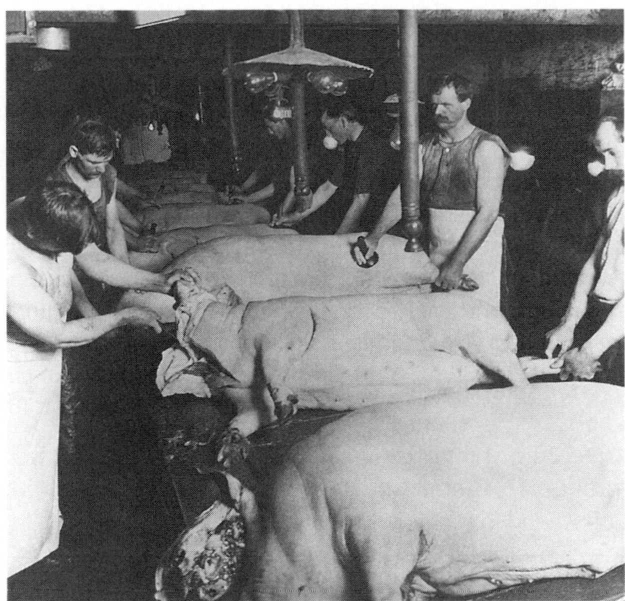

Slaughterhouse workers scrape hog carcasses at a Swift & Co. plant in Chicago, Illinois.

Public uproar from *The Jungle* and Neill and Reynolds's report forced Roosevelt and Congress to confront the meatpackers. In 1906, Congress passed and Roosevelt signed the *Meat Inspection Act* and the *Pure Food and Drug Act,* both of which committed the federal government to guarantee the safety of meat and other food and drugs for Americans.

Primary Source

The Jungle [excerpt]

SYNOPSIS: In this excerpt, readers hear the shrieks of hogs and cattle hoisted into the air and see the flash of knives that slashed their necks, leaving them in midair to bleed to death. Workers, speckled with blood, labored in blood half an inch thick.

At the same instant the ear was assailed by a most terrifying shriek; the visitors started in alarm, the women turned pale and shrank back. The shriek was followed by another, louder and yet more agonizing—for once started upon that journey, the hog never came back; at the top of the wheel he was shunted off upon a trolley, and went sailing down the room. And meantime another was swung up, and then another, and another, until there was a double line of them, each dangling by a foot and kicking in frenzy—and squealing. The uproar was appalling, perilous to the eardrums; one feared there was too much sound for the room to hold—that the walls must give way or the ceiling crack. There were high squeals and low squeals, grunts, and wails of agony; there would come a momentary lull, and then a fresh outburst, louder than ever, surging up to a deafening climax. It was too much for some of the visitors—the men would look at each other, laughing nervously, and the women would stand with hands clenched, and the blood rushing to their faces, and the tears starting in their eyes.

Meantime, heedless of all these things, the men upon the floor were going about their work. Neither squeals of hogs nor tears of visitors made any difference to them; one by one they hooked up the hogs, and one by one with a swift stroke they slit their throats. There was a long line of hogs, with squeals and lifeblood ebbing away together; until at last each started again, and vanished with a splash into a huge vat of boiling water.

It was all so very businesslike that one watched it fascinated. It was porkmaking by machinery, porkmaking by applied mathematics. And yet somehow the most matter-of-fact person could not help thinking of the hogs; they were so innocent, they came so very trustingly; and they were so very human in their protests—and so perfectly within their rights! They had done nothing to deserve it; and it was adding insult to injury, as the thing was done here, swinging them up in this cold-blooded, impersonal way, without a pretense of apology, without the homage of a tear. Now and then a visitor wept, to be sure; but this slaughtering machine ran on, visitors or no visitors. It was like some horrible crime committed in a dungeon, all unseen and unheeded, buried out of sight and of memory.

One could not stand and watch very long without becoming philosophical, without beginning to deal in symbols and similes, and to hear the hog-squeal of the universe. Was it permitted to believe that there was nowhere upon the earth, or above the earth, a heaven for hogs, where they were requited for all this suffering? Each one of these hogs was a separate creature. Some were white hogs, some were black; some were brown, some were spotted; some were old, some young; some were long and lean, some were monstrous. And each of them had an individuality of his own, a will of his own, a hope and a heart's desire; each was full of self-confidence, of self-importance, and a sense of dignity. And trusting and strong in faith he had gone about his business, the while a black shadow hung over him and a horrid Fate waited in his pathway. Now suddenly it had swooped upon him, and had seized him by the leg. Relentless, remorseless, it was; all his protests, his screams, were nothing to it—it did its cruel will with him, as if his wishes, his feelings, had simply no existence at all; it cut his throat and watched him gasp out his life. And now was one to believe that there was nowhere a god of hogs, to whom this hog-personality was precious, to whom these hog-squeals and agonies had a meaning? Who would take this hog into his arms and comfort him, reward him for his work well done, and show him the meaning of his sacrifice? Perhaps some glimpse of all this was in the thoughts of our humble-minded Jurgis, as he turned to go on with the rest of the party, and muttered: "*Dieve*—but I'm glad I'm not a hog!"

The carcass hog was scooped out of the vat by machinery, and then it fell to the second floor, passing on the way through a wonderful machine with numerous scrapers, which adjusted themselves to the size and shape of the animal, and sent it out at the other end with nearly all of its bristles removed. It was then again strung up by machinery, and sent upon another trolley ride; this time passing between two lines of men, who sat upon a raised platform, each doing a certain single thing to the carcass as it came to him. One scraped the outside of a leg; another scraped the inside of the same leg. One with a swift stroke cut the throat; another with two swift strokes severed the head, which fell to the floor and vanished through a hole. Another made a slit down the body; a second opened the body wider; a third with a saw cut the breastbone; a fourth loosened the entrails; a fifth pulled them out—and they also slid through a hole in the floor. There were men to scrape each side and men to scrape the back; there were men to clean the carcass inside, to trim it and wash it. Looking down this room, one saw, creeping slowly, a line of dangling hogs a hundred yards in length; and for every yard there was a man, working as if a demon were after him. At the end of this hog's progress every inch of the carcass had been gone over several times; and then it was rolled into the chilling room, where it stayed for twenty-four hours, and where a stranger might lose himself in a forest of freezing hogs.

Before the carcass was admitted here, however, it had to pass a government inspector, who sat in the doorway and felt of the glands in the neck for tuberculosis. This government inspector did not have the manner of a man who was worked to death; he was apparently not haunted by a fear that the hog might get by him before he had finished his testing. If you were a sociable person, he was quite willing to enter into conversation with you, and to explain to you the deadly nature of the ptomaines which are found in tubercular pork; and while he was talking with you you could hardly be so ungrateful as to notice that a dozen carcasses were passing him untouched. This inspector wore an imposing silver badge, and he gave an atmosphere of authority to the scene, and, as it were, put the stamp of official approval upon the things which were done in Durham's.

Jurgis went down the line with the rest of the visitors, staring open-mouthed, lost in wonder. He had dressed hogs himself in the forest of Lithuania; but he had never expected to live to see one hog dressed by several hundred men. It was like a wonderful poem to him, and he took it all in guilelessly—even to the conspicuous signs demanding immaculate cleanliness of the employees. Jurgis was vexed when the cynical Jokubas translated these signs with sarcastic comments, offering to take them to the secret rooms where the spoiled meats went to be doctored.

The party descended to the next floor, where the various waste materials were treated. Here came the entrails, to be scraped and washed clean for sausage casings; men and women worked here in the midst of a sickening stench, which caused the visitors to hasten by, gasping. To another room came all the scraps to be "tanked," which meant boiling and pumping off the grease to make soap and lard; below they took out the refuse, and this, too, was a region in which the visitors did not linger. In still other places men were engaged in cutting up the carcasses that had been through the chilling rooms. First there were the "splitters," the most expert workmen in the plant, who earned as high as fifty cents an hour, and did not a thing all day except chop hogs down the middle. Then there were "cleaver men," great giants with muscles of iron; each had two men to attend him—to slide the half carcass in front of him on the table, and hold it while he chopped it, and then turn each piece so that he might chop it once more. His cleaver had a blade about two feet long, and he never made but one cut; he made it so neatly, too, that his implement did not smite through and dull itself—there was just enough force for a perfect cut, and no more. So through various yawning holes there slipped to the floor below—to one room hams, to another forequarters, to another sides of pork. One might go down to this floor and see the pickling rooms, where the hams were put into vats, and the great smoke rooms, with their airtight iron doors. In other rooms they prepared salt pork—there were whole cellars full of it, built up in great towers to the ceiling. In yet other rooms they were putting up meats in boxes and barrels, and wrapping hams and bacon in oiled paper, sealing and labeling and sewing them. From the doors of these rooms went men with loaded trucks, to the platform where freight cars were waiting to be filled; and one went out there and realized with a start that he had come at last to the ground floor of this enormous building.

Then the party went across the street to where they did the killing of beef—where every hour they turned four or five hundred cattle into meat. Unlike the place they had left, all this work was done on one floor; and instead of there being one line of carcasses which moved to the workmen, there were fifteen or twenty lines, and the men moved from one to another of these. This made a scene of intense activity, a picture of human power wonderful to watch. It was all in one great room, like a circus amphitheater, with a gallery for visitors running over the center.

Along one side of the room ran a narrow gallery, a few feet from the floor; into which gallery the cattle were driven by men with goads which gave them electric shocks. Once crowded in here, the creatures were prisoned, each in a separate pen, by gates that shut, leaving them no room to turn around; and while they stood bellowing and plunging, over the top of the pen there leaned one of the "knockers," armed with a sledge hammer, and watching for a chance to deal a blow. The room echoed with the thuds in quick succession, and the stamping and kicking of the steers. The instant the animal had fallen, the "knocker" passed on to another; while a second man raised a lever, and the side of the pen was raised, and the animal, still kicking and struggling, slid out to the "killing bed." Here a man put shackles about one leg, and pressed another lever, and the body was jerked up into the air. There were fifteen or twenty such pens, and it was a matter of only a couple of minutes to knock fifteen or twenty cattle and roll them out. Then once more the gates were opened, and another lot rushed in; and so out of each pen there rolled a steady stream of carcasses, which the men upon the killing beds had to get out of the way.

The manner in which they did this was something to be seen and never forgotten. They worked with furious intensity, literally upon the run—at a pace with which there is nothing to be compared except a football game. It was all highly specialized labor, each man having his task to do; generally this would consist of only two or three specific cuts, and he would pass down the line of fifteen or twenty carcasses, making these cuts upon each. First there came the "butcher," to bleed them; this meant one swift stroke, so swift that you could not see it—only the flash of the knife; and before you could realize it, the man had darted on to the next line, and a stream of bright red was pouring out upon the floor. This floor was half an inch deep with blood, in spite of the best efforts of men who kept shoveling it through holes; it must have made the floor slippery, but no one could have guessed this by watching the men at work.

The carcass hung for a few minutes to bleed; there was no time lost, however, for there were several hanging in each line, and one was always ready. It was let down to the ground, and there came the "headsman," whose task it was to sever the head, with two or three swift strokes. Then came the "floorsman," to make the first cut in the skin; and then another to finish ripping the skin down the center; and then half a dozen more in swift succession, to finish the skinning. After they were through, the carcass was again swung up; and while a man with a stick examined the skin, to make sure that it had not been cut, and another rolled it up and tumbled it through one of the inevitable holes in the floor, the beef proceeded on its journey. There were men to cut it, and men to split it, and men to gut it and scrape it clean inside. There were some with hose which threw jets of boiling water upon it, and others who removed the feet and added the final touches. In the end, as with the hogs, the finished beef was run into the chilling room, to hang its appointed time.

Further Resources

BOOKS

Dell, Floyd. *Upton Sinclair: A Study in Social Protest.* Philadelphia: Folcroft, 1969.

Harte, James L. *This Is Upton Sinclair.* Emmaus, Penn.: Rodale, 1938.

Sinclair, Upton. *The Autobiography of Upton Sinclair.* New York: Harcourt, Brace, 1962.

Thompson, Frank H. *The Jungle Notes: Including Sinclair's Life and Career, Background in Social History.* Lincoln, Nebr.: Cliff's Notes, 1970.

Yoder, Jon A. *Upton Sinclair.* New York: Ungar, 1975.

PERIODICALS

Goode, Stephen. "Utopian Sinclair." *Insight on the News,* July 31, 2000, 24–26.

McChesney, Robert W., and Scott, Ben. "Upton Sinclair and the Contradictions of Capitalist Journalism." *Monthy Review: An Independent Socialist Magazine,* May 2002, 1–14.

"Upton Sinclair and the Jungle." *Workforce,* January 2002, 36.

WEBSITES

The Jungle by Upton Sinclair. Available online at http://www.roggeman.com/jungle (accessed March 15, 2003).

"Upton Sinclair." E Literature: Author List. Available online at http://www.eliterature.com.ar/sinclair_upton; website home page: http://www.eliterature.com.ar (accessed March 15, 2003).

"Upton Sinclair." Spartacus Educational. Available online at http://www.spartacus.schoolnet.co.uk/Jupton.htm; website home page: http://www.spartacus.schoolnet.co.uk (accessed March 15, 2003).

"Upton Sinclair: *The Jungle.*" Marxists.org Internet Archive. Available online at http://www.marxists.org/reference/archive/sinclair-upton/works/jungle; website home page: http://www.marxists.org (accessed March 15, 2003).

FDA-Federal Meat Inspection Act

Law

By: James Wilson

Date: 1906

Source: Wilson, James. *FDA-Federal Meat Inspection Act.* U.S. Food and Drug Administration. Available online at http://www.fda.gov/opacom/laws/meat.htm; website home page: http://www.fda.gov (accessed March 15, 2003).

About the Author: James Wilson (1835–1920), born in Scotland, immigrated to the United States in 1852. He served two terms in the U.S. House of Representatives. In 1897, President William McKinley (served 1897–1901) appointed Wilson secretary of agriculture, a position he held until 1913, making him the longest-serving agriculture secretary in U.S. history. In addition to authoring the *Meat Inspection Act* in 1906, Wilson convinced Congress to add the Bureaus of Chemistry, Plant Industry, and Soils to the U.S. Department of Agriculture. ■

Introduction

The U.S. meatpacking industry that arose during the nineteenth century centered in Chicago, which sat astride the hog-raising lands of the Midwest and the cattle ranges south and west of hog territory. The industry fed Americans and people overseas. To meet the demand for beef and pork, meatpackers had to process thousands of carcasses a day.

The speed of this process encouraged sloppiness and unsanitary practices. The result was contaminated meat that came to national attention in 1900 when Theodore Roosevelt, who had fought in the Spanish-American War (1898), testified before Congress that he and his troops became ill from eating the U.S. Army's canned meat rations. Roosevelt declared that he would rather eat his hat

Government inspectors examine hogs at a meat packing plant in Chicago in 1906, following the passage of the law which provided for Federal approval on all meat destined for interstate commerce. Upton Sinclair charged that many inspectors were on the payrolls of the stock yards. © BETTMANN/CORBIS. REPRODUCED BY PERMISSION.

than another tin of meat, a declaration that made newspaper headlines. Soon thereafter, newspapers began to report on the quality of beef and pork.

The *Appeal to Reason,* a socialist newspaper, in 1905 hired novelist Upton Sinclair to investigate the meatpackers. The novel that resulted from his observations, *The Jungle* (1906), revealed that workers added dead and putrid rats, feces, hair, and bones to the vats along with the carcasses of hogs and cattle.

The novel was an immediate sensation. Newspapers carried reports that news of the novel's contents had prompted President Roosevelt (served 1901–1909) to throw his breakfast sausages out a White House window. Roosevelt dispatched Charles P. Neill, the U.S. labor commissioner, and James B. Reynolds, a New York attorney, to investigate the meatpackers. They reported that the conditions were worse than what Sinclair had written.

Significance

Attention now focused on the meatpackers and Congress. The tradition in the United States had been to allow business to regulate itself. The meatpackers hid behind this tradition, arguing that they could clean up their industry without governmental oversight. The argument might have worked had the public not been outraged and had Roosevelt not calculated that he could enhance his reputation as a crusader of the people by taking on the meatpackers.

With an energy few previous presidents had displayed, Roosevelt demanded congressional action. The meatpackers, of course, lobbied Congress to do nothing, but steady pressure from newspaper editors and from Roosevelt forced Congress on June 30, 1906, to pass the *Meat Inspection Act.*

The act declared contaminated meat "injurious to the public welfare" and empowered the U.S. Department of Agriculture to inspect "all cattle, sheep, swine, and goats" before they entered slaughterhouses and to permit no diseased animal to be processed for meat. Moreover, the Department of Agriculture had authority to inspect slaughterhouses for sanitary practices and to inspect meat from them to ensure its wholesomeness for human consumption.

The act was a victory for public health and for the principle that government had an obligation to protect Americans from health hazards. It also heightened the role of the federal government as an agent of public health and demonstrated that public welfare, at least in this case, trumped the right of business to maximize profit.

Primary Source

FDA-Federal Meat Inspection Act [excerpt]

SYNOPSIS: In this excerpt, Congress authorizes the U.S. Department of Agriculture to inspect livestock before slaughter to ensure that no diseased animals enter the food supply, to inspect slaughterhouses to make certain that their operations are sanitary, and to guarantee the wholesomeness of meat that leaves slaughterhouses for distribution to consumers worldwide.

That for the purpose of preventing the use in interstate or foreign commerce, as hereinafter provided, of meat and meat food products which are unsound, unhealthful, unwholesome, or otherwise unfit for human food, the Secretary of Agriculture, at his discretion, may cause to be made, by inspectors appointed for that purpose, an examination and inspection of all cattle, sheep, swine, and goats before they shall be allowed to enter into any slaughtering, packing, meat-canning, rendering, or similar establishment, in which they are to be slaughtered and the meat and meat food products thereof are to be used in interstate or foreign commerce; and all cattle, swine, sheep, and goats found on such inspection to show symptoms of disease shall be set apart and slaughtered separately from all other cattle, sheep, swine, or goats, and when so slaughtered the carcasses of said cattle, sheep, swine, or goats shall be subject to a careful examination and inspection, all as provided by the rules and regulations to be prescribed by the Secretary of Agriculture as herein provided for.

That for the purposes hereinbefore set forth the Secretary of Agriculture shall cause to be made by inspectors appointed for that purpose, as hereinafter provided, a post-mortem examination and inspection of the carcasses and parts thereof of all cattle, sheep, swine, and goats to be prepared for human consumption at any slaughtering, meat-canning, salting, packing, rendering, or similar establishment in any State, Territory, or the District of Columbia for transportation or sale as articles of interstate or foreign commerce; and the carcasses and parts thereof of all such animals found to be sound, healthful, wholesome, and fit for human food shall be marked, stamped, tagged, or labeled as "Inspected and passed;" and said inspectors shall label, mark, stamp, or tag as "Inspected and condemned," all carcasses and parts thereof of animals found to be unsound, unhealthful, unwholesome, or otherwise unfit for human food; and all carcasses and parts thereof thus inspected and condemned shall be destroyed for food purposes by the said establishment in the presence of an inspector, and the Secretary of Agriculture may remove inspectors from any such establishment which fails to so destroy any such condemned carcass or part thereof, and said inspectors, after said first inspection shall, when they deem it necessary, reinspect said carcasses or parts thereof to determine whether since the first inspection the same have become unsound, unhealthful, unwholesome, or in any way unfit for human food, and if any carcass or any part thereof shall, upon examination and inspection subsequent to the first examination and inspection, be found to be unsound, unhealthful, unwholesome, or otherwise unfit for human food, it shall be destroyed for food purposes by the said establishment in the presence of an inspector, and the Secretary of Agriculture may remove inspectors from any establishment which fails to so destroy any such condemned carcass or part thereof.

The foregoing provisions shall apply to all carcasses or parts of carcasses of cattle, sheep, swine, and goats, or the meat or meat products thereof which may be brought into any slaughtering, meat-canning, salting, packing, rendering, or similar establishment, and such examination and inspection shall be had before the said carcasses or parts thereof shall be allowed to enter into any department wherein the same are to be treated and prepared for meat food products; and the foregoing provisions shall also apply to all such products which, after having been issued from any slaughtering, meat-canning, salting, packing, rendering, or similar establishment, shall be returned to the same or to any similar establishment where such inspection is maintained.

That for the purposes hereinbefore set forth the Secretary of Agriculture shall cause to be made by inspectors appointed for that purpose an examination and inspection of all meat food products prepared for interstate or foreign commerce in any slaughtering, meat-canning, salting, packing, rendering, or similar establishment, and for the purposes of any examination and inspection said inspectors shall have access at all times, by day or night, whether the establishment be operated or not, to every part of said establishment; and said inspectors shall mark, stamp, tag, or label as "Inspected and passed" all such products found to be sound, healthful, and wholesome, and which contain no dyes, chemicals, preservatives, or ingredients which render such meat or meat food products unsound, unhealthful, unwholesome, or unfit for human food;

and said inspectors shall label, mark, stamp, or tag as "Inspected and condemned" all such products found unsound, unhealthful, and unwholesome, or which contain dyes, chemicals, preservatives, or ingredients which render such meat or meat food products unsound, unhealthful, unwholesome, or unfit for human food, and all such condemned meat food products shall be destroyed for food purposes, as hereinbefore provided, and the Secretary of Agriculture may remove inspectors from any establishment which fails to so destroy such condemned meat food products: *Provided,* That, subject to the rules and regulations of the Secretary of Agriculture, the provisions hereof in regard to preservatives shall not apply to meat food products for export to any foreign country and which are prepared or packed according to the specifications or directions of the foreign purchaser, when no substance is used in the preparation or packing thereof in conflict with the laws of the foreign country to which said article is to be exported; but if said article shall be in fact sold or offered for sale for domestic use or consumption then this proviso shall not exempt said article from the operation of all the other provisions of this Act.

That when any meat or meat food product prepared for interstate or foreign commerce which has been inspected as hereinbefore provided and marked "Inspected and passed" shall be placed or packed in any can, pot, tin, canvas, or other receptacle or covering in any establishment where inspection under the provisions of this Act is maintained, the person, firm, or corporation preparing said product shall cause a label to be attached to said can, pot, tin, canvas, or other receptacle or covering, under the supervision of an inspector, which label shall state that the contents thereof have been "inspected and passed" under the provisions of this Act; and no inspection and examination of meat or meat food products deposited or inclosed in cans, tins, pots, canvas, or other receptacle or covering in any establishment where inspection under the provisions of this Act is maintained shall be deemed to be complete until such meat or meat food products have been sealed or inclosed in said can, tin, pot, canvas, or other receptacle or covering under the supervision of an inspector, and no such meat or meat food products shall be sold or offered for sale by any person, firm, or corporation in interstate or foreign commerce under any false or deceptive name; but established trade name or names which are usual to such products and which are not false and deceptive and which shall be approved by the Secretary of Agriculture are permitted.

The Secretary of Agriculture shall cause to be made, by experts in sanitation or by other competent inspectors, such inspection of all slaughtering, meat canning, salting, packing, rendering, or similar establishments in which cattle, sheep, swine, and goats are slaughtered and the meat and meat food products thereof are prepared for interstate or foreign commerce as may be necessary to inform himself concerning the sanitary conditions of the same, and to prescribe the rules and regulations of sanitation under which such establishments shall be maintained; and where the sanitary conditions of any such establishment are such that the meat or meat food products are rendered unclean, unsound, unhealthful, unwholesome, or otherwise unfit for human food, he shall refuse to allow said meat or meat food products to be labeled, marked, stamped, or tagged as "inspected and passed."

That the Secretary of Agriculture shall cause an examination and inspection of all cattle, sheep, swine, and goats, and the food products thereof, slaughtered and prepared in the establishments hereinbefore described for the purposes of interstate or foreign commerce to be made during the nighttime as well as during the daytime when the slaughtering of said cattle, sheep, swine, and goats, or the preparation of said food products is conducted during the nighttime.

Further Resources

BOOKS

Leffingwell, Albert. *American Meat: Its Methods of Production and Influence on Public Health.* New York: Schulte, 1910.

Libecap, Gary D. *The Rise of the Chicago Packers and The Origin of Meat Inspection and Antitrust.* Cambridge, Mass.: National Bureau of Economic Research, 1991.

Robertson, William. *Meat and Food Inspection.* Chicago: Keener, 1908.

PERIODICALS

"Between the Bread: Tougher Meat Inspection Necessary." *The Philadelphia Inquirer,* November 12, 2002, B4.

Purdum, Todd S. "Meat Inspection Facing Overhaul, First in 90 Years." *New York Times,* July 7, 1996, A1.

WEBSITES

"Federal Meat Inspection Act of 1906." U.S. House Committee on Agriculture. Available online at http://agriculture.house.gov/glossary/federal_meat_inspection_act_of_1906.htm; website home page: http://agriculture.house.gov (accessed March 15, 2003).

"Federal Meat Inspection Act of 1906." U.S. Department of Agriculture, Food and Safety Inspection Service. Available online at http://www.fsis.usda.gov/OFO/HRDS/STATE/food%20law/Aovervw/sld011.htm; website home page: http://www.fsis.usda.gov (accessed March 15, 2003).

"The Theodore Roosevelt Administration: Meat Inspection Act, 1906." U-S-History.com. Available online at http://www.u-s-history.com/pages/h918.html; website home page: http://www.u-s-history.com (accessed March 15, 2003).

AUDIO AND VISUAL MEDIA

Packer to Consumer. Creative Educational Videos. Videocassette, 1988.

Pure Food and Drug Act

Law

By: Harvey W. Wiley

Date: 1906

Source: Wiley, Harvey W. *Pure Food and Drug Act.* Matrix. Available online at http://coursesa.matrix.msu.edu/~hst203/documents/pure.html; website home page: http://coursesa.matrix.msu.edu (accessed March 15, 2003).

About the Author: Harvey W. Wiley (1844–1930) received his doctorate in chemistry from Harvard University in 1873. He was a professor of chemistry at Purdue University between 1874 and 1883 and chief of the Bureau of Chemistry in the U.S. Department of Agriculture between 1883 and 1912. He was also the author of the *Pure Food and Drug Act* of 1906. ■

Introduction

The safety and wholesomeness of food and drugs suffered a crisis of confidence at the beginning of the twentieth century. Two movements exposed contaminated and impure foods and ineffective and dangerous drugs.

The first movement was in 1900, when Theodore Roosevelt testified before Congress that he and his troops became ill eating the canned meat the U.S. Army served as rations during the Spanish-American War (1898). Following this congressional investigation, newspapers began to report on the quality of beef and pork.

In 1905, Upton Sinclair was hired by the *Appeal to Reason,* a socialist newspaper, to investigate the meatpackers. He eventually published his observations in *The Jungle* (1906), which revealed the filth that contaminated U.S. meat and caused a public uproar.

The second movement was sparked by writer Samuel Hopkins Adams, who in 1905 published a series of magazine articles that attacked the drug industry as a fraud. Many drugs had no medicinal value, wrote Adams. Instead, they filled patients with alcohol and opium. Some drugs were nothing more than diuretics, eliminating fluids from a person at the very time he or she needed to be hydrated to fight infection. Such drugs worsened rather than improved health. He stated that drug manufacturers cared nothing for the truth and advertised medicinal benefits they knew their drugs lacked.

Significance

The crisis peaked in 1906 when an outraged public demanded action. Roosevelt, by now president (served 1901–1909), saw an opportunity to enhance his reputation as a crusader for the public. Opposing Roosevelt and the public were the meatpackers and drug manufacturers. They pointed to the American tradition in which business regulated itself without governmental oversight, and they lobbied Congress to do nothing. But public uproar and Roosevelt's steady pressure forced Congress to act.

On June 30, 1906, Congress passed the *Meat Inspection Act,* which empowered the U.S. Department of Agriculture to ensure the safety and wholesomeness of U.S. meat. Had Congress gone no further, business might have been able to declare victory. True, the act put meatpackers under Department of Agriculture oversight, but other food manufacturers and all drug manufacturers could continue business as usual.

That day, however, Roosevelt also signed the *Pure Food and Drug Act.* The act empowered the Departments of the Treasury, Agriculture, and Commerce to inspect any "specimen" of food and drug for purity and truth in safety and labeling. Should the departments find manufacturers selling impure food and drugs or falsely advertising them, the act empowered federal courts to fine violators $500 and imprison them for a year.

Like the *Meat Inspection Act,* the *Pure Food and Drug Act* put public health above the right of business to maximize profit. The act reinforced the role of the federal government as protector of public health. It also demonstrated that a president backed by public support could compel business to guarantee the safety and wholesomeness of its products.

Primary Source

Pure Food and Drug Act [excerpt]

SYNOPSIS: The *Pure Food and Drug Act* empowered the Departments of the Treasury, Agriculture, and Commerce to inspect food and drugs for safety and labeling and for purity and truth. If the manufacturers were found to be selling impure food and drugs or falsely advertising them, the act empowered federal courts to fine and imprison violators.

For preventing the manufacture, sale, or transportation of adulterated or misbranded or poisonous or deleterious foods, drugs, medicines, and liquors, and for regulating traffic therein, and for other purposes.

Be it enacted by the Senate and House of Representatives of the United States of America in Congress assembled, That it shall be unlawful for any person to manufacture within any territory or the District of Columbia any article of food or drug which is adulterated or misbranded, within the meaning of this Act; and any person who shall violate any of the provisions of this section shall be guilty of a misdemeanor, and for each offense shall, upon conviction thereof, be fined not to exceed five hundred dollars or shall be sentenced to one year's imprisonment, or both such fine and imprisonment, in the discretion of the court, and for each subsequent offense and conviction thereof shall be fined not less than one thousand dollars or sentenced to one year's imprisonment, or both such fine and imprisonment, in the discretion of the court.

Sec. 2. That the introduction into any State or Territory or the District of Columbia from any other State or Territory or the District of Columbia, or from any foreign country, or shipment to any foreign country of any article of food or drugs which is adulterated or misbranded, within the meaning of this Act, is hereby prohibited; and any person who shall ship or deliver for shipment from any State or Territory or the District of Columbia to any other State or Territory or the District of Columbia, or to a foreign country, or who shall receive in any State or Territory or the District of Columbia from any other State or Territory or the District of Columbia, or foreign country, and having so received, shall deliver, in original unbroken packages, for pay or otherwise, or offer to deliver to any other person, any such article so adulterated or misbranded within the meaning of this Act, or any person who shall sell or offer for sale in the District of Columbia or the Territories of the United States any such adulterated or misbranded foods or drugs, or export or offer to export the same to any foreign country, shall be guilty of a misdemeanor, and for such offense be fined not exceeding two hundred dollars for the first offense, and upon conviction for each subsequent offense not exceeding three hundred dollars or be imprisoned not exceeding one year, or both, in the discretion of the court: Provided, That no article shall be deemed misbranded or adulterated within the provisions of this Act when intended for except to any foreign country and prepared or packed according to the specifications or directions of the foreign purchaser when no substance is used in the preparation or packing thereof in conflict with the laws of the foreign country to which said article is intended to be shipped; but if said article shall be in fact sold or offered for sale for domestic use or consumption, then this proviso shall not exempt said article from the operation of any of the other provisions of this Act.

Dr. Harvey W. Wiley, the Department of Agriculture's chief chemist, published findings on the widespread use of harmful preservatives in the meat-packing industry.

Sec. 3. That the Secretary of the Treasury, the Secretary of Agriculture, and the Secretary of Commerce and Labor shall make uniform rules and regulations for carrying out the provisions of this Act, including the collection and examination of specimens of foods and drugs manufactured or offered for sale in the District of Columbia, or in any Territory of the United States, or which shall be offered for sale in unbroken packages in any State other than that in which they shall have been respectively manufactured or produced, or which shall be received from any foreign country, or intended for shipment to any foreign country, or which may be submitted for examination by the chief health, food, or drug officer of any State, Territory, or the District of Columbia, or at any domestic or foreign port through which such product is offered for interstate commerce, or for export or import between the United States and any foreign port or country.

Sec. 4. That the examinations of specimens of foods and drugs shall be made in the Bureau of Chemistry of the Department of Agriculture, or under the direction and supervision of such Bureau, for the purpose of determining from such examinations whether such articles are adulterated or misbranded within the meaning of this Act; and if it shall appear from any such examination that any of such specimens is adulterated or misbranded within the meaning of this Act, the Secretary of Agriculture shall cause notice thereof to be given to the party from whom such sample was obtained. Any party so notified shall be given an opportunity to be heard, under such rules and regulations as may be prescribed as aforesaid, and if it appears that any of the provisions of this Act have been violated by such party, then the Secretary of Agriculture shall at once certify the facts to the proper United States district attorney, with a copy of the results of the analysis or the examination of such article duly authenticated by the analyst or officer making such examination, under the oath of such officer. After judgment of the court, notice shall be given by publication in such manner as may be prescribed by the rules and regulations aforesaid.

Sec. 5. That is shall be the duty of each district attorney to whom the Secretary of Agriculture shall report any violation of this Act, or to whom any health or food or drug officer or agent of any State, Territory, or the District of Columbia shall present satisfactory evidence of any such violation, to cause appropriate proceedings to be commenced and prosecuted in the proper courts of the United States, without delay, for the enforcement of the penalties as in such case herein provided.

Sec. 6. That the term “drug,” as used in this Act, shall include all medicines and preparations recognized in the United States Pharmacopoeia or National Formulary for internal or external use, and any substance or mixture of substances intended to be used for the cure, mitigation, or prevention of disease of either man or other animals. The term “food,” as used herein, shall include all articles used for food, drink, confectionery, or condiment by man or other animals, whether simple, mixed, or compound.

Sec. 7. That for the purposes of this Act an article shall be deemed to be adulterated:

In case of drugs:

First. If, when a drug is sold under or by a name recognized in the United States Pharmacopoeia or National Formulary, it differs from the standard of strength, quality, or purity, as determined by the test laid down in the United States Pharmacopoeia or National Formulary official at the time of investigation: Provided, That no drug defined in the United States Pharmacopoeia or National Formulary shall be deemed to be adulterated under this provision if the standard of strength, quality, or purity be plainly stated upon the bottle, box, or other container thereof although the standard may differ from that determined by the test laid down in the United States Pharmacopoeia or National Formulary.

Second. If its strength or purity fall below the professed standard or quality under which it is sold.

In the case of confectionery:

If it contain terra alba, barytes, talc, chrome yellow, or other mineral substance or poisonous color or flavor, or other ingredient deleterious or detrimental to health, or any vinous, malt or spirituous liquor or compound or narcotic drug.

In the case of food:

First. If any substance has been mixed and packed with it so as to reduce or lower or injuriously affect its quality or strength.

Second. If any substance has been substituted wholly or in part for the article.

Third. If any valuable constituent of the article has been wholly or in part abstracted.

Fourth. If it be mixed, colored, powdered, coated, or stained in a manner whereby damage or inferiority is concealed.

Fifth. If it contain any added poisonous or other added deleterious ingredient which may render such article injurious to health: Provided, That when in the preparation of food products for shipment they are preserved by any external application applied in such manner that the preservative is necessarily removed mechanically, or by maceration in water, or otherwise, and directions for the removal of said preservative shall be printed on the covering or the package, the provisions of this Act shall be construed as applying only when said products are ready for consumption.

Sixth. If it consists in whole or in part of a filthy, decomposed, or putrid animal or vegetable substance, or any portion of an animal unfit for food, whether manufactured or not, or if it is the product of a diseased animal, or one that has died otherwise than by slaughter.

Further Resources

BOOKS

Kline, Mahlon N. *Digest of National Food and Drugs Act and Regulations.* Philadelphia: Smith, Kline and French, 1907.

Robertson, William. *Meat and Food Inspection.* Chicago: Keener, 1908.

U.S. Department of Agriculture. *Decisions of Courts in Cases Under the Federal Food and Drugs Act.* Washington, D.C.: U.S. Government Printing Office, 1934.

PERIODICALS

"Early Drug Laws." *Congressional Quarterly Researcher,* July 28, 2000, 604–607.

"Safer and Healthier Foods." *Morbidity and Mortality Weekly Report,* October 15, 1999, 905–913.

"Stamp Marks Early Public Health Law." *FDA Consumer,* March–April 1998, 4.

Weisberger, Bernard A. "Dr. Wiley and His Poison Squad." *American Heritage,* February–March 1996, 14–16.

WEBSITES

"Harvey Washington Wiley." U.S. Food and Drug Administration, Center for Drug Evaluation and Research. Available online at http://www.fda.gov/cder/about/history/BioWiley.htm; website home page: http://www.fda.gov (accessed March 15, 2003).

"The Pure Food and Drug Act." Forces International. Available online at http://www.forces.org/articles/files/whiteb/white02.htm; website home page: http://www.forces.org (accessed March 15, 2003).

"Pure Food and Drug Act." U-S-History.com. Available online at http://www.u-s-history.com/pages/h917.html; website home page: http://www.u-s-history.com (accessed March 15, 2003).

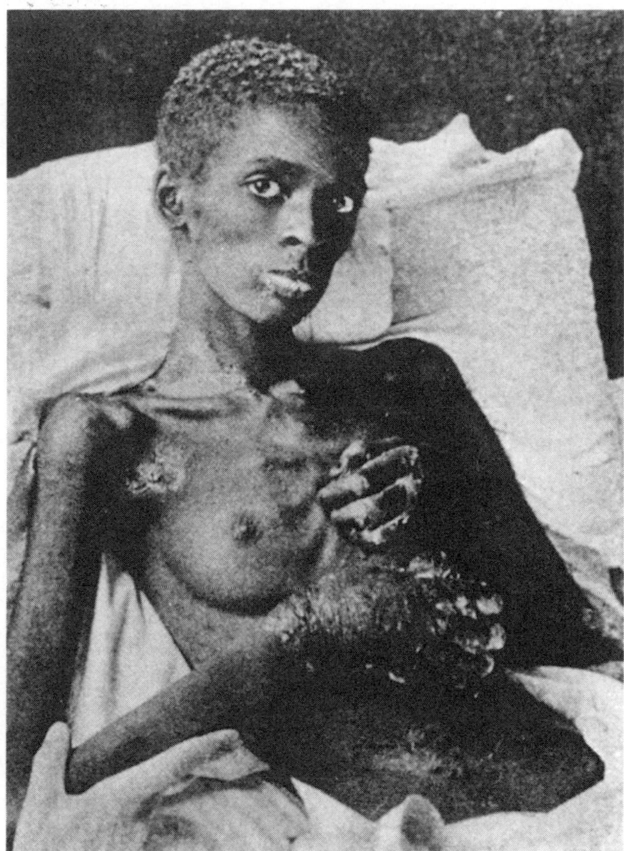

A Pellagra victim from South Carolina. **REPRINTED FROM DAPHNE A. ROE, *A PLAGUE OF CORN; THE SOCIAL HISTORY OF PELLAGRA,* CORNELL UNIVERSITY PRESS, 1973.**

"An Epidemic of Acute Pellagra"

Journal article

By: George H. Searcy

Date: July 6, 1907

Source: Searcy, George H. "An Epidemic of Acute Pellagra." *Journal of the American Medical Association,* July 6, 1907, 37–38.

About the Author: George H. Searcy (1871–1947) received his doctorate in medicine from the University of Pittsburgh in 1895. His interest in the diseases of poverty led him to study patients at the Mount Vernon Insane Hospital, an asylum for blacks in Alabama, where he attributed the incidence of pellagra to a microbe in corn. Although this idea was wrong, it focused attention on corn, a culprit in the disease. ■

Introduction

U.S. scientists discovered the first vitamin in 1914, with others to follow. By 1940, nutritionists had come to understand that humans needed a minimum intake of calories, protein, vitamins, and minerals for good health. The next year, the National Academy of Sciences and the U.S. Department of Agriculture issued the first dietary guidelines of protein, calories, vitamins, and minerals: the Recommended Daily Allowances.

Before the 1940s, nutritionists and physicians had difficulty identifying diseases that arose from dietary deficiencies. Pellagra was a classic case, resulting from a deficiency of niacin, a vitamin discovered in the 1920s.

The human body can process niacin from foods or synthesize it from the amino acid tryptophan. In the absence of sufficient niacin or tryptophan, humans suffer from pellagra. In its early stages, pellagra causes fatigue, weakness, weight loss, headaches, indigestion, backaches, and skin inflammations. Severe cases produce dark, scaly dermatitis, as though the victim suffers from acute sunburn. The mouth, tongue, and lips redden and become sore, making it difficult for victims to eat. Victims experience nausea, vomiting, and diarrhea. They may also appear confused and disoriented, mental states that may deepen into hallucinations and paranoia. Death follows unless victims consume sufficient niacin or tryptophan, a fact no physician could have known in 1907.

Around 1900, pellagra was endemic to the southern United States where corn was a dietary staple. Corn is naturally low in both niacin and tryptophan, and milling reduces the amount of these nutrients even further. Other staples—bacon fat and molasses—added neither niacin nor tryptophan to southern diets. This diet was the norm for the poor. Pellagra thus emerged as a disease of poverty as much as of diet.

Significance

George H. Searcy drew attention to pellagra in 1907 when he reported several cases, a majority of which were fatal, at Mount Vernon Insane Hospital. Searcy cautioned physicians against drawing the popular but incorrect inference that pellagra resulted from mental illness.

With remarkable prescience, Searcy identified the culprit in the patients' nutrient-poor diet. He sent a sample of corn meal to a Department of Agriculture plant pathologist in Washington, D.C., who declared the meal "unfit for human use" because it was full of bacteria and fungi.

Searcy went wrong, however, when he suspected, on the basis of the plant pathologist's report, that a microbe in corn caused pellagra. The explanation was simpler, though Searcy could not have known it then: corn is deficient in both niacin and tryptophan. As such, corn needed no microbe to cause disease.

Regardless, Searcy came close to recognizing dietary deficiency as a culprit for, by his orders, those who developed symptoms switched their diet to potatoes and wheat bread, foods that restored their health, partially because they contained sufficient amounts of niacin and tryptophan.

Searcy's work established a link between diet and disease and helped elevate the study of nutrition to a science. He also established a link between poverty, which was often the cause of a poor diet, and disease. This connection bothered southerners, who did not want anyone calling attention to poverty, much less racism, in the South. This opposition made it difficult for medicine to fight the intertwined evils of poverty and disease, and only in the 1960s would President Lyndon B. Johnson (served 1963–1969), himself a southerner, demand progress against poverty and disease by declaring war on poverty.

Primary Source

"An Epidemic of Acute Pellagra" [excerpt]

SYNOPSIS: In this excerpt, Searcy reports eighty-eight cases of pellagra, with fifty-seven of them being fatal, at Mount Vernon Insane Hospital. He discusses the symptoms, diagnosis, pathology, prognosis and treatment, and general observations. Ultimately, he identifies corn meal as a cause of pellagra. The real reason for what caused pellagra—a diet deficient in both niacin and tryptophan—was not fully understood until the 1940s.

Last summer at the Mount Vernon Insane Hospital, the hospital for colored insane in Alabama, there appeared a few cases of a disease which had been noticed every summer since the patients had been moved there from Tuscaloosa in 1901. Some three or four cases of this disease would occur during each summer and they usually proved fatal. The true nature of the disease was not recognized, and in most instances it was supposed to be a condition of general debility. . . .

There occurred at the Mount Vernon Hospital during the late summer and early fall of 1906 eighty-eight cases of acute pellagra, with fifty-seven deaths—a mortality of about 64 per cent. . . .

A sample of the meal used at the Mount Vernon Hospital, which was supposed to be the best western meal, was sent to the pathologist in charge of the laboratory of plant pathology at Washington, and he reported the meal wholly unfit for human use; that it was made of moldy grain and contained quantities of bacteria and fungi of various sorts, some of which were identified.

In addition to the eating of damaged corn, the sun has been supposed to have much to do with the cause of pellagra, as the cutaneous lesions appear in those places exposed to the sun's rays, as back of hands, back of feet, face and neck. It is now generally accepted, however, that the chemical rays simply have more or less influence on the severity of the skin lesions and do not cause them. . . .

One case in the epidemic at Mount Vernon, in which the patient wore a band around his wrist, showed a severe erythema above and below the band, but beneath it the skin was but slightly affected. In some cases there is no doubt that the sun makes the skin lesions more severe, but severe skin lesions do occur in those who wear shoes and are exposed to the sun but little. . . .

It is generally accepted now, however, that pellagra is caused by eating a substance formed by the growth of certain organisms in corn. This substance attacks the central nervous system, affecting trophic centers, and the chemical rays of the sun influence, more or less, the severity of the lesions in those regions whose trophic centers are affected and which are exposed to the sun.

Symptoms of Acute Pellagra

The disease appears mostly in the summer months and first manifests itself by lassitude, weakness and a general run-down condition. The digestive tract becomes disarranged, giving rise to more or less gastric and intestinal disturbances with toxemia. The characteristic signs all appear about the same time. These are the skin lesions and those symptoms arising from the alimentary tract. The mouth becomes somewhat sore and red and there is a profuse flow of saliva accompanied by digestive disturbances, more or less diarrhea and considerable toxemia.

About the same time there appears a congestion or erythema in one or more well-defined locations, as the back of the hands and lower forearms, dorsal surface of the feet, back of the neck and on the face about the cheek bones. The skin in these regions becomes red and congested, with no pain and but slight itching or burning sensations. In a few days either vesicles and bullæ form, under which the surface is raw, weeping and not infrequently fissured, or the epidermis dries and desquamates, leaving a slightly-pigmented surface, or in some cases the skin becomes dry, thick and more heavily pigmented. In those cases where vesicles and bullæ form these break and the epidermis peels off, leaving a raw surface, which, if the patient survives, gradually heals over, leaving a thin, silk-like and slightly darker skin.

When the salivation and the dermatitis appear the patient usually takes to bed from general weakness, complaining but little of any pain or discomfort, and showing more or less dulness and depression, and as the disease progresses this dull condition becomes more marked. The temperature rarely goes more than a degree and a half above normal, and the pulse follows the temperature curve very closely. The fatal cases may prove rapidly so, in a week or ten days from the time they take to bed, or they may run on several weeks, the pulse gradually getting weaker and a little more rapid and the patient finally dying from general weakness.

When recovery follows, convalescence is very slow, the patient remaining weak and more or less dull a month or more, and even for several months remains below normal.

Diagnosis

The disease is to be differentiated from scurvy, acrodynia, purpura, erythema multiforme and allied conditions by the characteristic signs. These are the parts affected: back of hands, lower forearms, face and dorsal surface of feet; the character of the skin lesion, a dermatitis followed by vesiculation or desquamation with some pigmentation; the disturbances of the alimentary tract, salivation and more or less diarrhea; the depression; the toxemia and the absence of any pain and of any swelling or hemorrhage of the gums. If to these is added the fact that the patient has lived largely on corn products the diagnosis becomes more certain.

Pathology

The pathologic findings, as far as worked out, are pachymeningitis, some sclerosis of the brain and cord, fatty degeneration of the internal organs and those changes in the skin which follow varying degrees of erythema.

Prognosis and Treatment

The prognosis in acute cases, as in the Mount Vernon epidemic, is always unfavorable, death ensuing in most cases in from two to three weeks; others run longer. Recovery in any case is very slow, the patient remaining for months feeble and more or less depressed.

As for the treatment, there are no specific remedies. The essential management consists in placing the patient in good hygienic surroundings and trying to improve the general health by good nourishing food and such tonics as may seem indicated. Arsenic, iron and pepsin preparations were the remedies on which most support was placed and which sometimes seemed to influence the disease favorably. . . .

No nurses had the disease. They handled the patients, slept in the halls near them, and the chief difference in their way of living was in the diet. They ate little corn bread, mostly flour bread, biscuits, etc., and had a little more variety of diet.

As soon as the nature of the disease was determined and the true cause suspected the patients were taken off corn bread and grits and wheat bread and potatoes substituted. The rest of their diet was continued as before. No new cases, except the one in the test case, appeared after about ten days. A set of eight patients was kept on the former diet with corn bread and grits as a test. One of these developed the disease, another began to show symptoms, and all became in such poor general health that their diet was changed also.

Since attention has been called to this disease some four or five cases have been recognized in the

Hospital for the Insane at Tuscaloosa. I believe that when it becomes generally known that pellagra may occur in this country we will have more cases reported, especially in the south, where corn bread and grits are so largely used.

Reports from Italy show that the disease often occurs in jails, poorhouses, asylums, etc., where corn products are used so largely as diet, and also among the peasants who use a great deal of corn; and it is shown that in southern Italy, where the grain ripens earlier and better, there is not so much pellagra as in the provinces north of Rome.

I have been informed that much of the western corn crop of 1905 was badly damaged by wet weather at harvesting time, and since it is known that pellagra may occur in this country it behooves the government to see, under the pure food laws, that no damaged corn is used for food purposes.

I will say that the grits sent to Washington for examination came up to the standard, and during the winter this food has been added again to the diet at Mount Vernon. No new cases have developed since last summer; some of the old cases are still hanging on, and it remains to be seen whether any new cases will develop or the old ones relapse this coming summer.

Further Resources

BOOKS

Carpenter, Kenneth J., ed. *Pellagra.* Stroudsburg, Penn.: Hutchinson Ross, 1981.

Etheridge, Elizabeth W. *The Strange Hunger: A Social History of Pellagra in the South.* Ann Arbor, Mich.: University Microfilms, 1967.

Harris, Henry F. *Pellagra.* New York: Macmillan, 1919.

Niles, George N. *Pellagra: An American Problem.* Philadelphia: Saunders, 1916.

Professional Guide to Diseases. 6th ed. Springhouse, Penn.: Springhouse, 1998.

Roe, Daphne A. *A Plague of Corn: The Social History of Pellagra.* Ithaca, N.Y.: Cornell University Press, 1973.

PERIODICALS

Karthikeyan, Kaliaperumal, and Devinder M. Theppa. "Pellagra and Skin." *International Journal of Dermatology,* August 2002, 476–482.

WEBSITES

"Colloidal Minerals: Niacin." Colloidal Mineral Health Resource Center. Available online at http://www.eagle-min.com/faq/faq100.htm; website home page: http://www.eagle-min.com (accessed March 15, 2003).

"MEDLINEplus Medical Encyclopedia: Pellagra." MEDLINEplus Health Information. Available online at http://www.nlm.nih.gov/medlineplus/ency/article/000342.htm; website home page: http://www.nlm.nih.gov/medlineplus (accessed March 15, 2003).

"Pellagra." *World Book Medical Encyclopedia.* Available online at http://www.rush.edu/worldbook/articles/016000a/016000085.html; website home page: http://www.rush.edu/worldbook (accessed February 5, 2003).

"People and Discoveries: Pellagra Shown to Be Dietary Disease." Public Broadcasting Service. Available online at http://www.pbs.org/wgbh/aso/databank/entries/dm15pa.html; website home page: http://www.pbs.org (accessed March 15, 2003).

"Pellagra." *World Book Medical Encyclopedia.* Available online at http://www.rush.edu/worldbook/articles/016000a/016000085.html; website home page: http://www.rush.edu/worldbook (accessed February 5, 2003).

Letter to Commissioner of Indian Affairs Francis E. Leupp

Letter

By: Susan La Flesche Picotte

Date: November 15, 1907

Source: Picotte, Susan La Flesche. Letter to Commissioner of Indian Affairs Francis E. Leupp, November 15, 1907. U.S. National Library of Medicine. Available online at http://www.nlm.nih.gov/exhibition/if_you_knew/images.dir/letter-1a.jpg, http://www.nlm.nih.gov/exhibition/if_you_knew/images.dir/letter-1b.jpg; website home page: http://www.nlm.nih.gov (accessed March 15, 2003).

About the Author: Susan La Flesche Picotte (1865–1915), graduating first in her class, received her doctorate in medicine from the Women's Medical College of Pennsylvania in 1889. The first American Indian woman physician, Picotte treated American Indians on the Omaha Reservation in Nebraska from 1889 to 1893, when her own health began to deteriorate. She also worked to raise awareness in the Bureau of Indian Affairs of the American Indians' medical needs. ■

Introduction

American Indians crossed from Siberia to North America some thirteen thousand years ago, at the end of the last Ice Age. Thereafter cut off from the people of Europe, Asia, and Africa, they did not develop resistance to the diseases that afflicted the Old World. The Spanish, arriving in the sixteenth century, and the English, in the seventeenth century, brought with them smallpox, tuberculosis, influenza, measles, and other diseases to which American Indians had no immunity. Pandemics swept the New World, killing as much as 90 percent of American Indians.

Europeans regarded these deaths as evidence that American Indians were inherently sickly and could only survive if they adopted Western medicine. Physicians stressed the importance of sanitary conditions in preventing the spread of diseases among American Indians. In 1909, physician Henry R. Wheeler of the Fort Hall Agency in Idaho reported to the Bureau of Indian Affairs his efforts at teaching American Indians to bathe themselves and their infants regularly, to eat a wholesome diet, and to take in fresh air. Wheeler reported 277 cases of illness at the agency that year; 131 cases were due to the mumps and 5 to tuberculosis. He blamed American Indian reliance on "the 'Old Medicine Man'" for fatal cases of pneumonia and influenza on the reservation. His message was clear: American Indians who clung to their traditions were helpless against disease. Only those who adopted modern medicine could fight illness.

Significance

Susan La Flesche Picotte had adopted modern medicine, a fact that led one of her medical school professors to praise her as a model for "her people." In a 1907 letter to Francis E. Leupp, the commissioner of Indian Affairs, Picotte described the stress of being the only physician for an entire tribe of American Indians on a Nebraska reservation. In the first sentence, she admitted to having "broken down from overwork." She asked the commissioner for two more people to lessen the workload. She felt an urgency in her request, writing that her poor health would prevent her from working "for 6 months."

Meanwhile, tuberculosis spread through the reservation, afflicting American Indians "something terrible." She reported that it struck the lungs, kidneys, brain, blood, and glands and that children were particularly vulnerable to the disease. She assured the commissioner she had done "all [she] could to prevent infection and contagion" and that she would be grateful to him for the Bureau of Indian Affairs' help in fighting the disease.

Picotte's letter demonstrates the difficulties of practicing medicine among American Indians in the first decade of the twentieth century. Picotte, short of manpower and resources, had to beg the Bureau of Indian Affairs for help. Bureaucrats in Washington, D.C., rather than Picotte, made the decisions regarding medical care for American Indians, and Picotte's letter implies that the political elite in Washington did not regard American Indian health as a priority.

There is a sense of isolation in her letter. Picotte was a woman physician at a time when men monopolized the profession. More than that, she was the first American Indian woman physician and was responsible for the care of an entire tribe. Although her letter is not explicit, the reservation agent and nurse already stationed at the reservation were likely white, leaving her as the only American Indian in a capacity to make decisions. Also, she could not turn to other American Indians for guidance because they had no medical knowledge.

Susan La Fleshe Picotte was the first Native American woman M.D. NATIONAL ANTHROPOLOGICAL ARCHIVES, SMITHSONIAN INSTITUTION, PHOTO NO. 4503.

Primary Source

Letter to Commissioner of Indian Affairs Francis E. Leupp

SYNOPSIS: In this letter, Picotte describes her work as an American Indian physician on a Nebraska reservation in 1907. Short of manpower and resources, she is struggling to battle an epidemic of tuberculosis that is ravaging the reservation. Her only recourse is to beg the Bureau of Indian Affairs for help.

Nov. 15, 1907

St. Vincent's Hospital
Sioux City, Iowa
Hon. Francis E. Leupp

Dear Sir:

I am an Omaha Indian and have been working as medical missionary among the Omahas but have broken down from overwork. Altho' I have been here several weeks I have kept in touch with affairs at Macy.

I know what a small figure our affairs cut with-all the Department has on its hands, but I also know that if you knew the conditions and circumstances, to be remedied you would do all you could to remedy them.

I understand Mr. Commons, our Agent, has been cut off from a stenographer.

It takes most of his time answering necessary correspondence and the affairs of the Indians have to be neglected.

Mr. Commons is a good man, and does all he can for the Indians, but under the circumstances he can't do clerical work and attend to the Indians' wants too, so we need a stenographer. Mr. Commons has told me nothing of this.

Second: We need another Field Matron besides the one we have now, Miss Collett. She is doing fine work and the Indians like her very much, but there is more than enough work for another one. We would like to have Miss Sallie Hagan, who is day school teacher, and is known to Maj. Lanabe personally. The Indians are working better and so drinking much less they are beginning to get interested in the church and now is the time when they are beginning to climb up, that they need the most help and this help can be given to them thru the field matrons. We would want Miss Hagan, for the Indians like her and she is sympathetic, and they would allow her to do things for them, they would not allow anyone else to do.

I asked Mr. Commons and Maj. Hutchings if they tho't the Government would allow us one—they spoke of a man but it's essentially a woman's work, and the man would have to be a second Henry Drummond, (and such men are scarce) in order to work successfully among the Indians.

I had intended to do so much work this fall—the Doctor tells me I cannot do any medical work for 6 mos. and I feel that something must be done for the people such as our field matron is doing now, real missionary work, for you can't rush at the Indians with an open Bible anymore than you can the white people.

Will you please give us Miss Hagan beside Miss Collett?

Third: The spread of Tuberculosis among my people is something terrible—it shows itself in the lungs, kidneys, alimentary track, blood, brain and glands—so many many, of the young children are marked with it in some form. The physical degeneration in 20 years among any people is terrible. I have talked with them and done all I could to prevent infection and contagion, but I want to know if the Gov't can't do for us, what it did for the Sioux, in preventing the spread of this White-Plague.

The financial outlay for any of these three requests is but small compared to the amount of good it will bring forth to my people.

Most Respectfully—
Susan La Flesche Picotte, M.D.

Further Resources

BOOKS

Ferris, Jeri. *Native American Doctor: The Story of Susan LaFlesche Picotte.* Minneapolis, Minn.: Carolrhoda, 1991.

Tong, Benson. *Susan La Flesche Picotte, M.D.: Omaha Indian Leader and Reformer.* Norman: University of Oklahoma Press, 1999.

PERIODICALS

Noelke, Virginia. "Susan La Flesche Picotte, M.D." *Isis,* December 2001, 799–801.

Parker, Judy. "A Doctor for Her People." *Jack and Jill,* June 2002, 32–34.

Reese, Linda. "Susan La Flesche Picotte, M.D." *American Indian Quarterly,* Spring 1999, 100–102.

WEBSITES

"'If You Knew the Conditions . . . ': Health Care to Native Americans." U.S. National Library of Medicine. Available online at http://www.nlm.nih.gov/exhibition/if_you_knew/if_you_knew_01.html; website home page: http://www.nlm.nih.gov (accessed March 15, 2003).

"Indian School Hospitals Under the Office of Indian Affairs (c.1883–c.1916)." U.S. National Library of Medicine. Available online at http://www.nlm.nih.gov/exhibition/if_you_knew/if_you_knew_05.html; website home page: http://www.nlm.nih.gov (accessed March 15, 2003).

"Reservation and Hospital Care Under the Office of Indian Affairs (c.1890–1925)." U.S. National Library of Medicine. Available online at http://www.nlm.nih.gov/exhibition/if_you_knew/if_you_knew_06.html; website home page: http://www.nlm.nih.gov (accessed March 15, 2003).

"Susan La Flesche Picotte (1865–1915)." U.S. National Library of Medicine. Available online at http://www.nlm.nih.gov/exhibition/if_you_knew/if_you_knew_12.html; website home page: http://www.nlm.nih.gov (accessed March 15, 2003).

"United States 19th-Century Doctors' Thoughts About Native American Medicine." U.S. National Library of Medicine. Available online at http://www.nlm.nih.gov/exhibition/if_you_knew/if_you_knew_04.html; website home page: http://www.nlm.nih.gov (accessed March 15, 2003).

"The Conduct of a Plague Campaign"

Journal article

By: Rupert Blue

Date: February 1, 1908

Source: Blue, Rupert. "The Conduct of a Plague Campaign." *Journal of the American Medical Association,* February 1, 1908, 327–329.

About the Author: Rupert Blue (1868–1948) was born in Richmond County, North Carolina, and received his doctorate in medicine from the University of Maryland in 1892. The following year, he joined the Marine Hospital Service as an assistant surgeon. He worked with health officials throughout the United States in combating plague and yellow fever. Between 1912 and 1920, he was the U.S. surgeon general. ■

Introduction

The bacterium *Yersinia pestis* causes plague. The bacterium lives in the gut of the flea *Xenopsylla cheopis,* which transmits the bacterium to mammals by biting them, much as female mosquitoes transmit malaria, yellow fever, and the West Nile Virus by biting humans. Plague is usually a disease of small mammals like rodents. Infected fleas can transmit plague to humans, though both the spread of the disease and its lethality vary with outbreaks of plague.

Plague exists in three forms. The first is bubonic plague, whose symptoms include fever and swollen lymph nodes, which humans have since antiquity called "buboes," hence the name "bubonic plague." In virulent cases, the buboes appear black, thereby giving the victims a frightening appearance. The second form is pneumonic plague, in which bacteria infect the lungs. The lungs secrete mucus to protect them from bacteria, but because bacteria of this form of plague spread so rapidly, the lungs are forced to secrete too much mucus, so much so that the victim drowns in it. Pneumonic plague spreads rapidly through coughing and is more lethal than bubonic plague. The third form is septicemic plague, in which bacteria spread throughout the blood. Medieval accounts describe victims who bled through the mouth, nose, and even eyes. They were likely victims of septicemic plague, which is highly lethal and is perhaps the most frightening manifestation of plague. Medieval accounts record victims who writhed in pain and saw hallucinations before death.

Historical accounts indicate that plague was endemic to ancient Asia, spreading along the trade routes to Europe. Plague afflicted the Roman Empire in the second century A.D. A larger outbreak struck Europe in 542, and the greatest pandemic killed as much as half of Europe's population between 1347 and 1351, though some historians doubt plague was the culprit. Of the three forms, only pneumonic plague can spread rapidly enough to cause high mortality. Pneumonic plague spreads during winter, yet the disease that struck fourteenth-century Europe raged during the summer months and abated with cool weather.

Significance

Europeans brought plague along with other diseases to the New World in the sixteenth century. Typical of a mortality rate that is normally low for humans, plague took fewer lives than smallpox, malaria, dysentery, typhus, tuberculosis, typhoid, and yellow fever. The danger lay in the transmission of plague from rats harboring fleas on a merchant ship. The commercial cities—New York City, Philadelphia, and Charleston in the east and San Francisco in the west—ran the most risk of outbreaks. Because plague appears to have arisen in Asia, San Francisco was vulnerable to infestation from a Chinese merchant vessel.

In March 1900, a Chinese American, likely a dockworker, died of plague in San Francisco, the first casualty of the new century. Twenty-one additional cases surfaced that year in the city. By the end of 1902, the number rose to one hundred. Plague ebbed early in 1904 with a second outbreak in 1906.

In his 1908 article "The Conduct of a Plague Campaign," Rupert Blue discussed what the public health officials were doing in San Francisco to eradicate plague. Blue focused attention on the destruction of rats, depriving fleas of the hosts, thereby lessening the number of fleas that could infect humans.

The Citizens' Health Committee of San Francisco vigorously applied Blue's measures in 1906, checking plague's spread in the city and ending the final outbreak of the disease in San Francisco during the decade. Plague has erupted periodically since, but never with the high degree of mortality of earlier centuries.

Primary Source

"The Conduct of a Plague Campaign" [excerpt]

SYNOPSIS: In this excerpt, Blue outlines the steps public health officials took in San Francisco to stamp out plague. He urges health officials to scrutinize every home where they suspect plague, to identify sanctuaries for rats and have those rats exterminated, to evacuate buildings with confirmed cases of plague and sanitize them, and to destroy buildings with repeated cases of plague.

To be successful, the campaign of eradication must be based on a knowledge of the etiology, mode of transmission and the causes of the continuance of the disease. First of all, the campaign should be conducted by a trained corps of medical men having

Health officials examine rats to determine if they are carrying bubonic plague in New Orleans, 1914. © CORBIS. REPRODUCED BY PERMISSION.

few local affiliations or prejudices, able to devote their entire time to the work, and backed by the strong arm of the government. No matter how earnest and conscientious the local authorities may be in the discharge of their duties, their plans of operation do not always meet with that acceptance and approbation which is accorded an outsider. Personal and political differences often arise to hamper the best efforts of an honest and capable board of health, and often render futile the plans which would have ensured a successful issue. Given a special plague department, heartily backed by the local authorities, and the people they represent, provide them with sufficient funds and power to act, and the stamping out of the disease is almost certain.

The duties of this department, briefly summarized are: The location and determination of plague cases, both human and rodent; the tracing of the source of infection in each case, and the destruction of the infecting agents. The destruction of rat habitations as far as possible; the abolition of the means of rat sustenance; and the protection of all places of human residence against the ingress of rodents. . . .

The following excerpt from the instructions issued to medical officers in the field outlines the routine measures for plague infected localities:

Upon the occurrence of a case of plague in a block, and when the infection is thought to have been contracted in that locality, concentrate a sufficient force to carry out, in as short a time as possible, the following measures in addition to the disinfection of the infected house.

A rapid sanitary survey of the infected and contiguous blocks. (a) Note the cases of sickness at the time and for the past six weeks in each house; (b) number of stables, their condition as to sewer connections, character of flooring, number of stalls, and the meat markets and bakeries for the same conditions; (c) sanitary condition of occupied premises and vacant lots with regard to rat food and harboring places; (d) note the prevalence of rats, and especially if dead rats have been seen recently. The inspector will enter every house in search of this information and impress on householders the necessity of destroying rats and rat-food, and of making their homes rat-proof. If a case of plague has gone unrecognized in the family, as shown by the sanitary history of the house, the facts should at once be reported to headquarters.

The rat-holes and runs in the infected and adjoining houses should be flooded with carbolic solution (1 to 40) or bichlorid of mercury solution (1 to 500) and then treated as follows: Holes in wooden floors to be sealed with tin or sheet metal; brick or concrete, with cement; earthen holes to be filled with broken glass and brick.

(a) Place poisons, preferably phosphorus and arsenic pastes, in holes and runs in the infected and contiguous blocks; (b) place traps, both spring and cage, over the same ground. (c) Danysz' virus of high virulence should be placed in cellars, kitchens and households generally.

Depopulation of infected sections with the destruction of infected buildings has succeeded in several instances in the present epidemic in stopping the march of the disease. This applies particularly to the irregular camps in the North Beach and Lobos Square districts. In dark, damp places, without adequate means of ventilation, alterations should be made to correct these insanitary evils. Limewashing is an old but effective measure, and may be applied by spray pumps or brushes.

When plague continues to manifest itself in a house, or a locality after a thorough disinfection has been done, make a careful search in the neighborhood for the cause of the continuance. All harboring places and places in which rat-food is found in abundance should be looked on with suspicion. Defective wooden floors, and walls of the infected house and the adjoining houses may be torn out and a search made for rat cadavers. Stables and restaurants may be treated in a like manner. In 1903, 87 dead rats were found in the walls of a Chinese restaurant. Eleven rats showed plague infection. After the destruction of this focus no further cases occurred. . . .

It is a curious fact that the morbidity and mortality rate from plague in rats is frequently low. This fact probably assists in keeping the disease alive, for if it spread rapidly among the rats they would soon be exterminated and the chief source of infection to human beings would cease. Under the closest observation during the Hong Kong epidemic only 7 per cent of the rats examined had plague, while in the present epidemic in San Francisco the percentage has been found to be less than one per cent. The disease also exists in chronic forms in rats, the bacteria being encapsulated in the viscera and cervical and inguinal glands. The service laboratory in Chinatown, during the previous epidemic, demonstrated the virulence of the organisms recovered from the bodies of such rats. These rats were found alive, emaciated to be sure, but still ambulatory foci for the spread of the infection. This, in my opinion, is one of the principal causes of the continuance of the disease and the long intermissions between cases. . . .

This knowledge suggests several important measures in plague eradication; namely: 1. All houses should be made rat-proof. 2. The screening and protection of food. 3. Disinfection of infected houses to destroy bacteria as well as suctorial and scavenger insects. . . .

The fact is often overlooked that it is as important to find and eradicate plague infection among rats as it is among human beings. Careful search, then, should be made for the cadavers of rats during plague times. Those that have died recently should be sent in for bacteriologic examination; bodies in which putrefaction has occurred should be burned. The measures that should be adopted to stamp out rat-plague are the same as those recommended for human plague. Every rat focus should be considered as a possible human focus, and the most active measures instituted immediately on its discovery. Rat contacts should be kept under observation and inspected daily for a period of seven days.

All defective buildings in which rats dead of plague have been found should be vacated at once to prevent the occurrence of the disease among human beings. The same rule applies to adjoining houses. Buildings in which plague continues to appear, in spite of the measures enumerated above, should be vacated and destroyed. These rules are in addition to careful general sanitation, the disinfection of infected houses, and the isolation of those sick of the disease.

Of the means employed in San Francisco for the destruction of the rat, trapping and poisoning on a large scale are chiefly relied on. Two varieties of traps are used, the cage and the spring, or snap-traps.

These are apportioned between the laborers, one of whom cares for from 30 to 40 traps in a forenoon, the afternoon being used in placing poisons. Cheese, bacon, fish, sausage, green fruits and vegetables are used for bait. The poisons used have included plaster-of-Paris flour, phosphorus and arsenic pastes. The latter two are the most reliable. . . .

As previously stated, all rat food and harboring places should be destroyed. The city should be given a thorough cleaning, the piles of debris removed and lumber piled two feet above ground. All places of human residence should be made rat-proof by the concreting of basements, the screening of all windows and entrances near the ground level, and the careful fitting of plumbing to the holes through which it enters and leaves the house. Stables and markets are a great menace. All stables should be concreted, connected with sewers, have proper manure boxes and metal-lined containers for feed and grain. The stable which does not conform to the above should be condemned and vacated. Warehouses should be similarly rat-proofed and the articles stored therein protected against the lodgment of rats.

In view of the danger of the shipment of infected rats in freight, the wharves and piers should be constructed of stone or concrete and all goods stored thereon placed on platforms elevated from one to two feet above the floor level. Long piers extending into the harbor of a city in which plague prevails should be protected by a drawbridge which can be elevated at night. A less expensive arrangement for the accumulation and temporary storage of cargoes could be made by sectioning off a part of a wharf by rat-proof fences and placing suitable guards on the ceilings, girders and rafters.

There can be no doubt that rats and similar vermin mechanically transfer other diseases from the sewers to human dwellings. Therefore, I would recommend the rat-proofing of sewers. Wherever possible, the old brick and mortar sewer should be replaced by concrete, metal or vitrified clay sewers of proper diameter. The junction of the soil pipe and the main is the weakest point and one brick out of place in this locality forms a point of ingress and egress for the sewer rat who gorges himself with all manner of filth and pollution to return and disseminate the disease germs to man. To prevent stagnation of contents, the sewers should be flushed frequently. This also washes out large numbers of dead rats that have died of plague and may infect their kindred which are liable to feed on these carcasses.

Further Resources

BOOKS

Link, Vernon B. *A History of Plague in the United States of America.* Washington, D.C.: U.S. Government Printing Office, 1955.

Professional Guide to Diseases. 6th ed. Springhouse, Penn.: Springhouse, 1998.

Rail, Chester D. *Plague Ecotoxicology: Including History Aspects of the Disease in the Americas and the Eastern Hemisphere.* Springfield, Ill.: Thomas, 1985.

PERIODICALS

Markel, Howard. "In the Wake of the Plague." *New England Journal of Medicine,* July 25, 2002, 297–299.

Titball, R. W. "*Yersinia pestis* and Plague." *Biochemical Society Transactions,* February 2003, 104–107.

WEBSITES

CDC Plague Home Page. Available online at http://www.cdc.gov/ncidod/dvbid/plague (accessed March 17, 2003).

"Plague." Center for Civilian Biodefense Strategies, Johns Hopkins University. Available online at http://www.hopkins-biodefense.org/pages/agents/agentplague.html; website home page: http://www.hopkins-biodefense.org (accessed March 17, 2003).

"Plague." Communicable Disease Surveillance and Response, World Health Organization. Available online at http://www.who.int/csr/disease/plague/en; website home page: http://www.who.int/csr/en/ (accessed March 17, 2003).

"The Plague." Decameron Web, Brown University. Available online at http://www.brown.edu/Departments/Italian_Studies/dweb/plague/index.shtml; website home page: http://www.brown.edu/Departments/Italian_Studies/dweb (accessed March 17, 2003).

"Plague." Medical Microbiology, Kirksville College of Osteopathic Medicine. Available online at http://www.kcom.edu/faculty/chamberlain/website/lectures/lecture/plague.htm; website home page: http://www.kcom.edu/faculty/chamberlain (accessed March 17, 2003).

"Plague in Action." Vess Research. Available online at http://www.larrythecrocodile.com/action.htm (accessed March 17, 2003).

"Soil Pollution: The Chain Gang As a Possible Disseminator of Intestinal Parasites and Infections"

Journal article

By: Charles Wardell Stiles

Date: May 23, 1913

Source: Stiles, Charles Wardell. "Soil Pollution: The Chain Gang As a Possible Disseminator of Intestinal Parasites and

Infections." *Public Health Reports,* 28, no. 21, May 23, 1913, 985–986.

About the Author: Charles Wardell Stiles (1867–1941) was famous for his work to cure hookworm. He taught at the Johns Hopkins Medical School for forty years, as well as at Georgetown University, and was the U.S. assistant surgeon general from 1910 to 1930. He investigated many animal diseases, such as trichinosis and parasitic worms. He served for nearly forty years on the International Commission on Zoological Nomenclature. He coauthored the Index-Catalog of Medical and Veterinary Zoology, which was published between 1902 and 1920. ■

Introduction

The prison system began much later than the arrival of Europeans in the New World. The early colonists very often used public punishments, such as forcing people to stand in the stocks. These were wooden structures that were locked around the hands and head of a prisoner who would then stand in them for hours or days. Other early punishments included whipping and being forced to wear letters, including the infamous scarlet letter, meaning that one had to wear an "A" if convicted of adultery. For the serious crimes, there was capital punishment. Both in Europe and in United States, capital punishment was used for a wide variety of crimes—at least 222 crimes in England carried the possible penalty of death.

In much of the North, a new type of prison was being developed in the early nineteenth century. These new prisons focused more on the reform of the criminal and the desire for rehabilitation more than punishment. Harsh rules were still used; for example, silence was ordered for work details so that the workers could "reflect" on what they had done wrong. This desire was more prevalent in the North than in the South, which had always been more decentralized, and in which fewer prisons were built. One way the South avoided prisons was to allow slave masters to discipline their slaves before the Civil War (1861–1865). Another way was through the frequency of lynchings. Many "crimes" in the South after the Civil War led to lynchings rather than prison terms, especially if an African American was the accused. Soon after the Civil War, to reduce prison costs further, the South started convict leasing. This was a practice of leasing or renting convicts to corporations for a fee. The system was generally quite brutal, with 20 percent of the prisoners dying each year. Due to complaints about this and opposition to it by the workers whose wages were undercut by the convicts, states moved to chain gangs, who worked on state projects and lived in harsh conditions.

Significance

The high level of pollution and poor quality of life described in Charles Wardell Stiles's 1913 article "Soil Pollution" typified the chain gang and demonstrated how brutal the chain gang system was. Chain gangs were not only dehumanizing to the convicts, but destructive to the environment as well. Soil pollution due to improper outhouses continued to be a concern throughout the South for the rest of the twentieth century. The general spread of sewage treatment systems, along with increased zoning requirements that required the use of proper septic systems, decreased this concern. However, these improved conditions were not always present, and soil pollution due to poor septic systems still persists in some areas.

Chain gangs were used throughout the South until the 1960s when the last ones were phased out. An increasing protest against them, along with a larger concern for the rights of inmates that was encouraged by the U.S. Supreme Court, led to their abolishment. Another reason for their end was the movie *Cool Hand Luke,* starring Paul Newman, which protested chain gangs.

Attitudes toward prisoners began to change again though, and in the 1990s a "get tough on crime" attitude swept through the United States. As part of this attitude, several states reintroduced chain gangs in the mid-1990s to work on roads and collect garbage. These chain gangs, though, are usually given access to a portable toilet, removing the soil pollution concern, even as it raises human rights issues.

Primary Source

"Soil Pollution: The Chain Gang As a Possible Disseminator of Intestinal Parasites and Infections"

SYNOPSIS: This article begins by arguing that by examining how a society treats its prisoners, one learns about the society at large. It then recounts Stiles's observations of two different chain gangs. The first was inadequately cared for and had no bathroom facilities. The second, claiming to be the best jail in the land, had an unsanitary privy. Stiles discusses how both jail arrangements spread pollution and calls for change.

The civilization and refinement of any community may be judged from a number of different points of view, one of which is the method it follows in handling its convicts—men and women who are so absolutely in its power that they are unable to protect themselves.

If a given community subjects its convicts to conditions that result in the possibility of spreading disease, unnecessarily, either among the criminals themselves or among the community in which they are being held in confinement, a question may legitimately arise as to the progress that community

Prisoners often worked in chain gangs under physically harsh and unsanitary conditions. **THE LIBRARY OF CONGRESS.**

has made in the onward march of refinement and civilization.

During the past 20 years I have had a number of opportunities to observe prisoners in penitentiaries, prison farms, jails, and chain gangs, and have been seriously impressed with the average lack of cleanliness among the criminals and their guards, although the opportunities for rigid discipline rendered it possible to make these penal institutions admirable schools in which the State might easily give to its charges some good lessons in cleanliness, hygiene, and sanitation. With few exceptions the authorities not only failed to see and to utilize the opportunity offered, but they actually permitted things to occur which were dangerous to the communities. Two examples of "chain gangs" recently (1912) visited will suffice to bring out the points in question.

In the county of X there was a chain gang of about 20 negroes working on the road. At night the men were huddled together in a cage, the only protection for which was a small tree. There were mattresses for less than half of the men, and the others had only thin blankets as beds. When the negroes returned from work they were huddled together in the cage, in which, according to the statement of the men and the keeper, they not only slept, but they also ate. Buckets without covers or disinfectants were placed in the cage for use in urinating and defecating. The excreta were carried to a small stream into which the material was thrown. The kitchen was near the cage and at the time of my visit was swarming with flies.

The guards—five white men—occupied a small house close by. There was no privy either for them or for the several "trusties" who were not in the cage. Soil pollution was practiced back of the camp and ample opportunity was present for the spread of fecal material to the food both of the guards and of the convicts.

The washing facilities consisted of a tub which was filled with water and in which all the prisoners washed.

The less said about the food the better, especially since this short article is not supposed to deal with that side of the question.

The county of Y boasts of what is said to be one of the best jails and convict camps in the State. The jail possibly deserves its reputation. The camp has some good features and is far superior to the camp of the county of X. The kitchen was swarming with flies. According to statements made by the "trusties," they and the guards went to the woods near by to defecate. Most of the men were working down the road some distance, close to a house occupied by a white family. Out of respect to the women and children in this household, a temporary cloth privy was erected for the convicts. Be it said to the credit of both the white and the negro prisoners, this privy was used by them. There was, however, no pail in the privy. The men defecated on the ground and made a pretense of covering the excreta with dirt; part of it was in fact covered, part was trampled down by the prisoners' shoes, part was carried away on the prisoners' shoes, part was being carried by flies to the near-by house to be devoured in the food by the white family living there.

Here we have two institutions (and there are many others equally bad) under the direction of the civil authorities of supposed civilized communities; in these institutions discipline is enforced but the prisoners are not only permitted but compelled to live under conditions of filth that are ideal for the spread of soil-pollution diseases. It is not necessary to prove that disease exists among the prisoners observed, or that cases of disease have actually spread from these camps to families in these localities. It is sufficient to show that the civil authorities in question (in a State where the State board of health is making heroic efforts to suppress soil pollution and soil-pollution diseases) are not only setting a very poor example to the people, but are actually feeding their convicts upon their own excreta and are at the same time feeding the convict guards and nearby families upon the same condiment.

What an encouragement this to public health officers who are fighting against the spread of disease; what a commentary upon the regard the authorities in question have for the health of the women and children under their protection; what an example of refinement and twentieth century civilization!

Further Resources

BOOKS

Barlow, Ronald S. *The Vanishing American Outhouse: A History of Country Plumbing.* El Cajon, Calif.: Windmill, 1989.

Degler, Stanley. *A Study of County Convict Road Work.* Montclair, N.J.: Patterson Smith, 1969.

WEBSITES

"Florida Reintroduces Chain Gangs." Amnesty International News and Reports Library. Available online at http://www.web.amnesty.org/ai.nsf/index/AMR510021996; website home page: http://www.web.amnesty.org (accessed March 17, 2003).

AUDIO AND VISUAL MEDIA

Mervyn LeRoy et al. *I Am a Fugitive From a Chain Gang.* MGM/UA Home Video. Videocassette, 1992.

"Early History, in Part Esoteric, of the Hookworm (Uncinariasis) Campaign in Our Southern United States"

Journal article

By: Charles Wardell Stiles

Date: August 1939

Source: Stiles, Charles Wardell. "Early History, in Part Esoteric, of the Hookworm (Uncinariasis) Campaign in Our Southern United States." *The Journal of Parasitology,* 25, no. 4, August 1939, 283, 296–308.

About the Author: Charles Wardell Stiles (1867–1941) was famous for his work to cure hookworm. Educated at the University of Leipzig, among other institutions, he worked at the Bureau of Animal Industry before he taught at Johns Hopkins Medical School and Georgetown University. He investigated many animal diseases, such as trichinosis and parasitic worms; and worker's health issues, such as mine sanitation and the health of cotton mill workers. He spearheaded new rules in zoological classifications and helped to form the Rockefeller Sanitary Commission. ■

Introduction

Hookworm was less studied and less noticed than the epidemic diseases that spread across the American South in the nineteenth century. One reason for this is that hookworm, unlike cholera or malaria, rarely killed directly, and especially not in large numbers. Some did die from the lasting effects of hookworm, but this was not directly due to the hookworm. Rather, it was because the hookworm-ravaged victim would fall prey to a disease that someone free of hookworm would be strong enough to shake off.

Hookworm first immigrated to the New World in the early seventeenth century and thrived in the warm climate of the South. After the Civil War (1861–1865), it spread across the region, infecting up to 40 percent of the populace. A person infected with hookworm became weak and listless, and many people assumed that those without shoes and good clothes were naturally lazy, so they did not look to any other cause, such as hookworm. By the 1880s, a cure had been found for hookworm, even though it was not a pleasant treatment. One was given thymol (carbolic acid) followed up by Epsom salts, which rid the body of hookworms. The key item after treatment was the prevention of reinfection, by ensuring that proper outhouses were built (even if pit toilets), followed by the wearing of shoes.

Charles Wardell Stiles, the author of the 1939 article "Early History, in Part Esoteric, of the Hookworm (Uncinariasis) Campaign in Our Southern United States," had been educated in Europe, where he became knowledgeable about the disease. He was sure that many of the problems that rural southerners faced were due to this disease, and his interest was shared by Walter Hines Page of the Rockefeller Foundation. Stiles and Page met while both were working on the federal government's Country Life Commission and Page put Stiles into contact with people connected with the Rockefeller Foundation, which resulted in the formation of the Rockefeller Sanitary Commission.

Significance

In 1909, the Rockefeller Sanitary Commission was formed to combat hookworm. Stiles worked with this commission, but was never given the responsibility for overseeing it on a daily basis. Wickliffe Rose was handed this charge as the administrative secretary of the commission. He organized conferences to inform southern populations about the problem and worked hard to remove their opposition to the program. Many in the South saw the commission's work as mere Yankee meddling. Regardless, Rose was able to encourage most of the southern states to follow his lead and an intensive survey of the problem was undertaken. Dispensaries, often traveling ones, were created to allow treatment with thymol and Epsom salts and education and privies were constructed, although these latter two aspects of the program lagged. Substantial progress had been made by the time the commission was ended in 1914.

After the success of the Rockefeller Sanitary Commission in the United States, Rose used the same program overseas through the International Health Division of the Rockefeller Foundation. As the crusade against hookworm made significant and effective progress, the International Health Division's attention was given to other diseases, including the flu, tuberculosis, typhus, and malaria.

The hookworm crusade was viewed as effective in the United States and public statements, including some from the Rockefeller Sanitary Commission, had stated that hookworm had been eradicated. However, investigations, including some by Stiles in the 1920s, found that more than one-quarter of people in much of the South still had hookworm. As recently as 1965, this disease was still common throughout the United States. Regardless, the Rockefeller Sanitary Commission drew attention to

Dr. Charles Wardell Stiles (center by tent post) at a North Carolina field clinic for hookworm. **STILES, DR. CHARLES W. (CENTER), c. 1900, PHOTOGRAPH.**

the problem and caused a sizable decrease in the pervasiveness of hookworm infection and disease.

Primary Source

"Early History, in Part Esoteric, of the Hookworm (Uncinariasis) Campaign in Our Southern United States" [excerpt]

SYNOPSIS: In the following excerpt, Stiles discusses his reasons for writing this article and his involvement in the early years of fighting the disease in the United States. He delineates his attempts to discuss the situation in medical journals and gives practical examples of his experiences. He also details his fund-raising efforts, which took time, but eventually resulted in the Rockefeller Foundation's support for an anti-hookworm project. Stiles then outlines his campaign with the Rockefeller money to fight the disease.

Recent literature contains several accounts of the origin of the hookworm campaign in our Southern States. As some of the data have been presented by authors who were not connected with the movement, it is not unnatural that discrepancies have crept into the publications.

Because of my intimate connection with the early history of the movement, repeated requests have been made of me to supplement the existing accounts, paying particular attention to the earlier years and (for the sake of historic accuracy) clearing up certain points of discrepancy. The chief reason why these requests have not thus far had results is my antipathy to using the perpendicular pronoun. In now complying with the requests, humble apology is herewith presented for using the first person singular so frequently; but unfortunately this technique can not be avoided entirely. The important points are *a* that the campaign took place, *b* that tens of thousands of patients were treated, and *c* that preventive measures have been instituted. The question as to who did what, when and why, is of infinitely secondary interest. . . .

In December, 1902, at Wyman's request, I presented a paper before the Pan-American Sanitary Conference at Washington, D. C., giving the results obtained in the survey. An aftermath of this address was exceedingly amusing and more important. A newspaper reporter (who has since been identified [personal letter] by Mark Sullivan as Mr. Irving C. Norwood) was present, and he reported the address with the headline that the "Germ of Laziness" had been discovered. This press story was published throughout the world, causing amusement in some circles and indignation in some quarters. My interpretation is that this newspaper reporter contributed an exceedingly valuable piece of work in disseminating knowledge concerning hookworm disease. The "Germ of Laziness" became common information. It would have taken scientific authors years of hard work to direct as much attention to this subject as Mr. Norwood did through his use of the expression "Germ of Laziness." Public health workers and the laity owe him a debt of gratitude.

Wyman, who was ahead of his time in public health matters, immediately agreed with me as to the importance of starting a campaign in the United States against this infection. As first move in this direction, he detailed me to meetings of various state medical societies. At these meetings, papers were presented on the subject, microscopic diagnosis was demonstrated, and patients were exhibited. This plan initiated the field campaign (in this country) against hookworm disease by promptly familiarizing many physicians with the new findings. In these addresses emphasis in respect to prevention was placed on two points in particular, namely, treatment of the sick and improvement of the sanitation. One favorite expression was to the effect that the eradication of hookworm disease should be based upon "20 per cent. thymol and epsom salts [treatment] combined with 80 per cent. sanitation [prevention]."

In marked contrast to the favorable reaction of the physicians in general, a sadly amusing or amusingly sad incident once occurred, namely, a couple of backwoods physicians protested to the program committee against my preaching a doctrine which inevitably would reduce their income by resulting in a decrease in disease! . . .

The first clinic in this country, as far as I can recall, to specialize for any length of time on hookworm disease was conducted at Columbia, S.C., by Dr. William Weston who had established a cotton-mill clinic about 1901, specializing on malaria. As soon [1902] as the results of the survey of 1902 became known to him, he turned his special attention in this clinic to hookworm disease, and a paper (which has been very generally overlooked) was published in 1907 in which he emphasized the importance of hookworm disease in the cotton mills and reported having treated [1902–1907] "between three and four hundred cases with practically uniform good results."

Wyman and I agreed that the second most important step was to cut off the foci of infection by improving the sanitation of the homes where infection, once introduced, spread to various members of the family, and especially to improve the sanitation at the public schools and churches where infection, once introduced, spread to different families. In harmony with this idea, a portion of Bulletin 10 (1903), Hygienic Laboratory, was given up to a discussion of sanitary privies. When the manuscript was forwarded for publication, it was returned with the request that this portion of the discussion be eliminated as it was considered that this chapter was exceedingly undignified, in fact disgusting, and had no place in a scientific article on public health. It required considerable argument to prove to the "powers that be" that this portion of the Bulletin represented the key in any plan for restricting the disease; finally the manuscript appeared in print as originally written. . . .

A number of practical points and many very amusing incidents came to light in this side of the campaign. It is to be recalled that in those days there was a great popular prejudice in rural districts against privies. The point of view was that not only were they unpleasant places but that nature's way of disposing of excreta was to expose it to the rays of the sun or to hide it in the brush. At a conservative estimate, eighty per cent of the Southern rural schools and churches did not have even a "sunshine" ("surface open in back") toilet, and the subject was not supposed to be discussed in public. . . .

During these efforts to improve sanitation, I made so many public addresses and wrote so many articles on sanitary privies that the noted chemical wit of government service (Dr. Harvey W. Wiley) gave to me the nickname of "Herr Geheimrath" (namely, "Privy Councillor").

A difficulty which soon developed was that when a family followed the advice of the health authorities and installed toilets, constipation very commonly resulted and people then reverted to "dog sanitation" as compared with "cat sanitation." This resulted in the important observation that the seats of most toilets were too high. . . .

At Columbia, S.C., Dr. Weston, the late Dr. Coward, and I conducted a clinic in the Olympia Mill Kindergarten School and treated a considerable number of cases. The cotton mill authorities provided a public health nurse and furnished the drugs.

One cotton mill president offered to place at my disposal $50,000 to be used in combatting the disease in cotton mills, but unfortunately, the offer could not be accepted because as a government officer I was investigating the mills, and the danger was present that this kind offer might be subject to misinterpretation from certain unfriendly quarters. Thus another chance for doing good evaporated.

Probably the most difficult problem in public health work is to put into practical application the theoretical knowledge we possess which can be utilized to reduce unnecessary death, suffering, and disease, and to increase health and happiness. Mr. Rockefeller financed a campaign of this nature and for this purpose. The South can never adequately express its debt of gratitude to him. He it was who by his altruistic generosity financed (on the advice of that wonderful analytical mind, the late Frederick T. Gates) the hookworm campaign which lies at the basis of the general public health progress made in our Southern States during the present century, for this campaign made the South health-minded. When he attached his signature to that letter he spelled health and happiness to hundreds of thousands of persons living in the South and to millions yet unborn. It is therefore eminently fitting that in enumerating the factors operative in public health advancement in the South, John D. Rockefeller should be named as among the first. . . .

Later Mr. Rockefeller's office sent telegrams or verbal messages to the twelve men in question inviting them to meet at his office on October 26, 1909, and at this meeting it was announced that Mr. Rockefeller had decided to give a sum of money up to a million dollars to finance the work. The board organized as the Rockefeller Sanitary Commission for the Eradication of Hookworm Disease, replied to Mr. Rockefeller's letter, selected an executive committee, talked over general plans, and adjourned. Mr. Gates and I spent the rest of the day discussing plans. He gave an announcement to the Associated Press, authorized me to send telegrams of announcement to the Surgeons-General of the United States Army, Navy, and Public Health Service and to all of the southern State Boards of Health. He also authorized me to approach Surgeon-General Wyman on the plan of detailing officers from his service to aid the work in the respective states, and he agreed not to press the question of my resigning from government service. . . .

■ ■ ■

My part of the work consisted largely in traveling all over the South to give technical and popular addresses to professional and lay audiences and to help in clinics as occasion presented. For instance, during the first year of this work I gave 246 addresses on the subject of hookworm disease.

It was exceedingly interesting to note how certain local Chambers of Commerce, one in particular, tried to concentrate the administrative work in its locality.

Mr. Gates, who always had his telescope focused on "all corners of the earth" and whose central idea in life was to accomplish good for humanity, recommended to Mr. Rockefeller the establishment of the Rockefeller Foundation, one subdivision of which was the International Health Board. Although the work by the Rockefeller Commission ceased, this Board took over some phases of the Commission's campaign and even extended the hookworm work to foreign countries.

The cooperative work for rural sanitation, by the results of its campaign in building sanitary privies, became an important factor in inhibiting the spread of hookworm disease. The various state boards of health have carried on the work, but not so intensively for hookworm disease as when working with the Rockefeller Commission, since the state boards naturally had to combine this part of their work with other duties.

One factor in improving sanitation on the farms and thus inhibiting hookworm infection has had more influence than seems to be generally appreciated. Reference is made to the demonstration work in various lines conducted by the U. S. Department of Agriculture. Agents of this organization have visited thousands of farms, and a number of these persons have spread the gospel of improvement in sanitation. . . .

The final obsequies were somewhat tragic. There were somewhere between 100 and 150 persons, chiefly physicians, on the pay roll, the $1,000,000 had not been exhausted, and the work had not been completed. A difference of opinion arose between Mr. Gates on the one hand and Mr. Rockefeller, Jr., and myself on the other, as to the advisability of continuing the work. As Mr. Rockefeller, Jr., expressed it; "Let us complete the job." Mr. Gates, on the other hand, felt that it was time for the Southern State Boards of Health to shoulder the full duties which theoretically belonged to them. Mr. Rose was instructed to survey the situation and to report at the next meeting of the Executive Committee. His report was presented at the next meeting as the combined recommendation of the Southern State Boards. As a result, the Commission ended its days, much to the regret expressed by Mr. Rockefeller, Jr., and myself. Later it developed that the Southern Boards had understood that the Commission had already voted to cease work and that the Boards were called upon simply to advise as to the details of closing up the work. Accordingly, the final vote by the Commission to close the work was based upon the erroneous premise that this action was advised by the Southern State Boards of Health; and the reports of the latter were predicated upon the erroneous premise that the Commission had taken a final vote to close.

Further Resources

BOOKS

Acheson, Roy M. *Wickliffe Rose of the Rockefeller Foundation: 1862–1914, the Formative Years.* Cambridge, Mass.: Killycarn, 1992.

Ettling, John. *The Germ of Laziness: Rockefeller Philanthropy and Public Health in the New South.* Cambridge, Mass.: Harvard University Press, 1981.

Pawlowski, Zbigniew S., G. A. Schad, and G. J. Stott. *Hookworm Infection and Anemia: Approaches to Prevention and Control.* Geneva: World Health Organization, 1991.

Schad, G. A., and Kenneth S. Warren. *Hookworm Disease: Current Status and New Directions.* London: Taylor and Francis, 1990.

Washburn, Benjamin Earle. *As I Recall: The Hookworm Campaigns Initiated by the Rockefeller Sanitary Commission and the Rockefeller Foundation in the Southern United States and Tropical America.* New York: Office of Publications, Rockefeller Foundation, 1960.

WEBSITES

"Hookworm Infection." Division of Parasitic Diseases, Centers for Disease Control and Prevention. Available online at http://www.cdc.gov/ncidod/dpd/parasites/hookworm/default.htm; website home page: http://www.cdc.gov/ncidod/dpd/ (accessed March 17, 2003).

Abraham Flexner: An Autobiography

Autobiography

By: Abraham Flexner

Date: 1940

Source: Flexner, Abraham. *Abraham Flexner: An Autobiography.* New York: Simon & Schuster, 1960, 70–71, 74–78, 80–81.

About the Author: Abraham Flexner (1866–1959) was a Louisville native who graduated at nineteen with a bachelor's degree from Johns Hopkins University. After founding his own prepatory school and spending time in Europe, he wrote a study of American medical schools, which changed medical education forever. He eventually became the assistant secretary of the General Education Board and then founded the Institute for Advanced Study at Princeton University in 1930. He served as director of that school until 1939. ■

Introduction

The United States, being a colony of Great Britain, not surprisingly based its early medical education on British policies. However, there were few hospitals and colleges, so the British model could not be fully followed. In Britain, a mix of college education and apprenticeships were used, but in the colonies most future doctors were trained through apprenticeships of up to three years. The apprentice paid a fee and helped the doctor, and the doctor gave him training, room, board, and books to read. Medical schools were started in the late eighteenth century, but they had few pupils. In the nineteenth century, more schools were added, and after the Civil War (1861–1865), medical schools boomed, with over a hundred schools in operation by 1875.

In 1846, the American Medical Association was formed and it pushed for stricter licensing procedures with little effect. The biggest impact came almost entirely from the American medical students who had trained abroad. After viewing English and German medical training, they realized how far behind the United States was and began pushing for its improvement.

One force encouraging reform that grew up around the turn of the twentieth century was the Johns Hopkins Medical School, which studied the European approach and set up a medical school based on the European model. By requiring an undergraduate degree to enter medical school and maintaining a full-time faculty, it became the model for others to follow.

Around this same time, large amounts of money were donated by patrons to improve medical and graduate education. Such donations created Johns Hopkins Medical School and also created the Carnegie Foundation. The latter group chartered Abraham Flexner to study medical education in the United States.

Significance

Flexner's report was based on his visitation of every single medical school in the United States and his description of the conditions at each one. Of all the schools studied, only three—Johns Hopkins, Harvard University, and Western Reserve (forerunner of Case Western Reserve University in Cleveland)—were described as fitting the standards, which included full-time faculty, laboratory resources, a bachelor's degree for admission, and ties to a university. Within ten years of Flexner's report, almost half of the medical schools had closed. The Rockefeller Foundation helped fund graduate education by awarding over $70 million, all of which went to the better schools. An unfortunate side effect was that this funding also limited the number of schools women and minorities could attend.

In the 1930s, full-time clinical faculty personnel were added to medical schools and the curriculums were standardized. During the 1940s, medical school programs were shortened and training was sped up to provide more doctors. In the 1950s, medical schools benefited from federal money pouring into biomedical research; as more faculty were hired, more attention was paid to that area. In the 1960s, medical schools began admitting more students as a need for more doctors was seen.

In the 1960s and 1970s, as more people graduated from college, the number of applications to medical schools increased, so the medical schools began to work with one another more effectively. A single application form for many colleges was created and the Medical College Admission Test, a standardized test, was created as well. Medical schools also began to recruit more women and minorities. Perhaps the biggest development of the past half-century, in both medical school and postmedical school education, was the development of specialization. Flexner's report did not foresee all this, but it did spark a huge improvement in medical education.

Abraham Flexner's report on medical schools led to improvements in their standards. THE LIBRARY OF CONGRESS.

Primary Source

Abraham Flexner: An Autobiography [excerpt]

SYNOPSIS: In his autobiography, Flexner discusses how he came to study American medical schools, the good support he received from the Carnegie Foundation, the standards he set for medical education, and how he came to write the famous "Bulletin Number Four," including an excerpt from it. Flexner then gives some examples of the inadequate medical education he saw throughout the United States and the varied reaction he received at some of the schools he visited.

In Heidelberg during the summer, reflecting at leisure upon my experience with boys and girls prepared in Louisville for various colleges and upon what I had seen at Harvard and abroad, I settled down to write my first book, *The American College.* It was a severe criticism of the elective system, the lecture system, and assistantships, as I had observed them at Harvard during the year 1905–1906. Its roots, however, went farther back, for I had noticed all too frequently that the boys whom I had sent to eastern colleges lost rather than gained enthusiasm for scholarship in the course of their college careers. After our return to America in 1908, the book was published by the Century Company and fell quite flat, for no one was prepared to act on the sweeping criticism which I made. The elder Dean Russell once pinned a rose on my coat lapel by saying that I was twenty-five years ahead of my time. Certain it is that many suggestions contained in the little volume, and quite ignored for years after its publication, have now become matters of course. At the time of publication, though it brought about no reforms, it had for me several fortunate results. In the first place, among its earliest readers was Charles P. Howland, and a meeting suggested by him proved the beginning of one of my most intimate and important friendships in New York. It also fell into the hands of the late Dr. Henry S. Pritchett, who had become president of the recently established Carnegie Foundation for the Advancement of Teaching.

It had occurred to me that I might find congenial occupation at the Carnegie Foundation, and I asked President Remsen, Mr. Gilman's successor, for a card of introduction to Dr. Pritchett. When I presented this introduction Dr. Pritchett allowed me to read a speech which he had written for delivery at Brown University and in which he had taken much the same line that was advocated in my little book. When I next saw him he asked me whether I would like to make a study of medical schools. As our family resources had been depleted during the preceding three years, I was, I confess, prepared to do almost anything of a scholarly nature; but it occurred to me that Dr. Pritchett was confusing me with my brother Simon at the Rockefeller Institute, and I called his attention to the fact that I was not a medical man and had never had my foot inside a medical school.

He replied, "That is precisely what I want. I think these professional schools should be studied not from the point of view of the practitioner but from the standpoint of the educator. I know your brother, so that I am not laboring under any confusion. This is a layman's job, not a job for a medical man."

Dr. Pritchett thus anticipated the habitual characterization of the General Education Board by its chief, Dr. Buttrick, as "the layman's contribution to education." I had my doubts at the beginning of my work, but they have long since disappeared, partly, I think, because of early contacts with medical men in Lousiville. Time and again it has been shown that an unfettered lay mind, if courageous, imaginative, and determined to master relationships, is, in the very nature of things, best suited to undertake a general survey. It was, for example, not a professional soldier, but rather a layman, Richard Burdon Haldane—afterward Viscount Haldane—who reorganized the British army. At the same time, as I shall tell later, he presided as chairman of the commission to plan the reorganization of the University of London. The expert has his place, to be sure; but if I were asked to suggest the most promising way to study legal education, I should seek a layman, not a professor of law; or for the sound way to investigate teacher training, the last person I should think of employing would be a professor of education. Dr. Pritchett was right: even though I might well have been the wrong choice, the proper person to study medical education was a layman with general educational experience, not a professor in a medical school.

Dr. Pritchett's offer carried with it a modest compensation but, fortunately, an unlimited expense account. About December 1, 1908, I set to work on my survey of medical education in the United States and Canada. Throughout I struck from the shoulder, naming names and places. Pritchett stood behind me like a stone wall. Who else would have done so, then or now? . . .

I began by reading everything on which I could lay my hands that dealt with the history of medical education in Europe and America. The most important and stimulating volume was Billroth's *Lehren und Lernen der medizinischen Wissenschaften,* of which many years later the General Education Board financed an admirable translation, which was printed by the Macmillan Company under the title of *The Medical Sciences in the German Universities,* and which has been widely distributed.

I went to Chicago, for two reasons: first, to confer on the general situation in medical education with Dr. George H. Simmons, secretary of the American Medical Association, an able administrator and editor; second, to read the reports prepared for the Council on Medical Education of the association by Dr. N. P. Colwell. Colwell's reports were creditable and painstaking documents, which, however, as Dr. Pritchett foresaw, had to be extremely diplomatic, because they were prepared by a committee of physicians about medical schools, the faculties of which consisted of their fellow physicians. Dr. Colwell and I made many inspection trips together, but, whereas he was under the necessity of proceeding cautiously and tactfully, I was fortunately in a position to tell the truth with utmost frankness.

Having finished my preliminary reading, I went to Baltimore—how fortunate for me that I was a Hopkins graduate—where I talked at length with Drs. Welch, Halsted, Mall, Abel, and Howell, and with a few others who knew what a medical school ought to be, for they had created one. I had a tremendous advantage in the fact that I became thus intimately acquainted with a small but ideal medical school embodying in a novel way, adapted to American conditions, the best features of medical education in England, France, and Germany. Without this pattern in the back of my mind, I could have accomplished little. With it I began a swift tour of medical schools in the United States and Canada—155 in number, every one of which I visited. I had no fixed method of procedure. I have never used a questionnaire. I invariably went and saw the schools and talked with teachers of medicine and the medical sciences and their students. I do not mean in this connection to summarize the work, which was subsequently published as "Bulletin Number Four" of the Carnegie Foundation for the Advancement of Teaching, but I may bring out a few facts of first importance.

"Bulletin Number Four" begins:

> [The American medical school] began soundly as a supplement to the apprentice-

ship system still in vogue during the seventeenth and eighteenth centuries. The likely youth of that period, destined to a medical career, was at an early age indentured to some reputable practitioner, to whom his service was successively menial, pharmaceutical, and professional: he ran his master's errands, washed the bottles, mixed the drugs, spread the plasters, and finally, as the stipulated term drew toward its close, actually took part in the daily practice of his preceptor, bleeding his patients, pulling their teeth, and obeying a hurried summons in the night. The quality of the training varied within large limits with the capacity and conscientiousness of the master. Ambitious spirits sought, therefore, a more assured and inspiring discipline. Beginning early in the eighteenth century, having served their time at home, they resorted in rapidly increasing numbers to the hospitals and lecture halls of Leyden, Paris, London, and Edinburgh. The difficulty of the undertaking proved admirably selective; for the students who crossed the Atlantic gave a good account of themselves. Returning to their native land, they sought opportunities to share with their less fortunate or less adventurous fellows the rich experience gained as they "walked the hospitals" of the old world in the footsteps of Cullen, Munro, and the Hunters. The voices of the great masters of that day thus re-echoed in the recent western wilderness. High scientific and professional ideals impelled the youthful enthusiasts, who bore their lighted torches safely back across the waters.

Out of these early essays in medical teaching, the American medical school developed. As far back as 1750 informal classes and demonstrations, mainly in anatomy, are matters of record. Philadelphia was then the chief center of medical interest. There, in 1762, William Shippen the younger, after a sojourn of five years abroad, began in the very year of his return home, a course of lectures on midwifery. In the following autumn he announced a series of anatomical lectures "for the advantage of the young gentlemen now engaged in the study of physics in this and the neighboring provinces, whose circumstances and connections will not admit of their going abroad for improvement to the anatomical schools in Europe; and also for the entertainment of any gentlemen who may have the curiosity to understand the anatomy of the Human Frame." From these detached courses the step to an organized medical school was taken at the instigation of Shippen's friend and fellow student abroad, John Morgan, who in 1765 proposed to the trustees of the College of Philadelphia the creation of a professorship in the theory and practice of medicine. At the ensuing commencement, Morgan delivered a noble and prophetic discourse, still pertinent, upon the institution of medical schools in America. The trustees were favorable to the suggestion; the chair was established, and Morgan himself was its first occupant. Soon afterward Shippen became professor of anatomy and surgery. Thirteen years previously the Pennsylvania Hospital, conceived by Thomas Bond, had been established through the joint efforts of Bond himself and Benjamin Franklin. Realizing that the student "must Join Examples with Study, before he can be sufficiently qualified to prescribe for the sick, for Language and Books alone can never give him Adequate Ideas of Diseases and the best methods of Treating them," Bond now argued successfully in behalf of bedside training for the medical students. "There the Clinical professor comes in to the Aid of Speculation and demonstrates the Truth of Theory by Facts," he declared in words that a century and a half later still warrant repetition; "he meets his pupils at stated times in the Hospital, and when a case presents adapted to his purpose, he asks all those Questions which lead to a certain knowledge of the Disease and parts Affected; and if the Disease baffles the power of Art and the Patient falls a Sacrifice to it, he then brings his Knowledge to the Test, and fixes Honour or discredit on his Reputation by exposing all the Morbid parts to View, and Demonstrates by what means it produced Death, and if perchance he find something unexpected, which Betrays an Error in Judgment, he like a great and good man immediately acknowledges the mistake, and, for the benefit of survivors, points out other methods by which it might have been more happily treated." The writer of these sensible words fitly became our first professor of clinical medicine, with unobstructed access to the one hundred and thirty patients then in the hospital wards. Subsequently the faculty of the new school was increased and greatly strengthened when Adam Kuhn, trained by Linnaeus, was made professor of materia medica, and Benjamin Rush, already at twenty-four on the threshold of his brilliant career, became professor of chemistry.

But the sound start was soon forgotten:

The rapid expansion of the country, with the inevitable decay of the apprentice system in consequence, must necessarily have lowered the terms of entrance upon the study. But for a time only: the requirements of medical education would then have slowly risen with the general increase in our educational resources. Medical education would have been part of the entire movement instead of an exception to it. The number of schools would have been well within the number of actual universities, in whose development as respects endowments, laboratories, and libraries they would have partaken; and the country would have been spared the demoralizing experience in medical education from which it is but now painfully awakening.

Quite aside from the history, achievements, or present merits of any particular independent medical school, the creation of the type was the fertile source of unforeseen harm to medical education and to medical practice. Since that day medical colleges have multiplied without restraint, now by fission, now by sheer spontaneous generation. Between 1810 and 1840, twenty-six new medical schools sprang up; between 1840 and 1876, forty-seven more; and the number actually surviving in 1876 has been since then much more than doubled. First and last, the United States and Canada have in little more than a century produced four hundred and fifty-seven medical schools, many, of course, short-lived, and perhaps fifty still-born. One hundred and fifty-five survived in 1907. Of these, Illinois, prolific mother of thirty-nine medical colleges, still harbored in the city of Chicago fourteen; forty-two sprang from the fertile soil of Missouri, twelve of them still "going" concerns; the Empire State produced forty-three, with eleven survivors; Indiana, twenty-seven, with two survivors; Pennsylvania, twenty, with eight survivors; Tennessee, eighteen, with nine survivors.

The schools were essentially private ventures, money-making in spirit and object. A school that began in October would graduate a class the next spring; it mattered not that the course of study was two or three years; immigration recruited a senior class at the start. Income was simply divided among the lecturers, who reaped a rich harvest, besides, through the consultations which the loyalty of their former students threw into their hands. "Chairs" were therefore valuable pieces of property, their prices varying with what was termed their "reflex" value: only recently a professor in a now defunct Louisville school, who had agreed to pay $3000 for the combined chair of physiology and gynecology, objected strenuously to a division of the professorship assigning him physiology, on the ground of "failure of consideration"; for the "reflex" which constituted the inducement to purchase went obviously with the other subject. No applicant for instruction who could pay his fees or sign his note was turned down. State boards were not as yet in existence. The school diploma was itself a license to practice. The examinations, brief, oral, and secret, plucked almost none at all; even at Harvard, a student for whom a majority of nine professors "voted" was passed. The man who had settled his tuition bill was thus practically assured of his degree, whether he had regularly attended lectures or not. Accordingly, the business throve. Rivalry between different so-called medical centers was ludicrously bitter. Still more acrid were—and occasionally are—the local animosities bound to arise in dividing or endeavoring to monopolize the spoils. Sudden and violent feuds thus frequently disrupted the faculties. But a split was rarely fatal: it was more likely to result in one more school. Occasionally, a single too-masterful individual became the strategic object of a hostile faculty combination. Daniel Drake, indomitable pioneer in medical education up and down the Ohio Valley, thus tasted the ingratitude of his colleagues. As presiding officer of the faculty of the Medical College of Ohio, at Cincinnati, cornered by a cabal of men, only a year since indebted to him for their professorial titles and profits, he was compelled to put a motion for his own expulsion and to announce to his enemies a large majority in its favor. It is pleasant to record that the indefatigable man was not daunted. He continued from time to time to found schools and to fill professorships—at Lexington, at Philadelphia, at Oxford in Ohio, at Louisville, and finally again in that beloved Cincinnati, where he had been so hardly served. In the course of a busy and fruitful career, he had occupied eleven different chairs in six different schools, several of which he had himself founded; and he had besides traversed the whole country, as it then was, from Canada and the Great Lakes to the Gulf, and as far westward as Iowa, collecting material for his great work, historically a classic, *The Diseases of the Interior Valley of North America*. . . .

Amusing incidents were frequent. I recall the fact that when, in Salem, Washington, I asked the dean of the medical school whether the school possessed a physiological laboratory, he replied, "Surely. I have it upstairs; I will bring it to you." He went up and brought down a small sphygmograph—an instrument designed to register the movement of the pulse.

On another occasion I visited one morning an osteopathic school in Des Moines with the dean of the school and found every door locked, though on the outside each bore a name—ANATOMY, PHYSIOLOGY, PATHOLOGY, etc. The janitor could not be found—probably not altogether an accident. Having expressed my satisfaction, I was driven to the railroad station and left, as the dean supposed, to take the next train to Iowa City. Instead, after waiting until he got out of sight, I returned to the school, found the janitor, gave him five dollars, in return for which he opened every door. The equipment in every one of the rooms was identical. It consisted of a desk, a small blackboard, and chairs; there were no charts, no apparatus—nothing

The State University of North Carolina gave the first two years of its medical course at Chapel Hill, while the two clinical years were given at Raleigh. The medical-school building at Raleigh was filthy and absolutely without equipment. I employed a photographer, who took photographs of every room in the building. When I returned to New York, Dr. Pritchett sent these photographs to the president of the university with a letter saying that they would be reproduced in facsimile in the forthcoming report. The president, who had probably never visited the medical school, was horrified. After a hurried visit to Dr. Pritchett, he called the regents together, and the clinical years were abolished, so that it became unnecessary to mention them in the bulletin that was subsequently printed.

Bowdoin College maintained a slight connection with the Medical School of Maine at Portland. It was a disgraceful affair. When I showed Dr. Pritchett my brief account of it, he was quietly amused, for the president of the college was one of the trustees of the Carnegie Foundation. However, following our custom, we sent the report to him. He came down to New York in great indignation, saying, first, that he understood that I was not a medical man; second, that Professor Councilman, head of the department of pathology at Harvard, had visited the school recently and praised it highly. I suggested that Dr. Pritchett send the report to Councilman and obtain his opinion. Councilman replied characteristically, "What could I do? They gave me a good dinner with lots to drink and smoke and then asked me to make a speech. I just had to be nice about it. But," he added slyly, "even Flexner will break down when it comes to Louisville!"—a prophecy, which, however, I belied. Armed with this letter, Dr. Pritchett stood back of my report. Later I met Dr. Edville G. Abbott, who was professor of orthopedics in the Portland school. He told me that when my report was read to the faculty, one of the members remarked pettishly that I had spent only a day looking at the school. "That," Dr. Abbott intervened, "is where we were lucky!"

Further Resources

BOOKS

American Medical Association. *Caring for the Country: A History and Celebration of the First 150 years of the American Medical Association.* Chicago: American Medical Association, 1997.

Bonner, Thomas Neville. *Iconoclast: Abraham Flexner and a Life in Learning.* Baltimore, Md.: Johns Hopkins University Press, 2002.

Burrow, James Gordon. *AMA: Voice of American Medicine.* Baltimore, Md.: Johns Hopkins University Press, 1963.

Flexner, Abraham, and Charles Vevier. *Flexner: 75 Years Later—A Current Commentary on Medical Education.* Lanham, Md.: University Press of America, 1987.

Johnson, James A., and Walter J. Jones. *The American Medical Association and Organized Medicine: A Commentary and Annotated Bibliography.* New York: Garland, 1993.

Wheatley, Steven Charles. *The Politics of Philanthropy: Abraham Flexner and Medical Education.* Madison: University of Wisconsin Press, 1988.

WEBSITES

"The Flexner Report in Context." Galen II, University of California, San Francisco Digital Library. Available online at http://www.library.ucsf.edu/ucsfhistory/themes/themes_flexner.html; website home page: http://www.library.ucsf.edu/ (accessed March 17, 2003).

10

Religion

PETER J. CAPRIOGLIO

Entries are arranged in chronological order by date of primary source. For entries with one primary source, the entry title is the same as the primary source title. Entries with more than one primary source have an overall entry title, followed by the titles of the primary sources.

CHRONOLOGY

PRIMARY SOURCES

Important Events in Religion, 1900–1909

1900

- *The Christian Oracle*, a journal circulated by the Disciples of Christ, changes its name to *Christian Century*. The journal became interdenominational in 1916.
- Nannie Helen Burroughs founds the Women's Auxiliary Convention of the National Baptist Convention, U.S.A., Inc. She gives an influential speech titled "How the Sisters Are Hindered From Helping."
- Congregationalist preacher and Social Gospel theologian Washington Gladden runs for city council in Columbus, Ohio, and wins a two-year term.
- On January 8, Mormon church president Lorenzo Snow releases a statement saying the Church had "positively abandoned the practice of polygamy, or the solemnization of plural marriages. . . ."
- On January 25, the House of Representatives votes 268-50 to unseat Congressman-elect Brigham H. Roberts of Utah because of his having three wives and an undetermined number of children. The Mormon church had officially prohibited polygamy in 1890.
- On February 13, Katherine Tingley founds a utopian settlement at Point Loma, California, which includes a theosophical school and an artistic community.
- On June 1, Carry Nation, a Woman's Christian Temperance Union member and the wife of a heavy drinker, smashes windows and other glassware at a saloon in Kiowa, Kansas. She would be arrested for similar agitations several times before her death in 1911.
- On July 24, Reverdy C. Ransom, pastor of the Bethel African Methodist Episcopal Church in Chicago, establishes the Institutional A.M.E. Church and Social Settlement on Dearborn Street near Thirty-ninth Street. The church, modeled on Jane Addams's Hull House, was the first of its kind for African Americans.
- On December 18, Baptist pastor Charles Thomas founds the Colored Men's Branch of the YMCA on West 53rd Street in New York City.

1901

- John Alexander Dowie's Christian Catholic Church purchases sixty-six hundred acres on the shore of Lake Michigan and founds the city of Zion, Illinois.
- Henry McNeal Turner, bishop of the African Methodist Episcopal Church, founds *Voice of the People,* a periodical devoted to the church and to African American activism.
- On January 1, Agnes Ozman, a student at Charles Parham's Bible School in Topeka, Kansas, receives baptism of the Spirit and allegedly begins speaking in tongues. She becomes the first modern Christian to experience the phenomenon known as glossolalia.
- On April 1, Jacob Beilhart and his communal Spirit Fruit Society (founded 1899) establish a farm near Lisbon, Ohio.
- On December 10, the American Federation of Catholic Societies holds its first meeting in Cincinnati, Ohio. The AFCS was founded to coordinate Christian education and social reform efforts of lay organizations and parishes.
- On December 29, Alma White, the wife of a minister, founds her own Holiness Church after she is forbidden by the Methodists to hold revival meetings. Begun as the Methodist Pentecostal Church and later renamed the Pillar of Fire Church, by 1936 it will have forty-six congregations, $4 million in assets, and more than four thousand members. White later becomes the first female bishop of any Christian church.

1902

- Solomon Schechter arrives in New York to take over the presidency of the Jewish Theological Seminary, becoming a major figure in Conservative Judaism.
- William James publishes *The Varieties of Religious Experience,* a pioneering work in the psychological study of religion.
- The last of a series of prophetic conferences originally organized by Dwight L. Moody in 1880 is held in Northfield, Massachusetts.
- The National American Woman Suffrage Association sets up a Committee on Church Work to help promote the cause of suffrage within male-dominated religious bodies.
- On May 15, the Christian Union, a Holiness group in Appalachia that had been reduced to about twenty members, reorganizes itself as the Holiness Church at Camp Creek in order to provide organizational stability and prevent "fanaticism" and loss of membership.
- On July 4, Swami Vivekananda, who had spoken at the World's Parliament of Religions in Chicago in 1893 and founded the Vedanta Society, the first Hindu mission in the United States, dies in India.

1903

- Pogroms in Russia (1903–1906) lead to a massive wave of Jewish immigration to the United States.
- William Walker Atkinson, a proponent of New Thought, adopts the name Swami Ramacharaka and begins publishing works that popularize Hinduism.
- Former professional baseball player and YMCA lecturer Billy Sunday is ordained a Presbyterian minister. His independent revivalistic career begins soon after.
- Eliza Healy, known as Sister Mary Magdalen, becomes principal of a school in Saint Albans, Vermont. At the same

time, she is named superior of the convent, becoming the first African American nun to hold so high a position.

- The Seventh-Day Adventists move their national headquarters from Battle Creek, Michigan, to Washington, D.C.
- On February 10, George A. Coe, professor of philosophy at Northwestern University; John Dewey, professor of philosophy at the University of Chicago; and others meet in Chicago and establish the Religious Education Association, an interfaith group devoted to designing morally responsible but not doctrinally specific curricula.
- On July 20, Pope Leo XIII dies in Rome. He is succeeded by Giuseppe Melchiorre Sarto, who takes the name Pius X.

1904

- Archbishop Patrick J. Ryan establishes the Catholic Missionary Society of Philadelphia. Among its first acts is the opening of Madonna House, a settlement house primarily for Italian Catholic immigrants.
- Western Theological Seminary in Chicago (now Seabury-Western in Evanston) is closed but is later reopened and reenergized by Charles Palmerston Anderson, the bishop of Chicago. By 1910 the seminary is flourishing.
- Evangeline Booth becomes field commander for the Salvation Army, a post she would hold until 1934.
- On April 6, Joseph F. Smith, President of the Church of Jesus Christ of Latter-Day Saints, delivers an official statement before the LDS general conference in which he expressly prohibits the practice of polygamy.
- On July 3, Theodor Herzl, the Hungarian Jew who founded modern political Zionism with his book *The Jewish State,* dies at the age of forty-six.
- On September 7, the Polish National Catholic Church comes into existence when a group of parishes meets in Scranton, Pennsylvania, to establish a synod that is independent of the Roman Catholic Church.

1905

- English revivalist F. B. Meyer, a central figure in the great Welsh Keswick revival of 1903, gives a series of lectures in Los Angeles. His visit encourages a number of Holiness believers to pray for a massive Pentecostal revival.
- Former pastor Thomas Dixon Jr. publishes *The Clansman,* adding fuel to the nascent Ku Klux Klan revival.
- African Methodist Episcopal preacher Reverdy C. Ransom gives a famous speech, "The Spirit of John Brown," at the second annual meeting of W. E. B. Du Bois's Niagara movement. According to Du Bois, Ransom's eloquence "led to the eventual founding of the National Association for the Advancement of Colored People."
- On June 18, the Federation of American Zionists adopts a resolution at its eighth annual convention stating that Palestine would be the best place to establish a Jewish colony. Their position affirms the platform of the International Zionist Congress, which had previously declined a British offer to help establish a colony in East Africa.

1906

- John A. Ryan, a Catholic priest, publishes *A Living Wage,* which fuels the minimum-wage-law movement.
- The Seventh-Day Adventists establish the College of Medical Evangelists (later Loma Linda University) in Loma Linda, California.
- On April 9, the Pentecostal movement has its official beginning when William J. Seymour, a Holiness preacher from Texas, receives baptism in the Holy Spirit and launches the Apostolic Faith Gospel Mission on Azusa Street in Los Angeles.
- On April 18, the San Francisco earthquake adds fervor to revivalist and Pentecostal movements throughout California.

1907

- Walter Rauschenbusch, a Baptist minister in New York City's "Hell's Kitchen," publishes *Christianity and the Social Crisis*. The book will inspire what becomes known as the Social Gospel movement.
- The Catholic Board for Mission Work among Colored People is founded. The board funds nuns and lay teachers in African American schools in the South.
- Harold Bell Wright publishes the popular novel *The Shepherd of the Hills*, which was inspired by the faith of people he had met in the Ozarks.
- The Church of Christ (Holiness), U.S.A., is founded by Charles Price Jones. Jones and Charles H. Mason had founded the Church of God in Christ in 1894, but after Mason's conversion to Pentecostalism, Jones split off to found the new Holiness denomination.
- On March 26, the First Presidency of the Church of Jesus Christ of Latter-Day Saints publishes *An Address: The Church of Jesus Christ of Latter-Day Saints to the World,* affirming the patriotism of American Mormons and renouncing all "quasi-political notions of kingdom."
- On June 6, Dropsie College for Hebrew and Cognate Learning, a postgraduate college for rabbinical and biblical studies, is chartered in Philadelphia.
- On July 17, Primitive Baptists meet in Huntsville, Alabama, to form the National Primitive Baptist Convention of the U.S.A. The convention establishes a Sunday school union and publishing board, a National Women's Auxiliary Convention, and an industrial and theological college at Winston-Salem, North Carolina.
- On September 8, Pope Pius X issues the encyclical *Pascendi dominici gregis,* condemning theological modernism.

1908

- Mary Baker Eddy's *The Christian Science Monitor* begins publishing in Boston, Massachusetts.
- Mary Lewis Tate, a self-appointed preacher since 1903, speaks in tongues after experiencing a miraculous recovery from illness. She subsequently founds the Church of the Living God, the Pillar and Ground of Truth, a Pentecostal denomination in Alabama.

- William J. Seymour of the Azusa Street Mission and Charles H. Mason hold revival services in Washington, D.C., leading to the founding of the Apostolic Faith Church of God.
- An African American Catholic priest, Father John Dorsey, with three white priests and several African American laymen, forms the Knights of Peter Claver in Mobile, Alabama. Modeled on the Knights of Columbus, the new fraternity is named for a Spanish Jesuit saint who, in the seventeenth century, had cared for sick slaves arriving on ships in Cartagena, Colombia.
- On April 13, the New England Methodist Episcopal Conference votes to remove its ban on dancing, card playing, and theatergoing.
- On May 10, two churches (one in West Virginia and one in Pennsylvania) hold the first formal observances of Mother's Day during their services. They are the result of a request from Anna Jarvis, who wished to honor the anniversary of her mother's death.
- On May 26, Hazrat Mirza Ghulam Ahmad, founder of the Ahmadiyya movement, one of the first Islamic missions to come to the United States, dies in Pakistan.
- On June 29, Pope Pius X issues the encyclical *Sapienti consilio,* declaring that the United States is no longer a missionary area, thereby removing the American church from the jurisdiction of the Congregation for the Propagation of the Faith in Rome.
- On October 13, the Pentecostal Church of the Nazarene (now Church of the Nazarene) is established from the union of several American holiness churches.
- On November 24, W. E. Fuller, the only African American charter member of the Fire Baptized Holiness Church in Georgia, oversees a meeting of a splinter group, the Colored Fire Baptized Church (now the Fire Baptized Holiness Church of God of the Americas) in Greer, South Carolina. The split occurs because of the rise of Jim Crow laws, which make it increasingly difficult for the church to find places to hold interracial services.
- On December 2, the Federal Council of Churches of Christ in America, representing thirty-three Protestant denominations and twelve million church members, is established in Philadelphia. The council adopts a Social Creed, calling for a series of labor reform measures.
- On December 27, dressed in white gowns "made specially for the occasion," followers of doomsday prophet Lee J. Spangler sit atop a mountain in Nyack, New York, awaiting the end of the world.

1909

- *The Reference Bible* edited by Cyrus I. Scofield, an extremely popular resource for the doctrines of dispensational premillennialism, is published.
- Amzi C. Dixon, pastor of the Moody Church in Chicago, meets layman Lyman Stewart and agrees to help him publish *The Fundamentals,* the classic statement of conservative Protestantism that first appeared in 1910.
- Unitarian educator Charles W. Eliot steps down as president of Harvard University, which he had substantially liberalized and secularized. Shortly before leaving, he writes an essay titled "The Religion of the Future," in which he predicted that secular benevolent societies would provide the model for a substantially modified twentieth-century Christianity.
- Jehovah's Witnesses establish their world headquarters in a Brooklyn building (to be renamed the Brooklyn Tabernacle) that was the former parsonage of nineteenth-century Congregationalist preacher Henry Ward Beecher.

"Total Abstinence"

Speech

By: Bessie Laythe Scovell

Date: 1900

Source: Scovell, Bessie Laythe. "President's Address," *Minutes of the Twenty-Fourth Annual Meeting of the W.C.T.U. of the State of Minnesota.* St. Paul, Minn.: W.J. Woodbury, 1900.

About the Author: Bessie Laythe Scovell grew up in Chatfield, Minnesota, and earned a bachelor's degree from the State University of Minnesota. She was a schoolteacher for three years and assistant editor of the *Duluth Evening Journal.* She joined the Minnesota Woman's Christian Temperance Union in 1895 and served as its president from 1897 to 1909. ■

Introduction

In the late nineteenth century, concern grew among American clergy and laity that alcohol use was getting out of control. Families were being neglected, violence toward women and children was becoming more common, and men could not function at their jobs. Churches responded to this social problem by crusading against alcohol locally and seeking legislation on a national level.

Women attempted to combat the problem of alcoholism by forming the Woman's Christian Temperance Union (WCTU), also known as the National Woman's Christian Temperance Union, in 1874. The WCTU was an offshoot of a meeting of the Woman's Temperance Crusade held at the Chautauqua Sunday School Assembly in that year. Just a year before, the group had launched a campaign in which women went into saloons, prayed and sang religious hymns, and urged drinkers to stop their destructive habit. Covering over twenty-three states, the Temperance Crusade managed to close thousands of businesses that sold alcohol. During the 1874 meeting, members determined that there was an urgent need for a national temperance organization. These discussions resulted in the formation of the National Woman's Christian Temperance Union in Cleveland, Ohio.

WTCU members defined temperance as "moderation in all things healthful; total abstinence from all things harmful." They chose total abstinence from alcohol in their personal lives and established as their watchword the protection of the home. Bessie Laythe Scovell, a leader of the WCTU movement and president of the Minnesota Woman's Christian Temperance Union, delivered a rallying call in her "President's Address: Total Abstinence" at the annual meeting of the Minnesota WCTU in 1900. Scovell discussed one of the primary goals of the Minnesota and National WCTU: legislation to prohibit alcohol, as well as tobacco, gambling, and pornography. She urged the members to continue with their petition work and letters to the U.S. congressional representatives urging them to take legislative action to combat these societal ills.

Significance

The WCTU grew rapidly in numbers and influence. By working through churches, schools, and other groups, the group created enough anti-alcohol sentiment to enable passage of the Eighteenth Amendment to the U.S. Constitution, prohibiting "the manufacture, sale, or transportation of intoxicating liquors within, the importation thereof into, or the exportation thereof from the United States and all territory subject to the jurisdiction thereof for beverage purposes." The amendment, proposed on December 18, 1917, and ratified on January 16, 1919, remained in force until 1933, when a successful countermovement resulted in the Twenty-First Amendment, ratified on December 5, 1933, which repealed the Eighteenth Amendment. The Twenty-First Amendment also promised federal help to "dry" states (those that prohibited alcohol) in enforcing their own laws. This federal promise was a partial victory for the WCTU.

As of 2002 the WCTU, headquartered in Evanston, Illinois, had affiliated groups in seventy-two countries and about half a million members.

Primary Source

"Total Abstinence" [excerpt]

SYNOPSIS: In these excerpts from her address to the Minnesota WCTU in 1900, Scovell, state president of the organization, warned that only total abstinence from alcohol and other dangerous substances would help relieve the family and society of its ills. She asked WCTU members to continue working diligently toward that objective.

An unexpected voice from the wilderness of nations was raised in France last spring by Rev. Latty, Bishop of Chalons, who sent a note of warning against "light wine" as the curse of the country in his Lenten pastoral letter. This Roman Catholic clergyman calls attention to the fact that France is in the last ranks of sobriety as a nation; that there are 450,000 saloons or one for every forty men; that women drunkards are common in many parishes; and the most serious cause for alarm he finds is the teaching the children are receiving at the hands of their parents. He says that many children are breakfasted on bread soaked in brandy, and often carry a bottle of brandy to school to moisten their mid-day lunch. May these people hear the voice of this brave bishop's warning, and save themselves from physical and national decay. My journey abroad this summer has convinced me that to establish total abstinence in the nations of Europe will take many years of shining of the white light of truth down into the darkened customs of the people. Then, too, these people with the customs of wine drinking centuries back of them are coming to our own country, bringing their customs with them. I came home convinced that this warfare which we wage is to be a life struggle. We may as well establish ourselves and prepare for our life's business. Many of our members enlist for a short time, thinking the whole matter of intemperance will soon be settled and then they shall rest. In a few years they get weary and discouraged and fall out of the ranks. My sisters, the King for whom we fight needs a standing army, ever ready for service. There is more hope in our own nation today than in any other. Yet we must strengthen our department of work among foreigners. We must meet the foreigners early and give them our customs before they have established theirs of the old world upon us. Nothing must be too hard for us to do. Some of us must consecrate ourselves to learn a language and devote ourselves to a certain people. Nothing will so endear us to the homesick foreigner as to be able to speak to him in his mother tongue, understand the history of his nation and to teach him the language and history of the new. We have 6,000,000 Germans in our country today. We must have a regiment of American workers, who will learn the German language, love the German people, work among the German children and young people until we get them to love clear brains better than beer. There must be others who for the love of country and dear humanity will learn the Scandinavian language and be real neighbors to the many people of this nationality who have come to make homes in America. Again others must learn the French and Italian and various dialects, even, that the truths of personal purity and total abstinence be taught to these who dwell among us. We must feel it a duty to teach these people the English language to put them in sympathy with our purposes and our institutions. To the women who will do this will come great opportunities for service. Do not think I am discouraged in the warfare when I say these things. I came home feeling greater necessity to work in this cause than ever before and as determined as ever to give a life to this cause. I firmly believe in the final triumph of total abstinence and the annihilation of the liquor business, but I also believe we shall work many years yet, must go deeper into science, lay still broader foundations, make greater sacrifices than we have yet made, must study to prepare ourselves for more effective service.

We have been deeply disappointed with the inaction of congress this year in regard to the canteen. This means that Attorney General Griggs' opinion is sustained by the president and Secretary Root and congress sustains the president. Yet the public press has wittingly and unwittingly been at work quickening the conscience of the people. I quote from the New Enterprise: "There is no question about suppressing army canteens if congress and the president want to suppress them. It is merely a question of desire." The friends of the president generally state "that personally Mr. McKinley would like to suppress the canteen." We are to conclude then that politically Mr. McKinley does not dare suppress it and since his political desires are stronger than his personal, the canteen, with all its blighting influence to our soldier boys, will be maintained. Therefore, if your boy is in the army, he may be sacrificed for the sake of the party and the party candidate and not for the sake of the country as your fond patriotism would like to believe. Again and again has my blood boiled at the reports from missionaries and others of the hundreds of American saloons being established throughout our new possessions. According to the United States Bureau of Statistics dated July 20th, the export of malt liquors, brandy, whisky and other liquors for the Philippines altogether was three times greater in March than it was last November, although the government claims to have reduced the number of saloons. And shame of shames, our military authorities in the Philippines have introduced that open and official sanction of prostitution which was prohibited in the British army through the protest and investigation of American women. My sisters, our work for purity the coming year must engage our most earnest attention. The White Cross flag must follow the Red if our soldiers are to be protected from the most awful disease and death. The managing editor of one of the leading Manila daily papers, while riding past the national

Members of the Women's Christian Temperance Union march in support of prohibition, Washington D.C., c. 1909. At the annual meeting of the Minnesota chapter of the WCTU, president Bessie Laythe Scovell's address warned of the neccessity of abstinence from alcohol and focused on the sustained effort needed to accomplish this objective. GETTY IMAGES. REPRODUCED BY PERMISSION.

cemetery at Malate recently, said deliberately while pointing to the great number of fresh mounds: "Far more of our boys who are lying there met their death through bad women and drink than through the bullets of the Filipinos."

Encouragement

Through the clouds of national sin and shame, however, come a few gleams of hope to those who love humanity. By vote of congress, Brigham H. Roberts, the Mormon polygamist, was not allowed a seat in that body, was sent back to the ones who elected him, a rebuke to perfidious Utah. The facts revealed by the investigation of the Roberts case go to show that while the cancer was seared over for a time, it was not taken out root and branch as we had supposed when Utah was admitted as a state. The anti-polygamy fight is not over. We must see that every polygamous federal official is removed from office and that an anti-polygamy amendment to the national constitution is carried. Since women are given the credit of having aroused our national congress on this subject let us not rest until the work is finished. As W.C.T.U. women we must go on with our petition work and personal letters to the coming session of congress. Another gleam of encouragement is the circular issued by the commissioner of internal revenue, "prohibiting the use of manufacturers of cigars, cigarettes or tobacco put up in packages, of labels containing any promise or offer of, or any order or certificate for any gift, prize, premium, payment or reward. This to take effect Sept. 1, 1900." This will help, not only to stop smoking contests for the sake of the premium, but will also stop fostering the gambling and lottery spirit, as well as keep the impure pictures often contained in these packages from the eyes of the users of the poisonous weed.

In Minneapolis this last spring an ordinance was passed by the city council which prohibits the wine-room partitions in the saloons of that city, to take effect July 1st. This was a stroke toward lessening the awful immorality which is the natural outgrowth of the whole saloon system, and wine-rooms in particular. It was only a step to be sure, but it was a step. May the thought soon get into the minds of men, if saloons can be regulated, their existence can be prevented.

The presidential campaign is again upon us with all party candidates personally decent, reputable men. We are glad that political parties have seemed to catch the thought that their chiefs must be men whose "known virtue is from scandal free." Each candidate for president and vice president, as far as we know, is a good "homey" man, devoted to wife and family. I am glad I can think this much good of each one. But I am sorry to say that not all the parties to which these candidates belong are good "homey" parties. Some of them forget the wife and the family when they are silent upon the great evil that threatens the home more than any other—the traffic in alcoholic liquors. To be silent, to shut the eyes to the awfulness of this curse cannot cure the evil.

As to the methods of election by most political parties, too, there is grave doubt. When we think of the millions of dollars expended every four years to elect a president, the bad blood stirred up, the buying of ballots with bad beer, etc., etc., makes us more firmly believe in the W.C.T.U. method of election, which a la Kipling would be:

Where no one works for money, and no one works for fame;
But each for the joy of the working and each in her separate star,
Does the work as she sees it for the God of things as they are.

I am glad, too, that a man has demonstrated the truth that money does not need to be expended in order to be elected, and his success may point the way to similar achievements for even presidents. Dr. Washington Gladden, pastor of the First Congregational church of Columbus, Ohio, was elected to the city council of that city on the independent ticket in April of this year. Dr. Gladden did not take an active part in the campaign, declaring that he would neither spend a penny nor ask a single man to vote for him. It was distinctly understood that Dr. Gladden stood for:

1. Non-partisan municipal government.
2. Absolute fairness and justice to all parties.
3. Efficient and economical administration.
4. Placing only competent men in office.
5. Publicity in transacting public business.

Dr. Gladden said, after his election: "The result has one or two lessons for practical politicians. It proves that a candidate does not need to make a personal canvass in order to secure his own election. If I had gone about my ward begging people to vote for me I should have been defeated. There are quite a number of people in this country who greatly prefer to vote for a candidate who will not solicit their votes. Another point for the practical politician is the fact that it is not necessary to pay for political work. There are plenty of people who are ready to work for what they believe in without being paid for it. Americans are not all mercenaries. Give them a fair chance to work for better government in the city and they will not need to be hired. The most cheering result of this campaign is the demonstration that elections can be carried even against big odds without the use of money."

We might also add that a man of convictions standing for great principles can be elected without any party. This gives him freedom from without consulting his party. We long for the good old sentiment: "I the party lash and must give a chance for true manliness to develop, a quality the practical politician scarce dare assert at the present time would rather be right than president," to come into politics, which would develop statesmen rather than politicians, and with James Russell Lowell,

I honor the man who is willing to sink
Half his present repute for the freedom to think,
And, when he has thought, be his case strong or weak,
Will risk t' other half for the freedom to speak.

Coming more closely to our lines of work, we note that the Jewish Associated Charities of Chicago have decided to abolish henceforth all balls, fairs and charity bazaars as methods of swelling their funds and have resolved to give of their means according to their ability, and promised that their already magnificent philanthropies shall not suffer by the change. This is a note of encouragement to our department of Proportionate and Systematic Giving, and an example worthy of imitation by all charity organizations.

Edward Everett Hale has substituted water for wine at communion in his church in Boston, believing that the contents of the cup is a matter following the customs of the people. He believes that America has established water drinking as a custom, and hence he makes the change. That woman's cause is steadily marching on is evinced by the fact that the M.E. General Conference, in session in Chicago last May, voted to admit women as delegates.

The department of Temperance and Labor is being also helped by outside organizations. The Consumers' League, which has been gaining ground among women since 1896, has now a national organization. It seeks to educate conscience among those who buy, toward the laborer who produces the goods and the ones who stand behind counters and deliver our goods after the purchase is made. Women of wealth and fashion are studying into the conditions of the sweat shops and are insisting that garments be made in factories where there is light and fresh air and steam or electric power for running the machines; that the laborers be treated from a more humane standpoint; that eight or ten hours be a day's work and that a living wage be paid. More and more manufacturers are beginning to see that it is for their own interests that their employees have decent homes and pleasant environments.

Had I time, I might speak of many more signs of encouragement that makes me feel that

Man to man the world o'er
Shall brothers be for a' that.

Further Resources

BOOKS

Scovell, Bessie Laythe. *Yesteryears: A History of the Minnesota W.C.T.U. 1877–1939.* Minneapolis, Minn.: Bruce, 1939.

Tyler, Helen E. *Where Prayer and Purpose Meet: The WCTU Story, 1874–1949.* Evanston, Ill.: Signal Press, 1949.

Willard, Frances Elizabeth. *Woman and Temperance: Or, the Work and Workers of the Woman's Christian Temperance Union.* New York: Arno, 1972.

WEBSITES

Woman's Christian Temperance Union. "Friends of WCTU." Available online at http://www.wctu.org/friends.html; website home page: http://www.wctu.org/ (accesssed January 10, 2003). This site provides links to affiliated WCTU organizations.

Woman's Christian Temperance Union. "The History of the WCTU." Available online at http://www.wctu.org/history.html; website home page: http://www.wctu.org/ (accessed January 10, 2003).

Religious Opposition to Imperialism

"A Prayer for the Use of Anti-Imperialists"; "Clergymen Address Voters"

Prayer; Statement

By: Herbert Seely Bigelow
Date: 1900

Source: "A Prayer for the Use of Anti-Imperialists." *The Public* 3 (Aug. 25, 1900). Available online at http://www.boondocksnet.com/ai/ailtexts/hbs_prayer2.html; "Clergymen Address Voters." *The Public* 3 (November 3, 1900). Available online at http://www.boondocksnet.com/ai/ailtexts/clergy00.html. Website home page: Zwick, Jim, ed. "Anti-Imperialism in the United States, 1898–1935." http://www.boondocksnet.com/ai/ (accessed January 10, 2003).

About the Author: Herbert Seely Bigelow (1870–1951) was the activist pastor of the Vine Street Congregational Church, later the nondenominational People's Church, in Cincinnati, Ohio. He served on the executive committee of the Cincinnati Anti-Imperialist League and was a vice president of the national American Anti-Imperialist League. His book, *The Religion of Revolution* (1916), contained sermons on social issues. ■

Introduction

Herbert Seely Bigelow, like many prominent Americans in education, religion, and business, opposed American territorial acquisition. At the American Anti-Imperialist League meeting held on October 17, 1899, in Chicago, Illinois, the delegates approved a platform in which they "earnestly condemned" the policy of President William McKinley in the Philippines. The president had ordered American troops to suppress the Filipino nationalist movement led by Emilio Aguindaldo, who in January 1899 had declared the independence of the Philippines. The United States, according to McKinley, desired to maintain its presence in that country.

The league's platform cited political and religious reasons for opposing McKinley's foreign policy, especially toward the Philippines. One statement in the platform emphasized this opposition: "We hold, with Abraham Lincoln, that 'no man is good enough to govern another man without that man's consent. When the white man governs himself, that is self-government, but when he governs himself and also governs another man, that is more than self-government—that is despotism. . . . Those who deny freedom to others deserve it not for themselves, and under a just God cannot long retain it.'"

An avid advocate of the social gospel movement, Bigelow was committed to fighting what he considered to be the injustices of imperialism. The social gospel movement, which began in the late nineteenth century and flourished in the early twentieth century, was a movement by American Protestants and other Christians to build a social order in line with Christian principles. Bigelow, along with other leaders of this movement, was dedicated to making ethics and social renewal central to Christianity and society. Many of the advocates of the social gospel sought reform of the capitalist system, improvement of the conditions of the working classes, the end of imperialism, and the establishment of international justice and peace.

In *The Religion of Revolution,* Bigelow included his social gospel sermons. In one of them, "The Religion of Inspired Politics," he presented his basic beliefs about the role of religion in politics: "We need Good Samaritans who have, besides the vision, the faith that this can be done; men who, with consecrated enthusiasm and a sound comprehension of economic laws, will work passionately for a truer freedom than the world has yet known. This is what we call the religion of inspired politics."

Significance

Many Christians expressed surprise, and sometimes dismay, after hearing about the role Christian ministers such as Bigelow were playing in the anti-imperialism movement. For these ministers, it was a very different public role and one with which their congregations were not familiar. While Bigelow and other league members did not succeed in ending U.S. control over the Philippines, they did make Americans more aware of what the government was doing in that area of the world.

The Philippines had come under U.S. control in 1898 after the Spanish-American War. In 1935 a commonwealth was established, but full independence was not granted until 1946.

Primary Source

Religious Opposition to Imperialism

SYNOPSIS: The prayer against imperialism was offered by Bigelow at the opening of the Anti-Imperialist Congress at Indianapolis on August 15, 1900. The second document, issued on October 30, 1900, is an official statement signed by thirty-five ministers, including Bigelow, expressing their belief that war against the Filipinos was not right because it was "a war of conquest."

"A Prayer for the Use of Anti-Imperialists"

Almighty God, may the spirit of truth preside over the deliberations of this convention. We know that the judgment of man is fallible; but we believe there can be no honest difference as to the cardinal principles that govern moral conduct. We seek to prepare ourselves for the work that is before us by making sure of our devotion to those simple precepts that must appeal with equal force to all those who are pure in heart. We believe that Thou hast created of one blood all the nations of the earth. We believe, therefore, that we do not err in judgment merely, but that we commit sin if we treat any of Thy creatures as we would not wish to be treated. We believe that in Thy sight all men have the same right to live, and that when we take the lives of others we do that which we know to be wrong. We believe that the right to live means also the right of self-government, by which men secure their lives; and we believe that when we kill other men to keep them from adopting our political faith, we do that which we would all acknowledge to be a crime if our moral judgment were not perverted by pride or prejudice or corrupted by greed of gain.

We believe that these self-evident moral principles apply with equal force whether we act collectively as a nation or whether we act as individuals. We believe that what is wrong for a man to do is wrong also for the nation. We believe that when a government commits any act which is wrong for the individual citizen, the citizen who votes to support that nation becomes involved in moral guilt and that his loyalty to such a government is treason against the law of heaven. We do not believe that good ever comes out of evil. We believe that national prosperity must be founded upon national righteousness, and that every departure from the path of rectitude must be atoned for either by national repentance or national ruin.

Grant us a Christian citizenship. Hasten the day when men shall cease to vote for policies which they would not execute. May we feel the reproach of increasing armies, and learn to loathe the man who glories in war. May we have too much faith in the sovereignty of Thy laws to fancy that we may lay the foundations of civilization upon the ruins of popular liberty. May we sheathe our dripping sword for shame, and be content to pave the way for the advance of civilization by the practice of plain and simple justice. May the physical courage of the battlefield find a nobler expression in the moral courage to trust the divine intuitions of the soul—to speak the truth and do the right always.

In this and in every moral conflict may we be guided by an unclouded inner light, which, if trusted, will lead us all aright and keep our hearts in accord with the eternal forces that make for righteousness and peace.

"Clergymen Address Voters"

We, the undersigned ministers of religion, declare our deep conviction that the war against the Filipinos is not right. We regard it as a war of conquest, and directly within Mr. McKinley's definition of "criminal aggression."

We refuse to accept the undemocratic conclusion that because the American people can by might govern colonies, they ought to do so. We deny that either the president or congress may rightfully gov-

American soldiers in Caloocan City with a captured cannon during the Philippine Insurrection. Many prominent Americans opposed American territorial acquisition. © CORBIS. REPRODUCED BY PERMISSION.

ern anywhere outside the protecting constraints of the constitution. We agree with Benjamin Franklin, "that neither the obtaining nor the retaining of any trade is an object for which men may justly shed each other's blood." We feel bound to withhold our approval of the immoral use of the public authority, even to accomplish an assumed moral end.

We hold that what is immoral for men to do acting singly is immoral for them to do acting collectively as a nation. Each step in a course of action must be moral if the end is not to be tainted with immorality. No end can justify immoral means to secure it. It is too late to maintain the doctrine that in the sacred name of religion we may kill some men in order to convert those who survive. "Love, not force, was the weapon of the Nazarene; sacrifice for others, not exploitation of them, was His method of reaching the human heart."

We desire to see America exercise her influence as a "world power" in a new rather than in the old way. We view with grave apprehension the tendency to make her what other nations are. We desire to see her become the supreme moral factor in the world's progress. Any great and permanent increase of her military establishment, with the cultivation of the military spirit among us, will indicate moral deterioration.

Herbert S. Bigelow, Cincinnati.
Henry H. Barber, Meadville, Pa.
Thomas Scott Bacon, Maryland.
William T. Brown, Rochester, N.Y.
William M. Brown, Bishop of Arkansas.
Robert C. Bryant, Lisbon, N.H.
Ellison Capers, Bishop of South Carolina.
Joseph H. Crooker, Ann Arbor, Mich.
Lewis J. Duncan, Milwaukee, Wis.
Quincy Ewing, Greenville, Miss.
John Faville, Peoria, Ill.
W. C. Gannett, Rochester, N.Y.
N. P. Gilman, Meadville, Pa.
Frank O. Hall, North Cambridge, Mass.
John M. Henderson, Gerlaw, Ill.
Jenkin Lloyd Jones, Chicago.
Louis George Landenberber, St. Louis.
Charles R. Brown, Oakland, Cal.
William R. Lord, Portland, Ore.
T. Emory Lyon, Chicago.
Joseph May, Philadelphia.
James Ryan, Bishop of Alton.
John F. Spalding, Bishop of Colorado.
John Lancaster Spalding, Bishop of Peoria.
J. T. Sunderland, Oakland, Cal.
J. L. Stern, Cumberland, Md.
William M. Salter, Chicago.
Hiram W. Thomas, Chicago.
Joseph Brown Turner, Dover, Del.
Gustavus Tuckerman, St. Louis.
Earl W. Wilber, Pennsylvania.
L. L. West, Winona, Minn.
Francis M. Whittle, Bishop Diocese of Virginia.
Albery A. Whitman, Atlanta, Ga.
H. M. Timmons, Cincinnati.

Further Resources

BOOKS

Bigelow, Herbert Seely. *The Religion of Revolution.* Cincinnati, Ohio: D. Kiefer, 1916.

Fann, K.T., ed. *Readings in U.S. Imperialism.* Boston: P. Sargent, 1971.

Rozwenc, Edwin Charles. *The United States and the New Imperialism, 1898–1912.* Lexington, Mass.: Heath, 1968.

WEBSITES

Ferraro, Vincent. "Documents Relating to American Foreign Policy: 1898–1914." Available online at http://www.mtholyoke.edu/acad/intrel/to1914.htm; website home page: http://www.mtholyoke.edu/acad/intrel/feros-pg.htm (accessed January 10, 2003).

Geocities.com. "United States Interventionism: Some Notes." Available online at http://www.geocities.com/Athens/Ithaca/9852/usimp.htm; website home page: http://www.geocities.com (accessed January 10, 2003).

Small Planet Communications. "An On-Line History of the United States: The Age of Imperialism." Available online at http://www.smplanet.com/imperialism/toc.html; website home page: http://www.smplanet.com/index.html (accessed January 10, 2003).

Graves de Communi Re (On Christian Democracy)

Papal encyclical

By: Pope Leo XIII

Date: January 18, 1901

Source: Papal Encyclicals Online. "Graves de Communi Re." Available online at http://www.papalencyclicals.net/Leo13/l13grcom.htm (accessed January 10, 2003).

About the Author: Pope Leo XIII (1810–1903) was born in Carpineto, Italy, with the birth name Vincenzo Giocchino Pecci. Ordained a priest in 1837, he was named a cardinal in 1853. He was elected pope in 1878 and served until his death in 1903. He was noted for opening the archives of the Vatican for historical investigations in 1883 and for his encyclicals addressing social and religious concerns of the time. ■

Introduction

Pope Leo XIII's goal in *Graves de Communi Re* was for Roman Catholics to distinguish clearly between two movements—social democracy and Christian democracy—that some Catholics and other Christians thought were essentially the same. The pope believed that there was no common ground between them, for they were polar opposites in their philosophy and objectives; in his view, they differed from each other "as much as the sect of socialism differs from the profession of Christianity."

Social democracy was a political movement that worked toward a peaceful and gradual transformation of capitalism to socialism through democratic methods. The movement, which developed in the latter part of the nineteenth century and whose roots were in Europe, gradually found itself attracting American social reformers, theologians, and religious activists. In the pope's view, though, the more extreme adherents of social democracy advocated such excesses "as to maintain that there is really nothing existing above the natural order of things and that the acquirement and enjoyment of corporal and external goods constitute man's happiness." Their aim, he said, was "putting all government in the hands of the masses, reducing all ranks to the same level, abolishing all distinction of class, and finally introducing community of goods. Hence, the right to own private property is to be abrogated, and whatever property a man possesses, or whatever means of livelihood he has, is to be common to all."

Christian democracy, according to the pope, was radically different. Because it is Christian, it "is built, and necessarily so, on the basic principles of divine faith, and it must provide better conditions for the masses, with the ulterior object of promoting the perfection of souls made for things eternal." In addition, in the functioning of Christian democracy, "justice is sacred; it must maintain that the right of acquiring and possessing property cannot be impugned, and it must safeguard the various distinctions and degrees which are indispensable in every well-ordered commonwealth. Finally, it must endeavor to preserve in every human society the form and the character which God ever impresses on it."

This was not the first time Pope Leo XIII had addressed such social issues. In a 1891 encyclical, *Rerum Novarum* (On the Condition of Labor), he called for societal protections for the poor and the weak. He warned, however, that these protections should not involve socialism and class struggle. He also affirmed the God-given right of individuals to own private property and to organize into associations to improve their working and living standards.

Significance

More conservative American and European Catholics were relieved by the pope's encyclical. Their fears that socialism was going to transform their societies were somewhat eased by his words. More liberal Catholics, in contrast, were disappointed by the pope's admonitions about social democracy but found comfort in his view of Christian democracy: that it was the responsibility of the nonpoor to help the poor through individual efforts and charitable contributions as well as through social policies and programs.

In promoting Christian democracy, Pope Leo XIII viewed the Roman Catholic Church as backing major reforms to help improve the condition of the poor, but not at the expense of the loss of freedom for the individual. As he had stated in *Rerum Novarum,* "It must not be supposed that the Church so concentrates her energies on caring for souls as to overlook things which pertain to mortal and earthly life."

Primary Source

Graves de Communi Re (On Christian Democracy) [excerpt]

SYNOPSIS: In these excerpts, Pope Leo XIII maintains that there is a wide difference between social democracy and Christian democracy. He warns that socialism threatens not only temporal possessions but also morality and religion. Christian democracy, rather than social democracy, would help liberate and care for the poor without the excesses of socialism.

1. The grave discussions on economical questions which for some time past have disturbed the peace of several countries of the world are growing in frequency and intensity to such a degree that the minds of thoughtful men are filled, and rightly so, with worry and alarm. These discussions take their rise in the bad philosophical and ethical teaching which is now widespread among the people. The changes, also, which the mechanical inventions of the age have introduced, the rapidity of communication between places, and the devices of every kind for diminishing labor and increasing gain, all add bitterness to the strife; and, lastly, matters have been brought to such a pass by the struggle between capital and labor, fomented as it is by professional agitators, that the countries where these disturbances most frequently occur find themselves confronted with ruin and disaster.

2. At the very beginning of Our pontificate We clearly pointed out what the peril was which confronted society on this head, and We deemed it Our duty to warn Catholics, in unmistakable language, how great the error was which was lurking in the utterances of socialism, and how great the danger was that threatened not only their temporal possessions, but also their morality and religion. That was the purpose of Our encyclical letter Quod Apostolici Muneris which We published on the 28th of December in the year 1878; but, as these dangers day by day threatened still greater disaster, both to individuals and the commonwealth, We strove with all the more energy to avert them. This was the object of Our encyclical Rerum Novarum of the 15th of May, 1891, in which we dwelt at length on the rights and duties which both classes of society—those namely, who control capital, and those who contribute labor—are bound in relation to each other; and at the same time, We made it evident that the remedies which are most useful to protect the cause of religion, and to terminate the contest between the different classes of society, were to be found in the precepts of the Gospel.

Pope Leo XIII, late 1800s. Pope Leo XIII's 1901 encyclical *Graves De Communi Re* warns Catholics against the threats of socialism and advocates Christian democracy.

3. Nor, with God's grace, were Our hopes entirely frustrated. Even those who are not Catholics, moved by the power of truth, avowed that the Church must be credited with a watchful care over all classes of society, and especially those whom fortune had least favored. Catholics, of course, profited abundantly by these letters, for they not only received encouragement and strength for the excellent undertakings in which they were engaged, but also obtained the light which they needed in order to study this order of problems with great sureness and success. Hence it happened that the differences of opinion which prevailed among them were either removed or lessened. In the order of action, much

has been done in favor of the proletariat, especially in those places where poverty was at its worst. Many new institutions were set on foot, those which were already established were increased, and all reaped the benefit of a greater stability. Such are, for instance, the popular bureaus which supply information to the uneducated; the rural banks which make loans to small farmers; the societies for mutual help or relief; the unions of working men and other associations or institutions of the same kind. Thus, under the auspices of the Church, a measure of united action among Catholics was secured, as well as some planning in the setting up of agencies for the protection of the masses which, in fact, are as often oppressed by guile and exploitation of their necessities as by their own indigence and toil.

4. This work of popular aid had, at first, no name of its own. The name of Christian Socialism, with its derivatives, which was adopted by some was very properly allowed to fall into disuse. Afterwards, some asked to have it called the popular Christian Movement. In the countries most concerned with this matter, there are some who are known as Social Christians. Elsewhere, the movement is described as Christian Democracy and its partisans as Christian Democrats, in opposition to what the socialists call Social Democracy. Not much exception is taken to the first of these two names, i.e., Social Christians, but many excellent men find the term Christian Democracy objectionable. They hold it to be very ambiguous and for this reason open to two objections. It seems by implication covertly to favor popular government and to disparage other methods of political administration. Secondly, it appears to belittle religion by restricting its scope to the care of the poor, as if the other sections of society were not of its concern. More than that, under the shadow of its name there might easily lurk a design to attack all legitimate power, either civil or sacred. Wherefore, since this discussion is now so widespread, and so bitter, the consciousness of duty warns Us to put a check on this controversy and to define what Catholics are to think on this matter. We also propose to describe how the movement may extend its scope and be made more useful to the commonwealth.

5. What Social Democracy is and what Christian Democracy ought to be, assuredly no one can doubt. The first, with due consideration to the greater or less intemperance of its utterance, is carried to such an excess by many as to maintain that there is really nothing existing above the natural order of things, and that the acquirement and enjoyment of corporal and external goods constitute man's happiness. It aims at putting all government in the hands of the masses, reducing all ranks to the same level, abolishing all distinction of class, and finally introducing community of goods. Hence, the right to own private property is to be abrogated, and whatever property a man possesses, or whatever means of livelihood he has, is to be common to all.

6. As against this, Christian Democracy, by the fact that it is Christian, is built, and necessarily so, on the basic principles of divine faith, and it must provide better conditions for the masses, with the ulterior object of promoting the perfection of souls made for things eternal. Hence, for Christian Democracy, justice is sacred; it must maintain that the right of acquiring and possessing property cannot be impugned, and it must safeguard the various distinctions and degrees which are indispensable in every well ordered commonwealth. Finally, it must endeavor to preserve in every human society the form and the character which God ever impresses on it. It is clear, therefore, that there is nothing in common between Social and Christian Democracy. They differ from each other as much as the sect of socialism differs from the profession of Christianity. . . .

9. Let there be no question of fostering under this name of Christian Democracy any intention of diminishing the spirit of obedience, or of withdrawing people from their lawful rulers. Both the natural and the Christian law command us to revere those who in their various grades are shown above us in the State, and to submit ourselves to their just commands. It is quite in keeping with our dignity as men and Christians to obey, not only exteriorly, but from the heart, as the Apostle expresses it, "for conscience' sake," when he commands us to keep our soul subject to the higher powers. It is abhorrent to the profession of Christianity that any one should feel unwilling to be subject and obedient to those who rule in the Church, and first of all to the bishops whom (without prejudice to the universal power of the Roman Pontiff) "the Holy Spirit has placed to rule the Church of God which Christ has purchased by His Blood." He who thinks or acts otherwise is guilty of ignoring the grave precept of the Apostle who bids us to obey our rulers and to be subject to them, for they watch as having to give an account of our souls. Let the faithful everywhere implant these principles deep in their souls, and put them in practice in their daily life, and let the ministers of the Gospel meditate them profoundly, and incessantly labor, not merely by exhortation but especially by example, to teach them to others.

10. We have recalled these principles, which on other occasions We had already elucidated, in the hope that all dispute about the name of Christian Democracy will cease and that all suspicion of any danger coming from what the name signifies will be put at rest. And with reason do We hope so; for, neglecting the opinions of certain men whose views on the nature and efficacy of this kind of Christian Democracy are not free from exaggeration and from error, let no one condemn that zeal which, in accordance with the natural and divine laws, aims to make the condition of those who toil more tolerable; to enable them to obtain, little by little, those means by which they may provide for the future; to help them to practice in public and in private the duties which morality and religion inculcate; to aid them to feel that they are not animals but men, not heathens but Christians, and so to enable them to strive more zealously and more eagerly for the one thing which is necessary; viz., that ultimate good for which we are born into this world. This is the intention; this is the work of those who wish that the people should be animated by Christian sentiments and should be protected from the contamination of socialism which threatens them. . . .

18. Let it be understood, therefore, that this devotion of Catholics to comfort and elevate the mass of the people is in keeping with the spirit of the Church and is most conformable to the examples which the Church has always held up for imitation. It matters very little whether it goes under the name of the Popular Christian Movement or Christian Democracy, if the instructions that have been given by Us be fully carried out with fitting obedience. But it is of the greatest importance that Catholics should be one in mind, will, and action in a matter of such great moment. And it is also of importance that the influence of these undertakings should be extended by the multiplication of men and means devoted to the same object.

19. Especially must there be appeals to the kindly assistance of those whose rank, wealth, and intellectual as well as spiritual culture give them a certain standing in the community. If their help is not extended, scarcely anything can be done which will help in promoting the well-being of the people. Assuredly, the more earnestly many of those who are prominent citizens conspire effectively to attain that object, the quicker and surer will the end be reached. We would, however, have them understand that they are not at all free to look after or neglect those who happen to be beneath them, but that it is a strict duty which binds them. For, no one lives only for his personal advantage in a community; he lives for the common good as well, so that, when others cannot contribute their share for the general good, those who can do so are obliged to make up the deficiency. The very extent of the benefits they have received increases the burden of their responsibility, and a stricter account will have to be rendered to God who bestowed those blessings upon them. What should also urge all to the fulfillment of their duty in this regard is the widespread disaster which will eventually fall upon all classes of society if his assistance does not arrive in time; and therefore is it that he who neglects the cause of the distressed masses is disregarding his own interest as well as that of the community. . . .

25. There remains one thing upon which We desire to insist very strongly, in which not only the ministers of the Gospel, but also all those who are devoting themselves to the cause of the people, can with very little difficulty bring about a most commendable result. That is to inculcate in the minds of the people, in a brotherly way and whenever the opportunity presents itself, the following principles; viz.: to keep aloof on all occasions from seditious acts and seditious men; to hold inviolate the rights of others; to show a proper respect to superiors; to willingly perform the work in which they are employed; not to grow weary of the restraint of family life which in many ways is so advantageous; to keep to their religious practices above all, and in their hardships and trials to have recourse to the Church for consolation. In the furtherance of all this, it is of great help to propose the splendid example of the Holy Family of Nazareth, and to advise the invocation of its protection, and it also helps to remind the people of the examples of sanctity which have shone in the midst of poverty, and to hold up before them the reward that awaits them in the better life to come. . . .

Further Resources

BOOKS

Quardt, Robert. *The Master Diplomat, from the Life of Leo XIII.* Staten Island, N.Y.: Alba House, 1964.

Wallace, Lillian Parker. *Leo XIII and the Rise of Socialism.* Durham, N.C.: Duke University Press, 1966.

Watzlawik, Joseph. *Leo XIII and the New Scholasticism.* Detroit, Mich.: Cellar Book Shop, 1966.

WEBSITES

Benigni, U. "Pope Leo XIII." *Catholic Encyclopedia.* Available online at http://www.newadvent.org/cathen/09169a.htm; website home page: http://www.newadvent.org (accessed January 10, 2003).

Defending the Faith, Christ's Faithful People. "Leo XIII." Available online at http://www.cfpeople.org/Books/Pope/POPEp254.htm; website home page: http://www.cfpeople.org/CFPMain.htm (accessed January 10, 2003).

The Vatican. "Leo XIII." Available online at http://www.vatican.va/holy_father/leo_xiii/ (accessed January 10, 2003).

"Unity of the Human Race"

Magazine article

By: J. W. Sanders

Date: July 1902

Source: Sanders, J. W. "Unity of the Human Race." *African Methodist Episcopal Church Review,* July 1902, 427. Available online at http://dbs.ohiohistory.org/africanam/det.cfm?ID=2275; website home page: http://www.ohiohistory.org/index.html (accessed May 15, 2003).

About the Organization: The African Methodist Episcopal Church was founded by a group of African American Methodists in 1787 to protest racial segregation. The *African Methodist Episcopal Church Review,* one of the church's publications, contained information about the church itself, African American issues, and perspectives on race and racism. It advocated self-determination for people of color and highlighted the accomplishments of people of African descent. ■

Introduction

The Emancipation Proclamation issued by President Abraham Lincoln (served 1861–1865) on January 1, 1863, declared freedom for slaves in the rebellious Confederate states. Later, the Thirteenth Amendment abolishing slavery was ratified on December 6, 1865. Although the Civil War had ended, it left bitter relationships between whites and blacks, Northerners and Southerners, and antislavery groups and pro-slavery groups.

"Unity of the Human Race" appeared at a time when African Americans, both in the South and North, continued to face racial discrimination and a climate of intolerance and hatred, sometimes resulting in deadly violence. Sanders's article was an attempt to challenge prejudice and widely held notions of racial inferiority by affirming the church's belief that all people were united under God. One's culture, race, or religion did not matter in the eyes of God because he created all people to live together in harmony, friendship, and respect. The article not only urged Americans to accept that a common bond ties all Americans together, regardless of their physical or cultural traits, but also spoke to the human condition around the world. Sanders reminded Americans of God's universal requirement to accept one's brothers and sisters on an equal basis and with love.

Significance

The article is an important example of the African Methodist Episcopal Church's mission: to reach out on critical religious and social issues by publishing the *Church Review.* Its audience was not just church members but also African Americans throughout the country, people living in Africa, and white Americans who supported its basic beliefs concerning the equality of all people. In addition to the written word, the church maintained active evangelistic programs and succeeded in recruiting thousands of new members after the Civil War. From 1890 to 1916 the church grew from 494,777 members in 2,481 congregations to 548,355 members in 6,636 congregations.

Through its political involvement during Reconstruction (1865–1867), more than fifty members of the church's clergy held office in the legislatures of Alabama, Florida, Georgia, South Carolina, and other states. The struggle for civil rights had begun. Through the efforts of the *Church Review* and the active involvement of the church's laity and clergy, the church became a leading force in the civil rights movement of the twentieth century. The church today still has a leadership role in religious, social, and political matters in black communities and is one of the larger Protestant denominations in the United States, with membership of about 2,500,000 in about 6,200 churches.

Primary Source

"Unity of the Human Race"

SYNOPSIS: Sanders's article addresses the reasons for believing that all human beings, regardless of race, religion, or culture, are unified under God in a common bond. Science, he points out, has observed that humans are far more similar to each other than they are dissimilar. He also notes the importance of the roles of the inner spirit and the environment in shaping how children think about the world in which they live.

One might at first thought say, "What does it matter if a Chinaman disclaims any genetic connection with a Malay? or, if perchance, a Caucasian denies having any racial connection whatever with the Negro, as is often done?" It matters much every way. In the first place, we observe there are two forces playing ceaselessly on the hearts of the children. One, an internal force, we will call inspiration; the second, the external power of friendly environment. Now, the proper conception of the truth of the "oneness of man" leads to the encouragement of peoples who are down, by causing the exercise of the brotherly instincts of the dominant race; the improper conception leads to the paralysis of every aspiration of the lower races to rise from a state of inferiority. It means either that I am to be recognized as a man and brother, and thus be offered every inducement and encouragement to scale the heights, or that by all the strength of a dominant race I am to be held in subjection and made subservient to those who rule.

Now, if you will for a moment consider, you will readily discover that the full acceptance of the "unity of man" does not obtain among the vanguard of the nations whose potent influence dominates the earth.

There are nine millions of Afro-Americans in this country, and they are popularly considered inferior to others in mental, moral and spiritual power. And this inferiority is not looked upon as an accident of birth, or as resulting, from a lack of opportunities, but is viewed as the unchangeable status of a race under the ban of God's displeasure. Nor should there arise in the souls of the sons of Ham thoughts and longings never so lofty, is it to be considered for a moment that the dark-skinned child of fate—who was to fair-skinned Israel, "but a hewer of wood and drawer of water"—should ever aspire, even after the year of jubilee, to purify himself and walk into the congregation and take his seat with others. They say God has set barriers in nature with a "Thus far shalt thou come, but no farther."

So that no Negro need expect to develop that culture, refinement, Christian grace and elegance necessary to exact from the proud Caucasian a hearty reception to places of honor. We are to inquire whether the color of a man's skin and the texture of his hair, which are the two chief marks of difference in a physiological sense, are the results of climatic influences, or are they indicative of a different order of being? I have heard it preached that Negroes have no brain to speak of, could only learn enough to serve their masters. They had no souls; Christ did not die for them; it was nonsense to talk of the stocky mothers with dark skins and thick lips having any racial connection with the white race. Dr. John Miley has given us the benefit of exhaustive research. He says, at some length, "Let us compare notes along two general lines. First—Physical; Second—Mental; and if we find that the differences along these lines are only superficial, and the result of environment or circumstances, then the objections raised against the doctrine of the unity of man will fall to the ground." This is largely a question of science, says he, or, at least, we must go to science for a knowledge of the facts. The unity of the human race is a question of the unity of species. Definitions setting forth the idea of species greatly differ, but the following will cover the idea we wish to convey approximately— "Species is a collection of individuals more or less resembling each other, which may be regarded as having descended from a single pair by an uninterrupted and natural succession of families." Herein is found two fundamental facts: First—Resemblance; Second—Genetic connection. The idea of genetic connection is the deeper idea.

MEAN, BUT FUTILE.
President Harrison's Spite can not Disturb the Growing Harmony between the Whites and Negros of the South.

An African American man and a white man walk together in this political cartoon from an 1890s issue of *Judge*. J.W. Sanders addressed racial harmony in a 1902 article that asserted the unity of the human race under God.

There are wide variations, particularly in size, form and color. We are to inquire, whether these variations are consistent with a common parentage. While some hold four or five, up to sixty, different origins of the human family, the weight of scientific authority is for a unity of origin. This question of species is common to the manifold forms of vegetable and animal life. Fixation of racial types is no disproof of unity. There are numerous instances of physiological change as a result of new conditions. Let us cite a few: 200 years ago the Irish were driven from Armagh and the South of Down, and have become prognathous like the Australians. The Yankees are descendants of the English, and yet they have a type of their own. Certain tribes of Indians have permanently changed the shapes of their heads by bandaging them in infancy. The Jews are confessedly of one origin, and yet we have the Polish Jews who are light-haired, and the dark Jew of the Nile Valley. Again, the Portuguese, who settled in East India in the sixteenth century, are now as dark as the Hindus themselves. Also we find that Africans become lighter as they go up the Aluvial River banks to higher ground; and, on the contrary, the coast tribes, who drive out the Negroes of the interior and take their territory, end by becoming Negroes themselves. Hence, we argue that there is a oneness of races in physical characteristics. The distinctions are superficial and the result of local influences. The human body is one in chemical elements, one in anatomical structure, one in physiological construction, one in pathological susceptibilities, one in psychological endowment. Of course, you could set in wide contrast the barbaric Negro against the Christian Caucasian, but lo and behold! there are differences almost as great even among the same Caucasian race. But that is understood to be only accidental, or superficial. There are the same sensibilities, with their marvelous adjustments to manifold relations of mind in all; the same moral and religious nature. While it may sink to barbarism and idolatry in the white man, it may rise to the highest moral and Christian life in the Mongolian and the Negro. Here is a vast law of nature, that like shall produce like. Throughout the different orders of created beings this great law holds good; and nature sets bars in the way of the infraction of this law, both in animal and vegetable life. The law of hybridity contravenes when sacrilegious hands are laid on this law to disturb its orderly workings, so that strict sterility is seen when an attempt is made to bring together different species, as in the case of the horse and the mule. [Genesis] "And God said let the earth bring forth grass, the herb yielding seed, and the fruit tree yielding fruit after his kind whose seed is in itself upon the earth, and it was so." Now, if science speaks to me in her many toned and yet harmonious voices that in all essential physical points all races of men are one, if the voice of psychology tells me that all men, in mental endowments, are one, and if the voice of revelation tells me that there is no respect of persons with God, I have but to buckle on my armor and move up the line, in spite of all powers that oppose. But I have not introduced a witness in this case, which, perhaps, is the most convincing of all, for it is found in the chambers of one's own soul. It is that of consciousness. A voice within speaks to each man upon whom the light of God's truth has shone and tells him that the same God who circled the heavens upon which to sit, has made each man—all men—to work out for himself a glorious destiny; and this voice is so convincing that, though a dozen kings should meet a peasant and should decry the noble aspirations swelling his breast methinks the humble man would smile at the usurpers and would turn from them feeling that in true dignity and inherent worth he was on a par with the mightiest potentate beneath the sun. I must understand, however, if I am to achieve any noble results in life, it must be through earnest personal efforts. We must work, work, work as a race, and we shall gradually rise in the scale of being.

"The planets at their Maker's will
  Move onward in their cars,
For Nature's wheel is never still:
  Progressive as the stars,
The moments fly on lightning's wing:
  And life's uncertainty, too—
We've none to waste on foolish things,
  There's work enough to do."

Further Resources

BOOKS

Gregg, Howard D. *History of the African Methodist Episcopal Church: (The Black Church in Action).* Nashville, Tenn.: AMEC, 1980.

Payne, Daniel A. *History of the African Methodist Episcopal Church.* Nashville, Tenn.: AMEC Sunday School Union/ Legacy, 1998.

Wright, R.R. *The Bishops of the African Methodist Episcopal Church.* Nashville, Tenn.: Henry A. Belin, Jr., 1963.

WEBSITES

African Methodist Episcopal Church. "History." Available online at http://www.ame-church.com/aboutus.html#history; website home page: http://www.ame-church.com/index.php (accessed May 16, 2003).

African Methodist Episcopal Church. "A.M.E. Today." Available online at http://www.ame-today.com (accessed May 16, 2003).

The Varieties of Religious Experience

Lecture

By: William James

Date: 1902

Source: James, William. *The Varieties of Religious Experience: A Study in Human Nature.* New York: Longmans, Green, 1902. Available online at http://www.psywww.com /psyrelig/james/james15.htm (accessed April 15, 2003).

About the Author: William James (1842–1910) was born in New York City and in 1869 received his doctorate from Harvard, where he taught philosophy and psychology from 1872 to 1907. In 1890 he published *Principles of Psychology,* which also contained his views on philosophy. In addition, he was noted for his interest in the psychology of the religious experience. ■

Introduction

At the turn of the twentieth century, there was an ongoing academic battle between theologians who affirmed their belief in God and scientists who rejected any belief in the supernatural as being superstitious, exploitative, or, at the very least, wishful thinking. William James saw a need to take an objective look at these arguments and then present his analysis of them. That is what he attempted to accomplish in *The Varieties of Religious Experience,* which began as a series of lectures.

James defined *religion* as the feelings, acts, and experiences of individuals in their solitude as they contemplate whatever they may consider to be divine—not what takes place in a building. His goal in the lectures was the scientific examination and evaluation of the religious experiences of humanity from anthropological, psychological, and philosophical perspectives. Although at times he seemed skeptical about these experiences, he did not dismiss them as false or invalid. Rather, he raised significant, relevant questions concerning religion and suggested possible clues or answers to them.

In one, for example, he examined the functions of philosophy and religion. He pointed out that religion was "more enthusiastic than philosophy," that it was characterized by "enthusiasm in solemn emotion," and that it had the ability to overcome unhappiness. In another, which dealt with the reality of the unseen, he argued that people possessed a sense of reality other than that given by the normal senses. From this sense of reality, they can "sense a divine presence." In the "The Religion of Healthy Mindedness," he proposed that happiness was humanity's chief concern. In explaining "The Sick Soul" in one of his lectures, he stated that belief in a supernatural religion provided relief.

Significance

William James's book soon developed into a classic text on the psychology and philosophy of religion. Reviewers of twentieth-century literature have often listed it as one of the best works of nonfiction. Praise for the book, however, was not necessarily universal in the early 1900s. Some scientists believed that James was "pro-religion" and not critical or skeptical enough in his analysis. They believed his book to be more philosophical and less scientific. Some religious leaders and theologians criticized James for being "antireligion" and favoring religious skeptics while denigrating believers. The theologian may read *Varieties of Religious Experience* as a book primarily analyzing personal religious experience; the psychologist may see it as one of the first books to study religion with psychological methods.

In his *Varieties of Religious Experience* (1902), the American psychologist and philosopher William James discusses the characteristics and nature of religion and its role in human lives.

Primary Source

The Varieties of Religious Experience [excerpt]

SYNOPSIS: James's book consisted of lectures originally presented at "The Gifford Lectures on Natural Religion" in 1901 and 1902 at the University of Edinburgh in Scotland. The following excerpts are from his last lecture, in which he presented conclusions regarding his study of religion. He postulated that religion is primarily a biological reaction, that the religions of humanity need not be identical, and that "the science of religions" can only suggest, not proclaim, a religious creed. He also stated his fundamental hypothesis: The subconscious self intermediated between nature and the higher region or "God."

. . . Summing up in the broadest possible way the characteristics of the religious life, as we have found them, it includes the following beliefs:

1. That the visible world is part of a more spiritual universe from which it draws its chief significance;

2. That union or harmonious relation with that higher universe is our true end;

3. That prayer or inner communion with the spirit thereof—be that spirit 'God' or 'law'—is a process wherein work is really done, and spiritual energy flows in and produces effects, psychological or material, within the phenomenal world.

Religion includes also the following psychological characteristics:

4. A new zest which adds itself like a gift to life, and takes the form either of lyrical enchantment or of appeal to earnestness and heroism.

5. An assurance of safety and a temper of peace, and, in relation to others, a preponderance of loving affections.

In illustrating these characteristics by documents, we have been literally bathed in sentiment. In re-reading my manuscript, I am almost appalled at the amount of emotionality which I find in it. After so much of this, we can afford to be dryer and less sympathetic in the rest of the work that lies before us. . . .

Is the existence of so many religious types and sects and creeds regrettable?

To [this] I answer 'No' emphatically. And my reason is that I do not see how it is possible that creatures in such different positions and with such different powers as human individuals are, should have exactly the same functions and the same duties. No two of us have identical difficulties, nor should we be expected to work out identical solutions. Each, from his peculiar angle of observation, takes in a certain sphere of fact and trouble, which each must deal with in a unique manner. One of us must soften himself, another must harden himself; one must yield a point, another must stand firm, in order the better to defend the position assigned him. If an Emerson were forced to be a Wesley, or a Moody forced to be a Whitman, the total human consciousness of the divine would suffer. The divine can mean no single quality, it must mean a group of qualities, by being champions of which in alternation, different men may all find worthy missions. Each attitude being a syllable in human nature's total message, it takes the whole of us to spell the meaning out completely. So a 'god of battles' must be allowed to be the god for one kind of person, a god of peace and heaven and home, the god for another. We must frankly recognize the fact that we live in partial systems, and that parts are not interchangeable in the spiritual life. If we are peevish and jealous, destruction of the self must be an element of our religion; why need it be one if we are good and sympathetic from the outset? If we are sick souls, we require a religion of deliverance; but why think so much of deliverance, if we are healthy-minded? Unquestionably, some men have the completer experience and the higher vocation, here just as in the social world; but for each man to stay in his own experience, whatever it be, and for others to tolerate him there, is surely best. . . .

But, you may now ask, would not this one-sidedness be cured if we should all espouse the science of religions as our own religion? In answering this question I must open again the general relations of the theoretic to the active life.

Knowledge about a thing is not the thing itself. You remember what Al-Ghazzali told us in the Lecture on Mysticism,—that to understand the causes of drunkenness, as a physician understands them, is not to be drunk. A science might come to understand everything about the causes and elements of religion, and might even decide which elements were qualified, by their general harmony with other branches of knowledge, to be considered true; and yet the best man at this science might be the man who found it hardest to be personally devout. . . .

■ ■ ■

The world of our experience consists at all times of two parts, an objective and a subjective part, of which the former may be incalculably more extensive than the latter, and yet the latter can never be omitted or suppressed. The objective part is the sum total of whatsoever at any given time we may be thinking of, the subjective part is the inner 'state' in which the thinking comes to pass. . . .

Let us agree, then, that Religion, occupying herself with personal destinies and keeping thus in contact with the only absolute realities which we know, must necessarily play an eternal part in human history. The next thing to decide is what she reveals about those destinies, or whether indeed she reveals anything distinct enough to be considered a general message to mankind. . . .

Both thought and feeling are determinants of conduct, and the same conduct may be determined either by feeling or by thought. When we survey the whole field of religion, we find a great variety in the thoughts that have prevailed there; but the feelings on the one hand and the conduct on the other are almost always the same, for Stoic, Christian, and Buddhist saints are practically indistinguishable in their lives. The theories which Religion generates, being thus variable, are secondary; and if you wish to grasp her essence, you must look to the feelings and the conduct as being the more constant elements. It is between these two elements that the short circuit exists on which she carries on her principal business, while the ideas and symbols and other institutions form loop-lines which may be perfections and improvements, and may even some day all be united into one harmonious system, but which are not to be regarded as organs with an indispensable function, necessary at all times for religious life to go on. This seems to me the first conclusion which we are entitled to draw from the phenomena we have passed in review. . . .

At this purely subjective rating, therefore, Religion must be considered vindicated in a certain way from the attacks of her critics. It would seem that she cannot be a mere anachronism and survival, but must exert a permanent function, whether she be with or without intellectual content, and whether, if she have any, it be true or false.

We must next pass beyond the point of view of merely subjective utility, and make inquiry into the intellectual content itself.

First, is there, under all the discrepancies of the creeds, a common nucleus to which they bear their testimony unanimously?

And second, ought we to consider the testimony true?

I will take up the first question first, and answer it immediately in the affirmative. The warring gods and formulas of the various religions do indeed cancel each other, but there is a certain uniform deliverance in which religions all appear to meet. It consists of two parts:

1. An uneasiness; and
2. Its solution.

1. The uneasiness, reduced to its simplest terms, is a sense that there is something wrong about us as we naturally stand.

2. The solution is a sense that we are saved from the wrongness by making proper connection with the higher powers. . . .

■ ■ ■

God is the natural appellation, for us Christians at least, for the supreme reality, so I will call this higher part of the universe by the name of God. We and God have business with each other; and in opening ourselves to his influence our deepest destiny is fulfilled. The universe, at least those parts of it which our personal being constitutes, takes a turn genuinely for the worse or for the better in proportion as each one of us fulfills or evades God's demands. As far as this goes I probably have you with me, for I only translate into schematic language what I may call the instinctive belief of mankind: God is real since he produces real effects. . . .

The real effects in question, so far as I have as yet admitted them, are exerted on the personal centres of energy of the various subjects, but the spontaneous faith of most of the subjects is that they embrace a wider sphere than this. Most religious men believe (or 'know,' if they be mystical) that not only they themselves, but the whole universe of beings to whom the God is present, are secure in his parental hands. There is a sense, a dimension, they are sure, in which we are all saved, in spite of the gates of hell and all adverse terrestrial appearances. God's existence is the guarantee of an ideal order that shall be permanently preserved. This world may indeed, as science assures us, some day burn up or freeze; but if it is part of his order, the old ideals are sure to be brought elsewhere to fruition, so that where God is, tragedy is only provisional and partial, and shipwreck and dissolution are not the absolutely final things. Only when this farther step of faith concerning God is taken, and remote objective consequences are predicted, does religion, as it seems to me, get wholly free from the first immediate subjective experience, and bring a real hypothesis into play. A good hypothesis in science must have other properties than those of the phenomenon it is immediately invoked to explain, otherwise it is not prolific enough. God, meaning only what enters into the religious man's experience of union, falls short of being an hypothesis of this more useful order. He needs to enter into wider cosmic relations in order to justify the subject's absolute confidence and peace.

That the God with whom, starting from the hither side of our own extra-marginal self, we come at its remoter margin into commerce should be the absolute world-ruler, is of course a very considerable over-belief. Over-belief as it is, though, it is an article of almost every one's religion. Most of us pretend in some way to prop it upon our philosophy, but the philosophy itself is really propped upon this faith. What is this but to say that Religion, in her fullest exercise of function, is not a mere illumination of facts already elsewhere given, not a mere passion, like love, which views things in a rosier light. It is indeed that, as we have seen abundantly. But it is something more, namely, a postulator of new facts as well. The world interpreted religiously is not the materialistic world over again, with an altered expression; it must have, over and above the altered expression, a natural constitution different at some point from that which a materialistic world would have. It must be such that different events can be expected in it, different conduct must be required.

This thoroughly 'pragmatic' view of religion has usually been taken as a matter of course by common men. They have interpolated divine miracles into the field of nature, they have built a heaven out beyond the grave. It is only transcendentalist metaphysicians who think that, without adding any concrete details to Nature, or subtracting any, but by simply calling it the expression of absolute spirit, you make it more divine just as it stands. I believe the pragmatic way of taking religion to be the deeper way. It gives it body as well as soul, it makes it claim, as everything real must claim, some characteristic realm of fact as its very own. What the more characteristically divine facts are, apart from the actual inflow of energy in the faith-state and the prayer-state, I know not. But the over-belief on which I am ready to make my personal venture is that they exist. The whole drift of my education goes to persuade me that the world of our present consciousness is only one out of many worlds of consciousness that exist, and that those other worlds must contain experiences which have a meaning for our life also; and that although in the main their experiences and those of this world keep discrete, yet the two become continuous at certain points, and higher energies filter in. By being faithful in my poor measure to this over-belief, I seem to myself to keep more sane and true. I can, of course, put myself into the sectarian scientist's attitude, and imagine vividly that the world of sensations and of scientific laws and objects may be all. But whenever I do this, I hear that inward monitor of which W. K. Clifford once wrote, whispering the word 'bosh!' Humbug is humbug, even though it bear the scientific name, and the total expression of human experience, as I view it objectively, invincibly urges me beyond the narrow scientific bounds. Assuredly, the real world is of a different temperament,—more intricately built than physical science allows. So my objective and my subjective conscience both hold me to the over-belief which I express. Who knows whether the faithfulness of individuals here below to their own poor over-beliefs may not actually help God in turn to be more effectively faithful to his own greater tasks? . . .

Further Resources

BOOKS

Allen, Gay Wilson. *William James: A Biography.* New York: Viking, 1967.

McDermott, John J., ed. *The Writings of William James: A Comprehensive Edition.* New York: Modern Library, 1967.

Townsend, Kim. *Manhood at Harvard: William James and Others.* New York: Norton, 1996.

PERIODICALS

Curley, Augustine J. "Varieties of Religion Today: William James Revisited." *Library Journal,* February 1, 2002, 108.

Taylor, Charles. "Risking Belief: Why William James Still Matters." *Commonweal,* March 8, 2002, 14.

Zaleski, Carol. "A Letter to William James." *The Christian Century,* January 16, 2002, 32.

WEBSITES

Emory University. "William James." Available online at http://www.emory.edu/EDUCATION/mfp/james.html; website home page: http://www.emory.edu/EDUCATION/mfp/Index.html (accessed January 10, 2003). This site contains numerous links to primary and secondary sources.

Goodman, Russell. "William James." *Stanford Encyclopedia of Philosophy.* Available online at http://plato.stanford.edu/entries/james/; website home page: http://plato.stanford.edu/ (accessed May 15, 2003).

Pragmatism Cybrary. "William James Society." Available online at http://www.pragmatism.org/societies/william_james.htm; website home page: http://www.pragmatism.org/default.htm (accessed January 10, 2003).

The Souls of Black Folk

Nonfiction work

By: W.E.B. Du Bois

Date: 1903

Source: Du Bois, W.E.B. *The Souls of Black Folk.* Chicago: A.C. McClurg, 1903. Available online at http://www.bartleby.com/114/10.html; website home page: http://www.bartleby.com/ (accessed May 16, 2003).

About the Author: W.E.B. (William Edward Burghardt) Du Bois (1868 1963) was born in Great Barrington, Massachusetts, and attended Harvard University, completing a bachelor's degree in 1888, a master's three years later, and a doctorate in 1895. For the next fifteen years he taught economics and history at Atlanta University. In 1910, Du Bois and others organized the National Association for the Advancement of Colored People (NAACP). ■

Introduction

During slavery and postslavery times, African American churches became important institutions for organizing social life. During the eighteenth century, slaves were generally allowed into the white churches in a subordinate status, where they were exposed to white preachers. As the number of African American converts to christianity grew in the nineteenth century, the numbers of African American ministers also expanded.

Since African Americans were frequently denied access to the larger white community and its resources, they had to build their own institutions and social structures. Most of the churches in the white community tended to ignore the needs of black people and generally not include them in their congregations. In those that did, blacks were often relegated to second-class status and not allowed full and equal participation in activities. In response to these inequalities, African American Christians formed their own congregations.

In the late nineteenth century, the social gospel movement was beginning to develop in America. Its advocates sought to follow the words of Jesus by working to bring about solutions to social problems, but many people in white churches were not interested in extending their social concerns to the black community. Some ministers, like Solomon Washington Gladden, did want to take that religious movement to African Americans, but his viewpoints and efforts were in the minority among Christians. For the most part, African Americans were left to develop their own social gospel movement within their own churches and communities. In the early 1900s, an African Methodist Episcopal Church minister, Bishop Reverdy Ransom, worked toward the creation of settlement houses in Chicago and New York. He was a leading example of the relevancy and importance of the African American church to the African American community.

Significance

Through their own church institutions and programs, African American Christians reached the disenfranchised in their communities. These churches not only provided spiritual guidance but also were critical in helping African Americans create a sense of community identity and belonging. They also functioned as places where people could build unity, create social networks, and make contacts to help in their everyday lives. They gave members a sense of hope and optimism that life would get better. Their ministers and congregations often did help significantly in meeting the needs of the people by communicating employment opportunities, providing mutual aid when facing illness and hardship, and fostering appreciation of their own American traditions as well as African heritage.

In the twenty-first century, many African American denominations are still vital and meaningful to their members. Five large Christian denominations that have predominantly African American membership are the National Baptist Convention U.S.A., the Church of God in Christ, the National Baptist Convention of America, the African Methodist Episcopal Church, and the African Methodist Episcopal Zion Church. According to the National Council of the Churches of Christ, these denominations currently have over twenty-one million members.

Primary Source

The Souls of Black Folk [excerpt]

SYNOPSIS: The following excerpts are from Chapter 10, entitled "Of the Faith of the Fathers." Du Bois describes the characteristics of the typical black church and asserts that the church was the "social center of life" in the black community. He notes that there was a black church for every sixty black families in America.

It was out in the country, far from home, far from my foster home, on a dark Sunday night. The road wandered from our rambling log-house up the stony bed of a creek, past wheat and corn, until we could hear dimly across the fields a rhythmic cadence of song,—soft, thrilling, powerful, that swelled and died sorrowfully in our ears. I was a country school-teacher then, fresh from the East, and had never seen a Southern Negro revival. To be sure, we in Berkshire were not perhaps as stiff and formal as they in Suffolk of olden time; yet we were very quiet and subdued, and I know not what would have happened those clear Sabbath mornings had some one punctuated the sermon with a wild scream, or interrupted the long prayer with a loud Amen! And so most striking to me, as I approached the village and the little plain church perched aloft, was the air of intense excitement that possessed that mass of black folk. A sort of suppressed terror hung in the air and seemed to seize us,—a pythian madness, a demoniac possession, that lent terrible reality to song and word. The black and massive form of the preacher swayed and quivered as the words crowded to his lips and flew at us in singular eloquence. The people moaned and fluttered, and then the gaunt-cheeked brown woman beside me suddenly leaped straight into the air and shrieked like a lost soul, while round about came wail and groan and outcry, and a scene of human passion such as I had never conceived before.

Those who have not thus witnessed the frenzy of a Negro revival in the untouched backwoods of the South can but dimly realize the religious feeling of the slave; as described, such scenes appear grotesque and funny, but as seen they are awful. Three things characterized this religion of the slave,—the Preacher, the Music, and the Frenzy. The Preacher is the most unique personality developed by the Negro on American soil. A leader, a politician, an orator, a "boss," an intriguer, an idealist,—all these he is, and ever, too, the centre of a group of men, now twenty, now a thousand in number. The combination of a certain adroitness with deep-seated earnestness, of tact with consummate ability, gave him his preëminence, and helps him maintain it. The type, of course, varies according to time and place, from the West Indies in the sixteenth century to New England in the nineteenth, and from the Mississippi bottoms to cities like New Orleans or New York.

The Music of Negro religion is that plaintive rhythmic melody, with its touching minor cadences, which, despite caricature and defilement, still remains the most original and beautiful expression of human life and longing yet born on American soil. Sprung from the African forests, where its counterpart can still be heard, it was adapted, changed, and intensified by the tragic soul-life of the slave, until, under the stress of law and whip, it became the one true expression of a people's sorrow, despair, and hope.

Finally the Frenzy or "Shouting," when the Spirit of the Lord passed by, and, seizing the devotee, made him mad with supernatural joy, was the last essential of Negro religion and the one more devoutly believed in than all the rest. It varied in expression from the silent rapt countenance or the low murmur and moan to the mad abandon of physical fervor,—the stamping, shrieking, and shouting, the rushing to and fro and wild waving of arms, the weeping and laughing, the vision and the trance. All this is nothing new in the world, but old as religion, as Delphi and Endor. And so firm a hold did it have on the Negro, that many generations firmly believed that without this visible manifestation of the God there could be no true communion with the Invisible.

These were the characteristics of Negro religious life as developed up to the time of Emancipation. Since under the peculiar circumstances of the black man's environment they were the one expression of his higher life, they are of deep interest to the student of his development, both socially and psychologically. Numerous are the attractive lines of inquiry that here group themselves. What did slavery mean to the African savage? What was his attitude toward the World and Life? What seemed to him good and evil,—God and Devil? Whither went his longings and strivings, and wherefore were his heart-burnings and disappointments? Answers to such questions can come only from a study of Negro religion as a development, through its gradual changes from the heathenism of the Gold Coast to the institutional Negro church of Chicago.

Moreover, the religious growth of millions of men, even though they be slaves, cannot be without potent influence upon their contemporaries. The Methodists and Baptists of America owe much of their condition to the silent but potent influence of their millions of Negro converts. Especially is this noticeable in the South, where theology and religious philosophy are on this account a long way behind the North, and where the religion of the poor whites is a plain copy of Negro thought and methods. The mass of "gospel" hymns which has swept through American churches and well-nigh ruined our sense of song consists largely of debased imitations of Negro melodies made by ears that caught the jingle but not the music, the body but not the soul, of the Jubilee songs. It is thus clear that the study of Negro religion is not only a vital part of the history of the Negro in America, but no uninteresting part of American history.

The Negro church of to-day is the social centre of Negro life in the United States, and the most characteristic expression of African character. Take a typical church in a small Virginian town: it is the "First Baptist"—a roomy brick edifice seating five hundred or more persons, tastefully finished in Georgia pine, with a carpet, a small organ, and stained-glass windows. Underneath is a large assembly room with benches. This building is the central club-house of a community of a thousand or more Negroes. Various organizations meet here,—the church proper, the Sunday-school, two or three insurance societies, women's societies, secret societies, and mass meetings of various kinds. Entertainments, suppers, and lectures are held beside the five or six regular weekly religious services. Considerable sums of money are collected and expended here, employment is found for the idle, strangers are introduced, news is disseminated and charity distributed. At the same time this social, intellectual, and economic centre is a religious centre of great power. Depravity, Sin, Redemption, Heaven, Hell, and Damnation

A seeker "gets religion" at a Negro revival meeting. In "Of the Faith of the Fathers" W.E.B. DuBois describes the characteristics of such churches and asserts that the church was the "social center of life" in the black community. © CORBIS. REPRODUCED BY PERMISSION.

are preached twice a Sunday with much fervor, and revivals take place every year after the crops are laid by; and few indeed of the community have the hardihood to withstand conversion. Back of this more formal religion, the Church often stands as a real conserver of morals, a strengthener of family life, and the final authority on what is Good and Right.

Thus one can see in the Negro church to-day, reproduced in microcosm, all that great world from which the Negro is cut off by color-prejudice and social condition. In the great city churches the same tendency is noticeable and in many respects emphasized. A great church like the Bethel of Philadelphia has over eleven hundred members, an edifice seating fifteen hundred persons and valued at one hundred thousand dollars, an annual budget of five thousand dollars, and a government consisting of a pastor with several assisting local preachers, an executive and legislative board, financial boards and tax collectors; general church meetings for making laws; subdivided groups led by class leaders, a company of militia, and twenty-four auxiliary societies. The activity of a church like this is immense and far-reaching, and the bishops who preside over these organizations throughout the land are among the most powerful Negro rulers in the world.

Such churches are really governments of men, and consequently a little investigation reveals the curious fact that, in the South, at least, practically every American Negro is a church member. Some, to be sure, are not regularly enrolled, and a few do not habitually attend services; but, practically, a proscribed people must have a social centre, and that centre for this people is the Negro church. The census of 1890 showed nearly twenty-four thousand Negro churches in the country, with a total enrolled membership of over two and a half millions, or ten actual church members to every twenty-eight persons, and in some Southern States one in every two persons. Besides these there is the large number who, while not enrolled as members, attend and take part in many of the activities of the church. There is an organized

Negro church for every sixty black families in the nation, and in some States for every forty families, owning, on an average, a thousand dollars' worth of property each, or nearly twenty-six million dollars in all.

Such, then, is the large development of the Negro church since Emancipation. The question now is, What have been the successive steps of this social history and what are the present tendencies? First, we must realize that no such institution as the Negro church could rear itself without definite historical foundations. These foundations we can find if we remember that the social history of the Negro did not start in America. He was brought from a definite social environment,—the polygamous clan life under the headship of the chief and the potent influence of the priest. His religion was nature-worship, with profound belief in invisible surrounding influences, good and bad, and his worship was through incantation and sacrifice. The first rude change in this life was the slave ship and the West Indian sugar-fields. The plantation organization replaced the clan and tribe, and the white master replaced the chief with far greater and more despotic powers. Forced and long-continued toil became the rule of life, the old ties of blood relationship and kinship disappeared, and instead of the family appeared a new polygamy and polyandry, which, in some cases, almost reached promiscuity. It was a terrific social revolution, and yet some traces were retained of the former group life, and the chief remaining institution was the Priest or Medicine-man. He early appeared on the plantation and found his function as the healer of the sick, the interpreter of the Unknown, the comforter of the sorrowing, the supernatural avenger of wrong, and the one who rudely but picturesquely expressed the longing, disappointment, and resentment of a stolen and oppressed people. Thus, as bard, physician, judge, and priest, within the narrow limits allowed by the slave system, rose the Negro preacher, and under him the first Afro-American institution, the Negro church. This church was not at first by any means Christian nor definitely organized; rather it was an adaptation and mingling of heathen rites among the members of each plantation, and roughly designated as Voodooism. Association with the masters, missionary effort and motives of expediency gave these rites an early veneer of Christianity, and after the lapse of many generations the Negro church became Christian.

Two characteristic things must be noticed in regard to this church. First, it became almost entirely Baptist and Methodist in faith; secondly, as a social institution it antedated by many decades the monogamic Negro home. From the very circumstances of its beginning, the church was confined to the plantation, and consisted primarily of a series of disconnected units; although, later on, some freedom of movement was allowed, still this geographical limitation was always important and was one cause of the spread of the decentralized and democratic Baptist faith among the slaves. At the same time, the visible rite of baptism appealed strongly to their mystic temperament. To-day the Baptist Church is still largest in membership among Negroes, and has a million and a half communicants. Next in popularity came the churches organized in connection with the white neighboring churches, chiefly Baptist and Methodist, with a few Episcopalian and others. The Methodists still form the second greatest denomination, with nearly a million members. The faith of these two leading denominations was more suited to the slave church from the prominence they gave to religious feeling and fervor. The Negro membership in other denominations has always been small and relatively unimportant, although the Episcopalians and Presbyterians are gaining among the more intelligent classes to-day, and the Catholic Church is making headway in certain sections. After Emancipation, and still earlier in the North, the Negro churches largely severed such affiliations as they had had with the white churches, either by choice or by compulsion. The Baptist churches became independent, but the Methodists were compelled early to unite for purposes of episcopal government. This gave rise to the great African Methodist Church, the greatest Negro organization in the world, to the Zion Church and the Colored Methodist, and to the black conferences and churches in this and other denominations.

The second fact noted, namely, that the Negro church antedates the Negro home, leads to an explanation of much that is paradoxical in this communistic institution and in the morals of its members. But especially it leads us to regard this institution as peculiarly the expression of the inner ethical life of a people in a sense seldom true elsewhere. Let us turn, then, from the outer physical development of the church to the more important inner ethical life of the people who compose it. The Negro has already been pointed out many times as a religious animal,—a being of that deep emotional nature which turns instinctively toward the supernatural. Endowed with a rich tropical imagination and a keen, delicate appreciation of Nature, the transplanted African lived in a world animate with gods and devils, elves and witches; full of strange influences,—of Good to be implored, of Evil to be propitiated. Slavery, then, was to him the dark triumph of Evil over him. All the hateful powers of the Underworld were striving against him, and a spirit of revolt and revenge filled his heart. He called up all the resources of heathenism to aid,—exorcism and witchcraft, the mysterious Obi worship with its barbarous rites, spells, and blood-sacrifice even, now and then, of human victims. Weird midnight orgies and mystic conjurations were invoked, the witch-woman and the voodoo-priest became the centre of Negro group life, and that vein of vague superstition which characterizes the unlettered Negro even to-day was deepened and strengthened.

Further Resources

BOOKS

Aptheker, Herbert, ed. *Prayers for Dark People: W.E.B. Du Bois.* Amherst, Mass: University of Massachusetts Press, 1980.

Fontenot Chester J., Jr., and Mary Alice Morgan, eds. *W.E.B. Du Bois and Race: Essays Celebrating the Centennial Publication of The Souls of Black Folk.* Macon, Ga.: Mercer University Press, 2001.

Zuckerman, Phil, ed. *Du Bois on Religion.* Walnut Creek, Calif.: AltaMira Press, 2000.

PERIODICALS

Adell, Sandra. "W.E.B. Du Bois on Race and Culture." *African American Review,* Winter 1999, 702.

Early, Gerald. "A Homeless Mind." *National Review,* December 4, 2000.

White, Jack E. "Race Warrior: W.E.B. Du Bois: A Frank Look at His Fight for Equality." *Time,* October 30, 2000, 86.

WEBSITES

African American Perspectives. "W.E.B. Du Bois: Biography." Available online at http://memory.loc.gov/ammem/aap/dubois.html; website home page: http://www.memory.loc.gov/ammem/aap/aaphome.html (accessed January 11, 2003).

Hale, Steven. "Works by W.E.B. Du Bois on the Internet." Available online at http://www.dc.peachnet.edu/~shale/humanities/composition/assignments/dubois.html (accessed May 16, 2003).

University of Massachusetts. "W.E.B. Du Bois Papers." Available online at http://www.library.umass.edu/spcoll/dubois.html; website home page: http://www.library.umass.edu/spcoll/spec.html (accessed January 11, 2003).

"Remarks of Dr. Washington Gladden"

Speech

By: Washington Gladden

Date: 1903

Source: "Remarks of Dr. Washington Gladden." In Du Bois, W.E. Burghardt, ed. *The Negro Church: Report of a Social Study Made Under the Direction of Atlanta University; Together with the Proceedings of the Eighth Conference for the Study of the Negro Problems.* Atlanta, Ga.: The Atlanta University Press, 1903, 204–207. Available online at http://docsouth.unc.edu/church/negrochurch/dubois.html (accessed January 11, 2003).

About the Author: Solomon Washington Gladden (1836–1918) was born in Pottsgrove, Pennsylvania, and in 1859 graduated from Williams College. In 1882 he became the pastor of the First Congregational Church of Columbus, Ohio, where he served for the rest of his life. He authored more than three dozen books and frequently expressed his support of the social gospel movement. ■

Introduction

In 1903, Gladden addressed an audience of students, teachers, ministers, and others at an Atlanta University conference examining the nature and condition of black churches in America. A leading proponent of the social gospel movement and called by some its father, Gladden spoke about the application of social gospel principles to African Americans and their churches.

The social gospel movement in America had developed in the last quarter of the nineteenth century. Its basic tenet was that God wished truly religious people, both laity and clergy, to work to bring about social changes that would help their neighbors in need. It was not enough for Christians to love and worship God, lead a moral life, go to church services, and take care of personal and family responsibilities. The truly moral Christian was expected to work toward social renewal. This was the message that Gladden delivered to his congregation in Ohio, to the young people gathered at Atlanta University, and to any group in the nation that asked him to speak.

Gladden firmly believed that societal conflicts could be healed by going beyond purely Christian denominational concerns. What was needed was a social gospel that would preach the theological reasons for finding moral and practical solutions to the problems of the day. He felt that drawn-out theological debates about questions that no one could really answer were not as important as devising the best solutions to social and human problems.

The social gospel movement had been addressing the needs of laborers and the working classes, including African Americans, in their attempts to make inroads into the political and social structure of the larger white society. While ministering in the industrial city of Springfield, Massachusetts, in the mid- and late 1870s, Gladden had seen the importance of the social gospel to those who helped poverty-stricken workers and the labor unions they were trying to organize. His active support of these

Washington Gladden sought to encourage social responsibility among those in his congregations. THE LIBRARY OF CONGRESS.

efforts became an important characteristic of his social gospel thought. Gladden wished that the same advocacy of the social gospel could be applied to African Americans who were seeking political and social progress for themselves. He believed that the principles that guided the labor movement could be applied to African Americans in their efforts to bring about change.

Significance

Gladden's speech was an important step in helping to lay a theological foundation for the involvement of Christians in the effort to help improve the lives of African Americans. By advocating the active involvement of Christians in political and social causes, he helped establish religious roots for the civil rights movement in the twentieth century.

Given the religious conservatism of the time, Gladden's advocacy of the social gospel did not meet with approval from many Christians. His message was a difficult one to accept because it required taking risks. For Christian black and white people to openly advocate and work toward the advancement of African Americans, especially in the South, meant facing ostracism and even personal danger. Despite these risks, however, some Christians were inspired by Gladden's words and tried to apply the social gospel. Gladden's commitment to applying the principles of the social gospel to the major social issues of his day, including the rights of African Americans, made him a historical force in stirring the conscience of Christian Americans.

Primary Source

Remarks of Dr. Washington Gladden

SYNOPSIS: In his remarks, included as a chapter in W.E.B. Du Bois's report, *The Negro Church,* Gladden urged African Americans to participate in political affairs and to consider work in the ministry in order to purify "the ideals of the Christian church."

You are citizens, by the definition of the constitution, and you are bound to be good citizens—intelligent citizens, law-abiding citizens, loyal citizens. From these obligations I am sure you do not wish to escape. You mean to do your part in contributing to the peace, the order, the security, the welfare of this great commonwealth in which you live.

In my counsels to the young people of Columbus, O., I went on to say that those to whom the duties as well as the rights of citizenship are entrusted ought not only to fit themselves for their discharge, but to discharge them solemnly and conscientiously, when the time comes for their performance. What shall I say to you who find yourselves obstructed in the performance of these duties? I do not wish to make any inflammatory suggestions; I doubt whether the question of your political rights can be settled by violence. But this much I am safe in saying: people who are thoroughly fitted for good citizenship, and who show by their conduct that they have the disposition and the purpose to be good citizens, are not going to be permanently excluded, in any part of this country, from the responsibilities and duties of citizenship. That is as sure as tomorrow's sun-rising. It cannot be that in the United States of America, young men who are thoroughly intelligent, who know what citizenship means, who love their country, who are working to build up its prosperity and to secure its peace and who are ready to shed their blood in its defence, are going to be forbidden to take any part in its government.

What I have said, therefore, applies to you, I think, even more closely than to the young people of my own state. To you, in an exceptional and impressive way, this truth ought to come home. The more strenuously men oppose your participation in political affairs, the more zealous and dilligent [sic] ought you to be in qualifying yourselves to take part in them. You are not wholly shut out from such duties and whenever you have a chance to exercise them, let every man see that they are performed with exceptional intelligence and exceptional conscientiousness; that the black man holds the suffrage as a high and sacred trust; that he cannot be bribed or led astray by the arts of the demagogue; that he puts aside his own personal interests when he votes; that he will not even use the suffrage as a means of extorting benefits for his own race at the expense of the rest of the community, but will always keep in view the general welfare; that he is always and everywhere a patriot in his political action; that when he holds an office he discharges its duties more faithfully and honestly than the white man does. I have heard of some instances of this nature since I came to Atlanta of men in public station whose white neighbors testify concerning them that their conduct is blameless and their service of the highest order. Let such instances be multiplied. Hold up the standard everywhere; rally round it all your people. Let it be your constant endeavor, your highest ambition to infuse this spirit, this purpose, into the thought and the life of all colored men. Before such a purpose as that the barriers of political exclusiveness are sure to go down.

Do not understand me as justifying or excusing those exclusions. I think they are utterly many. But I am pointing out to you the kind of weapons with which you can surely batter them down.

And now, very briefly, what can we say of the relations of the young people to the church? Here are these 1,210,481 young people under twenty-one. They are all citizens of Georgia; they all belong to the state. Do they all belong to the church? No; I fear not. They all belong to God; they are all His children; they owe Him love and reverence; if they are filial children, prodigal children, they are all God's children; they cannot, if they renounce and forswear it, rid themselves of the obligation of allegiance to Him. We may say of them, that they all belong in one sense to the kingdom of God. . . .

Here again I find myself in some doubt as to the fitness of these words to your peculiar circumstances. To those of you who live in Atlanta I can speak with confidence for I know that you can find a church here of which all that I say is true, in which you can find the kind of instruction and inspiration you need, to which you can attach yourselves with intelligent enthusiasm, with which you can join in the work of uplifting humanity. I suppose that there are churches of the same sort in many of the Southern cities in which you could be welcome. Doubtless there are a great many churches in all the Southern states which are far below this ideal, in which the religious instruction you would receive would be imperfect, in which the prevailing idea of religion would be one that no intelligent and conscientious person could accept. Many of you will find yourselves in communities in which the only churches are of this kind. I am not familiar enough with the situation in such communities to give you any very positive counsel respecting your conduct. I had hoped that I might be able to attend the whole of this conference, and that then I might be able to gain some information which would enable me to form a clearer judgment upon these questions.

What I say about it now must be very provisional and tentative.

1. In the first place, it seems to me that you are bound to do all you can for the purification of the ideal of the Christian church. What the Christian church is, what it ought to stand for, you have some clear idea. You know that it stands, above all things, for pure conduct and high character; that its members ought to be men and women of blameless lives; that its ministers ought to be examples of virtue and honor and nobility. You know that conversion is no mere ebullition of religious emotion; that it is a change of mind and heart and life; a change from untruth to veracity, from impurity to chastity, from selfishness to unselfishness, from the spirit which is always asking, "How much am I going to get out of this?" to the spirit which is always saying, "Where can I give the most to those who are neediest?" You know that a Christian church ought not to be a company of men and women whose main business is having a good time—by getting happy and convincing themselves that they are sure of going to heaven—but whose main business is bringing heaven down to earth by showing men how to live such clean, beautiful, unselfish lives that the wilderness and the solitary place are glad for them, and that flowers of Paradise spring up in their path wherever they go. And I think it is your first duty to enforce this high and true ideal of what a church ought to be upon all the people with whom you come in contact. You will have to be wise about it. It will not do to be harsh and censorious in your judgments of the ideas and practices of those whom you are trying to lead into the light; you must persuade them by lifting up higher ideals before them, rather than by condemning and denouncing their ways. But I am

sure that the young men and women who go out from such schools as this can do much, if they are wise and kind, to purify and elevate the ideals of the church in the communities where they live.

2. In some cases, doubtless, it will be found impracticable to improve the conditions of the existing churches, and it will, therefore, be necessary to organize new churches in which the essentials of Christianity can be maintained and exemplified. This will call for hard and self-condemning work. It will demand faith and courage and patience and gentleness; but it may be work of the highest value and productiveness, and you must be ready for it.

3. Finally, let me express my belief that no other kind of work can be more vital or more fruitful in the elevation of the Negro race than the work of the ministry when it is exercised with intelligence and fidelity and devotion to the highest standards of Christian conduct and character.

There are few positions in which a young man can do more harm than in the leadership of a church which is the exponent of nothing better than a mere emotional religionism; in which pietism is divorced from character and made the cover of all kinds of immoralities. But, on the other hand, there are few positions in which a young man can do more good than as the pastor of a church in which clean living and unselfish service are exemplified; a church which stands for all the great verities of manhood and womanhood and lifts up a standard around which the elements that make for social and civic righteousness may gather and do heroic battle for God and home and native land. I do not believe that such churches as these are likely, in the present order of things, to be very popular all at once. It is probable that young men who undertake to organize and lead them will have to be content with the hard work and small compensation. They can find softer places and better salaries in churches where the standards are different. But no man can afford to lower his ideals for the sake of self or popularity. The elevation of the Negro race will wait a long time under such leadership. But men who are not looking for such berths, men to whom life means service, can find, in the Christian ministry, a great opportunity to serve their race and their country.

Such are the ideals which will, I trust, commend themselves to your choice as you go out to the work of life. For men and women with such purposes and aims the church has need and the state has need, and great rewards are waiting for them. I want you to win success, the true success—that which is won not by outstripping our neighbors but by helping them to get on their feet and keep in the way of life. That is not what the world means by success, but it is the only true success, believe me. Now is the time for you to get this truth firmly fixed in your own minds, not only as a pleasing sentiment, but as a working theory of life.

Further Resources

BOOKS

Dorn, Jacob H. *Washington Gladden: Prophet of the Social Gospel.* Columbus, Ohio: Ohio State University Press, 1967.

Gladden, Washington. *Applied Christianity: Moral Aspects of Social Questions.* New York: Arno, 1976.

———. *Being a Christian: What It Means and How to Begin.* Freeport, N.Y.: Books for Libraries Press, 1972.

WEBSITES

Cyber Hymnal. "Washington Gladden." Available online at http://www.cyberhymnal.org/bio/g/l/gladden_w.htm; website home page: http://www.cyberhymnal.org/ (accessed May 16, 2003).

Net Biography. "Biography of Washington Gladden." Available online at http://www.sacklunch.net/biography/G/WashingtonGladden.html; website home page: http://www.sacklunch.net/ (accessed May 16, 2003).

Neil, Chris. "Congregationalists Lead Social Gospel Movement against 'Gospel of Wealth.'" Available online at http://www.cpcucc.org/cpcnews/1998.05/history.htm; website home page: http://www.cpcucc.org/ (accessed May 16, 2003).

"How Can We as Women Advance the Standing of the Race?"

Journal article

By: Annie H. Jones

Date: July 1904

Source: Jones, Annie H. "How Can We as Women Advance The Standing of the Race?" *National Association Notes* 7, no. 11, July 1904, 9–13. Available online at http://womhist.binghamton.edu/nacw/doc16.htm; website home page: http://womhist.binghamton.edu/index.html (accessed May 16, 2003).

About the Organization: The National Association of Colored Women's Clubs (NACWC) was founded in 1896 in Washington, D.C., with the motto "Lifting As We Climb." The major objectives of the NACWC were the promotion of the family life of black women and the elevation of their social status. Josephine St. Pierre Ruffin, a founder of the organization, emphasized "the training of our children," "the moral education of the race," and "temperance and morality." Annie H. Jones contributed her views to the association. ■

Introduction

Annie H. Jones observed that the church and the state were two great institutions that could improve humankind, but she also held that it was not reasonable to expect these institutions to do the job by themselves. A third agency was necessary: charitable efforts by community associations like women's clubs.

The church was one of the most influential institutions in the life of most African American communities, both in the South and in the North, during the times of slavery and after slavery ended. In both eras, many white Christians felt it was their responsibility to bring their religion to African Americans. Sometimes African Americans were allowed to worship in white churches, but more often than not, they were forced to establish their own churches. Since whites for the most part did not want to mix with African Americans, African American churches were allowed to develop. Thus, African American churches grew in importance in the community because, relative to other institutions in their lives, churches had more freedom to develop.

The state, too, could help improve people's lives. Jones, like other African American leaders, encouraged the states to do more to help educate their children. Eventually in the South, schooling for African Americans was allowed to develop, but only on a limited and segregated basis.

A third important agency for the development of African Americans, according to Jones, was community organizations, like women's clubs. The NACWC, established in 1896, concentrated on issues of major concern to African American women: the family, temperance, employment, segregation, poverty, suffrage, politics, safety, and the role of women. In her first presidential address, delivered in Nashville, Tennessee, in 1897, Mary Church Terrell, the first president of the NACWC, stressed the special role that women played in the advancement of African Americans: "the work which we hope to accomplish can be done better, we believe, by the mothers, wives, daughters, and sisters of our race than by the fathers, husbands, brothers, and sons."

Significance

The NACWC is one of the oldest national African American secular organizations in existence today. For over a hundred years of continuous service to humanity, the State of Rhode Island General Assembly honored the NACWC on April 9, 2002, through a formal resolution. Introduced by Representative Maxine B. Shavers, the resolution noted that the NACWC was and is "a key institution through which women have asserted political influence within the black community and in the larger society. . . . The NACWC is a great fellowship of women united for service to lift the standards of the home and extending their service to help make better communities. The activities and contributions of the club women help to improve the quality of the life for all people, especially those in the African American community."

The resolution goes on, "The Rhode Island Association of Colored Women's Clubs was founded on July 21, 1903. Sixteen representatives from eleven states answered the call. It was in local women's clubs that African American women found a means to pool their resources and coordinate their efforts. In locality after locality, they raised funds, launched charitable initiatives, and gained the respect of the male power structure. As a national umbrella organization, the National Association of Colored Women's Clubs provides an invaluable overview of the black women's club movement."

Primary Source

"How Can We as Women Advance the Standing of the Race?"

SYNOPSIS: In this article, Annie H. Jones expressed her views concerning the "two great agencies of human improvement," church and state. She believed that the "moral and intellectual standard of the race" could be advanced by these agencies and philanthropic efforts by churches, women's associations, and other organizations.

There is hope for people who recognize their own deficiencies and needs.

It is a trite saying but none the less a true one that "Self Satisfaction is the bane of all progress."

But where an individual or a race realizes its imperfections and resolutely sets to work to overcome them, there is no power under heaven that can keep that individual or that race from progressing.

Possibly we may be pardoned if a little of the prayer of the Pharisee creeps into our minds and we say inwardly: "We thank thee Lord that we are not as some races and peoples who are satisfied with their blankets and hunting grounds, and simply ask to be let alone. We thank thee for our very unrest, our dissatisfaction; we want all—everything that the most favored race on earth has, all the comfort, the privilege, the education, the culture, the liberty, the religion. NOTHING ELSE WILL SATISFY."

We have sometimes been trammeled with the remark that we sang so long: "You may have all the world, give me Jesus"—and we were taken at our word and everything taken from us. That makes a good joke for a speaker until we remember that the hymn was born of the conditions of slavery. Nothing else was allowed the slave—he could not even call

After emancipation, most African Americans found themselves facing poverty, prejudice, and lack of education. Annie H. Jones, representing the National Association of Colored Women's Clubs, asserted that moral and intellectual improvement depended on efforts by both the church and state. © MICHAEL MASLAN HISTORIC PHOTOGRAPHS/CORBIS. REPRODUCED BY PERMISSION.

wife and child his own. But the fact that we pay taxes on $460,000,000 worth of property, according to the statistics of the dominant race, would seem to indicate that we can show a clear title to something other than mansions in the skies.

No race feels more keenly than our own the disgrace that comes to it from the crimes of large untrained elements, the lower millions, even though we may know that the lower element is increasing even among the proud Anglo-Saxons with their thousands of years of training. We know, too, that there is a legitimate reason for the large number of criminals in our ranks. Let us note the conditions: A race newly emancipated with the heritage of 300 years of enforced degradation, and a feeling of injustice and wrong lying deep under the joy of freedom, is turned adrift to battle with responsibility, poverty, prejudice, in a country where competition is keen and civilization is high, where the struggle for existence and the "survival of the fittest" were not only theories but facts.

In the daily struggles of this race both parents had to toil from dawn to dark; the home—there could be none worthy the name—simply a place noisome and dark, where children were fed partly clothed, their training was obtained principally on the streets or in the alleys; a few years or a few months school sufficed and they early joined the great army of breadwinners, without a trade, without education, without training. Then place these same youths in the large cities to which they are lured, principally by the hope of employment at unskilled labor, but there in contact with the dregs of American civilization—the slum element of the great cities—for poverty and prejudice will permit them in no other part.

What is the legitimate result? The criminals of today are the children of those conditions. They missed the severe discipline of slavery, that their elders had, and missed the kindly, wholesome discipline of homes. We can expect nothing else of such conditions than a harvest of crime. There must be time for the formation of homes where children can receive moral and social training. To these the schools must add mental and moral training.

It is easy to give statistics in criminology. Figures may not lie[;] neither do they tell all the truth. Like Ananias and Sapphira they keep a part of the price.

A race cannot rise above its womanhood. Because of her finer sensibilities, a woman is capable of being worse than a man or better than a man. The status of its womanhood is the measure of the progress of the race.

To purify the stream we start with the source. Hence the question, "How can we as women advance the standing of the race?"

The two great agencies of human improvement are the Church and the State.

The State places the means of education within the means of the majority, it offers an education to those who are willing and able to take advantage of it. It makes no provision for the large number who from poverty or ignorance take no steps to avail themselves of its advantages. The State punishes for violation of laws; in its juvenile measures it is reformatory.

The teacher as an employee of the State in its educational work, labors with those who are in the school. Occasionally she goes beyond her pupils to their homes. Rarely does she go beyond these boundaries. To do this requires the missionary or the philanthropic spirit, which is usually not more abundant in this profession than in others. In fact it is less abundant because its ranks are constantly being recruited from the young.

The second great agency of improvement is the Church.

Our largest churches are usually so burdened with debt that the time and strength of the pastor and people are almost entirely taken in securing the necessary dollars to meet obligations. He is an exceptional minister who has any time to spare from looking after the sick and needy of his members to go into the highways and hedges—which means today the tenement houses and alleys of our crowded cities—to better the condition of the large element who never find their way into a church and at whose doors lie the greater part of the crime committed—he finds it impossible.

This is not often the fault of the minister. As a rule he finds the huge debt, ready-made, awaiting him; in fact the strongest, best and most resourceful of our men are the ones who are sent where the financial burdens are heaviest.

To what then must we look for better agencies of improvement?

We must look to SOCIETY, to its organized charities. The experience[d], the thoughtful, the philanthropic from all professions and churches must organize for this immense task. They can work in the churches. There should be societies within the churches whose work is entirely outside its membership, a city missionary department whose work is as necessary as the missionary work in West and South Africa. They can work in the schools, organize the philanthropic element among the teachers who will extend their work beyond the school-room.

Much is being done by women's clubs, much more can be done in this kind of work. Their borders can be strengthened and enlarged. We should support morally and financially the woman who has the heart and capacity for this kind of work. If she is eloquent send her out into the State to arouse and organize clubs for carrying on the work. It is true in this work, as in the ministerial, that the "workman is worthy of his hire," and the woman who really works and accomplishes something should be supported, unless she is wealthy and desires to give her labor, a thing that can hardly happen among us.

It is too much to expect of our organizers and workers, that they leave their homes or give up opportunities of remunerative employment to do the work which needs to be done by our societies and leagues. We could not then expect efficient work. It is possible to secure means to support such persons by regular subscription; there are those who will give regularly certain amounts to do such work, but have not the time or the strength. Such will gladly contribute to have it done. Frequently the name charitable prevents the highest success in such labor. Call it social improvement, or social culture or home culture work. There are some in every smaller community who will find pleasure in this duty, but it is difficult for them to organize themselves. The experienced and sympathetic from our urban centers must lead in the work.

It is worth our while to study the means that are used by our wealthier and more experienced races for the amelioration of social conditions. Study the methods pursued by the Jewish people in their organized philanthropy, their emphasis upon the improvement of home life, their study of sanitary diseases and remedies; the practical advice of the Jewish Rabbi, upon hygienic and moral questions; their close personal oversight of the youth of the race.

The methods of this oldest of races will repay careful study and contrasts forcibly with the "laissez faire" policy followed by many peoples who have come upon the stage of civilization later.

To those of us who as teachers, mothers or guardians of youth in any way have authority, let me emphasize the idea of DISCIPLINE, KINDLY but FIRM.

A recent paper in one of our largest cities spoke of the lack of discipline of its youth as being the skeleton in the American closet. If this need is felt by a race with its centuries of culture and training back of it, how much more necessary for a people who stepped from the stern school of slavery into the broad arena of license—more than learning, more than wealth—we need the home training, the discipline that will make character. A very sad feature in our development is to see the laxity in respect to their children of parents who have culture and training. They are brought up with the "let alone" theory; i.e.: "Let the little fellow alone." It matters not how impudent, disobedient or how dishonest he is now, "when he gets older he will come allright; he will know better." Punishment is too much like slavery. It is old fogyism. How often do we see around us the sad results of this parental policy; saddest in these homes that should have produced something better.

The foundation of Mothers' Clubs is productive of great good. The experienced, unselfish mothers can be a help to many young or ignorant mothers; especially is this true if the mothers have sons and daughters who are an honor to the community. There can be a freedom and directness in the talk, mother with mother, that no amount of preaching, teaching, reading, or lecturing can secure. One of the most recent methods for social amelioration is what is known as the University Settlement. It is a well-known fact that forums, meetings and clubs usually fail to reach the class who needs them. If a meeting were called to discuss the prevention of disease or the best method of caring for children, the people who most need to know these things would be conspicuous by their absence. Hence the University Settlement or Social Set idea in which several benevolent persons or families go down to live in the thickly populated district of the cities among the people they desire to help. By living among the people, cultivating friendly relations with them, they become examples along sanitary, intellectual and moral lines, showing them how to meet the requirements of their narrower conditions, in health, happiness and intellectual advancement; how to do this in the limited means at their disposal, giving lessons in nursing and care of diseases, providing social entertainments, and means of instruction in various lines. Toynbee Hall in London was one of the first and Hull House in Chicago is the best known in this country.

Among the colored people two at least are being tried, Institutional Church in Chicago and a University Settlement in Philadelphia, the latter being under the patronage of the University of Pennsylvania.

If as women we are not able to embark in so large enterprises as this we can do much good on a smaller scale. Let the various clubs of women take up some particular work, let some visit and assist the sick, let others assist the orphans or the old folks' home, let another take in charge the education of some bright but needy girl or boy, let another give a yearly outing to the poor children in the community, or a Christmas tree with presents for the mission church with its poor children. Such work as this may be easily done by the smaller clubs while the larger ones do such work as the supporting of an orphans home, or the paying for a bed in a hospital or the support of a nurse training school or an old folks' home.

There is plenty of work to be done! Look especially for work that will be preventative of crime; work with the young in our great cities, especially with young girls.

We can advance the standard of the race by advancing our own moral and intellectual standard by individual effort and by organized efforts to further the standard of all with whom we may come in contact, thus one by one will a whole race be lifted.

Further Resources

BOOKS

Davis, Elizabeth Lindsay. *Lifting as They Climb.* New York: G.K. Hall, 1996.

Spain, Daphne. *How Women Saved the City.* Minneapolis, Minn.: University of Minnesota Press, 2001.

Wesley, Charles H. *The History of the National Association of Colored Women's Clubs: A Legacy of Service.* Washington, D.C.: The Association, 1984.

WEBSITES

Dublin, Thomas. "What Gender Perspectives Shaped the Emergence of the National Association of Colored Women, 1895–1920?: Introduction." Available online at http://womhist.binghamton.edu/nacw/intro.htm; website home page: http://www.womhist.binghamton.edu/index.html (accessed January 11, 2003).

Robertson, Nancy Marie. "Sources for National Association of Colored Women and African-American Clubwomen, Race, and Reform: 1996." Available online at http://www2.h-ne.msu.edu/~women/bibs/club.html; website home page:http://www.2.h-net.msu.edu/~women/ (accessed January 11, 2003).

Temple University, Center for African American History and Culture. "National Association of Colored Women's Clubs Records, 1895–1992." Available online at http://www.temple.edu/CAAHC/new_page_17.htm; website home page: http://www.temple.edu/ (accessed January 11, 2003).

Lamentabili Sane (Condemning the Errors of the Modernists)

Papal encyclical

By: Pope Pius X

Date: July 3, 1907

Source: Pope Pius X. *Lamentabili Sane.* Available online at http://www.newadvent.org/docs/df07ls.htm; website home page: http://www.newadvent.org/ (accessed May 16, 2003).

About the Author: Pope Pius X (1835–1914) was born near Treviso, Italy, as Giuseppe Sarto. He was ordained a priest in 1858, became a bishop in 1884, and was installed as a cardinal in 1893. He was elected pope in 1903 and served in that position until his death. He was noted for his interest in the poor, reforming the liturgy, and reorganizing canon law. He was canonized a saint in 1954. ■

Introduction

Modernism was a movement by some theologians that questioned the dogmatic theology of Christianity and the historical accuracy of the Bible. Arising in the late nineteenth century, this movement was an outgrowth of contemporary scientific theories and philosophical writings that challenged basic beliefs held by Christians for centuries. Modernists held, for example, that the Bible was not inspired by the will of God, that Jesus Christ was just a great human being and not divine, and that even the existence of God cannot be conclusively stated. All these theological views contradicted traditional Roman Catholic thinking and even the beliefs of other Christian groups. Catholic modernism was sometimes linked with Protestant liberalism, which also appeared in the late nineteenth century. Both movements were attempts by Christians to cast aside traditional religious beliefs in favor of modern culture and ways of thinking.

Pope Pius X and the hierarchy of the Roman Catholic Church viewed this movement as a threat to the theological foundations of the church. Consequently, the Office of the Holy Roman and Universal Inquisition, whose function was to oversee matters connected with the Catholic faith, conducted an investigation and compiled a list of the modernists' erroneous beliefs. On the basis of the office's findings, Pope Pius X issued *Lamentabili Sane* (Condemning the Errors of the Modernists)—a list of sixty-five beliefs that faithful Roman Catholics were prohibited from holding as true. Those who did were guilty of heresy, or holding beliefs in direct opposition to the traditional teachings of the church. The most serious penalty faced by heretics at that time was excommunication, or expulsion from the church.

Significance

The encyclical, for the most part, slowed the modernist movement within the church; its remaining supporters revised and toned down considerably their public statements. Three years later, on September 1, 1910, the church released the Oath Against Modernism, consisting of eight statements concerning the Roman Catholic faith that "all clergy, pastors, confessors, preachers, religious superiors, and professors in philosophical-theological seminaries" should take. Any person who took the vow would essentially be rejecting the sixty-five errors listed in the encyclical.

All clergy were expected to take the Oath Against Modernism until the era of the Second Vatican Council (1962–1965), when the requirement was abolished. This liberalizing change was controversial. Church conservatives saw it as potentially weakening the faith; liberals welcomed the change as a "breath of fresh air." On May 31, 1967, the Congregation for the Doctrine of the Faith substituted a brief Profession of Faith for the Oath Against Modernism.

Primary Source

Lamentabili Sane (Condemning the Errors of the Modernists)

SYNOPSIS: In this landmark encyclical, Pope Pius X warned all Roman Catholics—including the laity, clergy, teachers, and theologians—to avoid modernism, a movement that doubted the Bible's historical accuracy and questioned basic Christian theology. The pope rejected the heretical view that dogmas evolve and change according to the times and conditions of the world.

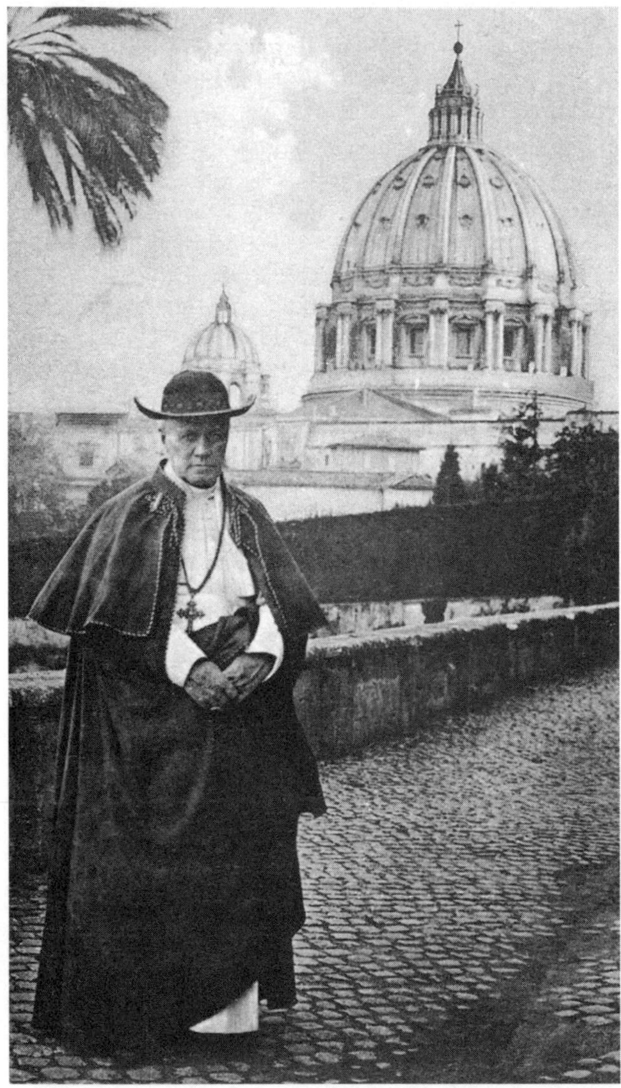

Pope Pius X found fault in the tenets of modernism and warned Catholics to avoid the movement which adversely affected the way the Bible was viewed. GETTY IMAGES. REPRODUCED BY PERMISSION.

With truly lamentable results, our age, casting aside all restraint in its search for the ultimate causes of things, frequently pursues novelties so ardently that it rejects the legacy of the human race. Thus it falls into very serious errors, which are even more serious when they concern sacred authority, the interpretation of Sacred Scripture, and the principal mysteries of Faith. The fact that many Catholic writers also go beyond the limits determined by the Fathers and the Church herself is extremely regrettable. In the name of higher knowledge and historical research (they say), they are looking for that progress of dogmas which is, in reality, nothing but the corruption of dogmas.

These errors are being daily spread among the faithful. Lest they captivate the faithful's minds and corrupt the purity of their faith, His Holiness, Pius X, by Divine Providence, Pope, has decided that the chief errors should be noted and condemned by the Office of this Holy Roman and Universal Congregation.

Therefore, after a very diligent investigation and consultation with the Reverend Consultors, the Most Eminent and Reverend Lord Cardinals, the General Inquisitors in matters of faith and morals have judged the following proposals to be condemned and proscribed. In fact, by this current decree, they are condemned and proscribed.

1. The ecclesiastical law which prescribes that books concerning the Divine Scriptures are subject to previous examination does not apply to critical scholars and students of scientific exegesis of the Old and New Testament.

2. The Church's interpretation of the Sacred Books is by no means to be rejected; nevertheless, it is subject to the more accurate judgment and correction of the exegetes.

3. From the ecclesiastical judgments and censures passed against free and more scientific exegesis, one can conclude that the Faith the Church proposes contradicts history and that Catholic teaching cannot really be reconciled with the true origins of the Christian religion.

4. Even by dogmatic definitions the Church's magisterium cannot determine the genuine sense of the Sacred Scriptures.

5. Since the Deposit of Faith contains only revealed truths, the Church has no right to pass judgment on the assertions of the human sciences.

6. The "Church learning" and the "Church teaching" collaborate in such a way in defining truths that it only remains for the "Church teaching" to sanction the opinions of the "Church learning."

7. In proscribing errors, the Church cannot demand any internal assent from the faithful by which the judgments she issues are to be embraced.

8. They are free from all blame who treat lightly the condemnations passed by the Sacred Congregation of the Index or by the Roman Congregations.

9. They display excessive simplicity or ignorance who believe that God is really the author of the Sacred Scriptures.

10. The inspiration of the books of the Old Testament consists in this: The Israelite writers handed down religious doctrines under a peculiar aspect which was either little or not at all known to the Gentiles.

11. Divine inspiration does not extend to all of Sacred Scriptures so that it renders its parts, each and every one, free from every error.

12. If he wishes to apply himself usefully to Biblical studies, the exegete must first put aside all preconceived opinions about the supernatural origins of Sacred Scripture and interpret it the same as any other merely human document.

13. The Evangelists themselves, as well as the Christians of the second and third generations, artificially arranged the evangelical parables. In such a way they explained the scanty fruit of the preaching of Christ among the Jews.

14. In many narrations the Evangelists recorded, not so much things that are true, as things which, even though false, they judged to be more profitable for their readers.

15. Until the time the canon was defined and constituted, the Gospels were increased by additions and corrections. Therefore there remained in them only a faint and uncertain trace of the doctrine of Christ.

16. The narrations of John are not properly history, but a mystical contemplation of the Gospel. The discourses contained in his Gospel are theological meditations, lacking historical truth concerning the mystery of salvation.

17. The fourth Gospel exaggerated miracles not only in order that the extraordinary might stand out but also in order that it might become more suitable for showing forth the work and glory of the Word Incarnate.

18. John claims for himself the quality of witness concerning Christ. In reality, however, he is only a distinguished witness of the Christian life, or of the life of Christ in the Church at the close of the First Century.

19. Heterodox exegetes have expressed the true sense of the Scriptures more faithfully than Catholic exegetes.

20. Revelation could be nothing else than the consciousness man acquired of his revelation to God.

21. Revelation, constituting the object of the Catholic faith, was not completed with the Apostles.

22. The dogmas the Church holds out as revealed are not truths which have fallen from heaven. They are an interpretation of religious facts which the human mind has acquired by laborious effort.

23. Opposition may, and actually does, exist between the facts narrated in Sacred Scripture and the Church's dogmas which rest on them. Thus the critic may reject as false facts the Church holds as most certain.

24. The exegete who constructs premises from which it follows that dogmas are historically false or doubtful is not to be reproved as long as he does not directly deny the dogmas themselves.

25. The assent of faith ultimately rests on a mass of probabilities.

26. The dogmas of the Faith are to be held only according to their practical sense; that is to say, as perceptive norms of conduct and not as norms of believing.

27. The divinity of Jesus Christ is not proved from the Gospels. It is a dogma which the Christian conscience has derived from the notion of the Messias.

28. While He was exercising His ministry, Jesus did not speak with the object of teaching He was the Messias, nor did His miracles tend to prove it.

29. It is permissible to grant that the Christ of history is far inferior to the Christ Who is the object of faith.

30 In all the evangelical texts the name "Son of God" is equivalent only to that of "Messias." It does not in the least way signify that Christ is the true and natural Son of God.

31. The doctrine concerning Christ taught by Paul, John and the Councils of Nicea, Ephesus and Chalcedon is not that which Jesus taught but that which the Christian conscience conceived concerning Jesus.

32. It is impossible to reconcile the natural sense of the Gospel texts with the sense taught by our theologians concerning the conscience and the infallible knowledge of Jesus Christ.

33. Everyone who is not led by preconceived opinions can readily see that either Jesus professed an error concerning the immediate Messianic coming or the greater part of His doctrine as contained in the Gospels is destitute of authenticity.

34. The critics can ascribe to Christ a knowledge without limits only on a hypothesis which cannot be historically conceived and which is repugnant to the moral sense. That hypothesis is that Christ as man possessed the knowledge of God and yet was unwilling to communicate the knowledge of a great many things to His disciples and posterity.

35. Christ did not always possess the consciousness of His Messianic dignity.

36. The Resurrection of the Savior is not properly a fact of the historical order. It is a fact of merely the supernatural order (neither demonstrated nor demonstrable) which the Christian conscience gradually derived from other facts.

37. In the beginning, faith in the Resurrection of Christ was not so much in the fact itself of the Resurrection, as in the immortal life of Christ with God.

38. The doctrine of the expiatory death of Christ is Pauline and not evangelical.

39. The opinions concerning the origin of the Sacraments which the Fathers of Trent held and which certainly influenced their dogmatic canons are very different from those which now rightly exist among historians who examine Christianity.

40. The Sacraments had their origin in the fact that the Apostles and their successors, swayed and moved by circumstances and events, interpreted some idea and intention of Christ.

41. The Sacraments are intended merely to recall to man's mind the ever-beneficent presence of the Creator.

42. The Christian community imposed the necessity of Baptism, adopted it as a necessary rite, and added to it the obligation of the Christian profession.

43. The practice of administering Baptism to infants was a disciplinary evolution, which became one of the causes why the Sacrament was divided into two, namely, Baptism and Penance.

44. There is nothing to prove that the rite of the Sacrament of Confirmation was employed by the Apostles. The formal distinction of the two Sacraments of Baptism and Confirmation does not pertain to the history of primitive Christianity.

45. Not everything which Paul narrates concerning the institution of the Eucharist (I Cor. 11:23–35) is to be taken historically.

46. In the primitive Church the concept of the Christian sinner reconciled by the authority of the Church did not exist. Only very slowly did the Church accustom herself to this concept. As a matter of fact, even after Penance was recognized as an institution of the Church, it was not called a Sacrament since it would be held as a disgraceful Sacrament.

47. The words of the Lord, "Receive the Holy Spirit; whose sins you shall forgive, they are forgiven them; and whose sins you shall retain, they are retained" (John 20:22–23), in no way refer to the Sacrament of Penance, in spite of what it pleased the Fathers of Trent to say.

48. In his Epistle (Chapter 5:14–15) James did not intend to promulgate a Sacrament of Christ but only commend a pious custom. If in this custom he happens to distinguish a means of grace, it is not in that rigorous manner in which it was taken by the theologians who laid down the notion and number of the Sacraments.

49. When the Christian supper gradually assumed the nature of a liturgical action those who customarily presided over the supper acquired the sacerdotal character.

50. The elders who fulfilled the office of watching over the gatherings of the faithful were instituted by the Apostles as priests or bishops to provide the necessary ordering of the increasing communities and not properly for the perpetuation of the Apostolic mission and power.

51. It is impossible that Matrimony could have become a Sacrament of the new law until later in the Church since it was necessary that a full theological explication of the doctrine of grace and the Sacraments should first take place before Matrimony should be held as a Sacrament.

52. It was far from the mind of Christ to found a Church as a society which would continue on earth for a long course of centuries. On the contrary, in the mind of Christ the kingdom of heaven together with the end of the world was about to come immediately.

53. The organic constitution of the Church is not immutable. Like human society, Christian society is subject to a perpetual evolution.

54. Dogmas, Sacraments and hierarchy, both their notion and reality, are only interpretations and evolutions of the Christian intelligence which have increased and perfected by an external series of additions the little germ latent in the Gospel.

55. Simon Peter never even suspected that Christ entrusted the primacy in the Church to him.

56. The Roman Church became the head of all the churches, not through the ordinance of Divine Providence, but merely through political conditions.

57. The Church has shown that she is hostile to the progress of the natural and theological sciences.

58. Truth is no more immutable than man himself, since it evolved with him, in him, and through him.

59. Christ did not teach a determined body of doctrine applicable to all times and all men, but rather inaugurated a religious movement adapted or to be adapted to different times and places.

60. Christian Doctrine was originally Judaic. Through successive evolutions it became first Pauline, then Joannine, finally Hellenic and universal.

61. It may be said without paradox that there is no chapter of Scripture, from the first of Genesis to the last of the Apocalypse, which contains a doctrine absolutely identical with that which the Church teaches on the same matter. For the same reason, therefore, no chapter of Scripture has the same sense for the critic and the theologian.

62. The chief articles of the Apostles' Creed did not have the same sense for the Christians of the first age as they have for the Christians of our time.

63. The Church shows that she is incapable of effectively maintaining evangelical ethics since she obstinately clings to immutable doctrines which cannot be reconciled with modern progress.

64. Scientific progress demands that the concepts of Christian doctrine concerning God, creation, revelation, the Person of the Incarnate Word, and Redemption be re-adjusted.

65. Modern Catholicism can be reconciled with true science only if it is transformed into a non-dogmatic Christianity; that is to say, into a broad and liberal Protestantism.

The following Thursday, the fourth day of the same month and year, all these matters were accurately reported to our Most Holy Lord, Pope Pius X. His Holiness approved and confirmed the decree of the Most Eminent Fathers and ordered that each and every one of the above-listed propositions be held by all as condemned and proscribed.

Peter Palombelli
Notary, Congregation for the Propagation of the Faith

Further Resources

BOOKS

Dal-Gal, Girolamo. *Pius X: The Life-Story of the Beatus: The New Italian Life of Pius X.* Dublin, Ireland: Gill, 1953.

Giordani, Igino. *Pius X: A Country Priest.* Milwaukee, Wis.: Bruce, 1954.

Sullivan, William Laurence. *Letters to His Holiness: Pope Pius X by a Modernist.* Chicago, Ill.: Open Court, 1914.

WEBSITES

Benigni, U. "Pope Pius X." *Catholic Encyclopedia.* Available online at http://www.newadvent.org/cathen/12137a.htm; website home page: http://www.newadvent.org/ (accessed January 12, 2003).

The Vatican (the Holy See). "The Holy Father: Pius X." Available online at http://www.vatican.va/holy_father/pius_x/; website home page: http://www.vatican.va/ (accessed May 16, 2003).

Reuben Quick Bear v. Leupp

Supreme Court decision

By: Melville Weston Fuller

Date: May 18, 1908

Source: Find Law for Legal Professionals U.S. Supreme Court. *Reuben Quick Bear v. Leupp,* 210 U.S. 50 (1908). Available online at http://caselaw.lp.findlaw.com/scripts/getcase.pl?navby=case&court=US&vol=210&page=50; website home page: http://www.findlaw.com/casecode/ (accessed May 16, 2003).

About the Author: Melville Weston Fuller (1833–1910) was born in Augusta, Maine. After receiving his law degree from Harvard, he practiced law in Chicago, where he was active in Democratic Party politics. In 1888 President Grover Cleveland (served 1885–1889 and 1893–1897) appointed him Chief Justice of the U.S. Supreme Court, where he served until his death. ■

Introduction

In *Reuben Quick Bear v. Leupp* (1908), more than four dozen members of the Sioux tribe sued U.S. government officials who, as trustees for the tribe, were using money from a treaty trust fund to pay the Bureau of Catholic Indian Missions to provide schools for the tribe. The plaintiffs included Reuben Quick Bear and other members of the Sioux Tribe of the Rosebud Agency in South Dakota. The defendants were Commissioner of Indian Affairs Francis E. Leupp, Secretary of the Interior Ethan Allen Hitchcock, Treasury Secretary George Bruce Cortelyou, and others.

The plaintiffs asked that a permanent injunction be issued against the Commissioner of Indian Affairs and the Secretary of the Interior "to restrain them from paying or authorizing the payment of, either by themselves or by any of their subordinate officers or agents whatever, any moneys of either the Sioux treaty fund or the interest of the Sioux trust fund, or any other fund appropriated, either by permanent appropriation or otherwise, for the uses of the Sioux tribe, to the Bureau of Catholic Indian Missions of Washington or to any other sectarian organization whatever, for the support, education, or maintenance of any Indian pupils of the said Sioux tribe, at the St. Francis Mission Boarding School or any other sectarian school on the said Rosebud reservation or elsewhere." Put simply, the plaintiffs were asking that trust fund money not be used to fund education in religious schools.

Supreme Court Chief Justice Melville Fuller delivered a 1908 opinion of the Court that allowed trust funds to pay for American Indians' tuition to private schools. THE LIBRARY OF CONGRESS.

In his decision, Chief Justice Fuller held that "the Catholic missions schools in question were erected many years ago at the cost of charitable Catholics, and with the approval of the authorities of the government of the United States, whose policy it was then [to] encourage the education and civilization of the Indians through the work of religious organizations." On this basis the Court ruled that funds set aside in trust for the Sioux tribe, with the federal government acting as trustee, could be legally used to pay tuition costs at a religious school. The Court considered this constitutionally valid even though the money would go to a church-sponsored school.

Significance

Opponents believed that by using the tribe's money to help pay tuition costs at a Catholic school, the government would be indirectly supporting the establishment of a church in violation of the First Amendment, which says that Congress shall "make no law respecting the establishment of religion." In previous decisions the Supreme Court had interpreted the amendment as prohibiting any kind of government aid or endorsement of religious institutions.

In this case, however, the Court concluded that the First Amendment did not apply because the money actually belonged to the tribe; it came from a treaty fund agreement between the tribe and the U.S. government, and since the government was holding the money in trust, it was not the government's money. Once the money was granted by treaty to the Sioux tribe and was no longer the property of the federal government, it could be used to pay tuition at religious-based schools.

Primary Source

Reuben Quick Bear v. Leupp [excerpt]

SYNOPSIS: In these excerpts, the Supreme Court ruled that money held by the federal government as trustee could be used to pay American Indians' tuition at private religious schools. The separation of church and state did not apply in this case because the money belonged to the tribe, not the federal government. The money was being used by the tribe in its own behalf for education. It did not matter that the school had a religious affiliation. The case was argued February 26–27, 1908, and was decided May 18, 1908.

The appellants filed their bill in equity in the supreme court of the district of Columbia, alleging that:

1. The plaintiffs are citizens of the United States, and members of the Sioux tribe of Indians of the Rosebud agency, in the state of South Dakota, and bring this suit in their own right as well as for all other members of the Sioux tribe of Indians of the Rosebud agency.

2. The defendants are citizens of the United States and residents of the District of Columbia, and are sued in this action as the Commissioner of Indian Affairs, the Secretary of the Interior, the Secretary of the Treasury, the Treasurer of the United States, and the Comptroller of the Treasury, respectively.

3. That by article 7 of the Sioux treaty of April 29, 1868 . . . , continued in force for twenty years after July 1, 1889, by 17 of the act of March 2, 1889 . . . the United States agreed that for every thirty children of the said Sioux tribe who can be induced or compelled to attend school, a house shall be provided, and a teacher competent to teach the elementary branches of an English education shall be furnished, who will reside among said Indians, and faithfully discharge his or her duties as a teacher.

4. That, for the purpose of carrying out the above provision of the said treaty during the fiscal year ending June 30, 1906, the following appropriation was made by the act of March 3, 1905 . . .

> For support and maintenance of day and industrial schools, including erection and repairs of school buildings in accordance with article seven of the treaty of April twenty-nine, eighteen hundred and sixty-eight, which article is continued in force for twenty years by section seventeen of the act of March second, eighteen hundred and eighty-nine, two hundred and twenty-five thousand dollars.The fund so appropriated is generally known as the Sioux treaty fund.

5. That 17 of the said act of March 2, 1889, further provides as follows:

> And in addition thereto there shall be set apart out of any money in the Treasury not otherwise appropriated, the sum of three million of dollars, which said sum shall be deposited in the Treasury of the United States to the credit of the Sioux Nation of Indians as a permanent fund, the interest of which at five per centum per annum, shall be appropriated, under the direction of the Secretary of the Interior, to the use of the Indians receiving rations and annuities upon the reservations created by this act, in proportion to the numbers that shall so receive rations and annuities at the time that this act takes effect, as follows: One half of said interest shall be so expended for the promotion of industrial and other suitable education among said Indians, and the other half thereof in such manner and for such purposes, including reasonable cash payments per capita as, in the judgment of said Secretary, shall, from time to time, most contribute to the advancement of said Indians in civilization and self-support.This fund of $3,000,000 is generally known as the Sioux trust fund.

6. That the interest on the said Sioux trust fund is paid annually by the United States in accordance with the provisions of the second clause of the act of April 1, 1880 . . . reading as follows:

> And the United States shall pay interest semiannually, from the date of deposit of any and all such sums in the United States Treasury, at the rate per annum stipulated by treaties or prescribed by law, and such payments shall be made in the usual manner, as each may become due, without further appropriation by Congress.

7. That the act of June 7, 1897 . . . , contains the following provision:

> And it is hereby declared to be the settled policy of the government to hereafter make no appropriation whatever for education in any sectarian school. . . .

Wherefore the plaintiffs ask relief, as follows:

1. That a permanent injunction issue against the said Francis E. Leupp, Commissioner of Indian Affairs, to restrain him from executing any contract with the said Bureau of Catholic Indian Missions of Washington, District of Columbia, or any other sectarian organization whatever, for the support, education, or maintenance of any Indian pupils of the said Sioux tribe at the said St. Francis Mission Boarding School, or any other sectarian school on the said Rosebud reservation or elsewhere, and that a permanent injunction issue against the said Francis E. Leupp, Commissioner of Indian Affairs, and the said . . . Secretary of the Interior, to restrain them from paying or authorizing the payment of, either by themselves or by any of their subordinate officers or agents whatever, any moneys of either the said Sioux treaty fund or the interest of the said Sioux trust fund, or any other fund appropriated, either by permanent appropriation or otherwise, for the uses of the said Sioux tribe, to the said Bureau of Catholic Indian Missions of Washington, District of Columbia, or to any other sectarian organization whatever, for the support, education, or maintenance of any Indian pupils of the said Sioux tribe, at the said St. Francis Mission Boarding School or any other sectarian school on the said Rosebud reservation or elsewhere.

2. And for a permanent injunction against the drawing, countersigning, and paying "any warrants in favor of the said Bureau of Catholic Indian Missions of Washington, District of Columbia, or any other sectarian organization whatever, for the support, education, and maintenance of any Indian pupils of the said Sioux tribe at the said St. Francis Mission Boarding School, or any other sectarian school on the said Rosebud reservation or elsewhere, payable out of any money appropriated, either by permanent appropriation or otherwise, for the uses of the said Sioux tribe."

And for general relief. The defendants answered:

1. Admitting "that the plaintiffs are citizens of the United States, and members of the Sioux tribe of Indians, but aver that the said Indians are only nominal plaintiffs, the real plaintiff being the Indian Rights Association, who have had this suit brought for the purpose of testing the validity of the contract hereinafter referred to."

2. Admitting "that they are residents of the District of Columbia, and are sued in this action as Commissioner of Indian Affairs, the Secretary of the Interior, the Secretary of the Treasury, the Treasurer of the United States, and the Comptroller of the Treasury, respectively. These defendants, as officers of the government of the United States, have

no interest in the controversy raised by the bill, except to perform their duties under the law, and they, therefore, as such officers, respectfully submit the validity of the contract hereinafter referred to, and the payments thereunder, to the judgment of this honorable court. The real defendant in interest is the "Bureau of Catholic Indian Missions,"—a corporation duly incorporated by chapter 363 of the acts of assembly of Maryland for the year 1894, for the object, inter alia, of educating the American Indian directly, and also indirectly, by training their teachers and others, especially to train their youth to become self-sustaining men and women, using such methods of instruction in the principles of religion and of human knowledge as may be best adapted to these purposes.

> As the object of the bill filed is to test the validity of a contract made between the Commissioner for Indian Affairs and the said "Bureau of Catholic Indian Missions," and the validity of the payment of the money thereunder, this answer will set forth the facts and the statutes of the United States under which it is contended that such contract and the payment of money thereunder are valid. . . .

Mr. Chief Justice Fuller delivered the opinion of the court:

We concur in the decree of the court of appeals of the District, and the reasoning by which its conclusion is supported, as set forth in the opinion of Wright, J., speaking for the court. . . .

The validity of the contract for $27,000 is attacked on the ground that all contracts for sectarian education among the Indians are forbidden by certain provisos contained in the Indian appropriation acts of 1895, 1896, 1897, 1898. But if those provisos relate only to the appropriations made by the government out of the public moneys of the United States, raised by taxation from persons of all creeds and faiths, or none at all, and appropriated gratuitously for the purpose of education among the Indians, and not to "tribal funds," which belong to the Indians themselves, then the contract must be sustained. The difference between one class of appropriations and the other has long been recognized in the annual appropriation acts. The gratuitous appropriation of public moneys for the purpose of Indian education has always been made under the heading, "Support of Schools;" whilst the appropriation of the "treaty fund" has always been under the heading, "Fulfilling Treaty Stipulations and Support of Indian Tribes;" and that from the "trust fund" is not in the Indian appropriation acts at all. One class of appropriations relates to public moneys belonging to the government; the other to moneys which belong to the Indians and which is administered for them by the government. From the history of appropriations of public moneys for education of Indians, set forth in the brief of counsel for appellees, and again at length in the answer, it appears that before 1895 the government, for a number of years, had made contracts for sectarian schools for the education of the Indians, and the money due on these contracts was paid, in the discretion of the Commissioner of Indian Affairs, from the "tribal funds" and from the gratuitous public appropriations. But in 1894 opposition developed against appropriating public moneys for sectarian education. Accordingly, in the Indian appropriation act of 1894, under the heading of "Support of Schools," the Secretary of the Interior was directed to investigate the propriety of discontinuing contract schools, and to make such recommendations as he might deem proper. The Secretary suggested a gradual reduction in the public appropriations on account of the money which had been invested in these schools, with the approbation of the government. He said: "It would be scarcely just to abolish them entirely,—to abandon instantly a policy so long recognized,"—and suggested that they should be decreased at the rate of not less than 20 per cent a year. Thus, in a few years they would cease to exist; and during this time the bureau would be gradually prepared to do without them, while they might gather strength to continue without government aid. . . .

Some reference is made to the Constitution, in respect to this contract with the Bureau of Catholic Indian Missions. It is not contended that it is unconstitutional, and it could not be. . . . But it is contended that the spirit of the Constitution requires that the declaration of policy that the government "shall make no appropriation whatever for education in any sectarian schools" should be treated as applicable, on the ground that the actions of the United States were to always be undenominational, and that, therefore, the government can never act in a sectarian capacity, either in the use of its own funds or in that of the funds of others, in respect of which it is a trustee; hence, that even the Sioux trust fund cannot be applied for education in Catholic schools, even though the owners of the fund so desire it. But we cannot concede the proposition that Indians cannot be allowed to use their own money to educate their children in the schools of their own choice because the government is necessarily undenominational, as it cannot make any law respecting an establishment of religion or prohibiting the free exercise thereof. The court of appeals well said:

> The "treaty" and "trust" moneys are the only moneys that the Indians can lay claim to as matter of right; the only sums on which they are entitled to rely as theirs for education; and while these moneys are not delivered to them in hand, yet the money must not only be provided, but be expended, for their benefit, and in part for their education; it seems inconceivable that Congress shall have intended to prohibit them from receiving religious education at their own cost if they desire it; such an intent would be one to prohibit the free exercise of religion amongst the Indians, and such would be the effect of the construction for which the complainants contend.

The . . . trust cannot be deprived of their rights by the trustee in the exercise of power implied.

Decree affirmed.

Further Resources

BOOKS

Stroup, Herbert Hewitt. *Church and State in Confrontation.* New York: Seabury, 1967.

Wilson, John Frederick, ed. *Church and State in American History.* Boston, Mass: Heath, 1965.

Wilson, John F., and Donald L. Drakeman, eds. *Church and State in American History: The Burden of Religious Pluralism.* Boston, Mass.: Beacon, 1987.

WEBSITES

Separation of Church and State Home Page. "The Position of the Different Sides in the Separation Debate." Available online at http://members.tripod.com/~candst/tnppage/view3.htm; website home page: http://www.members.tripod.com/~candst/tnppage/tnpidx/htm (accessed January 12, 2003).

Spielman, Michael. "The Church/State Debate," September 1997. Available online at http://loxafamosity.com/states/0997.html; website home page: http://www.loxafamosity.com/index.html (accessed January 12, 2003).

Rudimental Divine Science

Theological work

By: Mary Baker Eddy

Date: 1908

Source: Eddy, Mary Baker. *Rudimental Divine Science.* Boston: Christian Science Publishing Society, 1908. Available online at http://www.mbeinstitute.org/Prose_Works/Rudimental_Divine_Science.html; website home page: http://www.mbeinstitute.org (accessed January 12, 2003).

About the Author: Mary Baker Eddy (1821–1910) was born in Bow, New Hampshire. Because of her poor health and gender, she received little formal education but expressed a keen desire to write poetry and study religion. She founded the Christian Science movement in Lynn, Massachusetts, and presented the basics of Christian Science in 1875 in her book *Science and Health.* The First Church of Christ, Scientist was founded in Boston in 1879. ■

Mary Baker Eddy was healed of a serious injury as she read one Biblical account of Jesus' healings. She thus discovered what she called the "science of Christianity" and founded the Christian Science movement. © CORBIS. REPRODUCED BY PERMISSION.

Introduction

In searching for a way to deal with her own physical afflictions, Mary Baker Eddy established a Bible-based system of spiritual healing, Christian Science. In *Rudimental Divine Science,* she outlined the basic theology of Christian Science, which rested upon the belief that since people were created in God's image, they had an innately spiritual human nature that was a reflection of the Creator. Because of this gift from God, people were endowed with the intelligence to overpower evil and infirmities. Prayer and spiritual healing were two important parts of Christian Science.

Eddy had already formally introduced the public to the tenets of Christian Science in her 1875 book, *Science and Health,* later revised and republished as *Science and Health with Key to the Scriptures.* She published *Rudimental Divine Science* in 1908 principally to make it easier for the beginner to grasp her basic principles. The book could be likened to the catechism traditionally used by Catholics to teach the basics of the faith to the young and to converts.

In the decades following the publication of *Science and Health,* Eddy dedicated her life to the growth of her church by seeking new adherents and to its internal development by strengthening the organizational structure. In 1876, she formally organized her followers into the Christian Scientists' Association. With the chartering of the Church of Christ, Scientist in 1879, the Christian Science movement became a fully established and publicly recognized religious organization.

The years following the establishment of the Church of Christ, Scientist were times of rapid growth in the church. There were so many congregations across the nation that in 1886 a national association was founded to coordinate their activities. In 1881, Eddy established the Massachusetts Metaphysical College to train practitioners of Christian Science.

Significance

Rudimental Divine Science helped to introduce more people to Christian Science because of its methodical and clear manner of approaching Eddy's theology. Some people, however, did not accept this new theology. Clergy members openly disagreed with her interpretations of Christianity, and many people were skeptical about the effectiveness of spiritual healing and were concerned that people would choose spiritual healing over traditional medicine. But many of Eddy's followers remained loyal because her vision of reality and wellness appealed to them.

Despite Eddy's detractors, the faith spread. In the same year as the publication of *Rudimental Divine Science* (1908), the *Christian Science Monitor* was born and published its first edition on November 28. Eddy's beliefs strongly affected the philosophy and content of the new newspaper, which developed a focus on moral and social problems. This focus would be the first step in the healing process espoused by Christian Science. By becoming more aware of the world's problems through a rational and scientific approach to them, the followers of Christian Science believed they could help alleviate them.

At the beginning of the twenty-first century, there were about two thousand branch churches of Christian Science in seventy-nine countries. The Mother Church is still located in Boston (The First Church of Christ, Scientist). *Science and Health with Key to the Scriptures* has been a best-seller for over 125 years, with over 10 million copies sold.

Primary Source

Rudimental Divine Science [excerpt]

SYNOPSIS: In these excerpts, Mary Baker Eddy, the founder of the Christian Science movement, summarizes the basic characteristics of the theology of Christian Science in a question-and-answer format. The dedication states: "This little book is tenderly and respectfully dedicated to all loyal students, working and waiting for the establishment of the science of mind-healing."

How would you define Christian Science?

As the law of God, the law of good, interpreting and demonstrating the divine Principle and rule of universal harmony.

What is the Principle of Christian Science?

It is God, the Supreme Being, infinite and immortal Mind, the Soul of man and the universe. It is our Father which is in heaven. It is substance, Spirit, Life, Truth, and Love,—these are the deific Principle.

Do you mean by this that God is a person?

The word *person* affords a large margin for misapprehension, as well as definition. In French the equivalent word is *personne.* In Spanish, Italian, and Latin, it is *persona.* The Latin verb *personare* is compounded of the prefix *per* (through) and *sonare* (to sound). In law, Blackstone applies the word *personal* to bodily presence, in distinction from one's appearance (in court, for example) by deputy or proxy.

Other definitions of *person,* as given by Webster, are "a living soul; a self-conscious being; a moral agent; especially, a living human being, a corporeal man, woman, or child; an individual of the human race." He adds, that among Trinitarian Christians the word stands for one of the three subjects, or agents, constituting the Godhead.

In Christian Science we learn that God is definitely individual, and not a person, as that word is used by the best authorities, if our lexicographers are right in defining *person* as especially a finite human being; but God is personal, if by *person* is meant infinite Spirit.

We do not conceive rightly of God, if we think of Him as less than infinite. The human person is finite; and therefore I prefer to retain the proper sense of Deity by using the phrase an individual God, rather than a personal God; for there is and can be but one infinite individual Spirit, whom mortals have named God.

Science defines the individuality of God as supreme good, Life, Truth, Love. This term enlarges our sense of Deity, takes away the trammels assigned to God by finite thought, and introduces us to higher definitions.

Is healing the sick the whole of Science?

Healing physical sickness is the smallest part of Christian Science. It is only the bugle-call to thought and action, in the higher range of infinite goodness. The emphatic purpose of Christian Science is the healing of sin; and this task, sometimes, may be harder than the cure of disease; because, while mortals love to sin, they do not love to be sick. Hence their comparative acquiescence in your endeavors to heal them of bodily ills, and their obstinate resistance to all efforts to save them from sin through Christ, spiritual Truth and Love, which redeem them, and become their Saviour, through the flesh, from the flesh,—the material world and evil.

This Life, Truth, and Love—this trinity of good—was individualized, to the perception of mortal sense, in the man Jesus. His history is emphatic in our hearts, and it lives more because of his spiritual than his physical healing. His example is, to Christian Scientists, what the models of the masters in music and painting are to artists.

Genuine Christian Scientists will no more deviate morally from that divine digest of Science called the Sermon on the Mount, than they will manipulate invalids, prescribe drugs, or deny God. Jesus' healing was spiritual in its nature, method, and design. He wrought the cure of disease through the divine Mind, which gives all true volition, impulse, and action; and destroys the mental error made manifest physically, and establishes the opposite manifestation of Truth upon the body in harmony and health.

By the individuality of God, do you mean that God has a finite form?

No. I mean the infinite and divine Principle of all being, The everpresent I AM, filling all space, including in itself all Mind, the one Father-Mother God. Life, Truth, and Love are this trinity in unity, and their universe is spiritual, peopled with perfect beings, harmonious and eternal, of which our material universe and men are the counterfeits.

Is God the Principle of all science, or only of Divine or Christian Science?

Science is Mind manifested. It is not material; neither is it of human origin. All true Science represents a moral and spiritual force, which holds the earth in its orbit. This force is Spirit, that can "bind the sweet influences of the Pleiades," and "loose the bands of Orion."

There is no material science, if by that term you mean material intelligence. God is infinite Mind, hence there is no other Mind. Good is Mind, but evil is not Mind. Good is not in evil, but in God only. Spirit is not in matter, but in Spirit only. Law is not in matter, but in Mind only.

Is there no matter?

All is Mind. According to the Scriptures and Christian Science, all is God, and there is naught beside Him. "God is Spirit;" and we can only learn and love Him through His spirit, which brings out the fruits of Spirit and extinguishes forever the works of darkness by His marvellous light.

The five material senses testify to the existence of matter. The spiritual senses afford no such evidence, but deny the testimony of the material senses. Which testimony is correct? The Bible says: "Let God be true, and every man a liar." If, as the Scriptures imply, God is All-in-all, then all must be Mind, since God is Mind. Therefore in divine Science there is no material mortal man, for man is spiritual and eternal, he being made in the image of Spirit, or God.

There is no material sense. Matter is inert, inanimate, and sensationless,—considered apart from Mind. Lives there a man who has ever found Soul in the body or in matter, who has ever seen spiritual substance with the eye, who has found sight in matter, hearing in the material ear, or intelligence in non-intelligence? If there is any such thing as matter, it must be either mind which is called matter, or matter without Mind.

Matter without Mind is a moral impossibility. Mind in matter is pantheism. Soul is the only real consciousness which cognizes being. The body does not see, hear, smell, or taste. Human belief says that it does; but destroy this belief of seeing with the eye, and we could not see materially; and so it is with each of the physical senses.

Accepting the verdict of these material senses, we should believe man and the universe to be the football of chance and sinking into oblivion. Destroy the five senses as organized matter, and you must either become non-existent, or exist in Mind only; and this latter conclusion is the simple solution of the problem of being, and leads to the equal inference that there is no matter.

The sweet sounds and glories of earth and sky, assuming manifold forms and colors,—are they not tangible and material?

As Mind they are real, but not as matter. All beauty and goodness are in and of Mind, emanating from God; but when we change the nature of beauty and goodness from Mind to matter, the beauty is marred, through a false conception, and, to the material senses, evil takes the place of good.

Has not the truth in Christian Science met a response from Prof. S.P. Langley, the young American astronomer?

He says that "color is in us," not "in the rose;" and he adds that this is not "any metaphysical subtlety," but a fact "almost universally accepted, within the last few years, by physicists."

Is not the basis of Mind-healing a destruction of the evidence of the material senses, and restoration of the true evidence of spiritual sense?

It is, so far as you perceive and understand this predicate and postulate of Mind-healing; but the Science of Mind-healing is best understood in practical demonstration. The proof of what you apprehend, in the simplest definite and absolute form of healing, can alone answer this question of how much you understand of Christian Science Mind-healing. Not that all healing is Science, by any means; but that the simplest case, healed in Science, is as demonstrably scientific, in a small degree, as the most difficult case so treated.

The infinite and subtler conceptions and consistencies of Christian Science are set forth in my work Science and Health.

Is man material or spiritual?

In Science, man is the manifest reflection of God, perfect and immortal Mind. He is the likeness of God; and His likeness would be lost if inverted or perverted. According to the evidence of the so-called physical senses, man is material, fallen, sick, depraved, mortal. Science and spiritual sense contradict this, and they afford the only true evidence of the being of God and man, the material evidence being wholly false.

Jesus said of personal evil, that "the truth abode not in him," because there is no material sense. Matter, as matter, has neither sensation nor personal intelligence. As a pretension to be Mind, matter is a lie, and "the father of lies;" Mind is not in matter, and Spirit cannot originate its opposite, named matter.

According to divine Science, Spirit no more changes its species, by evolving matter from Spirit, than natural science, so-called, or material laws, bring about alteration of species by transforming minerals into vegetables or plants into animals,—thus confusing and confounding the three great kingdoms. No rock brings forth an apple; no pine-tree produces a mammal or provides breast-milk for babes.

To sense, the lion of to-day is the lion of six thousand years ago; but in Science, Spirit sends forth its own harmless likeness.

How should I undertake to demonstrate Christian Science in healing the sick?

As I have given you only an epitome of the Principle, so I can give you here nothing but an outline of the practice. Be honest, be true to thyself, and true to others; then it follows thou wilt be strong in God, the eternal good. Heal through Truth and Love; there is no other healer.

In all moral revolutions, from a lower to a higher condition of thought and action, Truth is in the minority and error has the majority. It is not otherwise in the field of Mind-healing. The man who calls himself a Christian Scientist, yet is false to God and man, is also uttering falsehood about good. This falsity shuts against him the Truth and the Principle of Science, but opens a way whereby, through willpower, sense may say the unchristian practitioner can heal; but Science shows that he makes morally worse the invalid whom he is supposed to cure.

By this I mean that mortal mind should not be falsely impregnated. If by such lower means the health is seemingly restored, the restoration is not lasting, and the patient is liable to a relapse,— "The last state of that man is worse than the first."

The teacher of Mind-healing who is not a Christian, in the highest sense, is constantly sowing the seeds of discord and disease. Even the truth he speaks is more or less blended with error; and this error will spring up in the mind of his pupil. The pupil's imperfect knowledge will lead to weakness in practice, and he will be a poor practitioner, if not a malpractitioner.

The basis of malpractice is in erring human will, and this will is an outcome of what I call mortal mind,—a false and temporal sense of Truth, Life, and Love. To heal, in Christian Science, is to base your practice on immortal Mind, the divine Principle of man's being; and this requires a preparation of the heart and an answer of the lips from the Lord.

The Science of healing is the Truth of healing. If one is untruthful, his mental state weighs against his healing power; and similar effects come from pride, envy, lust, and all fleshly vices.

The spiritual power of a scientific, right thought, without a direct effort, an audible or even a mental argument, has oftentimes healed inveterate diseases.

The thoughts of the practitioner should be imbued with a clear conviction of the omnipotence and omnipresence of God; that He is All, and that there can be none beside Him; that God is good, and the producer only of good; and hence, that whatever militates against health, harmony, or holiness, is an unjust usurper of the throne of the controller of all mankind. Note this, that if you have power in error, you forfeit the power that Truth bestows, and its salutary influence on yourself and others. . . .

Further Resources

BOOKS

Beasley, Norman. *Mary Baker Eddy.* New York: Duell, Sloan and Pearce, 1963.

Caldwell, Sallie Bowman. *Mary Baker Eddy.* Boston, Mass.: Christian Science Publishing Society, 1942.

Thomas, Robert David. *With Bleeding Footsteps: Mary Baker Eddy's Path to Religious Leadership.* New York: Knopf, 1994.

PERIODICALS

Gottschalk, Steven. "Mary Baker Eddy." *The Christian Century*, January 6, 1999, 32.

"*Mary Baker Eddy: Speaking for Herself.*" *Publishers Weekly*, September 9, 2002, 62.

WEBSITES

Christian Science Education Center. "A Biographical Sketch: Mary Baker Eddy." Available online at http://www.endtime.org/intro/mbe.html; website home page: http://www.endtime.org/ (accessed January 12, 2003).

Cornerstone Books. "Mary Baker Eddy." Available online at http://website.lineone.net/~cornerstone/eddy.htm; website home page: http://cornerstone.wwwhubs.com/ (accessed May 16, 2003).

First Church of Christ, Scientist. "Mary Baker Eddy." Available online at http://www.tfccs.com/gv/MBE/MBEMain.html; website home page: http://www.tfccs.com (accessed January 12, 2003).

Some Aspects of Rabbinic Theology

Theological work

By: Solomon Schechter

Date: 1909

Source: Schechter, Solomon. *Some Aspects of Rabbinic Theology.* New York: Macmillan, 1909. Reprint, *Aspects of Rabbinic Theology.* New York: Schocken Books, 1961.

About the Author: Solomon Schechter (1847–1915) was born in Focsani, Romania. Educated in Austria and Germany, he lectured in Jewish studies in 1890 at Cambridge University in England. In 1901, he joined the Jewish Theological Seminary of America in New York City, where he was regarded as a major scholar of Conservative Judaism. ■

Introduction

Solomon Schechter, one of the twentieth century's greatest Jewish scholars, once noted that "Conservative Judaism united what is desirable in modern life with the precious heritage of our faith . . . that has come down to us from ancient times." His goal in writing *Some Aspects of Rabbinic Theology* was to select certain areas of that "precious heritage of our faith" for examination. As both a theologian and a historian, he persistently provided ways of understanding and communicating the religious consciousness of the Jewish people. He believed in the importance of the study of the Bible and tradition. Through the examination of tradition, he believed, one can see how the Bible has repeated itself throughout Jewish history.

Using the Talmud (the authoritative body of Jewish tradition, civil law, and ceremonial law) and the Midrash (commentary from ancient times on the significance of Hebrew scriptures) for his sources, Schechter concentrated on the principles and dogmas that have been consistent in Judaism for many centuries. The book includes chapters on God and the world, God and Israel, the invisible kingdom of God, the universal visible kingdom of God, and the national kingdom of God. He also discussed the Torah (the law of God as revealed to Moses and recorded in the first five books of the Hebrew scriptures) from the standpoint of law, the joy of the law, the law of holiness, and the law of goodness. He detailed the theological implications of sin as rebellion, man's victory over evil by the grace of God, forgiveness from God, reconciliation with God, and repentance.

One concept to which Schechter gave particular attention was holiness. In his view, holiness involved the highest achievement of the law, the deepest experience of the law, and the realization of righteousness. The ideals of holiness originated "in the concept of the kingdom, the central idea of Rabbinic theology, and in Israel's consciousness of its close relation to his God, the King." His presentation of this and similar concepts was considered to be a classic example of the nature of this type of religious thinking.

Significance

The importance of *Some Aspects of Rabbinic Theology* rested on Schechter's clear way of presenting difficult religious concepts, providing guidance for both Jewish and Christian students of Judaism. Although written more than ninety years ago, the book continues to be a clear, practical, and useful dissertation on the essentials of Rabbinic Judaism. Professor Ismar Schorsch, chancellor of the Jewish Theological Seminary of America, said that Schechter "labored to mediate the dynamic otherness of Judaism to Christian America in unalloyed, clear and graceful prose." Louis Ginzberg, a famous Jewish author, noted that Schechter showed "the special Jewish conception of God and the universe, the special Jewish interpretation of the Bible." Dr. Alfred Gottschalk,

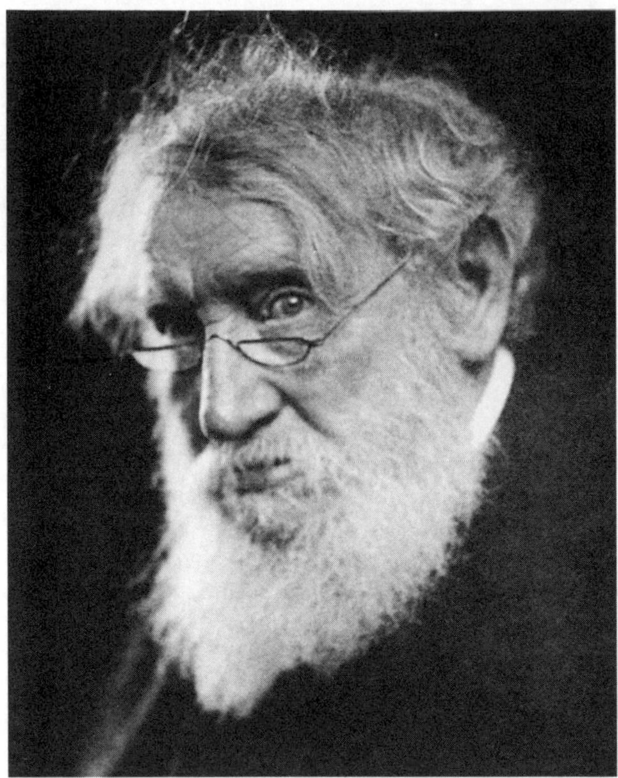

Solomon Schechter's *Some Aspects of Rabbinic Theology* (1909) was the first approach to a methodical presentation of Jewish theology. **THE LIBRARY OF CONGRESS.**

president of Hebrew Union College–Jewish Institute of Religion, stated that Schechter's work "still speaks to every generation of students of the Jewish tradition."

Primary Source

Some Aspects of Rabbinic Theology [excerpt]

SYNOPSIS: In the following excerpts from the introduction to *Some Aspects of Rabbinic Theology,* Schechter presents his rationale for outlining a Jewish theology and the materials and traditions on which such a theology should be based. He includes a discussion of miracles, dismissing attempts to minimize their significance in Judaism and noting that the miracles recorded in the Bible have parallels found in the Rabbinic literature. He emphasizes that miracles were an essential element of Rabbinic Judaism, just as they were for Christianity.

My object in choosing the title "Some Aspects of Rabbinic Theology" is to indicate that from the following chapters there must not be expected either finality or completeness. Nor will there be made any attempt in the following pages at that precise and systematic treatment which we are rightly accustomed to claim in other fields of scientific inquiry. I have often marvelled at the certainty and confidence with which Jewish legalism, Jewish transcendentalism, Jewish self-righteousness, are delineated in our theological manuals and histories of religion; but I have never been able to emulate either quality. I have rather found, when approaching the subject a little closer, that the peculiar mode of old Jewish thought, as well as the unsatisfactory state of the documents in which this thought is preserved, "are against the certain," and urge upon the student caution and sobriety. In these introductory paragraphs I shall try to give some notion of the difficulties that lie before us.

To begin with the difficulties attaching to the unsatisfactory state of Rabbinic documents. A prominent theologian has, when referring to the Rabbis, declared that one has only to study the Mishnah to see that it was not moral or spiritual subjects which engrossed their attention, but the characteristic hair-splitting about ceremonial trifles. There is an appearance of truth in this statement. The Mishnah, which was *compiled* about the beginning of the third century of the C.E., consists of sixty-one (or sixty-three) tractates, of which only one, known by the title of "The Chapters of the Fathers," deals with moral and spiritual matters in the narrower sense of these terms. Still this is not the whole truth, for there are also other tractates, occupying about one-third of the whole Mishnah, which deal with the civil law, the procedure of the criminal courts, the regulation of inheritance, laws regarding property, the administration of oaths, marriage, and divorce. All these topics, and many similar ones relating to public justice and the welfare of the community as the Rabbis understood it, are certainly not to be branded as ceremonial trifles; and if the kingdom of God on earth means something more than the mystical languor of the individual, it is difficult to see on what ground they can be excluded from the sphere of religion. But, apart from this consideration—for it seems that theologians are not yet agreed in their answer to the question whether it is this world, with all its wants and complications, which should be the subject for redemption, or the individual soul, with its real and imaginary longings—there runs, parallel with this Mishnah, a vast literature, known under the name of Agadah, scattered over a multitude of Talmudical and Midrashic works, the earliest of which were compiled even before or about the time of the Mishnah, and the latest of which, while going down as far as the tenth or even the eleventh century, still include many ancient elements of Rabbinic thought. In these *compilations* it will be found that the minds of the so-called triflers were engrossed also with such subjects as God, and man's relation to God; as righteousness and sin, and the origin of evil; as suffering and repentance and immortality; as the election of Israel, Messianic aspirations, and with many other cognate subjects lying well within the moral and spiritual sphere, and no less interesting to the theologian than to the philosopher. . . .

There is . . . the interesting subject of miracles, which plays such an important part in the history of every religion. Despite the various attempts made by semi-rationalists to minimise their significance, the frequent occurrence of miracles will always remain, both for believers and sceptics, one of the most important tests of the religion in question; to the former as a sign of its superhuman nature, to the latter as a proof of its doubtful origin. The student is accordingly anxious to see whether the miraculous formed an essential element of Rabbinic Judaism. Nor are we quite disappointed when we turn over the pages of the Talmud with this purpose in view. There is hardly any miracle recorded in the Bible for which a parallel might not be found in the Rabbinic literature. The greatest part of the third chapter of the Tractate Taanith, called also the "Chapter of the Saints," is devoted to specimens of supernatural acts performed by various Rabbis. But miracles can only be explained by more miracles, by regular epidemics of miracles. The whole period which saw them must become the psychological phenomenon to be explained, rather than the miracle-workers themselves. But of the Rabbinical miracles we could judge with far greater accuracy if, instead of the few specimens still preserved to us, we were in possession of all those stories and legends which once circulated about the saints of Israel in their respective periods.

Another problem which a fuller knowledge of these ancient times might have helped us to solve is this: With what purpose were these miracles worked, and what were they meant to prove? We are told in 1 Corinthians (I:22), that "the Jews ask for signs as the Greeks seek for wisdom." As a fact, however, in the whole of Rabbinic literature, there is not one single instance on record that a Rabbi was ever asked by his colleagues to demonstrate the soundness of his doctrine, or the truth of a disputed Halachic case, by performing a miracle. Only once do we hear of a Rabbi who had recourse to miracles for the purpose of showing that his conception of a certain Halachah was the right one. And in this solitary instance the majority declined to accept the miraculous intervention as a demonstration of truth, and decided against the Rabbi who appealed to it. Nor, indeed, were such supernatural gifts claimed for *all* Rabbis. Whilst many learned Rabbis are said to have "been accustomed to wonders," not a single miracle is reported for instance of the great Hillel, or his colleague, Shammai, both of whom exercised such an important influence on Rabbinic Judaism. On the other hand, we find that such men, as, for instance, Choni Hammaagel, whose prayers were much sought after in times of drought, or R. Chaninah b. Dosa, whose prayers were often solicited in cases of illness, left almost no mark on Jewish thought, the former being known only by the wondrous legends circulating about him, the latter being represented in the whole Talmud only by one or two moral sayings. "Signs," then, must have been as little required from the Jewish Rabbi as from the Greek sophist. But if this was the case, we are actually left in darkness about the importance of miracles and their meaning as a religious factor in those early times. Our chances of clearing up such obscure but important points would naturally be much greater if some fresh documents could be discovered.

. . . any attempt at an orderly and complete system of Rabbinic theology is an impossible task; for not only are our materials scanty and insufficient for such a purpose, but, when handling those fragments which have come down to us, we must always be careful not to labour them too much, or to "fill them with meaning" which their author could never have intended them to bear, against which all his other teachings and his whole life form one long, emphatic protest, or to spin from the harmless repetition by a Rabbi of a gnostic saying or some Alexandrinic theorem the importance of which he never understood, a regular system of Rabbinic theology. All that these fragments can offer us are some aspects of the theology of the Rabbis, which may again be modified by other aspects, giving us another side of the same subject. What we can obtain resembles rather a complicated arrangement of theological checks and balances than anything which the modern divine would deign to call a consistent "scheme of salvation." Still, I am inclined to think that a religion which has been in "working order" for so many centuries—which contains so little of what we call theology, and the little theology of which possesses so few fixities (whilst even these partake more of the nature of experienced realities than of logically demonstrated dogmas)—that this religion forms so unique and interesting a phenomenon as to deserve a more thorough treatment than it has hitherto received. It is not to be dismissed with a few general phrases, only tending to prove its inferiority.

This brings me to one other introductory point which I wish to suggest by the word *Aspects.* Aspects, as we know, vary with the attitude we take. My attitude is a Jewish one. This does not, I hope, imply either an apology for the Rabbis, or a polemic tendency against their antagonists. Judaism does not give as its *raison d'être* the shortcomings of any of the other great creeds of the civilised world. Judaism, even Rabbinic Judaism, was there before either Christianity or Mohammedanism was called into existence. It need not, therefore, attack them, though it has occasionally been compelled to take protective measures when they have threatened it with destruction. But what I want to indicate and even to emphasise is, that my attitude towards Rabbinic theology is necessarily different from that taken by most commentators on the Pauline Epistles. I speak advisedly of the commentators on Paul; for the Apostle himself I do not profess to understand. Harnack makes somewhere the remark that in the first two centuries of Christianity no man understood Paul except that heathen-Christian Marcion, and he misunderstood him. Layman as I am, it would be presumptuous on my part to say how far succeeding centuries advanced beyond Marcion. But one thing is quite clear even to every student, and this is that a curious alternative is always haunting our exegesis of the Epistles. Either the theology of the Rabbis must be wrong, its conception of God debasing, its leading motives materialistic and coarse, and its teachers lacking in enthusiasm and spirituality, or the Apostle to the Gentiles is quite unintelligible. I need not face this alternative, and may thus be able to arrive at results utterly at variance with those to be found in our theological manuals and introductions to the New Testament.

The question as to how far the theology of the Rabbis could be brought into harmony with the theology of our age is a matter of apologetics, and does not exactly fall within the province of these essays. With a little of the skill so often displayed by the writers of the life and times of ancient heroes, particularly New Testament heroes, it would certainly not be an impossible task to draw such an ideal and noble picture of any of the great Rabbis, such as Hillel, R. Jochanan ben Sakkai, or R. Akiba, as would make us recognise a nineteenth-century altruist in them. Nor would it require much ingenuity to parade, for instance, R. Abuhah as an accomplished geologist, inasmuch as he maintained that before the creation of *our* world God was ever constructing and destroying worlds; or again, to introduce as a perfect Hegelian that anonymous Rabbi who boldly declared that it was Israel's consciousness of God which was "the making of God": or finally, to arrogate for R. Benaha the merit of having been the forerunner of Astruc, because he declared that the Pentateuch was delivered not as a complete work, but in a series of successive scrolls. Indeed, the Rabbinic literature has already been described as a "wonderful mine of religious ideas from which it would be just as easy to draw up a manual for the most orthodox as to extract a vade-mecum for the most sceptical." But I have not the least desire to array the ancient Rabbis in the paraphernalia of modern fashion, and to put before the reader a mere theological masquerade, or to present the Talmud as a rationalistic production which only by some miracle escaped the vigilant eye of the authorities, who failed to recognise it as a heretical work and exclude it from the Synagogue. The "liberty of interpretation," in which so many theologians indulge, and which they even exalt as "Christian freedom," seems to me only another word for the privilege to blunder, and to deceive oneself and others.

To show, however, that Rabbinic theology is, with the least modicum of interpretation or re-interpretation, equal to the highest aspirations of the religious man of various modes of thought, occasional illustrations have been given from the works of philosophers and mystics, thus proving the latent possibilities of its application by various schools in different ages. As to "modernity," it entirely depends whether there is still room in its programme for such conceptions as God, Revelation, Election, Sin, Retribution, Holiness, and similar theological ideas; or is it at present merely juggling with words to drop them at the first opportunity? If this latter be the case, it will certainly find no ally in Rabbinic theology, or for that matter, in any other theology.

Further Resources

BOOKS

Bentwich, Norman. *Solomon Schechter: A Biography.* Cambridge, N.Y.: Cambridge University Press, 1938.

Fierstien, Robert E., ed. *Solomon Schechter in America: A Centennial Tribute.* New York: The Joint Convention Committee, 2002.

Marty, Martin E. *Modern American Religion,* vol. 1. Chicago, Ill.: University of Chicago Press, 1986.

WEBSITES

Schechter, Solomon. "The Dogmas of Judaism." Chapter 6 of *Studies in Judaism, First Series.* Jewish Publication Society of America, 1896. Available online at http://www.sacred-texts.com/jud/studies.htm; website home page: http://www.sacred-texts.com/index.htm (accessed May 16, 2003).

"Attempts at Religious Legislation from 1888–1945"

Congressional record

By: United States Congress

Date: 1949

Source: "Attempts at Religious Legislation from 1888–1945." *American State Papers on Freedom in Religion,* 4th ed. Washington, D.C.: The Religious Liberty Association, 1949. Available online at http://members.tripod.com/~candst/1888-49.htm (accessed April 15, 2003).

About the Author: The U.S. Congress, the legislative branch of the American government, is divided into the House of Representatives and the Senate. Legislation may be introduced in either body. Legislation passed by one body is then sent to the other. If both pass the legislation, it is submitted to the president for action. ■

Introduction

Sunday was, and still is for most Christians, the traditionally observed day of rest and religious observance. Mandatory Sunday closings are often referred to as "blue laws," a term applied to any laws devised by lawmakers to enforce their definition of morality. The label had a historical meaning as well: "Blue laws," the first printed laws of New Haven Colony during the colonial days, were printed on blue paper or bound in blue. In tracing the meaning of "blue laws," some historians also include the colonial laws of Massachusetts.

From 1900 to 1909 at least twenty-eight pieces of legislation were introduced dealing with mandatory Sunday closings of businesses. In addition, at least seven pieces of legislation were introduced advocating restoration of the motto "In God We Trust" on coins and paper money. That motto was placed on United States coins because of religious sentiment at the time of the Civil War. Legislation approved by Congress on March 3, 1865, allowed the Treasury Department to place the motto on all gold and silver coins, but the motto was missing on the double-eagle gold coin and the eagle gold coin shortly after they appeared in 1907. Congress received many complaints about the missing motto, especially from religious groups. An act of May 18, 1908, required that the motto appear on all coins upon which it had previously appeared, including all gold coins and silver dollar coins, half-dollar coins, and quarter-dollar coins. Since 1909, one-cent coins, and, since 1916, ten-cent coins have also had the motto struck on them.

Significance

In the period 1888 to 1945, the number of religious-based bills introduced to Congress totaled 142. Ninety-three of these bills related to Sunday closings. Most of them were not reported (handed from subcommittee to full committee for consideration), but a few were approved, resulting in some mandatory Sunday closings and the restoration of the "In God We Trust" motto on currency.

The Sabbath was a day traditionally set aside for religious worship, but the definition of "Sabbath" varied according to a person's religious beliefs. For some, the Sabbath was the first day of the week, Sunday; for others, it was the seventh day of the week, Saturday. For some Christians, as well as non-Christians who observed Saturday as their Sabbath—Seventh-day Adventists and Jews, for example—Sunday closings would still apply to them.

Sunday closings were inconvenient for some people, and in some cases meant economic hardship. If a Seventh-day Adventist or Jew did not work on Saturday, then Sunday closings might have resulted in that person working only five days a week instead of the usual six. Later in the twentieth century, many state Sunday closings laws were modified, repealed, or not enforced, but these laws still exist in some states.

In the case of the currency inscription of "In God We Trust," atheists and others who believed in the complete separation of church and state have raised objections, but Congress has not responded to their wishes with legislation to stop the practice.

Primary Source

"Attempts at Religious Legislation from 1888–1945" [excerpt]

SYNOPSIS: From 1900 to 1909, at least twenty-eight pieces of legislation dealing with mandatory Sunday closings of businesses and at least seven pieces of legislation addressing a proposal to restore "In God We Trust" on coins and paper money were introduced. Most of these were not reported, but a few were approved. [Note: S. stands for Senate; H. R. for House of Representatives; S. Res. for Senate Resolution; H. J. Req. for House Joint Resolution; the numbers following these indicate the number of the bill; matter following the number of the bill gives the title or description of the bill; the name, date, committee, etc., following this indicate who introduced it, when it was introduced, the committee to which it was referred, the fate of the measure, and the volume and page in the *Congressional Record* where reference to bill may be found. Thus, C. R. 19:4455 means *Congressional Record,* volume 19, p. 4455.]

Fifty-sixth Congress 1900–1901

Sunday Closings: passed H. R. 9829. "To provide for celebrating the 100th anniversary of the purchase of the Louisiana Territory . . . in . . . St. Louis." Lane of Iowa, March 21, 1900; to Special Committee on Centennial of the Louisiana Purchase; amended and favorably reported: passed House February 18, 1901, without Sunday-closing condition; referred to Senate Committee on Industrial Expositions; reported favorably (Senate Report 2382); passed Senate February 23, 1901, with Senator Teller's amendment: "That as a condition precedent to the payment of this appropriation the directors shall contract to close the gates to visitors on Sundays during the whole duration of the fair"; went to conference, House nonconcurring in Sunday-closing amendment (I-1. R. Report 2976); went to second conference, House receding from nonconcurrence, and both houses agreeing, March 1, 1901, to bill as passed by Senate. Approved March 3, 1901. C. R. 34:2872–4. (See U. S. Stat., vol. 31, part 1, pp. 1440–1445.)

Sunday Closings: not reported H. R. 10592. "To further protect the first day of the week as a day of rest in the District of Columbia." Allen of Maine, April 10, 1900; to Committee on District of Columbia; not reported. C. R. 33:3995.

Fifty-seventh Congress 1902

Sunday Closings: not reported S. 5334. "Requiring places of business in the District of Columbia to be closed on Sunday." McMillan of Michigan, April 19, 1902; to Committee on District of Columbia: not reported. C. R. 35:4422.

Sunday Closings: not reported H. R. 13970. "Requiring places of business in the District of Columbia to be closed on Sunday." Jenkins of Wisconsin, April 24, 1902; to Committee on District of Columbia; not reported. C. R. 35:4655.

Sunday Closings: not reported H. R. 14110. "To further protect the first day of the week as a day of rest in the District of Columbia." Allen of Maine, April 30, 1902; to Committee on District of Columbia; not reported. C. R. 35:4905.

Sunday Closings: not reported S. 5563. "To further protect the first day of the week as a day of rest in the District of Columbia." Dillingham of Vermont, May 1, 1902; to Committee on District of Columbia; not reported. C. R. 35:4909.

Fifty-eighth Congress 1903–1904

Sunday Closings: not reported H. R. 4859. "To further protect the first day of the week as a day of rest in the District of Columbia." Allen of Maine, November 24, 1903; to Committee on District of Columbia; not reported. C. R. 37:472.

Sunday Closings: not reported H. R. 11819. "Requiring certain places of business in the District of Columbia to be closed on Sunday." Wadsworth of New York, February 4, 1904; to Committee on District of Columbia; reported favorably; amended and passed House; referred to Senate Committee on District of Columbia; not reported. C. R. 38:1646, 4077, 4375, 4414.

Fifty-ninth Congress 1905–1907

Sunday Closings: not reported H. R. 3022. "To prevent Sunday banking in post offices in the handling of money orders and registered letters." Sibley of Pennsylvania, December 5, 1905; to Committee on Post Offices and Post Roads; not reported. C. R. 40:112.

Sunday Closings: reported adversely and indefinitely postponed S. 1653. "To prevent Sunday banking in post offices in the handling of money orders and registered letters. " Penrose of Pennsylvania, December 14, 1905; to Committee on Post Offices and Post Roads; reported adversely and indefinitely postponed. C. R. 40:385, 2747.

Sunday Closings: not reported H. R. 10510. "To further protect the first day of the week as a day of rest in the District of Columbia." Allen of Maine, January 5, 1906; to Committee on District of Columbia; not reported. C. R. 40:747.

Sunday Closings: did not come to vote H. R. 12610. "To authorize the United States Government to participate in the Jamestown Tercentennial Exposition." Maynard of Virginia, January 20, 1906; to Committee on Industrial Arts and Expositions; reported with amendments, with proviso, "that as a condition precedent to the appropriations herein provided for, the Jamestown Exposition Company shall contract to close exhibits and places of amusement to visitors on Sundays"; did not come to vote. C. R. 40: 1336, 5486, 5637.

Sunday Closings: passed the House but not reported by Senate Committee H. R. 16483. "Requiring certain places of business in the District of Columbia to be closed on Sunday." Wadsworth of New York, March 9, 1906; passed House June 11, 1906, but not reported by Senate Committee. C. R. 40:3655, 8268–71, 8307.

Sunday Closings: not reported H. R. 16556. "To prohibit labor on buildings, and so forth, in the District of Columbia on the Sabbath day." Heflin of Al-

Opening ceremonies of the U.S. 59th Congress, 2nd session, 1906. The line of separation between church and state has been defined and redefined several times in U.S. history. In this Congress alone there were nine pieces of religious-based legislation introduced. **REPRODUCED FROM THE COLLECTIONS OF THE LIBRARY OF CONGRESS.**

abama, March 12, 1906; to Committee on District of Columbia; not reported. C. R. 40:3711.

Sunday Closings: reported with amendment, but not brought to vote S. 5825. "To authorize the United States Government to participate in the Jamestown Tercentennial Exposition," with proviso, "That as a condition precedent to the payment of the appropriations herein provided for, the Jamestown Exposition Company shall contract to close exhibits and places of amusements to visitors on Sundays." Daniel of Virginia, April 23, 1906; to select Committee on Industrial Expositions; reported with amendment, but not brought to vote. C. R. 40:5682, 7589.

Sunday Closings: approved H. R. 19844. United States Sundry Civil bill, appropriating two hundred fifty thousand dollars to the Jamestown Tercentennial Exposition. June 29, 1906, House and Senate agreed to bill with following proviso: "That, as a condition precedent to the payment of this appropriation in aid of said exposition, the Jamestown Exposition Company shall agree to close the grounds of said exposition to visitors on Sunday during the period of said exposition." Approved June 30, 1906. C. R. 40:9673–4. (See U. S. Stat., vol. 34, part 1, pp. 764–768.)

Sunday Closings: considered and agreed to S. Res. 215. "That the Postmaster General be directed to inform the Senate by what authority post offices are required to be kept open on Sunday, together with the regulation of Sunday opening, as to the extent of the business that may be transacted, and also what the provisions are for clerical help, and whether postal clerks and carriers are required to work more than six days per week." Burkett of Nebraska, January 9, 1907; considered and agreed to. C. R. 41:804.

Sixtieth Congress 1907–1909

Sunday Closings: not reported H. R. 327. "To restore the inscription 'In God we trust' upon the coins of the United States of America." O. M. James of Kentucky, December 2, 1907; to Committee on Coinage, Weights, and Measures; not reported. C. R. 42:18.

Sunday Closings: not reported H. R. 353. "Requiring the motto 'In God we trust' to be inscribed on all forms of moneys hereafter issued by the United States." Sheppard of Texas, December 2, 1907; to Committee on Coinage, Weights, and Measures; not reported. C. R. 42: 19.

Sunday Closings: not reported H. R. 4897. "To further protect the first day of the week as a day of rest in the District of Columbia." Allen of Maine, December 5, 1907; to Committee on District of Columbia; not reported. C. R. 42:186.

Sunday Closings: not reported H. R. 4929. "Prohibiting labor on buildings, and so forth, in the District of Columbia on the Sabbath day." Heflin of Alabama, December 5, 1907; to Committee on District of Columbia; not reported. C. R. 42:186.

Sunday Closings: not reported S. 1519. "To prevent Sunday banking in post offices in the handling of money orders and registered letters. " Penrose of Pennsylvania, December 9, 1907; to Committee on Post Offices and Post Roads; not reported. C. R. 42:209.

In God We Trust: not reported H. R. 11295. "Authorizing the continuance of the inscription of a motto ["In God we trust"] on the gold and silver coins of the United States." Moore of Pennsylvania, December 21, 1907; to Committee on Coinage, Weights, and Measures; not reported. C. R. 42:467.

Sunday Closings: not reported H. R. 13471. "Prohibiting work in the District of Columbia on the first day of the week, commonly called Sunday." Lamar of Missouri, January 13, 1908; to Committee on District of Columbia; not reported. C. R. 42:666.

In God We Trust: not reported H. R. 13648. "Requiring the motto 'In God we trust' to be inscribed on all coins of money hereafter issued by the United States, as formerly." Reale of Pennsylvania, January 14, 1908; to Committee on Coinage, Weights, and Measures; not reported. C. R. 42:706.

Sunday Closings: not reported S. 3940. "Requiring certain places of business in the District of Columbia to be closed on Sunday. "Johnston of Alabama, January 14, 1908; to Committee on District of Columbia; hearing on bill before Senate subcommittee, April 15, 1908; amended and reintroduced by Mr. Johnston, May 1, 1908, as S. 3940, with Calendar No. 605 [report No. 5961 attached; reported favorably; passed Senate May 15, 1908; introduced in House May 16, 1908; hearing on bill before House District Committee, February 15, 1909; not reported by House Committee. C. R. 42:676, 5514, 6434.

In God We Trust: not reported H. R. 14400. "Requiring the motto 'In God we trust' to be restored to certain coins." Ashbrook of Ohio, January 20, 1908; to Committee on Coinage, Weights, and Measures; not reported. C. R. 42:899.

Sunday Closings: not reported H. R. 15239. "Requiring certain places of business in the District of Columbia to be closed on Sunday." Langley of Kentucky, January 27, 1908; to Committee on District of Columbia; not reported. C. R. 42:1166.

In God We Trust: not reported H. R. 15439. "Providing for the restoration of the motto 'In God we trust' on certain denominations of the gold and silver coins of the United States." Wood of New Jersey, January 28, 1908; to Committee on Coinage, Weights, and Measures; not reported. C. R. 42:1257.

In God We Trust: not reported H. R. 16079. "Providing for the restoration of the motto 'In God we trust' on certain denominations of the gold and silver coins of the United States." McKinney of Illinois, February 3, 1908; to Committee on Coinage, Weights, and Measures; not reported. C. R. 42:1505.

In God We Trust: not reported H. R. 17144. "Providing for the restoration of the motto 'In God we trust' on certain denominations of the gold and silver coins of the United States." Foster of Illinois, February 14, 1908; to Committee on Coinage, Weights, and Measures; not reported. C. R. 42:2051.

In God We Trust: approved H. R. 17296. "Providing for the restoration of the motto 'In God we trust' on certain denominations of the gold and silver coins of the United States," McKinley of Illinois, February 17, 1908; to Committee on Coinage, Weights, and Measures; reported favorably; passed House March 16; referred to Senate Committee on Finance March 17; reported favorably; passed Senate May 13. Approved May 18, 1908. C. R. 42:2106, 3384, 6189. (See U. S. Stat., vol. 35, part 1, p. 164.)

Sunday Closings: not reported H. R. 19965. "For the proper observance of Sunday as a day of rest " [in the District of Columbia]. Hay of Virginia, March 27, 1908; to Committee on District of Columbia; not reported. C. R. 42:4058.

Sunday Closings: not reported S. 6535. "For the proper observance of Sunday as a day of rest in the District of Columbia " (first section did not mention Sunday, or first day of week, and so prohibited labor on all days). Johnson of Alabama, April 7, 1908; to Committee on District of Columbia; hearing on this and the original S. bill No. 3940 before it was remodeled, before Senate subcommittee February 15, 1909; not reported. C. R. 42:4458.

Sunday Closings: not reported S. 6853. "To amend an act entitled 'An act to license billiard and pool tables in the District of Columbia, and for other purposes'" requiring that "all such places shall be closed during the entire twenty-four hours of each and every Sunday." Gallinger of New Hampshire, April 28, 1908; to Committee on District of Columbia; not reported. C. R. 42:5324.

Further Resources

BOOKS

Connecticut. *The Code of 1650.* Hastings, Minn.: Hungry Point Farm, 1972.

Connecticut. *The Code of 1650: (being a compilation of the earliest laws and orders of the General Court of Connecticut: also, the constitution, or civil compact, entered into and adopted by the towns or Windsor, Hartford, and Wethersfield in 1638–9: to which is added some extracts from the laws and judicial proceedings of New-Haven Colony, commonly called blue laws).* Littleton, Colo.: F.B. Rothman, 1998.

Laband, David N. *Blue Laws: The History, Economics, and Politics of Sunday-Closing Laws.* Lexington, Mass.: Lexington Books, 1987.

WEBSITES

Bergen County, New Jersey. "Blue Laws." Available online at http://www.bergen.org/AAST/Projects/Forum/Issues/bluelaws/; website home page: http://www.bergen.org (accessed January 10, 2003).

Commonwealth of Massachusetts. "Massachusetts Blue Laws." Available online at http://www.state.ma.us/dlwd/bluelaws.html; website home page: http://www.state.ma.us/dlwd/index.htm (accessed January 10, 2003).

U.S. Department of the Treasury. "Fact Sheets: Currency & Coins: History of In God We Trust.'" Available online at http://www.treas.gov/education/fact-sheets/currency/in-god-we-trust.html; website home page: http://www.treas.gov/index.html (accessed January 10, 2003).

11

SCIENCE AND TECHNOLOGY

CHRISTOPHER CUMO

Entries are arranged in chronological order by date of primary source. For entries with one primary source, the entry title is the same as the primary source title. Entries with more than one primary source have an overall entry title, followed by the titles of the primary sources.

Important Events in Science and Technology, 1900–1909

1900

- Marie Curie discovers that an atom can spontaneously break apart, releasing energy. Scientists call this phenomenon "radioactivity."
- Sigmund Freud publishes *On the Interpretation of Dreams* in German.
- In April, Thomas Alva Edison invents the nickel-alkaline storage battery.
- On May 14, Dutch botanist Hugo de Vries announces his discovery of Austrian monk Gregor Mendel's three laws of genetics. Later in 1900, two other scientists, Carl Correns and Erich Tschermak, claim the same discovery.
- In July, geologists at the University of Berlin in Germany invent the modern pendulum seismograph for the detection of earthquakes. U.S. universities, led by the University of California, Berkeley, build seismographs in their geology departments.
- On July 2, the first zeppelin dirigible flies in Germany.
- In October, the U.S. Army builds its first dirigible. The army will use dirigibles for reconnaissance.
- On November 15, steel magnate Andrew Carnegie founds the Carnegie Institute of Technology in Pittsburgh, Pennsylvania. It will become Carnegie-Mellon University, a center for education and research in engineering and science.
- On December 14, German physicist Max Planck announces the basis of quantum theory: energy is not a continuum but instead comes in discrete amounts called quanta. In 1923, American physicist Arthur Holly Comptom will extend Planck theory to gamma rays.

1901

- Freud publishes *The Psychopathology of Everyday Life,* explaining "Freudian slips" of the tongue. Freud believes that misstatements, "Freudian slips," reveal a person's true thoughts about a person or event.
- In January, Percival Lowell, founder of the Lowell Observatory (1894) in Flagstaff, Arizona, announces that his examination of Mars reveals canals. Intelligent beings must have built them, Lowell reasons, evidence that Mars once harbored life and perhaps still does.
- In January, Dutch biologist Hugo de Vries publishes the first volume of his theory of genetic mutation. He calls his idea "saltation," meaning a genetic change so large that it produces a new species.
- On February 17, General Electric founds the first corporate research laboratory.
- In March, bicycle manufacturers and amateur aviators Wilbur and Orville Wright begin glider flights to observe and master the aerodynamics of flying.
- In April, Thaddeus Cahill exhibits his electric typewriter at the Pan-American Exhibition in Buffalo.
- In June, Congress establishes the National Bureau of Standards.
- On June 2, Andrew Carnegie announces his intention to donate $10 million to promote scientific research.
- In July, Japanese American chemist Jokichi Takamine and chemist-pharmacologist John Jacob Abel announce their isolation of adrenaline, a human hormone.
- In September, John D. Rockefeller establishes the Rockefeller Institute for Medical Research in New York City.
- On December 12, Guglielmo Marconi receives the first transatlantic radio communication.

1902

- The DuPont and Parke-Davis companies establish research laboratories.
- Dutch physician Eugene Dubois withdraws Java Man from scientific scrutiny, stung by criticism from Henry Fairfield Osborn at the American Museum of Natural History that Java Man is the ancestor of the gibbon rather than of humans. Dubois had discovered Java Man, a femur and part of a skull, in Java (today Indonesia) in 1897 and had hailed him our earliest ancestor.
- French auto manufacturer Louis Renault invents the drum brake; Englishman Frederick W. Lanchester invents the disc brake.
- Yale University mathematical physicist Josiah Willard Gibbs publishes *Elementary Principles of Statistical Mechanics,* in which he uses statistics to describe the motion of atoms and molecules.
- The vacuum cleaner and power lawn mower are invented in England.
- In March, German chemist Richard Zsigmondy invents the ultramicroscope, making possible the observation of molecules in a colloidal liquid.
- In April, electrical engineer and mathematician Charles Steinmetz patents the magnetite lamp.
- In May, British physicists Ernest Rutherford and Frederick Soddy publish an article that describes radioactivity as the release of energy from the nucleus of an atom. The idea that the nucleus of an atom can release energy lays the foundation for the U.S. building of the first atomic bomb in July 1945 and for the production of electricity by nuclear power.
- In June, Russian physiologist and psychologist Ivan Pavlov publishes his discovery of conditioned reflexes.
- On December 18, German Arthur Korn invents the photofax machine to transmit news photographs by telegraph.

1903

- The U.S. Navy buys German "Slaby-Arco" radio sets to equip its battleships and tests them in maneuvers.
- Reginald A. Fessenden invents the electrolytic radio detector, capable of receiving the human voice.
- Willem Einthoven, the Dutch physiologist who invented the string galvanometer, defines its application for electrocardiograms.
- British philosophers and mathematicians Bertrand Russell and Alfred North Whitehead publish *The Principles of Mathematics,* an attempt to prove that all mathematics are the logical extension of a small number of axioms.
- In January, President Theodore Roosevelt, from a Marconi station in Wellfleet, Massachusetts, exchanges greetings with England's King Edward VII via a wireless telegraph.
- In July, Liberty Hyde Bailey becomes Dean of the College of Agriculture at Cornell University in Ithaca, New York. Bailey will use his position to advocate science as the solutions to the problems of American agriculture.
- On October 7, Smithsonian Institution director Samuel P. Langley's airplane, launched from a houseboat, fails to fly. Langley's plane will fail a second time nine days before the Wrights' success.
- In November, Thomas Edison perfects the electroplating technique of making master record molds.
- On December 17, the Wright brothers fly successfully at Kitty Hawk, North Carolina.

1904

- Invented in Germany, the phonograph record replaces Thomas Edison's wax cylinder.
- In January, Englishman John A. Fleming invents the diode vacuum tube.
- In February, Charles D. Perrine discovers the sixth moon of Jupiter.
- In February, a group of civil and mechanical engineers, many of them West Point graduates, found the United Engineering Society.
- In March, the U.S. begins, under the leadership of U.S. president Theodore Roosevelt, to dig a canal across the isthmus of Panama. The Panama Canal will allow ships to cross from the Atlantic to the Pacific without having to go around the southern tip of South America.
- On May 8, French physicist Jules-Henri Poincaré delivers a lecture on the principles of mathematical physics at the International Congress of Arts and Sciences in Saint Louis. Poincaré emphasizes the importance of statistics in physics, as Yale University mathematical physicist J. Willard Gibbs had in 1902.
- In October, Japanese physicist Hantaro Nagaoka proposes a model of the structure of the atom by comparing the motion of electrons to that of the rings of the planet Saturn. Physicists will revise this model during the 1920s, demonstrating that electrons do not follow a circular orbit around an atom's nucleus, but, rather, occupy regions around the nucleus of an atom.
- On December 20, George Ellery Hale and the Carnegie Institution establish Mount Wilson Observatory near Pasadena, California. Hale becomes the observatory's first director.

1905

- English physiologist Ernest Starling coins the term *hormone* to describe chemical messengers produced by the endocrine glands.
- Sigmund Freud publishes *Jokes and their Relation to the Unconscious* and *Three Essays on the Theory of Sexuality,* both in German. Critics found the second too explicit in its sexual content.
- On June 30, Albert Einstein publishes a paper announcing his Special Theory of Relativity. Its essence is the proposition that time ticks at different rates for objects moving at different speeds.
- In July, University of Chicago physicist Robert Andrews Millikan calculates the charge on an electron. The charge is miniscule, implying that an electron is tiny. This work will win Millikan the 1924 Nobel Prize in physics.
- On August 30, a solar eclipse occurs and is best visible in Spain.
- On September 27, Albert Einstein publishes a paper announcing that mass and energy can transpose one into the other. Because the speed of light is 186 billion billion miles per second squared, a tiny mass yields enormous energy. This equation expresses the energy released in a nuclear explosion or by a nuclear power plant.
- In December, Albert Einstein publishes two papers. One extends Max Planck's quantum theory to light. The other asserts that tiny particles in liquid are atoms in random motion, colliding with one another and the sides of a container, just as atoms in a gas. Einstein calls this action Brownian Motion.

1906

- In January, the U.S. Department of Agriculture establishes the Bureau of Plant Industry, which would oversee all USDA crop-breeding experiments and would coordinate such experiments with the land-grant colleges and agricultural experiment stations.
- On March 16, Congress passes the Adams Act, giving each agricultural experiment station fifteen thousand dollars a year to conduct "basic" research: science that seeks knowledge for its own sake rather than for practical use.
- In May, Percival Lowell at the Lowell Observatory in Flagstaff, Arizona, determines that irregularities in Neptune's orbit are caused by an unidentified planet beyond Neptune. American astronomer Clyde Tombaugh will find that planet in 1930, naming it Pluto, the first two letters of which commemorate *P*ercival *L*owell.
- On December 11, British physicist John Joseph Thomson receives the Nobel Prize in physics for discovering the electron in 1902.
- On December 24, the first radio broadcast originates from Brant Rock, Massachusetts.

1907

- On January 14, Telharmonic Hall opens in New York City.
- On January 18, Lee De Forest develops the triode radio tube.
- On March 15, the Indiana legislature grants state courts the power to authorize surgeons to sterilize criminals, "idiots," and the insane. The law stems from a belief that that children of criminals will inherit criminality genes and themselves become criminals, obligating the state to protect the public by sterilizing criminals.
- On December 12, Albert Michelson, a German immigrant and U.S. Naval Academy graduate, wins the Nobel Prize in physics, becoming the first American Nobel laureate, for his study of the properties of sunlight.

1908

- The electric razor is introduced.
- In March, the Holt Company of California manufactures the first tractor with moving treads.
- In March, Henry Fairfield Osborn becomes president of the American Museum of Natural History in New York City. Osborn will use his position to popularize evolution in general and human evolution in particular.
- On March 2, G.H. Hardy works out a mathematical law governing the frequency of a dominant genetic trait in a population. It becomes known as the Hardy-Weinberg law.
- In August, Dutch physicist Heike Kamerlingh Onnes produces temperature and pressure so low that helium liquefies.
- On October 1, Henry Ford introduces the Model T, or "Tin Lizzie," the most popular of early motorcars.
- On November 8, George Ellery Hale discovers magnetic fields in sunspots.
- On December 7, engineers and astronomers install a sixty-inch reflecting telescope at Mount Wilson Observatory.
- On December 11, Ernest Rutherford of England receives the Nobel Prize in chemistry for his study of radioactivity.
- On December 21, Wilbur Wright wins the Michelin Cup in France by flying 77 miles in 2 hours, 20 minutes.

1909

- German evolutionary biologist August Weismann publishes his *Theory of Selection,* in which he argues, correctly, that organisms pass genes to offspring. Those genes that confer a survival advantage tend to pass to the next generation in greater number than genes that confer no advantage.
- On April 6, U.S. Navy commander Robert Peary reaches the North Pole.
- On June 29, John D. Rockefeller charters the Rockefeller Foundation.
- On July 25, Louis Blériot flies across the English Channel.
- In August, Dutch zoologist Wilhelm Johannsen defines *gene, genotype,* and *phenotype..*
- In August, Columbia University embryologist Thomas Hunt Morgan begins to breed *Drosophila,* the common fruit fly, to study the transmission of genes from generation to generation. This work will lead Morgan and his research team to establish that genes lie in a line on chromosomes.
- In August, Charles Doolittle Walcott, head of the Smithsonian Institution, discovers the Burgess Shale in Canada. The Shale is the fossilized remains of soft-bodied marine invertebrates some 550 million years old, and among the earliest evidence of multicellular life on Earth.
- In September, in his only visit to the United States, Sigmund Freud lectures at Clark University in Worcester, Massachusetts.
- On November 24, commemorative celebrations in the U.S., Britain and continental Europe mark the fiftieth anniversary of the publication of Charles Darwin's *On the Origin of Species* and the centennial of Darwin's birth.
- On December 11, Guglielmo Marconi and Karl F. Braun share the Nobel Prize in physics for wireless telegraphy and the radio.

The Velocity of Light

Monograph

By: Albert A. Michelson

Date: 1902

Source: Michelson, Albert A. *The Velocity of Light.* Vol. 9 of *The Decennial Publications.* Chicago: University of Chicago Press, 1902, 7–9.

About the Author: Albert Abraham Michelson (1852–1931) was born in what is today Germany. He immigrated with his family to Panama, then to San Francisco. In 1873 he graduated from the Naval Academy at Annapolis, Maryland, where he stayed to teach physics. In 1881 he resigned from the navy to accept a professorship at the Case Institute of Applied Science in Cleveland, Ohio. In 1907 he became the first American to win a Nobel Prize in physics. ■

Introduction

In the seventeenth century Isaac Newton passed white light through a prism, refracting it into a spectrum of colors. Light, he reasoned, must consist of particles of different sizes, with each size corresponding to a color. Particles of a particular size create the sensation of a particular color when they strike the retina.

This view of light and color perception prevailed until the nineteenth century, when British mathematician, physicist, and linguist Thomas Young passed light through two slits onto a screen. As the light passed through the slits, it broadened into two overlapping cones. If light consisted of particles, the area of overlap would have received twice as many particles as the other areas, creating a bright region where the particles overlapped. Instead, Young saw a series of bright and dark bands in the region of overlap. Light, he concluded, must be a wave rather than an aggregate of particles such that wherever two crests or troughs of the waves coincided on the screen, they reinforced one another, creating a bright band of light. Wherever a crest coincided with a trough, the two waves cancelled one another in a band of dark.

But the question remained how light could travel through space, for physicists believed that waves—sound, for example—could not travel through a vacuum. Space, therefore, must not be a vacuum but instead consist of a medium that Aristotle had called the ether.

Significance

Physicists, however, had no evidence that the ether existed. Michelson supposed that if it did, it must produce drag as the Earth passes through it, just as air produces drag on a car traveling along a road, slowing it down. Michelson tried several times to measure this reduction in light's speed and hence the ether's drag, but every attempt failed to register any change.

Albert Einstein saw the implications of Michelson's experiments—that the ether must not exist and that light's speed must be constant. As tame as these implications seem, the second revolutionized physics. Einstein held that if light's speed is constant, it must not vary for any observer no matter his position and speed. A wave of light will recede from an observer traveling near light speed as rapidly as from one traveling at just one mile per hour. This can only be true if space shrinks and time ticks more slowly for the observer traveling near light speed. Thus, space and time are relative, not absolute—the essence of Einstein's Special Theory of Relativity (1905), which built on Michelson's work.

Primary Source

The Velocity of Light [excerpt]

SYNOPSIS: In this excerpt Albert Michelson describes the apparatus he used in his attempt to detect the ether. A cautious scientist, he drew no conclusions from his experiments. The results of his experiments, though, hit physicists like a thunderbolt three years later, when Einstein announced his Special Theory of Relativity.

The following plan suggested itself during the experiments upon the "relative motion of the earth and the luminiferous ether": [*Amer. Jour. Sci.,* XXXIV (1887), November.]

The essential feature is the combination of a grating with a revolving mirror, which combination acts as a toothed wheel; the grating space representing the distance between the teeth, the radius being the distance from the revolving mirror to the grating.

It was proposed to utilize this combination in an attempt to solve the problem of the "relative motion" by measuring the velocity of light *in one direction,* that is, without returning the light to the source. This was before the celebrated work of Hertz showed that the electrical impulses (which were to be used to establish the required phase relation between the two revolving mirrors) would be affected in the same way as would the light-waves themselves. It may also be noted in this connection that

Diagram of Experimental Setups for Measuring the Speed of Light

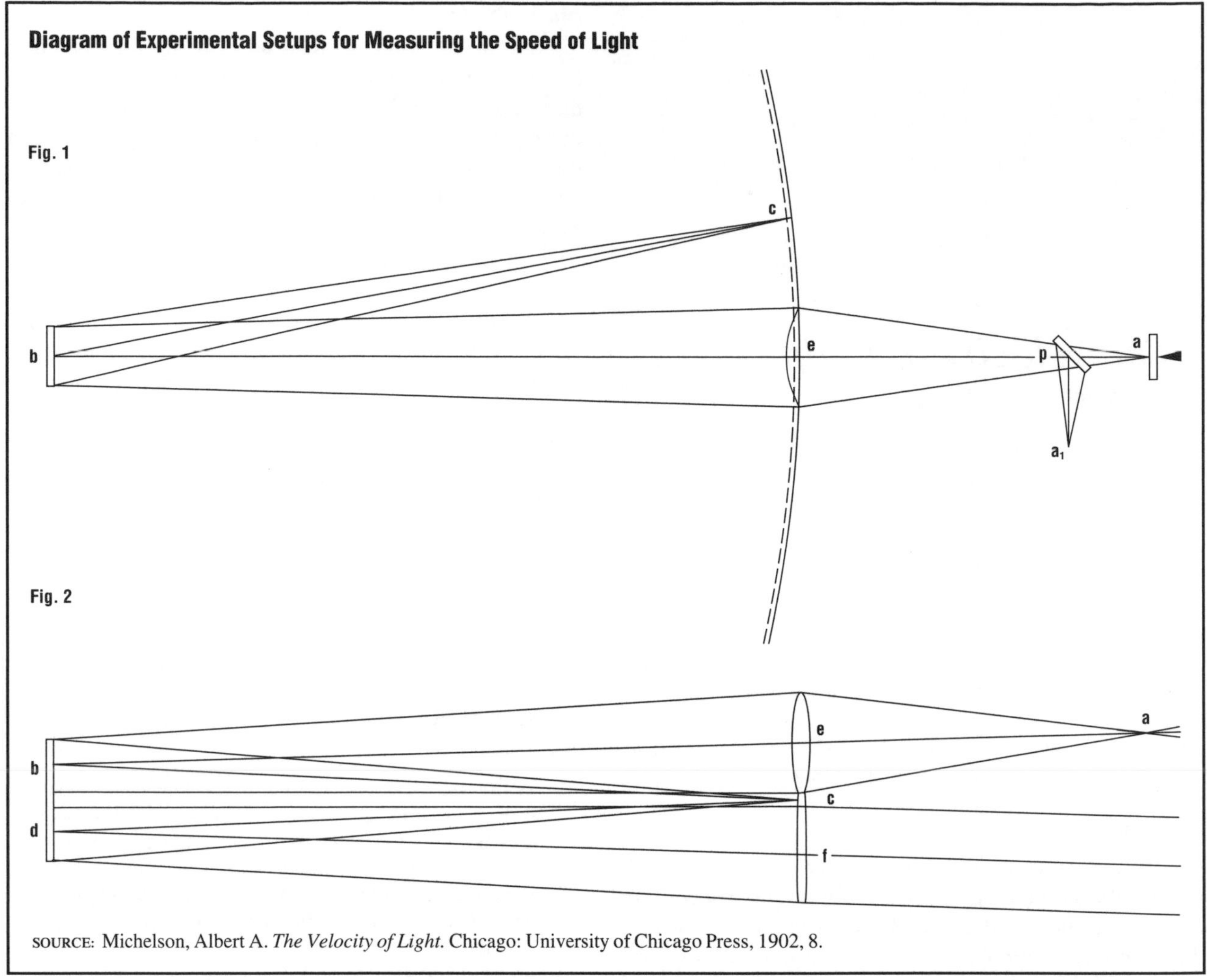

SOURCE: Michelson, Albert A. *The Velocity of Light.* Chicago: University of Chicago Press, 1902, 8.

the method proposed in the same article, and illustrated by Fig. 1, is also not sound. [It may also be worth mentioning that some preliminary experiments, made about two years ago, have shown that it is not entirely impossible to employ a mechanical method of keeping the two revolving mirrors in a constant phase relation. For instance, it was shown that the vibrations of a tuning-fork could be transmitted over a mile of piano wire with a diminution of amplitude of less than one-half.]

The plan proposed is virtually a combination of the methods of Foucault and Fizeau; the essential feature of the observation of eclipses corresponding to the latter method, while the production of the eclipses is brought about by a revolving beam of light as in the former method.

Figs. 1 and 2, in which the lettering is the same, will illustrate the essential features, subject to such minor modifications as experiment may suggest. The light starts from a slit at *a,* passes through a lightly silvered glass plate *P* and a lens *e,* and falls upon the upper half of the revolving mirror *b.* Thence it proceeds to the grating *c,* upon the surface of which it forms an image of the slit. It is thence reflected to the lower half *d* of the revolving mirror, which reflects the beam through the lens *f* to the distant mirror upon the surface of which the second image of the slit is formed. The light then retraces its course and returns to its source at *a,* part being reflected to *a* 1 for convenience of observation by the eyepiece. The limit of closeness of the grating space is determined by the aperture of the revolving mirror viewed from *c.*

If the "radius" *bc* is 3m. and the revolving mirror is 6cm. wide, this angle will be 0.02; and the breadth of the diffraction image at *c* will be of the order $\lambda/.02$, or, say, 0.025mm. The grating space should therefore be at least 0.05mm., and, probably better,

Albert Michelson uses an appartus to measure the speed of light. © BETTMANN/CORBIS. REPRODUCED BY PERMISSION.

0.1mm. If the number of revolutions is 250, and the distance to the fixed mirror be 3km., the displacement of the first image over the grating surface will be 18cm., corresponding to 1,800 eclipses. There need be no difficulty in counting the order of the eclipse observed, if the speed is gradually increased to its final value. The fractions could probably be observed correctly to something like 2 per cent., so that this element of the computation for *V* could be measured to something like 1 part in 100,000.

This same, or even a higher, order of accuracy may be obtained in the measurement of all the other elements. Previous experiments have shown that the speed of the mirror may be obtained by means of a rated tuning-fork to within 1 in 100,000. The measurement of the distance may be made directly on a base line especially prepared for such work to within 1 in 200,000.

Finally, the grating may be calibrated to an order of accuracy depending on the angle subtended by the diffraction fringes, i.e., 1/40 × 1/3000, or less than 1 in 100,000.

It seems not unreasonable to hope that, with proper care and patience, the value of this great fundamental constant of nature may be found to within 5km. or less.

It will be noted that in the form of experiment here proposed the more serious of the difficulties pointed out by M. Cornu no longer exist, or are very much diminished, while the possible accuracy is greatly increased. It may be hoped, therefore, that the result of this combination of the methods of Foucault and Fizeau will be to reconcile the difference which thus far seem to exist between the results of the work of their respective followers.

Further Resources

BOOKS

Jaffe, Bernard. *Michelson and the Speed of Light.* Garden City, N.Y.: Doubleday, 1960.

Livingston, Dorothy Michelson. *The Master of Light: A Biography of Albert A. Michelson.* New York: Scribner's, 1973.

Miller, Arthur I. *Albert Einstein's Special Theory of Relativity.* Reading, Mass.: Addison-Wesley, 1981.

Pyenson, Lewis. *The Young Einstein: The Advent of Relativity.* Boston: Hilger, 1985.

PERIODICALS

Cassidy, David. "Understanding the History of Special Relativity." *Historical Studies in the Physical and Biological Sciences,* March 1986, 177–195.

Handschy, M. A. "Reexamination of the 1887 Michelson-Morley Experiment." *American Journal of Physics,* July 1982, 987–990.

Halton, Gerald. "On the Origins of the Special Theory of Relativity." *American Journal of Physics,* December 1960, 627–636.

Hunt, Bruce. "Experimenting on the Ether." *Historical Studies in the Physical and Biological Sciences,* October 1986, 111–134.

Swenson, Loyd S. "Albert A. Michelson." *Dictionary of Scientific Biography* 12, 1973, 371–374.

WEBSITES

"Albert Abraham Michelson—Biography." Nobel e-Museum. Available online at http://www.nobel.se/physics/laureates/1907/michelson-bio.html; website home page: http://www.nobel.se (accessed January 5, 2003).

Elementary Principles in Statistical Mechanics

Monograph

By: J. Willard Gibbs

Date: 1902

Source: Gibbs, J. Willard. *Elementary Principles in Statistical Mechanics.* New York: Scribner's, 1902. Reprint, Woodbridge, Conn.: Ox Bow Press, 1981, vi–viii.

About the Author: Josiah Willard Gibbs (1839–1903) was born in New Haven, Connecticut, and received a Ph.D. in engineering in 1863 from Yale University. After studying mathematics and physics in Europe, he became professor of mathematical physics at Yale in 1871. Thereafter he seldom left New Haven, living the rest of his life in the house where he had been born. ■

Introduction

The seventeenth-century classical physics of Isaac Newton culminated in the nineteenth century in three grand theories that absorbed the attention of J. Willard Gibbs: thermodynamics, kinetic theory, and statistical mechanics. At mid-century scientists had formalized the first law of thermodynamics, which says that the total energy in a closed system (a system to which nothing is added or subtracted) remains constant, though energy may be converted from one form to another (as, for example, when an athlete transforms the chemical energy from food into the energy of motion and heat). Then in 1850 the German physicist Rudolf Clausius formalized the second law of thermodynamics, called entropy, based on the observation of French engineer Sadi Carnot that heat flows from an area of greater concentration to one of lesser concentration. Since heat is a form of energy, energy must flow from greater to lesser concentration over time. Since order of a system is one measure of energy, disorder must increase over time in a closed system.

In 1860 British mathematician and physicist James Clerk Maxwell asserted that a gas (and by extension all matter) is an aggregate of atoms in random motion such that the greater the energy (in the form of heat) of the gas, the greater the velocity of the atoms, the more numerous their collisions, and the further apart they will be assuming their presence in an elastic container. This is the kinetic theory of gases. Statistical mechanics, the branch of statistics that describes the behavior of large numbers of atoms in motion, flowed from kinetic theory. Maxwell and Austrian physicist Ludwig Boltzmann understood that not all atoms in a system at uniform temperature and pressure move at the same speed—that is, have the same energy. Yet the energy of the atoms will converge on an average, and it is this average that one measures in the temperature and pressure of, say, water boiling in a pot.

Significance

Gibbs unified the first and third theories by deriving the laws of thermodynamics from statistical mechanics. This meant a unification of all three theories because statistical mechanics is an outgrowth of kinetic theory. Gibbs's work thus represented the culmination of the nineteenth-century synthesis of thermodynamics, kinetic theory, and statistical mechanics. His contribution was to find solutions to the problems of nineteenth-century physics rather than to originate new ideas. In this he typified American science between 1900 and 1909, which attempted to refine ideas from the previous century.

As conventional as Gibbs was in this respect, in other ways he was an oddity. Before Gibbs American science was descriptive rather than theoretical. Most American biologists, for example, immersed themselves in the workaday world of taxonomy or plant breeding; physicists contented themselves with the precise measurement of physical constants. The descriptive nature of American science in 1900 meant that it was seldom mathematical. Gibbs distinguished himself among American scientists by being a theoretician. His papers were so laden with equations that he had trouble finding American publishers. Only when translators issued his work in German did physicists in large numbers recognize the import of his work.

Primary Source

Elementary Principles in Statistical Mechanics [excerpt]

SYNOPSIS: In this excerpt from the preface Gibbs announces his intention of deriving the laws of thermodynamics from statistical mechanics. He also makes the subtle point that his mathematical models cannot reveal what matter is, only how it behaves.

But although, as a matter of history, statistical mechanics owes its origin to investigations in thermodynamics, it seems eminently worthy of an independent development, both on account of the elegance and simplicity of its principles, and because it yields new results and places old truths in a new light in departments quite outside of thermodynamics. Moreover, the separate study of this branch of mechanics seems to afford the best foundation for the study of rational thermodynamics and molecular mechanics.

The laws of thermodynamics, as empirically determined, express the approximate and probable behavior of systems of a great number of particles, or, more precisely, they express the laws of mechanics for such systems as they appear to beings who have not the fineness of perception to enable them to appreciate quantities of the order of magnitude of those which relate to single particles, and who cannot repeat their experiments often enough to obtain any but the most probable results. The laws of statistical mechanics apply to conservative systems of any number of degrees of freedom, and are exact. This does not make them more difficult to establish than the approximate laws for systems of a great many degrees of freedom, or for limited classes of such systems. The reverse is rather the case, for our attention is not diverted from what is essential by the peculiarities of the system considered, and we are not obliged to satisfy ourselves that the effect of the quantities and circumstances neglected will be negligible in the result. The laws of thermodynamics may be easily obtained from the principles of statistical mechanics, of which they are the incomplete expression, but they make a somewhat blind guide in our search for those laws. This is perhaps the principal cause of the slow progress of rational thermodynamics, as contrasted with the rapid deduction of the consequences of its laws as empirically established. To this must be added that the rational foundation of thermodynamics lay in a branch of mechanics of which the fundamental notions and principles, and the characteristic operations, were alike unfamiliar to students of mechanics.

Josiah Willard Gibbs was professor of mathematical physics at Yale and at times worked without pay. **HULTON ARCHIVE. REPRODUCED BY PERMISSION.**

We may therefore confidently believe that nothing will more conduce to the clear apprehension of the relation of thermodynamics to rational mechanics, and to the interpretation of observed phenomena with reference to their evidence respecting the molecular constitution of bodies, than the study of the fundamental notions and principles of that department of mechanics to which thermodynamics is especially related.

Moreover, we avoid the gravest difficulties when, giving up the attempt to frame hypotheses concerning the constitution of material bodies, we pursue statistical inquiries as a branch of rational mechanics. In the present state of science, it seems hardly possible to frame a dynamic theory of molecular action which shall embrace the phenomena of thermodynamics, of radiation, and of the electrical manifestations which accompany the union of atoms. Yet any theory is obviously inadequate which does not take account of all these phenomena. Even if we confine our attention to the phenomena distinctively thermodynamic, we do not escape difficulties in as simple a matter as the number of degrees of freedom of a diatomic gas. It is well known that while theory would assign to the gas six degrees of freedom per molecule, in our experiments on specific heat we cannot account for more than five. Certainly, one is building on an insecure foundation, who rests his work on hypotheses concerning the constitution of matter.

Difficulties of this kind have deterred the author from attempting to explain the mysteries of nature, and have forced him to be contented with the more modest aim of deducing some of the more obvious propositions relating to the statistical branch of mechanics. Here, there can be no mistake in regard to the agreement of the hypotheses with the facts of nature, for nothing is assumed in that respect. The only error into which one can fall, is the want of agreement between the premises and the conclusions, and this, with care, one may hope, in the main, to avoid.

Further Resources

BOOKS

Bumstead, Henry A., and Ralph G. Van Name, eds. *The Collected Works of J. Willard Gibbs.* New Haven, Conn.: Yale University Press, 1948.

Donnan, F. G., and Arthur Haas. *A Commentary on the Scientific Writings of J. Willard Gibbs.* New Haven, Conn.: Yale University Press, 1936.

Harman, P. M. *Energy, Force, and Matter: The Conceptual Development of Nineteenth-Century Physics.* New York: Cambridge Univesity Press, 1982.

Rukeyser, Muriel. *Willard Gibbs.* Garden City, N.Y.: Doubleday, Doran, 1942.

Wheeler, Lynde P. *Josiah Willard Gibbs: The History of a Great Mind.* New Haven, Conn.: Yale University Press, 1951.

PERIODICALS

Cardwell, D. S. L., and Richard L. Hills. "Thermodynamics and Practical Engineering in the Nineteenth Century." *History of Technology,* June 1976, 1–20.

Sheynin, O. B. "On the History of the Statistical Method in Physics." *Archive for History of Exact Sciences,* 78, 1985, 351–382.

WEBSITES

"J. Willard Gibbs." Laboratory of Experimental and Computational Biology. Available online at http://www-lecb.ncifcrf.gov/~toms/gibbs.html; website home page: http://www-lecb.ncifcrf.gov (accessed January 5, 2003).

Diary Entry of December 17, 1903

Diary

By: Orville Wright

Date: December 17, 1903

Source: Wright, Orville. Diary entry of December 17, 1903. In McFarland, Marvin W., ed. *The Papers of Wilbur and Orville Wright.* Vol. 1: 1899–1905. New York: McGraw-Hill, 1953, 394–396.

About the Author: Wilbur Wright (1867–1912) was born on a farm in Indiana. The family moved to Dayton, Ohio, where his brother Orville was born in 1871. The two ran a print shop from 1889 to 1892 and began manufacturing bicycles in 1895. In 1899 they started tinkering with gliders, adding a gasoline engine in 1903 to achieve the first powered flight at Kitty Hawk, North Carolina. Wilbur died in 1912 and Orville in 1948. ■

Introduction

Until the early twentieth century, flight was possible only with gliders, hot-air balloons, and dirigibles. Although Smithsonian Institution director Samuel P. Langley, an advocate of the steam engine, remarked in 1891 that "Mechanical flight is possible with engines we now possess," the steam engine and electric motor were too heavy for the horsepower they generated. Starting in 1887 Langley tinkered with model airplanes as heavy as thirty pounds, and in 1896 he actually flew a model with a twelve-foot wingspan, a one-horsepower steam engine, and twin propellers three thousand feet along the Potomac River. That year, too, American engineer Octave Chanute began experimenting with gliders, designing one with two pairs of wings, a prototype of the biplane. In 1903 Langley built a full-size airplane, the Aerodrome, and hired Charles M. Manly to pilot it. That fall Manly twice tried to fly it but failed both times.

Significance

Nine days after Manly's second failure Wilbur and Orville Wright made their historic flight at Kitty Hawk, North Carolina. It was the gasoline-powered engine, rather than Langley's steam engine, that made their flight possible. Their success launched the twentieth century as the age of aviation and stimulated a frenzy of interest in the airplane. In 1907, Alexander Graham Bell formed the Aerial Experiment Association to promote the design of larger and safer planes. Bell regarded the Wrights' planes as hazardous because they required great speed to get aloft.

This interest in aviation paid dividends the next decade, as European and American armies used the airplane for reconnaissance and in combat during World War

Wright brothers' first flight. Kitty Hawk, North Carolina. December 17, 1903. **THE LIBRARY OF CONGRESS.**

I (1914–1918). The military use of airplanes prompted governments to pour money into their construction, yielding a surplus for civilian use after the war. During the 1920s Americans began to glimpse the potential of the airplane, using it to dust crops and deliver mail. Charles Lindbergh's transatlantic flight in 1927 proved that the airplane could travel vast distances with a speed that had before been impossible. The advent of the jet engine after World War II (1939–1945) ushered in the modern era of aviation. Manufacturers could now build jet planes large enough to carry hundreds of passengers. Flight had become a reality for all Americans, not the privileged few.

Primary Source

Diary entry of December 17, 1903 [excerpt]

SYNOPSIS: In this excerpt Orville Wright describes the Wright brothers' historic flight on December 17, 1903. That day they made four flights, each of which they recorded in methodical language. Nowhere in this excerpt does one glimpse the excitement and sense of historic importance that the Wright brothers must have felt.

When we got up a wind of between 20 and 25 miles was blowing from the north. We got the machine out early and put out the signal for the men at the station. Before we were quite ready, John T. Daniels, W. S. Dough, A. D. Etheridge, W. C. Brinkley of Manteo, and Johnny Moore of Nags Head arrived. After running the engine and propellers a few minutes to get them in working order, I got on the machine at 10:35 for the first trial. The wind, according to our anemometers at this time, was blowing a little over 20 miles (corrected) 27 miles according to the Government anemometer at Kitty Hawk. On slipping the rope the machine started off increasing in speed to probably 7 or 8 miles. The machine lifted from the truck just as it was entering on the fourth rail. Mr. Daniels took a picture just as it left the tracks. I found the control of the front rudder quite difficult on account of its being balanced too near the center and thus had a tendency to turn itself when started so that the rudder was turned too far on one side and then too far on the other. As a result the machine would rise suddenly to about 10 ft. and then as suddenly, on turning the rudder, dart for the ground. A sudden dart when out about 100 feet from the end of the tracks ended the flight. Time about 12 seconds (not known exactly as watch was not promptly stopped). The lever for throwing off the engine was broken, and the skid under the rudder cracked. After repairs, at 20 min. after 11 o'clock Will made the second trial. The course was about like mine, up and down but a little longer over the ground though about the same in time. Dist. not measured but about 175 ft. Wind speed not quite so strong. With the aid of the station men present, we picked the machine up and carried it back to the starting ways. At about 20 minutes till 12 o'clock I made the third trial. When out about the same distance as Will's, I met with a strong gust from the left which raised the left wing and sidled the machine off to the right in a lively manner. I immediately turned the rudder to bring the machine down and then worked the end control. Much to our surprise, on reaching the ground the left wing struck first, showing the lateral control of this machine much more effective than on any of our former ones. At the time of its sidling it had raised to a height of probably 12 to 14 feet. At just 12 o'clock Will started on the fourth and last trip. The machine started off with its ups and downs as it had before, but by the time he had gone over three or four hundred feet he had it under much better control, and was traveling on a fairly even course. It proceeded in this manner till it reached a small hummock out about 800 feet from the starting ways, when it began its pitching again and suddenly darted into the ground. The front rudder frame was badly broken up, but the main frame suffered none at all. The distance over the ground was 852 feet in 59 seconds. The engine turns was 1071, but this included several seconds while on the starting ways and probably about a half second after landing. The jar of landing had set the watch on machine back so that we have no exact record for the 1071 turns. Will took a picture of my third flight just before the gust struck the machine.

Further Resources

BOOKS

Augelucci, Enzo. *Airplane: From the Dawn of Flight to the Present Day.* New York: Greenwich House, 1971.

Bilstein, Roger E. *Flight in America, 1900–1983: From the Wrights to the Astronauts.* Baltimore, Md.: Johns Hopkins University Press, 1984.

Boyne, Walter J. *The Smithsonian Book of Flight.* Washington, D.C.: Smithsonian Books, 1987.

Freudenthal, Elsbeth E. *Flight into History: The Wright Brothers and the Air Age.* Norman, Okla.: University of Oklahoma Press, 1949.

Moolman, Valerie. *The Road to Kitty Hawk.* Alexandria, Va.: Time-Life Books, 1980.

Scott, Phil. *The Pioneers of Flight: A Documentary History.* Princeton, N.J.: Princeton University Press, 1999.

PERIODICALS

Horgan, James. "Aeronautics at the World's Fair of 1904." *Missouri Historical Society Bulletin,* April 1968, 215–246.

Walcott, C. D. "Biographical Memoir of Samuel P. Langley, 1834–1906." *National Academy of Sciences Biographical Memoirs,* April 1912, 247.

WEBSITES

Gates, Bill. "The Wright Brothers." The 100 Most Influential People of the 20th Century. *Time.* Available online at http://www.time.com/time/time100/scientist/profile/wright.html; website home page: http://www.time.com (accessed January 5, 2003).

Wright, Orville. "How We Made the First Flight." Aviation Enthusiast Corner. Available online at http://www.aero-web.org/history/wright/first.htm; website home page: http://www.aero-web.org (accessed January 5, 2003).

Experiments with Alternate Currents of High Potential and High Frequency

Lecture

By: Nikola Tesla

Date: 1904

Source: Tesla, Nikola. *Experiments with Alternate Currents of High Potential and High Frequency.* New York: McGraw-Hill, 1904, 3–4.

About the Author: Nikola Tesla (1856–1943) was born in Smiljan, Croatia, and immigrated to the United States in 1884. The next year he sold his patent rights to his alternating-current dynamos, transformers, and motors to George Westinghouse. In 1891 he invented the Tesla coil, an induction coil used in radio. ■

Introduction

Chemical cells produced the first electric currents, but they were an expensive way of generating voltage, making long-distance electrical transmission out of the question. Physicists spent much of the nineteenth century trying to find an inexpensive alternative. In 1820 Dutch physicist Hans Christian Oersted deflected a compass needle by passing an electric current through a copper wire, proving that an electric current could produce a magnetic field. British physicist Michael Faraday realized that if an electric current could produce a magnetic field, then a magnetic field could in turn generate an electric current. In 1831 he induced an electric current by spinning a coil of wire between the north and south poles of a magnet.

This arrangement produced alternating current: the periodic reversal of the direction in which electricity flows. The current begins at point zero, grows to a maximum, then decreases to zero. At the point at which it passes zero it reverses direction, reaches a maximum in the opposite direction, and returns again to zero. Alternating current in effect traces a sine curve, which each repetition of the curve representing one cycle. American inventor Thomas Edison opposed alternating current because he believed that current that reverses direction gets nowhere. In his view it was better to produce direct current: a flow of electricity that does not reverse direction and thus travels from point A to point B.

Significance

As sensible as direct current seemed to Edison, its transmission required the generation of high voltage, making it costly. Alternating current circumvented this problem by generating high frequency (a large number of cycles per second with each cycle at low voltage) rather than high voltage. The obstacle to alternating current was not cost but its complex mathematics. By 1880, though, mathematicians and physicists had solved the mathematical problems and perfected the dynamo (electric generator), opening an era of inexpensive electricity. Nikola Tesla joined American inventor George Westinghouse in championing alternating current with the same enthusiasm Edison had lavished on direct current. Much to Edison's chagrin, the economics of transmission favored Tesla and Westinghouse, and today alternating current generates most electricity. (The electricity from batteries and fuel cells is an exception.) Cycles of 60 per second are common for domestic and commercial power, though radar and microwave transmission requires several thousand cycles per second and television signals require 100 million cycles per second.

The significance of inexpensive electricity to Americans would be hard to overstate, for it is used to power home appliances, light homes and businesses, heat buildings where natural gas is scarce, and cool buildings during summer. Yet electricity is no panacea to U.S. energy problems. Nuclear and hydroelectric power account for only 5 percent of the nation's electricity. Coal and natural gas account for the rest, but neither can last indefinitely, both spew greenhouse gases into the atmosphere, and coal burning causes acid rain. Americans have learned to harness the power of electricity but at peril to the environment.

Nikola Tesla, inventor of induction motor and proponent of alternating current as the best method of electric power transmission.

Primary Source

Experiments with Alternating Currents of High Potential and High Frequency [excerpt]

SYNOPSIS: In this excerpt Tesla champions alternating current as the best method of transmitting electricity over long distances. Like many American scientists and inventors in the early twentieth century, Tesla emphasized the value of practical knowledge rather than theory for its own sake.

This investigation, then, it goes without saying, deals with alternating currents, and, to be more precise, with alternating currents of high potential and high frequency. Just in how much a very high frequency is essential for the production of the results presented is a question which, even with my present experience, would embarrass me to answer. Some of the experiments may be performed with low frequencies; but very high frequencies are desirable, not only on account of the many effects secured by their use, but also as a convenient means of obtaining, in the induction apparatus employed, the high potentials, which in their turn are necessary to the demonstration of most of the experiments here contemplated.

Of the various branches of electrical investigation, perhaps the most interesting and immediately the most promising is that dealing with alternating currents. The progress in this branch of applied science has been so great in recent years that it justifies the most sanguine hopes. Hardly have we become familiar with one fact, when novel experiences are met with and new avenues of research are opened. Even at this hour possibilities not dreamed of before are, by the use of these currents, partly realized. As in nature all is ebb and tide, all is wave motion, so it seems that in all branches of industry alternating currents—electric wave motion—will have the sway.

One reason, perhaps, why this branch of science is being so rapidly developed is to be found in the interest which is attached to its experimental study. We wind a simple ring of iron with coils; we establish the connections to the generator, and with wonder and delight we note the effects of strange forces which we bring into play, which allow us to transform, to transmit and direct energy at will. We arrange the circuits properly, and we see the mass of iron and wires behave as though it were endowed with life, spinning a heavy armature, through invisible connections, with great speed and power—with the energy possibly conveyed from a great distance. We observe how the energy of an alternating current traversing the wire manifests itself—not so much in the wire as in the surrounding space—in the most surprising manner, taking the forms of heat, light, mechanical energy, and, most surprising of all, even chemical affinity. All these observations fascinate us, and fill us with an intense desire to know more about the nature of these phenomena. Each day we go to our work in the hope of discovering—in the hope that some one, no matter who, may find a solution of one of the pending great problems—and each succeeding day we return to our task with renewed ardor; and even if we *are* unsuccessful, our work has not been in vain, for in these strivings, in these efforts, we have found hours of untold pleasure, and we have directed our energies to the benefit of mankind.

Further Resources

BOOKS

Asimov, Isaac. *The History of Physics.* New York: Walker, 1966.

Hughes, Thomas P. *Networks of Power: Electrification in Western Society, 1880–1930.* Baltimore, Md.: Johns Hopkins University Press, 1979.

MacLaren, Malcolm. *The Rise of the Electrical Industry during the Nineteenth Century.* Princeton, N.J.: Princeton University Press, 1943.

Sharlin, Harold I. *Making of the Electrical Age.* New York: Abelard-Schuman, 1963.

PERIODICALS

Devons, Samuel. "The Search for Electromagnetic Induction." *Physics Teacher,* May 1978, 625–631.

Finn, Bernard S. "History of Electrical Technology: The State of the Art." *Isis,* Autumn 1976, 31–35.

Hughes, Thomas P. "The Electrification of America: The System Builders." *Technology and Culture,* January 1979, 124–161.

———. "How Did the Heroic Inventors Do It?" *American Heritage of Invention and Technology,* August 1985, 18–25.

WEBSITES

Kosanovic, Bogdan R. "Nikola Tesla." Department of Neurological Surgery, University of Pittsburgh. Available online at http://www.neuronet.pitt.edu/~bogdan/tesla

Adolescence: Its Psychology

Reference work

By: G. Stanley Hall

Date: 1905

Source: Hall, G. Stanley. *Adolescence: Its Psychology.* New York: D. Appleton, 1905, ix, xiii, 2–3.

About the Author: Granville Stanley Hall (1844–1924) was born in Ashfield, Massachusetts, and received his Ph.D. in psychology from Harvard University in 1878. In 1884, he founded the first experimental psychology laboratory in the United States at Johns Hopkins University. In 1888, he became president of Clark University in Massachusetts and used his position to invite Sigmund Freud to lecture at the university in 1909. ■

Introduction

In 1866 German naturalist Ernest Haeckel announced the theory of recapitulation, an interpretation of Charles Darwin's theory of evolution by natural selection. Darwin believed nature adapted species ever more closely to their environment, and it was this adaptation that evolved new species. Darwin was careful, though, not to suggest that evolution has a direction from lower to higher forms. Haeckel, in contrast, was the most prominent of several naturalists to impose direction on evolution. He ordered species from simplest to most complex, asserting that species always evolved toward greater complexity. His view that the most complex species were higher by definition than simpler ones flattered human vanity because it meant that humans represented the culmination of eons of evolution and were the goal toward which evolution had aspired.

Haeckel saw evolution as an additive process. It worked by adding more complex stages of development to what had been simpler species. An amphibian was higher than a fish, for example, because in its development it progressed through a fish stage. Humans were at life's pinnacle because they passed through the stages of all other classes of organisms: bacterium, fish, amphibian, reptile, bird, and mammal. Each individual, Haeckel believed, recapitulated (repeated) in its embryological development the adult stages through which the human species had passed in its ascent. For Haeckel and his supporters, gill slits in the human embryo, for example, proved that humans had passed through a fish stage.

Significance

G. Stanley Hall, who considered psychology a subfield of biology, embraced a modified version of recapitulation. The individual, not merely the embryo, repeated in its development the stages of more primitive species. The theory of recapitulation, though, was on the defensive by the time Hall published *Adolescence.* Socially progressive biologists rejected it because racists used it to claim that whites were superior to blacks and to justify racial oppression. Other biologists pointed out that the theory was unscientific because it did not generate any hypothesis that one could test. It explained the presence of gill slits in human embryos, for example, without providing a way to prove or disprove whether humans passed through a fish stage. This shortcoming was particularly serious after biologists in 1900 rediscovered the work of Gregor Mendel, who showed that genes code for traits. Mendel's work provided another explanation: that human embryos share gill slits with fish because humans and fish, in sharing a common ancestor, shared genes that produced gill slits.

Hall thus weakened his own treatment of adolescence by tying it to an outmoded theory. Yet he deserves credit for defining adolescence as a stage in human development. While he did not coin the term *adolescence,* he was the first to subject it to scientific scrutiny. He thus legitimized the study of adolescence as a subject no less important than the study of childhood and adulthood.

G. Stanley Hall legitimized the study of adolescence as a subject no less important than the study of childhood and adulthood. **THE LIBRARY OF CONGRESS.**

Primary Source

Adolescence: Its Psychology [excerpt]

SYNOPSIS: In this excerpt Hall defines adolescence as a stage in human development. Human development was in turn the result of recapitulation—that is, humans repeated in their development the adult stages of their ancestral and more primitive species. Humans thus passed through primitive stages in their ascent to life's apex as nature's most complex species and the culmination of evolution.

The years from about eight to twelve constitute an unique period of human life. The acute stage of teething is passing, the brain has acquired nearly its adult size and weight, health is almost at its best, activity is greater and more varied than ever before or than it ever will be again, and there is peculiar endurance, vitality, and resistance to fatigue. The child develops a life of its own outside the home circle, and its natural interests are never so independent of adult influence. . . .

Adolescence is a new birth, for the higher and more completely human traits are now born. The qualities of body and soul that now emerge are far newer. The child comes from and harks back to a remoter past; the adolescent is neo-atavistic, and in him the later acquisitions of the race slowly become prepotent. Development is less gradual and more saltatory, suggestive of some ancient period of storm and stress when old moorings were broken and a higher level attained. . . .

In this process the individual in a general way repeats the history of its species, passing slowly from the protozoan to the metazoan stage, so that we have all traversed in our own bodies ameboid, helminthoid, piscian, amphibian, anthropoid, ethnoid, and we know not how many intercalary stages of ascent. How these lines of heredity and growth along which all the many thousand species, extant and extinct, these viatica of the holy spirit of life, the consummate products of millennia of the slow travail of evolution, have been unfolded, we know scarcely more than we do what has been the impelling force, or will to live, which seems so inexhaustible and insistent. Certain it is that the cellular theory needs to be supplemented by assuming, both in the organism as a whole and in the species, powers that can not be derived from the cells. Probably, too, the original cause of phylogenetic evolution was no inherent and specific nisus, but, as we know it, was due to a struggle for survival forced upon organisms by their environment.

The early stages of growth are telescoped into each other almost indistinguishably, so that phylogenetically the embryo lives a thousand years in a day, and the higher the species the more rapid relatively is the transit through the lower stages. This law of tachygenesis may perhaps be expressed somewhat as follows: Heredity, which slowly appears as a substitute for the external causes that have produced a given series of characters, tends to produce that succession with increasing economy and speed and also to become in a way more independent of the causes which originally determined it.

Further Resources

BOOKS

Brush, Stephen G. *The History of Modern Science: A Guide to the Second Scientific Revolution, 1800–1950.* Ames, Iowa: Iowa State University Press, 1988.

Gould, Stephen Jay. *Ever Since Darwin: Reflections in Natural History.* New York: Norton, 1977.

Hulse, Stewart H, and Bert F. Green, eds. *One Hundred Years of Psychological Research in America: G. Stanley Hall and the Johns Hopkins Tradition.* Baltimore, Md.: Johns Hopkins University Press, 1986.

Mayr, Ernst. *The Growth of Biological Thought: Diversity, Evolution, and Inheritance.* Cambridge, Mass.: Harvard University Press, 1982.

Ross, Dorothy. *G. Stanley Hall: The Psychologist as Prophet.* Chicago: University of Chicago Press, 1972.

PERIODICALS

Beatty, John. "What's in a Word? Coming to Terms in the Darwinian Revolution." *Journal of the History of Biology,* April 1982, 215–239.

Coleman, William. "Limits of the Recapitulation Theory." *Isis,* Spring 1973, 341–350.

Schwarz, Hans. "Darwinism Between Kant and Haeckel." *Journal of the American Academy of Religion,* March 1981, 581–602.

WEBSITES

"Dr. G. Stanley Hall Biographical Note." Robert H. Goddard Library, Clark University. Available online at http://www.clarku.edu/offices/library/archives/HallBio.htm; website home page: http://www.clarku.edu (accessed January 5, 2003).

Adams Act

Law

By: Henry Cullen Adams

Date: March 16, 1906

Source: U.S. Congress. *Adams Act.* 34 Stat. 63. March 16, 1906. In Knoblauch, Harold C., Ernest M. Law, and W. P. Meyer. *State Agricultural Experiment Stations: A History of Research Policy and Procedure.* Washington, D.C.: U.S. Government Printing Office, May 1962, 221–222.

About the Author: Henry Cullen Adams (1850–1906) was born in Verona, New York, but moved to Wisconsin, where he served in the Wisconsin State Assembly from 1883 to 1887. In 1902 he won election to the U.S. House of Representatives, where he served two terms and sponsored the law bearing his name that doubled federal appropriations to agricultural experiment stations. ■

Introduction

The tension between applied science and pure research has been a long-standing one in American history. The goal of applied research is the discovery of useful knowledge—a cure for cancer, for example. The goal of pure research is knowledge for its own sake, without practical application. Throughout American history the proponents of applied science have held the upper hand. In the eighteenth century the prestige of Thomas Jefferson and Benjamin Franklin, the nation's most prominent scientists, set the scientific agenda. Both believed that America needed scientists whose knowledge would contribute practical benefits to this new nation. They envisioned scientists working with farmers, for example, to increase crop yields. Moreover, they wanted America to establish its own traditions apart from Europe. They saw the European tradition of pure science as old-fashioned and therefore unsuited to a bold new nation.

During the nineteenth century a minority of scientists began to insist that pure research was as legitimate as applied science. They promoted this view through scientific societies, notably the American Association for the Advancement of Science, established in 1848. They believed that scientists should have the freedom to choose their own research paths without the artificial restriction that they lead to useful knowledge. Technicians might pursue practical matters, but scientists had a higher calling: to discover truth for its own sake. Nonetheless, the dawn of the twentieth century was the era of the automobile, the airplane, and the electric railway—and of practical men like Henry Ford, the Wright brothers, and Luther Burbank.

Significance

In 1906, Congress attempted to tip the balance more in favor of pure research by passing the Adams Act. The act gave up to $15,000 a year to each state agricultural experiment station to fund "original researches." This was a remarkable turnabout, for Congress and the states had originally charged them with doing applied research in the tradition of Jefferson and Franklin. The Adams Act was therefore a victory for pure research, which had been pursued by a few scientists in such disciplines as physics and geology but not agriculture.

Yet the Adams Act was a victory for applied science as well. In 1914 biologist Elmer McCollum, using funds provided by the Adams Act, discovered the first vitamin, which led to vitamin-fortified milk during the 1920s. In the 1940s the Adams Act funded microbiologist Salman Waksman's discovery of the first antibiotic effective against tuberculosis. These successes validate Jefferson's and Franklin's insight that American science is practical at its core—or at least suggest that the boundaries between pure and applied research can be uncertain.

Primary Source

Adams Act

SYNOPSIS: This passage is the full text of the Adams Act. The essential point is in the first paragraph: Congress will fund pure research at the agricultural experiment stations, institutions that the state legislatures and Congress had originally charged with discovering practical knowledge.

AN ACT To provide for an increased annual appropriation for agricultural experiment stations and regulating the expenditure thereof

Be it enacted by the Senate and House of Representatives of the United States of America in Congress assembled, That there shall be, and hereby is, annually appropriated, out of any money in the Treasury not otherwise appropriated, to be paid as hereinafter provided, to each State and Territory, for the more complete endowment and maintenance of agricultural experiment stations now established or which may hereafter be established in accordance with the act of Congress approved March second, eighteen hundred and eighty-seven, the sum of five thousand dollars in addition to the sum named in said act for the year ending June thirtieth, nineteen hundred and six, and an annual increase of the amount of such appropriation thereafter for five years by an additional sum of two thousand dollars over the preceding year, and the annual amount to be paid thereafter to each State and Territory shall be thirty thousand dollars, to be applied only to paying the necessary expenses of conducting original researches or experiments bearing directly on the agricultural industry of the United States. having due regard to the varying conditions and needs of the respective States or Territories.

Sec. 2. That the sums hereby appropriated to the States and Territories for the further endowment and support of agricultural experiment stations shall be annually paid in equal quarterly payments on the first day of January, April, July, and October of each year by the Secretary of the Treasury upon the warrant of the Secretary of Agriculture, out of the Treasury of the United States, to the treasurer or other officer duly appointed by the governing boards of said experiment stations to receive the same, and such officers shall be required to report to the Secretary of Agriculture on or before the first day of September of each year a detailed statement of the amount so received and of its disbursements, on schedules prescribed by the Secretary of Agriculture. The grants of money authorized by this act are made subject to legislative assent of the several States and Territories to the purpose of said grants: *Provided,* That payment of such in stallments of the appropriation herein made as shall become due to any State or Territory before the adjournment of the regular session of legislature meeting next after the passage of this act shall be made upon the assent of the governor thereof, duly certified by the Secretary of the Treasury.

Sec. 3. That if any portion of the moneys received by the designated officer of any State or Territory for the further and more complete endowment, support, and maintenance of agricultural experiment stations as provided in this act shall by any action or contingency be diminished or lost or be misapplied, it shall be replaced by said State or Territory to which it belongs, and until so replaced no subsequent appropriation shall be apportioned or paid to such State or Territory; and no portion of said moneys exceeding five per centum of each annual appropriation shall be applied, directly of indirectly, under any pretense whatever, to the purchase, erection, preservation, or repair of any building or buildings, or to the purchase or rental of land. It shall be the duty of each of said stations annually, on or before the first day of February, to make to the governor of the State or Territory in which it is located a full and detailed report of its operations, including a statement of receipts and expenditures, a copy of which report shall be sent to each of said stations to the Secretary of Agriculture, and to the Secretary of the Treasury of the United States.

Sec. 4. That on or before the first day of July in each year after the passage of this act the Secretary of Agriculture shall ascertain and certify to the Secretary of the Treasury as to each State and Territory whether it is complying with the provisions of this act and is entitled to receive its share of the annual appropriation for agricultural experiment stations under this act and the amount which thereupon each is entitled, respectively, to receive. If the Secretary of Agriculture shall withhold a certificate from any State or Territory of its appropriation, the facts and reasons therefore shall be reported to the President, and the amount involved shall be kept separate in the Treasury until the close of the next Congress, in order that the State or Territory may, if it shall so desire, appeal to Congress from the determination of the Secretary of Agriculture. If the next Congress shall not direct such sum to be paid, it shall be covered into the Treasury; and the Secretary of Agriculture is thereby charged with the proper administration of this law.

Sec. 5. That the Secretary of Agriculture shall make an annual report to Congress on the receipts and expenditures and work of the agricultural experiment stations in all of the States and Territories, and also whether the appropriation of any State or Territory has been withheld; and if so, the reason therefor.

Sec. 6. That Congress may at any time amend, suspend, or repeal any or all of the provisions of this act.

Approved March 16, 1906.

Further Resources

BOOKS

Daniels, George H. *Science in American Society: A Social History.* New York: Knopf, 1971.

Dupree, A. Hunter. *Science in the Federal Government.* Cambridge, Mass.: Harvard University Press, 1957.

Oleson, Alexandra, and Sanborn C. Brown. *The Pursuit of Knowledge in the Early American Republic.* Baltimore, Md.: Johns Hopkins University Press, 1976.

True, Alfred C. *A History of Agricultural Experimentation and Research in the United States, 1607–1925.* Washington, D.C.: U.S. Government Printing Office, 1937.

Van Tassel, David, and Michael G. Hall, eds. *Science and Society in the United States.* Homewood, Ill.: Dorsey, 1966.

PERIODICALS

Danbom, David B. "The Agricultural Experiment Station and Professionalism: Scientists' Goals for Agriculture, 1887–1910." *Agricultural History,* Spring 1986, 246–255.

Marcus, Alan I. "The Wisdom of the Body Politic: The Changing Nature of Publicly Sponsored American Agricultural Research Since the 1830s." *Agricultural History,* Summer 1988, 4–26.

Rosenberg, Charles E. "The Adams Act: Politics and the Cause of Scientific Research." *Agricultural History,* January 1964, 3–21.

Shryock, Richard. "American Indifference to Basic Science during the 19th Century." *Archives Internationales d'Histoire des Sciences,* March 1948, 50–65.

WEBSITES

"Agriculture Experiment Station WWW Sites." Iowa Agriculture and Home Economics Experiment Station. Available online at http://www.ag.iastate.edu/iaexp/aes.html; website home page: http://www.ag.iastate.edu (accessed January 5, 2003).

Pragmatism

Nonfiction work

By: William James

Date: 1907

Source: James, William. *Pragmatism.* New York: Longmans, Green, 1907. Reprinted in James, William. *Pragmatism and Four Essays from The Meaning of Truth.* New York: World, 1955, 79–80.

About the Author: William James (1842–1910) was born in New York City and received an M.D. from Harvard Medical School in 1869. A polymath interested in science, philosophy, psychology, and religion, he taught philosophy and psychology at Harvard University and was a founder of Pragmatism, a philosophical movement that influenced intellectuals at the turn of the century. ■

Introduction

During the eighteenth and early nineteenth centuries natural history (what we now call biology) and theology were closely intertwined. Their relationship rested on the Design Argument: the premise that organisms are too intricate in their adaptation to the environment to have arisen by mechanistic forces. Bats, for example, navigate dark caves and track and capture insects by emitting high-frequency sounds whose echo they hear. Surely, the Design Argument runs, such precise adaptation cannot have arisen by happenstance. God must have designed bats and, by extension, all other species.

The Design Argument was strongest in England and the United States. In 1802, for example, Anglican cleric William Paley reasoned that just as the intricacy of a watch is proof that a watchmaker designed it, the intricacy of organisms is proof that God designed life. In the United States naturalist Louis Agassiz championed the Design Argument. Yet by the 1830s not all scientists accepted the Design Argument. By then geologists understood that mass extinctions had punctuated the history of life. If God had designed species, they asked, why had so many gone extinct? Why had he created organisms with vestigial organs? Why had he designed parasites and pestilence?

Significance

William James understood that the Design Argument might have collapsed from its own internal contradictions had not Charles Darwin killed it—and in killing it ushered in a revolution that was as much theological and philosophical as scientific. At the core of the revolution was Darwin's substitution of natural selection for design. In Darwin's model, more organisms are born in each generation than will survive to sexual maturity. Organisms are not carbon copies of one another; they differ, and those with traits that adapt them to their environment (bats with acute ears for example) have the greatest probability of surviving to pass these traits on to their offspring. Bacteria and fleas were as successful in their adaptation to the environment as were humans. Over numerous generations organisms become successively more adapted to their environment, not because God had not fit them to their environment but because nature, in the struggle for survival, had adapted them to their environment by culling out the unfit. Organisms were remnants of species that extinction had not yet claimed.

Accordingly, the diversity and complexity of life could be explained not by God's intervention but by natural selection, which did not even require God's existence. Nature was an arena of mechanistic forces, not the handiwork of God. Theology and philosophy could no longer use science to defend the existence of God. By 1900 William James understood that theology and philosophy would have to make their way in the world alone. Science could no longer help them.

Primary Source

Pragmatism [excerpt]

SYNOPSIS: In this excerpt William James argues that Charles Darwin's influence on theology and philosophy was as large as that on science. He roots Darwin's philosophical significance in his dethroning of the Design Argument. He expresses astonishment that, in retrospect, the Design Argument had lasted so long and been so influential.

Let me pass to a very cognate philosophic problem, the *question of design in nature.* God's existence has from time immemorial been held to be proved by certain natural facts. Many facts appear as if expressly designed in view of one another. Thus the woodpecker's bill, tongue, feet, tail, etc., fit him wondrously for a world of trees, with grubs hid in their bark to feed upon. The parts of our eye fit the

William James, psychologist and founder of the philosophical movement known as pragmatism. AP/WIDE WORLD PHOTOS. REPRODUCED BY PERMISSION.

laws of light to perfection, leading its rays to a sharp picture on our retina. Such mutual fitting of things diverse in origin argued design, it was held; and the designer was always treated as a man-loving deity.

The first step in these arguments was to prove that the design *existed.* Nature was ransacked for results obtained through separate things being co-adapted. Our eyes, for instance, originate in intra-uterine darkness, and the light originates in the sun, yet see how they fit each other. They are evidently made *for* each other. Vision is the end designed, light and eyes the separate means devised for its attainment.

It is strange, considering how unanimously our ancestors felt the force of this argument, to see how little it counts for since the triumph of the darwinian theory. Darwin opened our minds to the power of chance-happenings to bring forth 'fit' results if only they have time to add themselves together. He showed the enormous waste of nature in producing results that get destroyed because of their unfitness.

According to the Design Argument, God's existence can be held to be proved by certain natural facts that appear as if they have been designed in view of one another. For example, the woodpecker's bill, tongue, feet, etc., work wondrously for finding grubs hidden in trees.

He also emphasized the number of adaptations which, if designed, would argue an evil rather than a good designer. *Here,* all depends upon the point of view. To the grub under the bark the exquisite fitness of the woodpecker's organism to extract him would certainly argue a diabolical designer.

Further Resources

BOOKS

Barzun, Jacques. *A Stroll with William James.* New York: Harper & Row, 1983.

Cravens, Hamilton. *The Triumph of Evolution.* Philadelphia: University of Pennsylvania Press, 1978.

Durant, John, ed. *Darwinism and Divinity: Essays on Evolution and Religious Belief.* New York: Blackwell, 1985.

Mayr, Ernst. *The Growth of Biological Thought: Diversity, Evolution, and Inheritance.* Cambridge, Mass.: Harvard University Press, 1982.

Ruse, Michael. *The Darwinian Revolution: Science Red in Tooth and Claw.* Chicago: University of Chicago Press, 1979.

Wiener, Philip P. *Evolution and the Founders of Pragmatism.* Cambridge, Mass.: Harvard University Press, 1949.

PERIODICALS

Bowler, Peter J. "Darwinism and the Argument from Design: Suggestions for a Reevaluation." *Journal of the History of Biology,* October 1977, 29–43.

Halliday, R. J. "God and Natural Selection: Some Recent Interpretations of the Relation of Darwinism to Protestant Belief." *History of European Ideas,* May 1981, 237–246.

Schwarz, Hans. "The Significance of Evolutionary Thought for American Protestant Theology: Late 19th Century Resolutions and 20th Century Problems." *Zygon,* Spring 1981, 261–284.

WEBSITES

Goodman, Russell. "William James." *Stanford Encyclopedia of Philosophy.* Available online at http://plato.stanford.edu/entries/james; website home page: http://plato.stanford.edu (accessed January 6, 2003).

"William James." Division of Educational Studies, Emory University. Available online at http://www.emory.edu/EDUCATION/mfp/james.html; website home page: http://www.emory.edu (accessed January 6, 2003). *This website contains links to a wide range of primary and secondary material about James and his work.*

Plant-Breeding: Being Six Lectures upon the Amelioration of Domestic Plants

Nonfiction work

By: Liberty Hyde Bailey

Date: 1907

Source: Bailey, Liberty Hyde. *Plant-Breeding: Being Six Lectures upon the Amelioration of Domestic Plants,* 4th ed. New York: Macmillan, 1907, 155–157.

About the Author: Liberty Hyde Bailey (1858–1954) was born in South Haven, Michigan, and in 1884 became professor of horticulture at Michigan State University, where he established the first horticultural laboratory in the United States. In 1888, he joined the faculty at Cornell University, first as professor of botany and horticulture and later as dean of the College of Agriculture. He was the author of sixty-six books and seven hundred articles. ■

Introduction

Throughout the nineteenth century theories of heredity fell into two camps. Scientists in the first camp, such as French naturalist Jean-Baptiste Lamarck, held that the environment affects heredity. In 1809, for example, Lamarck announced two laws of heredity. First, offspring inherit traits their parents acquired from the environment. For example, a giraffe that stretches its neck to reach leaves in a tree passes this additional length to its progeny. Second, organs grow with use and atrophy with disuse, and organisms pass these strengthened or weakened organs to their offspring. Thus, for example a mole that lives in dark burrows will pass weakened eyes to its offspring. So commonplace did these ideas seem that few naturalists challenged them. Even Charles Darwin took them for granted.

In the second camp German cytologist August Weismann stood almost alone in denying that the environment could affect heredity. In the 1880s Weismann announced that the cell's nucleus contained hereditary information and that organisms passed this information to offspring through gametes (sex cells). He knew that some insect species form gametes while still in the larval stage, concluding that the environment could not have had enough time to affect the gametes. He came close to the correct view that the cell's nucleus contains particles (genes) that code for traits and that the environment cannot change these particles, though he did not take the decisive step of proposing their existence.

Significance

Unkown to Weismann, Austrian monk Gregor Mendel had done so. Scientists, however, ignored his work until three Europeans rediscovered his 1866 paper on pea hybrids in 1900. Traditional accounts have not credited Americans in this rediscovery, but in 1907 Liberty Hyde Bailey claimed a minor role for himself. He wrote that Dutch botanist Hugo de Vries had discovered Mendel's paper in the bibliography of an article Bailey had published in 1892.

The fact that Bailey, aware of Mendel's paper in 1892, did not grasp its importance reveals two aspects of American science in the first decade of the twentieth century. First, Bailey, a horticulturist, was preoccupied with practical knowledge, as were virtually all other American biologists, who tended to work for the U.S. Department of Agriculture, at agricultural experiment stations, or, like Bailey, at agricultural and mechanical colleges. Mendel's paper, theoretical from start to finish, could not have interested Bailey, and only a handful of biologists paid attention to it. Second, Mendel's paper was mathematical; yet few American biologists at the time had a background in mathematics. Bailey typified the training of American biologists: He had a broad background in languages (hence his ability to read Mendel in the original German) but only an elementary acquaintance with mathematics. The practical bent of American biology between 1900 and 1909 de-emphasized mathematics because of its abstraction. For most American biologists at the time, calculus had little to do with, say, breeding a new variety of corn. Thus, most knew too little mathematics to absorb Mendel's ideas.

Liberty H. Bailey, noted botanist and one of the rediscoverers of Gregor Mendel's laws of heredity. **THE LIBRARY OF CONGRESS.**

Primary Source

Plant-Breeding: Being Six Lectures upon the Amelioration of Domestic Plants [excerpt]

SYNOPSIS: Bailey recounts the rediscovery of Gregor Mendel's 1866 paper on pea hybridization in 1900 by three European scientists. In contrast to traditional accounts, Bailey credited himself with leading one of them, Hugo de Vries, to the paper. Yet Bailey did not recognize the import of Mendel's ideas until de Vries and others made them plain in 1900.

Heredity: Mendel

De Vries made a thorough search of the literature of plant evolution. In an American publication he saw a reference to an article on plant hybrids by G. Mendel, published in 1865 in the proceedings of a natural history society of Brünn in Austria. On looking up this paper he was astonished to find that it discussed fundamental questions of hybridization and heredity, and that it had remained practically unknown for a generation. In 1900 he published an account of it, and this was soon followed by independent discussions by Correns, Tschermak, and Bateson. In May, 1900, Bateson gave an abstract of Mendel's work before the Royal Horticultural Society of England; and later the society published a translation of Mendel's original paper. It is only within the present year, however (1902), that a knowledge of Mendel's work has become widespread in this country. Perhaps the agencies that are most responsible for dissemination of the Mendelian ideas in America are the instruction given by Webber and others in the Graduate School of Agriculture at Columbus last summer, and the prolonged discussion before the International Conference on Plant-Breeding at New York last fall (1902). Lately, several articles on the subject have appeared from our scientific press. . . .

Mendel's work is important because it cuts across many of the current notions respecting hybridization. As De Vries's discussions call a halt in the current belief regarding the gradualness and slowness of evolution, so Mendel's call a halt in respect to the common opinion that the results of hybridizing are largely chance, and that hybridization is necessarily only an empirical subject. Mendel found uniformity and constancy of action in hybridization, and to explain this uniformity he proposed a theory of heredity.

Further Resources

BOOKS

Magnor, Lois. *A History of the Life Sciences.* New York: Dekker, 1979.

Mayr, Ernst. *The Growth of Biological Thought: Diversity, Evolution, and Inheritance.* Cambridge, Mass.: Harvard University Press, 1982.

Olby, Robert C. *Origins of Mendelism.* Chicago: University of Chicago Press, 1985.

Robinson, Gloria. *A Prelude to Genetics: Theories of a Material Substance of Heredity.* Lawrence, Kans.: Coronado, 1979.

PERIODICALS

MacRoberts, Michael H. "Was Mendel's Paper on *Pisum* Neglected or Unknown?" *Annals of Science* 93, 1985, 339–345.

Ravin, A.W. "Genetics in America: A Historical Overview." *Perspectives in Biology and Medicine,* June 1978, 214–231.

WEBSITES

"Liberty Hyde Bailey, 1858–1954." Horticulture and Crop Science in Virtual Perspective, Ohio State University. Available online at http://www.hcs.ohio-state.edu/hort/history/126.html; website home page: http://www.hcs.ohio-state.edu (accessed January 6, 2003).

Comparative Physiology of the Brain and Comparative Psychology

Nonfiction work

By: Jacques Loeb

Date: 1907

Source: Loeb, Jacques. *Comparative Physiology of the Brain and Comparative Psychology.* New York: G. P. Putnam's Sons, 1907, 10–11.

About the Author: Jacques Loeb (1859–1924) was born in Mayen, Prussia (now Germany), and received an M.D. from the University of Strasbourg in 1884. In 1891 he immigrated to the United States, where he held professorships at Bryn Mawr College in Pennsylvania, the University of Chicago, and the University of California, Berkeley. In 1910, he became a medical researcher at Rockefeller University in New York City. ■

Introduction

Charles Darwin stimulated the development of psychology as a science by affirming that humans were part of the animal kingdom, not separate from it, making every aspect of human behavior appropriate for scientific, as opposed to theological, scrutiny. Yet from the beginning psychologists sought a compromise that elevated humans above other animals without claiming that they were the product of divine creation. This compromise was to single out humans as alone among animals in having a mind, which the brain generated of its own complexity. Mind differed from brain in lacking a material basis. Brain was an object, whereas mind was a construct.

Sigmund Freud, perhaps the most influential psychologist in 1900, illustrated the uneasiness of this compromise. A physician, Freud sought to root his psychology in the brain. Yet he hypothesized the existence of mental states that bore no obvious relation to the brain. He believed every human had an unconscious into which he or she repressed memories and urges that society would condemn as sexual deviance if they had free play in the conscious mind. Freud never tried to root the unconscious in the brain, believing instead that it was a product of the brain, not part of it.

Significance

Freud's beliefs provoked a reaction in the United States, whose Calvinist roots tended to equate sex with sin. American scientists who objected to the sexual content of Freud's theories attacked them by doubting the existence of an unconscious. In extreme form this position doubted the existence of mind. Brain alone existed, and all mental processes were the brain's neurological activity.

Jacques Loeb held this extreme view. He believed that what we call consciousness is simply the brain's neurological activity. What Freud called the unconscious was nothing more than speculation. In rooting mental processes in the brain, Loeb was a reductionist, meaning that he sought to reduce all phenomena, no matter how complex, to an aggregate of simpler physical processes. An idea, for example, is nothing more than an electrical pattern in the brain. Language and behavior can be reduced to electricity, which in turn is simply neurological activity. Humans can be reduced to an aggregate of neurons, which are themselves aggregates of molecules, which are aggregates of atoms. Extreme reductionism ends by reducing humans to the interaction of atoms. Though such a position offends philosophers and theologians, reductionism is at the core of modern science. In his reductivist tendency to derive psychology from the brain's physiology, Loeb was more modern in his outlook than most of his contemporaries.

Jacques Loeb, physiologist and proponent of a purely mechanistic explanation for consciousness.

Primary Source

Comparative Physiology of the Brain and Comparative Psychology [excerpt]

SYNOPSIS: In this excerpt Loeb doubts the existence of "soul, consciousness, will." All three are products of the mind, a construct Loeb rejects. He sought to reduce mental states to "physiological processes." Characteristic of Loeb is his skepticism about the existence of consciousness on the grounds that one cannot trace it to molecules and atoms.

The physiology of the brain has been rendered unnecessarily difficult through the fact that metaphysicians have at all times concerned themselves with the interpretation of brain functions and have introduced such metaphysical conceptions as soul, consciousness, will, etc. One part of the work of the physiologist must consist in the substitution of *real* physiological processes for these inadequate conceptions. . . .

6. Thus far we have not touched upon the most important problem in physiology, namely, which mechanisms give rise to that complex of phenomena which are called psychic or conscious. Our method of procedure must be the same as in the case of instincts and reflexes. We must find out the elementary physiological processes which underlie the complicated phenomena of consciousness. Some physiologists and psychologists consider the purposefulness of the psychic action as the essential element. If an animal or an organ reacts as a rational man would do under the same circumstances, these authors declare that we are dealing with a phenomenon of consciousness. In this way many reflexes, the instincts especially, are looked upon as psychic functions. Consciousness has been ascribed even to the spinal cord, because many of its functions are purposeful. We shall see in the following chapters that many of these reactions are merely tropisms which may occur in exactly the same form in plants. Plants must therefore have a psychic life, and, following the argument, we must ascribe it to machines also, for the tropisms depend only on simple mechanical arrangements. In the last analysis, then, we would arrive at molecules and atoms endowed with mental qualities.

We can dispose of this view by the mere fact that the phenomena of embryological development and of organisation in general show a degree of purposefulness which may even surpass that of any reflex or instinctive or conscious act. And yet we do not consider the phenomena of development to be dependent upon consciousness.

Further Resources

BOOKS

Brush, Stephen G. *The History of Modern Science: A Guide to the Second Scientific Revolution, 1800–1950.* Ames, Iowa: Iowa State University Press, 1988.

Gay, Peter. *Freud for Historians.* New York: Oxford University Press, 1985.

Pauly, Philip J. *Controlling Life: Jacques Loeb and the Engineering Ideal.* New York: Oxford University Press, 1987.

Sulloway, Frank. *Freud: Biologist of the Mind.* New York: Basic Books, 1979.

PERIODICALS

Fleming, Donald. "Loeb, Jacques."*Dictionary of Scientific Biography.* 1973, 445–447.

McCarthy, Timothy. "Freud and the Problem of Sexuality." *Journal of the History of the Behavioral Sciences.* 1981, 332–339.

WEBSITES

"Jacques Loeb (1859–1924)." Lefalophodon: An Informal History of Evolutionary Biology Web Site. Available online at http://www.nceas.ucsb.edu/~alroy/lefa/Loeb.html; website home page: http://www.nceas.ucsb.edu/~alroy/lefa/lophodon.html (accessed January 6, 2003).

Genetics and the Debate Over Acquired Traits

The Training of the Human Plant

Nonfiction work

By: Luther Burbank

Date: 1907

Source: Burbank, Luther. *The Training of the Human Plant.* 1907. Reprint, New York: Century, 1916, 81–82.

About the Author: Luther Burbank (1849–1926) was born in Lancaster, Massachusetts, and was a self-taught plant breeder. In 1876, he established a fruit and vegetable farm in Santa Rosa, California, where he bred new varieties of fruits and vegetables. His work won praise from Dutch botanist Hugo de Vries and from Henry Ford and Thomas Edison, all of whom visited his farm.

"Darwin and Paleontology"

Lecture

By: Henry Fairfield Osborn

Date: January 1, 1909

Source: Osborn, Henry Fairfield. "Darwin and Paleontology." In *Fifty Years of Darwinism: Modern Aspects of Evolution.* New York: Henry Holt, 1909, 235–237.

About the Author: Henry Fairfield Osborn (1857–1935) was born in Fairfield, Connecticut, and taught at Princeton University, first as an assistant professor of natural sciences and then as professor of comparative anatomy. In 1891, he joined the faculty at Columbia University as professor of biology and zoology and was named curator of mammalian paleontology at the American Museum of Natural History in New York City. ■

Introduction

For 150 years evolutionists debated whether offspring can inherit traits their parents had acquired from the environment—for example, large muscles acquired by lifting weights. In 1794 Charles Darwin's grandfather, the physician Erasmus Darwin, floated the idea that offspring can inherit acquired traits, and in an unsystematic way the idea was popular in the late eighteenth century. Its most energetic proponent was French naturalist Jean-Baptiste Lamarck, who believed that organs develop from use and atrophy from disuse and are passed to offspring in strengthened or weakened form. According to this view, bats, for example, have acute ears because their ancestors needed them in dark caves. This need caused these proto-bats to develop acute ears, which they passed to their offspring.

German cytologist August Weismann held the minority view in rejecting the inheritance of acquired traits. In the 1880s he proposed that the nucleus of each cell contains hereditary information and that the gametes (sex cells) pass this information to offspring. He observed that several species of insect develop their gametes while larvae, in effect putting them in storage until they reached sexual maturity. He reasoned that the environment would not have had enough time to imprint traits on the gametes so early in the insect's life. In separating the gametes from the somatic (non-sex) cells, Weismann argued that nothing that happened to the body could affect the gametes and the hereditary information they contained.

Significance

The debate spilled over into the early twentieth century. Proponents of the inheritance of acquired traits, including Luther Burbank, were in the majority. Burbank's obsession with breeding crops convinced him that plants responded to their environment by becoming, for example, tolerant of drought in an arid climate or of frost in a cold climate. Plants, having acquired these traits, passed them to their seeds. Henry Fairfield Osborn disagreed, though he was less sure of his position than Burbank was of his, conceding that Lamarck might have been right.

Only in the 1930s would biologists begin to abandon Lamarck. During that decade biologists in England built statistical models in which natural selection shifted the frequency of genes in a population over time. This shift in gene frequencies modified traits and, given enough time, evolved new species. Natural selection alone was sufficient to explain an organism's traits, and by the 1950s the Lamarckian argument had collapsed. During that decade chemists proved that the flow of genetic information is one way, from DNA to RNA to the construction of amino acids and enzymes outside the cell's nucleus. The environment cannot imprint a trait on DNA because genetic information does not flow from the environment to DNA.

Primary Source

The Training of the Human Plant [excerpt]

SYNOPSIS: Luther Burbank defended the inheritance of acquired traits with his usual verve—to the point of being dogmatic.

Environment the Architect of Heredity

Heredity is not the dark specter which some people have thought—merciless and unchangeable, the embodiment of Fate itself. This dark, pessimistic belief which tinges even the literature of to-day comes, no doubt, from the general lack of knowledge of the laws governing the interaction of these two ever-present forces of heredity and environment wherever there is life.

My own studies have led me to be assured that heredity is only the sum of all past environment, in other words environment is the architect of heredity; and I am assured of another fact: acquired characters *are* transmitted and—even further—that *all* characters which *are* transmitted have been acquired, not necessarily at once in a dynamic or visible form, but as an increasing latent force ready to appear as a tangible character when by long-continued natural or artificial repetition any specific tendency has become inherent, inbred, or "fixed," as we call it. . . .

Repetition

Repetition is the best means of impressing any one point on the human understanding; it is also the means which we employ to train animals to do as we wish, and by just the same process we impress plant life. By repetition we fix any tendency, and the more times any unusual environment is repeated the more indelibly will the resultant tendencies be fixed in plant, animal, or man, until, if repeated often enough in any certain direction, the habits become so fixed and inherent in heredity that it will require many repetitions of an opposite nature to efface them.

Luther Burbank, self-taught plant breeder and proponent of the biological theory of the inheritance of acquired traits. June 5, 1909. **THE LIBRARY OF CONGRESS.**

Primary Source

"Darwin and Paleontology" [excerpt]

SYNOPSIS: Henry Fairfield Osborn opposed the concept of the inheritance of acquired traits. But his cautious approach stemmed from an awareness that he was in the minority.

Failure of Attempted Explanation of Adaptive Origins by Transmission of Acquired Characters

In seeking explanation of this definiteness or adaptiveness of direction in the origin of certain new parts, it was natural to first have recourse to the doctrine of the transmission of acquired characters, because it is a well-known principle that certain organs are definitely directed or guided along adaptive lines by use. By reference to my papers of 1889 and 1890, it will be seen that it was in seeking an explanation of *direction,* I was led to support the Lamarckian principle. I do not propose to discuss this enormous question here. Cope concentrated his whole energy on trying to demonstrate Lamarckianism from paleontology, but ended in a logical failure, or *non sequitur,* because the explanation will not apply to *all* cases. Here again I believe that experimental zoölogy rather than paleontology is the best field of research, and that the Lamarckian principle should not be finally abandoned until it is tested by a prolonged series of experiments extending over many years. It is well known that Darwin, for the very reason that he thought he saw in it a working explanation of a directing influence on heredity, finally adopted the Lamarckian principle and proposed his hypothesis of pangenesis. This was also the ground of my first conclusion of 1889, yet owing in the first instance to a trenchant criticism by Poulton, I have for the time abandoned this Lamarckian interpretation, since quite apart from the difficulties in the field of heredity, paleontology appears to offer many objections to it. The objections are simply these: that a very large number of new, definite, orthogenetic characters which could not have been acquired in ontogeny arise at birth, among them the cusps of the teeth. Since the Lamarckian doctrine either fails or need not be invoked to explain these definite adaptive origins in the teeth, and apparently also in the horns, why invoke it for other adaptive phenomena?

Further Resources

BOOKS

Barthelemy-Madaule, Madeleine. *Lamarck the Mythical Precursor.* Cambridge, Mass.: MIT Press, 1982.

Bowler, Peter J. *The Eclipse of Darwinism: Anti-Darwinian Evolution Theories in the Decades around 1900.* Baltimore, Md.: Johns Hopkins University Press, 1983.

Burkhardt, Richard. *The Spirit of System, Lamarck and Evolutionary Biology.* Cambridge, Mass.: Harvard University Press, 1977.

Jordanova, L.J. *Lamarck.* New York: Oxford University Press, 1984.

Mayr, Ernst. *The Growth of Biological Thought: Diversity, Evolution, and Inheritance.* Cambridge, Mass.: Harvard University Press, 1982.

PERIODICAL

Churchill, F.B. "The Weismann-Spencer Controversy over the Inheritance of Acquired Characters." *Proceedings of the XVth International Congress of History of Science* 15, 1977, 450–468.

WEBSITES

"Henry Fairfield Osborn (1857–1935)." Museum of Paleontology, University of California, Berkeley. Available online at http://www.ucmp.berkeley.edu/history/osborn.html; website home page: http://www.ucmp.berkeley.edu (accessed January 6, 2003).

"Luther Burbank (1849–1926)." Sonoma County Parks and Recreation. Available online at http://www.parks.sonoma.net/burbstory.html; website home page: http://www.parks.sonoma.net (accessed January 6, 2003).

General Lectures on Electrical Engineering

Lecture

By: Charles Steinmetz

Date: 1908

Source: Steinmetz, Charles Proteus. *General Lectures on Electrical Engineering,* 3rd ed. Schenectady, N.Y.: Robson & Adee, 1908, 149–150.

About the Author: Charles Proteus Steinmetz (1865–1923) was born in Breslau, Germany (now Wroclaw, Poland). He studied mathematics as a doctoral candidate at the University of Breslau, but university officials expelled him for advocating socialism. To escape arrest for his radicalism, he immigrated to the United States, where he rose to chief engineer for General Electric. He was the author of twelve books and some 150 articles. ■

Introduction

The harnessing of electricity as a source of power was an achievement of the nineteenth century. In 1831 British physicist Michael Faraday created a prototype of the dynamo (the electric generator), but not until 1880 did engineers and mathematicians perfect it, opening an era of inexpensive electricity. Electricity made possible the lightbulb and the telephone, but its effect on transportation was no less momentous. The dynamo also made possible the electric railway, which replaced the horse-drawn trolley in American cities along both coasts, around the Great Lakes, and in the South, which embraced the electric railway as a means of mass transit in the 1890s—though Seattle and San Francisco were exceptions in clinging to the steam-powered cable car. During the 1890s and the first decade of the new century engineers built more powerful electric motors, replaced the small four-wheeled car with the large eight-wheeled car to carry more people, and built cars with durable steel rather than wood. Cities financed the construction of electric railways and ran them in the public interest, setting inexpensive fares and maintaining track and cars.

Significance

Charles Steinmetz, who delivered his lecture in 1908, regarded the future of the electric railway as secure. He had reason for confidence. Cities were then extending

Electric streetcars in New Orleans. Circa 1900. © CORBIS. REPRODUCED BY PERMISSION.

track into the countryside, spurring the growth of the first suburbs, and their investment in track and cars evidenced a long-term commitment to the electric railway. Yet by the 1910s electric railways faced financial distress. Cities had set fares at a flat rate that did not keep pace with the rising cost of wages and materials. They might have weathered the lean times had they not faced competition from the car, for also in 1908 Henry Ford unveiled the Model T. By 1914 he was manufacturing 250,000 a year, and when he finally halted production in 1927 he had sold 15 million. The electric railway could not compete with the Model T, which gave Americans the freedom to go anywhere anytime, without being tied to the schedules and destinations of the electric railway. An equally serious competitor was the bus. Though buses cost more per mile than electric railways, bus companies did not have the costs of constructing and maintaining track, which made the electric railway less economical. By the 1930s cities were building mass transit around the bus rather than the electric railway.

The electric railway illustrates the complex interaction among technology, transportation, and economics. The car and bus replaced the electric railway not because they were superior technologies but because they were either cheaper or more convenient. Given the fluidity of technology, the surprise is not that the car replaced the electric railway but that nothing has challenged the car since the Model T.

Primary Source

General Lectures on Electrical Engineering [excerpt]

SYNOPSIS: In this excerpt Steinmetz outlines the technical requirements of the electric railway. His interest was in its challenges for the engineer, the problems the engineer deemed ripe for solution. As a means of transportation, the electric railway did not interest him. Nor does he seem aware that the car would rapidly challenge and ultimately replace the electric railway.

Electric Railway

Train Characteristics

The performance of a railway consists of acceleration, motion and retardation, that is, starting, running and stopping.

The characteristics of the railway motor are:

1. Reliability.

2. Limited available space, which permits less margin in the design, so that the railway motor runs at a higher temperature, and has a shorter life, than other electrical apparatus. The rating of a railway motor is therefore entirely determined by its heating. That is, the rating of a railway motor is that output which it can carry without its temperature exceeding the danger limit. The highest possible efficiency is therefore aimed at, not so much for the purpose of saving a few percent of power, but because the power lost produces heat and so reduces the motor output.

3. Very variable demands in speed. That is, the motor must give a wide range of torque and speed at high efficiency. This excludes from ordinary railway work the shunt motor and the induction motor.

The power consumed in acceleration usually is many times greater than when running at constant speed, and where acceleration is very frequent, as in rapid transit service, the efficiency of acceleration is therefore of foremost importance, while in cases of infrequent stops, as in long distance and interurban lines, the time of acceleration is so small a part of the total running time, that the power consumed during acceleration is a small part of the total power consumption, and high efficiency of acceleration is therefore of less importance.

Typical classes of railway service are:

1. Rapid transit, as elevated and subway roads in large cities.

Characteristics are high speeds and frequent stops.

2. City surface lines, that is, the ordinary trolley car in the streets of a city or town.

Moderate speeds, frequent stops, and running at variable speeds, and frequently even at very low speeds, are characteristic.

3. Suburban and interurban lines. That is, lines leading from cities into suburbs and to adjacent cities, through less densely populated districts.

Characteristics are less frequent stops, varying speeds, and the ability to run at fairly high speeds as well as low speeds.

4. Long distance and trunk line railroading.

Characteristics are: infrequent stops, high speeds, and a speed varying with the load, that is, with the profile of the road.

5. Special classes of service, as mountain roads and elevators.

Characteristics are fairly constant and usually moderate speed; a constant heavy load, so that the power of acceleration is not so much in excess of that of free running; and usually frequent stops. This is the class of work which can well be accomplished by a constant speed motor, as the three-phase induction motor.

Further Resources

BOOKS

Cavin, Ruth. *Trolleys: Riding and Remembering the Electric Interurban Railways.* New York: Hawthorn, 1976.

Fischler, Stanley I. *Moving Millions: An Inside Look at Mass Transit.* New York: Harper & Row, 1979.

Hammond, John Winthrop. *Charles Proteus Steinmetz.* New York: Century, 1924.

Hilton, George W., and John F. Due. *The Electric Interurban Railway in America.* Stanford, Calif.: Stanford University Press, 1960.

Johnson, Emory R. *Elements of Transportation: A Discussion of Steam Railroad, Electric Railway, and Ocean and Inland Water Transportation.* Port Washington, N.Y.: Kennikat, 1970.

Miller, John Anderson. *Fares Please: A Popular History of Trolleys, Streetcars, Buses, Elevateds, and Subways.* New York: Dover, 1960.

PERIODICALS

Faust, Clifford A. "The Trolley Bus." *Electric Railway Journal.* June 4, 1931, 5–32.

Harte, Charles Rufus. "Boom Days of the Electric Railways." *Transit Journal.* September 15, 1934, 31–42.

Sprague, Frank J. "Birth of the Electric Railway." *Transit Journal.* September 15, 1934, 22–29.

WEBSITES

Flynn, Tom. "Charles Proteus Steinmetz, Inventor." Yonkers Historical Society. Available online at http://www.yonkershistory.org/stein.html; website home page: http://www.yonkershistory.org (accessed January 6, 2003).

"Mutation"

Lecture

By: Charles B. Davenport

Date: January 1, 1909

Source: Davenport, Charles B. "Mutation." One of a series of centennial addresses in honor of Charles Darwin, given before the American Association for the Advancement of Science, Baltimore, January 1, 1909. Printed in *Fifty Years of Darwinism: Modern Aspects of Evolution.* New York: Henry Holt, 1909, 160–161.

About the Author: Charles Benedict Davenport (1866–1944) was born in Stamford, Connecticut, and received a Ph.D. in zoology from Harvard University in 1892. He taught there until 1899, when he became professor of zoology at the University of Chicago. From 1904 to 1934, he directed the department of genetics for the Station for Experimental Evolution at Cold Spring Harbor, New York, where he founded the Eugenics Record Office. ■

Introduction

Life reproduces in two ways: cell division and sex. In contrast to cell division, sex produces organisms that differ from one another. Biologists have long debated whether these differences are continuous or discontinuous. In other words, are variations so slight that they form a continuum of gradual change, or are they large enough that they form a series of discrete traits? Human skin color is an example of continuous variation, since shades grade gradually from dark to light. The presence or absence of wisdom teeth is an example of a discontinuous variation. One either has them or not.

Depending on the evidence, different biologists have favored one type over the other. Charles Darwin headed the camp of biologists (then called naturalists) who favored continuous variation. This view agreed with his belief that evolution was a gradual process, because only gradual variation among organisms could lead to gradual change. In contrast, Dutch botanist Hugo de Vries favored discontinuous variation. In 1901, he announced that an evening primrose had produced offspring so different from itself that they had to be considered a new species. De Vries called the discontinuous variation that led to the sudden origin of a new species a mutation. Neither de Vries nor Darwin, though, had gotten to the root of variation. This task fell to Gregor Mendel, an Austrian monk who had realized in 1866 that discrete units (genes) account for variation among organisms. The more two organisms differ in their genes, the more they will vary in appearance, and vice versa.

Significance

The term "mutation" has had a fluid history, its definition depending on the preconceptions and scientific specialty of its user. Charles Davenport tried to reconcile de Vries's notion of mutation with Mendel's idea of the gene by defining it as the addition or loss of one or more genes. Columbia University embryologist Thomas Hunt Morgan restricted the term to the addition of a gene, and in the 1920s his former student Herman J. Muller offered a fourth definition: a mutation is a change in a gene's chemistry. Others defined it as a change in the chemistry of a chromosome, of the structure containing genes, or of a gene. Still others observed that genes and chromosomes had the ability to repair chemical changes, leading them to define it as an unrepaired chemical change in a chromosome or gene.

The word mutation suffered from an additional complication between 1900 and 1909, as Davenport makes clear. He was unsure whether the existence of mutations strengthened or weakened Darwin's concept of natural selection. It was clear that mutations were a source of variation and that variation provided the raw material for natural selection. Among organisms that differ, nature will select for survival those whose variations best adapt them to their environment. Yet Darwin had staked his theory on continuous variation, whereas Davenport followed de Vries in believing that mutations produced discontinuous variation.

Davenport's article thus reveals that American biology was in theoretical flux between 1900 and 1909. No one knew how to combine the ideas of Darwin, Mendel, and de Vries in a convincing synthesis. Yet the fact that a handful of American biologists were willing to debate theory was significant at a time when so many American biologists avoided theory in favor of practical knowledge.

Primary Source

"Mutation" [excerpt]

SYNOPSIS: In this excerpt from "Mutation," Davenport defines a mutation as the addition or loss of one or more genes. Davenport followed Hugo de Vries in emphasizing the discontinuity of mutations and was therefore uncertain whether the existence of mutations strengthened or weakened Charles Darwin's theory of evolution by natural selection, a theory Darwin tied to a belief in continuous, rather than discontinuous, variation.

Mutation Defined

First of all it is necessary to define mutation in de Vries' sense and to show its relation to other evolutionary principles. Mutation in any strain is a change in the unhybridized germ-plasm of that strain which is characterized by the acquisition or loss of one or more unit characters. There has already been presented to you the evidence for unit characters, a conception first clearly elucidated by Darwin. I think it may fairly be said that the mutation theory rests on the doctrine of unit characters and applies only so far as that doctrine applies. As even the most extreme neo-Darwinian school recognizes such units with their representatives (determinants of Weismann) in the egg, and as in evolution there must be the acquisition or loss of at least some one character, it might be expected that the idea of mutation as defined above would find universal acceptance. But it has not done so. The difference of opinion relates to the *gradient* of the transition by which a new unit character is introduced or an old one disappears. Mutation in de Vries' sense implies the sudden appearance, complete in the first generation, of the new unit character and its germinal representative, the pangene or determinant. Mutation is regarded by many who call themselves Darwinians as an innovation and as opposed to Darwin's fundamental assumptions. For the neo-Darwinian conceives the determinant as gradually changing in evolution and exhibiting in the adult forms of successive generations the same continuous series that an organ shows in its ontogenetic development.

Further Resources

BOOKS

Allen, Garland E. *Life Science in the Twentieth Century.* New York: Cambridge University Press, 1978.

Garber, Edward D., ed. *Genetic Perspectives in Biology and Medicine.* Chicago: University of Chicago Press, 1985.

Magner, Lois. *A History of the Life Sciences.* New York: Dekker, 1979.

Mayr, Ernst. *The Growth of Biological Thought: Diversity, Evolution, and Inheritance.* Cambridge, Mass.: Harvard University Press, 1982.

Robinson, Gloria. *A Prelude to Genetics: Theories of a Material Substance of Heredity.* Lawrence, Kans.: Coronado, 1979.

PERIODICALS

Meijer, Onno G. "Hugo de Vries No Mendelian?" *Annals of Science* 78, 1985, 189–232.

Ravin, A.W. "Genetics in America: A Historical Overview." *Perspectives in Biology and Medicine,* July 1978, 214–231.

WEBSITES

Human Gene Mutation Database. University of Wales College of Medicine. Available online at http://archive.uwcm.ac.uk/uwcm/mg/hgmd0.html; website home page: http://www.uwcm.ac.uk/home.htm (accessed January 6, 2003).

"The Cell in Relation to Heredity and Evolution"

Lecture

By: Edmund B. Wilson

Date: January 1, 1909

Source: Wilson, Edmund B. "The Cell in Relation to Heredity and Evolution." One of a series of centennial addresses in honor of Charles Darwin, given before the American Association for the Advancement of Science, Baltimore, January 1, 1909. Printed in *Fifty Years of Darwinism: Modern Aspects of Evolution.* New York: Henry Holt, 1909, 98–100.

About the Author: Edmund Beecher Wilson (1856–1939) was born in Geneva, Illinois, and became a professor of zoology at Columbia University in 1891. He studied embryology, with a focus on cell biology, and became an advocate of the chromosome theory of inheritance. He established that sex chromosomes determine the sex of an organism. ■

Introduction

At times, technology stimulates science. The microscope, for example, invented by Dutch spectacle makers around 1590, opened the field of cell biology, or cytology. This science developed gradually, though, and for more than half a century the microscope was more a curiosity than a research tool. In 1665, English physicist and naturalist Robert Hooke coined the term *cell* for the walled structures he saw in thin slices of magnified cork. Later in the century, others found cells in magnified tissues of plants and animals but had no inkling of their function. In the 1830s, German botanist Matthias J. Schleiden discovered that plants are composed entirely of cells, and in 1839 German zoologist Theodor Schwann extended this insight to animals.

Later researchers began to focus on the cell's structure and function, particularly the structure at its center, which scientists in the 1870s termed the nucleus. In 1879, English cytologist Walter Flemming discovered that the nucleus contains tiny threads, which he called chromatin. By then, Flemming understood that chromosomes (the term coined in 1888 by William Waldeyer), after having first doubled, halve during the division of somatic (nonsex) cells. In 1892, German cytologist August Weismann applied this insight to meiosis, the division of cells to form gametes (sex cells). He observed that each gamete receives half the chromosomes of the parent cell. When two gametes (a sperm and an egg, for example) unite, they restore the full complement of chromosomes. Each somatic cell in humans has forty-six chromosomes, but each sperm and egg has twenty-three chromosomes. The union of sperm and egg restores the complete set of forty-six chromosomes.

Significance

The rediscovery in 1900 of Gregor Mendel's theory of particulate inheritance complicated the progress of cytology. Mendel had inferred that discrete units (genes) code for traits in pea plants. This work implied that genes code for traits in all life. But the relationship between genes and chromosomes, which both appeared to have a role in heredity, remained uncertain. American biologists gave only tentative answers to this question between 1900 and 1909. Wilson correctly believed that the chromatin (chromosomes) contained hereditary information, but he was unsure of the relationship between genes and chromosomes, and his inability to elucidate this relationship left a central problem of heredity unsolved. The solution would await the work of Thomas Hunt Morgan and his team at Columbia University. Between 1909 and 1927, they established that genes code for traits, as Mendel had believed, and are in a line on chromosomes.

Wilson's work demonstrated that American biology was in theoretical flux between 1900 and 1909. But this was no sign of weakness, for scientists always work on the edge of the unknown and always have more questions than answers. What is important is that during this decade a handful of American biologists began asking theoretical questions in a science that was otherwise preoccupied with practical knowledge. The largest employers of biologists during this decade were the U.S. Department of Agriculture, agricultural experiment stations, and agricultural and mechanical colleges, and their agendas were practical rather than theoretical. The fact that Wilson was grappling with theoretical problems was a sign of maturity in American science.

Primary Source

"The Cell in Relation to Heredity and Evolution" [excerpt]

SYNOPSIS: In this excerpt from "The Cell in Relation to Heredity and Evolution," Wilson writes that the chromatin (chromosomes) in the nucleus of each cell contains hereditary information. Yet he was unable to untangle the relationship between genes and chromosomes, a central problem in biology after 1900.

The Physical Basis of Heredity

It is now universally admitted that the physical basis of heredity is contained in the germ-cell. Is this basis formed by the entire living energid, or may we distinguish in the cell a particular species-substance or idioplasm, that is at least theoretically separable from the other cell-constituents? This question has not yet been answered with certainty. The cell-system forms an enormously complex moving equilibrium, which must in one way be regarded as a single and indivisible unit. From this point of view it may justly be maintained that the basis of heredity and of the vital activities generally is represented by the cell-system in its totality. But such a position, philosophically correct though it may be, cuts us off from the possibilities of exact analysis. We have every right to inquire in what way the energies of cell-life are distributed in the system and how they are related; and the question whether certain elements of the system may possess an especial and primary significance for the determination of the cell-activities forms a legitimate part of this inquiry.

I stand with those who have followed Oscar Hertwig and Strasburger in assigning a special significance to the nucleus in heredity, and who have recognized in the chromatin a substance that may in a certain sense be regarded as the idioplasm. This view is based upon no single or demonstrative proof. It rests upon circumstantial and cumulative evidence, derived from many sources. The irresistible appeal which it makes to the mind results from the manner in which it brings together under one point of view a multitude of facts that otherwise remain disconnected and unintelligible. What arrests the attention when the facts are broadly viewed is the unmistakable parallel between the course of heredity and the history of the chromatin-substance in the whole cycle of its transformation. In respect to some of the most important phenomena of heredity it is only in the chromatin that such a parallel can be accurately traced. It is this substance, in the form of chromosomes, that shows the association of exactly equivalent maternal and paternal elements in the fertilization of the egg. In it alone do we clearly see the equal distribution of these elements to every part of the body of the offspring. In the perverted forms of development that result from double fertilization of the egg and the like it is only in the abnormal distribution of the chromatin-substance by multipolar division that we see a physical counterpart of the derangement of development. Only in the chromatin-substance, again, do we see in the course of the maturation of the germ-cells a redistribution of elements that shows a parallel to the astonishing disjunction and redistribution of the factors of heredity that are displayed in the Mendelian phenomenon.

Further Resources

BOOKS

Allen, Garland E. *Life Science in the Twentieth Century.* New York: Cambridge University Press, 1978.

Hughes, Arthur. *A History of Cytology.* New York: Abelard-Schuman, 1959.

Magner, Lois. *A History of the Life Sciences.* New York: Dekker, 1979.

Mayr, Ernst. *The Growth of Biological Thought: Diversity, Evolution, and Inheritance.* Cambridge, Mass.: Harvard University Press, 1982.

PERIODICALS

Baxter, Alice Levine. "Edmund B. Wilson as a Preformationist: Some Reasons for His Acceptance of the Chromosome Theory." *Journal of the History of Biology,* March 1976, 29–57.

Bechtel, William. "The Evolution of Our Understanding of the Cell: A Study in the Dynamics of Scientific Progress." *Studies in History and Philosophy of Science,* February 1984, 309–336.

Gilbert, Scott. "The Embryological Origins of the Gene Theory." *Journal of the History of Biology,* June 1978, 307–351.

WEBSITES

"Edmund B. Wilson (1856–1939)." Lefalophodon: An Informal History of Evolutionary Biology Web Site. Available online at http://www.nceas.ucsb.edu/~alroy/lefa/EBWilson.html; website home page: http://www.nceas.ucsb.edu/~alroy/lefa/lophodon.html (accessed January 6, 2003).

The Evolution of Worlds

Nonfiction work

By: Percival Lowell

Date: 1909

Source: Lowell, Percival. *The Evolution of Worlds.* New York: Macmillan, 1909, 1–3.

About the Author: Percival Lowell (1855–1916) was born in Boston. He published four novels on Asian culture before turning to astronomy. He built an observatory at Flagstaff, Arizona, through which he scanned Mars, popularizing the notion that intelligent life once inhabited it. Lowell predicted the existence of Pluto twenty-five years before its discovery. ■

Introduction

The question of the origin and end of the universe fascinated the ancients, all of whom had creation myths, such as the Hebrew story of creation in Genesis, to account for its origin. For Christian scholars Christ's Parousia, or Second Coming, described the universe's end. Yet the twelfth-century Muslim philosopher Averroes warned that no evidence supported the claim that the universe had a beginning and one day would end. It was as logical to suppose the universe to be eternal as to suppose it bounded in time. The great sixteenth- and seventeenth-century Western astronomers—Nicolaus Copernicus, Galileo Galilei, Johannes Kepler, and Isaac Newton—described how the universe behaved, not how or when it had begun or would end.

But the philosophical predisposition to bound the universe in time was too strong to derail. In the eighteenth century German philosopher Immanuel Kant and French astronomer Pierre-Simon Laplace proposed that the stars and planets had condensed from hot gases. During the nineteenth century scientists built a circumstantial case for the universe's origin by showing that both sunlight and heated elements on earth produced the same spectrum of lines, suggesting that both the sun and the Earth—and by extension, the stars and other planets—were made of the same elements. If the Earth had a beginning, a long-standing tenet of science and philosophy, so too must the other planets and stars—and the universe as well.

Significance

This conclusion did not settle matters, for it left unanswered how and when the universe began and said nothing about how and when it would end. To complicate matters, at the beginning of the twentieth century, American geologist T.C. Chamberlin and astronomer F. R. Moulton rejected the notion that the stars and planets had condensed from hot gases, for the speed of their molecules would have been too great, they believed, for the gases to have coalesced into a planet. In *The Evolution of Worlds* Percival Lowell had to admit that in the first decade of the century astronomers had no hypothesis of how and when the universe had begun or would end.

The state of astronomy between 1900 and 1909 illustrates the turbulence of this decade for the physical sciences. In 1900 German physicist Max Planck undermined the belief that energy is a continuum with his quantum theory, and in 1905 Albert Einstein overthrew the notion that space and time are absolutes with his Special Theory of Relativity. That year Einstein also contradicted the belief that light was a wave, instead arguing that it consisted of particles. In the 1890s American physicist Albert Michelson had predicted that physicists were on the threshold of a complete understanding of nature. During the first decade of the twentieth century Lowell and other scientists lost this confidence.

Astronomers would not venture a theory of the origin of the universe until 1927, when French astronomer Georges Lemaître advanced the Big Bang Theory, and they remain divided on how it will end. One camp believes that gravity will cause the matter in the universe to collapse into a dense point: the reverse of the Big Bang (sometimes called the Big Crunch). Another camp believes that the amount of matter is too small for this collapse. Rather, matter will spread apart indefinitely, converting into energy in accord with Einstein's famous equation, energy equals mass times the speed of light squared. The universe will thus end as a uniform sheen of energy.

Primary Source

The Evolution of Worlds [excerpt]

SYNOPSIS: In this excerpt Lowell admits that astronomers did not know in 1909 how or when the universe had begun or would end. Nevertheless, Lowell held the philosophical position that the universe is bounded by time, an idea as old as the creation account in Genesis.

Birth of a Solar System

Astronomy is usually thought of as the study of the bodies visible in the sky. And such it largely is when the present state of the universe alone is considered. But when we attempt to peer into its past and to foresee its future, we find ourselves facing a new side of the heavens—the contemplation of the invisible there. For in the evolution of worlds not simply must the processes be followed by the mind's eye, so short the span of human life, but they begin and end in what we cannot see. What the solar system sprang from, and what it will eventually become, is alike matter devoid of light. Out of darkness into darkness again: such are the bourns of cosmic action.

The stars are suns; past, present, or potential. Each of those diamond points we mark studding the heavens on a winter's night are globes comparable with, and in many cases greatly excelling, our own ruler of the day. The telescope discloses myriads more. Yet these self-confessed denizens of space form but a fraction of its occupants. Quite as near, and perhaps much nearer, are orbs of which most of us have no suspicion. Unimpressing our senses and therefore ignored by our minds, bodies people it which, except for rare occurrences, remain forever invisible. For dark stars in countless numbers course hither and thither throughout the universe at speeds as stupendous as the lucent ones themselves.

Had we no other knowledge of them, reasoning would suffice to demonstrate their existence. It is the logic of unlimited subtraction. Every self-shining star is continually giving out light and heat. Now such an expenditure cannot go on forever, as the source of its replenishing by contraction, accretion, or disintegration is finite. Long to our measures of time as the process may last, it must eventually

Percival Lowell, astronomer and popularizer of the notion of life on Mars, performing astronomical observations. Mt. Stromlo Observatory, Australia. **REPRODUCED BY PERMISSION OF THE LOWELL OBSERVATORY.**

have an end and the star finally become a cold dark body, pursuing as before its course, but in itself inert and dead; an orb grown *orbéd,* in the old French sense. So it must remain unless some cosmic catastrophe rekindle it to life. The chance of such occurrence in a given time compared with the duration of the star's light-emitting career will determine the number of dark stars relative to the lucent ones. The chance is undoubtedly small, and the number of dark bodies in space proportionally large. Reasoning, then, informs us first that such bodies must exist all about us, and second that their multitude must be great.

Further Resources

BOOKS

Asimov, Isaac. *The Universe: From Flat Earth to Quasar.* New York: Avon-Discus, 1971.

Hoyt, William Graves. *Lowell and Mars.* Tuscon, Ariz.: University of Arizona Press, 1976.

Motz, Lloyd, and Jefferson Hane Weaver. *The Story of Physics.* New York: Plenum, 1989.

Singh, Jagjit. *Great Ideas and Theories of Modern Cosmology.* New York: Dover, 1970.

PERIODICALS

Brush, Stephen G. "Looking Up: The Rise of Astronomy in America." *American Studies,* November 1979, 41–67.

Mendillo, Michael, David DeVorkin, and Richard Berendzen. "History of American Astronomy." *Astronomy,* June 1976, 20–63.

———. "The Universe Unfolds: 1900–1950." *Astronomy,* May 1976, 87–95.

Rothenberg, Marc. "History of Astronomy." *Osiris* 63, 1985, 117–131.

WEBSITES

"Percival Lowell." Lowell Observatory home page. Available online at http://www.lowell.edu/AboutLowell/plowell.html; website home page: http://www.lowell.edu (accessed January 6, 2003).

12

SPORTS

JESSIE BISHOP POWELL

Entries are arranged in chronological order by date of primary source. For entries with one primary source, the entry title is the same as the primary source title. Entries with more than one primary source have an overall entry title, followed by the titles of the primary sources.

Important Events in Sports, 1900–1909

1900

- On January 29, Byron Bancroft "Ban" Johnson regroups the former minor Western League into the American League in Chicago. It consists of Chicago, Cleveland, Detroit, Indianapolis, Kansas City, Milwaukee, and Minneapolis. The new league quickly becomes a threat to the dominant National League.
- On April 19, James J. Caffrey of Hamilton, Ontario, wins the fourth annual Boston Marathon with a time of 2:39:44.0.
- On May 3, Jimmy Boland rides Lieutenant Gibson to victory in the twenty-sixth annual Kentucky Derby.
- From May 20 to October 28, Paris hosts the Summer Olympic Games, called the International Meeting of Physical Training and Sport, as an adjunct to the Paris Exhibition. The United States wins twenty gold medals and France wins twenty-nine gold metals.
- From June 12 to June 15, the first Grand American Championship for trap shooting is held in New York. Rollo O. "Pop" Heikes of Dayton, Ohio wins.
- From August 8 to August 10, in the first Davis Cup Challenge tennis tournament the United States defeats Great Britain three matches to none.
- On October 5, Harry Vardon of Great Britain wins the sixth annual U.S Open Golf Tournament held at the Chicago Golf Club.

1901

- From January 8 to January 11, the American Bowling Congress holds the first National Bowling Championship in Chicago. Forty-one teams, representing seventeen cities from nine states, compete for a purse of $1,592.
- On April 19, James J. Caffrey of Hamilton, Ontario, becomes the first repeat winner of the fifth annual Boston Marathon in 2:29:23.6.
- On April 29, Jimmy Winkfield rides His Eminence to victory in the twenty-seventh annual Kentucky Derby.
- On May 12, Joe Gans captures the world lightweight boxing title, which he holds until 1908.
- On June 15, Willie Anderson defeats Alex Smith in a playoff round by one stroke to win the U.S. Open Golf Tournament, held at the Myopia Hunt Club in South Hamilton, Massachusetts.
- On August 21, Joe "Iron Man" McGinnity, pitcher for the Baltimore Orioles, is expelled from major-league baseball for stepping on umpire Tom Connolly's toes, spitting in his face, and punching him. McGinnity is fined, officially rebuked, and reinstated because he is very popular with the fans.
- From September 28 to October 4, the U.S. yacht *Columbia* successfully defends the America's Cup against the British challenger, *Shamrock II.*
- On December 18, Joe Walcott wins the world welterweight boxing title by knocking out Rube Ferns in the fifth round.

1902

- On January 1, Michigan defeats Stanford 49–0 in the first Rose Bowl football game. Beginning in 1916, the Rose Bowl becomes an annual event.
- On April 19, Samuel A. Mellor of Yonkers, New York, wins the sixth annual Boston Marathon with a time of 2:43:12.0.
- On May 3, Jimmy Winkfield rides Alan-a-Dale to his second consecutive victory in the Kentucky Derby.
- On August 8, the United States, led by William A. Larned, defeats Great Britain, three matches to two, to win a second consecutive Davis Cup tennis challenge.
- On October 11, Laurie Auchterlonie wins the U.S. Open Golf Tournament at the Garden City Golf Club on Long Island, New York.

1903

- The Portage Lakers of Houghton, Michigan, the first professional hockey team formed in the United States, win twenty-four of twenty-six games in their first year. They win the International Hockey League championship.
- On April 20, John C. Lorden of Cambridge, Massachusetts, wins the seventh annual Boston Marathon in 2:41:29.8.
- On April 22, Jack Root wins the world light heavyweight boxing title over Charles "Kid" McCoy.
- On May 2, Hal Booker rides Judge Himes to victory in the twenty-ninth annual Kentucky Derby.
- On June 27, Willie Anderson defeats David Brown in a playoff round by two strokes to win a second U.S. Open Golf Tournament.
- On August 8, Great Britain's Doherty brothers, Hugh and Reginald, defeat the United States four matches to one to win the third Davis Cup tennis challenge.
- On August 14, Jim Jeffries defeats the former champion James J. Corbett in the tenth round, thus retaining his world heavyweight boxing title.
- From August 22 to September 2, the U.S. yacht *Reliance* successfully defends the America's Cup against the British yacht *Shamrock III.*
- From October 1 to October 13, Boston Red Socks (then Pilgrims) defeat Pittsburgh five games to three in the first World Series played between the National League and American League champions.
- On November 4, Bob Fitzsimmons wins the world light heavyweight boxing title, outpointing George Gardner in twenty rounds.

- Harvard Stadium, the first stadium built for football and the largest reinforced steel structure in the world, is formally opened.

1904

- The Gold Cup, the premier event of the American Power Boat Association, is held for the first time on the Hudson River.
- On January 12, Henry Ford sets a world land-speed record of 91.37 miles per hour.
- On February 22, the National Ski Association holds the first national ski jumping championship in Ishpeming, Michigan.
- On April 19, Michael Spring of New York City wins the eighth annual Boston Marathon in 2:38:04.4.
- On April 29, Aaron "Dixie Kid" Brown defeats Joe Walcott for the world welterweight boxing championship.
- On May 2, Frank Prior rides Elwood to victory in the Kentucky Derby.
- On May 5, Boston pitcher Denton T. "Cy" Young pitches his second no-hit game and baseball's first perfect game in the American League, beating Philadelphia 3-0.
- From July 1 to November 23, St. Louis holds the first Summer Olympic Games in the United States. The Americans win 80 gold, 86 silver, and 72 bronze medals.
- On July 9, Willie Anderson wins his third U.S. Open Golf Tournament.
- During the fall, John McGraw, the tempermental manager of New York Giants, calls off the World Series between the Giants and the Boston Red Sox.

1905

- American May G. Sutton wins the Wimbledon singles title and becomes the first foreigner to win the British championship.
- On April 5, Yale wins the first intercollegiate wrestling tournament against Columbia, Penn, and Princeton. The school discontinued the sport in 1991.
- On April 19, United States Olympian Frederick Lorz of Yonkers, New York, wins the ninth annual Boston Marathon in 2:28:25.
- On May 10, Jack Martin rides Agile to victory in the thirty-first annual Kentucky Derby.
- On July 3, Marvin Hart wins the world heavyweight boxing championship by knocking out Jack Root in the twelfth round.
- On September 22, twenty-five year old Willie Anderson wins his fourth and last U.S. Open Golf championship. He dies in 1910.
- On October 1, President Theodore Roosevelt hosts a conference of academic and athletic officials from Harvard, Princeton, and Yale to curb the brutality of college football.
- From October 9 to October 14, the New York Giants of the National League defeat the Philadelphia Athletics of the American League four games to one in the second World Series. Christy Mathewson pitched three shutouts in a week.
- On December 20, Bob Fitzsimmons is knocked out by Philadelphia Jack O'Brien in the world light heavyweight title bout. O'Brien holds the title until his retirement in 1912.
- On December 28, the Intercollegiate Athletic Association of the United States is founded in New York with sixty-two institutions to establish rules and requirements for intercollegiate athletics.

1906

- University of Oregon's Daniel J. Kelley sets a new world record of 9.6 seconds in the 100-yard dash.
- On February 26, swimmer Charles M. Daniels equals the world record of 57.6 seconds for 100 yards to become the first American to swim the distance in less than 60 seconds.
- On April 19, eighteen-year old Timothy Ford of Cambridge, Massachusetts, wins the tenth annual Boston Marathon in 2:45:45.0.
- From April 22 to May 2, Athens hosts the Summer Olympic Games to celebrate the tenth anniversary of their revival. The United States wins twelve gold medals and France wins fifteen gold medals.
- On May 2, Roscoe Troxler rides Sir Huon to victory in the thirty-second annual Kentucky Derby.
- On May 23, Frank Gotch regains the world heavyweight wrestling title by defeating Tom Jenkins.
- On June 29, Alex Smith defeats his brother Willie in the U.S. Open Golf Tournament.
- From October 9 to October 14, the Chicago White Sox of the American League defeat the Chicago Cubs of the National League four games to one in the World Series.

1907

- Hawaiian George Douglas Freeth introduces surfing to the U.S. mainland at Redondo Beach, California.
- On February 7, Asario Autio wins the first national cross-country skiing championship.
- On April 19, Thomas Longboat, an Onandaga Native American from Hamilton, Ontario, wins the eleventh annual Boston Marathon in 2:24:24.
- On May 6, Andy Minder rides Pink Star to victory in the thirty-third Kentucky Derby.
- On June 21, Alex Ross wins the U.S. Open Golf Tournament in Philadelphia.
- On October 7, in the opening game of the World Series, the Chicago Cubs and the Detroit Tigers tie 3-3. The Cubs tie the game in the twelfth inning when Tiger catcher Bob Schmidt commits a passed ball on a third strike, allowing the running from third base to score. The game is called due to darkness. The Cubs go on to sweep the Tigers 4-0.
- On November 28, John Hayes wins the first Yonkers Marathon in New York.

1908

- Irving Brokaw, who studied figure skating in Europe, returns to the United States and begins to promote the sport.

- From February 14 to July 30, a United States team wins the Great Automobile Race from New York City to Paris, France. The Americans beat the second-place Germans by 169 days.
- On February 22, Stanley Ketchel knocks out Jack (Twin) Sullivan for the middle heavyweight title, in twenty rounds, in San Francisco.
- On April 3, Frank Gotch defends his world heavyweight wrestling championship against the "Russian Bear," George Hackenschmidt, who quits after two hours and one minute.
- On April 20, Thomas P. Morrissey of Yonkers, New York, wins the twelfth annual Boston Marathon in 2:25:43.2.
- From April 27 to October 31, London holds the Summer Olympic Games as an adjunct to its World's Fair. The United States wins 15 of 28 events.
- On April 30, Abe Attell knocks out Tommy Sullivan in the fourth round to win the world featherweight boxing title.
- On May 5, Arthur Pickens rides Stone Street to victory in the thirty-fourth annual Kentucky Derby.
- On July 4, Oscar "Battling" Nelson knocks out Joe Gans in seventeen rounds for the world lightweight title.
- On August 8, Fred McLeod wins the U.S. Open Golf Tournament by one stroke over Willie Smith at the Myopia Hunt Club in South Hamilton, Massachusetts.
- On September 7, twenty-year-old Walter Johnson of the Washington Senators pitches a complete game shutout against New York. This is Mathewson's third complete game shutout in the four-game series.
- In Fall, the National Collegiate Athletic Association assumes control of college basketball rules from the Amateur Athletic Union and the Springfield, Massachusetts, YMCA.
- The college of Washington and Lee begins the practice of identifying football players with numbered jerseys.
- On October 2, Addie Joss of the Cleveland Indians pitches a perfect game against the Chicago White Sox.
- From October 10 to October 14, the National League's Chicago Cubs defeat the Detroit Tigers of the American League four games to one in the World Series. The Cubs are the first team to record three consecutive World Series appearances and two consecutive World Series victories.
- On November 21, Cornell University wins the first ICAA cross-country championship over eight other colleges.
- On December 26, Jack Johnson becomes the first African American world heavyweight boxing champion, defeating Tommy Burns in fifteen rounds in Sydney, Australia.

1909

- The United States wins the Westchester Cup, polo's most prestigious trophy, from Great Britain.
- On March 15, Edward P. Weston, age seventy, completes a walk from New York to San Francisco in 107 days, 7 hours.
- On April 19, Henri Renaud of Nashua, New Hampshire, wins the thirteenth annual Boston Marathon in 2:53:36.8.
- On May 3, Vincent Powers rides Wintergreen to victory in the thirty-fifth annual Kentucky Derby.
- From June 1 to June 29, the first transcontinental automobile race, consisting of six cars, is held from New York City to Seattle. A Ford vehicle is the winner.
- On June 24, George Sargent wins the U.S. Open Golf Tournament with the decade's best score of 290 strokes.
- On August 23, Glenn H. Curtiss wins the Bennett Cup and the Prix de la vitesse at the first International Aviation Meet at Rheims, France, setting a new speed record of 43.34 miles per hour.
- On September 4, after platform diving is added to the events at the men's national swimming championship, George Gaidzik wins the title. He captures the next two as well.
- In fall, the value of the field goal in football is reduced from four to three points.
- On October 8, the Pittsburgh Pirates of the National League defeat the Detroit Tigers of the American League four games to three to win the World Series. This is Ty Cobb's last World Series, even though he continued to play until for the Tigers until 1928.

"Boston's Champion Team"

Newspaper article

By: *The New York Times*

Date: October 14, 1903

Source: "Boston's Champion Team." *The New York Times,* October 14, 1903, 10.

About the Organization: Founded in 1850 as the *Daily Times, The New York Times* was originally a relatively obscure local paper. By the early part of the twentieth century, it had evolved into a widely known, well respected news source. Its banner, "All the News That's Fit to Print," is recognized across the United States and throughout the world. ■

Introduction

The first professional baseball club was formed in 1869, when the Cincinnati Red Stockings had a full roster of paid players. In 1876 William Hulbert, who owned the Chicago Cubs, founded baseball's National League. The teams included the Chicago White Stockings, the Boston Red Caps, the Cincinnati Red Stockings, the St. Louis Brown Stockings, the Philadelphia Athletics, the New York Mutuals, the Louisville Grays, and the Hartfield Dark Blues. The National League got a rival in 1901, when the American League was formed by Ban Johnson (1864–1931). Some early American League Teams were drawn from the National League, and others came from Johnson's Western League. The first clubs of the American League were the Baltimore Orioles, the Boston Somersets, the Chicago White Stockings, the Cleveland Blues, the Detroit Tigers, the Milwaukee Brewers, the Philadelphia Athletics (Philadelphia's National League team became the Phillies), and the Washington Nationals. Johnson stole many of the National League's top players to give his league good status in the 1901 and 1902 seasons. The two leagues liberally stole each others' players and glory until they made peace in 1903. At this time, professional baseball was largely a game of bunting, base stealing, and well-placed hits with few stars. Known as the "dead-ball era" for this reason, it was more a game of teams than of players at the turn of the twentieth century.

It was in 1889 that National League President Abraham G. Mills, with the vocal support of the extremely influential Albert Spalding, reportedly insisted that baseball was a game of wholly American origins. Others, including the well known sportswriter Henry Chadwick, disagreed, but the myth arose that Abner Doubleday developed the game in 1839. Doubleday should probably be better remembered for firing the first Union gun at Fort Sumter at the start of the Civil War (1861–1865). However, the legend stuck and was extremely popular in the late nineteenth and early twentieth centuries.

Significance

As early as 1884, baseball teams were meeting for unofficial post-season championship matches in what became known as the "Fall Classic." At that time, the National League champion played against the champion of a league called the American Association, which folded in 1891. However, the intense rivalry between the American and National Leagues in the early 1900s initially made it impossible to pit the winners of each league against each other in a post-season series.

Fortunately, the 1903 American League Boston team (by then called the Boston Pilgrims; it would not be "Red Sox" until 1907) and National League Pittsburgh Pirates agreed to meet in a best-of-nine postseason series to determine which team was baseball's world champion. Not only did this ensure popularity with fans, it also helped cool the ferocious fighting between the two major leagues. The Pirates's roster featured shortstop Honus Wagner, one of the first five players inducted into the Baseball Hall of Fame. The Pilgrims roster, on the other hand, featured pitcher Cy Young, the winningest pitcher of all time. In his major league career, 1890–1911, Young won more games (511) and pitched more innings (7,375) than any other pitcher to this date. Ironically, because he pitched so many games, he also lost more games (315) than any other pitcher.

The Pirates took an early lead in the series, winning games one, three, and four. However, Boston, after winning only game two of the first four matchups, went on to defeat Pittsburgh in games five, six, seven, and eight of the series, making them the first ever World Series champions. The number of games in the World Series would be reduced to seven the next time that it was played. The National League New York Giants refused to play the Boston Pilgrims in 1904. Since 1905, the World Series has been played annually, missing only 1994 because of a player strike. Baseball's origin in the British game of Rounders (as opposed to the version crediting Doubleday) was verified in 1939.

Primary Source

"Boston's Champion Team" [excerpt]

SYNOPSIS: This article reports on the Boston win over the Pirates in game eight, summarizing some of the

The first game of the first World Series between the Boston Pilgrims and Pittsburgh Pirates, played in Boston, Massachussetts in 1903. Boston went on to win the best-of-nine World Championship. AP/WIDE WORLD PHOTOS. REPRODUCED BY PERMISSION.

best plays of the game. Of particular note is that the final Pittsburgh player to strike out in this final game of the first World Series was Honus Wagner, who, the article later notes, played well as Pittsburgh's shortstop in the game. The teams are referred to according to the league they represented—the "Boston Americans" and "Pittsburg Nationals," of the American and National Leagues, respectively.

Pittsburg Unable to Score in the Deciding Game of the Championship Baseball Series

Boston, Oct. 13.—The Boston Americans shut out the Pittsburg Nationals to-day and won the world's baseball championship, to the almost frenzied delight of 7,000 enthusiasts. While the attendance at all the previous games of the series has been larger than to-day, the demonstration which followed Dineen's striking out of "Hans" Wagner in the ninth equaled any college football game.

Phillippi, who was such an enigma to the Bostons in the first few games, essayed to pitch for the visitors for the sixth time. He was not only batted hard, but he saw his rival, Dineen, carry off the honors by holding the Nationals down to four scattered hits, which, backed by perfect fielding, prevented a single Pittsburg man getting further than third base. Dineen struck out seven men, and his support by Criger contributed materially to the success of the game. The latter's bluff throw to second in the fourth inning, followed by a quick snap of the ball to Collins, catching Leach off the bag, was the best piece of work in the game.

Other features were mainly contributed by the visitors, and Boston's score would undoubtedly have been larger but for the great running catches of Beaumont and Clarke, Wagner's work at short, and Leach's at third base. For the home team, Parent's hauling down of a liner from Clarke's bat roused the greatest enthusiasm.

Further Resources

BOOKS

Helyar, John. *Lords of the Realm: The Real History of Baseball.* New York: Villard, 1994.

Rader, Benjamin G. *Baseball: A History of America's Game.* Urbana, Ill.: University of Illinois Press, 1992.

Ritter, Lawrence S. *The Glory of Their Times: The Story of the Early Days of Baseball Told by the Men Who Played It.* New York: MacMillan, 1966.

WEBSITES

Major League Baseball. "Boston Red Sox History." Available online at http://boston.redsox.mlb.com/NASApp/mlb/bos

/history/bos_history_timeline.jsp; website home page: http://mlb.com (accessed May 15, 2003).

National Baseball Hall of Fame and Museum, Inc. "National Baseball Hall of Fame and Museum." Available online at http://baseballhalloffame.org (accessed March 15, 2003).

AUDIO AND VISUAL MEDIA

Spalding, Albert G. *Story of the Boston Red Sox: An Account of the Beginnings of Professional Baseball in America.* North Hollywood, Calif.: Center for Cassette Studies. Audiocassette, 1972.

Bill Reid's Diary

Diary

By: Bill Reid

Date: September 20 and November 25, 1905

Source: Reid, Bill. Diary entries, September 20 and November 25, 1905. Reprinted in *Big-time Football at Harvard, 1905: The Diary of Coach Bill Reid.* Ronald A. Smith, ed. Urbana: University of Illinois Press, 1994, 128–130, 316–318.

About the Author: Bill Reid (1878–1976) would become an influential member of the National Collegiate Athletics Association (NCAA), starting at its establishment in 1906 as the Intercollegiate Athletic Association of the United States (IAAUS). However, after an impressive record as Harvard's football coach, he accepted employment as assistant headmaster at his father's Belmont School in California. He later had a failed career as a bond salesman. Reid was elected into the Football Hall of Fame in 1970. ■

Introduction

In the first few years of the twentieth century, football was dominated by Ivy League schools and was accurately considered a dangerously violent sport. Indeed, it was not unusual for young men to die playing the game.

Changes to football in the nineteenth century helped improve the game, but did little to protect the players from each other. Although the number of players per team was reduced, the football field's size was set, and the downs system was introduced, some dangerous elements of play remained in place. Particularly dangerous were so called "mass-movements" where the team with the ball would attempt to surge forward and force the other team aside en masse. Players on both sides would interlock arms to attempt to hold up or break through the opposing ranks. Additionally, players wore little or no protective gear, and tackling below the waist was legalized in the latter part of the nineteenth century, increasing the sport's danger even more.

Bill Reid was a student at Harvard starting in 1897. As a student, he played baseball and football, defeating Yale in both baseball (from 1899 to 1901) and in football in 1898. In 1899, the Yale-Harvard game ended in a tie, and in 1900, Reid refused to play football owing to injuries and a dispute with the coach and captain. (Harvard lost, 22-0.) In 1901, Reid coached the Harvard football team to a victory over Yale.

In 1905, Reid was invited to coach again at Harvard, this time as the team's first paid leader. At a salary of seven thousand dollars, he was paid only slightly less than Harvard's president. His team lost to Yale in that year's match-up. In that same year, President Roosevelt (served 1901–1909) called a meeting at the White House to discuss the game's problems with prominent coaches and an elite group of others from Ivy League schools. However, the changes resulting from this meeting were minor and designed more to appease Roosevelt than to actually protect the players.

Significance

In November of 1905, Union College halfback Harold Moore died of a cerebral hemorrhage, prompting a rift in football's rules committee. Up until that point, intercollegiate football had been dominated by those who supported only minimal changes to the game. After Moore's death, a large number of football coaches, college presidents, and boards argued for significant reform in how football was played.

Headed by New York University's Chancellor Henry M. MacCracken, a group of thirteen schools called for a national meeting in December of that year. The December meeting produced the formation of the Intercollegiate Athletic Association of the United States (IAAUS) in 1906. That body, which took the name of National Collegiate Athletic Association (NCAA) in 1910, would go on to become the governing association, not only of football, but of all college sports, and it remains in place nearly one hundred years later.

For football, this meeting represented a crucial turning point. Changes included the introduction of a new neutral zone between opposing lines and an end to the practice of interlocking arms. Additionally, there was an expansion in the number of yards to be gained from five to ten, and the forward pass, previously widely opposed as a desperate effort likely to result in the loss of the ball, was made a palatable option. Although the game would not become significantly less dangerous until safety equipment was introduced, it would never again have a season in which eighteen players died, as was the case in 1905.

Primary Source

Bill Reid's Diary [excerpt]

SYNOPSIS: In the first excerpt, Reid discusses a day of training the team, emphasizing that players must catch with their hands, rather than their bodies, a

Yale-Harvard football game in December 1905. **THE LIBRARY OF CONGRESS.**

principle still important to the game. In the second excerpt, Reid summarizes the 1905 Yale-Harvard game, which Harvard lost, including the Burr-Quill incident, in which a Yale player struck a Harvard player unconscious and broke his nose without receiving a penalty.

Wednesday, September 20, 1905

Morning:

I left Cohasset at 8:02 this morning and came out to Cambridge at once. There I found that Boyd, who had said that he could not afford to come in and out from one of the suburban towns and pay for his meals also, had been straightened out by [Francis] Goodhue so that he is now rooming with one of the other fellows and does not have to travel back and forth.

The weather was muggy and so we decided to make the work very light. I found, also, that a good many of the men had pretty sore feet, due apparently to either the thinness of the soles of their shoes, or to the fact that the morning's and afternoon's practices had been pretty long and the men had been subjected to bruising processes on the bottom of their feet, due to their being on their cleats so long. This being the case we determined to make the morning work lighter hereafter and perhaps to cut it out altogether some day this week. It would be well for succeeding coaches to look out for this sort of sore foot trouble, since some of the men have developed very sensitive corns with some puffs at times, even with the careful way in which we have handled them. I gave the men a long talk before they went down on the field, including a few minutes discussion of the rules and a very brief outline of the Yale system of defence, showing how certain plays cannot work against the Yale Defence and how others can. I also gave several examples of cases where very serious results had happened through the inability of a man to tell just what he should do at a given instant through ignorance of the rules. I told them the story about Brewster of Cornell, who lost the Princeton-Cornell game by catching a punt on his own one yard line and then deliberately turning around and touching it behind his own goal line, thinking all the time that he was only making a touch back. I showed the men also how it was necessary to think all the time in order to outwit the other fellows if possible, and by their brains overcome physical disadvantages. The talk was pretty general and too long, but I had the undivided attention of the entire squad during the whole time. Taking the men on to the field, I took the most promising men on the squad and had each man fall on the ball six times; once on each shoulder with the ball rolling parallel with them. Then I gave them practice in holding the ball for a buck and for an end run. I forgot to say that before the men came out of the house I gave them a set of signals which we shall start off with this year, and which I expect to work in permanently. I spent considerable time coaching Foster and Leonard on their feet. Foster seems to have good form now except in dropping the ball from his hands to his feet, when it is very likely to turn in the air. He is also likely to drop the ball too far out. Leonard is likely to drop the ball too far on the outside of his foot so that it goes off to one side every now and then. He also does not get quite enough height to the ball. By throwing the ball too far from his body, Foster was getting very poor results for two particular reasons: In the first place the ball fell so far from his body that he was wholly unable to reach it unless he had his leg out straight so that when he hit the ball he was unable to get any snap into his blow, with the consequence that the ball travelled very poorly. Then, too, he was unable to get any height at all. The ball must be kept fairly near the body in order that the knee snap may be secured. This is a valuable point to keep in mind in coaching the kickers. While Foster and Leonard were kicking, I had Nesmith and Kempner catching. These two men have been catching with their arms cramped too close to their body instead of pretty free, with the result that the ball frequently hit them on the body before they were able to get their hands on it. I had Nesmith keep his arms away from his body and he quickly grasped the idea and in a very few kicks seemed to have the new principle pretty well in mind. Kempner's greatest trouble seems to be in judging the ball. Those that he judges properly [he] catches high; those that he misjudges he fumbles badly. It should be kept in mind in coaching catchers that the ball must be caught with the arms and hands with the body as a back ground, and not with the body with the hands and arms as a back ground. The hands and arms are capable of giving with the catch, while it is very difficult to give an elasticity to the body. I had one or two men doing some work in drop kicks and goals also. . . .

November 25, 1905

. . . There were two things during the game which caused a great deal of discussion, one of them the disqualification of Morse for striking Wendell. I do not think that Morse hit Wendell intentionally, unless Wendell was doing some holding which he had no business to do. The other case was that of Burr and Quill, which happened in the first half. In this half Yale had kicked out once and Burr had tried for a field goal but missed it. A few minutes later Yale had to kick out on a touch back and Burr himself caught the ball and made a fair catch distinctly. As he caught the ball Quill, the Yale back, came along and struck him square in the face; whether with his fist, the heel of his hand, or his open hand, I do not know, but at any rate he struck him a hard blow, knocking Burr senseless for a moment and breaking his nose. A perfect storm of hisses came forth and Major [Henry L.] Higginson told me to take the team off the field at once, which I did not do. To my astonishment, Dashiell did not rule out Quill[,] and McClung did not recognize the fair catch, which may perhaps have lost us the game, as the ball was caught on about the 40 yard line and almost directly in front of the goal post. [After a fair catch, a team could attempt a field goal from that point unhindered by the opposition. This little-known rule is still in existence. Referee "Bum" McClung claimed that no heel mark was left, a rule for making a fair catch.] Whether Burr would have gotten it over or not is a question, of course, but there was at any rate a good chance of it. It was the failure on the part of Dashiell to penalize this foul that I think caused him to penalize Morse's small act in the second half, in an endeavor to square himself if possible.

In the second half the Yale players used their fists a great deal more than they did in the first half. Wendell said he was struck squarely in the body at the very kick off. Other men complained in like way. Not one of our men lost his temper and we had the satisfaction of having all the blame credited to Yale, who before the game had been boasting that Harvard had been criticizing Yale's players too much and had better look after her own, that Yale had not had anyone disqualified in seven or eight years. When Morse was disqualified Shevlin tried to get Knowlton to agree to let Morse stay in, which Dashiell would not allow, and of course, which Knowlton would not have agreed to. This was an interesting side light on the remark that Camp and Shevlin made to me regarding the not having of Edwards as an official. They could not think of having anyone as an official who would do as Edwards had done the year before in the Penn game, allow two men one of either side, who were disqualified, both to remain in the game; yet here they were trying to have their own man stay in when none of our men had been disqualified. I am rather sorry for Morse but [there] was so much banging on the part of the Yale team made me quite willing that anyone of them should be disqualified as a punishment for the illegal practice.

In this game for the first time in a long while I saw a Yale team apparently "up a tree" and there were numerous consultations on plays and Shevlin was running back and forth very much disturbed at the signals and plays, and apparently very much upset because things were not going the way he expected them to go.

When Nichols dropped his kick a great sigh came from the Harvard stands and many people broke out crying—I felt like it myself.

At the close of the game Walter Camp came out and congratulated me. I was not in the mood for congratulations because I thought the game ought to have been a tie. On all sides as the crowd moved out I heard expressions of admiration for our team's work, and many expressions in which the speaker said that he would rather be a Harvard player than a Yale player after the mean game which Yale had played.

We got into the Locker Building after a time and the whole college came around it and cheered, showing the greatest enthusiasm. The team inside was heart broken and many of them were crying. I stayed until I had spoken to them all and had seen some of the coaches and then went out with a newspaper man from the Globe and drove home.

Further Resources

BOOKS

Baldwin, Robert. *College Football Records: Division I-A and the Ivy League, 1869–1984.* Jefferson, N.C.: McFarland, 1987.

Perrin, Tom. *Football: A College History.* Jefferson, N.C.: McFarland, 1987.

Whittingham, Richard. *Rites of Autumn: The Story of College Football.* New York: Free Press, 2001.

———. *Saturday Afternoon: College Football and the Men Who Made the Day.* New York: Workman, 1985.

WEBSITES

"Ivy Leaguers in the College Football Hall of Fame." Ivy League Sports. Available online at http://www.ivyleaguesports.com/documents/fbhhall.asp; website home page: http://www.ivyleaguesports.com (accessed March 16, 2003).

"General Health of Girls in Relation to Athletics"

Speech

By: Katherine D. Blake

Date: March 30, 1906

Source: Blake, Katherine D. "General Health of Girls in Relation to Athletics." Paper read before the Public School Physical Training Society, New York, March 30, 1906. In *American Physical Education Review* 11, no. 3, September 1906, 171–174.

About the Author: Katherine D. Blake (1858–1950) was the daughter of Lille Devereux Blake, a pioneer in the movement for women's suffrage. Katherine herself led various women's groups, including the Association of Women School Principals of New York and the teacher's section of the New York State Women's Suffrage Association. Blake traveled to Russia in 1929 to meet with Soviet educators, and in 1932 presented a disarmament petition to President Herbert Hoover (served 1929–1933) at the International Disarmament Conference in Geneva, Switzerland. ■

Introduction

In the 1890s, the emergence of women into the white collar workforce began to have a favorable impact on how women were viewed in the workplace. However, prevailing attitudes still dictated that engaging in competitive sports was unhealthy for ladies. Indeed, until the late 1800s, any exercise at all was considered a man's pursuit, largely inappropriate for women. Clothing was another of the chief hindrances to women's participation in sports in the mid- to late 1800s. Upholstered Victorian dresses with heavy corsets were common, especially in the South, and they made exercise difficult if not outright impossible for many young women.

Attitudes about dress began to change around the same time as did attitudes about the relationship of women's health to sport. The introduction of Swedish gymnastics began to change public opinion to suggest that exercise in controlled quantities would be healthy for young women (even young ladies), and, in the right amount, would not make them too competitive or mannish. Cycling was one popular form of exercise for ladies, especially as bloomers began to appear as the appropriate dress of choice for exercising women. Basketball was also considered appropriate for young women, if played by the appropriate rules.

While many women were restricted to ladylike games that matched Victorian ideals of women's behavior—such as croquet—some women were breaking new ground in a variety of sports. Women's field hockey became extremely popular in 1901, eventually eclipsed by basketball. Women's baseball enjoyed success in the "bloomer girls" era from the 1890s to the 1930s. However, the players of this sport never mustered enough public support to counter the impression that women were physically inferior to men, and the leagues eventually disbanded. Though certainly considered unladylike in the extreme, one Lizzie Arlington signed a contract with a minor league baseball team in 1898.

Significance

Because even the reformers advocating women's sports did not accept women's equality with men, sexist attitudes prevailed. Whether because of biology or culture, most people in the 1900s felt a woman was physically inferior to a man. Women were considered more delicate and graceful, and their participation in men's sports was either discouraged or outright forbidden. Where a women's equivalent of a sport existed, its rules were almost always modified to meet the expectation that women were less capable athletes, more likely than men to be injured by rough games.

Additionally, although the clothing women wore to play such sports had changed dramatically, it remained considerably more restrictive than men's uniforms. Where they were permitted to do so, women wore bloomers, but many still had to have long, tangle-prone skirts that made running awkward. Men, who did not need to protect their modesty, wore either pants or shorts. However, in the early twentieth century, women gained the right to vote. Along with this came some equality in other matters, and attitudes regarding women's dress further relaxed. Thus women did gain the right to play in appropriate dress fairly early in the twentieth century.

However, other elements of sports would remain male-oriented for much of the twentieth century, largely because the ingrained attitudes about female physical inferiority went unchallenged by sporting (and other) authorities. Moreover, many women wanted to preserve an aura of feminine uniqueness, even as they fought the repressive boundaries such attitudes imposed upon them. Women were considered morally superior to men, and sports figures did not, in this era, attempt to shed that image. Indeed, such sexism carried the weight of fact when it was presented by authorities throughout the field. Eventually, however, the rise of organized women's sports and the passage of Title IX helped to create a sphere in which women could become accomplished athletes with professional leagues in the latter part of the twentieth century.

As director of physical education at Smith College, Senda Berenson organized the first women's collegiate basketball game. SMITH COLLEGE ARCHIVES, SMITH COLLEGE. REPRODUCED BY PERMISSION.

Primary Source

"General Health of Girls in Relation to Athletics"

SYNOPSIS: In this speech, Blake asserts a difference between athletics and gymnastics, considering gymnastics to be any health building exercise but athletics to be merely a competition of physical fitness designed purely for entertainment. She considers athletics too dangerous for both girls and boys, and points out that girls should be allowed to play in clothing that enables free movement. Finally, she argues that gymnastic exercise should be encouraged instead of overcompetitive athletics for both girls and boys to shape them into better citizens.

Before discussing the topic of the "General Health of Girls in Relation to Athletics," let me carefully distinguish the difference between gymnastics and athletics. In the dictionary that I regard as the most accurate and careful, I find: "Gymnastics, the art of developing by means of gymnastic exercises, bodily strength and agility: athletics, games and sports that depend wholly or partly on feats of physical strength; feats of strength performed for their own sake and not as an incident of any game; especially outdoor feats in which the maintenance of health is not the prime object."

In brief, gymnastics are physical exercise that tend to develop health; while athletics are similar exercises indulged in for sport and caring nothing for the upbuilding of health. Indeed, athletic contests do not admit any except the exceptionally vigorous. The weak who need development are excluded, and so far from tending toward health, the participants are frequently injured, maimed and even killed.

When I consider these things, I feel like saying that I believe that the general health of girls will be better conserved by having no relation to athletics, and when I say girls, I mean boys also, for they are as delicate, as precious as girls and more prone to recklessness. You see, I am regarding my subject as a layman, an outsider, not as an expert teacher of athletics; and I cannot help being appalled at the stories that come to me of the dangers of athletics. One man said to me only two days ago, "My boy shall never play football. I have a football knee that troubles me all the time and I suppose it will be stiff as I grow old. I wonder how my mother let us play. She had four boys. Perhaps she had boys to spare. But my boy shan't play."

Your distinguished president told me that there was more heart trouble as a result of basketball than from football, and only a short time ago a boy was killed in a match game of basketball. Have we any right to permit such waste? Is it not our duty to impress upon the youth under our care that "a sacred burden is this life we bear," that it is the first duty of each one of us to realize that we have no right to play recklessly with our health—to take part in any games that are likely to injure us for life? To impress this will not be difficult, for children are not merely willing but eager to do what we wish, most anxious to secure our approbation. Their health-developing

Two shots of a game of basketball at Smith College, c. 1903. At times games were played out on grass fields and some hoops, like this one, had closed nets with a string attached to them. When a basket was scored, the string would be pulled, popping the ball out of the hoop. **SMITH COLLEGE ARCHIVES, SMITH COLLEGE. REPRODUCED BY PERMISSION.**

gymnastics are done admirably and enjoyed, and gymnastic games can well be substituted for injurious athletics.

In the list of questions sent out for discussion by the Society, I have looked in vain for two which seemed to be vital, yet I could not find them. One relates to girls only, and as your sessions are devoting themselves to the study of athletic problems applied to girls and women, I will put it first. Should girls be permitted to exercise in clothing that is unhygienic and preventive of free movement? I feel very strongly upon this subject, as I am convinced that in our schools of to-day there are many girls who are exercising under conditions such as to render their gymnastic work not merely of no use, but positively detrimental. I should be glad if some authoritative action could be taken forbidding exercise under such conditions in the future.

The second question applies equally to boys and girls and may be stated as: What should be the character of the games that should be encouraged and taught in our schools? The old saying, "If I may write the songs of a nation, I care not who makes its laws," might well be paraphrased, "If you let me make the games of a nation, I care not who makes its laws." The games we teach our boys and girls leave lasting impressions on their later years. The dolls we give our little girls train them toward loving motherhood. Are we not blind when we give our boys soldier caps and guns, that we do not realize that we are training them for that most stupid of all national pastimes—war? The men that are trained in football as it has been played, are the men that make predatory trusts and insurance scandals possible. We are a body of educators and we dare not shut our eyes to the importance of the problem that lies before us. For what are we training our boys and girls? It ought to be our proud aim to teach them to make life noble, to be kind and helpful to all about them. Do our present games do this? I cannot regard as valuable any game or athletic contest which requires an unusual sacrifice of young men or maidens, like the Minotaur of old. The young have no right to die: it is their duty to live and be valuable to the community which has reared them. If they must die, it should be in some worthy cause, not in the capture of a silver-plated trophy.

Competition is a divine and beautiful thing, but it should be competition not of man against man, but of man against physical forces. It is glory to conquer time, space, distance, chemical combinations, the secrets of the stars, but not to conquer another human being. Altruism should be the keynote of physical education. There should be team work to train toward co-operation, but it should be the team against time, rather than against another team. The relay race with its opportunity for each to play her part in her own little place to the best of her ability is almost an ideal contest, when time is offered as an opponent instead of another team. The danger of over-stimulus is removed when the competition ceases to be personal. So also are removed envy, hatred, malice, and all uncharitableness.

The relay principle can be quite readily applied to a number of games of ball, and ball games properly constructed give admirable training in most desirable attributes: quickness of eye, accuracy, forethought, dexterity. No games should be tolerated in which a foul may not be easily, instantly detected. This would prohibit all the dangerous "rough and tumble" games which are so disastrous. Rules about fouls should be absolutely clear, so as to preclude controversy; and fouls should be punished by a corresponding gain to the other side—in which case they become undesirable.

We in the public schools are not obliged, as some of the colleges have been, to make athletic contests over-important as a means of advertising. Already overcrowded, we do not need to attract pupils in this way; and we should be able to approach this problem in an unbiased, scientific spirit. How powerful an influence games play in our lives is shown by the way in which we speak of life itself as a game, of business in the same manner. Let us then choose games for our children that may train them in quickness of eye, grace, precision, accuracy, and forethought, games whose rules may instil the love of honor and altruism in their hearts, games in which there can be no danger to life or limb, so that the element of brutality or bravado may be removed from both contestants and spectators—so shall we mould them into men and women who will go forth into the world to help one another, and to conquer the hard conditions of life, and change this city from a city of selfishness into the abode of generosity.

Further Resources

BOOKS

Guttmann, Allen. *Women's Sports: A History.* New York: Columbia University Press, 1991.

Macy, Sue. *Winning Ways: A Photohistory of American Women in Sports.* New York, Holt, 1996.

Smith, Lissa, ed. *Nike Is a Goddess: The History of Women in Sports.* New York. Atlantic Monthly Press, 1998.

PERIODICALS

"Katherine Blake, Educator, was 92." Obituary of Katherine Blake. *The New York Times,* February 3, 1950, 23.

Sargent, Dudly Allen. "What Athletic Games, if Any, Are Injurious for Women in the Form in Which They Are Played by Men?" *American Physical Education Review* 11, no. 3, September 1906, 174–179.

WEBSITES

"History of Women in Sports Timeline." American Association of University Women, St. Lawrence County Branch. Available online at http://www.northnet.org/stlawrenceaauw/timeline.htm; website home page: http://www.northnet.org/stlawrenceaauw/ (accessed March 15, 2003).

Struna, Nancy. "Women's Pre-Title IX Sports In the United States." *Women's Sport's Foundation History,* April 26, 2001. Available online at http://www.womenssportsfoundation.org/cgi-bin/iowa/issues/history/article.html?record=769; website home page: http://www.womenssportsfoundation.org (accessed March 15, 2003).

"Inter-School Athletics"

Speech

By: Elma L. Warner

Date: March 31, 1906

Source: Warner, Elma L. "Inter-School Athletics." Paper read before the Public School Physical Training Society, Brooklyn, New York, March 31, 1906. In *American Physical Education Review* 11, no. 3, September 1906, 182–186.

About the Author: Elma L. Warner was a member of the Public School Physical Training Society in Brooklyn during the early twentieth century. ■

Introduction

Cycling was one popular form of exercise for ladies in the late nineteenth century, especially as bloomers began to appear as the appropriate dress of choice for women while engaged in exercise. Another popular sport for young ladies, starting when Senda Berenson introduced the game at Smith College in 1892, was basketball. Berenson's rules were based on those of the game's originator, James Naismith, but with a heavy emphasis on keeping the game appropriate for young ladies. Thus, the rules avoided all roughness (a quality Berenson felt inexcusable in women) and emphasized team play over competitiveness. For example, Berenson partitioned the floor into three segments, assigned players to each of the segments, and prohibited players to leave their section of the floor.

Other women's basketball originators were even more restrictive. In the American South, Clara Baer outlawed dribbling because it encouraged too much competition. She renamed her game Basquette and published her own set of rules in 1895. Women's sports were to concentrate on players' improving their health while engaging in team play. Small doses of exercise might indeed be healthy for women, but the men's game of basket ball (the sport was originally two words) was considered far too rough for young ladies to play.

Significance

Because the women's game focused so heavily on teamwork rather than competition, inter-school play was generally discouraged, whether at the high school or college level. Instead, intramural play was the most popular, with teams from different classes playing against one

Spectators and players await the start of a freshman and sophomore basketball game at Smith College, c. 1903. Basketball was one of the most popular sports for women at the turn of the century. SMITH COLLEGE ARCHIVES, SMITH COLLEGE. REPRODUCED BY PERMISSION.

another. However, intercollegiate play was not unheard of, and it was these games that led to a meeting in 1899 designed to standardize the rules for women's basketball. Until that time, different groups, particularly colleges, played with their own variations on the men's rules. They all had different rules concerning snatching the ball, dribbling, bounce passing, and shooting. Meetings between colleges with different standards usually resulted in disputes and confusion. Thus, Bertha Alice Foster called the 1899 Physical Training Meeting to standardize the rules.

At the meeting, Senda Berenson was appointed editor of the women's rules, and standardized rules for women's play were generally agreed upon. The court was officially divided into three parts and snatching of the ball and dribbling more than three times were prohibited. Indeed, until 1971, women were restricted from crossing the half-court line.

Although the move for standardization came from intercollegiate play, most women's basketball in the first decade of the 1900s remained intramural. High schools frequently used the men's rules when playing other schools, to the disapproval of those who considered such competition unfeminine. Many women wanted to preserve the aura of feminine uniqueness, and competitive games seemed to encroach on that mystique. Women were perceived as physically inferior and morally superior to men, and most of the early pioneers in women's sports wanted to reinforce these perceptions with their games. However, ultimately, it was the rise of organized women's sports, particularly women's basketball, along with the eventual passage of Title IX, which helped to create a sphere in which women could become accomplished athletes with professional leagues in the latter part of the twentieth century.

Primary Source

"Inter-School Athletics"

SYNOPSIS: Warner highlights some of the benefits and drawbacks of inter-school competition between girls' high school basketball teams. Her chief focus is on the negative effects of such games, such as roughness and physical exhaustion. Particularly, she objects to girls in inter-school competitions playing by the men's rules, as these rules encourage roughness and partisanship such as cheering and hissing from the crowd, which she considers inappropriate to women's games.

The interest in athletics for girls, particularly the question of interscholastic competition, is steadily growing. The action of our Society in choosing this topic for discussion at the present convention is a timely one. We are all anxious for public expressions of experience and opinion on various phases of the subject.

In New York and vicinity the attitude taken toward interscholastic competition by students, faculty, parents, and press, is widely different. Among the students, both boys and girls, the interest is strong. In a recent examination a class of girls was asked to state whether they preferred interscholastic or inter-class games, and to give reason for their preference. A student taking inter-scholastic side writes, "I think it is better to select the best players in school and play other schools. If we had class teams, we might pay more attention to our team than our studies, which would not be good for the school. Then if you had but one set of girls to train, it would not be so hard for you." Another pupil favoring inter-class work writes, "Each class should have its own team and then these teams could play each other. This would enable more girls to play and make healthy and jolly-looking girls, for I really think that there are many girls who would like to play but who are too bashful to practice with regular teams who play so well. Inter-class games would bring the classes together more and it would be a comfort to know that we were going to have a little fun after our lessons are over." A large majority of students voted for a combination of the two methods.

The faculty of each school show only slight interest in the girls' games. Evidently some are of President Jordan's opinion that "athletics and games are only by-play, most worthy and valuable for many reasons, but nevertheless only an adjunct to the real work of the school, which is education." It is needless to take up the educational value of games before this audience. In a season of inter-school games I have seen but three teachers and one principal at a game.

In the majority of cases, a girl's mother has never seen a game of basketball, hockey, etc., and when she does witness a game, expresses strong disapproval. I have heard one man coach say that he would not allow a daughter of his to play in interscholastic competition under present conditions.

Of course, the press, like the poor, are always with us; and our girls receive a certain kind of notoriety from notices and pictures, which cannot be recommended.

The preparation of these contests between schools begins early in October, with the practice of the girls who desire to make teams. The requirements demand that a girl's standing in her studies be satisfactory. A few schools—not all—demand a physician's certificate of fitness. These certificates vary in wording to such an extent that I question whether all our physicians realize the demands made upon a girl engaged in athletic contests. However that may be, it places the responsibility where it should be. It is my belief that every school should insist upon each girl having a physician's certificate and that a certain definite form should be made out for physicians to sign.

The general rule for practice is two afternoons each week, play lasting from one hour to an hour and a half with rest periods. There are no uniform regulations, although girls are requested not to wear certain clothing, not to play at certain times, not to eat or drink injudiciously, not to dissipate. The observance of these requests is left to the girl's honor, but sometimes a girl fails to observe the more important of the rules, as well as the lesser ones. In some cases no attention is paid to the physical condition of a girl when she comes on the field. If her playing is poor, the reason is not sought. She is simply scolded and whipped—not literally—into making stronger effort. Particularly is this true when a man coach is in charge. This is a strong point against the employment of a man coach for athletics for girls.

I must touch on the question of coaches for our school girls. The prevailing method is not that of selection, but of chance. Any teacher in the school who will volunteer his services is put in charge, regardless of qualifications. In some cases, such teachers have been successful in working up a strong team, but the result to individual girls has not been beneficial, to say the least. When unable to secure a teacher, a student coach is sometimes employed. Teams coached by this method are lacking in responsibility, in refinement of speech and manner, and are rough, unfair, even dishonorable in playing. When a professional coach is employed, excellent play results, but girls show a lack of the spirit of courtesy and good will. It is a battle for victory not a game for the sake of sport. All athletic work for girls should be done under a properly trained woman coach, or if a student or professional coach is employed, under the actual supervision of the woman instructor of physical training.

In planning schedules, the manager, a member of the team, has full sway. All challenges are accepted and a date for a return game suggested. In no case are the age, weight, height or amount of training of challenging teams considered, nor their court, audience, or previous record. From ten to twenty games are played in a season.

In attending games, there is no rule of chaperonage. A teacher is supposed to accompany the team and should. The members of teams generally meet at some convenient place and then proceed together, but frequently late arrivals, with no knowledge of how to reach destination, wander about city and delay game thereby.

Admission to games varies. Generally it is by ticket, purchased at door for from ten to fifty cents. Occasionally admission is free; sometimes by invitation only. It is needless to draw conclusions as to the kind of audience obtained by various methods. The paid admission is advocated because it decreases size of audience and increases amount in treasury of athletic association. The former result may be obtained by issuing a limited number of cards of invitation and the tone of the occasion will be raised. The more we try to establish the spirit of hospitality and to make our audiences feel that they are our guests, the less liable we will be to a vulgar display of partisanship, shown by cheers, hisses, mechanical noises, audible comments on players and officials, coaching from side lines, and general rudeness. There is absolutely no reason for our contests for girls partaking of the same public character as those for boys and men.

Interscholastic games are not played on a neutral court, but one game on home court and one on opponent's court. Courts differ widely. Some are large, some small; some open space, some with interfering posts; some have slippery floors; some have windows, doors, apparatus, or steam pipes for boundary lines, causing minor accidents; some are damp and unheated; some lack dressing rooms and toilet facilities. If we have inter-school games, they should all be played upon the best court obtainable, preferably neutral, so that but one game need be played between competing teams.

The officials of these games are the coaches of competing teams, who act as referee and umpire, while the timekeepers and scorers are chosen from student body. Non-partisan officials are preferable. The rules of play are men's rules, that is, no lines, five men on a team, twenty-minute halves, and interference allowed. In comparison with women's rules, this means a greater amount of running, fewer women to do the work, greater strain on individuals, and probability of much roughness. If men's rules are used, a non-interference rule should be made and time of holding ball lessened to three seconds. This would eliminate much of the roughness and yet necessitate quick passing.

In no case is there as strict an enforcement of rules as there should be. A good suggestion has been made to restrict fouling, namely, for each foul give point to opposite side, doing away with free throw for goal.

The rule of being ready to play at time appointed is never enforced, never penalized, and consequently always broken. After play has begun, too long a time is allowed for struggle over a "held ball," with resulting roughness. I have seen two girls, each holding tightly to the ball, pull and wrench and struggle for possession of it, until one threw the other completely off floor, with resulting shock that brought unconsciousness. Too much leniency is allowed in holding as regards players, and as regards ball "by hands only." Our girls can and should be trained to play a clean, open game, depending upon skilful catching, passing, throwing, and agility in running, jumping, and dodging for the winning of points.

"Time out" is frequently called for necessary repair to clothing; for breathlessness, for bleeding of nose or lips; for wrenched arms or legs; for bruised heads, faintness; in a few cases hysteria and even temper. I have seen very few halves played without several demands for "time out." This should not be necessary, if girls are in good physical condition and play an open, intelligent game.

A social element is introduced after the contest by a "spread" given by home team, sometimes followed by a short period of dancing. In this social hour the losing team must show the courage of defeat by being bright and lively, while the winning team must keep their joy and pride within bounds—chance for control on both sides. Too much cannot be said for the increasing of the social side of our work with girls.

It is difficult to speak definitely of the results of interscholastic games. Physically, we get the usual strained muscles, bumps and bruises, sometimes faintness, hysteria or melancholy immediately after the game. Occasionally a girl is completely exhausted and takes two or three days to recover her normal condition. I do not favor coddling our girls, but they should not be allowed to overtax their powers of endurance. The keen competition in match games means a much more severe strain on nerves and muscles than in ordinary play, and in the very great excitement girls do not realize that they are overdoing, until they drop.

My own experience in playing other schools is that such competition is not beneficial under present conditions. The competition in itself is too severe for girls of the high school age, and the use of men's rules entails too great a strain physically for any girl, when played without modifications. Some of our school principals argue that with the abolishment of inter-school competition all activity in athletics and games would cease, and that if the girls are not allowed to play by men's rules, the game would not hold their interest. By uniform action in the matter by all schools, and by the encouragement of athletics and games within each school, such an outcome would be avoided.

There is a very real need of doing everything practical to encourage an active play spirit in our girls. Too many of them are merely passive onlookers and a few are absolutely uninterested. Therefore, in our athletics and games for girls, let us work to gain the interest and activity of the many, rather than for the selection and training of the few for interscholastic competition.

Further Resources

BOOKS

Berlage, Gai Ingham. *Women in Baseball: The Forgotten History.* Westport, Conn: Praeger, 1994.

Sparhawk, Ruth M. *American Women in Sport, 1887–1987: A 100-Year Chronology.* Metuchen, N.J.: Scarecrow Press, 1989.

Stanley, Gregory Kent. *The Rise and Fall of the Sportswoman: Women's Health, Fitness, and Athletics, 1860–1900.* New York: P. Lang, 1996.

Vertinsky, Patricia. *The Eternally Wounded Woman: Women, Doctors, and Exercise in the Late Nineteenth Century.* New York: Manchester University Press, 1990.

PERIODICALS

Sargent, Dudly Allen. "What Athletic Games, if Any, Are Injurious for Women in the Form in Which They Are Played by Men?" *American Physical Education Review* 11, no. 3, September 1906, 174–179.

WEBSITES

Johnson, Scott. "Not Altogether Ladylike: The Premature Demise of Girls' Interscholastic Basketball in Illinois." Paper presented at the annual meeting of the North American Society for Sport History, June, 1992. Available online at http://www.ihsa.org/feature/hstoric/earlybkg.htm; website home page: http://www.ihsa.org (accessed May 13, 2003).

Middleton, Ken. "American Women's History: A Research Guide: Sports." Available online at http://www.mtsu.edu/~kmiddlet/history/women/wh-sports.html; website home page: http://www.mtsu.edu (accessed March 16, 2003).

AUDIO AND VISUAL MEDIA

McGimpsey, David. "Women in Baseball." A talk with Gai Berlage, author of "Women in Baseball: The Forgotten History." June 5, 2000. Talking History. Available online at http://talkinghistory.oah.org/arch2000.html; website home page: http://talkinghistory.oah.org (accessed May 13, 2003).

"Baseball Scores Over Crap Games"

Newspaper article

By: *The New York Times*

Date: August 25, 1907

Source: "Baseball Scores Over Crap Games." *The New York Times,* August 25, 1907, S4.

About the Organization: Founded in 1850 as the *Daily Times, The New York Times* was originally a relatively obscure local paper. By the early part of the twentieth century, it had evolved into a widely known, well respected news source. Its banner, "All the News That's Fit to Print," is recognized across the United States and throughout the world. ■

Introduction

At the turn of the twentieth century, black players were excluded from playing baseball on teams with their white counterparts. Bigotry kept the color line firmly in place, although a few slipped across to play in the white leagues. For example, Charlie Grant played for a short time for the Baltimore Orioles under the assumed American Indian identity of "Chief Tokahoma." However, the actions of major league star Ty Cobb and other white players who shared his racist attitudes generally prevented even those players who were willing to "pass" from being able to do so. White managers sometimes hired black players to fill roles other than team players. Andrew "Rube" Foster was the best black pitcher at the turn of the century; he would, in fact, go on to found the Negro National League in 1920. In 1903, the New York Giants' John McGraw is reported to have hired Foster to teach his players, including Christy Mathewson, to pitch.

As talent and enjoyment of the game certainly did not differentiate the black from the white players, black players formed teams and leagues of their own. In 1903, two of the best teams of these leagues played each other, and the Cuban "X" Giants beat the Philadelphia Giants in the first black World Series. This was the same year the Pirates lost to the Boston Pilgrims in the first Major League (i.e., white) World Series. Rube Foster pitched four games for the Giants in the nine-game series. Black teams did sometimes play against white teams, but Ty Cobb wasn't the only baseball player who considered it

As a rookie pitcher for the Chicago Union Giants, Andrew "Rube" Foster won 51 games in 1902. In 1910 he assembled the Chicago American Giants—considered to be the greatest black baseball talent ever assembled. NATIONAL BASEBALL HALL OF FAME LIBRARY, COOPERSTOWN, N.Y. REPRODUCED BY PERMISSION.

demeaning to play against a black man. In 1909, when the Leland Giants, then of Chicago, challenged the National League's second place Chicago Cubs to a crosstown game, two of the Cubs' players refused to play in the series. Rube Foster, who was playing for the Giants as well as managing them, pitched two of the three games in the narrow Cubs victory.

Significance

The stars of these black teams remain baseball's largely unsung heroes. How they would have performed in comparison to their white counterparts is unknown, as they were rarely given the opportunity to play against white teams. Moreover, the white community generally scorned black baseball, assuming it was inferior because of its players' race. Although some white reporters were openly admiring of black players, the predominant racist attitude was often apparent in newspaper sports stories, when white newspapers saw fit to cover a black game. The reporter who wrote "Baseball Scores Over Crap Games," for example takes a patronizing attitude towards the attendees of the baseball game he is recording, insisting that many of the crowd would otherwise be gambling were the game not umpired by boxing's heavyweight champion Jack Johnson. Although admitting that the game has some white attendees, by characterizing their speech with stereotypical emphasis on the word "Mistah," the reporter makes the fans' enjoyment of Johnson's celebrity presence sound like idol worship unheard of at white events.

Such racism demonstrates some of the entrenched attitudes against black players in this era. Fighting these attitudes would prove an uphill battle that required more than playing skill. When the Negro Leagues were founded in the 1920s, black players got access to formally organized sports leagues. However, it would be nearly two more decades before black and white players took the field as equals. In 1946, Jackie Robinson finally broke the color barrier when the Brooklyn Dodgers signed him. But not until 1971 did the Baseball Hall of Fame begin recognizing the accomplishments of Negro League players when it inducted Satchel Paige, who also played major league ball, as a Negro League Player. The next year, the Hall inducted two players who had played only for the Negro Leagues and never for the majors: Josh Gibson and Buck Leonard.

Primary Source

"Baseball Scores Over Crap Games" [excerpt]

SYNOPSIS: This is an article about a baseball game between the Cuban "X" Giants and Philadelphia Giants. Heavyweight boxing champ Jack Johnson umpired the game, and the article states he was responsible for the game's large crowd. Mentioning only a few game details, the article is primarily concerned with the crowd's enthusiastic response to Johnson after the game and the celebrity's subsequent "escape" to the street and subway.

Baseball Scores Over Crap Games

Colored Population Forsakes Favorite Sport to See Jack Johnson Umpire.

Was the Real Attraction

Spectators Make Him Hero at the Game Between Cuban and Philadelphia Giants.

Big "Jack" Johnson, the negro heavyweight pugilist, who recently scored a victory over Bob Fitzsimmons, was the real attraction at American League Park yesterday. The occasion was the baseball game between the Cuban Giants and the Philadelphia Giants for the benefit of the Colored Branch of the Young Men's Christian Association, which is trying to raise funds for a new building.

Johnson umpired the game, and "San Juan Hill" and the several other "quarters" of the city where crap games flourish were minus their pure sporting elements who attended the game on the hilltop.

Ordinarily Clarence Williams, who caught for the "Cubans," would have been sufficient to furnish the fun at an event of this sort, for Williams is Sixth Avenue's representative athlete, and he has his own way of playing ball, but Johnson had all the colored celebrities "faded" yesterday. The 2,500 or more spectators made the colored pugilist their especial idol, and would hardly restrain themselves during the progress of the game in their desire to honor him. To those present Jack Johnson was the only living representative of this pugilistic art, for his victory over the auburn-haired Australian and his throwing down the gauntlet to Champion J. J. Jeffries had placed him on a pinnacle far above ordinary colored mortals.

The scene after the game savored of a reception following a cakewalk. As the players departed for the clubhouse there was a concerted movement on the part of the spectators to the home plate, where Johnson stood, evidently waiting for some such demonstration. Men and women vied with each other in their desire to show "Mistah" Johnson how much they thought of him. They tagged at his coattails, pulled his arms in their eagerness to grasp his massive hands, patted him on the back, and told him he was the greatest representative of the colored race before the public. Nor were those who showered their adulations on the fistic umpire confined to his own race, as many white persons helped to swell the mob that wanted to show their respects to the vanquisher of Fitzsimmons.

Johnson showed no disposition to resent the impromptu homage, but accepted it as though due him. He finally eluded his well-wishers and reached the street, his clothes somewhat ruffled and pulled out of shape. Even there he was not safe from the crowd, which followed him, cheering all the way to the Subway station, which saved him from further molestation. It was a grand opportunity for the colored folk, and they did not fail to make much of it.

The inclement weather kept down the attendance to about 2,500, although it was stated that 4,000 tickets had been disposed of in advance of the game. Additional interest was lent to the game by the announcement that it counts in the championship series of the National Association of Professional Colored Clubs.

Williams kept the crowd in good humor. He shaded the irrepressible "Arlie" Latham on the coaching lines, and many of his remarks brought smiles to the ebony-hued visages in the stands.

Johnson seemed to be thoroughly at home in his position, although he had a number of close decisions to make. Once in a while some of the players would dispute him, but the brawny boxer would silence them with either a deprecatory wave of the hand or a significant look.

The game was interesting, and was won by the Cuban Giants by the score of 7 to 2. The Philadelphia Giants could not solve Bowman's curves, and the best they were able to do was to secure three hits, including a three-bagger by R. Williams, which gave the losers their first point in the sixth inning.

The fielding was sharp at times. Errors by the Philadelphians were costly, and helped the Cubans to make three of their runs.

Further Resources

BOOKS

Chadwick, Bruce. *When the Game Was Black and White: The Illustrated History of the Negro Leagues.* New York: Abbeville Press, 1992.

Holway, John B. *Blackball Stars: Negro League Pioneers.* Westport, Conn.: Meckler, 1988.

McKissack, Patricia C., and Frederick McKissack, Jr. *Black Diamond: The Story of the Negro Baseball Leagues.* New York: Scholastic, 1994.

Peterson, Robert. *Only the Ball Was White.* Englewood Cliffs, N.J.: Prentice-Hall, 1970.

Sammons, Jeffrey T. *Beyond the Ring: The Role of Boxing in American Society.* Chicago: University of Illinois Press, 1988.

WEBSITES

"Black Baseball's Negro Baseball Leagues." TK Publishers & Blackbaseball.com. Available online at http://www.blackbaseball.com (accessed March 16, 2003).

"Negro Leagues." MLB.com. Available online at http://mlb.mlb.com/NASApp/mlb/mlb/history/mlb_negro_leagues.jsp; website home page: http://mlb.com (accessed March 16, 2003).

"Athletes Aroused Over Point Scoring"

Newspaper article

By: *The New York Times*

Date: July 17, 1908

Source: "Athletes Aroused Over Point Scoring." *The New York Times,* July 17, 1908, 8.

About the Publication: Founded in 1850 as the *Daily Times, The New York Times* was originally a relatively obscure local paper. By the early part of the twentieth century, it had evolved into a widely known, well respected news source. Its banner, "All the News That's Fit to Print," is recognized across the United States and throughout the world. ■

Introduction

After Baron Pierre de Coubertin revived interest in the Olympics and established the International Olympic Committee (IOC) with himself as its secretary-general, the first Olympic games were held in Athens in 1896. The games were successful enough to warrant their continuation, so according to its policy of holding the games in a different city every four years, the IOC awarded the 1900 games to Paris over protests that the games should always be held in Athens. The French government was generally unenthusiastic about this honor and the games were not well organized.

The 1904 games in St. Louis, Missouri, had little international significance because most of the athletes were American and many foreign competitors could not travel the long distance to attend the games. These games had originally been awarded to Chicago in 1900, but that city lost its enthusiasm and St. Louis nominated itself instead. Similarly, the 1908 games were originally awarded to Rome, but Italy had to withdraw when financial problems and personality conflicts led to the dissolution of its organizing committee and when Mt. Vesuvius erupted in 1906, leading to two thousand deaths. Because Great Britain was already preparing to hold the Franco-British Exposition in London in 1908, London was awarded the games in Rome's stead.

Significance

From the beginning, the 1908 London Olympics were plagued with controversy. The British refused to let Ireland send its own delegation, which particularly angered the Americans, as many of the U.S. athletes were Irish American. America's flag bearer, Ralph Rose, an Irish American, refused to dip the American flag to King Edward VII and no American flag bearer has since dipped the flag to a foreign head of state. In addition, British officials were biased, particularly against the American competitors. Americans also felt the British method of determining the Olympic champion was biased, as the British only awarded points for gold medals in their computations, with no credit for a silver or bronze.

The 1908 Olympics did have some positive impact on future games. For instance, figure skating debuted at the 1908 Summer Games, as did hockey. (Winter Olympics as a separate sporting event would not begin until 1908.) Boxing made its first appearance as a medal sport—it had been a demonstration sport in 1904 in St. Louis. And the 1908 Olympics boasted 107 events and 2,035 competitors in contrast to the 89 events and 689 competitors at the 1904 St. Louis games. Moreover, the 1908 Olympics represented the first time Olympic participation was by nations rather than individuals. Therefore, the International Olympic Committee, for the first time in 1908, chose an official American team. Before that, colleges, clubs, and private individuals had all entered on their own.

In spite of British bias, American athletes achieved several Olympic accomplishments. The American four hundred–meter relay team won a gold medal. The team included John Taylor, the first black athlete to win Olympic gold. The United States' Ray Ewry also won his last two Olympic golds, for a career high of ten gold medals, the only athlete in Olympic history to win that many. To eliminate future problems with bias, the IOC made Olympic officiating international in 1912. However, controversies over judging bias have continued, most recently at the 2002 Winter Olympics in Salt Lake City when Canada—who lost to Russia by one vote—was later also awarded a gold medal in figure skating after it was discovered a French judge was pressured to vote for the Russians.

Primary Source

"Athletes Aroused Over Point Scoring" [excerpt]

SYNOPSIS: This article explains the ramifications of the British system of determining the Olympic Champion—to award a point for every first place and not to count second and third place finishes. It lists the events in which the United Kingdom, United States, and Sweden won first place, and it details the American complaint with the British system.

Athletes Aroused Over Point Scoring

English System of Marking Olympic Victories Would Make England Sure Winner.

Mr. Sullivan Takes Issue

American Commissioner Says United States Is Making a Fight in the Field Events Only.

London, July 16.—This was America's day in the Olympic sports at the Stadium, both big events which reached the finals, throwing the discus free style, and putting the shot being carried off by Martin J. Sheridan of the Irish-American Athletic Club of New York and Ralph Rose of the Olympic Club, San Francisco, respectively. The United Kingdom captured the third final, the 400 meters swimming event, in which H. Taylor added to the score of his country by beat-

The American Olympic team marches at the opening of the 1908 Olympic games. The flag bearer, Ralph Rose, refused to dip the flag to King Edward VII. © HULTON-DEUTSCH COLLECTION/CORBIS. REPRODUCED BY PERMISSION.

ing Beaurepaire, the Australian crack, and Scheff of Australia.

The final also was reached in the 1,000 meters cycle race, but this proved such a fiasco through the attempts of four of the participants, Schilles of France and Jones, Kingsbury, and Johnson of England, to force each other to take the pace that the judges declared the event off, it not being finished within the time limit.

Italy got her first gold medal to-day in the team gymnastic competition, receiving the greatest number of points against a great array of competitors.

No official announcement is obtainable as to how the British Olympic Association is going to decide the Olympic championship, but the system adopted by the London sporting papers in arriving at the respective positions of the various countries has been generally accepted. This system awards 1 point for each win, ignoring seconds and thirds, and includes all sports carried out under the auspices of the association, whether within the Stadium or outside of it.

Following this method of counting points, the countries would be placed in this order: United Kingdom, 20; United States, 8; Sweden, 3; Norway, 2, and Canada, France, Belgium, and Italy, 1 each. The United Kingdom's 20 points, according to this computation, are made up as follows: Men's doubles and singles and ladies singles in both the lawn tennis and covered court tennis competitions, polo competition, singles and doubles at racquets, individual rifle competition, individual miniature rifle competition at disappearing target, individual miniature rifle competition at moving target, team and individual competitions, miniature rifles at ordinary targets, team competition at clay birds, and the following wins in the Stadium: 3,500-meter walk, 20-kilometer cycle race, 660-yard cycle race, three-mile team race, and 400-meter swim.

The score of the United States is made up of the following wins: Rifle team competition, revolver team competition, individual double shot at running deer, Jay Gould's victory in court tennis competition, throwing the hammer, 1,500-meter flat race, throwing the discus, and putting the weight.

The Swedish points were scored by wins in the team and individual competitions at running deer and throwing the javelin; Norway, the team and individual rifle shooting at 300 meters; Canada, the individual competition at clay birds; France, the 2,000-kilometer tandem cycle race; Belgium, the individual revolver competition, and Italy, team gymnastic competition.

As the Summer section of the games will continue until October 19 and will include yachting, the Olympic regatta and figure skating, and as there will be a Winter section to include rugby and association football, hockey, lacrosse, and boxing, it will be the end of the year before the trophy for the championship in all sports can be awarded. If this method of counting points is followed by the British Olympic Association, England will win the trophy, for there are few countries taking part in these sports outside the Stadium.

The American athletic team, which is devoting its attention to the events within the Stadium, however, is not accepting this interpretation. James E. Sullivan, President of the Amateur Athletic Union and United States Commissioner to the Olympic games, said to The Associated Press to-night:

"We came here, as we went to Paris and Athens, with a field team, and are making a fight in the field events, caring nothing for the other sports. We asked that the championship trophy be put up for the field sports separately, but this request was not acceded to. So we will simply take the score in the field events, counting first, 5 points; second, 3 points, and third, 1 point; and figure out the American score on this basis."

Under the American system the score as it stands to-night is as follows:

America—Throwing the hammer, 8; team race, 3; discus, 9; putting the shot, 6; 1,500-meter race, 5. Total 31.

United Kingdom—Team race 5; putting the shot, 3; 1,500-meter race, 4; 3,500-meter walk, 8. Total—20.

Sweden, 5; Greece, 3; Canada, 1; Australia, 1; Norway, 1.

Commissioner Sullivan has received a reply to the letter which he sent to Lord Desborough, Chairman of the Council of the British Olympic Association, protesting against certain of the rules governing the contests and referring to other matters in connection with the games.

In his reply, Lord Desborough opens with an apology to the Americans for the failure to use a single American flag in the decoration of the Stadium on the opening day, the omission to do which, he says, has been remedied. He then takes up the complaints of the Americans regarding the conduct of the sports. The question of the pole vault was referred to the Amateur Athletic Association, which decided not to allow the Americans to dig a hole for the pole, but acceded to the request to have pits filled with sand for landing on.

With regard to the questions of heat drawings, Lord Desborough pointed out in his letter that the drawings had already been made in the various heats and could not be altered, although this had not been asked for. The Athletic Association, he said, had invited the American Committee to have a man in the arena during the progress of the events in which America was interested, and Mr. Matthew P. Halpin, the American manager, had been appointed to this post.

After reading Lord Desborough's letter, Commissioner Sullivan replied that if the drawings were already made, the Americans would like to see them before the day on which the events were to be contested, a privilege which heretofore had not been accorded them.

Lord Desborough and the British Olympic Council to-night gave a banquet to the second contingent of 400 athletes at the Holborn Restaurant. The guests included Lord Kinnaird and Lord Blyth.

Lord Desborough during the course of a speech congratulated all concerned in the courage they had shown in facing the adverse weather conditions and for the splendid records they had made. It is proposed to have three more banquets similar to those already given, so that all the athletes may be entertained.

Further Resources

BOOKS

Chronicle of the Olympics: 1896–1996. Boston: DK, 1996.

Guttmann, Allen. *The Olympics: A History of the Modern Games.* Urbana, Ill.: University of Illinois Press, 1992.

Kieran, John, Arthur Daley, and Pat Jordan. *The Story of the Olympic Games: 776 B.C. to 1976.* Philadelphia: Lippincott, 1977.

Leder, Jane, et al. *Grace & Glory: A Century of Women in the Olympics.* Chicago: Triumph, 1996.

WEBSITES

International Olympic Committee. Official Website of the Olympic Movement. Available online at http://www.olympic.org (accessed May 17, 2003).

"The Olympics Factbook." 1908. Rediff.com. Available online at http://www.rediff.com/sports/fact6.htm; website home page: www.rediff.com (accessed March 17, 2003).

"Summer Olympics 2000." ESPN.com. Available online at http://espn.go.com/oly/summer00; website home page: http://espn.com (accessed March 17, 2003).

United States Olympic Committee home page. Available online at http://www.olympic-usa.org (accessed May 17, 2003).

"70 Years, Many Magical Moments." Washintonpost.com. Available online at http://www.washingtonpost.com/wp-srv/sports/longterm/olympics1998/history.htm; website home page: http://www.washingtonpost.com (accessed May 17, 2003).

"Travers Defeats Travis in Fine Golf"

Newspaper article

By: *The New York Times*

Date: September 19, 1908

Source: "Travers Defeats Travis in Fine Golf." *New York Times,* September 19, 1908, 8

About the Publication: Founded in 1850 as the *Daily Times, The New York Times* was originally a relatively obscure local paper. By the early part of the twentieth century, it had evolved into a widely known, well respected news source. Its banner, "All the News That's Fit to Print," is recognized across the United States and throughout the world. ■

Introduction

Although golf was played in the United States as early as the 1780s, it did not become extremely popular in this country until one hundred years later. The first U.S. golfing clubs were organized in the late 1880s, starting with St. Andrews golf club in 1887. Golf was largely an upper class game, enjoyed by those who had the leisure time to play it. Moreover, it was largely a British game, with no American tradition to draw upon. With its first rules formalized in Scotland in 1744, golf had no historical ties to the United States, and it was largely dominated by British players.

Nonetheless, by 1894 there were sufficient clubs in America to justify the formation of an Amateur Golf Association to write rules, establish a national system of handicapping, and, perhaps most importantly for the game, hold national championships. Soon after its formation, the Amateur Golf Association renamed itself the United States Golf Association. It chose to hold both an amateur and an open (i.e., open to professional golfers who earned money teaching golf) competition. Blair McDonald won the amateur competition in 1895, and the first U.S. Open was won by an English professional, Horace Rawlins, who belonged to the Newport, Rhode Island, golf club, where the tournament was held. At that time, there were seventy-five clubs in the United States.

Jerome Travers won four U.S. Amateur golf championships, his first in 1907. AP/WIDE WORLD PHOTOS. REPRODUCED BY PERMISSION.

In just five years, that number swelled to more than a thousand U.S. clubs. Tournaments were (and continue to be) of two types: stroke and match play. In stroke play, the total number of strokes a player takes to get the ball into the hole is added up to determine his or her score, with the lowest score (the fewest strokes) winning. In match play, two players face off against each other at each hole. The player who gets the ball into the hole with the fewest strokes wins that hole, and the player who wins the most holes on the course wins the game.

Significance

In the first decade of the 1900s, golf was still dominated by British players. While touring the U.S. for the A.G. Spalding company, unsuccessfully promoting a ball named for him, the well known British player Harry Vardon increased interest in the game in the United States. The game was also helped along when Coburn Haskell developed the rubber core ball in 1898, although his patent was not held valid in the United Kingdom. In 1900, John Gammeter invented and patented a mechanism to mechanically wind the elastic around the rubber core and allow for economical mass production of rubber core golf balls. These balls, along with the wide variety of clubs players carried, reduced the skill needed to play golf, changed players' strategies, improved their scores, and altered course designs.

One of the few highly competitive games available to women in this era (along with tennis), the game of golf also began to produce American stars. Beatrix Hoyt won three consecutive amateur titles from 1896 to 1898. Walter Travis, though native to Australia, immigrated to the United States in 1885, and started playing golf when he was thirty-five years old. He won the U.S. amateur title in 1900 and 1901, and again in 1903. Another American, native born Jerome Travers, would become a golf star beginning at age seventeen in 1904. Travers and Travis's friendly but fierce rivalry attracted numerous individuals to golf in the United States and hinted at the potential for American domination of the sport that would come later in the century.

Primary Source

"Travers Defeats Travis in Fine Golf" [excerpt]

SYNOPSIS: The article below states that Jerome Travers will play against Max Behr to determine the U.S. Champion, as Travers has defeated Walter Travis. It explains that even though the Travers-Travis match-up was only a semi-final game, many members of the crowd considered it really to be the championship game. There follows a detailed account of the match, including some of each player's finest shots.

Travers Defeats Travis in Fine Golf

National Title Holder Wins Great Match for Amateur Championship.

Behr Beats Herreshoff

Big and Enthusiastic Gallery Follows Splendid Matches in Semi-Finals on the Garden City Courses.

Jerome D. Travers, the present National title holder in amateur golf, and Max Behr will play the concluding thirty-six hole round to-day at Garden City to determine the championship of the United States for the coming year. Travers is a trifle younger than his opponent, while Behr is a Yale student. Both are typical representatives of the best there is in golf and among the younger players of note they stand at the top. By defeating the veteran Walter J. Travis by two holes in one of the grandest golf contests ever seen in America the superiority of the young chaps over the old-timers seems to be well sustained. With the exception of Travis, all of the three semi-finalists were of the younger set, as Ferderick Herreshoff, who was beaten by Behr on the thirty-seventh hole, this concluding an exceptionally noteworthy day in a National championship, is still to go to college. Travers is a strong favorite to retain the title. Behr actually played the game of his life and his victory over Herreshoff was a general surprise.

It was easy to see in the size of and the keen interest in the crowd that the Travers-Travis match was universally regarded as the deciding championship round. More than fifteen hundred persons witnessed the play, and they were rewarded by golf of marked brilliancy, rare steadiness, with a succession of exciting features that will make the game go down in history as one of the greatest contests ever seen in this country.

More than a score of automobiles followed the players from green to green watching the play from the sandy roadway. President Daniel Chauncey and his committee, however, had little difficulty in controlling the crowd. Among those in the gallery were Miss Gladys Mills, Miss Beatrix Mills, Mrs. William A. Manice, a former metropolitan woman champion; Mrs. Arthur Brooks, Judge Gildersleeve, Judge Horace Russell, John Reid, the father of American golf; Col. George Harvey, Capt. Cook, who came up from Vicksburg to witness the championship; L. H. Graham, Louis Larocque, Findlay Douglas, John M. Ward, R. C. Watson, and Alex Smith.

The closeness of the morning eighteen rounds simply whetted the appetite of the increased afternoon crowd for the concluding half of the day's play. Travis led Travers by one hole and Behr finished one up on Herreshoff. Both Travers and Travis played the morning round in 76, and Travers did 77 in the afternoon. Travers usually got the longer drives but in putting Travis has never done better than a thirty-foot put that Travis ran down on the tenth green, winning the hole, plainly disconcerting the champion, but he got, as he remarked to a friend, a "nerve restorer" on the twelfth hole, when Travis made his only poor put of the day, missing an easy one of three feet to halve.

Beginning the morning play, the first five holes were halved in one under par golf, Travis missing a

"Travis Explains New Golfing Code: Says That Changes in Rules Imply a Decided Improvement in the Game"

In golfing circles it is but natural that the new code of rules which will go into effect with the new year has attracted widespread attention, for while there are no radical changes, a number of important amendments have been made to the old formula with which it will be absolutely necessary for golfers to be familiar. Some criticisms have been made to certain of the changes abroad, but the general consensus of opinion is that what changes have been authorized will make for the better conduct and appreciation of the game. The United States Golf Association, which sent a carefully prepared draft of recommendations last Spring to the Rules Committee of the Royal and Ancient Club of St. Andrews, Scotland will formally adopt the new code at its annual meeting early in January, and there is not the slightest indication that a single objection will be made to any portion of the accepted code.

Walter J. Travis, who has made as close a study of the technicalities of golf as any one in this country, has issued a unqualified indorsement of the new code, and as editor of The American Golfer, he says, in the current number:

"The new rules, as a whole, will be hailed with delight and universal approve by all loyal supporters and true lovers of the royal and ancient game, and their thanks will go forth not only to the Rules of Golf Committee of St. Andrews, but also to the present officials of the United States Golf Association, which organization for the first time in its history has been officially recognized and represented in the councils of the governing body. No one, in going carefully over the new rules, can fail to be profoundly impressed with the prodigious amount of thoughtful care bestowed on their compilation."

In dealing with some of the changes in detail, Mr. Travis says that they must be frankly admitted as distinctly in the line of improvements over the formal code. Railways and fences will no longer be regarded as hazards, but permanent grass within a hazard is to be considered part of the hazard. This omission in the old rules, says Mr. Travis, read in conjunction with the new rule simply means that at present when a ball is in a hazard, whether it be on grass or not, the club shall not be so led under penalty of the loss of the hole, implying that now all hazards must be carefully defined.

Mr. Travis approves heartily of the change which prevents a golfer from using the back of his hand to smooth down the line of his put. Commenting on this, he says:

"Loose impediments may be lifted from the putting green and dung. Worm casts, snow, and ice may be lightly scraped aside with a club, but otherwise the line of put must not be touched. Brushing with the hand means the loss of the hole. A very important change, and most excellent one."

"It is gratifying to note," adds Mr. Travis, "the reinstatement of the rule of etiquette in the regular code and also the addition of several desirable features including the duties of players looking for a lost ball. In this connection it will be observed that the section has been amplified which stipulates that player looking for a lost ball should allow other matches coming up to pass them; they should signal to the players following them to pass, and having given such signal they should not continue their play until these players have passed and are out of reach."

Other important alterations are: No one shall stand to mark the line of play through the green or from a hazard. Penalty, loss of the hole.

It is no longer necessary to drop a ball from the head. Face the hole, stand erect, and drop behind, over the shoulder.

Under no circumstances shall a practice swing be taken anywhere, except or the tee, when the ball is not in play, under penalty of loss of the hole.

Casual water on a putting green is now practically non-existent. When a ball is on a green a clear put to the hole is permissible, free from intervening water.

On the much mooted question as to whether stymies shall be played or not Mr. Travis says:

"Stymies form an integral part of the code, and, therefore, should be played. They are defensible on the ground that they are capable of being negotiated by the exercise of the lightest degree of skill. In match play competition. It is absolutely essential that all contestants should be compelled to play stymies, otherwise great injustice may be worked. The new rules make their playing compulsory under penalty of disqualification."

SOURCE: *The New York Times,* December 6, 1908, S3.

fifteen-foot put to win the first after a sliced drive. Perfect play gave the champion the sixth, Travis being bunkered twice and picking up. He won the next, tying the match, and took the ninth, Travers flubbing his approach, his first actually bad shot. This left Travis 1 up at the turn, but honors were squared at the eleventh, when Travis sliced his second in the bunker near the green, and took three puts, the only time he required more than two. The champion made one of the grandest approaches of the day at the thirteenth, landing on the green, 513 yards, in two, and won in 4 to 5, but Travis captured the next by a magnificent three, his ball being dead to the hole, 339 yards in two. Travers missed a put to halve the sixteenth hole, leaving Travis 1 up, and the last two were halved.

The first three holes in the afternoon were halved, Travis making long puts from 20 to 30 feet dead to the hole in each case. Travers won the fourth in a fine five, tying the game, and when he won the sixth the boy was 1 up. Travers lost the next, driving into the rough grass, but although Travis got in the sand he recovered finely. Travers made one of his finest puts on the eighth, running down from 15 feet for a half, and he won the ninth in three, 295 yards, laying his ball dead in two.

Beginning the homeward journey, Travis showed that his putting streak was still with him by running down a thirty-foot put, and when he captured the next the veteran was ahead. On this hole Travers got a miserable lie in high grass to the right of the green and missed his first stroke to get out. The short twelfth was one of the critical holes of the match. Travers was on the green from the tee, but his put was obstructed by the edge of the mound on the green. Travis also had a hob-back formation to put over. Travers overputted ten feet, while Travers ran up within three feet. Amid breathless silence the champion putted, and when his ball ran down the enthusiasm was expressed by loud clapping. Travis was evidently disconcerted at this for he missed, and losing the hole left honors even again. Travers made an unusually short drive to the next and then fell into the sand pit near the green, the veteran winning handily in 5, and the latter won the next, Travers driving into a sand bunker and, striking at his ball irritably, missed getting out, and had to take another.

There were only four more holes to go and things looked dubious for the champion, as he was two down. Few persons in the crowd would have believed that he could win the next four holes, but he did it in fine style. He had good luck on the fifteenth, for from a long approach his ball grazed a man's shoulder near the green and bounded off to the far edge, preventing a long roll into high grass. Travis was troubled by sand bunkers at the next. Both made beautiful drives at the seventeenth, Travis, from a long put, just missed going down by an inch and Travers won in 4 to 5, being one up with one more to go. Travers made a glorious drive over the pond, landing fifteen feet from the hole. Travis, driving for the lower end of the green, fell into the deep sand pit and, after playing two to get out, gave up the hole and the match.

Further Resources

BOOKS

Barkow, Al. *The Golden Era of Golf: How America Rose to Dominate the Old Scots Game.* New York: St. Martin's Press, 2000.

Labbance, Bob. *The Old Man: The Biography of Walter J. Travis.* Chelsea, Mich.: Sleeping Bear Press, 2000.

McCord, Robert R. *Golf: An Album of Its History.* Short Hills, N.J.: Burford, 1998.

Peper, George, et al., eds. *Golf in America, The First One Hundred Years.* New York: Abrams, 1988.

Wind, Herbert Warren. *The Story of American Golf, Its Champions and Its Championships.* New York: Knopf, 1975.

WEBSITES

"U.S. Open History." Available online at http://www.usopen.com/history; website home page: http://www.usopen.com (accessed March 17, 2003).

"Dorando Defeats Hayes in Marathon"

Newspaper article

By: *The New York Times*

Date: March 16, 1909

Source: "Dorando Defeats Hayes in Marathon." *The New York Times,* March 16, 1909, 7.

About the Publication: Founded in 1850 as the *Daily Times, The New York Times* was originally a relatively obscure local paper. By the early part of the twentieth century, it had grown into a widely known, well respected news source. Its banner, "All the News That's Fit to Print" is recognized across the United States and throughout the world. ■

Introduction

In the first decade of the 1900s, marathon racing was still a new form of endurance competition. Encouraged by national pride and the donation of a gold cup for the winner from French classicist and historian Michel Breal, the Organizing Committee of the Athens Olympics introduced the twenty-six mile race at the 1896 Olympics. Although ancient Olympians only raced about three miles at the most, the marathon was designed to celebrate the run of Pheidippides, the Greek soldier who, in 490 B.C.E., ran forty kilometers (about twenty-six miles) from Marathon to Athens to proclaim that the Greeks had defeated the Persians—and then dropped dead from the exertion.

After the Olympic marathon, other countries began holding marathons of their own, to prepare runners to enter future Olympic marathons. In the United States, the first-ever marathon was held in New York City on September 20, 1896. However, several members of the U.S.

CAN DORANDO BEAT HAYES? THE FAMOUS OLYMPIC RA... TO BE RE-RUN
AMERICA vs. ITALY
MARATHON
Match Race, 26 Miles, 385 Yards
HAYES VS. DORANDO
MADISON SQUARE GARDEN
THANKSGIVING EVE., NOV. 25
RACE STARTS 9 P. M.
Garden Box-Office Opens For Sale of Seats Friday, November 20, at 9 A. M.
PUO' DORANDO VINGERE HAYES? La FAMOSA OLYMPIA CORSA SARA' RIAPERTA

A poster advertises the return-race between Hayes and the Italian, Dorando Pietri, at Madison Square Garden, New York on November 25, 1908. © DAVID LEES/CORBIS. REPRODUCED BY PERMISSION.

Olympic Team were from the Boston Athletic Association, and so that city held its own marathon the following spring. The race was so popular that it became an annual event attracting runners from as far away as Canada. In 1906, Timothy Ford, a last-minute entrant whom many took for a joke because of his dress and attitude, won the race by six seconds. The marathon of the 1904 St. Louis Olympics further encouraged the race's growth, but it was the rivalry of the 1908 Olympics between Italian Dorando Pietri and Irish American John J. Hayes that assured the marathon its status as a professional sport in the United States.

Significance

The 1908 marathon, like that year's entire Olympic Games held in London, was plagued by controversy. First, the United States protested that a Canadian marathon runner was actually a professional, and therefore ineligible to run. The Canadian government, and ultimately Olympic officials, supported runner Longboat's claim to amateur status. However, this minor political scuffle was forgotten in the fervor of controversy that surrounded the race's results.

British runners started the race by running too fast and, tiring, fell back behind other runners. Italian Dorando Pietri maintained a competitive position from the beginning of the race, but Jack Hayes, after starting conservatively, saved his energy for the end of the race. By the time Pietri entered the London stadium to begin the final lap, he was in a state of near collapse. In this condition, he was additionally hampered by a change in elevation from level to downhill, a wildly cheering crowd, and the race's having been extended an additional 385 yards so that it would end directly opposite Queen Alexandra's royal box. He turned the wrong way inside the stadium and had to be corrected by officials. He then collapsed just past the twenty-six-mile mark and was helped to his feet by doctors and attendants. Four more times he fell, and when he finally reached the finish line, he collapsed once more and was removed from the stadium. The Americans argued he was carried across the finish line, and even the biased British judges couldn't deny that they had caught Pietri as he fell at the tape.

By contrast, Hayes's initial conservative pace allowed him to complete the last four hundred yards of the race behind Pietri without any collapses or assistance. In spite of the finish-line assistance Pietri had received, which was strictly against marathon rules, the British declared him the winner over Hayes. However, the International Olympic Committee supported an American protest of Pietri's victory, and Hayes was awarded the gold medal. Hayes's win, although not officially disputed, was certainly controversial.

Thus, the Madison Square Marathon, held the day before Thanksgiving in 1908, was widely considered a rematch between the two popular runners. New York's marathon enthusiasts rooted heavily for Jack Hayes, although Pietri had a large following as well. Pietri went on to defeat Hayes, which he insisted proved he could have beaten the American in London without intervention. He beat Hayes again the following March, lending support to his argument.

Primary Source

"Dorando Defeats Hayes in Marathon"

SYNOPSIS: The article notes the following for both John Hayes and Dorando Pietri at the 1909 Madison Square race. It provides details of the contest and leaves no doubt that Pietri was the more capable runner, although Hayes was the crowd favorite.

Dorando Defeats Hayes in Marathon

Italian Runner Leads American All the Way at Madison Square Garden.

Victor Shows Good Form

Breaks Records in Early Miles and Gains Two Laps in Eighteenth, After Which He Reduces His Speed.

Leader and Time for Each Mile

Miles Leader	H.M.S.	*Previous Race
1—Dorando	5:06	5:27
2—Dorando	10:42	11:18 1–5
3—Dorando	16:20	17:14 4–5
4—Dorando	22:00	23:17 3–5
5—Dorando	27:38	29:24 1–5
6—Dorando	33:24	35:22 3–5
7—Dorando	39:02	41:32 1–5
8—Dorando	44:55	47:41 4–5
9—Dorando	50:49	53:48 1–5
10—Dorando	56:46	1:00:06 1–5
11—Dorando	1:02:41	1:06:14 2–5
12—Dorando	1:08:41	1:12:29 4–5
13—Dorando	1:14:45	1:18:51 1–5
14—Dorando	1:20:54	1:25:21 4–5
15—Dorando	1:27:05	1:31:43 3–5
16—Dorando	1:33:04	1:35:07 3–5
17—Dorando	1:39:22	1:44:39 1–5
18—Dorando	1:45:53	1:50:12
19—Dorando	1:53:07	1:57:46 1–5
20—Dorando	2:00:33	2:04:23 4–5
21—Dorando	2:08:15	2:10:55 1–5
22—Dorando	2:16:08	2:17:35 2–5
23—Dorando	2:23:58	2:23:55
24—Dorando	2:31:42	2:30:31
25—Dorando	2:40:17	2:36:57 1–5
26—† Dorando	2:48:08	2:44:20 2–5

*Time for each mile in Dorando-Hayes race held Nov. 25, 1908.
†Twenty-six miles and 385 yards.

More than eight thousand persons saw Dorando Pietri, the Italian Marathon runner, defeat "Johnny" Hayes in their second professional Marathon contest in Madison Square Garden last night. Dorando ran a fast and easy race throughout and led at every mile. He finished in excellent condition, while Hayes, who showed visible evidences of distress in the last three miles, stopped in the sixth lap of the twenty-sixth mile. Dorando finished with an excellent burst of speed that elicited cheer upon cheer from the throng. The Italian colony was unusually well represented, and Dorando's victory was greeted with salvos of applause, the waving of scores of small Italian flags, and other manifestations of joyous enthusiasm. Dorando finished the twenty-sixth mile five laps in the lead.

For fifteen miles the men ran close together, Hayes occasionally trying to wrest the lead from his rival, and in the thirteenth mile he succeeded in holding the lead for one lap, but that was the best he could do, and even then he was barely three feet in front. Dorando was content with a lead of from three to four feet until 13½ miles had been covered, when he suddenly started off at a lively pace, and before completing a mile he gained a lap. He gained his second lap a little later, and then maintained the slow pace set by Hayes, trailing the Irish-American until the twenty-fifth mile, when Dorando set out to finish the race. Hayes was in bad shape. His left leg had been bothering him for some time. Dorando, on the other hand, appeared fully as fresh as at the start, and he frequently turned to his friends in the boxes to wave his hand or reply to their questions.

Hayes was utterly unable to keep up with Dorando when the latter let himself out. When Dorando started out to make a whirlwind finish, the final spark of physical endurance remaining in Hayes simmered out, and, with the crowd cheering Dorando to the echo, the little Irish-American gave up the struggle.

It was Hayes's second defeat by the Italian in the Garden, the first time being last November at the opening of the long series of professional Marathon races in this country. In three of these

Dorando Pietro is assisted across the finish line in the 1908 Olympic marathon in London. Pietri was first past the post after taking a wrong turn and receiving medical attention for a fall. He was disqualified for being helped across the line. © HULTON-DEUTSCH COLLECTION/CORBIS. REPRODUCED BY PERMISSION.

long distance races (twenty-six miles 385 yards,) therefore, in which these men have been rivals the Italian has triumphed twice.

The defeat of Hayes was a bitter disappointment to the American sportsmen, as Hayes had been training hard for this race, and it was confidently believed by hundreds of his friends that he would repeat his victory of the London Marathon.

As it was the third meeting of these redoubtable Marathon contestants and represented their "rubber" competition, interest in the outcome was naturally keen. Each man had plenty of supporters, but the majority sentiment was clearly with the little Irish-American, and he was the recipient of a wild outburst of cheers when he appeared on the track shortly after 9 o'clock.

Both men were in prime condition, Hayes being in far better physical condition for a hard race than on his initial appearance in the Garden, when, despite the fact that he was beaten, he finished the contest, being, in this respect, the only defeated professional to finish a dual Marathon event this season.

Early in the evening it was clearly demonstrated around Madison Square Garden that Marathon racing between two popular runners, possessing at the same time reputation, still holds a firm grip upon a large proportion of New York's sport-loving pub-

"Runner Dorando Here: Italian Athletes Say He will Beat Hayes on Thanksgiving Eve"

Dorando Pietri, the Italian long-distance runner, arrived in New York yesterday on the Kronprinzessin Cecilie of the North German Lloyd Line. Dorando was defeated by John J. Hayes of the Irish-American Athletic Club in the Olympic Marathon race, and is matched to meet Hayes in a race at the same distance at Madison Square Garden on Thanksgiving Eve. He is accompanied by his brother Ulpiano, who acts as his interpreter.

The Italians were received by deputations from the numerous societies in this city representing their native land and frantically embraced. On behalf of the Italian newspaper Il Progreso, it was stated that Dorando would get a silver cup and a purse containing $200 if he succeeded in defeating Hayes at Madison Square Garden next week.

Dorando, who is about the same size as Hayes, says he is confident of turning tables on the American. He declares that while he was tired out and dazed at the end of the Olympic race in England, he would have been able to cross the line unaided and declared the winner of the race, but the interference of officials caused his disqualification. In discussing the coming race he said:

> I am confident that I will beat Hayes when we meet again. He won the Marathon Race through the unwarranted interference of the British Olympic officials, and if they had let me get up myself I would have crossed the line first. I have not competed in a race since meeting Hayes, but my wind is good, and it will not take me very long to get into the best possible condition. I did no training on the steamship, as the sea was very rough and made me seasick.
>
> I have been beaten but twice in my career. I have won thirty events and broken several world's records in Paris, where I ran ten kilometers in two and a half hours. The report that I had broken my ankle is entirely without foundation. My brother fell and scratched his leg, and this was the basis of the report.

SOURCE: *The New York Times,* November 18, 1908, 7.

lic. There was a big throng clamoring for admission at the Madison Avenue entrance as early as 6 o'-clock, and when the doors were opened, about one and one-half hours later, a mad scramble set in for the upper galleries. Within half an hour standing room was at a premium in the "sky" gallery. The second gallery was filled soon after 8, and before 9 o'clock the boxes and arena seats presented almost as crowded appearance as in the first Dorando-Hayes race, Nov. 25. The rail within the main floor inclosure was lined five and six deep with young enthusiasts, most of them acknowledged rooters for little "Johnny" Hayes. The boxes contained a large proportion of women, and the big band kept the vast interior reverberating with patriotic melodies, contributing thereby to the good humor of the crowd. When the race started, at 9:22 o'clock, more than 6,000 persons were in the Garden, and the number was steadily augmented during the next hour.

Sheriff Tom Foley started the race, and at the crack of the pistol both men dashed off at a rattling good pace.

Further Resources

BOOKS

Benyo, Richard. *The Masters of the Marathon.* New York: Atheneum, 1983.

Cooper, Pamela. *The American Marathon.* Syracuse, N.Y.: Syracuse University Press, 1998.

Martin, David E. *The Marathon Footrace: Performers and Performances.* Springfield, Ill: Thomas, 1979.

Martin, David E., and Roger W. H. Gynn. *The Olympic Marathon.* Champagne, Ill: Human Kinetics, 2000.

Treadwell, Sandy. *The World of Marathons.* New York: Stewart, Tabori & Chang, 1987.

WEBSITES

"Boston Marathon Scrapbook: 1907 Boston Marathon." Community Newspaper Company. Available online at http://www.townonline.com/marathon/history/hist1907.htm; website home page: http://www.townonline.com/marathon (accessed March 18, 2003).

"Why Sir Thomas Lipton Has So Much Trouble Challenging for the Cup"

Newspaper article

By: Charles P. Tower

Date: October 31, 1909

Source: Tower, Charles P. "Why Sir Thomas Lipton Has So Much Trouble Challenging for the Cup." *The New York Times,* October 31, 1909, S3.

About the Author: Charles Putnam Tower (1854?–1919) was an avid boater and secretary of the Yacht Racing Association of Long Island Sound. He contributed frequent articles about boating and yacht racing to *The New York Times* in the 1900s and 1910s. In 1905 he helped found the Motor Boat Club of America and served as its temporary chairman. ■

Introduction

Like golfing, yachting was a sport for the rich man in the early twentieth century. Only those with the leisure time and money for the sport could afford to participate. Indeed, the costly yachts used in races were often no good for pleasure sailing, having no room for crew or passengers. The sport was popular worldwide before developing a following in the United States. John Cox Stephens began the first U.S. Yachting club in 1844.

In 1851, England's Prince Albert hosted a Royal Yacht Squadron Regatta, and an American team came across the ocean to compete, bringing along their boat, the *America.* Competing against fifteen British racing yachts, the Americans won the regatta. The silver cup they won, called the Hundred Guinea Cup by the British and the "America's Cup" by its winners, became the symbol of yachting challenge when the last surviving member of the syndicate that owned the *America* donated the winning cup to the New York Yachting club. His "Deed of Gift" specified several rules, among them that the challengers were required to reveal the length of their boats at the waterline, so that the defending champions would always know what they were up against.

Although in the early 2000s the Cup is held every three or four years, it was originally held only when there was a challenge, which meant that between 1851 and 1870, there was no America's Cup race, and from 1870 to 1900, the race was held ten times, with anywhere from one to six years between races. The America's Cup is the oldest international sporting event. The country that wins the America's Cup keeps it and hosts the next race For 132 years, from 1851 to 1983, the winning country was the United States.

Significance

Between 1899 and 1930, Sir Thomas Lipton, tea baron, challenged for the America's Cup five times. After losing the race in 1899, Lipton made two attempts for the Cup in the 1900s, in 1901 and in 1903. The 1903 race, in particular, resulted in some drastic changes in yachting rules.

Lipton's yachts were all named *Shamrock,* and in 1903, *Shamrock III* was defeated by an unwieldy American craft called the *Reliance.* The *Reliance* was what was

Raced against Sir Thomas Lipton, *Reliance,* dubbed a "freak" boat, won the 1903 America's cup.

known among yachting enthusiasts as a "freak" boat because its design was such that, although excellent for racing, it was otherwise unseaworthy, and was not likely to hold up in even moderately bad weather. The 1903 race specified a ninety-foot maximum length at the waterline, and *Reliance* was eighty-nine feet, eight inches long. But when the boat heeled (tilted in the wind), its overhangings submerged, giving her an overall length of 144 feet and a huge advantage over the British challenger. *Reliance* was so unseaworthy that two months after successfully defending the cup, the boat was broken up for scrap.

Because of the *Reliance* and other boats like it that took increasingly greater risks in order to skirt the race's rules, the New York Yachting club developed a new rule, called the "universal rule," which penalized some of the features that were the *Reliance's* chief advantages. However, this rule was not applied to the America's Cup. Sir Thomas Lipton objected to the New York Yachting Club's using the old rule for the America's Cup. He believed the universal rule would have given him the chance to win in both 1901 and 1903, and so was reluctant to challenge until the America's Cup race fell under that rule. In the end, he issued his challenge under the old rule, but the committee both accepted his challenge and agreed to apply the universal rule in 1913. However, due to the outbreak of World War I (1914–1918), the first

America's Cup using the universal rule did not take place until 1920.

Primary Source

"Why Sir Thomas Lipton Has So Much Trouble Challenging for the Cup"

SYNOPSIS: Charles P. Tower writes this article in an effort to justify the New York Yachting Club's singular refusal to apply the universal rule to the America's Cup. He explains the differences between the universal and old (Seawanhaka) rules, defines a "freak boat," and insists that the *Reliance* could cross the Atlantic and be ready to race.

Trying for the America's Cup as Simple as Rolling Off a Log When You Know How—Two Real Sharps Discuss This Interesting Proposition.

"Why doesn't the New York Yacht Club allow Sir Thomas Lipton to race for the America's Cup if he wants to?"

"Why should the club have two sets of rules, one for its ordinary racing and one for the America's Cup?"

"What is the difference between the two sets of rules?"

"What is the universal rule?"

"Why does Sir Thomas have to build a heavy boat, while we can build a light racing freak?"

"What is a freak boat, anyway?"

"Why doesn't the club give this Irishman a fair show?"

These are a few—only a very few—of the questions asked by people who don't know a bobstay from a boom crotch; who don't care a straw about yachting from one cup race to another, but who are fired up to the main touch with enthusiasm at the first suggestion of the possibility of a challenge for the America's Cup, and who get erroneous ideas from reading interviews with Sir Thomas or his friends, written by conscientious reporters who are doing the best they know, but who do not happen to be expert on the subject of the America's Cup

It may as well be said right here that the New York Yacht Club has never yet declined a challenge that has been made in proper form. The deed of gift stipulates that the challenger shall give the dimensions of his boat. The reason for this should be obvious to any one who engages in a contest of any sort. The club holding the cup is entitled to know "what it is up against." The dimensions required are load water line length, beam at the water line, extreme beam, and draught. But the New York Yacht Club has time and again waived all these, excepting load water line, because of the plea of intending challengers that to give all these dimensions would "give away" their boats in too great a degree. So the New York Yacht Club has said, "Give us your load water line length only, and let it go at that." In his challenge of two years ago—because of the rejection of which the New York Yacht Club has incurred more or less criticism—Lipton did not give the load water line length of his boat. He challenged for a race with a boat of the sixty-eight-foot class, as described in the so-called universal rule. Now the fact is that under that rule naval architects have so much liberty of action in the treatment of length, sail area, and displacement that boats of that class, rating close to the maximum, too, turned out by different designers, might vary anywhere from five to ten feet in length. Therefore Sir Thomas evaded the one thing stipulated in the deed of gift, which the club has always, and very properly, insisted on securing in a challenge. Incidentally the club expressed a preference for a race with boats of the maximum length—ninety feet on the water line—but that was not binding, inasmuch as the deed of gift specifically allows a challenge with a sloop of sixty-five feet L. W. L.

Now, as to the universal rule, and the manner in which it differs from any other. And, by the way, the term is a misnomer. The so-called "universal rule" of rating is simply a rule framed by a conference of delegates representing all the important yacht clubs and yacht-racing organizations on the Atlantic Coast between Marblehead and Philadelphia, called together by the New York Yacht Club. This rule was recommended to the clubs and yacht-racing associations, and was adopted by most of them, and especially by those in and around Massachusetts waters, Long Island Sound, Gravesend Bay, and Delaware River. In some part, too, if not all, the rule is in force on at least a part of the Great Lakes, but not all. But one has to go no further away from New York than Yonkers or the south shore of Long Island to find yacht clubs which know not the "universal rule," and which race under the old "Seawanhaka" rule or some slight modification of it. And it is the same Seawanhaka rule—so called because it was originated for the Seawanhaka-Corinthian Yacht Club, under which all cup challengers and defenders in recent years have been measured for the purpose of calculating time allowance. Under this rule the racing length of a yacht was ascertained by adding the square root, in feet, of her sail area to her load water line length, and dividing the sum by two. For example, the racing length of a yacht of 90 feet on the water line, carrying 16,000 square feet of sail, would be 126.5 (approximately the square root of 16,000) plus 90, her water-line length, making 216.5; divided by two, resulting in 108.25. And time allowance would be figured from a table made up on the principle that, other things being equal, the opportunities for speed of two boats vary as to the square roots of their water-line length, the principle being modified to such extent as to assume that "racing length," as above explained, was a more nearly accurate factor than water-line length.

That "freaks" were ultimately developed under this rule any boy that has sailed a boat will tell you. In a cynical way, a "freak" may be described as the other fellow's boat that goes faster than your own. Also, it may be said that the "freak" of three or four years ago is considered an old tub to-day. Nevertheless, the naval architects went to great excess, under the rule, in building boats of light displacement—meaning by that boats of lean body, with little room below decks, and with scow bows, so fashioned that when a boat was heeled over in sailing she had a longer side to sail on than could be had in a boat of ordinary form, with the sides at the water line forward coming together gradually. The designers went to extreme limits in the way of draught as well. Now you can build a strong boat of that kind, but it's expensive construction. Moreover, such a boat is not of the best for offshore sailing, and is not good for cruising, because of lack of accommodations. It is really fit only for racing. Wherefore—if it isn't your boat—it is a freak.

Now, where does all this come in, with regard to Sir Thomas Lipton's proposed challenge? Just here. Reliance, by the record, is the fastest sailing yacht ever built. Reliance was built under the old rule. Reliance, according to Sir Thomas, is a "light racing freak." Reliance, according to her admirers, is the strongest, as well as the fastest, boat ever built, and there is some reason for the contention, for N. G. Herreshoff, her designer, is a wizard as a constructing engineer simply. Doubtless she could cross the Atlantic and turn up ready for racing. But Sir Thomas confesses his inability to build a boat of the Reliance sort, bring her across, and stand a show of winning. Likewise, if Reliance were to be rated for time allowance under the present rule of measurement, she would have to give so much time allowance to a boat of ninety feet water line built under that rule that she would have no chance of winning. Why? Because such a boat would have "sharper ends" and would suffer no penalty for quarter beam length, while Reliance would be penalized heavily for excess of quarter beam length. Moreover, the new boat might have greater displacement, and probably would. Sir Thomas will take a chance against a new boat, built under the present rule, but he doesn't want to meet Reliance again unless she is rated for time allowance under that rule.

Yachting Glossary

BEAM: A boat's width.

BOOM: A pole known as a spar that juts out horizontally from the mast and holds the base of the mainsail.

KEEL: A lead filled bulb attached to the hull that increases the boat's stability.

DRAUGHT: Vertical distance from the waterline to the bottom of the keel.

HEEL: When the boat leans over due to wind pressure.

Further Resources

BOOKS

Conner, Dennis, and Michael Levitt. *The America's Cup: The History of Sailing's Greatest Competition in the Twentieth Century.* New York: St. Martin's, 1998.

Fisher, Bob. *Great Yacht Races.* New York: Stewart, Tarobi & Chang, 1984.

Phillips-Birt, Douglas Hextall Chedzey. *The History of Yachting.* New York: Stein and Day, 1974.

Whipple, Addison Beecher Colvin, et al. *The Racing Yachts.* Time-Life Books, 1980.

WEBSITES

"America's Cup Museum (1983): A History of the America's Cup." America's Cup Museum. Available online at http://acmuseum.com (accessed March 18, 2003).

"Cup History." The Official Site of the America's Cup. Available online at http://www.americascup.yahoo.com/section8.html; website home page: http://www.americascup.yahoo.com (accessed March 18, 2003).

"Walter Camp for More Open Football"

Newspaper article

By: *The New York Times*

Date: December 19, 1909

Source: "Walter Camp for More Open Football." *The New York Times,* December 19, 1909, S7.

About the Organization: Founded in 1850 as the *Daily Times, The New York Times* was originally a relatively obscure local paper. By the early part of the twentieth century, it had grown into a widely known, well respected news source. Its banner, "All the News That's Fit to Print," is recognized across the United States and throughout the world. ■

Introduction

Known as the father of American football, Walter Camp (1859–1925) was not only instrumental in significantly changing the game in the late nineteenth century, but had an additional impact in 1905 as a part of the rule-making meeting of the newly formed Intercollegiate Athletic Association of the United States (IAAUS), which would become the National Collegiate Athletic Association (NCAA) in 1910. Football in the first five years of the twentieth century was publicly perceived as a dangerously violent sport. Serious injuries were commonplace, and on many occasions young men died playing the game.

Camp's innovations in the nineteenth century helped improve the game, but did little to protect the players from each other. His changes at that time included reducing the number of players a team could have on the field from fifteen to ten, and setting the field's size at 110 yards. Camp introduced downs to the game in 1888, allowing players three downs to advance the ball five yards. The team with the ball would attempt to surge forward and force the other team aside en masse. These mass movements were one of the most dangerous elements of the game. Additionally, players wore little or no protective gear, and tackling below the waist was legalized in the latter part of the nineteenth century, increasing the sport's danger even more.

In 1905, President Roosevelt (served 1901–1909) called a meeting at the White House to discuss the game's problems with prominent coaches and an elite group of others from Ivy League schools. However, the changes that resulted from this meeting were minor.

Significance

Not satisfied with these ineffective changes, some more reform-minded individuals met to form the Intercollegiate Athletic Association of the United States (IAAUS), initially excluding the old-school members of the former rules committee such as Walter Camp. However, members of the old committee were invited to participate if they would agree to a more flexible stance on what changes could be made. Realizing the influential nature of this new organization, Camp encouraged members of the old committee to work with the new one and thus ultimately had some voice in the more radical changes that came from what would become the NCAA.

One of the greatest changes the NCAA introduced to the game was the forward pass. Camp disapproved of this move, but he was one of the first to demonstrate its effectiveness in game play. Previously, coaches had considered the forward pass a desperate move that was more likely to result in a turnover than in advancing the ball. Camp himself supported another change the NCAA endorsed: an increase in the number of yards to be gained from five to ten. The hope here was that such a change would reduce dependence upon mass moves. While the increase did not wholly eliminate such maneuvers, it did serve to somewhat decrease their deadly side effects.

Walter Camp would go on to be the secretary of the NCAA, a position he would hold for the rest of his life, and continue his participation in the sport's changes. For his entire life, Camp was committed to making football the best it could be. When he was forced to admit that the old-style rules were hampering rather than helping the game, he willingly assented to changes that would revolutionize football. Although the nature of the game was continuing to evolve in terms of strategy, many of the basic rules Camp helped to establish remain in place today in the early twenty-first century.

Primary Source

"Walter Camp for More Open Football"

SYNOPSIS: In this interview, Walter Camp discusses the value of critical input to playing football. He believes that critics who came to see the game played got a much better understanding of it and therefore were able to give better input. He argues for a game with more room for kicking, and he expresses concern over the sudden return to "mass plays" with weakened defense. A continuing theme of his remarks is his optimistic assessment of increased good sportsmanship.

Walter Camp for More Open Football

Would Like to See Game with More Opportunities for Kicking of Ball.

Manly Spirit of Players

Yale's Famous Expert Notes Increase of Sportsmanship and Good Feeling Among Opposing Contestants.

New Haven, Dec. 18.—That a very constantly growing spirit of sportsmanship is apparent in football and that this spirit will, with some necessary changes in the rules, aid in solving many of the existing problems of the gridiron, were two opinions expressed to-day by Walter Camp of Yale to a reporter for THE TIMES.

Along with this increase of sportsmanship and good feeling among opposing players, Mr. Camp said, there has never been a football season when the critics and opponents of the game have been so fair, tolerant, and openminded in their criticisms and denunciations. He said that those who had once been blindly set against football without ever having taken the time or the trouble to see a game had this year made careful personal investigations of actual conditions on the field. And as a consequence, he added, what they had to say was of far greater value than had ever before been the case.

Mr. Camp referred also to the marked tendency of the season just ended to give strategy precedence over mere strength. He pointed out that while the universities, colleges, and preparatory schools of the Central West had perhaps opened and diversified their game more than was the general rule in the East, still even in the East, where there had been a sudden return to mass plays, these were started from formations which made the progress of the ball far easier to watch than in any previous year.

Walter Camp, during his days as a Yale football player, circa 1879. **AP/WIDE WORLD PHOTOS. REPRODUCED BY PERMISSION.**

Lessons for Rules Committee.

Altogether, it was Mr. Camp's belief, that the fatalities of the year which were directly attributable to football were fecund with lessons for the intercollegiate Rules Committee, of which he is a member, to coaches, to players, and to public alike. He believed that all concerned would take due and proper heed from these sad accidents, and that, in so far as it was possible to rid any team game in which there was physical contact of its dangers, the constituted authorities would take every precaution to make the game a playable one.

"The spirit of football and its participants," Mr. Camp said, "was infinitely better and finer this year than it used to be. There was an almost total absence of the old charges of intentional injury to this player or that. That old way must either be rewritten or written out under the impetus of the new spirit. There has been evident all season an appreciably growing good fellowship on the gridiron, so that, once a game ended, the members of the erstwhile opposing elevens have fraternized, and this means that they had met on the highest plane of sportsmanship.

Clean Sportsmanship on Increase.

"For, naturally, there could have been no fraternizing after a hard game unless there had been clean playing all through it. The man does not live who can be friendly with an opponent who has employed foul tactics but a few hours before. The best enemies of dirty or illegal work were the fellow-players of the man guilty of it. The whole atmosphere was this year higher and finer than it has ever been before, and showed a steady improvement that bids fair to mark every succeeding season as more successful than the last.

"I saw numerous instances of this keen sportsmanship, both in the East and in the West. To cite two notable instances of it, because they recur readily to mind, let me refer to the manner in which little Bergen, the Princeton quarter back, stayed with our boys after the Princeton-Yale game. He stayed up here in New Haven, was with members of the Yale eleven against whom he had played the previous Saturday in a championship game. While he was here he was a visitor at Yale field, being admitted to practice and enjoying it keenly. We would have welcomed every other Princeton man that met us had it been his desire to stay up here.

"Out West I saw a great big guard, of massive build and the speed of an express train, do one of the nicest, cleanest things it has been my pleasure to witness on the gridiron for many a year. In a game whose winning or losing meant much to him he had been as careful of the bodies of his opponents as it is humanly possible to be in football.

How Western Guard Saved Opponent.

"In one play he put his opponent out of the way so that he could not interrupt the advance of the ball, but the man fell backward in rather awkward fashion and was apparently in considerable danger of being stepped on. Without an instant's hesitation after taking in the situation this big guard—it is needless to name him here—threw himself across the body of his vis-a-vis, covering him almost completely and forming such an arch over his body, temporarily out of balance, that no injury could possibly befall him.

"It is this sort of spirit which is growing and spreading very broadly among American universities and schools. It is the only kind of spirit which should exist, and the more its day of universal application is hastened, so much nearer is the day of the finest type of American manhood. Certainly the old feeling of hostility of one player for another has gone, and, regardless of on what teams they play, the men of the elevens of the present time are individual friends before, during, and after a game.

"In other words, we are having rivalry without bitterness, competition without unfairness, play without hostility, and sport without any accompaniment except a decent, earnest, proper, American desire to win cleanly and fairly. But we must lessen the liability to serious accident.

"There is another thing of which I have been very thoroughly convinced this year," Mr. Camp said. "The critics of football—or should I say its opponents?—have been much fairer and more temperate than they were five or six years ago."

"Do you attribute that to their better knowledge of the game?" he was asked.

"Yes, indeed," was Mr. Camp's reply, "but also to the fact that they have traveled around to see various teams play. They have taken their places along with other spectators at the big games and watched these contests in fair and open-mined manner. They have asked questions on points about which they freely admitted their ignorance, and did not assume an acquaintanceship with intricate phases of the sport, as they used to do.

Critics Know More About Game Now.

"They came, and they saw that, despite perhaps preconceived ideas, there was no intent on the part of one player to 'do up' another. They left, and they acknowledged that, while the game was perhaps dangerous, it was virile and manly. In place of the old attitude of bias there was honest criticism. And that is just what we need, just what we want, and just what every football player and lover should welcome."

"Just what phases of the game, Mr. Camp, do you think were developed most during the season just ended?"

"Well, the development of kicking and of catching kicks, the dispatch and recovery of forward passes, and, strange to relate for a season wherein the open game was most generally expected, a return to mass plays. These, starting from tandem formations, were usually directed at the tackle positions, so that even if the ball was carried into or through the line more frequently than was the case last season, the spectators had a much better opportunity to see its progress.

"The careful scrutiny of the season's records, after a close watching of the games themselves, points out the present need of the backs playing a considerable distance back of their line on defense to guard against the onside kick and the forward pass. As a direct result of this the tackles have been left without any support. And instructors were quick to take advantage of the opportunity thus afforded. Through feints of one sort or another they kept the defensive backs away from the defending forwards, and thereby made it easier to send plays through the line, particularly at tackle."

Mr. Camp Wants the Open Game.

"Does that signify that you are opposed to the open game, Mr. Camp?"

"Not at all," he replied. "I believe that the game should be opened even more than it has been, and there seems to be no doubt about the inadvisability of retaining some of the present rules. I should like to see a game with more kicking in it, or, should I say, more opportunities for kicking. At the present time a team hangs on to the ball as long as it can, preferring not to take any chances of the other eleven getting possession of it.

"Even if three out of four attempts with the forward pass are successful under the present rules the one use of it which fails may be so fraught with disaster as to counterbalance all the gains of the three successful attempts. I should like to see end running made more possible under American rules. And I think that then you would see a great deal of longer passing.

"As to the manner in which reforms may be consummated, as to just what changes there may be in the rules, you know as much as I do now. But neither you nor any other man can positively foresee the results of any changes so far as real play is concerned.

"Revision may be legislated, but only actual performances on the field in big games will determine whether or not the committee has been successful in accomplishing what it seeks to put through. In other words, we thought we had made the play open and safe enough before, and for two years it proved so. Now mass play has come back through the weakening of the defense. We will try again, and we will keep on trying, and that is the only way in the world of finding out just what can be done."

Further Resources

BOOKS

Nelson, David M. *The Anatomy of a Game: Football, the Rules, and the Men Who Made the Game.* Newark, N.J.: University of Delaware Press, 1994.

Powel, Harford, Jr. *Walter Camp: The Father of American Football: An Authorized Biography.* Boston: Little, Brown, 1926.

Valenzi, Kathleen D., and Michael W. Hopps. *Champion of Sport: The Life of Walter Camp, 1859–1925.* Charlottesville, Va.: Howell Press, 1990.

PERIODICALS

"Walter Camp and Grantland Rice."*Collier's* 74, no. 20, November 15, 1924, 29.

WEBSITES

"Walter Camp: The Father of American Football." Walter Camp Football Foundation. Available online at http://www.waltercamp.org (accessed March 18, 2003).

Fundamentals of Basketball

Handbook

By: James Naismith

Date: c. 1909

Source: Naismith, James. *Fundamentals of Basketball.* St. Louis, Mo.: Rawlings Manufacturing Co., c. 1909.

About the Author: James Naismith (1861–1939) was born in Almonte, Ontario, Canada. His parents died when he was eight, and he was raised by his uncle. While a student at the Y.M.C.A. training school in Springfield, Massachusetts, while also serving as its director of physical education, Naismith was assigned to invent a game to occupy athletes during the winter. The resulting game, basketball, became widely popular, but its originator was largely unrecognized until just a few years before his death. ■

Introduction

In the late nineteenth century, sports flourished primarily when they could be played outdoors. Thus, although spring, summer, and fall had baseball, lacrosse, soccer, and football, there was no widely enjoyable sport that could be played indoors in the winter, when outdoor sports were hampered by cold weather. Under instructions from Dr. Luther Gulick of the Y.M.C.A. training school in Springfield, Massachusetts, James Naismith developed the game of basketball in 1891 especially to fill this gap. Originally, the game was played with eighteen players (nine to each side) and used a soccer ball, together with peach baskets that were tacked to the bottom of a running track ten feet above the gymnasium floor.

By the early twentieth century, basketball had become increasingly popular, moving rapidly from its origins in Y.M.C.A.s to become a collegiate sport. In 1891, Springfield college students played the first college basketball game. In 1893, Senda Berenson introduced the game for women at Smith College. On January 18, 1896, the University of Chicago's basketball team defeated Iowa City's team in the first college basketball game played with five players to a side. Naismith introduced basketball to the University of Kansas in 1898 and coached its Jayhawks for the following nine years.

Significance

Naismith's original thirteen rules for the game have been revised significantly since their origin. Many of the revisions came early in the game's life. In addition to the size of teams shrinking from nine to five players, the bottoms were cut out of the peach baskets, speeding the play of the game. Originally, the game was played in two fifteen-minute halves with a five-minute break between them. Overall, the game has increased in length, even as its pace has quickened, and high school and professional games have evolved from two halves to four quarters. High school games have four eight-minute quarters, college games have two twenty-minute halves, and professional games utilize four twelve-minute quarters.

By the close of the nineteenth century, the real struggle in basketball was between those who wanted to keep the sport as one played by amateurs and others who wanted to use it to make profits. As the Amateur Athletic

James Naismith and the nine players of the Springfield College basketball team pose on the steps of their gymnasium in 1891. © BETTMANN/CORBIS. REPRODUCED BY PERMISSION.

Union (AAU) wrestled with schools and individual teams in attempts to stop them from using basketball for profit, various groups published their own versions of the rules, designed to distinguish themselves from the AAU. In this way, college and professional basketball emerged as separate entities, distinct both from each other and from the AAU teams.

Somewhere in all of this controversy about how the game ought to be played, basketball escaped the doom of so many "designed" games. While most invented games failed to gain much popularity or following, basketball took hold of the nation. Perhaps one of the most significant signs that basketball had come to stay was the sport's development of its own ball. Instead of the soccer ball of Naismith's first players, basketball players of the early twentieth century used a basketball designed especially for this newly popular sport. The Overman Wheel Company (a bicycle manufacturer) made the first basketball in 1894, just three years after the sport was invented. By the 1900s, their basketball was the official ball for tournament play, and other sports equipment companies such as Rawlings wanted to compete. Though professional basketball would, for years, lag behind its college counterpart in popularity, by the 1900s it was clear that America had its own indoor sport.

Primary Source

Fundamentals of Basketball [excerpt]

SYNOPSIS: In the first excerpt, Naismith discusses the attributes athletes develop by playing basketball. In the second, he explains the evolution of basketball and then promotes his sponsor in writing this booklet, the Rawlings Manufacturing Company.

Attributes Developed by Basketball

Basketball is not now, nor was it ever intended to be, a complete system of physical education. Its main purpose was recreation and development of certain factors that are particularly developed by games. It was intended primarily for young men who had acquired their physical development. Its place in a system of physical education is to develop certain factors that are not obtained by manual labor, or heavy work of any kind.

On account of the fact that it is intrinsically interesting it has, in many cases, been substituted for all other forms of motor activity. This is an error, especially with young boys, in a system of physical education.

Basketball has a place in a scheme of physical education, first, because it is attractive in itself, and second, because it develops certain attributes as well, if not better, than most other forms of physical activity. These attributes are mainly development of the nerve control of the individual rather than the development of brawn. Games have been called the laboratory for the development of ethical and moral attributes, and they may become such if properly conducted.

The Attributes That Can Be Best Developed by Basketball Are:

1. Agility, or the power of the body to put itself into any position with quickness, ease and accuracy. This is especially developed by the movements of the body to elude the opponent, keep the ball away from him, get into a position to make a pass, a shot, or a dribble.

2. Accuracy—Goals are made by passing a ten inch ball through an eighteen inch opening set at a right angle to the backboard, and ten feet in the air. In order to do this it is necessary to give the ball the right direction, the right elevation, to let go of the ball at the right time—all of which makes for extreme accuracy.

3. Alertness—In some games there may be a letting down of attention as no further activity occurs until a signal is given, but in basketball the attention must be in such a condition as to be ready to operate at any time. The ball travels about so fast that the player must be awake and ready to act at any time while the game is in progress.

4. Cooperation—In no other game is cooperation so necessary as there are only five players and each is dependent on the other players. Two players cooperating can always beat one, three can beat two, four can beat three, and if one does not cooperate, the team is one man short.

5. Initiative—In basketball it is impossible to plan what the next move is going to be, consequently the player must react to the conditions without time to make up his mind as to which is the best plan. When he meets an entirely new condition he cannot depend on the coach to tell him, but must meet the emergency until he has time to formulate a plan of procedure. I consider this one of the most valuable attributes, and the present dependence on the coach destroys this attribute.

6. Skill—In few games that are easy to learn is there need for so great an amount of skill. Skill is the ability to use the right muscle groups at the time when they are most needed, and in the proper sequence, and with the correct amount of force, and this with a moving team mate and against a moving opponent.

7. Reflex judgment—This is the ability to make the arms and legs do the right thing without a mental process to tell which of several things to do. The eye sees an open space towards which a team mate is running and the ball is passed in such a way that he is able to get it in the most favorable position to pass, shoot, or dribble. The Kansas University record for sight and touch reaction is held by basketball men. No prettier sight can be seen in athletics than one player touching the ball to another, who touches it to a third, who tosses it into the goal, the whole done quicker than the mind could possibly devise the play.

8. Speed—The ability to move the body from one location to another in the shortest time possible. Basketball is a series of sprints, rather than a continuous running. According to experiments made, a player is in action less than 40% of the actual playing time. But he must move at a maximum speed to get there before the other player. This entails quick starting, and rapid movement, with the body in perfect control, as he may need to change his course to avoid another player who comes at any angle into his path.

9. Self-confidence—Each player must be able to carry on by himself if necessary. There are times when he cannot depend on his team mates to do even the things that they are better qualified for than himself, but he must perform of himself. He must be, to the greatest extent possible, an all round performer.

10. Self-sacrifice—In basketball there is no place for the egotist or for the one who is not willing to let another have all the credit if that will further the game. The unit in basketball is the team, not the individual player, and the one who would try to get glory at the sacrifice of the game is a hindrance to the team. These two in their proper place, though apparently contradictory, depend on the judgment of the player as to which he will do.

11. Self-control—He must be able to subordinate his feelings to his reflexes as any interference will interrupt the proper performance of his skill and he will be unable to do his best work. The one who permits his feelings to interfere is not only a hindrance to his team, but he is occupying the place of another man who would do this. There are so few players on a team that one player not doing his best is a greater reduction in the relative strength of the team than in some games where the ratio is less.

12. Sportsmanship—On account of the proximity of the spectators to the players and the fact that they can observe not only every movement, but also every player, he must observe the rules of the game. The officials must be impartial and competent to retain the respect of the crowd, and to keep the game under control. The players have found out that it pays to observe the rules and accept the decision of the officials. . . .

The Evolution of the Ball

That there must be a ball of some kind was the first factor settled in making the game of basketball. All of the so-called team games have a ball of some kind, or something that takes the place of a ball. One of the requirements of the game we sought was that it should be easy to learn, so that men who had had little experience in athletics could get the benefit of the game. Most of the games played with a small ball require some kind of an intermediate apparatus, such as tennis, hockey, lacrosse, etc. This makes the game more difficult to learn. A large ball is handled by the hands and requires little practice to be able to begin playing. There were two large balls in use at that time. The Rugby football was large and oblate in form and especially adapted for carrying it in the arms, but was not so valuable when carrying the ball was prohibited. The Soccer ball was round and the same in all directions, and was more easily handled with the hands. It could be handled in any position and could be thrown, batted or bounced with greater accuracy. Consequently, it was chosen as the best adapted for the purpose.

The first rule book specified that "the ball shall be an ordinary Association football." The goals were then fifteen inches in diameter. The first change made in the ball was in 1895–96, where the rule reads: Rule II, Section 1. "The ball shall be round; it shall be made of a rubber bladder covered with a leather case; it shall be not less than 30, nor more than 32 inches in circumference."

Sec. 3. The ball made by the Overman Wheel Company shall be the official ball.

Sec. 4. The official ball must be used in all match games.

In 1897 another clause was added. Rule II, Section 1. The limit of variableness shall be not more than one-fourth of an inch in three diameters. It shall weigh not less than 18 nor more than 20 ounces.

Sec. 4. The official ball shall be used in all match games.

In 1903: Rule II, Sec. 4. The official ball must be used in all match games. The Referee may, in all match games, and shall, in all serial championships, declare all games void where this rule is violated.

Sec. 4. The official ball must be used in all league games and by all affiliated teams.

In the first issue of the Collegiate rules, 1905–06, this rule concerning the official ball is inserted as a footnote. From that time, the choice of the ball has been left in the hands of the conferences or teams. This has led to a marked improvement in the ball.

In 1909 the manufacturers maintained that a ball of the specified weight could not be made to stand the strain to which they were subjected and the weight of the ball was increased from 18–20 ounces to 20–23 ounces. Official size and weight of official balls are now as follows: Shall measure not less than 30, nor more than 31 inches in circumference and shall weigh not less than 20 nor more than 22 ounces.

Rawlings Official Balls Conform to These Rules

When the different makes of balls all met these requirements the makers began to introduce certain refinements. At first the quality of the material and the way in which it kept its shape were the main points of attention. Later refinements resulted in changes in the structure of the ball. The early balls were all made with the lacing and the stem valve on the same side of the ball, and this resulted in a lopsided ball, one side being heavier than the others. As the skill of the players increased and the competition became keener, there was an attempt to counterpoise the ball. This was effected mainly by the introduction of the outside valve inserted in the side opposite to the lacing, which divided the weight. It also made it easier to keep the ball inflated to the proper pressure, thus eliminating the element of chance which always favors the unskilled team. The weight of the lacing was reduced as much as possible and an approximation to balance was acquired. The latest achievement is found where the lacing is invisible and a true balance established, so that it rolls, bounces, or rests at any position.

The Rawlings No. AXL Official Concealed Lace Basketball, I believe, is a decided advance in basketball construction.

Further Resources

BOOKS

Anderson, Dave. *The Story of Basketball.* New York: Morrow, 1988.

Isaacs, Neil David. *All the Moves: A History of College Basketball.* Philadelphia: Lippincott, 1975.

McCallum, John Dennis. *College Basketball, U.S.A., since 1892.* New York: Stein and Day, 1978.

Webb, Bernice Lawson. *The Basketball Man: James Naismith.* Lawrence, Kans.: University Press of Kansas, 1973.

WEBSITES

"Dr. James Naismith." Dr. James Naismith Foundation. Available online at http://collections.ic.gc.ca/naismith (accessed May 13, 2003).

Naismith, James. "Dr. James Naismith's 13 Original Rules of Basketball." Available online at http://www.ncaa.org/champadmin/basketball/original_rules.html; website home page: http://www.ncaa.org (accessed May 13, 2003).

"How to Play Shortstop"

Essay

By: John "Honus" Wagner

Date: 1949

Source: Wagner, Honus. "How to Play Shortstop." *The Official Encyclopedia of Baseball.* New York: A.S. Barnes, 1976, 667–668. Condensed from Wagner, Honus. "How to Play Shortstop." *The Sporting News,* April 13, 1949.

About the Author: Johannes Peter "Honus" Wagner (1874–1955), known as the "Flying Dutchman" for his heritage and amazing speed, played most of his professional career for the Pittsburgh Pirates. Wagner was a versatile player who set numerous records in his long career. After retiring from baseball in 1917, Wagner came back to coach for the Pirates from 1933 to 1951. He was one of the original five Baseball Hall of Fame inductees in 1936. ■

Introduction

By 1900, professional baseball had existed for thirty-one years, but it was largely a game of bunting, base stealing, and well-placed hits, relying on good defense and pitching. Honus Wagner honed all of these skills to perfection, making him one of the game's most versatile players. At five feet, eleven inches, and two hundred pounds, with bowed legs and a barrel chest, Wagner looked awkward even when playing his best, but his awkward appearance masked excellent speed and coordination. Over the course of his career, he played every position except catcher, sometimes multiple times in a season.

He was born Johannes Peter Wagner, and got the nickname "Honus," or "Hans" as a child because of his awkward appearance. He began working in the mines of his hometown in Pennsylvania when he was twelve, and every Sunday, and on many summer evenings, he and his four brothers played baseball. In 1893, he and his brother

Honus Wagner crouches into position as if to field a ground ball in this 1911 photo, during his days as a Pittsburgh Pirate. THE LIBRARY OF CONGRESS.

Al "Butts" Wagner played for Mansfield in the semipro Allegheny League. In 1897, he joined the major league Louisville Colonels. That year he maintained a .324 batting average, the first of seventeen consecutive seasons in which he had a batting average greater than .300. However, the Colonels folded after the 1899 season, and Wagner, like many of its players, ended up on the Pittsburgh Pirates.

Significance

The Pirates tried Wagner at several positions, finally discovering his sensational talent at shortstop in 1901. By 1903 this was his regular position, and it is the one for which he is best remembered. As a shortstop, he became one of baseball's first stars, along with Ty Cobb. However, unlike Cobb, Wagner was well liked by his colleagues, and he is still considered by many to be the greatest shortstop in baseball history.

Wagner earned his star status through his versatility and skill. Although all of his records were subsequently

Honus Wagner's Resignation Letter From the Pittsburgh Pirates, 1908

My Dear Barney,

I will not be with your team this season, but wish you a pennant winner and will always be plugging for Cap and the boys to win.

It is certainly hard for me to lay aside the uniform which I have been wearing since 1897, but every dog has his day, and the sport has become too strenuous for me.

I can look back and see that I was lucky in landing with you in Louisville, and that I made no mistake in staying with your Pittsburg team during war times. I was offered nearly double the amount I asked from you then, but I have been a gainer by it, as my salary has always remained the same. Besides, I have had the satisfaction of knowing that my boss appreciated the fact that I always gave the club the best I had.

I wish to thank you for your treatment of me while a member of your team, and assure you that I highly appreciate the same. Again, wishing you success, I am

Very truly yours,
John H. Wagner

SOURCE: Wagner, Honus. Letter to Barney Dreyfuss, March 1908. Reprinted in DeValeria, Dennis, and Jeanne Burke DeValeria. *Honus Wagner: A Biography.* New York: Holt, 1996, 172.

broken, when he retired Wagner held the records for the most games, at-bats, hits, runs, runs batted in (RBIs), stolen bases, total bases, and extra-base hits. Between 1901 and 1909, he played 1,044 games as the Pirates' shortstop with a total of only 422 errors. This number of errors appears high to a modern fan of the game, but in the early 1900s baseball gloves were not as good as they are now, and fielders consequently committed more errors. Between 1900 and 1909, Wagner played in 1,391 games, had 4,246 at-bats, 1,847 hits, 1,014 runs, and maintained an overall batting average of .352. He was the National League Batting Champion eight times over the course of his seventeen-year career, and his career batting average is .329.

Wagner was ahead of his time in at least one of his social stances. He had the American Tobacco Company recall his baseball card in 1910 because he did not want to be associated with tobacco products and seen as a bad influence on children. His team lost the first-ever World Series to the Boston Pilgrims in 1903, but they went on to win the series six years later in 1909, playing against the Detroit Tigers and Ty Cobb. Wagner came back to manage the Pirates from 1933 to 1951. In 1936, he was one of the first players elected to the Hall of Fame, and he tied with Babe Ruth for the second-most votes.

Primary Source

"How to Play Shortstop" [excerpt]

SYNOPSIS: In this short essay, an abridged version of an article that appeared in *The Sporting News* in April 1949, Wagner summarizes the most important elements of playing shortstop. He relates the rules a shortstop should always follow, such as thinking out each play before it happens. He proceeds to advise players on the shortstop's role in specific plays, such as double plays and long hits. Wagner's advice is still largely relevant to modern players, especially in his warning that it is wiser to be certain of one out than to lose two.

A shortstop must have a good arm as the prime requisite. Next, he must be fast, able to shift his feet and ready to move in any direction.

Keep trying. Don't be afraid of making an error. Seek the advice of older players, the coaches and manager. Above all, never lose sight of the ball.

Always keep in mind the number of outs, which bases are occupied and the score. Study each hitter. On a fast runner, you must handle the ball cleanly and hurry the throw. Shift for each batter, according to where he is most likely to hit.

Think out each play before it happens. If you boot the ball, think where you're going to throw it even before you pick it up, so no time is lost.

The hardest play for a shortstop to make is going to his right for a deep hit ball. Set yourself when you get your hands on the ball, and be in a position to throw to first. Another tough play is the slowly hit ball coming right at you, especially with a fast batter. Play this on your barehanded side so as to get the ball away quickly, picking the ball up and throwing it without hesitation in virtually a single motion.

In starting a double play, remember it is wiser to make sure of one out than lose two. Grab the ball and feed it to the second baseman letter-high. If the ball goes to your right, or deep, put something on the throw to second. If it's a grounder near second, flip it underhand to the second baseman.

When pivoting in a double play, be in motion when receiving the ball, step on second base with the right foot and remain on balance by stepping forward with the left before finally throwing to first.

With a runner on first, the shortstop covers second on a bunt. With runners on first and second, keep the runner as close to second as possible by feinting him back. To pick a runner off second, stand about five feet behind the line and slowly work your way up close behind him. Break for the bag when the runner is leaning toward the next base, so as to catch him off balance.

The shortstop takes most of the relays on long hits to the outfield; otherwise, he directs the player who does take the relay, as to where the throw should go. With a runner on first and a hit to right field, the shortstop stands about 25 feet in front of third base, on the grass, awaiting and guiding the throw from the outfielder. If there is a chance for the third baseman to catch the runner coming from first, he yells to the shortstop, "Let it go!" The shortstop bluffs the catch, to discourage the batter from advancing during the ensuing play, but lets the ball go through to the third baseman.

Other tips: Shortstop gets pitching signs from catcher and relays them to outfielders by hand or voice signal . . . Whether short or second baseman covers base on attempted steal depends on batter and type of pitch . . . Tag a runner with almost the same motion you get the ball, then get rid of the ball as fast as you can . . . Size up a pop fly and yell for it as soon as you feel sure you can get it; otherwise yell for either the left or center fielder to take it.

Further Resources

BOOKS

Hageman, William. *Honus: The Life and Times of a Baseball Hero.* Champagne, Ill.: Sagamore, 1996.

Hittner, Arthur D. *Honus Wagner: The Life of Baseball's "Flying Dutchman."* Jefferson, N.C.: McFarland, 1996.

Ritter, Lawrence S. *The Glory of Their Times: The Story of the Early Days of Baseball Told by the Men Who Played It.* New York: MacMillan, 1966.

WEBSITES

"Honus Wagner Statistics." Baseball-Reference.com. Available online at http://www.baseball-reference.com/w/wagneho01.shtml; website home page: http://www.baseball-reference.com (accessed March 20, 2003).

"The Official Honus Wagner Website." CMG Worldwide. Available online at http://www.honuswagner.com; website home page: http://www.cmgww.com (accessed March 20, 2003).

The Tumult and the Shouting: My Life in Sport

Autobiography

By: Grantland Rice

Date: 1954

Source: Rice, Grantland. *The Tumult and the Shouting: My Life in Sport.* New York: Barnes, 1954, 32–36.

About the Author: Henry Grantland Rice (1880–1954) sustained an injury that prevented him from developing a professional sports career, so he stayed involved with his passion through sportswriting. Rice established himself as a respected figure in that arena writing for newspapers in cities ranging from Nashville to Cleveland to New York City. His "Sportlight" column was nationally syndicated, and was the basis for a series of short films. He was also a film producer and narrator, radio broadcaster, editor, and poet. ■

Introduction

Until the mid-1850s, newspapers and magazines tended to consider sports an unworthy subject for coverage. However, publisher William Trotter Porter began extensive coverage of baseball around that time, and the subject was extremely popular with sports fans. Another prolific sportswriter of the nineteenth century was Henry Chadwick, who covered baseball extensively. The sports page prompted an increase in sales, encouraging editors to maintain the feature and inspiring other newspapers to add sports coverage. After the Civil War (1861–1865), when railroads enabled sports teams to travel from city to city, sportswriters became crucial connections between fans and their teams.

By the early part of the twentieth century, America's love affair with sports was solidifying into a marriage. Baseball was the national pastime; young men risked life and limb to play football; basketball filled the winter gap; and sportswriters followed their teams everywhere. Unlike many other reporters of the era, sportswriters saw large portions of the country just by following a particular team from one game to the next. Sizable newspapers often employed "stringers," who remained in large cities, submitting their stories via telegraph. The newspaper might also get some of its information from sources like the Associated Press. However, sportswriting had more flavor than most other types of reporting, so newspapers felt it worthwhile to send a reporter to all of a team's games to keep the fans back home up to speed.

Significance

In the 1900s, Grantland Rice was a young man whose sports injuries had cheated him out of a life as a professional player. He wanted to remain close to the game, however, and so started working as the *Nashville Daily*

Sports columnist Grantland Rice. © CORBIS. REPRODUCED BY PERMISSION.

News' sports editor at the sum of five dollars per week in 1901. He worked for increasingly larger papers until he was offered a job with the *Cleveland Daily News* that paid a weekly salary of fifty dollars. In that era, the five-dollar positions were far more common than the fifty-dollar variety, and Rice took the job.

Two years later, Rice returned to Nashville for even greater pay, and there experienced firsthand the other side of sportswriting: twelve- to eighteen-hour days to deliver a large volume of sportswriting with no assistant. Perhaps the only sportswriter to include his poetry with his writing, Rice achieved popularity and fame through his fair-handed reporting. Where other sportswriters often submitted biased accounts, slanted unreasonably in favor of their own teams and players (many were not above accepting bribes for taking sides on an issue), Rice attempted to play the middle ground. In 1911, he began writing a column called "The Sportlight," which was later syndicated by *The New York Tribune.*

Rice's work in the first decade of the twentieth century earned him the respect of fans and editors, and syndication of his column in the early 1910s increased his reputation throughout the nation. After serving in World War I (1914–1918), he returned to the United States to enjoy increased renown in the 1920s. One of his most famous pieces dubbed four Notre Dame football players the "Four Horsemen," and the nickname stuck for the rest of their careers. Rice began making short films from his "Sportlight" columns, and one of these won an Academy Award in 1943. He was one of America's most well known and respected sportswriters, and his colleagues called him the dean of his vocation. His contribution to American sportswriting spanned half a century and endures beyond his death.

Primary Source

The Tumult and the Shouting: My Life in Sport [excerpt]

SYNOPSIS: Having acquired a job at fifty dollars per week with the *Cleveland Daily News,* Rice settled into Cleveland and asked his fiancé, Katherine Hollis, to set their wedding date. In this excerpt, she joins in to describe their wedding, and Rice discusses their immediate return to his sports reporting and the grueling work which followed.

The Big Step

During the baseball season of '03 I became official scorer for the Atlanta Club of the Southern League. Atlanta was used by the old Cleveland Indians as spring-training quarters. Their star, Napoleon (Larry) Lajoie, and I became friends.

Philadelphia and the Giants clashed in the '05 World Series and I was sent North to cover the games. McGraw's Giants won as Christy Mathewson pitched three shutouts! I marvelled at the handsome righthander and wrote as much. Returning home, I found a letter from the *Cleveland News* offering me 50 dollars a week to handle their sports page. It took me less than a minute to accept. That was real money and for a fellow with marriage on his mind—money never hurt. I'd been going with a girl named Katherine Hollis from Americus, Georgia, long enough to realize she was to be the one. I invaded Cleveland only to walk into a fight. Half the *News* people, apparently, wanted a midwest writer named Bill Phelon for the job. Phelon and I found ourselves fighting for the same bone. A few years later I was to discover what a tremendously gifted writer and magnificent screwball Phelon was, but at this particular time we must have had little use for each other. Phelon moved on to Chicago; I moved into Cleveland. The paychecks started rolling in and I told Kit to set our wedding date.

Right here I think my bride should be allowed to describe her own wedding. Kit, will you take over?

"Well, you may wonder how Granny and I met in the first place. I'd gone up to Atlanta from my home,

Americus, to visit a girl friend. It was Saturday and we were taken to an amusement park by her brother and a friend. I was riding the merry-go-round—sidesaddle—and having a gay time when I noticed a tall, blond young fellow standing to one side watching me. He was smiling and he looked awfully nice.

"The next day Granny Rice came to call and we took a walk out into the country. I remarked on the fine-looking overcoat he was wearing. 'It's not mine,' he said. 'It belongs to my pal, Bill Newman.'

"A few days later, he came calling for me again—this time with a rented horse and buggy—and took me for a ride. I recall he wasn't very sure of himself . . . or the horse. It started to rain. There was a clap of thunder and the horse bolted and started running———away! Granny couldn't stop him, and the next thing both of us were pitched out of the cart. The horse galloped clear out of sight. We 'hitched' a ride back to Atlanta on a milk wagon.

"After that we began to see more and more of each other. . . . and when he finally visited me at Americus and proposed, perhaps I wasn't quite as surprised as I should have been. But I was awfully proud—and happy.

"The date was set for April 11, 1906, and we were to be married in Americus at the Methodist Church. Granny was off at spring training with the ball team but got a short leave of absence. His younger brother John was the best man. John was to arrive on the wedding morn from Nashville. When the great day arrived, Kate Hollis, one of eight Hollis children, was ready.

"It was an evening affair. As the strains of 'Here Comes the Bride' pealed from the old church organ, I took my brother-in-law's arm (my father had died when I was a baby) and proceeded down the aisle, cloud walking. As I approached the little side door where my groom, a knight in a rented cutaway, was to claim me, there was no Grantland! I whispered to my escort to slow down. There was I, waiting at the church—I knew just how the poor girl in that old song felt!

"After an eternity, the door swung open and out flew the groom—coat tails flapping, with brother John in his wake. He had arrived at the zero hour. Exhilarated with the reunion with John, Mr. Rice apparently had almost forgotten his own wedding!"

—Well, let Kit have her inning. Truth of the matter is, I hadn't almost forgotten the occasion. I had hovered around that church for nearly an hour before Kit and her entourage arrived. And Kit, from the moment I slipped that gold band on your finger, you've been my constant sidekick—at least in my thoughts—no matter how many the miles that have often separated us.

Our honeymoon was spent catching up with the Cleveland team, which had gone to Louisville, Kentucky, where the Indians were playing some exhibition games en route north. We caught up with them in the town that let loose the Kentucky Derby back in 1875—five years before I was born—and then proceeded to Cleveland with the club to open the 1906 season. Napoleon (Larry) Lajoie, Cleveland's playing manager, presented Kit with a huge barrel of china. For a bride about to set up light housekeeping in a Cleveland flat she hadn't yet picked out, my bride had enough chinaware to stock a hotel.

Cleveland was a good baseball town—still is. The Indians roared off to what seemed an insurmountable lead in 1906. Then the injury landslide started and the roof caved in. Lajoie, our star second baseman, was painfully spiked but continued and hit .355. However, Larry couldn't do it alone—Chicago and New York edged us out.

That fall the *News* upped me to 60 dollars a week. Several weeks later I was offered 70 dollars a week to return to Nashville. I accepted and in the spring of 1907 Kit, our brand-new baby, Florence, and I moved into my mother's house. I remember Kit berated me as we climbed the porch steps. It seems I was carrying Floncy under one arm like a football. She wasn't much larger.

The following four years—from 1907 through 1910—were my toughest. Luke Lea was starting a new paper, The *Nashville Tennessean,* with my friend, ex-Sewanee coach Herman Suter, as editor. Suter had lured me back home. My only assignments were:

1. To get out two pages of sports daily and four pages on Sunday, with no assistant.
2. To write a column of verse and paragraphs on the editorial page, after the manner of F. P. Adams, Burt Leston Taylor, Judd Mortimer Lewis and some others. This was seven days a week.
3. To cover the theatre—Nashville being a one-night stand—practically each night.

This meant being at the office at 8:00 A.M. and returning home about 2:00 A.M. It also meant around 30,000 words, excluding some 20 sets of verse each week, but verse, usually, was easier to write than prose. I knew many stretches of 18 hours a day, with 12 hours a day the rule. I wonder what the Newspaper Guild would have said about that.

As a youngster, Keats and Shelley had been my particular favorites; but as I hit 20, I had discovered a fellow named Rudyard Kipling. The meter and jungle drums inherent in Kipling's verse captured my ear and my imagination and never let go. My dear and departed pal O. B. Keeler of the *Atlanta Journal* could recite my stuff by the yard—but whatever verse I've written, more than 6,000 pieces, I've forgotten almost as quickly as I wrote it. Believe me, it just flowed.

Further Resources

BOOKS

Fountain, Charles. *Sportswriter: The Life and Times of Grantland Rice.* New York: Oxford University Press, 1993.

Harper, William A. *How You Played the Game: The Life of Grantland Rice.* Columbia, Mo.: University of Missouri Press, 1998.

Rice, Grantland. *Base-ball Ballads.* Nashville, Tenn.: Tennessean, 1910. Reprinted Finch Press, 1972. *Contains a collection of Rice's verse written throughout his career.*

PERIODICALS

Graham, Frank. "My Friend Grantland Rice." *Sport,* November 1954, 284–292.

Reverend Edmund C. Joyce, C.S.C. Sports Research Collection, University Library of Notre Dame. *This is a collection of general interest magazines containing articles on announcing college All-America football teams, 1896–1962. See specifically Grantland Rice's articles in "Collier's."*

"Walter Camp and Grantland Rice." *Collier's* 74, no. 20, November 15, 1924, 29.

WEBSITES

"Grantland Rice: Dean of American Sports." BaseballLibrary.com. Available online at http://www.pubdim.net/baseballlibrary/ballplayers/R/Rice_Grantland.stm; website home page: http://www.pubdim.net/baseballlibrary (accessed March 20, 2003).

My Life in Baseball: The True Record

Memoir

By: Ty Cobb, with Al Stump

Date: 1961

Source: Cobb, Ty, with Al Stump. *My Life in Baseball: The True Record.* New York: Doubleday, 1961, 75–79, 81.

About the Author: Ty Cobb (1886–1961) was one of the first professional baseball players to become independently wealthy. He negotiated tough contracts with baseball owners and invested his money carefully. Though a gifted player who set many records, some of which have yet to be surpassed, Cobb was a stubborn man whose personal prejudices interfered with his relationships, both personal and professional. He officially retired from baseball in 1928 and was the first of the original five players inducted into the Hall of Fame in 1936. ■

Introduction

By 1900, professional baseball had existed for thirty-one years, but it was largely a game of bunting, base stealing, and strategy. There were not many star players, so teams relied much on good defense and well-placed hits to score a few runs. Ty Cobb would be one of the first players to bring change to the so-called "dead-ball" era with his high batting average, skill in base-stealing, and ability to score. In 1904, Cobb played for the Tourists of Augusta, Georgia, but was released after two games. He then played for a semi-professional team in Anniston, Alabama, until being invited back to the Tourists in August. The following August, he was called up to play for the Detroit Tigers, the team he would stay with for all but two seasons of his professional career.

As well as Cobb played baseball, his career was heavily affected by his personal history. He was a violent man who came into frequent conflicts with colleagues and strangers alike. Some of his penchant for violence may have resulted from learning that his mother, apparently mistaking his father for an intruder, shot and killed the man. Cobb learned of his father's death the day before he was to leave for Detroit for his first appearance with the major league team. However, Cobb was a hard man to deal with even before his father's death, and he was hated by his manager while playing for the Tourists.

Significance

In the years from 1905 to 1909, Cobb established some of the hallmarks of his fame, including his tough contract negotiations, his sheer skill at the game, and his vicious attitude. In 1906 he requested a raise and received three hundred dollars more than he asked for. However, in 1908, he again asked for his salary to be raised, this time from twenty-four hundred to five thousand dollars. Tigers co-owner Frank Navin refused and the two settled in for a standoff. In the first decade of the 1900s, baseball was heavily controlled by the owners, and players had little bargaining power. However, Cobb knew he was skilled enough that the Tigers didn't want to lose him. And in the end, he was correct, forcing Navin to within two hundred of the five thousand–dollar goal. Although players in general would not gain equal footing with team management and owners until the 1970s, Cobb's successful negotiations did set a precedent for other stars in the early part of the twentieth century.

By the beginning of the 1910 season, Cobb had played in 595 games, with 2,267 at bats, 765 hits, 365 runs, and a batting average of .337. Over the course of his career, he would win twelve batting titles, and he had already won three of these in his first five years in the pros. His lifetime batting average of .366 is still the record, and his total number of hits, 4,189, was not surpassed until 1985 by Pete Rose, who required more at-bats for the feat. In the 1909 season, Cobb won the American League's triple crown with the league's highest batting average (.377), most runs batted in (107), and most home runs (nine). He stole seventy-six bases that year, and although he would deny the rumors after his retirement, when he was a player he supported suspicions that he sharpened his shoe spikes to slide into base and tear up the opposing player.

But marring these achievements were Cobb's virulent racism and his tendency to lash out at colleagues and strangers alike. He was handed only a suspended sentence when he attacked a black asphalt worker who yelled at him for walking too close to the asphalt he was spreading and some of it got on Cobb's pants. And Cobb was only the most outspoken of those who successfully opposed any manager's hiring "Indians" (who were actually light-skinned African Americans) in this time. After being hospitalized for an emotional breakdown in 1906 that resulted from his teammates' unkind treatment of him, Cobb held a lifetime of open warfare with those he felt were against his best interests.

Primary Source

My Life in Baseball: The True Record [excerpt]

SYNOPSIS: In this excerpt, Cobb summarizes his contract negotiations with Frank Navin for the 1908 season. He portrays himself as a hardworking man fighting against a cruel tightwad who has a personal grudge against him.

So, down South, that winter, it reached the newspapers that I'd asked for $5000 and a three-year contract for 1908. It also was publicized that I didn't like Navin's contractual power to release me within ten days after giving notice—if, for instance, I fell ill or was badly injured. This was a condition right on peonage and all ball-players were forced to live under it. We players had no equal right to abrogate the agreement—which, under all law, made it no contract at all. I demanded this clause be stricken from my contract.

But Navin bridled and acted as if I'd put a gun in his ribs. "Who does Cobb think he is?" he announced. "Our other stars, Sam Crawford and Bill Donovan, have signed their contracts at reasonable figures without a murmur, but Cobb seems to think he deserves special treatment. Well the creation cannot be greater than the creator—Cobb is not bigger than baseball."

Pretty grandiloquent stuff—and Navin's remarks put the fat in the fire. After two years of working for Detroit at $1800 and $2400, I intended to be pushed around no longer.

If $5000 seems a measly sum by modern standards to quibble over, keep in mind that Christy Mathewson was paid $6000 the year he won 37 games for the New York Giants, Cy Young never drew more than $3500 as the winningest pitcher of all time, Eddie Plank and Chief Bender worked for $4000 at their peak and Honus Wagner had to win five National League batting crowns before pushing his salary to $9000. Old-time ownership held you in a condition of bondage; those who challenged the front office were waived out of the game or dropped so fast it'd singe your hair to watch.

I came right back at Navin—retorting that a .350 average and the fact that I'd established myself at low pay made it obvious that I wasn't acting in a fractious matter. I made no threats. But Navin was full of them.

He bent the ear of the Associated Press with: "We have offered Cobb $3000 and a one-year contract, and to allow him to bluff us would be to court a hold-up by every other player. It would disorganize our club in the future far more than Cobb's absence for a season could do. It puts a premium on being a crab and a penalty on a man who treats the club with honor and respect.

"Cobb can have his contract back any time he wants it. We have the best outfield in baseball, as I figure it, with Crawford, Matty McIntyre and Davey Jones, and if Cobb doesn't get the point, let it be on his head. He surely won't be foolish enough to let us go to training camp in the spring without him."

No one has known it, until now, but Navin not only failed to pressure me into abandoning my holdout, he came within a hair of causing me to quit baseball permanently.

"Forget it, Tyrus," my family advised me. "Navin has called you a fathead, a bluffer, a crab, dishonorable and a lot of other things. No Cobb has to take that from anyone. Give up all this and do as your father wanted you to do."

My people were college-bred, they looked down on baseball as a low-life occupation and pleaded with me to chuck it all and enroll at a Southern uni-

Ty Cobb slides aggressively into third base to avoid the tag in a game played between 1905 and 1910. **NATIONAL BASEBALL HALL OF FAME LIBRARY, COOPERSTOWN, N.Y. REPRODUCED BY PERMISSION.**

versity in medicine or law. And for many weeks, while Navin pulled one nefarious trick after another, I seriously thought about taking their advice.

I've been called one of the hardest bargainers who ever held out, and I'm proud of it. One Navin had no regard for a mere boy, and resorted to every trickery he could think of to befuddle me. For what it's worth to players today who must fight over seven battle-fields to gain a decent paycheck, notice that he used three stratagems:

First, he circulated his conviction that Detroit's outfield and hitting would be plenty strong enough if Cobb sat on the sideline in 1908. "Let him go roll his little top," challenged Frank J.

This was to plant seeds of doubt and right in me—to lower my evaluation of myself. The belittling process scares many a man into capitulating.

Next, he arranged for friends of mine in and out of baseball to write and phone me, urging that I sign on his terms. Knowing I was a babe in years and impressionable, he didn't hesitate to use men of influence to pressure me. I've always considered that a despicable move. Navin was trying to make me think *If these men believe I'm wrong in asking $5000, perhaps I am.*

As his foxiest gambit, Navin coached a Detroit sportswriter to wire me: NAVIN SAYS IF SICK AND ACCIDENT CLAUSE ELIMINATED QUESTION OF SALARY WILL COUNT LITTLE. SAYS COME ON TO DETROIT AND TALK BUSINESS. WHAT DO YOU SAY? SEND REPLY COLLECT.

Willing to compromise to the extent of dropping the ten-day sick-or-hurt waiver I'd made, I took this to mean that the Tigers were acceding to my request on pay. Happily, I pulled my bats out of storage and began boning them. I wired back: I ACCEPT YOUR PROPOSITION. SHALL I REPORT TO SPRING TRAINING CAMP?

Ty Cobb's Tips on How to Hit

The first item in scientific hitting is selection of bat. For a swing hitter (one who starts his bat far back and completes his swing with a full follow-through) I suggest a bat with the feel on the light side. For the one with a shorter, more compact swing, the bat should feel slightly heavy.

Next comes position. Never copy a batter with an exaggerated crouch. The best hitters stand up and have the look of a good hitter. In case your normal stance becomes uncomfortable while awaiting the delivery, breaking of the knees (a dip or slight squat) will relieve this. But of course you must always come back to the position first assumed.

The space between feet should be measured by how well balanced you feel. This will measure about 14 inches for players of average height. But don't think of this kind of thing in inches. Just stand so you feel balanced, and can step either into the pitch or away.

If you are able to put a little extra weight on the front foot and still feel balanced to step either way, so much the better. The ability to do this will assure proper stride and, when swinging, will bring the body and arms up to the ball more automatically. I emphasize the value of proper striding because over-striding is fatal. It causes uppercutting and fly balls, upsets coordination and costs freedom to step in or out.

A righthanded batter attempting to hit the ball to right, or opposite (from normal), field should use the closed stance. That means the left foot is about 4 inches closer to the plate than the right. Hitting to left field, his front foot is about 4 inches further away, or in open stance. The straightaway hitter lines up both feet with the line of the pitch.

I always had trouble hitting lefthanded pitching, especially curve ballers, until I went to the back line of the batter's box. That gave me the benefit of the extra inches from the pitcher, and the split-second extra time in which to judge the pitch.

Keep your arms, particularly the elbows, away from the body. This insures freedom of swing. I also recommend the elbow nearer the pitcher be raised and exaggerated. This, plus a slight bending of the body from the waist up, will give you better body balance, insures automatically hitting the ball out in front and brings your eyes in better focusing position.

Do all your "fixing" as to grip and stance before delivery, then forget about your swing. Watch the pitcher's every move and never let your eye leave the ball. Many batters are thrown out by a half-step, so once you've hit the ball, run with all the speed you have, no matter where the ball goes.

SOURCE: Cobb, Ty. "How to Hit." In *The Official Encyclopedia of Baseball.* New York: A.S. Barnes, 1976, 663. Condensed from *Famous Slugger Year Book.* Louisville, Ky.: Hillerich & Bradsby, 1950.

Navin now slugged me with this reply: "HAVE MADE NO PROPOSITION. TO WHAT DO YOU REFER?"

The thing soon became a nightmare of telegrams, rumor, threats, and intrigue, with the whole country choosing up sides pro and con. When I left Georgia for Detroit to see if I couldn't force a few straight cards to be dealt, sporting editor Tom Hamilton of the Augusta *Herald* brought the truth into the open:

WILL COBB BE VICTIM OF DOUBLE-CROSS? headlined Hamilton.

He said: "Navin intends to fake a contract out of Tyrus by luring him to Detroit with false promises, where he will be able to bring big guns to bear. Of course, most of the fans in America are hoping that Cobb wins out. But it's a 40-to-1 shot that the majority of his friends would have advised him to steer clear of the Navin lair and stay home until he had an iron-clad offer from Detroit's attorneys. The Lord help him up North."

In Detroit, I was given the treatment Hamilton expected—ex-Mayor George Codd, Fielding (Hurry-Up) Yost, the famed football coach of the University of Michigan, and other impressive names did some brainwashing before I entered Navin's sumptuous office to reach one of two decisions: quit baseball or stay with it under respectable salary terms. "You're a fool if you continue to hold out," they assured me.

A word about Navin, the man. We players called him "The Chinaman" for his cold, implacable expression. He'd begun as a bookkeeper in the office of Sam Angus, a Detroit insurance man and railroad contractor who owned the Tigers prior to my arrival in 1905. Angus sold out for $50,000 to William Hoover Yawkey, a grand fellow, but to whom a baseball club was but a plaything. Yawkey gave Navin $5000 worth of stock and jumped him to club secretary-treasurer.

As a clue to Navin, the jolly, generous Bill Yawkey would slip a $100 bill to some Tiger or other who'd helped win a game. Navin turned blue when that happened. "It'll spoil them," he'd protest.

Yawkey was a delight to play for. He hired ex-middleweight champ Tommy Ryan to travel and box with him and one night at the Hollenden Hotel, high in his cups, he bet Billy Lamb, a rugged customer, $10,000 that he could pin Lamb in a wrestling match. Lamb said he didn't have $10,000.

"Hell, then if I win, you owe me nothing!" boomed Yawkey. "If I lose, I owe you $10,000."

They stripped and in a minute, Lamb had Bill's shoulders pinned. Yawkey paid off, Lamb refused the money, and Bill became so affronted at his pal's refusal to help him discharge an honorable debt that Lamb finally had to accept the 10,000 simoleons.

After our 1907 pennant, Yawkey moved to New York and handed co-ownership of the Detroit Ball Club to Navin, even lending him $40,000 with which to purchase half the stock. And now, in full control, he intended to box young Tyrus Cobb's ears publicly.

He had quite an edge on me. I wasn't yet old enough to vote; Navin was thirty-seven, a graduate of the Detroit College of Law, and backed by years of immutable baseball tradition wherein Slave served Master.

In earlier days, Navin also had been a croupier in a gambling hall and he followed the horses avidly, thinking nothing of dropping $1000 on a race. But paying a ballplayer his worth pained Old Stone Face deeply. In his office that day, he puffed his checks and gave me an intimidating glower.

"What's this about you going outlaw?" he demanded.

"I've had offers," I replied. Navin knew damned well that I had, for they'd made coast-to-coast headlines. The president of the upstart new Union League, A. W. Lawson, had tendered me a $10,000 start-per-season contract—said to be the highest offer ever made to a ballplayer—and Jimmy Callahan, of a Chicago semipro league, had made a similar tempting bid. Neither being in Organized Baseball, I'd be branded an "outlaw"—beyond the pale forever, probably—if I accepted.

"Lawson is full of hot air. His league is on paper only, and nothing'll come of it," barked Navin.

"Maybe not," I said. "But to get to the point, I am willing to waive all other clauses in my contract and take a straight-out $5000 a season. It isn't a question of principle with me, Mr. Navin. I want the money because I've earned it. It's the only way my earning capacity can be satisfied for this year."

"Can't pay it," he said. "Impossible. I'll come up $1000 from $3000, and that's the absolute limit. Look at Sam Crawford—he doesn't get more than $4000 and he's been a star for seven years."

"What you do with Crawford is your business and his," I retorted, getting hot under the collar at Navin's latest diversion. "All I know is that a ballplayer starts out at small pay, gets old in a hurry in the service of the team and finishes his career making peanuts. I want mine while I'm producing for you."

Navin wouldn't budge and I walked out, caught a train back to Dixie and sat tight while the Tigers left for spring training in Hot Springs, Arkansas. Days dragged by and training was almost finished. It rained buckets in Arkansas. The Tigers looked bedraggled, rather than like defending league champions. Hughie Jennings had some blunt things to say to Navin about the loss of my services. . . .

Navin capitulated and offered a $4000 season's contract, plus an $800 bonus if I averaged .300 or better and fielded .900. I had no fear about qualifying for the bonus, and signed. I'd come within $200 of my demand, which was victory enough.

Further Resources

BOOKS

Kramer, Sydelle. *Ty Cobb: Bad Boy of Baseball.* New York: Random House, 1995.

Rader, Benjamin G. *Baseball: A History of America's Game.* Urbana, Ill.: University of Illinois Press, 1992.

Soos, Troy. *Hunting a Detroit Tiger.* New York: Kensington, 1997.

Stump, Al. *Cobb: A Biography.* Chapel Hill, N.C.: Algonquin Books of Chapel Hill, 1994.

WEBSITES

The Official Website of Ty Cobb. Available online at http://www.cmgww.com/baseball/cobb (accessed March 19, 2003).

"Ty Cobb." National Baseball Hall of Fame. Available online at http://www.baseballhalloffame.org/hofers_and_honorees/hofer_bios/cobb_ty.htm; website home page: http://www.baseballhalloffame.org (accessed March 19, 2003).

"Ty Cobb Museum: Stats." Ty Cobb Museum. Available online at http://www.tycobbmuseum.org/stats.shtml; website home page: http://www.tycobbmuseum.org (accessed March 19, 2003).

"Ty Cobb Statistics." Baseball-reference.com. Available online at http://www.baseball-reference.com/c/cobbty01.shtml; website home page: http://www.baseball-reference.com (accessed March 19, 2003).

General Resources

General

Albers, Everett C., and David Levy. *Behold Our New Century: Early Twentieth Century Visions of America: A Reader From the Great Plains Chautauqua Society.* Bismarck, N.D.: The Society, 1998.

Allen, Frederick Lewis. *The Big Change: America Transforms Itself.* New York: Harper, 1952.

Boorstin, Daniel. *The Americans: The Democratic Experience.* New York: Vintage, 1973.

Campbell, A.E. *America Comes of Age: The Era of Theodore Roosevelt.* New York: American Heritage Press, 1971.

Cashman, Sean Dennis. *America in the Age of Titans.* New York: New York University Press, 1988.

Chambers, John, II. *The Tyranny of Change: America in the Progressive Era, 1900–1917.* New York: St. Martin's Press, 1992.

Commager, Henry Steele. *The Progressive Era.* New York: Torstar, 1975.

Cooper, John Milton, Jr. *Pivotal Decades: The United States, 1900–1920.* New York, 1990.

Dawn of the Century: 1900–1910. Alexandria, Va.: Time-Life Books, 1998.

Durrett, Deane. *1900s.* San Jose: Kidhaven Press, 2004.

Hofstadter, Richard. *The Age of Reform: From Bryan to FDR.* New York: Vintage, 1955.

Katz, William Loren, and Laurie R. Lehman. *The The Cruel Years: American Voices at the Dawn of the Twentieth Century.* Boston: Enfield, 2003.

Kazin, Alfred. *An American Procession.* New York: Knopf, 1984.

Kolko, Gabriel. *The Triumph of Conservatism.* New York: Free Press, 1963.

Lesy, Michael. *Dreamland: America at the Dawn of the Twentieth Century.* New York: New York Press, 1997.

Lord, Walter. *The Good Years From 1900 to the First World War.* New York: Harper, 1960.

Schlereth, Thomas J. *Victorian America: Transformations in Everyday Life, 1876–1915.* New York: HarperCollins, 1991.

Segelem, Lee. *The Last Turn: America When the Last Century Changes.* San Jose: Writer's Showcase, 2001.

Stewart, Gail. *1900s.* New York: Crestwood House, 1989.

Wagenknecht, Edward. *American Profile.* Amherst: University of Massachusetts Press, 1982.

Wiebe, Robert. *The Search for Order, 1877–1920.* New York: Hill & Wang, 1967.

The Arts

Aaron, Daniel. *Writers on the Left.* New York: Harcourt, Brace & World, 1961.

Addison, Gayle, Jr. *Oak and Ivy: A Biography of Paul Laurence Dunbar.* Garden City, N.Y.: Anchor/Doubleday, 1971.

Arnason, H. H. *History of Modern Art: Painting · Sculpture · Architecture.* Englewood Cliffs, N.J.: Prentice-Hall/New York: Abrams, 1968.

Baur, John I. H., ed. *New Art in America: Fifty Painters of the 20th Century.* Greenwich, Conn.: New York Graphic Society, 1957.

Baym, Nina, et al. *The Norton Anthology of American Literature,* 4th ed., vol. 2. New York: Norton, 1994.

Bell, Bernard. *The Afro-American Novel and Its Tradition.* Amherst: University of Massachusetts Press, 1987.

Bernheim, Alfred L., and Sarah Harding. *The Business of the Theatre: An Economic History of the American Theatre, 1750–1932.* New York: Benjamin Blom, 1932.

Blair, Walter, and Hamlin Hill. *America's Humor.* New York: Oxford University Press, 1978.

Bowser, Eileen. *The Transformation of Cinema.* New York: Scribners, 1990.

Boyer, Paul S. *Purity in Print.* New York: Scribners, 1968.

Brockett, Oscar G., and Robert R. Findlay. *Century of Innovation: A History of European and American Theatre and Drama Since 1870.* Englewood Cliffs, N.J.: Prentice-Hall, 1984.

Charters, Ann. *Nobody: The Story of Bert Williams.* New York: Macmillan, 1970.

Christgau, Robert. *Grown Up All Wrong: 75 Great Rock and Pop Artists From Vaudeville to Techno.* Cambridge: Harvard University Press, 1998.

Craven, Wayne. *American Art: History and Culture.* New York: Harry N. Abrams, Inc., 1994.

Csida, Joseph, and June Bundy Csida. *American Entertainment: A Unique History of Show Business.* New York: Watson-Guptill, 1978.

Curtis, Susan. *Dancing to a Black Man's Tune: A Life of Scott Joplin.* Columbia: University of Missouri Press, 1994.

Duncan, Isadora. *The Art of the Dance,* edited by Sheldon Cheney. New York: Theatre Arts, 1928.

Dwight, Eleanor. *Edith Wharton, An Extraordinary Life.* New York: Abrams, 1994.

Elliott, Emory, ed. *Columbia Literary History of the United States.* New York: Columbia University Press, 1988.

Erenberg, Lewis *Steppin' Out: New York Nightlife and the Transformation of American Culture, 1890–1930.* Westport, Conn.: Greenwood Press, 1981.

Ewen, David. *All the Years of American Popular Music.* Englewood Cliffs, N.J.: Prentice-Hall, 1977.

Ewen, David. *New Complete Book of the American Musical Theater.* New York: Holt Rinehart and Winston, 1970.

Furia, Philip. *The Poets of Tin Pan Alley: A History of America's Great Lyricists.* New York: Oxford University Press, 1990.

Gerdts, William H. *American Impressionism.* New York: Abbeville Press, 1984.

Gregory, Horace, and Marza Zaturensha. *A History of American Poetry, 1900–1940.* New York: Harcourt, Brace, 1946.

Hazzard-Gordon, Katrina. *Jookin': The Rise of Social Dance Formations in African-American Culture.* Philadelphia: Temple University Press, 1990.

Homer, William Innes. *Alfred Stieglitz and the Photo-Secession.* New York: Little, Brown, 1983.

Hughes, Robert. *American Visions: The Epic History of Art in America.* New York: Alfred A. Knopf, 1997.

Kuritz, Paul. *The Making of Theatre History.* Englewood Cliffs, N.J.: Prentice Hall, 1988.

Lauter, Paul. *The Heath Anthology of American Literature,* vol. 2. Lexington, Mass.: Heath, 1990.

Lewis, R.W.B. *Edith Wharton: A Biography.* New York: Harper & Row, 1975.

Lingeman, Richard. *Theodore Dreiser: An American Journey.* London: John Wiley & Sons, 1993.

Loney, Glenn. *20th Century Theatre,* vol. 1 New York: Facts On File, 1983.

Madden, Ethan. *Better Foot Forward: The History of American Musical Theater.* New York: Grossman, 1976.

Magriel, Paul. *Chronicles of American Dance.* New York: Holt, 1948.

Mast, Gerald. *A Short History of the Movies,* rev. by Bruce F. Kawin. New York: Macmillan, 1992.

May, Henry F. *The End of American Innocence,* rev. ed. New York: Columbia University Press, 1992.

Meserve, Walter. *An Outline History of American Drama.* New York: Feedback Theatre Books & Prospero Press, 1994.

Morgan, Thomas L., and William Barlow. *From Cakewalks to Concert Halls: An Illustrated History of African-American Popular Music From 1895 to 1930.* Washington, D.C.: Elliott & Clark, 1992.

Musser, Charles. *Before the Nickelodeon: Edwin S. Porter and the Edison Manufacturing Company.* Berkeley: University of California Press, 1991.

Musser. *The Emergence of Cinema.* New York: Scribners, 1990.

Perkins, David. *A History of Modern Poetry: From the 1890s to the High Modernist Mode.* Cambridge, Mass.: Harvard University Press, 1976.

Peterson, Christina. *Alfred Stieglitz's Camera Notes.* New York: Norton, 1993.

Quartermain, Peter, ed. *American Poets, 1880–1945,* series 1–3; *Dictionary of Literary Biography,* vols. 45, 48, and 54. Detroit: Bruccoli Clark/Gale Research, 1986–1987.

Rideout, Walter B. *The Radical Novel in the United States 1900–1954.* Cambridge, Mass.: Harvard University Press, 1956.

Rose, Barbara. *American Art Since 1900.* New York: Praeger, 1968.

Rubin, Louis D., Jr., ed. *The History of Southern Literature.* Baton Rouge: Louisiana State University Press, 1985.

Ruyter, Nancy Lee Chalfa. *Reformers and Visionaries: The Americanization of the Art of Dance.* New York: Dance Horizons, 1979.

St. Denis, Ruth. *An Unfinished Life: An Autobiography.* New York: Harper, 1939.

Seller, Maxine Schwartz, ed. *Ethnic Theatre in the United States.* Westport, Conn.: Greenwood Press, 1983.

Sinclair, Andrew. *Jack: A Biography.* New York: Harper & Row, 1977.

Slide, Anthony. *The Encyclopedia of Vaudeville.* Westport, Conn.: Greenwood Press, 1994.

Smith, Eric L. *Bert Williams: A Biography of the Black Comedian.* Jefferson, N.C. & London: McFarland, 1992.

Business and the Economy

Beasley, Norman. *Main Street Merchant: The Story of the J.C. Penney Company.* New York: Whittlesey House, 1948.

Benson, Susan P. *Counter Cultures: Saleswomen, Managers, and Customers in American Department Stores, 1890–1940.* Urbana: University of Illinois Press, 1988.

Bogart, Ernest L., and Donald L. Kemmerer. *Economic History of the American People.* New York: Longmans, Green, 1942.

Boyer, Richard O., and Herbert M. Morais. *Labor's Untold Story.* Pittsburgh: UERMWA, 1955.

Brody, David. *Workers in Industrial America: Essays on the Twentieth-Century Struggle.* New York: Oxford University Press, 1980.

Brooks, John. *The Autobiography of American Business.* Garden City, N.Y.: Doubleday, 1974.

Carnegie, Andrew. *Autobiography.* Boston: Houghton Mifflin, 1920.

———. *The Gospel of Wealth and Other Timely Essays.* New York: Century, 1900.

Carosso, Vincent P. *The Morgans: Private International Bankers.* Cambridge: Harvard University Press, 1988.

Copley, Frank Barkley. *Frederick W. Taylor: Father of Scientific Management.* vols. 1 and 2. New York: Kelley, 1969.

Dubofsky, Melvyn. *Industrialization and the American Worker, 1865–1920.* Arlington Heights, Ill.: H. Davidson, 1985.

Dubofsky, Melvyn. *We Shall Be All: A History of the Industrial Workers of the World.* Chicago: Quadrangle, 1969.

Dulles, Foster Rhea. *Labor in America: A History.* New York: Crowell, 1949.

Ewen, Elizabeth. *Immigrant Women in the Land of Dollars: Life and Culture on the Lower East Side, 1890–1925.* New York: Monthly Review Press, 1985.

Ford, Henry. *My Life and Work.* Garden City, N.Y.: Doubleday, Page, 1922.

Freeman, Joshua, et al. *Who Built America? Working People and the Nation's Economy, Politics, Culture, and Society.* vol. 2. New York: Pantheon, 1992.

Great Stories of American Businessmen. New York: American Heritage Publishing, 1972.

Haywood, Bill. *Bill Haywood's Book: The Autobiography.* New York: International, 1929.

Hessen, Robert. *Steel Titan: The Life of Charles M. Schwab.* New York: Oxford University Press, 1975.

Lacy, Robert. *Ford: The Men and the Machine.* Boston: Little, Brown, 1986.

Mellon, Andrew. *Taxation: The People's Business.* New York: Macmillan, 1924.

Montgomery, David. *The Fall of the House of Labor: The Workplace, the State, and American Labor Activism, 1865–1925.* New York: Cambridge University Press, 1989.

Morgan, Gareth. *Images of Organization.* Newbury Park, Calif.: Sage, 1986.

Myers, Margaret. *A Financial History of the United States.* New York: Columbia University Press, 1970.

Nevins, Allan. *Ford: The Times, The Man, The Company.* New York: Scribners, 1954.

O'Connor, Harvey. *Mellon's Millions: The Biography of a Fortune.* New York: Day, 1993.

Patterson, James T. *America's Struggle Against Poverty, 1900–1980.* Cambridge: Harvard University Press, 1986.

Peiss, Kathy. *Cheap Amusements: Working Women and Leisure in Turn-of-the-Century New York.* Philadelphia: Temple University Press, 1986.

Penney, J.C. *Fifty Years With the Golden Rule.* New York: Harper, 1950.

———. *View From the Next Decade: Jottings From a Merchant's Daybook.* New York: Nelson, 1960.

Peterson, Joyce S. *American Automobile Workers, 1900–1933.* Albany: State University of New York Press, 1987.

Porter, Glenn. *The Rise of Big Business, 1860–1910.* New York: Crowell, 1973.

Rosenweig, Roy. *Eight Hours for What We Will: Workers and Leisure in an Industrial City, 1870–1920.* New York: Cambridge University Press, 1985.

Rozwenc, Edwin C., ed. *Roosevelt, Wilson and the Trusts.* Boston: Heath, 1950.

Satterlee, Herbert. *J. Pierpont Morgan: An Intimate Portrait.* New York: Macmillan, 1939.

Taft, Philip. *Organized Labor in American History.* New York: Harper & Row, 1964.

Taylor, Frederick Winslow. *Principles of Scientific Management.* New York: Harper, 1911.

Wall, Joseph Frazier. *Andrew Carnegie.* New York: Oxford University Press, 1970.

Websites

"Car Manufacturers, George Selden—Henry Ford in Patent Battle." Available online at http://inventors.about.com/library/weekly/aacarsseldona.htm.

"Findlaw: U.S. Constitution: Sixteenth Amendment." Available online at http://caselaw.findlaw.com/data/constitution/amendment16.

"Gold Standard Act—March 14, 1900." Available online at http://www.multied.com/documents/GoldStandard.html.

"Industrial Workers of the World." Available online at http://www.iww.org.

"International Ladies Garment Workers Union." Available online at http://www.nps.gov/elro/glossary/ilgwu.htm.

"Model T Ford Club of America." Available online at http://www.mtfca.com.

"The Nickelodeon's History." Available online at http://ct.essortment.com/nichelodeonshi_rqtl.htm.

"Railroad Legislation." Available online at http://www.u-s-history.com/pages/h921.html.

"Samuel Gompers." Available online at http://www.kentlaw.edu/ilhs/gompers.htm.

"U.S. Steel." Available online at http://www.usx.com/corp/index.htm.

Education

Anderson, James D. *The Education of Blacks in the South, 1860–1935.* Chapel Hill: University of North Carolina Press, 1988.

Beale, Howard K. *A History of Freedom of Teaching in American Schools.* Report of the Commission on the Social Studies, American Historical Association, part 16. New York & Chicago: Scribners, 1941.

Beatty, Barbara. *Preschool Education in America: The Culture of Young Children From the Colonial Era to the Present.* New Haven, Conn.: Yale University Press, 1995.

Berrol, Selma Cantor. *Julia Richman: A Notable Woman.* Philadelphia: Balch Institute Press, 1993.

Berube, Maurice R. *American School Reform: Progressive, Equality, and Excellence Movements, 1883–1993.* Westport, Conn.: Praeger, 1994.

Bourne, Randolph S. *The Gary Schools.* Cambridge, Mass.: MIT Press, 1970.

Button, H. Warren, and Eugene F. Provenzo Jr. *History of Education and Culture in America.* Englewood Cliffs, N.J.: Prentice-Hall, 1983.

Church, Robert L., and Michael W. Sedlak. *Education in the United States: An Interpretive History.* New York: Free Press, 1976.

Cremin, Lawrence A. *American Education: The Metropolitan Experience, 1876–1980.* New York: Harper & Row, 1988.

———. *The Transformation of the School: Progressivism in American Education, 1876–1957.* New York: Vintage, 1964.

Dabney, Charles William. *Universal Education in the South.* Chapel Hill: University of North Carolina Press, 1936.

Dawson, Howard A., and M.C.S. Noble Jr. *Handbook on Rural Education: Factual Data on Rural Education, Its Social and Economic Backgrounds.* Washington, D.C.: National Education Association of the United States, Department of Rural Education, 1961.

Dworkin, Martin. *Dewey on Education.* New York: Columbia University Teachers College Press, 1959.

Dykhuizen, George. *The Life and Mind of John Dewey.* Carbondale: Southern Illinois University Press, 1973.

Fishman, Stephen M. *John Dewey and the Challenge of Classroom Practice.* New York: Teachers College Press, 1998.

Graham, Patricia Albjerg. *S.O.S.: Sustain Our Schools.* New York: Hill & Wang, 1992.

Haley, Margaret A. *Battleground: The Autobiography of Margaret A. Haley.* Robert L. Reid, ed. Urbana: University of Illinois Press, 1982.

Harlan, Louis R. *Booker T. Washington: The Wizard of Tuskegee, 1901–1915.* New York: Oxford University Press, 1983.

———. *Separate and Unequal: Public School Campaigns and Racism in the Southern Seaboard States, 1901–1915.* Chapel Hill: University of North Carolina Press, 1958.

Hofstadter, Richard, and Wilson Smith. *American Higher Education: A Documentary History.* 2 vols. Chicago: University of Chicago Press, 1961.

Horowitz, Richard. *The Power and Passion of M. Carey Thomas.* New York: Knopf, 1994.

Horowitz, Richard, and Helen Lefkowitz. *Campus Life: Undergraduate Cultures From the End of the Eighteenth Century to the Present.* Chicago: University of Chicago Press, 1987.

James, Henry. *Charles W. Eliot: President of Harvard University, 1869–1909.* Boston: Houghton Mifflin, 1930.

James, Thomas. *Public versus Nonpublic Education in Historical Perspective.* Stanford, Calif.: Institute for Research on Educational Finance and Governance, School of Education, Stanford University, 1982.

Jonich, Geraldine. *The Sane Positivist: A Biography of Edward L. Thorndike.* Middletown, Conn.: Wesleyan University Press, 1968.

Karier, Clarence J. *Roots of Crisis: American Education in the Twentieth Century.* Chicago: Rand, McNally, 1973.

———. *Shaping the American Education State, 1900 to the Present.* New York: Free Press, 1975.

Kliebard, Herbert M. *The Struggle for the American Curriculum, 1893–1958.* New York: Routledge & Kegan Paul, 1987.

Krug, Edward A. *The Shaping of the American High School.* New York: Harper & Row, 1964.

Lagemann, Ellen Condliffe. *The Politics of Knowledge: The Carnegie Corporation, Philanthropy, and Public Policy.* Chicago: University of Chicago Press, 1989.

———. *Private Power for the Public Good: A History of the Carnegie Foundation for the Advancement of Teaching.* Middletown, Conn.: Wesleyan University Press, 1983.

Lazerson, Marvin, ed. *American Education in the Twentieth Century: A Documentary History.* New York: Teachers College Press, Columbia University, 1987.

Lewis, David Levering. *W.E.B. Du Bois: Biography of a Race, 1868–1919.* New York: Holt, 1993.

Lucas, Christopher J. *American Higher Education: A History.* New York: St. Martin's Press, 1994.

Margo, Robert A. *Race and Schooling in the South, 1880–1950: An Economic History.* Chicago: University of Chicago Press, 1990.

Maxcy, Spencer J. ed. *John Dewey and American Education.* Bristol: Thoemmes, 2002.

McLachlan, James. *American Boarding Schools: A Historical Study.* New York: Scribners, 1970.

McMillen, Neil R. *Dark Journey: Black Mississippians in the Age of Jim Crow.* Urbana: University of Illinois Press, 1989.

Morison, Samuel Eliot. *The Development of Harvard University Since the Inauguration of President Eliot, 1869–1929.* Cambridge: Harvard University Press, 1930.

Murphy, Majorie. *Blackboard Unions: The AFT and the NEA, 1900–1980.* Ithaca, N.Y.: Cornell University Press, 1990.

Perlmann, Joel. *Ethnic Differences: Schooling and Social Structure Among the Irish, Italians, Jews and Blacks in an American City, 1880–1935.* New York: Cambridge University Press, 1988.

Pulliam, John D. *History of Education in America.* 3rd ed. Columbus, Ohio: Merrill, 1986.

Seller, Maxine Schwartz, ed. *Women Educators in the United States, 1820–1993: A Bio-Bibliographical Sourcebook.* Westport, Conn.: Greenwood Press, 1994.

Sokal, Michael M. *Psychological Testing and American Society, 1890–1930.* New Brunswick, N.J.: Rutgers University Press, 1987.

Thayer, Vivian Trow. *Formative Ideas in American Education, From the Colonial Period to the Present.* New York: Dodd, Mead, 1965.

Torrance, Ridgely. *The Story of John Hope.* New York: Macmillan, 1948.

Tyack, David B. *The One Best System: A History of American Urban Education.* Cambridge: Harvard University Press, 1974.

Tyack, David B., and Elizabeth Hansot. *Managers of Virtue: Public School Leadership in America, 1820–1980.* New York: Basic Books, 1982.

Vassar, Rena L. *Social History of American Education.* Chicago: Rand, McNally, 1965.

Veysey, Laurence R. *The Emergence of the American University.* Chicago: University of Chicago Press, 1965.

Weaver, Warren. *U.S. Philanthropic Foundations: Their History, Structure, Management, and Record.* New York: Harper & Row, 1967.

Westbrook, Robert. *John Dewey and American Democracy.* Ithaca, N.Y.: Cornell University Press, 1991.

Zilversmit, Arthur. *Changing Schools: Progressive Education Theory and Practice, 1930–1960.* Chicago: University of Chicago Press, 1993.

Websites

"A Brief History of Francis W. Parker School." Available online at http://www.fwparker.org/about/history.html.

"John Dewey." Available online at http://www.johndewey.org.

"Marietta Johnson School of Organic Education." Available online at http://www.schoolfororganiceducation.org.

"Mary McLeod Bethune." Available online at http://www.usca.sc.edu/aasc/bethune.htm.

"The Pragmatism Cybrary: The Chicago School." Available online at http://www.pragmatism.org/genealogy/Chicago.htm.

"Schugurensky, Daniel. "History of Education: Selected Moments of the 20th Century." Available online at http://fcis.oise.utoronto.ca/daniel_schugurensky/ (accessed June 18, 2003).

"U.S. Supreme Court: Berea College v. Com. of Kentucky, 211 U.S. 45 (1908)." Available online at http://www.caselaw.lp.findlaw.com/cgi-in/getcase.pl?court=US&vol=211&invol=45.

Fashion and Design

Arwas, Victor. *Glass: Art Nouveau to Art Deco.* New York: Abrams, 1987.

Batterberry, Michael and Ariane Batterberry. *Mirror, Mirror: A Social History of Fashion.* New York: Holt, Rinehart & Winston, 1977.

Brockman, Helen L. *The Theory of Fashion Design.* New York: Wiley, 1965.

Burchard, John, and Albert Bush-Brown. *The Architecture of America: A Social and Cultural History.* Boston: Atlantic Monthly/Little, Brown, 1961.

Calloway, Stephen. *Twentieth-Century Decoration: The Domestic Interior From 1900 to the Present Day.* London: Weidenfeld & Nicolson, 1988.

Calloway, Stephen, and Elizabeth Cromley, eds. *The Elements of Style.* New York: Simon & Schuster, 1991.

The Changing American Woman: Two Hundred Years of American Fashion. New York: Fairchild, 1976.

Clark, Clifford Edward, Jr.. *The American Family Home, 1800–1960.* Chapel Hill: University of North Carolina Press, 1986.

Condit, Carl W. *The Chicago School of Architecture.* Chicago: University of Chicago Press, 1964.

Contini, Mila. *Fashion: From Ancient Egypt to the Present Day.* New York: Odyssey, 1965.

de Marly, Diana. *Fashion for Men: An Illustrated History.* New York: Holmes & Meier, 1985.

———. *The History of Haute Couture, 1850–1950.* New York: Holmes & Meier, 1980.

Dolan, Maryanne. *Vintage Clothing, 1880–1960: Identification and Value Guide.* Florence, Ala.: Books Americana, 1984.

Ewing, Elizabeth. *History of Twentieth Century Fashion,* rev. and updated ed. London: Batsford, 1992; Lanham, Md.: Barnes & Noble, 1992.

Fairbanks, Jonathan L., and Elizabeth Bidwell Bates. *American Furniture: 1620 to the Present.* New York: Marek, 1981.

Ginsburg, Madeleine. *Victorian Dress in Photographs.* New York: Holmes & Meier, 1982.

Hunt Jr., William Dudley. *Encyclopedia of American Architecture.* New York: McGraw-Hill, 1980.

Jones, Edgar R. *Those Were the Good Old Days: A Happy Look at American Advertising, 1880–1930.* New York: Simon & Schuster, 1989.

Ley, Sandra. *Fashion for Everyone: The Story of Ready-to-Wear, 1870–1970.* New York: Scribners, 1975.

Lloyd, Valerie. *McDowell's Directory of Twentieth Century Fashion.* Englewood Cliffs, N.J.: Prentice-Hall, 1985.

Maddex, Diane, ed. *Master Builders: A Guide to Famous American Architects.* Washington, D.C.: Preservation Press, 1985.

McAlester, Virginia, and Lee McAlester. *A Field Guide to American Houses.* New York: Knopf, 1992.

Milbank, Caroline Rennolds. *New York Fashion: The Evolution of American Style.* New York: Thames & Hudson, 1989.

Nash, Eric Peter. *Frank Llyod Wright: Force of Nature.* New York: Smithmark Pulishers, 1996.

Pool, Mary Jane, ed. *20th-Century Decorating, Architecture & Gardens: 80 Years of Ideas & Pleasure From House & Garden.* New York: Holt, Rinehart & Winston, 1980.

Rogers, Meyric R. *American Interior Design: The Traditions and Development of Domestic Design From Colonial Times to the Present.* New York: Norton, 1947.

Roth, Leland M. *A Concise History of American Architecture.* New York: Icon Editions/Harper & Row, 1979.

Ryan, Mary Shaw. *Clothing: A Study in Human Behavior.* New York: Holt, Rinehart & Winston, 1966.

Schoeffler, O.E., and William Gale. *Esquire's Encyclopedia of 20th Century Men's Fashion.* New York: McGraw-Hill, 1973.

Sichel, Marion. *History of Men's Costume.* London: Batsford, 1984.

Smith, C. Ray. *Interior Design in 20th Century America: A History.* New York: Harper & Row, 1986.

Stickley, Gustav. *Craftsman Homes.* New York: Gramercy Books, 1909. (Reprinted by Random House, 1995.)

Stowell, Donald, and Erin Wertenberger. *A Century of Fashion 1865–1965.* Chicago: Encyclopaedia Britannica, 1987.

Trahey, Jane. *The Mode in Costume.* New York: Scribners, 1958.

———. *Harper's Bazaar: One Hundred Years of the American Female.* New York: Random House, 1967.

Twombly, Robert. *Frank Lloyd Wright: His Life and His Architecture.* New York: Wiley, 1978.

Tyrrell, Anne V. *Changing Trends in Fashion: Patterns of the Twentieth Century 1900–1970.* London: Batsford, 1986.

Whiffen, Marcus, and Frederick Koeper. *American Architecture, 1607–1976.* Cambridge, Mass.: MIT Press, 1981.

Government and Politics

Cherny, Robert W. *A Righteous Cause: The Life of William Jennings Bryan.* Boston: Little, Brown, and Company 1985.

Coletta, Paolo E. *The Presidency of William Howard Taft.* Lawrence: University Press of Kansas, 1973.

Gifford Pinchot & The Making of Modern Environmentalism. Washington, D.C.: Island Press, 2001.

Gould, Lewis L. *The Presidency of Theodore Roosevelt.* Lawrence: University Press of Kansas, 1991.

Harbaugh, William Henry. *Power and Responsibility: The Life and Times of Theodore Roosevelt.* New York: Farrar, Straus & Cudahy, 1961.

Harlan, Louis R. *Booker T. Washington: The Making of a Black Leader, 1856–1901.* New York: Oxford University Press, 1972.

Jergens, George. *News From the White House: The Presidential-Press Relationship in the Progressive Era.* Chicago: University Chicago Press, 1981.

Levine, Lawrence W. *Defender of the Faith.* Cambridge: Harvard University Press, 1965.

McCullough, David G. *The Path Between the Seas: The Creation of the Panama Canal, 1870–1914.* New York: Simon & Schuster, 1977.

Morris, Edmund. *The Rise of Theodore Roosevelt.* New York: Coward, 1979.

Rosen, Ruth. *The Lost Sisterhood: Prostitutes in America, 1910–1918.* Baltimore, Md.: John Hopkins University Press, 1982.

Salvatore, Nick. *Eugene V. Debs: Citizen and Socialist.* New York: Chelsea House, 1982.

Sinclair, Andrew. *Era of Excess: A Social History of the Prohibition Movement.* New York: Harper & Row, 1962.

Thelen, David P. *Robert M. La Follette and the Insurgent Spirit.* Boston: Little, Brown, 1976.

Washington, Booker T. *Up From Slavery: An Autobiography.* Garden City, N.Y.: Doubleday, 1963.

Zimmerman, Warren. *First Great Triumph: How Five Americans Made Their Country a World Power.* New York: Farrar, 2002.

Law and Justice

Abraham, Henry J. *Justices, Presidents, and Senators: A History of the U.S. Supreme Court Appointments From Washington to Clinton.* Rowman & Littlefield, 1999.

Baker, Liva. *The Justice From Beacon Hill: The Life and Times of Oliver Wendell Holmes, Jr.* New York: HarperCollins, 1991.

Franklin, John Hope, and Alfred A. Moss Jr. *From Slavery to Freedom: A History of African Americans.* New York: Knopf, 2000.

Hall, Kermit L., ed. *The Oxford Companion to the Supreme Court.* New York: Oxford University Press, 1992.

Harrison, Maureen, and Steve Gilbert, eds. *Landmark Decisions of the United States Supreme Court II.* Beverly Hills, Calif.: Excellent Books, 1992.

Kelly, Alfred H., Winfred A. Harbison, and Herman Belz. *The American Constitution: Its Origins and Development.* vol. II. 7th ed. New York: Norton, 1991.

Lichtenstein, Nelson. *State of the Union: A Century of American Labor (Politics and Society in Twentieth-Century America).* Princeton, N.J.: Princeton University Press, 2002.

Mikula, Mark F., and L. Mpho Mabunda, eds. *Great American Court Cases.* Farmington Hills, Mich.: Gale Group, 2000.

Palmer, Kris E., ed. *Constitutional Amendments: 1789 to the Present.* Farmington Hills, Mich.: Gale Group, 2000.

Renshaw, Patrick. *The Wobblies: The Story of IWW and Syndicalism in the United States.* Chicago: Ivan R. Dee, Inc. 1999.

West's Encyclopedia of American Law. 2d ed. 12 vols. St. Paul, Minn.: West Publishing Co.

Websites

"The Last Days of a President: Films of McKinley and the Pan-American Exposition, 1901." Available online at http://memory.loc.gov/ammem/papr/mckhome.html; website home page: http://www.loc.gov (accessed April 20, 2003).

"The Oyez Project of Northwestern University, a U.S. Supreme Court Multimedia Database." Available online at http://www.oyez.com; (accessed April 20, 2003).

"The Presidents of the United States." Available online at http://www.whitehouse.gov/history/presidents/; website home page: http://www.whitehouse.gov (accessed April 20, 2003).

"The Trial of Bill Haywood." Available online at http://www.law.umkc.edu/faculty/projects/ftrials/haywood/haywood.htm; website home page http://www.law.umkc.edu/faculty/projects/ftrials/ftrials.htm (accessed April 20, 2003).

"The Trial of Sheriff Joseph Shipp." Available online at http://www.law.umkc.edu/faculty/projects/ftrials/shipp/shipp.html; website home page: http://www.law.umkc.edu/faculty/projects/ftrials/ftrials.htm (accessed April 20, 2003).

"U.S. Supreme Court Opinions." Available online at http://www.findlaw.com/casecode/supreme.html; website home page: http://www.findlaw.com (accessed April 19, 2003).

"Website of the Theodore Roosevelt Association." Available online at http://www.theodoreroosevelt.org/ (accessed April 20, 2003).

Lifestyles and Social Trends

Balkin, Richard, et al., eds. *Victorian America, 1876 to 1913.* New York: Facts on File, 1996.

Carson, Mina J. *Settlement Folk: Social Thought and the American Settlement Movement, 1885–1930.* Chicago: University of Chicago Press, 1990.

Cashman, Sean. *America in the Age of the Titans: The Progressive Era and World War I.* New York: New York University Press, 1988.

Chambers, John Whiteclay II. *The Tyranny of Change: America in the Progressive Era, 1890–1920.* New Brunswick, N.J.: Rutgers University Press, 2000.

Chudacoff, Howard P. *The Age of the Bachelor.* Princeton, N.J.: Princeton University Press, 2000.

Crunden, Robert M. *Ministers of Reform: The Progressives' Achievement in American Civilization, 1889–1920.* Champaign: University of Illinois Press, 1985.

Daniels, Roger. *Not Like Us: Immigrants and Minorities in America, 1890–1924.* Chicago: Ivan R. Dee, 1997.

Davis, Allen F. *Spearheads for Reform: The Social Settlements & the Progressive Movement, 1890 to 1914.* New Brunswick, N.J.: Rutgers University Press, 1985.

Diner, Steven J. *A Very Different Age: Americans of the Progressive Era.* New York: Hill and Wang, 1998.

Dubofsky, Melvin. *Industrialism and the American Worker, 1865–1920.* Arlington Heights, Ill.: Harlan Davidson, 1985.

Enstad, Nan. *Ladies of Labor, Girls of Adventure.* New York: Columbia University Press, 1999.

Fairclough, Adam. *Better Day Coming: Blacks and Equality, 1890–2000.* New York: Viking, 2001.

Georgano, Nick. *The American Automobile: A Centenary, 1893–1993.* New York: Smithmark, 1992.

Hale, Grace E. *Making Whiteness: The Culture of Segregation in the South, 1890–1940.* New York: Vintage Books, 1999.

Hays, Samuel P. *The Response to Industrialism 1885–1914.* 2d ed. Chicago: University of Chicago Press, 1996.

Ichioka, Yuji. *The Issei: The World of the First Generation Japanese Immigrants, 1885–1924.* New York: The Free Press, 1990.

Immell, Myra, ed. *The 1900s.* San Diego, Calif.: Greenhaven Press, 2000.

Jacobson, Matthew F. *Whiteness of a Different Color: European Immigrants and the Alchemy of Race.* Cambridge: Harvard University Press, 1999.

Jackson, Kenneth. *Crabgrass Frontier: The Suburbanization of the United States.* New York: Oxford University Press, 1985.

Kisseloff, Jeff. *You Must Remember This: An Oral History of Manhattan From the 1890s to World War Two.* Baltimore: John Hopkins University Press, 2000.

Jones, Jacqueline. *Labor of Love, Labor of Sorrow: Black Women, Work and the Family From Slavery to the Present.* New York: Basic Books, 1985.

Kasson, John F. *Amusing the Millions: Coney Island at the Turn of the Century.* New York: Hill & Wang, 1978.

Kessler-Harris, Alice. *Out to Work: A History of Wage-Earning Women in the United States.* New York: Oxford University Press, 1982.

Kraut, Alan. *The Huddled Masses: The Immigrant in American Society, 1880–1921.* Arlington Heights, Ill.: Harlan Davidson, 1982.

Leach, William. *Land of Desire: Merchants, Power, and the Rise of a New American Culture.* New York: Random House, 1993.

Lender, Mark Edward, and James Kirby Martin. *Drinking in America.* New York: Free Press, 1987.

Lesy, Michael. *Dreamland: America at the Dawn of the Twentieth Century.* New York: New Press, 1997.

Lewis, David L. *W.E.B. Du Bois: Biography of a Race, 1868–1919.* New York: H. Holt, 1993.

Ling, Peter J. *America and the Automobile: Technology, Reform and Social Change.* Manchester, U.K.: Manchester University Press, 1990.

Mintz, Steven, and Susan Kellogg. *Domestic Revolutions: A Social History of American Family Life.* New York: Free Press, 1988.

Nasaw, David. *Going Out: The Rise and Fall of Public Amusements.* New York: Basic Books, 1995.

Pegram, Thomas R. *Battling Demon Rum: The Struggle for a Dry America, 1800–1933.* Chicago: Ivan R. Dee, 1998.

Powers, Madelon. *Faces Along the Bar: Lore and Order in the Workingman's Saloon, 1870–1920.* Chicago: University of Chicago Press, 1998.

Robinson, David, and Martin Scorsese. *From Peepshow to Palace.* New York: Columbia University Press, 1995.

Rosenberg, Rosalind. *Divided Lives: American Women in the Twentieth Century.* New York: Hill & Wang, 1992.

Satter, Beryl. *Each Mind a Kingdom: American Women, Sexual Purity, and the New Thought Movement, 1875–1920.* Berkeley: University of California Press, 1999.

Scharff, Virginia. *Taking the Wheel: Women and the Coming of the Motor Age.* New York: Free Press, 1991.

Smith, Karen Manners. *New Paths to Power: American Women 1890–1920.* New York: Oxford University Press, 1994.

Starr, Franklin, and Isidore Starr. *The Negro in Twentieth Century America.* New York: Random House, 1967.

Strasser, Susan. *Never Done: A History of American Housework.* New York: Pantheon, 1982.

Van Slyck, Abigail A. *Free to All: Carnegie Libraries & American Culture, 1890–1920.* Chicago: University of Chicago Press, 1998.

Wiebe, Robert H. *The Search for Order 1877–1920.* New York: Hill & Wang, 1980.

Woodward, C. Vann. *The Strange Career of Jim Crow,* 3rd rev. ed. New York: Oxford University Press, 1974.

Websites

"American Cultural History, 1900–1909." Available online at http://kclibrary.nhmccd.edu/decade00.html (accessed April 22, 2003).

"American Variety Stage: Vaudeville and Popular Entertainment, 1870–1920." Available online at http://memory.loc.gov/ammem/vshtml/vshome.html (accessed April 22, 2003).

"Bijou Dream." Available online at http://pages.zdnet.com/kinema/index.html (accessed April 22, 2003).

"A Biography of America: A Vital Progressivism." Available online at http://www.learner.org/biographyofamerica/prog19/index.html html (accessed April 22, 2003).

"By Popular Demand: Votes for Women's Suffrage: Pictures, 1850–1920." Available online at http://memory.loc.gov/ammem/vfwhtml/vfwhome.html (accessed April 22, 2003).

"The Early 1900s: Primary Sources From American Popular Culture." Available online at http://www.authentichistory.com/1900s.html (accessed April 22, 2003).

"Gateway to African American History, 1900–1940." Available online at http://charter.uchicago.edu/AAH/19001940.htm (accessed April 22, 2003).

"The Nickelodeons." Available online at http://www.cinemaweb.com/silentfilm/bookshelf/17_sep_2.htm (accessed April 22, 2003).

"Temperance & Prohibition." Available online at http://prohibition.history.ohio-state.edu/Contents.htm (accessed April 22, 2003).

The Media

Brady, Kathleen. *Ida Tarbell: Portrait of a Muckraker.* New York: Putnam, 1984.

Chalmers, David Mark. *The Muckrake Years.* New York: Van Nostrand, 1974.

Douglas, Susan J. *Inventing American Broadcasting, 1899–1922.* Baltimore: Johns Hopkins University Press, 1987.

Emery, Edwin, and Michael Emery. *The Press and America: An Interpretive History of the Mass Media.* Boston: Allyn and Bacon, 1996.

Filler, Louis. *The Muckrakers.* University Park: Pennsylvania State University Press, 1976.

Fitzpatrick, Ellen. *Muckraking: Three Landmark Articles.* New York: Bedford Books/St. Martin's Press, 1994.

Gelatt, Roland. *The Fabulous Phonograph: From Edison to Stereo.* New York: Appleton-Century, 1966.

Griffith, Sally Foreman. *Hometown News: William Allen White and the Emporia Gazette.* New York: Oxford University Press, 1989.

Kaplan, Justin. *Lincoln Steffens, A Biography.* New York: Simon & Schuster, 1974.

Marschall, Richard. *America's Great Comic Strip Artists.* New York: Abbeville Press, 1989.

Miller, Sally M., ed. *The Ethnic Press in the United States: A Historical Analysis and Handbook.* Westport, Conn.: Greenwood Press, 1987.

Peterson, Theodore. *Magazines in the Twentieth Century.* Urbana: University of Illinois Press, 1956.

Ponce De Leon, Charles L. *Self-Exposure: Human-Interest Journalism and the Emergence of Celebrity in America, 1890–1940.* Chapel Hill: University of North Carolina Press, 1992.

Robinson, Jerry. *The Comics: An Illustrated History of Comic Strip Art.* New York: Putnam, 1974.

Schlipp, Madelon Golden, and Sharon M. Murphy. *Great Women of the Press.* Carbondale: Southern Illinois University Press, 1983.

Schudson, Michael. *Discovering the News: A Social History of American Newspapers.* New York: Basic Books, 1978.

Serrin, Judith, and William Serrin, eds. *Muckraking!: The Journalism That Changed America.* New York: New Press, 2002.

Swanberg, W.A. *Citizen Hearst.* New York: Scribners, 1961.

Tebbel, John. *Between Covers: The Rise and Transformation of Book Publishing in America.* New York: Oxford University Press, 1987.

———. *A History of Book Publishing in the United States.* vol. 2, *The Expansion of an Industry, 1865–1919.* New York & London: R. R. Bowker, 1975.

Thomas, Dana Lee. *The Media Moguls: From Joseph Pulitzer to William S. Paley, the Wheelings and Dealings of America's News Merchants.* New York: Putnam, 1981.

Websites

"America at Work, America at Leisure: Motion Pictures, 1894–1915." Available online at http://memory.loc.gov/ammem/awlhtml/awlhome.html (accessed April 22, 2003).

"Child Labor in America, 1908–1912: The Photographs of Louis W. Hine." Available online at http://historyplace.com/unitedstates/childlabor/index.html (accessed April 22, 2003).

"Dime Novels and Penny Dreadfuls." Available online at http://historyplace.com/unitedstates/childlabor/index.html (accessed April 22, 2003).

"United States Early Radio History." Available online at http://EarlyRadioHistory.us/ (accessed April 22, 2003).

"Voices of the 20th Century: Sounds From the Past." Available online at http://www.ibiscom.com/vofrm.htm (accessed April 22, 2003).

Medicine and Health

Abram, Ruth J., ed. *Send Us a Lady Physician: Women Doctors in America, 1835–1920.* New York: Norton, 1985.

Bates, Barbara. *Bargaining for Life: A Social History of Tuberculosis, 1876–1938.* Philadelphia: University of Pennsylvania Press, 1992.

Bean, William Bennett. *Walter Reed: A Biography.* Charlottesville: University Press of Virginia, 1982.

Bender, Arnold E. *A Dictionary of Food and Nutrition.* NewYork: Oxford University Press, 1995.

Bordley, James, and A. McGehee Harvey. *Two Centuries of American Medicine, 1776–1976.* Philadelphia: Saunders, 1976.

Brandt, Allan M. *No Magic Bullet: A Social History of Venereal Disease in the United States Since 1880.* New York: Oxford University Press, 1985.

Burrow, James G. *AMA: Voice of American Medicine.* Baltimore: Johns Hopkins University Press, 1963.

Caldwell, Mark. *The Last Crusade: The War on Consumption, 1862–1954.* NewYork: Antheneum, 1988.

Carpenter, Kenneth J., ed. *Pellagra.* Stroudsburg, Pa.: Hutchinson Ross, 1981.

Cassedy, James H. *Medicine in America: A Short History.* Baltimore: Johns Hopkins University Press, 1991.

Dolan, Edward. *Walter Reed, Vanquishing Yellow Fever.* Chicago: Britannica Books, 1962.

Duffy, John. *The Healers: The Rise of the Medical Establishment.* New York: McGraw-Hill, 1976; republished as *The Healers: A History of American Medicine.* Urbana: University of Illinois Press, 1979.

Etheridge, E. W. *The Butterfly Caste: A Social History of Pellagra in the South.* Westport, Conn.: Greenwood Press, 1972.

Ettling, John. *The Germ of Laziness: Rockefeller Philanthropy and Public Health in the New South.* Cambridge: Harvard University Press, 1981.

Fishbein, Morris. *A History of the American Medical Association, 1847–1947.* Philadelphia: Saunders, 1947.

Flexner, Abraham. *Medical Education in the United States and Canada: A Report to the Carnegie Foundation for the Advancement of Teaching.* New York: Carnegie Foundation, 1910.

Gibson, John M. *Physician to the World: The Life of General William C. Gorgas.* Tuscaloosa: University of Alabama Press, 1989.

Lederer, Susan E. *Subjected to Science: Human Experimentation in America Before the Second World War.* Baltimore: Johns Hopkins University Press, 1995.

Libecap, Gary. D. *The Rise of the Chicago Packers and the Origin of Meat Inspection and Antitrust.* Cambridge, Mass: National Bureau of Economic Research, 1991.

Parascandola, John. *The Development of American Pharmacology: John J. Abel and the Shaping of a Discipline.* Baltimore: Johns Hopkins University Press, 1992.

Professional Guide to Diseases. 6th ed. Springhouse, Pa.: Springhouse, 1998.

Rail, Chester D. *Plague Ecotoxicology: History Aspects of the Disease in the Americas and the Eastern Hemisphere.* Springfield, Ill.: Thomas, 1985.

Reilly, Philip. *The Surgical Solution: A History of Involuntary Sterilization in the United States.* Baltimore: Johns Hopkins University Press, 1991.

Roe, D.A. *A Plague of Corn: The Social History of Pellagra.* Ithaca, N.Y.: Cornell University Press, 1973.

Teller, Michael E. *The Tuberculosis Movement: A Public Health Campaign in the Progressive Era.* Westport, Conn.: Greenwood Press, 1988.

Tong, Benson. *Susan La Flesche Picotte, M.D.: Omaha Indian Leader and Reformer.* Norman, Oklahoma: University of Oklahoma Press, 1999.

Wheatleys, Steven Charles. *The Politics of Philanthropy: Abraham Flexner and Medical Education.* Madison: University of Wisconsin Press, 1988.

Websites

"CDC Plague Home Page." Available online at http://www.cdc.gov/ncidod/dvbid/plague.

"FDA—Federal Meat Inspection Act." Available online at http://www.fda.gov/opacom/laws/meat.htm.

"The History of the Bicycling Craze." Available online at http://www.cruzio.com/bedard/bike/history/bikehist.html.

Lombardo, Paul. "Eugenic Sterilization Laws." Available online at http://www.eugenicsarchives.org/html/eugenics/essay8text.html.

"Medicine and Madison Avenue—Timeline." Available online at http://scriptorium.lib.duke.edu/mma/timeline.html.

"MEDLINEplus Medical Encyclopedia: Pellagra." Available online at http://www.nlm.nih.gov/medlineplus/ency/articles/000342.htm.

"Pure Food and Drug Act." Available online at http://www.coursesa.matrix.msu.edu/hst203/documents/pure.html.

"Reservation and Hospital Care Under the Office of Indian Affairs (c. 1890–1925)." Available online at http://www.nlm.nih.gov/exhibitions/if_you_knew/if_you_knew_06.html.

Sinclair, Upton. "The Jungle." Available online at http://www.roggeman.com/jungle.

"Tuberculosis Resources." Available online at http://www.epmc.columbia.edu/tbcpp.

"United States Cancer Mortality From 1900 to 1992." Available online at http://www.healthsentinel.com/Vaccines/DiseaseAndRelatedData_files/she.

"Yellow Fever/Reed Commission Exhibit." Available online at http://hcs.virginia.edu/hs-library/historical/yelfev/tabcom.html.

Religion

Abell, Aaron I. *American Catholicism and Social Action: A Search for Social Justice, 1865–1950.* Garden City, N.Y.: Hanover House, 1960.

Ahlstrom, Sydney E. *A Religious History of the American People.* New Haven, Conn.: Yale University Press, 1972.

Albanese, Catherine L. *America: Religions and Religion.* 2d ed. Belmont, Calif.: Wadsworth, 1992.

Allen, Gay Wilson. *William James: A Biography.* New York: Viking, 1967.

Anderson, Robert Mapes. *Vision of the Disinherited: The Making of American Pentecostalism.* Peabody, Mass.: Hendrickson, 1979.

Dolan, Jay P. *The American Catholic Experience.* Garden City, N.Y.: Doubleday, 1985.

Gaustad, Edwin Scott. *A Religious History of America.* rev. ed. San Francisco: HarperCollins, 1990.

Haaland, C. Carlyle. "Shinto and Indigenous Chinese Religion," in *Encyclopedia of the American Religious Experience.* edited by Charles H. Lippy and Peter Williams. New York: Scribners, 1988.

Hutchinson, William R. *The Modernist Impulse in American Protestantism.* Cambridge, Mass.: Harvard University Press, 1976.

Jehovah's Witnesses: Proclaimers of God's Kingdom. Brooklyn: Watch Tower Bible & Tract Society of New York, 1993.

Marsden, George M. *Fundamentalism and American Culture: The Shaping of Twentieth Century Evangelicalism, 1870–1925.* New York: Oxford University Press, 1980.

Marty, Martin E. *Modern American Religion.* vol. 1, *The Irony of It All, 1893–1919.* Chicago: University of Chicago Press, 1986.

Melton, J. Gordon, ed. *Religious Leaders of America.* Detroit: Gale Research, 1991.

Miller, William R., ed. *Contemporary American Protestant Thought, 1900–1970.* Indianapolis: Bobbs-Merrill, 1973.

Noorbergen, Rene. *Ellen G. White: Prophet of Destiny.* New Canaan, Conn.: Keats, 1972.

Penton, M. James. *Apocalypse Delayed: The Story of Jehovah's Witnesses.* Toronto: University of Toronto Press, 1985.

Prebish, Charles S. "Buddhism," in *Encyclopedia of the American Religious Experience.* Lippy, Charles H., and Peter Williams, ed.. New York: Scribners, 1988.

Sandeen, Ernest. *The Roots of Fundamentalism: British and American Millenarianism, 1800–1930.* Chicago: University of Chicago Press, 1970.

Thomas, Robert David. *"With Bleeding Footsteps": Mary Baker Eddy's Path to Religious Leadership.* New York: Knopf, 1994.

Weber, Timothy P. *Living in the Shadow of the Second Coming: American Premillennialism, 1875–1982.* Grand Rapids, Mich.: Academic Books, 1983.

Wilson, P.W. *General Evangeline Booth of the Salvation Army.* New York: Scribners, 1948.

Science and Technology

Archer, Gleason L. *History of Radio to 1926.* New York: American Historical Society, 1938.

Benison, Saul, A. Clifford Barger, and Elin L. Wolfe. *Walter B. Cannon: The Life and Times of a Young Scientist.* Cambridge: Harvard University Press, 1987.

Bilstein, Roger E. *Flight in America: From the Wrights to the Astronauts.* Baltimore: Johns Hopkins University Press, 1984.

Bowler, Peter J. *The Mendelian Revolution.* Baltimore: Johns Hopkins University Press, 1989.

Donovan, Frank. *Wheels for a Nation.* New York: Crowell, 1965.

Dreyer, Peter. *A Gardener Touched With Genius: The Life of Luther Burbank.* Berkeley: University of California Press, 1985.

Flink, James J. *America Adopts the Automobile, 1895–1910.* Cambridge, Mass.: MIT Press, 1970.

Ford, Henry. *My Life and Work.* Garden City, N.Y.: Doubleday, 1922.

Freidel, Robert, and Paul Israel. *Edison's Electric Light: Biography of an Invention.* New Brunswick, N.J.: Rutgers University Press, 1987.

Glick, Thomas F., ed. *The Comparative Reception of Relativity.* Dordrecht, Netherlands: D. Reidel, 1987.

Gould, Stephen J. *The Mismeasure of Man.* Now York: Norton, 1981.

———. *Wonderful Life: The Burgess Shale and the Nature of History.* New York: Norton, 1989.

Hale Jr., Nathan G. *Freud and the Americans: The Beginnings of Psychoanalysis in the United States, 1876–1917.* New York: Oxford University Press, 1971.

Hayes, J. Gordon. *Robert Edwin Peary: A Record of his Explorations, 1886–1909.* London: Grant Richards, 1929.

Hobbs, William Herbert. *Peary.* New York: Macmillan, 1936.

Howard, Fred. *Wilbur and Orville: A Biography of the Wright Brothers.* New York: Knopf, 1987.

Josephson, Matthew. *Edison: A Biography.* New York: McGraw-Hill, 1959.

Joslin, Rebecca R. *Chasing Eclipses: The Total Solar Eclipses of 1905, 1914, 1925.* Boston: Walton, 1925.

Kevles, Daniel J. *In the Name of Eugenics: Genetics and the Uses of Human Heredity.* New York: Knopf, 1985.

Kline, Ronald R. *Steinmetz: Engineer and Socialist.* Baltimore: Johns Hopkins University Press, 1992.

Kohler, Robert E. *Lords of the Fly: Drosophila Genetics and the Experimental Life.* Chicago: University of Chicago Press, 1994.

———. *Partners in Science: Foundations and Natural Scientists, 1900–1945.* Chicago: University of Chicago, 1991.

Lacey, Robert. *Ford: The Men and the Machine.* Boston: Little, Brown, 1986.

Milliard, André. *Edison and the Business of Invention.* Baltimore: Johns Hopkins University Press, 1990.

Mitchell, Samuel Alfred. *Eclipses of the Sun.* New York: Columbia University Press, 1923.

Morgan, T. H. *The Genetics of Drosophila.* The Hague: M. Nijhoff, 1925.

Morris, Richard Knowles. *John P. Holland, Inventor of the Modern Submarine.* Annapolis, Md.: United States Naval Institute, 1966.

Newman, Louise M., ed. *Man's Ideas/Women's Realities: Popular Science, 1870–1915.* New York: Pergamon Press, 1984.

Olby, Robert C. *Origins of Mendalism.* Chicago: University of Chicago Press, 1987.

Pauly, Philip L. *Controlling Life: Jacques Loeb and the Engineering Idea in Biology.* Berkeley: University of California Press, 1990.

Reingold, Nathan, and Ida H. Reingold. *Science in America.* Chicago: University of Chicago Press, 1981.

Ross, Dorothy. *G. Stanley Hall: The Psychologist as Prophet.* Chicago: University of Chicago Press, 1972.

Russett, Cynthia E. *Darwin in America: The Intellectual Response, 1865–1912.* San Francisco: Freeman, 1976.

Smith, Robert W. *The Expanding Universe: Astronomy's Great Debate, 1900–1931.* New York: Cambridge University Press, 1982.

Swenson, Loyd S. Jr. *The Ethereal Aether: A History of the Michelson-Morley-Miller Aether-Drift Experiments, 1880–1930.* Austin: University of Texas Press, 1972.

Wachhorst, Wynn. *Thomas Alva Edison: An American Myth.* Cambridge, Mass.: MIT Press, 1981.

Wohl, Robert. *A Passion for Wings: Aviation and the Western Imagination, 1908–1918.* New Haven, Conn.: Yale University Press, 1994.

Wright, Helen. *Explorer of the Universe: A Biography of George Ellery Hale,* 2d ed. Woodbury, N.Y.: American Institute of Physics, 1994.

Websites

"Albert A. Michelson—Biography." Available online at http://www.nobel.se/physics/laureates/1907/michelson-bio.html.

"Burgess Shale Fossils." Available online at http://www.geo.ucalgary.ca/macrae/Burgess_Shale.

"Charles Proteus Steinmetz, Inventor." Available online at http://www.yonkershistory.org/stein.html.

"Dr. J. Willard Gibbs." Available online at http://jwgibbs.cchem.Berkeley.edu/jwgibbs_bio.html.

"Experiment Stations—KS—Cyclopedia." Available online at http://skyways.lib.ks.us/genweb/archives/1912/e/experiment_stations.html.

"Liberty Hyde Bailey Loop." Available online at http://www.cfe.cornell.edu/plantations/bailey.html.

"Nikola Tesla." Available online at http://www.neuronet.pitt.edu/bogdan/tesla.

"Percival Lowell." Available online at http://www.lowell.edu/AboutLowell/plowell.html.

"Robert A. Millikan—Biography." Available online at http://www.nobel.se/physics/laureates/1923/millikan-bio.html.

"The Wright Brothers." Available online at http://www.time.com/time/time100/scientist/profile/wright.html.

Sports

Alexander, Charles C. *John McGraw.* New York: Viking, 1988.

———. *Ty Cobb.* New York: Oxford Press, 1985.

Axelson, G. W. *'Commy' The Life Story of Charles A. Comiskey.* Jefferson, N.C.: McFarland, 2003.

Berenson, Sendra. *Line Basketball for Women.* New York: A.G. Spalding, 1901.

Bernstein, Mark F. *Football: The Ivy League Origins of an American Obsession.* Philadelphia: University of Pennsylvania Press, 2001.

Burke, Robert. *Never Just A Game: Players, Owners and American Baseball to 1920.* Chapel Hill: University of North Carolina Press, 1994.

DeValeria, Dennis. *Honus Wagner: A Biography.* New York: Henry Holt, 1996.

Danzig, Allison. *The History of American Football: Its Great Teams, Players, and Coaches.* Englewood Cliffs, N.J.: Prentice-Hall, 1956.

Garraty, John Arthur. *Theodore Roosevelt; The Strenuous Life.* New York: American Heritage, 1967.

Gimore, Al-Tony. *Bad Nigger! The National Impact of Jack Johnson.* Port Washington, N.Y.: Kennikat Press, 1975.

Gorn, Elliot J. *The Manly Art: Bare-Knuckle Prize Fighting in America.* Ithaca, N.Y.: Cornell University Press, 1986.

Issacs, Neil D. *All the Moves: A History of College Basketball.* New York: Harper & Row, 1984.

Kaye, Ivan. *Good Clean Violence: A History of College Football.* Philadelphia: Lippincott, 1973.

Levy, Alan H. *Rube Waddell: The Zany, Brilliant Life of a Strike Out Artist.* Jefferson, N.C.: McFarland, 2000.

Levy, Lester S. *Take Me Out to the Ball Game and Other Favorite Song Hits, 1906–1908.* New York: Dover, 1984.

Mansch, Larry D. *Rube Marquard: The Life and Times of A Hall-of-Famer.* Jefferson, N.C.: McFarland, 1995.

Mathewson, Christy. *Pitching Pitch, or, Baseball From the Inside.* Lincoln: University of Nebraska Press, 1994.

Naismith, James. *Basketball: Its Origins and Development.* Urbana: University of Illinois Press, 1992.

Needham, Henry B. *The Double Squeeze.* Garden City: Doubleday, 1915.

Norris, James D. *Advertising and the Transformation of American Society, 1865–1920.* New York: Greenwood Press, 1990.

Petersen, Robert W. *Only the Ball Was White.* Englewood Cliffs, N.J.: Prentice-Hall, 1970.

Powell, Harford Jr. *Walter Camp: The Father of American Football.* Freeport, N.Y.: Books for Libraries Press, 1970.

Rader, Benjamin G. *American Sports: From the Age of Folk Games to the Age of Spectators.* Englewood Cliffs, N.J.: Prentice-Hall, 1983.

Riess, Steven A. *City Games: The Evolution of American Urban Society and the Rise of Sports.* Urbana: University of Illinois Press, 1989.

Roberts, Randy. *Papa Jack: Jack Johnson and the Era of White Hopes.* New York: Free Press, 1983.

Sammons, Jeffrey T. *Beyond the Ring: The Role of Boxing in American Society.* Urbana & Chicago: University of Illinois Press, 1988.

Schoor, Gene, and Henry Gilford. *Christy Mathewson: Baseball's Greatest Pitcher.* New York: Julian Messner, 1953.

Smith, Ronald A. *Sports and Freedom: The Rise of Big Time College Athletics.* New York & Oxford: Oxford University Press, 1988.

Spalding, Albert Goodwill. *America's National Game.* 1911.

Tavin, A.H. *A Century of Baseball: Odd and Humorous Tales of Players, Plays, and Incidents that Made Baseball Our National Sport.* Louisville, Ky.: Standard Printing, 1938.

Thomas, Henry. *Walter Johnson: Baseball's Big Train.* Washington, D.C.: Phenom Press, 1995.

Whittingham, Richard. *Rites of Autumn. The Story of College Football.* New York: Free Press, 2001.

Primary Source Type Index

Primary source authors appear in parentheses. Page numbers in italics indicate images, and those followed by the letter t *indicate tables.*

Primary source authors appear in parentheses. Page numbers in italics indicate images, and those followed by the letter *t* indicate tables.

Primary source authors appear in parentheses. Page numbers in italics indicate images, and those followed by the letter *t* indicate tables.

Reports

Short stories

Songs

Speeches

Statements

Supreme Court decisions

Tables

Textbooks

Theological works

Works of art

Primary source authors appear in parentheses. Page numbers in italics indicate images, and those followed by the letter *t* indicate tables.

General Index

Page numbers in bold indicate primary sources; page numbers in italic indicate images; page numbers in bold italic indicate primary source images; page numbers followed by the letter t *indicate tables. Primary sources are indexed under the entry name with the author's name in parentheses. Primary sources are also indexed by title. All primary sources can be identified by bold page locators.*

Page numbers in bold indicate primary sources; page numbers in italic indicate images; page numbers in bold italic indicate primary source images; page numbers followed by the letter *t* indicate tables.

Page numbers in bold indicate primary sources; page numbers in italic indicate images; page numbers in bold italic indicate primary source images; page numbers followed by the letter *t* indicate tables.

Page numbers in bold indicate primary sources; page numbers in italic indicate images; page numbers in bold italic indicate primary source images; page numbers followed by the letter *t* indicate tables.

Page numbers in bold indicate primary sources; page numbers in italic indicate images; page numbers in bold italic indicate primary source images; page numbers followed by the letter *t* indicate tables.

Page numbers in bold indicate primary sources; page numbers in italic indicate images; page numbers in bold italic indicate primary source images; page numbers followed by the letter *t* indicate tables.

I

Page numbers in bold indicate primary sources; page numbers in italic indicate images; page numbers in bold italic indicate primary source images; page numbers followed by the letter *t* indicate tables.

Page numbers in bold indicate primary sources; page numbers in italic indicate images; page numbers in bold italic indicate primary source images; page numbers followed by the letter *t* indicate tables.

Page numbers in bold indicate primary sources; page numbers in italic indicate images; page numbers in bold italic indicate primary source images; page numbers followed by the letter *t* indicate tables.

Page numbers in bold indicate primary sources; page numbers in italic indicate images; page numbers in bold italic indicate primary source images; page numbers followed by the letter *t* indicate tables.

Page numbers in bold indicate primary sources; page numbers in italic indicate images; page numbers in bold italic indicate primary source images; page numbers followed by the letter *t* indicate tables.

Page numbers in bold indicate primary sources; page numbers in italic indicate images; page numbers in bold italic indicate primary source images; page numbers followed by the letter *t* indicate tables.

Page numbers in bold indicate primary sources; page numbers in italic indicate images; page numbers in bold italic indicate primary source images; page numbers followed by the letter *t* indicate tables.

Page numbers in bold indicate primary sources; page numbers in italic indicate images; page numbers in bold italic indicate primary source images; page numbers followed by the letter *t* indicate tables.

Page numbers in bold indicate primary sources; page numbers in italic indicate images; page numbers in bold italic indicate primary source images; page numbers followed by the letter *t* indicate tables.

Page numbers in bold indicate primary sources; page numbers in italic indicate images; page numbers in bold italic indicate primary source images; page numbers followed by the letter *t* indicate tables.